Contents in Brief

Contents

Part 2 Internet Consumer Retailing   140

Part 3 Business-to-Business E-Commerce   235

Part 4 Other EC Models and Applications   336

Part 5 EC Support Services   469

Part 6 EC Strategy and Implementation 585

Online Chapters

Insights and Additions 17.4: Using Trading Assistants at eBay

Auction Rules

Strategic Issues

Auctions in B2B Exchanges

Case 17.3 **EC Application:** Online Grapes and Wine Auctions

Infrastructure for E-Auctions

Auctions on Private Networks

17.9 MOBILE E-AUCTIONS AND THE FUTURE OF AUCTIONS

Benefits and Limitations of Mobile Auctions

The Future of E-Auctions

MANAGERIAL ISSUES

SUMMARY

KEY TERMS

QUESTIONS FOR DISCUSSION

INTERNET EXERCISES

TEAM ASSIGNMENTS, PROJECTS, AND CLASS DISCUSSIONS

CLOSING CASE: DYNAMIC TRADING AT OCEANCONNECT.COM

ONLINE RESOURCES

REFERENCES

CHAPTER 18 BUILDING E-COMMERCE APPLICATIONS AND INFRASTRUCTURE

Developing a Web 2.0 Platform to Enable Innovative Market Research at Del Monte

18.1 A FIVE-STEP APPROACH TO DEVELOPING AN E-COMMERCE SYSTEM

Step 1: Identifying, Justifying, and Planning EC Systems

Step 2: Creating an EC Architecture

Step 3: Selecting a Development Option

Step 4: Installing, Testing, Integrating, and Deploying EC Applications

Step 5: Operations, Maintenance, and Updates

Managing the Development Process

18.2 DEVELOPMENT STRATEGIES FOR E-COMMERCE MAJOR APPLICATIONS

In-House Development: Insourcing

Buy the Applications (Off-the-Shelf Approach)

Outsourcing/Leasing EC Applications

Other Development Options

18.3 SELECTING A DEVELOPMENT METHOD

Software on Demand

Utility Computing

Application Service Providers (ASPs)

Software as a Service (SaaS)

Integrating with Web Services and Service-Oriented Architecture

Case 18.1 **EC Application:** MasterCard Capitalizes on Web 2.0's Reusability and Interoperability

Mashups

Development Tools

18.4 TECHNOLOGY SUPPORT: FROM BLOGGER.COM TO INFRASTRUCTURE SERVICES

Ajax

Really Simple Syndication (RSS) and Atom

Online Files

Technical Appendix

Online Tutorials

Entering the third millennium, we are experiencing one of the most important changes to our daily lives—the move to an Internet-based society. Internet World Statistics reported at the end of March 2009 that more than $1^1/_2$ billion people worldwide surf the Internet. According to Tryhorn et al. (2009) the number of Internet users worldwide using cell phone access alone was 1 billion at the end of 2008 (out of 4.1 billion cell phone users). The number of those people using desktop Internet is also increasing. The advent of less expensive computers ($200 or less) also contributes to the growth.

Internet World Stats (internetworldstats.com) reported in December 2008 that more than 73 percent of the North American population (which is almost 319 million) surf the Internet. More interesting is the fact that more than 93 percent of people between the ages of 12 and 18 surf the Internet on a regular basis. According to Pew/Internet, in 2008 the biggest increase in generational use of the Internet occurred in ages 70 to 75 with a 45 percent increase in older people going online (reported by *Marketing Charts* 2009). It is clear that these percentages will continue to increase, and similar trends exist in most other countries. As a result, much has changed at home, school, work, and in the government—and even in our leisure activities. Some of these changes are spreading around the globe. Others are just beginning in some countries. One of the most significant changes is in how we conduct business, especially in how we manage marketplaces and trading. For example, during the 2008/2009 recession, Amazon.com and other Internet companies were the few to increase both sales and profits.

Electronic commerce (EC) describes the manner in which transactions take place over networks, mostly the Internet. It is the process of electronically buying and selling goods, services, and information. Certain EC applications, such as buying and selling stocks and airline tickets on the Internet, are growing very rapidly, exceeding non-Internet trades. But EC is not just about buying and selling; it also is about electronically communicating, collaborating, and discovering information (sometimes referred to as *e-business*). It is about e-learning, e-government, social networks, and much more. EC is having an impact on a significant portion of the world, affecting businesses, professions, and, of course, people.

WHAT'S NEW IN THIS EDITION?

The following are the major changes in this edition:

▶ **New co-authors.** We welcome T. P. Liang (City University of Hong Kong and the National Sun Yat-Sen [Taiwan]) who brings expertise in several e-business areas. Deborrah C. Turban (Turban Company Inc., previously with the University of Santa Thomas in the Philippines) brings expertise in EC research and analysis.

▶ **Chapters with major changes.** Major changes have been made to the following chapters:

▶ Chapter 1 now includes social networks, virtual worlds, new business models, and other leading-edge topics.

▶ Chapter 2 includes extensive coverage of Web 2.0 tools and virtual worlds and their commercial applications.

▶ Chapter 4 includes new coverage of advertising models in social networking and marketing strategies.

- Old Chapters 5 and 6 have been combined to make one unified chapter on B2B EC.
- Chapter 6 includes the addition of several challenging innovations demonstrated in new applications.
- Chapter 9 includes an extensive coverage of business and enterprise social networks with many commercial applications.
- Chapter 10 was completely reorganized and updated with the most recent fraud and security reports available in 2009.
- Chapter 12 includes the addition of major innovations in e-supply chains and e-supply chain strategies. Also added were ERP and intelligent agents.
- Chapter 16 now covers the topic of Green EC.
- Chapter 18 was updated to include new technologies and developers' activities in social networks.

- **Chapters with less significant changes.** All data in the chapters were updated. About 25 percent of all cases have been replaced. About 20 percent of all end-of-chapter material has been updated and/or expanded. The Managerial Issues were significantly upgraded, as well as figures and tables. Duplications were eliminated and explanations of exhibits have been made more understandable. New topics were added in many of the sections to reflect the Web 2.0 and social networking revolution. We reduced both the size of most chapters and most of the older references were eliminated.
- **Online files.** The online files were updated and reorganized. Many new files have been added.
- **A new tutorial.** A new tutorial on Electronic Customer Relationship Management (e-CRM) was added.

THE IMPORTANCE OF EC

The impact of EC is not just in the creation of Web-based businesses. It is the building of a new industrial order. Such a revolution brings a myriad of opportunities, as well as risks. Bill Gates is aware of this, and the company he founded, Microsoft, is continually developing new Internet and EC products and services. Yet Gates has stated that Microsoft is always 2 years away from failure—that somewhere out there is an unknown competitor who could render its business model obsolete (Heller 2005). Bill Gates knows that competition today is not among products or services, but among business models. What is true for Microsoft is true for just about every other company. The hottest and most dangerous new business models out there are on the Web.

The years between 2006 and 2009 have been characterized by the emergence of Web 2.0 and social and enterprise networks, which expanded the boundaries of e-commerce from trading, information search, and collaboration with a business orientation, to personal life support, and then back to business, because companies are now adopting social computing technologies that were designed for individual use (such as blogs, wikis, file sharing, and social networks) to increase the effectiveness and efficiency of their operations. For example, during the economic crisis of 2008–2009, millions of job seekers used LinkedIn and other social networking sites to look for jobs.

Forrester Research reports that the easy connections that social computing has given us have made a major impact not only on the social structure that exists outside of the business world, but also on the global economy. Because of the pervasiveness of social computing, Forrester suggests that individuals take information from each other more often, rather than from institutional sources, such as mainstream media outlets and corporations. For a company to survive, Forrester suggests that its marketing initiatives must fundamentally change from a top-down information flow to one where communities and social computing initiatives are part of its products and services (reported by Blancharski 2006).

In revising Electronic Commerce *2008* to Electronic Commerce *2010*, we paid great attention to these developments. The reason is that the so-called social computing is changing not only our lives and the way we do business, but also the field of e-commerce itself. Appropriate applications appear in all chapters.

Another emerging factor is the interest in environmental issues and especially in what is known as "Green IT and EC," which in many cases impacts the way business is done. We elaborate on this in several chapters and especially in Chapters 9 and 16.

The purpose of this book is to describe what EC is—how it is being conducted and managed—as well as to assess its major opportunities, limitations, issues, and risks, all in the social-computing business environment. It is written from a managerial perspective. Because EC is an interdisciplinary topic, it should be of interest to managers and professional people in any functional area of business in all industries. People in government, education, health services, and other areas also will benefit from learning about EC.

Today, EC and e-business are going through a period of consolidation in which enthusiasm for new technologies and ideas is accompanied by careful attention to strategy, implementation, risks, and profitability. Most of all, people recognize that e-business has three parts; it is not just about *technology*, it is also about *commerce* and *people*.

This book is written by experienced authors who share academic as well as real-world practices. It is a comprehensive text that can be used in one-semester or two-semester courses. It also can be used to supplement a text on Internet fundamentals, MIS, or marketing.

FEATURES OF THIS BOOK

Several features are unique to this book.

MANAGERIAL ORIENTATION

Electronic commerce can be approached from two major aspects: technological and managerial. This text uses the second approach. Most of the presentations are about EC applications and implementation. However, we do recognize the importance of the technology; therefore, we present the essentials of security in Chapter 10 and the essentials of infrastructure and system development in Chapter 18, which is located on the book's Web site (www.pearsonglobaleditions.com/turban). We also provide some detailed technology material in the files, appendices, and tutorials on the book's Web site. Managerial issues are provided at the end of each chapter.

REAL-WORLD ORIENTATION

Extensive, vivid examples from large corporations, small businesses, of different industries and services, and government and nonprofit agencies from all over the world make concepts come alive. These examples show students the capabilities of EC, its cost and justification, and the innovative ways real corporations are using EC in their operations. Examples cover both large and small (SME) companies.

SOLID THEORETICAL BACKGROUND AND RESEARCH SUGGESTIONS

Throughout the book, we present the theoretical foundations necessary for understanding EC, ranging from consumer behavior to the economic theory of competition. Furthermore, we provide Web site resources, many exercises, and extensive references to supplement the theoretical presentations. At the end of each chapter, we provide a list of online resources in each chapter and current references.

MOST CURRENT CUTTING-EDGE TOPICS

The book presents the most current topics relating to EC, as evidenced by the many 2007 to 2009 citations. Topics such as social networking, e-learning, e-government, e-strategy, Web-based supply chain systems, collaborative commerce, mobile commerce, and EC economics are presented from the theoretical point of view as well as from the application side.

INTEGRATED SYSTEMS

In contrast to other books that highlight isolated Internet-based systems, we emphasize those systems that support the enterprise and supply chain management. Intra- and interorganizational systems are highlighted as are the latest innovations in global EC and in Web-based applications.

GLOBAL PERSPECTIVE

The importance of global competition, partnerships, and trade is increasing rapidly. EC facilitates export and import, the management of multinational companies, and electronic trading around the globe. International examples are provided throughout the book. Our authors and contributors are from six different countries.

INTERDISCIPLINARY APPROACH

E-commerce is interdisciplinary, and we illustrate this throughout the book. Major EC-related disciplines include accounting, finance, information systems, marketing, management, operations management, and human resources management. In addition, some nonbusiness disciplines are related, especially public administration, computer science, engineering, psychology, political science, and law. Finally, economics plays a major role in the understanding of EC.

EC FAILURES AND LESSONS LEARNED

In addition to EC success stories, we also present EC failures and, where possible, analyze the causes of those failures with lessons learned.

ONLINE SUPPORT

More than 150 files are available online to supplement text material. These include files on generic topics, such as data mining and intranets; cases; technically oriented text; and much more.

USER-FRIENDLINESS

While covering all major EC topics, this book is clear, simple, and well organized. It provides all the basic definitions of terms as well as logical conceptual support. Furthermore, the book is easy to understand and is full of interesting real-world examples and "war stories" that keep readers' interest at a high level. Relevant review questions are provided at the end of each section so the reader can pause to review and digest the new material.

ORGANIZATION OF THE BOOK

The book is divided into 16 chapters grouped into 6 parts. Two additional chapters (17 and 18), an appendix, and two tutorials are available as online supplements.

PART 1—INTRODUCTION TO EC

In Part 1, we provide an overview of today's business environment as well as the fundamentals of EC and some of its terminology (Chapter 1). A discussion of electronic markets and their mechanisms and impacts is provided in Chapter 2 where special attention is given to blogs, wikis, and virtual worlds. Also included in Chapter 2 is an appendix giving an in-depth look at build-to-order production.

PART 2—INTERNET CONSUMER RETAILING

In Part 2, we describe EC B2C applications in two chapters. Chapter 3 addresses e-tailing and electronic service industries (e.g., travel, e-banking). Chapter 4 deals with consumer behavior online, market research, and online advertising.

PART 3—BUSINESS-TO-BUSINESS E-COMMERCE

In Part 3, we examine the one-to-many B2B models including auctions, and the many-to-many models including exchanges (Chapter 5). An online file to Chapter 5 provides a discussion of the transition from traditional EDI to Internet-based EDI, and another online file provides additional material on extranets. Chapter 6 describes the e-supply chain, intrabusiness EC, and collaborative commerce.

PART 4—OTHER EC MODELS AND APPLICATIONS

Part 4 begins with several interesting applications, such as e-government, e-learning, and consumer-to-consumer EC, as presented in Chapter 7. Chapter 8 explores the developing applications in the world of wireless EC (m-commerce, l-commerce, and pervasive computing). Finally, in Chapter 9 we explore social networking with special attention given to business and enterprise networks.

PART 5—EC SUPPORT SERVICES

Chapter 10 begins with a discussion of the need to protect computer systems. It also describes various types of computer attacks including fraud, and then discusses how to minimize these risks through appropriate security programs. Chapter 11 describes a major EC support service—electronic payments. Chapter 12 concentrates on order fulfillment, ERP, intelligent agents, and other support services.

PART 6—EC STRATEGY AND IMPLEMENTATION

Chapter 13 discusses strategic issues in implementing and deploying EC. The chapter also presents global EC and EC for small businesses. Chapter 14 deals with the economics of EC, including balanced scorecards, metrics, and justification methods. Chapter 15 is unique; it describes how to build an *Internet company* from scratch, as well as how to build a storefront. It takes the reader through all the necessary steps and provides guidelines for success. Chapter 16 deals with legal, ethical, and societal issues concentrating on legal issues, compliance and Green IT and EC.

ONLINE PART 7—AUCTIONS AND APPLICATION DEVELOPMENT

Two online chapters conclude the book. Online Chapter 17 deals with auctions, bartering, and negotiations online, and Online Chapter 18 deals with EC applications development, including Web Services, Software as a Service, and other emerging technologies.

LEARNING AIDS

The text offers a number of learning aids to the student:

- **Chapter Outlines.** A listing of the main headings ("Content") at the beginning of each chapter provides a quick overview of the major topics covered.
- **Learning Objectives.** Learning objectives at the beginning of each chapter help students focus their efforts and alert them to the important concepts to be discussed.
- **Opening Cases.** Each chapter opens with a real-world example that illustrates the importance of EC to modern corporations. These cases were carefully chosen to call attention to the major topics covered in the chapters. Following each vignette, a short section titled "What We Can Learn . . . " links the important issues in the vignette to the subject matter of the chapter.
- **EC Application Cases.** In-chapter cases highlight real-world problems encountered by organizations as they develop and implement EC. Questions follow each case to help direct student attention to the implications of the case material.
- **Insights and Additions.** Topics sometimes require additional elaboration or demonstration. Insights and Additions boxes provide an eye-catching repository for such content.

- **Exhibits.** Numerous attractive exhibits (both illustrations and tables) extend and supplement the text discussion. Many are available online.

- **Review Questions.** Each section ends with a series of review questions about that section. These questions are intended to help students summarize the concepts introduced and to digest the essentials of each section before moving on to another topic.

- **Marginal Glossary and Key Terms.** Each Key Term is defined in the margin when it first appears. In addition, an alphabetical list of Key Terms appears at the end of each chapter with a page reference to the location in the chapter where the term is discussed.

- **Managerial Issues.** At the end of every chapter, we explore some of the special concerns managers face as they adapt to doing business in cyberspace. These issues are framed as questions to maximize readers' active engagement with them.

- **List of Online Resources.** At the end of each chapter we provide a list of the chapter's online files with a brief description of their content. In addition we provide a list of URLs relevant to the chapter.

- **Chapter Summary.** The chapter summary is linked one-to-one with the learning objectives introduced at the beginning of each chapter.

- **End-of-Chapter Exercises.** Different types of questions measure students' comprehension and their ability to apply knowledge. Questions for Discussion are intended to promote class discussion and develop critical-thinking skills. Internet Exercises are challenging assignments that require students to surf the Internet and apply what they have learned. Over 250 hands-on exercises send students to interesting Web sites to conduct research, investigate an application, download demos, or learn about state-of-the-art technology. The Team Assignments, Projects, and Class Discussions exercises are challenging group projects designed to foster teamwork.

- **Topics for class discussion.** This new feature, included in the "team assignments," lists three to five topics suggested for class discussion.

- **Closing Cases.** Each chapter ends with a comprehensive case, which is presented in somewhat more depth than the in-chapter EC Application Cases. Questions follow each case relating the case to the topics covered in the chapter.

SUPPLEMENTARY MATERIALS

The following support materials are also available.

ONLINE INSTRUCTOR'S RESOURCE CENTER: WWW.PEARSONGLOBALEDITIONS.COM/TURBAN

This convenient online *Instructor's Resource Center* includes all of the supplements: Instructor's Manual, Test Item File, TestGen, PowerPoint Lecture Notes, and Image Library (text art).

The **Instructor's Manual**, written by Jon Outland, includes answers to all review and discussion questions, exercises, and case questions. The **Test Item File**, written by Linda Volonino, is an extensive set of multiple-choice, true-false, and essay questions for each chapter. It is available in Microsoft Word, **TestGen**, and WebCT- and Blackboard-ready test banks.

The **PowerPoint Lecture Notes**, by Judy Lang, are oriented toward text learning objectives.

COMPANION WEB SITE: WWW.PEARSONGLOBALEDITIONS.COM/TURBAN

The book is supported by a companion Web site that includes:

- Online chapters (Chapter 17 and Chapter 18).
- Bonus EC Application Cases and Insights and Additions features can be found in each chapter's online files.

- One technology appendix on Web site design for EC.
- Two tutorials, one on preparing an EC business plan and one on e-CRM.
- All of the Internet Exercises from the end of each chapter in the text are provided on the Web site for convenient student use.

MATERIALS FOR YOUR ONLINE COURSE

Prentice Hall supports adopters using online courses by providing files ready for upload into both WebCT and Blackboard course management systems for our testing, quizzing, and other supplements. Please contact your local Prentice Hall representative for further information on your particular course.

ACKNOWLEDGMENTS

Many individuals helped us create this text. Faculty feedback was solicited via reviews and through individual interviews. We are grateful to them for their contributions.

Several individuals helped us with the administrative work. We thank the many students of Sun Yat-Sen University in Taiwan for their help in literature searches. We thank Daphne Turban, Sarah Miller, and all these people for their dedication and superb performance shown throughout the project.

We also recognize the various organizations and corporations that provided us with permissions to reproduce material. Special thanks go to Dion Hinchcliffe for allowing us to use his figures. Thanks also to the Pearson Prentice Hall team that helped us from the inception of the project to its completion under the leadership of Executive Editor Bob Horan. The dedicated staff includes Editorial Project Manager Kelly Loftus, Editorial Assistant Valerie Patruno, Production Managers Ann Pulido and Judy Leale, Art Director Janet Slowik, and Media Project Manager Denise Vaughn.

Last, but not least, we thank Judy Lang, who as coordinator and problem solver, contributed innovative ideas and provided the necessary editing.

CONTENT CONTRIBUTORS

The following individuals contributed material for this edition.

- Linda Lai of the Macau Polytechnic Institute of China updated Chapter 3 and contributed to Chapter 15.
- Carol Pollard of Appalachian State University updated Chapter 18, available on the book's Web site.
- Christy Cheung of Hong Kong Baptist University contributed material to Chapter 13.
- Judy Lang of Lang Associates updated material in several chapters and conducted supported research.
- Ivan C. Seballos II of De La Salle Lipa University, Philippines, contributed the new illustrations and helped in updating several chapters.
- Vipin Saini of National Sun Yat-Sen University in Taiwan conducted research on Internet marketing for Chapter 4.

REVIEWERS

We wish to thank the faculty who participated in reviews of this text and our other EC titles.

David Ambrosini, Cabrillo College

Timothy Ay, Villanova University

Deborah Ballou, University of Notre Dame

Christine Barnes, Lakeland Community College

Martin Barriff, Illinois Institute of Technology

Sandy Bobzien, Presentation College

Stefan Brandle, Taylor University

Joseph Brooks, University of Hawaii

Bruce Brorson, University of Minnesota

Clifford Brozo, Monroe College-New Rochelle

Stanley Buchin, Boston University

John Bugado, National University

Ernest Capozzolli, Troy State University

Mark Cecchini, University of Florida

Sandy Claws, Northern University

Jack Cook, State University of New York at Geneseo

Larry Corman, Fort Lewis College

Mary Culnan, Georgetown University

Chet Cunningham, Madisonville Community College

Roland Eicheleberger, Baylor University

Ted Ferretti, Northeastern University

Colin Fukai, Gonzaga University

Vickie Fullmer, Webster University

Dennis Galletta, University of Pittsburgh

Ken Griggs, California Polytechnic University

Varun Grover, University of South Carolina

Tom Gruen, University of Colorado at Colorado Springs

Norman Hahn, Thomas Nelson Community College

Harry Harmon, University of Central Missouri

James Henson, Barry University

Sadie Herbert, Mississippi Gulf Coast Community College

James Hogue, Wayland Baptist University

Brian Howland, Boston University

Chang Hsieh, University of Southern Mississippi

Paul Hu, University of Utah

Jin H. Im, Sacred Heart University

Bandula Jayatilaka, Binghamton University

Jeffrey Johnson, Utah State University

Kenneth H. Johnson, Illinois Institute of Technology

Robert Johnson, University of Connecticut

Morgan Jones, University of North Carolina

Charles Kelley, California Baptist University

Douglas Kline, Sam Houston State University

Mary Beth Klinger, College of Southern Maryland

Parag Kosalge, Grand Valley State University

Tanvi Kothari, Temple University

Joanne Kuzma, St. Petersburg College

Charles Lange, DeVry University

Chunlei Liu, Troy State University

Byungtae Lee, University of Illinois at Chicago

Lakshmi Lyer, University of North Carolina

Joseph Maggi, Technical College of the Lowcountry

Ross Malaga, Montclair State University

Steve Mann, Humphreys College

Michael McLeod, East Carolina University

Susan McNamara, Northeastern University

Mohon Menon, University of South Alabama

Stephanie Miller, University of Georgia

Ajay Mishra, State University of New York at Binghamton

Bud Mishra, New York University

Robert Moore, Mississippi State University

Lawrence Muller, LaGuardia Community College, CUNY

Suzy Murray, Piedmont Technical College

Mohammed M. Nadeem, National University

William Nance, San Jose State University

Lewis Neisner, University of Maryland

Katherine A. Olson, Northern Virginia Community College

Somendra Pant, Clarkson University

Wayne Pauli, Dakota State University

Craig Peterson, Utah State University

Sarah Pettitt, Champlain College

Dien D. Phan, University of Vermont

H.R. Rao, State University of New York at Buffalo

Catherine M. Roche, Rockland Community College

Jorge Romero, Towson University

Greg Rose, California State University at Chico

Linda Salchenberger, Loyola University of Chicago

George Schell, University of North Carolina at Wilmington

Sri Sharma, Oakland University

Daniel Shen, SUNY New Paltz

Seungjae Shin, Mississippi State University-Meridian

Sumit Sircar, University of Texas at Arlington

Elliot B. Sloane, Villanova University

Hongjun Song, University of Memphis

Kan Sugandh, DeVry Institute of Technology

John Thacher, Gwinnett Technical College

Goran Trajkovski, Towson University

Dothang Truong, Fayetteville State University

Linda Volonino, Canisius College

Andrea Wachter, Point Park University

Ken Williamson, James Madison University

John Windsor, University of North Texas

Gregory Wood, Canisius College

Walter Wymer, Christopher Newport University

James Zemanek, East Carolina University

INTERNATIONAL CONTRIBUTORS:

Maged Farouk, Arab Academy for Science, Technology and Maritime Transport, Egypt

Patrick Soh, Multimedia University Malaysia

INTERNATIONAL REVIEWERS:

Leila Halawi - The American University of Dubai

Kamel Rouibah - College of Business Administration, Kuwait University

May-Lin Yap - Universiti Teknologi MARA, Malaysia

Rathimala Kannan - Multimedia University, Malaysia

Sandy Lloyd - City College, London

Sunanda Sangwan - Nanyang Technological University, Singapore

REFERENCES

Heller, R. "Strengths and Weaknesses: Assess the Strengths and Weaknesses of Your Business, as Well as the Opportunities and Threats, with SWOT Analysis." *Thinking Managers*, 2005.

Internet World Stats. "Internet Usage Statistics: The Big Picture." April 9, 209. internetworldstats.com/stats.htm (accessed April 2009).

Marketing Charts. "Old and Young Use the Internet Differently." marketingcharts.com/interactive/generations-online-use-internet-differently-8145/pew-internet-generations-percentage-online-generations-by-age-january-2009jpg (accessed April 2009).

Tryhorn, C. "Nice Talking to You—Mobile Phone Use Passes a Milestone." *The Guardian* (London), March 3, 2009. guardian.co.uk/technology/2009/mar/03/mobile-phones1 (accessed April 2009).

OVERVIEW OF ELECTRONIC COMMERCE

Content

Learning Objectives

Upon completion of this chapter, you will be able to:

1. Define electronic commerce (EC) and describe its various categories.
2. Describe and discuss the content and framework of EC.
3. Describe the major types of EC transactions.
4. Discuss e-commerce 2.0.
5. Understand the elements of the digital world.
6. Describe the drivers of EC as they relate to business pressures and organizational responses.
7. Describe some EC business models.
8. Describe the benefits and limitations of EC to organizations, consumers, and society.

BEIJING 2008: A DIGITAL OLYMPICS

Known in China as "Superfish," Michael Phelps was on his way to achieving his goal of eight gold medals. His most difficult competition, and his final race, was the 100-meter butterfly. On PCs, cell phones, electronic billboards, and televisions, millions of viewers worldwide watched him win the event by .01 seconds. The results appeared on the screens almost in real time. If you did not see this exciting race, you can access it on YouTube. This was only one component in the "most wired," or digital, Olympics.

The Problem

It was not an easy task to manage 42 events in 7 different cities in China. Results had to be displayed worldwide not only on PCs and televisions, but also on jumbo public display screens in stadiums and streets in hundreds of cities and on millions of tiny mobile device screens.

But, this was only one problem. The Olympic organizers also had to manage the logistics of the participants and requirements of the media while also accommodating over 100 million tourists. The following are some of the specific requirements that the Beijing Olympic organizers had to meet:

- Record the performance of all athletes and determine the winners instantly, sometimes based on millisecond differences. These results then had to be disseminated around the globe in real time.

- China hosted about 300,000 athletes, referees, trainers, journalists, and other workers from more than 200 countries, speaking dozens of languages. All needed to have accommodations, transportation, and food.

- Nearly 8 million visitors from abroad and close to 120 million domestic travelers attended the Olympics. They needed accommodation, transportation, and so forth.

- Tickets to all events had to be issued, many in advance, and to people in other countries. Protection against counterfeiting was necessary.

- Approximately 1,000 percent more Web-delivered videos were needed in 2008 than were needed by the 2004 Olympics.

- The organizers anticipated a greater than 1,000 percent increase in page views, and even more in video watching. Sufficient infrastructure had to be in place.

- In real time, the system had to collect and filter more than 12 million monitored events and identify potential security threats.

- Real-time, transoceanic coverage, including digital videos, required sophisticated hardware, software, and networks.

- Many visitors preferred to shop online and have Olympic souvenirs shipped to their homes.

- Overall, it was necessary to securely process more than 80 percent more information compared with the 2004 Olympics in Athens, Greece.

- Traffic in Beijing can be a major problem and is a major air pollutant, so monitoring and controls were needed to minimize it.

These problems and requirements can be classified into seven categories:

1. Information collection and monitoring
2. Information dissemination to the world
3. Tickets and souvenirs management
4. Food and supplies along the supply chain
5. Security and privacy monitoring and protection
6. Transportation and pollution control
7. Social networking for the public

The $4 Billion IT and EC Solutions

To address the administrative problems just discussed, as well as many others, the organizers employed the latest information technology tools, including electronic commerce, the subject of this book. To explain how this was done, the seven requirements have been divided into five basic categories, as shown in Exhibit 1.1 (left side), which also shows the e-commerce solutions used (right side).

The following major e-commerce solutions were implemented:

- The International Olympic Committee (IOC) launched a YouTube channel to broadcast clips that were accessible in 77 developing countries. Viewers were able to watch free clips on demand from PCs, as well as news and commentaries. These clips were broadcast on television and display boards as well. Videos were

downloaded with Microsoft's Silverlight and Adobe's Flash.

- The instant display of the results was possible due to the use of sophisticated photo-finish cameras and computers. The system was capable of identifying winners accurately even when the difference was only milliseconds.

- Over 12 million tickets were available for the events. Many of these tickets were purchased online, using Beijing Gehue Ticketmaster, in what we call business-to-consumer (B2C) electronic commerce.

- All of the tickets were equipped with Radio Frequency Identification (RFID) tags that were loaded with information designed to prevent counterfeit tickets. (See Online File W1.1 for an introduction to RFID.)

- Millions watched the Olympics through online videos and Internet-enabled cell phones and other mobile devices.

WWW

EXHIBIT 1.1   EC Solutions at the Beijing Olympics

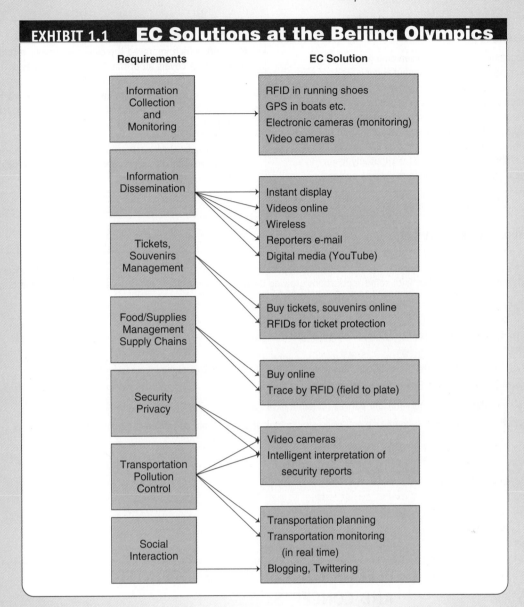

Requirements

- Information Collection and Monitoring
- Information Dissemination
- Tickets, Souvenirs Management
- Food/Supplies Management Supply Chains
- Security Privacy
- Transportation Pollution Control
- Social Interaction

EC Solution

- RFID in running shoes
- GPS in boats etc.
- Electronic cameras (monitoring)
- Video cameras

- Instant display
- Videos online
- Wireless
- Reporters e-mail
- Digital media (YouTube)

- Buy tickets, souvenirs online
- RFIDs for ticket protection

- Buy online
- Trace by RFID (field to plate)

- Video cameras
- Intelligent interpretation of security reports

- Transportation planning
- Transportation monitoring (in real time)
- Blogging, Twittering

- Using RFID tags, the Olympic coordinators ensured the safety of athletes' food by tracking the ingredients from farms to plates.

- Global Positioning Systems (GPS) were used to track the position of sailing and rowing boats five times per second for comparison purposes.

- RFID tags were attached to one shoe of each marathon runner. When the runners passed RFID readers at certain locations along the running route, their whereabouts were known as well as their exact time of arrival.

- More than 50 software applications supported the games management. For example, a workforce management tool was used to manage the work of hundreds of telecommunication technicians and others during the games.

- Bloggers were encouraged to blog. For example, the Bank of America sponsored a site called "America's Cheer" where athletes were blogging. Others blogged on *rotorblog.com*, as well as thousands of other sites. Twitter (see Chapter 2) was also a great source of coverage. Social networking capabilities were provided by the "Olympic Network TV Station."

- Electronic collaboration among over a dozen IT companies and especially Cisco Systems, Microsoft, and Limelight Networks ensured the successful execution of the supporting IT and EC systems.

The Results

The organizing committee clearly deserved a gold medal. Everything was perfect, even the computer-generated fireworks that were displayed in the video of the opening and closing ceremonies! The EC solutions were able to handle over 20 times more video screens than the 2004 Olympics, satisfying approximately 60 million unique users (vs. 11 million in 2004) who viewed more than 1 trillion pages (vs. 230 million in Athens). All of this was accomplished without any major problems. The Olympics helped create many new online communities that provided instant feedback to NBC and Microsoft, which improved the coverage. Finally, a social network that covers all of the Olympic games was developed at *olympic-network.net*. No other Olympics had such sophisticated information processing capabilities and superb EC applications. Even the illegal e-commerce market that was selling pirated Olympic merchandise was minimized.

Sources: Compiled from Taft (2008), *IT Strategy* (2008), *rotorblog.com* (miscellaneous dates), *InformationWeek* (2008a and 2008b), Burger (2008), and Magnier (2008).

WHAT WE CAN LEARN . . .

The opening case illustrates the increased use of e-commerce applications that result in improved performance. The differences compared to just 4 years earlier are incredible, with some applications growing by 1,000 percent. Some of the most notable e-commerce applications are:

- Selling products and services online to individuals (business-to-consumer)
- Buying foods and other supplies from suppliers (business-to-business) and tracing the shipment of the food (supply chain improvement)
- Extensive use of digital media for publicity, advertising, and entertainment (e-commerce services)
- Use of digital systems for security and control
- Electronic collaboration among multiple parties (collaborative commerce)

Now that you have an idea of e-commerce activities we can look at some formal definitions and concepts.

1.1 ELECTRONIC COMMERCE: DEFINITIONS AND CONCEPTS

Let's begin by looking at what the management guru Peter Drucker had to say about EC:

> *The truly revolutionary impact of the Internet Revolution is just beginning to be felt. But it is not "information" that fuels this impact. It is not "artificial intelligence." It is not the effect of computers and data processing on decision making, policymaking, or strategy. It is something that practically no one foresaw or, indeed even talked about 10 or 15 years ago; e-commerce—that is, the explosive emergence of the Internet as a major, perhaps eventually the major, worldwide distribution channel for goods, for services, and, surprisingly, for managerial and professional jobs. This is profoundly changing economics, markets and industry structure, products and services and their flow; consumer segmentation, consumer values and consumer behavior; jobs and labor markets. But the impact may be even greater on societies and politics, and above all, on the way we see the world and ourselves in it. (Drucker 2002, pp. 3–4)*

electronic commerce (EC)
The process of buying, selling, or exchanging products, services, or information via computer.

DEFINING ELECTRONIC COMMERCE

Electronic commerce (EC) is the process of buying, selling, transferring, or exchanging products, services, and/or information via computer networks, mostly the Internet and intranets. For an overview, see en.wikipedia.org/wiki/E-commerce. EC can also be defined from the following perspectives:

> **Business process.** From a business process perspective, EC is doing business electronically by implementing business processes over electronic networks, thereby substituting information for physical business processes.

> **Service.** From a service perspective, EC is a tool that addresses the desire of governments, firms, consumers, and management to cut service costs while improving the quality of customer service and increasing the speed of service delivery.

> **Learning.** From a learning perspective, EC is an enabler of online training and education in schools, universities, and other organizations, including businesses.

> **Collaborative.** From a collaborative perspective, EC is the framework for inter- and intraorganizational collaboration.

> **Community.** From a community perspective, EC provides a gathering place for community members to learn, transact, and collaborate. The most popular type of community is social networks, such as MySpace and Facebook.

EC is often confused with e-business.

DEFINING E-BUSINESS

Some people view the term *commerce* as describing only buying and selling transactions conducted between business partners. If this definition of commerce is used, the term *electronic commerce* would be fairly narrow. Thus, many use the term *e-business* instead. E-business refers to a broader definition of EC, not just the buying and selling of goods and services, but also servicing customers, collaborating with business partners, conducting e-learning, and conducting electronic transactions within an organization. However, others view e-business as comprising those activities that do not involve buying or selling over the Internet, such as collaboration and intrabusiness activities; that is, it is a *complement* of the narrowly defined e-commerce. Finally, some define e-business as dealing with organizations' internal activities only, whereas e-commerce deals with external activities only. In this book, we use the broadest meaning of electronic commerce, which is basically equivalent to the broadest definition of e-business. The two terms will be used interchangeably throughout the text.

e-business
A broader definition of EC that includes not just the buying and selling of goods and services, but also servicing customers, collaborating with business partners, and conducting electronic transactions within an organization.

OTHER EC CONCEPTS

Several other concepts are frequently used in conjunction with EC. The major ones are as follow.

Pure Versus Partial EC

EC can take several forms depending on the degree of digitization (the transformation from physical to digital) of (1) the product (service) sold, (2) the process (e.g., ordering, payment, fulfillment), and (3) the delivery method. The possible configurations of these three dimensions (Exhibit 1.2) determine different levels of EC. A product may be physical or digital, the process may be physical or digital, and the delivery method may be physical or digital. These alternatives create eight cubes, each of which has three dimensions. In traditional commerce, all three dimensions of the cube are physical (lower-left cube); in pure EC, all dimensions are digital (upper-right cube). All other cubes include a mix of digital and physical dimensions.

If there is at least one digital dimension, we consider the situation EC, but only partial EC. For example, purchasing a computer from Dell's Web site or a book from Amazon.com is partial EC, because the merchandise is physically delivered. However, buying an e-book from Amazon.com or a software product from Buy.com is pure EC, because the product, payment, and delivery to the buyer are all digital.

EXHIBIT 1.2   The Dimensions of Electronic Commerce

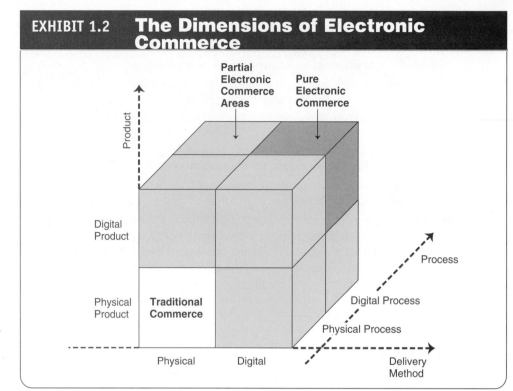

Source: Whinston, A. B., Stahl, D. O., and Choi, S. *The Economics of Electronic Commerce*. Indianapolis, IN: Macmillan Technical Publishing, 1997. Used with permission of the authors.

brick-and-mortar (old economy) organizations
Old-economy organizations (corporations) that perform their primary business off-line, selling physical products by means of physical agents.

virtual (pure-play) organizations
Organizations that conduct their business activities solely online.

click-and-mortar (click-and-brick) organizations
Organizations that conduct some e-commerce activities, usually as an additional marketing channel.

electronic market (e-marketplace)
An online marketplace where buyers and sellers meet to exchange goods, services, money, or information.

interorganizational information systems (IOSs)
Communications systems that allow routine transaction processing and information flow between two or more organizations.

intraorganizational information systems
Communication systems that enable e-commerce activities to go on within individual organizations.

EC Organizations

Purely physical organizations (companies) are referred to as **brick-and-mortar (old economy) organizations**, whereas companies that are engaged only in EC are considered **virtual**, or **pure-play, organizations**. **Click-and-mortar (or click-and-brick) organizations** are those that conduct some EC activities, usually as an additional marketing channel. Gradually, many brick-and-mortar companies are changing to click-and-mortar ones (see the closing case about Mary Kay).

ELECTRONIC MARKETS AND INTERORGANIZATIONAL AND INTRAORGANIZATIONAL INFORMATION SYSTEMS

EC can be conducted in an **electronic market (e-marketplace)** where buyers and sellers meet online to exchange goods, services, money, or information. Any individual can also open a market selling products or services online. Electronic markets are connected to sellers and buyers via the Internet but they may be supplemented by connecting interorganizational or intraorganizational information systems.

Interorganizational information systems (IOSs) are those where routine transaction processing and information flow take place between two or more organizations using a standard protocol, such as electronic data interchange (EDI). EC activities that take place within individual organizations are facilitated by **intraorganizational information systems**. These systems also are known as *intrabusiness EC*.

Section 1.1 ▶ REVIEW QUESTIONS

1. Define EC and e-business.
2. Distinguish between pure and partial EC.
3. Define click-and-mortar and pure play organizations.
4. Define electronic markets, IOSs, and intraorganizational information systems.

1.2 THE ELECTRONIC COMMERCE FIELD: CLASSIFICATION, CONTENT, AND HISTORY

Although some people still use a stand-alone computer exclusively, the vast majority of people use computers connected to a global networked environment known as the *Internet*, or to its counterpart within organizations, an *intranet*. An **intranet** is a corporate or government network that uses Internet tools, such as Web browsers, and Internet protocols.

Another computer environment is an **extranet**, a network that uses the Internet to link multiple intranets in a secure manner. A good example of how EC is done over these networks can be seen in the case of Dell (Online File W1.2).

The Dell case demonstrates several ways that businesses can use EC to improve the bottom line. Dell is not the only company that is doing business online. Thousands of other companies, from retailers to hospitals, are moving in this direction. In general, selling and buying electronically can be either business-to-consumer (B2C) or business-to-business (B2B). In B2C, online transactions are made between businesses and individual consumers, such as when a person purchases a computer at dell.com. In B2B, businesses make online transactions with other businesses, such as when Dell electronically buys components from its suppliers. Dell also collaborates electronically with its partners and provides customer service online (e-CRM). Several other types of EC were described in the opening case, and others will be described soon.

According to the U.S. Census Bureau e-commerce sales accounted for 3.2 percent of total U.S. retail sales in 2007, rising from 2.8 percent in 2006. eMarketer estimates that retail e-commerce sales will increase an average of 18.6 percent in 2008 and 2009 (reported by *International Trade Commission* 2008).

These activities comprise the essence of EC. However, EC can be explained better by viewing the following framework.

AN EC FRAMEWORK

The EC field is a diverse one, involving many activities, organizational units, and technologies (e.g., see Khosrow-Pour 2006). Therefore, a framework that describes its contents is useful. Exhibit 1.3 introduces one such framework.

As can be seen in the exhibit, there are many EC applications (top of exhibit), some of which were illustrated in Online File W1.2 about Dell; others will be shown throughout the book (see also Papazoglou and Ribbers 2006, en.wikipedia.org/wiki/electronic_commerce, Lee et al. 2006, and Jelassi and Enders 2005). To execute these applications, companies need the right information, infrastructure, and support services. Exhibit 1.3 shows that EC applications are supported by infrastructure and by the following five support areas: (shown as pillars in the exhibit):

> ▶ **People.** Sellers, buyers, intermediaries, information systems and technology specialists, other employees, and any other participants comprise an important support area.
>
> ▶ **Public policy.** Legal and other policy and regulatory issues, such as privacy protection and taxation, which are determined by governments. Included as part of public policy is the issue of technical standards, which are established by government and/or industry-mandated policy-making groups. Compliance with regulations is an important issue.
>
> ▶ **Marketing and advertisement.** Like any other business, EC usually requires the support of marketing and advertising. This is especially important in business-to-commerce (B2C) online transactions, in which the buyers and sellers usually do not know each other.
>
> ▶ **Support services.** Many services are needed to support EC. These range from content creation to payments to order delivery.
>
> ▶ **Business partnerships.** Joint ventures, exchanges, and business partnerships of various types are common in EC. These occur frequently throughout the *supply chain* (i.e., the interactions between a company and its suppliers, customers, and other partners).

intranet
An internal corporate or government network that uses Internet tools, such as Web browsers, and Internet protocols.

extranet
A network that uses the Internet to link multiple intranets.

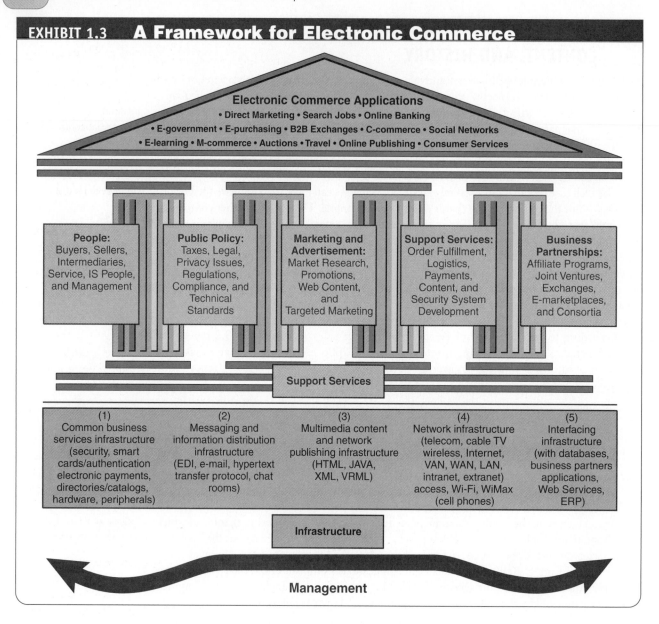

EXHIBIT 1.3   **A Framework for Electronic Commerce**

Electronic Commerce Applications
• Direct Marketing • Search Jobs • Online Banking
• E-government • E-purchasing • B2B Exchanges • C-commerce • Social Networks
• E-learning • M-commerce • Auctions • Travel • Online Publishing • Consumer Services

People:
Buyers, Sellers, Intermediaries, Service, IS People, and Management

Public Policy:
Taxes, Legal, Privacy Issues, Regulations, Compliance, and Technical Standards

Marketing and Advertisement:
Market Research, Promotions, Web Content, and Targeted Marketing

Support Services:
Order Fulfillment, Logistics, Payments, Content, and Security System Development

Business Partnerships:
Affiliate Programs, Joint Ventures, Exchanges, E-marketplaces, and Consortia

Support Services

(1) Common business services infrastructure (security, smart cards/authentication electronic payments, directories/catalogs, hardware, peripherals)

(2) Messaging and information distribution infrastructure (EDI, e-mail, hypertext transfer protocol, chat rooms)

(3) Multimedia content and network publishing infrastructure (HTML, JAVA, XML, VRML)

(4) Network infrastructure (telecom, cable TV wireless, Internet, VAN, WAN, LAN, intranet, extranet) access, Wi-Fi, WiMax (cell phones)

(5) Interfacing infrastructure (with databases, business partners applications, Web Services, ERP)

Infrastructure

Management

The infrastructure for EC is shown at the bottom of Exhibit 1.3. *Infrastructure* describes the hardware, software, and networks used in EC. All of these components require good *management practices.* This means that companies need to plan, organize, motivate, devise strategy, and restructure processes, as needed, to optimize the business use of EC models and strategies. Management also deals with strategic and operational decisions (see Chapter 13 and examples throughout the book).

This text provides details on the major components of the framework. The infrastructure of EC is described in the online Technical Appendix, on the book's Web site, in the Online Files, and in Online Chapter 18.

CLASSIFICATION OF EC BY THE NATURE, DIRECTION OF THE TRANSACTIONS, AND INTERACTIONS

A common classification of EC is by the nature of the transactions or the relationship among the participants. The following major types of EC transactions are listed on the following page with the place in the book where that they are presented.

Business-to-Business (B2B)

All of the participants in **business-to-business (B2B)** e-commerce are either businesses or other organizations (see Chapters 5 through 7). For example, suppliers sold food and other goods to the Beijing Olympics. Dell (Online File W1.2) sells its products to companies. Today, over 85 percent of EC volume is B2B (Mockler et al. 2006).

Business-to-Consumer (B2C)

Business-to-consumer (B2C) EC includes retail transactions of products or services from businesses to individual shoppers. The typical shopper at Wal-Mart online or at Amazon.com is an individual. This EC type is also called **e-tailing**. Selling Olympic tickets online is also B2C. Other examples can be found in Chapter 3 and in Case 1.1).

Business-to-Business-to-Consumer (B2B2C)

In **business-to-business-to-consumer (B2B2C)** EC, a business provides some product or service to a client business. The client business maintains its own customers, who may be its own employees, to whom the product or service is provided. One example of B2B2C is a company that pays AOL to provide its employees with Internet access rather than having each employee pay an access fee directly to AOL. Another example is Godiva (Case 1.1). The company sells chocolates directly to business customers. Those businesses may then give the chocolates as gifts to employees or to other businesses. Godiva may mail the chocolate directly to the recipients (with compliments of . . .). An interesting example of B2B2C can be found at wishlist.com.au. The term B2B frequently includes B2B2C as well.

Consumer-to-Business (C2B)

The **consumer-to-business (C2B)** category includes individuals who use the Internet to sell products or services to organizations and individuals who seek sellers to bid on products or services (see Chapters 2 and 17). Priceline.com is a well-known organizer of C2B transactions.

Intrabusiness EC

The **intrabusiness EC** category includes all internal EC organizational activities that involve the exchange of goods, services, or information among various units and individuals in that organization. Activities can range from selling corporate products to one's employees, to online training, and to collaborative design efforts (see Chapter 6). Intrabusiness EC is usually performed over intranets and/or corporate portals (gateways to the Internet).

Business-to-Employees (B2E)

The **business-to-employees (B2E)** category is a subset of the intrabusiness category in which an organization delivers services, information, or products to individual employees. A major category of employees is *mobile employees*, such as field representatives (see Chapter 8). EC support to such employees is also called *B2ME (business-to-mobile employees)*. The Beijing Olympics used wireless devices to maintain contact with employees. The Mary Kay closing case also demonstrates B2E.

Consumer-to-Consumer (C2C)

In the **consumer-to-consumer (C2C)** category (see Chapter 7), consumers transact directly with other consumers. Examples of C2C include individuals selling residential property, cars, and so on in online classified ads. The advertising of personal services over the Internet and the selling of knowledge and expertise online are other examples of C2C. In addition, many auction sites allow individuals to place items up for auction.

---

business-to-business (B2B)
E-commerce model in which all of the participants are businesses or other organizations.

business-to-consumer (B2C)
E-commerce model in which businesses sell to individual shoppers.

e-tailing
Online retailing, usually B2C.

business-to-business-to-consumer (B2B2C)
E-commerce model in which a business provides some product or service to a client business that maintains its own customers.

consumer-to-business (C2B)
E-commerce model in which individuals use the Internet to sell products or services to organizations or individuals who seek sellers to bid on products or services they need.

intrabusiness EC
E-commerce category that includes all internal organizational activities that involve the exchange of goods, services, or information among various units and individuals in an organization.

business-to-employees (B2E)
E-commerce model in which an organization delivers services, information, or products to its individual employees.

consumer-to-consumer (C2C)
E-commerce model in which consumers sell directly to other consumers.

CASE 1.1
EC Application
WANT TO BUY CHOCOLATE ONLINE? TRY GODIVA.COM

The Business Opportunity

The demand for high-quality chocolate has been increasing rapidly since the early 1990s. Several local and global companies are competing in this market. Godiva Chocolatier is a well-known international company based in New York whose stores can be found in hundreds of malls worldwide. The company was looking for ways to increase its sales. It had the courage to try online sales as early as 1994. The company was a pioneering first mover online that exploited an opportunity years before its competitors.

The Project

Teaming with Fry Multimedia (an e-commerce pioneer), Godiva.com (*godiva.com*) was created as a division of Godiva Chocolatier. The objective was to sell online both to individuals (B2C) and to businesses (B2B). Because its online activities began in 1994, the Godiva.com story parallels the dynamic growth of e-commerce.

Godiva.com went through difficult times—testing e-commerce technologies as they appeared; failing at times, but maintaining its commitment to online selling; and, finally, becoming the fastest-growing division of Godiva, outpacing projections. Godiva.com embodies a true success story. Here we present some of the milestones encountered.

The major driving factors in 1994 were Internet user groups of chocolate lovers, who were talking about Godiva and to whom the company hoped to sell its product online. Like other pioneers, Godiva had to build its Web site from scratch without EC-building tools. A partnership was made with *Chocolatier Magazine,* allowing Godiva.com to show-case articles and recipes from the magazine on its site in exchange for providing an online magazine subscription form for e-shoppers. The recognition of the importance of relevant content was correct, as was the need for fresh content. The delivery of games and puzzles, which was considered necessary to attract people to EC sites, was found to be a failure. People were coming to learn about chocolate and Godiva and to buy—not to play games. Another concept that failed was the attempt to make the Web site look like the physical store. It was found that different marketing channels should look different from one another.

Godiva.com is a user-friendly place to shop. Its major features include electronic catalogs, some of which are constructed for special occasions (e.g., Mother's Day and Father's Day); a store locator (how to find the nearest physical store and events at stores close to you); a shopping cart to make it easy to collect items to buy; e-cards; a gift selector and a gift finder; custom photographs of the products; a search engine by product, price, and other criteria; instructions on how to shop online (take the tour); a chocolate guide that shows you exactly what is inside each box; a place to click for live assistance or for a paper catalog; and the ability to create an address list for shipping gifts to friends or employees. The site also features "My Account," a personalized place where customers can access their order history, account, order status, and so on; general content about chocolate (and recipes); and tools for making shipping and payment arrangements.

Godiva.com sells both to individuals and to corporations. For corporations, incentive programs are offered, including address lists of employees or customers to whom the chocolate is to be sent—an example of the B2B2C EC model.

Godiva.com continues to add features to stay ahead of the competition. The site is now accessible using wireless technologies. For example, the store locator is available to wireless phone users, and Palm Pilot users can download mailing lists.

The Results

Godiva.com's online sales have been growing at a double-digit rate every year, outpacing the company's "old economy" divisions, as well as the online stores of competitors.

Sources: Compiled from Reda (2004) and from *godiva.com* (accessed November 2008).

Questions

1. Identify the B2B and B2C transactions in this case.
2. Why did Godiva decide to sell online? List the EC drivers in this case.
3. Visit *godiva.com*. How user-friendly is the site?
4. Describe B2B2C at Godiva.

Collaborative Commerce

collaborative commerce (c-commerce)
E-commerce model in which individuals or groups communicate or collaborate online.

When individuals or groups communicate or collaborate online, they may be engaged in **collaborative commerce,** or **c-commerce** (see Chapter 6). For example, business partners in different locations may design a product together (see the Boeing case at Online File W1.3), using screen-sharing; manage inventory online, as in the Dell case; or jointly forecast product demand. The various partners of the Beijing Olympics, some of which were in different countries, used EC for collaboration.

E-Learning

In **e-learning**, training or formal education is provided online (see Chapter 7). E-learning is used heavily by organizations for training and retraining employees (called *e-training*). It is also practiced at virtual universities.

e-learning
The online delivery of information for purposes of training or education.

E-Government

In **e-government** EC, a government entity buys or provides goods, services, or information from or to businesses (G2B) or from or to individual citizens (G2C) (see Chapter 7).

Many examples of the various types of EC transactions will be presented throughout this book.

Note that all the above, which started on wireline computers, are moving to wireless systems. Thus, the term e-commerce includes *mobile commerce* (*m-commerce*), which is examined in Chapter 8.

e-government
E-commerce model in which a government entity buys or provides goods, services, or information from or to businesses or individual citizens.

A BRIEF HISTORY OF EC

EC applications were first developed in the early 1970s with innovations such as *electronic funds transfer (EFT)* (see Chapters 7 and 11), whereby funds could be routed electronically from one organization to another. However, the use of these applications was limited to large corporations, financial institutions, and a few other daring businesses. Then came *electronic data interchange (EDI)*, a technology used to electronically transfer routine documents, which later expanded from financial transactions to other types of transactions (see Chapter 5 for more on EDI). EDI enlarged the pool of participating companies from financial institutions to manufacturers, retailers, services, and many other types of businesses. Such systems were called *interorganizational system (IOS)* applications, and their strategic value to businesses has been widely recognized. More new EC applications followed, ranging from travel reservation systems to stock trading.

The Internet began life as an experiment by the U.S. government in 1969, and its initial users were a largely technical audience of government agencies and academic researchers and scientists. Some of them started to place classifieds on the Internet. A major milestone in the development of EC was the introduction of the World Wide Web in the early 1990s. This allowed companies to have presence on the Internet with both text and photos. When the Internet became commercialized and users began flocking to participate in the World Wide Web in the early 1990s, the term *electronic commerce* was coined. EC applications rapidly expanded. A large number of so-called dot-coms, or *Internet start-ups*, also appeared. One reason for this rapid expansion was the development of new networks, protocols, and EC software. The other reason was the increase in competition and other business pressures (see discussion in Section 1.5).

Since 1995, Internet users have witnessed the development of many innovative applications, ranging from online direct sales to e-learning experiences. Almost every medium- and large-sized organization in the world now has a Web site, and most large U.S. corporations have comprehensive portals through which employees, business partners, and the public can access corporate information. Many of these sites contain tens of thousands of pages and links. In 1999, the emphasis of EC shifted from B2C to B2B, and in 2001 from B2B to B2E, c-commerce, e-government, e-learning, and m-commerce. In 2005, social networks started to receive quite a bit of attention, as did l-commerce and wireless applications. Given the nature of technology and the Internet usage, EC will undoubtedly continue to grow, shift, and change. More and more EC successes are emerging. For a comprehensive ready-reference guide to EC including statistics, trends, and in-depth profiles of over 400 companies, see Plunkett (2006) and en.wikipedia.org/wiki/E-commerce.

While looking at the history of EC, one must keep in mind the following issues.

The Interdisciplinary Nature of EC

Because EC is a new field, it is just now developing its theoretical and scientific foundations. From just a brief overview of the EC framework and classification, you can probably see that EC is related to several different disciplines. The major academic EC disciplines include the following: *computer science, marketing, consumer behavior, finance, economics, management information systems, accounting, management, human resource management, business law, robotics, public administration,* and *engineering.*

The Google Revolution

During its early years, EC was impacted by companies such as Amazon.com (Chapter 3), eBay (Chapter 17), AOL, and Yahoo! However, since 2001 no other company has probably had more of an impact on EC than Google. As will be seen in Chapter 4, Google related Web searches to targeted advertisements much better than its competitors did. Today, Google is much more than just a search engine; it employs several innovative EC models, is involved in many EC joint ventures, and impacts both organizational activities and individual lives, as described in Online File W1.4.

EC Failures

Starting in 1999, a large number of EC companies, especially e-tailing and B2B exchanges, began to fail (see disobey.com/ghostsites and Carton 2002). Well-known B2C failures include eToys, Xpeditor, MarchFirst, Drkoop, Webvan, and Boo. Well-known B2B failures include Chemdex, Ventro, and Verticalnet. (Incidentally, the history of these pioneering companies is documented in David Kirch's "The Business Plan Archive" [businessplanarchive.org].) A survey by *Strategic Direction* (2005) found that 62 percent of dot-coms lacked financial skills and 50 percent had little experience with marketing. Similarly, many companies failed to ensure they had the inventory and distribution setup to meet the fluctuating demand for their products. The reasons for these and other EC failures are discussed in detail in Hwang and Stewart (2006) and in Chapters 3, 5, and 13. In 2008, many start-ups related to Web 2.0 started to collapse (per blogs.cioinsight.com/knowitall/content001/startup_deathwatch_20.html).

Does the large number of failures mean that EC's days are numbered? Absolutely not! First, the dot-com failure rate is declining sharply. Second, the EC field is basically experiencing consolidation as companies test different business models and organizational structures. Third, some pure EC companies, including giants such as Amazon.com, are expanding operations and generating increased sales. Finally, the click-and-mortar model seems to work very well especially in e-tailing (e.g., Sears, Wal-Mart, Target, and Best Buy).

EC Successes

The last few years have seen the rise of extremely successful virtual EC companies such as eBay, Google, Yahoo!, VeriSign, AOL, and E-Trade. Click-and-mortar companies such as Cisco, Wal-Mart online, General Electric, IBM, Intel, and Schwab also have seen great success (see Papazoglou and Ribbers 2006 and Jelassi and Enders 2005). Additional success stories include start-ups such as Alloy.com (a young-adults-oriented portal), Blue Nile, Ticketmaster, FTD, Expedia, and Campusfood (see Online File W1.5).

For more on the history of e-commerce, see Tian and Stewart (2006). Although the history is interesting, let's see the forecasted future of EC.

THE FUTURE OF EC

Today's predictions about the future size of EC, provided by respected analysts such as AMR Research, Jupiter Media, Emarketer.com, and Forrester, vary. For example, according to Jupiter Media (2006), online retail (B2C) spending will increase from $81 billion in 2005 to $144 billion in 2010. By 2010, 71 percent of online users will use the Internet to shop, compared to 65 percent in 2005, and the Internet will influence nearly half of total retail sales, compared to just 27 percent in 2005. According to Forrester Research (2006), online sales reached $176 billion in 2005 and were expected to grow to $211 billion in 2006. Excluding travel, online sales account for nearly 5 percent of the U.S. retail market (vs. less than 2 percent in 2000). The number of Internet users worldwide was estimated at over 900 million in 2008. Experts predict that as many as 50 percent of all Internet users will shop online by 2010. EC growth will come not only from B2C, but also from B2B and from newer applications such as e-government, e-learning, B2E, and c-commerce. Overall, the growth of the field will continue to be strong into the foreseeable future. Despite the failures of individual companies and initiatives, the total volume of EC has been growing by 15 to 25 percent every year; as Lashinsky (2006) said, "The boom is back."

The rising price of petroleum, along with repercussions of the 2008–2009 financial meltdown, should motivate people to shop from home and look for bargains online where price comparison is easy and fast. However, a major potential EC limitation is bandwidth availability.

Finally, it seems that EC's future is now being shaped largely by social computing and networking, as will be illustrated next.

Section 1.2 ▶ REVIEW QUESTIONS

1. List the major components of the EC framework.
2. List the major transactional types of EC.
3. Describe the major landmarks in EC history.
4. List some EC successes and failures.
5. Summarize the future of EC.

1.3 E-COMMERCE 2.0: FROM WEB 2.0 TO ENTERPRISE SOCIAL NETWORKING AND VIRTUAL WORLDS

The first generation of EC involved mainly trading, e-services, and corporate-sponsored collaboration. We are moving now into the second generation of EC, which we call e-commerce 2.0. It is based on Web 2.0 tools, social networks, and virtual worlds, the result of social computing.

SOCIAL COMPUTING

Social computing is computing that is concerned with the intersection of social behavior and information systems. It is performed with a set of tools that includes blogs, mashups, instant messaging, social network services, wikis, social bookmarking and other *social software*, and marketplaces. Whereas traditional computing systems concentrate on supporting organizational activities and business processes and zero in on cost reduction and increases in productivity, social computing concentrates on improving collaboration and interaction among people and on user-generated content. It is a shift from traditional top-down management communication to a bottom-up strategy where individuals in communities become a major organizational power. In social computing and commerce, people can collaborate online, get advice from one another and from trusted experts, and find goods and services they really like.

Example. Advances in social computing are affecting travel decisions and arrangements. Travelers share information and warn others of bad experiences at sites such as tripadvisor.com.

The premise of social computing is to make socially produced information available to all. This information may be provided directly, as when systems show the number of users who have rated a book or a movie (e.g., at amazon.com and netflix.com). Or, the information may be provided indirectly, as is the case with Google's page rank algorithms, which sequences search results based on the number of page hits. In all of these cases, information that is produced by individuals is available to all, usually for free. Social computing is largely supported by Web 2.0 tools.

WEB 2.0

The term Web 2.0 was coined by O'Reilly Media in 2004 to refer to a supposed second generation of Internet-based services that let people generate and control content and collaborate and share information online in perceived new ways, such as social networking sites, wikis, communication tools, and folksonomies. O'Reilly Media, in collaboration with MediaLive International, used the phrase as a title for a series of conferences. Since then, it

social computing
An approach aimed at making the human–computer interface more natural.

Web 2.0
The second-generation of Internet-based services that let people collaborate and share information online in new ways, such as social networking sites, wikis, communication tools, and folksonomies.

has become a popular, ill-defined, and often criticized buzzword in the technical and marketing communities.

O'Reilly (2005) divided Web 2.0 into the following four levels:

▶ Level 3 applications, the most "Web 2.0" oriented, exist only on the Internet, deriving their effectiveness from interhuman connections and from the network effects that Web 2.0 makes possible and growing in effectiveness as people make more use of them. O'Reilly offered eBay, Craigslist, Wikipedia, del.icio.us, Skype, Dodgeball, and AdSense as examples of level 3 applications.

▶ Level 2 applications can operate offline but gain advantages from going online. O'Reilly cited Flickr as an example, which benefits from its shared photo database and from its community-generated tag database.

▶ Level 1 applications operate offline but gain features online. O'Reilly pointed to Writely (now Google Docs & Spreadsheets) and iTunes (because of its music store portion) as examples.

▶ Level 0 applications work as well offline as online. O'Reilly offered the examples of MapQuest, Yahoo! Local, and Google Maps.

O'Reilly (2005) also provided a road map. A comprehensive explanation of Web 2.0 and its tools, processes, and so on is provided in Exhibit 1.4. Note the complexity of the field. For more information on Web 2.0, see en.wikipedia.org/wiki/WEB_2.0. The major characteristics of Web 2.0 are presented in Online File W1.6. The major tools of Web 2.0 are described in Chapter 2, and the applications are described in most chapters, especially in Chapter 9. Also, browse at Don Hinchcliffe's Web 2.0 blog at web2.wsj2.com for Web 2.0 definitions, explanations, and applications.

social network
A category of Internet applications that help connect friends, business partners, or individuals with specific interests by providing free services such as photos presentation, e-mail, blogging, and so on using a variety of tools.

SOCIAL NETWORKS AND SOCIAL NETWORK SERVICES

The most interesting e-commerce application in recent years has been the emergence of social and enterprise social networks. Originating from online communities (Chapter 9), these networks are growing rapidly and providing for many new EC initiatives, revenue models, and business models.

A **social network** is a social structure composed of nodes (which are generally individuals or organizations) that are tied by one or more specific types of interdependency, such as values, visions, ideas, financial exchange, friendship, kinship, dislike, conflict, or trade. The structures are often very complex.

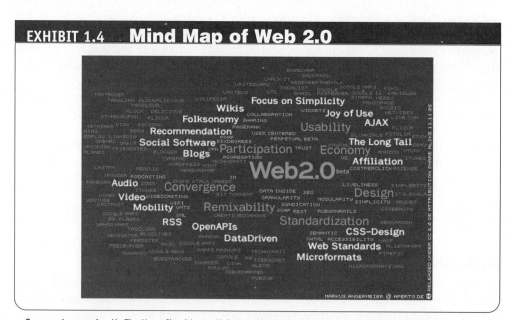

EXHIBIT 1.4 Mind Map of Web 2.0

Source: Angermeier, M. *The Huge Cloud Lense Web 2.0.* Kosmar.de, November 11, 2005. *kosmar.de/archives/ 2005/11/11/the-huge-cloud-lens-bubble-map-web20* (accessed July 2009). Reprinted by permission of Markus Angermeier.

In its simplest form, a social network can be described as a map of all relevant ties (connection) between the nodes. The network can also be used to determine the social capital of individual participants. These concepts are often displayed in a social network diagram, where nodes are the points and ties are the lines.

Participants in a *social network* congregate on a Web site where they can create their own homepage for free and on which they can write blogs and wikis; post pictures, videos, or music; share ideas; and link to other Web locations they find to be interesting. Social networkers chat using instant messaging and Twitter, and tag the content they post with their own key words, which makes the content searchable and facilitates the conduct of people-to-people transactions.

Social Network Services

In effect, in a social network there are *online communities* of people with similar interests. **Social network services (SNSs)**, such as MySpace and Facebook, provide a Web space for people to build their homepages, which they then host for free, and they also provide basic communication and other support tools for conducting different activities in the social network. These activities are referred to as *social networking*. Social networks are people oriented. For example, a 15-year-old Filipino singer named Pempengco thought her music career was doomed after she lost a local singing competition in 2006, but YouTube gave her a "cyber" of a lifetime when a video clip of her singing Jennifer Holliday's "And I'm Telling You I Am Not Going" caught the attention of TV host Ellen DeGeneres and Grammy Award winning producer David Foster. Initially, social networks were used for only social activities. However, as described in Chapter 9, today corporations are starting to have an interest in this EC feature (e.g., see linkedin.com, a network that connects businesses by industry, functions, geography, and areas of interest). For more on social networking, see De Jonge (2008) and en.wikipedia.org/wiki/Social_networking.

Finally, we define **social networking** as the creation or sponsoring of a social network service and any activity, such as blogging, done in a social network (external or internal).

The following are examples of representative social network services:

> ▶ Facebook.com: Facilitates socialization for people of all ages.
> ▶ YouTube.com and Metacafe.com: Users can upload and view video clips.
> ▶ Flickr.com: Users share and comment on photos.
> ▶ Friendster.com: Provides a platform to find friends and make contacts.
> ▶ Hi5.com: A popular global social network.
> ▶ Cyworld.nate.com: Asia's largest social networking Web site.
> ▶ Habbohotel.com: Entertaining country-specific sites for kids and adults.
> ▶ MySpace.com: The most visited social network Web site (see Case 1.2).

The following are representative capabilities and services provided by social network sites:

> ▶ Users can construct a Web page that they can use to present themselves to the larger community.
> ▶ Users can create a circle of friends who are linked together.
> ▶ The site provides discussion forums (by group, by topic).
> ▶ Photo, video, and document viewing and sharing (streaming videos, user-supplied videos) are supported.
> ▶ Wikis can be used to jointly create documents.
> ▶ Blogs can be used for discussion, dissemination of information, and much more.

social network service (SNS)
A service that builds online communities by providing an online space for people to build free homepages and that provides basic communication and support tools for conducting different activities in the social network.

social networking
The creation or sponsoring of a social network service and any activity, such as blogging, done in a social network (external or internal).

EC Application

MYSPACE: THE WORLD'S MOST POPULAR SOCIAL NETWORKING WEB SITE

An Overview
MySpace is an interactive social network of user-submitted blogs, profiles, groups, photos, MP3s, videos and an internal e-mail system. It has become an increasingly influential part of contemporary pop culture. The site claims to have over 100 million members (the world's fourth most popular English-language Web site) and draws 500,000 new members each week.

MySpace is also used by some independent musicians and filmmakers who upload songs and short films on their profiles. These songs and films can also be embedded in other profiles, an interconnectedness that adds to MySpace's appeal.

Contents of a MySpace Profile
Each member's profile contains two "blurbs": "About Me" and "Who I'd Like to Meet." Profiles also can contain optional sections about personal features such as marital status, physical appearance, and income. Profiles also contain a blog with standard fields for content, emotion, and media. Users can also upload images and videos to their MySpace page.

Users can choose a certain number of friends to be displayed on their profile in the "Top Friends" area. In 2006, MySpace allowed up to 24 friends to be displayed. The "Comments" area allows the user's friends to leave comments. MySpace users can delete comments or require all comments to be approved before posting. The site gives users some flexibility to modify their user pages, and "MySpace editors" are available to help.

The Major Capabilities of MySpace
MySpace has many capabilities and more are being added constantly. Here are some representative examples:

▶ Instant messenger (MySpace IM)
▶ Groups
▶ MySpace TV for video sharing
▶ MySpace Mobile for accessing MySpace with mobile devices
▶ MySpace News to display RSS feeds submitted by users
▶ MySpace classifieds for person-to-person advertising

Other capabilities include MySpace Books, MySpace Horoscopes, MySpace Jobs, MySpace Movies.

MySpace Celebrities
MySpace has led to the emergence of MySpace celebrities, popular individuals who have attracted hundreds of thousands of "friends," leading to coverage in other media. Some of these individuals have remained only Internet celebrities, others have been able to jump to television, magazines, and radio.

Major Issues Surrounding MySpace
The following are several major issues surrounding MySpace use.

Accessibility
Sometimes there are accessibility problems on users' profiles, because the site is set up so that anyone can customize the layout and colors of their profile page with virtually no restrictions. Poorly constructed MySpace profiles may freeze up Web browsers. Also, new features, such as song and video sharing through streaming media, and the huge number of MySpace users joining daily means that more users are online for longer periods; this increase in usage slows down the MySpace servers at peak times.

Restricting Access
Many schools and public libraries in the United Kingdom have begun to restrict access to MySpace because it has become "such a haven for student gossip and malicious comments" and because MySpace was consuming up to 40 percent of the daily Internet bandwidth, impeding delivery of Web-based courses. Regular administrative functions may also be slowed down.

Potential Damage to Students
The *Chicago Tribune*'s RedEye printed an article concerning MySpace and an individual's search for employment. The author argued that young college graduates compromise their chances of starting careers because of the content they post on their accounts. For example, an employer may not hire a highly qualified candidate because the candidate maintains an account that suggests overly "exuberant" behavior.

Security and Safety
MySpace allows registering users to be as young as 14. Profiles of users with ages set to 14 to 15 years are automatically private. Users whose ages are set at 16 or over do have the option to restrict their profiles, as well as the option of merely allowing certain personal data to be restricted to people other than those on their "friends list." The full profiles of users under age 18 are restricted to direct MySpace friends only.

MySpace Music
In September 2008, MySpace launched a joint venture with Universal, Sony BMG, and Warner Music called MySpace Music, a digital music service that enables MySpace users to listen to any song from the catalog of the participating media companies for free (but with on-screen ads).

Globalization and Competition
In 2006, News Corporation took MySpace to China, where it is spreading rapidly (in Chinese, of course). MySpace is available in many countries and languages.

(continued)

CASE 1.2 *(continued)*

Other Issues
Other issues affecting MySpace are musicians' rights and the user agreement, social and cultural issues, and legal issues. These and other issues are discussed in Chapter 16.

Competition and Income Source on MySpace
When News Corporation purchased MySpace in July 2005 for $580 million, many questioned the wisdom of paying so much for a site with no income and questionable advertisement revenue sources. However, in August 2006 Google paid MySpace more than the entire purchase sum for allowing Google to place its search and advertising on MySpace pages. This is helpful to MySpace, too, because now its users do not have to leave the site to conduct a Google search.

MySpace's major competitors are Xanga, Wayn, Reunion, Friendster, and Facebook. See Chapter 9 for details.

Sources: Compiled from Hupfer (2007), Sellers (2006), and *en.wikipedia.org/wiki/MySpace* (accessed November 2008).

Questions

1. Why does MySpace attract so many visitors?
2. List the major issues faced by the company.
3. What are the benefits to MySpace and Google from their collaboration?
4. Visit *myspace.com* and review some features not discussed in this case. Prepare a report.

▶ The site offers community e-mail and instant messaging (IM) capabilities.

▶ Experts can be made available to answer member queries.

▶ Consumers can rate and comment on products.

▶ The site provides an e-newsletter.

▶ Online voting may be available to poll member opinions.

▶ The site supports conference (group) chatting, combined with photo sharing.

▶ Message and bulletin board services are available for posting information to groups and anyone on the Web site.

▶ The site provides storage for content, including photos, videos, and music.

▶ Users can bookmark self-created content.

▶ Users can find other networks, friends, or topics of interest.

Not all networks have all these capabilities, but some have even more.

ENTERPRISE SOCIAL NETWORKS

Enterprise-oriented networks are social networks whose primary objective is to facilitate business. For example, YUB.com is a huge online shopping mall with about 6 million items. Users can also hang out at YUB.com with friends and meet others who are looking for discounts and bargains. Another example is craigslist.com, the classified ad super site, which offers many social-oriented features (see Chapter 2). Many B2B portals offer community services for thousands of members. EC is rapidly branching out to include enterprise social networks, as will be illustrated throughout the book, especially in Chapters 2 and 9.

enterprise-oriented networks
Social networks whose primary objective is to facilitate business.

Businesses are increasingly using enterprise social networks as a means of growing their circle of business contacts and promoting themselves online. Because businesses are expanding globally, social networks make it easier to keep in touch with other contacts around the world. Specific cross-border EC platforms and business partnering networks now make globalization accessible even for small and medium-sized companies and for individuals.

Corporations have been interacting or using social networks in the following major modes:

▶ Participating in existing public social networks such as Facebook, MySpace, Linkedin, and Second Life

▶ Creating private social networks for customers and business partners (e.g., Starbucks' mystarbucksidea.com)

▶ Offering internal private social networks for employees and alumni (e.g., Caterpillar Network and Oracle's Connect)

▶ Enhancing existing applications, such as e-mail and customer relationship management applications, by including the functionality commonly available in social networking systems (such as blogs and wikis)

▶ Developing tools or offering services for building and supporting social networks (e.g., IBM's Lotus Connections and Atlas)

With Web 2.0 tools, companies can engage users on a one-to-one basis in a way that old media, from flat Web sites to Super Bowl ads, was never able to accomplish. Community-based tools, such as small, integrated applications that run on top of a Web site's publishing platform, accomplish this direct communication by offering more ways for consumers to engage and interact. For example, a company can:

▶ Encourage consumers to rate and comment on products.

▶ Allow consumers to create their own topic areas and build communities (forums) around shared interests possibly related to a company's products.

▶ Hire bloggers or staff editors who can lead more company-formatted essays and discussions that allow, but are not driven by, customer comments.

▶ Provide incentives such as sweepstakes and contests for customers to get involved in new product (service) design and marketing campaigns.

▶ Encourage user-made videos about products/services and offer prizes for winning video ads. Capitalize on streaming videos.

▶ Provide interesting stories in e-newsletters.

Examples of Enterprise Social Networks

Enterprise social networks can be private (e.g., Carnival Lines) or public (e.g., Xing). Carnival Cruise Lines sponsors a social networking site (carnivalconnections.com) to attract cruise fans. Visitors use the site to exchange opinions, organize groups for trips, and much more. It cost the company $300,000 to set up the site, but Carnival anticipates that the cost will be covered by increased business. For details, see Fass (2006).

Originating in Germany, Xing.com (xing.com) is a business network that attracts millions of executives, sales representatives, and job seekers from many countries, mostly in Europe. The site offers secure services in 16 languages. Users can use the site to:

▶ Establish new business contacts.

▶ Systematically expand and manage their contacts' networks.

▶ Market themselves in a professional business context.

▶ Identify experts and receive advice on any topic.

▶ Organize meetings and events.

▶ Control the level of privacy and ensure that their personal data are protected.

For more on Xing.com, take the site's "Guided Tour." Services also are available for mobile device users.

VIRTUAL WORLDS AND SECOND LIFE

virtual world
A user-defined world in which people can interact, play, and do business. The most publicized virtual world is Second Life.

A special class of social networking is the *virtual world*. A **virtual world**, also known as a *metaverse,* is a 3D computer-based simulated environment built and owned by its residents. Community members inhabit virtual spaces and interact via *avatars*. These avatars, about 10 million of them in 2008, are usually depicted as textual, 2D, or 3D graphical presentations, although other forms are possible. The essentials of virtual worlds and a prime example of a virtual world, Second Life (secondlife.com), are presented in Chapter 2.

Until 2007, virtual worlds were most often limited to 3D games, including massively multiplayer online games. In addition to creating buildings, people can create and share cars, clothes, and many other items. More recently, they have become a new way for people to socialize, and even do business. There.com focuses more on social networking activities, such as chatting, creating avatars, interacting, playing, and meeting people.

How Students Make Money in a Virtual World

According to Alter (2008), the research firm Gartner Media estimates that by 2011 as many as 80 percent of all Internet users worldwide will have avatars, making animated online persons as common as e-mail and screen names are today. This means that there will be many jobs available to provide support to virtual worlds.

However, you do not have to wait until 2011 to make money in virtual worlds. If you cannot get a summer (or other) job, try a job in a virtual world. With summer jobs in short supply, more young people are pursuing money-making opportunities in virtual worlds. According to Alter (2008), a new breed of young entrepreneurs is honing their computer skills to capitalize on the growing demand for virtual goods and services.

Alter provides examples of six young and successful entrepreneurs:

▶ Mike Mikula, age 17, uses graphic design tools to build virtual buildings. His avatar in Teen Second Life, Mike Denneny, helps him to earn $4,000 a month as a builder and renovator of sites on Second Life.

▶ Ariella Furman, age 21, earns $2,000 to $4,000 a month using her avatar Ariella Languish in Second Life. She is a machinima, a filmmaker who works exclusively in Second Life. She directs avatars using a virtual producer and works in the virtual world for companies like IBM and Nestlé.

▶ John Eikenberry, age 25, earns $2,000 to $4,000 a month building Second Life neighborhoods, creating malls, coffee shops, and an auditorium over 16 landscaped acres called regions. His avatar is Lordfly Digeridoo in Second Life.

▶ Kristina Koch, age 17, is a character designer. Her avatar in Teen Second Life, Silver Bu, earns $600 to $800 a month using Second Life tools to add effects, such as shadows, to avatars. She and her boyfriend also design and sell virtual fairy wings and wizard's robes to dress avatars.

▶ Mike Everest, age 18, is a virtual hunter and trader, selling the skins of what he hunts. He also learned how to transform virtual ore into virtual weapons, which he sells. His avatar in the virtual world of Entropia Universe, Ogulak Da Basher, earns $200 to $1,000 a month. He is the family's primary money maker, and he was able to finance his brother's college education.

▶ Twins Andy and Michael Ortman, age 19, are inventors. Their avatars in Teen Second Life, Alpha Zaius and Ming Chen, earn about $2,500 a month each. The engineering majors work for Deep Think Labs, a virtual world development company based in Australia. They program Open Simulator, which allows companies and individuals to hold private meetings and training sessions in virtual environments similar to Second Life.

Section 1.3 ▶ REVIEW QUESTIONS

1. Define social computing and list its characteristics.
2. Define Web 2.0 and list its attributes.
3. Define social networks.
4. Describe the capabilities of social network services (SNSs).
5. Describe MySpace. Why is it so popular?
6. What is an enterprise social network?
7. Define virtual worlds and list their characteristics.
8. Describe some ways for student with computer skills to make money from virtual worlds.

1.4 THE DIGITAL WORLD: ECONOMY, ENTERPRISES, AND SOCIETY

The digital revolution is upon us. We see it every day at home and work, in businesses, schools, hospitals, on the roads, in entertainment and even in wars. We recognize here three elements: economy, enterprises, and society.

THE DIGITAL ECONOMY

digital economy

An economy that is based on digital technologies, including digital communication networks, computers, software, and other related information technologies; also called the *Internet economy,* the *new economy,* or the *Web economy.*

The **digital economy** refers to an economy that is based on digital technologies, including digital communication networks (the Internet, intranets, extranets, and VANs), computers, software, and other related information technologies. The digital economy is sometimes called the *Internet economy,* the *new economy,* or the *Web economy.* This platform displays the following characteristics:

- A vast array of digitizable products—databases, news and information, books, magazines, TV and radio programming, movies, electronic games, musical CDs, and software—are delivered over a digital infrastructure anytime, anywhere in the world. We are moving from analog to digital, even the media is getting digital (TVs as of February 2009).
- Consumers and firms conduct financial transactions digitally through digital currencies that are carried via networked computers and mobile devices.
- Microprocessors and networking capabilities are embedded in physical goods such as home appliances and automobiles.
- Information is transformed into a commodity.
- Knowledge is codified.
- Work and production are organized in new and innovative ways.

The term *digital economy* also refers to the convergence of computing and communications technologies on the Internet and other networks and the resulting flow of information and technology that is stimulating EC and vast organizational changes. This convergence enables all types of information (data, audio, video, etc.) to be stored, processed, and transmitted over networks to many destinations worldwide.

The digital economy is creating an economic revolution (see Chapter 14 and Shaw 2006), as was evidenced by the unprecedented economic performance and the longest period of uninterrupted economic expansion in U.S. history (1991–2000), combined with low inflation. Because of the growth of the Internet and its usage, hardware advances, progress in communications capabilities (e.g., VoIP, worldwide broadband adoption), advanced usage of digital media (e.g., Internet video, blogs, and wikis), and IT spending for better productivity, the future of the digital economy is looking promising.

Exhibit 1.5 describes the major characteristics of the digital economy. The digital revolution accelerates EC mainly by providing competitive advantage to organizations (Shaw 2006). A framework for understanding the business trends, emerging opportunities, and barriers to overcome with regards to the rapid developments that are taking place in the digital economy and EC can be found in Shaw (2006).

The digital revolution also enables many innovations, and new ones appear almost daily (e.g., see the Google case in Online File W1.4). The digital revolution provides the necessary technologies for EC and creates major changes in the business environment, as described in Section 1.5.

THE DIGITAL ENTERPRISE

digital enterprise

A new business model that uses IT in a fundamental way to accomplish one or more of three basic objectives: reach and engage customers more effectively, boost employee productivity, and improve operating efficiency. It uses converged communication and computing technology in a way that improves business processes.

The term *digital enterprise* has a number of definitions. It usually refers to an enterprise, such as Dell, Amazon.com, Google, or Ticketmaster, that uses computers and information systems to automate most of its business processes. The **digital enterprise** is a new business

EXHIBIT 1.5	**Major Characteristics of the Digital Economy**
Area	**Description**
Globalization	Global communication and collaboration; global electronic marketplaces and competition.
Digital system	From TV to telephones and instrumentation, analog systems are being converted to digital ones.
Speed	A move to real-time transactions, thanks to digitized documents, products, and services. Many business processes are expedited by 90 percent or more.
Information overload and intelligent search	Although the amount of information generated is accelerating, intelligent search tools can help users find what they need.
Markets	Markets are moving online. Physical marketplaces are being replaced by electronic markets; new markets are being created, increasing competition.
Digitization	Music, books, pictures, videos, and more (see Chapter 2) are digitized for fast and inexpensive distribution.
Business models and processes	New and improved business models and processes provide opportunities to new companies and industries. Cyberintermediation and no intermediation are on the rise.
Innovation	Digital and Internet-based innovations continue at a rapid pace. More patents are being granted than ever before.
Obsolescence	The fast pace of innovation creates a high rate of obsolescence.
Opportunities	Opportunities abound in almost all aspects of life and operations.
Fraud	Criminals employ a slew of innovative schemes on the Internet. Cybercons are everywhere.
Wars	Conventional wars are changing the cyberwars.
Organizations	Organizations are moving to digital enterprises.

model that uses IT in a fundamental way to accomplish one or more of three basic objectives: (1) reach and engage customers more effectively, (2) boost employee productivity, and (3) improve operating efficiency. It uses converged communication and computing technology in a way that improves business processes. The major characteristics of a digital enterprise are provided in Exhibit 1.6, where they are compared with those of a traditional enterprise.

The digital enterprise shifts the focus from managing individual information resources—devices, applications, and datasets—to orchestrating the services and workflows that define the business and ultimately deliver optimal value to customers and end users.

A digital enterprise uses networks of computers to facilitate the following:

▶ All internal communication is done via an intranet, which is the counterpart of the Internet inside the company.

▶ All business partners are reached via the Internet, or via a secured Internet, called an extranet, or via value-added private communication lines.

The vast majority of EC is done on computers connected to these networks. Many companies employ a **corporate portal**, which is a gateway for customers, employees, and partners to reach corporate information and to communicate with the company. The enterprise of the future will be the *digital enterprise*, according to an IBM study (2008). For additional details, see Chapter 6 and en.wikipedia.org/wiki/corporate_portal.

The major concern of many companies today is how to transform themselves into digital enterprises so that they can take part in the digital economy. For example, Harrington (2006)

corporate portal
A major gateway through which employees, business partners, and the public can enter a corporate Web site.

EXHIBIT 1.6   The Digital Versus Brick-and-Mortar Company

Brick-and-Mortar Organizations	Digital Organizations (Enterprises)
Selling in physical stores	Selling online
Selling tangible goods	Selling digital goods as well
Internal inventory/production planning	Online collaborative inventory forecasting
Paper catalogs	Smart electronic catalogs
Physical marketplace	Electronic marketplace
Use of telephone, fax, VANs, and traditional EDI	Use of computers, smartphones, the Internet, and extranets
Physical auctions, infrequently	Online auctions, everywhere, any time
Broker-based services, transactions	Electronic infomediaries, value-added services
Paper-based billing	Electronic billing
Paper-based tendering	Electronic tendering (reverse auctions)
Push production, starting with demand forecasting	Pull production, starting with an order (build-to-order)
Mass production (standard products)	Mass customization, build-to-order
Physical-based commission marketing	Affiliated, virtual marketing
Word-of-mouth, slow and limited advertisement	Explosive viral marketing, in particular in social networks
Linear supply chains	Hub-based supply chains
Large amount of capital needed for mass production	Less capital needed for build-to-order; payments can be collected before production starts
Large fixed cost required for plant operation	Small fixed cost required for plant operation
Customers' value proposition is frequently a mismatch (cost > value)	Perfect match of customers' value proposition (cost <= value)

describes why and how, as a CEO, he transformed the Thomson Corp. from a traditional $8 billion publishing business into an electronic information services provider and publisher for professionals in targeted markets. In 5 years, revenue increased over 20 percent and profit increased by more than 65 percent. For more on transformation to the digital economy, see Chapter 15 and Shaw (2006). If a transformation is successful, many companies will reach the status of our hypothetical toy company shown in Exhibit 1.7, which uses the Internet, intranets, and extranets in an integrated manner to conduct various EC and IT activities.

It may take 5 to 10 years for companies to become fully digitized like the hypothetical Toys, Inc. Major companies such as Schwab, IBM, Intel, and General Electric are moving rapidly toward such a state.

The term *enterprise* refers to any kind of organization, small or large. An enterprise can be a manufacturing plant, a hospital, a university, or even a city. They are all moving toward being digitized.

Example. In preparation for hearings on whether nuclear waste should be buried in the Yucca Mountains in Nevada, the Nuclear Regulatory Commission (NRC) has spent $6.2 million building the courtrooms in Nevada and Maryland (the commission's headquarters). The NRC is using voice-activated videoconferencing, digital video recorders, computer terminals on each desk (e.g., for viewing exhibits), flat-panel video monitors on the walls (for videoconferencing between the two locations), and searchable transcripts of the proceedings (to assist the judges and the lawyers). The hearings commenced in mid-2008. A diagram of the digital courtroom is shown in Exhibit 1.8.

THE DIGITAL SOCIETY

The final, and perhaps most important, element of the *digital world* is people and the way they live and interact. Clearly, the digital society has changed contemporary life with regard to almost any activity we can think of—work, play, shopping, entertainment, travel, medical care, education, and much more. Almost every day new digital applications are developed. Just think about your digital camera, your digital TV, your digital car, and

EXHIBIT 1.7 — The Digital Enterprise: How a Company Uses the Internet, Intranets, and Extranets

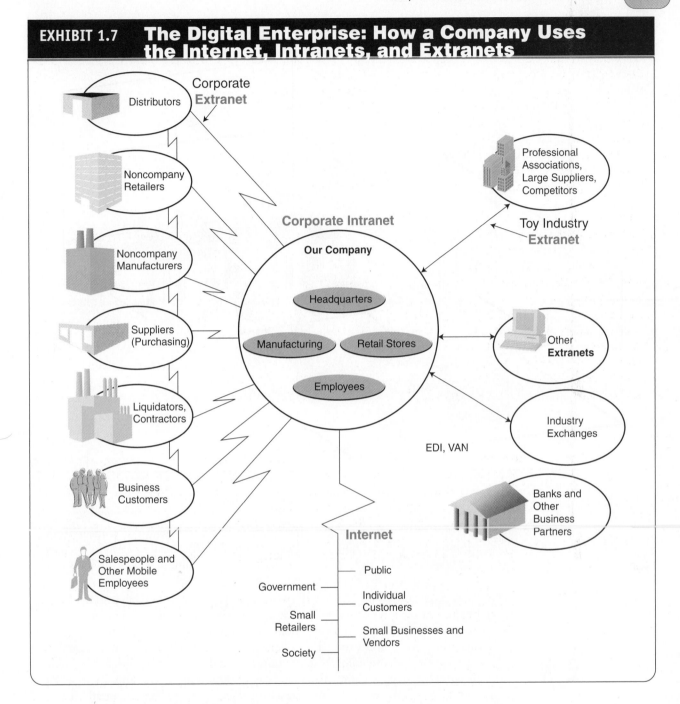

almost anything else. It is only natural that people are utilizing EC at an accelerating rate. Let's take a look at some examples:

▶ Kaboodle.com makes it easy to shop online with friends. You can share recommendations and discover new products and services from your community friends. Shopping at Kaboodle can be fun. You can discover many useful things from people with similar tastes and styles and discuss with them certain vendors and products. You can even simplify your life with a wish list.

▶ In 2008, high-school girls were able to solicit feedback from their friends regarding 70 different prom dresses that were displayed by Sears on Facebook. This enabled Sears to extend the shopping experience into the social sphere.

EXHIBIT 1.8   Futuristic Digital Courtroom

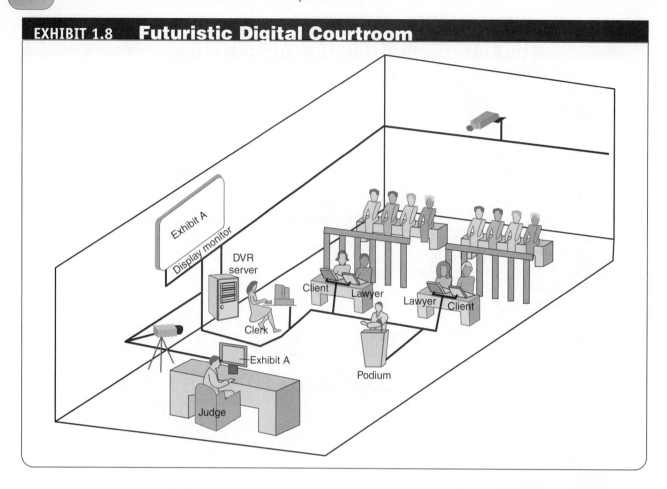

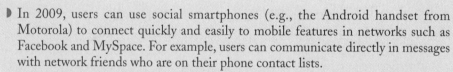

- In 2009, users can use social smartphones (e.g., the Android handset from Motorola) to connect quickly and easily to mobile features in networks such as Facebook and MySpace. For example, users can communicate directly in messages with network friends who are on their phone contact lists.

- According to Farivar (2004), VIP patrons of the Baja Beach Club in Barcelona, Spain, can have RFID chips, which are the size of a grain of rice, implanted into their upper arms, allowing them to charge drinks to a bar tab when they raise their arm toward the RFID reader. The RFID is a tiny tag that contains a processor and antenna; it can communicate wirelessly with a detecting unit in a reader over a short distance (see Online File W1.1 and Leobbecke 2006) "You don't call someone crazy for getting a tattoo," says Conrad Chase, director of Baja Beach Clubs International. "Why would they be crazy for getting this?"

- Dryers and washers in college dorms are hooked to the Web. Students can punch a code into their cell phones or sign in at esuds.net and check the availability of laundry machines. Furthermore, they can receive e-mail alerts when their wash and dry cycles are complete. Once in the laundry room, a student activates the system by swiping a student ID card or keying in a PIN number. The system automatically injects premeasured amounts of detergent and fabric softener, at the right cycle time.

- Using his blog site (oneredpaperclip.blogspot.com), Kyle MacDonald of Canada was able to trade a red paper clip into a three-bedroom house. He started by advertising in the barter section of craigslist.com that he wanted something bigger or better for one red paper clip. In the first iteration, he received a fish-shaped pen, and he posted on Craigslist again and again. Following many iterations and publicity on TV, after one year, received a house (see Chapter 17 for details).

▶ Camera-equipped cell phones are used in Finland as health and fitness advisors. A supermarket shopper using the technology can snap an image of the bar code on a packet of food. The phone forwards the code number to a central computer, which sends back information on the item's ingredients and nutritional value. The computer also calculates how much exercise the shopper will have to do to burn off the calories based on the shopper's height, weight, age, and other factors.

▶ Doggyspace.com allows dog lovers from around the globe to come together. You can build a page and a profile and post a video or photos to show off your dog, creating a social experience around the pets you care about. The site offers medical and other advice. Like in any other social network, people can create groups of friends with whom you share your doggy experiences.

▶ A remote medical monitoring system can help with early diagnosis of heart failure. A person stands on a special bathroom scale that can wirelessly transmit data to a clinician's screen. A computer analyzes the weight change and triggers an alarm for a suspected anomaly that predicts possible trouble. The medical technician then calls the person to discuss medication, the need to see a doctor, and so forth. The system keeps patients healthier and cuts health care costs.

▶ Similar remote monitoring devices are used to treat children with asthma, adults with mental disorders, patients with diabetes, and more. Some systems allow for real-time audio and video consultation with a physician. A unique system sells an electronic pill box that records whether and when patients take their medicine. Interested? Try Health Buddy from Health Hero Network (hhn.com) and visit the eWeek Health Care Center (eweek.com/c/s/Health-Care-IT) for the latest news, views, and analysis of technology's impact on health care.

▶ Online dating and matching services are becoming more popular. Companies such as eHarmony, Match.com, JDate, and Yahoo! Personal, are leading hundreds of other companies worldwide that are making matches. For example, Match.com has begun offering free profile and photo tips via an online video with Jay Manuel, of the television show *America's Next Top Model*. The company also sells services for $2 to $6 a month that offer advice on dating and ways to make profiles and photographs stand out.

Match.com views online dating as the candidates being on stage and being viewed by thousands of prospects. It suggests spending some time backstage getting ready. Several companies can help you to get ready, mostly for free (e.g., dating-profile.com and e-cyrano.com).

▶ Bicycle computers (by Bridgestone Cycle Co.) can automatically keep track of your travel distance, speed, time, and calorie consumption. Travel data are stored for 30 days, and you can transmit it to your computer. A community Web site allows you to share experiences. You can also find people to ride around the world with. Interested? See emeters.jp/try.html.

Additional examples of the digital world in everyday life are provided in Online File W1.7.

One of the most interesting phenomena of the digital society is the changes in the way that politicians interact with the public. This topic will be discussed in Chapter 7. However, as an example, note the extensive use of EC made by President Barack Obama. For example, Obama purchased Internet ads featured in 18 videogames through Microsoft's Xbox Live Service. His objective was to target young adult males, who are difficult to reach through traditional campaign advertising. For other innovative and pioneering EC initiatives used by President Obama, see Online File W1.8. It is estimated that these activities netted him at least 2 percent of the vote. Some claim that without such tactics Obama would have lost the election (Needle 2008).

Section 1.4 ▶ REVIEW QUESTIONS

1. Define the digital revolution and list its components.
2. List the characteristics of the digital economy.
3. Define a digital enterprise.
4. Compare traditional and digital enterprises.
5. Describe the digital society.
6. Visit doggyspace.com and dogtoys.com. Compare the two sites and relate their contents to the digital society.

1.5 ELECTRONIC COMMERCE DRIVERS AND THE CHANGING BUSINESS ENVIRONMENT

EC is driven by many technological, economic, and social factors. These are frequently related to global competition and rapid changes in the business environment.

THE DRIVERS OF EC AND ITS GROWTH

EC initiatives play an increasing role in supporting innovations and strategies that help companies to compete and flourish, especially companies that want to introduce changes rather than respond to them. What makes EC suitable for such a role is a *set of capabilities* and *developments*; the major capabilities and developments are summarized in Exhibit 1.9.

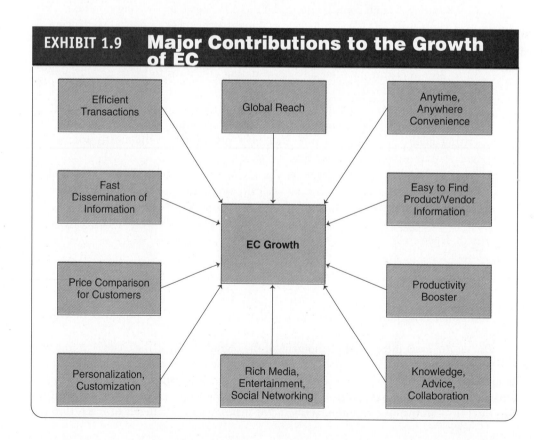

EXHIBIT 1.9 Major Contributions to the Growth of EC

The essentials of the capabilities that drive EC are the ability to:

- Provide efficient and effective business transactions.
- Provide global reach for selling, buying, or finding business partners.
- Conduct business anytime, from anywhere, in a convenient way. For example, there are more than 250 million wireless subscribers in the United States (Burns 2007).
- Disseminate information rapidly, frequently in real time (e.g., the Beijing Olympics).
- Compare prices.
- Customize products and personalize services.
- Use rich media in advertisement, entertainment, and social networking.
- Receive experts' and other users' advice quickly.
- Collaborate in different ways, both internally and externally.
- Share information and knowledge.
- Increase productivity and performance, reduce costs, and compress time (e.g., by having smarter applications).
- Easily and quickly find information about both vendors, products, and competitors.

Because EC technology is improving over time and decreasing in cost, its comparative advantage is increasing, further contributing to the growth of EC. EC growth is related to the changing business environment.

The Changing Business Environment

Economic, legal, societal, and technological factors have created a highly competitive business environment in which customers are becoming more powerful. These environmental factors can change quickly, vigorously, and sometimes in an unpredictable manner. Companies need to react quickly to both the problems and the opportunities resulting from this new business environment.

Because the pace of change and the level of uncertainty are expected to accelerate, organizations are operating under increasing pressures to produce more products, faster, and with fewer resources. For example, the financial/economic crisis of 2008–2009 has resulted in many companies going out of business or being acquired by other companies. It has also presented the opportunity for large banks to buy even larger ones. These business environment changes impact the manner in which companies operate, and many firms have restructured themselves and their information systems, as well as their EC model.

The new business environment is a result of advances in science and technology occurring at an accelerated rate. These advances create scientific knowledge that feeds on itself, resulting in more and more technology. The rapid growth in technology results in a large variety of more complex systems. As a result, the business environment has the following characteristics: a more turbulent environment, with more business problems and opportunities; stronger competition; the need for organizations to make decisions more frequently, either by expediting the decision process or by having more decision makers; a larger scope for decisions, because more factors (market, competition, political issues, and global environment) need to be considered; and more information and/or knowledge is needed for making decisions. Globalization is playing an even larger role in the environmental changes. Let's see how all of these impact organizational performance.

PERFORMANCE, BUSINESS PRESSURES, AND ORGANIZATIONAL RESPONSES

Most people, sports teams, and organizations are trying to improve their *performance*. For some, it is a challenge; for others, it is a requirement for survival. Yet for others it is the key to improved life, profitability, or reputation.

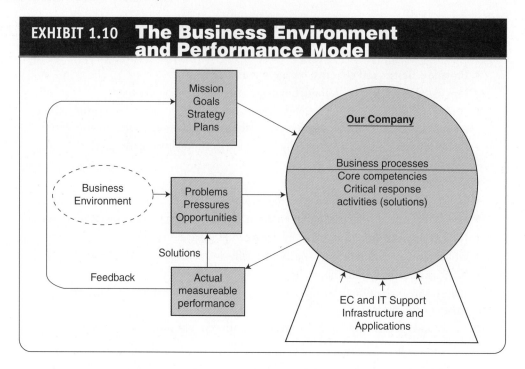

EXHIBIT 1.10   The Business Environment and Performance Model

Most organizations measure their performance periodically, comparing it to some metrics and to the organization's mission, objectives, and plans. Unfortunately, in business, performance often depends not only on what you do but also on what others are doing, as well as on forces of nature. In the business world, we refer to such events, in totality, as the *business environment*. Such an environment may create significant pressures that can impact performance in uncontrollable, or sometimes even in unpredictable, ways.

The Business Environment and Performance Impact Model

The model shown in Exhibit 1.10 illustrates how the business environment (left) creates pressures, problems, and opportunities that drive what organizations are doing in their business processes (the "our company" box). Other drivers are the organization's mission, goals, strategy, and plans. Business processes include competencies, activities, and responses to the environmental pressures that we call *critical response activities* or *solutions*. The business processes and activities result in measurable performance, which provides solutions to problems/opportunities, as well as feedback as to the attainment of the mission, strategy, goals, and plans.

Notice that in the exhibit EC and IT provide support to organizations' activities and to the resultant performance, countering the business pressures. We will demonstrate this cyclical process throughout the book. Now, let's examine the two major components of the model: business pressures and organizational responses.

Business Pressures

In this text, business pressures are divided into the following categories: market (economic), societal, and technological. The main types of business pressures in each category are listed in Exhibit 1.11. (Note that some of the business environment conditions create opportunities.)

Organizational Response Strategies

How can organizations operate in such an environment? How can they deal with the threats and the opportunities? To begin with, many traditional strategies are still useful in today's environment. However, because some traditional response activities may *not* work in today's turbulent and competitive business environment, many of the old solutions need to be modified, supplemented, or discarded. Alternatively, new responses can be devised. Critical response activities can take place in some or all organizational processes, from the daily processing of payroll and order entry to strategic activities such as the acquisition of a company. Responses can also occur in the supply chain, as demonstrated by the cases of Boeing (Online File W1.3), and Dell (Online File W1.2). A response activity can be a reaction to a specific pressure already

EXHIBIT 1.11 Major Business Pressures

Market and Economic Pressures	Societal Pressures	Technological Pressures
Strong competition	Changing nature of workforce	Increasing innovations and new technologies
Global economy	Government deregulation, leading to more competition	Rapid technological obsolescence
Regional trade agreements (e.g., NAFTA)	Compliance (e.g., Sarbanes-Oxley Act)	Increases in information overload
Extremely low labor costs in some countries	Shrinking government subsidies	Rapid decline in technology cost versus labor cost (technology becomes more and more attractive)
Frequent and significant changes in markets	Increased importance of ethical and legal issues	
Increased power of consumer	Increased societal responsibility of organizations	
Political and governmental	Rapid political changes	
	Terrorism	

in existence, or it can be an initiative that will defend an organization against future pressures. It can also be an activity that exploits an opportunity created by changing conditions.

Many response activities can be greatly facilitated by EC, and this fuels the growth of the field. In some cases, EC is the *only* solution to certain business pressures. Representative EC-supported response activities are provided in Exhibit 1.12 and in Online File W1.9.

EXHIBIT 1.12 Innovative Organizational Responses

Response Strategy	Descriptions
Strategic systems	Improve strategic advantage in industry.
Agile systems	Increase ability to adapt to changes and flexibility.
Continuous improvements and business process management	Using enterprise systems improve business processes. Introduce e-procurement.
Customer relationship management	Introduce programs to improve customer relationships using the Internet and EC models.
Business alliances and Partner Relationship Management (PRM)	Create joint ventures, partnerships, e-collaboration, virtual corporations, and others for win-win situations—even with competitors (see Online File W1.3).
Electronic markets	Use both private and public electronic markets to increase efficiency and effectiveness.
Cycle time reduction	Increase speed of operation and reduce time-to-market.
Empowering employees, especially at the front line (interacting with customers, partners)	Provide employees with computerized decision aids so they can make quick decisions on their own (see Davenport 2006).
Mass customization in a build-to-order system	Produce customized products (services), rapidly at reasonable cost to many, many customers (mass) as Dell does.
Intrabusiness use of automation	Many intrabusiness activities, from sales force automation to inventory management can be improved with e-commerce and m-commerce.
Knowledge management	Appropriate creation, storage, and dissemination of knowledge using electronic systems, increases productivity, agility, and competitiveness.
Customer selection, loyalty, and service	Identify customers with the greatest profit potential; increase likelihood that they will want the product or service offering; retain their loyalty.
Human capital	Select the best employees for particular tasks or jobs, at particular compensation levels.
Product and service quality	Detect quality problems early and minimize them.
Financial performance	Better understand the drivers of financial performance and the effects of nonfinancial factors.
Research and development	Improve quality, efficacy, and where applicable, safety of products and services.
Social networking	Innovative marketing, advertising, collaboration, and innovation using the power of the crowd.

1. List five of the major drivers of EC

2. List the components of the business environment impact model and explain the model.

3. List the major factors in today's business environment.

4. List some of the major response activities taken by organizations (consult Exhibit 1.12).

1.6 ELECTRONIC COMMERCE BUSINESS MODELS

business model

A method of doing business by which a company can generate revenue to sustain itself.

One of the major characteristics of EC is that it enables the creation of new business models (Prahahalad and Krishnan 2008). A **business model** is a method of doing business by which a company can generate revenue to sustain itself. The model also spells out where the company is positioned in the value chain; that is, by what activities the company adds value to the product or service it supplies. (The *value chain* is the series of value-adding activities that an organization performs to achieve its goals, such as making profit, at various stages of the production process.) One company may have several business models. Some models are very simple. For example, Wal-Mart buys merchandise, sells it, and generates a profit. In contrast, a TV station provides free broadcasting to its viewers. The station's survival depends on a complex model involving advertisers and content providers. Public Internet portals, such as Yahoo!, also use a complex business model.

Business models are a subset of a business plan or a business case. These concepts frequently are confused. (In other words, some equate a business model with a business plan.) However, as Chapter 13 and Online Tutorial T1 explain, business plans and cases differ from business models (also see Lee et al. 2006 and Currie 2004).

THE STRUCTURE AND PROPERTIES OF BUSINESS MODELS

Several different EC business models are possible, depending on the company, the industry, and so on.

A comprehensive business model is composed of the following elements:

▶ A description of the *customers* to be served and the company's relationships with these customers, including what constitutes value from the customers' perspective (*customers' value proposition*).

▶ A description of all *products* and *services* the business will offer and the markets in which they will be sold.

▶ A description of the *business process* required to make and deliver the products and services including distribution and marketing strategies.

▶ A list of the *resources* required and the identification of which ones are available, which will be developed in house, and which will need to be acquired (including human resources).

▶ A description of the organization's *supply chain*, including *suppliers* and other *business partners*.

▶ A list of the major competitors, their market share, and strengths/weaknesses.

▶ The competitive advantage offered by the business model.

▶ The anticipated organizational changes and any resistance to change.

▶ A description of the revenues expected (*revenue model*), anticipated costs, sources of financing, and estimated profitability (*financial viability*).

Models also include a *value proposition*, which is an analysis of the benefits of using the specific model (tangible and intangible), including the customers' value proposition cited earlier. A detailed discussion of and examples of business models and their relationship to business plans is presented in the Online Tutorial. For a list of components and key issues of EC business models, see Lee et al. (2006).

This chapter presents two of the models' elements that are needed to understand the material in Chapters 2 through 18: revenue models and value propositions.

Revenue Models

A revenue model outlines how the organization, or the EC project, will generate revenue. For example, the revenue model for Godiva's online EC initiative shows revenue from online sales. The major revenue models are:

> **Sales.** Companies generate revenue from selling merchandise or services over their Web sites. An example is when Wal-Mart, Amazon.com, or Godiva sells a product online.

> **Transaction fees.** A company receives a commission based on the volume of transactions made. For example, when a homeowner sells a house, he or she typically pays a transaction fee to the broker. The higher the value of the sale, the higher the total transaction fee. Alternatively, transaction fees can be levied *per transaction*. With online stock trades, for example, there is usually a fixed fee per trade, regardless of the volume.

> **Subscription fees.** Customers pay a fixed amount, usually monthly, to get some type of service. An example would be the access fee for AOL. Thus, AOL's primary revenue model is subscription (fixed monthly payments).

> **Advertising fees.** Companies charge others for allowing them to place a banner on their sites. This is how Google has made its fortune (see Chapter 4).

> **Affiliate fees.** Companies receive commissions for referring customers to others' Web sites.

> **Other revenue sources.** Some companies allow people to play games for a fee or to watch a sports competition in real time for a fee (e.g., see espn.go.com). Another revenue source is licensing fees (e.g., datadirect-technologies.com). Licensing fees can be assessed as an annual fee or a per usage fee. Microsoft takes fees from each workstation that uses Windows NT, for example.

A company uses its *revenue model* to describe how it will generate revenue and its *business model* to describe the *process* it will use to do so. Exhibit 1.13 summarizes five common revenue models.

The revenue model can be part of the value proposition or it may complement it.

Innovative revenue models for individuals. The Internet allows for innovative revenue models, some of which can be utilized even by individuals, as demonstrated by the following two examples.

Example 1: Buy low–sell high.   This strategy has been known for generations, but now you have a real chance. How about buying stuff cheap on Craigslist (or other online classified site) and resell it for a 50 to 200 percent profit on eBay! Try it, you might make money. Some people make it even bigger. The person who bought the domain name pizza.com for $20 in 1994 sold it for $2.6 million in April 2008.

Example 2: Traffic arbitrage.   This is a more complex implementation of buy low-sell high. The process is illustrated in Exhibit 1.14. Basically, you buy ad space on less expensive search engines (such as Microsoft's Ad Center). The search engine then directs traffic to your Web site via key words. Then you fill your personal Web site with Google's ads (see Chapter 4 for AdSense). When users come to your Web site and click on Google's ads, they are then directed to advertisers' Web sites. The advertisers pay Google for the referrals, and Google shares the fees with you.

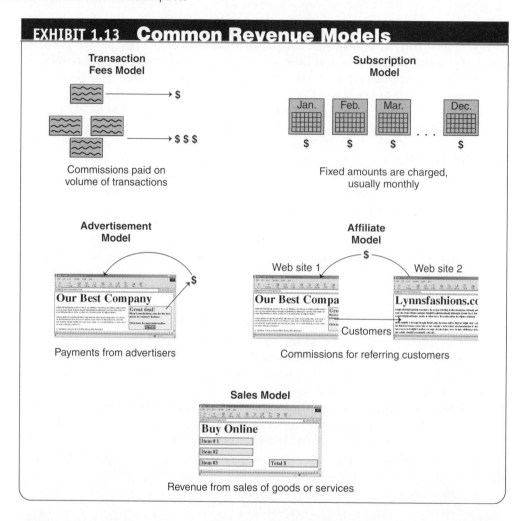

EXHIBIT 1.13 Common Revenue Models

Transaction Fees Model

Commissions paid on volume of transactions

Subscription Model

Jan. Feb. Mar. . . . Dec.

Fixed amounts are charged, usually monthly

Advertisement Model

Our Best Company

Payments from advertisers

Affiliate Model

Web site 1   Web site 2

Our Best Compa   Lynnsfashions.c

Customers

Commissions for referring customers

Sales Model

Buy Online

Item #1
Item #2
Item #3   Total $

Revenue from sales of goods or services

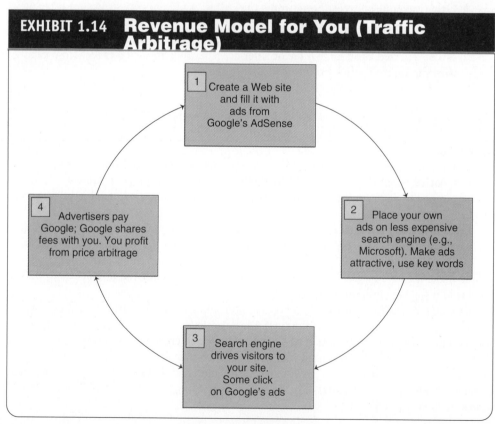

EXHIBIT 1.14 Revenue Model for You (Traffic Arbitrage)

1 Create a Web site and fill it with ads from Google's AdSense

2 Place your own ads on less expensive search engine (e.g., Microsoft). Make ads attractive, use key words

3 Search engine drives visitors to your site. Some click on Google's ads

4 Advertisers pay Google; Google shares fees with you. You profit from price arbitrage

Value Proposition

Business models also include a value-proposition statement. A **value proposition** refers to the benefits, including the intangible, nonquantitative ones, that a company can derive from using the model. In B2C EC, for example, a value proposition defines how a company's product or service fulfills the needs of customers. The *value proposition* is an important part of the marketing plan of any product or service.

Specifically, how do e-marketplaces create value? Amit and Zott (2001) identify four sets of values that are created by e-business: search and transaction cost-efficiency, complementarities, lock-in, and novelty. *Search and transaction cost-efficiency* enables faster and more informed decision making, wider product and service selection, and greater economies of scale—cost savings per unit as greater quantities are produced and sold (e.g., through demand and supply aggregation for small buyers and sellers). *Complementarities* involve bundling some goods and services together to provide more value than from offering them separately. Lock-in is attributable to the high switching cost that ties customers to particular suppliers. *Novelty* creates value through innovative ways for structuring transactions, connecting partners, and fostering new markets.

value proposition
The benefits a company can derive from using EC.

Functions of a Business Model

Business models have the following functions or objectives:

> ▶ Describe the major business processes of a company.
>
> ▶ Describe the business model's (the venture's) positioning within the value network linking suppliers and customers (includes identification of potential complementors and competitors). Also, describe the supply and value chains.
>
> ▶ Formulate the venture's competitive strategy and its long-range plans.
>
> ▶ Articulate a customer value proposition.
>
> ▶ Identify a market segment (who will use the technology for what purpose; specify the revenue-generation process; where the company will operate).
>
> ▶ Define the venture's specific value chain structure.
>
> ▶ Estimate the cost structure and profit potential.

TYPICAL EC BUSINESS MODELS

There are many types of EC business models. Examples and details of EC business models can be found throughout this text, in Rappa (2008), and Currie (2004). The following are the five most common models. Additional models are listed in Online File W1.10.

1. **Online direct marketing.** The most obvious model is that of selling products or services online. Sales may be from a *manufacturer* to a customer, eliminating intermediaries or physical stores (e.g., Godiva), or from *retailers* to consumers, making distribution more efficient (e.g., Wal-Mart). This model is especially efficient for digitizable products and services (those that can be delivered electronically). This model has several variations (see Chapters 3 and 5) and it uses different mechanisms (e.g., auctions, discussed in Chapter 17). It is practiced in B2C (where it is called *e-tailing*) and in some B2B types of EC.

2. **Electronic tendering systems.** Large organizational buyers, private or public, usually make large-volume or large-value purchases through a **tendering (bidding) system**, also known as a *reverse auction*. Such tendering can be done online, saving time and money. Pioneered by General Electric Corp., e-tendering systems are gaining popularity. Indeed, several government agencies mandate that most of their procurement must be done through e-tendering (see Chapter 5).

3. **Electronic marketplaces and exchanges.** Electronic marketplaces existed in isolated applications for decades (e.g., stock and commodities exchanges). But as of 1996, hundreds of e-marketplaces (old and new) have introduced new efficiencies to the trading process. If they are well organized and managed, e-marketplaces can provide significant benefits to both

tendering (bidding) system
Model in which a buyer requests would-be sellers to submit bids; the lowest bidder wins.

buyers and sellers. Of special interest are vertical marketplaces that concentrate on one industry (e.g., gnx.com for the retail industry and chemconnect.com for the chemical industry).

4. **Viral marketing.** According to the viral marketing model (see Chapter 4), an organization can increase brand awareness or even generate sales by inducing people to send influencing messages to other people or to recruit friends to join certain programs. It is basically Web-based *word-of-mouth* advertising, and it is popular in social networks.

5. **Social networking and Web 2.0 tools.** Many companies are deriving commercial benefits from social networking (Chapter 9) and Web 2.0 tools (see Chapter 2).

Section 1.6 ❱ REVIEW QUESTIONS

1. What is a business model? Describe its functions and properties.

2. Describe a revenue model and a value proposition.

3. Describe the following business models: direct marketing, tendering system, electronic exchanges, viral marketing, and social networking.

4. Identify business models related to buying and those related to selling.

1.7 THE BENEFITS, LIMITATIONS, AND IMPACTS OF ELECTRONIC COMMERCE

Few innovations in human history encompass as many benefits as EC does. The global nature of the technology, the opportunity to reach hundreds of millions of people, its interactive nature, the variety of possibilities for its use, and the resourcefulness and rapid growth of its supporting infrastructures, especially the Web, result in many potential benefits to organizations, individuals, and society. These benefits are just starting to materialize, but they will increase significantly as EC expands. It is not surprising that some maintain that the EC revolution is as profound as the change that accompanied the Industrial Revolution.

THE BENEFITS AND IMPACTS OF EC

EC provides benefits to *organizations, individual customers,* and *society.* These benefits are summarized in Exhibit 1.15.

THE LIMITATIONS AND BARRIERS OF EC

Barriers to EC can be classified as either technological or nontechnological. The major barriers are summarized in Exhibit 1.16.

According to a 2006 study (Harmony Hollow Software 2006), the major barriers to EC are (1) resistance to new technology, (2) implementation difficulties, (3) security concerns, (4) lack of technology skills, (5) lack of potential customers, and (6) cost. Van Toorn et al. (2006) believe that the barriers are sectoral barriers (e.g., government, private sector, international organizations), internal barriers (e.g., security, lack of technical knowledge, and lack of time and resources), and external barriers (e.g., lack of government support). Van Toorn et al. (2006) also list the top barriers with regards to global EC: cultural differences, organizational differences, incompatible B2B interfaces, international trade barriers, and lack of standards.

Ethical Issues

ethics
The branch of philosophy that deals with what is considered to be right and wrong.

Ethical issues create pressures or constraints on business operations. **Ethics** relates to standards of right and wrong, and *information ethics* relates to standards of right and wrong in information technology and EC practices. Ethical issues have the power to damage the image of an organization and morale of employees. Ethics is a difficult area, because ethical issues are not cut-and-dried. What is considered ethical by one person may seem unethical to another. Likewise, what is considered ethical in one country may be unethical in another.

Implementing EC use may raise ethical issues ranging from employee e-mail monitoring to invasion of privacy of millions of customers whose data are stored in private and public databases. In implementing EC, it is necessary to pay attention to these issues and recognize that some of

EXHIBIT 1.15 Benefits of E-Commerce

Benefit	Description
Benefits to Organizations	
Global reach	Locating customers and/or suppliers worldwide, at reasonable cost and fast.
Cost reduction	Lower cost of information processing, storage, distribution.
Facilitate problem solving	Solve complex problems that have remained unsolved.
Supply chain improvements	Reduce delays, inventories, and cost.
Business always open	Open 24/7/365; no overtime or other costs.
Customization/personalization	Make it to consumers' wish, fast and at reasonable cost.
Seller's specialization (niche market)	Seller can specialize in a narrow field (e.g., dog toys), yet make money.
Ability to innovate, use new business models	Facilitate innovation and enable unique business models.
Rapid time-to-market and increased speed	Expedite processes; higher speed and productivity.
Lower communication costs	The Internet is cheaper then VAN private lines.
Efficient procurement	Saves time and reduces costs by enabling e-procurement.
Improved customer service and relationship	Direct interaction with customers, better CRM.
Fewer permits and less tax	May need fewer permits and be able to avoid sales tax.
Up-to-date company material	All distributed material is up-to-date.
Help SME to compete	EC may help small companies to compete against large ones by using special business models.
Lower inventories	Using customization inventories can be minimized.
Lower cost of distributing digitizable product	Delivery online can be 90 percent cheaper.
Provide competitive advantage	Innovative business models.
Benefits to Consumers	
Ubiquity	Can shop any time from any place.
More products/services	Large selection to choose from (vendor, products, styles).
Customized products/services	Can customize many products and/or services.
Cheaper products/services	Can compare and shop for lowest prices.
Instant delivery	Digitized products can be downloaded immediately upon payment.
Information availability	Easy finding what you need, with details, demos, etc.
Convenient auction participation	Do auctions any time and from any place.
No sales tax	Sometimes.
Enable telecommuting	Can work or study at home.
Electronic socialization	Can socialize online in communities yet be at home.
Find unique items	Using online auctions, collectible items can be found.
Benefits to Society	
Enable telecommuting	Facilitate work at home; less traffic, pollution.
More public services	Make education, health, etc., available for more people. Rural area can share benefits; more services for the poor.
Improved homeland security	Facilitate domestic security.
Increased standard of living	Can buy more and cheaper goods/services.
Close the digital divide	Allow people in developing countries and rural areas to accept more services and purchase what they really like.

them may limit, or even prohibit, the use of EC. An example of this can be seen in the attempted implementation of RFID tags in retail stores due to the potential invasion of buyers' privacy.

Despite these barriers, EC is expanding rapidly. As experience accumulates and technology improves, the cost-benefit ratio of EC will increase, resulting in even greater rates of EC adoption.

WHY STUDY E-COMMERCE?

The academic area of e-commerce started around 1995 with only a few courses and textbooks. Today, many universities offer complete programs in e-commerce or e-business

EXHIBIT 1.16   Limitations of Electronic Commerce

Technological Limitations	Nontechnological Limitations
Lack of universal standards for quality, security, and reliability.	Security and privacy concerns deter customers from buying.
The telecommunications bandwidth is insufficient, especially for m-commerce, videos, and graphics.	Lack of trust in EC and in unknown sellers hinders buying.
Software development tools are still evolving.	People do not yet sufficiently trust paperless, faceless transactions.
It is difficult to integrate Internet and EC software with some existing (especially legacy) applications and databases.	Many legal and public policy issues, including taxation, have not yet been resolved or are not clear.
Special Web servers are needed in addition to the network servers, which add to the cost of EC.	National and international government regulations sometimes get in the way.
Internet accessibility is still expensive and/or inconvenient.	It is difficult to measure some of the benefits of EC, such as online advertising. Mature measurement methodologies are not yet available.
Order fulfillment of large-scale B2C requires special automated warehouses.	Some customers like to feel and touch products. Also, customers are resistant to the change from shopping at a brick-and-mortar store to a virtual store.
	People do not yet sufficiently trust paperless, faceless transactions.
	In many cases, the number of sellers and buyers that are needed for profitable EC operations is insufficient.
	Online fraud is increasing.
	It is difficult to obtain venture capital due to the failure of many dot-coms.

(e.g., majors in e-commerce, minors in e-commerce and certificate programs; see University of Virginia, University of Maine). Recently, e-commerce topics have been integrated into all functional fields (e.g., Internet marketing, electronic financial markets). The reason for this proliferation is that e-commerce is penetrating more and more business areas, services, and governments. Although you will encounter EC in your specialty discipline, you will find that EC applications frequently cross departmental and organizational boundaries. Therefore, learning about EC from an enterprise perspective, in a comprehensive way, will help you understand complex business processes, such as order fulfillment, both in your classes and when working. This is provided for you in this book.

However, there are also some very tangible benefits to increased knowledge of EC. First, your chances of getting a good (or better) job are higher. The demand for both technical and managerial EC skills is growing rapidly, and so are the salaries (e.g., see salary comparison sites such as salary.com, cbsalary.com, monster.com). Second, your chances for promotion could be higher if you understand EC and know how to seize its opportunities. Finally, it gives you a chance to become a billionaire, like the founders of Google, Facebook, and Yahoo!, or to make lots of money on eBay (see Joyner 2007). Even if you are not so lucky you can still make good money in Second Life (see Alter 2008 and Rymaszewski et al. 2008) or simply by selling on eBay, Yahoo!, or your own Web site. And you can do it while you are a student, as Lily, Shu, and Adrian did (see Case 1.3).

Section 1.7 ❯ REVIEW QUESTIONS

1. Describe some EC benefits to organizations, individuals, and society.
2. List the major technological and nontechnological barriers and limitations to EC.
3. Describe some of the benefits of studying EC.

1.8   OVERVIEW OF THIS BOOK

This book is composed of 16 chapters and 2 online chapters, grouped into 7 parts, as shown in Exhibit 1.17. The seventh part, which comprises two chapters, is available at the text's Web site. Additional content, including a tutorial, a technical appendix, and online supplemental material for each chapter, is also available online at the book's Web site.

CASE 1.3
EC Application
HOW COLLEGE STUDENTS BECOME ENTREPRENEURS

U.S. students Lily Kim, Shu Lindsey, and Adrian Mak use computers and the Internet extensively. They also do extensive writing (on paper) and especially like using ultra thin pens with a tip half the width of the average ballpoint. They learned about these pens when they visited Japan. Because these pens were not available in U.S. stores, they purchased them online directly from Japan. When they showed the pens to their friends (an example of the power of social marketing), they found that there was great interest in such pens in the United States.

Sensing the opportunity, in 2004 they decided to use their $9,000 savings to open a business, called JetPens (*jetpens.com*), selling pens they imported from Japan to their classmates. To keep costs low, they used open source free software (from osCommerce) to build and run the store. Soon after they opened an online storefront, they began advertising their products via e-mail to other students. By January 2009, they had about 5,000 registered users. To meet the demand, they initially kept an inventory of pens in their bedrooms, but now they rent storage space.

They also have a small advertising budget for Google ads. By using smart key words, their store ranks at the top of search engine discoveries when a user searches for "Japanese pens" (try a Google search to verify). This strategy is called *site optimization* (Chapters 4 and 15).

In 2007, the owners expanded the product line by adding interesting office supplies, including a best-selling eraser with 28 corners, which increased their sales volume to over 10,000 items per month. Other best sellers include a pen with a tip fine enough to write on a grain of rice, the Uni-ball Alpha Gel ballpoint pen with a squishy silicon-gel grip (this silicon gel is famous for keeping an egg from breaking when dropped from 5 feet), colorful and erasable gel pens that work just as well as pencils, and BeGreen environmentally friendly pens. To find friends and customers, they use Facebook, Flickr, and YouTube and they have a forum on the JetPens Web site.

By keeping a tight cap on operating expenses and using Internet advertising successfully, the young entrepreneurs have been able to do what many others have failed to do—generate a profit within 2 years and grow by hundreds of percentage points every year.

Sources: Compiled from Blakely (2007) and *jetpens.com* (accessed October 2008).

Questions

1. Go to *jetpens.com* and examine the catalog. What impresses you the most?
2. Evaluate the site's ease of use.
3. Do you think that a business like this can succeed as an independent online-only store? Why or why not?
4. What is the purpose of the site's JetPress RSS Feed?

Source: Used with permission of jetpens.com.

EXHIBIT 1.17 **Plan of the Book**

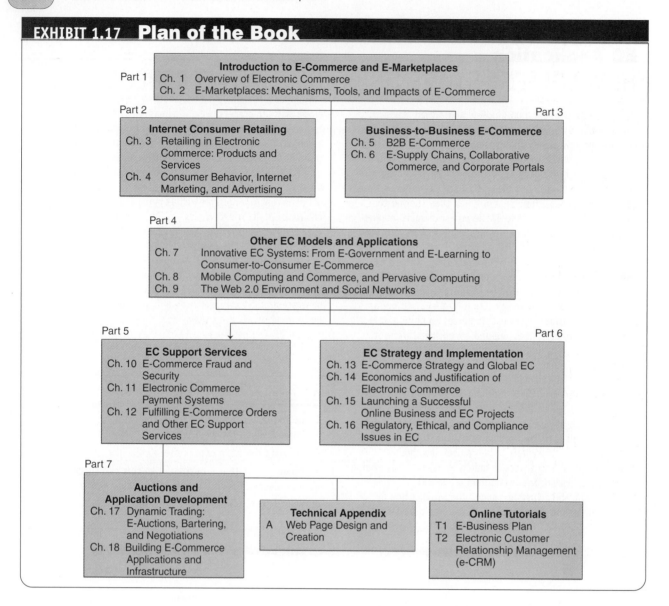

The specific parts and chapters of this textbook are as follows.

PART 1: INTRODUCTION TO E-COMMERCE AND E-MARKETPLACES

This section of the book includes an overview of EC and its content, benefits, limitations, and drivers, which are presented in Chapter 1. Chapter 2 presents electronic markets and their mechanisms, such as electronic catalogs and auctions. Chapter 2 also includes a presentation of Web 2.0 tools and mechanisms.

PART 2: INTERNET CONSUMER RETAILING

This section includes two chapters. Chapter 3 describes e-tailing (B2C), including some of its most innovative applications for selling products online. It also describes the delivery of services, such as online banking, travel, and insurance. Chapter 4 explains consumer behavior in cyberspace, online market research, and Internet advertising.

PART 3: BUSINESS-TO-BUSINESS E-COMMERCE

Part 3 is composed of two chapters. In Chapter 5, we introduce B2B EC and describe company-centric models (one buyer—many sellers, one seller—many buyers) as well as electronic exchanges (many buyers and many sellers). Chapter 6 examines e-supply chain topics, c-commerce, and corporate portals.

PART 4: OTHER EC MODELS AND APPLICATIONS

Several other EC models and applications are presented in Part 4. E-government, e-learning, C2C, and knowledge management are the major subjects of Chapter 7. In Chapter 8, we introduce the topics of mobile commerce. Finally, Chapter 9 examines social networking in the Web 2.0 environment.

PART 5: EC SUPPORT SERVICES

Part 5 examines issues involving the support services needed for EC applications. Chapter 10 delves into EC security. Of the many diverse Web support activities, we concentrate on three: payments (Chapter 11), CRM (Chapter 11), and order fulfillment (Chapter 12).

PART 6: EC STRATEGY AND IMPLEMENTATION

Part 6 includes four chapters on EC strategy and implementation. Chapter 13 examines e-strategy and planning, including going global and the impact of EC on small businesses. Chapter 14 deals with the economics of EC. Chapter 15 deals with creating, operating, and maintaining an Internet company. It also discusses initiating EC initiatives and creating EC content. Chapter 16 provides an examination of legal and societal issues in EC.

ONLINE PART 7: AUCTIONS AND APPLICATION DEVELOPMENT

Two additional complete chapters are available online at the book's Web site (pearsonglobaleditions.com/turban). Chapter 17 provides an overview of electronic auctions, and Chapter 18 addresses EC application development processes and methods, including the emerging topics of software as a service, Web Services, and service-oriented architecture (SOA).

ONLINE TUTORIALS

Online Tutorial T1 on business plans is available at the book's Web site (pearsonglobaleditions. com/turban).

Online Tutorial T2 on Electronic Customer Relationship Management is available on the book's Website (pearsonglobaleditions.com/turban).

ONLINE APPENDIX

A technical appendix on Web page design and creation is available at the book's Web site pearsonglobaleditions.com/turban.

ONLINE SUPPLEMENTS

A large number of Online Files organized by chapter number support the content of each chapter.

MANAGERIAL ISSUES

Many managerial issues are related to EC. These issues are discussed throughout the book and also are summarized in a separate section (like this one) near the end of each chapter. Some managerial issues related to this introductory chapter are as follows.

1. **Is it real?** For those not involved in EC, the first question that comes to mind is, "Is it real?" We believe that the answer is an emphatic "yes." The Internet is already an integral part of our lives. Banking from home, trading stocks online, and buying books from *Amazon.com* are now common practices for many people. The concern is not whether to start EC, but to what extent should it be developed and how to ensure the success of the e-business. Jack Welch, former CEO of General Electric, has commented, "Any company, old or new, that doesn't see this technology literally as important as breathing could be on its last breath" (McGee 2000).

2. **Why is B2B e-commerce so essential?** B2B EC is essential for several reasons. First, some B2B models are easier to implement than traditional off-line models. The value of transactions is larger in B2B, and the potential savings are larger and easier to justify in contrast to B2C, which has several major problems, ranging from channel conflict with existing distributors to a lack of a critical mass of buyers. Many companies can start B2B by simply buying from existing online stores and B2B exchanges or selling electronically by joining existing marketplaces or an auction house. The problem is determining where to buy or sell.

3. **What should be my business model?** Beginning in early 2000, the news was awash with stories about the failure of many dot-coms. Industry consolidation often occurs after a "gold rush." About 100 years ago, hundreds of U.S. companies tried to manufacture cars, following Ford Motor Company's success; only three survived. The important thing is to learn from the successes and failures of others, and discover the right business model for each endeavor. For lessons that can be learned from EC successes and failures, see Chapters 3, 5, and 15.

4. **How do we transform our organization into a digital one?** Once a company determines its strategy and decides to move to EC, it is necessary to plan how to implement the strategy. This process is described in Chapters 13 and 15. It is also discussed by Davenport et al. (2004) and at *digitalenterprise.org*.

5. **How should we evaluate the magnitude of business pressures and technological advancement?** A good approach is to solicit the expertise of research institutions, such as Gartner or Forrester Research, which specialize in EC. Otherwise, by the time you determine what is going on, it may be too late. The consulting arms of big certified public accounting companies may be of help too. (PricewaterhouseCoopers, Accenture, and others provide considerable EC information on their Web sites.) It is especially important for management to know what is going on in its own industry.

6. **How can we exploit social/business networking?** There are major possibilities here. Some companies even open their own social networks. Advertising is probably the first thing to consider. Recruiting can be a promising avenue as well. Offering discounted products and services should also be considered. Finally, the ultimate goal is associating the social network with commerce so that revenue is created.

7. **What should be my company's strategy toward EC?** In the early stage, a company needs to decide which part of the business should go online. Then the company should transform the traditional way of doing business to cooperate with the online business. This issue is revisited in Chapter 13, together with related issues such as the cost-benefit trade-offs of EC, integrating EC into the business, outsourcing, going global, and how SMEs can use EC. Another strategic issue is the prioritization of the many initiatives and applications available to a company.

8. **What are the top challenges of EC?** The top 10 technical issues for EC (in order of their importance) are security, adequate infrastructure, data access, back-end systems integration, sufficient bandwidth, network connectivity, up time, data warehousing and mining, scalability, and content distribution. The top 10 managerial issues for EC are budgets, project deadlines, keeping up with technology, privacy issues, the high cost of capital expenditures, unrealistic management expectations, training, reaching new customers, improving customer ordering services, and finding qualified EC employees. Most of these issues are discussed throughout this book.

SUMMARY

In this chapter, you learned about the following EC issues as they relate to the chapter's learning objectives.

1. **Definition of EC and description of its various categories.** EC involves conducting transactions electronically. Its major categories are pure versus partial EC, Internet versus non-Internet, and electronic markets versus interorganizational systems.

2. **The content and framework of EC.** The applications of EC, and there are many, are based on infrastructures and are supported by people; public policy and technical standards; marketing and advertising; support services, such as logistics, security, and payment services; and business partners—all tied together by management.

3. **The major types of EC transactions.** The major types of EC transactions are B2B, B2C, C2C, m-commerce, intrabusiness commerce, B2E, c-commerce, e-government, and e-learning.

4. **E-commerce 2.0.** This is the use of social computing in business, often through the use of Web 2.0 tools (such as blogs, wikis), as well as the emergence of enterprise social networking and commercial activities in virtual worlds. Social and business networks attract huge numbers of visitors. Many of the visitors are young (future EC customers). Therefore, advertisers are willing to spend money on advertising, either to an entire group or to individuals (e.g., using Google's technology).

5. **The elements of the digital world.** The major elements of the digital world are the digital economy, digital enterprises, and digital society. They are diversified and expanding rapidly.

6. **Drivers of EC.** EC is a major product of the digital and technological revolution, which enables companies to

simultaneously increase both growth and profits. This revolution enables digitization of products, services, and information. The business environment is changing rapidly due to technological breakthroughs, globalization, societal changes, deregulation, and more. The changing business environment forces organizations to respond. Many traditional responses may not be sufficient because of the magnitude of the pressures and the pace of the changes involved. Therefore, organizations must frequently innovate and reengineer their operations. In many cases, EC is driven by the needs of organizations to perform and even survive.

EC provides strategic advantage so organizations can compete better. Also, organizations can go into remote and global markets for both selling and buying at better prices. Organizations can speed time-to-market to gain competitive advantage. They can improve the internal and external supply chain as well as increase collaboration. Finally, they can better comply with government regulations.

7. **The major EC business models.** The major EC business models include online direct marketing, electronic tendering systems, name-your-own-price, affiliate marketing, viral marketing, group purchasing, online auctions, mass customization (make-to-order), electronic exchanges, supply chain improvers, finding the best price, value-chain integration, value-chain providers, information brokers, bartering, deep discounting, and membership.

8. **Benefits of EC to organizations, consumers, and society.** EC offers numerous benefits to all participants. Because these benefits are substantial, it looks as though EC is here to stay and cannot be ignored.

9. **Barriers to EC.** The barriers to EC can be categorized as technological and nontechnological. As time passes and network capacity, security, and accessibility continue to improve through technological innovations, the barriers posed by technological limitations will continue to diminish. Nontechnological barriers also will diminish over time, but some, especially the behavioral ones, may persist for many years in some organizations, cultures, or countries.

KEY TERMS

Brick-and-mortar (old economy) organizations	48	Corporate portal	63	Intrabusiness EC	51
Business-to-business (B2B)	51	Digital economy	62	Intranet	49
Business-to-business-to-consumer (B2B2C)	51	Digital enterprise	62	Intraorganizational information systems	48
		E-business	47		
Business-to-consumer (B2C)	51	E-government	53	Social computing	55
Business-to-employees (B2E)	51	E-learning	53	Social network	56
Business model	72	Electronic commerce (EC)	46	Social networking	57
Click-and-mortar (click-and-brick) organizations	48	Electronic market (e-marketplace)	48	Social network service (SNS)	57
		Enterprise-oriented networks	59	Tendering (bidding) system	75
Collaborative commerce (c-commerce)	52	E-tailing	51	Value proposition	75
		Ethics	76	Virtual (pure-play) organizations	48
Consumer-to-business (C2B)	51	Extranet	49	Virtual world	60
Consumer-to-consumer (C2C)	51	Interorganizational information systems (IOSs)	48	Web 2.0	55

QUESTIONS FOR DISCUSSION

1. Compare brick-and-mortar and click-and-mortar organizations.

2. Why is buying with a smart card from a vending machine considered EC?

3. Why is e-learning considered EC?

4. Why is it said that EC is a catalyst for fundamental changes in organizations?

5. How does EC facilitate customization of products and services? (Hint: see Online File W1.10.)

6. Discuss the relationships among the various components of a business model.

7. Explain how EC can reduce cycle time, improve employees' empowerment, and facilitate customer support.

8. Compare and contrast viral marketing with affiliate marketing. (Hint: see Online File W1.10.)

9. Explain how EC is related to supply chain management. (Hint: see Online File W1.10.)

10. Discuss the possibilities of commerce activities in social networks such as MySpace and Facebook.

11. Carefully examine the nontechnological limitations of EC. Which are company-dependent and which are generic?

12. Which of the EC limitations do you think will be more easily overcome—the technological or the nontechnological limitations? Why?

13. Why are virtual worlds such as Second Life related to EC?

14. Discuss how EC can cause business environment pressures (e.g., EC contributes to technological obsolescence).

15. Register at **ibm.com/enterpriseofthefuture** and download IBM's study "The Enterprise of the Future" (IBM 2008). In one page, summarize how the enterprise of the future differs from today's enterprise.

INTERNET EXERCISES

1. Visit **bigboxx.com** and identify the services the company provides to its customers. What type of EC is this? What business model(s) does Bigboxx use?

2. Visit **amazon.com** and locate recent information in the following areas:
   a. Find the five top-selling books on EC.
   b. Find a review of one of these books.
   c. Review the customer services you can get from Amazon.com and describe the benefits you receive from shopping there.
   d. Review the products directory.

3. Visit **priceline.com** and identify the various business models used by Priceline.com.

4. Enter **olympic-network.net** and **socialmediaportal.com** and find entries related to the Beijing Olympic's use of e-commerce. Prepare a report.

5. Go to **ups.com** and find information about recent EC projects that are related to logistics and supply chain management. How is UPS using wireless services?

6. Go to **nike.com** and design your own shoes. Next visit **office.microsoft.com** and create your own business card. Finally, enter **jaguar.com** and configure the car of your dreams. What are the advantages of each activity? The disadvantages?

7. Try to save on your next purchase. Visit **letsbuyit.com**, **kaboodle.com**, **yub.com**, and **buyerzone.com**. Which site do you prefer? Why?

8. Enter **espn.go.com** and identify and list all of the revenue sources on the site.

9. Enter **lala.com** and listen to some of the commercial-free digital songs offered (cost 10¢). What other digital products and services so they offer? Write a summary.

10. Enter **philatino.com**, **stampauctioncentral.com**, and **statusint.com**. Identify the business model(s) and revenue models they use. What are the benefits to sellers? To buyers?

11. Enter **lowes.com**. View the "design it" online feature and the animated "How Tos." Examine the Project Calculators and Gift Advisor features. Relate these to the business models and other EC features of this chapter.

12. Enter **airtroductions.com** and **triplife.com**. Compare their capabilities.

13. Go to **zipcar.com**. What can this site help you do?

14. Enter **digitalenterprise.org**. Prepare a report regarding the latest EC models and developments.

15. Visit some Web sites that offer employment opportunities in EC (such as **execunet.com** and **monster.com**). Compare the EC salaries to salaries offered to accountants. For other information on EC salaries, check *Computerworld*'s annual salary survey, **unixl.com**, and **salary.com**

TEAM ASSIGNMENTS, PROJECTS, AND CLASS DISCUSSIONS

1. Create an online group for studying EC or a particular aspect of EC that interests you. You can do this via Google Groups, a social network of your choice, or Yahoo! Groups. Each member of the group must have an e-mail account. Go to Yahoo! Groups **groups.yahoo.com** and log in. At the bottom of the page, there is a section titled "Create your own Group."

   Step 1: Click on "Start a Group Now."
   Step 2: Select a category that best describes your group (use the Search Group Categories, or

use Browse Group Categories tool). You must find a category.

Step 3: Describe the purpose of the group and give it a name.

Step 4: Set up an e-mail address for sending messages to all group members.

Step 5: Each member must join the group (select "profile"); click on "Join this Group."

Step 6: Go to Word Verification Section; follow instructions.

Step 7: Finish by clicking "Continue."

Step 8: Select a group moderator. Conduct a discussion online of at least two topics of the group's interest.

Step 9: Arrange for messages from the members to reach the moderator at least once a week.

Step 10: Find a similar group (use Yahoo!'s "find a group" and make a connection). Write a report for your instructor.

2. Enter **teradatastudentnetwork.com** (ask your instructor for a password). Find the Web Seminar "Turning Active Enterprise Intelligence into Competitive Advantage," by Imhoff, Hawkings, and Lee (2006). Identify the business environment pressures and real-time responses. Finally, identify how EC strategies can support the organizations described. Prepare a report.

3. Each team will research two EC success stories. Members of the group should examine companies that operate solely online and some that extensively utilize a click-and-mortar strategy. Each team should identify the critical success factors for their companies and present a report to the other teams (see Online File W1.11 for some resources).

4. Each team selects an enterprise social network such as Linkedin, Xing, or Viadeo. Each team presents the essentials of the site, the attributes, etc. Each team will try to convince other students why their site is superior (see Online File W1.11 for some resources).

5. Enter the customer video library at **citrix.com**. Each team member reviews an EC-related case. Relate each case to the nature of EC transaction and to the business model used.

6. All class members that are not registered in Second Life need to register and create their avatars. Let each team address one of the following areas:

- Trading virtual properties
- Creating buildings, projects, stores
- Shopping and retail outlets
- Virtual jobs
- Learning and training
- Other topics

a. Prepare a description of what is going on in that area.

b. Have members' avatars interact with other avatars. Write a report about your experience.

c. What can you learn from this project?

7. Address the following topics in a class discussion:

a. How can EC be a business pressure and an organizational response?

b. Some claim that digital businesses eliminate the "human touch." Discuss.

c. Why do companies frequently change their business models? What are the advantages? The disadvantages?

Closing Case

MARY KAY'S EC SYSTEMS

Founded in 1962, Mary Kay (*marykay.com*) has about 1.8 million consultants selling its cosmetics and fragrances in 34 countries. In 2008, the company had about $2.4 billion in wholesale sales.

As a company that has based its reputation on personal contacts in door-to-door visits and home gatherings, one might think that Mary Kay would not benefit from EC. Actually, the opposite is true. Currently, more than 95 percent of Mary Kay's independent salespeople place orders via the Internet.

The Problem

The cosmetics market is very competitive, but it is growing rapidly, especially in developing countries. Mary Kay is trying to capitalize on this trend. The Mary Kay business

model enables rapid growth into new markets. By the early 2000s, consultants found that more and more customers wanted to shop online. With a long and global supply chain and the need to manage almost 2 million consultants, it was clear that automation was needed, but Mary Kay's existing computer system was old and lacked Web or e-commerce applications. Therefore, a major overhaul of the information systems was needed. Finally, it became clear that the emergence of social computing might provide a golden opportunity for Internet marketing by the company.

The Solution

Mary Kay's IT department is now split into three divisions: e-commerce, supply chain, and back-office support. Because of pressure from the consultants, the restructuring focused on e-commerce.

The company's goals and objectives were set based on industry best practices. Recall from Exhibit 1.5 that goals and objectives determine what, how, and when the company is operated, and these also apply to EC initiatives. Mary Kay's EC solution included the creation of an electronic service desk that supports consultants in 30 countries in a standardized way. Mary Kay also introduced a global electronic ordering system, called Atlas, that allows the consultants to communicate with company warehouses. An intelligent data repository that dynamically maintains a logical model of the EC environment that can be accessed by Mary Kay IT staff.

Mary Kay and its consultants are also making extensive use of social computing. The following are some representative examples of how Mary Kay uses social computing:

▶ The company posts job opening announcements on several sites, including MySpace Jobs (*jobs.myspace.com*).

▶ Movies and videotapes are available on YouTube (*youtube.com*) and on *movies.go.com*.

▶ Several blogs are available, both for and against the company (e.g.,*marykayandrews.com/blog*)

▶ Auctions and fixed price items are available for sale on eBay.

▶ Mary Kay provides a consultant locator on the Internet (*marykay.com/locator*).

All of these developments are supported by an extensive hardware and software infrastructure, including a wireless remote management system at the 760,000 square-foot corporate headquarters, an extensive wide area network (WAN, see Chapter 8), and a large data center. Some of the EC systems are used enterprise wide (e.g., service desk, ticketing system for consultants for events, and service requests made by consultants). Others are functional (e.g., accounting, finance, marketing, and inventory control). The company uses an intranet for internal communications as well as dozens of other EC applications.

In addition to providing better support to consultants, the EC initiatives produced other benefits, such as greater efficiency, reduced costs and downtime, and improved service. In terms of human resources, it enabled the company to handle its rapid growth without a substantial increase in staffing. The changes also have allowed EC personnel to focus on strategic tasks. Mary Kay found that its engineers and technical people now have time to spend on new innovations.

Sources: Compiled from Rubin (2007), *Channel Insider* (2008), LGC Wireless (2008), Dubie (2006), and *marykay.com* (accessed November 2008).

Questions

1. List the drivers of EC at Mary Kay.

2. List the business pressures faced by Mary Kay. How did Mary Kay respond to them?

3. What new EC models did Mary Kay implement?

4. What types of EC transactions is Mary Kay involved in?

5. What social networking activities is Mary Kay involved in?

6. What were the benefits of the new EC initiative to Mary Kay and its employees and customers?

ONLINE RESOURCES
available at pearsonglobaleditions.com/turban

Online Files

W1.1   What Is a Radio Frequency Identification (RFID) System?

W1.2   Application Case: Dell—Using E-Commerce for Success

W1.3   Application Case: Boeing Using E-Commerce for Collaboration

W1.4   Application Case: Google Is Changing Everything

W1.5   Application Case: Campus Food—Student Entrepreneurs

W1.6   Major Characteristics of Web 2.0

W1.7   Examples of Innovative EC Applications

W1.8   How Obama Used EC to Win

W1.9   Response Activities by Organizations

W1.10   Representatives EC Business Models

W1.11   Resources for E-Commerce

Other Resources

Online Chapters

Online Tutorials

Online Tutorial T1 on business plans is available at the book's Web site (*pearsonglobaleditions.com/turban*).

Online Tutorial T2 on electronic customer relationship management is available at the book's Web site (*pearson globaleditions.com/turban*).

Online Appendix

A technical appendix is available at the book's Web site (*pearsonglobaleditions.com/turban*).

Web Sites

Electronic Resource Guide: Electronic Commerce (*libserv2. rutgers.edu/rul/rr_gateway/research_guides/busi/ecomm.shtml*): Offers resources and links to Internet statistics: see clickZstats, Nielsen/NetRatings, U.S. Census Bureau, ComScore.

Social Computing Magazine (*socialcomputingmagazine.com*)

REFERENCES

Alter, A. "My Virtual Summer Job." *smSmallBiz.com*, May 21. 2008. **smsmallbiz.com/profiles/My_Virtual_Summer_Job.html** (accessed March 2009).

Amit, R., and C. Zott. "Value Creation in E-Business." *Strategic Management Journal*, 22, no. 6 (2001).

Blakely, L. "Making Their Point." *Business 2.0*, April 23, 2007.

Burger, A. K. "The Olympics, Part 2: Gold-Medal Network Performance." *E-Commerce Times*, August 16, 2008. **ecommercetimes.com/story/64180.html?wlc=1222501114** (accessed March 2009).

Burns, E. "U.S. Wireless Subscriptions Surge Past 250 Million." *Clickz.com*, November 27, 2007. **clickz.com/showPage.html?page=3627705** (accessed March 2009).

Carton, S. *The Dot.Bomb Survival Guide*. New York: McGraw-Hill, 2002.

Channel Insider. "Mary Kay Gets IT Makeover." April 25, 2008. **channelinsider.com/c/a/News/Mary-Kay-Gets-IT-Makeover** (accessed March 2009).

Currie, W. *Value Creation from E-Business Models*. Burlington, MA: Butterworth-Heinemann, 2004.

Davenport, T., J. Harris, and S. Cantrell. "Enterprise Systems and Ongoing Process Change." *Business Process Management Journal*, February 2004.

De Jonge, A. *Social Networks Around the World*. North Charleston, SC: Booksurge Publications, 2008.

Drucker, P. *Managing in the Next Society*. New York: Truman Talley Books, 2002.

Dubie, D. "Mary Kay Makes Over Its WAN." *Network World*, June 1, 2006. **networkworld.com/newsletters/accel/2006/0529netop2.html** (accessed March 2009).

Farivar, C. "New Ways to Pay." *Business 2.0*, July 1, 2004.

Fass, A. "TheirSpace.com." *Forbes*, May 6, 2006. forbes.com/forbes/2006/0508/122.html (accessed March 2009).

Forrester Research. "Retail First Look," **Forrester.com**, June 1, 2006. **forrester.com/FirstLook/Vertical/Issue/0,6454,600,00.html** (accessed March 2009).

Harmony Hollow Software. "What Are the Barriers of Implementing E-Commerce Solutions?" 2006. **harmonyhollow.net/webmaster-resources/ecommerce/15604.php** (accessed March 2009).

Harrington, R. "The Transformer" (an e-mail interview with *Baseline's* editor-in-chief, J. McCormic). *Baseline*, April 2006.

Hupfer, R., et al. *MySpace for Dummies*. Hoboken, NJ: Wiley Publishers, Inc., 2007.

Hwang, H. S., and C. Stewart. "Lessons from Dot-Com Boom and Bust." In Khosrow-Pour, M. (Ed.). *Encyclopedia of E-Commerce, E-Government, and Mobile Commerce*. Hershey, PA: Idea Group Reference, 2006.

IBM. "IBM Global CEO Study: The Enterprise of the Future." IBM special study, 2008.

InformationWeek. "Some Beijing Olympics Fireworks Faked." August 11, 2008a. **informationweek.com/news/personal_tech/TV_theater/showArticle.jhtml?articleID=210002310** (accessed March 2009).

InformationWeek. "YouTube to Broadcast Beijing Olympics, but Not in the U.S." August 5, 2008b. **informationweek.com/news/personal_tech/TV_theater/showArticle.jhtml?articleID=209903442** (accessed November 2008).

International Trade Commission. "Electronic Commerce 2008." **ita.doc.gov/investamerica/ecommerce.asp** (accessed April 2009).

IT Strategy. "IT's Role in the Beijing Olympics." August 28, 2008. **itstrategyblog.com/it%E2%80%99s-role-in-beijing-olympics** (accessed March 2009).

Jelassi, T., and A. Enders. *Strategies for e-Business*. Harlow, England: FT, Prentice Hall, 2005.

Joyner, A. *The eBay Billionaire's Club*. Hoboken, NJ: Wiley Publications, 2007.

Jupiter Media. "Jupiter Research Forecasts Online Retail Spending Will Reach $144 Billion in 2010, a CAGR of 12% from 2005." February 6, 2006. **jupitermedia.com/corporate/releases/06.02.06-newjupresearch.html** (accessed March 2009).

Khosrow-Pour, M. (Ed.) *Encyclopedia of E-Commerce, E-Government, and Mobile Commerce*. Hershey, PA: Idea Group Reference, 2006.

Lashinsky, A. "The Boom Is Back." *Fortune*, May 1, 2006.

Leobbecke, C. "RFID in the Retail Supply Chain." In Khosrow-Pour, M. (Ed.). *Encyclopedia of E-Commerce, E-Government, and Mobile Commerce*. Hershey, PA: Idea Group Reference, 2006.

Lee, C. S., Y. G. Chen, and Y.-H. Fan. "Structure and Components of E-commerce Business Model." In Khosrow-Pour, M. (Ed.) *Encyclopedia of E-Commerce,*

E-Government, and Mobile Commerce. Hershey, PA: Idea Group Reference, 2006.

LGC Wireless. "Mary Kay Puts a New Face on Wireless." LGC Wireless case study, 2008. **lgcwireless.org/ downloads/Case_Study_Mary_Kay.pdf** (accessed March 2009).

Magnier, M. "Beijing Olympics Visitors to Come Under Widespread Surveillance." *Los Angeles Times,* August 7, 2008.

McGee, M. K. "Chiefs of the Year: Internet Call to Arms." *InformationWeek,* November 27, 2000.

Mockler, R. J., D. G. Dologite, and M. E. Gartenfeld. "B2B E-Business." In Khosrow-Pour, M. (Ed.) *Encyclopedia of E-Commerce, E-Government, and Mobile Commerce.* Hershey, PA: Idea Group Reference, 2006.

Needle, D. "Huffington: Obama Not Elected Without Internet." *Internetnews.com,* November 7, 2008. **internet news.com/webcontent/article.php/3783741/Huffingt on+Obama+Not+Elected+Without+Internet.htm** (accessed April 2009).

O'Reilly, T. "What Is Web 2.0?" *OReillynet.com,* September 30, 2005.**oreillynet.com/pub/a/oreilly/tim/news/2005/ 09/30/what-is-web-20.html** (accessed March 2008).

Papazoglou, M. P., and P. M. A. Ribbers. *e-Business: Organizational and Technical Foundations.* West Sussex, England: Wiley 2006.

Plunkett, J. W. *Plunkett's E-Commerce and Internet Business Almanac 2006.* Houston, TX: Plunkett Research, Ltd., February 2006.

Prahahalad, C. K., and M. S. Krishnan. *The New Age of Innovation.* New York: McGraw-Hill, 2008.

Rappa, M. "Business Models on the Web." *Digitalenterprise. org,* 2006. **digitalenterprise.org/models/models.html** (accessed March 2009).

Reda, S. "Godiva.com's Story Parallels Dynamic Growth of E-Commerce." *Stores,* February 2004.

Rubin, C. "More Than Skin Deep." *Communication News,* March 2007.

Rymaszewski, M., et al. *Second Life: The Official Guide.* Indianapolis, IN: Wiley Publishers, Inc., 2008.

Sellers, P. "MySpace Cowboys." *Fortune,* September 4, 2006.

Shaw, M. *E-Commerce and the Digital Economy.* Armonk, NY: M.E. Sharpe, 2006.

Strategic Direction. "DotCom Boom and Bust: The Secrets of E-Commerce Failure and Success." February 2005.

Taft, D. K. "NBC Olympic Coverage Shines as Silverlight Proving Ground." *e-Week,* August 13, 2008.

Tian, Y., and C. Stewart. "History of E-Commerce." In Khosrow-Pour, M. (Ed.) *Encyclopedia of E-Commerce, E-Government, and Mobile Commerce.* Hershey, PA: Idea Group Reference, 2006.

Van Toorn, C., D. Bunker, K. Yee, and S. Smith. "The Barriers to the Adoption of E-Commerce by Micro Businesses, Small Businesses and Medium Enterprises." Sixth International Conference on Knowledge, Culture, and Change in Organisations, Prato, Tuscany, Italy, July 11–14, 2006.

CHAPTER 2

E-MARKETPLACES: MECHANISMS, TOOLS, AND IMPACTS OF E-COMMERCE

Content

Learning Objectives

Upon completion of this chapter, you will be able to:

1. Describe the major electronic commerce (EC) activities and processes and the mechanisms that support them.

2. Define e-marketplaces and list their components.

3. List the major types of e-marketplaces and describe their features.

4. Describe electronic catalogs, search engines, and shopping carts.

5. Describe the major types of auctions and list their characteristics.

6. Discuss the benefits, limitations, and impacts of auctions.

7. Describe bartering and negotiating online.

8. List the major Web 2.0 tools and their use in EC.

9. Understand virtual worlds and their use in EC.

10. Discuss competition in the digital economy.

11. Describe the impact of e-marketplaces on organizations, intermediation, and industries.

WEB 2.0 TOOLS AT EASTERN MOUNTAIN SPORTS

Eastern Mountain Sports (EMS) (*ems.com*) is a medium-sized specialty retailer (annual sales $200 million) that sells goods in more than 80 physical stores, through mail-order catalogs, and online. Operating in a very competitive environment, the company uses leading-edge information technologies. EMS is now introducing a complementary set of Web 2.0 tools in order to increase collaboration, information sharing, and communication among stores and their employees, suppliers, and customers. Let's see how this works.

The Business Intelligence Strategy and System

During the past few years, the company has implemented a business intelligence (BI) system (see Online File W4.2) that includes business performance management and dashboards. (A *dashboard* is a graphical presentation of results of reports about performance.) A BI system collects raw data from multiple sources, processes them into a data warehouse (or data mart), and conducts analyses that include comparing performance to operational metrics in order to assess the health of the business (see details in Turban et al. 2008).

The illustration shows how the system works. Point-of-sale (POS) information and other relevant data, which are available on an IBM mainframe computer, are loaded into Microsoft's SQL server and into a data mart (see Online File W4.2). The data are then analyzed with Information Builders' WebFOCUS 7.12 platform. The results are presented via a series of dashboards that users can view by using Web browsers. This allows users to access a unified, high-level view of key performance indicators (KPI) such as sales, inventory, and margin levels, and then drill down to granular details that analyze specific transactions.

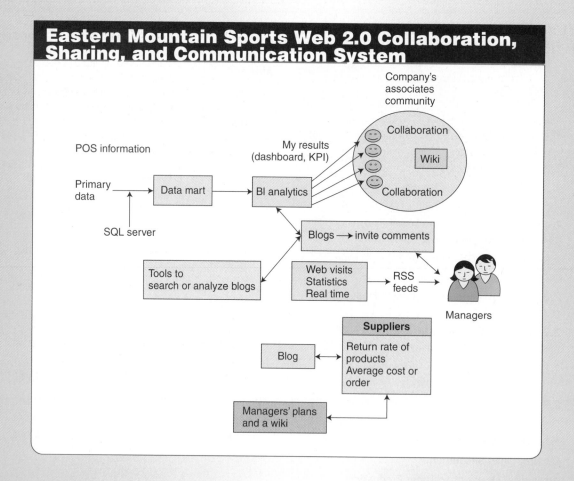

Eastern Mountain Sports Web 2.0 Collaboration, Sharing, and Communication System

The Web 2.0 Collaboration, Sharing, and Communication System

The company created a multifunctional employee workbench called *E-Basecamp*. E-Basecamp contains all information relevant to corporate goals integrated with productivity tools (e.g., Excel) and role-based content customized to each individual user. Then, EMS added a set of Web 2.0 tools. The system facilitates collaboration among internal and external stakeholders. EMS is using 20 operation metrics (e.g., inventory levels and turns). These metrics also cover e-tailing, where e-commerce managers monitor Web traffic and conversion rates on an hourly basis (Chapter 4). The dashboard shows deviations from targets by means of a color code. The system uses the following Web 2.0 tools:

- **RSS feeds.** RSS feeds (Chapter 7) are embedded into the dashboards to drive more focused inquiries. These feeds are the base for information sharing and online conversations. For example, by showing which items are selling better than others, users can collectively analyze the transaction characteristics and selling behaviors that produce the high sales. The knowledge acquired then cascades throughout the organization. For instance, one manager observed an upward spike in footwear sales at store X. An investigation revealed that store X employees had perfected a multistep sales technique that included recommending (both online and in stores) special socks, designed for specific uses along with an inner sole. The information was disseminated using the RSS feed. As a result, sales of footwear increased 57 percent in a year.

- **Wikis.** Wikis are used to encourage collaborative interaction throughout the company. Dashboard users are encouraged to post a hypothesis or request for help and then invite commentary and suggestions, almost like a notepad alongside the dashboard.

- **Blogs.** Blogs were created around specific data or a key metric. The blogs are used to post information and invite comment. Tools are then used to archive, search, and categorize blogs for easy reference. For example, store managers post an inquiry or explanation regarding sale deviations (anomalies). Keeping comments on blogs lets readers observe patterns they might have overlooked using data analysis alone.

Going to Business Partners Externally

Suppliers were added in the phase that began in late 2006. For example, suppliers can monitor the return rate of a product on the dashboard and invite store managers to provide explanations and suggestions using wikis or blogs. Assuming that proper security has been installed, suppliers can get data about how well their products sell in almost real time and can prepare better production plans.

The objective is to build a tighter bond with business partners. For instance, by attaching a blog to suppliers' dashboards, the suppliers can view current sales information and post comments to the blogs. Product managers use a wiki to post challenges for the next season (such as a proposed percentage increase in sales) and then ask vendors to suggest innovative ways to achieve these goals. Several of the customers and other business partners subscribe to RSS feeds.

Called *Extreme Deals* (big discounts for a limited time), blogs are also embedded into the EMS product lifecycle management (PLM) tool. This allows vendors to have virtual conversations with the product development managers.

The major impact of the Web 2.0 collaboration tools is that instead of having conversations occur in the hallway (where you need to be in the right place at the right time), conversations take place on blogs and wikis where all interested parties can participate.

Sources: Compiled from Nerille (2007) and from *ems.com* (accessed October 2008).

WHAT WE CAN LEARN . . .

Eastern Mountain Sports was successful in bolstering communication and collaboration both among its own managers and with its suppliers. They did so with Web 2.0 tools: blogs, wikis, and RSS feeds. These tools facilitated the company's business processes and their existing information systems. The Web 2.0 tools enhance the activities of e-commerce, business-to-employee (B2E) information sharing, and e-tailing (business-to-consumer). The Web 2.0 tools are the newest mechanisms of EC and are introduced in this chapter together with the more traditional mechanisms that support selling and buying online.

2.1   ELECTRONIC COMMERCE MECHANISMS: AN OVERVIEW

The many EC models and types of transactions presented in Chapter 1 are enabled by different mechanisms. To begin, the generic enablers of any information system include databases, networks, security, operating systems, and hosting services. Then come the special EC enablers that are presented in this chapter, and in Chapter 15, such as electronic markets, e-stores, and e-catalogs. Also, there are different methods for executing EC, such as buying at a fixed price or at an auction, and each method has a different mechanism. In this chapter, the major EC mechanisms are described so that you will understand what they are when you read about them in Chapters 3 through 16. An overview of these mechanisms is presented first, followed by a description of the purchasing process and the conduct of transactions in which these mechanisms are used.

EC ACTIVITIES AND MECHANISMS

Chapter 1 describes the major activities of EC. These are divided into six categories, which are listed on the left side of Exhibit 2.1. Each activity is supported by one or more EC mechanisms, which are shown on the right side of Exhibit 2.1, along with the sections in

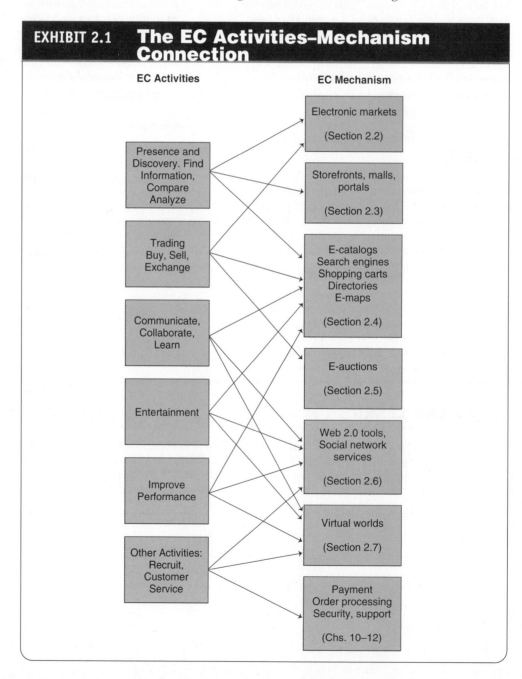

EXHIBIT 2.1   The EC Activities–Mechanism Connection

Chapter 2 where they are presented. Additional mechanisms exist for special activities, such as payment (Chapter 11), security (Chapter 10), order fulfillment (Chapter 12), and CRM (Chapter 11).

The conduct of activities and the support provided by the different mechanisms can be done in different ways. Next, we present one of these: selling and buying online.

SELLERS, BUYERS, AND TRANSACTIONS

Typically, a seller (retailer, wholesaler, or manufacturer) sells to customers. The seller buys either raw material (as a manufacturer) or finished goods (as a retailer) from suppliers. This process is illustrated in Exhibit 2.2.

The selling company, shown as "Our Company," appears in the center of the exhibit. Internally, processes and transactions are conducted in different functional areas and are supported by EC software. The customers place orders (in B2C or B2B), and the selling company fulfills them. Our Company buys materials, products, and so on from suppliers, distributors (B2B), or from the government (G2B) in a process called *e-procurement* (see Chapter 5). Sometimes intermediaries are involved in this process. Let's zero in on what happens during a typical purchasing process.

The Purchasing Process

Customers buy goods online in different ways. The most common way is purchasing from catalogs at fixed prices. Sometimes prices may be negotiated or discounted. Another way is dynamic pricing, which refers to nonfixed prices such as those in auctions or stock (commodity) markets. The buyers use the process illustrated in Exhibit 2.3.

The process starts with logging into a seller's Web site, registering (if needed), and entering into an online catalog or the buyer's "my account." E-catalogs can be very large, so a search mechanism may be needed. Also, the buyer should compare prices. Some sellers (e.g., American Airlines) provide comparisons with competing vendors. Otherwise, the buyer may need to leave the site or do price comparisons *before* entering into the specific seller's store. If not satisfied, the buyer will abandon the site. If satisfied, the buyer will select an item and place it in a *shopping cart*. The buyer may return to the catalog to choose more items. Each selected item is placed in the shopping cart. When shopping is complete, the buyer goes to a checkout page, where a shipment option is selected from a menu. Also, a payment option may be available. For example, newegg.com lets you pay by credit card, with PayPal, by check after billing, in installments, and so on. After checking all details for accuracy, the buyer submits the order.

The major mechanisms that support this process are described in the remainder of this chapter. The place where these processes occur is the e-marketplace.

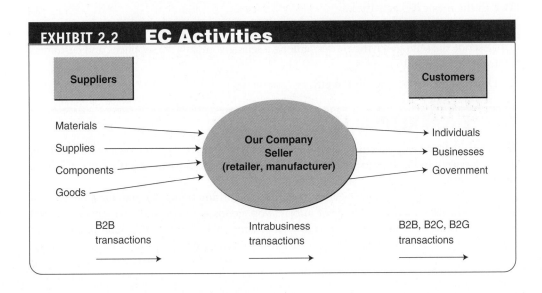

EXHIBIT 2.2   EC Activities

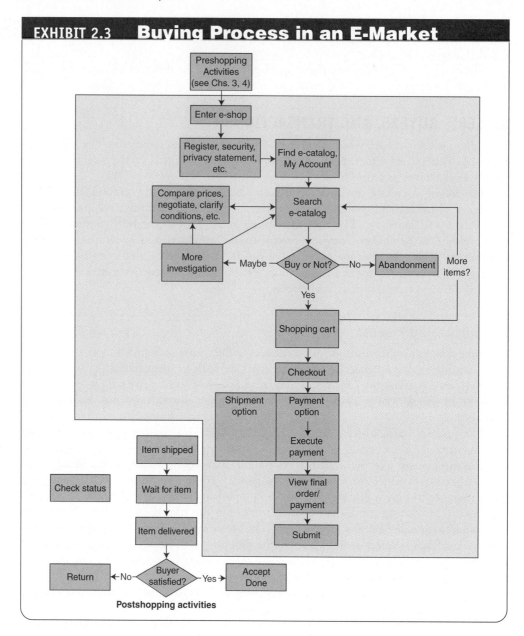

EXHIBIT 2.3   Buying Process in an E-Market

Section 2.1 ▶ REVIEW QUESTIONS

1. List the major EC activities.
2. List the major EC mechanisms.
3. Describe the selling–buying process among a selling company, its suppliers, and customers (consult Exhibit 2.2).
4. Describe the major steps in the buying process (consult Exhibit 2.3).

2.2 E-MARKETPLACES

Electronic markets play a central role in the economy, facilitating the exchange of information, goods, services, and payments. In the process, they create economic value for buyers, sellers, market intermediaries, and for society at large.

Markets (electronic or otherwise) have three main functions: (1) matching buyers and sellers; (2) facilitating the exchange of information, goods, services, and payments associated with market transactions; and (3) providing an institutional infrastructure, such as a legal and regulatory framework, that enables the efficient functioning of the market (see Exhibit 2.4).

EXHIBIT 2.4 Functions of a Market

Matching of Buyers and Sellers	Facilitation of Transactions	Institutional Infrastructure
• Determination of product offerings Product features offered by sellers Aggregation of different products • Search (of buyers for sellers and of sellers for buyers) Price and product information Organizing bids and bartering Matching seller offerings with buyer preferences • Price discovery Process and outcome in determination of prices Enabling price comparisons • Others Providing sales leads	• Logistics Delivery of information, goods, or services to buyers • Settlement Transfer of payments to sellers • Trust Credit system, reputations, rating agencies such as *Consumer Reports* and the BBB, special escrow and online trust agencies • Communication Posting buyers' requests	• Legal Commercial code, contract law, dispute resolution, intellectual property protection • Regulatory Rules and regulations, compliance, monitoring enforcement • Discovery Provides market information (e.g., about competition, government regulations)

Sources: Compiled from Bakos (1998) and from E-Market Services (2006).

ELECTRONIC MARKETS

The major place for conducting EC transactions is the electronic market (e-market). An **e-marketplace** is a virtual marketplace in which sellers and buyers meet and conduct different types of transactions. Customers exchange goods and services for money (or other goods and services if bartering is used). The functions of an e-market are the same as those of a physical marketplace; however, computerized systems tend to make electronic markets much more efficient by providing more updated information and diverse support services to buyers and sellers.

e-marketplace
An online market, usually B2B, in which buyers and sellers exchange goods or services; the three types of e-marketplaces are private, public, and consortia.

EC has increased market efficiencies by expediting or improving the functions listed in Exhibit 2.4. Furthermore, EC has been able to significantly decrease the cost of executing these functions.

The emergence of *electronic marketplaces* (also called *e-marketplaces, virtual markets,* or *marketspaces*), especially Internet-enabled ones, changed several of the processes used in trading and supply chains. These changes, driven by technology, resulted in:

- Greater information richness of the transactional and relational environment
- Lower information search costs for buyers
- Diminished information asymmetry between sellers and buyers
- Less time between purchase and possession of physical products purchased in the e-marketplace
- Greater temporal proximity between time of purchase and time of possession of digital products purchased in the e-marketplace
- The ability of buyers, sellers, and the virtual market to be in different locations
- The ability for EC to leverage capabilities with increased effectiveness and lower transaction and distribution costs, leading to more efficient "friction-free" markets. An example of such efficiency is provided in Case 2.2. For more on e-marketplaces, see Li and Du (2005).

marketspace
A marketplace in which sellers and buyers exchange goods and services for money (or for other goods and services), but do so electronically.

E-MARKETPLACE COMPONENTS AND PARTICIPANTS

A **marketspace** includes electronic transactions that bring about a new distribution of goods and services. The major components and players in a marketspace are customers, sellers, products and services (physical or digital), infrastructure, a front end, a back end, intermediaries and other business partners, and support services. A brief description of each follows:

▶ **Customers.** More than 2 billion people worldwide who surf the Web are potential buyers of the goods and services offered or advertised on the Internet. These consumers are looking for bargains, customized items, collectors' items, entertainment, socialization, and more. They are in the driver's seat. They can search for detailed information, compare, bid, and sometimes negotiate. Organizations are the largest consumers, accounting for more than 85 percent of EC activities.

▶ **Sellers.** Millions of storefronts are on the Web, advertising and offering a huge variety of items. These stores are owned by companies, government agencies, or individuals. Every day it is possible to find new offerings of products and services. Sellers can sell direct from their Web sites or from e-marketplaces.

▶ **Products and services.** One of the major differences between the marketplace and the marketspace is the possible digitization of products and services in a marketspace. Although both types of markets can sell physical products, the marketspace also can sell **digital products**, which are goods that can be transformed to digital format and instantly delivered over the Internet. In addition to digitization of software and music, it is possible to digitize dozens of other products and services, as shown in Online File W2.1. Digital products have different cost curves than those of regular products. In digitization, most of the costs are fixed, and variable costs are very low (see Chapter 14). Thus, profits will increase very rapidly as volume increases, once the fixed costs are paid.

▶ **Infrastructure.** The marketspace infrastructure includes electronic networks, hardware, software, and more. (EC infrastructure is presented in Online Chapter 18.)

▶ **Front end.** Customers interact with a marketspace via a **front end**. The components of the front end can include the seller's portal, electronic catalogs, a shopping cart, a search engine, an auction engine, and a payment gateway. (For details, see Beynon-Davies 2004.)

▶ **Back end.** All the activities that are related to order aggregation and fulfillment, inventory management, purchasing from suppliers, accounting and finance, insurance, payment processing, packaging, and delivery are done in what is termed the **back end** of the business. (For details, see Beynon-Davies 2004.)

▶ **Intermediaries.** In marketing, an **intermediary** is typically a third party that operates between sellers and buyers. Intermediaries of all kinds offer their services on the Web. The role of these electronic intermediaries is frequently different from that of regular intermediaries (such as wholesalers), as will be seen in Section 2.9 and throughout the text, especially in Chapters 3 and 5. For example, online intermediaries create and manage the online markets. They help match buyers and sellers, provide some infrastructure services, and help customers and/or sellers institute and complete transactions. They also support the vast number of transactions that exist in providing services. Most of these online intermediaries operate as computerized systems.

▶ **Other business partners.** In addition to intermediaries, several types of partners, such as shippers, use the Internet to collaborate, mostly along the supply chain.

▶ **Support services.** Many different support services are available, ranging from certification and escrow services (to ensure security) to content providers.

digital products
Goods that can be transformed to digital format and delivered over the Internet.

front end
The portion of an e-seller's business processes through which customers interact, including the seller's portal, electronic catalogs, a shopping cart, a search engine, and a payment gateway.

back end
The activities that support online order fulfillment, inventory management, purchasing from suppliers, payment processing, packaging, and delivery.

intermediary
A third party that operates between sellers and buyers.

TYPES OF E-MARKETPLACES

In general conversation, the distinction between a mall and a marketplace is not always clear. In the physical world, malls are often viewed as collections of stores (i.e., shopping centers) where the stores are isolated from each other and prices are generally fixed. In contrast, marketplaces, some of which are located outdoors, are often viewed as places where many vendors compete and shoppers look for bargains and are expected to negotiate prices (e.g., the International Marketplace in Honolulu).

On the Web, the term *marketplace* has a different and distinct meaning. If individual customers want to negotiate prices, they may be able to do so in some storefronts or malls. We distinguish two types of e-marketplaces: private and public.

Private E-Marketplaces

Private e-marketplaces are those owned and operated by a single company. As can be seen in the Raffles Hotel case (Online File W2.2), private markets are either sell-side or buy-side. In a **sell-side e-marketplace**, a company, Cisco for example, will sell either standard or customized products to individuals (B2C) or to business (B2B); this type of selling is considered to be one-to-many. In a **buy-side e-marketplace**, a company purchases from many suppliers; this type of purchasing is considered to be *many-to-one*, and it is B2B activity. For example, Raffles Hotel buys its supplies from approved vendors that come to its e-market. Private marketplaces may be open only to selected members and are not publicly regulated. We will return to the topic of private e-marketplaces in Chapters 3 (B2C) and 5 (B2B).

sell-side e-marketplace
A private e-marketplace in which one company sells either standard and/or customized products to qualified companies.

buy-side e-marketplace
A private e-marketplace in which one company makes purchases from invited suppliers.

Public E-Marketplaces

Public e-marketplaces are usually B2B markets. They often are owned by a third party (not a seller or a buyer) or by a group of buying or selling companies (a consortium), and they serve many sellers and many buyers. These markets also are known as *exchanges* (e.g., a stock exchange). They are open to the public and are regulated by the government or the exchange's owners. An example of a public marketplace, NTE.net, is provided in Online File W2.3. Public e-marketplaces are presented in detail in Chapter 5.

Section 2.2 ▶ REVIEW QUESTIONS

1. Define e-marketplace and describe its attributes.
2. What is the difference between a physical marketplace and an e-marketplace (marketspace)?
3. List the components of a marketspace.
4. Define a digital product and provide five examples.
5. Describe private versus public e-markets.

2.3 CUSTOMER INTERACTION MECHANISMS: STOREFRONTS, MALLS, AND PORTALS

Several kinds of possible interactions exist among sellers, buyers, and e-marketplaces. The major B2C e-marketplaces are *storefronts* and *Internet malls*. Let's elaborate on these, as well as on the gateways to e-marketplaces—portals.

ELECTRONIC STOREFRONTS

An electronic or Web **storefront** refers to a single company's Web site where products and services are sold. It is an electronic store. The storefront may belong to a manufacturer (e.g., geappliances.com and dell.com), to a retailer (e.g., walmart.com and wishlist.com.au), to individuals selling from home, or to another type of business. Note that companies that sell services (such as insurance) may refer to their storefronts as portals. An example of a service-related portal is a hotel reservation system, as shown in Online File W2.2.

A storefront includes several mechanisms that are necessary for conducting online sales. The most common mechanisms are an *electronic catalog*; a *search engine* that helps the consumer find products in the catalog; an *electronic cart* for holding items until checkout; *e-auction facilities* where auctions take place; a *payment gateway* where payment arrangements can be made; a *shipment court* where shipping arrangements are made; and *customer services*, which include product and warranty information. The first three mechanisms are described in Section 2.4; e-auctions are described in Section 2.5 and in Chapter 17; payment mechanisms are described in Chapter 11; and shipments are discussed in Chapter 12. Customer

storefront
A single company's Web site where products or services are sold.

Source: Courtesy of Seeds of Change. Used with permission.

services, which can be fairly elaborate, are covered throughout the book and especially in Chapter 11 (see CRM).

ELECTRONIC MALLS

In addition to shopping at individual storefronts, consumers can shop in electronic malls (e-malls). Similar to malls in the physical world, an **e-mall (online mall)** is an online shopping location where many stores are located. For example, Hawaii.com (hawaii.com) is an e-mall that aggregates Hawaiian products, services, and providers. It contains a directory of vacation services and product categories and the vendors in each category. When a consumer indicates the category he or she is interested in, the consumer is transferred to the appropriate independent *storefront*. This kind of mall does not provide any shared services; it is merely a directory. Other malls, such as Choice Mall (choicemall.com), do provide shared services. Some malls are actually large click-and-mortar retailers; others are virtual retailers (e.g., buy.com).

> **e-mall (online mall)**
> An online shopping center where many online stores are located.

Visualization and Virtual Realty in Shopping Malls

To attract users to shopping malls, vendors use rich media, including virtual reality (VR). Lepouras and Vassilakis (2006) proposed an architecture for a virtual reality mall. Recently a similar presentation was made in virtual worlds (Section 2.7).

TYPES OF STORES AND MALLS

Stores and malls are of several different types:

- **General stores/malls.** These are large marketspaces that sell all kinds of products. Examples are amazon.com, choicemall.com, walmart.com, spree.com, and the major public portals (yahoo.com, aol.com, and msn.com). All major department and discount stores also fall into this category.
- **Specialized stores/malls.** These sell only one or a few kinds of products, such as books, flowers, wine, cars, or pet toys. Amazon.com started as a specialized e-bookstore but today is a generalized store. 1800flowers.com sells flowers and related gifts; cars.com sells cars; fashionmall.com/beautyjungle specializes in beauty products, tips, and trends; and cattoys.com sells cat toys. Visit newegg.com for computer electronics and endless.com for shoes and apparel.

▶ **Regional versus global stores.** Some stores, such as e-grocers or sellers of heavy furniture, serve customers that live nearby. For example, parknshop.com serves the Hong Kong community only; it will not deliver outside of Hong Kong. However, some local stores will sell to customers in other countries if the customer is willing to pay shipping, insurance, and other costs (e.g., see hothothot.com).

▶ **Pure-play online organizations versus click-and-mortar stores.** Stores may be pure online (i.e., virtual or pure-play) organizations, such as Blue Nile, Amazon.com, Buy.com, Newegg.com or Cattoys.com. They do not have physical stores. Others are physical stores that also sell online (e.g., Wal-Mart with walmart.com, 1-800-Flowers.com with 1800flowers.com, and Woolworths with woolworths.com.au). This second category is called *click-and-mortar*. Both categories will be described further in Chapter 3.

WEB (INFORMATION) PORTALS

With the growing use of intranets and the Internet, many organizations encounter information overload at a number of different levels. Information is scattered across numerous documents, e-mail messages, and databases at different locations and in disparate systems. Accessing relevant and accurate information is often a time- and effort-consuming task and requires access to multiple systems.

As a consequence, organizations lose a lot of productive employee time. One solution to this problem is the use of Web portals. A *portal* is an information gateway that is used in e-marketplaces, e-stores, and other types of EC (e.g., in intrabusiness and e-learning). Advanced search and indexing techniques (such as Google's Desktop) have been developed to address information overload. A **Web portal** is a single point of access, through a Web browser, to critical business information located inside and outside (via Internet) of an organization. Many Web portals can be personalized for the users. Note that wireless devices are becoming portals for enterprise and Internet access. For more on portals, see en.wikipedia.org/wiki/Web_portal.

Web portal
A single point of access, through a Web browser, to critical business information located inside and outside (via Internet) of an organization.

Types of Portals

Portals can be described in many ways and assume many shapes. One way to distinguish among them is to look at their content, which can vary from narrow to broad, and their community or audience, which also can vary. The major types of portals are as follows:

▶ Commercial (public) portals. These portals offer content for diverse communities and are the most popular portals on the Internet. Although they can be customized by the user, they are still intended for broad audiences and offer fairly routine content, some in real time (e.g., a stock ticker and news about a few preselected items). Examples of such sites are yahoo.com, aol.com, and msn.com.

▶ **Corporate portals.** Corporate portals provide organized access to rich content within relatively narrow corporate and partners' communities. They also are known as *enterprise portals* or *enterprise information portals*. Corporate portals appear in different forms and are described in detail in Chapter 6.

▶ **Publishing portals.** These portals are intended for communities with specific interests. These portals involve relatively little customization of content, but provide extensive online search features and some interactive capabilities. Examples of such sites are techweb.com and zdnet.com.

▶ **Personal portals.** These target specific filtered information for individuals. They offer relatively narrow content and are typically very personalized, effectively having an audience of one. Personalized portals, or home pages, pioneered by Netvibes (netvibes.com) is an alternative to a regular Web portal. It is offered by Yahoo!, Google, and many more. Netvibes lets individuals assemble their favorite widgets, Web sites, blogs, e-mail accounts, social networks, search engines, instant messenger, photos, videos, podcasts, and everything else they enjoy on the Web—all in one place. Today, Netvibes is a global multilanguage global community of users who are taking control of their digital lives by personalizing their Web experience. Netvibes is also a widget platform that is used by thousands of publishers around the world.

mobile portal
A portal accessible via a mobile device.

- **Mobile portals. Mobile portals** are portals that are accessible from mobile devices (see Chapter 8 for details). An increasing number of portals are accessible via mobile devices. One example of such a mobile portal is i-Mode, which is described in Chapter 8.

voice portal
A portal accessed by telephone or cell phone.

- **Voice portals. Voice portals** are Web sites, usually portals, with audio interfaces. This means that they can be accessed by a standard telephone or a cell phone. AOLbyPhone is an example of a service that allows users to retrieve e-mail, news, and other content from AOL via telephone. It uses both speech recognition and text-to-speech technologies. Companies such as Tellme (tellme.com) and BeVocal (bevocal.com) offer access to the Internet from telephones, and also tools to build voice portals. Voice portals are especially popular for 1-800 numbers (enterprise 800 numbers) that provide self-service to customers with information available in Internet databases (e.g., find flight status at delta.com).

- **Knowledge portals.** Knowledge portals enable access to knowledge by knowledge workers and facilitate collaboration (see Chapter 7).

THE ROLES AND VALUE OF INTERMEDIARIES IN E-MARKETPLACES

Intermediaries (brokers) play an important role in commerce by providing value-added activities and services to buyers and sellers. There are many types of intermediaries. The most well-known intermediaries in the physical world are wholesalers and retailers.

The two types of *online intermediaries* are brokers and infomediaries.

Brokers

A *broker* is a company that facilitates transactions between buyers and sellers. The following are different types of brokers:

- **Buy/sell fulfillment.** A corporation that helps consumers place buy and sell orders (e.g., eTrade).
- **Virtual mall.** A company that helps consumers buy from a variety of stores (e.g., Yahoo! Stores).
- **Metamediary.** A firm that offers customers access to a variety of stores and provides them with transaction services, such as financial services (e.g., Amazon zShops).
- **Bounty.** An intermediary that will locate a person, place, or idea for a fee (e.g., bountyhunt.com for bail enforcement agents).
- **Comparison agent.** A company that helps consumers compare different stores (e.g., bizrate.com).
- **Shopping facilitator.** A company that helps consumers use online shops by providing currency conversion, language translation, payment features, delivery solutions, and potentially a user-customized interface (e.g., myorbital.com).
- **Matching services.** These match people, sellers to buyers, buyers to products, and so forth.

infomediaries
Electronic intermediaries that provide and/or control information flow in cyberspace, often aggregating information and selling it to others.

Infomediaries

In cyberspace, some intermediaries provide and/or control information flow. These electronic intermediaries are known as **infomediaries.** The information flows to and from buyers and sellers via infomediaries, as shown in Online File W2.4. Infomediaries are Web sites that gather and organize large amounts of data and act as intermediaries between those who want the information and those who supply the information (see webopedia.com/term/infomediary.html). There are two types of infomediaries:

▶ The first offers consumers a place to gather information about specific products and companies before making purchasing decisions. It is a third-party provider of unbiased information; it does not promote or try to sell specific products in preference over other products or act on behalf of any vendors (e.g., autobytel.com, cars.com, and bizrate.com).

▶ The second is not necessarily Web-based. It provides vendors with consumer information that will help the vendor develop and market products. The infomediary collects personal information from the buyers and sells that data to businesses.

CASE 2.1
EC Application
TRADEEGYPT.COM

The main challenge facing Egyptian export promoters is establishing Egypt as a target source on the map of international exporting countries. In order for Egyptian products to acquire a share of the international marketplace, it is fundamental that Egyptian firms promote the export sector by means of a professional, efficient global marketing campaign.

Export Gateway Online (EGO) is an Egyptian company established in 2001 with the specific purpose of enhancing the export of Egyptian products. Its strategy was to utilize IT platforms and the explosive online B2B marketplace. EGO launched TradeEgypt.com after spending 2 years conducting research to identify the main services of value to prospective customers.

EGO recognized that the online marketplace was the most cost-effective way of achieving its objective, utilizing innovative, state-of-the-art marketing techniques and effectively executing the art of Internet marketing. To do that, TradeEgypt.com advertises on 168 portal and trade-related Web sites and has established affiliate agreements with major trade portals (e.g., Alibaba.com, Europages.com, Tradefeeds.com, and FITA.org).

The primary function of TradeEgypt.com is to offer a virtual marketplace where Egyptian exporters can meet and interact with global importers, local producers, and international suppliers of raw materials to negotiate opportunities and develop commercial relationships. TradeEgypt.com promotes itself not just as a directory or database for trade, but also as a facilitator to the export process and a "one-stop shop" for all exporter needs and requirements for success.

TradeEgypt.com offers a variety of marketplace services, including the following:

▶ **Lead center.** A company can post and view offers to buy or sell, publish an online profile, and create a products catalog.

▶ **Catalog center.** Catalogs of Egyptian exporters and manufacturers and of non-Egyptian exporters.

▶ **Company listing.** Listings for importers and exporters, shippers and forwarders, and a variety of service providers, including inspection companies, packagers, customs clearance services, law firms, insurance and warehousing companies, and banks.

▶ **Shipping information center.** Information about cargo lines, information about container specifications, a container calculator, INCOTERMS (internationally accepted definitions for the terms of sale), and shipment tracing services.

▶ **Business guide and tools.** Information about trade and export laws and regulations, trade agreements, and Ministry of Foreign Affairs programs. The service also offers a multiunit converter package (for weight, volume, distance, speed, and temperature).

▶ **Resource library.** Provides trade data, import and export statistics, an economic bulletin board, economic and financial indicators, an investment profile for Egypt, and a directory of national and international telephone numbers and port and airport codes.

▶ **Business directory.** Details of Egyptian commercial services, Egyptian embassies abroad, Egyptian trade points, foreign embassies, international trade organizations, Egyptian airports, port authorities, banks, business associations, chambers of commerce, and local airline offices.

▶ **On-demand market research reports.** Subscribers to TradeEgypt.com can order credit reports on certain companies, as well as customs reports, international standards and specifications for products, import–export statistics, and country profiles.

After serving 2,464 Egyptian exporters, attracting 27,627 foreign importers, and generating thousands of trade leads and international business opportunities in 2007, TradeEgypt.com has now widened its exclusive services to accommodate the needs of Egyptian importers with over 10,000 self-registered global sellers and suppliers who are specifically interested in establishing trade relations with Egyptian importers.

TradeEgypt.com has also developed international alliances with recognizable trade facilitators in over 35 key countries worldwide to set up a Consortium of Excellence. This consortium ensures that TradeEgypt.com clients' products

(continued)

CASE 2.1   (continued)

receive a fair chance at competing effectively, professionally, and efficiently within the global arena. TradeEgypt.com has become a regional partner to Alibaba.com (the world's largest online B2B marketplace).

TradeEgypt.com has also allocated a considerable amount of effort in terms of search engine optimization to ensure all of the keywords related to subscribers are in a priority position. TradeEgypt.com has managed to achieve a first two-page rank on the major search engines, such as Yahoo!, Google, and MSN, for more than 12,000 keywords.

EGO has access to large databases of information and has demonstrated an excellent understanding of the needs and requirements of Egyptian exporters and manufacturers. In recognition of this, the Ministry of Communication and Information Technology (MCIT) in Egypt, the United States Agency for International Development (USAID), and Microsoft Egypt have awarded the company the task of providing the

content, design, development, and management of the exporter services section on Egypt's e-Government portal.

By 2009, TradeEgypt.com had 42,876 registered members and was ranked the 14th most popular B2B marketplace within its category by Ranking.com. TradeEgypt.com gets an average of 9,489,925 hits per month and an average of 133,442 visits per month.

Source: *www.tradeegypt.com*

Questions

1. Visit *TradeEgypt.com* and learn about the full range of marketplace services it provides. What are its revenue models?

2. What impact can TradeEgypt.com have on trade and exports in a developing country like Egypt?

The advantage of this approach is that consumer privacy is protected and some infomediaries offer consumers a percentage of the brokerage deals.

Producers and consumers may interact directly in an e-marketplace: Producers provide information to customers, who then select from among the available products. In general, producers set prices; sometimes, prices are negotiated. However, direct interactions are sometimes undesirable or unfeasible. In that case, intermediation is needed. Intermediaries, whether human or electronic, can address five important limitations of *direct interaction*, which are shown in Online File W2.5.

Distributors in B2B

A special type of intermediary in e-commerce is the B2B *e-distributor*. These intermediaries connect manufacturers with business buyers (customers), such as retailers (or resellers in the computer industry). **E-distributors** basically aggregate the catalogs or product information from many manufacturers, sometimes thousands of them, in one place—the intermediary's Web site. An example is W.W. Grainger (see Chapter 5 for details).

e-distributor
An e-commerce intermediary that connects manufacturers with business buyers (customers) by aggregating the catalogs of many manufacturers in one place—the intermediary's Web site.

Section 2.3 ▶ REVIEW QUESTIONS

1. Describe electronic storefronts and e-malls.
2. List the various types of stores and e-malls.
3. What are information portals? List the major types.
4. List the roles of intermediaries in e-markets.
5. Describe e-distributors.

2.4 ELECTRONIC CATALOGS, SEARCH ENGINES, AND SHOPPING CARTS

To enable selling online, a Web site usually needs *EC merchant server software* (see Online Chapter 18). Merchant software includes many functionalities. An example can be seen in OsCommerce.com, which is an open-system software (see oscommerce.com *and* en.wikipedia.org/wiki/OsCommerce). The basic functionality offered by such software includes electronic catalogs, search engines, and shopping carts.

ELECTRONIC CATALOGS

**electronic catalogs
(e-catalogs)**
The presentation of product information in an electronic form; the backbone of most e-selling sites.

Catalogs have been printed on paper for generations. Recently, electronic catalogs on CD-ROM and the Internet have gained popularity. **Electronic catalogs (e-catalogs)** consist of a product database, directory, and a presentation function. They are the backbone of most e-commerce sales sites. For merchants, the objective of electronic catalogs is to advertise and promote products and services. For the customer, the purpose of such catalogs is to locate information on products and services. Electronic catalogs can be searched quickly with the help of search engines, and they can be interactive (Cox and Koelzer 2006). For example, *Change My Image* from Infinisys (infinisys.co.jp) allows you to insert your photo and then change the hairstyle and color. Electronic catalogs can be very large; for example, the U.S. Library of Congress Web catalog (catalog.loc.gov) contains millions of records.

Most early online catalogs were replications of text and pictures from printed catalogs. However, online catalogs have evolved to become more dynamic, customized, and integrated with selling and buying procedures, shopping carts, order taking, and payment. The tools for building them are being integrated with merchant suites and Web hosting (e.g., see smallbusiness.yahoo.com/merchant). An example of a product catalog can be seen at jetpens.com (see Case 1.3 in Chapter 1).

Electronic catalogs can be classified according to three dimensions:

1. **The dynamics of the information presentation.** Catalogs may be static or dynamic. In static catalogs, information is presented in text and static pictures. In dynamic catalogs, information is presented in motion pictures, videos, or animation, possibly with supplemental sound. Dynamic catalogs can be real time, changing frequently, such as with prices of stocks (and commodities) on stock exchange tickers.

2. **The degree of customization.** Catalogs may be standard or customized. In standard catalogs, merchants offer the same catalog to any customer. In customized catalogs, content, pricing, and display are tailored to the characteristics of specific customers. See the discussion and example of how this is done at Office Max in Online File W2.6.

3. **Integration with business processes.** Catalogs can be classified according to the degree of integration with the following business processes or features: order taking and fulfillment; electronic payment systems; intranet workflow software and systems; inventory and accounting systems; suppliers' or customers' extranets; and paper catalogs. For example, when a customer places an order at amazon.com, the order is transferred automatically to a computerized inventory-availability check. Many sellers advise you on the availability of items and delivery dates.

Although used only occasionally in B2C commerce, customized catalogs are used frequently in B2B e-commerce. For example, e-catalogs can show only the items that the employees in a specific organization are allowed to purchase and can exclude items the buying company's managers do not want their employees to see or to buy. E-catalogs can be customized to show the same item to different customers at different prices, reflecting discounts or purchase-contract agreements. They can even show the buyer's ID number for the item, model, or stock-keeping unit (SKU) number, rather than the seller's ID numbers. For a comprehensive discussion of online catalogs, see jcmax.com/advantages.html and purchasing.about.com.

Online Catalogs Versus Paper Catalogs

The advantages and disadvantages of online catalogs are contrasted with those of paper catalogs in Exhibit 2.5. Although online catalogs have significant advantages, such as ease of updating, the ability to be integrated with the purchasing process, coverage of a wide spectrum of products, interactivity, customization, and strong search capabilities, they also have disadvantages and limitations. To begin, customers need computers and Internet access to view online catalogs. However, as computer availability and Internet access continue to grow, many paper catalogs will be supplemented by, if not actually replaced by, electronic ones. The number of print newspapers and magazines may have diminished due to online ones, but the future of print will not be to disappear entirely. Paper catalogs probably will not disappear altogether either. There seems to be room for both media, at least in the near future. However, in B2B paper catalogs may disappear more quickly.

Example. RadioShack (radioshack.com) builds and maintains electronic catalogs based on its customers' paper catalogs. The catalogs include search capabilities, the ability to feature large numbers of products, enhanced viewing capabilities, updating, and support.

EXHIBIT 2.5	Comparison of Online Catalogs with Paper Catalogs	
Type	**Advantages**	**Disadvantages**
Paper catalogs	• Easy to create without high technology • Reader is able to look at the catalog without computer system • More portable than electronic	• Difficult to update changed product information promptly • Only a limited number of products can be displayed • Limited information through photographs and textual description is available • No possibility for advanced multimedia such as animation and voice
Online catalogs	• Easy to update product information • Able to integrate with the purchasing process • Good search and comparison capabilities • Able to provide timely, up-to-date product information • Provision for globally broad range of product information • Possibility of adding on voice and animated pictures • Long-term cost savings • Easy to customize • More comparative shopping • Ease of connecting order processing, inventory processing, and payment processing to the system	• Difficult to develop catalogs, large fixed cost • Need for customer skill to deal with computers and browsers

EC SEARCH ACTIVITIES, TYPES, AND ENGINES

Search activities are popular in EC, and many tools for conducting searches are available. Here we describe only the essentials. First, though, we look at the major types of searches.

Types of EC Searches

The three major types of EC search are *Internet/Web search*, *enterprise search*, and *desktop search*.

Internet/Web Search. This is the standard search that involves any documents on the Web. According to Pew Internet and other statistical sites, finding information is one of the topmost important activities on the Web.

Enterprise Search. An **enterprise search** is the practice of identifying and enabling specific content across the enterprise to be indexed, searched, and displayed to authorized users. It describes the application of search technology to information *within* an organization. This is in contrast to the other two main types of horizontal search environment: Web search and desktop search.

The major challenge faced by enterprise search is the need to index documents from a variety of sources, such as file systems, intranets, document management systems, e-mail, and

enterprise search

The practice of identifying and enabling specific content across the enterprise to be indexed, searched, and displayed to authorized users.

databases, and then present a consolidated list of relevance-ranked documents from these various sources. Access controls are vital if users are to be restricted to documents within the various document repositories of the enterprise.

Desktop Search. A **desktop search** is conducted by tools that search only the contents of a user's own computer files. The emphasis is on finding all the information that is available on the user's PC, including Web browser histories, e-mail archives, music, chats, photos, and word-processed documents.

One main advantage of desktop search programs is that search results come up in a few seconds. A variety of desktop search programs are available, such as Spotlight from Apple Computer, XI Enterprise, and Google's Desktop (see desktop.google.com). Desktop search is very useful: It is an efficient productivity tool that helps to increase information security.

Each search discussed here is accomplished with search engines and intelligent agents.

Search Engines

A **search engine** is a computer program that can access databases of Internet or intranet resources, search for specific information or keywords, and report the results. For example, customers tend to ask for information (e.g., requests for product information or pricing) in same general manner. This type of request is repetitive, and answering such requests is costly when done by a human. Search engines deliver answers economically and efficiently by matching questions with FAQ (frequently asked question) templates, which respond with "canned" answers.

Google, AltaVista, and Lycos are popular search engines. Portals such as AOL, Yahoo!, and MSN have their own search engines. Special search engines organized to answer certain questions or search in specified areas include Ask.com, Northern Light, Mama, and Looksmart. Thousands of different public search engines are available (see searchengineguide.com). These can be very specialized with different capabilities (see Martin 2008). In addition, hundreds of companies have search engines on their portals or storefronts. Endeca InFront (from endeca.com) is a special search engine for online catalogs.

Software (Intelligent) Agents

Unlike a search engine, a software (intelligent) agent can do more than just "search and match." It has capabilities that can be used to perform routine tasks that require intelligence. For example, it can monitor movements on a Web site to check whether a customer seems lost or ventures into areas that may not fit the customer's profile. If it detects such confusion, the agent can notify the customer and provide assistance. Software agents can be used in e-commerce to support tasks such as conducting complex searches, comparing prices, interpreting information, monitoring activities, and working as an assistant. Users can even chat or collaborate with intelligent agents as is done in Second Life, where the agents are avatars that "understand" natural language interface.

Voice-Powered Search

To ease searching, especially when using a cell phone, Google introduced a voice-powered tool that allows you to skip the keyboard altogether. The first product was included as part of iPhone's mobile search application. It allows you to talk into your phone, ask any question, and the results of your query are offered on your iPhone.

SHOPPING CARTS

An **electronic shopping cart** is an order-processing technology that allows customers to accumulate items they wish to buy while they continue to shop. In this respect, it is similar to a shopping cart in the physical world. The software program of an electronic shopping cart allows customers to select items, review what has been selected, make changes, and then finalize the list. Clicking on "buy" will trigger the actual purchase.

Shopping carts for B2C are fairly simple (visit amazon.com to see an example), but for B2B a shopping cart may be more complex.

Shopping-cart software is sold or provided for free as an independent component (e.g., ecommerce.networksolutions.com and easycart.com). It also is embedded in merchants'

desktop search
Search tools that search the contents of a user's or organization's computer files, rather than searching the Internet. The emphasis is on finding all the information that is available on the user's PC, including Web browser histories, e-mail archives, and word-processed documents, as well as in all internal files and databases.

search engine
A computer program that can access databases of Internet resources, search for specific information or keywords, and report the results.

electronic shopping cart
An order-processing technology that allows customers to accumulate items they wish to buy while they continue to shop.

servers, such as smallbusiness.yahoo.com/merchant. Free online shopping carts (trials and demos) are available at volusion.com and gomerchant.com.

For more on shopping carts, see Chapter 15 and Online Chapter 18.

Product Configuration

A key characteristic of EC is the self-customization of products and services, as done by Dell. Manufacturers need to produce customized products in economic and rapid ways so that the price of the products will be competitive. *Product configuration* systems support the acquisition of customer requirements while automating the order-taking process, and they allow customers to configure their products by specifying their technical requirements. Sophisticated product configuration systems use artificial intelligence (AI) tools because they need to support interaction with the customers and understand their needs.

Section 2.4 ▶ REVIEW QUESTIONS

1. List and briefly describe the dimensions by which electronic catalogs can be classified.
2. List the benefits of electronic catalogs.
3. Explain how customized catalogs are created and used.
4. Compare search engines with software intelligent agents.
5. Describe an electronic shopping cart.

2.5 AUCTIONS, BARTERING, AND NEGOTIATING ONLINE

One of the most interesting market mechanisms in e-commerce is electronic auctions (Nissanoff 2006). They are used in B2C, B2B, C2C, G2B, G2C, and more.

DEFINITION AND CHARACTERISTICS

auction

A competitive process in which a seller solicits consecutive bids from buyers (forward auctions) or a buyer solicits bids from sellers (backward auctions). Prices are determined dynamically by the bids.

An **auction** is a market mechanism that uses a competitive process by which a seller solicits consecutive bids from buyers (forward auctions) or a buyer solicits bids from sellers (reverse auctions). Prices are determined dynamically by the bids. A wide variety of online markets qualify as auctions using this definition. Auctions, an established method of commerce for generations, deal with products and services for which conventional marketing channels are ineffective or inefficient, and they ensure prudent execution of sales. For example, auctions can expedite the disposal of items that need to be liquidated or sold quickly. Rare coins and other collectibles are frequently sold at auction.

There are several types of auctions, each with its own motives and procedures. (For details, see Chapter 17.) Auctions can be done *online* or *offline*. They can be conducted in *public* auction sites such as at eBay. They also can be done by invitation to *private* auctions.

This section presents information about auctions that is necessary for understanding related material in Chapters 3 through 5.

TRADITIONAL AUCTIONS VERSUS E-AUCTIONS

Traditional, physical auctions are still very popular. However, the volume traded on e-auctions is significantly larger and continues to increase.

Limitations of Traditional Offline Auctions

Traditional offline auctions, regardless of their type, have several limitations. They usually last only a few minutes, or even seconds, for each item sold. This rapid process may give potential buyers little time to make a decision, so they may decide not to bid. Therefore, sellers may not get the highest possible price; bidders may not get what they really want or they may pay too much for the item. Also, in many cases the bidders do not have much time to examine the goods. Bidders have difficulty learning about auctions and cannot compare what is offered at each location. Bidders must usually be physically present at auctions; thus, many potential bidders are excluded.

Similarly, it may be difficult for sellers to move goods to an auction site. Commissions are fairly high because a location must be rented, the auction needs to be advertised, and an auctioneer and other employees need to be paid. Electronic auctioning removes these deficiencies.

Electronic Auctions

The Internet provides an infrastructure for executing auctions electronically at lower cost, with a wide array of support services, and with many more sellers and buyers. Individual consumers and corporations both can participate in this rapidly growing and very convenient form of e-commerce. Forrester Research projects that the Internet auction industry will reach $65.2 billion in sales by 2010 (*Edgar Online* 2006).

Electronic auctions (e-auctions) are similar to offline auctions except that they are done online. E-auctions have been in existence since the 1980s over LANs (e.g., flowers; see Saarinen et al. 2006). Host sites on the Internet, which were started in 1995, serve as brokers, offering services for sellers to post their goods for sale and allowing buyers to bid on those items.

Major online auctions, such as eBay, offer consumer products, electronic parts, artwork, vacation packages, airline tickets, and collectibles, as well as excess supplies and inventories being auctioned off by B2B marketers. Another type of B2B online auction is increasingly used to trade special types of commodities, such as electricity transmission capacities and gas and energy options. Furthermore, conventional business practices that traditionally have relied on contracts and fixed prices are increasingly being converted into auctions with bidding for online procurements (e.g., Raffles Hotel, Online File W2.2). Some examples of innovative auctions are provided next.

electronic auctions (e-auctions)
Auctions conducted online.

Innovative Auctions

Examples of innovative implementations of e-auctions are as follows:

> ▶ Every year, Warren Buffett, the famous U.S. stock investor and investment guru, invites a group of eight people to lunch with him. The eight pay big money for the pleasure. The money is donated to the needy in San Francisco. In the past, Buffett charged $30,000 per group. As of July 2003, Buffett places the invitation on an online auction (eBay). In 2003, bidders pushed the bid from $30,000 to $250,100. The winning bid in 2008 was $2,110,000. One of the winners commented that he was willing to pay whatever was needed so that he could express to Buffett his appreciation for investment guidance. Before the auction, he had no chance to be invited.
>
> ▶ A Harley-Davidson motorcycle autographed by celebrities and offered by talk-show host Jay Leno fetched $800,100 on eBay to benefit tsunami victims.
>
> ▶ JetBlue airlines started to auction flights in September 2008 on eBay. The initial offer was 300 flights and six vacation packages, with opening bids set between 5¢ and 10¢ (yes, cents) The flights are to more than 20 destinations, including four "mystery" JetBlue Getaways, vacation packages to undisclosed locations.
>
>   The 3-, 5-, and 7-day auctions included 1- and 2-person roundtrip, weekend flights in September from cities including Boston, Chicago, New York, Orlando, Salt Lake City, Fort Lauderdale, and Southern California.
>
>   Although no one was lucky enough to get a flight for 5 or 10 cents, many auctions gave the winners a flight that was 10 to 20 percent cheaper than regular prices.
>
> ▶ Richard Dan operates an eBay store in Maui, Hawaii, called Safedeal (see the trading assistants list on ebay.com). Initially he was selling unclaimed items from his pawnbroker business. Now he is also one of eBay's 40,000 "trading assistants." Web Auction Hawaii and other trading assistants handle advertisements, auction listings, appraisals, descriptions, authentication, payments, shipments, insurance, and more. Dan also advises sellers as to which eBay category is the best for their particular item. Dan is helping nonprofit organizations, estate administrators, and others to sell just about anything, including the four mules he helped sell in September 2004. Dan's basic charge is $25 per item plus a 25 percent commission. (He only handles items with an expected price of more than $200.)

DYNAMIC PRICING AND TYPES OF AUCTIONS

dynamic pricing
Prices that change based on supply and demand relationships at any given time.

One major characteristic of auctions is that they are based on dynamic pricing. **Dynamic pricing** refers to prices that are not fixed but that are allowed to fluctuate as supply and demand in a market change. In contrast, catalog prices are fixed, as are prices in department stores, supermarkets, and most electronic storefronts.

Dynamic pricing appears in several forms. Perhaps the oldest forms are negotiation and bargaining, which have been practiced for many generations in open-air markets. It is customary to classify dynamic pricing into four major categories based on how many buyers and sellers are involved. These four categories are outlined in the following text and are discussed more fully in Chapter 17.

One Buyer, One Seller

In this configuration, one can use negotiation, bargaining, or bartering. The resulting price will be determined by each party's bargaining power, supply and demand in the item's market, and (possibly) business environment factors.

One Seller, Many Potential Buyers

forward auction
An auction in which a seller entertains bids from buyers. Bidders increase price sequentially.

In this configuration, the seller uses a **forward auction**, an auction in which a seller entertains bids from multiple buyers. (Because forward auctions are the most common and traditional form, they often are simply called *auctions*.) The four major types of forward auctions are *English* and *Yankee* auctions, in which bidding prices increase as the auction progresses, and *Dutch* and *free-fall* auctions, in which bidding prices decline as the auction progresses. Each of these can be used for either liquidation or for market efficiency (see Chapter 17).

One Buyer, Many Potential Sellers

reverse auction (bidding or tendering system)
Auction in which the buyer places an item for bid (tender) on a request for quote (RFQ) system, potential suppliers bid on the job, with the price reducing sequentially, and the lowest bid wins; primarily a B2B or G2B mechanism.

Two popular types of auctions in which there is one buyer and many potential sellers are reverse auctions (tendering) and "name-your-own-price" auctions.

Reverse Auctions. When there is one buyer and many potential sellers, a **reverse auction** (also called a **bidding** or **tendering system**) is in place. In a reverse auction, the buyer places an item he or she wants to buy for bid (or *tender*) on a *request for quote* (RFQ) system. Potential suppliers bid on the item, reducing the price sequentially (see Exhibit 2.6). In electronic bidding in a reverse auction, several rounds of bidding may take place until the bidders do not reduce the price further. The winner is the one with the lowest bid (assuming

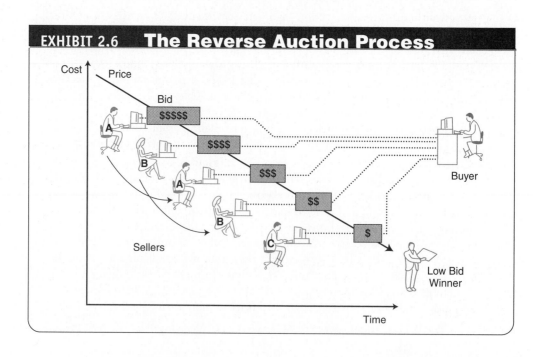

EXHIBIT 2.6   The Reverse Auction Process

that only price is considered). Reverse auctions are primarily a B2B or G2B mechanism. (For further discussion and examples, see Chapter 5.)

The Name-Your-Own-Price Model. Priceline.com pioneered the **"name-your-own-price" model.** In this model, a would-be buyer specifies the price (and other terms) that he or she is willing to pay to any willing and able seller. For example, Priceline.com presents consumers' requests to sellers, who fill as much of the guaranteed demand as they wish at prices and terms requested by buyers. Alternately, Priceline.com searches its own database that contains vendors' lowest prices and tries to match supply against requests. Priceline.com asks customers to guarantee acceptance of the offer if it is at or below the requested price by giving a credit card number. This is basically a C2B model, although some businesses use it, too (see Chapter 17 for details).

"name-your-own-price" model
Auction model in which a would-be buyer specifies the price (and other terms) he or she is willing to pay to any willing and able seller. It is a C2B model that was pioneered by Priceline.com.

Many Sellers, Many Buyers

When there are many sellers and many buyers, buyers and their bidding prices are matched with sellers and their asking prices based on the quantities on both sides. Stocks and commodities markets are typical examples of this configuration. Buyers and sellers may be individuals or businesses. Such an auction is called a **double auction** (see Chapter 17 for details).

double auction
An auction in which multiple buyers and their bidding prices are matched with multiple sellers and their asking prices, considering the quantities on both sides.

BENEFITS, LIMITATIONS, AND IMPACTS OF E-AUCTIONS

E-auctions are becoming important selling and buying channels for many companies and individuals. E-auctions enable buyers to access goods and services anywhere auctions are conducted. Moreover, almost perfect market information is available about prices, products, current supply and demand, and so on. These characteristics provide benefits to all.

Benefits of E-Auctions

According to Nissanoff (2006), the auction culture will revolutionize the way customers buy, sell, and obtain what they want. A listing of the benefits of e-auctions to sellers, buyers, and e-auctioneers is provided in Exhibit 2.7.

EXHIBIT 2.7   Benefits of E-Auctions

Benefits to Sellers	Benefits to Buyers	Benefits to E-Auctioneers
• Increased revenues from broadening bidder base and shortening cycle time. Can sell anywhere globally. • Opportunity to bargain instead of selling at a fixed price. Can sell any time and conduct frequent auctions. • Optimal price setting determined by the market (more buyers, more information). • Sellers can gain more customer dollars by offering items directly (saves on the commission to intermediaries; also, physical auctions are very expensive compared with e-auctions). • Can liquidate large quantities quickly. • Improved customer relationship and loyalty (in the case of specialized B2B auction sites and electronic exchanges).	• Opportunities to find unique items and collectibles. • Entertainment. Participation in e-auctions can be entertaining and exciting. • Convenience. Buyers can bid from anywhere, even with a cell phone; they do not have to travel to an auction place. • Anonymity. With the help of a third party, buyers can remain anonymous. • Possibility of finding bargains, for both individuals and organizations.	• Higher repeat purchases. Jupiter Research (*jupiterresearch.com*) found that auction sites, such as eBay, tend to garner higher repeat-purchase rates than the top B2C sites, such as Amazon.com. • High "stickiness" to the Web site (the tendency of customers to stay at sites longer and come back more often). Auction sites are frequently "stickier" than fixed-priced sites. Stickier sites generate more ad revenue for the e-auctioneer. • Easy expansion of the auction business.

Limitations of E-Auctions

E-auctions have several limitations. The most significant limitations are minimal security, the possibility of fraud, and limited participation.

Minimal Security. Some of the C2C auctions conducted on the Internet are not secure because they are done in an unencrypted environment. This means that credit card numbers could be stolen during the payment process. Payment methods such as PayPal (paypal.com) can be used to solve the problem (see Chapter 11). In addition, some B2B auctions are conducted over highly secure private lines.

Possibility of Fraud. Auction items are in many cases unique, used, or antique. Because the buyer cannot see the items, the buyer may get defective products. Also, buyers can commit fraud by receiving goods or services without paying for them. Thus, the fraud rate on e-auctions is relatively high. For a discussion of e-auction fraud and fraud prevention, see Chapter 17.

Limited Participation. Some auctions are by invitation only; others are open to dealers only. Limited participation may be a disadvantage to sellers, who usually benefit from as large a pool of buyers as possible.

Impacts of Auctions

Because the trade objects and contexts for auctions are very diverse, the rationale behind auctions and the motives of the different participants for setting up auctions are quite different. The following are some representative impacts of e-auctions.

Auctions as a Coordination Mechanism. Auctions are used increasingly as an efficient coordination mechanism for establishing price equilibrium. An example is auctions for the allocation of telecommunications bandwidth.

Auctions as a Social Mechanism to Determine a Price. For objects that are not traded in traditional markets, such as unique or rare items, or for items that may be offered randomly or at long intervals, an auction creates a marketplace that attracts potential buyers, and often experts. By offering many of these special items at a single place and time and by attracting considerable attention, auctions provide the requisite exposure of purchase and sale orders, and hence liquidity of the market in which an optimal price can be determined. Typical examples are auctions of fine arts or rare items, as well as auctions of communications frequencies, Web banners, and advertising space. For example, wine collectors can find a global wine auction at winebid.com.

Auctions as a Highly Visible Distribution Mechanism. Some auctions deal with special offers. In this case, a supplier typically auctions off a limited number of items, using the auction primarily as a mechanism to gain attention and to attract those customers who are bargain hunters or who have a preference for the gambling dimension of the auction process. The airline seat auctions by Cathay Pacific, American Airlines, and Lufthansa fall into this category (see Saarinen et al. 2006).

Auctions as an EC Component. Auctions can stand alone, or they may be combined with other e-commerce activities. An example of the latter is the combination of group purchasing with reverse auctions, as described in Online File W2.7.

Auctions for Profit for Individuals. As illustrated in Chapter 1, individuals can make money by selling things that they buy at bargain prices on eBay. If you are interested in learning how to do this, read Joyner (2007) and Weber (2008).

ONLINE BARTERING

bartering
The *exchange* of goods and services.

Bartering, the exchange of goods and services, is the oldest method of trade. Today, it is done primarily between organizations. The problem with bartering is that it is difficult to find trading partners. Businesses and individuals may use classified ads to advertise what they need and what they offer, but they still may not be able to find what they want. Intermediaries may be helpful, but they are expensive (20% to 30% commission) and very slow.

e-bartering (electronic bartering)
Bartering conducted online, usually in a bartering exchange.

E-bartering (electronic bartering)—bartering conducted online—can improve the matching process by attracting more partners to the barter. In addition, matching can be done faster, and as a result, better matches can be found. Items that are frequently bartered online include office space, storage, and factory space; idle facilities; and labor, products, and banner ads. (Note that e-bartering may have tax implications that need to be considered.)

E-bartering is usually done in a **bartering exchange**, a marketplace in which an intermediary arranges the transactions. These exchanges can be very effective. Representative bartering Web sites include allbusiness.com, intagio.com, and barterdepot.com. The process works like this: First, the company tells the bartering exchange what it wants to offer. The exchange then assesses the value of the company's products or services and offers it certain "points" or "bartering dollars." The company can use the "points" to buy the things it needs from a participating member in the exchange.

Bartering sites must be financially secure. Otherwise, users may not have a chance to use the points they accumulate. (For further details see virtualbarter.net and barternews.com.)

> **bartering exchange**
> A marketplace in which an intermediary arranges barter transactions.

ONLINE NEGOTIATING

Dynamic prices also can be determined by *negotiation*. Negotiated pricing commonly is used for expensive or specialized products. Negotiated prices also are popular when large quantities are purchased. Much like auctions, negotiated prices result from interactions and bargaining among sellers and buyers. However, in contrast with auctions, negotiation also deals with nonpricing terms, such as the payment method and credit. Negotiation is a well-known process in the offline world (e.g., in real estate, automobile purchases, and contract work). In addition, in cases where there is no standard service or product to speak of, some digital products and services can be personalized and "bundled" at a standard price. Preferences for these bundled services differ among consumers, and thus they are frequently negotiated. A simple peer-to-peer (P2P) negotiation can be seen at ioffer.com (see Chapter 17). For more on negotiation in P2P money lending, see the ZOPA and Prosper cases in Chapter 9. *Online (electronic) negotiation* may be more effective and efficient than offline negotiation. Due to customization and bundling of products and services, it is often necessary to negotiate both prices and terms for online sales. E-markets allow such online negotiations to be conducted virtually for all products and services. Three factors may facilitate online negotiation: (1) the products and services that are bundled and customized, (2) the computer technology that facilitates the negotiation process, and (3) the software (intelligent) agents that perform searches and comparisons, thereby providing quality customer service and a base from which prices can be negotiated. Chemconnect, a large B2B exchange, allows parties to negotiate online (see Chapter 5).

Section 2.5 ▶ REVIEW QUESTIONS

1. Define auctions and describe how they work.
2. Describe the benefits of electronic auctions over traditional (offline) auctions.
3. List the four types of auctions.
4. Distinguish between forward and reverse auctions.
5. Describe the "name-your-own-price" auction model.
6. List the major benefits of auctions to buyers, sellers, and auctioneers.
7. What are the major limitations of auctions?
8. List the major impacts of auctions on markets.
9. Define bartering and describe the advantages of e-bartering.
10. Explain the role of online negotiation in EC.

2.6 WEB 2.0 TOOLS AND SERVICES: FROM BLOGS TO WIKIS

The Web 2.0 environment is usually associated with its tools. The major tools and services are listed in Exhibit 2.8. For a comprehensive list see Kathy Schrock's Guide for Educators at school.discoveryeducatiuon.com/schrockguide/edtools.html and kathyschrock.net/web20.

The increased importance of social networking and Web 2.0 computing resulted in many innovative tools and services. Social networking, for example, is penetrating into enterprises and even becoming a B2B phenomenon (see Chapters 5 and 9). However, according to

EXHIBIT 2.8   Social-Networking Software Tools

Tools for Online Communication
- Instant messaging
- VoIP and Skype
- Text chat
- Internet forums
- Blogs or weblogs
- Wikis
- Collaborative real-time editor
- Prediction markets

Types of Services
- Social network services
- Social network search engines
- Social guides
- Social bookmarking
- Social citations
- Social libraries
- Virtual worlds and Massively-Multiplayer Online Games (MMOGs)
- Other specialized social applications
- Politics and journalism
- Content management tools

Emerging Technologies
- Peer-to-peer social networks
- Virtual presence
- Mobile tools for Web 2.0

Tools for Individuals
- Personalization
- Customization
- Search
- RSS
- File-sharing tools

Web 2.0 Development Tools
- Mushups
- Web services (Online Chapter 16)

Sources: Compiled from *en.wikipedia.org/wiki/Social_software* (accessed April 2009), Hinchcliffe (2006, Weblogs, Inc. (2007), and authors' experience.

Harvard Business School professor Andrew McAfee (Farber 2008), we need to keep in mind that most Web 2.0 tools (or Enterprise 2.0 tools) are new, and their acceptance depends on shifts in perspective on the part of business leaders and decision makers. Enterprise 2.0 tools have no inherent respect for organizational boundaries, hierarchies, or job titles. They facilitate self-organization and emergent rather than imposed structure. They require line managers, compliance officers, and other stewards to trust that users will not deliberately or inadvertently use them inappropriately.

According to a Forrester survey, companies are spending money mostly on wikis, blogs, RSS, tagging, podcasting and social networking (Farber 2008).

In this chapter we will cover blogs, wikis, micro-blogging, and Twitter (in this section) and virtual worlds in Section 2.7.

BLOGGING (WEBLOGGING)

blog
A personal Web site that is open to the public to read and to interact with; dedicated to specific topics or issues.

The Internet offers the opportunity for individuals to publish on the Web using a technology known as *Weblogging*, or *blogging*. A **blog** is a personal Web site, open to the public, in which the owner expresses his or her feelings or opinions. Blogs became very popular after the terrorist attacks of September 11, 2001. People were looking for as many sources of information as possible and for personal connections to the tragedy. Blogs comfort people in times of stress. They offer a place where people feel their ideas are noticed, and they can result in two-way communication and collaboration, group discussion, and so on. As seen in the EMS opening case, blogs can be used in the enterprise. Blogs are written usually by individuals, but some are written by two or more authors.

Many blogs provide commentary or news on a particular subject; others function as more personal online diaries. A typical blog combines text, images, and links to other blogs, Web pages, and other media related to its topic. The ability for readers to leave comments in an interactive format is an important part of many blogs. Most blogs are primarily textual, although some focus on art (artlog), photographs (photoblog), sketches (sketchblog), music (MP3 blog), or audio (podcasting, which is part of a wider network of social media). *Microblogging* is another type of blogging, one that consists of blogs with very short posts. A **vlog** (or **video blog**) is a blog with video content. As of December 2007, blog search engine Technorati was tracking more than 112 million blogs. With the advent of video blogging, the word *blog* has taken on an even looser meaning than that of any other media wherein the subject expresses his opinion or simply talks about something. Notice that almost 10,000 fake or spam blogs are created daily (out of 150,000 to 200,000) in total. The number of blogs is estimated to double every year. Most blogs are written in English and Japanese.

vlog (or video blog)
A blog with video content.

The totality of blogs is known as the *blogosphere*. The most common types of blogs are *professional blogs*, which focus on professions, job aspects, and career building; *personal blogs*, which often take the form of an online diary containing thoughts, poems, experiences, and other personal matters; *topical blogs*, which focus on a certain topic or niche (see the list at en.wikipedia.org/wiki/Blog), discussing specific aspects of the chosen subject; and *business blogs*, which are discussions about business and/or the stock market. Other types of blogs include, but are not limited to, *science blogs, culture blogs,* and *educational blogs.* Flynn (2006) estimates that one new blog is created every second (two blogs per second in 2008). There were more than 2 million daily postings on the blogosphere as of June 2008. The January 1, 2007, issue of *Time* was dedicated to blog communities. It described the story of 15 citizens—including a French rapper, a relentless reviewer, and a lonely girl—who are members of the new digital democracy.

Building Effective Blogs

It is becoming easier and easier to build blogs. Programs from blogger.com, pitas.com, and others are very user-friendly. Blog space is free; the goal is to make it easy for users to create their own blogs. *Bloggers* (the people who create and maintain blogs) are handed a fresh space on their Web site to write in each day. They can easily edit, add entries, and broadcast whatever they want by simply clicking "send." Blogging software such as WordPress or Movable Type helps bloggers update their blogs easily. Free blog generators, such as Blogger, let users host their content on Google servers without having to install any software or obtain a domain name. Vlogs are often distributed through RSS feeds.

The crucial features that distinguish a blog from a regular Web page, according to Rapoza (2006), are trackbacks, blogrolls, pings, feedblitz (an e-mail list management solution), and RSS feeds. Bloggers also use a special terminology. See samizdata.net for a dictionary of blog terms.

Datta (2006) suggests seven principles for building effective blogs:

1. Focus intently on a narrow niche, ideally one whose audience has a predilection for high-margin products.
2. Set up blogs so that each post gets its own permanent URL.
3. Think of a blog as a database, not a newspaper-like collection of dispatches.
4. Blog frequently and regularly, at least a half-dozen posts every weekday.
5. Use striking images that liven up the pages and attract readers.
6. Enable comments and interact with readers.
7. Make friends with other bloggers, online and off.

Micro-Blogging and Twitter

micro-blogging
A form of blogging that allows users to write messages (usually up to 140 characters) and publish them, either to be viewed by anyone or by a restricted group that can be chosen by the user. These messages can be submitted by a variety of means, including text messaging, instant messaging, e-mail, MP3, or just on the Web.

Micro-blogging is a form of blogging that allows users to write messages (usually up to 140 characters) and publish them, either to be viewed by anyone or by a restricted group that can be chosen by the user. These messages can be submitted by a variety of means, including text messaging, instant messaging, e-mail, MP3, or just on the Web.

The content of a micro-blog differs from that of a regular blog due to the limited space per message. Many micro-blogs provide short messages about personal matters.

A new service known as Pownce integrates micro-blogging with file sharing and event invitations. Another service, Spoink, integrates blogging, podcasting, telephony, and short message service (SMS) texting; it supports all major mobile audio, video, and picture formats.

The popular social-networking Web sites Facebook, MySpace, Xing, and LinkedIn have a micro-blogging feature called "status update." The most popular service is Twitter. There are more than 100 competitors of Twitter worldwide. The main competitor to Twitter has been Jaiku (although this has since been acquired by Google and has been closed to public registrations).

Twitter

Twitter
A free micro-blogging service that allows its users to send and read other users' updates.

tweets
Text-based posts up to 140 characters in length posted to Twitter.

Twitter is a free micro-blogging service that allows its users to send and read other users' updates, otherwise known as **tweets**, which are text-based posts up to 140 characters in length.

Updates are displayed on the user's profile page and delivered to other users who have signed up to receive them. The sender can restrict delivery to those in his or her circle of friends (delivery to everyone being the default). Users can receive updates via the Twitter Web site, SMS, RSS, e-mail, or through an application such as Twitterrific or Facebook. Four gateway numbers are currently available for SMS: short codes for India, the United States, and Canada, as well as a United Kingdom–based number for international use. Several third parties offer posting and receiving updates via e-mail. A special version is available for Japanese users. For details, see en.wikipedia.org/wiki/Twitter.

As of October 2008, Twitter claims to have more than 3,200,000 registered accounts. Socialtext (socialtext.com) offers a version of Twitter for the enterprise. For Twitter as a communication and collaboration tool, see Chapters 6 and 8.

Commercial Uses of Blogs

The blog concept has transferred quickly to the corporate world. According to the 2006 Workplace E-Mail, Instant Messaging & Blog Survey from the American Management Association (AMA) and the ePolicy Institute, 8 percent of U.S.–based organizations operate business blogs. Of that number, 55 percent operate external, or "facing out," blogs to communicate with customers and other third parties, as was done in the opening case of this chapter. Another 48 percent have established internal blogs to enhance employee communication with one another (many operate both). Even CEOs are diving into the blogosphere, with 16 percent using blogs to build trust-based relationships, polish corporate reputations, promote social causes, and accomplish other professional goals. Blogging provides the opportunity to supplement corporate public relations, press releases, and brochures with more personal, "from the heart" talk and offer convenient links to related sources. A skillfully written, content-rich business blog can help organizations position executives as industry thought leaders, build brand awareness, facilitate two-way communication, and accomplish other important business goals (Weber 2007). Blogs have gone from self-indulgent hobbies to flourishing businesses with the Web 2.0 wave. See Sloan and Kaihla (2006) for a survey of commercial uses of blogs. The following examples illustrate how companies use blogs for different purposes.

Example 1: Stonyfield Farm Adopts Blogs for Public Relations. Stonyfield Farm (stonyfield.com) is the third largest organic company in the world, producing more than 18 million cups of yogurt each month. The company's core values are promoting healthy food and protecting the environment. It guarantees the use of only natural ingredients in its products and donates 10 percent of its profit each year to efforts that protect the earth.

The company employs "word-of-mouth" marketing approaches that are compatible with its grassroots "people-friendly" image. Recently, Stonyfield turned to blogs to further personalize its relationship with its customers and connect with even more people. The blogs provide the company with what the management calls a "handshake" with customers. Stonyfield publishes four different blogs on its Web site: (1) "Healthy Kids" encourages healthy food consumption in public schools; (2) "Strong Women Daily" features fitness, health tips, and stress-coping strategies; (3) "Baby Babble" provides a forum for child development and balancing work with family; and (4) "The Bovine Bugle" provides reports from organic dairy farms.

Stonyfield hires a journalist and almanac writer to post new content to each of the blogs daily, five days a week. When readers subscribe to the blogs, they will receive automatic updates, and they can also respond to the postings. The blogs have created a positive response for the Stonyfield brand by providing readers with topics that inspire them and pique their interests. They are also, of course, persuaded to try and buy Stonyfield products. The management believes that blogs are an excellent method of public relations.

Example 2: Arianna Huffington Makes a New Business Model from Blogging. Arianna Huffington (with her partner Kenneth Lerer) assembled a group of bloggers into a liberal gossip/commentary site, *The Huffington Post* (known as *HuffPo*). It is considered a citizen-powered online blog that covers politics, education, religion, and world affairs. The site attracts many visitors, but it has been blamed for allowing the posting of controversial and hate speech. Huffington removes such comments as soon as they come to the attention of the blog's moderators. However, this points to the issue of user-created content control (see the Wikipedia case in Chapter 9).

Despite the controversy, the site is blooming financially. For example, Barry Diller, the CEO of one of the world's largest EC companies, IAC Interactive Corp. (iac.com), partnered with HuffPo when he launched a comedy Web site.

With relatively little money, Huffington and her partners created a new business model for building communities around news content. Unlike a conventional newspaper that devotes the majority of its resources to basic news gathering, *The Huffington Post* instead devoted its scant editorial budget to hiring a few key editors, staff bloggers, and political reporters who post links to the day's stories and fill the site with a gossipy and slightly indignant sensibility, while giving the endless parade of invited bloggers co-star status on the Arianna Show. By fall 2007, some 1,600 bloggers (including very famous people such as John Kerry and Governor Bill Richardson) accepted Huffington's invitation to write. They are given a password to log into the site's publishing system and blog at will.

Using Blogging to Facilitate Collaboration

Organizations use mainly blogs, wikis, and RSS feeds to facilitate collaboration, communication, and information sharing internally as well as externally. They use an intranet (internally) and an extranet (externally). Here are a few examples:

- Dresdner Kleinwort bank (Germany) is using wikis to supplement regular collaboration tools within its global teams. The wikis also provide a complete audit trail (see socialtext.com).
- According to Weinstein (2006), wikis, blogs, and intranet knowledge bases are used by many companies to facilitate training of both individuals and groups (classes).
- Procter & Gamble uses RSS feeds for news and business information dissemination, wikis for collaboration, blogs for communication and sharing, and more. They even launched a social network that makes it easier to find people with needed expertise (Hoover 2007).
- Stormhoek Vineyards, a small South African winery, tripled its sales in 2 years by using a wiki and blogs to create groups for wine-tasting parties (see Chapter 9).
- Motorola is using 4,400 blogs and 4,200 wiki pages; 2,600 people actively do content tagging and social bookmarking (Hoover 2007).
- McDonald's blog, called "Open for Discussion," brings together all those interested in social responsibility for the company. The blog is maintained by a professional corporate blogger. Customers, suppliers, and employees make contributions.

Potential Risks of Corporate Blogs

Some people see risks in corporate blogging. Two obvious examples are the risk of revealing trade secrets and of making statements that are or could be construed as libel or defamation. Many companies have corporate policies on blogging. Groove Networks is one such example; the company even has corporate lawyers review the contents of its blogs.

According to Flynn (2006), blog-related risks can be minimized by establishing a strategic *blog management* program that incorporates the 3-Es of electronic risk management:

1. Establish comprehensive, written rules and policies. Make sure employees understand that all company policies apply to the blogosphere, regardless of whether employees are blogging at the office or from home.

2. Educate employees about blog-related risks, rules, and regulations. Be sure to address rights and privacy expectations, as well as the organization's blog-related risks and responsibilities.

3. Enforce blog policy with disciplinary action and technology. Take advantage of blog search engines to monitor the blogosphere and to keep track of what is being written about your company.

For a comprehensive discussion of corporate blogs, their risk, and how to mitigate this risk, see Cox et al. (2008) and Chapter 9.

Bloggers and Politics

Bloggers are getting more and more active in politics. In France, politicians pursued millions of voters in the blogosphere during the 2007 presidential elections.

In the 2008 presidential election in the United States, President Obama received considerably much more help from bloggers than his opponents (see Online File W1.8).

MECHANISM AIDS FOR WEB 2.0 TOOLS: TAGS, FOLKSONOMY, AND SOCIAL BOOKMARKS

When you blog, you may see a notice that reads "Browse This Blog's Tags," followed by a list of keywords. Tags are one of the most useful aids to Web 2.0 tools. (See en.wikipedia.org/wiki/Tag_(metadata) for details.)

Tags

tag
A nonhierarchical keyword or term assigned to a piece of information (such as an Internet bookmark, digital image, video clip, or any computer document).

A **tag** is a nonhierarchical keyword or term assigned to a piece of information (such as an Internet bookmark, digital image, video clip, or any computer document). This kind of metadata (data about data) helps describe an item as a keyword and allows it to be found by browsers when searching. Tags are chosen informally and personally by the item's creator or by its viewer, depending on the system. On a Web site in which many users tag many items, this collection of tags becomes a *folksonomy*.

Folksonomy

folksonomy (collaborative tagging, social classification, social indexing, social tagging)
The practice and method of collaboratively creating, classifying, and managing tags to annotate and categorize content.

Folksonomy (also known as **collaborative tagging, social classification, social indexing, or social tagging**) is the practice and method of collaboratively creating, classifying, and managing tags to annotate and categorize content. In contrast to traditional subject indexing, keywords (metadata) are generated not only by experts but also by creators and consumers of the content. Usually, freely chosen keywords are used instead of a controlled vocabulary. *Folksonomy* (from *folk* + *taxonomy*) is a user-generated taxonomy. For additional information see en.wikipedia.org/wiki/Folksonomy.

Social Bookmarking

social bookmarking
Web service for sharing Internet bookmarks. The sites are a popular way to store, classify, share, and search links through the practice of folksonomy techniques on the Internet and intranets.

Social bookmarking is a method for Internet users to store, organize, search, and manage bookmarks of Web pages on the Internet with the help of metadata.

In a social-bookmarking system, users save links to Web pages that they want to remember and/or share. These bookmarks are usually public and can be saved privately, shared only with specified people, groups, or networks, and so forth. People can usually view these bookmarks chronologically, by category or tags, or via a search engine.

Social-bookmarking services (such as Blink) encourage users to organize their bookmarks with informal tags instead of the traditional browser-based system of folders. They also enable viewing bookmarks associated with a chosen tag, and even include information about the number of users who have bookmarked them.

As these services have matured and grown more popular, extra features such as ratings and comments on bookmarks, the ability to import and export bookmarks from browsers, e-mailing of bookmarks, Web annotation, and groups or other social network features have been added. For details, see en.wikipedia.org/wiki/Social_bookmarking.

WIKIS

A **wiki (wikilog)** can be viewed as an extension of a blog. Whereas a blog usually is created by an individual (or maybe a small group) and may have an attached discussion board, a *wikilog*, *wikiblog*, or *wiki* is essentially a blog that enables everyone to participate as a peer. Anyone may add, delete, edit, or change content. It is like a loose-leaf notebook with a pencil and eraser left in a public place. Anyone can read it, scrawl notes, tear out a page, and so on. Creating a wikilog is a *collaborative process*. For description and details, see Meatball wiki at usemod.com/cgi-bin/mb.pl?WikiLog. Wikis can be implemented in many ways. One way is through contribution by many, like Wikipedia (see Chapter 9). A similar concept is employed by the CIA in their "Intellipedia." For further discussion, see en.wikipedia.org/wiki/wiki. A commercial use of a wiki was presented in the opening case. For a comprehensive list of wikis see webtrends.about.com/od/wiki/a/guide_to_wikis.htm.

> **wiki (wikilog)**
> A blog that allows everyone to participate as a peer; anyone may add, delete, or change content.

Section 2.6 ▶ REVIEW QUESTIONS

1. Define blogs and bloggers.
2. Discuss the critical features that distinguish a blog from a user-produced regular Web page.
3. Describe the potential advantages and risks of blogs.
4. Discuss the commercial uses of blogs and wikis.
5. Define tags, folksonomy, and social bookmarking.
6. Define wikis.

2.7 VIRTUAL WORLDS AS AN ELECTRONIC COMMERCE MECHANISM

Virtual worlds, which were introduced and defined in Chapter 1, are being used more in EC applications (White 2008). According to en.wikipedia.org/wiki/Virtual_world, in virtual worlds the *computer-simulated* world offers the use of visual stimuli that in turn can manipulate elements of the modeled world and thus create *telepresence*, to a certain degree. The modeled world may motivate situations and rules based on the real world or some fantasy world. Examples of rules are *gravity, topography, locomotion, real-time actions*, and *communication*. With the use of avatars, communication among users includes text, graphical icons, visual gesture, sound, and so forth.

These animated characters are software agents with personalities. **Avatars** are animated computer representations of humanlike movements and behaviors in a computer-generated 3D world. Advanced avatars can "speak" and display behaviors such as gestures and facial expressions. They can be fully automated to act like robots. The purpose of avatars is to introduce believable emotions so that the computerized agents gain credibility with users. For example, the real estate giant RE/MAX uses hundreds of virtual sales agents as avatars. For a demonstration of avatars in business, see pulse.3d.com.

> **avatars**
> Animated computer characters that exhibit humanlike movements and behaviors.

Avatars are aimed at making the human–computer interface more natural. Studies conducted by Extempo Systems (Hayes-Roth 1999) showed that interactive characters can improve customer satisfaction and retention by offering personalized, one-to-one service.

They also can help companies get to know their customers and support advertising. For more on avatars, see en.wikipedia.org/wiki/avatars_(computing).

BUSINESS ACTIVITIES AND VALUE IN VIRTUAL WORLDS

As businesses compete in the real world, they also compete in virtual worlds. Many companies and organizations now incorporate virtual worlds as a new form of advertising and sales (see the Scion closing case in Chapter 4). An example of this would be Apple Computer creating a virtual store within Second Life. This allows users to browse Apple's latest innovative products. You cannot actually purchase a product (yet), but having these "virtual stores" is a way for vendors to access a different clientele and customer demographic as customers examine products in 3D and exchange opinions and recommendations. The use of advertising within "virtual worlds" is a relatively new idea. Extensive educational activities and training are going on in virtual worlds (see Chapter 7). Using a virtual world, companies can reduce cost and time constraints.

There are several types of business activities in virtual worlds:

▶ Creating and managing a virtual business (see Terdiman 2008 for guidelines on how to do this)

▶ Conducting regular business activities (e.g., advertising, marketing, collaboration) within the framework of the virtual world

▶ Providing services for those who build, manage, or make money with virtual properties

For example, in a cover story in *BusinessWeek*, Hof (2008) discusses the various opportunities for conducting business in Second Life. Specifically, he introduces seven residents who are making substantial amounts of money. These include the Anshe Chung avatar, known as the "Rockefeller of Second Life," who buys virtual land from Second Life, "develops" it, and sells or rents it globally. Her business has grown so rapidly that she employs 20 people to design and program the development projects.

Following are two examples of how companies are using virtual worlds to bolster their physical businesses:

Example 1: Collaboration. More than 2,000 IBM employees signed up as members of Second Life, using the site to share ideas and work on projects. IBM holds an "alumni block party" in Second Life, allowing current and former employees from around the globe to get together in virtual meetings. IBM purchases islands for use as meeting places and technology showcases, and for experiments in virtual reality business. For example, IBM has set up a Circuit City store and a Sears appliance store as virtual commerce demonstration projects. IBM allows greater interactivity with products than a conventional store will allow. Users can, for example, customize appliances.

Example 2: Research and Marketing. Starwood Hotels constructed a prototype of the new Aloft brand hotels before they appeared in the real world in 2008. The company purchased two islands: Aloft, for the hotel prototype, and Argali, where visitors viewed the development project. Working from a preliminary architectural sketch, the designers begin roughing out the layout, furnishings, and textures of the hotel, which were then refined in response to feedback from the *brick-and-mortar* architects and from Second Life residents who were invited to critique the design and layout. Then, the developers began remodeling the hotel in response to feedback from Second Life residents.

Using virtual worlds gives companies the opportunity to gauge customer reaction and receive feedback about new products or services. This can be crucial because it will give the companies insight into what the market and customers want from new products, which can give them a competitive edge. For more, see the closing case of this chapter as well as Chapter 9.

Section 2.7 ▶ REVIEW QUESTIONS

1. Define virtual worlds.
2. Describe avatars. Why do we use them?
3. List some business activities in virtual worlds. Categorize them by type.

Sears in Second Life

Source: flickr.com/photos/cynpeccable/1054312323. Used with permission.

2.8 COMPETITION IN THE DIGITAL ECONOMY AND ITS IMPACT ON INDUSTRIES

The mechanisms described in the previous sections help in creating EC applications that in turn impact our economy and organizations. One of the major economic impacts of EC is its contribution to competitive advantage.

COMPETITION IN THE INTERNET ECOSYSTEM

The Internet economy has low barriers to entry, and so e-business is expanding rapidly. As the Internet ecosystem evolves both technologically and in population, it will be even easier and likelier for countries, companies, and individuals to participate in it. Already, a $1.5 trillion technical infrastructure is in place, ready and available for anyone to use at any time—free of charge. New ideas and ways of doing things can come from anywhere at any time in the Internet economy. Therefore, some of the old rules of competition no longer apply.

Competitiveness Factors

EC competition is very intense because online transactions enable the following:

> **Lower search costs for buyers.** E-markets reduce the cost of searching for product information (e.g., sellers, models, prices), frequently close to zero. This can significantly impact competition, enabling customers to find less expensive (or better) products and forcing sellers, in turn, to reduce prices and/or improve customer service. Sellers who provide information to buyers can exploit the Internet to gain a considerably larger market share. For example, companies including Wal-Mart and Walgreens developed intelligent search tools that increased their online sales on their sites by 25 to 50 percent.

> **Speedy comparisons.** Not only can customers find inexpensive products online, but they also can find them quickly. For example, a customer does not have to go to several bookstores to find the best price for a particular book. Using shopping search engines such as allbookstores.com, or shopping.com for consumer products, customers can find what they want and compare prices. Companies that sell online at competitive prices and provide that information to search engines will gain a competitive advantage.

▶ **Lower prices.** Buy.com, Half.com, and other companies can offer low prices due to their low costs of operation (no physical facilities, minimum inventories, and so forth). If volume is large enough, prices can be reduced by 40 percent or more (see Case 2.2).

▶ **Customer service.** Amazon.com and Dell, for example, provide superior customer service. As will be shown in Chapters 3 and 12, such service is an extremely important competitive factor.

▶ **Barriers to entry are reduced.** Setting up a Web site is relatively easy, fast, and inexpensive, and doing so reduces the need for a sales force and brick-and-mortar stores. Therefore, it is easy to start an online business. However, companies must view this as both a threat (e.g., Where will our next competitor come from?) and an opportunity (e.g., Can we use our core competencies in new areas of business?).

▶ **Virtual partnerships multiply.** With easy access to the Web and the ability to share production and sales information easily, the ability of a firm to create a virtual partnership to exploit an EC opportunity increases dramatically (recall the Boeing case in Online File W1.3).

▶ **Market niches abound.** The market-niche strategy is as old as the study of competitive advantage. What has changed is that without the limits imposed by physical storefronts, the number of business opportunities is as large as the Web. The challenge strategists face is to discover and reap the benefits from profitable niches before the competition does so.

differentiation
Providing a product or service that is unique.

▶ **Differentiation.** Differentiation involves providing a product or service that is not available elsewhere. For example, Amazon.com differentiates itself from other book retailers by providing customers with information that is not available in a physical bookstore, such as communication with authors, almost real-time book reviews, and book recommendations. An example of customization of wedding rings is provided in Case 2.2.

CASE 2.2

EC Application

HOW BLUE NILE, INC., IS CHANGING THE JEWELRY INDUSTRY

Blue Nile, Inc. (*bluenile.com*), a pure-play online e-tailer that specializes in diamonds and jewelry, capitalized on online diamond sales as a dot-com start-up in 1999. The company provides a textbook case of how EC fundamentally undercuts the traditional way of doing business.

The Opportunity
Using the B2C EC model—knocking out expensive stores and intermediaries and then slashing prices (up to 35% less than rivals to gain market share), Blue Nile captured a high market share in a short time, making a sizable profit by inducing more people to buy online.

How did the start-up defy the conventional wisdom that diamonds could not be sold online? Basically, Blue Nile offers a huge selection of diamonds and more information on diamonds than a jewelry expert offers in a physical store. In October 2008, Blue Nile offered about 33,000 round diamonds that could be used to build a customized wedding ring. No

physical store can offer so many diamonds. It also features educational guides in plain English and provides independent (and trusted) quality ratings for every stone. A customer can look over a rating scale for cut, clarity, color, and so on and then conduct a price comparison with Diamond.com (*diamond.com*) and other online stores. Most important is the 30-day money-back guarantee (now an online industry standard). This provides customers with a comfort level against fraud and gives Blue Nile a competitive edge against stores that take the stones back but charge a fee to do so.

The Results
Blue Nile sales reached $129 million in 2003 (a 79% increase over 2002), with a net income of $27 million. In 2007, sales exceeded $320 million (40% annual growth). The company became the eighth-largest specialty jewelry company in the United States and went public in 2004 (one of the most successful IPOs of 2004).

(continued)

CASE 2.2   (continued)

To sell $320 million in jewelry, a traditional retail chain needs 300 stores and close to 3,000 employees. Blue Nile does it with one 10,000-square-foot warehouse and 190 staffers. The company also bypasses the industry's tangled supply chain, in which a diamond may pass through five or more intermediaries before reaching a retailer. Blue Nile deals directly with original suppliers, such as Thaigem.com.

This is one reason why some 465 small jewelry stores in the United States closed in 2003 alone. By 2008, large jewelry store chains were closing many of their physical stores. The survivors specialize in custom-crafted pieces. Large rivals try to fight back, streamlining the supply chain, emphasizing customer service, and even trying to sell some products online.

The future seems to be clear, as summarized by Roger Thompson, a small jeweler in Lambertville, New Jersey, who said, "Anyone with half a brain, who wants a diamond engagement ring, will go to the Internet." So, he stopped

selling diamonds. In the meantime, grooms make proposals with Blue Nile rings, saving $3,000 to $5,000.

Note that the competition in the jewelry business is very strong, not only from jewelry retailers, but also from general e-tailers such as *overstock.com*, *ice.com*, and *amazon.com*.

Sources: Compiled from Rivlin (2007), *BusinessWeek Online* (2006), *RedOrbit.com* (2006), and *bluenile.com* (accessed December 2008).

Questions

1. Using the classifications of EC (Section 1.3, Chapter 1), what can you say about Blue Nile?

2. In what ways is the company changing its industry?

3. What are the critical success factors of the company?

4. Research Blue Nile's affiliate marketing program via Linkshare. How does this program help Blue Nile?

In addition, EC provides for personalization or customization and personalization of products and services.

Customization, Personalization, and Competition

The terms *customization* and *personalization* are frequently used interchangeably. However, some distinguish between the two by defining **customization** as creating a product to the specification of the buyer. For example, if you order a computer from Dell, they will make it as you wish (from a list of options). This creates the *build-to-order production process* and the concept of *mass customization*. (See Section 2.9 and Appendix 2A.)

Personalization refers to the ability to tailor a service or Web content to specific user preferences. For example, Amazon.com notifies customers by e-mail when new books on their favorite subjects or by their favorite authors are published. Several sites track news or stock prices based on the consumer's preferences. For example, Google will e-mail all news regarding certain topics (e.g., Chinese stocks and companies) to a user. The aim of personalization is to increase the usability of complex information by customizing the presentation, making the user interface more intuitive and easier to understand, and reducing information overload by tailoring content and navigation. For personalization techniques, see Anke and Sundaram (2006).

Personalization Tools. Personalization can be done by EC vendors (such as Amazon.com) and by individuals. Users can create highly personalized pages for themselves that are constantly updated with information such as news articles and stock prices, view photos, use a calculator, and perform similar actions, all in one page. Users can also post necessary tools as modules, which appear as small square or rectangular objects, with the content or functionality inside. Users can arrange the modules on their sites. Users can also produce a wide variety of modules and upload software made available for free. Pages can be personalized online or offline.

One such personalization tool is My Yahoo! This tool can be used to combine page segments featuring Yahoo!'s own news and information with segments containing RSS feeds. Microsoft's My MSN is another tool.

The best known mini-application for the desktop is Apple's Dashboard, which allows Macintosh users to install tiny programs called *widgets* that perform searches, display photo slideshows, track stocks, play music, and more. Microsoft Windows' Vista operating system has a comparable system called *Sidebar*. Netvibes (netvibes.com) offers the best features of My Yahoo! and Dashboard. Modules can be added easily and are arranged in a menu. For graphics-rich content, users can use Pageflakes (pageflakes.com).

Here is how personalization is done at Amazon.com:

Example: Amazon.com. Amazon.com's catalog includes several million items. Easy navigation and personalization are provided as well. For instance, when a customer looks up

customization
Creation of a product or service according to the buyer's specifications.

personalization
The ability to tailor a product, service, or Web content to specific user preferences.

a book on a certain topic, it recommends popular books on the same topic ("customers who bought this book also bought . . ."). In addition, it recommends five authors in the customer's area of interest. Recommendations appear several times during surfing of the site. Amazon.com also bundles a similar book with the book the customer is interested in for a large discount. For details, see the opening case in Chapter 3.

Consumers like differentiation and personalization and are frequently willing to pay more for them. Differentiation reduces the substitutability between products, benefiting sellers who use this strategy. Also, price cutting in differentiated markets does not impact market share very much: Many customers are willing to pay a bit more for customized or personalized products or services.

IMPACT ON COMPETITION

Several competitive factors have become less important as a result of EC. For example, the size of a company may no longer be a significant competitive advantage (as will be discussed later). Similarly, location (geographical distance from the consumer) plays a less significant role in EC, and language is becoming less important as translation programs remove some language barriers. Finally, digital products are not subject to normal wear and tear, although some become obsolete.

It can also be said that competition between companies is being replaced by competition between *networks*. The company with better communication networks, online advertising capabilities, and relationships with other Web companies (e.g., having an affiliation with suppliers, with Google, or with Amazon.com) has a strategic advantage. It can also be said that competition is now mostly between *business models*. The company with the better business model will win. Finally, e-competition may lead to perfect markets.

Perfect Competition

All in all, EC supports market efficiencies and could result in almost perfect competition. In a perfect market, a *commodity* (an undifferentiated product) is produced when the consumer's willingness to pay equals the marginal cost of producing the commodity and neither sellers nor buyers can influence supply or demand conditions individually. The following are necessary for *perfect competition*:

- Many buyers and sellers must be able to enter the market at little or no entry cost (no barriers to entry).
- Large buyers or sellers are *not able* to individually influence the market.
- The products must be homogeneous (commodities). (For customized products, therefore, there is no perfect competition.)
- Buyers and sellers must have comprehensive information about the products and about the market participants' demands, supplies, and conditions.

Porter's Competitive Analysis in an Industry

Porter's *competitive forces model* (2001) identifies five major forces of competition that determine an industry's structural attractiveness. These forces, in combination, determine how the economic value created in an industry is divided among the players in the industry. Such industry analysis helps companies develop their competitive strategy.

Because the five forces are affected by both the Internet and e-commerce, it is interesting to examine how the Internet influences the industry structure portrayed by Porter's model. Porter divided the impacts of the Internet into either positive or negative impacts for the industry. As shown in Exhibit 2.9, most of the impacts are negative (marked by a minus sign). Of course, there are variations and exceptions to the impacts shown in the exhibit, depending on the industry, its location, and its size. A negative impact means that competition will intensify in most industries as the Internet is introduced, causing difficulties to a company that controls or strongly influences its industry. Because the strength of each of the five forces varies considerably from industry to industry, it would be a mistake to draw general conclusions about the impact of the Internet on long-term industry profitability; each industry is affected in different ways. Nevertheless, an examination of a wide range of industries in which

EXHIBIT 2.9 **Porter's Competitive Forces Model: How the Internet Influences Industry Structure**

Threat of substitute products or services

(+) By making the overall industry more efficient, the Internet can expand the size of the market

(–) The proliferation of Internet approaches creates new substitution threats

Bargaining power of suppliers

Rivalry among existing competitors

Buyers

| Bargaining power of channels | Bargaining power of end users |

(–) Procurement using the Internet tends to raise bargaining power over suppliers, though it can also give suppliers access to more customers

(–) The Internet provides a channel for suppliers to reach end users, reducing the leverage of intervening companies

(–) Internet procurement and digital markets tend to give all companies equal access to suppliers, and gravitate procurements to standardized products that reduce differentiation

(–) Reduced barriers to entry and the proliferation of competitors downstream shifts power to suppliers

(–) Reduces differences among competitors as offerings are difficult to keep proprietary

(–) Migrates competition to price

(–) Widens the geographic market, increasing the number of competitors

(–) Lowers variable cost relative to fixed cost, increasing pressures for price discounting

(+) Eliminates powerful channels or improves bargaining power over traditional channels

(–) Shifts bargaining power to end consumers

(–) Reduces switching costs

Barriers to entry

(–) Reduces barriers to entry such as the need for a sales force, access to channels, and physical assets; anything that Internet technology eliminates or makes easier to do reduces barriers to entry

(–) Internet applications are difficult to keep proprietary from new entrants

(–) A flood of new entrants has come into many industries

Source: "Porter's Competitive Forces Model: How the Internet Influences Industry Structure" from "Strategy and the Internet," by M. E. Porter, March 2001 © 2001 by the Harvard Business School Publishing Corp. *Harvard Business Review.* Reprinted by permission.

the Internet is playing a role reveals some clear trends, as summarized in Exhibit 2.9. The Internet can boost an industry's efficiency in various ways, expanding the overall size of the market by improving its position relative to traditional substitutes. Thus, the Internet means stronger competition, especially for commodity-type products (e.g., toys, books, CDs); because of this, many dot-com companies collapsed between 2000 and 2003. To survive and prosper in such an environment, a company needs to use innovative strategies.

Examples of how e-commerce is changing entire industries are financial services, especially stock trading, cyberbanking, and e-mortgages. Zopa.com (Chapter 9) may change money lending by moving some of it from banks to a person-to-person level. Obviously, retailing is changing, and so are travel, entertainment, and more. An emerging change is in classified ads, as demonstrated in Case 2.3.

EC IMPACT ON WHOLE INDUSTRIES

In addition to its impact on individuals and organizations, EC is reshaping entire industries. Major changes are taking place in the way that business is done. For example, Blue Nile, described earlier, is changing the jewelry retail business. Also, the travel and hospitality industry is going through a major transition. The health-care industry is also undergoing dramatic changes. For instance, Suomi (2006) identifies the following major emerging changes in the health-care industry:

▶ Patient self-care is growing rapidly.

▶ The amount of free online medical information is exploding.

▶ Patient empowerment is gaining importance (more information, more choices).

▶ Electronic interaction is increasing among patients, hospitals, pharmacies, and so forth.

▶ The number of digital hospitals and other health-care facilities is increasing.

▶ Data collected about patients is growing in amount and quality.

▶ Access to patient data is easy and can be shared.

▶ Elder care and special types of care are improving significantly due to wireless systems.

▶ The need to protect patient privacy and to contain cost is increasing.

Therefore, the whole health-care industry may change. For example, home care may increase.

CASE 2.3
EC Application

CRAIGSLIST: THE ULTIMATE ONLINE CLASSIFIED SITE

If you want to find (or offer) a job, housing, goods and services, social activities, and much more in more than 500 cities in five languages and in more than 50 countries worldwide, go to Craigslist (*craigslist.org*). The site has much more information than you will find in all the newspapers in the individual cities. For example, more than 500,000 new jobs are listed from the more than 10 million new classified ads received by Craigslist every month. Each month there are more than 50 million visitors to the site. Craig Newmark, the founder of Craigslist, has said that everything is for sale on the site except the site itself. Although many other sites offer free classifieds, no other site even comes close to Craigslist.

In addition, Craigslist features dozens of topical discussion forums with more than 100 million user postings. No wonder that Craigslist has more than 4 billion page views per month, making it the seventh most visited site in the English language. Craigslist is considered by many as one of the few Web sites that could change the world because it is simply a free notice board with more than 4 billion readers (Naughton 2008). For more information, see *craigslist.org/about/factsheet*.

Users cite the following reasons for the popularity of Craigslist:

▶ It gives people a voice.
▶ It promotes a sense of trust, even intimacy.
▶ It is consistent and champions down-to-earth values.
▶ It illustrates simplicity.
▶ It has social-networking capabilities.
▶ It can be used for free in most cases (you can post free ads except for business, for rent, or for sale ads in few large cities).
▶ It is effective and well visited. The site serves more than 10 million page views per month.

As an example of the site's effectiveness, we provide the personal experience of one of the authors, who needed to rent his condo in Los Angeles. The usual process would take 2 to 4 weeks and $400 to $700 in newspaper ads, plus ads in the local online for rent services, to get the condo rented. With Craigslist, it took less than a week at no cost. As more people discover Craigslist, the traditional newspaper-based classified ad industry will probably be the loser; ad rates may become lower, and fewer ads will be printed.

eBay owns 25 percent of Craigslist. Craigslist charges for "help wanted" ads and apartment broker listings in some larger cities. In addition, Craigslist may charge ad placers, especially when an ad has rich media features. Classified advertising is Craigslist's real money-making opportunity. According to Copeland (2006), the offline classifieds generate $27 billion in annual revenues, and online classifieds could quadruple that amount in 4 years. Both Google and Microsoft are attempting to control this market.

Craigslist has revolutionized traditional commerce by facilitating direct buyer–seller interaction for free in an online context. The free posting, immediacy of the Internet, and sheer scope of buyers and sellers allow for goods and services to be found, bought, and/or exchanged far more quickly than any physical market could allow. This levels the playing field for small businesses looking for a fast and cheap way to promote their business.

Fans and advocates of Craigslist applaud its altruistic and noncommercial nature. The unobtrusive moderation of ads and user movement is a welcome respite from an online environment where one seemingly can't go two page-views without being bombarded by online ads. The deadpan gray color of the homepage and its basic ".org" domain contribute to its grassroots appeal. Establishing a noncorporate culture is a value for Newmark, the founder of the site. Despite Craigslist's phenomenal expansion, however, some

(continued)

CASE 2.3   (continued)

people contend that the site is missing out on millions of dollars of potential revenue by not going the way of Facebook and selling ad space or consumer information. Newmark so far has resisted an onslaught of advertising offers and multimillion-dollar buyouts. An exception is eBay, which has a 25 percent stake in the company.

Further questions regarding the future of Craigslist have to do with the very hands-off mentality that made this site famous. Specifically, critics charge that users post illegitimate and possibly illegal ads on the site, and the Craigslist staff are unable to effectively police this practice. Some users have complained about questionable ads being posted, especially in the "jobs" section. This would include pyramid schemes and under-the-counter work. Craigslist also attracts criminals seeking to commit fraud by misleading the gullible into accepting false checks. Some con artists knowingly overpay for items via checks and then arrange to have the overpaid amount wired back to them by the seller, just before it is discovered that the check was never good to begin with. The seller is now without the money "refunded" as well as the item sold. The anonymity of Craigslist's users and the lack of ratings systems create an environment where deceitful users cannot be held accountable for their actions.

Another concern is that erotic services make up a significant portion of the total traffic on the site. There is a fear that many of the sexual encounters facilitated using Craigslist

have been with underage girls. With the sheer volume of users and ads posted per day, such policing is not possible given the modest workforce of only 24 that the site employs.

In addition, many supporters contend that attempts to control Craigslist may simply cause users to relocate to a different, less-regulated site. Surely the design of Craigslist shouldn't be too difficult to duplicate. However, its brand is extremely strong.

Sources: Compiled from *craigslist.org* (accessed April 2009), Brandon (2006), Naughton (2008), Copeland (2006), *Time* (2006), and *en.wikipedia.org/wiki/craigslist* (accessed April 2009).

Questions

1. Identify the business model used by Craigslist.
2. Visit *craigslist.org* and identify the social network and business network elements.
3. Why is Craigslist considered a site that "changes the world"?
4. What do you like about the site? What do you dislike about it?
5. What are some of the risks and limitations of using this site?

Section 2.8 ❱ REVIEW QUESTIONS

1. Why is competition so intense online?
2. Describe Porter's competitive forces model in the Internet and EC environment.
3. Describe the impact of competition on whole industries.
4. How does Craigslist influence the classifieds industry and its competitors?

2.9 IMPACTS OF ELECTRONIC COMMERCE ON BUSINESS PROCESSES AND ORGANIZATIONS

Little statistical data or empirical research on the full impact of EC is available because of the relative newness of the field. Therefore, the discussion in this section is based primarily on experts' opinions, logic, and some actual data.

Existing and emerging Web technologies are offering organizations unprecedented opportunities to rethink strategic business models, processes, and relationships. These e-opportunities can be divided into three categories: e-marketing (Web-based initiatives that improve the marketing of existing products; see Zimmerman 2007); e-operations (Web-based initiatives that improve the creation of existing products); and e-services (Web-based initiatives that improve service industries and customer service). The discussion here is also based in part on the work of Bloch et al. (1996), who approached the impact of e-marketplaces on organizations from a value-added point of view. Their model, which is shown in Exhibit 2.10, divides the impact of e-marketplaces into three major categories: improving direct marketing, transforming organizations, and redefining organizations. This section examines each of these impacts.

IMPROVING MARKETING AND SALES

Traditional direct marketing is done by mail order (catalogs) and telephone (telemarketing). According to the Direct Marketing Association, actual sales generated by direct mail totaled

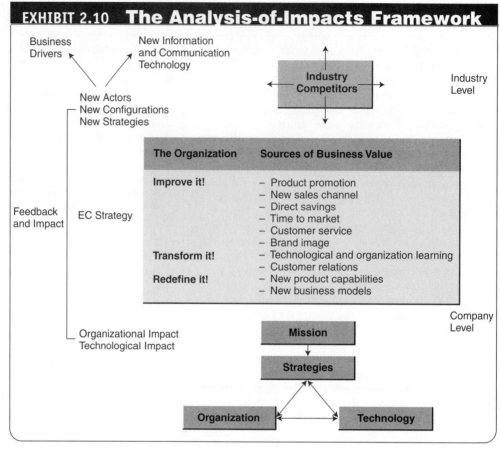

EXHIBIT 2.10 The Analysis-of-Impacts Framework

Source: M. Bloch, Y. Pigneur, and A. Segev "Leveraging Electronic Commerce for Competitive Advantage: A Business Value Framework." *Proceedings of the Ninth International Conference on EDI-IOS,* Bled, Slovenia, June 1996. Reprinted by permission of Yves Pigneur.

$960 billion in 2007. This figure is small, but growing rapidly. Zimmerman (2007), Zappala and Gray (2006), and others describe the impacts of e-marketplaces on B2C direct marketing as shown in Online File W2.8.

For digital products—software, music, and videos—the changes brought by e-markets is dramatic. Already, these are delivered over the Internet. The ability to deliver digitized products electronically affects (eliminates) packaging and greatly reduces the need for specialized distribution models.

New sales models such as shareware, freeware, and pay-as-you-use are emerging. Although these models currently exist only within particular sectors, such as the software and publishing industries, they will eventually pervade other sectors.

The impacts of e-marketplaces on marketing are summarized in Exhibit 2.11.

All of these impacts of e-markets on direct marketing provide companies, in some cases, with a competitive advantage over those that use only traditional direct-sales methods, as vividly illustrated in the Blue Nile case. Furthermore, because the competitive advantage is so large, e-markets are likely to replace many nondirect marketing channels. Some people predict the "fall of the shopping mall," and many retail stores and brokers of services (e.g., stocks, real estate, and insurance) are labeled by some as soon-to-be-endangered species.

TRANSFORMING ORGANIZATIONS

A second impact of e-marketplaces is the transformation of organizations. Here, we look at three key topics: organizational learning, changing the nature of work, and disintermediation and reintermediation (Anandarajan et al. 2006).

Technology and Organizational Learning

Rapid progress in EC will force a Darwinian struggle: To survive, companies will have to learn and adapt quickly to the new technologies. This struggle will offer them an opportunity

EXHIBIT 2.11 **The Changing Face of Marketing**

	Old Model—Mass and Segmented Marketing	New Model—One-to-One and Customization
Relationships with customers	Customer is mostly a passive recipient.	Customer is an active coproducer. Target marketing is to individuals.
Customer needs	Articulated	Articulated and inferred
Segmentation	Mass market and target segments	Segments looking for customized solutions and segmented targets; one-to-one targets
Product and service offerings	Product line extensions and modification	Customized products, services, and marketing; personalization
New product development	Marketing and R&D drive new product development.	R&D focuses on developing the platforms that allow consumers to customize based on customer inputs.
Pricing	Fixed prices and discounting	Customer influencing pricing (e.g., Priceline.com; auctions); value-based pricing models, e-auctions, e-negotiations (i-offer)
Communication	Advertising and PR	Integrated, interactive, and customized marketing communication, education, and entertainment; use of avatars
Distribution	Traditional retailing and direct marketing	Direct (online) distribution and rise of third-party logistics services
Branding	Traditional branding and cobranding	The customer's name as the brand (e.g., My Brand or Brand 4 ME)
Basis of competitive advantage	Marketing power	Marketing finesse and "capturing" the customer as "partner" while integrating marketing, operations, R&D, and information
Communities	Discount to members in physical communities	Discounts to members of e-communities; social networking
Advertising	TV, newspapers, billboards	Innovative, viral, on the Web, wireless devices

Sources: Compiled from Wind (2001), Kioses et al. (2006), and Singh (2006).

to experiment with new products, services, and business models, which may lead to strategic and structural changes. These changes may transform the way in which business is done. We believe that as EC progresses, it will have a large and durable impact on the strategies of many organizations. New technologies will require new organizational structures and procedures. For instance, the structure of the organizational unit dealing with e-marketspaces might be different from the conventional sales and marketing departments.

In summary, corporate change must be planned and managed. Before getting it right, organizations may have to struggle with different experiments and learn from their mistakes.

The Changing Nature of Work

The nature of some work and employment will be restructured in the Digital Age; it is already happening before our eyes. For example, driven by increased competition in the global marketplace, firms are reducing the number of employees to a core of essential staff and outsourcing whatever work they can to countries where wages are significantly lower. The upheaval brought on by these changes is creating new opportunities and new risks and is forcing people to think in new ways about jobs, careers, and salaries.

Digital Age workers will have to be very flexible. Few will have truly secure jobs in the traditional sense, and many will have to be willing and able to constantly learn, adapt, make decisions, and stand by them. Many will work from home.

The Digital Age company will have to view its core of essential workers as its most valuable asset. It will have to constantly nurture and empower them and provide them with every means possible to expand their knowledge and skill base (Anandarajan et al. 2006). One area where work is changing is intermediation.

Disintermediation and Reintermediation

Intermediaries are agents that mediate between sellers and buyers. Usually, they provide two types of services: (1) They provide relevant information about demand, supply, prices, and requirements and, in doing so, help match sellers and buyers; (2) They offer value-added services such as transfer of products, escrow, payment arrangements, consulting, or assistance in finding a business partner. In general, the first type of service can be fully automated and thus is likely to be assumed by e-marketplaces, infomediaries, and portals that provide free or low-commission services. The second type requires expertise, such as knowledge of the industry, the products, and technological trends, and it can only be partially automated.

Intermediaries that provide only (or mainly) the first type of service may be eliminated; this phenomenon is called **disintermediation**. An example is the airline industry and its push for buying electronic tickets directly from the airlines. As of 2004, most airlines require customers to pay $5 or more per ticket if they buy a ticket from an agent or by phone, which is equivalent to the agent's commission. This is resulting in the *disintermediation* of travel agents from the purchasing process. In another example, discount stockbrokers that only execute trades manually are disappearing. However, brokers who manage electronic intermediation are not only surviving but may also be prospering (e.g., eTrade). This phenomenon, in which disintermediated entities or newcomers take on new intermediary roles, is called *reintermediation* (see Chapters 3 and 5).

Disintermediation is more likely to occur in supply chains involving several intermediaries, as illustrated in the Blue Nile case.

REDEFINING ORGANIZATIONS

Following are some of the ways in which e-markets redefine organizations.

New and Improved Product Capabilities

E-markets allow for new products to be created and for existing products to be customized in innovative ways. Such changes may redefine organizations' missions and the manner in which they operate. Customer profiles, as well as data on customer preferences, can be used as a source of information for improving products or designing new ones.

Mass Customization

The concepts of personalization and customization were introduced in Section 2.8. A related topic is mass customization.

Mass customization enables manufacturers to create specific products for each customer based on the customer's exact needs (see Appendix 2A at the end of this chapter). For example, Motorola gathers customer needs for a pager or a cellular phone, transmits the customer's specifications electronically to the manufacturing plant where the device is manufactured, and then sends the finished product to the customer within a day. Dell pioneered this approach in building their products. Many other companies are following Dell's lead: Mattel's My Design lets fashion-doll fans custom-build a friend for Barbie at Mattel's Web site; the doll's image is displayed on the screen before the person places an order. Nike allows customers to customize shoes, which can be delivered in a week. Lego.com allows customers to configure several of their toys. Finally, De Beers allows customers to design their own engagement rings. Until the 2008 financial crisis, the automobile industry was customizing its products and expecting to save billions of dollars in inventory reduction alone every year by producing made-to-order cars. You can design your own T-shirt, Swatch watch, and many more products and services. Configuring the details of the customized products, including the final design, ordering, and paying for the products, is done online. Also known as *build-to-order*, customization can be done on a large scale, in which case it is called *mass customization*. For a historical discussion of the development of the idea of mass customization, see en.wikipedia.org/wiki/mass_customization. With the use of mass-customization methods, the cost of customized products is at or slightly above the comparable retail price of standard products. Exhibit 2.12 shows how customers can order customized Nike shoes.

Build-to-Order Manufacturing. **Build-to-order (pull system)** is a manufacturing process that starts with an order (usually customized). Once the order is paid for, the

disintermediation
Elimination of intermediaries between sellers and buyers.

mass customization
A method that enables manufacturers to create specific products for each customer based on the customer's exact needs.

build-to-order (pull system)
A manufacturing process that starts with an order (usually customized). Once the order is paid for, the vendor starts to fulfill it.

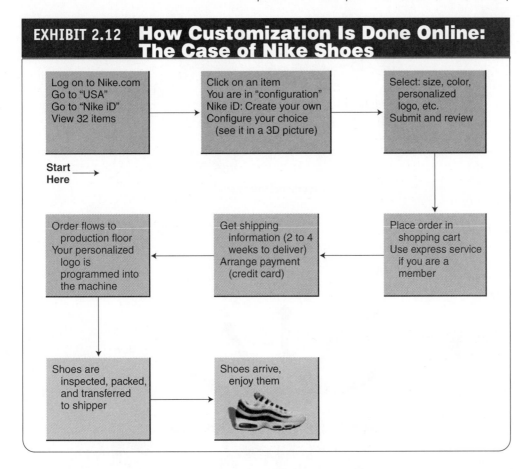

EXHIBIT 2.12 How Customization Is Done Online: The Case of Nike Shoes

Log on to Nike.com
Go to "USA"
Go to "Nike iD"
View 32 items

Click on an item
You are in "configuration"
Nike iD: Create your own
Configure your choice
(see it in a 3D picture)

Select: size, color,
personalized
logo, etc.
Submit and review

Start Here →

Order flows to
production floor
Your personalized
logo is
programmed into
the machine

Get shipping
information (2 to 4
weeks to deliver)
Arrange payment
(credit card)

Place order in
shopping cart
Use express service
if you are a
member

Shoes are
inspected, packed,
and transferred
to shipper

Shoes arrive,
enjoy them

vendor starts to fulfill it. This changes not only production planning and control but also the entire supply chain and payment cycle. For example, manufacturing or assembly starts only after an order is received. For more on build-to-order production, see Appendix 2A at the end of this chapter. For additional impacts on manufacturing, finance, and HRM see Online File W2.9.

Improving the Supply Chain

One of the major benefits of e-markets is the potential improvement in supply chains. A major change is the creation of a hub-based chain, as shown in Exhibit 2.13 (in comparison with a traditional supply chain—upper part of the exhibit). Chapter 6 elaborates on this topic. One such topic is self-service.

Self-Service. One of the major changes in the supply chain is to transfer some activities to customers and/or employees through self-service. This strategy is used extensively in call centers (e.g., track your package at UPS or FedEx), with self-configuration of products (e.g., Dell, Nike), by having customers use FAQs, and by allowing employees to update personal data online. Shifting activities to others in the supply chain saves money and increases data accuracy and accountability.

Impacts on Manufacturing

EC is changing manufacturing systems from mass-production lines to demand-driven, just-in-time manufacturing. These production systems are integrated with finance, marketing, and other functional systems, as well as with business partners and customers. Using Web-based ERP systems (supported by software such as SAP R/3), companies can direct customer orders to designers and/or to the production floor within seconds. Production cycle time can be cut by 50 percent or more in many cases, even if production is done in a different country from where the designers and engineers are located. (Recall the Boeing case in Online File W1.3.)

EXHIBIT 2.13   Changes in the Supply Chain

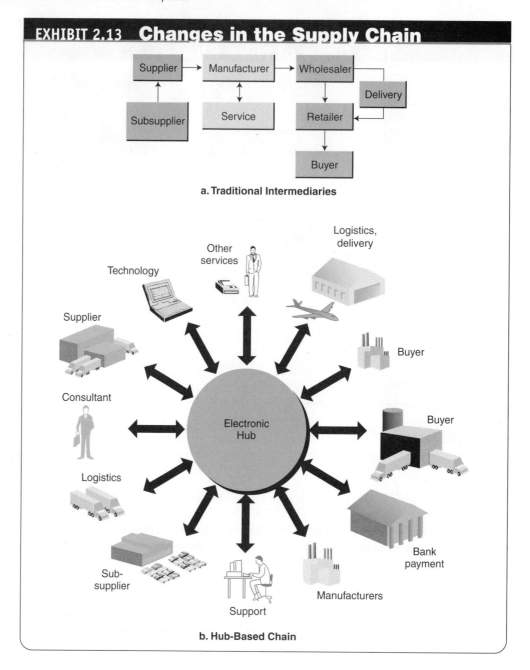

a. Traditional Intermediaries

b. Hub-Based Chain

Section 2.9 ▶ REVIEW QUESTIONS

1. List the major parts of Bloch et al.'s value-added model.
2. Describe how EC improves direct marketing.
3. Describe how EC transforms organizations.
4. Describe how EC redefines organizations.
5. Describe the concept of build-to-order (customization).

MANAGERIAL ISSUES

Some managerial issues related to this chapter are as follows.

1. **What about intermediaries?** Many EC applications will change the role of intermediaries. This may create a conflict between a company and its distributors. It may also create opportunities. In many cases, distributors will need to change their roles. This is a sensitive issue that needs to be planned for during the transformation to the e-business plan.

2. **Should we auction?** A major strategic issue is whether to use auctions as a sales channel. Auctions do have some limitations, and forward auctions may create

conflicts with other distribution channels. If a company decides to use auctions, it needs to select auction mechanisms and determine a pricing strategy. These days, auctions often allow an immediate purchase with a fixed price. These decisions determine the success of the auction and the ability to attract and retain visitors on the site. Auctions also require support services. Decisions about how to provide these services and to what extent to use business partners are critical to the success of high-volume auctions.

3. **Should we barter?** Bartering can be an interesting strategy, especially for companies that lack cash, need special material or machinery, and have surplus resources. However, the valuation of what is bought or sold may be hard to determine, and the tax implications in some countries are not clear.

4. **How do we compete in the digital economy?** Although the basic theories of competition are unchanged, the rules are different. The speed of changes in competitive forces can be rapid, and the impact of new business models can be devastating.

The competition between pure online retailers and hybrid players will continue. Manufacturers tend to build to order and support direct marketing to remove unnecessary inventory (e.g., Dell). The fundamental changes happen in the digital products and services sectors, where variable costs are low but illegal copies proliferate. Note that the online music and software businesses have declined. As Bill Gates once said, "Competition is not among companies, but among business models" (Financial Analysts Meeting 1998).

5. **What organizational changes will be needed?** Companies should expect organizational changes in all functional areas once e-commerce reaches momentum. Change is particularly evident in the financial services sector, where services can broadly be replaced by the Internet. Electronic procurement changes the business process among businesses in organizations as affiliate programs change the paradigm of marketing and business partnerships. Finally, the trends toward build-to-order and demand-driven manufacturing will continue to expand.

SUMMARY

In this chapter, you learned about the following EC issues as they relate to the chapter's learning objectives.

1. **Activities and mechanisms.** The major activities are information dissemination and presence, trading, collaboration, entertainment, and search. The major mechanisms are marketplaces, storefronts, shopping carts, catalogs, Web 2.0 tools, and virtual worlds. The role of intermediaries will change as e-markets develop: Some will be eliminated (disintermediation); others will change their roles and prosper (reintermediation). In the B2B area, for example, e-distributors connect manufacturers with buyers by aggregating electronic catalogs of many suppliers. New value-added services that range from content creation to syndication are mushrooming.

2. **E-marketplaces and their components.** A marketspace, or e-marketplace, is a virtual market that does not suffer from limitations of space, time, or borders. As such, it can be very effective. Its major components include customers, sellers, products (some digital), infrastructure, front-end processes, back-end activities, electronic intermediaries, other business partners, and support services.

3. **The major types of e-marketplaces.** In the B2C area, there are storefronts and e-malls. In the B2B area, there are private and public e-marketplaces, which may be vertical (within one industry) or horizontal (across different industries). Different types of portals provide access to e-marketplaces.

4. **Electronic catalogs, search engines, and shopping carts.** The major mechanisms in e-markets are electronic catalogs, search engines, software (intelligent) agents, and electronic shopping carts. These mechanisms facilitate EC by providing a user-friendly shopping environment.

5. **Types of auctions and their characteristics.** In forward auctions, bids from buyers are placed sequentially, either in increasing mode or in decreasing mode. In reverse auctions, buyers place an RFQ and suppliers submit offers in one or several rounds. In "name-your-own-price" auctions, buyers specify how much they are willing to pay for a product or service and an intermediary tries to find a supplier to fulfill the request.

6. **The benefits and limitations of auctions.** The major benefits for sellers are the ability to reach many buyers, to sell quickly, and to save on commissions to intermediaries. Buyers have a chance to obtain bargains and collectibles while shopping from their homes. The major limitation is the possibility of fraud.

7. **Bartering and negotiating.** Electronic bartering can greatly facilitate the swapping of goods and services among organizations, thanks to improved search and matching capabilities, which is done in bartering

exchanges. Software agents can facilitate online negotiation.

8. **Web 2.0 tools.** The major tools discussed in this chapter are blogs, wikis, and Twitter. Web 2.0 tools are used for several purposes, most commonly to improve communication and collaboration, to initiate viral marketing (word-of-mouth), to create branding awareness, and to foster interpersonal relationships.

9. **Virtual worlds.** These environments provide entertainment, trading virtual property, discussion groups, learning, training, and much more. Everything is simulated, animated, and supported by avatars. Thousands of companies have established presences in virtual worlds, especially in Second Life, offering mainly dissemination of information and advertising.

10. **Competition in the digital economy.** Competition in online markets is very intense due to the increased power of buyers, the ability to find the lowest price, and the ease of switching to another vendor. Global competition has increased as well.

11. **The impact of e-markets on organizations.** All functional areas of an organization are affected by e-markets. Broadly, e-markets improve direct marketing and transform and redefine organizations. Direct marketing (manufacturers to customers) and one-to-one marketing and advertising are becoming the norm, and mass customization and personalization are taking off. Production is moving to a build-to-order model, changing supply chain relationships and reducing cycle time.

KEY TERMS

Auction	106	E-distributor	102	Mobile portal	100
Avatars	117	E-mall (online mall)	98	"Name-your-own-price" model	109
Back end	96	E-marketplace	95	Personalization	121
Bartering	110	Electronic auctions (e-auctions)	107	Reverse auction (bidding, tendering	
Bartering exchange	111	Electronic catalogs (e-catalogs)	102	system)	108
Blog	112	Electronic shopping cart	105	Search engine	105
Build-to-order (pull system)	128	Enterprise search	104	Sell-side e-marketplace	97
Buy-side e-marketplace	97	Folksonomy (collaborative tagging,		Social bookmarking	116
Customization	121	social classification, social		Storefront	97
Desktop search	105	indexing, social tagging)	116	Tag	116
Differentiation	120	Forward auction	108	Tweets	114
Digital products	96	Front end	96	Twitter	114
Disintermediation	128	Infomediaries	100	Vlog (video blog)	113
Double auction	109	Intermediary	96	Voice portal	100
Dynamic pricing	108	Marketspace	95	Web portal	99
E-bartering (electronic		Mass customization	128	Wiki (wikilog)	117
bartering)	110	Micro-blogging	114		

QUESTIONS FOR DISCUSSION

1. Compare marketplaces with marketspaces. What are the advantages and limitations of each?

2. Compare and contrast competition in traditional markets with that in digital markets.

3. Explain why sell-side and buy-side marketplaces in the same company are usually separated, whereas in an exchange they are combined.

4. Discuss the need for portals in EC.

5. Discuss the advantages of dynamic pricing over fixed pricing. What are the potential disadvantages of dynamic pricing?

6. The "name-your-own-price" model is considered a reverse auction. However, this model does not include RFQs or consecutive bidding. Why is it considered a reverse auction?

7. Some say that blogs and wikis are going to eliminate e-mail. Discuss.

8. Compare wikis and blogs.

9. Discuss how wikis, blogs, and virtual worlds can be used for collaboration.

10. Discuss the competitive advantage of Craigslist in classifieds.

11. Discuss the value of a virtual world as an EC environment. Why does it attract users? Why does it attract companies?

12. Discuss the reasons why Twitter is becoming so popular.

13. Discuss the potential risks of using Web 2.0 tools.

INTERNET EXERCISES

1. Visit **bluenile.com**, **diamond.com**, and **jewelry-exchange.com**. Compare the sites. Comment on the similarities and the differences.

2. Go to **cisco.com**, **google.com**, and **cio.com** and locate information about the status of the "virtual close." Write a report based on your findings.

3. Visit **ticketmaster.com**, **ticketonline.com**, and other sites that sell event tickets online. Assess the competition in online ticket sales. What services do the different sites provide?

4. Examine how bartering is conducted online at **tradeaway.com**, **buyersbag.com**, **u-exchange.com**, and **intagio.com**. Compare and contrast the functionalities and ease of use of these sites.

5. Enter **blogger.com** and find its capabilities. Then enter **blogsearch.google.com** and find what this site helps you to do. Write a report.

6. Enter **mfgquote.com** and review the process by which buyers can send RFQs to merchants of their choice. Evaluate all of the online services provided by the company. Write a report based on your findings.

7. Enter **bloomsburgcarpet.com**. Explain how the site solves the problem of sending carpet sample books to representatives all over the country.

8. Enter **respond.com** and send a request for a product or a service. Once you receive replies, select the best deal. You have no obligation to buy. Write a short report based on your experience.

9. Enter Web 2.0 Journal at **web2.sys-con.com** and find recent material on wikis and blogs. Write a report.

10. Enter **yahoo.com** and find what personalization methods it offers.

11. Enter The Timberland Company (**timberland.com**) and design a pair of boots. Compare it to building your own sneakers at **nike.com** Compare these sites to **zappos.com/shoes.zhtml**.

12. Enter **cars.com**. List all services available to sellers and to buyers of cars. Compare it to **carsdirect.com**. Also, identify the revenue sources of the sites.

13. Enter **craigslist.org**. From what you know about the design of Web sites and from comparisons with **monster.com**, what suggestions would you make to improve the site?

14. Enter **ups.com**.
    a. Find out what information is available to customers before they send a package.
    b. Find out about the "package tracking" system; be specific.
    c. Compute the cost of delivering a 10" × 20" × 15" box, weighing 40 pounds, from your hometown to Long Beach, California. Compare the fastest delivery against the lowest cost.
    d. Prepare a spreadsheet for two different types of calculations available on the site. Enter data for two different calculators. Use Excel.

15. Enter **nichemarketsolutions.com/template.asp** and find the tools it makes for EC activities described in this chapter. Also find other EC mechanisms. Prepare a list.

16. Register at Second Life, and enter the site.
    a. Find what IBM and Coca-Cola are doing on the site.
    b. Find out what three universities that you are familiar with are doing on the site.
    c. Write a report.

17. Create an avatar in Second Life. Let your avatar interact with avatars of some companies. Why do we consider an avatar as a mechanism for EC? Write a report.

TEAM ASSIGNMENTS, PROJECTS, AND CLASS DISCUSSIONS

1. Reread the Blue Nile case and discuss the following:
    a. What are the key success factors for Blue Nile?
    b. Amazon.com makes only a 15 percent margin on the jewelry products it sells. This enables Amazon.com to sell diamond earrings for $1,000 (traditional jewelers charge $1,700 for the same). Do you think that Amazon.com will succeed in selling this type of jewelry as Blue Nile did in selling expensive engagement rings?
    c. Competition between Blue Nile and Amazon.com will continue to increase. In your opinion, which one will win (visit their Web sites and see how they sell jewelry)?
    d. Why is "commoditization" so important in the diamond business?
    e. Compare the following three sites: **diamond.com**, **ice.com**, and **bluenile.com**.
    f. Follow the performance of Blue Nile's stock since 2004 (symbol: NILE, go to **money.cnn.com**).

2. Read the opening case about EMS and answer the following questions.

   a. Why not just have meetings and send e-mails rather than using blogs, wikis, and RSS feeds?

   b. What are the benefits to EMS of combining its BI system with the Web 2.0 tools?

   c. In what ways is corporate performance bolstered?

   d. How can customers of the retail stores utilize the Web 2.0 tools?

   e. Can the company use any other Web 2.0 technologies? What and how?

3. Assign each group to a large e-tailer (e.g., Amazon.com, Walmart.com, Target.com, Dell.com, Apple.com, and HP.com). Trace the purchasing process. Look at the catalogs, search engines, shopping carts, and any other mechanism that improves e-shopping. Make a presentation that will include recommendations for improving the existing process.

4. Enter **en.wikipedia.org/wiki/Businesses_and_organizations_in_Second_Life** and view the list of businesses. Identify some virtual companies and explore several in depth. Find what product (service) they offer and how much they charge if they sell their product (service). Then, identify several companies that are related to real-world businesses. (e.g., SL Bay auctions allow you to purchase real-world items with Linden dollars).

5. Build your own business in Second Life (SL). This can be each member or each group. Using the company cited in question 4, determine what business you want to build. Then obtain a copy of Terdiman's book (2008) or a similar guide. Register at SL and go to work. In your project do the following:

   a. Select a business category and develop a business strategy.

   b. Develop a business plan and model (see the Online Tutorial) for your virtual enterprise.

   c. Choose where to set up your business.

   d. Conduct a budget and cash flow analysis (see Appendix B in Terdiman 2008).

   e. Buy virtual land and other virtual properties.

   f. Develop marketing and advertising plans (examine the competition)!

   g. Look for any possible revenues; make a pricing decision.

   h. Examine the possibility of running your business in "Teen SL."

   i. Plan all support business using the SL tools.

   j. Watch for legal issues and other risks.

   k. Build the business (using the SL tools).

   l. Build a supporting blog. How would you use it for viral marketing?

6. Address the following topics in a class discussion:

   a. Compare and contrast competition in traditional markets with that in digital markets.

   b. Some say that blogs and wikis are going to eliminate e-mail. Discuss.

Closing Case

SECOND LIFE

In 2003, a 3D virtual world called Second Life (SL) was opened to the public. The world is entirely built and owned by its residents. In 2003, the virtual world consisted of 64 acres. By 2009 it had grown to about 100,000 acres and was inhabited by millions of residents from around the planet (see *secondlife.com*). The virtual world consists of a huge digital continent, people, entertainment, experiences, and opportunities.

Thousands of new residents join each day and *create their own avatars* through which they travel around the Second Life world meeting people, communicating, having fun, and buying virtual land and other virtual properties where they can open a business or build a personal space limited only by their imaginations and their ability to use the virtual 3D applications. Avatars have unique names and move around in imaginative vehicles including helicopters, submarines, and hot-air balloons.

Second Life is dedicated to creativity, and everything in Second Life is resident-created. Residents retain the rights to their digital creations and can buy, sell, and trade with other residents in Second Life marketplaces. Residents can also socialize and participate in group activities. Virtual businesses succeed due to the owners' ingenuity, artistic ability, entrepreneurial expertise, and reputation.

Residents get some free virtual land (and they can buy more) where they build a house, a city, or a business. They can then sell the virtual properties or the virtual products or services they create. Residents can also sell real-world products or services. For example, Copeland and Kelleher (2007) report that more than 25,000 aspiring entrepreneurs trade virtual products or services at Second Life. Stevan Lieberman, an attorney, is one of these. He uses his expertise in intellectual property and the site to solicit work—mainly from programmers who are looking to patent their code.

Second Life is managed by Linden Labs, which provides Linden dollars that can be converted to U.S. dollars. Second Life uses several Web 2.0 tools such as blogs, wikis, RSS, and tags (from *del.icio.us*). These tools are described here and in Chapters 9 and 18.

Many organizations use Second Life for 3D presentations of their products. Even governments open virtual embassies on "Diplomacy Island," located on the site. Many universities offer educational courses and seminars in virtual classrooms [see "EduIslands" on SL site, Chapter 7, and Appendix A at Rymaszewski et al. (2008)].

Roush (2007) describes how to combine Second Life with Google Earth. Such combinations enable investigation of phenomena that would otherwise be difficult to visualize or understand. Shopping for virtual goods is popular in SL. You can start at the GNUbie Store (bargain prices), New Citizens Incorporates (NCI), and Free Dove. Second Life friends will help you to choose! You can shop outside SL (for real goods) yet pay Linden dollars, the currency of SL (see shop.onrez.com and slexchange.com). For SL fashion selection, try secondstyle.com. Also sluniverse.com/php/shop lets you quickly and easily search and shop for many items. You can even use a shopping cart on this site.

Note: We suggest you build your own virtual business on SL in order to experience real-life thrills. For suggestions on how to profit in SL see Chapter 13 in Rymaszewski et al. (2008). You can work as a musician, hunter, financial speculator, or a writer. You can also work in many other virtual jobs—you are only limited by your imagination.

Example. For awhile now, real-world organizations have been taking a growing interest in Second Life. Educational institutions were the first to recognize the potential of the virtual world to act as a new communications, advertising, and learning platform, and they were quickly followed by corporations doing what most corporations do: Look for profit. Appendix C of Rymaszewski et al. (2008) provides information about real-life brand presence and retail outlets SL.

At the time of this writing, corporate activity in Second Life is still in its infancy. Although an impressive number of companies have made or are in the process of making a foray into the virtual world, many treat it as an experiment whose only sure payoff is the media publicity it generates in the real world. However, to others—perhaps more visionary—Second Life offers very tangible advantages: A visit to *secondlifegrid.net/slfe/business-virtual-world* will educate you in depth on how organizations

utilize SL's virtual environment. For readers interested in the corporate take on the virtual world, Rymaszweski et al. (2008) presents three voices from three countries, representing companies in different fields of business.

The most common commercial activities on SL are:

- Marketing and advertising
- Designing and prototyping
- Market research
- Sales
- Corporate communication
- Broadcasting and entertainment
- Travel and tourism

For details, see Chapter 9 and Robbins and Bell (2008).

An increasing number of businesses are using the virtual world. For example, IBM uses it as a location for meetings, training, and recruitment. American Apparel was the first major retailer to set up shop in Second Life. The Mexican Tourism Board and Morocco Tourism are examples of 3D presentations of major tourist attractions. Many companies use Second life as a hot place to go to try new business ideas (see Rosedale 2007). For example, you can test-drive a Toyota Scion, toymakers prototype toys, and anyone can become a virtual architect.

Sources: Compiled from Copeland and Kelleher (2007), Robbins and Bell (2008), Rosedale (2007), and Rymaszewski et al. (2008), Roush (2007), and *secondlife.com* (accessed November 2008).

Questions

1. Enter the Second Life site (*secondlife.com*) and identify EC activities there. (You need to register for free and create an avatar.)

2. Which types of transactions are observable at the site?

3. Which business models are observable at the site?

4. If you were a travel agent, how would you utilize the site?

5. Have your avatar communicate with five others. Write a report on your experience.

ONLINE RESOURCES
available at pearsonglobaleditions.com/turban

Online Files

W2.1   Examples of Digital Products

W2.2   Application Case: How Raffles Hotel is Conducting E-Commerce

W2.3   Application Case: NTE Exchange

W2.4   Intermediaries and the Information Flow Model

W2.5   Limitations of Direct Seller-Buyer Interactions of Intermediaries

W2.6   Application Case: Electronic Catalogs at OfficeMax

W2.7   Application Case: Reverse Mortgage Auctions in Singapore

W2.8   EC Impact on B2C Direct Marketing

W2.9   Impact of EC on Functional Areas of Organizations

Comprehensive Educational Web Sites

wiki.secondlife.com/wiki/video_tutorials

vectec.org/old_web/researchcenter

allthingsweb2.com

REFERENCES

Anandarajan, M., et al., (Eds.). *The Internet and Workplace Transformation.* Armonk, NY: M.E. Sharpe, Inc., 2006.

Anderson, D. M. *Build-to-Order and Mass Customization.* Cambria, CA: CIM Press Publishers, 2008.

Anke, J., and D. Sundaram. "Personalization Techniques and Their Application." In M. Khosrow-Pour, (Ed.). *Encyclopedia of E-Commerce, E-Government, and Mobile Commerce.* Hershey, PA: Idea Group Reference, 2006.

Bakos, Y. "The Emerging Role of Electronic Marketplaces on the Internet." *Communications of the ACM* (August 1998).

Beynon-Davies, P. *@-business.* New York: Palgrave-Macmillan, 2004.

Bloch, M., Y. Pigneur, and A. Segev. "Leveraging Electronic Commerce for Competitive Advantage: A Business Value Framework." *Proceedings of the Ninth International Conference on EDI-IOS,* June 1996, Bled, Slovenia.

Brandon, E. "Finding an Apartment on Craigslist: Five Tips." *U.S. News & World Report,* July 10, 2006.

BusinessWeek Online. "Business Week's Hot Growth Companies: Blue Nile." 2006. businessweek.com/hot_growth/2006/company/10.htm (accessed November 2008).

Copeland, M. V. "The Big Guns' Next Target: eBay." CNNMoney.com, January 31, 2006. money.cnn.com/magazines/business2/business2_archive/2006/01/01/8368106/index.htm (accessed November 2008).

Copeland, M. V., and K. Kelleher, "The New New Careers." *Business 2.0,* May 2007.

Cox, J. L., E. R. Martinez, and K. B. Quinlan. "Blogs on the Corporation: Managing the Risk, Reaping the Benefits." *Journal of Business Strategy,* 29, no. 3 (2008).

Cox, B. G., and W. Koelzer. *Internet Marketing: Strategy, Implementation, and Practice,* 3rd ed. Upper Saddle River, NJ: Prentice Hall, 2006.

Datta, S. "The 7 Habits of Highly Effective Bloggers." *Business 2.0,* September 2006.

Edgar Online. "Growth of Online Commerce and Online Auction Market." March 17, 2006. sec.edgar-online.com/2006/03/17/0001047469-06-003660/Section9.asp (accessed November 2008).

E-Market Services. "Why Use E-Markets?" *E-marketservices.com,* 2006. emarketservices.com/start/Knowledge/eMarket-Basics/Why-use-eMarkets/index.html (accessed November 2008).

Farber, D. "2009: The Year of Enterprise Social Networks." *ZDNet,* February 14, 2008. blogs.zdnet.com/BTL/?p=7997 (accessed November 2008).

Financial Analysts Meeting, Seattle, Washington, July 23, 1998.

Flynn, N. *Blog Rules: A Business Guide to Managing Policy, Public Relations, and Legal Issues.* Saranac Lake, NY: AMACOM, 2006.

Hayes-Roth, B. "Smart Interactive Characters: Automating One-to-One Customer Service." *New Architect,* September 1999. webtechniques.com/archives/1999/09/hayesroth (accessed November 2008).

Hinchcliffe, D. "Profitably Running an Online Business in the Web 2.0 Era." *SOA Web Services Journal,* November 29, 2006. web2.wsj2.com (accessed February 2009).

Hof, R. D. "My Virtual Life." *BusinessWeek,* May 1, 2008.

Hoover, J. N. "Enterprise 2.0." *InformationWeek,* February 26, 2007.

Joyner, A. *The eBay Billionaires Club,* Hoboken, NJ: Wiley, 2007.

Khosrow-Pour, M. (Ed.). *Encyclopedia of E-Commerce, E-Government, and Mobile Commerce.* Hershey, PA: Idea Group Reference, 2006.

Kioses, E., K. Pramatari, and G. Doukidis. "Factors Affecting Perceived Impact of E-Marketplaces." *Proceedings of the 19th Bled eConference,* Bled, Slovenia, June 5–7, 2006.

Lepouras, G., and C. Vassilakis. "Adaptive Virtual Reality Shopping Malls." In M. Khosrow-Pour, (Ed.). *Encyclopedia of E-Commerce, E-Government, and Mobile Commerce.* Hershey, PA: Idea Group Reference, 2006.

Li, E. Y., and T. C. Du, (Eds.). *Advances in Electronic Business,* volume 1. Hershey, PA: Idea Group Publishing, 2005.

Martin, R. "The Right Search Tool." *InformationWeek,* September 29, 2008.

Naughton, J. "Web Sites That Changed the World." IndiaStudyChannel.com, August 14, 2006. indiastudychannel.com/resources/10578-Websites-that-changed-world.aspx (accessed November 2008).

Nerille, J. "X-treme Web 2.0." *Optimize Magazine,* January 2007.

Nissanoff, D. *Future Shop: How the New Auction Culture Will Revolutionize the Way We Buy, Sell, and Get Things We Really Want.* New York: The Penguin Press, 2006.

O'Buyonge, A. A., and L. Chen. "E-Health Dot-Coms' Critical Success Factors." In M. Khosrow-Pour, (Ed.). *Encyclopedia of E-Commerce, E-Government, and Mobile Commerce.* Hershey, PA: Idea Group Reference, 2006.

Parry, G., and A. P. Graves. *Build to Order: The Road to the 5-Day Car.* London: Springer Verlag, 2008.

Porter, M. E. "Strategy and the Internet." *Harvard Business Review* (March 2001).

Radarajan, P. R., and M. S. Yadav. "Marketing Strategy and the Internet: An Organizing Framework." *Academy of Marketing Science,* 30, no. 4 (Fall 2002).

Rapoza, J. "Microsoft Takes Web Development Leap." *eWeek,* 2006.

RedOrbit.com. "Blue Nile Launches New Interactive Diamond Search." March 27, 2006. redorbit.com/news/entertainment/445262/blue_nile_launches_new_interactive_diamond_search (accessed November 2008).

Rivlin, G. "When Buying a Diamond Starts with a Mouse." *New York Times,* January 7, 2007.

Robbins, S., and M. Bell. *Second Life for Dummies.* Hoboken, NJ: Wiley, 2008.

Rosedale, P. "Alter Egos." *Forbes*, May 7, 2007.

Roush, W. "Second Earth." *Technology Review*, July/August 2007.

Rymaszewski, M., et al. *Second Life: The Official Guide*, 2nd ed. Indianapolis, IN: Wiley, 2008.

Saarinen, T., M. Tinnild, and A. Tseng, (Eds.). *Managing Business in a Multi-Channel World: Success Factors for E-Business.* Hershey, PA: Idea Group, Inc., 2006.

Singh, A. M. "Evolution of Marketing to E-Marketing." In M. Khosrow-Pour, (Ed.). *Encyclopedia of E-Commerce, E-Government, and Mobile Commerce.* Hershey, PA: Idea Group Reference, 2006.

Sloan, P., and P. Kaihla. "Blogging for Dollars." *Business 2.0*, September 2006.

Suomi, R. "Governing Health Care with IT." In M. Khosrow-Pour, (Ed.). *Encyclopedia of E-Commerce, E-Government, and Mobile Commerce.* Hershey, PA: Idea Group Reference, 2006.

Terdiman, D. *The Entrepreneur's Guide to Second Life*, Indianapolis, IN: Wiley, 2008.

Time. "50 Coolest Web Sites 2006." August 23, 2006.

Turban, E., et al. *Business Intelligence: A Managerial Approach.* Upper Saddle River, NJ, Prentice Hall, 2008.

Weber, S. *eBay 101: Selling on eBay for Part Time or Full Time Income.* Falls Church, VA: Web Books, 2008.

Weber, S. *Plug Your Business.* Falls Church, VA: Weber Books, 2007.

Weblogs, Inc. "The Social Software Weblog," 2007. **socialsoftware.weblogsinc.com** (accessed February 2009).

Weinstein, M. "On Demand Is in Demand." *Training Magazine*, October 2006.

White, B. A. *Second Life: A Guide to Your Virtual World.* Indianapolis, IN: Que Publishers (A Pearson Publishing Company), 2008.

Wind, Y. "The Challenge of Customization in Financial Services." *Communications of the ACM* (2001).

Zappala, S., and C. Gray. *Impact of E-Commerce on Consumers and Small Firms.* Surrey, UK: Ashgate Publishing Co., 2006.

Zimmerman, J. *Web Marketing for Dummies.* Indianapolis, IN: Wiley, 2007.

BUILD-TO-ORDER PRODUCTION

The concept of build-to-order means that a firm starts to make a product or service only after an order for it is placed. It is also known as *demand-driven manufacturing (DDM)*, *customization*, *personalization*, and *pull technology* (Anderson 2008). This concept is as old as commerce itself and was the only method of production until the Industrial Revolution. According to this concept, if a person needs a pair of shoes, he or she goes to a shoemaker, who takes the person's measurements. The person negotiates quality, style, and price and pays a down payment. The shoemaker buys the materials and makes a customized product for the customer. Customized products are expensive, and it takes a long time to finish them. The Industrial Revolution introduced a new way of thinking about production.

The Industrial Revolution started with the concept of dividing work into small parts. Such division of labor makes the work simpler, requiring less training for employees. It also allows for specialization. Different employees become experts in executing certain tasks. Because the work segments are simpler, it is easier to automate them. As machines were invented to make products, the concept of build-to-market developed. To implement build-to-market, it was necessary to design standard products, produce them, store them, and then sell them.

The creation of standard products by automation drove prices down, and demand accelerated. The solution to the problem of increased demand was mass production. In mass production, a company produces large amounts of standard products at a very low cost and then "pushes" them to consumers. Thus began the need for sales and marketing organizations. Specialized sales forces resulted in increased competition and the desire to sell in wider, and more remote, markets. This model also required the creation of large factories and specialized departments such as accounting and personnel to manage the activities in the factories. With mass production, factory workers personally did not know the customers and frequently did not care about customers' needs or product quality. However, the products were inexpensive and good enough to fuel demand, and thus the concept became a dominant one. Mass production also required inventory systems at various places in the supply chain, which were based on forecasted demand. If the forecasted demand was wrong, the inventories were incorrect. Thus, companies were always trying to achieve the right balance between not having enough inventory to meet demand and having too much inventory on hand.

As society became more affluent, the demand for customized products increased. Manufacturers had to meet the demand for customized products to satisfy customers. As long as the demand for customized product was small, it could be met. Cars, for example, have long been produced using this model (see the Toyota and others' experiences in Parry and Graves 2008). Customers were asked to pay a premium for customization and wait a long time to receive the customized product, and they were willing to do so. Note that the process starts with product configuration (Anderson 2008) namely, the customer decides what the product is going to look like, what operations it will perform, and what capabilities it will have (e.g., the functionalities in Dell).

Slowly, the demand for customized products and services increased. Burger King introduced the concept of "having it your way," and manufacturers sought ways to provide customized products in large quantities, which is the essence of mass customization, as pioneered by Dell. Such solutions were usually enhanced by some kind of information technology. The introduction of customized personal computers (PCs) by Dell was so successful that many other industries wanted to try mass customization. EC can facilitate customization, even mass customization. In many cases, EC is doing it via personalization. To understand how companies can use EC for customization, let's first compare mass production, also known as *push system*, and mass customization, also known as a *pull system*, as shown in Exhibit 2A.1.

Notice that one important area in the supply chain is order taking. Using EC, a customer can self-configure the desired product online. The order is received in seconds. Once the order is verified and payment arranged, the order is sent electronically to the production floor. This saves time and money. For complex products, customers may collaborate in real time with the manufacturer's designers, as is done at Cisco Systems. Again, time and money are saved and errors are reduced due to better communication and collaboration. Other contributions of EC are that the customers' needs are visible to all partners in the order fulfillment chain (fewer delays, faster response time), inventories are reduced due to rapid communication, and digitizable products and services can be delivered electronically.

A key issue in mass customization is knowing what the customers want. In many cases, the seller can simply ask the customer to configure the product or service. In other cases, the seller tries to predict what the customer wants. EC is very helpful in this area due to the use of online market research methods such as collaborative filtering (see Chapter 4 and Holweg and Pil 2001). Using collaborative filtering, a company can discover what each customer wants without asking the customer directly. Such market research is accomplished more cheaply by a machine than by human researchers.

EXHIBIT 2A.1 Push Versus Pull Production Systems

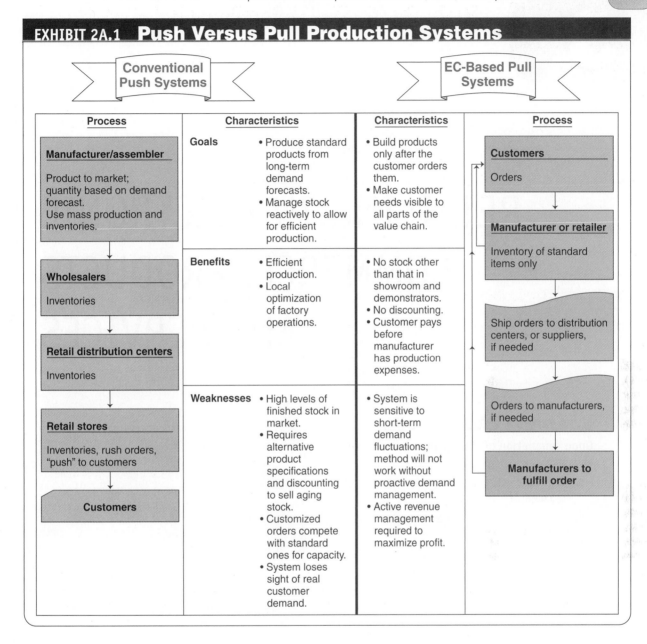

From the production point of view, EC also can enable mass customization. In the factory, for example, IT in general and e-commerce in particular can help in expediting the production changeover from one item to another. Also, because most mass production is based on the assembly of standard components, EC can help a company create the production process for a product in minutes and identify needed components and their location. Furthermore, a production schedule can be generated automatically, and needed resources can be deployed, including money. This is why many industries are planning to move to build-to-order using EC. By doing so, they are expecting huge cost reductions, shorter order-to-delivery times, and lower inventory costs.

Mass customization on a large scale is not easy to attain (Anderson 2008; Larco et al. 2007), but if performed properly, it may become the dominant model in many industries.

REFERENCES

Holweg, M., and F. Pil. "Successful Build-to-Order Strategies Start with the Customer." *MIT Sloan Management Journal*, 43, no. 1 (2001).

Larco, J. A., R. Dekker, and U. Kaymak. "Distributed Services with Foreseen and Unforeseen Tasks: The Mobile

Re-Allocation Problem." *Social Science Research Network*, July 12, 2007.

Parry, G., and A. P. Graves. *Build to Order: The Road to the 5-Day Car.* London: Springer Verlag, 2008.

CHAPTER

3

RETAILING IN ELECTRONIC COMMERCE: PRODUCTS AND SERVICES

Learning Objectives

Upon completion of this chapter, you will be able to:

1. Describe electronic retailing (e-tailing) and its characteristics.

2. Define and describe the primary e-tailing business models.

3. Describe how online travel and tourism services operate and their impact on the industry.

4. Discuss the online employment market, including its participants, benefits, and limitations.

5. Describe online real estate services.

6. Discuss online stock-trading services.

7. Discuss cyberbanking and online personal finance.

8. Describe on-demand delivery of groceries and similar products/services.

9. Describe the delivery of digital products and online entertainment.

10. Discuss various online consumer aids, including comparison-shopping aids.

11. Describe disintermediation and other B2C strategic issues.

Content

AMAZON.COM: E-TAILING GROWS DESPITE THE SLUMPING ECONOMY

The Opportunity

Amazon.com (*amazon.com*) reported that its annual profit for 2008 had doubled, with a 41 percent revenue increase, despite adverse U.S. and global economic conditions.

Entrepreneur Jeff Bezos faced an opportunity rather than a business problem. In the early 1990s, Bezos saw the huge potential for retail sales over the Internet and identified books as the most logical product for e-tailing. In July 1995, Bezos started Amazon.com, an e-tailing pioneer, offering books via an electronic catalog from its Web site. Over the years, the company has recognized that it must continually enhance its business models and online storefront by expanding its product selection, improving the customer experience, and adding services and alliances. In addition, the company recognized early on the importance of order fulfillment and warehousing. It has invested hundreds of millions of dollars in building physical warehouses designed for shipping small packages to hundreds of thousands of customers. Amazon.com's challenge was, and remains, how to succeed where many have failed—namely, how to sell consumer products online, at a profit, and show a reasonable rate of return on investment.

The Solution: Reaching Out to Customers

In addition to its initial electronic bookstore, Amazon has expanded its offerings to a vast array of products and services segmented into three broad categories: media (books, music, DVDs, etc.); electronics and other merchandise (including its new wireless reading device, "Kindle"; office supplies; cameras; toys; etc.); and other (nonretail activities, such as Web services, Amazon Enterprise Solutions, etc.). Key features of the Amazon.com superstore are easy browsing, searching, and ordering; useful product information, reviews, recommendations, and personalization; broad selection; low prices; secure payment systems; and efficient order fulfillment.

The Amazon.com Web site has a number of features that make the online shopping experience more enjoyable. Its "Gift Ideas" section features seasonally appropriate gift ideas and services. AmazonConnect allows customers to select their favorite authors, read about them, and then receive e-mails from those authors.

Amazon also offers various marketplace services. Amazon Auctions hosts and operates auctions on behalf of individuals and small businesses throughout the world. The Shops service hosts electronic storefronts for a monthly fee, offering small businesses the opportunity to have customized storefronts supported by the richness of Amazon's order-fulfillment processing. Customers can use Web-enabled cell phones, PDAs, or Pocket PCs to access Amazon.com and shop anywhere, anytime. Amazon.com also can be accessed via AT&T's #121 voice service.

Amazon is recognized as an online leader in creating sales through customer intimacy and customer relationship management (CRM), which are cultivated by informative marketing front ends and one-to-one advertisements. In addition, sales are supported by highly automated, efficient back-end systems. When a customer makes a return visit to Amazon, a cookie file (see Chapter 4) identifies the user and says, for example, "Welcome back, Sarah Shopper," and then proceeds to recommend new books from the same genre of the customer's previous purchases and a range of other items. It also provides detailed product descriptions and ratings to help consumers make informed purchase decisions. The site has an efficient search engine and other shopping aids. Amazon.com has a superb warehousing system that gives the company an advantage over the competition.

Customers can personalize their accounts and manage orders online with the patented "1-Click" order feature. 1-Click includes an electronic wallet (see Chapter 11), which enables shoppers to place an order in a secure manner without the need to enter their address, credit card number, and other information each time they shop and allows customers to view their order status, cancel or combine orders that have not yet entered the shipping process, edit the shipping options and addresses on unshipped orders, modify the payment method for unshipped orders, and more.

In 1997, Amazon.com started an extensive associates program. By 2009, the company had more than 2 million partners worldwide that refer customers to Amazon.com. Amazon.com pays a 4 to 10 percent commission on any resulting sale. Starting in 2000, Amazon.com has undertaken alliances with major "trusted partners" that provide knowledgeable entry into new markets. For example, clicking "Office Supplies" allows customers either to select from Amazon.com's office supplies or to browse those of Office Depot; clicking "Health and Personal Care" allows customers to benefit from great deals offered by Weight Watchers. In yet another extension of its services, in September 2001 Amazon signed an agreement with Borders Group Inc., providing Amazon's users with the option of picking up their merchandise at Borders' physical bookstores (In-Store pickup). Amazon.com also is becoming a Web fulfillment contractor for national chains such as Target. Amazon also has its own search engine, called A9 (*a9.com*), and offers a range of Web services to developers (Amazon Web Services).

The Results

In 1999, *Time* magazine named Bezos "Person of the Year," recognizing the company's success in popularizing online shopping. In January 2002, Amazon declared its first profit—for the 2001 fourth quarter. Since then, the company has remained profitable. Annual sales for Amazon.com have trended upward, driven largely by product diversification and its international presence. This pioneer e-tailer now offers over 17 million book, music, and DVD/video titles to some 20 million customers.

Amazon also offers several features for international customers, including over 1 million Japanese-language

titles. Amazon.com maintained its position as the number one e-tailer in 2008, generating revenues of $19.2 billion, with a net income of $645 million. In 2009, the Amazon.com Web site attracted at least 615 million visitors. Like all businesses, Amazon.com, the king of e-tailers, which has shown all others the potential of B2C EC, will continue to walk the fine line of profitability, at least in the short run.

Sources: Compiled from Reuters (2008), Dignan (2008), and *amazon.com* (accessed February 2009).

Source: Courtesy of Amazon.com. Used with permission.

WHAT WE CAN LEARN . . .

The case of Amazon.com, the most recognized and the largest e-tailer in the world, demonstrates the evolution of e-tailing, some of the problems encountered by e-tailers, and the solutions employed by Amazon.com to expand its business. It also is indicative of a key trend in Internet retailing: that the biggest online retailers are still growing and becoming more dominant, with the top 500 e-retailers accounting for 61 percent ($83.6 billion) of all online sales in 2007 (Hanks 2007). E-tailing, as demonstrated by the Amazon case, continues its double-digit, year-over-year growth rate despite the global economic downturn. This is, in part, because sales are shifting away from stores and also because online shoppers are, in general, more affluent. However, some experts argue that online retailers will need to better understand customer behavior and preferences if they are to achieve a better convergence between technological capability and customer desires. In this chapter, we will look at the delivery of both products and services online to individual customers. We also discuss e-tailing successes and failures.

3.1 INTERNET MARKETING AND ELECTRONIC RETAILING

The Amazon.com case illustrates how commerce can be conducted on the Internet. Indeed, the amount and percentage of goods and services sold on the Internet is increasing rapidly, despite the failure of many dot-com companies. According *Internet Retailer* (2007a), approximately 45 percent of adult U.S. Internet users shop online and/or research offline sales online. With estimates of 220 million Internet users in the United States, this suggests that in 2008 there were approximately 100 million online shoppers in that country. However, as the number of Internet users reaches saturation, the rate of increase of online shoppers will slow. One of the challenges for electronic retailers, therefore, is to increase the amount spent online. As discussed in Chapters 1 and 2, companies have many reasons to market and sell their goods and services online. Innovative marketing strategies and a deep understanding of online consumer behavior and preferences will be required for sustained success in a competitive online environment.

This chapter presents an overview of Internet retailing, its diversity, prospects, and limitations. (For a more detailed analysis, see Soopramanien and Robertson 2007.) Retailing, especially when conducted in a new medium, must be supported by an understanding of consumer buying behavior, market research, and advertising, topics that will be presented in Chapter 4. Let's begin our discussion of EC products and services with an overview of electronic retailing.

OVERVIEW OF ELECTRONIC RETAILING

A retailer is a sales *intermediary*, a seller that operates between manufacturers and customers. Even though many manufacturers sell directly to consumers, they usually supplement their sales through wholesalers and retailers (a *multichannel approach*). In the physical world, retailing is done in stores (or factory outlets) that customers must visit in order to make a purchase. Companies that produce a large number of products, such as Procter & Gamble, must use retailers for efficient distribution. However, even if a company sells only a relatively few products (e.g., Kodak), it still might need retailers to reach a large number of customers.

Catalog sales offer companies and customers a relief from the constraints of space and time: Catalogs free a retailer from the need for a physical store from which to distribute products, and customers can browse catalogs on their own time. With the ubiquity of the Internet, the next logical step was for retailing to move online. Retailing conducted over the Internet is called **electronic retailing**, or **e-tailing**, and those who conduct retail business online are called **e-tailers**. E-tailing also can be conducted through auctions. E-tailing makes it easier for a manufacturer to sell directly to the customer, cutting out the intermediary (e.g., Godiva in Chapter 1). This chapter examines the various types of e-tailing and related issues.

The concept of retailing and e-tailing implies sales of goods and/or services to individual customers—that is, B2C EC. However, the distinction between B2C and B2B EC is not always clear. For example, Amazon.com sells books mostly to individuals (B2C), but it also sells to corporations (B2B). Amazon.com's chief rival in selling books online, Barnes & Noble (barnesandnoble.com), has a special division that caters only to business customers. Wal-Mart (walmart.com) sells to both individuals and businesses (via Sam's Club). Dell sells its computers to both consumers and businesses from dell.com, Staples sells to both markets at staples.com, and insurance sites sell to both individuals and corporations.

SIZE AND GROWTH OF THE B2C MARKET

The statistics for the volume of B2C EC sales, including forecasts for future sales, come from many sources. Reported amounts of online sales *deviate substantially* based on how the numbers are derived, and thus it is often difficult to obtain a consistent and coherent picture of the growth of EC. Some of the variation stems from the use of different definitions and classifications of EC. For example, when tallying financial data some analysts include the investment costs in Internet infrastructure, whereas others include only the value of the actual transactions conducted via the Internet. Another issue is how the items for sale are categorized. Some sources combine certain products and services; others do not. Some sources include online travel sales in the data for EC retail; others do not. Sometimes different time periods are used in the measurement. When reading data about B2C EC sales, therefore, it is very important that care is taken in interpreting the figures.

electronic retailing (e-tailing)
Retailing conducted online, over the Internet.

e-tailers
Retailers who sell over the Internet.

EXHIBIT 3.1   Representative Sources of EC Statistics

BizRate (*bizrate.com*)

Business 2.0 (*money.cnn.com/ magazines/business2*)

comScore (*comscore.com*)

ClickZ Network (*clickz.com*)

Ecommerce Info Center (*ecominfocenter.com*)

eMarket (*emarket.com*)

Forrester Research (*forrester.com*)

Gartner (*gartner.com*)

Gomez (*gomez.com*)

InternetRetailer (*internetretailer.com*)

Lionbridge (*lionbridge.com*)

Nielsen Online (*nielsen-online.com*)

Shop.org (*shop.org*)

Omniture SiteCatalyst (*omniture.com*)

Pew Internet (*pewinternet.com*)

Yankee Group (*yankeegroup.com*)

U.S. Census Bureau (*census.gov/estats*), and (*census.gov/mrts/www/data*)

The sites listed in Exhibit 3.1 provide statistics on e-tailing as well as on other Internet and EC activities. Typical statistics used in describing e-tailing and consumer behavior include Internet usage by demographic (online sales by age, gender, country, etc.); online sales by item; online sales by vendor; and buying patterns online.

The following are some general statistics about U.S. online sales from Forrester Research (Mulpuru et al. 2008). U.S. online retail sales topped $175 billion in 2007, comprising about 6 percent of total retail sales and delivering 21 percent greater growth over 2006 online sales. Online retail sites get 4.6 million visitors a minute, and 72 million people shopped sometime during a day in 2007. B2C e-commerce sales are projected to reach $335 billion by 2012. On average, e-tailing sales are expected to grow at an annual rate of 14 percent from 2008 to 2012, compared to only 2.6 percent for brick-and-mortar stores. E-commerce is expected to account for nearly 13 percent of total U.S. retail sales by 2012. Beyond promoting a rapid increase in e-commerce transactions, the Web also plays a prominent role in influencing brick-and-mortar retail sales. In 2007, retailers reported that 27 percent of store sales were either directly or indirectly influenced by the Web. In 2008, online product research generated $3.95 in offline sales for every $1 in e-commerce sales; that number is expected to increase to $4.68 by 2012. The major e-tailers, by descending order of sales, are Amazon.com, Staples, Home Depot, Dell, HP, Office Max, Apple Computers, Sears, CDW, and Newegg.com.

WHAT SELLS WELL ON THE INTERNET

With approximately 100 million shoppers online in the United States in 2008, e-tailers appreciate the need to provide excellent choice and service to an ever-increasing cohort of potential customers. Hundreds of thousands of items are available on the Web from numerous vendors. Exhibit 3.2 shows categories that are all selling well online. For some current trends in B2C, see Online File W3.1.

CHARACTERISTICS AND ADVANTAGES OF SUCCESSFUL E-TAILING

Many of the same basic principles that apply to retail success also apply to e-tail success. Sound business thinking, visionary leadership, thorough competitive analysis and financial analysis, and the articulation of a well-thought-out EC strategy are essential. So, too, is ensuring appropriate infrastructure, particularly a stable and scalable technology infrastructure to support the online and physical aspects of EC business operations. Newly required capabilities (e.g., capabilities in logistics and distribution) might need to be obtained through external strategic alliances. Offering quality merchandise at good prices, coupled with excellent service, and cross-channel coordination and integration in which customers can almost seamlessly operate between the online and physical environments of a business are also important elements in successful e-tailing. In a sense, the online and traditional channels are not very different. However, e-tailers can offer expanded consumer services not offered by traditional retailers. For a comparison of e-tailing and retailing, including advantages, see Exhibit 3.3.

EXHIBIT 3.2   What Sells Well on the Internet?

Category	Description
Travel	Expedia and Travelocity are major players in this category. Online travel agents offer a range of services, including travel booking, hotel reservations, car rentals, and vacation packages.
Computer hardware and software	Dell and Gateway are the major online vendors of computer hardware and software. Computer hardware and software is the largest category of products sold online.
Consumer electronics	Consumer electronics include digital cameras, printers, scanners, and wireless devices. Consumer electronics is the second largest category of products sold online.
Office supplies	B2C and B2B sales of office supplies are increasing rapidly, all over the world, as companies increasingly use the Internet to place orders for stationery and the like.
Sport and fitness goods	Sporting goods sell very well on the Internet. However, it is difficult to measure the exact amount of sales because only a few e-tailers sell sporting goods exclusively online (e.g., *fogdog.com*).
Books and music (CDs, DVDs)	Amazon.com and Barnesandnoble.com are the major sellers of books. However, hundreds of other e-tailers sell books on the Internet, especially specialized books (e.g., technical books, children's books).
Toys and hobbies	In 2007, online sales of toys dropped again due to toy recalls, specifically those toys made in China (*Biz Report* 2007).
Health and beauty	A large variety of health and beauty products—from vitamins to cosmetics and fragrances—are sold online by most large retailers and by specialty stores.
Entertainment	This is another area where dozens of products, ranging from tickets to events (e.g., *ticketmaster.com*) to paid fantasy games (see Section 3.7), are embraced by millions of shoppers worldwide.
Apparel and clothing	With the possibility of buying customized shirts, pants, and even shoes, the online sale of apparel also is growing. Guaranteed returns policies and improving features on fitting clothing without first trying it on have increased the customers' comfort zone for buying apparel online.
Jewelry	Online sales of jewelry are booming. Claims of prices about 40 percent less than would be paid in traditional stores, the trend toward online jewelry sales is likely to continue.
Cars	The sale of cars over the Internet is just beginning (people still like to "kick the tires"), but could be one of the top sellers on the Internet in the near future. Customers like the build-to-order capabilities, but even selling used cars online has advantages and is increasing rapidly. Support services such as financing, warranties, and insurance also are selling well online.
Services	Sales in service industries, especially travel, stock trading, electronic banking, real estate, and insurance, are increasing—more than doubling every year in some cases.
Food and drugs	Innovative delivery solutions help with food sales. Ordering prescription drugs online may save time and even money. Many online pharmacies provide information about drug interactions. Some even e-mail alerts when a drug is recalled or a generic equivalent becomes available.
Pet supplies	Pet supplies is a new category in the top-seller list. As family pets become more and more integrated as a member of the family, online spending on toys, edible treats, food, pet accessories, and veterinary products and services is soaring.
Others	Many other products, ranging from prescription drugs to custom-made shoes are offered on the Internet. Many items are specialized or niche products.

Sources: *Biz Report* (2007) and Mulpuru et al. (2008).

With all else being equal in the online environment, goods with the following characteristics are expected to facilitate higher sales volumes:

▶ High brand recognition (e.g., Lands' End, Dell, Sony)
▶ A guarantee provided by highly reliable or well-known vendors (e.g., Dell, L.L.Bean)
▶ Digitized format (e.g., software, music, or videos)
▶ Relatively inexpensive items (e.g., office supplies, vitamins)
▶ Frequently purchased items (e.g., groceries, prescription drugs)

EXHIBIT 3.3 Retailing Versus E-Tailing

Factor	Retailers	E-Tailers
Physical expansion (when revenue increases as the number of visitors grows)	• Expansion of retailing platform to include more locations and space	• Expansion of e-commerce platform to include increased server capacity and distribution facilities
Physical expansion (when revenue does not increase as the number of visitors grows)	• May not need physical expansion • Expand marketing effort to turn "window shoppers" into effective shoppers	• May still need physical expansion to provide sustainable services • Expand marketing to turn "pane shoppers" into effective shoppers
Technology	• Sales automation technologies such as POS systems	• Front-end technologies • Benefit from browsing • Back-end technologies • "Information" technologies
Customer relations	• More stable due to nonanonymous contacts • More tolerable of disputes due to visibility • "Physical" relationships	• Less stable due to anonymous contacts • More intolerant of disputes due to invisibility • "Logical" relationships
Cognitive shopping overhead	• Lower cognitive shopping overhead due to easy-to-establish mutual trust	• Higher cognitive shopping overhead due to hard-to-establish mutual trust
Competition	• Local competition	• Global competition
Customer base	• Fewer competitors • Local area customers • No anonymity • Fewer resources needed to increase customer loyalty • Customers remain loyal for future purchases	• More competitors • Wide area customers • Anonymity • More resources needed to increase customer loyalty • Customers shift loyalty
Supply chain cost	• High, interruption	• Lower
Customization and personalization	• Expensive and slow	• Fast, efficient
Price changing and price discrimination	• Expensive to do, not done so often	• Inexpensive, anytime
Adaptability to market trends	• Slow	• Rapid

Sources: Compiled from Kwon and Lennon (2009) and Ha and Stoel (2009).

▶ Commodities with standard specifications (e.g., books, CDs, airline tickets), making physical inspection unimportant

▶ Well-known packaged items that cannot be opened even in a traditional store (e.g., foods, chocolates, vitamins)

The next section examines business models that have proven successful in e-tailing.

Section 3.1 ▶ REVIEW QUESTIONS

1. Describe the nature of B2C EC.
2. What sells well in B2C?
3. What are the characteristics of high-volume products and services?
4. Describe the major trends in B2C.

3.2 E-TAILING BUSINESS MODELS

In order to better understand e-tailing, let's look at it from the point of view of a retailer or a manufacturer that sells to individual consumers. The seller has its own organization and must also buy goods and services from others, usually businesses (B2B in Exhibit 3.4). As also shown in Exhibit 3.4, e-tailing, which is basically B2C (right side of the exhibit), is done between the seller (a retailer or a manufacturer) and the buyer. The exhibit shows other EC transactions and related activities that may impact e-tailing. In this section, we will look at the various B2C models and their classifications.

CLASSIFICATION BY DISTRIBUTION CHANNEL

A business model is a description of how an organization intends to generate revenue through its business operations. More specifically, it is an analysis of the organization's customers and, from that, a discussion of how that organization will achieve profitability and sustainability by delivering goods and services (value) to those customers. E-tailing business models can be classified in several ways. For example, some classify e-tailers by the scope of items handled (general purpose versus specialty e-tailing) or by the scope of the sales region covered (global versus regional), whereas others use classification by revenue models (see Chapter 1). Here we will classify the models by the distribution channel used, distinguishing five categories:

1. **Direct marketing by mail-order retailers that go online.** Most traditional mail-order retailers, such as QVC, Sharper Image, and Lands' End, simply added another distribution channel—the Internet. Several of these retailers also operate physical stores, but their main distribution channel is direct marketing.

2. **Direct marketing by manufacturers.** Manufacturers, such as Dell, Nike, Lego, Godiva (Chapter 1), and Sony, market directly online from company sites to individual customers. Most of these manufacturers are click-and-mortar, also

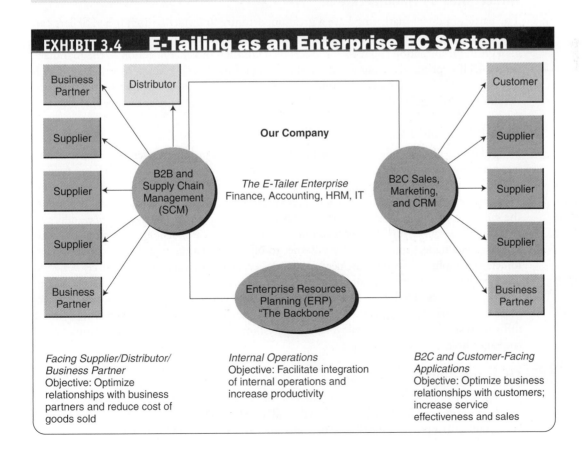

EXHIBIT 3.4   E-Tailing as an Enterprise EC System

Facing Supplier/Distributor/Business Partner
Objective: Optimize relationships with business partners and reduce cost of goods sold

Internal Operations
Objective: Facilitate integration of internal operations and increase productivity

B2C and Customer-Facing Applications
Objective: Optimize business relationships with customers; increase service effectiveness and sales

selling in their own physical stores or via retailers. However, the manufacturer may be a pure-play company (e.g., Dell).

3. **Pure-play e-tailers.** These e-tailers do not have physical stores, only an online sales presence. Amazon.com is an example of a pure-play e-tailer.

4. **Click-and-mortar retailers.** These are of two sorts, depending on how the businesses were originally founded. Originally, click-and-mortar referred to traditional businesses that developed Web sites to support their business activities in some way (e.g., walmart.com, homedepot.com, and sharperimage.com). For details, see en.wikipedia.org/wiki/Bricks_and_clicks. However, we are now seeing the reverse trend. A small number of successful e-tailers are now creating physical storefronts, leveraging the brand power of the online environment to support more traditional trading activities via stores. For example, Dell, a pioneer of e-tailing and one of the largest sellers of computers online, has also opened physical stores.

5. **Internet (online) malls.** As described in Chapter 2, these malls include large numbers of independent storefronts.

We will examine each of these distribution channel categories in the pages that follow.

Direct Marketing by Mail-Order Companies

direct marketing

Broadly, marketing that takes place without intermediaries between manufacturers and buyers; in the context of this book, marketing done online between any seller and buyer.

In a broad sense, **direct marketing** describes marketing that takes place without intermediaries. Direct marketers take orders directly from consumers, bypassing traditional wholesale or retail distribution.

Firms with established, mature mail-order businesses have a distinct advantage in online sales, given their existing payment processing, inventory management, and order-fulfillment operations, as shown in Online File W3.2.

Direct Sales by Manufacturers

The parties in direct marketing have a great opportunity to influence each other. Sellers can understand their markets better because of the direct connection to consumers, and consumers gain greater information about the products through their direct connection to the manufacturers. Dell is primarily using direct marketing combined with a build-to-order approach (see Appendix 2A for more on build-to-order), customizing its products. Insights and Additions 3.1 describes the process by which customers can configure and order cars online.

Pure-Play E-Tailers

virtual (pure-play) e-tailers

Firms that sell directly to consumers over the Internet without maintaining a physical sales channel.

Virtual (pure-play) e-tailers are firms that sell directly to consumers over the Internet without maintaining a physical sales channel. Amazon.com is a prime example of this type of e-tailer. Virtual e-tailers have the advantage of low overhead costs and streamlined processes. However, one drawback can be a lack of established infrastructure (or back office) to support the online front-office activities. Virtual e-tailers are *general purpose* or *specialized* e-tailers.

General e-tailers, such as Amazon.com (see the opening case), selling a vast range of goods and services online, capitalize on the Internet to offer such variety to a diverse group of customers geographically without the need to maintain a large physical retail (storefront) network.

Specialty e-tailers can operate in a very narrow market, as does Cattoys.com (cattoys.com), described in Online File W3.3, or Rugman.com (rugman.com), which offers more than 12,000 Oriental and Persian rugs online. Such specialized businesses would find it difficult to survive in the physical world, because they would not have enough customers and could not hold the variety of stock.

click-and-mortar retailers

Brick-and-mortar retailers that offer a transactional Web site from which to conduct business.

Click-and-Mortar Retailers

A **click-and-mortar retailer** is a combination of both the brick-and-mortar retailer and an online transactional Web site. Many click-and-mortar retailers started life as a traditional storefront with a physical retail presence only and over time adopted an online transactional

Insights and Additions 3.1 Selling Cars Online: Build-to-Order

The world's automobile manufacturers operate in complex enterprises with thousands of suppliers and millions of customers. Their traditional channel for distributing cars has been the automobile dealer, who orders cars and then sells them from the lot. When a customer wants a particular feature or color ("options"), the customer might have to wait weeks or months until the "pipeline" of vehicles has that particular car on the production line.

In the traditional system, the manufacturers conduct market research in order to estimate which features and options will sell well, and then they make the cars they wish to sell. In some cases, certain cars are ultimately sold from stock at a loss when the market exhibits insufficient demand for a particular vehicle. The automakers have long operated under this "build-to-stock" environment, building cars that are carried as inventory during the outbound logistics process (ships, trucks, trains, and dealers' lots). General Motors (GM) estimates that it holds as much as $40-billion worth of unsold vehicles in its distribution channels. Other automakers hold large amounts as well.

Ford, GM, and Toyota, along with other automakers around the world, have announced plans to implement a build-to-order program, much like the Dell approach to building computers. These auto giants intend to transform themselves from build-to-stock companies to build-to-order companies, thereby cutting inventory requirements in half, while at the same time giving customers the vehicle they want in a short period (e.g., 1 to 2 weeks).

However, according to Weiner (2006) this transformation has so far been "doomed to failure by rigid production processes, inflexible product structures, the lack of integrated logistics processes, and inadequate networking of manufacturers, suppliers and customers." Only when a network of suppliers produce standard modules for cars using standardized processes and IT systems will the dream of a truly agile and responsive supply chain delivering build-to-customer-order capability be realized.

As an example of this trend toward build-to-order mass customization in the new car market, Jaguar car buyers can build a dream car online. On Jaguar's Web site (*jaguar.com*), consumers are able to custom configure their car's features and components, see it online, price it, and have it delivered to a nearby dealer. Using a virtual car on the Web site, customers can view in real time more than 1,250 possible exterior combinations out of several million, rotate the image 360 degrees, and see the price updated automatically with each selection of trim or accessories. After storing the car in a virtual garage, the customer can decide on the purchase and select a dealer at which to pick up the completed car. (Thus, conflicts with the established dealer network channel are avoided.) The Web site helps primarily with the research process—it is not a fully transactional site. The configuration, however, can be transmitted to the production floor, thereby reducing delivery time and contributing to increased customer satisfaction. Similar configuration systems are available from all the major car manufacturers. Customers can electronically track the progress of the car, including visualization of the production process in the factory. Another Web site with similar functionality is *hummer.com*.

Sources: Compiled from *jaguar.com* (accessed February 2009), *hummer.com* (accessed February 2009), and Weiner (2006).

---

capability as well (mortar-only to click-and-mortar; e.g., walmart.com). Another type of click-and-mortar business is those that started their business online and then expanded to physical storefronts as well (click-only to click-and-brick; e.g., expedia.com).

Brick-and-mortar retailers conduct business in the physical world, in traditional brick-and-mortar stores. Traditional retailing frequently involves a single distribution channel, the physical store. In some cases, traditional sellers also might operate a mail-order business.

In today's digital economy, click-and-mortar retailers sell via stores, through voice phone calls to human operators, over the Internet through interactive Web sites, and via mobile devices. A firm that operates both physical stores and an online e-tail site is said to be a click-and-mortar business selling in a **multichannel business model** (see Agatza 2008). Examples of retailers going from brick-only to brick-and-click are department stores, such as Macy's (macys.com) and Sears (sears.com), as well as discount stores, such as Wal-Mart (walmart.com) and Target (target.com). It also includes supermarkets and all other types of retailing.

Expedia in the travel industry and Dell in the computer industry are examples of companies moving from click-only to click-and-brick. For many years, some catalog companies, such as Argos in the United Kingdom, have had storefronts, but these served to display catalogs, to offer advice, and to accept orders and payments for goods, which were then delivered via the usual catalog-delivery modes. This is precisely the approach Dell has adopted in opening its physical stores in Dallas and New York. Dell has for some time operated kiosks

brick-and-mortar retailers
Retailers who do business in the non-Internet, physical world in traditional brick-and-mortar stores.

multichannel business model
A business model where a company sells in multiple marketing channels simultaneously (e.g., both physical and online stores).

in shopping malls in the United States, but the physical stores add a new dimension to their move to click-and-mortar. Various models of computers are on display in the stores, and Dell staff is available to offer advice and support and to assist customers in personalizing their purchases. However, the stores hold no inventory, so interested customers must still place their orders online from within these stores, assisted by Dell staff. The difference from the Web site is that customers are able to touch and feel and compare different Dell models before buying. Dell has not really altered its direct-to-customer model, because the physical stores do not currently have the capability to transact directly.

Retailing in Online Malls

Online malls, as described in Chapter 2, are of two types: referring directories and malls with shared shopping services.

Referring Directories. This type of mall is basically a directory organized by product type. Catalog listings or banner ads at the mall site advertise the products or stores. When users click on the product and/or a specific store, they are transferred to the storefront of the seller, where they then complete the transaction. Examples of referring directories can be found at bedandbreakfast.com. The stores listed in a directory either own the site collectively or they pay a subscription fee or a commission to the third party (e.g., a portal) that advertises their logos. This type of e-tailing is basically a kind of affiliate marketing.

Malls with Shared Services. In online malls with shared services, a consumer can find a product, order and pay for it, and arrange for shipment. The hosting mall provides these services, but they usually are executed by each store independently. (To see the variety of services provided, consult smallbusiness.yahoo.com.) The buyer must repeat the process in each store visited in the mall, but it is basically the same process. The storefront owners pay rent and/or transaction fees to the owner. Both manufacturers and retailers sell in such malls. Yahoo! provides a rich example of this type of shared-services mall. When a user goes to Yahoo!, clicks on "shopping," then "all categories," "pets," "dogs," and then "dog toys," for example, a large range of dog toys, sourced from many different e-tailers, is displayed for shoppers. You can see the name of the company selling the item, the price and availability, and so on. In addition, when two e-tailers supply the same product, users are provided with a comparison of the price at each of those stores. Alternatively, users can go directly to one of the vendors' sites; in this case, users will not know that they are in the Yahoo! environment until the checkout process. Other malls with shared services are firststopshops.com and shopping.msn.com.

Ideally, the customer would like to go to different stores in the same mall, use one shopping cart, and pay only once. This arrangement is possible in Yahoo! stores (smallbusiness.yahoo.com/ecommerce).

OTHER B2C MODELS AND SPECIAL RETAILING

Several other business models are used in B2C. They are discussed in various places throughout the book. Some of these models also are used in B2B, B2B2C, G2B, and other types of EC. A summary of these other models is provided in Exhibit 3.5. Representative special B2C services are discussed in Online File W3.4.

B2C IN SOCIAL NETWORKS

In the era of Web 2.0, setting up an e-tailer and waiting for customers to log on is no longer enough. Instead, companies are being more proactive, finding ways to engage customers, build relationships, and create communities. This trend, known as *social commerce*, has been brought about by the merging of Web 2.0 technologies, e-business opportunities, and online communities. What differentiates social commerce from an ordinary e-business site is the social elements involved. Social commerce is concerned with the creation of places where people can collaborate online, solicit advice from trusted individuals, create content, and avail themselves of goods and services. Thus, the research and purchasing cycle are shrunk by the establishment of a single destination powered by the power of many.

B2C sites such as Amazon.com (amazon.com) and Netflix (netflix.com) provide consumers with rich social context and relevancy to the purchases that they are making. The companies have promoted three activities that shoppers can do collectively via wikis, blogs,

EXHIBIT 3.5   Other B2C Business Models

Model Name	Description	Location in Book
Transaction brokers	Electronically mediate between buyers and sellers. Popular in services, the travel industry, the job market, stock trading, and insurance (e.g., *hotels.com*).	Chapter 3
Information portals	Besides information, most portals provide links to merchants, for which they are paid a commission (affiliate marketing). Some provide hosting and software (e.g., *store.yahoo.com*), some also sell.	Chapters 3, 5
Community portal and social networks	Combines community services with selling or affiliate marketing (e.g., *virtualcommunities.start4all.com*). Also see *facebook.com* and *myspace.com*.	Chapters 4, 9
Content creators or disseminators	Provide content to the masses (news, stock data). Also participate in the syndication chain (e.g., *espn.com, reuters.com,* and *cnn.com*).	Chapter 15
Viral marketing	Use e-mail or SMS to advertise. Also can sell direct or via affiliates (e.g., *blueskyfrog.com*).	Chapters 4, 9
Market makers	Create and manage many-to-many markets (e.g., *chemconnect.com*); also auction sites (e.g., *ebay.com* and *dellauction.com*). Aggregate buyers and/or sellers (e.g., *ingrammicro.com*).	Chapters 5 and 17
Make (build)-to-order	Manufacturers that customize their products and services via online orders (e.g., *dell.com, nike.com,* and *jaguar.com*).	Chapters 2, 3, 12
B2B2C	Manufacturer sells to a business, but delivers to individual customers (e.g., *godiva.com*).	Chapters 2, 3
Service providers	Offer online payments, order fulfillment (delivery), and security (e.g., *paypal.com* and *escrow.com*).	Chapters 10, 11, 12

and other online tools: find, collect, and share/recommend. These three acts comprise the phenomenon of online group shopping. Such sites have a mechanism for intergroup feedback in that they allow users to leave a short review of the product they bought as well as the services obtained from the sellers. Meanwhile, other participants rely on group members who have previously rated the product/service and/or seller. The B2C e-commerce relies on word-of-mouth among social network participants.

Section 3.2 ▶ REVIEW QUESTIONS

1. List the B2C distribution channel models.
2. Describe how mail-order firms are going online.
3. Describe the direct marketing model used by manufacturers.
4. Describe virtual e-tailing.
5. Describe the click-and-mortar approach.
6. Describe e-malls.

3.3   TRAVEL AND TOURISM (HOSPITALITY) SERVICES ONLINE

Online travel bookings and associated travel services are one of the most successful e-commerce implementations. In 2008, U.S. travel sales booked online reached $105 billion, up 12 percent from 2007 (Grau 2008). It is expected that U.S. online leisure and business travel sales will grow to $163 billion by 2012 (Grau 2008). According to Jupiter Research, half of all leisure travelers book online and 43 percent of those use the Internet to research their trips (reported in Leggatt 2007). The most popular types of Web sites are online travel agencies (such as Expedia, Travelocity, and Priceline), search engine Web sites (such as Google and Yahoo!), and company-owned Web sites for airlines, hotels, and the like. This outstanding performance is underpinned by increased Web traffic of more than 10 percent to major travel sites, higher conversion of visitors to sales, and increased average value per sale, all suggesting that people are becoming more confident and trusting of booking travel-related services online (*Internet Retailer* 2006). By 2009, growth in the number of new customers had stopped, but purchases per customer increased due to the fact that people were taking more short vacations and fewer longer ones.

Some major travel-related Web sites are expedia.com, travelocity.com, zuji.com (now owned by Travelocity but operating separately), and priceline.com. Online travel services also are provided by all major airlines (e.g., britishairways.com); vacation services (e.g., blue-hawaii.com); large, conventional travel agencies (e.g. expedia.com); trains (e.g., amtrak.com); car rental agencies (e.g., autoeurope.com); hotels (e.g., marriott.com); commercial portals (e.g., cnn.com/travel); and tour companies (e.g., atlastravelweb.com). Publishers of travel guides such as Lonely Planet (lonelyplanet.com) provide considerable amounts of travel-related information on their Web sites, as well as selling travel services there. The online ticket consolidator ebookers.com and the travel information broker tiscover.com are linking up to create a comprehensive online travel resource.

The revenue models of online travel services include direct revenues (commissions), revenue from advertising, lead-generation payments, consultancy fees, subscription or membership fees, revenue-sharing fees, and more. With such rapid growth and success, the travel industry seems to have matured beyond initial concerns such as trust, loyalty, and brand image. However, competition among online travel e-tailers is fierce, with low margins, little customer loyalty, and increasing commoditization of products and services. Thus, guaranteed best rates and various loyalty programs are likely to be popular ways of affecting customer behavior.

Three important trends will drive further changes in the online travel industry. First, online travel agents may try to differentiate themselves through customer-service messaging and other related services, presenting themselves as adding value to the customer. Second, the number of travel meta search facilities, or "travel bots"—online sites or services that search through a range of related sites to find the best price or compare the value of travel products for a consumer—is likely to increase (Kim et al. 2009). Third, online travel companies are likely to increasingly use the growing phenomenon of social networking sites (such as myspace.com) to provide content to would-be travelers and also use these sites to study the behavior of potential customers (see discussion later in this section).

SERVICES PROVIDED

Virtual travel agencies offer almost all of the services delivered by conventional travel agencies, from providing general information to reserving and purchasing tickets, accommodations, and entertainment. In addition, they often provide services that most conventional travel agencies do not offer, such as travel tips provided by people who have experienced certain situations (e.g., a visa problem), electronic travel magazines, fare comparisons, city guides, currency conversion calculators, fare tracking (free e-mail alerts on low fares to and from a city and favorite destinations), worldwide business and place locators, an outlet for travel accessories and books, experts' opinions, major international and travel news, detailed driving maps and directions (see infohub.com), chat rooms and bulletin boards, and frequent-flier deals. In addition, some offer several other innovative services, such as online travel auctions.

SPECIAL SERVICES ONLINE

Many online travel services offer travel bargains. Consumers can go to special sites, such as those offering standby tickets, to find bargain fares. Lastminute.com (lastminute.com) offers very low airfares and discounted accommodation prices to fill otherwise-empty seats and hotel rooms. Last-minute trips also can be booked on americanexpress.com, sometimes at a steep discount. Special vacation destinations can be found at priceline.com, tictactravel.com, stayfinder.com, and greatrentals.com. Flights.com (flights.com) offers cheap tickets and also Eurail passes. Travelers can access cybercaptive.com for a list of thousands of Internet cafes around the world. Similar information is available via many portals, such as Yahoo! and MSN.

Also of interest are sites that offer medical advice and services for travelers. This type of information is available from the World Health Organization (who.int), governments (e.g., cdc.gov/travel), and private organizations (e.g., tripprep.com, medicalert.org, and webmd.com).

Other special services include:

▶ **Wireless services.** Several airlines (e.g., Cathay Pacific, Delta, and Qantas) allow customers with cell phones with Internet access to check their flight status, update frequent-flier miles, and book flights. British Air offers a broadband Internet connection for passengers on board. Customers of Qantas (qantas.com.au) can send and receive in-flight e-mails, SMSs, and calls via their own mobile phones and personal electronic devices, such as BlackBerries.

▶ **Direct marketing.** Airlines sell electronic tickets over the Internet. When customers purchase electronic tickets online (or by phone), all they have to do is print the boarding pass from their computer's printer or upon arrival at the airport enter their credit card at an *electronic kiosk* to get a boarding pass. Alternatively, travelers can get a boarding pass at the ticket counter. Using direct marketing techniques, airlines are able to build customer profiles and target specific customers with tailored offers.

▶ **Alliances and consortia.** Airlines and other travel companies are creating alliances to increase sales or reduce purchasing costs. For example, some consortia aggregate only fares purchased over the Internet. Several alliances exist in Europe, the United States, and Asia. For example, zuji.com is a travel portal dedicated to Asia-Pacific travelers. It is a consortium of regional airlines, Travelocity, some hotel chains, and car-rental providers that specializes in tour packages in the region. The company also has a booking engine for travel agents, enabling them to store their customers' e-mail addresses (a B2B2C service).

Travel-Oriented Social Networks

Since 2005, online leisure travelers' use of social computing technologies, such as blogs, RSS, wikis, and user reviews, for researching travel has skyrocketed. Travel e-businesses, marketing executives, and managers realized that social computing was increasingly playing a larger role in corporate online strategy, even if all a company did was monitor what travelers were saying about a certain company in third-party forums. Companies that implement social computing technologies on their own Web sites probably need to view it primarily as supporting business goals, such as improving customer communication or increasing engagement of customers, and less as a sales or customer service tool.

As travelers forge connections and share information with like-minded travelers online, their needs and expectations change. They want more relevance and more correct information. Social computing has shifted online travel from passive selling to active customer engagement, which affects how travel companies and agents distribute and market their products (Epps 2007). Several social networks have travel channels that cater to travelers. One such network is wikia.com, which features a travel channel. In a special report, Harteveldt (2006) provided guidelines for travel e-commerce and for marketing executives and managers on how travelers embrace social computing technologies. Case 3.1 shows an example of a social network for travelers.

Travel Recommendation. One of the characteristics of Web 2.0 is personalization support. For an example of how it is being done in the travel industry, see Online File W3.5.

BENEFITS AND LIMITATIONS OF ONLINE TRAVEL SERVICES

The benefits of online travel services to travelers are enormous. The amount of free information is tremendous, and it is accessible at any time from any place. Substantial discounts can be found, especially for those who have time and patience to search for them. Providers of travel services also benefit: Airlines, hotels, and cruise lines are selling otherwise-empty spaces. Also, direct selling saves the provider's commission and its processing.

Online travel services do have some limitations. First, many people do not use the Internet. Second, the amount of time and the difficulty of using virtual travel agencies can be significant, especially for complex trips and for inexperienced Internet surfers. Finally, complex trips or those that require stopovers might not be available online because they require specialized knowledge and arrangements, which may be better done by a knowledgeable, human travel agent. Therefore, the need for travel agents as intermediaries remains, at least for the immediate future.

CASE 3.1
EC Application
WAYN: A SOCIAL NETWORK FOR TRAVELERS

WAYN (which stands for "Where Are You Now?") is a social networking Web site (*wayn.com*) with a goal of uniting travelers from around the world. WAYN was launched in London in May 2003. It has grown from 45,000 to about 12 million members as of 2009, adding 20,000 new members each day. Approximately 2 million members are based in the United Kingdom. It also is strong in the United States, Canada, Australia, New Zealand, and other countries in Western Europe.

As with many other social networking services, WAYN enables its users to create a personal profile and upload and store photos. Users can then search for others with similar profiles and link them to their profiles as friends. It also is possible to send and receive messages using discussion forums. Because it is designed for travelers, members are able to search for contacts based on a particular location. Using a world map, users can visually locate where each of their contacts is situated around the world. The goal of the service is for members to keep friends informed of where they are while traveling and, in turn, to be able to locate their friends.

In addition, users can send SMSs to any of their contacts worldwide; chat online using WAYN's Instant Messenger; and plan trips and notify their friends about them. Using WAYN, users can create discussion groups, ask for recommendations,

and send smiley icons to all. Finally, chat bots (avatars) are dynamic and fully active, representing one of the best ways of meeting people in the WAYN community.

WAYN is one of the very few sites that did not lose new subscriptions after introducing fees for its premier membership service, making it one of the few social networking communities that has managed to quickly become profitable.

WAYN is now popular in 220 countries, becoming a global brand. It is not aimed at any particular age group, but it seems to be most popular with the 18-to-25 age group. It also has a strong position among the 35-to-45-plus age group. Members can find out who will be traveling to their next intended destination, at the same time as they are.

Sources: Butcher (2008), *wayn.com* (accessed February 2009), and *en.wikipedia.org/wiki/WYAN* (accessed February 2009).

Questions

1. Visit *wayn.com*. What options do you find most exciting on the site?

2. Why has WAYN been so successful even though the site requires subscription fees?

CORPORATE TRAVEL

The corporate travel market is huge and has been growing rapidly in recent years. Corporations can use all of the travel services mentioned earlier. However, many large corporations receive additional services from large travel agencies. To reduce corporate travel costs, companies can make arrangements that enable employees to plan and book their own trips. Using online optimization tools provided by travel companies, such as those offered by American Express (americanexpress.com), companies can try to reduce travel costs even further. Travel authorization software that checks availability of funds and compliance with corporate guidelines is usually provided by travel companies such as American Express. Expedia Inc. (expedia.com), Travelocity (travelocity.com), and Orbitz (orbitz.com) also offer software tools for corporate planning and booking.

An example of how a major corporation uses online corporate travel services is described in Online File W3.6. For further discussion, see B2B travel in Chapter 5.

IMPACT OF EC ON THE TRAVEL INDUSTRY

It was not uncommon in the mid-late 1990s for people to forecast the demise of travel agents, arguing that all travel agency services would be replaced by the rise of travel superstores on the Internet (e.g., see Bloch and Segev 1997).Others suggested that only the value-added activities of travel agencies that could not be automated would be performed by travel organizations that would serve certain targeted markets and customers (also see Van der Heijden 1996). Travel superstores, providing many products, services, and entertainment, might enter the industry, as well as innovative individuals operating as travel agents and undertaking some aspects of service tasks from their homes.

The Internet has had a large impact on the role of travel agents. This has occurred through direct impacts, with customers increasingly using the Internet to make bookings. It has also occurred somewhat indirectly, with airlines and hotel chains, for example, encouraging customers to book direct or through online wholesalers, bypassing travel agents. However, others argue that travel agents will become the "leisure consultants" of the future, gaining an advantage through their overall knowledge of the industry and their independent advice. In these cases, both a physical and virtual presence are seen as essential, and investing in content (information, travel advice, and the like) is seen as an absolute requirement for success in this competitive market (Vermeulen and Seegersa 2009).

Major companies, such as Expedia and Orbitz, provide excellent service via their Web sites and search through their own extensive databases and networks to offer attractive deals and packages to customers. Rapid growth of late, however, has occurred in the use of travel search engines, or travel bots. The use of intelligent agents in travel services is discussed in Online File W3.7.

Section 3.3 ▶ REVIEW QUESTIONS

1. What travel services are available online that are not available offline?

2. List the benefits of online travel services to travelers and to service providers.

3. What role do software (intelligent) agents have in online travel services? What future applications may be possible? (See Online File W3.7.)

4. How do social networks facilitate travel?

3.4 EMPLOYMENT PLACEMENT AND THE JOB MARKET ONLINE

The job market is very volatile, and supply and demand are frequently unbalanced. Traditionally, job matching has been done in several ways, ranging from ads in classified sections of newspapers to the use of corporate recruiters, commercial employment agencies, and headhunting companies. The job market has now also moved online. The online job market connects individuals who are looking for a job with employers who are looking for employees with specific skills. It is a very popular approach, and, increasingly, both job seekers and prospective employers are turning away from traditional print-based advertising and recruitment methods in preference of online advertisements and recruitment activities. In addition to online job ads and placement services available through specialized Web sites (such as careerbuilder.com), larger companies are increasingly building career portals on their corporate Web sites as a way of trimming recruitment costs and reducing the time to fill vacancies (Beerworth 2006). Advantages of the online job market over the traditional one are listed in Exhibit 3.6.

EXHIBIT 3.6 Traditional Versus Online Job Markets

Characteristic	Traditional Job Market	Online Job Market
Cost	Expensive, especially in prime space	Can be very inexpensive
Life cycle	Short	Long
Place	Usually local and limited if global	Global
Context updating	Can be complex, expensive	Fast, simple, inexpensive
Space for details	Limited	Large
Ease of search by applicant	Difficult, especially for out-of-town applicants	Quick and easy
Ability of employers to find applicants	May be very difficult, especially for out-of-town applicants	Easy
Matching of supply and demand	Difficult	Easy
Reliability	Material can be lost in mail	High
Communication speed between employees and employers	Can be slow	Fast
Ability of employees to compare jobs	Limited	Easy, fast

THE INTERNET JOB MARKET

The Internet offers a rich environment for job seekers and for companies searching for hard-to-find employees. Nearly all *Fortune* 500 companies now use the Internet for some of their recruitment activities, and studies reveal that online resources are now the most popular way to find suitably qualified applicants for job vacancies. Online job recruitment revenues and volume overtook print ad classifieds and in 2008 were estimated to reach $6 billion (Fisher 2008). More than 40,000 online job boards are now operating in the United States alone. The U.S. market is dominated by three major players: Monster, Careerbuilder, and Yahoo! HotJobs, which together comprise about 55 percent of the market.

The following parties use the Internet job market:

- **Job seekers.** Job seekers can reply to employment ads. Or, they can take the initiative and place their resumes on their own homepages or on others' Web sites, send messages to members of newsgroups asking for referrals, and use the sites of recruiting firms, such as careerbuilder.com, Yahoo! HotJobs (hotjobs.yahoo.com), and monster.com. For entry-level jobs and internships for newly minted graduates, job seekers can go to collegerecruiter.com. Job seekers can also assess their market value in different U.S. cities at wageweb.com and use the Web to compare salaries and conditions, obtain information about employers, and get career advice. Passive job seekers, those just keeping an eye on opportunities, are using this medium, as well as those actively seeking new employment.

- **Employers seeking employees.** Many organizations, including public institutions, advertise openings on their Web sites. Others advertise job openings on popular public portals, online newspapers, bulletin boards, and with recruiting firms. Employers can conduct interviews and administer interactive intelligence, skills, and psychological tests on the Web. Forty percent of large U.S. firms are using computerized assessments to screen new hires or to identify up-and-comers for training and development. The tests are designed to predict success by measuring behavioral or personality traits and comparing a candidate's profile with those of people who have succeeded in similar jobs (Rose 2008). LinkedIn offers several tools that help recruiters to find employees registered at the site. Also see Yahoo!'s Resumix (at viviente.com/resumix/website).

- **Classified ads.** Classified ads for job openings and job seekers are available at craigslist.org, kijiji.com, linked.com, and in the online classified sections of many newspapers. Also, several social networks allow posting of job openings.

- **Job agencies.** Hundreds of job agencies are active on the Web. They use their own Web pages to post available job descriptions and advertise their services in e-mails and at other Web sites. Job agencies and/or employers use newsgroups, online forums, bulletin boards, Internet commercial resume services, and portals such as Yahoo! HotJobs and AOL. Most portals are free; others, such as MktgLadder (marketing.theladders.com), charge membership fees but offer many services.

- **Government agencies and institutions.** Many government agencies advertise openings for government positions on their Web sites and on other sites; some are required by law to do so. In addition, some government agencies use the Internet to help job seekers find jobs elsewhere, as is done in Hong Kong and the Philippines. An initiative by the Australian Government, Jobsearch (jobsearch.gov.au), the largest free job board in the country, offers free advertising to employers. It claims the largest candidate database in Australia and has over 1 million visitors per month, with an average of 80,000 jobs on offer at any one time. It links this online presence to an Australia-wide network of touch-screen kiosks. Employers are notified when a candidate's resume matches an advertised job (*Jobsearch.gov.au* 2009).

A Consortium of Large Employers and College Career Advisors

Most large employers, such as GE, IBM, and Xerox, spend hundreds of thousands of dollars annually on commissions to online job companies and on recruitment activities. For colleges, an important performance metric is the employability of their graduates; hence, providing career advice and services is an important part of campus life. To save money, a number of leading companies joined a nonprofit consortium that created a career portal called jobcentral.com. The National Association of Colleges and Employers created other sites, including the NACELink Network (nacelink.com). These nonprofit associations now have merged to form JobCentral, providing people at all education levels timely information about careers and employment opportunities nationwide (*JobCentral.com* 2009). The site is used primarily to catalog job postings from the sites of the member employers. It also provides a rich resource of information about occupations, career development, relocation information, and the like. Having the job postings of a number of large employers in one place makes it easy for job searchers to explore available openings.

Online Job Markets on Social Networking

In today's age of Web 2.0, the wide reach of social networking sites such as MySpace and LinkedIn can get people hired faster. As demonstrated in Exhibit 3.7, job referral social networking sites (e.g., jobster.com and bluechipexpert.com) solve the problem of finding the right people for the job in hours. The sites provide job seekers opportunities to promote their areas of expertise as well as help them get "found" by employers. The added incentive of getting paid for every successful referral makes it even more worthwhile to join these networks. The site's algorithms enable headhunters to sort qualified applicants by different criteria. When an offer is

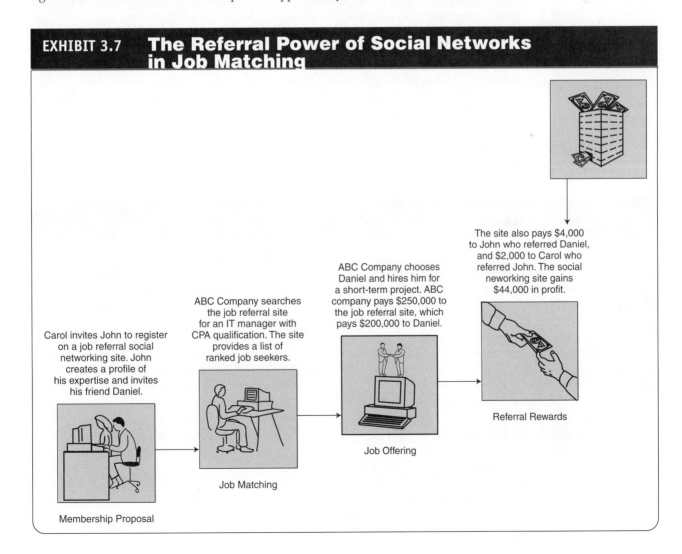

EXHIBIT 3.7   The Referral Power of Social Networks in Job Matching

Carol invites John to register on a job referral social networking site. John creates a profile of his expertise and invites his friend Daniel.

Membership Proposal

ABC Company searches the job referral site for an IT manager with CPA qualification. The site provides a list of ranked job seekers.

Job Matching

ABC Company chooses Daniel and hires him for a short-term project. ABC company pays $250,000 to the job referral site, which pays $200,000 to Daniel.

Job Offering

The site also pays $4,000 to John who referred Daniel, and $2,000 to Carol who referred John. The social neworking site gains $44,000 in profit.

Referral Rewards

made, the job referral site receives payment on behalf of the employees, including a referral fee. Social networking commerce has certainly found its niche in the online job recruitment industry.

Global Online Portals

The Internet is very helpful for anyone looking for a job in another country. An interesting global portal for Europe is described in Online File W3.8. An interesting global site for placing/finding jobs in different countries is xing.com (see Internet Exercise 10). A similar service is provided by linkedin.com.

BENEFITS AND LIMITATIONS OF THE ELECTRONIC JOB MARKET

As indicated earlier, the electronic job market offers a variety of benefits for both job seekers and employers. These major advantages are shown in Exhibit 3.8.

Probably the biggest limitation of the online job market is the fact that some people do not use and do not have access to the Internet, although this problem has declined substantially. Nonetheless, the potential for an ever-increasing gap between those with skills and access to the Internet and those without is of concern. To overcome this problem, companies might use both traditional advertising approaches and the Internet. However, the trend is clear: Over time, more and more of the job market will be on the Internet. One solution to the problem of limited access is the use of in-store Internet kiosks, as used by companies such as Home Depot or Macy's.

Interestingly, the reverse of lack of access is a major limitation of online recruiting. Many companies find that they are flooded with applicants when they advertise online, most of who are not really suited to the position advertised. Screening all these applications can be a time-consuming and costly process. However, the use of intelligent agents (see Online File W3.9) offers a solution to this problem for many organizations.

Security and privacy are another limitation. Resumes and other online communications are usually not encrypted, so one's job-seeking activities might not be secure, and thus confidentiality and data protection cannot be guaranteed. It also is possible that someone at a job seeker's current place of employment (possibly even his or her boss) might find out that that person is job hunting. LinkedIn, for example, provides protection of privacy, enabling job seekers to determine who can see their resume online. The electronic job market can also create high turnover costs for employers by accelerating employees' movement to better jobs. Finally, finding candidates online is more complicated than most people think, mostly due to

EXHIBIT 3.8	Advantages of the Electronic Job Market for Job Seekers and Employers
Advantages for Job Seekers	**Advantages for Employers**
Can find information on a large number of jobs worldwide	Can advertise to a large numbers of job seekers
Can communicate quickly with potential employers	Can save on advertisement costs
Can market themselves directly to potential employers (e.g., *quintcareers.com*)	Can reduce application-processing costs by using electronic application forms
Can write and post resumes for large-volume distribution (e.g., Personal Search Agent at *careerbuilder.com*, *brassring.com*)	Can provide greater equal opportunity for job seekers
Can search for jobs quickly from any location	Increased chance of finding highly skilled employees
Can obtain several support services at no cost (e.g., *hotjobs.yahoo.com* and *monster.com* provide free career-planning services)	Can describe positions in great detail
Can assess their market value (e.g., *wageweb.com* and *rileyguide.org*; look for salary surveys)	Can conduct interviews online (using video teleconferencing)
Can learn how to use their voice effectively in an interview (*greatvoice.com*)	Can arrange for testing online
Can access newsgroups that are dedicated to finding jobs (and keeping them)	Can view salary surveys for recruiting strategies

the large number of resumes available online. The LinkedIn search engine can help employers quickly find the appropriate candidate.

Section 3.4 ▶ REVIEW QUESTIONS

1. What are the driving forces of the electronic job market?
2. What are the major advantages of the electronic job market to the candidate? To employers?
3. Describe the role of intelligent agents in the electronic job market. (See Online File W3.9.)
4. Why is LinkedIn so useful for job seekers and for employees?

3.5 REAL ESTATE, INSURANCE, AND STOCK TRADING ONLINE

Online financial services are exploding on the Internet and are being embraced by customers. Internet and related technologies are more than just new distribution channels. They are a different way of providing financial services (Smith 2008). The major financial services are presented in this and the following section.

REAL ESTATE ONLINE

The increasing presence and realization of e-commerce possibilities and opportunities in the real estate business is creating a momentum and a readiness for change and slowly adding pressure to transform the old ways of doing things in this previously stable and conservative business. Changes are reaching a tipping point, beyond which the nature of the real estate business will be altered. The changes have been some time in coming, but after a long period of quantitative changes experts are beginning to see some fundamental qualitative changes in the industry (Knox 2006). However, some argue that online real estate services have disrupted the industry and have contributed to credit fraud by borrowers, a significant factor of the subprime mortgage crisis started in the United States in late 2007.

To get some idea of the changes, consider the following statistics. In 2006, when total advertising spending in real estate was $11.5 billion, online spending had grown to $2 billion, or 17.7 percent of the total. By 2010, when online spending is predicted to pass $3 billion, online spending is forecast to surpass newspaper print advertising in terms of market share (Borrell Associates 2006). According to the *New York Times* (2007), in 2007 real estate companies spent 26 percent more on online ads than in 2006. The increase in Internet real estate advertising is understandably influencing buying behavior. Studies by the National Association of Realtors (NAR) have shown that over 80 percent of real estate buyers begin their searches for properties on the Internet (*Realtors Magazine* 2009).

In the face of such increases in consumer knowledge and control of the early parts of the identification and purchase of properties, some U.S. realtors have tried to restrict public access to some of the databases of properties, such as the local Multiple Listing Services. In many localities, local brokers have tried to restrict access to such databases to members of a professional association, such as the NAR.

In summary, e-commerce and the Internet are slowly but surely having an ever-increasing impact on the real estate industry. For example, despite the changes that are beginning to emerge, real estate agents have not been disintermediated. Homebuyers today tend to use both real estate agents and the Internet. In 2006, 81 percent of homebuyers who used the Internet to look for a property also used a real estate agent (Knox 2006). Thus, despite the fact that the Internet is shaking up the real estate industry, the emerging pattern is more complex than the simple disintermediation of agents. For examples, see *New York Times* (2007).

Zillow, Craigslist, and Other Web 2.0 Real Estate Services

Craigslist and Zillow are examples of Web 2.0 free real estate services that have been intended to disintermediate unnecessary middlemen, such as newspaper and classified advertising.

Zillow (zillow.com) is a Seattle-based online real estate service company founded in 2005 by the former Microsoft executives and founders of Expedia. The site's "Make Me Move" function allows users to shop for homes that are not necessarily for sale. Homeowners who may have no intention of moving, but who certainly would for the right price, can list information about their homes on "Make Me Move" so that gutsy buyers can try to make a deal. A homeowner can post a "Make Me Move" price without exposing any personal information. Zillow then enables interested buyers to contact the owner through an e-mail "anonymizer." The service is free. The company also provides free listings for all homeowners and realtors. Listings can include photos, and realtors can also create Web sites for each listing. Another Web 2.0 function of Zillow is the Real Estate wiki, which has hundreds of articles on buying, selling, financing, or any topic an owner/buyer might need. Wiki visitors can edit or comment on articles or create new articles.

Craigslist (craigslist.org) is a centralized network of online communities, featuring free online classified advertisements—with jobs, housing, and personals for sale/barter/wanted, services, community, and pets categories—and forums on various topics. The site serves over 30 million unique visitors and generates 9 billion page views per month, putting it at 47th place among Web sites worldwide and 9th place among U.S. Web sites as of August 2008. Craigslist has become a powerhouse site for advertising real estate listings, with more and more agents turning to the site for added exposure to buyers looking online. Property listings are free to list on Craigslist in all markets except New York, where brokers must pay $10 per listing. The classifieds site recently put forth a proposal to limit the HTML that can be used in listings as a way to help ward off spam. Some real estate folks have been discussing the proposal and how it would impact various real estate listings services should it go through.

For more about real estate applications and services offered online, see Online File W3.10.

INSURANCE ONLINE

Although the uptake of EC in the insurance industry is relatively slow in some countries, an increasing number of companies use the Internet to offer standard insurance policies, such as auto, home, life, or health, at a substantial discount, mostly to individuals. Furthermore, third-party aggregators offer free comparisons of available policies. Several large insurance and risk-management companies offer comprehensive insurance contracts online. Although many people do not trust the faceless insurance agent, others are eager to take advantage of the reduced premiums. For example, a visit to insurance.com will show a variety of different policies. At answerfinancial.com customers and businesses can compare car insurance offerings and then make a purchase online. At travel-insurance-online.com, customers can book travel insurance. Another popular insurance site is insweb.com. Many insurance companies use a dual strategy, keeping human agents but also selling online. Like the real estate brokers, insurance brokers send unsolicited e-mails to millions of people. It is estimated that Web insurance transactions cost about 50 cents each to process, compared with up to $8 for those that are paper-based (McDougall 2007).

ONLINE STOCK TRADING

In the late 1990s, online trading was an exciting innovation in the financial services industry. However, the dot-com crash and increasing competition saw consolidation, cost-cutting, and price reduction become the order of the day.

The commission for an online trade is between $1 and $19, compared with an average fee of $100 from a full-service broker and $25 from a non-Internet discount broker. With online trading, there are no busy telephone lines, and the chance for error is small, because there is no oral communication in a frequently noisy environment. Orders can be placed from anywhere, at any time, day or night, and there is no biased broker to push a sale. Furthermore, investors can find a considerable amount of free information about specific companies or mutual funds. Many services provided to online traders including online statements, extensive research on companies, and even tutoring on how to trade.

Several discount brokerage houses initiated extensive online stock trading, notably Charles Schwab in 1995. Full-service brokerage companies, such as Merrill Lynch, followed in 1998–1999. By 2008, more than 30 percent of stock trades are executed automatically via the Internet (*InformationWeek* 2008).

How does online trading work? Let's say an investor has an account with Schwab. The investor accesses Schwab's Web site (schwab.com), enters an account number and password, and clicks stock trading. Using a menu, the investor enters the details of the order (buy, sell, margin or cash, price limit, or market order). The computer tells the investor the current (real-time) "ask" and "bid" prices, much as a broker would do over the telephone, and the investor can approve or reject the transaction. The flow chart of this process is shown in Exhibit 3.9.

Some companies, including Schwab, are now also licensed as exchanges. This allows them to match the selling and buying orders of their own customers for many securities in 1 to 2 seconds.

Some well-known companies that offer online trading are E*TRADE and Ameritrade. E*TRADE offers many finance-related services using multimedia software.

The most innovative collection of online brokerage services is that of E*TRADE. In 1999, E*TRADE broadened its services by starting its own portfolio of mutual funds. E*TRADE is expanding rapidly into several countries, enabling global stock trading. E*TRADE now allows you to trade online in seven different countries, taking care of the currency exchange.

With the rapid pace of adoption of mobile handsets, mobile banking will become more and more popular. Mobile banking services enable users to receive information on their account balances via SMS and to settle payments for bills and purchase stocks (Dahlberg et al. 2008).

See Online File W3.11 for more on investment information available online.

The Risk of Trading in an Online Stock Account

The major risk of online trading is security. Although all trading sites require users to have an ID and password, problems may still occur. For example, in 2004 it was discovered that hackers could steal users' ID numbers and passwords when they used the Windows operating system. The problem has been corrected. Problems of this nature also can occur when conducting online trading or online banking, our next topic.

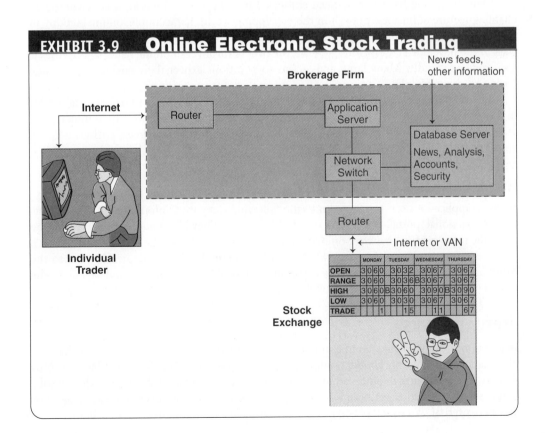

EXHIBIT 3.9 Online Electronic Stock Trading

Section 3.5 ▶ REVIEW QUESTIONS

1. List the major online real estate applications.
2. What are the advantages of online stock tracking?
3. What investment information is available online? (See Online File W3.11.)
4. What are some of the risks of trading stocks online?

3.6   BANKING AND PERSONAL FINANCE ONLINE

electronic (online) banking or e-banking
Various banking activities conducted from home or the road using an Internet connection; also known as cyberbanking, virtual banking, online banking, and home banking.

Electronic (online) banking, or **e-banking**, also known as cyberbanking, virtual banking, or home banking, includes various banking activities conducted via the Internet from home, business, or on the road rather than at a physical bank location. Consumers can use e-banking to check their accounts, pay bills online, secure a loan electronically, and much more. In 2007, online banking boasts more than 84 million users, and is forecasted to reach 110 million by 2010 (Forzley 2007).

E-banking saves users time and money. For banks, it offers an inexpensive alternative to branch banking and a chance to enlist remote customers. Many physical banks now offer home banking services, and some use EC as a major competitive strategy. One such U.S. bank is Wells Fargo (wellsfargo.com). In Hong Kong, a leading bank is the Bank of East Asia (hkbea-cyberbanking.com). In the United States, HSBC offers online banking activities including checking accounts. Many banks offer wireless services (see Chapter 8).

An emerging innovation in online banking is peer-to-peer (P2P) online lending. Zopa in the United Kingdom and Prosper in the United States offer P2P online lending (see Chapter 9). However, despite the global credit crunch of 2008–2009 and the fact that neither has a government-backed guarantee, Zopa and Prosper are enjoying a boom. For example, in the third quarter of 2008 new borrowers of Zopa soared by nearly 50 percent, to 3,700, compared with the previous quarter (Keegan 2008). The default rate of these P2P lenders is very low, because the borrowers and the lenders know each other through social networking. Disintermediation of the banks also allows the lenders to get much more and the borrowers to pay much less.

Online banking has not only been embraced in the developed world; it is becoming an enabling feature of business growth in the developing world. For example, online banking in China is increasing rapidly in popularity, especially among China's new educated middle class in the developed cities. Consequently, the overall turnover of online banking activities is also growing rapidly. Many large and global corporations expect their business to become click-and-mortar banks.

The Bank of China and the China Merchants Bank started their online banking service in 1998. These online service offerings were followed by online offerings by China's other major banks and a number of smaller banks. These services have been enthusiastically embraced by China's new business classes.

HOME BANKING CAPABILITIES

Banking applications can be divided into the following categories: informational, administrative, transactional, portal, and others (see Exhibit 3.10). They also found that the larger the bank, the more services that were offered online.

Electronic banking offers several of the EC benefits listed in Chapter 1, both to the banks and to their customers, such as expanding the bank's customer base and saving on the cost of paper transactions.

VIRTUAL BANKS

In addition to regular banks' adding online services, *virtual banks* have emerged; these have no physical location but only conduct online transactions. Security First Network Bank (SFNB) was the first such bank to offer secure banking transactions on the Web. Amidst the consolidation that has taken place in the banking industry, SFNB has since been purchased and now is a part of RBC Centura (rbccentura.com). Another representative virtual bank in the

EXHIBIT 3.10 Online Banking Applications

Application Type	Information/Services Provided
Informational	General bank information and history
	Financial education information
	Employment information
Administrative	Interest rate quotes
	Financial calculators
	Current bank and local news
	Account information access
	Open new account online
	Applications for services
	Move all banking online
	Personal finance software applications
Transactional	Account transfer capabilities
	Transfer funds housed at different financial institutions
	Bill-pay services
	Corporate services (e.g., cash management, treasury)
	Online insurance services
	Online brokerage services
	Real-time funds transfer
	Online trust services
Portal	Links to financial information
	Links to community information
	Links to local businesses
	Links to nonlocal businesses (and/or advertisers)
Others	Wireless capabilities
	Search function

Sources: Compiled from Acharya et al. (2008) and Cash Edge (2006).

United States is First Internet Bank (firstib.com). Virtual banks exist in many other countries (e.g., bankdirect.co.nz). In some countries, virtual banks are involved in stock trading, and some stockbrokers are doing online banking (e.g., see etrade.com). More than 97 percent of the hundreds of pure-play virtual banks failed by 2003 due to lack of financial viability. Many more failed during 2007–2008. The most successful banks seem to be of the click-and-mortar type.

A word of caution about virtual banking: Before sending money to any cyberbank, especially those that promise high interest rates for your deposits, make sure that the bank is a legitimate one. Several cases of fraud already have occurred.

INTERNATIONAL AND MULTIPLE-CURRENCY BANKING

International banking and the ability to handle trades in multiple currencies are critical for international trading. Although some international retail purchasing can be done by providing a credit card number, other transactions may require international banking support. Examples of such cross-border support include the following:

▶ Tradecard and MasterCard have developed a multiple-currency system for global transactions (see tradecard.com). This system is described in Chapter 11.

▶ Bank of America (bankofamerica.com) and most other major banks offer international capital funds, cash management, trades and services, foreign exchange, risk management investments, merchant services, and special services for international traders.

▶ Fxall.com is a multidealer foreign exchange service that enables faster and cheaper foreign exchange transactions. Special services are being established for stock market traders who need to pay for foreign stocks (e.g., at Charles Schwab).

ONLINE FINANCIAL TRANSACTION IMPLEMENTATION ISSUES

As one would expect, the implementation of online banking and online stock trading can be interrelated. In many instances, one financial institution offers both services. The following are some implementation issues for online financial transactions. For an example, see Xu et al. (2006).

Securing Financial Transactions

Financial transactions for home banking and online trading must be very secure. In Chapter 11, we discuss the details of secure EC payment systems. In Case 3.2, we give an example of how a bank provides security and privacy to its customers.

Access to Banks' Intranets by Outsiders

Many banks provide their large business customers with personalized service by allowing them access to the bank's intranet. For example, Bank of America allows its business customers access

---

CASE 3.2

EC Application

SECURITY FOR ONLINE BANK TRANSACTIONS

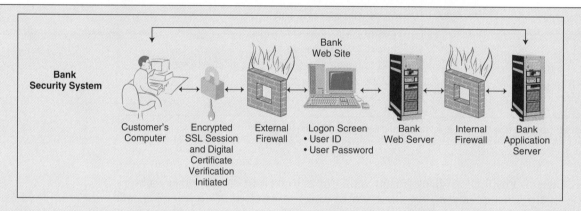

Banks provide extensive security to their customers. The following describes some of the safeguards provided.

Customers accessing a bank system from the outside must go through encryption provided by SSL (Secure Socket Layer) and digital certificate verification (see Chapter 10). The verification process assures users each time they sign on that they are indeed connected to their specific bank. The customer inquiry message then goes through an external firewall. Once the log-on screen is reached, a user ID and a password are required. This information flows through a direct Web server and then goes through an internal firewall to the bank's application server.

Information is shared among a bank's family of partners only for legitimate business purposes. Sharing information with outside companies is done with extreme care.

Banks do not capture information provided by customers when conducting "what-if" scenarios using planning tools (to ensure privacy). Most banks use cookies to learn about their customers; however, customers can control both the collection and use of the information. In addition, most banks provide suggestions on how users can increase security (e.g., "Use a browser with 128-bit encryption").

With the increased use of mobile devices (Chapter 8), the threat of security risks has increased. Banks are coming up with innovative solutions. For example, in January 2009 Bank of America introduced its "Safe Pass Card," a device that can generate a six-digit, one-time pass code that is necessary to complete an online transaction. The pass code is delivered via a text message to your mobile device.

Sources: Compiled from various security statements of online bank Web sites, including *cooperativebank.co.uk* (accessed February 2009) and *anz.com* (accessed February 2009).

Questions

1. Why is security so important for a bank?
2. Why is there a need for two firewalls?
3. Who is protected by the bank's security system—the customer, the bank, or both? Elaborate.
4. What might be the limitations of such a system?

to accounts, historical transactions, and other data, including intranet-based decision-support applications, which may be of interest to large business customers. Bank of America also allows its small business customers to apply for loans through its Web site.

Imaging Systems

Several financial institutions (e.g., Bank of America and Citibank) allow customers to view images of all of their incoming checks, invoices, and other related online correspondence. Image access can be simplified with the help of a search engine.

Fees Online Versus Fees for Offline Services

Computer-based banking services are offered free by some banks, whereas others charge $5 to $10 a month. Also, some banks charge fees for individual transactions (e.g., fee per check, per transfer, and so on). Financial institutions must carefully think through the pricing of online and offline services. Fee issues must take into account the costs of providing the different types of services, the organization's desire to attract new customers, and the prices offered by competitors.

Risks

Online banks, as well as click-and-mortar banks, might carry some risks and problems, especially in international banking. The first risk that most people think of is the risk of hackers getting into their account. In addition, some believe that virtual banks carry *liquidity* risk (the risk of not having sufficient funds to pay obligations as they come due) and could be more susceptible to panic withdrawals. Regulators are grappling with the safeguards that need to be imposed on e-banking.

PERSONAL FINANCE ONLINE

Individuals often combine electronic banking with personal finance and portfolio management. Also, brokerage firms such as Schwab offer personal finance services such as retirement planning. However, vendors of specialized personal finance software offer more diversified services. For example, both Intuit's Quicken and Microsoft's Money offer the following capabilities: bill paying and electronic check writing; tracking of bank accounts, expenditures, and credit cards; portfolio management, including reports and capital gains (losses) computations; investment tracking and monitoring of securities; stock quotes and past and current prices of stocks; personal budget organization; record keeping of cash flow and profit and loss computations; tax computations and preparations; and retirement goals, planning, and budgeting.

Online Billing and Bill Paying

The era of e-payment is around the corner. The number of checks the U.S. Federal Reserve System processes has been decreasing while the volume of commercial automated clearinghouse (ACH) transactions has been increasing. Many people prefer to pay monthly bills, such as telephone, utilities, rent, credit cards, cable, and so on, online. The recipients of such payments are equally eager to receive money online because online payments are received much more regularly and quickly and have lower processing costs.

Another method to pay bills over the Internet is electronic bill presentment and payments (EBPP). With this method, the consumer makes payments at each biller's Web site either with a credit card or by giving the biller enough information to complete an electronic withdrawal directly from the consumer's bank account. The biller makes the billing information available to the customer (presentment) on its Web site or the site of a billing hosting service. Once the customer views the bill, he or she authorizes and initiates payment at the site. The payment can be made with a credit/debit card or an ACH debit. The biller then initiates a payment transaction that moves funds through the payment system, crediting the biller and debiting the customer. See Chapter 11 for more about EBPP.

Online billing and bill paying can be classified into B2C, B2B, or C2C. This section has focused largely on B2C services, which help consumers save time and payees save on processing costs. However, large opportunities also exist in B2B services, which can save businesses about 50 percent of billing costs. In Hong Kong, for example, Citicorp enables automatic payments by linking suppliers, buyers, and banks on one platform.

Taxes

One important area in personal finance is advice about and computation of taxes. In the United States alone, dozens of sites are available to help people in their federal tax preparations. Many sites will help people legally cut their taxes. For U.S. citizens, the following list offers some sites worth checking:

- irs.gov: The official Web site of the Internal Revenue Service.
- webtax.com: A massive directory of tax-related information, research, and services.
- fairmark.com: A tax guide for investors.
- moneycentral.msn.com/tax/home.asp: A useful reference and educational site.
- quicken.com/taxes: Emphasizes tax planning.
- taxaudit.com: Offers advice on minimizing taxes.
- taxprophet.com: Provides tax advice in an entertaining manner.
- 1040.com: Information about deduction rules.
- unclefed.com: Offers advice on audits.

Section 3.6 ▶ REVIEW QUESTIONS

1. List the capabilities of online banking. Which of these capabilities would be most beneficial to you?
2. Discuss some implementation issues of financial services.
3. List the major personal finance services available online.

3.7 ON-DEMAND DELIVERY OF PRODUCTS, DIGITAL ITEMS, ENTERTAINMENT, AND GAMING

This section examines B2C delivery issues related to on-demand items, including perishable products, as well as the delivery of digitizable items, entertainment, and games.

ON-DEMAND DELIVERY OF PRODUCTS

Most e-tailers use common logistics carriers to deliver products to customers. They might use the postal system within their country or they might use private shippers such as UPS, FedEx, or DHL. Delivery can be made within days or overnight if the customer is willing to pay for the expedited shipment.

e-grocer
A grocer that takes orders online and provides deliveries on a daily or other regular schedule or within a very short period of time.

on-demand delivery service
Express delivery made fairly quickly after an online order is received.

Some e-tailers and direct marketing manufacturers own a fleet of delivery vehicles and incorporate the delivery function into their business plan in order to provide greater value to the consumer. These firms will either provide regular deliveries on a daily or other regular schedule or they will deliver items within very short periods of time, usually 1 hour. They might also provide additional services to increase the value proposition for the buyers. An example is Bigboxx.com (bigboxx.com), presented in Online File W5.1. An online grocer, or **e-grocer**, is a typical example of businesses in this category. Home delivery of food from restaurants is another example. In addition, another class of firms (groceries, office supplies, repair parts, and pharmaceutical products) promises virtually instantaneous or at least same-day delivery of goods to consumers.

Whether the delivery is made by company-owned vehicles or is outsourced to a carrier, an express delivery model is referred to as an **on-demand delivery service**. In such a model, the delivery must be done fairly quickly after an order is received. (For more on this topic, see Chapter 12.) A variation of this model is same-day delivery. According to this model, delivery is done faster than "overnight" but slower than the 30 to 60 minutes expected with on-demand delivery. E-grocers often deliver using the same-day delivery model.

The Case of E-Grocers

In the United States, online grocery sales amounted to $7.3 billion in 2008 and are expected to reach $13.7 billion, 2 percent of total grocery sales, in 2012. (Mulpuru et al 2008). It is a very competitive market, and margins are very thin. Many e-grocers are click-and-mortar retailers that operate in the countries where they have physical stores, such as Woolworths in Australia (woolworths.com.au) and Albertsons (albertsons.com) in the United States. (For statistics on the grocery industry, see retailindustry.about.com/library.)

All e-grocers offer consumers the ability to order items online and have them delivered to their homes. Some e-grocers offer free regular "unattended" weekly delivery (e.g., to the customer's garage), based on a monthly subscription model. Others offer on-demand deliveries (if the customer is at home) with a surcharge added to the grocery bill and sometimes an additional delivery charge. One e-grocer sells only nonperishable items shipped via common carrier, a model also adopted by Amazon.com with its recent foray into online grocery sales. Many offer additional services, such as dry-cleaning pickup and delivery. Other add-on features include "don't run out" automatic reordering of routine foods or home office supplies, as well as fresh flower delivery, movie rentals, meal planning, recipe tips, multimedia features, and nutritional information.

Today, it is possible to shop for groceries from cell phones, BlackBerries, and PDAs (see Chapter 8). For e-grocery implementation issues, see Online File W3.12.

FRESHDIRECT

FreshDirect is an online grocer that delivers to residences and offices in the New York City metropolitan area. The company uses SAP AG software to process thousands of orders placed on its Web site every night. Orders are dispatched to the kitchen, bakery, and deli as well as to fresh storage rooms, produce ripening rooms, and production areas within the company's refrigerated facility. All order components are custom-cut, packaged, weighed, and priced. In the case of dry goods or frozen foods, items are picked from storage before being placed inside bins that travel along conveyors to the sorting area. There, products in a customer's order are scanned and gathered in corrugated fiberboard boxes. The boxes are labeled, recorded, and loaded into refrigerated delivery trucks. FreshDirect adopts a *just-in-time* manufacturing practice that reduces waste and improves quality and freshness.

ONLINE DELIVERY OF DIGITAL PRODUCTS, ENTERTAINMENT, AND MEDIA

Certain goods, such as software, music, or news stories, can be distributed in a physical form (such as hard copy, CD-ROM, DVD, and newsprint), or they can be digitized and delivered over the Internet. For example, consumers can purchase shrink-wrapped CD-ROMs containing software (along with the owner's manual and a warranty card) or pay for the software at a Web site and immediately download it onto their computers (usually through File Transfer Protocol [FTP], a fast way to download large files).

As described in Chapter 2, products that can be transformed to digital format and delivered over the Internet are called *digital products*. Exhibit 3.11 provides examples of digital products that can be distributed either physically or digitally. Each delivery method has advantages and disadvantages for both sellers and buyers. Customers, for example, may prefer the formats available through physical distribution. They perceive value in holding a physical CD-ROM or music CD as opposed to a downloaded file. In addition, the related packaging of a physical product can be significant. In some cases, customers enjoy the "liner notes" that accompany a music CD. Paper-based software user manuals and other materials also have value and may be preferred over online help features. However, customers might have to wait days for physical products to be delivered.

For sellers, the costs associated with the manufacture, storage, and distribution of physical products (DVDs, CD-ROMs, paper magazines, etc.) can be enormous. Inventory management also becomes a critical cost issue, and so does delivery and distribution. The need for retail intermediaries requires the establishment of relationships with channel partners and revenue-sharing plans. Direct sales of digital content through digital download, however,

EXHIBIT 3.11   Distribution of Digital Versus Physical Products

Type of Product	Physical Distribution	Digital Distribution
Software	Boxed, shrink-wrapped	FTP, direct download, e-mail
Newspapers, magazines	Home delivery, postal mail	Display on Web, "e-zines"
Greeting cards	Retail stores	E-mail, URL link to recipient
Images (e.g., clip-art, graphics)	CD-ROM, magazines	Web site display, downloadable
Movies	DVD, VHS, NTSB, PAL	MPEG3, streaming video, RealNetwork, AVI, QuickTime, etc.
Music	CD, cassette tape	MP3, WAV, RealAudio downloads, wireless devices, iTunes

allow a producer of digital content to bypass the traditional retail channel, thereby reducing overall costs and capturing greater profits. However, retailers often are crucial in creating demand for a product through in-store displays, advertising, and human sales efforts, all of which are lost when the producer disintermediates the traditional channel.

A major revolution in the online entertainment industry occurred when Napster introduced the P2P file-sharing of music (see Online File W3.13). Another major phenomenon in the online delivery of entertainment is YouTube (see Chapter 9).

ONLINE ENTERTAINMENT

Online entertainment is growing rapidly. Online entertainment is now the most popular medium in the United States among young people between the ages of 8 and 17. More than 50 percent of the U.S. youngsters prefer to be entertained online, whereas less than 20 percent prefer to watch television. There are many kinds of Internet entertainment. It is difficult to precisely categorize them because there tends to be a mixture of entertainment types, delivery modes, and personal taste and choice in deciding whether something is entertainment or not. Some online entertainment can be regarded as interactive, in that the user can interact, often in a somewhat conversational way, with the software and thus change the outcome or shape the direction of the entertainment activity. The global online games market is worth more than $4 billion and is predicted to grow at a compound annual growth rate of 25.2 percent over the 2008–2011 forecast period, reaching $11.8 billion and representing approximately one-third of the total games software market by 2011 (Strategy Analytics 2007).

The major forms of traditional entertainment are television, film, radio, music, games, reading, and gambling. All of these are now available over the Internet. However, some have become much more popular in the new environment because the capabilities of modern technology mean that the experience can be enhanced for people who enjoy that activity. For example, online games offer multimedia experiences with colorful animations and sound and allow the player to affect the course and outcome of the game. Examples of online entertainment and services are described in Exhibit 3.12. For a more detailed summary of online entertainment, see Online File W3.14. For information on entertainment in the Web 2.0 environment, see Chapter 9.

Adult Entertainment

Online adult entertainment is probably the most profitable B2C model and accounts for a huge percentage of Internet usage. Adult content sites succeed because they offer three things unavailable in an offline store: anonymity, instant gratification, and choice (Caslon Analytics 2008). According to Nielsen Online, in October 2008 approximately a quarter of employees visited Internet porn sites during working hours, a 23-percent increase from October 2007 (Kuchment and Springen 2008). With little or no advertising effort to attract viewers, many of these sites are making good money. According to reports by market research firms that monitor the industry, such as Forrester, IDC, DataMonitor, Jupiter Media, and

NetRating, viewers eagerly pay substantial subscription fees to view adult sites. See Online File W3.14 for more online services and products for adults.

EXHIBIT 3.12	Examples of Online Entertainment and Services	
Online Entertainment	**Entertainment-Related Services**
Web browsing	Event ticketing
Internet gaming	Restaurant reservations
Fantasy sports games	Information retrieval
Single and multiplayer games	Retrieval of audio and video entertainment
Adult entertainment	
Card games	
Social networking sites	
Participatory Web sites	
Movies, TV online	
Live events	
Virtual worlds: (trading, creating, etc.)	

Internet Gambling

Internet gaming includes all forms of gaming, including arcade gaming, lotteries, casino gaming, promotional incentives, and so on. In 2008, online gambling revenue continued to increase despite of bad economic times. One study indicated that although the offline market is anticipated to produce only a modest average development rate of 2.2 percent until 2012, the online market is going to accomplish average expansion rates of 10.3 percent per annum until 2012, hitting a total market volume of $24.4 billion, or 6.3 percent of the gaming market (Baranzelli 2008). The ease of access and take-up of broadband services throughout the world in recent years has been vital to the expansion of online gaming.

Online Dating Services

Online dating is a dating system that allows individuals, couples, and groups to make contact and communicate with each other over the Internet, usually with the objective of developing a personal romantic or sexual relationship. Online dating services usually provide unmoderated matchmaking over the Internet through the use of personal computers or cell phones. As a paid content category, online dating services are the third largest attractor of Internet users after music and games, earning 10 percent of the online audience in 2007. According to one study (*Jupiter Research Corporation 2007*), online dating sites are projected to increase revenue from $900 million in 2007 to $1.9 billion in 2012, an increase of 16 percent over 5 years.

Section 3.7 ▶ REVIEW QUESTIONS

1. Explain on-demand delivery service.
2. Describe e-grocers and how they operate.
3. What are the difficulties in shopping online for groceries?
4. Describe digital goods and their delivery.
5. What are the benefits and the limitations of digital delivery?
6. What are the major forms of online entertainment? (See Online File W3.14.)
7. Do you think people of different age groups and social classes might be attracted to different types of online entertainment?

3.8 ONLINE PURCHASE-DECISION AIDS

Many sites and tools are available to help consumers with online purchasing decisions. Wal-Mart, for example, equipped its online store with an intelligent search engine. Consumers must decide which product or service to purchase, which site to use for the purchase (a manufacturer site, a general-purpose e-tailer, a niche intermediary, or some other site), and what other services to employ. Some sites offer price comparisons as their primary tool (e.g., pricerunner.com and shopzilla.com); others evaluate services, trust, quality, and other factors. Shopping portals, shopping robots ("shopbots"), business ratings sites, trust verification sites, and other shopping aids also are available.

SHOPPING PORTALS

shopping portals
Gateways to e-storefronts and e-malls; may be comprehensive or niche oriented.

Shopping portals are gateways to storefronts and e-malls. Like any other portal, they can be comprehensive or niche oriented. Comprehensive, or general-purpose, portals have links to many different sellers and present and evaluate a broad range of products. An example of a comprehensive portal is eCOST.com (ecost.com). Several public portals also offer shopping opportunities and comparison aids. Examples are shopping.com, shopping.yahoo.com, shopping.msn.com, and shopping.aol.com. eBay is a shopping portal because it offers shopping at fixed prices as well as auctions. All have clear shopping links from the main page of the portal, and they generate revenues by directing consumers to their affiliates' sites. Some of these portals even offer comparison tools to help identify the best price for a particular item. Several of these evaluation companies have purchased shopbots (see the following discussion) or other, smaller shopping aids and incorporated them into their portals.

Some shopping portals also offer specialized niche aids with information and links for purchasers of automobiles, toys, computers, travel, or some other narrow area. Such portals also help customers conduct research. Examples include review.zdnet.com and shopper.cnet.com for computer equipment. The advantage of niche shopping portals is their ability to specialize in a certain line of products and carefully track consumer tastes within a specific and relevant market segment. Some of these portals seek only to collect the referral fee from their affiliation with sites they recommend. Others have no formal relationship with the sellers; instead, they sell banner ad space to advertisers who wish to reach the communities who regularly visit these specialized sites. In other cases, shopping portals act as intermediaries by selling directly to consumers, although this might harm their reputation for independence and objectivity.

SHOPBOTS SOFTWARE AGENTS

shopping robots (shopping agents or shopbots)
Tools that scout the Web on behalf of consumers who specify search criteria.

Savvy Internet shoppers may bookmark their favorite shopping sites, but what if they want to find other stores with good service and policies that sell similar items at lower prices? **Shopping robots** (also called **shopping agents** or **shopbots**) are tools that scout the Web for consumers who specify search criteria. Different shopbots use different search methods. For example, mySimon (mysimon.com) searches the Web to find the best prices and availability for thousands of popular items. This is not a simple task. The shopbot might have to evaluate different SKU (stock-keeping unit) numbers for the same item, because each e-tailer may have a different SKU rather than a standardized data-representation code. In addition to price, pricegrabber.com includes product details and features, product reviews from merchants and consumers, and additional information about the store selling the item.

Some agents specialize in certain product categories or niches. For example, consumers can get help shopping for cars at autobytel.com, carsdirect.com, autovantage.com, and autos.msn.com. Zdnet.com searches for information on computers, software, and peripherals. A shopping agent at mysimon.com helps consumers find the best price for products from online stores. A shopping agent for books is isbn.nu. In addition, agents such as pricegrabber.com are able to identify customers' preferences. Shopping.com (shopping.com) (now owned by eBay) allows consumers to compare over 1,000 different merchant sites and seeks lower prices on their behalf. Negotiation agents are even available to assist auction bidders by automating the bid process using the bidder's instructions. See Wang (2006) for a comparison of shopping bots.

"SPY" SERVICES

In this context, "spy" services are not the CIA or MI5 (mi5.gov.uk). Rather, they are services that visit Web sites for customers, at their direction, and notify them of their findings. Web surfers and shoppers constantly monitor sites for new information, special sales, ending time of auctions, stock updates, and so on, but visiting the sites to monitor them is time consuming. Several sites will track stock prices or airline special sales and send e-mails accordingly. For example, cnn.com, pcworld.com, and expedia.com will send people personalized alerts. Spectorsoft.com enables users to create a list of "spies" that visit Web sites; the spy sends an e-mail when it finds something of interest. Users can choose predesigned spies or create their own. Special searches are provided by web2mail.com, which responds to e-mail queries. Of special interest is Yahoo! Alerts (alerts.yahoo.com), an index of e-mail alerts for many different things, including job listings, real estate, travel spetials, and auctions. Users set up alerts so that they hit their in-boxes periodically or whenever new information is available. The alerts are sent via e-mail and come with commercial ads.

Of course, one of the most effective ways to spy on Internet users is to introduce cookies and spyware in their computers (see Chapter 4 for details).

Wireless Shopping Comparisons

Users of mySimon (all regular services) and AT&T Digital PocketNet service have access to wireless shopping comparisons. Users who are equipped with an AT&T Internet-ready cell phone can find the service on the AT&T main menu; it enables shoppers to compare prices any time from anywhere, including from any physical store.

BUSINESS RATINGS SITES

Many Web sites rate various e-tailers and online products based on multiple criteria. Bizrate.com (bizrate.com), Consumer Reports Online (consumerreports.org), Forrester Research (forrester.com), and Gomez Advisors (gomez.com) are such well-known sites. At Gomez.com, the consumer can actually specify the relative importance of different criteria when comparing online banks, toy sellers, e-grocers, and so on. Note that different raters provide different rankings. Alexa Internet, Inc. (alexa.com) is a California-based subsidiary company of Amazon.com that is best known for operating a Web site that provides information on Web traffic to other Web sites. Alexa ranks sites based on tracking information of users of its Alexa Toolbar for Internet Explorer and from integrated sidebars in Mozilla and Netscape. Online File W3.15 discusses ResellerRatings (resellerratings.com), an interesting example of a business ratings site.

TRUST VERIFICATION SITES

With so many sellers online, many consumers are not sure whom they should trust. A number of companies purport to evaluate and verify the trustworthiness of various e-tailers. One such company is TRUSTe (truste.com). The TRUSTe seal appears at the bottom of each TRUSTe-approved e-tailer's Web site. E-tailers pay TRUSTe for use of the seal (which they call a "trustmark"). TRUSTe's 1,300-plus members hope that consumers will use the seal as an assurance and as a proxy for actual research into their conduct of business, privacy policy, and personal information protection.

The most comprehensive trust verification sites are VeriSign and BBBOnline. VeriSign (verisign.com) tends to be the most widely used. Other sources of trust verification include Secure Assure (secureassure.com), which charges yearly license fees based on a company's annual revenue. In addition, Ernst and Young, the global public accounting firm, has created its own service for auditing e-tailers in order to offer some guarantee of the integrity of their business practices.

OTHER SHOPPING TOOLS

Other digital intermediaries assist buyers or sellers, or both, with the research and purchase processes. For example, escrow services (e.g., escrow.com and fortis-escrow.com) assist buyers and sellers in the exchange of items and money. Because buyers and sellers do not see or know each other, a trusted third party frequently is needed to facilitate the proper exchange of money and goods. Escrow sites may also provide payment-processing support, as well as letters of credit (see Chapter 11).

Other decision aids include communities of consumers who offer advice and opinions on products and e-tailers. One such site is epinions.com, which has searchable recommendations on thousands of products. Pricescan.com is a price-comparison engine, and pricegrabber.com is a comparison shopping tool that covers over 1 million products, and Onlineshoes.com specializes in all types of shoes. Other software agents and comparison sites are presented in Online File W3.16.

Another shopping tool is a *wallet*—in this case, an *electronic wallet*, which is a program that contains the shopper's information. To expedite online shopping, consumers can use electronic wallets so that they do not need to reenter the information each time they shop. Although sites such as Amazon.com offer their own specialized wallets, Microsoft has a universal wallet in its Passport program (see Chapter 10 for details).

Section 3.8 ❱ REVIEW QUESTIONS

1. Define shopping portals and provide two examples.
2. What are shopbots?
3. Explain the role of business and Web site rating and site verification tools in the purchase-decision process.
4. Why are escrow services and electronic wallets useful for online purchases?
5. Describe the role of search engines to support shopping.

3.9 PROBLEMS WITH E-TAILING AND LESSONS LEARNED

There are a number of challenges in creating a successful e-tailing business. A few companies do not even try e-tailing, although these numbers are declining. The reasons that retailers give for not going online include: their product is not appropriate for Web sales, lack of significant opportunity, high cost, technological immaturity, online sales conflict with core business, and the like. Others try e-tailing but do not succeed. E-tailing offers some serious challenges and tremendous risks for those who fail to provide value to the consumer, who fail to establish a profitable business model, or who fail to properly execute the model they establish. The road to e-tail success is littered with dead companies that could not deliver on their promises. The shakeout from mid-2000 to late-2002 caused many companies to fail; others learned and adapted. It is fair to say that the much more balanced, analytical, and sober perspective of late offers a much better appreciation of the issues, challenges, risks, and potential benefits of EC.

Online File W3.17 provides a sample of failed B2C companies. Some enduring principles can be distilled from the failures, and these "lessons learned" are discussed next.

Although thousands of companies have evolved their online strategies into mature Web sites with extensive interactive features that add value to the consumer purchase process, many sites remain simple "brochureware" sites with limited interactivity. Many traditional companies are in a transitional stage. Mature transactional systems include features for payment processing, order fulfillment, logistics, inventory management, and a host of other services. In most cases, a company must replicate each of its physical business processes and design many more that can only be performed online. Today's environment includes sophisticated access to order information, shipping information, product information, and more through Web pages, touchtone phones, Web-enabled cell phones, and PDAs over wireless networks. Faced with all of these variables, the challenges to implementing EC can be daunting.

The real gains for traditional retailers come from leveraging the benefits of their physical presence and the benefits of their online presence. Web sites frequently offer better prices and selection, whereas physical stores offer a trustworthy staff and opportunities for customers to examine items before purchasing. Large, efficient established retailers, such as Wal-Mart (walmart.com), Marks & Spencer (marksandspencer.com), and Nordstrom (nordstrom.com), are able to create the optimum value proposition for their customers by providing a complete offering of services.

A traditional brick-and-mortar store with a mature Web site that uses a click-and mortar strategy is able to do the following:

- **Speak with one voice.** A firm can link all of its back-end systems to create an integrated customer experience. The online experience should be an extension of the experience encountered in traditional transactions.

- **Leverage the multichannels.** The innovative retailer will offer the advantages of each marketing channel to customers from all channels. Whether the purchase is made online or at the store, the customer should benefit from the presence of both channels.

- **Empower the customer.** The seller needs to create a powerful 24/7 channel for service and information. Through various information technologies, sellers can give customers the opportunity to perform various functions interactively, at any time. Such functions include the ability to find store locations, product information, and inventory availability online.

Section 3.9 ▶ REVIEW QUESTIONS

1. What challenges do virtual e-tailers face?
2. What makes click-and-mortar companies successful?

3.10   ISSUES IN E-TAILING

The following are representative issues that need to be addressed when conducting B2C.

DISINTERMEDIATION AND REINTERMEDIATION

Disintermediation refers to the removal of organizations or business process layers responsible for certain intermediary steps in a given supply chain. As shown in part B of Exhibit 3.13,

disintermediation
The removal of organizations or business process layers responsible for certain intermediary steps in a given supply chain.

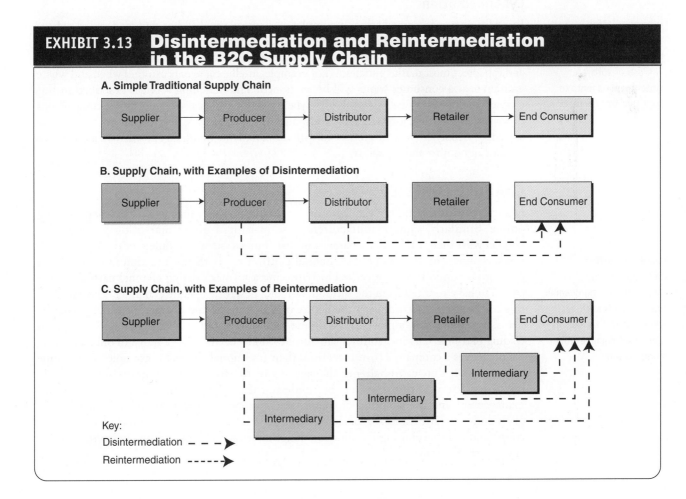

EXHIBIT 3.13   Disintermediation and Reintermediation in the B2C Supply Chain

A. Simple Traditional Supply Chain

Supplier → Producer → Distributor → Retailer → End Consumer

B. Supply Chain, with Examples of Disintermediation

Supplier → Producer → Distributor   Retailer   End Consumer

C. Supply Chain, with Examples of Reintermediation

Supplier → Producer → Distributor → Retailer   End Consumer   Intermediary   Intermediary   Intermediary

Key:
Disintermediation – – – ▶
Reintermediation - - - - - ▶

the manufacturer can bypass the wholesalers and retailers, selling directly to consumers. Also, e-tailers may drive regular retailers out of business. For a vivid case of such disintermediation, see the Blue Nile case in Chapter 2.

However, consumers might have problems selecting an online vendor; vendors might have problems delivering to customers; and both might need an escrow service to ensure the transaction. Thus, new online assistance might be needed, and it might be provided by new or by traditional intermediaries. In such cases, the traditional intermediaries fill new roles, providing *added value* and assistance. This process is referred to as **reintermediation**. It is pictured in part C of Exhibit 3.13. Thus, for the intermediary, the Internet offers new ways to reach new customers, new ways to bring value to customers, and perhaps new ways to generate revenues.

The intermediary's role is shifting to one that emphasizes value-added services, such as assisting customers in comparison shopping from multiple sources, providing total solutions by combining services from several vendors, and providing certifications and trusted third-party control and evaluation systems. For instance, in the world of online new and used car sales, electronic intermediaries assist buyers and/or sellers. These are new *reintermediaries*; intermediaries that have restructured their role in the purchase process. An example of the new roles of intermediaries is Edmunds (edmunds.com), which gives consumers a vast amount of information about cars, including price comparisons, ratings, the location of cars for sale, and the dealer's true costs.

Some reintermediaries cooperate with manufacturers or retailers to provide a needed service to the seller or distributor in the online environment. Other reintermediaries are virtual e-tailers that fill a unique niche. Intermediaries such as online retailers and shopping portals can also act as reintermediaries. The evolution and operation of these companies is critical to the success of e-commerce.

reintermediation
The process whereby intermediaries (either new ones or those that had been disintermediated) take on new intermediary roles.

Cybermediation

In addition to reintermediation, a completely new role in EC has emerged called **cybermediation**, or **electronic intermediation**. These terms describe special Web sites that use intelligent agents to facilitate intermediation. Cybermediators can perform many roles in EC and can affect most market functions. For example, intelligent agents can find when and where an item that a consumer wants will be auctioned. The matching services described in this chapter are done by *cybermediator agents*. Cybermediator agents also conduct price comparisons of insurance policies, long-distance calls, and other services. Cybermediation services are spreading rapidly around the globe, and with developments in intelligent software are likely to increase in number and capability.

cybermediation (electronic intermediation)
The use of software (intelligent) agents to facilitate intermediation.

CHANNEL CONFLICT

Many traditional retailers establish a new marketing channel when they start selling online. Similarly, some manufacturers have instituted direct marketing initiatives in parallel with their established channels of distribution, such as retailers or dealers. In such cases, channel conflict can occur. **Channel conflict** refers to any situation in which direct competition and/or damage caused by bypassing a former existing channel partner is perceived to have resulted from the introduction of a new, often online, channel. The extent of this conflict varies according to the nature of the industry and characteristics of particular firms, but sometimes, a move to sell online can damage old, valued relationships between trading partners. Channel conflict can also be said to occur when a move to online trading simply moves a company's customers from their traditional stores, for example, to an online environment, thus cannibalizing the sales from the former and potentially negatively impacting the traditional outlets by rendering them less profitable. However, careful management and the adoption of sound strategies can deliver a number of synergies for click-and-mortar e-tailers, especially those associated with encouraging cross-channel cooperation and exploiting the unique strengths of each channel to maximize the experience for the customer.

channel conflict
Situation in which an online marketing channel upsets the traditional channels due to real or perceived damage from competition.

DETERMINING THE RIGHT PRICE

Pricing a product or service on the Internet, especially by a click-and-mortar company, is complicated. On the one hand, prices need to be competitive on the Internet. Today's comparison engines will show the consumer the prices at many stores, for almost all commodity products, at almost no cost to the consumer. However, balanced against this is the fact that for some items, transaction costs will decrease, the cost of distribution will decrease, and supply chains may become more efficient and shorter, meaning that e-tailers might be able to compete in the aggressive online market space. On the other hand, prices should be in line with the corporate policy on profitability and, in a click-and-mortar company, in line with the offline channel's pricing strategy. To avoid price conflict, some companies have created independent online subsidiaries.

EC offers companies new opportunities to test prices, segment customers, and adjust to changes in supply and demand. We argue that companies are not taking advantage of these opportunities. Companies can make prices more precise (optimal prices); they can be more adaptable to changes in the environment; and they can be more creative and accurate regarding different prices to different segments. In addition, in one-to-one marketing (Chapter 4) a company can have personalized prices.

PRODUCT AND SERVICE CUSTOMIZATION AND PERSONALIZATION

One significant characteristic of many online marketing business models is the ability of the seller to create an element of *personalization* for each individual consumer.

The Internet also allows for easy self-configuration ("design it your way"). This creates a large demand for customized products and services. Manufacturers can meet that demand by using a *mass customization* strategy. As indicated earlier, many companies offer customized products from their Web sites (e.g., see the Dell case in Online File W1.2).

Although pure-play e-tailing is risky and its future is unclear, e-tailing is growing rapidly as a complementary distribution channel to traditional stores and catalogs. In other words, the *click-and-mortar model is winning currently and all evidence suggests that this trend will continue.* (See the closing case at the end of the chapter.)

FRAUD AND OTHER ILLEGAL ACTIVITIES

A major problem in B2C is the increasing rate of online fraud. This can cause losses to both buyers and sellers. For a more detailed and thorough discussion of online fraud, see the discussion of online fraud in Chapter 10.

HOW TO MAKE CUSTOMERS HAPPY

A critical success factor for B2C is to find what customers want, so the vendor can make them happy. In addition to price, customers want convenience, service, and quality, and they often want to enjoy the experience of online shopping. Merchants can find out what customers want through *market research*, the topic of our next chapter.

Section 3.10 ▶ REVIEW QUESTIONS

1. Define disintermediation.
2. Describe mediation issues, including disintermediation, reintermediation, and cybermediation.
3. Describe channel conflict and other conflicts that may appear in e-tailing.
4. Describe price determination in e-tailing.
5. Explain personalization and mass customization opportunities in e-tailing.

MANAGERIAL ISSUES

Some managerial issues related to this chapter are as follows.

1. **What should our strategic position be?** The most important decision for retailers and e-tailers is the overall *strategic position* they establish within their industry. What niche will they fill? What business functions will they execute internally, and which functions will be outsourced? What partners will they use? How will they integrate brick-and-mortar facilities with their online presence? What are their revenue sources in the short and long run, and what are their fixed and marginal costs? An e-business is still a business and must establish solid business practices in the long run in order to ensure profitability and viability. Manufacturers need to understand the importance and structure of their online marketing and sales channels in order to replace or combine their online operations with their traditional ones. We discuss such issues in Chapter 13.

2. **Limitations of e-tailing.** In Korea, Internet retailing has become the second most important distribution channel, exceeding the national sales volume of all department stores. The question is what the limit of e-tailing will be. The large e-mall volume has grown faster than individual online storefronts. The market concentration has already happened, making the entrance barrier to scale e-tailers very high. However, small businesses can easily start their online channel as part of a stable e-mall service platform. The opportunity can be cultivated by redefining the merchant's business plan with the addition of click-and-mortar strategies or of alliances with both online or offline partners.

   Because most easy sources of funding have dried up and revenue models are being scrutinized, vendor consolidation will continue until there is a greater stability within the e-tailing sector. Ultimately, there will likely be a smaller number of larger sellers with comprehensive general sites (e.g., Amazon.com) and many smaller, specialized niche sites.

3. **How should we introduce wireless shopping?** In some countries (e.g., Japan), shopping from cell phones is very popular (see Chapter 8). In other countries, mobile shopping is not popular, although the platform itself is available. Alternative channels and a culture of a variety of communication channels should be developed in different countries in order to develop mobile strategies. Also, because the younger generation prefers the mobile platform, the age effect on the platform should be monitored closely. Offering mobile shopping might not be simple or appropriate to all businesses.

4. **Do we have ethics and privacy guidelines?** Ethical issues are extremely important in an agentless system. In traditional systems, human agents play an important role in assuring the ethical behavior of buyers and sellers. Will online ethics and the rules of etiquette be sufficient to guide behavior on the Internet? Only time will tell. For example, as job-applicant information travels over the Internet, security and privacy become even more important. It is management's job to make sure that information from applicants is secure. Also, e-tailers need to establish guidelines for protecting the privacy of customers who visit their Web sites. Security and privacy must be high priorities.

5. **How will intermediaries act in cyberspace?** The role of online intermediary has become more and more important. In the banking, stock trading, job market, travel industry, and book sales sectors, the Internet has become a most important service channel. These intermediary services create new business opportunities and convenience for users.

6. **Should we try to capitalize on social networks?** Many individuals began trading or selling products and services on Facebook and other social networks. Although large companies are concentrating on advertising at the moment, some are experimenting with B2C sales (see Chapter 9).

SUMMARY

In this chapter, you learned about the following EC issues as they relate to the learning objectives.

1. **The scope and characteristics of e-tailing.** E-tailing, the online selling of products and services, is growing rapidly. Computers, software, and electronics are the major items sold online. Books, CDs, toys, office supplies, and other standard commodities also sell well. More successful are services sold online, such as airline tickets and travel services, stocks, and insurance.

2. **E-tailing business models.** The major e-tailing business models can be classified by distribution channel—a manufacturer or mail-order company selling direct to consumers, pure-play (virtual) e-tailing, a

click-and-mortar strategy with both online and traditional channels, and online malls that provide either referring directories or shared services.

3. **How online travel/tourism services operate.** Most services available through a physical travel agency also are available online. In addition, customers get much more information, much more quickly through online resources. Customers can even receive bids from travel providers. Finally, travelers can compare prices, participate in auctions and chat rooms, and view videos and maps.

4. **The online job market and its benefits.** The online job market is growing rapidly, with thousands and thousands of jobs matched with job seekers each year. The major benefits of online job markets are the ability to reach a large number of job seekers at low cost, to provide detailed information online, to take applications, and even to conduct tests. Also, using intelligent agents, resumes can be checked and matches made more quickly. Millions of job offers posted on the Internet help job seekers, who also can post their resumes for recruiters.

5. **The electronic real estate market.** The online real estate market is basically supporting rather than replacing existing agents. However, both buyers and sellers can save time and effort in the electronic market. Buyers can purchase distant properties much more easily and in some places have access to less expensive services. Eventually, commissions on regular transactions are expected to decline as a result of the electronic market for real estate and more sales "by owner" will materialize.

6. **Online trading of stocks and bonds.** One of the fastest growing online businesses is the online trading of securities. It is inexpensive, convenient, and supported by a tremendous amount of financial and advisory information. Trading is very fast and efficient, almost fully automated, and moving toward 24/7 global trading. However, security breaches are possible, so tight protection is a must.

7. **Cyberbanking and personal finance.** Branch banking is on the decline due to less expensive, more convenient online banking. The world is moving toward online banking; today, most routine banking services can be done from home. Banks can reach customers in remote places, and customers can bank with faraway institutions. This makes the financial markets more efficient. Online personal finance applications, such as bill paying, tracking of accounts, and tax preparation, also are very popular.

8. **On-demand delivery service.** On-demand delivery service is needed when items are perishable or when delivering medicine, express documents, or urgently needed supplies. One example of on-demand delivery is e-groceries; these may be ordered online and are shipped or ready for store pickup within 24 hours or less.

9. **Delivery of digital products.** Anything that can be digitized can be successfully delivered online. Delivery of digital products such as music, software, movies, and other entertainment online has been a success. Some print media, such as electronic versions of magazines or electronic books (see Chapter 7), also are having success when digitized and delivered electronically.

10. **Aiding consumer purchase decisions.** Purchase decision aids include shopping portals, shopbots and comparison agents, business rating sites, trust verification sites, and other tools.

11. **Disintermediation and other B2C strategic issues.** Direct electronic marketing by manufacturers results in disintermediation by removing wholesalers and retailers. However, online reintermediaries provide additional value, such as helping consumers make selections among multiple products and vendors. Traditional retailers may feel threatened or pressured when manufacturers decide to sell online; such direct selling can cause channel conflict. Pricing of online and offline products and services is one issue that always needs to be addressed.

KEY TERMS

Brick-and-mortar retailers	149	E-grocer	166	Reintermediation	174
Channel conflict	174	E-tailers	143	Shopping portals	170
Click-and-mortar retailers	148	Electronic (online) banking		Shopping robots (shopping	
Cybermediation (electronic		or e-banking	162	agents, shopbots)	170
intermediation)	174	Electronic retailing (e-tailing)	143	Virtual (pure-play) e-tailers	148
Direct marketing	148	Multichannel business model	149		
Disintermediation	173	On-demand delivery service	166		

QUESTIONS FOR DISCUSSION

1. What are Amazon.com's critical success factors? Is its decision to offer a much broader selection of items a good marketing strategy? With the broader selection, do you think the company will dilute its brand or extend the value proposition to its customers?

2. Discuss the advantages of established click-and-mortar companies such as Wal-Mart over pure-play e-tailers such as Amazon.com. What are the disadvantages of click-and-brick retailers as compared with pure-play e-tailers?

3. Discuss the importance of comparison tools, product reviews, and customer ratings in online shopping.

4. Discuss the advantages of a specialized e-tailer, such as DogToys.com (dogtoys.com). Could such a store survive in the physical world? Why or why not?

5. Discuss the benefits of build-to-order to buyers and sellers. Are there any disadvantages?

6. Why are online travel services a popular Internet application? Why do so many Web sites provide free travel information?

7. Compare the advantages and disadvantages of online stock trading with offline trading.

8. It is said that the service Zuji.com (zuji.com) provides to travel agents will lead to their reintermediation. Discuss.

9. Online employment services make it easy to change jobs; therefore, turnover rates may increase. This could result in total higher costs for employers because of increased costs for recruiting and training new employees and the need to pay higher salaries and wages to attract or keep them. What can companies do to ease this problem?

10. Compare the advantages and disadvantages of distributing digitizable products electronically versus physically.

11. Discuss each of the following as limiting factors on the growth of B2C EC: (a) Too much competition, (b) expensive technology, (c) need a computer to shop, (d) people need the social interaction in face-to-face shopping, (e) many people cannot afford an Internet access, (f) the EC market is already saturated.

INTERNET EXERCISES

1. Enter gcitrading.com/sharing-trading. Register for a free demonstration account. Receive $50,000 in fake money and trade in the stock market. See how well you can do with the software.

2. Many consumer portals offer advice and ratings of products or e-tailers. Identify and examine two separate general-consumer portals that look at other sites and compare prices or other purchase criteria. Try to find and compare prices for a digital camera, a microwave oven, and an MP3 player. Visit clusty.com. How can this site help you in your shopping? Summarize your experience. Comment on the strong and weak points of such shopping tools.

3. Almost all auto manufacturers allow consumers to configure their cars online. Visit a major automaker's Web site and configure a car of your choice (e.g., jaguar.com). Also visit one electronic intermediary (e.g., autobytel.com). After you decide what car you want, examine the payment options and figure your monthly payments. Print your results. How does this process compare with visiting an auto dealer? Do you think you found a better price online? Would you consider buying a car this way?

4. Visit amazon.com and identify at least three specific elements of its personalization and customization features.

Browse specific books on one particular subject, leave the site, and then go back and revisit the site. What do you see? Are these features likely to encourage you to purchase more books in the future from Amazon.com? Check the 1-Click feature and other shopping aids provided. List the features and discuss how they may lead to increased sales.

5. Visit landsend.com and prepare a customized order for a piece of clothing. Describe the process. Do you think this will result in better-fitting clothing? Do you think this personalization feature will lead to greater sales volume for Lands' End?

6. Make your resume accessible to millions of people. Consult asktheheadhunter.com or careerbuilder.com for help rewriting your resume. See monster.com for ideas about planning your career. Get prepared for a job interview. Also, use the Web to determine what salary you can get in the city of your choice.

7. Visit move.com, decisionaide.com, or a similar site and compute the monthly mortgage payment on a 30-year loan at 7.5 percent fixed interest. Also check current interest rates. Estimate your closing costs on a $200,000 loan. Compare the monthly payments of the fixed rate with that of an adjustable rate for the first year. Finally,

compute your total payments if you take the loan for 15 years at the going rate. Compare it with a 30-year mortgage. Comment on the difference.

8. Access the Virtual Trader game at virtualtrader.co.uk and register for the Internet stock game. You will be bankrolled with £100,000 in a trading account every month. You also can play investment games at investorsleague.com, fantasystockmarket.com, and etrade.com.

9. Compare the price of a Sony digital camera at shopping.com, mysimon.com, bottomdollar.com, bizrate.com, and pricescan.com. Which site locates the best deal? Where do you get the best information?

10. Enter xing.com and identify its job-related offerings. Prepare a list of support activities offered.

11. Compare the "build-your-own" at Nike (nike.com) with Timberland's Boot Studio (timberland.com).

12. Enter jobster.com and monster.com and compare the processes used by recruiting companies to find qualified candidates. Comment on the differences between the two sites. Also, compare the sites from a job seeker's perspective. Finally, compare the capabilities to those of LinkedIn (linkedin.com).

13. Enter Bazaarvoice (bazaarvoice.com) and find how consumers can engage in a dialog. Look at its Ask & Answer service. How is quality of content maintained. Write a report based on your findings.

14. Enter vivente.com/resumix/website, examine the capabilities of the tools, and write a report.

TEAM ASSIGNMENTS, PROJECTS, AND CLASS DISCUSSIONS

1. Each team will investigate the services of two online car-selling sites from the following list (or other sites). When teams have finished, they should bring their research together and discuss their findings.

   a. Buying new cars through an intermediary (autobytel.com, carsdirect.com, autoweb.com, or amazon.com)

   b. Buying used cars (autotrader.com)

   c. Buying used cars by auto dealers (manheim.com)

   d. Automobile ratings sites (carsdirect.com and fueleconomy.gov)

   e. Car-buying portals (thecarportal.com and cars.com)

   f. Buying antique cars (classiccars.com and antiquecars.com)

2. Each team will represent a broker-based area (e.g., real estate, insurance, stocks, job finding). Each team will find a new development that has occurred in the assigned area over the most recent 3 months. Look for the site vendor's announcement and search for more information on the development with google.com or another search engine. Examine the business news at bloomberg.com. After completing your research, as a team, prepare a report on disintermediation in your assigned area.

3. Each team will examine fantasy games at various sites. Each team should examine the type of game, the rules, and the cost. Play at least one time. Each team should write a report based on its experiences. (Hint: see Online File W3.14.)

4. Address the following topics in a class discussion:

   a. How should a company handle channel conflict with its distributors?

   b. Should online sales be an independent unit in a click-and-mortar firm?

   c. Will P2P lending disrupt banking?

   d. Would you use Monster.com or LinkedIn for recruiting?

Closing Case

WAL-MART POWERS ONLINE

Wal-Mart (walmart.com) is the largest retailer in the world, with $404 billion in sales for the fiscal year ending January 31, 2009. Wal-Mart employs more than 2 million people. The company has more than 7,000 stores around world. Each week, 180 million customers visit Wal-Mart stores worldwide, including 127 million in the United States (see walmartfacts.com for current statistics).

Wal-Mart maintains an intense strategic focus on the customer. Its standard company cheer ends with, "Who's number one? The customer." Wal-Mart has also established itself as a master of the retail process by streamlining its supply chain and undercutting competitors with low prices.

Wal-Mart has had an online presence since 1996. However, one problem with its strategy for growing online sales has been the demographics of its primary customer base. Wal-Mart's target demographic is households with $25,000 in annual income, whereas the median income of online consumers is perhaps $60,000. Despite these demographics, online sales (primarily in music, travel, and electronics) through *walmart.com* already account for about 10 percent of Wal-Mart's U.S. sales. Its long-time chief rival, Kmart, Inc., tried to attract its demographic audience to its Web site (*kmart.com*) by offering free Internet access. This appealed to its cost-conscious, lower-income constituency and provided the opportunity for those customers to access the site to conduct purchases. However, this move decreased company profits in the short run and was one of the factors that led Kmart to file for bankruptcy in 2002.

Wal-Mart also has concerns about cannibalizing its in-store sales. Its alliance with AOL is designed to provide cobranded low-cost Internet access to dwellers in both very rural and very urban areas, where there are no Wal-Mart stores nearby. The intent is to lure new market segments and thus cancel the effect of cannibalization. Ultimately, a hybrid e-tailer that can offer a combination of huge selection with the click-and-mortar advantages of nearby stores (e.g., merchandise pickup or returns) might prove to be the major force of online consumer sales.

In 2002, Walmart.com matured, offering order status and tracking, a help desk, a clear return policy and mechanisms, a store locator, and information on special sales and liquidations. Today, community services, such as photo sharing, are provided.

Wal-Mart only offers some of its merchandise online, but the selection is increasing, including items not available in some or all stores (e.g., spas, mattresses). In 2004, Wal-Mart started selling songs online for 88 cents each, competing with Apple's iTunes. Inexpensive items (e.g., those that sell for less than $5) are not available online. Also in 2004, during a 4-day Thanksgiving special, Wal-Mart began to court more affluent shoppers with new and more expensive items available only online. Products included cashmere sweaters and shiatsu massage chairs. The Web site averaged 8 million visitors each week prior to the promotion.

Wal-Mart had added many new products to its online catalog. International customers can buy Wal-Mart products directly from Wal-Mart (if shipping is available) or from affiliate sites. For example, see ASDA (*asda.co.uk*), a Wal-Mart owned U.K. company.

In 2006, a fake "Wal-Marting Across America" blog—a very rough attempt at teen social networking—became a learning experience for the company. Also in 2006, the company revamped its site for the first time since 2000. The site now features a new four-click checkout process and rich-media, including interactive functions in the toy section.

In 2007, Wal-Mart rolled out its new order online/pick up in store service. "Site to Store," enables customers to buy online and have products shipped for free to their store of choice. The new service also gives customers access to tens of thousands of products, many more than are available in stores. Delivery for such items is 7 to 10 days (*Internet Retailer* 2007c).

According to Nielsen/NetRatings, in 2007 Wal-Mart recorded the third-largest increase in Web traffic among the top 10 online shopping and travel sites. Site visits to Walmart.com in January 2007 were 23 million, up 25 percent over January 2006. For January 2007, Walmart.com was ranked the third most popular site by Nielsen/NetRatings in terms of the number of visits, behind eBay and Amazon.com (*Internet Retailer* 2007b).

Wal-Mart now adopts existing Web 2.0 social networks for its e-tailing activities. In late 2007, Wal-Mart launched "Roommate Style Match" on Facebook, a site that allows students to design their dorm rooms with their roommates. Facebook users who join the Wal-Mart group are able to take a quiz to determine their decorating style and get a list of "recommended products" they can buy at Wal-Mart to mesh their style with their roommate's. Students can also download a shopping list of dorm room items sold at Wal-Mart, link to Wal-Mart's Web site promoting "earth-friendly" products, or click on Soundcheck, Wal-Mart's Web site that shows musical performances by popular singers like Bon Jovi and Mandy Moore. It is believed that Wal-Mart will soon make use of blogs and other Web 2.0 tools to support its online sales (e.g., customer product reviews). Wal-Mart Watch (myspace.com/walmartwatch) is a page on MySpace where frustrated customers and employees get a chance to express their feelings.

In 2008, Wal-Mart continued to gain market share and clout as cash-strapped shoppers sought out its low prices. It reported a stronger-than-expected 3.4 percent rise in sales at its U.S. stores during the 2008 holiday shopping season (Maestri 2008).

Sources: Compiled from Maestri (2008), *Internet Retailer* (2007b), *Internet Retailer* (2007c), and *walmart.com* (accessed February 2009).

Questions

1. Compare *walmart.com* with *amazon.com*. What features do the sites have in common? Which are unique to Wal-Mart? To Amazon.com?

2. Will Wal-Mart become the dominant e-tailer in the world, replacing Amazon.com, or will Amazon.com dominate Wal-Mart online? What factors would contribute to Wal-Mart's success in the online marketplace? What factors would detract from its ability to dominate online sales the way it has been able to dominate physical retail sales in many markets?

3. Check the shopping aids offered at *walmart.com*. Compare them with those at *amazon.com*.

4. What online services can be purchased on Walmart.com?

5. Compare buying a song from Walmart.com versus buying it from Apple's iTunes.

6. Walmart.com sells movies online for a monthly fee. How do similar sellers compare?

7. Visit *walmart.com*, *target.com*, *marksandspencer.com*, and *sears.com*. Identify the common features of their online marketing and at least one unique feature evident at each site. Do these sites have to distinguish themselves primarily in terms of price, product selection, or Web site features?

8. Investigate the options for international customers on the Wal-Mart Web site.

ONLINE RESOURCES
available at pearsonglobaleditions.com/turban

WWW

Online Files

W3.1 Some Current Trends in B2C EC

W3.2 Application Case: Littlewoods Shop Direct Group: From Mail-Order Catalog to High Street to the Web

W3.3 Application Case: CatToys.Com, a Specialty E-Tailer

W3.4 Representative Special B2C Services

W3.5 Application Case: Content-Based Filtering at Eurovacations.com

W3.6 Application Case: Gateway's "Book-It-In-The-Box" E-Travel Solutions

W3.7 Intelligent Agents in Travel Services

W3.8 Application Case: The European Job Mobility Portal (EURES CV-Search) and Xing.Com

W3.9 Intelligent Agents in the Electronic Job Market

W3.10 Real Estate Applications

W3.11 Investment Information

W3.12 Application Case: Implementing E-Grocery

W3.13 Application Case: The Napster Experience: Its Rise, Collapse, and Revival

W3.14 Examples of Online Entertainment

W3.15 Application Case: Reseller Ratings: Making Online Retailers Accountable to Customers

W3.16 Representative Shopping Software Agents and Comparison Sites

W3.17 What Lessons can be Learned from these EC failures?

Comprehensive Educational Web Sites

youtube.com/watch?v=DbwiRLbBg6U
youtube.com/watch?v=P18xwbZFCxM
dictionary.zdnet.com/definition/B2C.html
isos.com.my/ecommerce/b2c.htm
marketresearch.com/map/research/b2c/622.html
managementhelp.org/infomgnt/e_cmmrce/e_cmmrce.htm

REFERENCES

Acharya, R. N., A. Kagan, and S. R. Lingam. "Online Banking Applications and Community Bank Performance." *International Journal of Bank Marketing* (October 2008).

Agatza, N. A. H., M. Fleischmann, and J. A. E. E. van Nunena. "E-Fulfillment and Multi-Channel Distribution—A Review." *European Journal of Operational Research* (June 2008).

Baranzelli, M. F. "Growing Revenue in Internet Gambling." *Online Casino Extra*, November 18, 2008. onlinecasinoextra.com/casino_news_1811.html (accessed February 2009).

Beerworth, R. "Online Recruitment Increases Exponentially." March 31, 2006. wiliam.com.au/wiliam-blog/online-recruitment-increases-exponentially (accessed February 2009).

Biz Report. "Toys Made in China Off Christmas Shopping Lists." *BizReport.com*, November 14, 2007. bizreport.com/2007/11/toys_made_in_china_off_christmas_shopping_lists.html (accessed February 2009).

Bloch, M., and A. Segev. "The Impact of Electronic Commerce on the Travel Industry." *Proceedings 30th Annual HICSS*, Maui, Hawaii, January 1997.

Borrell Associates. "2006 Update: Online Real Estate Advertising." *MarketResearch.com*, July 2006. marketresearch.com/product/display.asp?productid=1311602&g=1 (accessed February 2009).

Butcher, M. "WAYN Said to Be Close to Sale. The Price? $200m. The Buyer? AOL." *Tech Crunch*, January 16, 2008. uk.techcrunch.com/2008/01/16/wayn-said-to-be-close-to-sale-the-price-200m-the-buyer-aol (accessed February 2009).

Cash Edge. "Cash Edge Survey Confirms Consumer Demand for Value Added Online Banking Services." *News Blaze*, October 12, 2006. newsblaze.com/story/2006101206005100005.pz/topstory.html (accessed February 2009).

Caslon Analytics. "Caslon Analytics Profile: Adult Content Industries." *Caslon Analytics*, February 2008. caslon.com.au/xcontentprofile.htm (accessed February 2009).

Dahlberg, T., N. Mallat, J. Ondrus, and A. Zmijewska. "Past, Present and Future of Mobile Payments Research: A Literature Review." *Electronic Commerce Research and Applications* (Summer 2008).

Dignan, L. "Retail Stinks, but Amazon Doesn't; E-Tailer Delivers Strong Fourth Quarter." *ZDNet*, January 29, 2009. blogs.zdnet.com/BTL/?p=11928 (accessed February 2009).

Epps, S. R., H. H. Hartveldt, and B. McGowan. "How Social Computing Changes the Way You Sell Travel." *Forrester Research*, April 30, 2007. forrester.com/Research/Document/Excerpt/0,7211,42100,00.html (accessed February 2009).

Fisher, A. "30 Best Web Sites for Job Hunters." *Fortune Magazine*, May 9, 2008. money.cnn.com/2008/05/07/news/economy/best.websites.fortune/index.htm (accessed February 2009).

Forzley, M. "The Power of Pay." *Retail Merchandiser*, July/August 2007.

Grau, G. "U.S. Online Travel: Planning and Booking." *eMarketer*, August 2008. emarketer.com/Reports/All/Emarketer_2000502.aspx (accessed February 2009).

Ha, S., and L. Stoel. "Consumer E-Shopping Acceptance: Antecedents in a Technology Acceptance Model." *Journal of Business Research* (In press, 2009).

Hanks, J. "Internet Retailer 2007." *JeremyHanks.com*, June 6, 2007. jeremyhanks.com/2007/06/06/internet-retailer-2007 (accessed February 2009).

Hartveldt, H. H. "Travelers Embrace Social Computing Technologies." *Forrester Research Report*, October 23, 2006. forrester.com/Research/Document/Excerpt/0,7211,39928,00.html (accessed February 2009).

InformationWeek. "Marketcetera Platform, Open Source Software for Automated Stock Trading." April 21, 2008.

Internet Retailer. "Target Posts Largest July Traffic Gain Among Top 10 Shopping Sites." September 1, 2006. internetretailer.com/dailyNews.asp?id=19761 (accessed February 2009).

Internet Retailer. "45% of U.S. Adults Shop Online, but Security Concerns Hold Others Back." November 16, 2007a. internetretailer.com/internet/marketing-conference/72196-45-us-adults-shop-online-but-security-concerns-hold-others-back.html (accessed February 2009).

Internet Retailer. "Wal-Mart Moves Up in the Ranks of Shopping Destinations." February 23, 2007b. internetretailer.com/dailyNews.asp?id=21528 (accessed February 2009).

Internet Retailer. "Wal-Mart's New In-Store Pick-Up Service Might Not Be Fast, But It's Free." March 6, 2007c. internetretailer.com/dailyNews.asp?id=2164 (accessed February 2009).

JobCentral. "Welcome to JobCentral." February 2009. jobcentral.com/aboutus.asp (accessed February 2009).

Jupiter Market Research. "US Paid Content Forecast, 2007 to 2012." *Market Research*, January 29, 2008. marketresearch.com/product/display.asp?productid=1765727&g=1 (accessed February 2009).

Jupiter Research Corporation. "Online Dating in 2007." *Market Research*, February 2, 2007. marketresearch.com/product/display.asp?productid=1601597&SID=25013955-446132061-468369822&curr=USD&kw=Online%09dating&view=abs (accessed May 2009).

Keegan, V. "Zopa Shows Banks How to Do It Right." *The Guardian*, November 13, 2008. guardian.co.uk/technology/2008/nov/13/zopa-credit-crunch (accessed February 2009).

Kim, H. B., T. T. Kim, and S. W. Shin. "Modeling Roles of Subjective Norms and etrust in Customers' Acceptance of Airline B2C eCommerce Websites." *Tourism Management* (April 2009).

Knox, N. "It's Always 'OPEN HOUSE' as Real Estate Goes Online." *USA Today*, May 16, 2006.

Kuchment, A., and K. Springen. "The Tangled Web of Porn in the Office." *Newsweek*, November 29, 2008. newsweek.com/id/171279 (accessed February 2009).

Kwon, W. S., and S. J. Lennon. "What Induces Online Loyalty? Online Versus Offline Brand Images." *Journal of Business Research* (In Press, 2009).

Leggatt, H. "Half of Leisure Travelers Book Online." *BizReport*, October 17, 2007. bizreport.com/2007/10/half_of_leisure_travelers_book_online.html (accessed February 2009).

Maestri, N. "Walmart.com Offers 'Thousands' of Wiis from Monday." Reuters, December 7, 2008. reuters.com/article/technologyNews/idUSTRE4B608520081207 (accessed February 2009).

McDougall, P. "Web Lets Insurers Cut Costs, Improve Service." *InformationWeek*, September 17, 2007.

Mulpuru, S., C. Johnson, B. McGowan, and W. Scott. "U.S. eCommerce Forecast: 2008 to 2012." Forrester Research, January 18, 2008. forrester.com/Research/Document/Excerpt/0,7211,41592,00.html (accessed February 2009).

New York Times. "Real Estate Sales and Advertising Enter Cyberspace." December 17, 2007.

Realtors Magazine. "Market Research by Industry." *Realtors Magazine*, 2009. realtor.org/wps/wcm/connect/752953004bbaa1ca950bdff09f174b6c/Research+Book.pdf?MOD=AJPERES&CACHEID=752953004bbaa1ca950bdff09f174b6c (accessed May 2009).

Reuters. "Amazon Net Profit Doubles, Helped by Asset Sale." July 23, 2008. reuters.com/article/pressReleasesMolt/idUSWNAB207520080723 (accessed February 2009).

Rose, B. "More Employers Use Personality Tests to Screen Job Candidates." *Chicago Tribune,* January 14, 2008. archives.chicagotribune.com/2008/jan/14/business/chi-mon_space_0114jan14 (accessed February 2009).

Smith, A. "Online Payment Service Providers and Customer Relationship Management." *International Journal of Electronic Finance* (August 2008).

Soopramanien, D. G. R., and A. Robertson. "Adoption and Usage of Online Shopping: An Empirical Analysis of the Characteristics of 'Buyers,' 'Browsers,' and 'Non-Internet' Shoppers." *Journal of Retailing and Consumer Services* (January 2007).

Strategy Analytics. "Global Online Games Market Expected to Triple in Five Years." September 13, 2007. wi-fitechnology.com/displayarticle3007.html (accessed February 2009).

Van der Heijden, J. G. M. "The Changing Value of Travel Agents in Tourism Networks: Towards a Network Design Perspective." In Stefan Klein, et al. (Eds.), *Information and Communication Technologies in Tourism.* New York: Springer-Verlag, 1996.

Vermeulen, I. E., and D. Seegersa. "Tried and Tested: The Impact of Online Hotel Reviews on Consumer Consideration." *Tourism Management* (February 2009).

Wang, F. "E-Shoppers' Perception of Web-Based Decision Aid." In M. Khosrow-Pour (Ed.). *Encyclopedia of E-Commerce, E-Government, and Mobile Commerce.* Hershey, PA: Idea Group Reference, 2006.

Weiner, M. (2006) "The 5-Day Car: Ordered on Monday—Delivered on Friday." Ilipt.org, February 28, 2006. fraunhofer.de/fhg/Images/magazine_2-2006_28_tcm6-64704.pdf (accessed February 2009).

Xu, M. X., S. Wilkes, and M. H. Shah. "E-Banking Application and Issues in Abbey National PLC." In M. Khosrow-Pour, (Ed.). *Encyclopedia of E-Commerce, E-Government, and Mobile Commerce.* Hershey, PA: Idea Group Reference, 2006.

CONSUMER BEHAVIOR, INTERNET MARKETING, AND ADVERTISING

Learning Objectives

Upon completion of this chapter, you will be able to:

1. Describe the factors that influence consumer behavior online.

2. Understand the decision-making process of consumer purchasing online.

3. Describe segmentation and how companies are building one-to-one relationships with customers.

4. Explain how consumer behavior can be analyzed for creating personalized services.

5. Discuss the issues of e-loyalty and e-trust in electronic commerce (EC).

6. Describe consumer market research in EC.

7. Describe the objectives of Web advertising and its characteristics.

8. Describe the major advertising methods used on the Web.

9. Describe various online advertising strategies and types of promotions.

10. Describe permission marketing, ad management, localization, and other advertising-related issues.

11. Relate Web 2.0 and social networks to Internet market research and advertising.

Content

NETFLIX INCREASES SALES USING DVD RECOMMENDATIONS AND ADVERTISEMENTS

Netflix (*netflix.com*) is the world's largest online movie rental subscription company, offering 8.4 million members access to more than 100,000 DVD titles plus a growing library of more than 12,000 full-length movies and television episodes that are available for instant viewing on members' PCs in 2008. The company's appeal and success are built on providing the most comprehensive selection of DVDs, an easy way to choose movies, and fast, free delivery. Netflix distributes 2 million DVDs each day.

The Problem

Because of the large number of titles available on DVD, customers often had difficulty determining which ones they wanted to watch. In many cases, they chose the most recent and popular titles, which meant that Netflix had to maintain more and more copies of the same title. In addition, some unpopular titles were not renting well, even though they matched certain customers' preferences. For Netflix, matching titles with customers yet maintaining the right level of inventory is critical.

A second major problem facing Netflix is the competitive nature of the movie rental business. Netflix competes against Blockbuster and other rental companies, as well as against companies offering downloads of movies and videos. In 2008, Blockbuster started offering online movie rental subscription, including the most recent movies, increasing the direct competition with Netflix.

The Solution

Netflix reacted successfully to the first problem by offering a recommendation service called *CineMatch*. This software agent uses data mining tools to sift through a database of more than 2 billion film ratings, as well as through customers' rental histories. Using proprietary formulas, CineMatch recommends rentals to individuals. It is a personalized service, similar to the one offered by *amazon.com* that recommends books to customers. The recommendation is accomplished by comparing an individual's likes, dislikes, and preferences against people with similar tastes by using a variant of collaborative filtering (described later in this chapter). With the recommendation system, Netflix tells subscribers which DVDs they probably would like. CineMatch is like the geeky clerk at a small movie store who sets aside titles he knows you will like and tells you to return them whenever.

Netflix subscribers can also invite one another to become "friends" and make movie recommendations to each other, peek at one another's rental lists, and see how other subscribers have rated movies using a social network called *FriendsSM*. All these personalized functions make the online rental store very customer friendly.

To improve CineMatch's accuracy, in October 2006 Netflix began a contest offering $1 million to the first person or team to write a program that would increase the prediction accuracy of CineMatch by 10 percent. The company understands that this will take quite some time; therefore, it is offering a $50,000 Progress Prize each year the contest runs. This prize goes to the team whose solution shows the most improvement over the previous year's accuracy bar (see *netflixprize.com*).

Netflix is advertising extensively on the Web using several advertising techniques, especially placing static banner ads on reputed sites, permission e-mail, blogs, social networks, classifieds, Really Simple Syndication (RSS), and more.

The Results

As a result of implementing its CineMatch system, Netflix has seen very fast growth in sales and membership. The benefits of CineMatch include the following:

- **Effective recommendations:** Approximately 60 percent of Netflix members select their movies based on movie recommendations tailored to their individual tastes.
- **Customer satisfaction:** More than 90 percent of Netflix members say they are so satisfied with the Netflix service that they recommend the service to family members and friends.
- **Inventory:** Netflix has more than 100,000 titles and more than 55 million DVDs. Every 3 months, Netflix members rent more than 95 percent of the 100,000 titles in the Netflix library. On any given day, more than 46,000 of the 100,000 titles available at Netflix are in distribution. (Netflix

provides more than 9.4 million subscribers with access to more than 100,000 DVD titles plus a growing library of more than 12,000 choices that can be watched on their PCs. Netflix ships more than 2 million DVDs on a typical day and subscribers rate an average of 2 million movies a day).

- **Ratings:** Netflix has more than 2 billion movie ratings from members. The average member has rated about 200 movies.
- **Rental habits:** Netflix members say they rent twice as many movies per month than they did prior to joining the service. Netflix members add 2 million movies to their queues (movies they want to get) every day.
- **Volume:** If you stacked every movie Netflix ships (on average, 2 million DVDs per day) in a single pile, the stack would be taller than Mt. Everest within a week.
- **Environment:** If Netflix members drove to and from a rental store, they would consume 800,000 gallons

of gasoline and release more than 2.2 million tons of carbon dioxide emissions annually.

The domain Netflix.com attracted about 194 million visitors in 2008, according to a Compete.com survey. This is about five times the number of visitors to Blockbuster.com (*Compete.com* 2009).

CineMatch has become the company's core competence. Netflix's future relies heavily on CineMatch's making accurate recommendations and subscribers' accepting them, which is why the company strives to increase its accuracy.

Sources: Compiled from Flynn (2006), *wikipedia.org* (accessed March 2009), and *netflix.com* (accessed March 2009).

WHAT WE CAN LEARN . . .

This case illustrates that the use of online marketing is quite different from traditional marketing. In particular, Netflix uses intelligent agents in movie recommendation and gains a substantial advantage over its competitors. Netflix's CineMatch is designed to increase sales, customer satisfaction, and loyalty. The case also identifies some of the most popular advertising methods used in EC. These topics are the main subjects of Chapter 4.

4.1   LEARNING ABOUT CONSUMER BEHAVIOR ONLINE

Companies are operating in an increasingly competitive environment. Therefore, they treat customers like royalty as they try to lure them to buy their goods and services. Finding and retaining customers is a major critical success factor for most businesses, both offline and online. One of the keys to building effective customer relationships is an understanding of consumer behavior online. For an overview, see Markellou et al. (2006).

A MODEL OF CONSUMER BEHAVIOR ONLINE

For decades, market researchers have tried to understand consumer behavior, and have summarized their findings in various models. The purpose of a consumer behavior model is to help vendors understand how a consumer makes a purchasing decision. If a firm understands the decision process, it may be able to influence the buyer's decision, for example, through advertising or special promotions.

Before examining the consumer behavior model's variables, let's examine who the EC consumers are. Online consumers can be divided into two types: individual consumers (who get much of the media attention) and organizational buyers, who do most of the actual shopping in cyberspace in terms of dollar volume of sales. Organizational buyers include governments, private corporations, resellers, and public organizations. Purchases by organizational buyers are generally used to create the new major portion of our model by adding value to material or products. Also, organizational buyers may purchase products for resale without any further modifications. We will discuss organizational purchasing in detail in Chapter 5 (e-procurement) and focus on the individual consumer in this chapter.

The purpose of a consumer behavior model is to show factors that affect consumer behavior. Exhibit 4.1 shows the basic factors of a consumer behavior model. The model is composed of two major parts: influential factors and the consumer decision process. Influential factors are those that may affect consumers' intention to buy and their behavior, as shown in the center of the diagram.

- **Influential factors:** Five dimensions are considered to affect consumer behavior. They are consumer characteristics, environmental characteristics, merchant and intermediary characteristics (which are at the top of the diagram and are considered uncontrollable from the seller's point of view), product/service characteristics (which include market stimuli), and EC systems. The last two are mostly controlled by the sellers. Exhibit 4.1 identifies some of the variables in each influential dimension.

- **The attitude-behavior process:** This is shown in the center of the exhibit and is influenced by the five factors just discussed. This process starts with a positive attitude (intention to buy) and ends with the buyers' decisions to purchase and/or repurchase (dependent variables).

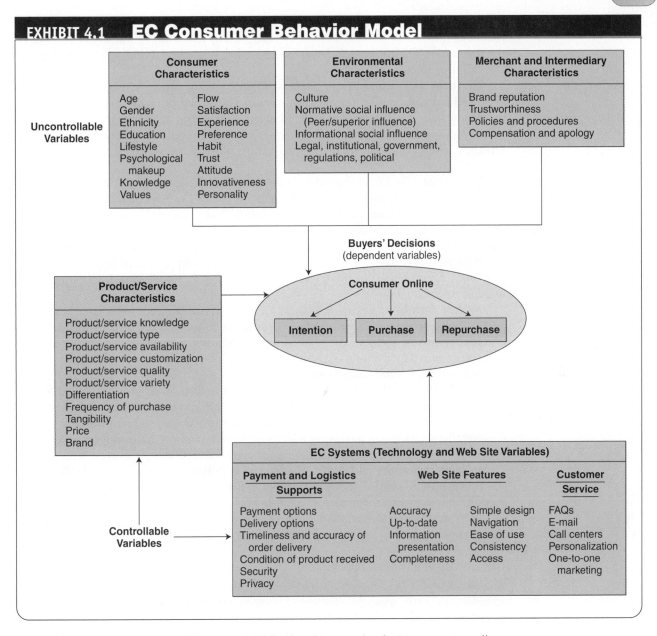

EXHIBIT 4.1   EC Consumer Behavior Model

This chapter examines the following model-related issues: the decision process, seller-customer-relationship building, and customer service.

Major Influential Factors

These are grouped as follows:

Personal Characteristics. Personal characteristics, which are shown in the top-left portion of Exhibit 4.1, refer to *demographic* factors, individual *preferences*, and *behavioral* characteristics. Several Web sites provide information on customer buying habits online (e.g., emarketer.com, clickz.com, and comscore.com). The major demographics that such sites track are gender, age, marital status, educational level, ethnicity, occupation, and household income, which can be correlated with Internet usage and EC data. A survey on the trend of global Internet shopping (Crampton 2005) revealed that the gender of online shoppers is roughly balanced. However, when it comes to certain products and services, the differences are significant. In some countries including China, Sweden, and Austria, more women than men are making their purchases online.

Psychological variables such as personality and lifestyle characteristics are studied by marketers. These variables are briefly mentioned in several places throughout the text. The reader who is interested in the impact of lifestyle differences on online shopping should see Wang et al. (2006).

Product/Service Factors. The second group of factors is related to the product/service itself. Whether a consumer decides to buy is affected by the nature of the product/service in the transaction. These may include the price, quality, design, brand, and other related attributes of the product.

Merchant and Intermediary Factors. Online transactions may also be affected by the merchant that handles the product/service. This group of factors includes merchant reputation, size of transaction, trust in the merchant, and so on. For example, people feel more secure when they purchase from Amazon.com (due to its reputation) than from a no-name seller. Other factors such as marketing strategy and advertising can also play a major role.

EC Systems. The EC platform for online transactions (e.g., security protection, payment mechanism, and so forth) offered by the merchant may also have effects. Liang and Lai (2002) reported that consumers are more likely to buy from well-designed e-tailers. EC design factors can be divided into motivational and hygiene factors. Motivational factors were found to be more important than hygiene factors in attracting online customers.

Motivational factors. Motivational factors are the functions available on the Web site to provide direct support in the transactional process (e.g., search engine, shopping carts, multiple payment methods).

Hygiene factors. Hygiene factors are functions available on the Web site whose main purpose is to prevent possible trouble in the process (e.g., security and product tracking).

Environmental Factors. The environment in which a transaction occurs may affect a consumer's purchase decision. As shown in Exhibit 4.1, environmental variables can be grouped into the following categories:

Social variables. People are influenced by family members, friends, coworkers, and "what's in fashion this year." Therefore, social variables (such as customer endorsement, word-of-mouth) play an important role in EC. Of special importance in EC are Internet communities (see Chapter 9) and discussion groups, in which people communicate via chat rooms, electronic bulletin boards, and newsgroups. These topics are discussed in various places in the text.

Cultural/community variables. It makes a big difference in what people buy if a consumer lives near Silicon Valley in California or in the mountains in Nepal. Chinese shoppers may differ from French shoppers, and rural shoppers may differ from urban ones.

Other environmental variables. These include aspects such as available information, government regulations, legal constraints, and situational factors.

The Behavior Process Model

Several influential factors affect buying decisions. A classic model for describing advertising effectiveness is the Attention-Interest-Desire-Action (AIDA) model. This hierarchical model, developed by E. St. Elmo Lewis in 1898, was used to describe the process consumers employ when making decisions based on an advertising message. It argues that consumer processing of an advertising message includes the following four stages:

1. A–Attention (Awareness): The first step is to attract the attention of the customer.
2. I–Interest: A message may raise customer interest by demonstrating features, advantages, and benefits.
3. D–Desire: Customers may be convinced that they want and desire the product or service and that it will satisfy their needs.
4. A–Action: Finally, the consumer will take action toward purchasing.

Now, some researchers also add another letter to form AIDA(S), where:

5. S–Satisfaction: Customer satisfaction will generate higher loyalty and lead to repurchase after using a product/service.

Another well-known model for interpreting the internal psychological process of the consumer buying decision is the *attitude-behavior model,* which includes three major constructs: *attitude, intention,* and *behavior.* A favorable attitude would lead to a stronger buying intention, which in turn would result in the actual buying behavior. Previous research has shown that the linkages among the three constructs are quite strong. For example, Ranganathan and Jha (2007) found that past online shopping experiences have the strongest associations with online purchase intention, followed by customer concerns, Web site quality, and computer self efficacy. Therefore, developing a positive consumer attitude plays a central role in the final purchase decision.

Section 4.1 ▶ REVIEW QUESTIONS

1. Describe the major components and structure of the consumer online purchasing behavior model.
2. List some major personal characteristics that influence consumer behavior.
3. List the major environmental variables of the purchasing environment.
4. List and describe five major merchant-related variables.
5. Explain the major stages in the AIDA model.
6. Describe the relationships among attitude, intention, and actual behavior in the behavior process model.

4.2 THE CONSUMER PURCHASING DECISION-MAKING PROCESS

In Section 4.1 we concentrated on consumer behavior online and described a process that includes a buying decision. Here we explore this decision.

A GENERIC PURCHASING-DECISION MODEL

From the consumer's perspective, a general purchasing-decision model consists of five major phases. In each phase, we can distinguish several activities and, in some, one or more decisions. The five phases are (1) need identification, (2) information search, (3) evaluation of alternatives, (4) purchase and delivery, and (5) postpurchase behavior. Although these phases offer a general guide to the consumer decision-making process, one should not assume that every consumer's decision-making process will necessarily proceed in this order. In fact, some consumers may proceed to a point and then revert to a previous phase, or they may skip a phase altogether. The phases are discussed more completely next.

1. **Need identification.** The first phase occurs when a consumer is faced with an imbalance between the actual and the desired states of a need. A marketer's goal is to get the consumer to recognize such imbalance and then convince the consumer that the product or service the seller offers will fill this gap.

2. **Information search.** After identifying the need, the consumer searches for information on the various alternatives available to satisfy the need. Here, we differentiate between two decisions: what product to buy (**product brokering**) and from whom to buy it (**merchant brokering**). These two decisions can be separate or combined. In the consumer's search for information, catalogs, advertising, promotions, and reference groups influence decision making. During this phase, online product search and comparison engines, such as shopping.com, buyersindex.com, and mysimon.com, can be very helpful.

3. **Alternative evaluation.** The consumer's information search will eventually generate a smaller set of preferred alternatives. From this set, the would-be buyer will further evaluate the alternatives and, if possible, negotiate terms. In this phase, a consumer will use the collected information to develop a set of criteria. These criteria will help the consumer evaluate and compare alternatives.

4. **Purchase and delivery.** After evaluating the alternatives, the consumer will make the purchasing decision, arrange payment and delivery, purchase warranties, and so on.

5. **Postpurchase behavior.** The final phase is a postpurchase phase, which consists of customer service and evaluation of the usefulness of the product (e.g., "This product is really great!" or "We really received good service when we had problems."). If the customer is satisfied with the product and services, loyalty will increase and repeat purchases will occur afterward.

product brokering
Deciding what product to buy.

merchant brokering
Deciding from whom (from what merchant) to buy a product.

Several other purchasing-decision models have been proposed. Of special interest is a model proposed by Chaudhury et al. (2001). In this model, the buying decision is influenced by how much time is available and the locale (space) where the purchasing is done. In this context, space is the equivalent to shelf space in a physical store—namely, how well a product is presented online and where it is presented on the Web site. Space also can refer to whether products are sold via wireline or wireless devices. The model distinguishes four scenarios: "less time and more space," "more time and less space," "more time and more space," and "less time and less space." For example, the space on a small banner ad is more limited than the space on a large pop-up ad. For each scenario, the vendors can develop different Web sites.

CUSTOMER DECISION SUPPORT IN WEB PURCHASING

The preceding generic purchasing-decision model was widely used in research on consumer-based EC. In the Web-based environment, decision support is available in each phase. The framework shown in Exhibit 4.2 shows that each of the phases of the purchasing model can be supported by both consumer decision support system (CDSS) facilities and Internet and Web facilities. The CDSS facilities support the specific decisions in the process. Generic EC technologies provide the necessary mechanisms as well as enhance communication and collaboration. Specific implementation of this framework and explanations of some of the terms are provided throughout this chapter and the entire text.

The planner of B2C marketing needs to consider the Web purchasing models in order to better influence the customer's decision-making process (e.g., by effective one-to-one advertising and marketing).

Online File W4.1 shows a model for a Web site that supports buyer decision making and searching. This model revises the generic model by describing the purchasing framework. The model is divided into three parts. The first includes three stages of buyer behavior (see top of exhibit): identify and manage buying criteria, search for products and merchants, and compare alternatives. Below these activities are seven boxes with decision support system (DSS) design options (such as product representation), the options to support searching, and the options to compare alternatives.

EXHIBIT 4.2 Purchase Decision-Making Process and Support System

Steps in the Decision-Making Process	CDSS Support Facilities	Generic Internet and Web Support Facilities
Need recognition	Agents and event notification	Banner advertising on Web sites URL on physical material Discussions in newsgroups
Information search	Virtual catalogs Structured interaction and question/answer sessions Links to (and guidance on) external sources	Web directories and classifiers Internal search on Web site External search engines Focused directories and information brokers
Evaluation, negotiation, selection	FAQs and other summaries Samples and trials Models that evaluate consumer behavior Pointers to and information about existing customers	Discussions in newsgroups Cross-site comparisons Generic models
Purchase, payment, and delivery	Ordering of product or service Arrangement of delivery	Electronic cash and virtual banking Logistics providers and package tracking
After-purchase service and evaluation	Customer support via e-mail and newsgroups	Discussions in newsgroups

Source: O'Keefe and McEachern (1998).

The second part of the model (on the right) has three boxes: price, shipping, and finance. These become relevant when alternatives are compared. The third part, at the bottom of the exhibit, is composed of three boxes. The model demonstrates the flow of data and the decisions that support EC.

PLAYERS IN THE CONSUMER DECISION PROCESS

Several different players may play roles in various phases of the consumer decision process. The following are five major roles:

- **Initiator.** The person who first suggests or thinks of the idea of buying a particular product or service.
- **Influencer.** A person whose advice or view carries some weight in making a final purchasing decision.
- **Decider.** The person who ultimately makes a buying decision or any part of it—whether to buy, what to buy, how to buy, or where to buy.
- **Buyer.** The person who makes an actual purchase.
- **User.** The person who consumes or uses a product or service.

A single person may play all the roles if the product or service is for personal use. In this case, the marketer needs to understand and target that individual. In many situations, however, different people may play different roles, For example, a newly graduated engineer proposed to buy a car for his mother, which was followed by suggestions from his father and friends. Finally, he followed his father's suggestion to buy the car. When more than one individual comes into play, it becomes more difficult to properly target advertising and marketing. Different marketing efforts may be designed to target people playing different roles.

Section 4.2 ▶ REVIEW QUESTIONS

1. List the five phases of the generic purchasing-decision model.
2. Use an example to explain the five phases in the generic purchasing-decision model.
3. Describe the supporting functions available in Web-based purchasing.
4. Describe the major players in a buy decision.

4.3 MASS MARKETING, MARKET SEGMENTATION, AND ONE-TO-ONE MARKETING

One of the greatest benefits of EC is its ability to match products (services) with individual consumers. Such a match is a part of *one-to-one marketing*, which treats each customer in a unique way to fit marketing and advertising with the customer's profile and needs. Let's first see how the one-to-one approach evolved from the traditional marketing approaches.

FROM MASS MARKETING TO ONE-TO-ONE MARKETING

Three basic approaches are used in marketing and advertising: mass marketing, market segmentation, and one-to-one marketing.

Mass Marketing and Advertising

Marketing efforts traditionally were targeted to everyone (the "masses"). For example, using a newspaper or TV ad usually means one-way interpersonal communication to who sees it. Such an effort may be effective for brand recognition or for introducing a new product or service. It can be conducted on the Internet as well.

In 2005, Ford Motor Company unveiled a roadblock approach on the Internet to promote its F-150 truck. (A "roadblock" refers to running a commercial on all major TV channels at exactly the same time, so viewers cannot switch channels to escape the commercial.) On the day of the launch, Ford placed static banner ads for 24 hours on the three leading Internet portals—AOL, MSN, and Yahoo!—introducing a 3-month campaign. Some 50 million Web surfers saw Ford's banner. Millions of them clicked on the banner, pouring onto Ford's Web site at a rate that reached 3,000 per second. Ford claimed that the traffic led to a 6 percent increase in sales over the first 3 months of the campaign.

Market Segmentation

market segmentation
The process of dividing a consumer market into logical groups for conducting marketing research and analyzing personal information.

Market segmentation refers to the practice of promoting a product or service to a subset of customers or prospects. One advantage of market segmentation is that advertising and marketing efforts can match segments better than the "mass," providing a better response rate. Also, the expense of reaching the segments may be lower, and marketing efforts can be faster (e.g., e-mails are sent to fewer people, or banner ads are placed on fewer Web sites). The Internet enables more effective market segmentation (see Section 4.4), but it enables an even better approach, in that of close relationship marketing, of one-to-one.

Statistical and data mining methods are often used to identify valuable segments for promotion or advertising. Modern companies assign a variety of segments to their customers, often dynamically defining segments and temporarily regrouping customers for specific campaigns. By segmenting customers, companies could begin more specialized communications about their products. Much of this relies on the company's understanding its business strategies to the extent that they know their most desirable segments. For instance, if a bank has organized its Web site on deriving most of its profits from fee-income products offered in its investment services line of business, customers for this bank will likely have different preferences and characteristics from those banks offering only savings accounts. Segmenting customers based on their preferred line of business or desired product features can reveal interesting facts about their different preferences and behaviors.

A simple way to do segmentation online is to go to a specialized Web site or portal and advertise to its visitors. For example, by going to ivillage.com, you reach mostly women. Advertising in Internet communities and social networks usually provides you with market segmentation. Increasingly, advertising is being placed on social networking sites (such as MySpace or Facebook). Note that U.S. spending on social network advertising is expected to rise to $2.15 billion in 2010 (*eMarketer* 2006). Some Weblogs that focus on specific niches (e.g., paidcontent.org, fark.com) have received a generous amount of dollars from advertisers.

Relationship and One-to-One Marketing (Relationship Marketing)

As consumers began purchasing online, more data became available about them. Data analysts began associating products with the customers who were buying them. And it was through these analytic activities that companies began to understand that their customer data could be valuable for one-to-one marketing.

Although segmentation can focus on a group of customers, it may not be good enough because most of the competitors adopt similar strategies. It may be advisable, therefore, to shift the target for marketing from a group of consumers to each individual. Instead of selling a single product to as many customers as possible, marketers are trying to sell as many products as possible to one customer—over a long period of time. To do this, marketers need to concentrate on building unique relationships with individual customers on a one-to-one basis. **One-to-one marketing**, also referred to as **relationship marketing**, is a way for marketing departments to get to know their customers more intimately by understanding their preferences and then providing personalized advertisement and marketing, thus increasing the odds of retaining customers.

one-to-one marketing (relationship marketing)
Marketing that treats each customer in a unique way.

One-to-one means not only communicating with customers as individuals, but possibly developing custom products and tailored messages based on the customer's explicit and implicit needs as well. It relies on a two-way dialog between a company and its customers in order to foster a true relationship, and allows customers to express desires that the company can help fulfill. The major characteristics of one-to-one marketing as compared to mass marketing and market segmentation are illustrated in Exhibit 4.3.

HOW ONE-TO-ONE RELATIONSHIPS ARE PRACTICED

Although some companies have had one-to-one marketing programs for years, it may be much more beneficial to institute a corporate-wide policy of building one-to-one

EXHIBIT 4.3 From Mass Marketing to Segmentation to One-to-One

Factor	Mass Marketing	Market Segmentation	Relationship Marketing (One-to-One)
Interactions	Usually none, or one-way	Usually none, or with a sample	Active, two-way
Focus	Product	Group (segment)	Customer-focused (one)
Recipient	Anonymous	Segment profiles	Individuals
Campaigns	Few	More	Many
Reach	Wide	Smaller	One at a time
Market Research	Macro in nature	Based on segment analysis or demographics	Based on detailed customer behaviors and profiles

relationships around the Web. This can be done in several ways. For example, Gartner, Inc., an IT consulting company, proposed a new marketing cycle of relationship building (illustrated in Exhibit 4.4). It views relationships as a two-way street: The process can start at any point in the cycle. Usually, though, it starts with "Customer receives marketing exposure" (at the top of the exhibit). The customer then decides on how to respond to the marketing exposure (e.g., whether to buy the product online or offline; if online, whether to buy as individual or to use group purchasing). When a sale is made, customer information is collected (lower-right corner) and then placed in a database. Then, a customer's profile is developed, and the so-called four P's of marketing (Product, Place, Price, and Promotion) are planned based on the profile, on a one-to-one basis. For example, appropriate advertisements are prepared that will hopefully lead to another purchase

EXHIBIT 4.4 The New Marketing Model

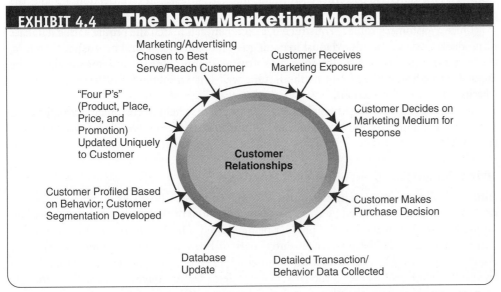

Source: Nelson, S. "The New Marketing Relationship Model," Gartner, Inc., July 22, 1996. © Gartner, Inc. Used with permission.

by the customer. Once a purchase is made, the detailed transaction is added to the database and the cycle is repeated. All of this can, and should, be done in the Web environment.

One of the benefits of doing business over the Internet is that it enables companies to better communicate with customers and better understand customers' needs and buying habits. These improvements, in turn, enable companies to enhance and frequently personalize their future marketing efforts. For example, Amazon.com can e-mail customers announcements of the availability of books in their areas of interest as soon as they are published; Expedia.com will ask consumers where they are likely to fly to and then e-mail them information about special discounts to their desired destination. Details on these key concepts that are part of *personalization* are discussed in Section 4.4.

Section 4.3 ▶ REVIEW QUESTIONS

1. Define and describe mass marketing.
2. Define market segmentation. How is segmentation done?
3. Define one-to-one marketing. What are its advantages?
4. Describe the marketing relationship process.
5. How is the knowledge of a customer profile used by the advertisers?

4.4 PERSONALIZATION AND BEHAVIORAL MARKETING

Internet marketing facilitates the use of market segmentation and one-to-one marketing. Here we address three key issues related to one-to-one marketing: personalization, behavioral targeting, and collaborative filtering.

PERSONALIZATION IN E-COMMERCE

personalization

The matching of services, products, and advertising content with individual consumers and their preferences.

user profile

The requirements, preferences, behaviors, and demographic traits of a particular customer.

cookie

A data file that is placed on a user's hard drive by a remote Web server, frequently without disclosure or the user's consent, which collects information about the user's activities at a site.

Personalization refers to the matching of services and advertising content to individuals and their preferences. The matching process is based on what a company knows about the individual user. This knowledge is usually referred to as a *user profile*. The **user profile** defines customer preferences, behaviors, and demographics. It can be generated by getting information directly from the user; observing what people are doing online through the use of tools such as a **cookie** (a data file that is placed on a user's hard drive by a remote Web server, frequently without disclosure or the user's consent, that collects information about the user's activities at a site; see cookiecentral.com and Insights and Additions 4.1); building profiles from previous purchase patterns; performing marketing research (see Section 4.5 and the Netflix case); and making inferences (see the Netflix case).

Once a customer profile is constructed, a company can match the profile with a database of products, services, or ads. Manual matching is time-consuming and expensive; therefore, the matching process is usually done by software agents. One-to-one matching can be applied through several different methods. One well-known method is *collaborative filtering* (discussed later in this section).

Many vendors provide personalization techniques that help in customer acquisition and retention. Examples of such vendors are Omniture (omniture.com) and Magnify 360 (magnify360.com).

Using Personalized Techniques to Increase Sales

Amazon makes recommendations on the basis of a customer's browsing and buying history, on items viewed or purchased by customers who have bought the product being viewed, and on items that seem related to the product being viewed. On Amazon, reviews, recommendations, and rankings become an essential part of browsing and shopping experiences. Another company, MotherNature.com (mothernature.com) is using data and text mining to analyze each site visit based on the customer's preferences and buying habits. They are able to track everything from the success rate of online promotions to trends that can be used in site personalization.

Insights and Additions 4.1 Cookies in E-Commerce

The use of cookies is a well-known method that enables the identification of customers' future visits on the same computers (see *en.wikipedia.org/wiki/cookies* and *pcworld. com/resource/browse/0,cat,1384,sortIdx,1,00.asp* for more on cookies).

Are cookies bad or good? The answer is "both." When users revisit Amazon.com or other sites, customers are greeted by their first name. How does Amazon.com know a user's identity? Through the use of cookies! Vendors can provide consumers with considerable personalized information if they use cookies that signal a consumer's return to a site. A variation of cookies is known as *e-sugging* ("SUG-ing," from "selling under the guise of research"). For example, consumers who visit travel sites may get more and more unsolicited travel-related e-mails and pop-up ads.

Cookies can provide marketers with a wealth of information, which then can be used to target ads to them.

Thus, marketers get higher rates of "click-throughs," and customers can view the most relevant information. Cookies can also prevent repetitive ads because vendors can arrange for a consumer not to see the same ad twice. Finally, advanced data mining companies, such as NCR and Sift, can analyze information in cookie files so companies can better meet the customers' needs.

However, some people object to cookies because they do not like the idea that "someone" is watching their activity on the Internet. Users who do not like cookies can disable them. However, some consumers may want to keep the friendly cookies. For example, many sites recognize a person as a subscriber so that they do not need to register. Internet Explorer (IE) gives users control over third-party cookies. (Go to "Internet Options" under "Tools" and select "Private tab," click "Advanced," and put a check mark next to "Override automatic cookie handling." Then, direct IE to accept cookies.)

BEHAVIORAL MARKETING AND COLLABORATIVE FILTERING

One of the most popular ways of matching customers with ads is by using technologies based on customer behavior on the Web. We discuss here the essentials of this approach, which is known as *behavioral targeting*, and provide brief information on one method for doing it.

Behavioral Targeting

Behavioral targeting uses information collected about an individual's Web-browsing behavior, such as the pages they have visited or the searches they have made, in order to select an advertisement to display to that individual. Many vendors believe that this can help them deliver online advertisements to the users who then would be influenced by the ads. Behavioral targeting can be used on its own or in conjunction with other forms of targeting, such as using factors like location of the customers, demographics, or the surrounding content. Representative vendors of behavioral targeting tools are predictad.com, adlink.com, adaptlogic.com, boomerang.com, criteo.com, and valueclick.com. For more information see en.wikipedia.org/wiki/behavioral_targeting.

behavioral targeting
Targeting that uses information collected about an individual's Web-browsing behavior, such as the pages they have visited or the searches they have made, to select an advertisement to display to that individual.

Collaborative Filtering

It would be useful if the company could predict what products or services are of interest to a customer without asking the customer directly. **Collaborative filtering** is a method that attempts to do just that; it uses the preferences and activities of customers with similar characteristics to build user profiles of new customers and make product recommendations to them. Many personalization systems are based on collaborative filtering (e.g., backflip.com and choicestream.com). The statement "Those who bought this item also bought the following items:" is a typical statement generated by collaborative filtering, which intends to persuade a consumer by pointing to preferences of other consumers.

collaborative filtering
A market research and personalization method that uses customer data to predict, based on formulas derived from behavioral sciences, what other products or services a customer may enjoy; predictions can be extended to other customers with similar profiles.

Other Methods

In addition to collaborative filtering, other methods for identifying users' profiles are:

▶ **Rule-based filtering.** A company asks consumers a series of yes/no or multiple-choice questions. The questions may range from personal information to the specific information the customer is looking for on a specific Web site. Certain behavioral patterns are predicted using the collected information. From this information, the collaborative filtering system derives behavioral and demographic rules such as, "If customer age is greater than 35, and customer income is above $100,000, show Jeep Cherokee ad. Otherwise, show Mazda Protégé ad."

▶ **Content-based filtering.** With this technique, vendors identify customer preference by the attributes of the product(s) they intend to buy. Based on user preferences, the vendor's system will recommend additional products with similar attributes to the user. For instance, the system may recommend a text-mining book to customers who have shown interests in data mining, or recommend more action movies after a consumer rented one.

▶ **Activity-based filtering.** Filtering rules can also be built by watching the user's activities on the Web.

For more about personalization and filtering, see en.wikipedia.org/wiki/collaborative_filtering.

Legal and Ethical Issues in Collaborative Filtering

Information often is collected from users without their knowledge or permission. This raises several ethical and legal questions, including invasion of privacy issues. Several vendors offer permission-based personalization tools. With these, companies request the customer's permission to receive questionnaires and ads. (See Chapter 16 for more on privacy issues, and Section 4.10 for information about permission marketing.)

Section 4.4 ▶ REVIEW QUESTIONS

1. Define personalization.
2. List some benefits of personalization.
3. Define behavioral targeting.
4. Define collaborative filtering.

4.5 LOYALTY, SATISFACTION, AND TRUST IN EC

Good online marketing can generate positive effects, which are generally observed as customer satisfaction, loyalty, and trust in the merchant.

CUSTOMER LOYALTY

One of the major objectives of one-to-one marketing is to increase customer loyalty (recall the Netflix case). *Customer loyalty* refers to a deep commitment to rebuy or repatronize a preferred product/service continually in the future, thereby causing repetitive same-brand or same brand-set purchasing, despite situational influences and marketing efforts having the potential to cause switching behavior. Customer acquisition and retention is a critical success factor in e-tailing. The expense of acquiring a new customer can be more than $100; even for Amazon.com, which has a huge reach, it is more than $15. In contrast, the cost of maintaining an existing customer at Amazon.com is $2 to $4.

Attracting and retaining loyal customers remains the most important issue for any selling company, including e-tailers. Increased customer loyalty can bring cost savings to a company in various ways: lower marketing and advertising costs, lower transaction costs, lower customer turnover expenses, lower failure costs such as warranty claims, and so on. Customer loyalty also strengthens a company's market position because loyal customers are kept away from the competition. In addition, customer loyalty can lead to high resistance to competitors, a decrease in price sensitivity, and an increase in favorable word-of-mouth.

Loyalty programs were introduced more than 100 years ago and are widely used among airlines, retailers, hotel chains, casinos, car rentals, restaurants, and credit card companies. But now, loyalty programs have been computerized and expanded to all kinds of businesses. For example, Octopus Hong Kong (octopuscards.com), a stored-value card operator, launched a reward program for consumers aimed at increasing card usage across Hong Kong. Reward points are gained by purchasing at a number of leading merchants across the territory, including

Wellcome, Watsons, UA Cinemas, and McDonald's. Each Octopus card can store up to 1,000 rewards points, which can be redeemed on the next purchase. FANCL (fancl.com), a Japanese cosmetics and health-care company, offers the "FANCL point program" where consumers earn FANCL points that are saved for gift redemption.

However, the introduction of Internet technologies and social networking has the potential to undermine brands and discourage customer loyalty. The customers' ability to shop, compare, get quick advice from friends, and switch to different vendors becomes easier, faster, and less expensive given the aid of search engines and other technologies. Furthermore, customers are less loyal to the brand because of the lower switching costs for them to take advantage of special online offers and promotions, as well as to try new things.

It is interesting to note that companies have found that loyal customers end up buying more when they have an optional Web site from which to shop. For example, W. W. Grainger, a large industrial-supply company, found that loyal B2B customers increased their purchases substantially when they began using Grainger's Web site (grainger.com). (See Chapter 5 for more information.) Also, loyal customers may refer other customers to a site, especially with word-of-mouth in social networks. Therefore, it is important for EC companies to increase customer loyalty. The Web offers ample opportunities to do so.

E-Loyalty

E-loyalty refers to a customer's loyalty to an e-tailer or a manufacturer that sells directly online or to loyalty programs delivered online or supported electronically. Companies can foster e-loyalty by learning about their customers' needs, interacting with customers, and providing superb customer service. A major source of information about e-loyalty is e-loyaltyresource.com. One of its major services is an online journal, the *e-Loyalty Resource Newsletter*, which offers numerous articles describing the relationships among e-loyalty, customer service, personalization, CRM, and Web-based tools. Another source of information is colloquy.com, which concentrates on loyalty marketing.

In an online environment, merchant ratings can be the source of interpersonal communication and are obtained from other consumers, not just friends and family. It is interesting to note that positive customer reviews have considerable impact on repurchase intention. It is not the total number of reviews that influences customer repurchase intention, but the percentage of positive reviews. This increases e-loyalty.

Also, online ratings and word-of-mouth may undermine the effects of competitors' low prices. For example, Amazon.com has higher prices than Half.com, but Amazon.com is still preferred by many customers. The difference is that Amazon.com has customer reviews and other personalization services, and Half.com does not.

Business Intelligence and Analytical Software for E-Loyalty. Businesses are getting better at analyzing customer data to determine satisfaction level and the potential for cross-selling products. It also helps to gain insights fast enough to stop unhappy customers before they leave the site. For example, online delivery service eCourier works with approximately 2,000 clients that expect to be able to use the company's Web site to have packages picked up and delivered anywhere in central London within an hour. eCourier is using software called *SeeWhy* that generates customer data more quickly; it has the ability to report what's happening with customers instantly. When a new booking enters eCourier's database, the information is duplicated and saved in a repository within SeeWhy. The software then compares it with previous information and trends, and if it notices an anomaly, it takes action. When an account manager calls a customer to notify that customer about the anomaly, the customer appreciates the gesture even if the anomaly is the fault of eCourier. It gives them the feeling that their account is being watched and that eCourier is offering proactive and personalized customer service. Such a service can increase e-loyalty.

SATISFACTION IN EC

Satisfaction is one of the most important success measures in the B2C online environment. Customer satisfaction is associated with several key outcomes (e.g., repeat purchase, positive word-of-mouth, and so on) and it can lead to higher customer loyalty. A survey indicates that 80 percent of highly satisfied online consumers would shop again within 2 months, and

e-loyalty
Customer loyalty to an e-tailer or loyalty programs delivered online or supported electronically.

90 percent would recommend Internet retailers to others. However, 87 percent of dissatisfied consumers would permanently leave their Internet retailers without any complaints (Cheung and Lee 2005).

Satisfaction has received considerable attention in studies of consumer-based EC. For example, ForeSee Results, an online customer satisfaction measurement company, developed the American Customer Satisfaction Index (ACSI) (theasci.org) for measuring customer satisfaction with EC. The Customer Respect Group (customerrespect.com) also provides an index to measure customers' online experiences. The Customer Respect Index (CRI) includes the following components: simplicity, responsiveness, transparency, principles, attitude, and privacy.

Researchers have proposed several models to explain the formation of satisfaction with online shopping. For example, Cheung and Lee (2005) proposed a framework for consumer satisfaction with Internet shopping by correlating the end-user satisfaction perspective with the service quality viewpoint. The framework is shown in Exhibit 4.5.

The ability to predict consumer satisfaction can be useful in designing Web sites as well as advertising and marketing strategies. However, Web site designers should also pay attention to the nature of Web site features. Different features have different impacts on customer (dis)satisfaction. If certain Web site features, such as reliability of content, loading speed, and usefulness, fail to perform properly, customer satisfaction will drop dramatically. In contrast, if features such as those make the usage enjoyable, entertaining, and useful, they could result in a significant jump in customer satisfaction.

TRUST IN EC

trust
The psychological status of willingness to depend on another person or organization.

Trust is the psychological status of depending on another person or organization to achieve a planned goal. When people trust each other, they have confidence that their transaction partners will keep their promises. However, both parties in a transaction assume some risk. In the electronic marketplace, sellers and buyers do not meet face to face. The buyer can see a picture of the product but not the product itself. Promises of quality and delivery time can be easily made—but will they be kept? To deal with these issues, EC vendors need to establish high levels of trust with current and potential customers. Trust is particularly important in global EC transactions due to the difficulty of taking legal action in cases of a dispute or fraud and the potential for conflicts caused by differences in culture and business environments.

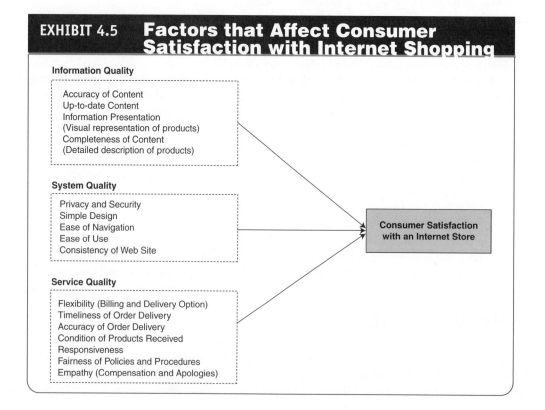

EXHIBIT 4.5   Factors that Affect Consumer Satisfaction with Internet Shopping

Information Quality

- Accuracy of Content
- Up-to-date Content
- Information Presentation (Visual representation of products)
- Completeness of Content (Detailed description of products)

System Quality

- Privacy and Security
- Simple Design
- Ease of Navigation
- Ease of Use
- Consistency of Web Site

Service Quality

- Flexibility (Billing and Delivery Option)
- Timeliness of Order Delivery
- Accuracy of Order Delivery
- Condition of Products Received
- Responsiveness
- Fairness of Policies and Procedures
- Empathy (Compensation and Apologies)

Consumer Satisfaction with an Internet Store

In addition to sellers and buyers trusting each other, both must have trust in the EC computing environment and in the EC infrastructure. For example, if people do not trust the security of the EC infrastructure, they will not feel comfortable about using credit cards to make EC purchases.

EC Trust Models

Several models have been put forth to explain the EC–trust relationship. For example, Lee and Turban (2001) examined the various aspects of EC trust and developed the model shown in Exhibit 4.6. According to this model, the level of trust is determined by numerous variables (factors) shown on the left side and in the middle of the exhibit. The exhibit illustrates the complexity of trust relationships, especially in B2C EC.

How to Increase Trust in EC

Consumer trust is fundamental to successful online retailing; it is considered the "currency" of the Internet. The following are representative strategies for building consumer trust in EC.

Affiliate with an Objective Third Party. This approach aims at building consumer trust by affiliating the customer with trusted third parties. Internet stores can put hypertext links on their Web sites to trusted targets, including reputable companies or well-known portals. These reputable companies are able to transfer brand equity to the Internet stores because companies with brand names facilitate trust. Internet stores can also use third-party seals of approval such as TRUSTe (truste.com) and BBBOnline (bbbonline.org), the online version of the Better Business Bureau. Escrow providers and reputation finders (e.g., cyberalert.com and cymfony.com) also are useful. These agencies provide business-critical intelligence on how brands are being used on the Internet as well as research about spying on businesses.

Working against EC trust are stories about fraud on the Internet, especially when unknown parties are involved. In Chapters 10 and 16, we describe measures to reduce fraud and increase trust.

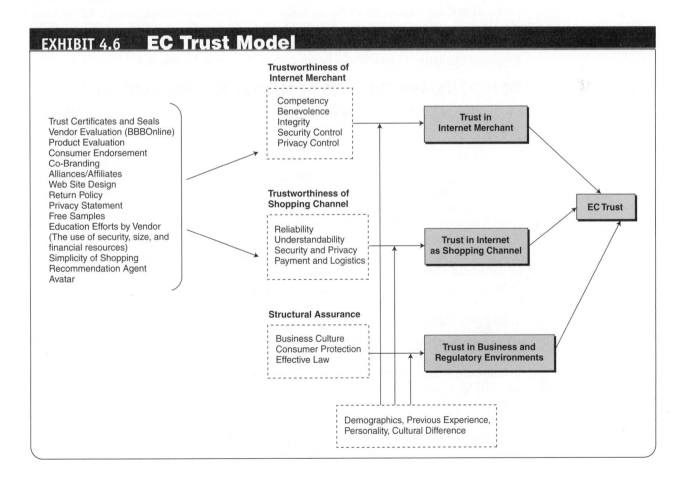

EXHIBIT 4.6   EC Trust Model

Establish Trustworthiness. Trustworthiness can be achieved through three key elements: *integrity, competence*, and *security*. Integrity conveys an overall sense of the ability of the Internet store to build an image of strong justice and fulfill all of the promises that have been made to the customers (i.e., offering a money-back guarantee with the products and clearly stating the guarantee policy on the Web site). Another indicator of trustworthiness is an Internet store's competence. Stores can promote the perception of competence by delivering a professional Web site. A professional appearance should include the basic features that facilitate navigation, including correct grammar and spelling, full and accurate information, and good use of graphic design. The Web site should include some advanced features that provide support to users, such as an internal search engine, quick order ability, order tracking, and an online chat room. Finally, EC security mechanisms can help solidify trust. Dell was the first PC manufacturer to launch an online secure shopping guarantee to online shoppers making purchases at its Web site.

Section 4.5 ▶ REVIEW QUESTIONS

1. Describe loyalty and e-loyalty.
2. Describe the use of business intelligence and analytical software for e-loyalty.
3. Describe the issue of trust in EC and how to increase it.
4. What influences consumer satisfaction online? Why do companies need to monitor it?
5. How can trust be increased in EC?

4.6   MARKET RESEARCH FOR EC

In order to sell products well, it is important to conduct proper market research to find information and knowledge about consumers and products. The market researcher's goal is to discover marketing opportunities and issues, to establish marketing plans, to better understand the purchasing process, and to evaluate marketing performance. On the Web, its purpose is also to investigate the market and behavior of online customers. Market research includes gathering information about topics such as the economy, industry, firms, products, pricing, distribution, competition, promotion, and consumer purchasing behavior. Here we focus on the latter. In Chapter 13, we will look at some other market research topics: the need to research the market, the competition, the technology, the business environment, and much more.

OBJECTIVES AND CONCEPTS OF MARKET RESEARCH ONLINE

Investigation of EC markets can be conducted through conventional methods or it can be done with the assistance of the Internet. Although telephone or shopping mall surveys will continue, interest in Internet research methods is on the rise. Market research that uses the Internet frequently is faster and more efficient and allows the researcher to access a more geographically diverse audience than those found in offline surveys (see FAQs at casro.org). Also, on the Web, market researchers can conduct a very large study much more cheaply than with other methods. Even telephone surveys can cost as much as $50 per respondent. This may be too expensive for a small company that needs several hundred respondents. An online survey will cost a fraction of a similarly sized telephone survey and can expedite research considerably, as shown in Case 4.1. The increased sample size can theoretically increase the accuracy and the predictive capabilities of the results. Hewson et al. (2003) provide a comprehensive review of online market research technologies, methods, tools, issues, and ethical considerations.

What Are Marketers Looking For in EC Market Research?

By looking at a personal profile that includes observed behaviors on the Web, it is possible for marketers to explain and predict online buying behavior. For example, companies want to know why some customers are online shoppers whereas others are not. Major factors that are used for predicting customer online purchasing behavior are (in descending order of importance): product information requested, number of related e-mails, number of orders made, products/services ordered, and gender.

Typical questions that online market research attempts to answer are: What are the purchase patterns for individuals and groups (market segmentation)? What factors encourage

---

CASE 4.1
EC Application

INTERNET MARKET RESEARCH EXPEDITES
TIME-TO-MARKET AT PROCTER & GAMBLE

For decades, Procter & Gamble (P&G) and Colgate-Palmolive have been competitors in the market for personal care products. Developing a major new product from concept to market launch used to take more than 5 years. First, a concept test was conducted: The companies sent product photos and descriptions to potential customers, asking whether they might buy the product. If the feedback was negative, they tried to improve the product concept and then repeated the previous concept test. Once positive response was achieved, sample products were mailed out, and the customers were asked to fill out detailed questionnaires. When customers' responses met the companies' internal hurdles, the companies would start with mass TV advertising.

However, thanks to the Internet, it took P&G only 3½ years to get Whitestrips, a teeth-brightening product, onto the market and to a sales level of $200 million a year—considerably quicker than it had taken in the past with other oral care products. In September 2000, P&G threw out the old marketing test model and instead introduced Whitestrips on the Internet, offering the product for sale on P&G's Web site. The company spent several months studying who was coming to the site and buying the product and collecting responses to online questionnaires, which was much faster than the old mail-outs.

The online research, which was facilitated by data mining conducted on P&G's huge historical data (stored in a data warehouse) and the new Internet data, identified the most enthusiastic groups. These included teenage girls, brides-to-be, and young Hispanic Americans. Immediately, the company started to target these segments with appropriate advertising.

The Internet created a product awareness of 35 percent, even before any shipments were made to stores. This buzz created a huge demand for the product by the time it hit the shelves.

In 2006, P&G began using on-demand solutions from RightNow Technologies (*rightnow.com*), including survey tools that execute opinion polls among selected segments of consumers who have opted into the company's market research programs.

As of 2008, P&G started to experiment with feedback collected at Facebook and other social networks. Such an information solicitation can be beneficial for successful promotion of products since people can spread the word around by word-of-mouth.

From these experiences, P&G learned important lessons about flexible and creative ways to approach product innovation and marketing. The whole process of studying the product concept, segmenting the market, and expediting product development has been revolutionized.

Sources: Compiled from *TMCnet* (2006), Buckley (2002), and *pg.com* (accessed March 2009).

Questions

1. How did P&G reduce time-to-market?
2. How was data mining used?
3. What research methods were used?

---

online purchasing? How can we identify those who are real buyers from those who are just browsing? How does an individual navigate—do consumers check information first or do they go directly to ordering? What is the optimal Web page design? Knowing the answers to questions such as these helps a vendor to advertise properly, to price items, to design the Web site, and to provide appropriate customer service. Online market research can provide such data about individuals, groups, and the entire organization.

Internet-based market research is often done in an interactive manner, allowing personal contact with customers, and it provides marketing organizations with a greater ability to understand the customer, the market, and the competition. For example, it can identify early shifts in product and customer trends, enabling marketers to identify new trends and marketing opportunities and to develop products that customers really want to buy. It also tells management when a product or a service is no longer popular. To learn more about market research on the Web, see the tutorials at webmonkey.com.

REPRESENTATIVE MARKET RESEARCH APPROACHES

Of the many market research approaches, we selected some that are more useful for EC.

Market Segmentation Research

For years, companies used direct mail to contact customers. However, they frequently did so regardless of whether the products or services were appropriate for the specific

EXHIBIT 4.7	Consumer Market Segmentation in the United States (A Partial List)
Market Segmentation	**Bases/Descriptors**
Geographic	Region; size of city, province, or Standard Metropolitan Statistical Area (SMSA); population density; climate; language
Demographic	Age, occupation, gender, education, family size, religion, race, income, nationality, urban (or suburban or rural)
Psychographic (lifestyle)	Social class, lifestyle, personality, activities, VALS typology (see *sric-bi.com/VALS/presurvey.shtml*)
Cognitive, affective, behavioral	Attitudes, benefits sought, loyalty status, readiness stage, usage rate, perceived risk, user status, innovativeness, usage situation, involvement, Internet shopping experience
Profitability	Valued customers are placed in a special category
Risk score	Low-risk customers are in a special category

individuals on the company's mailing list. For example, a retailing company may need to send out four mailings to 1 million customers each year. The cost of the direct mailings is $1.25 million or $1.25 per customer. Assuming that only 1 percent responds, this means the cost per responding customer is $125. Obviously, this type of direct marketing usually is not cost-effective.

One way to reduce the cost is to conduct market segmentation to increase the response rate. A consumer market can be segmented in several ways, for example, by geography, demographics, psychographics, and benefits sought, as shown in Exhibit 4.7.

For EC markets, Brengman et al. (2005) proposed segmenting Internet shoppers based on their Web-usage-related lifestyle, themes of Internet usage, Internet attitude, and psychographic and demographic characteristics. The researchers identified four online shopping segments (tentative shoppers, suspicious learners, shopping lovers, and business users) and four online nonshopping segments (fearful browsers, positive technology muddlers, negative technology muddlers, and adventurous browsers). By isolating and identifying combinations of attributes that make markets, prospects, and customers unique, marketers use strategies developed to appeal to targeted segments. One segment that is being targeted is the so-called Internet generation, or NetGen, the generation that has been raised with the power of the Internet. Internet marketing and advertising is more appropriate for the NetGen than traditional advertising.

Market segmentation is done with the aid of tools such as data modeling and data warehousing. Using data mining and Web mining (see Online File W4.2), businesses can look at consumer buying patterns to slice segments even finer. This is not an easy process, and it requires considerable resources and computer support. Most successful market segmentation stories involve large companies. For example, Royal Bank of Canada segments its 10 million customers at least once a month to determine credit risk, profitability, and so on. This market segmentation has been very successful: The response to Royal Bank of Canada advertising campaigns has increased from 3 to 30 percent. Market segmentation can be very effective in the Web environment, especially when used with appropriate statistical tools. For more on market segmentation surveys, see sric-bi.com/VALS/presurvey.shtml.

To perform online marketing, it is necessary to know what the customer wants or needs. Such information can be collected by the following approaches:

▶ Soliciting information from customers online (e.g., via interviews, questionnaires, use of focus groups, or blogging).

▶ Observing what customers are doing on the Web by transaction logs and cookies.

▶ Using data mining or collaborative filtering techniques to analyze available data.

Insights and Additions 4.2 Market Research by Comscore, Inc.

Comscore Media Metrix is providing Internet audience measurement for advertising agencies, publishers, marketers, and financial analysts. It is using proprietary data collection technology and online data solicitation methodology. Comscore Media Metrix is counting unique visitors across the digital world daily. Powered by a global panel of consumers, Comscore Media Metrix 2.0 delivers highly accurate and comprehensive audience ratings and estimates. This provides an accurate demographic view of Internet users, allowing Web sites to analyze their online efforts and compare them to that of competitors. Media Metrix 2.0 targets specific online audiences to improve advertising and marketing performance (more clicks, better conversions); uses accurate and detailed demographic data to improve sales and partnership proposals; identifies and studies competitors' online activities in order to formulate strategies for gaining market share,

providing a complete view of users' online efforts, allowing for strategic and sound decisions; and utilizes panel-based methodology to provide greater insights into the online behavior of consumers.

Comscore Video Metrix enables its clients to understand the rapidly growing online video market and effectively target advertising in this dynamic and evolving medium (video ads are discussed later in this chapter). Video Metrix identifies and counts the total unique viewers and the number of videos viewed, duration, and videos seen per viewer. Inside Research (*insideresearch.com*) has recognized Comscore as the fastest growing global market research firm. As the provision of online video content continues to grow, it is vital for the industry to have a comparative measure of all the competing entities in this segment of the Internet advertising market.

Online Sampling Methods

Specific methods for collecting online data include e-mail communication with individual customers, moderated focus groups conducted in chat rooms, questionnaires placed on Web sites, and tracking customers' movements on the Web. A typical Internet-based market research process is shown in Online File W4.3. Professional pollsters and marketing research companies frequently conduct online voting polls (e.g., see cnn.com and acnielsen.com). For example, Comscore (comscore.com) offers reporters access to "apples-to-apples" comparisons that measure the entire network of sites owned by each major Internet portal or vendor (e.g., Google, Fox interactive media, Yahoo!, Viacom digital, MSN). For more information on market research, see Insights and Additions 4.2.

Online Surveys

An online survey is a major method for collecting EC data. It has many advantages, including lower overall preparation and administration costs, greater speed in survey distribution and collection, better control of the questionnaire filling process (which may lead to fewer response errors, more complete responses, and easier follow-up), and more flexibility in the questionnaire design. However, online surveys also have some weaknesses, including potential lack of anonymity, data privacy and security concerns, technological competency variation of the potential respondents, and being impersonal.

Web-Based Surveys. A special type of online survey is placing the questions on the Web and inviting potential customers to reply. For example, Mazda North America used a Web-based survey to help design its Miata line. Web surveys may be passive (a fill-in questionnaire) or interactive (respondents download the questionnaires, add comments, ask questions, and discuss issues).

Several tools for Web-based survey are available. For example, SuperSurvey (supersurvey.com) provides online surveys with 50 templates and 20-plus question types to create customized surveys. Surveys can be created in any language, including multibyte languages such as Chinese and Arabic. Advanced validation protocols, randomization, and filtering options help to ensure the integrity of survey results.

Online Focus Groups. Several research firms create panels of qualified Web regulars to participate in online focus groups. For example, NPD Group's panel (npd.com) consists of a pod of 15,000 consumers recruited online and verified by telephone. NPD recruits participants in advance by telephone and takes the time to help them connect to the Internet, if necessary. Use of preselected focus group participants helps to overcome some of the research problems (e.g., small sample size and partial responses) that sometimes limit the effectiveness of Web-based surveys. Greenfield Online (greenfieldonline.com) picks users from its own database and then calls them periodically to verify that they are who they say they are.

Hearing Directly from Customers

Instead of using focus groups, a company may ask customers directly what they think about a product or service. Companies can use chat rooms, newsgroups, blogs, wikis, podcasts, and electronic consumer forums to interact with consumers. For example, toymaker Lego used a market research vendor to establish a direct survey on an electronic bulletin board where millions of visitors read each other's comments and share opinions about Lego toys. The research vendor analyzed the responses daily and submitted the information to Lego. Netflix is using this approach extensively by inducing customers to report their likes and dislikes, as described earlier in this chapter. Software tools that can be used to hear directly from customers include Brand Advocacy Insights (used by Lego) from Informative, Inc. (satmatrix.com), Betasphere (voc-online.com), InsightExpress (insightexpress.com), and Survey (survey.com).

Data Collection in the Web 2.0 Environment

Collecting data in the Web 2.0 environment provides new and exciting opportunities. Here are some methods:

- **Polling.** People like to vote (e.g., for American Idol!), expressing preferences (see Netflix case). They provide opinions on products, services, and so forth.
- **Blogging.** Bloggers can raise issues or induce others to express opinions.
- **Chatting.** Community members love to chat in public chat rooms. By following what goes on there, collection of current data is assured.
- **Live chat.** Here, interactive data from customers in real time is collected.
- **Chatterbots.** These can be partially interactive. Logs of communications can be analyzed. Sometimes, people are more honest when they chat with an avatar.
- **Collective wisdom.** This is a kind of brainstorming. Researchers can find out what arguments people are having and the degree of the disagreements.
- **Find expertise.** Expertise is frequently found in the Web 2.0 environment, many times for free.
- **Folksonomy.** This social tagging makes data easier to find and access.
- **Data in videos, photos, and other media.** Places where these media are shared contribute to valuable data collection.

Observing Customers' Movements Online

To avoid some of the problems of online surveys, especially the giving of false or biased information, some marketers choose to learn about customers by observing their behavior rather than by asking them questions. Many marketers keep track of consumers' Web movements by using methods such as transaction logs (log files) or cookie files.

transaction log
A record of user activities at a company's Web site.

Transaction Logs. A transaction log records user activities at a company's Web site. A transaction log is created from the computer log file of user actions that have occurred. With log file analysis tools, it is possible to get a good idea of where visitors are coming from, how often they return, and how they navigate through a site. The transaction-log approach is especially useful if the visitors' names are known (e.g., when they have registered with the site). In addition, data from the shopping cart database can be combined with information in the transaction log to reveal more insights.

clickstream behavior
Customer movements on the Internet.

Note that as customers move from site to site, they establish their **clickstream behavior**, a pattern of their movements on the Internet, which can be seen in their transaction logs. Both ISPs and individual Web sites are capable of tracking a user's clickstream.

For example, Internet Profile Corporation (IPC) (ipro.com) collects data from a company's client/server logs and provides the company with periodic reports that include statistical data such as where customers come from or how many customers have gone straight from the homepage to placing an order. IPC also translates the Internet domain names of visitors into real company names. This way, a company knows from which Web page its customers are coming.

Cookies, Web Bugs, and Spyware. Cookies and Web bugs can be used to supplement transaction-log methods. As discussed earlier, cookies allow a Web site to store data on the user's PC; when the customer returns to the site, the cookies can be used to find what the customer did in the past. Cookies are frequently combined with **Web bugs**, tiny graphics files embedded in e-mail messages and on Web sites. Web bugs transmit information about the user and his or her movements to a monitoring site.

Spyware is software that gathers user information through an Internet connection without the user's knowledge. Originally designed to allow freeware authors to make money on their products, spyware applications are typically bundled together with freeware for download onto users' machines. Many users do not realize that they are downloading spyware with the freeware. Sometimes the freeware provider may indicate that other programs will be loaded onto the user's computer in the licensing agreement (e.g., "may include software that occasionally notifies users of important news"). Spyware stays on the user's hard drive and continually tracks the user's actions, periodically sending information on the user's activities to the owner of the spyware. It typically is used to gather information for advertising purposes. Users cannot control what data are sent via the spyware, and unless they use special tools, they often cannot uninstall the spyware, even if the software it was bundled with is removed from the system. Effective tools for fighting spyware include Ad-aware (lavasoftusa.com), Spykiller (spykiller.com), and Webwasher Spyware from Secure Computing (securecomputing.com). For more on spyware and banners, see Online File W4.4.

Representative vendors that provide tools for tracking customers' movements are Tealeaf Technology, Inc. (tealeaf.com, log files), Acxiom Corp. (acxiom.com, data warehousing), and Stat Counter (statcounter.com, real-time tracking).

The use of cookies and Web bugs is controversial. Many believe that they invade the customer's privacy (see privacyfoundation.org). Tracking customers' activities without their knowledge or permission may be unethical or even illegal.

Clickstream Analysis. Clickstream data are data generated in the Web environment; they provide a trail of a user's activities (the user's clickstream behavior) in a Web site. These data include a record of the user's browsing patterns: every Web site and every page of every Web site the user visits; how long the user remains on a page or site; in what order the pages were visited; and even the e-mail addresses of mail that the user sends and receives. By analyzing clickstream data, a firm can find out, for example, which promotions are effective and which population segments are interested in specific products. The list of information provided by clickstream data is available in Online File W4.5.

Several companies offer tools that enable such an analysis. For example, WebTrends 7 and higher features several advanced tools for analyzing clickstream data (e.g., see webtrends.com).

In addition, clickstream data can be maintained in a clickstream database or data warehouse for further analysis. Despite storing many terabytes of clickstream data and investing heavily in Web analytic tools, very few companies understand how to use the data effectively.

Web Analytics and Mining. Web analytics services and software have grown beyond simply reporting which page was clicked and how long a visitor stayed there. They now offer more advanced functions that retailers are finding indispensable. For example, options from Coremetrics (coremetrics.com) and others are enabling retailers to make site adjustments on the fly, manage online marketing campaigns and e-commerce initiatives, and track customer satisfaction. Also, if a company redesigns its Web site, it can gain almost-instant feedback on how the new site is performing. Web analytics can be done on a customer-by-customer or prospect-by-prospect basis, helping marketers decide which products to promote and merchandisers achieve a better understanding of the nature of demand. For tutorials on data mining and Web mining, see autonlab.org/tutorials.

Web Mining. Web mining refers to the use of data mining techniques for discovering and extracting information from Web documents. Web mining explores both Web

Web bugs
Tiny graphics files embedded in e-mail messages and in Web sites that transmit information about users and their movements to a Web server.

spyware
Software that gathers user information over an Internet connection without the user's knowledge.

clickstream data
Data that occur inside the Web environment; they provide a trail of the user's activities (the user's clickstream behavior) in the Web site.

Web mining
Data mining techniques for discovering and extracting information from Web documents; explores both Web content and Web usage.

content and Web usage. The usage analysis is derived from clickstream data. Web mining is having the potential to change the way we access and use the information available on the Web.

LIMITATIONS OF ONLINE MARKET RESEARCH AND HOW TO OVERCOME THEM

One problem with online market research is that too much data may be available. To use data properly, one needs to organize, edit, condense, and summarize it. However, such a task may be expensive and time-consuming. The solution to this problem is to automate the process by using data warehousing and data mining. The essentials of this process, known as *business intelligence*, are provided in Online File W4.2, and in Turban et al. (2008).

Some of the limitations of online research methods are accuracy of responses, loss of respondents because of equipment problems, and the ethics and legality of Web tracking. In addition, focus group responses can lose something in the translation from an in-person group to an online group. A researcher may get people online to talk to each other and play off of each other's comments, but eye contact and body language are two interactions of traditional focus group research that are lost in the online world. However, just as it hinders the two-way assessment of visual cues, Web research can actually offer some participants the anonymity necessary to elicit an unguarded response. Finally, a major limitation of online market research is the difficulty in obtaining truly representative samples.

Concerns have been expressed over the potential lack of representativeness in samples of online users. Online shoppers tend to be wealthy, employed, and well educated. Although this may be a desirable audience for some products and services, the research results may not be extendable to other markets. Although the Web-user demographic is rapidly diversifying, it is still skewed toward certain population groups, such as those with convenient Internet access (at home or work). Another important issue concerns the lack of clear understanding of the online communication process and how online respondents think and interact in cyberspace.

It is important for a company to identify the intended target audience or demographic so that the right kind of sampling can be performed. Web-based surveys typically have a lower response rate than e-mail surveys, and there is no respondent control for public surveys. If target respondents are allowed to be anonymous, it may encourage them to be more truthful in their opinions. However, anonymity may result in the loss of valuable information about the demographics and characteristics of the respondents. Finally, there are still concerns about the security of the information transmitted, which also may have an impact on the respondents' truthfulness. To overcome some of the limitations of online market research, companies may outsource their market research to large and experienced companies that have specialized market research departments and expertise.

BIOMETRIC MARKETING

One problem with Web analytics, Web mining, clickstream data, and so on is the representativeness. That is, we observe and follow a computer, not knowing who is actually moving the mouse. Many households have several users; thus, the data collected may not represent any one person's preferences (unless, of course, we are sure that there is one and only one user, as in the case of smart cell phones). A potential solution is suggested by Pons (2006) in the form of biometric marketing.

biometrics
An individual's unique physical or behavioral characteristics that can be used to identify an individual precisely (e.g., fingerprints).

A **biometric** is one of an individual's unique physical or behavioral characteristics that can be used to identify an individual precisely (e.g., fingerprints; see list in Chapter 10). By applying the technology to computer users, we can improve security and learn about the user's profile precisely. The question is how to do it. Indeed, there are programs by which users identify themselves to the computer by biometrics, and these are spreading rapidly. Utilizing the technology for marketing involves social and legal acceptability. For these reasons, advertisers are using methods that target individuals without knowing their profiles. An example is search engine–based methods, such as Adwords used by Google (see Section 4.8).

Some researchers are wildly optimistic about the prospects for market research on the Internet; others are more cautious.

1. Describe the objectives of market research.
2. Define and describe market segmentation.
3. Describe how market research is done online and the methods used by Comscore.
4. Describe the role of Weblogs and clickstream analysis.
5. Define cookies, Web bugs, and spyware and describe how they can be used in market research.
6. Describe how the issue of privacy relates to online market research.
7. Describe how biometrics and cell phones can improve market research and advertising.
8. Describe the limitations of online market research.

4.7 WEB ADVERTISING

Advertising on the Web plays an extremely important role in e-commerce. Internet advertising is growing very rapidly, and companies are changing their advertising strategies to gain a competitive edge. According to a McKinsey global survey of marketers (McKinsey 2007), online ads are also useful for brand building directly through response ads. Spending is expected to increase on all types of online advertising methods, including Web 2.0 tools over the next 3 years.

OVERVIEW OF WEB ADVERTISING

Advertising is an attempt to disseminate information in order to affect buyer–seller transactions. In traditional marketing, advertising was impersonal, one-way mass communication that was paid for by sponsors. Telemarketing and direct mail ads were attempts to personalize advertising to make it more effective. These direct marketing approaches worked fairly well but were expensive and slow and seldom truly one-to-one interactive. The cost–benefit was poor. For example, say a direct mail campaign costs about $1 per person and has a response rate of only 1 to 3 percent. This makes the cost per responding person in the range of $33 to $100. Such an expense can be justified only for high-ticket items (e.g., cars).

One of the problems with direct mail advertising was that the advertisers knew very little about the recipients. Market segmentation by various characteristics (e.g., age, income, gender) helped a bit but did not solve the problem. The Internet introduced the concept of interactive marketing, which enables marketers and advertisers to interact directly with customers. In interactive marketing, a consumer can click an ad to obtain more information or send an e-mail to ask a question. Besides the two-way communication and e-mail capabilities provided by the Internet, vendors also can target specific groups and individuals on whom they want to spend their advertising dollars. The Internet enables truly one-to-one advertising. A comparison of mass advertising, direct mail advertising, and interactive online advertising is shown in Online File W4.6. An example of cultivating customer relationships and e-loyalty on a one-to-one basis can be found in Online File W4.7.

The two major business models for advertising online are (1) using the Web as a channel to advertise a firm's own products and services and (2) making a firm's site a public portal site and using captive audiences to advertise products offered by other firms. For example, the audience might come to a P&G Web site to learn about Tide, but they might also get additional ads for products made by Coca-Cola.

interactive marketing
Online marketing, facilitated by the Internet, by which marketers and advertisers can interact directly with customers, and consumers can interact with advertisers/vendors.

The Advertising Cycle

With closed-loop campaign management, companies are treating advertisement as a cyclical process, as shown in Exhibit 4.8. The cyclical process entails carefully planning a campaign to determine who the target audience is and how to reach that audience. Then, analyzing a campaign after its completion assists a company in understanding the campaign's success. This new knowledge is then used when planning future campaigns.

ad views
The number of times users call up a page that has a banner on it during a specific period; known as *impressions* or *page views*.

button
A small banner that is linked to a Web site; may contain downloadable software.

page
An HTML (Hypertext Markup Language) document that may contain text, images, and other online elements, such as Java applets and multimedia files; may be generated statically or dynamically.

click (click-through or ad click)
A count made each time a visitor clicks on an advertising banner to access the advertiser's Web site.

CPM (cost per mille, i.e., thousand impressions)
The fee an advertiser pays for each 1,000 times a page with a banner ad is shown.

conversion rate
The percentage of clickers who actually make a purchase.

click-through rate
The percentage of visitors who are exposed to a banner ad and click on it.

click-through ratio
The ratio between the number of clicks on a banner ad and the number of times it is seen by viewers; measures the success of a banner in attracting visitors to click on the ad.

hit
A request for data from a Web page or file.

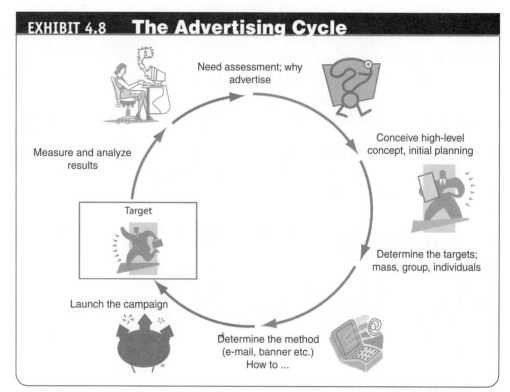

EXHIBIT 4.8   **The Advertising Cycle**

Need assessment; why advertise

Conceive high-level concept, initial planning

Determine the targets; mass, group, individuals

Determine the method (e-mail, banner etc.) How to ...

Launch the campaign

Target

Measure and analyze results

Before we describe the various steps of the cycle as it is implemented in Web advertising, let's learn some basic advertising terminology.

SOME INTERNET ADVERTISING TERMINOLOGY

The following list of terms and their definitions in the marginal glossary will be of use as you read about Web advertising.

- Ad views
- Button
- Page
- Click (click-through or ad click)
- CPM (cost per mille, i.e., thousand impressions)
- Conversion rate
- Click-through rate
- Click-through ratio
- Hit
- Visit
- Unique visit
- Stickiness

WHY INTERNET ADVERTISING?

The major traditional advertising media are television, newspapers, magazines, and radio. However, the market is changing as many consumers are spending more time on the Internet and using mobile phones. Internet advertising is getting more attention. According to *eMarketer*, online ad spending is expected to reach $42.0 billion in 2011 from $21.4 billion in 2007 (reported in *New Media Trend Watch* 2009).

Companies advertise on the Internet for several reasons. To begin with, television viewers are migrating to the Internet. Internet users are spending time online that they previously spent viewing television. Worldwide, Internet users are spending significantly less time watching television and more time using the Internet. This trend will continue, especially as Internet-enabled cell phones become commonplace. In addition, many Internet users are well educated and have high incomes. These Internet surfers are a desired target for many advertisers.

Advertising Online and Its Advantages

The major advantages of using the Internet over mass advertising are precise targeting, interactivity, rich media (grabs attention), cost reduction, efficiency, and customer acquisition. In comparison to traditional media, the Internet is the fastest growing communication medium by far. Worldwide, the number of Internet users surpassed 1 billion in 2005; the 2 billion Internet user milestone is expected in 2011 (*Computer Industry Almanac* 2006). Of course, advertisers are interested in a medium with such potential reach, both locally and globally.

Other reasons why Web advertising is growing rapidly include:

▶ **Cost.** Online ads are sometimes cheaper than those in other media. In addition, ads can be updated at any time with minimal cost.

▶ **Richness of format.** Web ads can effectively use the convergence of text, audio, graphics, and animation. In addition, games, entertainment, and promotions can be easily combined in online advertisements. Also, services such as mysimon.com enable customers to compare prices and, using a PDA or cell phone, do it at any time from anywhere.

▶ **Personalization.** Web ads can be interactive and targeted to specific interest groups and/or individuals; the Web is a much more focused medium.

▶ **Timeliness.** Internet ads can be fresh and up-to-the-minute.

▶ **Location-basis.** Using wireless technology and GPS, Web advertising can be location based; Internet ads can be sent to consumers whenever they are in a specific time and location (e.g., near a restaurant or a theater).

▶ **Linking.** It is easy to link from an online ad to a storefront—one click does it.

▶ **Digital branding.** Even the most price-conscious online shoppers are willing to pay premiums for brands they trust. These brands may be click-and-mortar brands (e.g., P&G) or dot-coms such as Amazon.com. British Airways places many Internet banner ads; however, these ads are not for clicking on to buy: They are all about branding, that is, establishing British Airways as a brand.

Each advertising medium, including the Internet, has its advantages and limitations. Online File W4.8 compares the advantages and limitations of Internet advertising against traditional advertising media. The combination of television–Web synergy can help attract more attention than either medium on its own. It has been found that a TV campaign increases brand awareness by 27 percent, whereas a combined TV and online campaign increases it by 45 percent. A TV campaign increases intent to purchase by 2 percent, whereas a combined TV and online campaign increases it by 12 percent.

ADVERTISING NETWORKS

One of the major advantages of Internet advertising is the ability to customize ads to fit individual viewers. This kind of personalized advertisement can tailor its content or format to the individual's preference. Specialized firms have sprung up to offer this service to companies that wish to locate customers through targeted advertising. Called **advertising networks** (or *ad server networks*), these firms offer special services such as brokering banner ads for sale, bringing together online advertisers and providers of online ad space, and helping target ads to consumers who are presumed to be interested in categories of advertisements based on consumer profiles. DoubleClick (a Google company) is a premier company in this area. DoubleClick created an advertising network for 1,500 companies. It prepares thousands of ads for its clients every week, following the process shown in Online File W4.9.

One-to-one targeted advertising and marketing may be expensive, but it can be very rewarding. For example, successful targeted online ads proved very effective for selling Lexus

visit
A series of requests during one navigation of a Web site; a pause of a certain length of time ends a visit.

unique visit
A count of the number of visitors entering a site, regardless of how many pages are viewed per visit.

stickiness
Characteristic that influences the average length of time a visitor stays in a site.

advertising networks
Specialized firms that offer customized Web advertising, such as brokering ads and targeting ads to select groups of consumers.

cars, at a cost of $169 per car sold. Targeting ads to groups based on market segmentation rather than to individuals also can be very cost-effective, depending on the advertising method used.

Section 4.7 ▶ REVIEW QUESTIONS

1. Define Web advertising and the major terms associated with it.
2. Describe the reasons for the growth in Web advertising.
3. Describe emerging Internet advertising approaches.
4. List the major benefits of Web advertising.
5. Explain the role of ad networks in Web advertising.

4.8 ONLINE ADVERTISING METHODS

A large number of online advertising methods exist. The following are a few major ones.

BANNERS

banner
On a Web page, a graphic advertising display linked to the advertiser's Web page.

A **banner** is a graphic display that is used for advertising on a Web page. The size of the banner is usually 5 to 6.25 inches in length, 0.5 to 1 inch in width, and is measured in pixels. A banner ad is linked to an advertiser's Web page. When users "click" the banner, they are transferred to the advertiser's site. Advertisers go to great lengths to design a banner that catches consumers' attention. Banners often include video clips and sound. Banner advertising including pop-up banners is the most commonly used form of advertising on the Internet.

keyword banners
Banner ads that appear when a predetermined word is queried from a search engine.

There are several types of banners. **Keyword banners** appear when a predetermined word is queried from a search engine. They are effective for companies that want to narrow their target audience. **Random banners** appear randomly, not as a result of some action by the viewer. Companies that want to introduce new products (e.g., a new movie or CD) or promote their brand use random banners. Static banners are always on the Web page. Finally, pop-up banners appear when least expected, as will be described later.

random banners
Banner ads that appear at random, not as the result of the user's action.

If an advertiser knows something about a visitor, such as the visitor's user profile, it is possible to match a specific banner with that visitor. Obviously, such targeted, personalized banners are usually most effective.

In the near future, banner ads will greet people by name and offer travel deals to their favorite destinations. Such *personalized banners* are being developed, for example, by Dotomi (dotomi.com). Dotomi delivers ads to consumers who opt in to view its system. Initial results show a 14 percent click-through rate, which measures the success of a banner in attracting visitors to click, versus 3 to 5 percent with nonpersonalized ads.

Benefits and Limitations of Banner Ads

The major benefit of banner ads is that, by clicking on them, users are transferred to an advertiser's site, frequently directly to the shopping page of that site. Another advantage of using banners is the ability to customize them for individual surfers or a market segment of surfers. Also, viewing of banners is fairly regular, because in many cases customers are forced to see banner ads while waiting for a page to load or before they can get the free information or entertainment that they want to see (a strategy called *forced advertising* and it is banner spam, see Chapter 16). Finally, banners may include attention-grabbing multimedia.

The major disadvantage of banners is their cost. If a company demands a successful marketing campaign, it will need to allocate a large percentage of its advertising budget to place banners on high-volume Web sites. Another drawback is that a limited amount of information can be placed on the banner. Hence, advertisers need to think of a creative but short message to attract viewers.

However, it seems that viewers have become somewhat immune to banners and simply do not notice them as they once did. The click-through rate has been declining over time. Because of these drawbacks, it is important to decide where on the screen to place banners. For more on the efficient use of banner ads, see Online File W4.10.

Banner Swapping and Banner Exchanges

Banner swapping means that company A agrees to display a banner of company B in exchange for company B's displaying company A's banner. This is probably the least expensive form of banner advertising, but it is difficult to arrange. A company must locate a site that will generate a sufficient amount of relevant traffic. Then, the company must contact the owner/Webmaster of the site and inquire if the company would be interested in a reciprocal banner swap. Because individual swaps are difficult to arrange, many companies use banner exchanges.

Banner exchanges are markets where companies can trade or exchange placement of banner ads on each other's Web sites. A multicompany banner match may provide a better match, and it will be easier to arrange than a two-company swap. For example, company A can display B's banner effectively, but B cannot display A's banner optimally. However, B can display C's banner, and C can display A's banner. Such bartering may involve many companies. Banner exchange organizers arrange the trading, which works much like an offline bartering exchange. Firms that are willing to display others' banners join the exchange. Each time a participant displays a banner for one of the exchange's other members, it receives a credit. After a participant has "earned" enough credits, its own banner is displayed on a suitable member's site. Most exchanges offer members the opportunity to purchase additional display credits.

Examples of exchanges are linkswap.co.uk, click4click.com, and exchange-it.com. For auctions related to banners, see thefreeauction.com/exchange. Banner exchanges are not without their disadvantages. To begin with, some charge high fees, charging members either money or ad space, or both. Second, some banner exchanges will not allow certain types of banners. In addition, tax issues may arise for companies that barter their banners.

POP-UP AND SIMILAR ADS

One of the most annoying phenomena in Web surfing is the increased use of pop-up, pop-under, and similar ads. A **pop-up ad**, also known as *ad spawning*, appears due to the automatic launching of a new browser window when a visitor enters or exits a site, when a delay occurs, or when other triggers cause the display. A pop-up ad appears in front of the active window. A **pop-under ad** is an ad that appears underneath (in back of) the current browser window. When users close the active window, they see the ad. Pop-ups cover the user's current screen and may be difficult to close. Pop-up and pop-under ads are controversial: Many users strongly object to this advertising method, which they consider to be intrusive. Most browsers provide an option that allows the viewer to block pop-up windows. Legal attempts have also been made to control pop-ups because they are basically a form of spam (see Chapter 16).

Several other tactics, some of them very aggressive, are being used by advertisers, and their use is increasing (see Online File W4.11). These tactics may be accompanied by music, voice, and other rich multimedia.

E-MAIL ADVERTISING

Sending company or product information to people or companies that appear on mailing lists has become a popular way to advertise on the Internet. E-mail messages may be combined with brief audio or video clips to promote a product; some messages provide links that users can click on to make a purchase. E-mail continues to enjoy popularity among consumers and has become acknowledged as a legitimate and relied-upon marketing channel.

The advantages of e-mail advertising are its low cost and the ability to reach a wide variety of targeted audiences. E-mail is an interactive medium that can combine advertising and customer service. It can include a direct link to any URL, so it acts like a banner. A consumer may be more likely to respond to e-mail messages related to discounts or special sales. Most companies have a database of customers to whom they can send e-mail messages. However, using e-mail to send ads (sometimes floods of ads) without the receivers' permission is considered spamming.

The quantity of e-mail that consumers receive is exploding. In light of this, marketers employing e-mail must take a long-term view and work toward motivating consumers to continue to read the messages they receive. As the volume of e-mail increases, consumers' tendency to screen and block messages will rise as well. Most e-mail services permit users to block messages from specific sources.

A list of e-mail addresses can be a very powerful tool for a company, helping it to target a group of people that it knows something about. For information on how to create a mailing list, consult groups.yahoo.com (the service is free) or topica.com.

E-mail can also be sent to a PDA and to other mobile devices. Mobile phones, in particular, offer advertisers a real chance to advertise interactively and on a one-to-one basis with consumers—anytime, anyplace. In the future, e-mail ads will be targeted to individuals based not only on their user profiles but also on their physical location at any point in time. See Chapter 8 for a description of this concept, known as *l-commerce*. For more information on l-commerce, see Online File W4.12.

E-Mail Hoaxes. E-mail hoaxes are very popular; some of them have been going on for years (e.g., Neiman Marcus's cookie recipe, the Nigerian treasure, the Koran and the Iraq invasion). Some of these are scams. For details, see ftc.gov and Chapter 10.

Fraud. Fraud also is a consideration. For example, a person may receive an e-mail stating that his or her credit card number is invalid or that his or her MSN service will be terminated unless another credit card number is sent in reply to the e-mail. For protection against such fraudulent practices, see scambusters.org and Chapters 10 and 16.

E-Mail Advertising Methods and Successes

E-mail advertising can be done in many different ways, as shown in Online File W4.13.

NEWSPAPER-LIKE AND CLASSIFIED ADS

In 2001, the Internet Advertising Bureau, an industry trade group, adopted five standard ad sizes for the Internet. These standardized ads, which are larger and more noticeable than banner ads, look like newspaper or magazine ads, so advertisers like them. Tests found that users read these ads four times more frequently than banners.

Classified Ads

Another newspaper-like ad is the classified ad. These ads can be found on special sites (e.g., craigslist.org and superpages.com), as well as on online newspapers, exchanges, and portals. In many cases, posting regular-size classified ads is free, but placing them in a larger size or with some noticeable features is done for a fee. For examples, see traderonline.com and advertising.microsoft.com.

SEARCH ENGINE ADVERTISEMENT

Search engines are a good mechanism for most people to find information and, therefore, a good platform for online advertising. The two major forms of search engine advertising are listing URLs and keyword advertising.

URL Listing

Most search engines allow companies to submit their Internet addresses, called URLs (Universal Resource Locators), for free so that these URLs can be searched electronically. Search engine spiders crawl through each site, indexing its content and links. The site is then included as a candidate for future searches. Because there are quite a few search engines, advertisers who use this method should register URLs with as many proper search engines as possible. In some cases, URLs may be searched even if they are not submitted.

The major advantage of using search engines as an advertising tool is that it is free. Anyone can submit a URL to a search engine and be listed. Searchers for a company's products will most likely receive a list of sites that mention the products, including the company's own site. Search engine advertisement has become the most popular online advertising method, mainly thanks to Google.

However, the URL method has several drawbacks. The major one is location: The chance that a specific site will be placed at the top of a search engine's display list (say, in the first 10 sites) is very slim. Furthermore, even if a company's URL makes it to the top, others can quickly displace it. Second, different search engines index their listings differently; therefore, making the top of several lists is difficult. The searcher may have the correct keywords, but if the search engine indexed the site listing using the "title" or "content description" in the meta tag, then the effort could be fruitless. A meta tag is a coding statement (in HTML) that describes the content of a Web page and is used by search engines in indexing.

Keyword Advertising

Google has created a new advertising technology by linking an advertisement with the user's keywords. Advertisers choose the keywords to which their advertisements will link. Advertisements appear on the screen along with the search results when the chosen keywords are searched. This can substantially increase the likelihood that the advertisement will be viewed because of its high relevance to user interests. In fact, more than 90 percent of Google's revenue is generated from this creative technology. Furthermore, Google allows the advertisers to bid for the order of appearance. Advertisers who pay more will appear higher on the list.

Improving a Company's Search Engine Ranking (Optimization)

Because the URL appearing at the top of the search engine results usually receives more attention, each company wants its URL to be placed at the top. **Search engine optimization (SEO)** is the method of increasing site rank on search engines. To do so, the optimizer needs to know the ranking algorithm of the search engine (which may be different for different search engines) and best search phrases, and then tailor the ads accordingly.

In Google's ranking, for example, certain rules apply: Google ranks Web sites by their linkage popularity and tends to give weights to links from major companies, trade groups, government organizations, and sites built on the .edu domain. Wordtracker is a tool that helps find phrases that people tend to type when looking for a specific product. Wordtracker, however, has its own shortcomings: Popular phrases may not always be the best match for your target customers.

Another solution is to buy keyword ads on the page that contains Google's results of a search. Using Google Analytics or another system, users can track which phrases best convert into sales.

Finally, ads that appear on the side and top of the search results are attention-grabbers, but they are expensive (see AdWords, later in this section). Several companies provide services that optimize Web content so that a site has a better chance of being discovered by a search engine—for example, Web Position from WebTrends (webtrends.com). More tips for improving a site's listing in various search engines can be found at searchenginewatch.com. For further details, see Chapter 15.

search engine optimization (SEO)
The craft of increasing site rank on search engines; the optimizer uses the ranking algorithm of the search engine (which may be different for different search engines) and best search phrases, and tailors the ad accordingly.

GOOGLE—THE ONLINE ADVERTISING KING

No other EC company can match the success of Google and its meteoric rise. Google is considered by many to be not only changing the Internet but also the world. Google uses several varieties of search engine advertising methods that are generating billions of dollars in revenue and profits. In Insights and Additions 4.3, we describe two of these methods.

ADVERTISING IN CHAT ROOMS

Vendors also advertise to members of social networks. Sites such as Facebook offer targeted advertising opportunities, and vendors usually offer discounts to members on advertised products. Ads also link users to other sites that might be of interest to community members. Advertisers sometimes use online fantasy sports (e.g., available at Yahoo!) to send ads to specific sports fans in specific leagues. According to *eMarketer* (2006), online fantasy sports attract millions of visitors every month.

Vendors frequently sponsor chat rooms. The sponsoring vendor places a chat link on its site, and the chat vendor does the rest (e.g., talkcity.com), including placing the advertising that pays for the session. The advertising in a chat room merges with the activity in the room, and the user is conscious of what is being presented.

The main difference between an advertisement that appears on a static Web page and one that comes through a chat room is that the latter allows advertisers to cycle through

Insights and Additions 4.3 Google's Major Advertisement Methods

Google uses its Internet search technology to serve advertisements based on Web site content, the user's geographical location, and other factors. The major methods are AdWords and AdSense.

AdWords

AdWords is a self-service ad server that uses relevance-ranking algorithms similar to the ones that make the search engine so effective. Advertisers tell Google how much they want to spend and then "buy" pertinent keywords. When Web surfers type in a term that matches the advertiser's keyword, the advertiser is listed in a banner near the search results with the heading "Sponsored Links." Each time a user clicks the advertiser's banner ad, Google subtracts the cost-per-click for the advertiser's prepaid account; when the account's daily ad budget is depleted, Google stops displaying the ad.

The system is easy to use and remarkably effective. The click-through rate is about 15 percent, which is more than 10 times the rate of the average banner ad. According to industry experts, many Google advertisers have experienced a 20 to 25 percent increase in online sales.

Each time a visitor clicks on an ad (which takes the visitor to the advertiser's site), the site owner shares the commission paid by the advertiser with Google. The advertisers also participate in the AdWords program.

Despite its success, AdWords by itself does not provide the best one-to-one targeting. This may be achieved in many cases through a complementary program—AdSense.

AdSense

Google's AdSense is an affiliate program in which Google offers Web site owners a chance to earn a commission for their willingness to place ads of other advertisers on their sites. AdSense automatically delivers an advertiser's text and image ads that are precisely matched to each affiliate site. This is a major improvement over matching individuals based on their preferences, which is less accurate in many cases and much more expensive. The matching (called *contextual matching*) is based on a proprietary algorithm (Google filed for more than 60 patents on these and other innovations). The key is the quality and appearance of both the pages and the ads, as well as the popularity of the site. Hundreds of thousands participate in the affiliate program. Google provides the affiliates with analytics that help convert visitors to customers.

AdSense uses Google's relevance-scoring algorithms. Web site owners can enroll as affiliates in this program to enable ads of text, image, and more recently, video advertisements to be on their Web sites. These ads generate revenue for Google on either a per-click or per-impression basis. The revenue is shared with the Web site owners (affiliates).

AdSense has become a popular method of placing advertising on Web sites because the advertisements are less intrusive than most other banners, and the content of the advertisements is often more relevant to the Web site. For an example of a site using AdSense, see RTC (*rtcmagazine.com*). Google's success is attributed to the quality of the matches, the large number of advertisers in its network, the ability to use ads in many languages, and the ability to understand the content of Web sites. Characteristics and demographics of the visitors that Google knows are considered in the match. This is also true of Google's competitors (e.g., MSN, with its AdCenter methodology). Similar programs are offered by eBay and Yahoo! (see eBay AdContex and Yahoo!'s Content Match). The closer the match, the less intrusive the ad is to the visitor, and the better the chance of the visitor's clicking on the ad.

Sources: Compiled from *adwords.google.com/select, google.com/adsense,* and *en.wikipedia.org/wiki/AdSense* (all sites accessed January 2009).

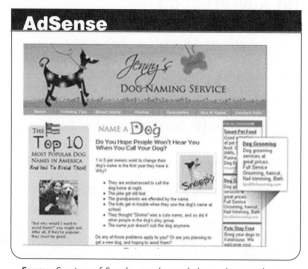

Source: Courtesy of Google. *google.com/adsense* (accessed January 2009).

messages and target the chatters again and again. Also, advertising can become more thematic in a chat room. An advertiser can start with one message and build upon it to a climax, just as an author does with a good story. For example, a toymaker may have a chat room dedicated to electronic toys. The advertiser can use the chat room to post a query such as, "Can anyone tell me about the new Electoy R3D3?" In addition, a company can go to competitors' chat rooms and observe the conversations there.

Chat rooms also are used as one-to-one connections between a company and its customers. For example, Mattel (mattel.com) sells about one-third of its Barbie dolls to collectors. These collectors use the chat room to make comments or ask questions that are then answered by Mattel's staff.

OTHER FORMS OF ADVERTISING

Online advertising can be done in several other ways, ranging from ads in newsgroups to ads in computer kiosks. For example, to celebrate National Tomato Month, Hunt's supplemented its Web site with a promotional game, recipes, and an online affinity program to target specific tomato-based foods and recipes, Hunt's saw a 400 percent increase in site traffic and a 41 percent increase in affinity program membership.

In addition, a site's domain name may be used for brand recognition. This is why some companies pay millions of dollars to keep certain domain names under their control (see alldomains.com) or to buy popular names (e.g., tom.com was purchased for $8 million). Known as *domainers*, some individuals buy thousands of names and then run ads on them with Google, charging advertisers. As of 2006, the use of video clips in online ads has been increasing. For example, see qvc.com (featured products), edmunds.com (cars), and so on. As will be shown in Chapter 8, advertising on cell phones and other mobile devices is increasing rapidly.

Advertising in Online Newsletters

Free online newsletters are abundant in e-commerce; one example is *Ecommerce Times* (ecommercetimes.com). This informative newsletter solicits ads from companies (see "How to Advertise"). Ads are usually short, and they have a link to details. They are properly marked as "Advertisement."

Posting Press Releases Online

Millions of people visit popular portals such as Yahoo!, MSN, AOL, or Google every day, looking for news. Thus, it makes sense to try to reach an audience through such sites. Indeed, Southwest Airlines was successful in selling $1.5 million in tickets by posting four press releases online. However, it is not as simple as it sounds. For a discussion of how to place online press releases, see the case study at MarketingSherpa (marketingsherpa.com).

Video Ads

Video ads are growing rapidly, mainly due to the popularity of YouTube and similar sites. According to *Reuters* (2007), online video is expected to grow at nearly 40 percent annually through 2011 while TV viewing continues to fall. According to Comscore, people watched 12 billion videos online in May 2008 alone. Video ads appear all over the Web, both as unsolicited pop-ups, or when you give permission to see a demo or information about a product. Video ads become very popular in the Web 2.0 environment and social networking.

Podcasting has begun to capture the public imagination. Content creators are now providing a growing stream of intriguing and diverse content for downloading on MP3 players or on personal computers, allowing consumers to control the time and place of their viewing or listening. And even advertising is emerging in podcasts. With the growth of online participation, consumers exert greater influence over the products and brands considered for purchase.

Two-minute YouTube clips were just the beginning as television comes to the Internet to become the network of tomorrow. For example, Diggnation (see digg.com) is a weekly tech/Web culture show based on the top social bookmarking news stories site. Diggnation drew about 250,000 viewers a week in 2008 and was among the most popular free video podcasts on Apple's iTunes service—alongside offerings from ABC, the BBC, and CNN.

Revision3 (revision3.com) appeals to niche audiences interested in the geek culture; its advertisers can target their messages to smaller, more relevant groups of buyers.

Advergaming

Advergaming is the practice of using games, particularly computer games, to advertise or promote a product, an organization, or a viewpoint. Web-enabled game consoles are giving advertisers new ways to target the young generation. Advergaming normally falls into one of three categories:

▶ A company provides interactive games on its Web site in the hope that potential customers will be drawn to the game and spend more time on the Web site or simply become more product (or brand) aware. The games themselves usually feature the company's products prominently. An example is shown at Intel's Web site (itmg2.intel.com).

▶ Games are published in the usual way, but they require players to investigate further. The subjects may be commercial, political, or educational. Examples include America's Army (americasarmy.com/downloads), intended to boost recruitment for the United States Army.

▶ With some games, advertising appears within the actual game. This is similar to subtle advertising in films, whereby the advertising content is within the "world" of the movie or game. An example is cashsprint.com, which puts advertising logos directly on the player's racing vehicle and around the racetrack.

Example 1: In 2006, Cadillac tried a novel approach to get young male car buyers excited about its tricked-out V-series collection of luxury vehicles. Irrespective of advertising in magazines, TV commercials, or online display ads, the automaker took its campaign to Xbox (xbox360.com). Through an arrangement with Xbox live, customers were invited to download and put through their paces three virtual V-series cars in a popular high-speed driving game called "Project Gotham Racing 3." Within 6 months, more than 240,000 players snagged the game. This Cadillac success story offers a beacon of hope at a time when advertisers are struggling to get the attention of the mass audiences.

Example 2: Moola.com is an advertisers-sponsored family of games that work like this: Players receive free credit to wager against other players in return for watching a 10-, 15-, or 30-second video advertisement and sometimes answering a trivia question related to the ad (to make sure they watched the ad). Players are given one penny by Moola to begin betting. They may only bet in doubling amounts (1 cent, 2 cents, 4 cents, 8 cents, 16 cents, 32 cents, etc.). Moola emphasizes that by doubling winnings 30 times, a player will earn more than $10 million. When players lose all of their money, Moola provides a penny to begin again. These players may then "cash out" the accumulated winnings for real cash once the equivalent of at least $10 has been reached. Moola offers several games as well as tournaments.

Advergames promote repeat traffic to Web sites and reinforce brands in compelling ways. Users choose to register to be eligible for prizes that can help marketers collect customer data. Gamers may invite their friends to participate, which could assist promotion from word-of-mouth or viral marketing. For further discussion, see en.wikipedia.org/wiki/Advergaming and adverblog.com.

Section 4.8 ▶ REVIEW QUESTIONS

1. Define banner ads and describe their benefits and limitations.
2. Describe banner swapping and banner exchanges.
3. Describe the issues surrounding pop-ups and similar ads.
4. Explain how e-mail is used for advertising.
5. Describe advertising via classified ads.
6. Describe video ads and their growing popularity.
7. Describe the search engine optimization technique.
8. Describe Google's AdWords and AdSense.
9. Define advergaming and describe how it works.

4.9   ADVERTISING STRATEGIES AND PROMOTIONS

Several advertising strategies can be used over the Internet. In this section, we will present the major strategies used.

SOCIAL NETWORK ADVERTISING

Social network advertising describes online advertising that focuses on social networking sites. One of the major benefits of advertising on a social networking site is that advertisers can take advantage of the *users' demographic information* and target to the users' ads appropriately. *eMarketer* estimated that $2 billion were spent in 2008 on social network advertising worldwide and that this market will continue to grow, reaching $3.8 billion in spending by 2011 (reported by *Marketing Charts* 2008).

> **social network advertising**
> Online advertising that focuses on social networking sites.

Many claim that social network advertising will revolutionize the online advertising market. There is no doubt that social network advertising is a significantly new way of reaching customers; however, the market is far from being mature. The new forms of advertisement are more difficult to plan, measure, and quantify than regular Internet ads. Here we cover only some topics; others are covered in Online File W4.14.

Types of Social Network Advertising

According to en.wikipedia.org/wiki/Social_network_advertising, the three major classifications of social network advertising are as follows:

- ▸ **Direct advertising that is based on your network of friends.** This can be the most effective—but also the most controversial—format. An example is the Facebook Beacon Project. Based on an action your friend has taken, you might see a message in your news feed saying, "Bob has just bought a RadioHead CD from Music World." This can be an extremely effective mode of viral advertisement because people often make decisions to purchase something or do something based on their close group of friends. However, this form of advertising can be seen as exploiting the personal relationships you have with your friends; it also raises privacy concerns.

- ▸ **Direct advertising placed on your social network site.** This concept is similar to placing banner ads on any other site. An ad like this may be seen as a brick on a MySpace page or as a banner in a Facebook profile. However, there are two differences. One difference is that social network advertisers can take advantage of demographic data on your profile and target ads directly to you. Second, these ads can be placed by developers on their application pages through ad networks such as AdParlor. Again, this raises the issue of privacy.

- ▸ **Indirect advertising by creating "groups" or "pages."** With this innovative marketing technique, a company will create a "group" that users can join. The advertiser will target the "subscribers" or "fans" of this group to promote a contest, a new product, or simply just to increase brand awareness. These groups can grow quickly and become a very effective marketing tool. See the Scion case at the end of this chapter for an interesting example of innovative advertising to a market segment.

Sponsored Reviews by Bloggers

Companies are soliciting the help of paid bloggers to briefly mention their brands in regular blog entries or in video chips. For example, Apogee (apogee.com), instead of pouring money into search results as big companies do to get noticed, decided to explore the growing popularity of online communities (blogs and social networks) to get people talking about its Web site. For as little as $12.50 per post, Apogee's name and description of its business appear on blogs across the Web.

For more on social network advertising, see Social Network Advertising (socialadblog.com).

VIDEO ADS ON THE WEB AND IN SOCIAL NETWORKING

Web 2.0 inspired the phenomenon of the short, snappy video delivery. Marketers are eager to find ways to add consumer-generated videos into their ads because consumers identify with and enjoy real people doing real things. For example, KFC is among companies that are using consumer-generated videos and combining several of them to tell a story. Then, they show the story as an online ad or on television. For instance, homemade videos of the foam eruptions that come from dropping Mentos into a two-liter bottle of Diet Coke became a huge hit on video sites (see eepybird.com/dcm1.html).

YouTube has emerged as the largest advertising platform for video ads. By one estimate, YouTube currently has approximately 5 million videos and is growing at the rate of about 1 million videos a year. YouTube is already allowing marketers from brands like Wendy's (wendys.com) and Dove (dove.us) to upload videos to YouTube, just like anybody else. YouTube also began adding conventional ads to some of its videos and splitting the revenue with users who provide the content. Google AdSense's ad distribution network also offers ad-supported video clips.

Tracking the Success of an Online Video Campaign

Web video analytics

A way of measuring what viewers do when they watch an online video.

According to en.wikipedia.org/wiki/Online_video_analytics, online video analytics, also known as **Web video analytics**, is a way of measuring what viewers do when they watch an online video. A video is any length of video stream, such as a movie clip, video advertisement, movie trailer, television show, or full-length movie. Companies that provide Web video analytics are able to answer questions such as:

▶ How long did the viewer watch a particular video?

▶ Did the viewers pass it along to a friend? Embed it in their homepage? Bounce out as soon as they clicked "play"?

▶ If there was an ad overlay with the video, did they watch it? If so, for how long? Did they click through to complete a sale proposed by the ad?

▶ Where do the viewers come from who watch videos on a particular site?

Using an analytics platform is an ideal way to track a campaign's success because it gives marketers real-time intelligence that allows them to continually optimize the campaign and ensure the highest ROI. Representative methods are as follows:

▶ *Analytics software* combines data from several sites. If advertisers are running a multiplatform campaign, they can assess the entire campaign via one analytics dashboard.

▶ *Search engine* rankings also are a quick way to gauge an online campaign's success. Search engines now crawl and rank sites based on blended content, including images, video, and audio.

▶ Another benchmark of success is the *traction* video content gets on sites such as youtube.com, metacafe.com, and blinkx.com, which allow viewers to tag, bookmark, rank, and comment on videos. Such feedback is a valuable way to gauge how video content is being perceived online.

▶ *Brand interaction* is another effective way to monitor the success of an online video campaign. Tracking how long viewers watch an advertisement, what percentage of the video clip viewers watch, and how often they see an advertisement can provide valuable information to online marketers.

VIRAL MARKETING

viral marketing

Word-of-mouth marketing by which customers promote a product or service by telling others about it.

Viral marketing or advertising refers to word-of-mouth marketing in which customers promote a product or service by telling others about it. This can be done by e-mails, by text messaging, in conversations facilitated in chat rooms, via instant messaging, by posting messages in newsgroups, and in electronic consumer forums. Having people forward messages to friends, asking them, for example, to "check out this product," is an example of viral marketing. This marketing approach has been used for generations, but now its speed and reach are multiplied by the Internet. This ad model can be used to build brand awareness at a minimal cost, because the people who pass on the messages are paid very little or nothing for their efforts.

Viral marketing has long been a favorite strategy of online advertisers pushing youth-oriented products. For example, advertisers might distribute, embedded within a sponsor's e-mail, a small game program that is easy to forward. By releasing a few thousand copies of the game to some consumers, vendors hope to reach hundreds of thousands of others. Viral marketing also was used by the founder of Hotmail, a free e-mail service that grew from zero to 12 million subscribers in its 18 initial months and to more than 50 million subscribers in about 4 years. Each e-mail sent via Hotmail carried an invitation for free Hotmail service. Also known as *advocacy marketing*, viral marketing, if properly used, can be effective, efficient, and relatively inexpensive. For further details, see en.wikipedia.org/wiki/Viral_marketing and en.wikipedia.org/wiki/Types_of_viral_campaigns.

One of the downsides of this strategy is that several e-mail hoaxes have been spread this way. Another danger of viral advertising is that a destructive virus can be added to an innocent advertisement-related game or message.

Viral Marketing in Social Networks

Social networks are a natural and ideal place for viral marketing. For example, Sears (sears.com) has been using social networking and e-commerce to drive prom-season sales. Sears kicked off a campaign that lets shoppers share their dress selections with friends on Facebook. There they have the option of sharing one of about 70 prom dresses with their Facebook friends. Choosing that option will either prompt users to select friends or place a photo of a model wearing the dress in their profile, along with a product description and a message requesting opinions. Prom dress selection is an important decision for high school girls who want to get feedback from a circle of trusted peers before buying.

OTHER ADVERTISING STRATEGIES

Affiliate Marketing and Advertising

We introduced the concept of *affiliate marketing* in Chapters 1 and 3, the revenue sharing model by which an organization refers consumers to the selling company's Web site. **Affiliate marketing** is used mainly as a revenue source for the referring organization and as a marketing tool for sellers. However, the fact that the selling company's logo is placed on many other Web sites is free advertising as well. Consider Amazon.com, whose logo can be seen on more than 1 million affiliate sites! Moreover CDNow (a subsidiary of Amazon.com) and Amazon.com both are pioneers in the "get paid to view" or "listen to" commercials also used in affiliate marketing.

> **affiliate marketing**
> A marketing arrangement by which an organization refers consumers to the selling company's Web site.

Ads as a Commodity (Paying People to Watch Ads)

With the ads-as-a-commodity approach, people are paid for time spent viewing an ad. This approach is used at mypoints.com, clickrewards.com, and others. At MyPoints.com, interested consumers read ads in exchange for payment from the advertisers. Consumers fill out data on personal interests, and then they receive targeted banners based on their personal profiles. Each banner is labeled with the amount of payment that will be paid if the consumer reads the ad. If interested, the consumer clicks the banner to read it, and after passing some tests as to its content, is paid for the effort. Readers can sort and choose what they read, and the advertisers can vary the payments to reflect the frequency and desirability of the readers. Payments may be cash (e.g., $0.50 per banner) or product discounts. This method is used with smartphones, too (see Chapter 8). For further details, see en.wikipedia.org/wiki/Online_advertising and en.wikipedia.org/wiki/Payment_conventions.

Selling Space by Pixels

Million Dollar Homepage (milliondollarhomepage.com) was created by 21-year-old student Alex Tew in the United Kingdom. The Web site sold advertising space on a first page grid, much as real estate is sold, displaying a total of 1 million pixels at $1 per pixel. The site was launched in August 2005 and sold out by January 13, 2006. Within a short time, people started to sell pixels in other countries (e.g., milliondollarhomepage.com.au, one of several Australian sites). Also, people who bought pixels at $1 each were selling them at higher prices through auctions. This is an innovative way of owning ad space because once you buy it, it's there forever. Incidentally, MillionDollarHomepage.com has been subjected to a distributed denial-of-service (DDoS) attack (Chapter 10) by malicious hackers, who have caused the site to be extremely slow to load or completely unavailable. Blackmailers at first asked for $5,000 to avert an attack on the site. The DDoS attack was launched after Tew declined to pay, and the hackers then demanded $50,000 to stop attacking. A further refusal to pay prompted the attackers to deface the site, replacing the regular page with a message stating: "Don't come back, you sly dog!" The police solved the problem.

Personalized Ads

The Internet has too much information for customers to view. Filtering irrelevant information by providing consumers with customized ads can reduce this information overload. BroadVision (broadvision.com) provides a customized ad service platform called *BroadVision eMarketing*. The heart of eMarketing is a customer database, which includes registration data and information gleaned from site visits. The companies that advertise via one-to-one use the database to send customized ads to consumers. Using this feature, a marketing manager can customize display ads based on user profiles. The product also provides market segmentation.

Webcasting

A free Internet news service that broadcasts personalized news and information, including seminars, in categories selected by the user.

Another model of personalization can be found in **Webcasting**, a free Internet news service that broadcasts personalized news and information as well as e-seminars. Users sign into the Webcasting system and select the information they would like to receive, such as sports, news, headlines, stock quotes, or desired product promotions. The users receive the requested information along with personalized ads based on their expressed interests and general ads based on their profile.

Adobe (adobe.com) with the help of Yahoo! launched an opt-in service that enables online commercial publishers to drive new revenue by including timely, contextual ads next to Adobe's Portable Document Format (PDF)–based content. The service has the potential to offer readers access to free content, enhanced with ads that match their interests. Every time the PDF content is viewed, contextual ads are dynamically matched to the content of the document. For details, see advision.webevents.yahoo.com/adobe.

ONLINE EVENTS, PROMOTIONS, AND ATTRACTIONS

In the winter of 1994, the term *EC* was hardly known, and people were just starting to discover the Internet. One company, DealerNet, which was selling new and used cars from physical lots, demonstrated a new way of doing business: It started a virtual car showroom on the Internet. It let people "visit" dozens of dealerships and compare prices and features. At that time, this was a revolutionary way of selling cars. To get people's attention, DealerNet gave away a car over the Internet.

This promotion received a lot of offline media attention and was a total success. Today, such promotions are regular events on thousands of Web sites. Contests, quizzes, coupons (see coolsavings.com), and giveaways designed to attract visitors are as much a part of online marketing as they are of offline commerce. Some innovative ideas used to encourage people to pay attention to online advertising are provided in Online File W4.15.

Live Web Events

Live Web events (concerts, shows, interviews, debates, videos), if properly done, can generate tremendous public excitement and bring huge crowds to a Web site. Some of the best practices for successful live Web events are:

- Carefully planning content, audience, interactivity level, preproduction, and schedule
- Executing the production with rich media if possible
- Conducting appropriate promotion via e-mails, affinity sites, and streaming media directories, as well as conducting proper offline and online advertisement
- Preparing for quality delivery
- Capturing data and analyzing audience response so that improvements can be made

A global event can allow a product to debut in disparate locations. For example, Cisco Systems unveiled one of its products (ASR 1000 router) with the flair of an in-person event in 2008. It was covered by e-mail campaign and traditional media coverage but also by content distribution to bloggers and by ads in social networking sites such as Facebook. The company bought banner ads on prominent sites to drive traffic to marketing materials on their site. It also built a game around the new product and invited top prospects to take part in telepresence sessions that put them at a virtual table. The events and the marketing campaign created a strong response.

MOBILE MARKETING AND ADVERTISING

As will be seen in Chapter 8, the number of applications of *mobile commerce* (m-commerce) in marketing and advertising is growing rapidly, with advertising on cell phones and PDAs on the rise. One area is that of pervasive computing—the idea that computer chips can be embedded in almost any device (clothing, tools, appliances, homes, and so on), and then the device can be connected to a network of other devices. An interesting application of this is digital ads atop 12,000 taxis in various U.S. cities. The ads also include public service announcements. The technology comes from Vert (vert.net).

Vert displays live content and advertising messages very effectively by targeting specific postal codes, neighborhoods, and individual city blocks. Ads can be scheduled for specific times during the day (e.g., promote coffee during the morning commute). Ads are beamed to Vert-equipped taxis like a cell phone signal. GPS satellites pinpoint where the cab is traveling, allowing ads to change from block to block.

Mobile Advertising

Mobile advertising (m-advertising) refers to ads sent to and presented on mobile devices. M-advertising can be seen as a part of m-commerce. M-advertising enables the advertisers to send unique, personalized, and customized ads to mobile devices.

mobile advertising (m-advertising)
Ads sent to and presented on mobile devices.

Advertising on mobile phones is currently a tiny business. In 2008, the estimated spending on mobile ads was $1.72 billion worldwide, but it is expected to grow to $12 billion by 2013 (according to Informa Telecoms and Media, reported by Lev-Ram 2008). Most of the industry's efforts have focused on inserting ads in mobile portals accessible through cell phone browsers. At the moment, most mobile advertisement takes the form of text messages. However, telecom firms are also beginning to deliver ads to handsets alongside video clips, photos, music, and game downloads, through mobile devices. The 3 billion mobile phones around the world can potentially reach a much bigger audience than personal computers. Also, most people carry their mobile phones with them everywhere, so they can be reached anytime.

Examples. In September 2007, Blyk (blyk.co.uk), a then-new mobile operator, launched its service in Britain. It offered subscribers 217 free text message and 43 free minutes of voice calls per month as long as they agreed to receive six advertisements by text message every day. To sign up for the service, customers must fill out a questionnaire about their hobbies and habits so advertisers can target their messages very precisely. In the United States, Virgin Mobile (virginmobileusa.com) tried something similar with its "Sugar Mama" program, which offers subscribers the choice between receiving an ad via text message or viewing a 45-second advertisement when browsing the Internet, in exchange for 1 free minute of talk time.

Vodafone (vodafone.com), a large mobile operator in Europe, sees mobile advertising as a lucrative source of additional income. It gave an option of downloading footage from *Big Brother*, a popular television show, in exchange for viewing a promotional video clip.

Apple's iPhone now runs thousands of software programs, available at Apple's Application Store. More than 100 million applications were downloaded by users in 5 months (July to

Source: Courtesy of Vert Incorporated.

December 2008). Those numbers have caught the attention of advertisers, who see social networking widgets, restaurant locators, mobile games, and other applications as prime targets.

Only 20 percent of the more than 3,000 software programs on Apple's Application Store are free, but they make about 90 percent of the downloads. A growing number of them, such as the popular mobile game "Tap Tap Revenge" and "Pandora Radio" (a personalized music service), are already experimenting with ads. Play a round of "Tap Tap," for instance, and you will likely see a banner ad for Jaguar cars on the bottom of your screen. Mobile ad networks like AdMob (admob.com) already have launched iPhone-specific ad services.

Some of the mobile phones that are equipped with GPS technology could be used to alert people to the availability and discounts of stores or restaurants that they are walking or driving by (see *l-commerce*, Chapter 8). Tying ads to online searches from mobile phones is another promising venture. A subscriber typing in "pizza," for instance, could receive ads for nearby pizza parlors with a discount coupon, along with his search results.

Mobile Marketing

For mobile marketing, several other issues need to be examined. For instance, is the product suitable for marketing on mobile devices? Will the location-based advertisement create the expected effect? Young consumers have been notoriously difficult for advertisers to reach; the mobile platform provides the perfect mechanism for reaching young consumers. For example, a large retailer might send electronic coupons to the phones of teenagers at a shopping mall to promote a new product.

In reality, the success of mobile ads campaigns has been mixed, because many companies don't understand or know what truly influences young consumers. Will they, for instance, be enticed by receiving electronic coupons on their cell phones, or will they be annoyed? Unsolicited messages to mobile devices interrupt the device holder. A survey by Tsang et al. (2004) indicated that most consumers hold a negative attitude toward receiving mobile advertising. Incentive programs are necessary for creating a positive attitude toward mobile ads.

Section 4.9 ▶ REVIEW QUESTIONS

1. Describe social network advertising.
2. Describe video ads and their explosion.
3. Describe viral marketing and discuss viral marketing in social networks.
4. Discuss the process and value of affiliate marketing.
5. How does the ads-as-a-commodity strategy work?
6. Describe other kinds of online advertising methods.
7. Describe mobile advertising.
8. List some typical Internet promotions.

4.10 SPECIAL ADVERTISING AND IMPLEMENTATION TOPICS

The following are major representative topics related to Internet advertising.

spamming
Using e-mail to send unwanted ads (sometimes floods of ads).

permission advertising (permission marketing)
Advertising (marketing) strategy in which customers agree to accept advertising and marketing materials (known as *opt-in*).

PERMISSION ADVERTISING

One of the major issues in one-to-one advertising is the flooding of users with unwanted (junk) e-mail, banners, pop-ups, and so forth. One of the authors of this book experienced a flood of X-rated ads. Each time such an ad arrived, he blocked receipt of further ads from this source. That helped for a day or two, but then the same ads arrived from another e-mail address. Most e-mail providers can place software agents to identify and block such junk mail. This problem, the flooding of users with unsolicited e-mails and other type of ads, is referred to as **spamming** (see Chapter 16). Spamming typically upsets consumers and, when blocked, may keep useful advertising from reaching them.

One solution used by advertisers is **permission advertising** or **permission marketing** (or the *opt-in approach*), in which users register with vendors and agree to accept advertising (see returnpath.net). For example, the authors of this book agreed to receive a large number of e-commerce newsletters, knowing that some would include ads. This way, we can keep abreast of what is happening in the field. We also agreed to accept e-mail from research companies, newspapers, travel agencies, and more. These vendors push, for free, very valuable information to us. The accompanying ads pay for such services. Note that Netflix asks permission to send users recommendations, but it does not ask whether it can use historical purchasing data to create recommendations (see Team Assignment 5).

SOME IMPLEMENTATION ISSUES

Although creative ideas are important to Internet marketing and advertising, implementation is at least equally important for a campaign to be successful. Here we present some representative implementation issues.

Admediation

Conducting promotions, especially large-scale ones, may require the help of vendors who specialize in promotions, such as Mypoints.com and those listed in Online File W4.15. These are called **admediaries**. A model showing the role of these vendors is shown in Exhibit 4.9. The exhibit concentrates on e-mail and shows the role of the admediaries.

admediaries
Third-party vendors that conduct promotions, especially large-scale ones.

Running promotions on the Internet is similar to running offline promotions. Some of the major considerations when implementing an online ad campaign include the following:

- The target audience needs to be clearly understood and should be online surfers.
- The traffic to the site should be estimated, and a powerful enough server must be prepared to handle the expected traffic volume.
- Assuming that the promotion is successful, what will the result be? This assessment is needed to evaluate the budget and promotion strategy.
- Consider co-branding; many promotions succeed because they bring together two or more powerful partners.

Companies combine several advertising methods as a result of market research. And if they have several Web sites, they may use different methods on each site.

Ad Exchanges

An advertising exchange is an open and transparent marketplace that facilitates the buying and selling of online advertising. It matches the need of advertisers and the capacity of ad providers. Advertising exchanges may use auctions to sell ads and directly connect advertisers and publishers. We have seen increased interest because of their transparency. Exchanges enable advertisers to bid for the type of ad and demographic that they would like to reach.

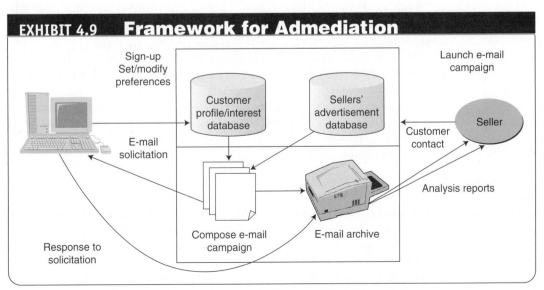

EXHIBIT 4.9   Framework for Admediation

Source: "A Framework for Admediation," Gopal et al., 2001, Fig 1, p. 92. Used with permission.

Advertisement as a Revenue Model

Many of the dot-com failures from 2000 to 2002 were caused by a revenue model that contained advertising income as the major or a major revenue source. Many small portals failed, but several large ones are dominating the field: Google, AOL, Yahoo!, and MSN. However, even these heavy-traffic sites only started to show a significant profit after 2004. Too many Web sites are competing for the advertising money. Thus, almost all portals are adding other sources of revenue.

However, if careful, a small site can survive by concentrating on a niche area. For example, nflrush.com is doing well. It pulls millions of dollars in advertising and sponsorship by concentrating on NFL fans. The site provides comprehensive and interactive content, attracting millions of visitors.

Measuring Online Advertising's Effectiveness

One managerial issue is how to measure the effectiveness of online advertising. A related issue is how to charge for ads. These two topics are presented in Online File W4.16.

AD MANAGEMENT

ad management

Methodology and software that enable organizations to perform a variety of activities involved in Web advertising (e.g., tracking viewers, rotating ads).

The activities involved in Web advertising, which range from tracking viewers to rotating ads, require a special methodology and software known as *ad management* software. **Ad management** software lets an advertiser send very specific ads on a schedule and target ads to certain population segments, which can be very small. For example, an advertiser can send an ad to all male residents of Los Angeles County between the ages of 26 and 39 whose income level is more than $30,000. The advertiser can even refine the segment further by using ethnic origin, type of employment, or home ownership.

When selecting ad management software, a company should look for the following features, which will optimize their ability to advertise online:

- **The ability to match ads with specific content.** Being able to match ads with Web content would allow an advertiser, for example, to run an ad from a car company in an article about the Indy 500 (Indy500.com).
- **Tracking.** Of course, the advertiser will need to deliver detailed metrics (performance measures) to its customers, showing impression rates, click-through rates, and other metrics. Tracking of viewing activity is essential in providing such metrics.
- **Rotation.** Advertisers may want to rotate different ads in the same space.
- **Spacing impressions.** If an advertiser buys a given number of impressions over a period of time, the software should be able to adjust the delivery schedule so that they are spread out evenly.

A variety of ad management software packages are available, including some from application service providers (ASPs) and some freeware. AdManager (from atlassolutions.com) is a comprehensive package that delivers all of the features just discussed.

One topic in ad management is campaign management, that is, management of an entire marketing and advertising campaign. Campaign management tools fall into two categories: those that are folded into CRM (customer relationship management), which consist mainly of marketing automation, and those that are targeted, stand-alone campaign management products. Companies such as DoubleClick provide partial management. More comprehensive management is provided by Atlas DMT's Digital Marketing suite (see atlassolutions.com/solutions_admanager.aspx).

LOCALIZATION

localization

The process of converting media products developed in one environment (e.g., country) to a form culturally and linguistically acceptable in countries outside the original target market.

Localization is the process of converting media products and advertisement material developed in one environment (e.g., a country) to a form culturally and linguistically acceptable outside the original target market. It is usually done by a set of internationalization guidelines. Web page translation (Chapter 13) is just one aspect of internationalization. However, several other aspects also are important. For example, a U.S. jewelry manufacturer that displayed its products on a white background was astonished to find that this display might not appeal to customers in some countries where a blue background is preferred.

If a company aims at the global market (and there are millions of potential customers out there), it must make an effort to localize its Web pages. This may not be a simple task because of the following factors:

▶ Many countries use English, but the English used may differ in terminology, spelling, and culture (e.g., the United Kingdom versus Australia).

▶ Some languages use accented characters. If text includes an accented character, the accent will disappear when converted into English, which may result in an incorrect translation.

▶ Hard-coded text and fonts cannot be changed, so they remain in their original format in the translated material.

▶ Graphics and icons look different to viewers in different countries. For example, a U.S. mailbox resembles a European trashcan.

▶ When translating into Asian languages, significant cultural issues must be addressed, for example, how to address older adults in a culturally correct manner.

▶ Dates that are written mm/dd/yy (e.g., June 8, 2007) in some countries are written dd/mm/yy (e.g., 8 June 2007) in many other countries. Therefore, "6/8" would have two meanings (June 8 or August 6), depending on the location of the writer.

▶ Consistent translation over several documents can be very difficult to achieve. (For free translation in six languages, see freetranslation.com.)

Automatic Versus Manual Web Page Translation

Certain localization difficulties result in a need for experienced human translators, who are rare, expensive, and slow. Therefore, companies are using automatic translation software, at least as an initial step to expedite the work of human translators. (See Chapter 13 for further discussion and references.) When ads are translated, manual translation is virtually a must.

Using Internet Radio for Localization

Internet radio Web sites provide music, talk, and other entertainment, both live and stored, from a variety of radio stations. The big advantage of Internet radio is that there are few limits on the type or number of programs it can offer, as compared with traditional radio stations. It is especially useful in presenting programming for local communities. For example, KIISFM (kiisfm.com) is a Los Angeles site that features music from up-and-coming L.A. bands, live concerts, interviews with movie stars, and so forth. About 40 percent of the site's traffic comes from listeners in California, and the rest from listeners around the world. The company that powers the KIISFM Web site also operates sites focused on country music, Latin music, and so forth. Advertisers can reach fairly narrow audience segments by advertising on a particular Internet radio site.

Internet radio
A Web site that provides music, talk, and other entertainment, both live and stored, from a variety of radio stations.

AD CONTENT

The content of ads is extremely important, and large companies use ad agencies to help in content creation for the Web just as they do for other advertising media. A major player in this area is Akamai Technologies (akamai.com). The company points out how the right content can drive traffic to a site. Akamai also describes how to evaluate third-party vendors and determine what content-related services are important.

Content is especially important to increase stickiness. Customers are expensive to acquire; therefore, it is important that they remain at a site, read its content carefully, and eventually make a purchase. The writing of the advertising content itself is, of course, important (see adcopywriting.com and Chapter 15). Therefore, large companies are using ad agencies. AgencyFinder (agencyfinder.com) maintains a huge database of agencies.

INTELLIGENT AGENTS APPLICATIONS

Intelligent agents (also called *software agents*) are computer software designed for performing certain tasks automatically. They have been widely used in e-commerce to overcome information overload on the Internet. In general, they can be used to facilitate the consumer in all stages of the purchasing process. Exhibit 4.10 shows a framework for classifying different types of software agents based on the six stages in the purchase decision process. A more detailed description of software agents is available in Online File W4.17. For some examples, see Online File W4.18.

Major types of EC agents include:

▶ Agents that support needs identification
▶ Agents that support product brokering
▶ Agents that support merchant brokering
▶ Agents that support purchase and delivery
▶ Agents that support after-sales service and evaluation

EXHIBIT 4.10 **The Purchase Decision-Making Process: Agent Classification**

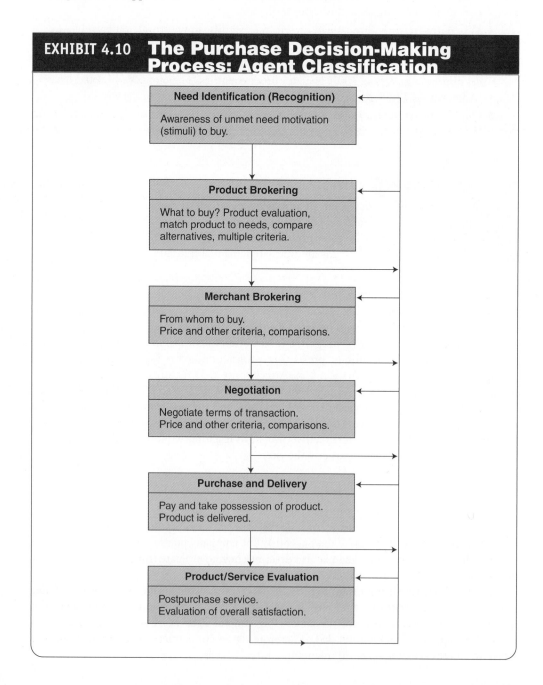

For a general discussion of intelligent and software agents, see Section 12.5 in Chapter 12.

Section 4.10 ▶ REVIEW QUESTIONS

1. Describe permission advertising.
2. Describe admediation and exchanges.
3. What is ad management?
4. What is localization? What are the major issues in localizing Web pages?
5. What is the importance of ad content?

MANAGERIAL ISSUES

Some managerial issues related to this chapter are as follows.

1. **Do we focus on value-creating customers?** Understanding customers, specifically what they need and how to respond to those needs, is the most critical part of consumer-centered marketing. This was not possible before the solutions for database marketing, one-to-one marketing, and customer relationship marketing became available. What tools do we use to satisfy and retain customers, monitor the entire process of marketing, sales, maintenance, and follow-up services? Do we focus these resources effectively to the VIP customers who contribute to enhancing the corporate value?

2. **Which Internet marketing/advertising channel do we use?** An increasing number of online methods are available from which to choose. These include banners, search engines, blogging, social networks, and more. Angel (2006) proposed a methodology for Internet marketing channel selection that might be adopted to assess these alternatives with a matrix for selection and implementation.

3. **What metrics do we use to guide advertisers?** A large amount of information has been developed to guide advertisers as to where to advertise, how to design ads, and so on. Specific metrics such as CPM (cost per thousand impressions), click-through rate, stickiness, and actual purchase rate may be used to assess the effectiveness of advertising and calculate the ROI from an organization's online advertising campaign. The metrics can be monitored by third-party monitoring companies.

4. **What is our commitment to Web advertising?** Once a company has committed to advertising on the Web, it must remember that a successful program is multifaceted. It requires input and vision from marketing, cooperation from the legal department, and strong technical leadership from the corporate information systems (IS) department. A successful Web advertising program also requires coordination with non-Internet advertising and top management support.

5. **Should we integrate our Internet and non-Internet marketing campaigns?** Many companies are integrating their TV and Internet marketing campaigns. For example, a company's TV or newspaper ads direct the viewers/readers to the Web site, where short videos and sound ads, known as *rich media*, are used. With click-through ratios of banner ads down to less than 0.5 percent at many sites, innovations such as the integration of offline and online marketing are certainly needed to increase click-through rates and ratios.

6. **Who will conduct the market research?** B2C requires extensive market research. This research is not easy to do, nor is it inexpensive. Deciding whether to outsource to a market research firm or maintain an in-house market research staff is a managerial concern. If a company owns a large-scale customer database, the research on the internal database itself can be an important market research tool, and data mining techniques will be helpful.

7. **Should we use intelligent agents?** Any company engaged in EC must examine the possibility of using intelligent agents to enhance customized service, and possibly to support market research and match ads with relevant consumers. Commercial agents that conduct collaborative filtering and basket analysis are available on the market at a reasonable cost.

8. **What ethical issues should we consider in online marketing?** Several ethical issues relate to online advertising. One issue that receives a great deal of attention is spamming (Chapter 16). Another issue is the selling of mailing lists and customer information. Some people believe not only that a company needs the consent of customers before selling a list, but also that the company should share the profits with customers derived from the sale of such lists. Using cookies without an individual's consent is considered by many to be an unethical issue. The negative impacts of advertising need to be considered.

SUMMARY

In this chapter, you learned about the following EC issues as they relate to the chapter's learning objectives.

1. **Factors influencing online consumer behavior.** Consumer behavior in EC is similar to that of any consumer behavior, but it has some unique features. It is described in a stimuli-based decision model that is influenced by factors that include the consumer's personal characteristics, environmental characteristics, product/service features, merchant and intermediary, and the EC systems (logistics, technology, and customer service). All of these characteristics and systems interact to influence the decision-making process and produce an eventual buyer decision.

2. **The online consumer decision-making process.** The goal of marketing research efforts is to understand the consumers' online decision-making processes and formulate an appropriate strategy to influence their behavior. For each step in the process, sellers can develop appropriate strategies. The Attention-Interest-Desire-Action model can help us design ad and marketing efforts for different purposes.

3. **Market segmentation and building one-to-one relationships with customers.** In segmentation, attention to advertising and marketing is given to a segment (e.g., female customers, customers in a certain country) for improving marketing effectiveness. EC offers companies the opportunity to build one-to-one relationships with customers that are not possible in other marketing systems. Product customization, personalized service, and getting the customer involved interactively (e.g., in feedback, order tracking, and so on) are all practical in cyberspace. In addition, advertising can be matched with customer profiles so that ads can be presented on a one-to-one basis.

4. **Online personalization.** Using personal Web pages, customers can interact with a company, learn about products or services in real time, or get customized products or services. Companies can allow customers to self-configure the products or services they want. Customization also can be done by matching products with customers' profiles. Personalization includes recommendation of products (services) and delivering content that customers want.

5. **Increasing loyalty and trust.** Customers can switch loyalty online easily and quickly. Therefore, enhancing e-loyalty (e.g., through e-loyalty programs) is a must. Similarly, trust is a critical success factor that must be nourished. Creating loyalty is difficult since customers can switch easily to competitors. Building trust is very difficult since people do not know or see each other. Trust is influenced by many variables.

6. **EC customer market research.** Several fast and economical methods of online market research are available. The two major approaches to data collection are (1) soliciting voluntary information from the customers and (2) using cookies, transaction logs, or clickstream data to track customers' movements on the Internet and find what their interests are. Understanding market segmentation by grouping consumers into categories is also an effective EC market research method. However, online market research has several limitations, including data accuracy and representation of the statistical population by a sample.

7. **Objectives and characteristics of Web advertising.** Web advertising attempts to attract surfers to an advertiser's site. Once at the advertiser's site, consumers can receive information, interact with the seller, and in many cases, are easily given a chance to place an order. With Web advertising, ads can be customized to fit groups of people with similar interests (segmentation) or even individuals (one-to-one). In addition, Web advertising can be interactive, is easily updated, can reach millions at a reasonable cost, and offers dynamic presentation and rich multimedia.

8. **Major online advertising methods.** Banners are the most popular online advertising method. Other frequently used methods are pop-ups and similar ads (including interstitials), e-mail (including e-mail to mobile devices), classified ads, registration of URLs with search engines, and advertising in chat rooms. Some of these are related to search results obtained through search engines such as keyword advertising (especially Google). Social network communities provide new opportunities for marketing by enabling segmentation, viral marketing, user-generated ads, and more. Advertising in videos is gaining popularity as well.

9. **Various advertising strategies and types of promotions.** The major advertising strategies are ads associated with search results (text links), affiliate marketing, pay incentives for customers to view ads, viral marketing, ads customized on a one-to-one basis, and online events and promotions. Web promotions are similar to offline promotions. They include giveaways, contests, quizzes, entertainment, coupons, and so on. Customization and interactivity distinguish Internet promotions from conventional ones. It is also important that marketing projects need to be localized to meet different cultures.

10. **Permission marketing and ad management.** In permission marketing, customers are willing to accept ads in exchange for special (personalized) information or monetary incentives. Ad management deals with planning, organizing, and controlling ad campaigns and ad use. Ads can be localized to culture, country, and so forth.

11. **Social networking, Web 2.0, market research, and advertising.** Market research can be facilitated by feedback from bloggers, chats in social networks, recommendations of friends, polling of members' opinions, and so forth. Advertising is enhanced by user-generated ad content, viral marketing, better segmentation, and reading affinity with small groups.

KEY TERMS

QUESTIONS FOR DISCUSSION

1. How can you describe the process of the purchase decision when the customer is online and looking for an iPhone? What can an online store do to attract this customer to purchase from the store?

2. What would you tell an executive officer of a bank about the critical success factors for increasing the loyalty of banking customers by using the Internet?

3. Why is personalization becoming an important element in EC? What techniques can be used to learn about consumer behavior? How can it be used to facilitate customer service? Please find an example.

4. Explain why online trust is more difficult to achieve than offline trust.

5. Discuss the similarities and differences between data mining, text mining, and Web mining. (Hint: To answer this question, you will need to read Online File W4.2.)

6. How can research on satisfaction and dissatisfaction help online sellers? What may affect online customer satisfaction?

7. Discuss why B2C marketing and advertising methods may not fit B2B.

8. Relate banner swapping to a banner exchange.

9. Discuss why banners are popular in Internet advertising. What kinds of products may be suitable for banners and what may not?

10. Discuss the situations in which market research and advertising are useful.

11. Discuss the advantages and limitations of listing a company's URL with various search engines.

12. How might a social network community (such as LinkedIn or Facebook) be used for advertising?

13. How might a chat room be used for advertising?

14. Is it ethical for a vendor to enter a chat room operated by a competitor and pose queries?

15. Explain why online ad management is critical. What are the major concerns for a company managing its own online ad program?

16. Examine some Web avatars and try to interact with them. Discuss the potential benefits and drawbacks of using avatars as an advertising medium (see Online File W4.17).

17. Explain the advantages of using chatterbots. Are there any disadvantages? (See Online File W4.17.)

18. Discuss the benefits of using software agents in marketing and advertising. To determine whether a bargaining agent online (an agent that can interact with potential customers to settle a discount price) can help the online shop's sales, see Online File W4.18.

19. Discuss whether avatars can increase trust (see Online File W4.17).

20. Discuss SRI Consulting's VALS tool. Enter sric-bi.com/VALS. View their activities and discuss how they can facilitate online market segmentation.

21. When you buy a banner ad, you actually lease space for a specific time period. At milliondollarhomepage.com, you buy space forever. Compare and discuss.

INTERNET EXERCISES

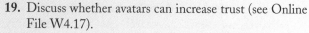

1. Enter netflix.com/Affiliates?hnjr=3. Describe the value of the program as a marketing channel.

2. Surf homedepot.com and check whether (and how) the company provides service to customers with different skill levels. Particularly, check the "kitchen and bath design center" and other self-configuration assistance. Relate this to market research.

3. Examine a market research Web site (e.g., acnielsen.com or claritas.com). Discuss what might motivate a consumer to provide answers to market research questions.

4. Enter mysimon.com and share your experiences about how the information you provide might be used by the company for marketing in a specific industry (e.g., the clothing market).

5. Enter marketingterms.com and conduct a search by keywords as well as by category. Check the definitions of 10 key terms in this chapter.

6. Enter 2020research.com, infosurv.com, and marketingsherpa.com and identify areas for market research about consumers.

7. Enter selfpromotion.com and find some interesting promotion ideas for the Web.

8. Enter selfpromotion.com and nielsen-online.com. What Internet traffic management, Web results, and auditing services are provided? What are the benefits of each service? Compare the services provided and the prices.

9. Compare the advertisements and promotions at thestreet.com and marketwatch.com. Write a report.

10. Enter adweek.com, wdfm.com, ad-tech.com, adage.com, and other online advertising Web sites to find new developments in Internet advertising. Write a report based on your findings.

11. Enter clairol.com to determine your best hair color. You can upload your own photo to the studio and see how different shades look on you. You can also try different hairstyles. This site also is for men. How can these activities increase branding? How can they increase sales?

12. What resources do you find to be most useful at targetmarketingmag.com, clickz.com, admedia.org, marketresearch.com, and wdfm.com? Describe useful information for online marketing that you have found from these Web sites.

13. Enter doubleclick.com and examine all of the company's products. Prepare a report.

14. Enter sitepal.com and check out each of the chatterbots listed under "reasons for using SitePal." In your opinion, which of these bots best accomplished the goal of the site? Why?

15. Enter zoomerang.com and learn how it facilitates online surveys. Examine the various products, including those that supplement the surveys. Write a report.

16. Enter pewInternet.org and pewresearch.org. What research do they conduct that is relevant to B2C? To B2B? Write a report.

17. Enter loomia.com. Describe their recommendation engines. Compare this with the recommendation engine of amazon.com.

18. Enter whattorent.com and compare the recommandation system to Netflix. Write a brief comparison.

TEAM ASSIGNMENTS, PROJECTS, AND CLASS DISCUSSIONS

1. Enter harrisinteractive.com, infosurv.com, and similar sites. Have each team member examine the free marketing tools and related tutorials and demos. Each team will try to find a similar site and compare the two. Write a report discussing the team's findings.

2. Each team will choose one advertising method and conduct an in-depth investigation of the major players in

that part of the ad industry. For example, direct e-mail is relatively inexpensive. Visit **the-dma.org** to learn about direct mail. Then visit **ezinedirector.com, venture direct.com**, and similar sites. Each team will prepare and present an argument as to why its method is superior.

3. In this exercise, each team member will enter **uproar.com** or similar sites to play games and win prizes. What could be better? This site is the destination of choice for game and sweepstakes junkies and for those who wish to reach a mass audience of fun-loving people. Relate the games to advertising and marketing.

4. Let the team try the services of **constantcontact.com**. Constant Contact offers a turnkey e-mail marketing package solution. In less than 5 minutes, you can set up an e-mail sign-up box on your Web site. As visitors fill in their names and e-mail addresses, they can be asked to check off topics of interest (as defined by you) to create targeted groups.

Constant Contact provides a system for creating custom e-mail newsletters that can be sent to your target users on a predetermined schedule. The site manages your mailings and provides reports that help you assess the success of your efforts. Pricing is based on the number of subscribers: less than 50 and the service is free. Write a report summarizing your experiences.

5. Enter **autonlab.org** and download tools for conducting data mining analysis (these downloads are free). Get data on customer shopping and analyze it. Write a report.

6. Address the following topics in a class discussion:

a. **Netflix.com, amazon.com**, and others view historical purchases as input available for use in their recommendation systems. Some believe that this is an invasion of privacy. Debate this issue.

b. Some say that you cannot provide one-to-one advertising without violating privacy. Discuss.

c. Some say that people come to social networks to socialize and they will not accept ads. Discuss.

d. What strategic implication do you see for companies that use videos, mobile devices, and social networks as platforms for advertising?

Closing Case

TOYOTA SCION GOES SOCIAL FOR ADVERTISING AND MARKET RESEARCH

The Problem

The automotive industry is a global multibillion-dollar business where competition is very intense. Both General Motors (GM) and Toyota are competing to be the world's #1 car manufacturer. At stake is not only how many cars can be sold, but also how much profit can be made and how to survive in economic downturns.

Toyota has been known for decades for its manufacturing innovations. Now it's taken an innovative lead on the Web. Here, we look at one of its newest brands, the Scion, geared toward Generation Y (Gen Y), which includes those born between 1980 and 1994. As of 2009, Gen Y and Gen X (the generation before Gen Y) combined are expected to account for at least 40 percent of vehicle sales. The problem faced by Scion is how to reach Gen Y and Gen X people.

Using Social Computing

Scion is using segmented advertising as its major media-based strategy in social networks. The company also uses search engine marketing, mass advertising, and one-to-one targeted marketing, all of which are aimed at increasing brand recognition.

Here are some representative activities:

▸ Scion uses display ads that reach urban audiences via sites such as *blastro.com* and *hiphopdx.com* (Rodgers

2007). Scion works with these sites to develop ad content in a way to make it attractive to the sites' membership. This ranges from photo galleries to social networking profile pages to offering interactive features.

▸ In August 2007, Scion launched *Club Scion*, a three-story virtual nightclub with dance floors, music, and hot tubs. Each level of the club reflects a different Scion model, which includes the xA hatchback, xB SUV, and tC sports coupe.

▸ Scion maintains a presence in several large virtual worlds, including *secondlife.com, whyville.com, there.com*, and *gaia.com*. Each virtual world lends itself to a different marketing strategy. In *Whyville*, where users tend to fall between ages 8 and 15, the company launched a virtual driver's education program. Since *there.com* is populated by older teens, Scion made sure to create a more provocative social environment.

▸ Toyota made effective use of the Internet by using live chat to attract the 18- to 24-year-old audience. The campaign includes the use of *microapplication ads* that allow consumers to stencil designs over the picture of the Scion.

To capitalize on wireless technology, in 2004 Toyota launched a mobile *advergame* (game to advertise a product), called "Scion Road Trip." Players earn virtual

Source: Courtesy of Toyota Motor Sales. Used with permission.

miles when they send e-cards to friends and get back responses. The campaign lasted for several months.

▶ For the 2008 xB SUV, Scion created a special Web site (*want2bsquare.com*). Visitors to the site can earn points by playing games, watching videos, and e-mailing others about the site. The site features eight *microsites*, including user community features; each has a unique theme and its own design. There are microsites that focus on music; resemble a Monty Python set; feature a haunted house; and include a town square and an urban zoo.

▶ Toyota targets children as a means to influence their parents. In April 2007, Toyota began placing its Scion on *whyville.net*, an online interactive community populated almost entirely by 8- to 15-year-olds. Toyota hopes Whyvillians will do two things: influence the users' parents' car purchases and grow up to buy Toyotas themselves. The power of younger consumers has grown stronger in recent years. According to *MediaBuyerPlanner.com* (2006), a study by Packaged Facts showed that 39 percent of parents of 10- and 11-year-olds say their children have a significant impact on brand purchases.

▶ Finally, like several other automakers, Scion is creating its own broadband channel. These channels are a way to move from push to pull marketing, where the consumer decides what materials to view and when. A content-rich, broadband-friendly site is an always-on marketing channel to which people will return.

▶ Toyota created its own social network site called *Scion Speak,* where Scion lovers can socialize, communicate, and play. Scion owners can choose from hundreds of symbols and create customized logos for their cars. They can then download the logo and make window decals, or have them painted onto their cars (for a fee).

The Results

According to *MarketingVox.com* (2007a), Scion has 80 percent brand recognition, a very high value. As of April 2007, Scion was the #1 brick-and-mortar e-tailer among consumers 35 years old and younger. Scion had not even made it into the top 25 sites in 2006; the amazing jump to the #1 ranking was due to the interactive and community-oriented nature of the Scion online experiences.

The Scion Web site is highly personalized. Sophisticated customization tools allow people to build their own virtual cars on the site. This online information is then integrated offline—a local dealership locates the desired or similar vehicle for each virtual car builder and contacts them for a test drive. Other digital frills like a social network for Scion car buyers and a Web site that plays music and lists concert information create superb brand experiences. Let's look at some of the specific advertising activities.

▶ The brand's Scion City in *Second Life* generated 10,000 blog posts between April and June 2007 and is the third most recognized brand behind Reuters in *Second Life* awareness.

▶ The on-site chat feature gets hundreds of conversations per week. Prior to the chat, users are asked a few questions, one of which is where they live. Interestingly, Toyota found that many of the chatters reside in areas where Scion is not even available, providing valuable information for dealer expansion plans.

▶ *The New York Times* reported that visitors to the site had used the word "Scion" in online chats more than 78,000 times; hundreds of virtual Scions were purchased using "clams," the currency of Whyville; and the community meeting place "Club Scion" was visited 33,741 times.

▶ SMS (*short messaging service* or *text message*) is being used to alert players of their accrued virtual miles and weekly contest events.

Sources: Compiled from *scion.com* (accessed March 2009), Bosman (2006), *MediaBuyerPlanner.com* (2006), *MarketingVox.com* (2007a, 2007b, and 2007c), and Rodgers (2007).

Questions

1. Identify all advertising actions and relate them to the methods described in this chapter.

2. Identify all activities that can be considered market research.

3. What can increase loyalty?

4. Identify personalization methods provided by Scion.

5. Find advertisement and market research activities conducted by Scion that are not cited in this case.

ONLINE RESOURCES
available at pearsonglobaleditions.com/turban

WWW

Online Files

W4.1   Overview of Design Space for Online Decision Support

W4.2   Business Intelligence: From Data Collection to Data Mining and Analysis

W4.3   Internet-Based Market Research Process

W4.4   Spyware

W4.5   List of Information Provided by Clickstream Data

W4.6   From Mass Advertising to Interactive Advertising

W4.7   Application Case: 1-800-Flowers.com Uses Data Mining to Foster Customer Relationship Management

W4.8   Advantages and Limitations of Internet Advertising

W4.9   Application Case: Targeted Advertising—The DoubleClick Approach

W4.10 Click-Through and Conversion Ratios

W4.11 Pop-up Advertising Methods

W4.12 What Is Involved in Localization?

W4.13 E-Mail Advertising Methods

W4.14 Marketing and Advertising in the Web 2.0 Environment

W4.15 How to Attract Web Surfers

W4.16 Economics of Advertisement

W4.17 Software Agents in Marketing and Advertising Applications

W4.18 Examples of Intelligent Agents

Comprehensive Educational Web Sites

marketresearch.com: E-commerce market research reports (for free)

ecommerce-guide.com/news/research: Comprehensive collection of resources

Internet.com: Many resources (for small business, in particular)

emarketer.com: Statistics, news, products, laws

wilsoweb.com/research: Case studies, articles, tutorials, videos, and more; the research room may require fees

lib.unc.edu/reference/busecon/ecommerce.html: List of EC resources

ecommercetimes.com: News and analysis

clickz.com/stat: EC statistics

cio.com/white-papers

REFERENCES

Angel, G. "The Art and Science of Choosing Net Marketing Channels." *E-Commerce Times*, September 21, 2006. ecommercetimes.com/story/53141.html (accessed November 2006).

Bosman, J. "Hey, Kid, You Want to Buy a Toyota Scion?" *The New York Times*, June 14, 2006. nytimes.com/2006/06/14/business/media/14adco.html?_r=2&oref=slogin&oref=slogin (accessed March 2009).

Brengman, M., M. Geuens, S. M. Smith, W. R. Swinyard, and B. Weijters. "Segmenting Internet Shoppers Based on Their Web-Usage-Related Lifestyle: A Cross-Cultural Validation." *Journal of Business Research* 58 (2005).

Buckley, N. "E-Route to Whiter Smile." *Financial Times*, August 26, 2002.

Chaudhury, A., D. Mallick, and H. R. Rao. "Web Channels in E-Commerce." *Communications of the ACM* (January 2001).

Cheung, C. M. K., and M. K. O. Lee. "The Asymmetric Impact of Website Attribute Performance on User Satisfaction: An Empirical Study." *e-Service Journal* 3, no. 3 (2005).

Compete. "Netflix Outruns Blockbuster 5 to 1." January 2009. siteanalytics.compete.com/netflix.com+blockbuster.com/?metric=uv (accessed March 2009).

Computer Industry Alamanac. "Worldwide Internet Users Top 1 Billion in 2005. USA Reach Newly 200M Internet Users." January 4, 2006. c-i-a.com/pr0106.htm (accessed February 2009).

Crampton, T. "10% of Population Has Shopped on Web, Study Shows." *International Herald Tribune*, October 2005. iht.com/articles/2005/10/18/business/eshop.php (accessed November 2006).

eMarketer. "Social Network Ad Space: Sorry, Sold Out!" November 3, 2006.

Flynn, L. J. "Like This? You'll Hate That (Not All Web Recommendations Are Welcome)." *The New York Times*, January 23, 2006.

Gopal, R. D., A. K. Tripathi , and Z. D. Walter. "Admediation: New Horizons in Effective Email Advertising." *The Communications of the ACM*, 44(12), 2001.

Hewson, C., et al. *Internet Research Methods*. London: Sage, 2003.

Lee, M., and E. Turban. "Trust in B2C Electronic Commerce: A Proposed Research Model and Its Application." *International Journal of Electronic Commerce* 6, no. 1 (2001).

Lev-Ram, M. "Ad Industry Eyes the iPhone." *Fortune*, October 9, 2008. money.cnn.com/2008/10/08/technology/mobile_ads.fortune/index.htm (accessed March 2009).

Liang, T. P., and H. J. Lai. "Effect of Store Design on Consumer Purchase: An Empirical Study of Online Bookstores." *Information & Management*, 39, no. 6 (2002).

Markellou, P., M. Rigou, and S. Sirmakessis. "A Closer Look to the Online Consumer Behavior." In Khosrow-Pour, (Ed.). *Encyclopedia of E-Commerce, E-Government, and Mobile Commerce.* Hershey, PA: Idea Group Reference, 2006.

Marketing Charts. "Social Network Ad Spend Doesn't Yet Match Hype." May 19, 2008. marketingcharts.com/interactive/social-network-ad-spend-doesnt-yet-match-hype-4637 (accessed March 2009).

MarketingVox. "Automakers Look to Create Own Broadband Channels." July 10, 2007a. marketingvox.com/automakers-look-to-create-own-broadband-channels-031267 (accessed March 2009).

MarketingVox. "Scion Joins Fourth—Yes, Fourth—Virtual World." August 16, 2007b. marketingvox.com/scion-joins-fourth-yes-fourth-virtual-world-032282 (accessed March 2009).

MarketingVox. "Scion's Online Strategy Favors Niche over Reach." July 5, 2007c. marketingvox.com/scions-online-strategy-favors-niche-over-reach-031136 (accessed March 2009).

McKinsey Quarterly. "How Businesses Are Using Web 2.0: A McKinsey Global Survey." March 2007. mckinseyquarterly.com/How_businesses_are_using_Web_20_A_McKinsey_Global_Survey_1913 (accessed March 2009).

MediaBuyerPlanner. "Toyota Targets Kids, Hopes to Influence Parents." June 14, 2006. mediabuyerplanner.com/2006/06/14/toyota_targets_kids_hopes_to (accessed March 2009).

NewMedia TrendWatch. "eCommerce." February 19, 2009. newmediatrendwatch.com/world-overview/101-ecommerce (accessed March 2009).

O'Keefe, R.M., and T. McEachern. "Web-Based Customer Decision Support System." *Communications of the ACM*, March 1998.

Pons, A. P. "Biometric Marketing: Targeting the Online Consumer." *Communications of the ACM* (August 2006).

Ranganathan, C., and S. Jha. "Examining Online Purchase Intentions in B2C E-Commerce: Testing an Integrated Model." *Information Resource Management Journal*, 20, no. 4 (2007).

Reuters. "U.S. Web Video Ads Seen Up to $4.3 Billion in 2011: Study." July 25, 2007. reuters.com/article/InternetNews/idUSN2544002420070725?feedType=RSS (accessed March 2009).

Rodgers, Z. "Scion Goes Urban, Eschewing Big Reach Buys." *Clickz.com*, July 3, 2007. clickz.com/showPage.html?page=3626318 (accessed March 2009).

TMCnet. "Procter & Gamble Applies Right Now to Deliver Superior Consumer Experience." August 30, 2006. tmcnet.com/usubmit/2006/08/30/1846211.htm (accessed October 2006).

Tsang, M., S. C. Ho, and T. P. Liang. "Consumer Attitudes Toward Mobile Advertising: An Empirical Study." *International Journal of Electronic Commerce*, 8, no. 3 (Spring 2004).

Turban, E., et al. *Business Intelligence: A Managerial Approach.* Upper Saddle River, NJ: Prentice Hall, 2008.

Wang, E. T. G., H. Y. Yeh, and J. J. Jiang. "The Relative Weights of Internet Shopping Fundamental Objectives: Effect of Lifestyle Differences." *Psychology and Marketing*, 23, no. 5 (2006).

CHAPTER 5

B2B E-COMMERCE

Content

Learning Objectives

Upon completion of this chapter, you will be able to:

1. Describe the B2B field.
2. Describe the major types of B2B models.
3. Discuss the characteristics of the sell-side marketplace, including auctions.
4. Describe the sell-side models.
5. Describe the characteristics of the buy-side marketplace and e-procurement.
6. Explain how reverse auctions work in B2B.
7. Describe B2B aggregation and group purchasing models.
8. Describe other procurement methods.
9. Define exchanges and describe their major types.
10. Describe B2B portals.
11. Describe third-party exchanges.
12. Describe partner relationship management (PRM).
13. Describe how B2B can benefit from social networking and Web 2.0.
14. Describe Internet marketing in B2B, including organizational buyer behavior.

AUCTION FOR SUPPLIES HELPS PORTSMOUTH HOSPITALS

Portsmouth Hospitals NHS Trust is one of the largest trusts in the United Kingdom, providing health-care services for almost 1 million people throughout Portsmouth and South East Hampshire.

The Problem

Like many other public health-care facilities, Portsmouth Hospitals attempts to deliver quality health care within a "never enough" budget. Any cost-saving measure can help add more beds and services. The hospitals needed a new 20-bed ward. The problem was to cut costs without reducing the quality of care. An obvious place to begin was the administrative services, and one such area was the back-office purchasing processes.

The Solution

The target was pharmaceutical supplies, and the idea was to use e-auctions. The goals were:

- To purchase standard products at the lowest prices
- To release cash for frontline services
- To demonstrate benefits of auctions to suppliers
- To shorten the procurement cycle by streamlining sourcing
- To cut the cost of purchasing administration of traditional tendering processes

As a buyer, the NHS Trust used *reverse auctions* (Chapter 2), whereby suppliers are invited to place bids on what the buyer needs. Online auctions were seen by the Trust as an opportunity to negotiate savings on the cost of supplies it purchased in bulk, particularly when consolidating spending with other Trusts across the south of England (for more on group purchasing, see Section 5.7). Driving competition between suppliers by increasing price transparency through real-time bidding would ensure the lowest prices and most favorable trading conditions.

The first auction was conducted on a platform provided by an electronic auctioneer (UKprocure) that was powered by Oracle's Exchange and Sourcing products. The auctioneer provided both training and administrative support.

Being the first pharmaceutical auction in the United Kingdom, the process required extensive preparations. UKprocure worked with the Trust to put together a project plan and to familiarize suppliers with the processes and regulations surrounding online bidding.

Knowledge transfer was a key part of the preparation, with procurement and supply managers at the Trust being involved at every stage. On the day of the auction, 26 suppliers submitted a total of 185 tendered bids outlining their best deals for pharmaceutical supplies. Suppliers had to bid lower than the reserve price, with each having a 30-minute window to better the preceding offer. Supplier anonymity was assured, because the names of bidders were shown only to buyers at the Trust. At the end of the auction, Portsmouth and the successful suppliers agreed upon the lowest mutually acceptable purchase price.

The Results

The £640,000 (US$936) annual savings generated by combining the traditional procurement process with a reverse auction represented a 12 percent price reduction for the Trust. Online auctions also save the purchasing organizations substantial sums in administration by eliminating the need to evaluate tenders manually and help shorten the procurement cycle. The savings enabled the Trust to fund a 20-bed ward within 12 months of starting the auctions.

Suppliers also benefited from the reduced administrative and lower transaction costs afforded by online auctions. Seeing what prices are being offered for the same or similar products increases suppliers' market intelligence and can help improve their competitive advantage.

The trust expanded the auctions to clinical supplies and nonclinical items. It also experimented auctioning from its own Web site.

Sources: Compiled from OCG (2004) and *portshosp.nhs.uk* (accessed January 2009).

WHAT WE CAN LEARN . . .

This case demonstrates one method of electronic procurement, a reverse auction, which is very popular with public organizations, where tendering is usually mandatory.

Electronic auctions increase performance by reducing costs and expediting processes. It is an example of a B2B buy-side application, a type of application discussed in this chapter. Other buy-side and sell-side methods, as well as relationships among B2B partners, are also examined in this chapter. The chapter also delves into implementation issues such as group purchasing and the use of intermediaries in conducting auctions. Finally, the new activities of B2B in social networking are discussed.

5.1   CONCEPTS, CHARACTERISTICS, AND MODELS OF B2B E-COMMERCE

B2B EC has some special characteristics as well as specific models, components, and concepts. The major ones are described next.

BASIC B2B CONCEPTS

Business-to-business e-commerce (B2B EC), also known as *eB2B* (*electronic B2B*), or just B2B, refers to transactions between businesses conducted electronically over the Internet, extranets, intranets, or private networks (see Papazoglou and Ribbers 2006). Such transactions may take place between a business and its supply chain members, as well as between a business, a government, and any other business. In this context, a *business* refers to any organization, private or public, for profit or nonprofit. The major characteristic of B2B is that companies attempt to electronically automate trading or communication and collaboration processes in order to improve them. Note that B2B commerce is also done without the Internet.

Key business drivers for B2B are the need to gain competitive advantage; the availability of a secure broadband Internet platform and private and public B2B e-marketplaces; the need for collaboration between suppliers and buyers; the ability to save money, reduce delays, and improve collaboration; and the emergence of effective technologies for intra- and interorganizational integration (see en.wikipedia.org/Wiki/B2B_ecommerce).

business-to-business e-commerce (B2B EC) Transactions between businesses conducted electronically over the Internet, extranets, intranets, or private networks; also known as eB2B (electronic B2B) or just B2B.

MARKET SIZE AND CONTENT OF B2B

Market forecasters estimate that by 2012 the global B2B market (online and offline) could reach $15 trillion. Harris (2006) reports an Interactive Data Corporation (IDC) estimate of B2B online sales to be 10 percent of the total B2B market. Chemicals, computer electronics, utilities, agriculture, shipping and warehousing, motor vehicles, petrochemicals, paper and office products, and food are the leading items in B2B. According to the authors' experience and several sources, the dollar value of B2B comprises at least 85 percent of the total transaction value of e-commerce, and in some countries it is 90 percent. (Note: This figure is considered current in 2009.)

The B2B market, which went through major consolidation in 2000–2002, is growing rapidly. Different B2B market forecasters use different definitions and methodologies. Because of this, predictions frequently change and statistical data often differ. Therefore, we will not provide any more estimates here. Data sources that can be checked for the latest information on the B2B market are provided in Chapter 3 (Exhibit 3.1).

B2B EC is now in its fifth generation, as shown in Exhibit 5.1. This generation includes collaboration with suppliers, buyers, government, and other business partners, internal and external supply chain improvements, and expert (intelligent) sales systems. Just starting is B2B social networking, which could usher in the sixth generation of B2B. Note that older generations coexist with new ones. Also, some companies are still using only EC from early generations. This chapter focuses on topics from the second and third generations. Topics from the fourth and sixth generations are presented in Chapters 6 through 9.

THE BASIC TYPES OF B2B TRANSACTIONS AND ACTIVITIES

The number of sellers and buyers and the form of participation used in B2B determine the basic B2B transaction types:

▶ **Sell-side.** One seller to many buyers.
▶ **Buy-side.** One buyer from many sellers.
▶ **Exchanges.** Many sellers to many buyers.
▶ **Supply chain improvements and collaborative commerce.** This category includes activities other than buying or selling among business partners, for example, supply chain improvements, communicating, collaborating, and sharing of information for joint design, planning, and so on (see Chapter 6).

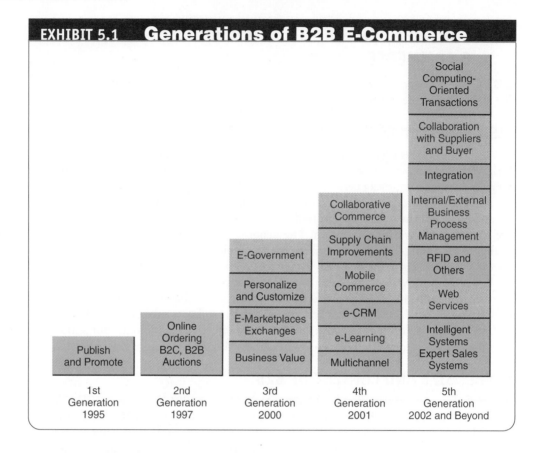

EXHIBIT 5.1   Generations of B2B E-Commerce

Exhibit 5.2 illustrates these four B2B types.

THE BASIC TYPES OF B2B E-MARKETPLACES AND SERVICES

The following are the basic types of B2B e-marketplaces.

One-to-Many and Many-to-One: Private E-Marketplaces

company-centric EC
E-commerce that focuses on a single company's buying needs (many-to-one, or buy-side) or selling needs (one-to-many, or sell-side).

In one-to-many and many-to-one markets, one company does either all of the selling (*sell-side market*) or all of the buying (*buy-side market*). Because EC is focused on a single company's buying or selling needs in these transactions, this type of EC is referred to as **company-centric EC**. Company-centric marketplaces—both sell-side and buy-side—are discussed in Sections 5.2 through 5.7.

In company-centric marketplaces, the individual sell-side or buy-side company has complete control over who participates in the selling or buying transaction and the supporting information systems. Thus, these marketplaces are essentially *private*. They may be at the sellers' Web sites or hosted by a third party (intermediary).

Many-to-Many: Exchanges

exchanges (trading communities or trading exchanges)
Many-to-many e-marketplaces, usually owned and run by a third party or a consortium, in which many buyers and many sellers meet electronically to trade with each other.

In many-to-many e-marketplaces, many buyers and many sellers meet electronically for the purpose of trading with one another. There are different types of such e-marketplaces, which are also known as **exchanges**, **trading communities**, or **trading exchanges**. We will use the term *exchanges* in this book. Exchanges are usually owned and run by a third party or by a consortium. They are described in more detail in Sections 5.7 and 5.9. Public exchanges are open to all interested parties (sellers and buyers), and thus are considered **public e-marketplaces**.

public e-marketplaces
Third-party exchanges open to all interested parties (sellers and buyers).

Supply Chain Improvers and Collaborative Commerce

B2B transactions are segments in the supply chain. Therefore, B2B initiatives need to be examined in light of other supply chain activities such as manufacturing, procurement of raw

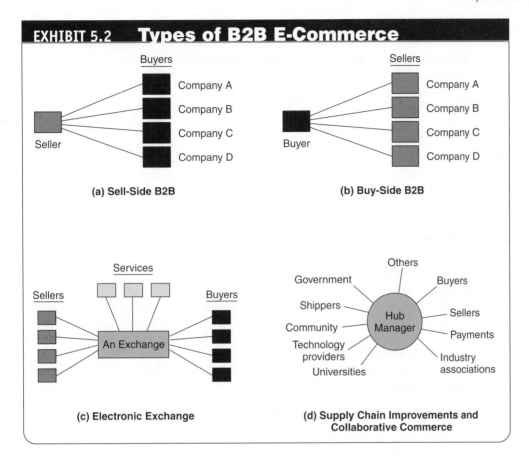

EXHIBIT 5.2   Types of B2B E-Commerce

(a) Sell-Side B2B

(b) Buy-Side B2B

(c) Electronic Exchange

(d) Supply Chain Improvements and Collaborative Commerce

materials and shipments, and logistics. Supply chain activities usually involve communication and collaboration.

Businesses deal with other businesses for purposes beyond just selling or buying. One example is that of *collaborative commerce*, which is communication, design, planning, and information sharing among business partners. To qualify as collaborative commerce, the activities that are shared must represent far more than just financial transactions. For example, they might include activities related to design, manufacture, or management.

B2B CHARACTERISTICS

Here we examine various qualities by which B2B transactions can be characterized.

Parties to the Transaction: Sellers, Buyers, and Intermediaries

B2B commerce can be conducted *directly* between a *customer* and a *manufacturer* or it can be conducted via an **online intermediary**. The intermediary is an online third party that brokers the transaction between the buyer and seller; it can be a virtual intermediary or a click-and-mortar intermediary. See Papazoglou and Ribbers (2006) for details. Some of the electronic intermediaries for consumers mentioned in Chapter 3 also can be referenced for B2B by replacing the individual consumers with business customers. Consolidators of buyers or sellers are typical B2B activities conducted by intermediaries (Section 5.3).

Types of Transactions

B2B transactions are of two basic types: *spot buying* and *strategic sourcing*. **Spot buying** refers to the purchasing of goods and services as they are needed, usually at prevailing market prices, which are determined dynamically by supply and demand. The buyers and the sellers may not even know each other. Stock exchanges and commodity exchanges (oil, sugar, corn, etc.) are examples of spot buying. In contrast, **strategic (systematic) sourcing** involves purchases based on *long-term contracts* and the parties know each other.

online intermediary
An online third party that brokers a transaction online between a buyer and a seller; may be virtual or click-and-mortar.

spot buying
The purchase of goods and services as they are needed, usually at prevailing market prices.

strategic (systematic) sourcing
Purchases involving long-term contracts that usually are based on private negotiations between sellers and buyers.

direct materials
Materials used in the production of a product (e.g., steel in a car or paper in a book).

indirect materials
Materials used to support production (e.g., office supplies or light bulbs).

MRO (maintenance, repair, and operation)
Indirect materials used in activities that support production.

vertical marketplaces
Markets that deal with one industry or industry segment (e.g., steel, chemicals).

horizontal marketplaces
Markets that concentrate on a service, material, or a product that is used in all types of industries (e.g., office supplies, PCs).

Spot buying can be conducted most economically on public exchanges. Strategic purchases can be supported more effectively and efficiently through direct buyer–seller offline or online negotiations, which can be done in private marketplaces or private trading rooms in public exchanges.

Types of Materials Traded

Two types of materials and supplies are traded in B2B: *direct* and *indirect*. **Direct materials** are materials used in making the products, such as steel in a car or paper in a book. The characteristics of direct materials are that their use is usually scheduled and planned for. They usually are not shelf items and are frequently purchased in large quantities after extensive negotiation and contracting.

Indirect materials are items, such as office supplies or light bulbs, that support production. They are usually used in **maintenance, repair, and operation (MRO)** activities. Collectively, they are known as *nonproduction materials*.

The Direction of the Trades

B2B marketplaces can be classified as *vertical* or *horizontal*. **Vertical marketplaces** are those that deal with one industry or industry segment. Examples include marketplaces specializing in electronics, cars, hospital supplies, steel, or chemicals. **Horizontal marketplaces** are those that concentrate on a service or a product that is used in all types of industries. Examples are office supplies, PCs, or travel services.

The various characteristics of B2B transactions are presented in summary form in Insights and Additions 5.1.

SUPPLY CHAIN RELATIONSHIPS IN B2B

In the various B2B transaction types, business activities are usually conducted along the supply chain of a company. The supply chain process consists of a number of interrelated subprocesses and roles. These extend from the acquisition of materials from suppliers, to the processing of a product or service, to packaging it and moving it to distributors and retailers. The process ends with the eventual purchase of a product by the end consumer. B2B can

Insights and Additions 5.1 Summary of B2B Characteristics

Parties to Transactions	Types of Transactions
Direct, seller to buyer or buyer to seller	Spot buying
Via intermediaries	Strategic sourcing
B2B2C: A business sells to a business, but delivers to individual consumers	
Types of Materials Sold	**Direction of Trade**
Direct materials and supplies	Vertical
Indirect (MROs)	Horizontal
Number and Form of Participation	**Degree of Openness**
One-to-many: Sell-side (e-storefront)	Private exchanges, restricted
Many-to-one: Buy-side	Private exchanges, restricted
Many-to-many: Exchanges	Public exchanges, open to all
Many, connected: Collaborative, supply chain	Private (usually), can be public

make supply chains more efficient and effective or it can change the supply chain completely, eliminating one or more intermediaries.

Historically, many of the segments and processes in the supply chain have been managed through paper transactions (e.g., purchase orders, invoices, and so forth). B2B applications are offered online so they can serve as supply chain enablers that offer distinct competitive advantages. Supply chain management also encompasses the coordination of order generation, order taking, and order fulfillment and distribution (see Chapters 6 and 12 for more discussion of supply chain management).

SERVICE INDUSTRIES ONLINE IN B2B

In addition to trading products between businesses, services also can be provided electronically in B2B. Just as service industries such as banking, insurance, real estate, and stock trading can be conducted electronically for individuals, as described in Chapter 3, so they can be conducted electronically for businesses. The major B2B services are:

- **Travel and hospitality services.** Many large corporations arrange their travel electronically through corporate travel agents. To further reduce costs, companies can make special arrangements that enable employees to plan and book their own trips online. For instance, American Express Business Travel (formerly Rosenbluth International) offers several tools to help corporate travel managers plan and control employee travel. In addition to traditional scheduling and control tools, it offers the following EC-based tools:
  - *TrackPoint* enables travel managers, as well as security and risk professionals, to pinpoint a traveler's whereabouts at any time.
  - *Travel Alert* and *Info Point* are information services that provide details about specific travel destinations. They are available free of charge to American Express Business Travel Clients.
  - *Travel Insight Plus* consulting service identifies specific opportunities for savings in air travel expenditure for a given organization. The consulting study compares the client company's air travel expenditure against that of its true peers—other organizations that travel similar routes, over similar periods, with comparable volumes. Savings are identified through two key comparisons: the difference between the client and peer group's average spending on a route as well as highlighting the number of peers that are paying a lower average fare than the client's.
  - American Express offers also a social network online.

  Expedia, Travelocity, Orbitz, and other online travel services provide both B2C and B2B services as well.

- **Real estate.** Commercial real estate transactions can be large and complex. Therefore, the Web might not be able to completely replace existing human agents. Instead, the Web can help businesses find the right properties, compare properties, and assist in negotiations. Some government-run foreclosed real estate auctions are open only to corporate real estate dealers and are conducted online.

- **Financial services.** Internet banking is an economical way of making business payments, transferring funds, or performing other financial transactions. For example, electronic funds transfer (EFT) is popular with businesses as are electronic letters of credit. Transaction fees over the Internet are less costly than any other alternative method. To see how payments work in B2B, see Chapter 11. Businesses can also purchase insurance online, both from pure online insurance companies and from click-and-mortar ones.

- **Online financing.** Business loans can be solicited online from lenders. Bank of America, for example, offers its commercial customers a matching service on IntraLoan (the bank's global loan syndication service), which uses an extranet to match business loan applicants with potential lending corporations. Several sites, such as garage.com, provide information about venture capital. Institutional investors use the Internet for certain trading activities.

▶ **Other online services.** Consulting services, law firms, health organizations, and others sell enterprise knowledge and special services online. Many other online services, such as the purchase of electronic stamps (similar to metered postage, but generated on a computer), are available online (see stamps.com). Also, recruiting and staffing services are done online.

THE BENEFITS AND LIMITATIONS OF B2B

The benefits of B2B are for buyers (B), sellers (S), or for both (J) and they depend on which model is used. In general, though, the major benefits of B2B (the beneficiaries are marked after each benefit) are that it:

▶ Creates new sales (purchase) opportunities (J)
▶ Eliminates paper and reduces administrative costs (J)
▶ Expedites processing and reduces cycle time (J)
▶ Lowers search costs and time for buyers to find products and vendors (B)
▶ Increases productivity of employees dealing with buying and/or selling (J)
▶ Reduces errors and improves quality of services (J)
▶ Makes product configuration easier (B)
▶ Reduces marketing and sales costs (S)
▶ Reduces inventory levels and costs (J)
▶ Enables customized online catalogs with different prices for different customers (J)
▶ Increases production flexibility, permitting just-in-time delivery (S)
▶ Reduces procurement costs (B)
▶ Facilitates customization via configuration (J)
▶ Provides for efficient customer service (B)
▶ Increases opportunities for collaboration (J)

B2B EC development has limitations as well, especially regarding channel conflict and the operation of public exchanges. Also, personal face-to-face interaction may be needed but unavailable. These will be discussed later in this chapter.

The development of B2B might eliminate the distributor or the retailer, which could be a benefit to the seller and the buyer (though not a benefit to the distributor or retailer). In previous chapters, such a phenomenon is referred to as *disintermediation* (Chapters 2 and 3).

THE CONTENT OF THE B2B FIELD

The B2B field is very diverse depending on the industry, products and services transacted, volume, method used, and more. The diversity can be seen in Exhibit 5.3 where we distinguish five major components: Our company that may be manufacturer, retailer, service provider, etc. It has many types of suppliers (left) and customers (right). Our company operations are supported by different services (bottom), and we may work with several intermediaries (top of exhibit).

In the remainder of the chapter, we will look at the various components of this exhibit as well as the major types of B2B structural models (sell-side, buy-side, exchanges) as well as at transaction models (e.g., auctions) and other B2B topics.

Section 5.1 ▶ REVIEW QUESTIONS

1. Define B2B.
2. Discuss the following: spot buying versus strategic sourcing, direct materials versus indirect materials, and vertical markets versus horizontal markets.

EXHIBIT 5.3 The Components of B2B

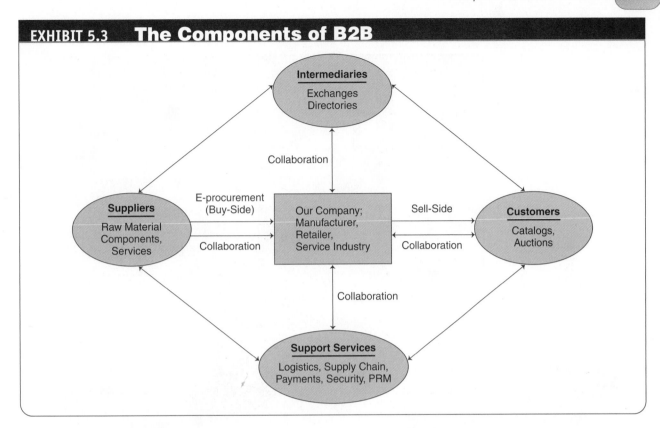

3. What are company-centric marketplaces? Are they public or private?

4. Define B2B exchanges.

5. Relate the supply chain to B2B transactions.

6. List the B2B online services.

7. List the benefits of B2B.

5.2 ONE-TO-MANY: SELL-SIDE E-MARKETPLACES

Many B2B activities involve online selling.

SELL-SIDE MODELS

In Chapter 3, we introduced the online-selling B2C model in which a manufacturer or a retailer sells electronically directly to consumers from a *storefront*. In a B2B **sell-side e-marketplace** a business sells products and services to business customers, frequently over an extranet. The seller can be a manufacturer selling to a wholesaler, to a retailer, or to an individual business. Intel, Cisco, and Dell are examples of such sellers. Or the seller can be a distributor selling to wholesalers, to retailers, or to businesses (e.g., W. W. Grainger). In either case, sell-side e-marketplaces involve one seller and many potential buyers. In this model, both individual consumers and business buyers might use the same sell-side marketplace (e.g., dell.com), or they might use different marketplaces. Exhibit 5.4 shows the different configuration of sell-side B2B marketplaces. The arrows indicate online or offline possible directions. The exhibit shows some, but not all of the possible intermediaries. For example, there could be value-added-retailers (VARs) who add some services and then sell it to the customers.

The architecture of this B2B model is similar to that of B2C EC. The major differences are in the process. For example, in B2B, large customers might be provided with customized catalogs and prices, and special trucks will deliver the goods (e.g., UPS or USPS in B2C). Usually, companies will separate B2C orders from B2B orders. One

sell-side e-marketplace
A Web-based marketplace in which one company sells to many business buyers from e-catalogs or auctions, frequently over an extranet.

EXHIBIT 5.4   Sell-Side Configuration Intermediations in B2B

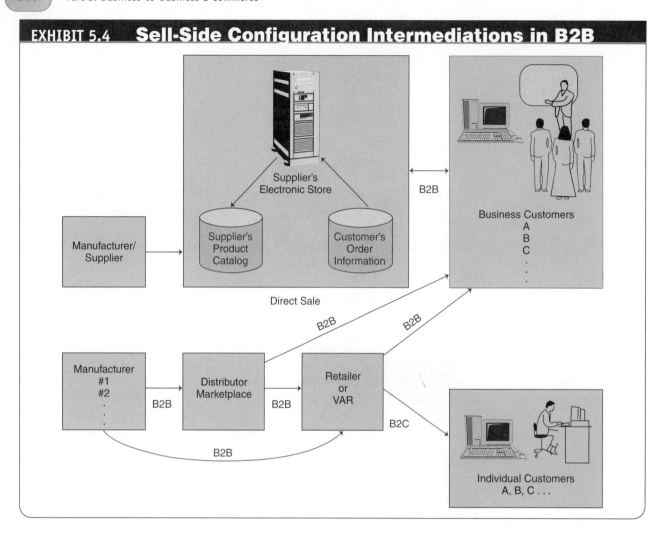

reason for this is that B2C and B2B orders have different *order-fulfillment processes* (see Chapter 12) and different pricing models (i.e., wholesale vs. retail pricing). Also, in B2B we use technologies such as RFID (see Chapter 6) and XML, which are not usually used in B2C.

The one-to-many model has three major marketing methods: (1) selling from *electronic catalogs*; (2) selling via *forward auctions*; and (3) one-to-one selling, usually under a *negotiated* long-term contract. Such one-to-one negotiating is familiar: The buying company negotiates price, quantity, payments, delivery, and quality terms with the selling company. We describe the first method in this section and the second method in Section 5.3.

B2B Sellers

Sellers in the sell-side marketplace may be click-and-mortar manufacturers or intermediaries (e.g., distributors or wholesalers). The intermediaries may even be pure online companies, as in the case of Bigboxx.com, described in Online File W5.1.

Customer Service

Online sellers can provide sophisticated customer services. For example, General Electric receives over 20 million calls a year regarding appliances. Although most of these calls come from individuals, many come from businesses. By using the Internet and automatic-response software agents (autoresponders), GE has reduced the cost of handling calls from $5 per call when done by phone to $0.20 per electronically answered call. Patton

(2006) estimated that a call handled by a human agent costs $2 to $10. If answered automatically (e.g., autoresponder, interactive voice response), the cost is between $.02 and $.20.

We now turn our attention to the first of the sell-side methods—selling online from electronic catalogs.

SALES FROM CATALOGS

Companies can use the Internet to sell directly from their online catalogs. A company may offer one catalog for all customers or a *customized catalog* for each large customer (usually both). However, this model may not be convenient for large and repetitive business buyers, because the buyer's order information is stored in the supplier's server and is not easily integrated with the buyer's corporate information system. To facilitate B2B direct sales, the seller can provide the buyer with a buyer-customized shopping cart (such as Bigboxx.com offers), which can store order information that can be integrated with the buyer's information system.

Many sellers provide separate pages and catalogs to their major buyers. For example, Staples, an office-supply vendor, offers its business customers personalized software catalogs of about 100,000 products and pricing at stapleslink.com.

Another example of B2B direct sales from catalogs is Microsoft, which uses an extranet to sell over $12 billion of software annually to its distributors and larger customers. Using Microsoft's extranet-based order-entry tool (MOET), buyers can check inventory, make transactions, and look up the status of orders. The online orders are automatically fed into the customer's SAP applications. The extranet handles over 1 million transactions per year. The system significantly reduces the number of phone calls, e-mails, and incorrect product shipments.

In selling online to business buyers, manufacturers might encounter a similar problem to that of B2C, namely conflict with the regular distribution channels, including corporate dealers (channel conflict). An interesting solution is illustrated in Case 5.1, where Gregg's Cycles sells online (both B2B and B2C). But it sells only peripheral products, such as parts and accessories, to consumers and provides a store locator where customers can buy its core product—bicycles—at brick-and-mortar distributors.

Configuration and Customization

As with B2C EC, B2B direct sales offer an opportunity for efficient customization (e.g., see the Cisco case in Online File W5.4.). As we will see in the case of Cisco, manufacturers can provide online tools for self-configuration, pricing, ordering, and so on. Business customers can self-configure customized products, get price quotes, and submit orders, all online.

Many click-and-mortar companies use a *multichannel distribution system*, in which the Internet is a supplemental channel that enables greater efficiency in the ordering process, as shown in the case of Whirlpool in Case 5.2.

Benefits and Limitations of Online Sales from Catalogs

Successful examples of the B2B online direct sales model include manufacturers, such as Dell, Intel, IBM, and Cisco, and distributors, such as Ingram Micro (which sells to value-added retailers; the retailer adds some service along with the product). Sellers that use this model can be successful as long as they have a superb reputation in the market and a large enough group of loyal customers.

Although the benefits of direct online sales are similar to that of B2C, there also are limitations. One of the major issues facing direct sellers is how to find buyers. Many companies know how to advertise in traditional channels but are still learning how to contact would-be business buyers online. Also, B2B sellers may experience channel conflicts with their existing distribution systems. Another limitation is that if traditional electronic data interchange (EDI)—the computer-to-computer direct transfer of business documents—is used, the cost to the customers can be high, and they will be reluctant to go

CASE 5.1

EC Application

GREGG'S CYCLES GOES ONLINE

Some high-quality bicycle manufacturers, such as Gregg's Cycles, do not sell their products online, nor do they allow their bicycles to be sold online by others. The manufacturer tries to avoid channel conflicts with its dealers and the independent bike shops that sell its bikes. Gregg's Cycles believes that selling bikes is as much about customer service as it is about the product.

Each bike sold in one of Gregg's stores is custom fitted to the customer. This type of customer service cannot be done online, because measurements and discussions must take place face-to-face. When Gregg's Cycles decided to build a Web site, it chose to display all its bikes online so that customers could see the huge selection as well as use the site as a resource to learn about the bikes. As a bonus, the software Gregg's chose, CartGenie (from J Street Technology), made it easy to sell online peripheral products, such as parts, clothing, accessories, and complementary products, such as snowboards and inline skates.

With the CartGenie software, the company is able to show the specs of each bike so that viewers can compare up to three bikes on one screen. Oftentimes, customers come into the company's physical stores armed with printouts from the Web site, knowing exactly what they want. In addition, the site displays inventory availability. If a store has the bike that the customer is looking for, the customer can come to the store to get it.

The online store now carries over 7,000 SKUs and caters to customers across the United States. Gregg's makes sure to mention its Web site address in all of its print ads and promotions. It also publishes an online newsletter to keep in touch with customers.

CartGenie enables bulk import of products to the corporate catalog, a most useful feature. Another useful feature is CartGenie Connect, which automatically updates pricing and availability. CartGenie Connect also takes information directly from the point-of-sale database and syncs it with the online database. With over 7,000 SKUs, it would be close to impossible for a person to keep the site up-to-date.

CartGenie is available in the Standard, Pro, and Enterprise Editions. Key features include:

- Full support for B2B and B2C selling
- Multiple retail and wholesale price levels
- A built-in comparison engine for doing side-by-side product comparisons
- A complete inventory control module
- Integrated UPS shipping calculator
- Volume discount pricing (for retailers, clubs, etc.)
- Search engine–friendly product catalog system
- Integration with PayPal
- Built-in product import utilities
- Full support for real-time credit card processing

The Web site also offers information on customizing bikes, bicycle repair, bike rental, blogging, store locations, job opportunities, coupons, bike events, and more. Customers love the Web site; the company gets favorable responses from most customers who send comments.

Sources: Compiled from Rincon (2006), *greggcycles.com* (accessed January 2009), and *jstreettech.com* (accessed January 2009).

Questions

1. Why is this a B2B sell-side case?
2. What are the benefits of this type of Web site for the company?
3. Relate the case to social networks.
4. How does CartGenie support the site?

online. The solution to this problem is the transfer of documents over extranets (see Online File W5.2) and an Internet-based EDI (see Online File W5.3). Finally, the number of business partners online must be large enough to justify the system infrastructure and operation and maintenance expenses.

ONLINE DIRECT SALES: THE EXAMPLE OF CISCO SYSTEMS

Cisco Systems (cisco.com) is the world's leading producer of routers, switches, and network interconnection services. Cisco's portal has evolved over several years, beginning with technical support for customers and developing into one of the world's largest direct sales EC sites. Today, Cisco offers about a dozen Internet-based applications to both end-user businesses and reseller partners.

Section 5.2 ▶ REVIEW QUESTIONS

1. List the types of sell-side B2B transaction models.
2. Distinguish between the use and nonuse of intermediaries in B2B sell-side transactions.
3. What are buy-side and sell-side transactions? How do they differ?

CASE 5.2
EC Application
WHIRLPOOL B2B TRADING PORTAL

Whirlpool (*whirlpool.com*) is a $20-billion global corporation based in Benton Harbor, Michigan. It is in the company's best interest to operate efficiently and to offer as much customer service for the members, (business partners) of its selling chain as possible. It is a complex job, because the partners are located in 170 countries. Middle-tier partners, who comprise 25 percent of the total partner base and 10 percent of Whirlpool's annual revenue, were submitting their orders by phone or fax because they were not large enough to have system-to-system computer connections direct (such as EDI) to Whirlpool.

To improve customer service for these dealers, Whirlpool developed a B2B trading partner portal (Whirlpool Web World), using IBM e-business solutions. The technologies enable fast, easy Web self-service ordering processes. Using these self-service processes, Whirlpool was able to cut the cost per order to under $5—a savings of 80 percent.

The company tested ordering via the Web by developing a portal for low-level products. It was so successful that Whirlpool created a second-generation portal, which allows middle-tier trade partners to place orders and track their status through a password-protected site.

Simultaneously, the company implemented SAP R/3 for order entry, which is utilized by the middle-tier partners on the second-generation portal. The company also is using IBM's Application Framework for e-business, taking advantage of its rapid development cycles and associated cost reductions.

Whirlpool's global platform provides its operations with resources and capabilities few other manufacturers can match. Whirlpool's global procurement, product development, and information technology organizations help the company's operations reduce costs, improve efficiencies, and introduce a continuous stream of relevant innovation to consumers.

Using the same IBM platform, Whirlpool launched a B2C site for U.S. customers for ordering small appliances and accessories. The site was so successful that the company realized a 100 percent ROI in just 5 months.

Sources: Compiled from IBM (2000) and *whirlpool.com* (accessed January 2009).

Questions

1. How do Whirlpool's customers benefit from the portal?
2. What are the benefits of the trading portal for Whirlpool?
3. Relate the B2B sell-side to a B2C storefront.

4. Describe customer service in B2B systems.
5. Describe direct online B2B sales process from catalogs.
6. Discuss the benefits and limitations of direct online B2B sales from catalogs.

5.3 SELLING VIA DISTRIBUTORS AND OTHER INTERMEDIARIES

Manufacturers can sell directly to businesses, and they do so if the customers are large buyers. However, frequently they use intermediaries to distribute their products to a large number of smaller buyers. The intermediaries (usually distributors) buy products from many manufacturers (see lower part of Exhibit 5.4) and aggregate them into one catalog from which they sell to customers or to retailers. Now, many of these distributors also are selling online via storefronts.

Some well-known online distributors for businesses are SAM's Club (of Wal-Mart), Avnet, and W. W. Grainger (Case 5.3). Most e-distributors sell in horizontal markets, meaning that they sell to businesses in a variety of industries. However, some specialize in one industry (vertical market), such as Boeing PART (see Online File W5.5). Most intermediaries sell at fixed prices; however, some offer quantity discounts, negotiated prices, or conduct auctions.

Section 5.3 ▶ REVIEW QUESTIONS

1. What are the advantages of using intermediaries in B2B sales?
2. What types of intermediaries exist in B2B?
3. What special services are provided to buyers by Boeing Parts? (See Online File W5.5.)
4. Compare an e-distributor in B2B to Amazon.com. What are the similarities? What are the differences?

CASE 5.3
EC Application

W. W. GRAINGER AND GOODRICH CORPORATION

W. W. Grainger has a number of Web sites, but its flagship is *grainger.com*. In 2008, of Grainger's $6.4 billion in annual sales, more than $1.5 billion was generated from e-commerce, with the majority of those sales placed through *grainger.com*.

More than 870,000 brand-name products from more than 3,000 suppliers are offered at *grainger.com*, and a growing number of Grainger's 1.8 million customers from 150 countries are ordering online. The Web site continues the same kind of customer service and wide range of industrial products provided by Grainger's traditional offline business with the additional convenience of 24/7 ordering, use of search engines, and additional services.

This convenience is what first attracted BFGoodrich Aerospace (now called Goodrich Corporation) in Pueblo, Colorado. In 2000, it found *grainger.com* to be one of the most convenient and easy purchasing sites to use. The purchasing agent of this relatively small Goodrich plant of approximately 250 employees used to call in an order to a supplier, give the salesperson a part number, and wait until the price could be pulled up. Goodrich's purchaser now can place orders online in a matter of minutes, and the purchaser's display has Goodrich's negotiated pricing built in.

Goodrich can get just about anything it needs from *grainger.com*. Grainger interfaces with other suppliers, so if Goodrich needs something specific that Grainger does not normally carry, Grainger will research and find the items through Grainger's Sourcing team. Consolidating their purchases through Grainger provided better prices.

Goodrich has achieved additional savings from the tremendous decrease in paperwork that has resulted from buying through *grainger.com*. Individuals in each department now have access to purchasing cards, which allow them to do some of their own ordering. Before, the central purchasing department had to issue purchase orders for every single item. Now, employees with purchasing cards and passwords can place orders according to the spending limits that have been set up based on their positions.

In 2002, the Goodrich Pueblo operation spent $200,000 for purchases from *grainger.com*, which reflected a 10 to 15 percent savings on its purchases. As a result, Goodrich signed a company-wide enterprise agreement that allows every Goodrich facility to order through *grainger.com*, with an expected savings of at least 10 percent.

Sources: Compiled from *en/Wikipedia.org/wiki/w._w._Grainger* (accessed January 2009), *grainger.com* (accessed January 2009), and Lucas (2005).

Questions

1. Enter *grainger.com* and review all of the services offered to online buyers. Prepare a list of these services.

2. Explain how Goodrich's buyers save time and money.

3. What other benefits does Goodrich enjoy by using *grainger.com*?

4. How was desktop purchasing (see details in Section 5.7) implemented at Goodrich Corporation?

Source: Courtesy of Grainger.com. Used with permission.

5.4 SELLING VIA E-AUCTIONS

Auctions are gaining popularity as a B2B sales channel (see Dasgupta et al. 2006). Some major B2B auction issues are discussed in this section.

USING AUCTIONS ON THE SELL SIDE

Many companies use *forward auctions* to sell their unneeded capital assets. In such a situation, items are displayed on an auction site (private or public) for quick disposal. Forward auctions offer the following benefits to B2B sellers:

▶ **Revenue generation.** Forward auctions support and expand online and overall sales. Forward auctions also offer businesses a new venue for quickly and easily disposing of excess, obsolete, and returned products (e.g., liquidation.com).

▶ **Cost savings.** In addition to generating new revenue, conducting auctions electronically reduces the costs of selling the auctioned items. These savings also help increase the seller's profits.

▶ **Increased "stickiness."** Forward auctions give Web sites increased "stickiness." As discussed in Chapter 4, stickiness is a characteristic that describes customer loyalty to a site, demonstrated by the number and length of visits to a site.

▶ **Member acquisition and retention.** All bidding transactions result in additional registered members, who are future business contacts. In addition, auction software aids enable sellers to search and report on virtually every relevant auction activity for future analysis and use.

Forward auctions can be conducted in two ways. A company can conduct its forward auctions from its own Web site or it can sell from an intermediary auction site, such as ebay.com. Let's examine these options.

AUCTIONING FROM THE COMPANY'S OWN SITE

For large and well-known companies that frequently conduct auctions, such as GM, it makes sense to build an auction mechanism on the company's own site. Why should a company pay a commission to an intermediary if the intermediary cannot provide the company with added value? Of course, if a company decides to auction from its own site, it will have to pay for infrastructure and operate and maintain the auction site. However, if the company already has an electronic marketplace for selling from e-catalogs, the additional cost for conducting auctions might not be too high. However, a significant added value that could be provided by intermediaries is the attraction of many potential buyers to the auction site.

USING INTERMEDIARIES IN AUCTIONS

Several intermediaries offer B2B auction sites (e.g., see asset-auctions.com and liquidation.com). An intermediary might conduct private auctions for a seller, either from the intermediary's or the seller's site. Or a company might choose to conduct auctions in a public marketplace, using a third-party hosting company (e.g., eBay, which has a special "business exchange" for small companies, see Chapter 17).

Using a third-party hosting company for conducting auctions has many benefits. The first is that no additional resources (e.g., hardware, bandwidth, engineering resources, or IT personnel) are required. Nor are there any hiring costs or opportunity costs associated with the redeployment of corporate resources. B2B auction intermediary sites also offer fast time-to-market: They enable a company to have a robust, customized auction up and running immediately. Without the intermediary, it can take a company weeks to prepare an auction site in-house.

Another benefit of using an intermediary relates to who owns and controls the auction information. In the case of an intermediary-conducted private auction, the intermediary sets up the auction to show the branding (company name) of the merchant rather than the intermediary's name. Yet, the intermediary does the work of collecting data on Web traffic, page views, and member registration; setting all the auction parameters (transaction fee structure, user interface, and reports); and integrating the information flow and logistics. Of course, if a company wants to dispose of unwanted assets without advertising to the public that it is doing so, an intermediary-conducted public auction would be the logical choice.

Another benefit of using intermediaries relates to billing and collection efforts, which are handled by the intermediary rather than the selling company. For example, intermediaries calculate merchant-specific shipping weights and charge customers for shipping of auctioned items. These services are not free, of course. They are provided as part of the merchant's commission to the intermediary; a cost often deemed worth paying in exchange for the ease of the service.

For an example of using an intermediary to liquidate old equipment, see Case 5.4.

EXAMPLES OF B2B FORWARD AUCTIONS

The following are examples of B2B auctions:

- Whirlpool Corp. sold $20 million in scrap metal in 2003 via asset-auctions.com, increasing the price received by 15 percent.
- SAM's Club (samsclub.com) auctions thousands of items (especially electronics) at auctions.samsclub.com. Featured auctions include the current bid, the number of bids, and the end date.
- ResortQuest, a large vacation rental company, uses auctionanything.com to auction rental space.

CASE 5.4
EC Application
HOW THE U.S. STATE OF PENNSYLVANIA SELLS SURPLUS EQUIPMENT

For many years, the Pennsylvania Department of Transportation (DOT) used a traditional offline auction process. As of October 2003, the U.S. state is holding online auctions to sell its surplus heavy equipment. The old, live in-person auction system generated about $5 million a year. Using the Internet, the DOT is generating at least a 20 percent increase in revenue.

The Commonwealth of Pennsylvania conducted its initial online sale of surplus DOT items in October 2003. The sale consisted of 77 items (including 37 dump trucks). Onsite inspection was available twice during the 2-week bidding period. The online sale allowed the Commonwealth of Pennsylvania to obtain an average price increase of 20 percent, while reducing labor costs related to holding a traditional on-site sale. On high-value specialty items (i.e., a bridge inspection crane and a satellite van), results exceeded the estimated sale prices by over 200 percent.

The auction was conducted by AssetAuctions (asset-auctions.com). The results of the auction were as follows:

- Total sales: $635,416.03.
- Half of the bidding activity occurred in the final 2 days.

- Every lot received multiple bids.
- Overtime bidding occurred in 39 lots.
- 174 bidders from 19 U.S. states and Mexico made about 1,500 bids in 5 days.
- 47 different buyers participated.

The Commonwealth of Pennsylvania now sells surplus equipment and properties using both AssetAuctions and eBay.

Sources: Material compiled from *asset-auctions.com* (accessed January 2009) and the Commonwealth of Pennsylvania (2006).

Questions

1. Why is heavy equipment amenable to such auctions?
2. Why did the state generate 20 percent more in revenues with the online auction?
3. Why do you need an intermediary to conduct such an auction?
4. Comment on the number of bidders and bids with an online auction as compared to an offline auction.

▶ At GovernmentAuctions.org (governmentauctions.org), businesses can bid on foreclosures, seized items, abandoned property, and more.

▶ Yahoo! conducts both B2C and B2B auctions of many items.

Section 5.4 ▶ REVIEW QUESTIONS

1. List the benefits of using B2B auctions for selling.
2. List the benefits of using auction intermediaries.
3. What are the major purposes of forward auctions, and how are they conducted?

5.5 ONE-FROM-MANY: BUY-SIDE E-MARKETPLACES AND E-PROCUREMENT

When a buyer goes to a sell-side marketplace, such as Cisco's, the buyer's purchasing department sometimes has to manually enter the order information into its own corporate information system. Furthermore, manually searching e-stores and e-malls to find and compare suppliers and products can be slow and costly. As a solution, large buyers can open their own marketplaces, as Portsmouth Hospitals did, called **buy-side e-marketplaces**, and invite sellers to browse and offer to fulfill orders. The term *procurement* is used to refer to the purchase of goods and services for organizations. It is usually done by *purchasing agents*, also known as *corporate buyers*.

buy-side e-marketplace
A corporate-based acquisition site that uses reverse auctions, negotiations, group purchasing, or any other e-procurement method.

PROCUREMENT METHODS

Companies use different methods to procure goods and services depending on what and where they buy, the quantities needed, how much money is involved, and more. The major procurement methods include the following:

▶ Conduct bidding in a system in which suppliers compete against each other. This method is used for large-ticket items or large quantities (Section 5.6).

▶ Buy directly from manufacturers, wholesalers, or retailers from their catalogs, and possibly by negotiation.

▶ Buy at private or public auction sites in which the organization participates as one of the buyers (Section 5.6).

▶ Buy from the catalog of an intermediary (e-distributor) that aggregates sellers' catalogs (Section 5.7).

▶ Buy from an internal buyer's catalog, in which company-approved vendors' catalogs, including agreed-upon prices, are aggregated. This approach is used for the implementation of *desktop purchasing*, which allows the requisitioners to order directly from vendors, bypassing the procurement department (Section 5.7).

▶ Join a group-purchasing system that aggregates participants' demand, creating a large volume. Then the group may negotiate prices or initiate a tendering process (Section 5.7).

▶ Buy at an exchange or industrial mall (Section 5.8).

▶ Collaborate with suppliers to share information about sales and inventory, so as to reduce inventory and stock-outs and enhance just-in-time delivery. (See Chapter 6 on collaborative commerce.)

Some of these activities are done in private marketplaces, others in public exchanges.

E-Procurement Organizations and Types

E-procurement methods can be organized into four segments: (1) Buy at own Web site, (2) buy at sellers' store, (3) buy at exchanges, and (4) buy at other e-market sites. Each segment includes several activities, as illustrated in Exhibit 5.5. Some of these will be described in Sections 5.6 through 5.9.

EXHIBIT 5.5   E-Procurement Methods

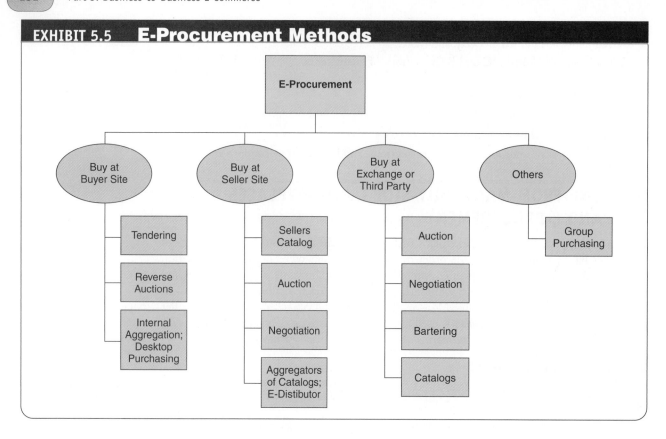

According to Wikipedia (en.wikipedia.org/wiki/E-procurement), the seven main types of e-procurement are as follows:

- **E-sourcing.** Identifying new suppliers for a specific category of purchasing requirements using Internet technology.
- **E-tendering.** Sending requests for information and prices to known suppliers and receiving the suppliers' responses and bids using Internet technology.
- **E-reverse auctioning.** Using Internet technology to buy goods and services from a number of known or unknown suppliers.
- **E-informing.** Gathering and distributing purchasing information both from and to internal and external parties using Internet technology.
- **Web-based ERP (electronic resource planning).** Creating and approving purchasing requisitions, placing purchase orders, and receiving goods and services by using a software system based on Internet technology.
- **E-marketsites.** Buying communities access favored suppliers' products and services, add products to shopping carts, create requisitions, seek approval, receive purchase orders, and process electronic invoices, integrating them into suppliers' supply chains and buyers' financial systems.
- **E-MRO (maintenance, repair, and operating).** The same as Web-based ERP except that the goods and services ordered are non–product-related MRO supplies.

procurement management

The planning, organizing, and coordinating of all the activities relating to purchasing goods and services needed to accomplish the organization's mission.

INEFFICIENCIES IN TRADITIONAL PROCUREMENT MANAGEMENT

Procurement management refers to the planning, organizing, and coordinating of all the activities pertaining to the purchasing of the goods and services necessary to accomplish the mission of an enterprise. It involves the B2B purchase and sale of supplies and services, as well as the flow of required information and networking systems. Approximately 80 percent of an organization's purchased items, mostly MROs, constitute 20 to 25 percent of the total purchase value. Furthermore, a large portion of corporate buyers' time is spent on non–value-added activities, such as entering data, correcting errors in paperwork, expediting delivery, or solving quality problems.

The procurement process may be lengthy and complex due to the many activities performed. The following are the major activities that may be evidenced in a single purchase:

> *Search for items* using search engines, catalogs, showrooms, and sales presentations.

> *Learn details of items and terms* using comparison engines and quality reports and research the items and vendors.

> *Negotiate or join group purchasing* using intelligent software agents (if available).

> *Sign agreement or contract* using contract management; arrange financing, escrow insurance, etc.

> *Create specific purchasing order(s)* using computerized system. Determine when and how much to order each time. Authorize corporate buyers.

> *Arrange packing, shipments, and deliveries* using electronic tracking, RFID, etc.

> *Arrange invoicing, payments, expense, management, and purchasing budgetary control* using software packages.

The traditional procurement process, shown in Exhibit 5.6, is often inefficient. For example, for high-value items, purchasing personnel spend a great deal of time and effort on procurement activities. These activities include qualifying suppliers, negotiating prices and terms, building rapport with strategic suppliers, and carrying out supplier evaluation and certification. If buyers are busy with the details of the smaller items (usually the MROs), they do not have enough time to properly deal with the purchase of the high-value items.

Other inefficiencies also may occur in conventional procurement. These range from delays to paying too much for rush orders. One procurement inefficiency is **maverick buying**. This is when a buyer makes unplanned purchases of items needed quickly, which results in buying at non–pre-negotiated, usually higher, prices.

To correct the situation, companies reengineer their procurement systems, implement new purchasing models, and, in particular, introduce e-procurement.

maverick buying
Unplanned purchases of items needed quickly, often at non–pre-negotiated higher prices.

e-procurement
The electronic acquisition of goods and services for organizations.

THE GOALS AND BENEFITS OF E-PROCUREMENT

Improvements to procurement have been attempted for decades, usually by using information technologies. The real opportunity for improvement lies in the use of **e-procurement**, the electronic acquisition of goods and services for organizations. For comprehensive coverage and

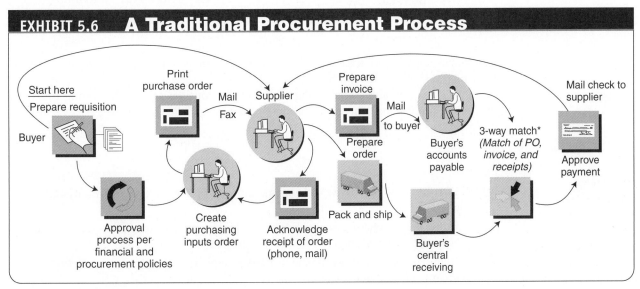

EXHIBIT 5.6   A Traditional Procurement Process

Source: *Ariba.com*, February 2001. Courtesy of Ariba Inc.

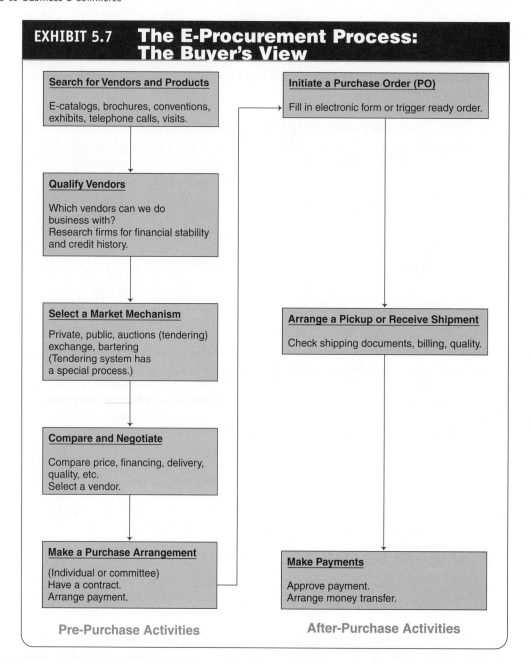

EXHIBIT 5.7   The E-Procurement Process: The Buyer's View

Search for Vendors and Products

E-catalogs, brochures, conventions, exhibits, telephone calls, visits.

Qualify Vendors

Which vendors can we do business with?
Research firms for financial stability and credit history.

Select a Market Mechanism

Private, public, auctions (tendering) exchange, bartering
(Tendering system has a special process.)

Compare and Negotiate

Compare price, financing, delivery, quality, etc.
Select a vendor.

Make a Purchase Arrangement

(Individual or committee)
Have a contract.
Arrange payment.

Initiate a Purchase Order (PO)

Fill in electronic form or trigger ready order.

Arrange a Pickup or Receive Shipment

Check shipping documents, billing, quality.

Make Payments

Approve payment.
Arrange money transfer.

Pre-Purchase Activities   **After-Purchase Activities**

case studies, see Saryeddine (2004). The general e-procurement process (with the exception of tendering) is shown in Exhibit 5.7.

By automating and streamlining the laborious routines of the purchasing function, purchasing professionals can focus on more strategic purchases, *achieving the following goals and benefits*:

▶ Increasing the productivity of purchasing agents (providing them with more time and reducing job pressure)
▶ Lowering purchase prices through product standardization, reverse auctions, volume discounts, and consolidation of purchases
▶ Improving information flow and management (e.g., supplier's information and pricing information)

- Minimizing the purchases made from noncontract vendors (minimizing maverick buying)
- Improving the payment process and savings due to expedited payments (for sellers)
- Establishing efficient, collaborative supplier relations
- Ensuring delivery on time, every time
- Slashing order-fulfillment and processing times by leveraging automation
- Reducing the skill requirements and training needs of purchasing agents
- Reducing the number of suppliers
- Streamlining the purchasing process, making it simple and fast (may involve authorizing requisitioners to perform purchases from their desktops, bypassing the procurement department)
- Streamlining invoice reconciliation and dispute resolution
- Reducing the administrative processing cost per order by as much as 90 percent (e.g., GM achieved a reduction from $100 to $10)
- Finding new suppliers and vendors that can provide goods and services faster and/or cheaper (improved sourcing)
- Integrating budgetary controls into the procurement process
- Minimizing human errors in the buying or shipping processes
- Monitoring and regulating buying behavior

For additional benefits, see Saryeddine (2004). For an example of a successful implementation, see Case 5.3. For implementation process and strategy, see Online File W5.6.

Section 5.5 ▶ REVIEW QUESTIONS

1. Define procurement and list the major procurement methods.
2. Describe the inefficiencies of traditional procurement.
3. Define e-procurement and list its goals.
4. List the major e-procurement segments and some activities in each.

5.6 BUY-SIDE E-MARKETPLACES: REVERSE AUCTIONS

One of the major methods of e-procurement is through reverse auctions. It can be done from the buyer's Web site, at an exchange, or via a specialized intermediary site. Recall from our previous chapters that a *reverse auction* is a tendering system in which suppliers are invited to bid on the fulfillment of an order and the lowest bid wins. In B2B usage of a reverse auction, a buyer may open an electronic market on its own server and invite potential suppliers to bid on the items the buyer needs. The "invitation" to such reverse auctions is a form or document called a **request for quote (RFQ)**. Traditional tendering usually implied one-time sealed bidding, whereas an e-reverse auction opens the auction to competing sequential bidding. See en.wikipedia.org/wiki/Reverse_auction for a comprehensive overview of reverse auctions.

request for quote (RFQ)
The "invitation" to participate in a tendering (bidding) system.

Governments and large corporations frequently mandate reverse auctions, which may provide considerable savings. To understand why this is so, see Online File W5.7, which compares the pre-Internet tendering process with the Web-based reverse auction process. The electronic process is faster and administratively much less expensive. It also can benefit buyers in locating the cheapest possible products or services.

CONDUCTING REVERSE AUCTIONS

As the number of reverse auction sites increases, suppliers will not be able to manually monitor all relevant tendering sites. This problem has been addressed with the introduction of online directories that list open RFQs. Another way to solve this problem is through the use of monitoring software agents. Software agents also can aid in the bidding process itself. Examples of agents that support the bidding process are auctionsniper.com and auctionflex.com.

Alternatively, third-party intermediaries may run the electronic bidding, as they do for forward auctions. General Electric's GXS (now an independent company, described in detail in Online File W5.7) is open to any buyer. Auction sites such as govliquidation.com, liquidation.com, and asset-auctions.com also belong to this category. Conducting reverse auctions in B2B can be a fairly complex process. This is why an intermediary may be beneficial.

The reverse auction process is demonstrated in Exhibit 5.8. As shown in the exhibit, the first step is for the would-be buyer to post bid invitations. When bids arrive, contract and purchasing personnel for the buyer evaluate the bids and decide which one(s) to accept. For further discussion, see Bush (2006).

E-Tendering by Governments

Most governments must conduct tendering when they buy or sell goods and services. Doing this manually is slow and expensive. Therefore, many are moving to e-reverse auctions.

GROUP REVERSE AUCTIONS

B2B reverse auctions are done in a private exchange or at an aggregator's site for a group of buying companies. Such *group reverse auctions* are popular in South Korea and usually involve large conglomerates. For example, the LG Group operates the LG MRO Auction for its members, and the Samsung Group operates iMarketKorea, as described in the closing case of this chapter.

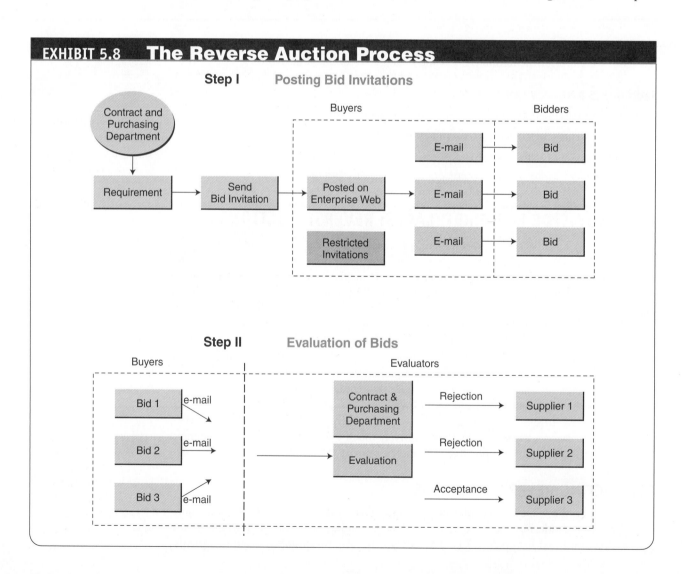

EXHIBIT 5.8   The Reverse Auction Process

Section 5.6 ▸ REVIEW QUESTIONS

1. Describe the manual tendering system.
2. How do online reverse auctions work?
3. List the benefits of Web-based reverse auctions.
4. Describe the business drivers of GE's TPN now (GXS) and its evolution over time. (See Online File W5.7.)

5.7 OTHER E-PROCUREMENT METHODS

Companies also have implemented other innovative e-procurement methods. Some common ones are described in this section.

AN INTERNAL PURCHASING MARKETPLACE: AGGREGATING SUPPLIERS' CATALOGS AND DESKTOP PURCHASING

Large organizations have many corporate buyers or purchasing agents that are usually located in different departments and locations. For example, Bristol-Myers Squibb Corporation has more than 3,000 corporate buyers located all over the world. These agents buy from a large number of suppliers. The problem is that even if all purchases are made from approved suppliers, it is difficult to plan and control procurement when many buyers purchase individually. In many cases, to save time, buyers engage in *maverick buying*, which is, unplanned, emergency-type buying. In addition, an organization needs to control the purchasing budget. This situation is especially serious in government agencies and multinational entities where many buyers and large numbers of purchases are involved.

One effective solution to such procurement problem is to aggregate the catalogs of all approved suppliers, combining them into a single internal electronic catalog. Prices can be negotiated in advance or determined by a tendering, so that the buyers do not have to negotiate each time they place an order. By aggregating the suppliers' catalogs on the buyer's server, it also is easier to centralize and control all procurement. Such an aggregation of catalogs is called an **internal procurement marketplace**.

> **internal procurement marketplace**
> The aggregated catalogs of all approved suppliers combined into a single internal electronic catalog.

Benefits of Internal Aggregated (Consolidated) Catalogs

Corporate buyers can use search engines to look through internal aggregated catalogs to quickly find what they want, check availability and delivery times, and complete electronic requisition forms. Another advantage of such aggregation is that a company can reduce the number of suppliers it uses. For example, Caltex, a multinational oil company, reduced the number of its suppliers from over 3,000 to 800. Such reduction is possible because the central catalog enables buyers at multiple corporate locations to buy from remote, but fewer, sellers. Buying from fewer sellers typically increases the quantities bought from each, lowering the per unit price.

Another example of a successful aggregation of suppliers' catalogs is that of MasterCard International, which aggregates more than 10,000 items from the catalogs of approved suppliers into an internal electronic catalog. The goal of this project is to consolidate buying activities from multiple corporate sites, improve processing costs, and reduce the supplier base. Payments are made with MasterCard's corporate procurement card. By 2006, the system was used by more than 2,500 buyers. MasterCard is continually adding suppliers and catalog content to the system (see MasterCard 2008).

Finally, internal catalogs allow for easy financial controls. As buyers make purchases, their account balances are displayed. Once the balance is depleted, the system will not allow new purchase orders to go through. Therefore, this model is especially popular in public institutions and government entities. The implementation of internal purchasing marketplaces is frequently done via a process known as *desktop purchasing*.

Desktop Purchasing

Desktop purchasing implies purchasing directly from internal marketplaces without the approval of supervisors and without the intervention of a procurement department. This is usually done by using a *purchasing card (P-card)* (see Chapter 11). Desktop purchasing reduces

> **desktop purchasing**
> Direct purchasing from internal marketplaces without the approval of supervisors and without the intervention of a procurement department.

the administrative cost and cycle time involved in purchasing urgently needed or frequently purchased items of small dollar value. This approach is especially effective for MRO purchases.

Microsoft built its internal marketplace, MS Market, for the procurement of small items. The aggregated catalog that is part of MS Market is used by Microsoft employees worldwide, whose purchasing totals over $3.5 billion annually. The system has drastically reduced the role and size of the procurement departments at Microsoft.

The desktop-purchasing approach also can be implemented by partnering with external private exchanges. For instance, Samsung Electronics of South Korea, a huge global manufacturer and its subsidiaries, has integrated its iMarketKorea exchange (see closing case at the end of this chapter) with the e-procurement systems of its buying agents. This platform can be easily linked with *group purchasing*, which is described later in this section.

BUYING AT SELLERS' E-AUCTIONS

Another popular approach to procurement is e-auctions. As described earlier sellers are increasingly motivated to sell surpluses and even regular products via auctions. In some cases, e-auctions provide an opportunity for buyers to find inexpensive or unique items fairly quickly. A prudent corporate buyer should certainly look at both those manufacturers and distributors that conduct auctions periodically (e.g., Dell) and at third-party auctioneers (e.g., eBay or auctions.yahoo.com). Auction aggregators can help purchasers find where and when auctions of needed items are being conducted. Auctions can be conducted at the seller's site, at an auctioneer's site, or at an exchange.

GROUP PURCHASING

group purchasing
The aggregation of orders from several buyers into volume purchases so that better prices can be negotiated.

Many companies, especially small ones, are moving to group purchasing. With **group purchasing**, orders from several buyers are aggregated into volume purchases so that better prices can be negotiated. Two models are in use: internal aggregation and external (third-party) aggregation.

Internal Aggregation of Purchasing Orders

Large companies, such as GE, spend billions of dollars on MROs every year. Company-wide orders, from GE companies and subsidiaries, for identical items are aggregated using the Web and are replenished automatically. Besides economies of scale (lower prices for large purchases) on many items, GE saves on the administrative cost of the transactions, reducing transaction costs from $50 to $100 per transaction to $5 to $10 (Rudnitsky 2000). With 5 million transactions annually at GE, this is a substantial savings.

External Aggregation for Group Purchasing

Many SMEs would like to enjoy quantity discounts but have difficulty finding others to join group purchasing to increase the procurement volume. Finding partners can be accomplished by an external third party such as BuyerZone (buyerzone.com), HIGPA (higpa.org), or the United Sourcing Alliance (usa-llc.com). The idea is to provide SMEs with better prices, selection, and services by aggregating demand online and then either negotiating with suppliers or conducting reverse auctions. The external aggregation group purchasing process is shown in Exhibit 5.9.

One can appreciate the importance of this market by taking into consideration some data about small businesses. In the United States, according to the U.S. Department of Commerce, 90 percent of all businesses have fewer than 100 employees, yet they account for over 35 percent of all MRO business volume (Small Business Administration 2009). Therefore, the potential for external aggregators is huge.

Several large companies, including large CPA firms, EDS, and Ariba, are providing similar aggregation services, mainly to their regular customers. Yahoo! and AOL also offer such services. A key to the success of these companies is a critical mass of buyers. An interesting strategy is for a company to outsource aggregation to a third party. For example, energysolutions.com provides group buying for community site partners in the energy industry.

Group purchasing, which started with commodity items such as MROs and consumer electronic devices, has now moved to services ranging from travel to payroll processing and Web hosting. Some aggregators use Priceline's "name-your-own-price" approach. Others try

EXHIBIT 5.9   The Group Purchasing Process

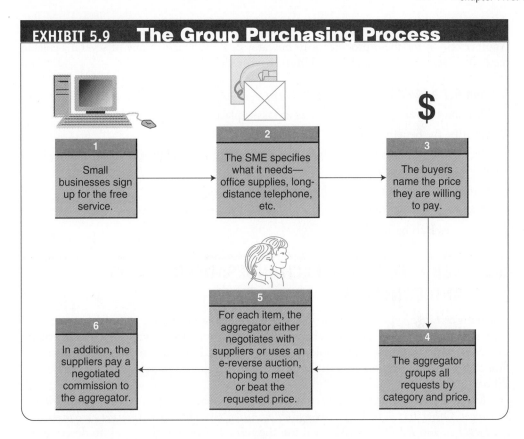

1 Small businesses sign up for the free service.

2 The SME specifies what it needs—office supplies, long-distance telephone, etc.

3 The buyers name the price they are willing to pay.

4 The aggregator groups all requests by category and price.

5 For each item, the aggregator either negotiates with suppliers or uses an e-reverse auction, hoping to meet or beat the requested price.

6 In addition, the suppliers pay a negotiated commission to the aggregator.

to find the lowest possible price (see njnonprofits.org/groupbuy.html). Similar approaches are used in B2C, and several vendors serve both markets.

BUYING AT SELLERS' SITES AND COLLABORATIVE COMMERCE

Section 5.3 described how companies use e-distributors as a sales channel (recall the case of W. W. Grainger). When buying small quantities, purchasers often buy from an e-distributor. If they buy online, it is considered e-procurement.

PURCHASING DIRECT GOODS

Until 2001, most B2B e-procurement implementations took place in the sell-side of large vendors (e.g., Cisco, Intel, and IBM) and in the procurement of MROs. In general, MROs comprise 20 to 50 percent of a company's purchasing budget. The remaining 50 to 80 percent of corporate purchases are for *direct materials* and *services*. Therefore, most companies would reap great benefits in using e-purchasing to acquire direct goods: Buyers would be able to purchase direct goods more quickly, reduce unit costs, reduce inventories, avoid shortages, and expedite their own production processes. Sourcing direct materials typically involves more complex transactions requiring negotiation and *collaboration* between the seller and buyer and greater information exchange. This leads us to collaborative commerce, which will be discussed in Chapter 6.

ELECTRONIC BARTERING

Bartering is the exchange of goods or services without the use of money. The basic idea is for a company to exchange its surplus for something that it needs. Companies can advertise their surpluses in classified ads and may find a partner to make an exchange, but in most cases a company will have little success in finding an exact match on its own. Therefore, companies usually ask an intermediary to help.

A bartering intermediary can use a manual search-and-match approach or it can create an electronic bartering exchange. With a **bartering exchange**, a company submits its surplus to the exchange and receives points of credit, which the company can then use to buy items that it needs. Popular bartering items are office space, idle facilities and labor, products, and even banner ads. Examples of bartering companies are u-exchange.com and itex.com.

bartering exchange
An intermediary that links parties in a barter; a company submits its surplus to the exchange and receives points of credit, which can be used to buy the items that the company needs from other exchange participants.

Buying in Exchanges

Another option for the e-procurer is to buy at a B2B exchange in one of several available methods. These options are described in the next section

Section 5.7 ▶ REVIEW QUESTIONS

1. Describe a buyer-operated procurement marketplace and list its benefits.
2. Describe the benefits of desktop purchasing.
3. Discuss the relationship of desktop purchasing with internal procurement marketplaces and with group purchasing.
4. Explain the logic of group purchasing and how it is organized.
5. Describe how e-distributors operate and discuss their appeal to buyers.
6. How does B2B bartering work?

5.8 B2B ELECTRONIC EXCHANGES: DEFINITIONS AND CONCEPTS

The term *exchange* implies many-to-many e-marketplaces. In the context of EC, exchanges are online trading venues. Many exchanges support community activities, such as distributing industry news, sponsoring online discussion groups, blogging, and providing research. Some also provide support services such as payments and logistics (see Papazoglou and Ribbers 2006).

Exchanges are known by a variety of names: *e-marketplaces, e-markets,* and *trading exchanges*. Other terms include *trading communities, exchange hubs, Internet exchanges, Net marketplaces,* and *B2B portals*. We will use the term *exchange* in this book to describe the general many-to-many e-marketplaces, but we will use some of the other terms in more specific contexts (e.g., see epiqtech.com/others-B2B-Exchanges.htm).

Despite their variety, all exchanges share one major characteristic: Exchanges are electronic trading-community meeting places for many sellers and many buyers, and possibly for other business partners, as shown in Exhibit 5.10. At the center of every exchange

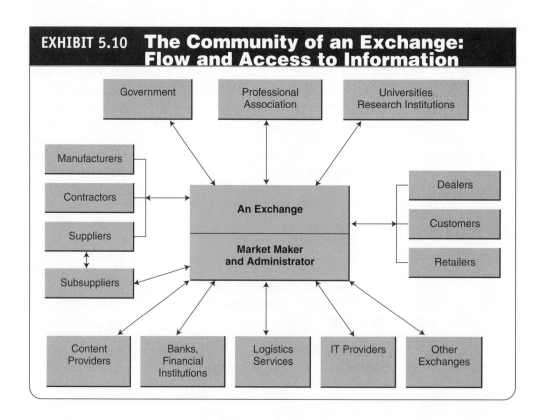

EXHIBIT 5.10 The Community of an Exchange: Flow and Access to Information

is a market maker, the third party that operates the exchange and, in many cases, may also own it.

In an exchange, just as in a traditional open-air marketplace, buyers and sellers can interact and negotiate prices and quantities. Generally, free-market economics rules the exchange community, as demonstrated by ChemConnect (see Case 5.5).

CASE 5.5

EC Application

CHEMCONNECT: THE WORLD COMMODITY CHEMICAL EXCHANGE

Today, buyers and sellers of chemicals and plastics can meet electronically in a large Internet public marketplace (founded in 1995) called ChemConnect (*chemconnect.com*), which was purchased by Intercontinental Exchange (ICE) in July 2007. Global chemical industry leaders, such as BP, Dow Chemical, BASF, Hyundai, Sumitomo, and many more, make transactions over ChemConnect every day in real time. They save on transaction costs, reduce cycle time, and find new markets and trading partners around the globe. It was the first B2B e-market in the chemical industry.

ChemConnect provides a link to the Global eXchange Services (GXS; *gxs.com*) trading marketplace, which manages a network about 100,000 trading partners worldwide. Members are producers, consumers, distributors, traders, and intermediaries involved in the chemical industry. ChemConnect offers its members a Trading Center with three trading places:

1. **Marketplace for buyers.** In this marketplace, buyers can find suppliers all over the world. They can post RFQs with reverse auctions, negotiate, and more.
2. **Marketplace for sellers.** This marketplace exposes sellers to many potential new customers. It provides automated tools for quick liquidation. More than 1,000 products are negotiated in auctions.
3. **Commodity markets platform.** This platform provides a powerful connection to the global spot marketplaces for chemicals, plastics, and related materials.

ChemConnect members can use the Trading Center to streamline sales and sourcing processes by automating requests for quotes, proposals, and new suppliers. The center enables a member to negotiate more efficiently with existing business partners as well as with new companies the member may invite to the table—all in complete privacy. The Trading Center is a highly effective way to get the best prices and terms available on the worldwide market. In addition, members can access a database containing more than 63,000 chemicals and plastics—virtually any product members are ever likely to look for. In addition to trading, the exchange provides back-end fulfillment services (e.g., payments, delivery).

All three trading places provide up-to-the-minute market information (mostly financial and news, via *bloomberg.com*) that can be translated into more than 30 different languages. Business partners provide several support services. For example, Citigroup and ChemConnect jointly offer several financial services for exchange members. ChemConnect also offers systems for connecting companies' back-end systems with their business partners and with ChemConnect itself.

The overall benefits of ChemConnect to its members are more efficient business processes, lower overall transaction costs, and time saved during negotiation and bidding. For example, conducting a reverse auction in a trading room enables buyers to save up to 15 percent of a product's cost in just 30 minutes. The same process using manual bidding methods would take several weeks or months.

ChemConnect continues to grow, adding members and increasing its trading volume each year. The company became profitable in 2004 (transaction volume in 2004 was over $10 billion) and was acquired by Intercontinental Exchange in 2007. One of the company's success factors is that 40 large chemical companies hold about one-third of the company's stock. Another factor is the fact that about 44 percent of the industry uses the exchange on a regular basis.

ChemConnect has expanded its coverage to become a more diversified company, offering midstream energy, such as ethanol, natural gas, and other commodities. It has also added negotiation solutions, collaboration hubs, data integration services, price discovery features, and more. Also, its community has been expanded. Participant companies include most large producers, consumers, distributors, traders, and transportation and logistics companies within each product class in addition to banks, hedge funds, and other interested financial institutions. Finally, it offers an infrastructure for negotiation (see *chemconnect.com/negotiation.html*).

Sources: Compiled from *chemconnect.com* (accessed January 2008), Angwin (2004), Rappa (2006), and *en.wikipedia.org/wiki/chemconnect* (accessed January 2009).

Questions

1. List the benefits of ChemConnect to trading companies.
2. Describe the different trading platforms.
3. List some of the capabilities of the system.

FUNCTIONS OF EXCHANGES

Exchanges have three major functions:

1. **Matching buyers and sellers.** The matching of buyers and sellers includes such activities as:
   - Establishing product offerings
   - Aggregating and posting different products for sale
   - Providing price and product information
   - Organizing bids, bartering, and auctions
   - Matching supplier offerings with buyer preferences
   - Enabling price and product comparisons
   - Supporting negotiations and agreements between buyers and suppliers
   - Providing directories of buyers and sellers

2. **Facilitating transactions.** Facilitating transactions includes the following activities:
   - Providing the trading platform and mechanisms such as arranging logistics of delivering information, goods, or services to buyers
   - Providing billing and payment information, including addresses
   - Defining terms and other transaction values
   - Inputting searchable information
   - Granting exchange access to users and identifying company users eligible to use the exchange
   - Settling transaction payments to suppliers, collecting transaction fees and providing other escrow services
   - Registering and qualifying buyers and suppliers
   - Maintaining appropriate security over information and transactions
   - Arranging for group (volume) purchasing

3. **Maintaining exchange policies and infrastructure.** Maintaining institutional infrastructure involves the following activities:
   - Ascertaining compliance with commercial code, contract law, export and import laws, and intellectual property law for transactions made within the exchange
   - Maintaining technological infrastructure to support volume and complexity of transactions
   - Providing interface capability to standard systems of buyers and suppliers
   - Obtaining appropriate site advertisers and collecting advertising and other fees

Services Provided by Exchanges

Exchanges provide many services to buyers and sellers. The types of services offered depend on the nature of the exchange. For example, the services provided by a stock exchange are completely different from those provided by a steel or food exchange or by an intellectual property or patent exchange. However, most exchanges provide the services shown in Exhibit 5.11.

dynamic pricing
A rapid movement of prices over time and possibly across customers, as a result of supply and demand matching.

DYNAMIC PRICING IN B2B EXCHANGES

The market makers in both vertical and horizontal exchanges match supply and demand in their exchanges, and this matching determines prices, which are usually *dynamic* and are based on changes in supply and demand. **Dynamic pricing** refers to a rapid movement of prices over time and possibly across customers. Stock exchanges are the prime example of

EXHIBIT 5.11 Services in Exchanges

The Exchange and Its Services

Sellers

A
B
C
D
•
•
•

- Buyer–seller registration, qualification, coordination
- Catalog management (conversion, integration, maintenance)
- Communication/protocol translation (EDI, XML, CORBA)
- Sourcing—RFQ, bid coordination (product configuration, negotiation)
- Security, anonymity
- Software: groupware, workflow
- Integration with members' back-office systems
- Auction management
- News, information, industry analysis
- Support services (financing, payment, insurance, logistics, tax, escrow, order tracking)
- Administration—profiles, statistics, etc.

Buyers

X
Y
Z
•
•
•

dynamic pricing. Another good example of dynamic pricing occurs in auctions, where prices vary all the time.

The typical process that results in dynamic pricing in most exchanges includes the following steps:

1. A company posts a bid to buy a product or an offer to sell one.

2. An auction (forward or reverse) is activated.

3. Buyers and sellers can see the bids and offers but might not always see who is making them. Anonymity often is a key ingredient of dynamic pricing.

4. Buyers and sellers interact with bids and offers in real time. Sometimes buyers join together to obtain a volume discount price (group purchasing).

5. A deal is struck when there is an exact match between a buyer and a seller on price, volume, and other variables, such as location or quality.

6. The deal is consummated, and payment and delivery are arranged.

ADVANTAGES, LIMITATIONS, AND THE REVENUE MODEL OF EXCHANGES

Exchanges have several benefits, including making markets more efficient, providing opportunities for sellers and buyers to find new business partners, cutting the administrative costs of ordering MROs, and expediting trading processes. They also facilitate global trade and create communities of informed buyers and sellers.

Despite these benefits, beginning in 2001, exchanges started to collapse, and both buyers and sellers realized that they faced the risks of exchange failure or deterioration. In the case of exchange failure, the risk is primarily a financial one—of suddenly losing the market in which one has been buying and selling and, therefore, having to scramble to find a new exchange or to find buyers and sellers on one's own. In addition, finding a new place to trade is an operational risk. Buyers also risk potentially poor product performance and receipt of incomplete information from degraded exchanges, which is a risk the sellers may face, too. For more on competition among buyers in online exchanges, see Bandyopadhyay et al. (2005).

The potential gains and risks of B2B exchanges for buyers and for sellers are summarized in Exhibit 5.12. As the exhibit shows, the gains outnumber the risks.

Revenue Models

Exchanges, like all organizations, require revenue to survive. Therefore, an exchange's owners, whoever they are, must decide how they will earn revenue. The following potential sources of revenue for exchanges are similar to those discussed Chapter 1.

EXHIBIT 5.12 **Potential Gains and Risks in B2B Exchanges**		
	For Buyers	**For Sellers**
Potential gains	• One-stop shopping, huge • Search and comparison shopping • Volume discounts • 24/7 ordering from any location • Make one order from several suppliers • Huge, detailed information • Access to new suppliers • Status review and easy reordering • Community participation • Fast delivery • Less maverick buying • Better partner relationship management	• New sales channel • No physical store is needed • Reduced ordering errors • Sell 24/7 • Community participation • Reach new customers at little extra cost • Promote the business via the exchange • An outlet for surplus inventory • Can go global more easily • Efficient inventory management • Better partner relationship management
Potential risks	• Unknown vendors; may not be reliable • Loss of customer service quality (inability to compare all services)	• Loss of direct CRM and PRM • More price wars • Competition for value-added services • Must pay transaction fees (including on seller's existing customers) • Possible loss of customers to competitors

▶ **Transaction fees.** Transaction fees are basically a commission paid by *sellers* for each transaction they make. Exchanges charge relatively low transaction fees per order in order to attract sellers. Therefore, to cover its expenses the exchange must generate sufficient volume, find other revenue sources, or raise its transaction fees.

▶ **Service fees.** Some exchanges have successfully changed their revenue model from commission (transaction fee) to "fee for service." Sellers are more willing to pay for value-added services than for commissions. Sometimes buyers also pay service charges to the exchange.

▶ **Membership fees.** A membership fee is a fixed annual or monthly fee. It usually entitles the exchange member to get some services free or at a discount. In some countries, such as China, the government may ask members to pay annual membership fees and then provide the participating sellers with free services and no transaction fees. This encourages members to use the exchange. The problem is that low membership fees might result in insufficient revenue to the exchange. However, high membership fees discourage participants from joining.

▶ **Advertising fees.** Exchanges also can derive income from fees for advertising on the information-portal part of the exchange. For example, some sellers may want to increase their exposure and will pay for special advertisements on the portal (like boxed ads in the yellow pages of telephone books).

▶ **Other revenue sources.** If an exchange is doing auctions, it can charge auction fees. License fees can be collected on patented information or software. Finally, market makers can collect fees for their services.

Section 5.8 ▶ REVIEW QUESTIONS

1. Define B2B exchanges and list the various types of public exchanges.
2. Differentiate between a vertical exchange and a horizontal exchange.
3. What is dynamic pricing? How does it work?

4. Describe the possible revenue models of exchanges.

5. List the potential advantages, gains, limitations, and risks of exchanges.

5.9   B2B PORTALS, DIRECTORIES, AND OWNERSHIP OF B2B MARKETPLACES

Two major varieties of B2B marketplaces exist: portals and directories.

B2B PORTALS

B2B portals are information portals for businesses. Some e-marketplaces act as pure information portals. They usually include *directories* of products offered by each seller, lists of buyers and what they want, and other industry or general information. Buyers then visit sellers' sites to conduct their transactions. The portal may get commissions for referrals or only derive revenue from advertisements. Thus, information portals sometimes have a difficult time generating sufficient revenues. Because of this, many information portals are beginning to offer, for a fee, additional services that support trading, such as escrow and shipments. An example of a B2B portal is MyBoeingFleet (myboeingfleet.com), which is a Web portal for airplane owners, operators, and MRO operators. Developed by Boeing Commercial Aviation Services, MyBoeingFleet provides customers (primarily businesses) direct and personalized access to information essential to the operation of Boeing aircraft.

Like exchanges, information portals may be horizontal (e.g., Alibaba.com, described in Case 5.6), offering a wide range of products to different industries. Or they may be vertical, focusing on a single industry or industry segment. Vertical portals often are referred to as **vortals**.

Some use the word *portal* when referring to an exchange. The reason for this is that many B2B portals are adding capabilities that make them look like exchanges. Also, many exchanges include information portals.

The two examples that follow illustrate some of the differences between *portals* and *exchanges*.

B2B portals
Information portals for businesses.

vortals
B2B portals that focus on a single industry or industry segment; "vertical portals."

Thomas Global

Thomas Global (thomasglobal.com) is a directory of over 700,000 manufacturers and distributors from 28 countries, encompassing over 11,000 products and service categories in 9 languages. It covers regional guides, such as Thomas Register of America (thomasnet.com), an information portal, which publishes a directory of millions of manufacturing companies. Thomas Register is basically an information portal for buyers using search engines, because it does not offer any opportunity for transactions on its site. For example, it does not offer a list of products with quantities needed (requests to buy) or offer what is available from sellers. A similar information-only service is provided by Manufacturing.Net (manufacturing.net).

Alibaba.com Corporation

Another intermediary that started as a pure information portal but that is moving toward becoming a trading exchange is Alibaba.com (alibaba.com). Launched in 1999, Alibaba.com initially concentrated on China. It includes a large, robust community of international buyers and sellers who are interested in direct trade without an intermediary. Initially, the site was a huge posting place for classified ads. Alibaba.com is a portal in transition, showing some characteristics of an information portal plus some services of an exchange. Today, Alibaba.com has two complementary markets, as described in Case 5.6.

CASE 5.6

EC Application
ALIBABA.COM

Alibaba.com Limited is the global leader in business-to-business (B2B) e-commerce and the flagship company of Alibaba Group. Founded in 1999, Alibaba.com makes it easy for millions of buyers and suppliers around the world to do business online through three marketplaces: a global trade marketplace (*alibaba.com*) for importers and exporters; a Chinese marketplace (*alibaba.com.cn*) for domestic trade in China; and, through an associated company, a Japanese marketplace (*alibaba.co.jp*), which facilitates trade to and from Japan. Together, its marketplaces form a community of 40 million registered users from more than 240 countries. Headquartered in Hangzhou, Alibaba.com has offices in more than 40 cities across Greater China as well as in Europe and the United States.

In 10 short years, Alibaba.com has grown into a premier e-commerce brand and a vibrant online marketplace for businesses from around the world. To date, Alibaba.com's international marketplace serves more than 8.6 million members, offering products in more than 3,500 different categories. Its Chinese marketplace facilitates domestic trade for 31.6 registered users in China, offering products in more than 6,000 different categories. Alibaba.com offers trade information in both breadth and depth and matches buyers and sellers 24/7.

Trust and safety are fundamental to e-commerce. Paid suppliers on Alibaba.com must pass an authentication and verification process conducted by an independent third party. Only those that have been successfully verified by the third party can obtain an Alibaba "TrustPass." Information such as the company's business registration, name, and address and the applicant's relationship with the business entity are verified. Alibaba.com's experience shows that over 85 percent of its buyers prefer to do business with verified members only.

Alibaba International (*alibaba.com*) is an English-language global trade marketplace, serving small and medium-sized enterprises (SMEs) in the international trade community. Alibaba.com offers a broad range of products and services to both suppliers and buyers. Basic features, such as standard supplier storefronts, product listings, and communication tools, are available for free. It also offers paid membership packages to verified suppliers. The subscription fee includes authentication and verification of the member's identity, which is performed by a third-party credit reporting agency. Alibaba.com is prospering from a business model dedicated to serving a vital, but disadvantaged, segment of China's economy: SMEs. Fewer than 1 million of the nation's 42 million small and medium-sized enterprises have Internet capability. Alibaba offers simple and efficient Internet solutions for such companies.

Alibaba China (*alibaba.com.cn*) is China's largest online Chinese-language marketplace for domestic trade. With more than 31.6 million registered users, Alibaba China is a trusted community of members who regularly meet, chat, search for products, and do business online. Just as in the international marketplace, customers pay an annual subscription fee for membership, which entitles them to post trade offers and products online.

In addition, Alibaba Group owns and maintains the following:

▶ *Yahoo.china.cn* is a leading Chinese-language portal. It offers search tools, an interactive community, and one of the most popular e-mail services in China. In 2008, it acquired China's leading classified listing Web site, Koubei.com, which then became Yahoo! Koubei.

▶ *Taobao.com* is China's largest Internet retail site. Taobao has 100 million registered users, and more than 1.5 million sellers have opened stores on the site. The annual transaction volume on Taobao (gross merchandise volume, or GMV) reached nearly $15 billion in 2008, expanding at a 3-year compound annual growth rate of more than 150 percent and exceeding the largest retailer in China in transaction volume. Alimama (*alimama.com*), an online advertising exchange and affiliate network for more than 400,000 publishers in China, was merged into Taobao in 2008.

▶ *Alipay.com* is China's leading third-party online payment platform. It enables individuals and businesses to execute payments online in a safe and secure manner. In August 2007, Alipay launched an online payment solution to help merchants worldwide sell directly to consumers in China, cooperating with more than 300 global retail brands and supports transactions in 12 major foreign currencies.

▶ *Alisoft.com* offers an Internet-based business management solution. It develops, markets, and delivers Internet-based business management software to SMEs in China. It commands more than 40 percent of the Software as a Service (SaaS) model, offering enterprise management tools, such as e-mail, customer support software, and information management software, and basic financial management tools, such as invoicing and bookkeeping.

To understand the capabilities of Alibaba.com, we need to explore its marketplace (take the multimedia tour!).

The Database

The center of Alibaba.com is its huge database, which is basically a horizontal information portal with offerings in a wide variety of product categories. The portal is organized into 44 major industry categories (as of 2009), including agriculture, apparel and fashion, automobiles, and toys. Each industry category is further divided into subcategories (over 700 in total). For example, the toy category includes items such as dolls, electrical pets, and wooden toys. Each subcategory includes classified postings organized into four groups: sellers, buyers, agents, and cooperation. Each group may include many companies. The postings are fairly short. Note that in all cases a user can click an ad for details. Some categories have thousands of product postings; therefore, a vertical search engine is provided to users to facilitate them

(continued)

CASE 5.6 *(continued)*

in redefining the search words. The search engine works by country, type of advertiser, and age of the postings.

Reverse Auctions

Alibaba.com also allows buyers to post RFQs. Would-be sellers can then send bids to the buyer, conduct negotiations, and accept a purchase order when one is agreed upon (all via the exchange). The RFQ process can be fully automated, partially automated, or done entirely manually. (To see how the process works, go to "My trade activity" and take the tour, initiate a negotiation, and issue a purchase order.)

Features and Services

Alibaba.com provides the following major features: free e-mail, instant messenger Trade Manager, Trust Service, FAQs, tutorials for traders, free e-mail alerts, news (basically related to importing and exporting), trade show information, legal information, arbitration, forums and discussion groups, trade trends, and so on. In addition, a member can create a personalized company Web page as well as a "product showroom"; members also can post their own marketing leads (where to buy and sell). Premium membership packages also provide premium storefronts, priority listing, dedicated training, and customer service, as well as a range of value-added services, including Product Showcase (private product showroom), Traffic Analyzer™, Buyer GPS™, Biz Trends, Buyer Country Locator, and company e-mail accounts. In the future, additional services will be added to increase the company's revenue stream.

Revenue Model

In order to attract buyers, sourcing on Alibaba.com is always free. Although it offers a number of tools and services for free, Alibaba.com offers a paid membership service to suppliers. Income is generated through paid memberships and value-added services. Alibaba.com competes with several global exchanges that provide similar services (e.g., see *asia-links.com* and *globalsources.com*).

In November 2008, Alibaba.com launched its new entry-level product—the Gold Supplier Starter Pack—designed for exporters that plan to shift their business online to achieve efficiencies in the current economic environment. The product, priced at $2,900 per year, offers basic storefront display and unlimited product listings. The original premium membership has been updated to enjoy more premium Web site features, such as additional Virtual Showrooms, which will enable suppliers to substantially increase the visibility of their key products. Companies must obtain third-party authentication and verification under the Quality Supplier Program before they can purchase the Gold Supplier Starter Pack. Although the global financial crisis will bring challenges to the real economy, the Gold Supplier Starter Pack appeals to a wide range of potential new customers. Someday in the future, Alibaba.com may be in a position that will enable it to make a great deal of money. Alibaba.com was strong enough to sustain losses until 2003, when it made $12 million profit. As of 2009, company profits were growing very rapidly. Total revenue for 2008 was $440 million, a 39 percent increase over 2007.

Going Public with an IPO

Alibaba.com's founder Jack Ma took the company public in November of 2007, using $1.7 billion in outside capital to deploy its business model on a full scale in order to show that e-commerce in China can make money (see Chandler

Source: Courtesy of Alibaba.com. Used with permission.

(continued)

2007). The influx of capital will allow Alibaba to continue building its customer base by offering the bulk of its services at no charge. And that may prove a winning strategy.

Sources: Compiled from *alibaba.com* (accessed May 2009), Alibaba.com (2009a), Alibaba.com (2009b), Alibaba.com (2009c), and Chandler (2007).

Questions

1. When the company's IPO started trading, hundreds of large corporations rushed to invest in it. Why?
2. Trace Alibaba.com's revenue sources.
3. List the major services provided by Alibaba.com.

Directory Services and Search Engines

The B2B landscape is huge, with hundreds of thousands of companies online. Directory services can help buyers and sellers manage the task of finding specialized products, services, and potential partners.

According to Killeen (2006), specialized search engines are becoming a necessity in many industries due to the information glut. The most useful search engines are those concentrating on vertical searches. Examples of vertical search engines and their services can be found at globalspec.com. In contrast to vertical searches, products such as Google Search provide search capabilities on many topics within one enterprise or on the Web in general.

OWNERSHIP OF B2B MARKETPLACES

Exchanges may be owned by a third-party operator. This arrangement is preferred by both sellers and buyers. Alternatively, an exchange may be owned by a few major sellers or buyers. This kind of arrangement is referred to as a *consortium*.

Third-Party Exchanges

Third-party exchanges are electronic intermediaries. In contrast with a portal such as Alibaba.com, the intermediary not only presents catalogs (which the portal does), but also tries to *match* buyers and sellers and encourages them to make transactions by providing electronic trading floors and rooms (which portals, in general, do not).

Third-party exchanges are characterized by two contradicting properties. On the one hand, they are *neutral* because they do not favor either sellers or buyers. On the other hand, because they do not have a built-in constituency of sellers or buyers, they sometimes have a problem attracting enough buyers and sellers to attain financial viability. Therefore, to increase their financial viability, these exchanges try to team up with partners, such as large sellers or buyers, financial institutions that provide payment schemes (as ChemConnect did with Citigroup), and logistics companies that fulfill orders.

Case 5.5 introduced ChemConnect, a neutral, public, third-party-owned vertical market maker. ChemConnect's initial success was well publicized, and dozens of similar third-party exchanges, mostly in specific industries, have been developed since. A thriving example of a third-party exchange is Agentrics.com, which is described in Case 5.7.

consortium trading exchange (CTE)

An exchange formed and operated by a group of major companies in an industry to provide industry-wide transaction services.

Consortium Exchanges

A subset of third-party exchanges is a **consortium trading exchange** (CTE), an exchange formed and operated by a group of major companies in one industry. The major declared goal of CTEs (also called *consortia*) is to provide industry-wide transaction services that support buying and selling. These services include links to the participants' back-end processing systems as well as collaborative planning and design services.

Markets operate in three basic types of environments, which are shown in the following list. The type of environment indicates which type of exchange is most appropriate.

CASE 5.7
EC Application
AGENTRICS: A GIANT RETAIL EXCHANGE

Agentrics (*agentrics.com*) is the world's largest exchange for retail and packaged consumer goods. It was formed from the mergers of several exchanges, including the World Wide Retail Exchange (WWRE) and GNX. As of November 2006, it had 250 members, including 17 of the world's 25 top retailers (e.g., Best Buy, Sears, Safeway, and Tesco). Its primary objective is to enable participating retailers and manufacturers to simplify, rationalize, and automate supply chain processes, thereby eliminating inefficiencies in the supply chain.

Today, Agentrics is the premier Internet-based B2B exchange in the retail e-marketplace. Utilizing the most sophisticated Internet technology available, the exchange enables retailers and manufacturers in the food, general merchandise, textile/home, and drugstore sectors to substantially reduce costs across product development, e-procurement, and supply chain processes. The exchange is used by more than 100,000 suppliers, partners, and distributors worldwide.

The exchange operates as an open, independently managed company that generates benefits for its members and ultimately the consumer. Agentrics is run as a private company with no plans of going public. Rather, it concentrates on bringing value to its members and customers.

Founding Principles
The following six principles guide the exchange's development and growth:

1. Openness
2. Commitment to utilizing the best available technology
3. Focus on improving efficiency and lowering costs for the retail industry
4. Operation as a neutral company
5. Equivalent fee structures for all participants
6. Confidentiality of transaction information

Value Proposition
Members realize value in seven key ways:

1. Low-cost product offerings that are robust, scalable, integrated, and fully supported
2. Shared technology investments and outsourced assets
3. Ability to access a global membership community and network with other retailers/manufacturers
4. Value-added services from a trusted source, at competitive costs
5. Participation in collaborative activities
6. Complex transactions and interactions made easy through automation
7. Standard-setting benefits for all B2B activities

The exchange offers about 20 different products and services. They are classified as those related to WWRE (e.g., global data synchronization, trading, sourcing, supply chain solutions) and those related to GNX (e.g., collaboration, performance and life cycle management, CPFR, and negotiation).

An example of one of the exchange's current efforts is its Global Data Synchronization project. Inaccurate product

Source: Courtesy of Agentrics.com. Used with permission.

(*continued*)

and item information costs the consumer goods industry more than $40 billion each year. Agentrics has developed a solution that enables retailers and suppliers to accurately maintain item information using industry standards and achieve a single point of entry into the Global Data Synchronization Network. The project is supported by WebMethods Corporation, which provides the necessary integration.

Sources: Compiled from *agentrics.com* (accessed January 2009); webMethods (2005); WWRE (2005); and *webmethods.com* (accessed January 2009).

Questions

1. Enter *agentrics.com* and find information about services offered, including auctions and negotiations. Write a report.

2. Enter *agentrics.com* and identify the services offered and the benefits to retailers and to suppliers. Write a summary.

3. Enter *webmethods.com* and find information about the item synchronization project (for WWRE). Summarize the benefits to retailers and to suppliers.

---

1. **Fragmented markets.** These markets have large numbers of both buyers and sellers. Examples include the life sciences and food industries. When a large percentage of the market is fragmented, third-party managed exchanges are most appropriate.

2. **Seller-concentrated markets.** In this type of market, several large companies sell to a very large number of buyers. Examples are the plastics and transportation industries. In this type of market, consortia may be most appropriate.

3. **Buyer-concentrated markets.** In this type of market, several large companies do most of the buying from a large number of suppliers. Examples are the automotive, airline, and electronics industries. Here, again, consortia may be most appropriate.

According to Richard and Devinney (2005), CTEs fared much better than independent third-party exchanges during the dot-com shakeout that took place between 2000–2002. Yet, of the hundreds of CTEs that existed all over the world in 2000, by 2002 many had folded or were inactive, including giants such as Covisint (see Online File W5.8). By 2006, CTEs had achieved stability, and some new exchanges arrived on the business scene. An example of a successful CTE is provided in Online File W5.9.

COMPARING THE MANY-TO-MANY B2B MODELS

Exhibit 5.13 summarizes the many-to-many models presented in this chapter.

EXHIBIT 5.13 **Comparing the Major B2B Many-to-Many Models**		
Name	**Major Characteristics**	**Types**
B2B portals and directories	• Community services, news, information • Communication tools • Classified ads • Employment markets • May support selling (buying) • Fixed prices • May do auctions	• Vertical (vortals), horizontal • Shopping directory, usually with hyperlinks
B2B trading exchanges	• Matches buyer/seller orders at dynamic prices, auctions • Provides trading-related information and services (payment, logistics) • Highly regulated • May provide general information, news, etc. • May provide for negotiations	• Vertical, horizontal • Forward auctions • Reverse auctions • Bid/ask exchanges

Section 5.9 ▶ REVIEW QUESTIONS

1. Define B2B portals.
2. Distinguish a vortal from a horizontal portal.
3. Describe some directory services in B2B.
4. What is a third-party–owned exchange?
5. Define consortium trading exchanges.

5.10 PARTNER AND SUPPLIER RELATIONSHIP MANAGEMENT

In order to succeed in B2B, and particularly in exchanges, it is necessary to have several support services.

PARTNER AND SUPPLIER RELATIONSHIP MANAGEMENT

Successful e-businesses carefully manage partners, prospects, and customers across the entire value chain, most often in a 24/7 environment. For benefits and methods, see Markus (2006). Therefore, one should examine the role of solution technologies, such as call centers and collaboration tools, in creating an integrated online environment for engaging e-business customers and partners. The use of such solutions and technology appears under two names: customer relationship management (CRM) and partner relationship management (PRM).

Corporate customers may require additional services. For example, customers need to have access to the supplier's inventory status report so they know what items a supplier can deliver quickly. Customers also may want to see their historical purchasing records, and they may need private showrooms and trade rooms. Large numbers of vendors are available for designing and building appropriate B2B relationship solutions. The strategy of providing such comprehensive, quality e-service for business partners is sometimes called **partner relationship management (PRM)**.

In the context of PRM, business customers are only one category of business partners. Suppliers, partners in joint ventures, service providers, and others also are part of the B2B community in an exchange or company-centric B2B initiative, as illustrated in Exhibit 5.10. PRM is particularly important to companies that conduct outsourcing (Hagel 2004). Companies with many suppliers, such as the automobile companies, may create special programs for them. Such programs are called *supplier relationship management* (SRM) (see Online File W5.10).

partner relationship management (PRM)
Business strategy that focuses on providing comprehensive quality service to business partners.

E-COMMUNITIES AND PRM

B2B applications involve many participants: buyers and sellers, service providers, industry associations, and others. Thus, in many cases the B2B implementation creates a community. In such cases, the B2B market maker needs to provide community services, such as chat rooms, bulletin boards, and possibly personalized Web pages.

E-communities are connecting personnel, partners, customers, and any combination of the three. E-communities offer a powerful resource for e-businesses to leverage online discussions and interaction in order to maximize innovation and responsiveness (e.g., see Case 5.6 on Alibaba.com). It is therefore beneficial to study the tools, methods, and best practices of building and managing e-communities. Although the technological support of B2B e-communities is basically the same as for any other online community, the nature of the community itself and the information provided by the community are different.

B2B e-communities are mostly communities of transactions or business networks, and, as such, members' major interests are trading and business-related information gathering. Most of the communities are associated with vertical exchanges; therefore, their needs may be fairly specific. However, it is common to find generic services such as classified ads, job vacancies, announcements, industry news, and so on. Communities promote partnering.

For further information, see About.com (2006). The newest variation of these communities is the business-oriented social network, described next.

Section 5.10 ▶ REVIEW QUESTIONS

1. Define PRM and describe its functions.
2. Define SRM.
3. Describe e-communities in B2B.

5.11 B2B IN THE WEB 2.0 ENVIRONMENT AND SOCIAL NETWORKING

Although a large number of companies conduct social networking that targets individual consumers (B2C), there is much less activity in the B2B arena. However, the potential is large, and new applications are added daily. The potential of B2B social networking depends on the companies' goals and the perceived benefits and risks involved.

THE OPPORTUNITIES

Companies that use B2B social networking may experience the following advantages:

- ▶ Discover new business partners.
- ▶ Improve recruitment (mostly B2C, but some B2B).
- ▶ Enhance their ability to learn about new technologies, competitors, and the business environment.
- ▶ Find sales prospects.
- ▶ Improve participation in industry association activities (including lobbying).

Some businesses are currently leveraging social networks and online communities to their advantage. For example, corporations are using social networks to:

- ▶ Create brand awareness (e.g., through the release of *widgets*, smart devices for customizing Web pages; see Chapter 18 for details).
- ▶ Advertise products and services and promote new ones.
- ▶ Create buzz about upcoming product releases.
- ▶ Drive traffic to their online Web properties in hopes of enticing users to engage with their sites, products, or solutions.
- ▶ Create social communities to encourage discussions among business partners (e.g., suppliers) about their products and/or act as a feedback mechanism about their products/services (for business improvements).
- ▶ Use social networks, such as Facebook and LinkedIn, to recruit new talent. Some HR departments are using social networks to obtain more insight into potential new hires.

More uses of B2B social networking are evidenced in what we call *enterprise social networking* (Chapter 9). We cover these topics briefly in this chapter.

THE USE OF WEB 2.0 TOOLS IN B2B

More companies are using blogs, wikis, RSS feeds, and other tools in B2B EC. For example, at Eastern Mountain Sport (opening case Chapter 2), the company uses blogs, RSS feeds, and wikis to communicate and collaborate with suppliers and distributors. Thousands of other companies are using (or experimenting with) these tools. For a study on the utilization of Web 2.0 tools in B2B EC, see New Media Institute (2006).

SOCIAL NETWORKS IN THE B2B MARKETPLACE

The importance of social networks has yet to be fully realized in the B2B marketplace. According to a 2008 study by KnowledgeStorm, 77 percent of respondents had little or no interaction with social networks (Spagnuolo 2008). Of the social networks frequented by business and EC professionals, LinkedIn (linkedin.com) was the most well known (see closing case in Chapter 9). Does this mean that B2B buyers and sellers are antisocial? Well, not really; it just means that because social networks are still fairly new they have not been used much for B2B applications. It may also indicate that there is a need for more B2B social network sites. Also, it is difficult to demonstrate tangible benefits from the use of B2B social networks, so firms may be reluctant to invest in them.

Businesses can use B2B social networking to improved knowledge sharing, collaboration, and feedback. Furthermore, social networking sites may also prove beneficial in aiding troubleshooting and problem-solving efforts. Companies (especially small ones), are using LinkedIn Answers, for example, for problem solving. B2B participants need to look into social networking as part of their overall EC strategy, otherwise they may miss an opportunity to reach the B2B audience and differentiate themselves from the competition.

According to eMarketer (2008), advertising on social networking sites will grow from $15 million in 2007 to $240 millions in 2012 (about a 13-fold increase). The same report attempted to answer the following key questions:

▶ How much will marketers spend on social network advertising aimed at a business audience?

▶ What types of B2B advertising can businesses do on social network sites?

▶ Why are companies creating social networks to market to business customers, vendors, distributors, and channel partners?

▶ What are the challenges of developing such networks?

EXAMPLES OF OTHER ACTIVITIES OF B2B SOCIAL NETWORKS

The following are examples of some social–network-oriented B2B activities:

▶ **American Express-sponsored Business Travel Social Network.** In October 2008, American Express launched an online social network, Business Travel Connexion (BTX, businesstravelconnexion.com), for the corporate travel industry. American Express hopes that BTX will be a dynamic network that will harness the collective intelligence of the business industry. It is designed for travel professionals who wish to become more informed and better equipped to optimize their travel and entertainment programs. The site offers an array of tools—blogs, photo albums, videos, galleries, community calendars, mobile alerts, a friends' list, and the ability to form subgroups—to leverage the power of social networking. For details, see Greengard (2008).

▶ **Corporate profiles on social networks.** LinkedIn and Facebook include substantial information on companies and their individual employees. In fact, employees' profiles can be part of a company's brand. For example, IBM currently has approximately 116,000 employees registered on LinkedIn; Microsoft has around 25,000 as of November 2008. In addition, some sites feature company profiles, with comments by employees and customers.

STRATEGY FOR B2B SOCIAL NETWORKING

Gaffney (2007) makes the following strategy suggestions for B2B social networking: participate, monitor, and use existing applications:

▶ **Participate.** Executives should become bloggers and social media participants. For example, an executive should create a LinkedIn profile (or another community) and post a few blog entries on industry-specific Web sites.

▶ **Monitor.** Social media monitoring is a big business. If you decide not to go with an automated report on how your company is mentioned in social media, assign an internal team to report on it.

▶ **Use existing applications.** Companies can find their own software applications to create a private B2B network or work with one of the public networks.

Eventually, companies will be able to use social networking more efficiently and decide what information should be made available to the entire network or to a more focused section of it. Companies want their employees to be more engaged on a long-term basis, which is precisely the direction in which enterprise social networking is moving.

The Future of Social Networking

Products such as Google's OpenSocial may spark interest from the B2B community with regard to social networking. OpenSocial is a programming standard that lets developers create applications that can run on a wide range of social networking platforms. More important, OpenSocial promises users the choice of which social networks they want to use for their applications (see Online Chapter 18).

Businesses must embrace social networking in order understand the needs and wants of their prospects and clients. Establishing trust with business partners and generating brand awareness will force B2B companies to become more involved in social networking.

Section 5.11 ▶ REVIEW QUESTIONS

1. List some of the reasons corporations are using social networking in B2B EC.
2. What are some of the benefits of social networking for B2B EC?
3. Discuss the strategies for B2B social networking.

5.12 INTERNET MARKETING IN B2B EC

B2B marketing is different from B2C marketing, which was discussed in Chapter 3 and in Sections 4.1 through 4.6. Major differences also exist between B2B and B2C EC with respect to the nature of demand and supply and the trading process. Here we discuss the corporate purchaser's buying behavior and the marketing and advertising methods used in B2B EC. More discussion of this topic is provided in Chapter 6.

ORGANIZATIONAL BUYER BEHAVIOR

Organizations buy large quantities of direct materials that they consume or use in the production of goods and services and in the company's operations. They also buy indirect materials, such as PCs, delivery trucks, and office supplies to support their production and operations processes.

Although the number of organizational buyers is much smaller than the number of individual consumers, their transaction volumes are far larger, and the terms of negotiations and purchasing are more complex. In addition, the purchasing process itself usually is more complex than the purchasing process of an individual customer. Also, the organization's buyer may be a group. In fact, decisions to purchase expensive items are usually made by a group. Therefore, factors that affect individual consumer behavior and organizational buying behavior are quite different.

A Behavioral Model of Organizational Buyers

The behavior of an organizational buyer is described by the model illustrated in Exhibit 5.14. A B2B module includes the organization's purchasing guidelines and constraints (e.g., contracts with certain suppliers) and the purchasing system used. Interpersonal influences, such as authority, and the possibility of group decision making must be considered.

THE MARKETING AND ADVERTISING PROCESSES IN B2B

The marketing and advertising processes for businesses differ considerably from those used for selling to individual consumers. For example, traditional (offline) B2B marketers use methods such as physical trade shows, advertisements in industry magazines, paper catalogs, and salespeople who call on existing customers and potential buyers.

In the digital world, these approaches may not be effective, feasible, or economical. Therefore, organizations use a variety of online methods to reach business customers. Popular methods include online directory services, matching services, the marketing and advertising

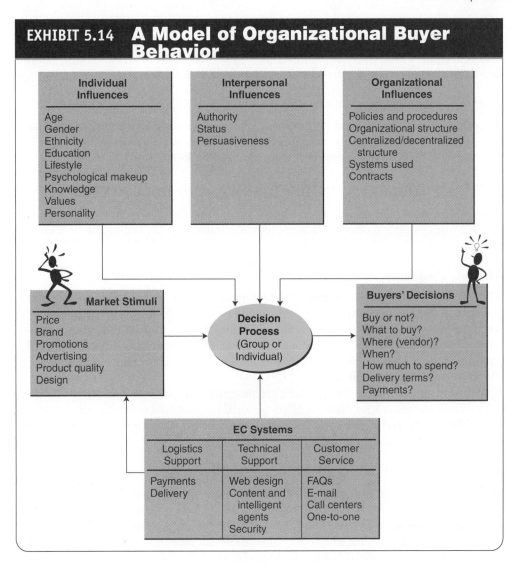

EXHIBIT 5.14 A Model of Organizational Buyer Behavior

Individual Influences
Age
Gender
Ethnicity
Education
Lifestyle
Psychological makeup
Knowledge
Values
Personality

Interpersonal Influences
Authority
Status
Persuasiveness

Organizational Influences
Policies and procedures
Organizational structure
Centralized/decentralized
  structure
Systems used
Contracts

Market Stimuli
Price
Brand
Promotions
Advertising
Product quality
Design

Decision Process
(Group or Individual)

Buyers' Decisions
Buy or not?
What to buy?
Where (vendor)?
When?
How much to spend?
Delivery terms?
Payments?

EC Systems

Logistics Support	Technical Support	Customer Service
Payments Delivery	Web design Content and intelligent agents Security	FAQs E-mail Call centers One-to-one

services of exchanges, cobranding or alliances, affiliate programs, online trade shows, online marketing services (e.g., see digitalcement.com), or e-communities. Several of these methods are discussed next.

METHODS FOR B2B ONLINE MARKETING

When a B2C niche e-tailer seeks to attract its audience of skiers, musicians, or cosmetic customers, it may advertise in traditional media targeted to those audiences, such as magazines or television shows, or use Internet ads. The same is true in B2B when trade magazines and directories are used. But when a B2B vendor wants to grow by adding new customers or products, it may not have a reliable, known advertising channel. How can it reach new customers?

Targeting Customers

A B2B company, whether a provider of goods or services, an operator of a trading exchange, or a provider of digital real-time services, can contact all of its targeted customers individually when they are part of a well-defined group. For example, to attract companies to an exchange for auto supplies, one might use information from industry trade association records or industry magazines to identify potential customers.

Another method of bringing new customers to a B2B site is through an affiliation service, which operates just as a B2C affiliate program does. A company pays a small commission every time the affiliate company "drives traffic" to the payer's site.

An important part of any marketing effort is advertising. Several of the advertising methods that will be presented later in this chapter are applicable both to B2C and B2B. For example, an ad server network provider, such as DoubleClick (doubleclick.com, now a Google company), can be used to target customers in B2B2C EC.

Electronic Wholesalers

One of the interesting B2B ventures is the e-wholesaler. Like click-and-mortar e-tailer Sam's Club, this kind of intermediary sells directly to businesses but does so exclusively online. An example is BigBoxx.com, described in Online File W5.1.

AFFILIATE PROGRAMS, INFOMEDIARIES, AND DATA MINING

Many more methods and approaches can be used in B2B marketing and advertising. Here we examine three popular methods: affiliate programs, infomediaries, and online data mining services.

Affiliate Programs

B2C affiliation services were introduced in Chapter 1. There are several types of affiliate programs. With the simplest type, which is used extensively in B2C EC, an affiliate puts a banner of another vendor, such as amazon.com, on its site. When a consumer clicks the vendor's banner, the consumer is taken to that vendor's Web site, and a commission is paid to the affiliate if the customer makes a purchase. Examples include the Netflix opening case in Chapter 4. The same method works for B2B.

With B2B, additional types of affiliate programs are possible. Schaeffer Research (schaeffersresearch.com), for example, offers financial institutions a content alliance program in which content is exchanged so that all obtain some free content. For more on B2B affiliate programs, see en.wikipedia.org/wiki/Affiliate_marketing.

Infomediaries and Online Data Mining Services

Marketing managers must understand current shopping behaviors in order to effectively advertise to customers in the future. Traditional B2C retailers evaluate point-of-sale (POS) data (e.g., grocery scanner data) and other available data to generate valuable marketing information. In today's online environment, more relevant information is available than ever before. However, the potential of the information can only be realized if the clickstream data can be analyzed and mined to produce constructive knowledge that can be used to improve services and marketing efforts. A new intermediary is emerging to provide such services to Web site owners who do not have the specialized knowledge and systems to perform such data mining on their own. As described in Chapter 2, these B2C and B2B intermediaries are called *infomediaries*.

Infomediaries start by processing existing information until new, useful information is extracted from it. This new information is sold to B2B customers or exchanged for more information, which is manipulated yet again, until even more valuable information can be extracted. B2B vendors use the information from infomediaries to identify likely buyers with much greater precision than ever before—leading to increased sales and drastically reduced marketing expenses. Representative infomediaries and data mining specialists are SAS Institute (sas.com), Unica NetTracker (unica.com), WebTrends (webtrends.com), NetIntellect (available from bizsecure.com), and SurfReport from netrics.com. For a discussion of data mining and an example of its use in B2B, see Online File W4.2.

One of the major objectives of market research is to provide tactics and strategies for EC advertising, as described in Section 4.9.

Section 5.12 ▶ REVIEW QUESTIONS

1. Distinguish between organizational buyers and individual consumers.
2. Describe B2B EC marketing and advertising methods.
3. Explain how affiliate programs and data mining work in B2B EC.

MANAGERIAL ISSUES

Some managerial issues related to this chapter are as follows.

1. **Which B2B model(s) should we use for e-procurement?** Among the various upstream B2B models, we need to match the suitable e-procurement goals with solution strategies depending upon whether the purchases are direct material or indirect material. Four typical goals that should be distinguished are interorganizational operational efficiency, minimum price, minimum inventory and stock-out, and purchase administrative cost. For each of these goals, the appropriate solution and system should be designed accordingly. Many third-party portal sites have provided mismatched solutions and failed their business. Handling many small and medium suppliers that do not have sophisticated systems is a challenging issue.

2. **Which B2B model(s) should we use for online B2B sales?** The big buyers usually have their own B2B procurement procedure and system. So the key issue for B2B sales is how to reconcile with the multiple buyers who adopt different EDI and ERP systems. The Enterprise Application Integration (EAI) solution transforms the internal data of multiple EDI formats used by different buyers. The integration of various types of EDI standards with ERP solutions is another challenge to overcome.

3. **Which exchange to join?** One of the major concerns of management is selecting exchanges in which to participate. At the moment, most exchanges are not tightly connected, so there may be a substantial start-up effort and cost for joining multiple exchanges. This is a multi-criteria decision that should be analyzed carefully. A related issue is whether to join a third-party public exchange or a consortium or to create a private exchange. Companies must take very seriously the issues listed in Exhibit 5.12. The risks of joining an exchange must be carefully weighed against the expected benefits. Joining an exchange may require a restructuring of the internal supply chain, which may be expensive and time consuming. Therefore, this possibility must be taken into consideration when deciding whether to join an exchange.

4. **Which solution vendor(s) should we select?** Vendors normally develop the B2B applications, even for large organizations. Two basic approaches to vendor selection exist: (1) Select a primary vendor such as IBM, Microsoft, or Oracle. This vendor will use its software and procedures and add partners as needed. (2) Use an integrator that will mix and match existing products and vendors to create "the best of breed" for your needs. See Online Chapter 18 for details.

5. **What is the organizational impact of B2B?** The B2B system will change the role of the procurement department by redefining the role and procedures of the department. The function of the procurement department may be completely outsourced. A procurement policy portfolio is necessary to balance strategic sourcing items and spot purchasing items and to design a supply relationship management system.

6. **What are the ethical issues in B2B?** Because B2B EC requires the sharing of proprietary information, business ethics are a must. Employees should not be able to access unauthorized areas in the trading system, and the privacy of trading partners should be protected both technically and legally. Control of partner relationship management is important in this regard.

7. **How shall we manage the suppliers?** Global suppliers can be evaluated periodically with regard to price, quality, and timely delivery. A supplier relationship management system can support the evaluation of suppliers. Management must decide whether to negotiate a quantity discount or to compel the suppliers to compete in reverse auctions.

8. **Which type of social network? Private (proprietary) or public?** There are successes and failures in both types. Some large companies have both types (e.g., Toyota, Coca-Cola, Disney). In most cases it is better to go with public networks such as LinkedIn and Facebook (see discussion in Chapter 9).

9. **Can we use B2C marketing methods and research in B2B?** Some methods can be used with adjustments; others cannot. B2B marketing and marketing research require special methods.

SUMMARY

In this chapter, you learned about the following EC issues as they relate to the learning objectives.

1. **The B2B field.** The B2B field comprises e-commerce activities between businesses. B2B activities account for 77 to 85 percent of all EC. B2B e-commerce can be done using different models.

2. **The major B2B models.** The B2B field is very diversified. It can be divided into the following segments: sell-side marketplaces (one seller to many buyers), buy-side marketplaces (one buyer from many sellers), and trading

exchanges (many sellers to many buyers). Intermediaries play an important role in some B2B models.

3. **The characteristics of sell-side marketplaces.** Sell-side B2B EC is the online direct sale by one seller (a manufacturer or an intermediary) to many buyers. The major technology used is electronic catalogs, which also allow for efficient customization, configuration, and purchase by customers. In addition, forward auctions are becoming popular, especially for liquidating surplus inventory. Sell-side auctions can be conducted from the seller's own site or from an intermediary's auction site. Sell-side activities can be accompanied by extensive customer service.

4. **Sell-side intermediaries.** The role of intermediaries in B2B primarily is to provide value-added services to manufacturers and business customers. They can also aggregate buyers and conduct auctions.

5. **The characteristics of buy-side marketplaces and e-procurement.** Today, companies are moving to e-procurement to expedite purchasing, save on item and administrative costs, and gain better control over the purchasing process. Major procurement methods are reverse auctions (bidding system); buying from storefronts and catalogs; negotiation; buying from an intermediary that aggregates sellers' catalogs; internal marketplaces and group purchasing; desktop purchasing; buying in exchanges or industrial malls; and e-bartering. E-procurement offers the opportunity to achieve significant cost and time savings.

6. **B2B reverse auctions.** A reverse auction is a tendering system used by buyers to get better prices from suppliers competing to fulfill the buyers' needs. Auctions can be done on a company's Web site or on a third-party auction site. Reverse auctions can dramatically lower buyer's costs, both product costs and the time and cost of the tendering process.

7. **B2B aggregation and group purchasing.** Increasing the exposure and the bargaining power of companies can be done by aggregating either the buyers or the sellers. Aggregating suppliers' catalogs into an internal marketplace gives buying companies better control of purchasing costs. In desktop purchasing, buyers are empowered to buy from their desktops up to a set limit without the need for additional approval. They accomplish this by viewing internal catalogs with pre–agreed-upon prices with the suppliers. Industrial malls specialize in one industry (e.g., computers) or in industrial MROs. They aggregate the catalogs of thousands of suppliers. A purchasing agent can place an order at an industrial mall, and shipping is arranged by the supplier or the mall owner. Buyer aggregation through group purchasing is very popular because it enables SMEs to get better prices on their purchases. In addition to direct purchasing, items can be acquired via bartering.

8. **Other procurement methods.** Common procurement methods include: internal marketplaces and desktop purchasing, buying at e-auctions, group purchasing, buying from distributors, bartering, and buying at exchanges.

9. **E-marketplaces and exchanges defined and the major types of exchanges.** Exchanges are e-marketplaces that provide a trading platform for conducting business among many buyers, many sellers, and other business partners. Types of public e-marketplaces include B2B portals, directories, third-party trading exchanges, and consortium trading exchanges. Exchanges may be vertical (industry oriented) or horizontal. They may target systematic buying (long-term relationships) or spot buying (for fulfilling an immediate need).

10. **B2B portals.** B2B portals are gateways to B2B community-related information. They are usually of a vertical structure, in which case they are referred to as *vortals*. Some B2B portals offer product and vendor information and even tools for conducting trades, sometimes making it difficult to distinguish between B2B portals and trading exchanges.

11. **Third-party exchanges.** Third-party exchanges are owned by an independent company and usually operate in highly fragmented markets. They are open to anyone and, therefore, are considered public exchanges. They try to maintain neutral relations with both buyers and sellers.

12. **Good relationship with business partners is critical to the success of B2B.** Similar to CRM in B2C, companies use Internet-based tools to support their relationships with their partners (known as PRM).

13. **B2B in Web 2.0 and social networks.** Although there are considerable B2C activities, B2B activities are just beginning. A major success has been seen in the use of blogs and wikis to collaborate with suppliers and customers. Large companies use social networking to create and foster business relationships. Smaller companies use social networking for soliciting experts' opinions. Other companies use it for finding business partners, business opportunities, employees, and sales leads as well as for generating sales leads.

14. **B2B Internet marketing methods and organizational buyers.** Marketing methods and marketing research in B2B differ from those of B2C. A major reason for this is that the buyers must observe organizational buying policies and frequently conduct buying activities as a committee. Organizations use modified B2C methods such as affiliate marketing. Buying decisions in B2B may be determined by a group, and purchasing is controlled by rules and constraints.

KEY TERMS

QUESTIONS FOR DISCUSSION

1. Explain how a catalog-based sell-side e-marketplace works and describe its benefits.

2. Discuss the advantages of selling through online auctions over selling from catalogs. What are the disadvantages?

3. Discuss the role of intermediaries in B2B. Distinguish between buy-side and sell-side intermediaries.

4. Discuss and compare all of the mechanisms that group-purchasing aggregators can use.

5. Should desktop purchasing only be implemented through an internal marketplace?

6. How do companies eliminate the potential limitations and risks associated with Web-based EDI? (See Online File W5.3.)

7. Suppose a manufacturer uses an outside shipping company. How can the manufacturer use an exchange?

8. Compare and contrast a privately owned exchange with a private e-marketplace.

9. How does ChemConnect change the market for commodity chemicals?

10. Compare external and internal aggregation of catalogs.

INTERNET EXERCISES

1. Enter gxs.com and review GXS Express's bidding process. Describe the preparations a company would have to make in order to bid on a job.

2. Enter inovis.com and view the capabilities of BizManager (inovis.com/solutions/software/biz-manager) and BizConnect (inovis.com/trybizconnect/form.jsp). Write a report.

3. Examine the following sites: ariba.com, trilogy.com, and icc.net. Match a B2B business model with each site.

4. Visit supplyworks.com and procuri.com. Examine how each company streamlines the purchase process. How do these companies differ from ariba.com?

5. Visit ebay.com and identify all of the activities related to its small business auctions. What services are provided by eBay?

6. Enter ondemandsourcing.com and view the demo. Prepare a list of benefits to small and midtier organizations.

7. Enter bitpipe.com and find recent B2B vendor reports related to e-procurement. Identify topics not covered in this chapter.

8. Visit iasta.com, purchasing.com, and cognizant.com examine the tools they sell for conducting various types of e-procurement. List and analyze each tool.

9. Enter bambooweb.com and find information about EDI. Prepare a report.

10. Enter thebuyinggroup.com, tidewatergpo.com, and other group purchasing sites. Report on B2B group buying activities.

11. Go to procurenet.com.au. Prepare a list of resources related to e-procurement.

12. Go to alibaba.com and sign up as a member (membership is free). Create a product and post it. Tell your instructor how to view this product.

13. Compare the services offered by globalsources.com with those offered by alibaba.com Assuming you are a toy seller, with which one would you register? Why? If you are a buyer of auto parts, which one would you join and why?

14. Enter chemconnect.com and view the demos for different trading alternatives. Examine the revenue model. Evaluate the services from both the buyer's and seller's points of view. Also, examine the site policies and legal guidelines. Are they fair? Compare chemconnect.com with chemicalonline.com and hubwoo.com. Which of these do you think will survive? Explain your reasoning.

15. Enter eBay's Business Industrial area (business.ebay.com or ebay.com and select "wholesale"). What kind of e-marketplace is this? What are its major capabilities?

16. Visit converge.com. What kind of exchange is this? What services does it provide? How do its auctions work?

17. Enter globalspec.com. Find information about vertical search engines. Summarize in a report.

18. Enter dir.yahoo.com/Business_and_Economy/Business_to_Business. Prepare a list of resources about exchanges and B2B directories.

19. Enter smallbusiness.yahoo.com/merchant/success_stories/testimonial3.php and summarize the sell-side case.

TEAM ASSIGNMENTS, PROJECTS, AND CLASS DISCUSSIONS

1. Predictions about the future magnitude of B2B and statistics on its actual volume in various countries keep changing. In this activity, each team will locate current B2B predictions and statistics for different world regions (e.g., Asia, Europe, North America). Using at least five sources, each team will find the predicted B2B volume (in dollars) for the next 5 years in its assigned region. Sources of statistics are listed in Exhibit 3.1 (page 144).

2. Each team should explore a different e-procurement method and prepare a summary paper for a class presentation. The paper should include the following about the e-procurement method:

   a. The mechanisms and technologies used
   b. The benefits to buyers, suppliers, and others (if appropriate)
   c. The limitations
   d. The situations for which each method is recommended

3. Form two teams (A and B) of five or more members. On each team, person 1 plays the role of an assembly company that produces television monitors. Persons 2 and 3 are domestic parts suppliers to the assembling company, and persons 4 and 5 play foreign parts suppliers. Assume that the TV monitor company wants to sell televisions directly to business customers. Each team is to design an environment composed of membership in exchanges they can use and present its results. A graphical display is recommended.

4. Enter isteelasia.com, metalworld.com, and lme.co.uk. Compare their operations and services. These exchanges compete in global markets. Examine the trading platforms, portal capabilities, and support services (e.g., logistics, payments, etc.) offered by each. In what areas do these companies compete? In what areas do they not compete? What are the advantages of isteelasia.com in dealing with Asian companies? Are regional exchanges needed? If it is good for Asia to have a regional exchange, why not have a Western European exchange, an Eastern European exchange, a Central American exchange, and so on? If regional exchanges are needed, can they work together? How? If there are too many exchanges, which are likely to survive? Research this topic and prepare a report.

5. Enter gtnexus.com and examine its offerings. Prepare a report on how exchanges can benefit from its services. How does GT Nexus facilitate supply chains? Can it help e-marketplaces?

6. Address the following topics in a class discussion:

   a. Discuss B2B opportunities in social networking.
   b. Discuss risk in B2B social networking.
   c. Discuss how globalization impacts B2B.
   d. Relate B2B to the four P's of marketing (product, pricing, placement, promotion).

Closing Case

IMARKETKOREA

Established in 2000, iMarketKorea (IMK) is South Korea's largest e-marketplace (exchange) specializing in MRO items for various industries and direct materials for the electronics industries. iMK's e-catalog includes over 1 million items. In 2008, sales revenues were $722 million, with 180,000 monthly purchase orders. IMK was originally established as the online procurement sourcing company of Samsung Group in 2000; since then it has expanded its customer groups to various industries, including manufacturing, finance, retail, universities, and hospitals. Since its inception, the company has grown rapidly (an average annual growth rate of 23%).

From a market for Samsung's 45 affiliated companies, IMK has grown to serve approximately 350 companies in 2008. Currently, 70 percent of customers are Samsung related, whereas 30 percent non-Samsung related. Many of the newly added customers are not Samsung affiliates, including some from outside South Korea. The site offers Korean, English, and Japanese options to registered users.

Initially, IMK concentrated on acting as a procurement agent to the Samsung companies. By 2007, however, the company shifted its mission to become a B2B procurement service provider, providing end-to-end

procurement and logistics services for a variety of industries.

Among its most popular services for buyers are payments, deliveries, purchasing, budget management, internal approval processes, inventory management, storage, and more. In addition, iMK helps to smooth its customers' supply chains (e.g., process improvement and workflow management). iMK also supports connectivity to enterprise systems (e.g., ERP, legacy systems). The system architecture and the major participants are shown in the following exhibit.

iMK's business model is interesting because IMK does not charge fees for its services, but rather shares in the reduced costs with its buying customers. In this manner, iMK removes the risk from the customer side. iMK pursues a 3S Leadership strategy: sourcing, service, and system leaderships. The strategic sourcing suites that iMK provides include SRM, Sourcing DSS, and e-catalog collaboration tools. They include features such as the following:

▶ Tools to calculate "total cost of ownership" (for purchasing)

▶ Strategic sourcing processes

IMK System Architecture

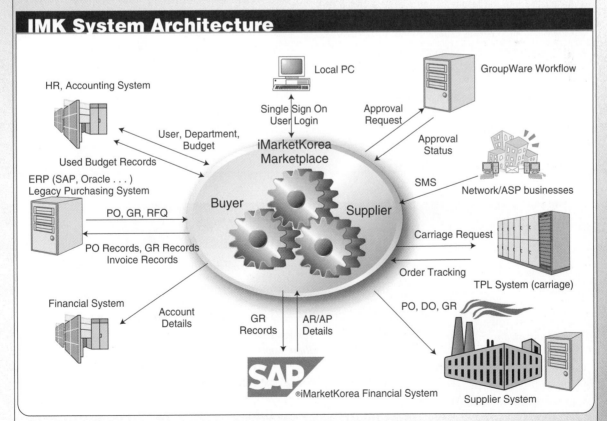

Source: iMarketKorea, "Purchasing Innovation: Value Proposition," 2009. *imarketkorea.co.kr/en_HD/DC9553ED_IMK_homepage_en_200408.pdf* (accessed April 2009).

▶ A scorecard grading system tool to perform a formal evaluation of suppliers (assessment, selection, monitoring)

▶ Knowledge sharing about best practices of procurement

▶ B2B auctions (forward and reverse, either as supporting the entire process or in helping customers take charge of the major activities, helping only with procedural matters during the auction)

▶ Spend management analysis and control tools

▶ Collaborative e-sourcing tools

▶ Decision support and optimization models for buyers

▶ Contract management features

▶ Integration of suppliers by selecting those who are reliable and sound and who are able to provide value (price matters, too, of course), leading to long-term strategic relationships (win-win situation)

▶ Risk assessment and management

▶ Item standardization for inventory and cost reduction at the suppliers' level, enabling better cataloging and faster and easier search (e.g., simultaneous search of many items)

▶ Analyzes replies to RFQs quickly, considering large amount of computerized information and knowledge

▶ Joint process improvement, attempting to reduce supplier's TCO (providing suppliers with a comprehensive program of how to do it)

The following are some recent iMK initiatives:

▶ An alliance with the Japanese Samitomo Corp. (a top online trading company), kicking off global business expansion. iMK is already exporting MROs to 12 countries.

▶ IMK exported over $87 million in MROs in 2008, plus $18 million in direct materials (a 37 % increase over 2007).

▶ In collaboration with Woori Bank, iMK opened B2C and B2B2C channels for selling gifts over the Internet to the bank's employees.

The results speak for themselves. iMK's customers have experienced the following benefits:

▶ On-time delivery has increased from 72 percent to 94.5 percent.

▶ Average lead-time has been reduced from 5.3 to 3.31 days.

▶ Catalog search speed has increased 40 percent.

▶ 12 to 18 percent savings in purchase prices.

▶ 30 to 50 percent savings in process costs.

▶ 5 to 15 percent savings in inventory management costs.

▶ 40 to 60 percent savings in reduced inventory.

All these savings have contributed to the success and growth of iMK.

Sources: Compiled from iMarketKorea (2006), iMarketKorea (2005), Lee and Lee (2007), and *imarketkorea.com* (accessed February 2009).

Questions

1. How do the support services benefit the exchange?

2. Relate this case to desktop purchasing.

3. Write a summary of the benefits of the exchange to buyers.

4. Write a summary of the benefits of the exchange to sellers.

5. Compare iMK to Alibaba.com. What are the similarities and the differences?

6. Much of iMK's success is attributed to the understanding of the Korean culture and business environment. Given that iMK wants to expand internationally, what could be some of its stumbling blocks?

7. Check the recent news and press releases (last 6 months) at *imarketkorea.com*. Identify expansion patterns.

ONLINE RESOURCES
available at pearsonglobaleditions.com/turban

Online Files

Comprehensive Educational Web Sites

b2btoday.com: B2B resources

optimizeandprophesize.com/jonathan_mendezs_blog: Optimize and Prophesize, Jonathan Mendez's blog

silicon.com: Case studies, publications

b2b.com: B2B topics, news, software, etc.

netb2b.com: B2B magazine

3.ibm.com/e-business/doc/content/case study: Case studies from IBM

REFERENCES

About.com. "B2B Trading Communities Evolution." 2006. logistics.about.com/library/weekly/aa060600a.htm (accessed January 2008).

Alibaba.com. "Corporate Overview." March 31, 2009c.

Alibaba.com. "Alibaba Group: Company Overview." 2009b. news.alibaba.com/specials/aboutalibaba/aligroup/index.html (accessed May 2009).

Alibaba.com. "Alibaba.com Announced Full Year 2008 Results." 2009a. news.alibaba.com/specials/aboutalibaba/aligroup/index.html (accessed May 2009).

Angwin, J. "Top Online Chemical Exchange Is an Unlikely Success Story." *Wall Street Journal Online*, January 8, 2004. webreprints.djreprints.com/907660072246.html (accessed January 2008).

Bandyopadhyay, S., J. M. Barron, and A. R. Chaturved. "Competition Among Sellers in Online Exchanges." *Information Systems Research* (March 2005).

Bush, D. "e-Sourcing Does Not Equal Reverse Auction." *E-Sourcing Forum*, March 24, 2006. esourcingforum.com/index.php?s=e-Sourcing+Does+Not+Equal+Reverse+Auction (accessed January 2008).

Chandler, C. "China's Web King." *Fortune*, November 23, 2007.

Commonwealth of Pennsylvania. "Pennsylvania's Surplus Property Programs." 2006. portal.state.pa.us/portal/server.pt?open=512&objID=1393&mode=2 (accessed January 2008).

Dasgupta, P., L. E. Moser, and P. M. Melliar-Smith. "Dynamic Pricing for E-Commerce," in Khosrow-Pour (2006).

eMarketer. "B2B Marketing on Social Networks." August 2008. emarketer.com/Report.aspx?code=emarketer_2000516 (accessed February 2009).

Gaffney, J. "Social Media Stepping Up as Source for Connecting B2B Networks." 2007. demandgenreport.com/archive.php?codearti=1154 (accessed February 2009).

Greengard, S. "Flying High with Social Networking." *Baseline*, November 2008.

Hagel, J. "Offshoring Goes on the Offensive." *McKinsey Quarterly*, no. 2 (2004).

Harris, L. "B2B Marketers Turn to Intelligent Search to Boost Profitability and Increase Buyer Satisfaction." *CXO*, 2005. cxoamerica.com/currentissue/article.asp?art=25456&issue=141 (accessed February 2009).

IBM. "Whirlpool's B2B Trading Portal Cuts per Order Cost Significantly." White Plains, NY: IBM Corporation Software Group, Pub. G325-6693-00, 2000.

iMarketKorea. "iMarketKorea Enters into Strategic Business Cooperation Agreement with Sumitomo Corporation Japan." January 25, 2006. imarketkorea.co.kr/en_HD/menu_05001-19view.jsp (accessed February 2009).

iMarketKorea. "iMarketKorea Opens Woori Bank e-Shop." December 19, 2005. imarketkorea.com/en_HD/menu_05001-17view.jsp (accessed February 2009).

Killeen, J. F. "The Value of Vertical Search for B2B Markets." *E-Commerce Times*, October 27, 2006. ecommercetimes.com/story/53931.html (accessed January 2008).

Lee, Z., and D. S. Lee. "Transition from a Buyer's Agent to a Procurement Service Provider in B2B iMarketKorea." In J. K. Lee, et al., *Premier E-Business Cases from Asia*. Singapore: Prentice Hall and Pearson Education South Asia, 2007.

Lucas, H. C. *Information Technology: Strategic Decision Making for Managers.* Hoboken, NJ: John Wiley and Sons, 2005.

Markus, L. "The Golden Rule." *CIO Insight*, July 2006.

MasterCard. "MasterCard Purchasing Card Program." *Mastercard.com*, 2006. mastercard.com/us/business/en/pdf/MC%20Sell%20Sheet%20Purchasing%2005 3006.pdf (accessed February 2009).

Microsoft. "Business Review: Eastman Chemical." 2000. download.microsoft.com/download/C/A/6/CA68EE 19-5D85-44C4-A0D2-47DB399C418B/Eastman Chemical_PeopleReady.doc (accessed February 2009).

New Media Institute. "Is the B2B Marketplace Utilizing Online Video, Social Networks, and Wikis?" November 13, 2006. newmedia.org/articles/43/1/Is-the-B2B-Marketplace-Utilization-Utilizing-Online-Video (accessed February 2009).

OCG. "Online Auction for Pharmaceutical Supplies Helps Portsmouth Hospitals NHS." 2004. ogc.gov.uk/case_studies_eprocurement_case_studies.asp (accessed January 2009).

Papazoglou, M., and P. Ribbers. *Building B2B Relationships—Technical and Tactical Implementations of E-Business Strategy.* Hoboken, NJ: Wiley & Sons, 2006.

Patton, S. "Answering the Call." *CIO.com*, June 1, 2006. cio.com.au/article/180389/answering_call (accessed February 2009).

Rappa, M. "Case Study: ChemConnect—Managing the Digital Enterprise." 2006. digitalenterprise.org/cases/chemconnect_text.html (accessed February 2009).

Richard, P. J., and T. M. Devinney. "Modular Strategies: B2B Technology and Architecture Knowledge." *California Management Review* (Summer 2005).

Rincon, A. "Gregg's Cycles Succeeds in E-Commerce by Not Selling Bikes Online." May 2005. onlinebusiness.about.com/od/casestudies/a/greggscycles.htm (no longer available online).

Rudnitsky, H. "Changing the Corporate DNA." *Forbes*, July 24, 2000.

Saryeddine, R. *E-Procurement: Another Tool in the Tool Box.* Ottawa, Ontario, Canada: The Conference Board of Canada, 2004.

Small Business Administration. sba.gov/advo/stats (accessed February 2009).

Spagnuolu, J. "Is the B2B Marketplace Utilizing Online Video, Social Networking, and Wikis?" November 13, 2008. newmedia.org/articles/43/1/Is-the-B2B-Mar ketplace-Utilizing-Online-Video-Social-Networks—Wikis/Page1.html (accessed February 2009).

webMethods. "WebMethods Helps Power WWRE's Global Data Synchronization Solution." WWRE Success Story, 2005. accessmylibrary.com/coms2/ summary_0286-24312890_ITM?email=ecommerce2008@gmail. com&library= (accessed March 2009).

WWRE. "WWRE Overview." 2005. worldwideretail exchange.org/cs/en_US/about/wr0100.html (accessed February 2009).

CHAPTER 6

E-SUPPLY CHAINS, COLLABORATIVE COMMERCE, AND CORPORATE PORTALS

Content

Learning Objectives

Upon completion of this chapter, you will be able to:

1. Define the e-supply chain and describe its characteristics and components.

2. List supply chain problems and their causes.

3. List solutions provided by e-commerce (EC) for supply chain problems.

4. Describe RFID supply chain applications.

5. Define c-commerce and list the major types.

6. Describe collaborative planning and collaboration, planning, forecasting, and replenishing (CPFR) and list the benefits of each.

7. Discuss integration along the supply chain.

8. Understand corporate portals and their types and roles.

9. Describe e-collaboration tools such as workflow software and groupware.

10. Describe Collaboration 2.0 technology and tools.

BOEING'S GLOBAL SUPPLY CHAIN FOR THE DREAMLINER 787

The Problem

Designing and manufacturing an aircraft is an immensely complex undertaking; the 787 Dreamliner project is said to be one of the largest, most complex, and challenging engineering projects being undertaken in the world. The supply chain involved in the design and production of this aircraft involves millions of different parts components and materials, and thousands of different suppliers, partners, contractors, and outsourcing vendors scattered across 24 countries working from 135 different sites. Absolute precision and meticulous attention to detail is required, and safety and quality are paramount. In addition to designing and producing new aircraft, the new production processes had to be designed, tested, and implemented. Close collaboration and communication among thousands of employees, information and knowledge management, and sound management of this complex global supply chain were essential to the project's success. In addition, competitive pressures, rising oil prices, and enhanced security requirements forced Boeing to significantly improve the old methods.

The Solution

Boeing had been increasingly relying on sophisticated information technology (IT) and EC solutions to support its operations. For example, it had been a user of CAD/CAM technologies since the early 1980s.

The Dreamliner, however, was to be a "paperless airliner," with EC being employed to support many critical activities. Boeing teamed with Dassault Systemes to create a Global Collaboration Environment (GCE), a product management life cycle solution, in order to support the virtual rollout of the new aircraft. The GCE enabled Boeing to digitally monitor the design, production, and testing of every aspect of the aircraft before the actual production started.

The GCE included the following components:

- **CATIA.** A collaborative 3D-design platform that enabled engineers worldwide to collaborate on the design of each and every part of the 787.

- **ENOVIA.** A system that supported the accessing, sharing, and managing of all information related to the 787 design in a secure environment.

- **DELMIA.** An environment for defining, simulating, and validating manufacturing and maintenance processes and establishing and managing workflows before actually building tools and production facilities.

- **SMARTEAM.** A Web-based system to facilitate collaboration, which included predefined and auditable processes and procedures, project templates, and best-practice methodologies all geared toward ensuring compliance with corporate and industry standards.

In addition, Boeing decided to integrate all databases associated with the Dreamliner, teaming up with IBM to employ a DB2 Universal Database for this purpose and ensuring partners access to the Dassault's suite of systems.

As the Dreamliner moved toward physical production using the new manufacturing processes (Boeing was to become the final assembler and integrator, rather than building much of the aircraft from scratch), excellent supply chain management was required to carefully coordinate the movement of components and systems across multiple-tier partners around the world. Boeing teamed with Exostar to provide software to support its supply chain coordination challenges. The Exostar supply chain management solution enables all suppliers access to real-time demand, supply, and logistics information so that crucial components and systems arrive at Boeing's production facilities just in time for assembly over a 3-day period. The Exostar solution includes the following functionalities: planning and scheduling; order placement and tracking purchase order changes; exchanging shipping information; managing inventory consumption across suppliers; managing returns; and providing a consolidated view of all activities in the manufacturing process. Business process exceptions can also be monitored across partners, allowing for informed evaluation of the impacts of these exceptions to take place across affected parties.

Finally, radio frequency identification (RFID) technologies were deployed in the aircraft to support finding parts and materials and for the maintenance activities. By tagging component parts, Boeing significantly reduced the costs.

The Results

The goal of the Dreamliner project was to produce a fuel efficient (and less polluting, hence environmentally responsible), cost-effective, quiet, and comfortable midsize aircraft that could travel long distances without stopping. It is a critical innovation for Boeing, which has in recent years struggled in the face of rising competition from Airbus. EC has played a critical role in supporting collaboration throughout this massive project, reducing the need for physical prototyping and testing, and making substantial impacts on the supply chain. EC has enabled faster decision making, better management of critical information and knowledge assets, increased sharing and exchange of product-related information and processes, reduced time-to-market, less rework, and reduced costs of manufacturing by reducing the final assembly time for the aircraft from 13 to 17 days to just 3 days.

Boeing had received nearly 900 orders for the plane by the end of 2007 and commitments in excess of $120 billion. Dreamliner was not completed on schedule, mainly due to

communication problems between different countries and the use of several languages. The new collaboration methods were just too new.

Sources: Compiled from Kumar and Gupta (2006), *Supply and Demand Chain Executive* (2006), *RFID Gazette* (2006), and *boeing.com* (accessed January 2009).

WHAT WE CAN LEARN . . .

In increasingly global industries, effective communication and collaboration are essential to an organization's success. Modern IT and Web-based systems have made collaboration, both internally and externally with key players along an industry supply chain, simpler, faster, and cheaper than ever before. Boeing recognized this and implemented a range of IT and EC technologies to facilitate the access, sharing, and storage of critical information related to the Dreamliner project. Vital, too, was its use of 3D virtual workspaces, removing the need for time-consuming and expensive physical prototyping of both aircraft components and the manufacturing process. The company also introduced EC to expedite design, reduce problems along the supply and value chains of the design process, and reduce cost, cycle time, and assembly time dramatically. This case demonstrates several applications of EC, IT, and a range of Web-enabled technologies: collaborative commerce and streamlining complex supply chains. These and related issues are the topics of this chapter.

6.1 E-SUPPLY CHAINS

Many people equate e-commerce with selling and buying on the Internet. However, although a company's success is clearly dependent on finding and retaining customers, its success may be far more dependent on what is behind the Web page rather than on what is on the Web page. In other words, the company's internal operations (the *back end*) and the company's relationships with suppliers and other business partners are as critical, and frequently much more complex, than customer-facing applications such as taking an order online. In many cases, these non-customer-facing applications are related to the company's supply chain.

It has been well-known for generations that the success of many organizations—private, public, and military—depends on their ability to manage the flow of materials, information, and money into, within, and out of the organization. Such a flow is referred to as a *supply chain*. Croza (2008) regards the supply chain as the competitive differentiator. Because supply chains may be long and complex and may involve many different business partners, we frequently see problems in supply chain operation. These problems may result in delays, products not being where they are required at the right time, customer dissatisfaction, lost sales, and high expenses that result from fixing the problems once they occur. World-class companies such as Wal-Mart, Dell, and Toyota attribute much of their success to effective supply chain management (SCM), which is largely supported by IT and e-commerce technologies.

This chapter focuses on supply chain issues related to e-commerce. In addition, it covers several related topics, such as collaboration and integration along the supply chain. The topic of financial supply chains (payment systems) is discussed in Chapter 11. Finally, a related topic of order fulfillment is presented in Chapter 12.

DEFINITIONS AND CONCEPTS

To understand e-supply chains, one must first understand nonelectronic supply chains. A **supply chain** is the flow of materials, information, money, and services from raw material suppliers through factories and warehouses to the end customers. A supply chain also includes the organizations and processes that create and deliver products, information, and services to the end customers. The term *supply chain* comes from the concept of how the partnering organizations are linked together.

As shown in Exhibit 6.1, a simple linear supply chain links a company that manufactures or assembles a product (middle of the chain) with its suppliers (on the left) and distributors and customers (on the right). The upper part of the exhibit shows a generic supply chain. The

supply chain
The flow of materials, information, money, and services from raw material suppliers through factories and warehouses to the end customers.

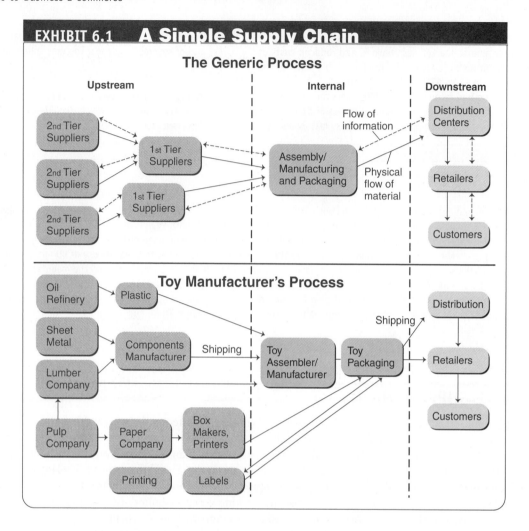

EXHIBIT 6.1   A Simple Supply Chain

bottom part of the exhibit shows a specific example of the toy-making process. The solid links in the exhibit show the flow of materials among the various partners. Not shown is the flow of returned goods (e.g., defective products) and money, which are flowing in the reverse direction. The broken links, which are shown only in the upper (generic) part of Exhibit 6.1, indicate the bidirectional flow of information.

A supply chain involves activities that take place during the entire product life cycle, "from dirt to dust," as some describe it. However, a supply chain is more than that, because it also includes the movement of information and money and the procedures that support the movement of a product or a service. Finally, the organizations and individuals involved are considered part of the supply chain as well. When looked at very broadly, the supply chain actually ends when the product reaches its after-use disposal—presumably back to Mother Earth somewhere.

The supply chain shown in Exhibit 6.1 is fairly simple. Supply chains can be much more complex, and they are of different types.

e-supply chain

A supply chain that is managed electronically, usually with Web technologies.

When a supply chain is managed electronically, usually with Web-based technologies, it is referred to as an **e-supply chain**. As will be shown throughout this chapter, improvements in supply chains are a major target for EC applications. However, before examining how e-supply chains are managed, it is necessary to better understand the basic composition of supply chains.

SUPPLY CHAIN PARTS

A supply chain can be broken into three major parts: upstream, internal, and downstream, as was shown in Exhibit 6.1:

▶ **Upstream supply chain.** The upstream part of the supply chain includes the activities of a company with its suppliers (which can be manufacturers, assemblers, or both, or service providers) and their connections with their suppliers (second-tier suppliers). The supplier relationship can be extended to the left in several tiers, all the way to the origin of the material (e.g., mining ores, growing crops). In the upstream supply chain, the major activity is *procurement*. **Procurement** is the process made up of a range of activities by which an organization obtains or gains access to the resources (materials, skills, capabilities, facilities) they need to accomplish their core business activities.

▶ **Internal supply chain and value chain.** The internal part of the supply chain includes all in-house processes used in transforming the inputs received from the suppliers into the organization's outputs. It extends from the time the inputs enter an organization to the time that the products go to distribution outside of the organization. In this part of the supply chain, the major concerns are production management, manufacturing, and inventory control. The activities along the internal supply chain are referred to as the company's *value chain* (see Chapter 13). The value chain is composed of a sequential set of primary activities (operations, outbound logistics, after-sales support and service, etc.) and support activities (administration, HR, finance, etc.) that an organization undertakes in order to deliver a good or service of value to their customers. The value chain can thus be seen as an integrator between customers (B2C) and suppliers (B2B) in that it transforms goods and services obtained from suppliers into goods and services of value to customers. The primary objective of the value chain is to add value along the internal supply chain.

▶ **Downstream supply chain.** The downstream part of the supply chain includes all the activities involved in delivering the products to the final customers. In the downstream supply chain, attention is directed at distribution, warehousing, transportation, and after-sale service.

A company's supply chain and its accompanying value chain encompass an array of business processes that create value by delivering goods or services to customers.

MANAGING SUPPLY CHAINS

Supply chain management (SCM) is a complex process that requires the coordination of many activities so that the shipment of goods and services from suppliers right through to customers is done efficiently and effectively for all parties concerned. SCM aims to minimize inventory levels, optimize production and increase throughput, decrease manufacturing time, optimize logistics and distribution, streamline order fulfillment, and overall reduce the costs associated with these activities (*SupplyChainManagement101* 2009). Managing supply chains can be difficult due to the need to coordinate several business partners, often in different countries and different time zones; several internal corporate departments; numerous business processes; and possibly many customers. In addition, complexity is added in industries where huge numbers of goods flow rapidly along the supply chain (think of supermarkets and the number and rate of items that flow on and off modern supermarket shelves). Managing medium to large supply chains manually is almost impossible. Information technology provides two types of software solutions: (1) SCM (including e-procurement) and (2) enterprise resource planning systems (ERP) (including e-business infrastructure, data warehouses, and the like) and its predecessors, material requirements planning (MRP) and manufacturing resource planning (MRP II). (These types of software are defined and described at Wikipedia.org.) A major requirement for any medium- to large-scale company that is moving to EC is integration among all activities conducted on the Web and the ERP/MRP/SCM solutions—in other words, creating an e-supply chain and managing it. As these software packages evolve and become increasingly integrated, we see a new umbrella term, *enterprise systems*, being used to embrace all the functionality of ERP, SCM, CRM, and e-business solutions.

E-Supply Chains and Their Management

Internet capabilities are having a profound impact on organizations' supply chains. Increasingly, companies are recognizing that the efficient and effective flow of information and materials along their supply chains is a source of competitive advantage and differentiation. **E-supply chain management (e-SCM)** is the collaborative use of technology to enhance B2B processes and improve speed, agility, real-time control, and customer satisfaction. It involves the use of information technologies to improve the operations of supply chain

---

procurement
The process made up of a range of activities by which an organization obtains or gains access to the resources (materials, skills, capabilities, facilities) they require to undertake their core business activities.

supply chain management (SCM)
A complex process that requires the coordination of many activities so that the shipment of goods and services from supplier right through to customer is done efficiently and effectively for all parties concerned. SCM aims to minimize inventory levels, optimize production and increase throughput, decrease manufacturing time, optimize logistics and distribution, streamline order fulfillment, and overall reduce the costs associated with these activities.

e-supply chain management (e-SCM)
The collaborative use of technology to improve the operations of supply chain activities as well as the management of supply chains.

activities (e.g., e-procurement), as well as the management of the supply chains (e.g., planning, coordination, and control). E-SCM is not about technology change alone; it also involves changes in management policies, organizational culture, performance metrics, business processes, and organizational structure across the supply chain. The success of an e-supply chain depends on the following:

> **The ability of all supply chain partners to view partner collaboration as a strategic asset.** Tight integration and trust among the trading partners generate speed, agility, and lower cost.

> **A well-defined supply chain strategy.** This includes a clear understanding of existing strengths and weaknesses, articulating well-defined plans for improvement, and establishing cross-organizational objectives for supply chain performance. Senior executives commitment is also essential and must be reflected through appropriate allocation of resources and priority setting.

> **Information visibility along the entire supply chain.** Information visibility refers to the information about inventories at various segments of the chain, demand for products, capacity planning and activation, synchronization of material flows, delivery times, and any other relevant information that must be visible to all members of the supply chain at any given time. To enable visibility, information must be managed properly—with strict policies, discipline, and daily monitoring. It must also be shared properly.

> **Speed, cost, quality, and customer service.** These are the metrics by which supply chains are measured. Consequently, companies must clearly define the measurements for each of these four metrics, together with the target levels to be achieved. The target levels should be attractive to the business partners.

> **Integrating the supply chain more tightly.** An e-supply chain will benefit from tighter integration, both within a company and across an *extended enterprise* made up of suppliers, trading partners, logistics providers, and the distribution channel.

Activities and Infrastructure of E-SCM

E-supply chain management processes and activities include the following:

Supply Chain Replenishment. Supply chain replenishment encompasses the integrated production and distribution processes. Companies can use replenishment information to reduce inventories, eliminate stocking points, and increase the velocity of replenishment by synchronizing supply and demand information across the extended enterprise. Real-time supply and demand information facilitates make-to-order and assemble-to-order manufacturing strategies across the extended enterprise. Supply chain replenishment is a natural companion to Web-enabled customer orders.

E-Procurement. As described in Chapter 5, e-procurement is the use of Web-based technology to support the key procurement processes, including requisitioning, sourcing, contracting, ordering, and payment. E-procurement supports the purchase of both direct and indirect materials and employs several Web-based functions, such as online catalogs, contracts, purchase orders, and shipping notices. E-procurement can improve the operation of the supply chain in various ways:

> Online catalogs can be used to eliminate redesign of components in product development.

> Visibility of available parts and their attributes enables quick decision making.

> Online purchase orders expedite the ordering process.

> Advanced-shipping notifications and acknowledgments streamline delivery.

From the purchaser's perspective, e-procurement can help better manage supplier relationships and accounts and allows for more effective tracking of orders. From the supplier's perspective, e-procurement enables them to respond more rapidly and effectively to the requirements of purchasers. Both purchasers and suppliers report that e-procurement can assist them in better managing their business process and cash flows.

information visibility
The process of sharing critical data required to manage the flow of products, services, and information in real time between suppliers and customers.

e-procurement
The use of Web-based technology to support the key procurement processes, including requisitioning, sourcing, contracting, ordering, and payment. E-procurement supports the purchase of both direct and indirect materials and employs several Web-based functions such as online catalogs, contracts, purchase orders, and shipping notices.

Supply Chain Monitoring and Control Using RFID. This is one of the most promising applications of RFID. We will return to this topic later in this chapter.

Inventory Management Using Wireless Devices. Many organizations are now achieving improvements in inventory management by using combinations of bar-coding technologies and wireless devices. For example, the auto industry is dependent on the supply of spare parts; in 2008, dealerships sold about $60 billion worth of spare parts. By combining bar coding and wireless technologies, dealers are now able to scan goods as they arrive and place them in inventory up to 50 percent faster than previously. Dealers have a much more accurate picture of their inventory levels and are now able to avoid running out of stock. In some industries, such as supermarkets and hospitals, reorder points have been automated so that when inventory gets down to a certain point the system will automatically generate an order for new stock without human intervention. MemorialCare in Southern California is just one of many hospitals that are using PDAs to enter inventory item counts and then load the data directly into the mainframe procurement system. This process is not only faster and less prone to error, but the data are also processed in real time, and orders (if needed) are generated automatically. The system is usually based on XML architecture. If orders are needed (based on the inventory count), the mainframe automatically transfers the order to an ERP system. This system creates purchase orders, e-mails them to the appropriate suppliers, generates invoices, and processes payments, all without any additional information.

Collaborative Planning. Collaborative planning is a business practice that combines the business knowledge and forecasts of multiple players along a supply chain to improve the planning and fulfillment of customer demand (VICS 2004). Collaborative planning requires buyers and sellers to develop shared demand forecasts and supply plans for how to support demand. These forecasts and supply plans should be updated regularly, based on information shared over the Internet. Such collaborative planning requires B2B workflow across multiple enterprises over the Internet, with data exchanged among partners dynamically. This topic is discussed further in Section 6.4.

Collaborative Design and Product Development. Collaborative product development involves the use of product design and development techniques across multiple companies to improve product launch success and reduce time-to-market (as demonstrated in the Boeing opening case). During product development, engineering and design drawings can be shared over a secure network among the contract firm, testing facility, marketing firm, and downstream manufacturing and service companies. Other techniques include sharing specifications, test results, and design changes and using online prototyping to obtain customer feedback. Development costs can be reduced by tightly integrating and streamlining communication channels. Lately, social networking has been used to solicit feedback from customers.

E-Logistics. *E-logistics* is the use of Web-based technologies to support the material acquisition, warehousing, and transportation processes. E-logistics enables distribution to couple routing optimization with inventory-tracking information. For example, Internet-based freight auctions enable spot buying of trucking capacity. Third-party logistics providers offer virtual logistics services by integrating and optimizing distribution resources. A company may even consider collaboration with its competitors to improve its supply chain. For an example of how Land O'Lakes collaborates with its competitors via an electronic market, see Online File W6.1. This topic will be discussed more fully in Chapter 12.

collaborative planning
A business practice that combines the business knowledge and forecasts of multiple players along a supply chain to improve the planning and fulfillment of customer demand.

Infrastructure for e-SCM

The key activities just described use a variety of infrastructure and tools. The following are the major infrastructure elements and tools of e-supply chains:

> ▶ **Electronic data interchange (EDI).** EDI (see Online File W5.3) is the major tool used by large corporations to facilitate supply chain relationships. Many companies are shifting from traditional EDI to Internet-based EDI.
>
> ▶ **Extranets.** These are described in Online File W5.2. Their major purpose is to support interorganizational communication and collaboration. For details on success factors for using extranets in e-SCM, see en/Wikipedia.org/wiki/Extranets.

▶ **Intranets.** These are the corporate internal networks for communication and collaboration.

▶ **Corporate portals.** These provide a gateway for external and internal collaboration, communication, and information search. They are described in Section 6.7.

▶ **Workflow systems and tools.** These are systems that manage the flow of information in organizations. They are described in Section 6.8.

▶ **Groupware and other collaborative tools.** Many tools facilitate collaboration and communication between two parties and among members of small as well as large groups. Various tools, some of which are collectively known as *groupware*, enable such collaboration, as described in Section 6.8. Blogs and wikis are beginning to play an important role (see the Eastern Mountain Sports opening case, Chapter 2). A major purpose of these tools is to provide *visibility* to all, namely, let people know where items are and when they arrive at certain locations.

▶ **Identification and tracking tools.** These tools are designed to identify items and their location along the supply chain. From a traditional bar code system, we are moving to RFID, as described in Section 6.3. Wireless and GPS technologies (Chapter 8) are also increasing in popularity.

Section 6.1 ▶ REVIEW QUESTIONS

1. Define the e-supply chain and list its three major parts.
2. Describe success factors of e-supply chain management.
3. List the eight processes or activities of e-supply chains.
4. List the major e-supply chain management infrastructures and enabling tools.
5. Describe a digital supply chain.
6. Describe visibility and tracking along the supply chain.

6.2 SUPPLY CHAIN PROBLEMS AND SOLUTIONS

Supply chains have been plagued with problems, both in military and business operations, for generations. These problems have sometimes caused armies to lose wars and companies to go out of business. The problems are most apparent in complex or long supply chains (e.g., global ones) and in cases where many business partners are involved. Complex and long supply chains involving multiple business partners are becoming more common in the contemporary business world as globalization and offshoring of manufacturing operations continue to intensify. Thus, the problems faced by those managing supply chains are becoming both more complex and more critical to company competitiveness and survival (Kotabe and Mol 2006). As this section will show, some remedies are available through the use of IT and EC.

TYPICAL PROBLEMS ALONG THE SUPPLY CHAIN

With increased globalization and offshoring, supply chains can be very long and involve many internal and external partners located in different places. Both materials and information must flow among several entities, and these transfers, especially when manually handled, can be slow and error prone.

In the offline world, there are many examples of companies that were unable to meet demand for certain products while having oversized and expensive inventories of other products. Similar situations exist online. Typical of the sorts of problems in EC that gain adverse publicity are when there is a supply–demand mismatch of goods, especially during a period of high demand, such as the holiday period. Another problem is often related to shipping. A lack of logistics infrastructure might prevent the right goods from reaching their destinations on time. Various uncertainties exist in delivery times, which depend on many factors ranging from vehicle failure to road conditions.

Pure EC companies may be likely to have more supply chain problems because they may not have a logistics infrastructure and may be forced to use external logistics services. This can be expensive, plus it requires more coordination and dependence on outsiders. For this reason, some large virtual retailers, such as Amazon.com, have developed physical warehouses and logistics systems. Other virtual retailers are creating strategic alliances with logistics companies or with brick-and-mortar companies that have their own logistics systems. Other problems along the EC supply chain mainly stem from the difficulty in coordinating several activities, internal units, and business partners.

For further information on the problems, issues, and challenges of contemporary supply chain management, see Coyle et al. (2008). A major problem along large supply chains is the *bullwhip effect*.

The Bullwhip Effect

The **bullwhip effect** refers to erratic shifts in orders up and down supply chains (see en.wikipedia.org/wiki/Bullwhip_effect). This effect was initially observed by Procter & Gamble (P&G) with their disposable diapers in offline retail stores. Although actual sales in stores were fairly stable and predictable, orders from distributors had wild swings, creating production and inventory problems for P&G and their suppliers. An investigation revealed that distributors' orders were fluctuating because of poor demand forecasts, price fluctuations, order batching, and rationing within the supply chain. All of this resulted in unnecessary inventories in various places along the supply chain, fluctuations in P&G orders to its suppliers, and the flow of inaccurate information. Distorted or late information can lead to tremendous inefficiencies, excessive inventories, poor customer service, lost revenues, ineffective shipments, and missed production schedules.

The bullwhip effect is not unique to P&G. Firms from HP in the computer industry to Bristol-Myers Squibb in the pharmaceutical field have experienced a similar phenomenon. Basically, even slight demand uncertainties and variabilities become magnified when viewed through the eyes of managers at each link in the supply chain. If each distinct entity makes ordering and inventory decisions with an eye to its own interest above those of the chain, stockpiling may be occurring simultaneously at as many as seven or eight different places along the supply chain as assurance against shortages. Such stockpiling can lead to as many as 100 days of inventory waiting "just in case." Companies may avoid the "sting of the bullwhip" if they take steps to share information along the supply chain. Such information sharing is implemented and facilitated by EDI, extranets, and collaborative technologies—topics discussed later in this chapter.

bullwhip effect
Erratic shifts in order up and down supply chains.

The Need for Information Sharing Along the Supply Chain

Information systems are the links that enable communication and collaboration along the supply chain. They represent one of the fundamental elements that link the organizations of the supply chain into a unified and coordinated system. In today's competitive business climate, EC and information technology are keys to the success, and perhaps even the survival, of any SCM initiative.

Case studies of some world-class companies, such as Wal-Mart, Dell, and FedEx, indicate that these companies have created very sophisticated information systems, exploiting the latest technological developments and creating innovative solutions. However, even world-class companies, such as Nike, may suffer from inappropriate information sharing resulting in poor forecasting and then severely underestimating the complexity of automating aspects of the supply chain (see the Nike case in Online File W6.2).

EC SOLUTIONS ALONG THE SUPPLY CHAIN

The connection between EC and supply chains has become more evident in recent years according to a survey conducted by Holsapple and Jin (2007). EC presents a new environment for managing the dynamics of supply chain relationships. The survey identified two main factors that differentiate the EC environment from the traditional business settings of supply chains: the greater scope of connectivity of organizations with their suppliers and customers, and the faster speed at which business activities occur. These two factors provide more visibility across the supply chain and engender new market structure and greater sense of uncertainty. According to Holsapple and Jin, this connection is facilitated by collaborative decision making in supply chains and by the support EC provides to collaborative decision making.

The following is a representative list of the major solutions provided by an EC approach and technologies for supply chain problems.

visibility
The knowledge about where materials and parts are at any given time, which helps solving problems such as delay, combining shipments, and more.

> ▶ *Visibility* increases along the supply chain. It is critical to know where materials and parts are at any given time. This is referred to as visibility. Such knowledge can help in solving problems such as delay, combining shipments, and more. Visibility is provided by several tools, such as bar codes, RFID (Section 6.3), collaborative devices (Section 6.8), and portals (Section 6.7). Visibility implies creating information transparency through effective integration of information flows across the multiple e-marketplaces that comprise the chain. Such visibility allows organizations to coordinate supply chain interactions efficiently in dynamic market conditions.
>
> ▶ *Order taking* can be done over the Internet, by EDI, by EDI/Internet, or over an extranet, and may be fully automated. For example, in B2B, orders are generated and transmitted automatically to suppliers when inventory falls below certain levels. The result is a fast, inexpensive, and more accurate (no need to rekey data) order-taking process. In B2C, Web-based ordering using electronic forms expedites the process, makes it more accurate (intelligent agents can check the input data and provide instant feedback), and reduces processing costs (see Chapters 3 and 5).
>
> ▶ *Order fulfillment* can become instant if the products can be digitized (e.g., software). In other cases, EC order taking interfaces with the company's back-office systems, including logistics. Such an interface, or even integration, shortens cycle time and eliminates errors. (See Chapter 12 for more on order fulfillment.)
>
> ▶ *Electronic payments* can expedite both the order fulfillment cycle and the payment delivery period. Payment processing can be significantly less expensive, and fraud can be better controlled. (See Chapter 11 for more on electronic payments.)
>
> ▶ *Managing risk* to avoid supply chain breakdown can be done in several ways. Carrying additional inventories is effective against the risk of stock-outs, and hence poor customer service, but can be expensive. Also, in certain cases the risk increases because products may become obsolete. (Managing inventories is described in Sections 6.3 through 6.5.)
>
> ▶ *Inventories can be minimized* by introducing a build-to-order manufacturing process as well as by providing fast and accurate information to suppliers. By allowing business partners to electronically track and monitor orders and production activities, inventory management can be improved and inventory levels and the expense of inventory management can be minimized. Inventories can be better managed if we know exactly where parts and materials are at any given time (e.g., by using RFID, Section 6.3). Inventories of retailers can be managed electronically by their suppliers (Section 6.4).
>
> ▶ *Collaborative commerce* among members of the supply chain can be done in many areas ranging from product design to demand forecasting. The results are shorter cycle times, minimal delays and work interruptions, lower inventories, and lower administrative costs. A variety of tools exist ranging from collaborative hubs and networks (Section 6.4) to collaborative planning (Section 6.5).

The Role of Mobility

Synchronizing supply chains with mobility is gaining in popularity. With increasing competition and globalization, companies are searching for solutions to have leaner supply chains. Mobility eliminates wasted time hidden in business processes.

Through mobility, computing power is moved from a stationary desktop computer to mobile devices—the tools workers need to automate business processes and capture data in real time—right at the point of work. Manual processes are replaced with real-time computing. Instead of issuing paperwork orders to employees, an electronic work order can be issued instantly and automatically by mobile-supported business systems. For a comprehensive review and list of dozens of activities along the supply chain that support mobility, see Motorola (2007) and business.motorola.com/hellomoto/enterprisemobilitysolutions/supplychain.html. One major tool of mobility is RFID.

Section 6.2 ▶ REVIEW QUESTIONS

1. Describe some typical problems along the supply chain.
2. Describe the reasons for supply chain–related problems.
3. Describe the bullwhip effect.
4. Describe the benefits of information sharing along the supply chain.
5. List some EC solutions to supply chain problems.

6.3 RFID AS A KEY ENABLER IN SUPPLY CHAIN MANAGEMENT

RFID has the potential to revolutionize supply chain management. Some of its limitations may be overcome by a new wireless standard—RuBee.

THE RFID REVOLUTION

One of the newest and most revolutionary solutions to supply chain problems is RFID. We introduced the concept of RFID in Chapter 1 (Online File W1.1). **Radio frequency identification (RFID)** tags can be attached to or embedded in objects, animals, or humans; these tags use radio waves to communicate with a reader for the purpose of uniquely identifying the object, transmitting data, storing information about the object, or locating an item. Eventually, RFID tags will be attached to every item. Tags are like bar codes, but they contain much more information. Also, they can be read from a longer distance (up to 50 feet). This can be done due to the tag's relatively small size (although they are mostly still too large for some small items) and relatively low cost. Cost has been a real issue, and one inhibitor of the uptake of RFID technology. In 2006, a major landmark was reached when Israeli RFID manufacturer SmartCode offered RFID tags for 5 cents per tag, providing orders were placed for 100 million tags at a time! This compares to Avery Dennison in the United States, which is offering tags at 7.9 cents for volumes of 1 million or more tags. Although few would be in a position to take up the SmartCode offer, it is an important signal that the cost of RFID technology is coming close to reaching a point where companies will be willing to invest in RFID because they can be more certain of achieving an ROI on their RFID investments. RFID tags for the 2008 Olympics (see Chapter 1) and for the 2010 World Trade Fair have been produced at about 3 cents each. However, cost is just one factor. Organizations still need to learn exactly how to effectively use the capabilities of RFID technology in their supply chains with the back-office systems and how business processes may need to be redesigned and retooled so that solid business benefits accrue from the use of this technology (for benefits, see Loebbecke 2006).

Given these developments, what effect will RFID have on supply chains? Let's look at Exhibit 6.2, which shows the relationship between a retailer (Wal-Mart), a manufacturer (such as P&G), and P&G's suppliers. Note that the tags are read as merchandise travels from the supplier to the retailer (steps 1 and 2). Note that the RFID transmits real-time information on the location of the merchandise. Steps 3–6 show the use of the RFID at the retailer, mainly to confirm arrivals (step 3) and to locate merchandise inside the company, control inventory, prevent theft, and expedite processing of relevant information (steps 4–6). It is no longer necessary to count inventories, and all business partners are able to view inventory information in real time. This transparency can go several tiers

radio frequency identification (RFID)
Tags that can be attached to or embedded in objects, animals, or humans and use radio waves to communicate with a reader for the purpose of uniquely identifying the object or transmitting data and/or storing information about the object.

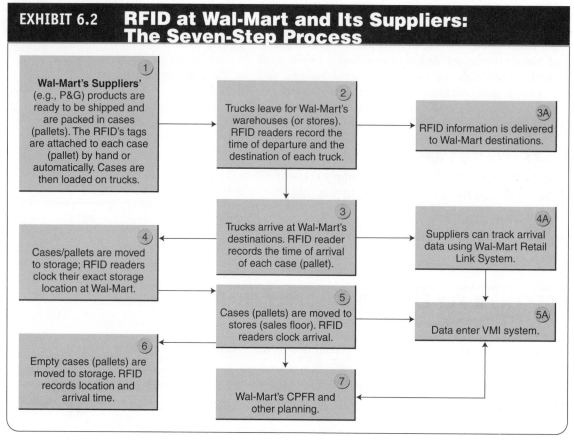

EXHIBIT 6.2   RFID at Wal-Mart and Its Suppliers: The Seven-Step Process

Source: Drawn by E. Turban.

down the supply chain. Additional applications, such as rapid checkout, which eliminates the need to scan each item, will be provided by RFID in the future.

RFID technology is presented in detail in Chapter 8, in Online File W1.1, and at en.wikipedia.org/wiki/RFID. The major applications are in the supply chain.

RFID APPLICATIONS IN THE SUPPLY CHAIN

Many potential and actual applications exist in enterprises using RFID (e.g., see Niederman et al. 2007). The following are examples of how RFID can be used in the supply chain.

RFID at Metro

Metro, a huge retailer from Germany, is using RFID tags in an attempt to speed the flow of goods from manufacturers in China to their arrival in Europe at the port of Rotterdam to distribution centers in Germany. Passive tags (see Online File W1.1) are being applied to cartons and cases of goods; active tags are also being applied to the containers in which those goods are packed for shipping. At various points en route to Germany, the active tags are read and record the arrival of the cargo, enabling a record to be kept of where goods are located at any point in time. This gives Metro greater insights into the flow of goods along their supply chain, with bottlenecks or points that slow the delivery of goods becoming quickly evident. This allows for a review of business processes and work practices to ensure speedier handling and delivery. In addition, these RFID tags are equipped with intrusion sensors, which give an indication of whether any attempt has been made to open the sealed containers during the journey. If the container is tampered with, the tags can trigger flashing lights or a siren to alert staff. Thus, Metro is able to detect any attempts to tamper with or pilfer stock (see Heinrich 2005).

The benefits of the RFID system to Metro are substantial. It is calculated that eliminating a single day from the supply chain will save Metro hundreds of thousands of dollars annually by reducing the amount of stock held in inventory. Estimates are that for large retailers (in excess of $1 billion in sales annually) each 1-day reduction in inventory can free up to $1 million in working capital (Sullivan 2006). For details, see future-store.org.

RFID at Starbucks

As Starbucks expands its range of fresh foods (such as salads, sandwiches, and the like) available at its outlets, the complexity and demands of managing this supply chain increase. Keeping the food fresh depends on keeping it at a steady cool state and in ensuring timely delivery. Starbucks is requiring its distributors to employ RFID tags to measure the temperature at the delivery trucks. These tags are programmed to record the temperature inside the truck every few minutes, and on return to the depot this temperature data can be downloaded and analyzed carefully. If there are unacceptable readings (e.g., the temperature is deemed to have risen too high), efforts are made to determine the cause and remedy the problem. This can then cause a redesign of critical business processes with regard to the transportation and handling of food (*RFID Journal* 2006). As RFID technology matures, it is conceivable, that in the future, the tags themselves will be able to detect variations in temperature and send a signal to a thermostat to activate refrigeration fans within the truck.

RFID at Deutsche Post

Deutsche Post owns 6 million shipping containers that it uses to hold and transport about 70 million letters and other items that pass through its distribution centers daily. In order to process these crates, Deutsche Post prints in excess of 500 million thick paper labels, all of which are thrown away after a single use. It was environmental concerns, rather than purely economic ones, that drove Deutsche Post's RFID initiative.

Deutsche Post uses passive RFID tags with a bi-stable display, meaning that the text displayed remains on-screen after power is removed and does not change until power is restored and the text is rewritten by an RFID interrogator. Tags on the crates must be readable from all angles and in all types of weather, requiring a robust tag. Furthermore, the tags need to last about 5 years in order for the application to be financially viable.

Deutsche Post developed a custom tag and RFID reader, and uses specialized software in this innovative application. Several other post offices around the world use RFID (e.g., Canada). For other applications and more details, refer to Loebbecke (2006) and Heinrich (2005).

RFID in the Government (U.S. Department of Defense)

Inventory tracking is a logistical challenge throughout the armed services and government agencies. At the same time, there is an urgent need to ensure the safety of military personnel and improve security worldwide. The end result is that RFID-based applications in the government and defense sectors are growing exponentially. RFID technology offers a viable solution with reliable, secure identification and tracking that integrates with existing enterprise mobility systems. For example, the U.S. Marine Corps uses RFID to improve flows in their supply chains.

RFID at Atlantic Beef Products (Ontario, Canada)

Cow's ears are tagged with RFID tags. After a cow is killed, its ear tags are scanned for food traceability. The carcass goes onto two leg hooks, each equipped with an RFID chip. They are synced to each animal's database record. The RFIDs replace bar codes, which could get contaminated with E. coli on the slaughter floor. The RFID helps track the movement of each cow and the meat produced at any time. The system won a gold medal from the Canadian IT organization.

RFID in Pharmaceuticals

MIT and SAP are examining the use of RFID in various industries, including pharmaceuticals and health-care delivery, as well as the necessary IT architecture to support such use. The goal is to be able to know where everything or anything is at any given time. The challenge, however, is in determining how such a scenario would play out—what the actual network would look like once companies up and down the supply chain collaboratively start exchanging information among trading partners and their partners' partners.

The Food and Drug Administration (FDA), for example, is interested in using RFID to find counterfeit drugs in the supply chain. An RFID chip with patient information (called

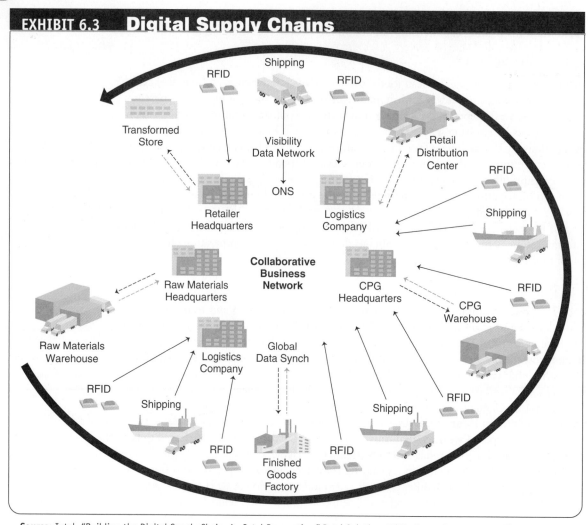

EXHIBIT 6.3   Digital Supply Chains

Source: Intel, "Building the Digital Supply Chain: An Intel Perspective," Intel Solutions White Paper, January 2005, Figure 5, p. 9.

SurgiChip, approved by the FDA) goes with the patient into surgery to help prevent errors. RFID tags are also used for patient identification throughout hospitals. Finally, many hospitals use RFID tags to find the whereabouts of pieces of portable equipment.

Theoretically, RFID can be read in many places along the supply chain, as illustrated in Exhibit 6.3.

For more examples of applications, see Online File W6.3 and Roberti (2007). For a successful implementation at Airbus, see Case 6.1.

Other Uses

⬧ RFID embedded in cell phones is beginning to replace credit cards, cash, train passes, keys to your car and home, business cards, and more (see Kharif 2006). DoCoMo of Japan introduced such a cell phone in 2004, and its use is growing rapidly.

⬧ RFID can be used in Sensor Networks (see Chapter 8).

LIMITATIONS AND CONCERNS OF RFID

RFID does have a number of limitations. For small companies, the cost of the system may be too high (at least for the near future). The lower-frequency systems (300 to 500Khz) required for passive tags are much cheaper but offer a decreased range. Radio frequency interference and the limited range of passive RFID tags also may be problematic, especially because passive tags are the most economically viable option for some businesses. These limitations should be minimized in the future as the cost of both passive and active RFID decreases and functionality increases. However, to date, many organizations have struggled to demonstrate

CASE 6.1
EC Application
AIRBUS IMPROVES PRODUCTIVITY WITH RFID

Because it is in constant competition with Boeing, the European aircraft manufacturer Airbus is looking for every opportunity to increase productivity, reduce costs, and make its production process more efficient. One of its latest efforts is the use of RFID technology, both in manufacturing and in maintenance of its airplanes. The initial deployment focused on automating the sourcing, logistics, manufacturing, and maintenance of the Airbus A380, the world's largest commercial aircraft, with IBM's RFID infrastructure software. The basic idea is to use RFID to track parts and tools, which are scattered over a large area; such information can eliminate delays. (Airbus had major delays in completing its A380, the two-decker, 525-seat airplane in 2008.)

Airbus hopes that RFID will become "as everyday as bar coding." The company experimented with the technology for 3 years before signing a multimillion-dollar deal with vendors to implement the technology. It also created a value chain visibility and RFID unit to implement the biggest private sector RFID deal ever.

Airbus has implemented process-improvement projects involving RFID to track parts inside warehouses as they move from one region to another, and as they are built into aircrafts, as well as to track how and where tools are used for manufacturing and maintenance. The new RFID software infrastructure lets Airbus employees and systems exchange information collected by RFID readers. The infrastructure also integrates RFID data with business systems such as Airbus's core ERP system (Chapter 10).

The software also manages data collected by bar codes, which remains an important part of Airbus's supply chain. RFID tags can hold more information and they do not require a line-of-sight reader, but they typically cost more than $1 per tag. So Airbus uses them only on rolling cages, pallets, cases, and high-cost parts.

Airbus expects the RFID to augment ongoing supply chain process improvements, saving money by reducing time spent searching for parts, reducing inventory, and improving employees' productivity.

Airbus is assessing a few pilot projects with suppliers tagging parts before shipping them, and the new software makes it possible to extend parts tracking from the supplier side to Airbus.

To close its RFID deal, Airbus had to navigate a still highly fragmented RFID industry. There are hundreds of vendors; each tells a different story, with different architectures and different payoffs. To sort it out, Airbus assigned a 25-person team of IT, business, and process analysts for about 2 years to develop a company-side RFID strategy and plans.

Airbus is employing RFID across two main categories: nonflyable and flyable.

▶ *Nonflyable* consists of ground-based processes, such as supply chain, transportation, logistics, manufacturing, and assembly-related applications.
▶ *Flyable* refers to all in-service processes, including operational, maintenance, and payload-tracking applications.

Sources: Compiled from Hayes-Weier (2008), *RFID Journal* (2007), and *Manufacturing Executive* (2009).

Questions

1. What are the drivers of the RFID project?
2. What information technologies were used in this project?
3. What categories of people are supported by RFID?
4. How can RFID provide visibility to Boeing?
5. Go to the link provided in the case sources and watch the Webcast. It will provide you with a virtual tour of Airbus's supply chain. Report on how RFID provides real-time visibility in the key processes.

---

the ROI of their RFID initiatives, raising the question of how long organizations will continue to invest in such technologies without gaining adequate returns.

Another major limitation of RFID currently is the restriction of the environments in which RFID tags are easily read. RFID tags do not work well in "harsh" environments, where reads are required in or around liquids and metals or around corners, for example. This means that RFID may not, in some cases, readily be used underwater or near items that are largely liquid (such as human beings and livestock, which are mostly water!), nor do they function well in warehouses or areas where large amounts of metals are present (e.g., metal-lined deep freezers or metal shelving). Another issue has arisen in real-world implementations of RFID—the accuracy of the readers. Some (but not all) organizations have reported achieving only 70 to 90 percent accuracy in their read rates and, of additional concern, achieving different levels of accuracy at different points along the supply chain. Using active tags with a relatively large read range on individual items can prove problematic where there are many other items stocked near the reader but not part of the shopping cart. However, accuracy is improving with time.

Concern over customer privacy (see Chapters 10 and 16) is another issue that remains a significant point of contention in arguments about the appropriateness of wide-scale implementation of RFID. First and foremost are security concerns related to the potential of RFID tags to be tracked long after their SCM purpose has been served. Following are some concerns regarding customer privacy and RFID tags:

▶ The customer buying an item with an RFID tag may not be able to remove the tag or may be unaware that an RFID tag is attached to the item.

▶ The presence of a tag might mean that it would still be capable of being read from some distance away without the knowledge of the purchaser or user of that item.

▶ If a purchase is made using a credit card, then the potential exists for the tag details to be linked directly to the personal details of the credit card holder.

Such concerns have lead to comments such as one U.S. politician remarking that "one day you realized your underwear was reporting your whereabouts!" (reported in en.wikipedia.org/wiki/RFID).

Public concern has not been allayed in this regard, with various incidents reported in the media involving linking RFID on products with smart shelves equipped with cameras, thus directly identifying the person buying an item (using a photographic record).

As with most immature technologies, agreeing on universal standards, as well as connecting the RFIDs with existing IT systems, is yet another issue. In 2008, however, the Gen 2 standard (a protocol for the exchange of information between the RFID tag and the reader) appears to be the major RFID standard. However, some feel that Gen 2 is inadequate technically with the increased adoption of RFID technologies, and they thus argue that Gen 3 will require a huge volume of item-level tagging and the alleviation of consumers' security concerns. In addition to technical standards, the players along the supply chain need to agree on how particular items are to be labeled and categorized. Take, for example, a common product such as aspirin. Aspirin is manufactured by a pharmaceutical company but distributed to major supermarkets and retailers, such as Wal-Mart, pharmacies, and other convenience stores. The supermarket may categorize aspirin as a fast-moving consumer good (FMCG), and the pharmacist would consider it a pharmacy item, thus posing problems for the manufacturer as to how to categorize and hence identify the item. The manufacturer may prefer to use HF RFID tags, the supermarket UHF RFID tags. Unless agreement on these sorts of issues can be reached by all key players along a supply chain, significant problems may occur. For more RFID implementation issues, see Niederman et al. (2007).

Alongside the concerns and limitations, there are many potential benefits, which are summarized in Online File W6.4.

RUBEE: AN ALTERNATIVE TO RFID?

In 2006, a new technology emerged that may act as an important complement to RFID in that it excels in situations where RFID has limitations. Known as *RuBee*, it relies on low-frequency magnetic waves to track products and transfer information. **RuBee** is defined as a bidirectional, on-demand, peer-to-peer radiating transceiver protocol (en.wikipedia.org/wiki/RuBee). It is currently being developed by the Institute of Electrical and Electronics Engineers (IEEE P1902.1). Online File W6.5 compares RuBee and RFID. Note that RuBee is not intended as a replacement for RFID but rather as a complement. As suggested in Online File W6.5, RFID is excellent for many applications, and indeed better than RuBee for some. However, RuBee tends to excel in areas where RFID has proven problematic; hence, it may prove vital in overcoming some of RFID's limitations. RuBee and RFID together may become partners in helping organizations better manage their global supply chains.

RuBee

Bidirectional, on-demand, peer-to-peer radiating transceiver protocol under development by the Institute of Electrical and Electronics Engineers.

Section 6.3 ▶ REVIEW QUESTIONS

1. Describe how RFID can be used to improve supply chains.
2. Explain how RFID works in a supplier–retailer system.
3. Briefly explain the differences between active and passive RFID tags. (Note: See Online File W 1.1.)
4. In what circumstances would it be better to use passive RFID tags? And in what circumstances might it be better to use active RFID tags?
5. What are some of the major limitations of RFID technology?
6. Describe RuBee and its capabilities.

6.4 COLLABORATIVE COMMERCE

Chapter 5 introduced B2B activities related mainly to selling and buying. Collaborative commerce is an e-commerce technology that can be used to improve collaboration within and among organizations, including in supply chains and their management.

ESSENTIALS OF COLLABORATIVE COMMERCE

Collaborative commerce (c-commerce) refers to the use of digital technologies that enable companies to collaboratively plan, design, develop, manage, and research products, services, and innovative EC applications. An example would be a manufacturer that is collaborating electronically with a supplier that designs a product or a part for the manufacturer, as was shown in the Boeing opening case. C-commerce implies communication, information sharing, and collaborative planning done electronically through tools such as groupware, blogs, wikis, and specially designed EC collaboration tools. Slobodow et al. (2008) advocate dual accountability between a buyer and its strategic suppliers through tools such as a two-way scoreboard (see Chapter 13), which provide a new approach to improving supply chain relationships. Major benefits cited are cost reduction, increased revenue, and better customer retention. These benefits are the results of fewer stock-outs, less exception and rush-order processing, reduced inventory throughout the supply chain, lower materials costs, increased sales volume, and increased competitive advantage. Two collaborative structures are hubs and networks.

collaborative commerce (c-commerce)
The use of digital technologies that enable companies to collaboratively plan, design, develop, manage, and research products, services, and innovative EC applications.

The Elements and Processes of C-Commerce

The elements of processes of c-commerce vary according to situations. Here our major concern is collaboration that involves a manufacturer (or assemblers) with its suppliers, designers, and other business partners as well as its customers and possibly government, along the supply chain. The major elements of the collaboration are illustrated in Exhibit 6.4. Notice that the collaboration is based on the analysis of internal and external data that are made visible via a portal. On the left side of the exhibit, we show the cyclical process of collaborative commerce. The people involved in this cycle use the information in the displays as well as the interactions among the major groups of participants.

COLLABORATION HUBS

One of the most popular forms of c-commerce is the *collaboration hub*, which is used by the members of a supply chain. A collaboration hub (c-hub) is the central point of control for an e-market. A single c-hub, representing one e-market owner, can host multiple collaboration spaces (c-spaces) in which trading partners use c-enablers to exchange data with the c-hub.

collaboration hub (c-hub)
The central point of control for an e-market. A single c-hub, representing one e-market owner, can host multiple collaboration spaces (c-spaces) in which trading partners use c-enablers to exchange data with the c-hub.

C-commerce activities usually are conducted between and among supply chain partners. Leightons Opticians, as shown in Online File W6.6, uses a hub to communicate among all its business partners and is thus able to improve customer service. Finally, in Online File W6.7, the case of Webcor, a company using special software to better collaborate with its partners electronically, is described.

There are several varieties of c-commerce, ranging from joint design efforts to forecasting. Collaboration can be done both between and within organizations. For example, a collaborative platform can help in communication and collaboration between headquarters and subsidiaries or between franchisers and franchisees. The platform provides e-mail, message boards and chat rooms, and online corporate data access around the globe, no matter what the time zone. The following sections demonstrate some types and examples of c-commerce.

COLLABORATIVE NETWORKS

Traditionally, collaboration took place among supply chain members, frequently those that were close to each other (e.g., a manufacturer and its distributor or a distributor and a retailer). Traditional collaboration results in a vertically integrated supply chain. However, as stated in Chapters 1 and 2, EC and Web technologies can *fundamentally change* the shape of the supply chain, the number of players within it, and their individual roles. The new supply chain can be a hub (recall Chapter 2) or even a network. A comparison between the traditional supply chain and the new one, made possible by Web technologies, is shown in

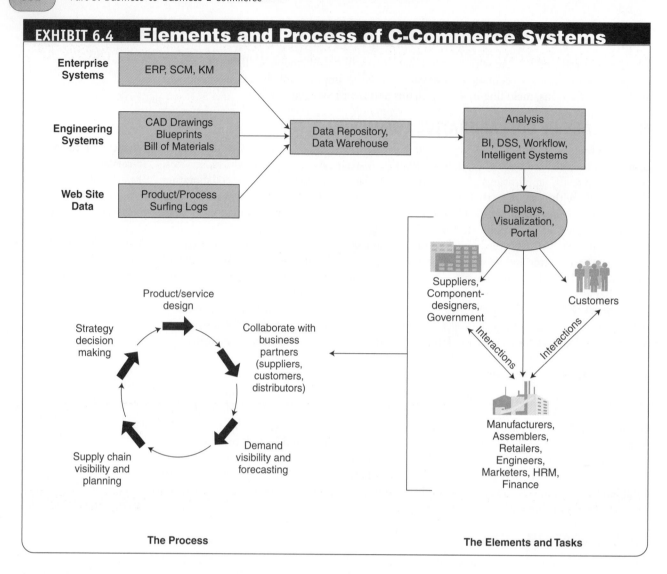

EXHIBIT 6.4 Elements and Process of C-Commerce Systems

The Process

The Elements and Tasks

Exhibit 6.5. Notice that the traditional chain in Exhibit 6.5A is basically linear. However, it may include advanced features such as CFPR (see description in Section 6.5). The *collaborative network* in Exhibit 6.5B shows that partners at any point in the network can interact with each other directly, bypassing traditional partners. Interaction may occur among several manufacturers or distributors, as well as with new players, such as software agents that act as aggregators, B2B exchanges, hubs, or logistics providers.

The collaborative network can take different shapes depending on the industry, the product (or service), the volume of information flow, and more.

REPRESENTATIVE EXAMPLES OF E-COLLABORATION

Leading companies such as Dell, Cisco, and HP use collaborative commerce strategically, enabling sophisticated business models while transforming their value chains. They also have implemented e-procurement and other mature collaboration techniques to streamline operations, reduce overhead, and maintain or enhance margins in the face of intense competition. For example, Dell implemented end-to-end integrated configuration and ordering, a single enterprise middleware backbone, and multi-tier collaborative planning. This has enabled Dell to support a make-to-order business model with best-in-class speed and efficiency. Cisco chose to support a virtual business model focusing on time-to-market and customer satisfaction. Cisco has integrated its order process with back-end processes, implemented purchase order automation, and enabled collaborative product development.

EXHIBIT 6.5A   Comparing the Traditional Collaborative Supply Chain and Collaborative Networks

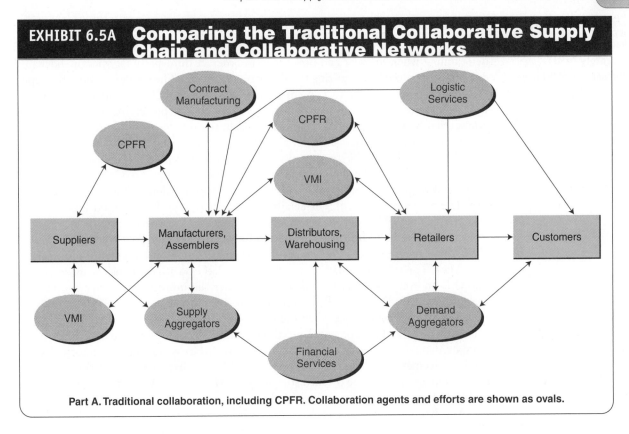

Part A. Traditional collaboration, including CPFR. Collaboration agents and efforts are shown as ovals.

EXHIBIT 6.5B   Supply Chain in Collaborative Networks

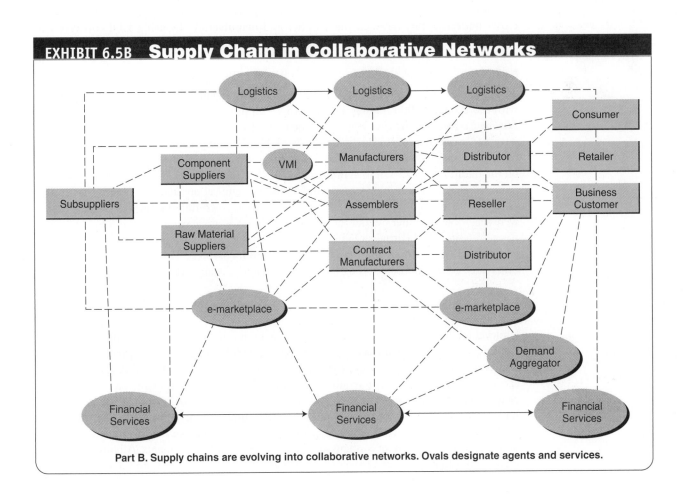

Part B. Supply chains are evolving into collaborative networks. Ovals designate agents and services.

Vendor-Managed Inventory

vendor-managed inventory (VMI)
The practice of retailers' making suppliers responsible for determining when to order and how much to order.

With **vendor-managed inventory (VMI)**, retailers make their suppliers fully responsible for determining when to order and how much to order. A third-party logistics provider (3PL) can also be involved by organizing the shipments as needed. The retailer provides the supplier with real-time information (e.g., point-of-sale data), inventory levels, and a threshold below which orders are replenished. The reorder quantities also are predetermined and usually recommended by the supplier. With this approach, the retailer is no longer burdened with inventory management, demand forecasting becomes easier, the supplier can see the potential need for an item before the item is ordered, there are no purchase orders, inventories are kept low, and out-of-stocks become infrequent. Today, it can be supported by CFPR and special software. VMI software solutions are provided by Sockeye Solutions (sockeyesolutions.com) and JDA Software (jda.com). For details, see Haines (2008). This method was initiated by Wal-Mart in the 1980s and has become popular. Let's look at an example.

Example: VMI and Information Sharing Between a Retailer (Wal-Mart) and a Supplier (P&G). Wal-Mart provides P&G access to sales information on every item P&G makes for Wal-Mart. The sales information is collected by P&G on a daily basis (or made visible to P&G) from every Wal-Mart store, and P&G uses the information to manage inventory replenishment for Wal-Mart. By monitoring the inventory level of each P&G item in every Wal-Mart store, P&G knows when the inventories fall below the threshold that triggers an automatic order and a shipment. Everything is done electronically. The benefit for P&G is accurate demand information; the benefit for Wal-Mart is adequate inventory. P&G has similar agreements with other major retailers; Wal-Mart has similar agreements with other major suppliers. For a more detailed study of Wal-Mart's use of VMI and other supply chain enablers, see the closing case at the end of this chapter.

As a symbiotic relationship, VMI makes it less likely that a business will unintentionally become out of stock of a good and also reduces inventory in the supply chain. VMI is one of the successful business models used by many large retailers. For example, Home Depot uses the technique with larger suppliers of manufactured goods. VMI helps foster a closer understanding between the supplier and manufacturer by using EDI software and statistical methodologies to forecast and maintain correct inventory in the supply chain.

Retailer–Supplier Collaboration: Target Corporation

Target Corporation (targetcorp.com) is a large retail conglomerate. It conducts EC activities with more than 20,000 trading partners. In 1998, then operating under the name *Dayton-Hudson Corporation*, the company established an extranet-based system for those partners that were not connected to its value-added network (VAN)-based EDI. The extranet enabled the company not only to reach many more partners but also to use many applications not available on the traditional EDI. The system (based on GXS's InterBusiness Partner Extranet platform; gxs.com) enabled the company to streamline its communications and collaboration with suppliers. It also allowed the company's business customers to create personalized Web pages that were accessible via either the Internet or GXS EDI VAN, as shown in Exhibit 6.6. Target now has a Web site called Partners Online (partnersonline.com), which it uses to communicate with and provide an enormous amount of information to its partners. This model is used by many other large corporations, including Caterpillar (Chapter 7) and Cisco Systems (Chapter 5).

Lower Transportation and Inventory Costs and Reduced Stock-Outs: Unilever

Unilever is a large global manufacturer of leading brands in food, home care, and personal care (unilever.com). Its 30 contract carriers deliver 250,000 truckloads of shipments every day. Unilever's Web-based database, the Transportation Business Center (TBC), provides the carriers with site-specification requirements when they pick up a shipment at a manufacturing or distribution center or when they deliver goods to retailers. TBC gives carriers all the vital information they need: contact names and phone numbers, operating hours, the number of dock doors at a location, the height of the dock doors, how to make an appointment to deliver or pick up shipments, pallet configuration, and other special requirements. All mission-critical information that Unilever carriers need to make pickups, shipments, and deliveries is now

EXHIBIT 6.6   Target's Extranet

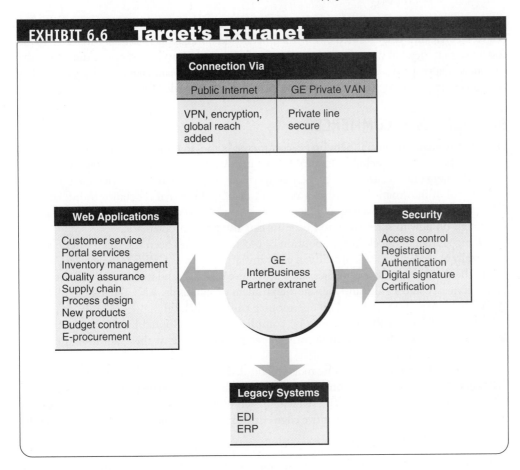

Connection Via

Public Internet	GE Private VAN
VPN, encryption, global reach added	Private line secure

GE InterBusiness Partner extranet

Web Applications

Customer service
Portal services
Inventory management
Quality assurance
Supply chain
Process design
New products
Budget control
E-procurement

Security

Access control
Registration
Authentication
Digital signature
Certification

Legacy Systems

EDI
ERP

available electronically 24/7. TBC also helps Unilever organize and automate its carrier selection processes based on contract provisions and commitments. When a primary carrier is unable to accept a shipment, TBC automatically recommends alternative carriers.

Reduction of Design Cycle Time: Clarion Malaysia

Clarion Malaysia, part of the global company Clarion Group, employs approximately 700 people in Malaysia. It manufactures audio electronic systems for cars.

Working with IBM through the implementation of CAD systems and collaborative product lifecycle management (PLM) technologies (see Section 6.5), Clarion has slashed its time-to-market from 14 months to about 9 months, while at the same time improving the quality of the products because more time can be spent in yielding superior designs. The application of the latest information technology has also supported much closer cooperation with and responsiveness to customers throughout the design process, better use of materials through the deployment of 3D modeling, and a 60 percent reduction in tooling preparation time (BNET 2006, IBM 2006). Another example of reduction of time-to-market is provided in Online File W6.8.

Reduction of Product Development Time: Caterpillar, Inc.

Caterpillar, Inc. (caterpillar.com) is a multinational, heavy-machinery manufacturer. In the traditional mode of operation, cycle time along the supply chain was long because the process involved the transfer of paper documents among managers, salespeople, and technical staff. To solve the problem, Caterpillar connected its engineering and manufacturing divisions with its suppliers, dealers, distributors, overseas factories, and customers through an extranet-based global e-collaboration system. By means of the collaboration system, a request for a customized tractor component, for example, can be transmitted from a customer to a Caterpillar dealer and on to designers and suppliers, all in a very short time. Customers also can use the extranet (accessible with wireless devices) to retrieve and modify detailed order information while the vehicle is still on the assembly line.

Remote collaboration capabilities between the customer and product developers have also decreased cycle time delays caused by rework time. In addition, suppliers also are connected to the system so that they can deliver materials or parts directly to Caterpillar's shops or directly to the customer, if appropriate. The system also is used for expediting maintenance and repairs. Other companies are also using EC technologies to reduce the time needed for product development.

BARRIERS TO C-COMMERCE

Despite the many potential benefits, c-commerce is moving ahead fairly slowly. Reasons cited in various studies include technical factors involving a lack of internal integration, standards, and networks; security and privacy concerns, and some distrust over who has access to and control of information stored in a partner's database; internal resistance to information sharing and to new approaches; and lack of internal skills to conduct c-commerce. Gaining agreement on how to share costs and benefits can also prove problematic.

A big stumbling block to the adoption of c-commerce has been the lack of defined and universally agreed-upon standards. Even early initiatives such as CPFR (see next section) are still in their infancy. New approaches, such as the use of XML and its variants and the use of Web Services, could significantly lessen the problem of standards. Also, the use of collaborative Web 2.0 tools that are based on open source could be helpful.

Finally, global collaboration may be complicated by additional barriers ranging from language incompatibility to cultural misunderstandings. Some of these additional barriers are described in Chapter 13.

Specialized c-commerce software tools will break down some of the barriers to c-commerce (see Section 6.8). In addition, as companies learn more about the major benefits of c-commerce—such as smoothing the supply chain, reducing inventories and operating costs, and increasing customer satisfaction and the competitive edge—it is expected that more will rush to jump on the c-commerce bandwagon.

C-commerce is a typical response to business pressures, as can be seen in the case of a global supply chain in the fashion retailing industry. The fashion retail supply chain poses some unique and very challenging decisions for managers, and the adoption of appropriate technologies to support such supply chains is obviously critical. Some fashion retailers are achieving extraordinary levels of success and are the envy of nearly all other players in this industry, even if they have not adopted all the prescriptions we have detailed here. Zara (zara.com) is one such example (see Online File W6.9).

Section 6.4 ▶ REVIEW QUESTIONS

1. Define c-commerce.
2. List the major types and characteristics of c-commerce.
3. Describe some examples of c-commerce.
4. Define collaborative networks and distinguish them from traditional supply chain collaboration.
5. Define VMI and list its benefits.
6. List some major barriers to c-commerce. How might these limitations be overcome?
7. How might e-collaboration support and improve industry supply chains?

6.5 COLLABORATIVE PLANNING, CPFR, APS, AND PLM

In collaborative planning, business partners—manufacturers, suppliers, distribution partners, and other partners—create initial demand (or sales) forecasts, provide changes as necessary, and share information, such as actual sales, and their own forecasts. Thus, all parties work according to a unified schedule aligned to a common view, and all have access to order and forecast performance that is globally visible through electronic links. Schedule, order, or product changes trigger immediate adjustments to all parties' schedules.

Collaborative planning is designed to synchronize production and distribution plans and product flows, optimize resource utilization over an expanded capacity base, increase customer responsiveness, and reduce inventories. It can be a complex process (see Exhibit 6.6).

Collaborative planning is a necessity in e-SCM (see vics.org/committees/cpfr). The planning process is difficult because it involves multiple parties and activities.

This section examines several aspects of collaborative planning and collaborative design.

COLLABORATIVE PLANNING, FORECASTING, AND REPLENISHMENT

Collaborative planning, forecasting, and replenishment (CPFR) is a business practice in which suppliers and retailers collaborate in planning and demand forecasting in order to ensure that members of the supply chain will have the right amount of raw materials and finished goods when they need them. The goal of CPFR is to streamline product flow from manufacturing plants all the way to customers' homes. Large manufacturers of consumer goods, such as P&G, have superb supply chains resulting from their use of CPFR.

The essentials of CPFR are shown in Exhibit 6.7. The process is discussed in Online File W6.10. Note that this is a cyclical process in which sellers, buyers, and end customers are considered. The process starts with strategy and planning, followed by demand and supply management, which results in execution. The results are analyzed, leading to reexamination of the strategy.

An interesting application of CPFR is that of West Marine, presented in Case 6.2. CPFR can be used with a company-centric B2B and with sell-side or buy-side marketplaces. For more on the benefits of CPFR, see cpfr.org/cpfr_pdf/index.html. Also, see en.wikipedia.org/wiki/CPFR.

collaborative planning, forecasting, and replenishment (CPFR)
Project in which suppliers and retailers collaborate in their planning and demand forecasting to optimize flow of materials along the supply chain.

ADVANCED PLANNING AND SCHEDULING

Advanced planning and scheduling (APS) systems are math-based computerized programs that identify optimal solutions to complex planning problems that are bound by constraints, such as limited machine capacity or labor. Using algorithms (such as linear programming), these systems are able to solve a wide range of problems, from operational (e.g., daily schedule) to strategic (e.g., network optimization). For details, see en.wikipedia.org/wiki/Advanced_Planning_&_Scheduling.

advanced planning and scheduling (APS) systems
Programs that use algorithms to identify optimal solutions to complex planning problems that are bound by constraints.

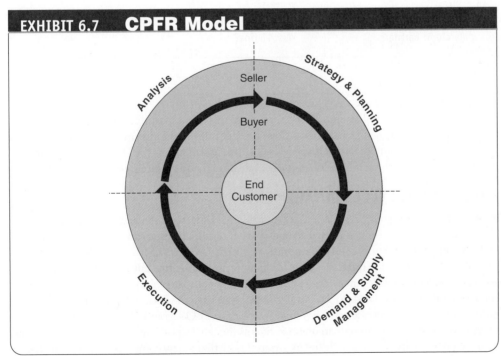

EXHIBIT 6.7   CPFR Model

Source: *VICS.org,* "Collaborative Planning, Forecasting, and Replenishment (CPFR): An Overview," May 18, 2004, Figure 1, p. 6. Permission of VICS; CPFR is a registered trademark of VICS.

CASE 6.2
EC Application
WEST MARINE: A CPFR SUCCESS STORY

West Marine is the largest boating-supply company in the United States. It has 400 stores and annual sales of $690 million. The company sells more than 50,000 different products, ranging from stainless-steel propellers and anchors to lifejackets and wetsuits, through its stores, Web site, catalog, and commercial sales arm.

West Marine has a dramatic story when it comes to its effective supply chain, which was guided and directed through its deep, intensive, and effective implementation of CPFR. West Marine is now regarded as having a showcase CPFR implementation; however, it wasn't always that way.

In 1997, West Marine acquired its East Coast competitor E&B Marine. As a result of the challenges of integrating the two companies, sales fell by almost 8 percent, and during the peak season out-of-stock situations rose by more than 12 percent over the previous year. Income dropped from $15 million in 1997 to little more than $1 million in 1998.

The situation was quite different when in 2003 West Marine purchased its largest competitor, BoatUS. West Marine successfully integrated BoatUS's distribution center in just 30 days. BoatUS's in-store systems were integrated into West Marine in just under 60 days. Further, supply chain performance and the bottom line were not affected.

So why was this second acquisition so much smoother? The difference was that by 2003 the company had an effective IT-enabled supply chain management system driven by CPFR.

In reviewing the CPFR implementation in West Marine, it is clear that a key success factor was West Marine's commitment to technology enablement. Through the CPFR information systems, data such as seasonal forecasts, promotional stock levels, and future assortment changes are calculated automatically. Joint forecasting and order fulfillment are enabled by information systems that are suitably integrated between supply chain partners.

As many similar case studies attest, such information sharing through integrated supply chain systems is one factor in successful supply chain management.

However, West Marine's successful CPFR implementation was not simply about the technology. Significant energy and resources were devoted to collaboration among the key supply chain personnel in West Marine and its supply chain partners. Joint skills and knowledge were developed along with the key elements of trust and joint understanding. These elements were built through joint education and training sessions as well as through the standard CPFR joint planning and forecasting sessions.

West Marine's CPFR program now involves 200 suppliers and more than 20,000 stock items, representing more than 90 percent of West Marine's procurement spending. Further, more than 70 of West Marine's top suppliers load West Marine's order forecasts directly into their production planning systems. In-stock rates at West Marine stores are well over 90 percent, forecast accuracy stands at 85 percent, and on-time shipments are now consistently better than 80 percent. Summing up West Marine's collaborative supply chain journey using CPFR, Larry Smith, senior vice president of planning and replenishment states, "The results, we believe, speak for themselves."

Sources: Compiled from Ayers and Odegaard (2007) and Smith (2006).

Questions

1. What were the major elements of West Marine's CPFR success?

2. What were the benefits of the CPFR implementation for West Marine?

The role of APS in EC is depicted in Exhibit 6.8.

Basically, APS supplements ERP in revolutionizing a manufacturing or distribution firm's supply chain, providing a seamless flow of order fulfillment information from consumers to suppliers. It helps integrate ERP, CRM, salesforce automation (SFA), knowledge management (KM), and more, enabling collaborative fulfillment and an integrated EC strategy.

PRODUCT LIFECYCLE MANAGEMENT

product lifecycle management (PLM)
Business strategy that enables manufacturers to control and share product related data as part of product design and development efforts.

Product lifecycle management (PLM) is a business strategy that enables manufacturers to control and share product-related data as part of product design and development efforts and in support of supply chain operations (e.g., see en.wikipedia.org/wiki/Product_Lifecycle_Management). Internet and other new technologies can automate the collaborative aspects of product development that even within one company can prove tedious and time-consuming if not automated. PLM is a big step for an organization, requiring it to integrate a number of different processes and systems (see Ayers and Odegoord 2007). Ultimately, information must be moved through an organization as quickly as possible to reduce cycle time and increase profitability. The faster different groups know that a new component or design change is on its way, the faster they can react and get it manufactured or reengineered and out the door,

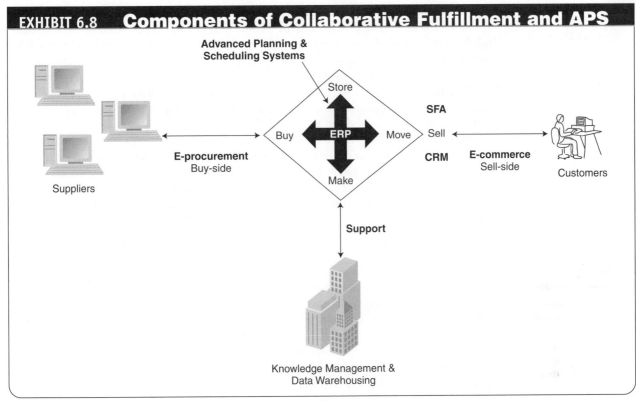

EXHIBIT 6.8   Components of Collaborative Fulfillment and APS

Source: Modified from *E-Procurement: From Strategy to Implementation,* by Neef, D., ©2001. Used by permission of Pearson Education, Inc., Upper Saddle River, NJ.

and the sooner the organization can realize revenue. PLM tools are offered by SAP (mySAP PLM), Matrix One, EDS, PTC, Dassault Systems, and IBM PLM.

SUPPORTING JOINT DESIGN

Collaborative efforts are common in joint design, as illustrated in the Boeing opening case. This is one of the oldest areas of electronic collaboration, which is becoming even more popular due to EC Web 2.0 tools, as discussed in Online File W6.11.

Section 6.5 ▶ REVIEW QUESTIONS

1. Define collaborative planning.
2. Define CPFR and describe its advantages.
3. Describe APS efforts.
4. Describe PLM.

6.6 SUPPLY CHAIN INTEGRATION

Supply chains from the suppliers' suppliers to the customers' customers need to be effective and efficient when viewed as a whole and, therefore, should be jointly planned and designed for overall optimality by all of the supply chain partners. Further, the supply chain needs to be operationally integrated so that procurement activities link seamlessly to order management activities, inventory activities link seamlessly to manufacturing activities, and so on. This implies attention to business process design and management that includes not only organizational business process redesign but also interorganizational business process redesign (Jeston and Nelis 2006).

HOW INFORMATION SYSTEMS ARE INTEGRATED

The integration issue can be divided into two parts: internal integration and integration with business partners (external). Internal integration includes connecting applications with databases and with each other and connecting customer-facing applications (front end) with order fulfillment and the functional information systems (back end). Internal integration is now commonly achieved through the implementation of an ERP and/or Web Services system. Integration with business partners connects an organization's systems with those of its external business partners, for example, a company's ordering system to its suppliers' fulfillment systems. Another example of integration with business partners would be connecting an organization's e-procurement system to the engineering departments of bidding companies. It is done with an ERP system (e.g., SAP) as well as with EDI, extranets, XML, and Web Services (Online Chapter 18).

Where a company has implemented an ERP system, it is necessary to connect the EC applications to the ERP system (see Siau and Tian 2004). An ERP system automates the flow of routine and repetitive information, such as submission of purchasing orders, billing, and inventory management. Increasingly, EC applications are incorporated into an ERP system's basic functionality.

Enabling Integration and the Role of Standards and Web Services

Web Services
An architecture enabling assembly of distributed applications from software services and tying them together.

Web Services is an architecture that enables the assembly of distributed applications from software services and ties them together. Integrating EC systems can be a complex task. As described in Online Chapter 18, integration involves connectivity, compatibility, security, and scalability. In addition, applications, data, processes, and interfaces must be integrated. Finally, a major difficulty is the connection of Web-based systems with legacy systems.

To ease the task of integration, vendors have developed integration methodologies and special software called *middleware* (see Online Chapter 18). In addition, major efforts are being undertaken to develop standards and protocols that will facilitate integration, such as XML. The topic of Web Services, one of the major goals of which is to facilitate seamless integration, is discussed in detail in Online Chapter 18.

INTEGRATION ALONG THE EXTENDED SUPPLY CHAIN

The discussion in Online File W6.12 provides an illustration of information integration along the extended supply chain—all the way from raw material to the customer's door. Such integration is possible with second-generation ERP systems (see en.wikipedia.org/wiki/Enterprise_resource_planning). Second-generation ERP systems include increasing amounts of SCM and CRM functionality, along with the internal ERP functionality.

A particular technology used in external supply chain integration is electronic data interchange (EDI). Large corporations have for some years used EDI to support their collaboration with partners. Increasingly, this EDI usage is becoming Internet based.

As an example of a corporation making extensive use of EDI, one can look at Boeing, which relies on hundreds of internal and external suppliers in dozens of different countries for the several million components needed to build a large airplane. Boeing is using EDI and other systems to facilitate collaboration with its partners.

Section 6.6 ▶ REVIEW QUESTIONS

1. Describe internal and external integration.
2. Explain the need to connect to an ERP system.
3. Describe the need for integrating standards and methodologies.

6.7 CORPORATE (ENTERPRISE) PORTALS

Portals and corporate portals were defined in Chapter 2. Corporate portals facilitate collaboration with suppliers, customers, employees, and others. This section provides in-depth coverage of corporate portals, including their support of collaboration and business process management.

CORPORATE PORTALS: AN OVERVIEW

corporate (enterprise) portal
A gateway for entering a corporate Web site, enabling communication, collaboration, and access to company information.

A **corporate (enterprise) portal** is a gateway to a corporate Web site and other information sources that enables communication, collaboration, and access to company information. A portal is a personalized, single point of access through a Web browser to critical business

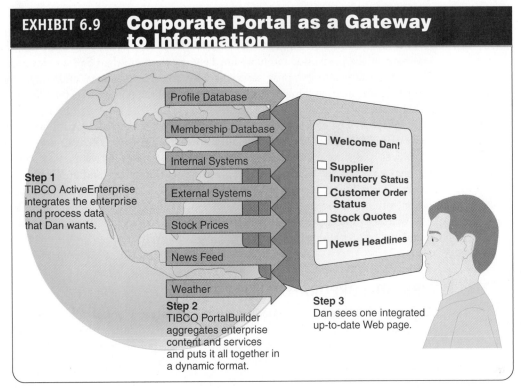

EXHIBIT 6.9   Corporate Portal as a Gateway to Information

Step 1
TIBCO ActiveEnterprise integrates the enterprise and process data that Dan wants.

Profile Database
Membership Database
Internal Systems
External Systems
Stock Prices
News Feed
Weather

☐ **Welcome Dan!**
☐ **Supplier Inventory Status**
☐ **Customer Order Status**
☐ **Stock Quotes**
☐ **News Headlines**

Step 2
TIBCO PortalBuilder aggregates enterprise content and services and puts it all together in a dynamic format.

Step 3
Dan sees one integrated up-to-date Web page.

Source: Courtesy of TIBCO Software, Inc., *tibco.com*.

information located inside and outside of an organization. In contrast with public commercial portals such as Yahoo! and MSN, which are gateways to general information on the Internet, corporate portals provide a single point of access to information and applications available on the intranets and extranets of a specific organization. Companies may have separate portals for outsiders and for insiders.

Corporate portals offer employees, business partners, and customers an organized focal point for their interactions with the firm. Through the portal, these people can have structured and personalized access to information across large, multiple, and disparate enterprise information systems, as well as the Internet. A schematic view of a corporate portal is provided in Exhibit 6.9.

Many large organizations are already implementing corporate portals. The reasons for doing so are to cut costs, to free up time for busy executives and managers, and to add to the bottom line. Corporate portals are especially popular in large corporations, as shown in the following examples:

Examples

P&G. The IT division of P&G developed a system for sharing documents and information over the company's intranet. The scope of this system later expanded into a global knowledge catalog to support the information needs of tens of thousands of its employees worldwide. Although the system helped provide required information, it also led to information overload. To solve this problem, P&G developed a corporate portal that provides personalized information to each employee. P&G's corporate portal, implemented by Plumtree, now owned by Oracle/BEA Systems, provides P&G's employees with marketing, product, and strategic information and with industry news documents numbering more than 1 million Web pages. The corporate portal can be accessed through a Web browser without having to navigate through all of the different divisions' Web sites. Employees can gain access to the required information through customized preset views of various information sources and links to other up-to-date information.

DuPont. DuPont implemented an internal portal to organize millions of pages of scientific information stored in information systems throughout the company. The initial version of the portal was intended for daily use by more than 550 employees to record product orders, retrieve progress reports for research products, and access customer-tracking information. However, today, DuPont uses the portal for its 60,000 employees in 30 business units in 70 countries.

Staples. The corporate portal for Staples, an office supply company, was launched in February 2000. It was immediately used by the company's 3,000 executives, knowledge workers, and store managers; by 2006, most of its employees were registered users. The portal serves as the interface to Staples' business processes and applications. It offers e-mail, scheduling, headlines on articles about the competition, new product information, internal news, job postings, and newsletters. The portal is used by top management as well as by managers of contracts, procurement, sales and marketing, human resources, and retail stores and by the company's three B2B Web sites.

TYPES OF CORPORATE PORTALS

Corporate portals are either generic or functional. Generic portals are defined by their audience (e.g., suppliers, employees). Functional portals are defined by the functionalities they offer. Portals are popular both in the private and the public sectors. See *BEA Systems* (2006) for an interesting array of both generic and functional portal applications.

Types of Generic Portals

The following five generic types of portals can be found in organizations.

Portals for Suppliers and Other Partners. Using such portals, suppliers can manage the inventories of their products that they sell to each specific customer online. They can view what they sold to the portal owner and for how much. They can see the inventory levels of the portal owner, and reorder material and supplies when they see that an inventory level is low; they can also collaborate with corporate buyers and other staff.

An example of a partners' portal is that of Samsung Electronic America's Digital IT. The company must keep in touch with 110,000 resellers and distributors. As part of its partner relationship management (PRM), Samsung developed a portal that enables it to personalize relationships with each partner (e.g., conduct promotions, provide special pricing, etc.). The portal helped to increase sales by 30 percent; related expenses dropped by 25 percent. For details, see Schneider (2004).

Customer Portals. Portals for customers can serve both businesses and individual customers. Customers can use these customer-facing portals to view products and services and to place orders, which they can later track. They can view their own accounts and see what is going on with their accounts in almost real time. They can pay for products and services, arrange for warranties and deliveries, and much more. These portals include a personalized part (e.g., under "My account"). For example, UNICCO Service Co., a cleaning, maintenance, and other services company, established a B2B customer portal, myUNICCO (my.unicco.com), for about 200 business customers who use the portal to track work quality, invoice processing, and compliance with contracts. The portal integrates many disparate software applications. It is also used by about 1,500 employees. For details of the portal and the benefits achieved, see Bennett (2007).

Employee Portals. Such portals are used for training, dissemination of company news and information, discussion groups, and more. Employee portals also are used for self-service activities, mainly in the human resources area (e.g., change of address forms, tax withholding forms, expense reports, class registration, and tuition reimbursement forms). Employees' portals are sometimes bundled with supervisors' portals in what are known as *workforce portals* (e.g., Workbrain Enterprise Workforce Management, workbrain.com).

Example. Shuffle Master is a casino equipment maker that depends on a large sales team that needed most accurate and timely information. Various enterprise software packages were attempted. However, they did not "talk" to each other; information was stale and not useful. The solution was an information portal for the employees built using Microsoft SharePoint server software that pulls data on demand from more than 60 databases, integrating them in one portal. For details, see Hildebrand (2006).

Executive and Supervisor Portals. These portals enable managers and supervisors to control the entire workforce management process—from budgeting to workforce scheduling. For example, Pharmacia (a Pfizer company) built a portal for its executives and managers worldwide, the Global Field Force Action Planner, which provides a single, worldwide view of the company's finances and performance. Business goals and sales figures are readily available on a consistent and transparent basis, allowing corporate management to evaluate and support field offices more effectively. Country managers also can share best practices with their peers and learn from other action plans, helping them to make better decisions.

Mobile Portals. Mobile portals are portals accessible via mobile devices, especially cell phones and PDAs. Most mobile portals are noncorporate information portals (i.e., they are commercial portals) such as DoCoMo's i-mode. (See the description of i-mode in Chapter 8.) Eventually, large corporations will introduce mobile corporate portals. Alternatively, they will offer access to their regular portals from wireless devices, which many already do (e.g., major airlines, banks, and retailers).

mobile portals
Portals accessible via mobile devices, especially cell phones and PDAs.

The Functionalities of Portals

Whoever their audience, the functionalities of portals range from simple information portals that store data and enable users to navigate and query those data, to sophisticated collaborative portals that enable collaboration.

Several types of functional portals exist: *Business intelligence portals* are used mostly by middle- and top-level executives and analysts to conduct business analyses and decision-support activities. For example, a business intelligence portal might be used to generate ad hoc reports or to conduct a risk analysis. *Intranet portals* are used mostly by employees for managing fringe benefits and for self-training. *Knowledge portals* are used for collecting knowledge from employees and for disseminating collected knowledge. (For an example of a business intelligence and knowledge management portal, see Kesner 2003.)

information portals
Portals that store data and enable users to navigate and query these data.

collaborative portals
Portals that allow collaboration.

CORPORATE PORTAL APPLICATIONS AND ISSUES

The top portal applications are as follows: knowledge bases and learning tools; business process support; customer-facing (frontline) sales, marketing, and services; collaboration and project support; access to data from disparate corporate systems; personalized pages for various users; effective search and indexing tools; security applications; best practices and lessons learned; directories and bulletin boards; identification of experts; news; and Internet access.

Exhibit 6.10 depicts a corporate portal framework. This framework illustrates the features and capabilities required to support various organizational applications.

Developing Portals

Before a company can develop a corporate portal, it must decide what the purpose and content of the portal will be and then justify it (Chapter 14). For some practical guidelines for determining a corporate portal strategy, see Smith (2004). Many vendors offer tools for building corporate portals as well as hosting services. Representative vendors are IBM, Microsoft, SAP, Oracle, BEA Systems, TIBCO (Portal Builder at tibco.com), Computer Associates (Jasmine II Portal at ca.com), Fujitsu (fujitsu.com), and Vignette (vignette.com).

Section 6.7 ▶ REVIEW QUESTIONS

1. What is a corporate portal?
2. List the types of corporate portals.
3. List five applications of portals.
4. List the major benefits of corporate portals.

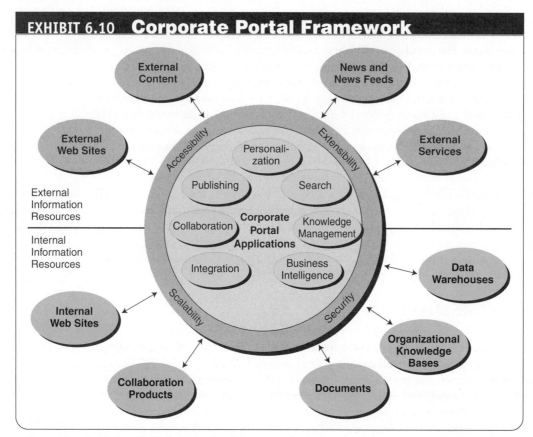

EXHIBIT 6.10 **Corporate Portal Framework**

Source: Compiled by N. Bolloju, City University of Hong Kong, from Aneja et al. (2000) and Koundadis (2000).

6.8 COLLABORATION-ENABLING ENVIRONMENTS AND TOOLS

As mentioned earlier, collaboration, knowledge management, and e-commerce are all vital ingredients in improving the performance of supply chains and organization. A large number of tools and methodologies are available that facilitate e-collaboration. The top business goals of the latest communication systems, known as *unified communication*, are to improve employee collaboration, increase employee efficiency, improve communication with customers to reduce travel expenses, improve global communication, and improve collaboration with suppliers (Thompson 2009). E-collaboration has many benefits, ranging from driving knowledge continuity to increase productivity, improve performance, and facilitate corporate strategies and decision making (see mindbuilt.com/ecs_benefits.php). According to Coleman and Levine (2008), there are more than 1,000 vendors of collaboration tools offering thousands of products. Here we cover only some representative ones. This section presents workflow technologies, groupware, and other collaboration-enabling tools, including Collaboration 2.0.

WORKFLOW TECHNOLOGIES AND APPLICATIONS

workflow

The movement of information as it flows through the sequence of steps that make up an organization's work procedures.

workflow systems

Business process automation tools that place system controls in the hands of user departments to automate information processing tasks.

Workflow is the movement of documents and tasks (and hence information) as they flow through the sequence of steps that make up an organization's work processes and procedures. Workflow embraces how tasks are to be structured and performed, who should perform them, how they should be logically ordered and sequenced, how tasks are to be tracked and monitored, and most important, what information is required and generated from all these tasks and how and where it needs to be recorded (en.wikipedia.org/wiki/Workflow). These are two major types of workflows: workflow systems and workflow management. They both create many applications, one of which is described in Online File W6.13.

Workflow systems essentially help organizations analyze, model, automate, and electronically enact aspects of workflow and task performance among workers both within and across multiple organizations in a supply chain. These types of systems may include features that enable task scheduling and prioritization, job routing, tracking and control, document imaging, document management, management reporting, and the like.

Workflow management involves the management of workflows so that documents, information, or tasks are passed from one participant to another in a way that is governed by the organization's rules or procedures to achieve required deadlines. Workflow management also involves tracking these tasks and documents, prioritizing tasks, and ensuring the allocation of adequate resources for the performance of these tasks. Workflow management involves all of the steps in a business process from start to finish, including all exception conditions. The key to workflow management is the tracking of process-related information and the status of each activity of the business process.

workflow management
The automation of workflows, so that documents, information, and tasks are passed from one participant to the next in the steps of an organization's business process.

COLLABORATION AND GROUPWARE: SOME BASIC CONCEPTS

Groupware refers to software products that support groups of people who share a common task or goal and collaborate on its accomplishment. Groupware implies the use of networks to connect people, even if they are in the same room. Many groupware products are available on the Internet or an intranet, enhancing the collaboration of a large number of people worldwide.

A number of different approaches and technologies are available for the support of groups on the Internet and intranets. Groupware tools and applications that support collaboration and conferencing are listed in Exhibit 6.11. We will present only some of them in this chapter.

groupware
Software products that support groups of people who share common tasks or goals and collaborate on their accomplishment.

EXHIBIT 6.11 Major Features in Collaboration and Conferencing Tools

General
- Built-in e-mail, messaging system, instant messaging
- Browser interface
- Joint Web-page creation
- Sharing of active hyperlinks
- File sharing (graphics, video, audio, or other)
- Built-in search functions (by topic or keyword)
- Workflow tools
- Use of corporate portals for communication, collaboration
- Shared screens
- Electronic decision rooms
- Peer-to-peer networks

Synchronous (same time)
- Webinar
- Webcast
- Videoconferencing, multimedia conferencing
- Audioconferencing
- Shared whiteboard, smart whiteboard
- Text chart
- Brainstorming, polling (voting), and other decision support (consensus builder, scheduler)

Asynchronous (different times)
- Threaded discussions
- Voice mail
- Users can receive/send e-mail, SMS
- Users can receive activity notification via e-mail
- Users can collapse/expand threads
- Users can sort messages (by date, author, or read/unread)
- Chat session logs
- Bulletin boards, discussion groups
- Use of blogs, wikis
- Web publishing
- Collaborative planning and/or design tools

We begin our presentation by introducing the concepts of unified communication, synchronous and asynchronous communication, virtual teams, and mass collaboration.

Synchronous Versus Asynchronous Communication

Collaboration tools may be *synchronous*, meaning that communication and collaboration are done in real time, or *asynchronous*, meaning that communication and collaboration are done by the participants at different times (e.g., by leaving a message on a bulletin board to be read and answered later), potentially from disparate locations. Web conferencing and instant messaging as well as Voice-over-Internet Protocol (VoIP) are associated with synchronous mode. Associated with asynchronous mode are *online workspaces* where participants can collaborate on joint designs or projects but work at different times. Vignette (vignette.com), Google (google.com), and Groove Networks (groove.net) allow users to set up online workspaces for sharing and storing documents. Many of the synchronous and some of the asynchronous tools offered by vendors are converging. Yahoo!, Google, and Skype, for example, offer text, voice, video, and photos on the same screen. Similar products are available for the enterprise. Groupware products are either stand-alone products that support one task (such as e-mail) or integrated kits that include several tools (such as e-mail and screen sharing). In general, groupware technology products are fairly inexpensive and can be easily incorporated into existing applications. Most of the software products are Web-based. The following describes some of the most common groupware collaboration tools.

Virtual Teams

virtual team
A group of employees using information and communications technologies to collaborate from different work bases.

A major objective of collaboration tools is to support *virtual teams*. A **virtual team**, also known as a *geographically dispersed team (GDT)*, is a group of individuals who work across time, space, and organizational boundaries with links strengthened by webs of communication technology. The members may have complementary skills and are committed to a common purpose, have interdependent performance goals, and share an approach to work for which they hold themselves mutually accountable. Virtual teams enable organizations to hire and retain the best people regardless of location. Members of virtual teams communicate electronically, so they may never meet face to face.

The Major Drivers of Virtual Teams. The explosion of virtual teams is driven by:

▶ Best employees may be located anywhere in the world.
▶ Workers demand personal flexibility (e.g., work at home).
▶ Workers demand increasing technological sophistication (can use sophisticated tools).
▶ A flexible organization is more competitive and responsive to the marketplace (faster executions).
▶ Workers tend to be more productive (i.e., they spend less time on commuting and travel).
▶ Trade and corporate activity are increasingly global in nature.
▶ The global workday is 24 hours versus 8 hours.
▶ Environments that require interorganizational cooperation as well as communication are emerging.

The Benefits of Virtual Teams. The benefits of virtual teams include:

▶ Some members of virtual teams do not need to come to the workplace; therefore, the company will not need to offer those workers office or parking space.
▶ Traveling expenses are reduced for employees.
▶ More people can be included in the labor pool, including part-timers and telecommuters.
▶ Air pollution and congestion are reduced because there is less commuting.
▶ Workers in organizations can be more flexible and work on flexible time.
▶ By working in virtual teams, physical handicaps are not a concern.
▶ Companies can procure the best talent without geographical restrictions.

Virtual teams have some limitations. Information technologies can remove some of them. For details, see en.wikipedia.org/wiki/Virtual_team.

Mass Collaboration

Mass collaboration is a form of collective action that occurs when large numbers of people work independently on a single project, often modular in its nature. Such projects typically take place on the Internet using social (Web 2.0) software and computer-supported collaboration tools such as wiki technologies.

A key aspect that distinguishes mass collaboration from other forms of large-scale collaboration is that the collaborative process is mediated by the content being created, as opposed to being mediated by direct social interaction like other forms of collaboration. Mass collaboration differs from mass cooperation and from online forums. For examples, and discussion, see en.wikipedia.org/wiki/Mass_collaboration.

ELECTRONIC MEETING SYSTEMS: FACE-TO-FACE SUPPORT AND VIRTUAL MEETINGS

Electronic meetings are an important area for collaboration. For decades, people have attempted to improve face-to-face meetings, which are known to have many potential pitfalls. Initially, people attempted to better organize group meetings by using a facilitator and established procedures (known as *group dynamics*). Numerous attempts have been made to use information technologies to improve meetings conducted in one room (see Nunamaker et al. 1997). The advancement of Web-based systems opens the door for improved electronically supported virtual meetings, where members are in different locations and even in different countries. Online meetings and presentation tools are provided by many companies, such as WebEx (webex.com).

One of the major benefits of electronic virtual meeting systems is the dramatic reductions in costs associated with business travel. For example, GoToMeeting allows you to give interactive animated presentations to remote customers and provides instant demos for a variety of situations.

Example. Clarity Corp. of Canada provides Internet-based business solutions (e.g., content management, workflow tools). It is a global company and its salespeople need to meet frequently with prospective clients. By using GoToMeeting tools, the company saves $60,000 to $120,000 annually on travel cost. In addition, productivity is up because the company can quickly generate meeting invitations complete with virtual meeting information. In addition, improvements in supporting technology, reductions in the price of the technology, and the acceptance of virtual meetings as a respected way of doing business are fueling the growth of virtual meetings.

Virtual meetings are supported by a variety of groupware tools. We begin our presentation of these tools with a discussion about the support provided to decision making, which is a major activity done in meetings. This is referred to as *group decision support systems*, and it supports both face-to-face meetings and virtual meetings.

virtual meetings
Online meetings whose members are in different locations, even in different countries.

Group Decision Support Systems

A group decision support system (GDSS) is an interactive, computer-based system that facilitates the solution of semistructured and unstructured problems by a group of decision makers. The goal of GDSSs is to improve the productivity of decision-making meetings, either by speeding up the decision-making process or by improving the quality of the resulting decisions, or both.

The major characteristics of a GDSS are as follows:

▶ Its goal is to support the group decision-making process by using IT tools to automate support subprocesses.

▶ It is a specially designed information system, not merely a configuration of already-existing system components. It can be designed to address one type of problem or a variety of group-level organizational decisions.

▶ It encourages idea generation, conflict resolution, and freedom of expression. It contains built-in mechanisms that discourage development of negative group behaviors, such as destructive conflict miscommunication and "groupthink."

▶ It aims to facilitate collaboration.

For more information, see Online File W6.14.

group decision support system (GDSS)
An interactive computer-based system that facilitates the solution of semistructured and unstructured problems by a group of decision makers.

Decision Theater

An interesting modern GDSS is the Decision Theater at Arizona State University in the U.S. The Decision Theater provides policy-makers and researchers access to state-of-the-art research-based analysis that can help them understand complicated variables for forecasting events. The theater consists of an interactive 3D environment using some of the most advanced graphics technologies, including a 260-degree, 7-screen panoramic display accommodating 25 people—an extraordinary benefit for collaborative and inclusive decision making. The true innovation of the theatre is that it is also user-friendly and accessible to local, regional, and national communities. The Decision Theater seeks to transform the ways decisions that impact our environment, health, workforce, and families are made. It is an immersive environment designed for collaboration. Participants are often arranged in a conference configuration to improve human engagement with each other and to interact with the visual information around them. They can take advantage of a variety of EC and IT tools to improve decision making, including 3D and geospatial visualization, simulation models, system dynamics, and computer-assisted tools for collecting participant input and collaboration. They also have access to the university's ongoing research databases in policy informatics, design, geography, computational science, business, psychology, and mathematics. For details, see decisiontheater.org.

REAL-TIME COLLABORATION TOOLS FOR VIRTUAL MEETINGS

The Internet, intranets, and extranets offer tremendous potential for real-time and synchronous interaction for people working in groups. Real-time collaboration (RTC) tools help companies bridge time and space to make decisions and to collaborate on projects. RTC tools support synchronous communication of graphical and text-based information. These tools are being used in distance training, product demonstrations, customer support, e-commerce, and sales applications. RTC tools can be purchased as stand-alone tools or used on a subscription basis (as offered by many vendors). One such tool is the *interactive whiteboard* (see Online File W6.15). Of special interest is the instant messenger tool that is used extensively in some companies (see en.wikipedia.org/wiki/Instant_messaging) and which can be used for teleconferencing as well (e.g., see messenger.yahoo.com).

Decision Theater at Arizona State University

Source: *decisiontheater.org/page/media.* Used with permission. Courtesy of Arizona State University.

Screen Sharing

In collaborative work, members frequently are in different locations. Using screen-sharing software, group members can work on the same document, which is shown on the PC screen of each participant. For example, two authors can work on a single manuscript. One may suggest a correction and execute it so that the other author can view the change. Collaborators can work together on the same spreadsheet or on the resultant graphics. Changes can be done by using the keyboard or by touching the screen. This capability can expedite the design of products, the preparation of reports and bids, and the resolution of conflicts.

A special screen-sharing capability is offered by Groove Networks (groove.net). Its product enables the joint creation and editing of documents on a PC (see Team Assignment 1).

screen-sharing software
Software that enables group members, even in different locations, to work on the same document, which is shown on the PC screen of each participant.

Sharing Documents and Workspaces

In addition to the conventional screen-sharing platforms, here are some other forms of sharing documents:

Examples. Sharing and collaboration by Google Docs and Office Live Workspace.

Sharing. Google Docs (docs.google.com) allows for easy sharing of files by just checking the checkbox next to the files and clicking *share* from the menu. Those who are invited to share can be invited as *collaborators* or *viewers*. Documents and presentations can be shared with 200 combined viewers, but spreadsheets have no limit.

Office Live Workspace. Office Live Workspace from Microsoft (office.microsoft.com) allows users to share documents or workspaces with others and mark them as *editors* or *viewers*. There is the option to allow "everyone to view this without signing in" and to "send me a copy of the sharing invitation." Files or workspaces can be shared with up to 100 others.

Collaboration. In Google Docs, collaborators can work together on files in real time. Ten people may edit and/or view a document or presentation at any given time. Fifty people can edit a spreadsheet at the same time.

Office Live Workspace allows for collaboration, but it is not real-time, online collaboration. If one user is editing a file, another will be informed that the file is "checked out." After one user finishes editing and saves the changes, the document is checked back in for other users to access.

Electronic teleconferencing is another major collaboration tool.

ELECTRONIC TELECONFERENCING

Teleconferencing is the use of electronic communication that enables two or more people at different locations to have a real-time conference. It is the simplest infrastructure for supporting a real-time virtual meeting. Several types of teleconferencing are possible. The oldest and simplest is a telephone conference call, wherein several people talk to each other from three or more locations. The biggest disadvantage of this is that it does not allow for face-to-face viewing. Also, participants in one location cannot see detailed graphs, charts, and pictures available at other locations very well. Although the latter disadvantage can be overcome by using a fax or scanning, this is a time-consuming, expensive, and frequently a poor-quality process. One solution is *video teleconferencing*.

teleconferencing
The use of electronic communication that allows two or more people at different locations to have a simultaneous conference.

Video Teleconferencing

In a video teleconference, participants in one location can see participants at other locations. Dynamic pictures of the participants can appear on a large screen or on a desktop computer. Originally, video teleconferencing was the transmission of live, compressed TV sessions between two or more points. Today, video teleconferencing (or *videoconferencing*) is a digital technology capable of linking various types of computers across networks.

With videoconferencing, participants can share data, voice, pictures, graphics, and animation. Data can be sent along with voice and video. Such data conferencing makes it possible to work on documents and to exchange computer files during videoconferences. This enables several geographically dispersed groups to work on the same project and to communicate by video simultaneously. Vendors of data conferencing tools include Microsoft, IBM (Lotus), NetSpoke, and WebEx.

video teleconference
Virtual meeting in which participants in one location can see participants at other locations on a large screen or a desktop computer.

data conferencing
Virtual meeting in which geographically dispersed groups work on documents together and exchange computer files during videoconferences.

Video teleconferencing offers various benefits. Two of them—providing the opportunity for face-to-face communication for participants that are in different locations and supporting several types of media during conferencing—have already been discussed. Video teleconferencing also improves employee productivity, cuts travel costs, conserves the time and energy of key employees, and increases the speed of business processes (such as product development, contract negotiation, and customer service). It improves the efficiency and frequency of communications and saves an electronic record of a meeting, enabling specific parts of a meeting to be reconstructed for future purposes. Video teleconferencing also makes it possible to hold classes at different locations. Finally, the tool can be used to interview candidates for employment.

Web Conferencing

Video conferencing can be done in special systems or simply on the Web. Such *Web conferencing* may include even thousands of people. It allows users to simultaneously view something on their computer screens, such as a sales presentation in Microsoft PowerPoint or a product drawing; interaction takes place via messaging or a simultaneous phone teleconference. Web conferencing is much cheaper than videoconferencing because it runs over the Internet. *Web seminars* that allow interactions and e-classroom are a special category.

The latest technological innovations support both B2B and B2C Web-conferencing applications. For example, banks in Alaska use video kiosks in sparsely populated areas instead of building branches that will be underutilized. The video kiosks operate on a bank's intranet and provide videoconferencing equipment for face-to-face interactions. A variety of other communication tools, such as online polls, whiteboards, and question-and-answer boards, may also be used. Such innovations can be used to educate staff members about a new product line or technology, to amplify a meeting with investors, or to walk a prospective client though an introductory presentation. People can use Web conferencing to view presentations, seminars, and lectures, and to collaborate on documents.

Web conferencing is becoming very popular. Almost all Web-conferencing products provide interactive whiteboarding and polling features and allow users to give presentations and demos and share applications. Popular Web-conferencing products are Centra EMeeting, Genesys Meeting Center, Microsoft Office Live Meeting, GoToMeetings (from Citrix), and WebEx Meeting Center. For information on the next generation of Web conferencing and its relationship to screen sharing, see Petersen (2007).

UNIFIED COMMUNICATION: INTEGRATION AND GROUPWARE SUITES

unified communication (UC)

Simplification of all forms of communication in the enterprise.

A *software suite* is created when several products are integrated into one system. It is known as **unified communication (UC)**, or *unified collaboration*. Integrating several technologies can save time and money for users. For example, Polycom (polycom.com) is combining video, voice, data, and Web-conferencing capabilities into a single solution. Polycom has formed an alliance with Microsoft to deliver collaborative solutions across a range of communication devices and applications to allow participants to connect and share information both inside and between organizations worldwide.

Unified communication allows an individual to send or receive a message on one medium and read it and reply to it on another. For example, one can receive a voice mail message and then read it in their e-mail box using a unified communications program.

The communication leveraged can include phone, e-mail, chat and IM, voice mail, video fax, teleconferencing, and presence awareness. The typical software program unifies these communication media so that any activity or message can be easily transferred to another. A successful implementation can automate and unifies all forms of human and device communications into a common user experience. Gains in efficiency can result through an optimization of business processes, enhancing human communications, reducing latency, managing flows, and eliminating device and media dependencies. For further details, see en.wikipedia.org/wiki/Unified_communications, and Coleman and Levine (2008).

Web Collaboration

Web collaboration solutions are emerging as one of the building blocks of those applications supporting knowledge workers' interactions-based business processes. For proof, scan the desktop of a successful, connected knowledge worker. You'll certainly find at least one instant messaging client, probably links to a Web-conferencing application or service, and possibly a shared workspace tool. In an echo of the user-driven PDA invasion of the late 1990s, knowledge workers are independently adopting collaboration tools because they meet an inescapable need. Web collaboration solutions facilitate and strengthen communication across departments, companies, and geographies; help knowledge workers build closer connections with customers and partners; and support them in making faster, more informed decisions.

Web-based online collaboration is growing rapidly with major support from most major vendors. For example, Lotus Sametime (from IBM) is an instant messaging system that is integrated with Web-conferencing tools from Web Dialogs. It is connected with the Lotus Connections communication system. Microsoft's SharePoint is another product; so are products from Cisco (with WebEx) and even Google with GAPE, a suite that includes Instant Messaging, Gmail, and related tools.

Example: How a Global Law Firm Collaborates. DLA Piper is a global law firms with 62 offices in 24 countries. The company's 32,000 attorneys, support employees, and clients need to communicate and collaborate with one another concerning legal documents, contracts, projects, and their administration.

A single legal case may involve as many as 300 lawyers from 40 different law firms for which documents need to be shared. Until 2007, the firm had been using e-mail and file sharing to share documents pertaining to cases. This proved to be both nonsecured and ineffective.

The solution was to use Web-based eRoom (from EMC Documentum) for sharing documents and files securely online. The EC system (eRoom and its complimentary software) creates redundancy and eliminates the hassles of e-mailing information back and forth.

The complementary software and hardware include Microsoft's Windows Server, HP Servers, Microsoft's SQL 2000 database, and several data security items (e.g., EMC's Authentica).

The e-collaboration system saves the firm more than 15,000 hours annually. It enables the easy creation of databases that are shared by all authorized people.

Web collaboration is often done with conferencing suites.

Collaboration Suites

Electronic teleconferencing is another major collaboration tool. Following are some additional examples of popular groupware suites.

Microsoft NetMeeting. Microsoft's groupware suite, NetMeeting, is a real-time collaboration package that supports whiteboarding, application sharing (of any Microsoft Windows application document), remote desktop sharing, file transfer, text chat, data conferencing, desktop audio, and videoconferencing. The NetMeeting suite is included in Windows 98 and more recent versions.

Windows Live Essentials. Out of the beta version in January 2009, Windows Live Essentials includes Messenger, Mail, Photo Gallery, Movie Maker, Writer (for blog services), Toolbar, Family Safety (to limit or block Web sites), Office Live Add-in (lets you save any of your Office documents directly to Microsoft Office Live Workspace, a Web-based program that lets you review, update, and comment on your documents from any computer that has an Internet connection), and Silverlight (a Web browser plug-in that enables rich Internet applications such as animation).

Lotus Notes/Domino. The Lotus Notes/Domino suite (from IBM) includes a document management system, a distributed client/server database, a basis for intranet and e-commerce systems, and a communication support tool. It enhances real-time communications with asynchronous electronic connections (e.g., e-mail and other forms of messaging). Group members using Lotus Notes/Domino may store all of their official memos, formal reports, and informal conversations related to particular projects in a shared database.

Lotus Notes Connections provides online collaboration capabilities, workgroup e-mail, distributed databases, bulletin whiteboards, text editing, (electronic) document management, workflow capabilities, instant virtual meetings, application sharing, instant messaging, consensus building, voting, ranking, and various application development tools. All of these capabilities are integrated into one environment with a graphic menu–based user interface. In 2007, Lotus added wikis, blogs, and other Web 2.0 tools to its products. See details in Taft (2007). At the beginning of 2009, there were more than 140 million Notes users worldwide (en.wikipedia.org/wiki/Lotus_Notes).

Lotus Sametime. IBM Lotus Sametime is an enterprise instant messaging, presence information awareness, and Web-conferencing application. Several related products exist. For example, Sametime Gateway adds support for communication with users of Google Talk, Yahoo! IM, and AOL. Another example is IBM Sametime 3-D, a mashup of IBM'S Lotus Sametime instant messaging and collaboration application with virtual worlds, such as OpenSim. IBM makes Sametime 3-D out of an enterprise application within the Lotus unified communications and collaborations suite.

Sametime 3-D lets users instant-message coworkers and launch into a 3D environment directly from within the Sametime chat session. The application creates a virtual meeting space on the fly, leveraging the typical properties found in a virtual environment, including avatars, presentation tools, and access to 3D objects.

Once Sametime 3-D is launched, collaborators can attach files, select a meeting space, type, and sign in using existing enterprise authentication tools. IBM will eventually allow meeting initiators to capture text chat, video record the meeting, and maintain a record of participants and materials. IBM Lotus Quick Place is integrated with Sametime, providing presence awareness of users available for conferencing.

GoToMeeting. GoToMeeting (from Citrix Corp.) allows PC and Mac users to host or attend online meetings anytime. Meeting organizers can start a meeting with one click or schedule meetings in seconds. There's no need to preinstall software or purchase separate accounts for attendees—they join your meeting instantly just by clicking the link you send them and participate as your free guests.

During your meeting, you can instantly share any file or application on your desktop, change presenters, or give keyboard and mouse control to attendees. Free integrated VoIP and phone conferencing make it easy to manage your audio connection, and you can even record meetings for future use or reference.

For information, watch the demo at gotomeeting.com and the GoToWebinar.

Microsoft SharePoint. This is a powerful and widely used collaboration and document management platform with comprehensive capabilities, but difficult to implement (Tucci 2008, *Collaboration 2.0* 2008). For details, see en.wikipedia.org/wiki/Microsoft_SharePoint#Collaborative_tools.

Novell GroupWise. Novell's GroupWise offers a wide range of communication and collaboration capabilities integrated with document management capabilities, including e-mail, calendaring, group scheduling, imaging, workflow, electronic discussions, and more.

Google's Collaboration Tools. The free Google Apps for Your Domain allows organizations to set up private-label versions of several of Google's collaboration services, including Gmail, Google Calendar, IM via Google Talk, and Google page creator. Basically, it's the Google services with your domain name instead of theirs. Here are some examples of free tools:

Google Calendar. Using Google Calendar, you can share private calendars (showing only what you want to show). Using Google's Docs, you can create Microsoft Office–compatible word-processing and spreadsheet files, invite people by e-mail to share documents, edit them simultaneously, and publish them to the world. Google Notebook allows users to compile libraries of clippings of parts or all of Web pages, including text, images, and links. The notebooks of reference and research materials can be shared.

Oracle Web Conferencing. This is a powerful suite that is combined with Oracle's service. It is a relatively new tool, but it is integrated with Oracle's enterprise applications.

EMC Documentum. EMC Documentum Knowledge Worker Solutions is a set of collaborative search technologies built on the Documentum repository, which provides a better way for knowledge workers to interact with information, people, and business processes that extend across organizational and information boundaries. It is based on eRoom software. By using these technologies, it is possible to create an agile organization for individuals, teams, and the enterprise at large so one can respond faster to evolving business requirements and changes. For details see *EMC/Documentum* (2008).

Cisco WebEx. WebEx (purchased by Cisco Systems for $2.9 billion) is a market leader in Web-conferencing technologies. Cisco is adding capabilities to WebEx in an attempt to compete with Microsoft's offering.

Other Representative Suites. Several companies offer similar collaboration tools. For example Zoho Notebook (from zoho.com) is a tool for collecting and collaborating on text line drawings, images, Web pages, video, RSS feeds, and other media.

Of special interest is Huddle Corp., which combines online collaboration, online project management, and document and idea sharing using social networking principles. You can add Huddle to your Facebook profile. With Huddle you can instantly create a network of collaborative team workspaces, each time bringing together the right team for the right activity. You can manage projects online; develop teams and relationships; or share ideas, files, and information. Because you are joining a network of workspaces, you can collaborate with hundreds of different people, allowing teams and organizations to meet globally in one place. To learn more, take the tour at huddle.net/what-is-huddle.

COLLABORATION 2.0

Collaboration 2.0 refers to the technology and tools used for collaboration in the Web 2.0 world and in Enterprise 2.0. These are in sync with social networking and user-generated content. For comprehensive coverage, see Coleman and Levine (2008). The major technologies used in Collaboration 2.0 follow.

Collaborative Workspace

A collaborative workspace or *shared workspace* is an interconnected environment in which all the participants in dispersed locations can access and interact with each other just as inside a single entity. The environment may be supported by electronic communications and groupware, which enable participants to overcome space and time differentials. These are typically enabled by a shared mental model, common information, and a shared understanding by all of the participants regardless of physical location. It is a part of a *collaborative environment* that includes tools such as e-mail, instant messaging, application sharing, video conferencing, workflow management, wikis, and blogs. For further information see en.wikipedia.org/wiki/Collaborative_workspace.

Online workspaces are used to support corporate development, project management, financing, collaborating with business partners, corporate governance, and for legal issues (such as contract management). The key benefits of using collaborative workspaces are:

▶ Fast, flexible access to information
▶ Reduced transaction and process time
▶ Cost savings on hardware and software
▶ Better control due to the ability to have a single document
▶ Better information security

Instant Messaging (IM)

Instant messaging technologies create the possibility of real-time text-based communication between two or more participants over the Internet or some form of internal network/intranet. What separates chat and instant messaging from e-mail is the perceived synchronicity of the communication by the user—chat happens in real time.

Many IM services have additional features, such as the immediate receipt of acknowledgement or reply, group chatting, conference services (including voice and video), webcam service, conversation logging and file transfer, and presence awareness.

IM is becoming popular in enterprise applications such as Live Chat. For comprehensive coverage, see en.wikipedia.org/wiki/Instant_messaging. An integral part of many IM systems is presence awareness.

Collaboration 2.0
The technology and tools used for collaboration in the Web 2.0 world and in Enterprise 2.0 that are in sync with social networking and user-generated content.

collaborative workspace
An interconnected environment in which all the participants in dispersed locations can access and interact with each other just as inside a single entity.

instant messaging
Technologies that create the possibility of real-time text-based communication between two or more participants over the Internet/intranet.

Presence Information and Awareness

presence information
Status indicator that conveys ability and willingness of a potential communication partner.

Presence information is a status indicator that conveys ability and willingness of a potential communication partner. A user's client provides presence information (presence state) via a network connection to a presence service, which is stored in what constitutes his or her personal availability record and can be made available for distribution to other users (called *watchers*) to convey availability for communication. Presence information has wide application in many communication services and is one of the innovations driving the popularity of instant messaging and VoIP applications. For details, see en.wikipedia.org/wiki/Presence_information.

Mobile Collaboration in the Web 2.0 Environment

With millions of employees on the road, it became necessary to develop mobile support systems. Probably the most important one is mobile e-mail. Ginevan (2008) provides an assessment of the benefits and risks (e.g., security) of mobile e-mail, including assessment of the major vendors, their groupware products, and the integration platforms and vendors. Several of these are Web 2.0 technologies.

Web 2.0 tools and environments are actively used by younger people who are active users of social networking and mobile devices. Here are two examples:

 ▶ **Mobile social networking service.** myGamma.com, by BuzzCity, is a mobile Internet community where people worldwide exchange ideas. Using mobiles, members interact via their personal profiles, blogs, discussion groups, and many other community features.
 ▶ **Mobile handset.** The 3 Skypephone mobile is a small handset with Skype functionality built in, the first of its kind in the world. Skype contacts and calls are completely integrated into the address book, adding presence awareness to the consumer's phonebook. The 3 Skypephone's Internet browser brings powerful applications to the mobile world, using a mixture of IP and 3G voice technology.

mobile instant messaging
Messaging service that transposes the desktop messaging experience to the usage scenario of being on the move.

Mobile Instant Messaging. Mobile instant messaging is a presence-enabled messaging service that aims to transpose the desktop messaging experience to the usage scenario of being on the move. Although several core ideas of the desktop experience apply to a connected mobile device, others do not. Users usually only look at their phone's screen; presence-status changes might occur under different circumstances., Several functional limits exist based on the fact that the vast majority of mobile communication devices are chosen by their users to fit into the palm of their hand.

Mobile Unified Communication. Unified communication, described earlier, is available to mobile users. For benefits, implementation, deployment options, products, and resources, see BlackBerry's E-Guide at research.pcpro.co.uk/detail/RES/1221059939_583.html.

Voice-over-IP and Instant Video

voice-over-IP (VoIP)
Communication systems that transmit voice calls over Internet Protocol–based networks.

Voice-over-IP (VoIP) refers to communication systems that transmit voice calls over Internet Protocol–based networks. Corporations are moving their phone systems to Internet standards to cut costs and boost efficiency. VoIP also is known as *Internet telephony*. Most browsers provide for VoIP capabilities. Users use their browsers to receive telephone calls initiated on the Internet (with a microphone and special VoIP software, which may be provided with the sender's browser). The market leader in VoIP is Skype, which offers unlimited free voice, video, and instant messaging communication between users, provided they also use the Yahoo! Messenger, Google, some social networks sites, and many others offer similar services (see about.skype.com/2008/04/skype_announces_unlimited_long.html).

The following are benefits of VoIP communications.

For the business:

 ▶ Allows chief information officers to explore different deployment options for company's communications needs
 ▶ Lowers total cost of ownership through voice/data convergence
 ▶ Lowers operational costs through use of integrated applications

> ▶ Reduces hardware requirements on the server side for certain applications (e.g., VoIP)
> ▶ Provides a holistic approach to security, enhanced by encryption and identity management
> ▶ Helps streamline workflows by empowering companies to communications-enable different business processes
> ▶ Enables optimized conferencing tools to replace business travel

For the user:

> ▶ Eliminates unwanted interruptions and unproductive actions by intelligently filtering communications
> ▶ Provides access to real-time presence information, which helps speed decision making
> ▶ Initiates ad hoc conferencing/collaboration sessions without the need to prearrange separate audio or videoconferencing bridges
> ▶ Enables participation in conferencing sessions quickly and easily via a variety of mobile devices

VoIP is offered today by many companies, and it is combined with data and video in what was described earlier as unified communication. Recently, UC become popular due to built-in Webcams and availability of services from Yahoo! Messenger, MSN, and Google.

Instant Video. The spread of VoIP and IM has led to the idea of linking people via both voice and video. Called *instant video*, the idea is for a kind of video chat room. It allows users to chat in real time and see the person(s) with whom they are communicating. A simple way to do this is to add video cameras (Webcam) to the participants' computers. A more sophisticated and better-quality approach is to integrate an existing online videoconferencing service with instant messaging software, creating a service that offers the online equivalent of a videophone.

Blogs, Wikis, Virtual Worlds, Forums, and Other Tools

Several other tools are used in Collaboration 2.0. We described blogs, wikis, micro blogs, and virtual worlds in Chapter 2. In Chapter 9, we will describe some tools that are used in social networking sites such as forums and discussion groups. DrKW (see Case 6.3) is an early adopter of blogs, wikis, instant messaging, and videoconferencing.

Other Tools. Other tools include Basecamp (basecamphq.com), which provides project management and collaboration tools; Writeboard (writeboard.com), which lets you share Web-based text documents; and Campfire (campfirenow.com), a Web-based group chat. Campfire includes a utility that can be used as a virtual blackboard for conference calls.

IMPLEMENTATION ISSUES FOR ONLINE COLLABORATION

Several implementation issues must be addressed when planning online collaboration. First, to connect business partners, an organization needs an effective collaborative environment. Such an environment is provided by groupware suites such as Lotus Notes/Domino or Cybozu Share360 (share360.com). Another issue is the need to connect collaborative tools with file management products on an organization's intranet. Two products that offer such connection capabilities are e/pop Web-conferencing and online meeting software (wiredred.com) and eRoom's server (documentum.com).

In addition, protocols are required to create a truly collaborative environment. Protocols are needed to integrate different applications and for standardizing communication. One such protocol is WebDAV (Web Distributed Authoring and Versioning protocol; see webdav.org).

CASE 6.3
EC Application

WIKIS, BLOGS, AND CHATS SUPPORT COLLABORATION AT DrKW

Dresdner Kleinwort Wasserstein (DrKW) is the international investment banking arm of Dresdner Bank. Headquartered in London and Frankfurt, DrKW provides capital market and advisory services, employing 6,000 people worldwide—in New York, Paris, Luxembourg, Tokyo, Singapore, and Hong Kong.

Because their employees are culturally diverse and geographically distributed, DrKW wanted them to have a full set of collaboration tools—not just e-mail and telephones. Blogs, wikis, instant messaging, chat, and audio/videoconferencing let workers select and switch communication modes depending on which mode is appropriate at any given time. DrKW installed a primitive open-source wiki in 1997. The company reviewed Socialtext products in March 2004 and ran a small pilot on the hosted service in July 2004. Based on the pilot, DrKW decided to upgrade to Socialtext Enterprise, which was installed in the third quarter of 2004.

DrKW chose Socialtext because it needed strong authentication, permissions, information sharing, and communication among the various company silos. DrKW is highly regulated, requiring that all bank communications be recorded, archived, searchable, and retrievable for auditors or other investigators. Those communications are business records, which must be retained according to financial regulations such as the Sarbanes-Oxley Act of 2002.

Usage and Benefits

The Information Strategy team was the first group to use Socialtext, followed by IT Security. The teams use it as a communications tool, collective discussion tool, and storehouse for documents and information. The User-Centered Design (UCD) team uses external-facing applications. The wiki allows team members to upload information easily, which encourages collaboration and increases transparency, which is not possible with e-mail messages. UCD also uses the wiki to explain its function and why it's important to the entire DrKW community.

The wiki tracks project development so that the teams and management know the status of projects and progress, who is doing what, and what actions should follow.

The Equity Delta1 equity financing team is one of the largest users of the wiki. This unit deals with loans, equity swaps, and so on. The wiki eliminates the burden of mountains of e-mails, shows the development of business plans, and stores commonly used information. The team creates an open forum where anyone can post views, comments, and questions on given subjects; publish and share white papers and bulletins; coordinate sales and marketing activities; and organize important team tasks.

One of the most enthusiastic user groups is Digital Markets, the division responsible for developing, deploying, and operating DrKW's online products and services. Digital Markets combines front office, support, and IT specialists in one unit. It has a wide cross-section of users who must all be brought together on the same page.

The E-Capital London Team develops back-end applications for the Digital Markets business line and supports a number of legacy systems. They share and develop new system specifications and product overviews, and help with documentation. The wiki provides an instantly editable collaboration platform that simplifies the publication process. The version history function is useful for product specs where it is important to retain a complete audit trail.

Users keep others informed by posting timely notes such as "this is what we're thinking about now." The limitation is that the wiki works only when everyone supports and is comfortable in such an open environment. Wikis fail in organizations where people are afraid to talk and publish. It works in DrKW, especially in Digital Markets where people willingly say, "Look, here it is." Their openness stimulates good debate and allows them to generate great ideas.

Sources: Compiled from Socialtext (2004) and *BusinessWeek Online* (2005).

Questions

1. What capabilities of the wiki are not available in regular e-mail?

2. Why are so many tools—blogs, wikis, instant messaging, chat, and audio/videoconferencing—needed?

3. How does the wiki increase employee productivity? What types of waste does it reduce?

4. What are some social, cultural, and ethical issues involved in the use of wikis for business collaboration?

Collaboration 2.0 tools are relatively inexpensive, and workers can use them without IT support or approval. Yet some question their usefulness. Executives, especially in IT, are still waiting to see more evidence of benefits.

Finally, note that online collaboration is not a panacea for all occasions or all situations. Oftentimes, a face-to-face meeting is a must. People sometimes require the facial cues and the physical closeness that no computer system can currently provide. (A technology called *pervasive computing* attempts to remove some of these limitations by interpreting facial cues.

For more, see Chapter 8.) However, face-to-face meetings may sometimes be improved by collaborative technologies, such as GDSS.

Section 6.8 ▶ REVIEW QUESTIONS

1. Define workflow systems and management.
2. Explain the types of workflow systems and the benefits of such systems.
3. List the major groupware tools.
4. Describe GDSSs and electronic meeting systems.
5. Define virtual teams and virtual meetings and describe how they are supported.
6. Describe the various types of electronic teleconferencing, including Web-based conferencing.
7. Describe VoIP, screen sharing, and collaborative workspace.
8. Describe integrated suites and their benefits.
9. Define virtual teams, mass collaboration, and unified communication.

MANAGERIAL ISSUES

Some managerial issues related to this chapter are as follows.

1. **How difficult is it to introduce e-collaboration?** Dealing with the technology may be the easy part. Tackling the behavioral changes needed within an organization and its trading partners may be the greater challenge. Change management requires an understanding of the new interdependencies being constructed and the new roles and responsibilities that must be adapted in order for the enterprise and its business partners to collaborate. Finally, e-collaboration costs money and needs to be justified. This may not be an easy task due to the intangible risks and benefits involved.

2. **How much can be shared with business partners?** Can they be trusted? Many companies are sharing forecast data and actual sales data. But when it comes to allowing real-time access to product design, inventory, and interface to ERP systems, there may be some hesitation. It is basically a question of security and trust. The more information that is shared, the better the collaboration. However, sharing information can lead to the giving away of trade secrets. In some cases, there is a cultural resistance against sharing (some employees do not like to share information even within their own organization). The value of sharing needs to be carefully assessed against its risks.

3. **Who benefits from vendor-managed inventory?** The vendor-managed inventory (VMI) system in collaborative planning, forecasting, and replenishment (CPFR) requires the supplier side to take the highest responsibility without the guarantee of sales. However, small suppliers may not have the ability to systematically manage inventory well. In this case, the large buyer will need to support the inventory management system on behalf of the suppliers. Sensitive issues must be agreed upon when initiating VMI. One such issue is who takes responsibility for unsold items due to the wrong demand forecast.

4. **What are the costs and benefits of RFID?** RFID in supply chain management has big potential, but the benefits and costs should be well designed. The cost of tagging and managing individual items rather than type of items can be costly; so, the most cost-effective combination of RFID and bar code portfolio will be necessary for quite a while.

5. **Who is in charge of our portal and intranet content?** Because content is created by many individuals, two potential risks exist. First, proprietary corporate information may not be secure enough, so unauthorized people may have access to it. Second, appropriate intranet "netiquette" must be maintained; otherwise, unethical or even illegal behavior may develop. Therefore, managing content, including frequent updates, is a must (see Chapter 13).

6. **Who will design the corporate portal?** Corporate portals are the gateways to corporate information and knowledge. Appropriate portal design is a must, not only for easy and efficient navigation but also because portals portray the corporate image to employees and to business partners who are allowed access to it. Design of the corporate portal must be carefully thought out and approved by management.

7. **Should we conduct virtual meetings?** Virtual meetings can save time and money and if properly planned can bring as good or even better results than face-to-face meetings. Although not all meetings can be conducted online, many can. The supporting technology is getting cheaper and better with time.

SUMMARY

In this chapter, you learned about the following EC issues as they relate to the chapter's learning objectives.

1. **The e-supply chain, its characteristics, and its components.** Digitizing and automating the flow of information throughout the supply chain and managing it via the Web results in an entity called the e-supply chain. The major parts of the e-supply chain are the upstream (to suppliers), internal (in-house processes), and downstream (to distributors and customers) components. E-supply chain activities include replenishment, procurement, collaborative planning, collaborative design/development, e-logistics, and use of exchanges or supply webs—all of which can be Internet based.

2. **Supply chain problems and their causes.** The major supply chain problems are too large or too small inventories, lack of supplies or products when needed, the need for rush orders, deliveries of wrong materials or to wrong locations, and poor customer service. These problems result from uncertainties in various segments of the chain (e.g., in transportation), from mistrust of partners and a lack of collaboration and information sharing, and from difficulties in forecasting demand (e.g., the bullwhip effect). Also, lack of appropriate logistics infrastructure can result in problems.

3. **Solutions to supply chains problems provided by EC.** EC technologies automate and expedite order taking, speed order fulfillment, provide for e-payments, properly control inventories, provide for correct forecasting and thus better scheduling, and improve collaboration among supply chain partners. Of special interest is the emerging RFID and RuBee technologies that could revolutionize supply chain management.

4. **RFID tags and Rubee.** Replacing bar codes with wireless technologies can greatly improve locating items along the supply chain quickly. These technologies have many benefits and few limitations. They will revolutionize supply chain management.

5. **C-commerce: Definitions and types.** Collaborative commerce (c-commerce) refers to a planned use of digital technology by business partners. It includes planning, designing, researching, managing, and servicing various partners and tasks, frequently along the supply chain. Collaborative commerce can be between different pairs of business partners or among many partners participating in a collaborative network.

6. **Collaborative planning and CPFR.** Collaborative planning concentrates on demand forecasting and on resource and activity planning along the supply chain. Collaborative planning tries to synchronize partners' activities. CPFR is a business strategy that attempts to develop standard protocols and procedures for collaboration. Its goal is to improve demand forecasting by collaborative planning in order to ensure delivery of materials when needed. In addition to forecasting, collaboration in design is facilitated by IT, including groupware. Product lifecycle management (PLM) enables manufacturers to plan and control product-related information.

7. **Integration along the supply chain.** Integration of various applications within companies and between business partners is critical to the success of companies. To simplify integration, one can use special software as well as employ standards such as XML. Web Services is a promising new approach for facilitating integration.

8. **Types and roles of corporate portals.** The major types of corporate portals are those for suppliers, customers, employees, and supervisors. There also are mobile portals (accessed by wireless devices). Functional portals such as knowledge portals and business intelligence portals provide the gateway to specialized knowledge and decision making. Corporate portals provide for easy information access, communication, and collaboration.

9. **Collaborative tools.** Hundreds of different collaboration tools are available. The major groups of tools are workflow and groupware. In addition, specialized tools ranging from group decision support systems (GDSSs) to devices that facilitate product design also are available.

10. **Collaboration 2.0.** Collaboration with Web 2.0 tools and in social networks adds a social dimension that could improve communication, participation, and trust. There are many new tools, some of which are being added to traditional collaboration tools. Better collaboration may improve supply chain operation, knowledge management, and performance.

KEY TERMS

QUESTIONS FOR DISCUSSION

1. Define e-supply chain and discuss its importance in supporting organizational performance.

2. Does a company's supply chain include the movement of money, materials, and information within the company? How are they interrelated?

3. Discuss the relationship between c-commerce and corporate portals.

4. Compare and contrast a commercial portal (such as Yahoo!) with a corporate portal.

5. Discuss the major considerations that must be taken into account when implementing VMI.

6. Discuss the difference between a portal, a marketplace, and an e-hub. Do you think that there are any significant differences?

7. Discuss the contribution of Web-enabled ERP systems to effective supply chain management.

8. Explain the need for groupware to facilitate collaboration.

9. Discuss the need for workflow systems as a companion to e-commerce.

10. It is said that c-commerce signifies a move from a transaction focus to a relationship focus among supply chain members. Discuss.

11. Discuss the need for virtual meetings.

12. Discuss how CPFR can lead to more accurate forecasting and how it can resolve the bullwhip effect.

13. Describe the advantages of RFID over a regular bar code in light of supply chain management.

14. Compare a collaborative hub and a collaborative network.

15. Enter mobileworldcongress.com and web20.telecom tv.com. List and discuss three mobile communication-related issues of current interest.

INTERNET EXERCISES

1. Enter ca.com/products and register. Take the Clever Path Portal Test Drive. (Flash Player from Macromedia is required.) Then enter ibm.com and bea.com. Prepare a list of the major products available for building corporate portals.

2. Enter bea.com. Find the white papers about corporate portals and their justification. Prepare a report based on your findings.

3. Enter doublediamondsoftware.com/product_ overview.htm. Identify all potential B2B applications and prepare a report about them.

4. Investigate the status of CPFR. Start at vics.org/committees/cpfr, google.com, and yahoo.com. Also enter supply-chain.org and find information about CPFR. Write a report on the status of CPFR.

5. Enter sap.com and bea.com, and find the key capabilities of their enterprise portals. List the benefits of using five of the capabilities of portals.

6. Enter nokia.com, motorola.com, and symbolic.com. Identify the B2E products you find at these sites. Prepare a list of the different products.

7. Enter i2.com and review its products. Explain how some of the products facilitate collaboration.

8. Enter collaborate.com and read about recent issues related to collaboration. Prepare a report.

9. Enter kolabora.com or mindjet.com. Find out how collaboration is done. Summarize the benefits of this site to the participants.

10. Enter vignette.com or cybozu.com and read the company vision for collaborative commerce. Then view the demo. Explain in a report how the company facilitates c-commerce.

11. Enter lotus.com and find the collaboration-support products. How do these products support groups?

12. Enter supplyworks.com and clickcommerce.com. Examine the functionalities provided for supply chain improvements (the inventory management aspects).

13. Enter 3m.com and smarttech.com. Find information about their whiteboards. Compare the products. (Hint: See Online File W6.15.)

14. Enter electronicssupplychain.org then click "Resources." Find new information on supply chain automation.

15. Enter epiqtech.com and find information about products related to this chapter.

16. Enter future-store.org and find the progress on the use of RFID and other tools in supply chain improvements in retailing.

17. Enter pocketvideo.com and microsoft.com/windows mobile/en-us/devices/default.mspx. Examine the demos. List the capabilities.

18. Learn about Lotus Sametime Standard by visiting www-01.ibm.com/software/lotus/sametime. Click "View the Screenshots."Prepare a report of the software's capabilities that support real-time collaboration.

19. Enter campfirenow.com. Explore its capabilities and write a report.

TEAM ASSIGNMENTS, PROJECTS, AND CLASS DISCUSSIONS

1. Have each team download a free copy of Groove from groove.net. Install the software on the members' PCs and arrange collaborative sessions. What can the free software do for you? What are its limitations?

2. Each team is assigned to an organization. The team members will attempt to identify several supply chains, their components, and the partners involved. Draw the chains and show which parts can be treated as e-supply chain parts.

3. Each team is assigned to a major vendor of corporate portals, such as BEA, TIBCO, IBM, or Oracle. Each team will check the capabilities of the corporate portal tools and try to persuade the class that its product is superior.

4. Each team is assigned to a major collaboration suite (from Lotus, Microsoft, Oracle, Cisco/WebEx, Google Apps, and so forth). Prepare a list of capabilities and present arguments for the superiority of the suite.

5. Each team studies a vendor that supports mobile communication, messaging, and collaboration (e.g., Microsoft, Sybase, Motorola, Nokia, Research-in-Motion). Prepare a report on the capabilities of the major products.

6. Address the following topics in a class discussion:

   a. Describe how the advent of the Internet in the late 1990s has affected supply chain management. Include in your answer the contribution of the Internet to the following aspects and challenges:
      ▶ Globalization
      ▶ Outsourcing, including business process outsourcing
      ▶ Increasingly demanding customers
      ▶ Diminishing product life cycles

   b. Discuss the proposition that competition in contemporary business is best described and conceptualized as competition between industry supply chains rather than between individual corporations.

   c. Discuss the importance of taking a holistic view of supply chain management rather than simply approaching supply chain management from a business-process and IT viewpoint.

   d. Is Collaboration 2.0 useful?

   e. What is the strategic value of mobile collaboration?

Closing Case

HOW WAL-MART USES EC IN ITS SUPPLY CHAIN

Wal-Mart Stores, Inc., is the world's largest public corporation by revenue and the largest private employer in the world (about 2,100,000 employees in 2008). Also in 2008, the company operated more than 7,000 stores around the world (discount, supercenters, neighborhood markets, and Sam's Clubs). Its revenue exceeded $400 billion, with net income of about $15 billion. For further details, see *en.wikipedia.org/wiki/Walmart* and *walmartfacts.com*. A major determinant of the success of Wal-Mart is its IT and EC-driven supply chain.

Wal-Mart's Supply Chain

Wal-Mart pioneered the world's most efficient technology-driven supply chain. Let's look at some of its components and innovations.

Wal-Mart invited its major suppliers to co-develop profitable supply chain partnerships. These partnerships are intended to amplify product flow efficiency and, in turn, Wal-Mart's profitability. A case in point is Wal-Mart's supplier relationship with P&G, a major supplier of consumer products. This relationship enables interoperation between the companies' systems at transactional, operational, and strategic levels. Since 1988, the relationship has evolved to yield tremendous value to both companies, and their mutual business has grown manifold. Examples of intercompany innovations are vendor-managed inventory (VMI), CPFR, and RFID. Let's look closer at Wal-Mart and some of its supply chain–related initiatives.

Inventory Management

Inventory management is done at the corporate and individual store levels. In both cases, computerized systems facilitate proper inventory levels and reordering of goods. Stores manage their inventories and order goods as needed instead of the company using a centralized control. By networking with suppliers, a quick replenishment order could be placed via Wal-Mart's own satellite communication system. This way, suppliers can quickly deliver the goods directly to the store concerned or to the nearest distribution center. The suppliers are able to reduce costs and prices due to better coordination. Wal-Mart invested $4 billion into a *retail link* collaboration system. About 20,000 suppliers use the retail link system to monitor the sales of their goods at individual stores and accordingly replenish inventory. The system has been upgraded several times with Web-enabled technologies. Wal-Mart also uses advanced EC-based communication and processing systems, and it has extensive disaster recovery plans, enabling the company to track goods and inventory levels when disaster strikes. This ensures uninterrupted service to Wal-Mart

customers, suppliers, and partners. With its major suppliers, Wal-Mart has VMI agreements.

Managing Distribution Centers and Forklift Management

Wal-Mart uses hundreds of distribution centers worldwide. Goods are transported to these centers from suppliers and then stored. When needed, goods are reorganized in trucks and delivered to the stores. Wal-Mart uses a computerized warehouse management system (WMS) to track and manage the flow of goods through its distribution centers. This system manages not only the forklifts within the distribution center, but also Wal-Mart's fleet of trucks.

Wireless Industrial Vehicle Management System

Forklifts and other industrial vehicles are the workhorses of material handling within the distribution centers and thus are critical factors in facility productivity. In each center, Wal-Mart installs a comprehensive wireless Vehicle Management System (VMS).

The major capabilities of this system (from I.D. Systems, Inc., *id-systems.com*) are listed here and organized by productivity and safety features:

Productivity Features:

- A two-way text messaging system that enables management to divert material-handling resources effectively and quickly to the point of activity where they are needed the most.
- Software that displays a graphical facility map, which enables not only near real-time visibility of vehicle/operator location and status, but also the ability to play back the trail of a vehicle movement over any slice of time. The system also helps to locate vehicles in real time.
- Unique data on peak vehicle utilization that enables optimal computerized fleet "right sizing." It also helps work assignments and communication, especially in response to unexpected changes and needs.

Safety Features:

- Electronic safety checklist system for identifying and responding to vehicles' problems.
- Access authorization to drive certain vehicles by trained drivers only.

- ▶ Impact sensing that provides a broad choice of automated management responses, from alerting a supervisor with visual or audible alarms, to generating a warning icon on a graphical software display of the facility, to sending an e-mail or text message to management.
- ▶ Automatic reporting and prioritization of emergency repair issues that are identified on electronic safety checklists, where operator responses are flagged by severity of the vehicle condition.
- ▶ Wireless, remote lock-out of vehicles that are unsafe or in need of repair.

For further details see the Wal-Mart case at *id-systems.com*.

Warehouse Management System

A *warehouse management system* (WMS) is a key part of the supply chain that primarily aims to control the movement and storage of material within a warehouse and process the associated transactions including receiving, shipping, and in-warehouse picking. The system also optimizes stock levels based on real-time information about the usage of parts and materials.

Warehouse management systems often utilize information technologies, such as bar code scanners, mobile computers, Wi-Fi, and RFID to efficiently monitor the flow of products. Once data has been collected, there is either a batch synchronization with, or real-time wireless transmission to, a central database. The database can then provide useful reports about the status of goods in the warehouse.

Warehouse management systems can be stand-alone systems, or modules in an ERP system (e.g., at SAP and Oracle) or in a supply chain management suite. The role and capabilities of WMS are ever-expanding. Many vendors provide WMS software (e.g., see *qssi-wms.com*). For a comprehensive coverage of WMS see Piasecki (2006).

Fleet and Transportation Management

Several thousands of company-owned trucks move goods from the distribution centers to stores. Wal-Mart uses several EC and IT tools for managing the trucks. These include a decision support system (DSS) for optimal scheduling, dispatching, and matching of drivers with vehicles; a computerized system for efficient purchasing and use of gasoline; a computerized preventive maintenance management system for efficient maintenance and repairs procedures; and a system that helps maximize the size of truck necessary for any given shipment. The company is experimenting with the use of a wireless GPS/GIS system for finding the trucks' locations at any given time.

Decisions about *cross-docking* are computerized. Cross-docking involves the elimination of the distribution center and instead uses a direct delivery to the customer after picking and sorting the goods from the suppliers. This is possible only if the suppliers ensure delivery within a specified time frame.

Going Green

Wal-Mart is spending $500 million a year to increase fuel efficiency in Wal-Mart's truck fleet by 25 percent over the next 3 years and plan to double it within 10 years.

WAL-MART and RFID Adoption

One of Wal-Mart's major initiatives in the supply chain area is pioneering the use of RFID. In the first week of April 2004, Wal-Mart launched its first live test of RFID tracking technology. Using one distribution center and seven stores, 21 products from participating vendors were used in the pilot test.

Wal-Mart set a January 2005 target for its top 100 suppliers to place RFID tags on cases and pallets destined for Wal-Mart stores. The system expanded to all major suppliers during 2006 through 2009, especially in the B2B Sam's Club stores. It improves flow along the supply chain, reduces theft, increases sales, reduces inventory costs (by eliminating overstocking), and provides visibility and accuracy throughout Wal-Mart's supply chain.

To encourage more suppliers to cooperate, in January 2008 Wal-Mart started to charge $2 per case or pallet not tagged (see Hayes-Weier 2008). In addition to requiring RFID tags from its suppliers, Wal-Mart is installing the technology internally. According to Scherago (2006), more than 2,000 Wal-Mart stores were RFID-enabled with gate readers and handhelds at loading docks, facility entrances, stock rooms, and sales floors by the end of 2006. According to Songini (2007), the emphasis now is on the use of RFID in stores rather than in distribution hubs.

The RFID initiative is an integral part of improving the company's supply chain (Scherago 2006). RFID along with a new EDI improves collaboration with the suppliers and helps reduce inventories. Companies that conformed early to Wal-Mart's RFID mandate enjoy benefits, too. For example, Daisy Brand, the manufacturer of sour cream and cottage cheese, started shipping RFID-tagged cases and pallets to Wal-Mart in the fall of 2004. Daisy says its investment in RFID has been a boon, helping it better manage the flow of its perishable products through Wal-Mart stores and ensuring that marketing promotions proceed as planned (Hayes-Weier 2008).

The next step in Wal-Mart's pilot is to mark each individual item of large goods with a tag. This plan raises a possible privacy issue: What if the tags are not removed from the products? People fear that they will be tracked after leaving the store. Wal-Mart can also use RFID for many other applications. For example, it could attach tags to shoppers' children, so when they are lost in the megastore, they could be tracked in seconds.

Conclusion

Wal-Mart's competitiveness and its future success depend upon EC and IT ability to deliver applications and systems that are agile and easy to adopt to changing market conditions, especially along the supply chain. Special attention needs to be paid to global operation and transportation. It is still difficult to find items in stores due to the lack of

Wal-Mart associates, as well as to check prices due to poor labeling in some cases. The future use of RFID can help the company overcome many of these problems.

Wal-Mart is using EC in many other applications. For example, the company has more than 30 million shoppers each day, which generates 800 million transactions (each item you buy adds one transaction regarding inventory levels and sale volume). Wal-Mart operates a huge data warehouse and uses business intelligence (BI) for reporting and analysis purposes.

Finally, Wal-Mart introduces more and more innovations. To increase the efficiency of money flow and customer service, Wal-Mart has introduced a smart network (Birchall 2008).

Sources: Birchall (2008), Hayes-Weier (2008), Piasecki (2006), Scherago (2006), and Songini (2007).

Questions

1. Why is Wal-Mart concentrating on supply chain projects?

2. Wal-Mart mandates RFID tags from all its large suppliers. Why are some suppliers not in compliance?

3. Investigate the options for international customers on the Wal-Mart Web site.

4. Compare *walmart.com* with *target.com*, *costco.com*, *kmart.com*, and other direct competitors. Write a report.

5. Envision how transaction processing systems (TPSs) are used in Wal-Mart stores. Go to Wal-Mart and pay with a check. How has EC improved the old way of paying with checks?

ONLINE RESOURCES
available at pearsonglobaleditions.com/turban

Online Files

W6.1   Application Case: Land O'Lakes Collaborates with Competitors to Improve Its Logistics

W6.2   Application Case: Nike's Supply Chain: Failure and Eventual Success

W6.3   Examples of RFID Implementation

W6.4   Benefits of RFID

W6.5   Comparison of RuBee and RFID

W6.6   Application Case: Leightons Opticians Sees the Value of Collaborative Hubs

W6.7   Application Case: Webcor: Supply Chain Hub

W6.8   Fila's Collaboration Software Reduces Time-to-Market and Product Cost

W6.9   Application Case: Zara: Fast Fashion Supply Chain Innovator

W6.10 The CPFR Process

W6.11 Application Case: Cadence Design Systems—Deploying a Corporate Portal on Its Intranet

W6.12 Seamless Integration of Business Partners' Systems

W6.13 Types of Workflow Applications

W6.14 Group Decision Support Systems

W6.15 Interactive Whiteboards

Comprehensive Educational Web Sites

rfidjournal.com: *The RFID Journal*

intranet.com/tutorials: Tutorials about collaboration and relates topics

collaboration20.com: Collection of news, articles, blogs, Web 2.0 glossary, and more

REFERENCES

Aneja, A., C. Rowan, and B. Brooksby. "Corporate Portal Framework for Transforming Content Chaos on Intranets." *Intel Technology Journal* Q1, 2000.

Ayers, J. B., and M. A. Odegaard. *Retail Supply Chain Management*. London, UK: Averbach Pubications, 2007.

BEA Systems. "State of the Portal Market 2006: Portals and the New Wisdom of the Enterprise." 2006. bea.com/content/news_events/white_papers/BEA_2006_State_of_the_Portal_Market_WP.pdf (accessed February 2009).

Bennett, E. "Clearing Up a Dirty Job. (Portal Software)." *Baseline*, February 2007.

Birchall, J. "Wal-Mart to Deploy 'Smart' Shop Network." *Financial Times*, September 4, 2008.

BNET. "Clarion Malaysia Reduces Design Time by 50 Percent with CATIA V5." May 2006. jobfunctions.bnet.com/abstract.aspx?docid=256355&tag=content;col1 (accessed February 2009).

BusinessWeek Online. "E-Mail Is So Five Minutes Ago." November 28, 2005. businessweek.com/magazine/

content/05_48/b3961120.htm (accessed February 2009).

Coleman, D., and S. Levine. *Collaboration 2.0*. Cupertino, CA: Happy About Books, 2008.

Collaboration 2.0. "Does SharePoint Pass the Test?" February 20, 2008. collaboration20.com/news?month=2008-02-01&public=true (accessed February 2009).

Coyle, J., et al. *Supply Chain Management: A Logistics Approach*. Mason, OH: Southwestern Publishing Co., 2008.

Croza, M. "Supply Chain—The Competitive Differentiator." *CMA Management* (June/July 2008).

EMC/Documentum. Knowledge Worker Solutions: Leveraging Social Collaboration and Information Management Technologies. A white paper. Applied Technology. EMC Corporation #3498, January 2008.

Ginevan, S. "Strategy: Securing Mobile Data." *Network Computing*, February 11, 2008. networkcomputing.com/channels/security/showArticle.jhtml?articleID=20640 1696 (accessed February 2009).

Haines, S. *The Product Manager's Desk References*. New York: McGraw-Hill, 2008.

Hayes-Weier, M. "Airbus' Sky-High Stakes on RFID." *InformationWeek*, April 18, 2008.

Hayes-Weier, M. "Sam's Club Suppliers Required to Use Tags or Face $2 Fee." *InformationWeek*, January 21, 2008.

Heinrich, C. *RFID and Beyond*. Indianapolis, IN: Wiley & Sons, 2005.

Hildebrand, C. "Betting on a Portal." *Baseline*, July 2006.

Holsapple, C. W., and H. Jin. "Connecting Some Dots: E-Commerce, Supply Chains, and Collaborative Decision Making," *Decision Line*, October 2007.

IBM. "Clarion Malaysia Reduces Design Time by 50 Percent with CATIA V5." 2006. www-01.ibm.com/software/success/cssdb.nsf/CS/JSTS-6Q2SA9?OpenDocument&Site= (accessed March 2009).

Jeston, J., and J. Nelis. *Business Process Management: Practical Guides to Successful Implementation*. Burlington, MA: Butterworth-Heinemann, 2006.

Kesner, R. M. "Building a Knowledge Portal: A Case Study in Web-Enabled Collaboration." *Information Strategy: The Executive Journal* (Winter 2003).

Kharif, O. "What's Lurking in That RFID Tag?" *BusinessWeekOnline*, March 16, 2006. businessweek.com/technology/content/mar2006/tc20060316_117677.htm (accessed February 2009).

Kotabe, M., and M. J. Mol. *Global Supply Chain Management*. North Hampton, MA: Edward Elgar Publishing, 2006.

Koundis, T., "Business Intelligence for Intelligent Business." *DM Review Magazine*, February 2000.

Kumar, M.V., and V. Gupta. "The Making of Boeing's 787 'Dreamliner.'" *ICFAI Center for Management Research*, Hyderabad, India, 2006, OPER/053.

Loebbecke, C. "RFID in the Retail Supply Chain." In M. Khosrow-Pour, (Ed.). *Encyclopedia of E-Commerce, E-Government, and Mobile Commerce*. Hershey, PA: Idea Group Reference, 2006.

Manufacturing Executive. "Webcase: Flying by Wire: Airbus Digitally Managed Supply Chain." managingautomation.com/webcastview.aspx?content_id=228218 (accessed February 2009).

Motorola. *Synchronizing the Distribution Supply Chain with Mobility*. A white paper. WP-Supply Chain, *Motorola Inc.*, December 2007.

Niederman, F., et al. "Examining RFID Applications in Supply Chain Management," *Communications of the ACM* (July 2007).

Nunamaker, J., R. O. Briggs, D. D. Mittleman, D. R. Vogel, and P. A. Balthazard. "Lessons from a Dozen Years of Group Support Systems Research: A Discussion of Lab and Field Findings." *Journal of Management Information Systems*, 13, no. 3 (1997).

Petersen, H. "Screen Sharing Performance of Web Conferencing Services." A white paper. Adobe Screen Sharing, September 2007. adobe.com/products/acrobatconnectpro/productinfo/features/turbo_screen sharing/turbo_screensharing_wp.pdf (accessed February 2009).

Piasecki, D. "Warehouse Management Systems (WMS)." *InventoryOps.com*, July 19, 2006. inventoryops.com/warehouse_management_systems.htm (accessed March 2009).

RFID Gazette. "RFID Used on Boeing's 787 Dreamliner." April 4, 2006. rfidgazette.org/2006/04/rfid_used_on_bo.html (accessed February 2009).

RFID Journal. "Starbucks Keep Fresh with RFID." December 13, 2006. rfidjournal.com/article/article print/2890/-1/1 (accessed February 2009).

RFID Journal. "Airbus to Present Case Study at RFID Journal Live! Europe 2007." September 5, 2007. rfidjournal.com/article/articleview/3596/1/1/definitions_off (accessed February 2009).

Roberti, M. "Kimberly-Clark Gets an Early Win." *RFID Journal* (March/April 2007).

Scherago, D. "Wal-Smart." *Retail Technology Quarterly* (January 2006).

Schneider, M. "Samsung's Partner Portal Delivers a 30 Percent Sales Increase." *CRM Magazine* (May 2004).

Siau, K., and Y. Tian. "Supply Chains Integration: Architecture and Enabling Technologies." *Journal of Computer Information Systems* (Spring 2004).

Slobodow, B., A. Omer, and W. C. Babuschak. "When Supplier Partnership Aren't." *MIT Sloan Management Review* (Winter 2008).

Smith, L. "West Marine: A CPFR Success Story." *Supply Chain Management Review* 10, no. 2 (2006).

Smith, M. A. "Portals: Toward an Application Framework for Interoperability." *Communications of the ACM* (October 2004).

Socialtext. "Dresdner Kleinwort Wasserstein (DrKW)." *Customer Success Story at Socialtext.com*, 2004. socialtext

.com/files/DrKWCase Study.pdf (accessed February 2009).

Songini, M. L. "Wal-Mart Shifts RFID Plans." *Computer world*, February 26, 2007.

Sullivan, L. "Metro Moves Tagging Up the Supply Chain." *RFID Journal*, December 6, 2006. rfidjournal.com/article/articleprint/2873/-1/1 (accessed February 2009).

Supply and Demand Chain Executive. "Exostar Marks One Year Enabling Boeing's 787 Supply Chain." December 19, 2006. sdcexec.com/online/article.jsp?id=9020&site Section=29 (accessed February 2009).

SupplyChainManagement101. "Info Guide to Supply Chain Management Software." supplychainmanagement101.com/?gg=us&kw=supply%20chain&gclid=CL6i5MqI3ocCFSMhYQodWX8Bog (accessed February 2009).

Taft, D. K. "IBM Lotus Takes Social Networking to New Heights." *eWeek*, January 23, 2007. eweek.com/article2/0,1895,2086494,00.asp (accessed February 2009).

Thompson, R. "The Basics of Building a Unified Communications Business." *BusinessSolutions.com*, January 26, 2009. bsminfo.com/index.php?option=com_content&task=view&id=404&Itemid=162 (accessed May 2009).

Tucci, L. "Implementing SharePoint Enterprise-Wide Requires Governance, Partner." *CIO News*, November 19, 2008.

VICS (Voluntary Interindustry Commercial Solutions). "CPFR Overview." 2004. vics.org/docs/committees/cpfr/CPFR_Overview_US-A4.pdf (accessed February 2009).

INNOVATIVE EC SYSTEMS: FROM E-GOVERNMENT AND E-LEARNING TO CONSUMER-TO-CONSUMER E-COMMERCE

Learning Objectives

Upon completion of this chapter, you will be able to:

1. Describe various e-government initiatives.

2. Understand e-government implementation issues.

3. Describe e-learning, virtual universities, and e-training.

4. Describe online publishing and e-books.

5. Describe knowledge management and dissemination as an e-business.

6. Describe C2C activities.

Content

CATERPILLAR INC. CHAMPIONS E-LEARNING

Caterpillar Inc. (CAT) is a large global manufacturer of heavy construction and mining equipment and a service provider to its products. It is also a major financial services provider. In 2008, CAT generated nearly $50 billion in revenue from the sale of its products and services.

The Problem

CAT has over 100,000 employees and sells through over 200 dealerships in 182 countries. The company has experienced explosive growth, more than doubling its size from 2003 to 2006. Reaching so many employees in so many locations and in different countries and time zones had become a major challenge for the company. In addition, with so many newcomers, as well as new and improved products and services, CAT needed to train new employees and retrain existing ones.

Another problem was knowledge drain. By early 2000, nearly half of CAT's senior leadership team and the general employee population were eligible to retire. Also, the industry is very competitive (e.g., competition from Japan is very strong), so employees and dealers need to have the skills and knowledge to succeed in the twenty-first-century workforce.

The Solution

The company spends more than $100 million a year on training and learning. It created a learning infrastructure that includes three major elements: governance, a learning technology infrastructure (mainly Web based), and an alignment strategy to create a lifelong culture of learning in accord with the firm's business goals. Caterpillar created Caterpillar University (CAT U) to meet its training and learning needs. CAT U uses a universal virtual collaboration tool, a synchronous online learning management system (LMS), and a knowledge network.

Caterpillar's LMS is a worldwide platform that supports both employees and dealers. A new release was implemented in 2007. The LMS has a learner-centric user interface that allows individual users to experience it in a customized fashion. It dynamically constructs each individual's learning plan on his or her desktop.

One of the biggest challenges facing any organization, let alone a large global one with a tightly integrated dealer network, is how to enable learning across an extended enterprise that includes employees, dealers, suppliers, and customers. CAT U enables e-learning through its knowledge management system, the Caterpillar Knowledge Network. Caterpillar employees, dealers, suppliers, and customers make use of the more than 4,000 communities of practice organized around specific business-related topics to exchange information, share files, ask questions, and contact subject-matter experts around the world. The knowledge network provides a deep mine of searchable data, giving users access to information created everywhere, anytime, in every area of the organization.

The company also created the CAT Knowledge Network to help preserve the knowledge of retiring executives and experts. Approximately 10,000 experts have been identified and listed. These experts' searchable "expert descriptions" serve as expertise locators for users within Caterpillar and throughout the value chain. Users can search online for experts by area of expertise.

In addition, the knowledge network includes "lessons learned," which capture past experiences in a formal template and are searchable, too. The knowledge network also includes a discussion bulletin board.

The network is also a powerful tool for making personal connections. Users no longer have to rely on a personal network built through years of experience and various job assignments; instead, they rely on a keyword search in the knowledge network. This allows a wheel-loader engineer in China, for instance, to quickly locate a transmission software expert in Europe.

Synchronous online learning allows the virtual delivery of learning across the globe. In this setting, a live instructor interacts with dispersed learners who are attending virtually. Online learning saves time and money by allowing information to be distributed quickly and by reducing travel costs. Conducting meetings via virtual collaboration has reduced travel costs. Between January and October of 2007, more than 2,100 classes were conducted using synchronous online learning and more than 300,000 meetings were conducted using virtual collaboration.

The Results

Caterpillar's learning technology enables its employees to quickly build both competence and confidence. In addition, the technology infrastructure is an important contributor to business sustainability by dramatically reducing travel and other expenses and increasing employee productivity. By aligning learning needs and strategies at the division and enterprise levels, Caterpillar is able to improve enterprise performance by providing the right skills and knowledge through learning. This increases engagement and increases discretionary effort, which leads to better performance. Engagement is the extent to which employees commit, rationally or emotionally, to the organization, how hard they work as a result of this commitment, and how long they intend to stay. This all leads to a bottom-line benefit, because better enterprise performance results in increased profitability. Finally, the knowledge-sharing platform was so successful that its software and procedures have been sold to many companies.

Sources: Compiled from Glynn (2008) and Boehle (2007).

WHAT WE CAN LEARN . . .

E-learning is an EC application that helps organizations teach and retrain a large number of learners to ensure that they can grow and handle their jobs effectively. E-learning at Caterpillar is based in part on the knowledge and best practices accumulated by employees over the years. This knowledge is managed in a knowledge management (KM) system and is accessible to learners and problem solvers electronically. E-learning and KM are two innovative systems introduced in this chapter that illustrate the benefits of EC. Other topics discussed in this chapter are e-government, online publishing and e-books, and consumer-to-consumer EC.

7.1 E-GOVERNMENT: AN OVERVIEW

Electronic government, or *e-government*, is a growing e-commerce application that encompasses many topics. This section presents the major e-government topics.

DEFINITION AND SCOPE

e-government

E-commerce model in which a government entity buys or provides goods, services, or information to businesses or individual citizens.

As e-commerce matures and its tools and applications improve, greater attention is being given to its use to improve the business of public institutions and governments (country, state, county, city, etc.). **E-government** is the use of information technology in general, and e-commerce in particular, to provide citizens and organizations with more convenient access to government information and services and to provide delivery of public services to citizens, business partners, and those working in the public sector. It also is an efficient and effective way of conducting government business transactions with citizens and businesses and within governments themselves. See Shark and Toporkoff (2008) and Wikipedia (en.wikipedia.org/wiki/E-Government) for details.

In this book, the term *e-government* will be used in its broader context—the bringing together of governments, citizens, and businesses in a network of information, knowledge, and commerce. In this broader view, e-government offers an opportunity to improve the efficiency and effectiveness of the functions of government and to make governments more transparent to citizens and businesses by providing access to more of the information generated by government, as well as facilitating transactions with and within governments.

Several major categories fit within this broad definition of e-government: government-to-citizens (G2C), government-to-business (G2B), government-to-government (G2G), internal efficiency and effectiveness (IEE), and government-to-employees (G2E). The performance objectives of the first four categories are provided in Exhibit 7.1. For a description of the range of e-government activities in the United States, see whitehouse.gov/omb/egov.

e-democracy (cyberdemocracy, digital democracy)

The use of EC and electronic communications technologies, such as the Internet, in enhancing democratic processes within a democratic country.

E-Democracy

E-democracy, which is sometimes referred to as **cyberdemocracy** or **digital democracy**, encompasses the use of EC and electronic communications technologies, such as the Internet, in enhancing democratic processes within a democratic country. E-democracy is still in its infancy, as well as the subject of much debate and activity by governments, civic-oriented groups, and societies around the world. For details on e-democracy, see Wikipedia (en.wikipedia.org/wiki/E-democracy) and Shark and Toporkoff (2008).

government-to-citizens (G2C)

E-government category that includes all the interactions between a government and its citizens.

GOVERNMENT-TO-CITIZENS

The **government-to-citizens (G2C)** category includes all of the interactions between a government and its citizens that can take place electronically. As described in the closing case

EXHIBIT 7.1 Categories of E-Government Performance Objectives

G2C

- Create easy-to-find single points of access to government services for individuals.
- Reduce the average time for citizens to find benefits and determine eligibility.
- Increase the number of citizens who use the Internet to find information on recreational opportunities.
- Meet the high public demand for information.
- Improve the value of government to citizen.
- Expand access to information for people with disabilities.
- Make obtaining financial assistance from the government easier, cheaper, quicker, and more comprehensible.

G2B

- Increase the ability for citizens and businesses to find, view, and comment on rules and regulations.
- Reduce burden on business by enabling online tax filing.
- Reduce the time to fill out export forms and locate information.
- Reduce time for businesses to file and comply with regulations.
- Make transactions with the government easier, cheaper, quicker, and more comprehensible.

G2G

- Decrease response times for jurisdictions and disciplines to respond to emergency incidents.
- Reduce the time to verify birth and death entitlement information.
- Increase the number of grant programs available for electronic application.
- Share information more quickly and conveniently between the national, regional, local, and tribal governments.
- Improve collaborations with foreign partners, including governments and institutions.
- Automate internal processes to reduce costs within the government by disseminating best practices across agencies.
- Plan IT investments more effectively.
- Secure greater services at a lower cost.
- Cut government operating costs.

IEE

- Increase availability of training programs for government employees.
- Reduce the average time to process clearance forms.
- Increase use of e-travel services within each agency.
- Reduce the time for citizens to search for government jobs.
- Reduce time and overhead cost to purchase goods and services throughout the government.

Sources: U.S. Government (2003), Lee et al. (2005), and Hyperion (2007).

about the governments of Singapore and Hong Kong in Online File W7.1, G2C can involve many different initiatives. The basic idea is to enable citizens to interact with the government from anywhere. G2C applications enable citizens to ask questions of government agencies and receive answers, pay taxes, receive payments and documents, and so forth. For example, in many U.S. states residents can renew driver's licenses, pay traffic tickets, and make appointments for vehicle emission inspections and driving tests. Governments also can disseminate information on the Web, conduct training, help citizens find employment, and more. In California, for example, drivers' education classes are offered online and can be taken anytime, anywhere.

Government services to citizens are provided via citizen portals. The services will vary depending on the country, on the level (city, province, country), and on the users' skills in using computers. An example of representative services in municipalities in Denmark is provided in Exhibit 7.2. For the diversity of services, see the Hong Kong case in Online File W7.1.

EXHIBIT 7.2   Sample G2C Municipal Services in Denmark

Service	Description
Your real estate	Information on your real estate holdings in a particular municipality.
Government housing eligibility	Self-calculate eligibility for government housing; online application is available.
Child care option	Child care options in your municipality; child care guides.
Facts and statistics	Data on your municipality of choice.
Change of address	Do it yourself and get a receipt online.
Pay tax and for services	Pay municipalities tax and pay for services (e.g., child care).
Calculate social benefits	Calculate available benefits (e.g., for elderly, children, pensions, maternity/paternity leave, sickness benefits for employees).
Budget preparation	Calculators for individuals and small businesses.
Tax calculations and matters	Calculate taxes; forms and guides are available.
Real estate information	Statistics, facts, and availability of real estate in Denmark, by municipality.
Building guides	Building guides for different municipalities; forms and guides.
Utility guides	Reports on water and electricity consumption in different cities.
Education	Information on how to sign up for wait lists for educational institutions.
Scholarships for nursery school	Applications for scholarships for nursery schools (not provided to everyone).
Real estate appraisers/ valuation	The official valuation of any real estate in Denmark.

Sources: Compiled from Henriksen (2006) and *dst.dk* (accessed February 2009).

The major features of government Web sites are phone and address information, links to other sites, publications, and databases. The major areas of G2C activities are tourism and recreation, research and education, downloadable forms, discovery of government services, information about public policy, and advice about health and safety issues. G2C is available now in many countries on mobile/wireless devices.

An interesting recent application is the use of the Internet by politicians, especially during election periods. For example, the French political parties pursued millions of voters in the blogosphere for the 2007 presidential election. In the United States, during the 2008 presidential election both major-party candidates sent e-mail messages to potential voters and had comprehensive information portals. Barack Obama even created a social network site (my.barackobama.com) and had pages on MySpace, Facebook, and Second Life, much earlier than his competitors who followed with similar activities (see Mark 2007). In South Korea, politicians log on to the Internet to recruit voters, because many people who surf the Internet rarely read newspapers or watch TV. The target audience of these politicians is 20- to 30-year-olds, the vast majority of whom surf the Internet. Pasdaq, the Seoul-based over-the-counter stock exchange, offers an Internet game that simulates the stock market and measures the popularity of some 300 politicians by allowing players to buy "stocks" in a politician. In one year, over 500,000 members signed up. Some politicians make decisions based on citizens' opinions collected on the Internet.

Another area of G2C activity is in solving constituents' problems. The government (or a politician) can use CRM-type software to assign inquiries and problem cases to the appropriate staff member. Workflow CRM software can then be used to track the progress of the problem's resolution.

E-Voting Machine

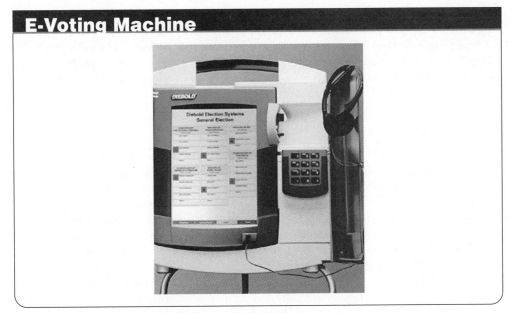

Source: TruthOut.org *truthout.org/092908VA* (accessed May 2009).

Note that over 20 countries block Web sites for political, social, or other reasons (e.g., China, Iran, Syria). For more on G2C, see nbc.gov/egov/g2c.html. Two popular examples of G2C are provided next.

Electronic Voting

Voting processes inherently are subject to error and also are historically subject to manipulation and fraud. In many countries, there are attempts to "rig" the votes; in others, the losers want to recount. Voting may result in major political crises, as happened in the Ukraine in November 2004. Problems with the U.S. 2000 and 2004 presidential elections have accelerated the trend toward electronic voting.

Voting encompasses a broad spectrum of technological and social problems that must be systematically addressed—from registration and voter authentication to the casting of ballots and subsequent tallying of results. Electronic voting automates some or all steps in the process (see photo).

Fully electronic voting systems have raised considerable controversy because of a variety of factors, such as the proprietary nature of the software, the weakness of the certification criteria, the inability of black-box testing to provide full assurances of correctness, the general secrecy of the evaluation process, vendor-commissioned evaluations, and the lack of any mechanism whereby independent recounting of the ballots and auditing of the vote totals can be performed.

The first country to use fully computerized balloting was Brazil. In the United States, for example, electronic systems have been in use since 1980 (mainly for counting the results); large-scale implementation of touch-screen systems occurred only in 2008. It is interesting to note that several states (e.g., California, Nevada) require that touch-screen machines be able to produce a printed record. A good voting machine should show the voter what he or she has entered and ask for confirmation, much like when purchasing a book online from Amazon.com, transferring funds, or selling stocks.

From a technology point of view, election fraud could be carried out by changing a program to count votes for X twice or not to count votes for Y at all (see Gibson and Brown 2006). Therefore, security and auditing measures are key to the success of e-voting. However, considering the amount of fraud that occurs with traditional, non–e-voting systems and the fact that e-security is improving (see Epstein 2007), e-voting eventually could be the norm. For more information on e-voting, see fcw.com.

Aspiring politicians are using blogs to promote themselves. Many continue to use blogs after being elected. Social networks, especially MySpace, Facebook, and YouTube, are being used to reach the voters directly, especially young voters. For example, Keen (2006) reported that Facebook (facebook.com) had over 1,400 candidate profiles for the November 2006 U.S. elections. All of the major-party presidential candidates had profiles for the 2008 election.

Electronic Benefits Transfer

One e-government application that is not new is electronic benefits transfer (EBT), which has been available since the early 1990s. The U.S. government, for example, transfers around $1,000 billion in benefits to its citizens annually. In 1993, the U.S. government launched an initiative to develop a nationwide EBT system to deliver government benefits electronically. Initially, the attempt was made to deliver benefits to recipients' bank accounts. However, more than 20 percent of these transfers go to citizens who do not have bank accounts. To solve this problem, the government initiated the use of smart cards (see Chapter 11). Benefit recipients can load electronic funds onto the cards and use the cards at automated teller machines (ATMs), point-of-sale locations, and grocery and other stores, just like other bank card users do. The advantage is not only the reduction in processing costs (from about 50 cents per paper check to 2 cents for electronic payment) but also the reduction of fraud. With biometrics (see Chapter 11) coming to smart cards and PCs, officials expect fraud to be reduced substantially.

For more information on EBT in government, see fns.usda.gov/FSP.

GOVERNMENT-TO-BUSINESS

government-to-business (G2B)
E-government category that includes interactions between governments and businesses (government selling to businesses and providing them with services and businesses selling products and services to government).

Governments seek to automate their interactions with businesses. Although we call this category **government-to-business (G2B)**, the relationship works two ways: government-to-business and business-to-government. Thus, G2B refers to e-commerce in which government sells products to businesses or provides them with services as well as to businesses selling products and services to government. Two key G2B areas are e-procurement and the auctioning of government surpluses. For other U.S. G2B initiatives, see nbc.gov/egov/g2b.html.

Government E-Procurement

Governments buy large amounts of MROs and other materials directly from suppliers. In many cases, RFQ (or tendering) systems are mandated by law. For years, these tenderings were done manually; the systems are now moving online. These systems employ reverse (buy-side auction systems), such as those described in Chapter 5. An example of a reverse auction used for G2B procurement in Hong Kong is described in Online File W7.1 and at info.gov.hk. For additional information about such reverse auctions, see gsa.gov. In the United States, for example, the local housing agencies of HUD (Housing and Urban Development), which provides housing to low-income residents, are moving to e-procurement (see Kumar and Peng 2006 and U.S. Department of Housing and Urban Development 2008). Governments provide all the support for such tendering systems.

The Procurement Marketing and Access Network from the Small Business Administration has developed a service called PRO-Net (pro-net.sba.gov), a searchable database that contracting officers in various U.S. government units can use to find products and services sold by small, disadvantaged, or women-owned businesses.

Group Purchasing

The U.S. government also uses online group purchasing, which was described in Chapter 1. For example, the eFAST service conducts reverse auctions for aggregated orders (see gsa.gov). Suppliers post group-purchasing offers, and the prices fall as more orders are placed. Alternatively, government buyers may post product requests that other buyers may review and join.

Forward E-Auctions

Many governments auction equipment surpluses or other goods, ranging from vehicles to foreclosed real estate. These auctions are now moving to the Internet. Governments can auction from a government Web site or they can use third-party auction sites such as ebay.com, bid4assets.com, or governmentauctions.org for this purpose. The U.S. General Services Administration (GSA) operates a property auction site online (auctionrp.com) where real-time auctions for surpluses and seized goods are conducted. Some of these auctions are restricted to dealers; others are open to the public (see governmentauctions.org).

GOVERNMENT-TO-GOVERNMENT

The **government-to-government (G2G)** category consists of EC activities between units of government, including those within one governmental body. Many of these are aimed at improving the effectiveness or the efficiency of the government. Here are a few examples from the United States:

> **Intelink.** Intelink is an intranet that contains classified information that is shared by the numerous U.S. intelligence agencies.

> **Procurement at GSA.** The GSA's Web site (gsa.gov) uses technologies such as demand aggregation and reverse auctions to buy for various units of the U.S. government. (See also governmentauctions.org and liquidation.com). The agency seeks to apply innovative Web-based procurement methods to government buying.

> **Federal Case Registry (Department of Health and Human Services).** This service helps state governments locate information about child support, including data on paternity and enforcement of child-support obligations. It is available at acf.hhs.gov/programs/cse/newhire/fcr/fcr.htm.

For more examples of G2G services, see govexec.com and nbc.gov/egov/g2g.html.

government-to-government (G2G)
E-government category that includes activities within government units and those between governments.

GOVERNMENT-TO-EMPLOYEES AND INTERNAL EFFICIENCY AND EFFECTIVENESS

Governments are introducing various EC models internally. Two areas are illustrated next.

Government-to-Employees (G2E)

Governments are just as interested as private-sector organizations are in providing services and information electronically to their employees. Indeed, because employees of national and regional governments often work in a variety of geographic locations, **government-to-employee (G2E)** applications may be especially useful in enabling efficient communication.

Example: G2E in the U.S. Navy. The U.S. Navy uses G2E to improve the flow of information to sailors and their families. Because long shipboard deployments cause strains on Navy families, in 1995 the Navy began seeking ways to ensure that quality-of-life information reaches Navy personnel and their loved ones all over the world. Examples of quality-of-life information include self-help, deployment support, stress management, parenting advice, and relocation assistance.

To help Navy families, the Navy developed Lifelines. Lifelines uses the Internet, simulcasting, teleconferencing, cable television, and satellite broadcasting to reach overseas personnel. The Navy has found that certain media channels are more appropriate for different types of information. Lifelines regularly features live broadcasts, giving forward-deployed sailors and their families welcome information and, in some cases, a taste of home. On the Web, several thousands of people access the Lifelines portal each day. In 2008, the portal covered dozens of topics ranging from jobs to recreation.

The government provides several other e-services to Navy personnel. Notable are online banking, personal finance services, and insurance. Education and training also are provided online. The Navy provides mobile computing devices to sailors while they are deployed at sea. The handheld devices offer both entertainment and information to Navy personnel on active duty. For details, see lifelines.navy.mil.

government-to-employees (G2E)
E-government category that includes activities and services between government units and their employees.

Internal Efficiency and Effectiveness (IEE)

These internal initiatives provide tools for improving the effectiveness and efficiency of government operations, and the processes are basically intrabusiness applications implemented in government units. For example, the U.S. Office of Management and Budget provides the following services:

- ▶ **E-payroll.** Consolidates systems at more than 14 processing centers across government.
- ▶ **E-records management.** Establishes uniform procedures and standards for agencies in converting paper-based records to electronic files.
- ▶ **E-training.** Provides a repository of government-owned courseware.
- ▶ **Enterprise case management.** Centralizes justice litigation case information.
- ▶ **Integrated acquisition.** Agencies share common data elements to enable other agencies to make better informed procurement, logistical, payment, and performance-assessment decisions.
- ▶ **Integrated human resources.** Integrates personnel records across government.
- ▶ **One-stop recruitment.** Automates national government information on career opportunities, resume submission and routing, and assessment. Streamlines the national hiring process and provides up-to-the-minute application status for job seekers.

Improving homeland security can be considered as IEE activity. The government is using different EC-related systems to improve security. For more information on security in e-government go to dhs.gov/index.shtm.

For more on using EC to improve the efficiency and effectiveness of government, see nbc.gov/egov/iee.html.

Section 7.1 ▶ REVIEW QUESTIONS

1. Define e-government.
2. What are the four major categories of e-government services?
3. Describe G2C.
4. Describe how EBT works.
5. Describe the two main areas of G2B activities.
6. How does government use EC internally and when dealing with other governments?

7.2 IMPLEMENTING E-GOVERNMENT

Like most other organizations, government entities want to move into the digital era and become click-and-mortar organizations. Therefore, one can find a large number of EC applications in government organizations. This section examines some of the issues involved in implementing e-government. Huang et al. (2006) review many implementation issues and trends in e-government. These are summarized in Online File W7.2.

THE TRANSFORMATION TO E-GOVERNMENT

The transformation from traditional delivery of government services to full implementation of online government services may be a lengthy process. The business consulting firm Deloitte & Touche conducted a study that identified six stages in the transformation to e-government. These stages do not have to be sequential, but frequently they are, as shown in Exhibit 7.3, with a seventh stage added by the authors. These stages are described in the following list.

- ▶ **Stage 1: Information publishing/dissemination.** Individual government departments set up their own Web sites. These provide the public with information about the specific department, the range of services it offers, and contacts for further assistance. The online presence helps reduce paperwork and the number of help-line employees needed.

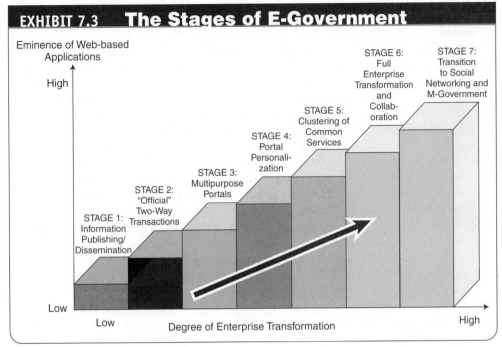

EXHIBIT 7.3   The Stages of E-Government

Source: Wong, W. Y. *At the Dawn of E-Government.* New York: Deloitte Research, Deloitte & Touche, 2000.

⟩ **Stage 2: "Official" two-way transactions with one department at a time.** With the help of secure Web sites, customers are able to submit personal information to and conduct monetary transactions with single government departments. In many countries, payments to citizens and from citizens to various government agencies can be performed online. Also, tax returns are filed online.

⟩ **Stage 3: Multipurpose portals.** Based on the fact that customer needs can cut across department boundaries, a portal enables customers to use a single point of entry to send and receive information and to process monetary transactions across multiple departments. For example, the government of South Australia's portal (sa.gov.au) features a "business channel" and a link for citizens to pay bills, manage bank accounts, and conduct personal stock trading. Singapore's ecitizen.gov.sg and gov.sg are also examples of such portals.

⟩ **Stage 4: Portal personalization.** In stage 4, government puts more power into the customers' hands by allowing them to customize portals with their desired features. The added benefit of portal personalization is that governments get a more accurate read on customer preferences for electronic versus nonelectronic service options.

⟩ **Stage 5: Clustering of common services.** As customers now view once-disparate services as a unified package through the portal, their perception of departments as distinct entities will begin to blur. Once a business restructuring needs to take place, they will recognize groups of transactions rather than groups of agencies.

⟩ **Stage 6: Full integration and enterprise transformation.** Stage 6 offers a full-service center, personalized to each customer's needs and preferences. At this stage, old walls defining silos of government services have been torn down, and technology is integrated across the new structure to bridge the shortened gap between the front and back offices. Full electronic collaboration among government agencies and between governments, citizens, and other partners will occur during this phase, which is in its planning stage.

⟩ **Stage 7: Transition to social computing.** The use of Web 2.0 tools, richer media, and social networking activities becomes routine. Also, there is a movement to the use of mobile government.

E-GOVERNMENT AND SOCIAL NETWORKING

Government agencies around the world are experimenting with social networking tools as well as with their own pages and presence on public social network sites. Governments are using Web 2.0 tools mainly for collaboration, dissemination of information, e-learning, online forums, and citizen engagement. An interesting example is the initiatives going on in Singapore, where social networking tools are being used to provide residents with the opportunity to voice their opinions on local matters (see chapter closing case about Singapore's e-government).

Some people believe that social networking will replace the current portal-based e-government and that the trend is clearly away from the "one-stop shop" portal. Government initiatives are very diversified with the Web 2.0 approach. For example, many governments own islands on Second Life on which they present diplomatic issues and advertise tourist attractions. Gartner Inc. cites a number of adventurous e-government Web 2.0 initiatives. With such initiatives, it is important to have strict security, accountability, and compliance functionality in place, which has proven challenging when implementing wikis and blogs. Gartner encourages e-government efforts to "experiment with innovative means to better serve and engage constituents," but it warns that "such pilots have to remain very well-focused and somewhat isolated from mainstream processes for at least the next two years." However, products such as Atlassian, which integrates with Microsoft SharePoint, have more than enough "control" to satisfy most government security requirements (reported by *Government Technology* 2008).

Note that politicians are using social networking extensively. For example, during the 2008 U.S. presidential election Democrat candidate Barack Obama created a page at LinkedIn, where he received thousands of connections and responses to his question, "What ideas do you have to keep America competitive in the years ahead?" Many of the responses were very interesting and insightful. Obama also added a LinkedIn interest group. One of the keys to Obama's success was that his LinkedIn profile was set up much like a "regular person" in tone and language, fitting with his strategy of not appearing to be an old-school Washington insider.

All the major-party candidates for the 2008 presidential election had official pages where videos were viewed by millions. They also created pages on Facebook and MySpace.

IMPLEMENTATION ISSUES OF E-GOVERNMENT

The following implementation issues depend on which of the seven stages of development a government is in and on its plan for moving to higher stages.

- **Transformation speed.** The speed at which a government moves from stage 1 to stage 7 varies, but usually the transformation is very slow. Some of the determining factors are the degree of resistance to change by government employees, the rate at which citizens adopt the new applications (see the following section), the available budget, and the legal environment.

- **G2B implementation.** G2B is easier to implement than G2C. In some countries, such as Hong Kong, G2B implementation is outsourced to a private company that pays all of the startup expenses for new businesses in exchange for a share of future transaction fees. As G2B services have the potential for rapid cost savings, they can be a good way to begin an e-government initiative.

- **Security and privacy issues.** Governments are concerned about maintaining the security and privacy of citizens' data. An area of particular concern is health care. From a medical point of view, it is necessary to have quick access to people's data, and the Internet and smart cards provide such capabilities; however, the protection of such data is very expensive. Deciding on how much security to provide is an important managerial issue. In the United States, the 2002 E-Government Act requires all U.S. agencies to conduct privacy assessments of all government information systems.

- **Business aspects.** Andersen (2006) points to the strategic management value of such initiatives. The author claims that the transformation of government to act "like business" requires internal analysis from a business point of view.

See Welch and Pandey (2006) for additional implementation issues.

Citizen Adoption of E-Government

One of the most important issues in implementing e-government is its adoption and usage by citizens. One of the major variables is "trust in e-government." Other variables, such as perceived ease of use and perceived usefulness, are generic to EC adoption. Moderating variables, such as culture, also are important.

M-GOVERNMENT

Mobile government, or **m-government**, is the wireless implementation of e-government applications (see en.wikipedia.org/M-government) mostly to citizens (e.g., Government of Canada Wireless Portal), but also to business. M-government uses wireless Internet infrastructure and devices. It is a value-added service, because it enables government to reach a larger number of citizens and is more cost-effective than other IT applications; it is convenient to users as well (per Trimi and Sheng 2008). In addition, governments employ large numbers of mobile workers who can be supported by wireless devices.

Proponents of m-government argue that it can help make public information and government services available "anytime, anywhere" and that the ubiquity of these devices mandates their employment in government functions. An example of such beneficial use of mobile technologies would be the sending of a mass alert to registered citizens via short message service, or SMS, in the event of an emergency.

Some implementation issues are:

▶ Wireless and mobile networks and related infrastructure, as well as software, must be developed.

▶ To increase citizen participation and provide citizen-oriented services, governments need to offer easy access to m-government information in several forms.

▶ Mobile phone numbers and mobile devices are relatively easily hacked, and wireless networks are vulnerable because they use public airwaves to send signals.

▶ Many countries have not yet adopted legislation for data and information practices that spell out the rights of citizens and the responsibilities of the data holders (government).

Several wireless applications suitable for e-government will be presented in Chapter 8. Notable are B2E applications, especially for field employees, and B2C information discovery, such as the U.S. Government 511 system. Another example is the city of Bergen, Norway, which provides wireless portable tourism services.

For implementation issues, success stories, applications, benefits, and more, see Massey and Taylor (2007).

mobile government (m-government)
The wireless implementation of e-government mostly to citizens but also to business.

Section 7.2 ▶ REVIEW QUESTIONS

1. List and briefly describe the seven stages of e-government development.

2. Describe some e-government implementation issues.

3. Describe m-government and its implementation issues.

7.3 E-LEARNING

The topic of e-learning is gaining much attention, especially because world-class universities such as MIT, Harvard, and Stanford in the United States and Oxford in the United Kingdom are implementing it. Exhibit 7.4 shows the forces that are driving the transition from traditional education to online learning. Details are provided in Online File W7.3. E-learning also is growing as a method for training and information delivery in the business world and is becoming a major e-business activity. In this section, we will discuss several topics related to e-learning (see Wagner 2008).

THE BASICS OF E-LEARNING: DEFINITIONS AND CONCEPTS

E-learning is the online delivery of information for purposes of education, training, or knowledge management (see elearnmag.org). It is a Web-enabled system that makes knowledge

e-learning
The online delivery of information for purposes of education, training, or knowledge management.

EXHIBIT 7.4   The Drivers of E-Learning

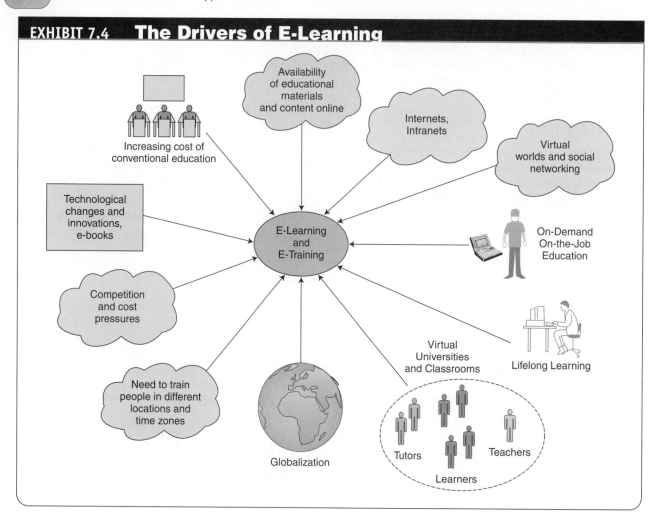

accessible to those who need it, when they need it, anytime, anywhere. It appears in a variety of formats, ranging from virtual classrooms to mobile learning (see Wagner 2008).

According to Wikipedia (en.Wikipedia.org/wiki/Elearning), e-learning can refer to any method of computer-enhanced learning. This could be as simple as the extension of traditional mail-order distance learning where CD-ROMs are used for media-rich interaction with the student. Alternatively, it can be extended all the way to fully interactive, institution-wide "managed learning environments" in which students communicate with professors and classmates, much as with face-to-face delivered courses. E-learning may include the use of Web-based teaching materials and hypermedia in general, multimedia CD-ROMs, Web sites, discussion boards, collaborative software, e-mail, blogs, wikis, chat rooms, computer-aided assessment, educational animation, simulations, games, learning management software, electronic voting systems, and more, and possibly in combination.

E-learning is also broader than the term *online learning*, which generally refers to purely Web-based learning. The term *m-learning* has been proposed when the material is delivered wirelessly to cell phones or PDAs.

E-learning can be useful both as an environment for facilitating learning at schools and as an environment for efficient and effective corporate training, as shown in Case 7.1

Technological advances, such as simulations, virtual worlds, and open-source software have reshaped the e-learning landscape. Rapid development tools enable organizations to create e-learning environments quickly and easily. Comprehensive sites about e-learning, including videos and PowerPoint presentations, are available at e-learningcenter.com and e-learningcentre.co.uk.

CASE 7.1

EC Application

E-LEARNING AT CISCO SYSTEMS

The Problem

Cisco Systems (*cisco.com*) is one of the fastest-growing high-tech companies in the world, selling devices that connect computers to the Internet and to other networks. Cisco's products are being upgraded or replaced continuously, so extensive training of employees and customers is needed. Cisco recognizes that its employees, business partners, and independent students seeking professional certification all require training on a continuous basis. Traditional classroom training was flawed by its inability to scale rapidly enough. Cisco offered in-house classes 6 to 10 times a year, at many locations, but the rapid growth in the number of students, coupled with the fast pace of technological change, made the training both expensive and ineffective.

The Solution

Cisco believes that e-learning is a revolutionary way to empower its workforce and its partners with the skills and knowledge needed to turn technological change to an advantage. Therefore, Cisco implemented e-learning programs that enable students to learn new software, hardware, and procedures. Cisco believes that once people experience e-learning, they will recognize that it is the fastest, easiest way to get the information they need to be successful.

To implement e-learning, Cisco created the Delta Force, which was made up of its CEO John Chambers, the IT unit, and the Internet Learning Solution Group. The group's first project was to build two learning portals, one for 40 partner companies that sell Cisco products and one for 4,000 systems engineers who deploy and service the products after the sale.

Cisco also wants to serve as a model of e-learning for its partners and customers, hoping to convince them to use its e-learning programs. To encourage its employees to use e-learning, Cisco:

▶ Makes e-learning a mandatory part of employees' jobs.
▶ Offers easy access to e-learning tools via the Web.
▶ Makes e-learning nonthreatening through the use of an anonymous testing and scoring process that focuses on helping people improve rather than on penalizing those who fail.
▶ Gives those who fail tests precision learning targets (remedial work, modules, exercises, or written materials) to help them pass and remove the fear associated with testing.
▶ Enables managers to track, manage, and ensure employee development, competency change, and, ultimately, performance change.
▶ Offers additional incentives and rewards such as stock grants, promotions, and bonuses to employees who pursue specialization and certification through e-learning.
▶ Adds e-learning as a strategic top-down metric for Cisco executives, who are measured on their deployment of IT in their departments.

For its employees, partners, and customers, Cisco operates E-Learning Centers for Excellence. These centers offer training at Cisco's office sites as well as at customers' sites via intranets and the Internet. Cisco offers a variety of training programs supported by e-learning. For example, Cisco converted a popular four-and-a-half-day, instructor-led training (ILT) course on Cisco's signature IOS (internetwork operating system) technologies into an e-learning program that blends both live and self-paced components. The goal was to teach seasoned systems engineers (SEs) how to sell, install, configure, and maintain those key IOS technologies and to do so in a way that would train more people than the 25 employees the on-site ILT course could hold.

The Results

With the IOS course alone, Cisco calculated its ROI as follows:

▶ It cost $12,400 to develop the blended course.
▶ The course saved each SE 1 productivity day and 20 percent of the travel and lodging cost of a 1-week training course in San Jose. Estimating $750 for travel and lodging and $450 for the productivity day, the savings totaled $1,200 per SE.
▶ Seventeen SEs attended the course the first time it was offered, for a total savings of $20,400. Therefore, in the first offering of the course, Cisco recovered the development costs and saved $8,000 over and above those costs.
▶ Since March 2001, the IOS Learning Services team has presented two classes of 40 SEs per month. At that rate, Cisco saves $1,152,000 net for just this one course every 12 months.

In 2004, over 12,000 corporate salespeople, 150,000 employees of business partners, and 200,000 independent students were taking courses at Cisco learning centers, many using the e-learning courses. By 2004, Cisco had developed over 100 e-learning courses and was planning to develop many more. According to Galagan (2002), e-learning is a major underpinning of Cisco's economic health.

Sources: Compiled from *cisco.com* (accessed September 2008) and Galagan (2002).

Questions

1. Use examples from the Cisco case to discuss the differences between e-learning and e-training.
2. What measures has Cisco adopted to encourage its employees to use e-learning?
3. Comment on the effectiveness of the e-learning programs of Cisco.

BENEFITS AND DRAWBACKS OF E-LEARNING

E-learning has many benefits. These benefits are presented in the following discussion and in Wagner (2008). However, it also has several drawbacks, thus making it a controversial topic.

Benefits of E-Learning

E-learning can be a great equalizer: By eliminating barriers of time, distance, and socioeconomic status, it can enable individuals to take charge of their own lifelong learning. In the information age, skills and knowledge need to be *continually updated* and refreshed to keep up with today's fast-paced business environment. E-learning of new content will help organizations and countries adapt to the demands of the Internet economy by training their workers and educating their citizens. E-learning can save money, reduce travel time, increase access to experts, enable large numbers of students to take classes simultaneously, provide on-demand education, and enable self-paced learning. It also may make learning less frustrating by making it more interactive and engaging (e.g., see Wagner 2008 and Roberts 2008).

More specific benefits of e-learning are as follows:

> **Time reduction.** As shown in the Cisco case, e-learning can reduce training time by 50 percent.

> **Large volume and diversity.** E-learning can provide training to a large number of people from diverse cultural backgrounds and educational levels even though they are at different locations in different time zones.

> **Cost reduction.** The cost of providing a learning experience can be reduced by 50 to 70 percent when classroom lectures are replaced by e-learning sessions.

> **Higher content retention.** E-learning students usually are self-initiated and self-paced. Their motive for acquiring more knowledge may be to widen their scope of view or to develop career skills. Such self-motivation may result in content retention that could be 25 to 60 percent higher than with traditional lecturer-led training.

> **Flexibility.** E-learners are able to adjust the time, location, content, and speed of learning according to their own personal schedules. For example, if necessary, they can refer back to previous lectures without affecting the learning pace of other students.

> **Updated and consistent material.** It is almost impossible to economically update the information in textbooks more frequently than every 2 or 3 years; e-learning can offer just-in-time access to timely information. E-learning may be more consistent than material presented in traditional classroom learning, because variations among teachers are eliminated.

> **Fear-free environment.** E-learning can facilitate learning for students who may not wish to join a face-to-face group discussion or participate in class. This kind of behavior usually is attributed to their reluctance to expose their lack of knowledge in public. E-learning can provide a fear-free and privacy-protected environment in which students can put forth any idea without fear of looking stupid.

Tutoring services that once required face time can now be profitably handled online and offshored to low-cost countries such as India. For more discussion of the benefits of e-learning, see e-learningguru.com and elearnmag.com. For current topics, see icl-conference.org and their International Conference.

E-Learning Management

One of the most effective tools for learning management is Blackboard (which was combined with WebCT). A brief description follows.

Example: Blackboard. Blackboard Inc. is the world's largest supplier of course management system software to educational institutions (2,200 universities in 60 countries in 2008).

There is a good chance that you will use the Blackboard framework when using this textbook. These products provide the Internet software needed for e-learning.

How do these products work? A publisher places a book's content, teaching notes, quizzes, and other materials on Blackboard in a standardized format. Instructors can access modules and transfer them into their own Blackboard sites, which can be accessed by their students.

Blackboard offers a complete suite of enterprise software products and services that power a total "e-education infrastructure" for schools, colleges, universities, and other education providers. Blackboard's two major lines of business are Course & Portal Solutions and Commerce & Access Solutions.

A professor can easily incorporate a book's content into the software that is used by thousands of universities worldwide. As of 2007, Blackboard also delivers corporate and government employee training programs in every major region of the world that increase productivity and reduce costs. For details, see blackboard.com and en.wikipedia.org/wiki/blackboard_Inc.

Drawbacks and Challenges of E-Learning

Despite the numerous benefits, e-learning does have some drawbacks. The following issues have been cited as possible drawbacks of e-learning:

▶ **Need for instructor retraining.** Some instructors are not competent in teaching by electronic means and may require additional training. It costs money to provide such training.

▶ **Equipment needs and support services.** Additional funds are needed to purchase multimedia tools to provide support services for e-learning creation, use, and maintenance.

▶ **Lack of face-to-face interaction and campus life.** Many feel that the intellectual stimulation that takes places through instruction in a classroom with a "live" instructor cannot fully be replicated with e-learning.

▶ **Assessment.** In the environment of higher education, one criticism is that professors may not be able to adequately assess student work completed through e-learning. There is no guarantee, for example, of who actually completed the assignments or exams.

▶ **Maintenance and updating.** Although e-learning materials are easier to update than traditionally published materials, there are practical difficulties (e.g., cost, instructors' time) in keeping e-learning materials up-to-date. The content of e-learning material can be difficult to maintain due to the lack of ownership of and accountability for Web site material. In addition, no online course can deliver real-time information and knowledge in the way a "live" instructor can.

▶ **Protection of intellectual property.** It is difficult and expensive to control the transmission of copyrighted works downloaded from the e-learning platform.

▶ **Computer literacy.** E-learning cannot be extended to those students who are not computer literate or do not have access to the Internet.

▶ **Student retention.** Without some human feedback, it may be difficult to keep some students mentally engaged and enthusiastic about e-learning over a long period of time.

Some of these drawbacks can be reduced by advanced technologies. For example, some online products have features that help stimulate student thinking. Offsetting the assessment drawback, biometric controls can be used to verify the identity of students who are taking examinations from home. However, these features add to the costs of e-learning.

From the learner's perspective, the challenge is simply to change the mind-set of how learning typically takes place. Learners must be willing to give up the idea of traditional classroom training, and they must come to understand that continual, lifelong learning will be as much a part of normal work life, past the college years, as voice mail and e-mail. From the teaching perspective, all learning objects must be converted ("tagged") to a digital format. This task can be difficult. Finally, another challenge for e-learning systems is the updating of the knowledge in them—who will do it and how often? Also, how will the cost of the updating be covered?

PREVENTING E-LEARNING FAILURES

Many of those who have tried e-learning have been pleased with it. In many cases, self-selection ensures that those who are likely to benefit from e-learning choose e-learning opportunities. For example, students who live at a great distance from school or who have family responsibilities during traditional school hours will be motivated to put in the time to make e-learning work. Similarly, employees for whom a training course at a distant site is a problem, either because of budget or personal constraints, are likely to be enthusiastic about e-learning programs.

E-learning does not work for everyone, though. It is believed that e-learning failures are due to the following issues (Impact Information 2006):

> ▶ **Believing that e-learning is always a cheaper learning or training alternative.** E-learning can be less expensive than traditional instruction, depending on the number of students. However, if only a few students are to be served, e-learning can be very expensive because of the high fixed costs.
>
> ▶ **Overestimating what e-learning can accomplish.** People sometimes do not understand the limitations of e-learning and, therefore, may expect too much.
>
> ▶ **Overlooking the shortcomings of self-study.** Some people cannot do self-study or do not want to. Others may study incorrectly.
>
> ▶ **Failing to look beyond the course paradigms.** The instructor needs to adapt course content for the e-learning environment with regard to pedagogy.
>
> ▶ **Viewing content as a commodity.** This results in a lack of attention to quality and delivery to individuals.
>
> ▶ **Ignoring technology tools for e-learning or fixating too much on technology as a solution.** A balanced approach is needed.
>
> ▶ **Assuming that learned knowledge will be applied.** This is difficult to accomplish successfully.
>
> ▶ **Believing that because e-learning has been implemented, employees and students will use it.** This is not always the case.

To prevent failure, companies and schools need to address these issues carefully and systematically.

DISTANCE LEARNING AND ONLINE UNIVERSITIES

distance learning
Formal education that takes place off campus, usually, but not always, through online resources.

The term **distance learning** refers to formal education that takes place off campus, often from home. The concept is not new. Educational institutions have been offering correspondence courses and degrees for decades. What is new, however, is the application of IT in general, and the Web in particular, to expand the opportunities for distance learning to the online environment. Neal (2007) describes the role of the Web 2.0 tools in distance learning in higher education, surveying implementation issues in terms of technology, course content, and pedagogy.

virtual university
An online university from which students take classes from home or other offsite locations, usually via the Internet.

The concept of **virtual universities**, online universities from which students take classes from home or an offsite location via the Internet, is expanding rapidly. Hundreds of thousands of students in dozens of countries, from the United Kingdom to Israel to Thailand, are studying in such institutions. A large number of existing universities, including Stanford

University and other top-tier institutions, offer online education of some form; for example, MIT is offering its entire 1,800 course curriculum online. Over 1.5 million independent learners (students, professors, self-learners) log on to the MIT OpenCourseWare site each month. Some universities, such as University of Phoenix (phoenix.edu), California Virtual Campus (cvc.edu), and the University of Maryland (umuc.edu/distance), offer hundreds of courses and dozens of degrees to students worldwide, all online. See distancelearn.about.com for more resources of distance learning and online universities. For a list of the top online MBA programs in the world, see onlinedegrees.com/Online-MBA-Degrees.html.

The virtual university concept allows universities to offer classes worldwide. Moreover, integrated degrees may soon appear by which students can customize a degree that will best fit their needs and take courses at different universities. Several other virtual schools include eschool.com.hk/hongkong, waldenu.edu, and trainingzone.co.uk.

ONLINE CORPORATE TRAINING

Like educational institutions, a large number of business organizations are using e-learning on a large scale (e.g., see Neal 2007). Many companies offer online training, as Cisco does. Some, such as Barclays Bank, COX Industries, and Qantas Airways, call such learning centers "universities." New employees at IBM Taiwan Corp. are given Web-based "electronic training," and KPMG Peat Marwick offers e-learning to its customers.

Corporate training is driven by multiple factors, as shown in Online File W7.4, and is often done via intranets and corporate portals. It has several variations, one of which is on-demand online training, which is offered by companies such as Citrix Systems (citrix.com). However, in large corporations with multiple sites and for studies from home the Internet is used to access the online material. For discussion of strategies for implementing corporate e-learning, see Chan and Ngai (2007) and Sener (2006). Vendors and success stories of online training and educational materials can be found at convergys.com and brightwave.co.uk.

Examples: Corporate Training. The following are a few examples of successful e-training:

▶ Sheetz operates approximately 300 convenience stores across 5 U.S. states. It uses e-training via a corporate portal to train and certify store associates in the proper procedures for alcohol sales. It uses a compliance-tracking tool from Compliance Solutions in the U.S. state of Virginia to monitor employee participation in the classes. The employees must know both government and corporate policies and regulations. The program helped to train about 1,000 employees in 2003, saving the company a considerable amount of money. Compliance Solutions prepares teaching materials for the entire industry.

▶ Shoney's Restaurant chain (over 400 restaurants) needs to provide training continuously to its thousands of employees, from busboys to managers. A multicasting solution (RemoteWare from XcelleNet) is used to offer computer-based training. With multicasting, files are sent by telephone line or satellite from a server to many remote computers at the same time. The system helps both in communication and information dissemination as well as in training. These capabilities have allowed Shoney's to use PCs located at the chain's sites for computer-based training (CBT). Each restaurant has one computer (with speakers) used exclusively for staff training. Training files containing video clips, animation, and spot quizzes are easily transferred to the restaurants' computers. The solution also offers management and evaluation tools (e.g., which employees have completed which courses and how they scored on tests). Course evaluation also is done online. Test results provide indications that aid in improving content. The cost is much lower than training offered via videotape or CD-ROM. Training material is kept up-to-date and is consistent across the corporation. High-quality training has helped the company reduce employee attrition, which means people stay longer at their jobs and provide better customer service.

▶ The University of Toyota (UOT), a division of Toyota Motor Sales, was established in 1999 to develop training for its 8,500 employees and 104,000 dealership associates. In addition to classroom training, UOT develops dozens of e-learning courses per year, all distributed via a commercially available learning management system (LMS). External vendors produce the majority of these courses. UOT uses a single set of development standards, benchmarks, purchasing specifications, and best practices to ensure standardization and quality of the work of the many vendors. This also helps in avoiding duplications and encourages the dissemination of new information among vendors. A major task was to coordinate all e-training efforts. Because each division (e.g., Lexus, Scion, etc.) is fairly independent in managing training, UOT arranges a corporate e-learning team from all divisions to work together with the vendors and the IT units. The best practices of each division are observed and shared among all. These efforts have been more than successful (Morrison 2008). The training is done via the UOT Web site (called E-source). Ease of use and clarity are achieved via standardization and detailed instructions are sent via a bimonthly e-mail bulletin. E-learning enables the elimination of delays in the deployment of new courses and increases learners' satisfaction.

IMPLEMENTING E-LEARNING AND E-TRAINING

Most schools and industries use e-learning as a supplementary channel to traditional classrooms. One facility that is used in industry is the learning center. A *learning center* is a focal point for all corporate training and learning activities, including online ones. Some companies have a learning center dedicated only to online training. However, most companies combine online and offline activities, as done by W. R. Grace and described in Online File W7.4. In industry, an increasing number of companies are using e-learning for teaching all skills, including managerial ones (see Roberts 2008). Large corporations refer to their learning centers as "universities."

For additional information about e-learning, see trainingmag.com, elearnmag.org, and astd.org/lc.

EDUTAINMENT

edutainment

The combination of education and entertainment, often through games.

Edutainment is a combination of education and entertainment, often through games. One of the main goals of edutainment is to encourage students to become active rather than passive learners. With active learning, a student is more involved in the learning process, which makes the learning experience richer and the knowledge gained more memorable. Edutainment embeds learning in an entertaining environment to help students learn almost without their being aware of it.

Edutainment covers various subjects, including mathematics, reading, writing, history, and geography. It is targeted at various age groups, ranging from preschoolers to adults, and it is also used in corporate training over intranets. Software Toolworks (toolworks.com, now a part of the Learning Company at broderbund.com) is a major vendor of edutainment products.

For over a decade, educational games have been delivered mostly on CD-ROMs. However, today increasing numbers of companies now offer online edutainment in a distance learning format (e.g., Knowledge Adventure products at sunburst.com and education.com). A major type of learning is associated with multiplayer electronic games and with virtual worlds.

SOCIAL NETWORKS AND E-LEARNING

Since its inception, social networking has been interrelated with learning. Social networks are virtual spaces where people of all ages can make contacts, share information and ideas, and build a sense of community. Like all technologies, they are built with tools that can serve many purposes.

Well-constructed social environments provide an excellent opportunity to model high-tech learning in a safe online environment, making it possible for employees to share their experiences with others. Several companies are using social networking for training and development (e.g., see advancinginsights.com).

Some students use MySpace, Facebook, and so forth, to connect with other learners. For example, learners can get together and study or hold a discussion online. Unfortunately the clutter and distractions found on these networks can make it difficult to focus on learning. Many MySpace users are seeking other virtual spaces geared to more specific needs, such as study or discussion.

Several social networks (or communities) are dedicated to learning and training (e.g., see e-learning.co.uk). For example, in 2008 Wi5Connect launched Commsocial, a Web 2.0

network platform, to fully leverage social networking's unique power to create "social communities" that can produce business value. The company also launched LearnSocial, which integrates social networking with LMS. Another example of a social network for learning is learnhub.com. Study Curve (studycurve.com) combines social networking and learning for middle schoolers through adults. Users can find experts to answer questions and rate the quality of their responses.

Many universities combine e-learning and social networks, and numerous professors have blogs and wikis for their classes.

LEARNING IN VIRTUAL WORLDS AND SECOND LIFE

A number of interesting learning initiatives have been implemented in virtual worlds, especially in Second Life (SL). Users can participate in simulations, role-plays, construction projects, and social events (see Robbins and Bell 2008 for details). Learners can use virtual worlds to explore ancient civilizations, gothic castles, or fantasy worlds. These places can be springboards to fiction writing, sociology studies, and historical reenactments.

Many people see SL and other virtual worlds as an opportunity to carry out learning projects that would be impossible in the real world because of constraints such as geography or cost. Others see it as a chance to engage a younger generation of learners, many of whom are impatient with traditional forms of education and training. Many see it as a way to advance the practice of learning itself, creating new pedagogies and extending and modifying old ones. Therefore, many refer to SL as the classroom of the future.

Learning in virtual worlds also offers the possibility of collaboration. With the growth in bandwidth, online games are not only multiplayer, but massively multiplayer when played on the Internet. It is no longer a matter of a learner interacting with a learning program. Now learners can interact with each other as well, across dispersed teams and communities of practice around the globe. This further extends the range of the types of learning that can, theoretically, take place in an online environment like SL. Learning a foreign language, team building, and leadership all benefit from group interaction. In addition, students report that they are learning more in SL than they would in the traditional classroom.

Learning in virtual worlds in general, and in Second Life in particular, is growing rapidly, with many activities and projects. According to Lagorio (2007), scores of universities have set up campuses on Second Life's islands, where classes meet and students interact in real time. They hold chat discussions and create multimedia presentations. Consider the following education-related SL applications:

▶ The New Media Consortium has created an experimental learning space called NMC Campus where members can explore learning and collaboration.

Source: Image by Jo Kay, via Flickr at: flickr.com/photos/33002318@N00/466962751. Used with permission.

- Info Island is an online space where users can explore innovative exhibits of information and participate in live in-world meetings with real-life authors. It also provides space for educators and nonprofit organizations.
- The International Spaceflight Museum is a great example of using SL to create something that would be almost impossible to build in real life.
- Aura Lily is a place where people with a passion for ancient Egypt can re-create artifacts and architecture of ancient Egypt using maps drawn by Napoleon's engineers.
- The Angel Learning Isle is a place for educators to meet, discuss, and create new courses (see the Gazebo of Knowledge there).
- Architecture professors bring their students to SL to build things that would either be too expensive or even physically impossible to create in the real world. The students can see each other while they are building and work collaboratively on projects.
- Psychologists and sociologists study what people choose to do in SL and why they are doing it.
- Ohio University Without Boundaries offers an SL virtual campus featuring multiple learning and collaboration opportunities for students on the Ohio campus and all over the world.
- Ball State and other schools have bought "land" on SL to build a campus. Ball State's Middletown Island has a tiki bar and lounge for dancing, a coffee shop, and dorms where students can "live" in SL without having to buy their own land. The students decorate their dorms with furnishings they buy in SL and then write about the experience for a composition class. And since anyone's avatar can look female or male (or not human at all), some students are writing about what it's like to be taken for the opposite gender.
- In a class taught at San Francisco State University, IT professor Sam Gill employs a virtual world to introduce students to business process management. Normally, students go to a McDonald's to see how it sells a burger. In SL, the students study a fictional business created by IBM.

The Second Life experience is particularly enhanced for distance learning. Of special interest is Harvard University Extension School.

Example: Harvard's Berkman Island. As of October 2008, several hundred universities have set up shops inside SL. In the fall semester of 2008, one Harvard University class held class meetings on Berkman Island within SL. Avatars representing the students and teachers gathered in an "outdoor" amphitheater, entered a virtual replica of Harvard Law School's Austin Hall, and traveled all over the digital world to complete assignments. Some

Ohio University's Second Life Campus

Source: Courtesy of Ohio University. Used with permission.

90 Harvard Law and Extension School students took the course, called "CyberOne: Law in the Court of Public Opinion," for real college credit. However, anyone on Earth with a computer connection could take the course for free. Students from as far away as South Korea and China participated. The students, who communicated via text messaging, were even able to have private one-to-one asides, just as they might in the real world.

Real-Life Education in Second Life

Second Life (SL) Educators (SLED) (see lists.secondlife.com/cgi-bin/mailman/listinfo/educators and Rymaszewski et al. 2007) was created to help educators find colleagues and collaborators in SL. SLED helps educators learn about the SL environment. It also sponsors meet-and-greet events in SL, helping real-life educators to connect with each other. SLED also advises educational institutions on how to create private virtual campuses in SL that are not open to the public.

Students and educators can work together in SL from anywhere in the world as part of a globally networked virtual classroom environment. Using SL as a supplement to traditional classroom environments provides new opportunities for enriching existing curricula. Many students would gladly schedule time for the virtual classroom. Educators should not be slow to step in and embrace this simple-to-use, interpersonal, and further-developing media.

VISUAL INTERACTIVE SIMULATION

An effective technology for e-training and e-learning is *visual interactive simulations* (VIS), which uses computer graphic displays to present the impact of decisions. It differs from regular graphics in that the user can adjust the decision-making process and see the results of the intervention. Some learners respond better to graphical displays, especially when it is done interactively. For example, VIS was used to examine the operations of a physician clinic environment within a physician network in an effort to provide high-quality, cost-effective health care in a family practice. The simulation system identified the most important input factors that significantly affected performance. These inputs, when properly managed, led to lower costs and higher service levels (Swisher et al. 2001).

VIS can represent a static or a dynamic system. Static models display a visual image of the result of one decision alternative at a time. Dynamic models display systems that evolve over time, and the evolution can be presented by animation. The learner can interact with the simulated model, watch the results develop over time, and try different activities or decision strategies.

The major potential benefits of such systems are:

⬧ Shortened learning time
⬧ Aids in teaching how to operate complex equipment
⬧ Enables self-paced learning, any place, any time
⬧ Aids in memorization
⬧ Lowers overall training costs
⬧ Records an individual's learning progress and improves upon it

Several companies provide the necessary software and learning procedures for VIS. One product is SimMAGIC from Hamastar Technology Co. (hamastar.com.tw). Exhibit 7.5 shows how the application is applied at a pharmaceutical company. Exhibit 7.6 provides a trainee progress chart.

E-LEARNING TOOLS AND MANAGEMENT

Many e-learning tools are available (e.g., see the directories of products and services at trainingmag.com). One of the facilitators of e-learning is Web 2.0 technologies, such as blogs and wikis (see wikipedia.com). The following are several examples of the use of Web 2.0 in e-learning:

⬧ IBM Workplace Collaborative Learning 2.0 software (ibm.com/software/workplace/collaborativelearning) is a Web-based tool that can be customized to fit a company's training needs. It uses customer-supplied job profile information to deliver role-based learning resources right to the users' desktops.

EXHIBIT 7.5 SimMagic Training Application

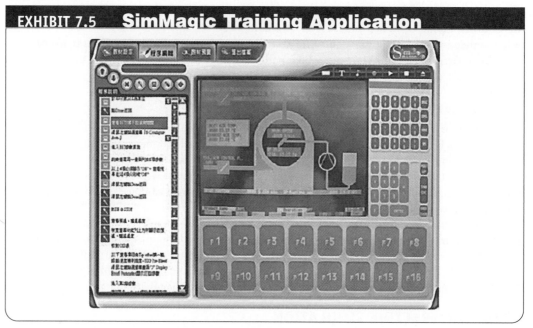

Source: Courtesy of Hamastar Technology. Used with permission.

▶ ComputerPREP (computerprep.com) offers almost 400 e-learning products, including a comprehensive library of Web-based classroom, distance-learning, and self-study curricula. Students can even combine products from different categories to customize their learning environments.

▶ Macromedia offers tools for wireless devices at adobe.com/software.

▶ eCollege (ecollege.com) offers an e-learning platform that includes free collaboration tools.

▶ Camtasia studio offers many e-learning tools, some of which instructors and students can use to create video tutorials (see techsmith.com/camtasia).

For additional information about e-learning, see trainingmag.com, elearnmag.org, and learningcircuits.org.

E-learning content can be facilitated with the aid of online publishing and e-books (Section 7.4), wikis and blogs (Chapter 2), and knowledge management (Section 7.5).

EXHIBIT 7.6 SimMagic Trainee Progress Chart

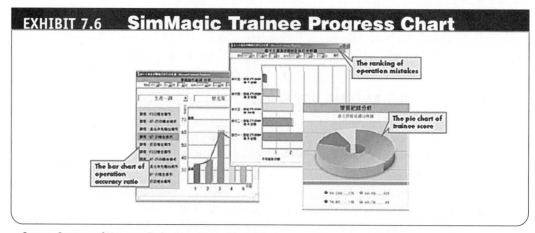

Source: Courtesy of Hamastar Technology. Used with permission.

Section 7.3 ❱ REVIEW QUESTIONS

1. Define e-learning and describe its drivers and benefits.
2. List some of the major drawbacks of e-learning and describe how they can be prevented.
3. Describe virtual universities and distance learning.
4. Define e-training and describe how it is done.
5. Describe the connection between learning and social networking.
6. Describe learning in virtual worlds.
7. List some e-learning tools and describe Blackboard and visual interactive simulation.

7.4 ONLINE PUBLISHING AND E-BOOKS

The movement of paper information to an electronic format has had a revolutionary impact on both the dissemination of information and learning. **Online publishing** is the electronic delivery of newspapers, magazines, books, news, music, videos, and other digitizable information over the Internet. Initiated in the late 1960s, online publishing was designed to provide online bibliographies and to sell knowledge that was stored in online commercial databases.

Today, online publishing has additional purposes. It facilitates e-learning, provides entertainment, disseminates knowledge, and supports advertising (because it is sometimes provided for free to attract people to sites where advertising is conducted). Publishers of traditional hard-copy media have expanded to add online operations. Magazine and newspaper publishers such as *Time*, *PC Magazine*, the *Wall Street Journal*, and *Adweek* all use online publishing to disseminate information online. Many magazines are offered only online; they are referred to as e-zines (e.g., technewsworld.com). Online publishing may be customized for the recipients.

online publishing
The electronic delivery of newspapers, magazines, books, news, music, videos, and other digitizable information over the Internet.

CONTENT PROVIDERS, PUBLISHERS, AND DISTRIBUTORS

Similar to offline publishing, online publishing involves several participants.

Content Providers and Distribution Methods

Content providers and distributors are those who provide and distribute content online. These services are offered by several specialized companies (e.g., akamai.com and mirror-image.com), as well as by news services such as the Associated Press and ABC News. Due to the difficulty of presenting multimedia, especially in wireless systems, content providers face major challenges when operating in an environment of less-developed infrastructures. Also, the issue of intellectual property payments is critical to the success of content distribution. If authors do not receive payments for or recognition of their work, content providers may face legal problems. However, even if payments are made, the providers' costs may be too high.

Many online content providers are starting to charge for content because advertising is proving insufficient to cover their expenses. In addition, more readers appear willing to pay for online publications. For example, the *New York Times* started to charge for articles in 2002.

Publishing of Music, Videos, Games, and Entertainment

The Internet is an ideal medium for publishing music, videos, electronic games, and related entertainment. As with content providers, a major issue here is the payment of intellectual property fees (see Chapter 16).

One of the most interesting new capabilities in this area is peer-to-peer networks over which people swap digital files, such as music or video files (Section 7.6). When such swapping is managed by a third-party exchange (e.g., Napster or Kazaa), the third party may be in violation of copyright law. For a discussion of the social and legal impacts of online music sharing activities, see Bhattacharjee et al. (2006). More and more people are willing to pay for digital music, as shown by the success of Apple's iTunes and similar programs.

Webcasting

One way that new or obscure musicians promote their work on the Web is by using **Webcasting**, or "live Webcasting shows." This is a free Internet news service that broadcasts personalized news and information, including seminars, in categories selected by the user. Some sites charge fees for such Webcasts. For example, onlineevents.com.au broadcasts Webcasts to inform clients about Australian and international entertainment activities. Affiliate clubs and artists get royalty payments based on how many people purchase and download a particular performance. CIO Insight (cioinsight.com) provides Webcasts on e-commerce topics. House of Blue's hob.com has been a pioneer in offering pay-per-view Webcasts.

Webcasting also can be used to broadcast public lectures. For example, CIO Insight and DM Review (dmreview.com) offer Webcast seminars, known as **Webinars**, or e-seminars. Many other sites offer e-seminars.

Podcasting

A **podcast** is a media file that is distributed by subscription (paid or unpaid) over the Internet using syndication feeds for playback on mobile devices or personal computers. As with the term *radio*, a podcast refers to both the content and the method of syndication. The host or author of a podcast is often called a *podcaster*. The term *podcast* is derived from Apple's portable music player, the iPod. A pod refers to a container of some sort; thus, the idea of broadcasting to a container, or pod, correctly describes the process of podcasting.

Though podcasters' Web sites may also offer direct download or streaming content, a podcast is distinguished from other digital audio formats by its ability to be downloaded automatically, using software capable of reading feed formats such as RSS. For more on podcasts, see en.wikipedia.org/wiki/Podcasts. For business applications of podcasts, see Gibson (2006).

ELECTRONIC BOOKS

An **electronic book**, or **e-book**, is a book in digital form that can be read on a computer screen, including handheld computers and a special reader. A major event in electronic publishing occurred on March 24, 2000, when Stephen King's book *Riding the Bullet* was published exclusively online. For $2.50, readers could purchase the e-book at amazon.com, ebooks.com, and other e-book providers. Several hundred thousand copies were sold in a few days. However, the publishing event did not go off without some problems. Hackers breached the security system and distributed free copies of the book. There are several distinct types of e-books, as described in Online File W7.5.

Publishers of e-books have since become more sophisticated, and the business of e-publishing has become more secure. E-books can be delivered and read in various ways:

- ▶ **Via Web access.** Readers can locate a book on the publisher's Web site and read it there. The book cannot be downloaded. It may be interactive, including links and rich multimedia.
- ▶ **Via Web download.** Readers can download the book to a PC.
- ▶ **Via a dedicated reader.** The book must be downloaded to a special device (an e-book reader).
- ▶ **Via a general-purpose reader.** The book can be downloaded to a general-purpose device, such as a Palm Pilot.
- ▶ **Via a Web server.** The contents of a book are stored on a Web server and downloaded for print-on-demand (see later discussion).

Most e-books require some type of payment. Readers either pay before they download a book from a Web site, or they pay when they order the special CD-ROM edition of a book. Amazon.com offers about 300,000 e-books, newspapers (including international ones), and much more. All are cheaper than the hard-copy version (e.g., new releases of books cost only $10).

Devices for Reading E-Books

The major device used to read an e-book is an e-book reader. Most e-book readers are lightweight (about 10 ounces) and convenient to carry. The major readers are:

- Kindle 2 from Amazon.com. This popular reader cost $359 in 2008, and it can hold over 200 titles. For capabilities, photos, and a video demonstration, go to amazon.com and search for "kindle 2.0." For more on Kindle, see Perenson (2009).
- The Sony PRS-200, which costs $400, can store 350 e-books in its internal memory. An older model, PRS-505, is available for $300. More content can be loaded onto special memory cards (in 2007) can store up to 100GB (see tigerdirect.com).

Several other aids are available to help readers who want to read large amounts of material online. For example, ClearType from Microsoft and CoolType from Adobe can be used to improve screen display, colors, and font sizes.

Advantages and Limitations of E-Books

For e-books to make an impact, they must offer advantages to both readers and publishers. Otherwise, there would be little incentive to change from the traditional format. E-books, like other books, can be used for pleasure reading and as textbooks to support learning (see Chu and Lam 2006).

Kindle 2.0

Source: Courtesy of Amazon.com. Used with permission.

The major advantage of e-books to readers is lower cost and portability. Readers can carry as many as 200 books wherever they go (and more when portable memory drives are used). Other advantages are easy search capabilities and links; easy downloading; the ability to quickly and inexpensively copy material, including figures; easy integration of content with other text; easy updating, no wear and tear on a physical book; ability to find out-of-print books; and books can be published and updated quickly, so they can be current up-to-the-minute.

E-books also can reduce some of the physical burdens of traditional books. A number of studies have shown that 6 out of 10 students ages 9 to 20 report chronic back pain related to heavy backpacks filled with books. Some schools have eliminated lockers for safety reasons, causing students to carry heavy backpacks not only to and from school, but all day long. A number of schools are experimenting with eliminating textbooks altogether and using an Internet-based curriculum or school materials on CD-ROMs.

The primary advantage that e-books offer publishers is lower production, marketing, and delivery costs, which have a significant impact on the price of books (e-textbooks are about 50% cheaper than print versions). Other advantages for publishers are lower updating and reproduction costs; the ability to reach many readers; the ease of combining several books, so professors can customize textbooks by using materials from different books by the same publisher; and lower advertising costs (see Chu and Lam 2006).

Of course, e-books have some limitations: They require hardware and software that may be too expensive for some readers; some people have difficulty reading large amounts of material on a screen; batteries may run down; and there are multiple, competing standards.

E-Book Issues

According to the Association of American Publishers (2008), e-book sales were up 26.1 percent for the year 2008. Despite persistent growth in the use of e-books and their functionalities, e-books generally are not selling well in relation to the overall size of the book market. Although e-books are easy to read, are generally platform independent, have high-resolution displays, and can be read using long-lasting batteries, customers are still reluctant to change their habits. The following issues, when resolved, will contribute to the ease of use and popularity of e-books:

> ▶ How to protect the publisher's/author's copyright.
> ▶ How to secure content (e.g., use encryption, employ Digital Rights Management [DRM]; see Chapter 16, and en.wikipedia.org/wiki/Digital_Rights_Management).
> ▶ How to distribute and sell e-books.
> ▶ How much to charge for an e-book versus a hard copy, and how to collect payment for e-books.
> ▶ How to best support navigation in an e-book.
> ▶ Which standards to use (e.g., see the Online Information Exchange Standard [ONIX] developed by EDItEUR [editeur.org/onix.html]).
> ▶ How to increase reading speed. On the average screen, reading is 25 percent slower than hard-copy reading.
> ▶ How to transform readers from hard-copy books to e-books; how to deal with resistance to change.
> ▶ How to design an e-book (e.g., how to deal with fonts, typefaces, colors, etc., online).
> ▶ How publishers can justify e-books in terms of profit and market share.

Free e-books and white papers on e-publishing are available from a large number of sites (e.g., free-ebooks.net and fictionwise.com). For more information on e-books, see netlibrary.com. Although e-books are only a minute fraction of the book industry, it is growing fast (doubling every 2 years, per Association of American Publishers 2008).

Digital Libraries

Many organizations are building digital libraries of e-books, journals, periodicals, and other materials. In fact, most universities no longer subscribe to paper periodicals. Electronic library items (books, journals, and periodicals) are cheaper, easier to handle, do not require storage space, and are amenable to electronic searches.

Google has been digitizing millions of print volumes to create to the Google Print database. Partnering with Google on this project are universities, including Harvard, Stanford, and Oxford, as well as the New York Public Library. The British Library in London has partnered with Microsoft, digitizing around 25 million pages of its books.

PRINT-ON-DEMAND

A recent trend in publishing is print-on-demand, which refers to customized printing jobs, usually in small quantities, possibly only one document or book. The process is especially attractive for small print jobs because both the total fixed setup cost and the per unit setup cost can be very low.

The print-on-demand process has three steps:

1. A publisher creates a digital master, typically in Adobe Systems' Acrobat format, and sends it to a specialized print-on-demand company. The files are stored on the printing company's network.

2. When an order is placed, a print-on-demand machine prints out the text of the document or book and then covers, binds, and trims it. The entire process can take about a minute for a 300-page book.

3. The book is packaged and shipped to the publisher or the consumer.

Most textbook publishers now offer print-on-demand textbooks, including Pearson Education, the publisher of this book.

Section 7.4 ▶ REVIEW QUESTIONS

1. Define online publishing and list some advantages it offers over traditional media.
2. List the major methods of online publishing.
3. What issues are involved in content creation and distribution?
4. Describe e-books and list their advantages and limitations.
5. List five e-book issues.
6. Describe print-on-demand.

7.5 KNOWLEDGE MANAGEMENT, LEARNING, AND ELECTRONIC COMMERCE

The term *knowledge management* frequently is mentioned in discussions of e-learning. Why is this? To answer this question, one first needs to understand what knowledge management is.

AN OVERVIEW OF KNOWLEDGE MANAGEMENT

Knowledge management and e-learning both use the same "coin of the realm"—knowledge. Whereas e-learning uses that "coin" for the sake of individual learning, knowledge management uses it to improve the functioning of an organization. Knowledge is one of the most important assets in any organization, and thus it is important to capture, store, and apply it. These are the major purposes of knowledge management. Thus, knowledge management (KM) refers to the process of capturing or creating knowledge, storing and protecting it, updating it constantly, disseminating it, and using it whenever necessary. For a comprehensive discussion of KM, see Holsapple (2003) and kmworld.com. For KM resources, see en.wikipedia.org/wiki/knowledge_management.

Knowledge is collected from both external and internal sources. Then it is examined, interpreted, refined, and stored in what is called an *organizational knowledge base*, the repository for

knowledge management (KM)

The process of capturing or creating knowledge, storing it, updating it constantly, disseminating it, and using it whenever necessary.

the enterprise's knowledge. A major purpose of an organizational knowledge base is to allow for *knowledge sharing*. Knowledge sharing among employees, with customers, and with business partners has a huge potential payoff in improved customer service, the ability to solve difficult organizational problems, shorter delivery cycle times, and increased collaboration within the company and with business partners. Furthermore, some knowledge can be sold to others or traded for other knowledge.

KM promotes an *integrated* approach to the process of handling an enterprise's information assets, both those that are documented and the tacit expertise stored in individuals' heads. The integration of information resources is at the heart of KM. EC implementation involves a considerable amount of knowledge—about customers, suppliers, logistics, procurement, markets, and technology. The integration of that knowledge is required for successful EC applications. These applications are aimed at increasing organizational competitiveness. The KM/EC connection will be described in more detail later in this section. First, though, let's examine KM types and activities.

Knowledge management programs are typically tied to organizational objectives such as performance, competitive advantage, innovation, development processes, best practices, communities of practice, transfer of lessons learned, and the general development of collaborative practices. Knowledge management is frequently linked to lifelong learning. Knowledge management also focuses on the management of knowledge as an asset and the development and cultivation of the channels through which knowledge is disseminated.

KM TYPES AND ACTIVITIES

Organizational knowledge is embedded in the following resources: (1) human capital, which includes employee knowledge, competencies, and creativity; (2) structured capital (organizational capital), which includes organizational structure and culture, processes, patents, and the capability to leverage knowledge through sharing and transferring; and (3) customer capital, which includes the relationship between organizations and their customers and other partners.

This organizational knowledge must be properly managed, and this is the purpose of KM. KM has the following major tasks:

> **Create knowledge.** Knowledge is created as people determine new ways of doing things or develop know-how. Sometimes external knowledge is brought in.
>
> **Capture knowledge.** New knowledge must be identified as valuable and be represented in a reasonable way.
>
> **Refine knowledge.** New knowledge must be placed in context so that it is actionable. This is where human insights (tacit qualities) must be captured along with explicit facts.
>
> **Store knowledge.** Useful knowledge must then be stored in a reasonable format in a knowledge repository so that others in the organization can access it.
>
> **Manage knowledge.** Like a library, the knowledge must be kept current. It must be reviewed to verify that it is relevant and accurate.
>
> **Disseminate knowledge.** Knowledge must be made available in a useful format to anyone in the organization who needs it, anywhere and anytime.

These tasks can be viewed as a cyclical process, as shown in Exhibit 7.7.

For a comprehensive list of KM activities and tools, see en.wikipedia.org/wiki/knowledge_management and kmworld.com.

Knowledge Sharing

Knowledge is of limited value if it is not updated and shared. The social networking boom discussed in Chapter 9 is based, in part, on the creation, updating, and sharing of online knowledge (or content). The ability to share knowledge decreases its cost and increases its

---

EXHIBIT 7.7 **The Knowledge Management System Cycle**

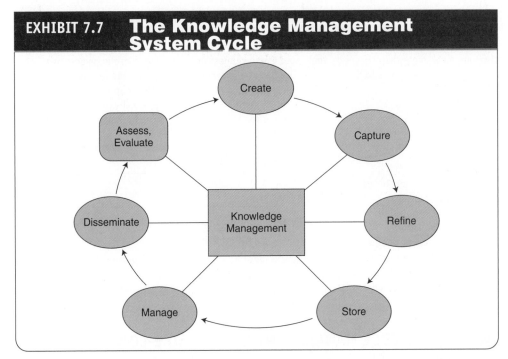

---

effectiveness for greater competitive advantage. Thus, a major purpose of KM is to increase knowledge sharing. Shared knowledge can also decrease risk and uncertainty. KM is about sharing a company's knowledge repository, but increasingly it is also about sharing the information stored in people's heads. An example of a knowledge sharing system at Infosystem is provided in Case 7.2. An example about KM at Xerox is provided in Online File W7.6.

CASE 7.2

Application Case

KNOWLEDGE MANAGEMENT AT INFOSYS TECHNOLOGIES

The Problem

A global software services company based in India, Infosys Technologies is a worldwide leader in outsourcing. With over 23,000 employees and globally distributed operations, Infosys develops IT solutions for some of the largest corporations in the world. During the past 10 years, Infosys has experienced annual growth of 30 percent. Infosys faced a challenge of keeping its large employee base up-to-date, staying ahead of both its competitors and clients, and ensuring that the lessons learned in one part of the organization were available to its consultants so they could reuse the knowledge accumulated in the company. The company's motto is "Learn once, use anywhere." The company's vision is that every instance of learning within Infosys should be available to every employee. But how does an organization turn such a vision into a reality?

The Solution

Infosys Technologies' effort to convert each employee's knowledge into an organizational asset started in the early 1990s and extended well into the first decade of 2000s. In the early 1990s, Infosys launched its *bodies of knowledge (BOK)* initiative, which involved encouraging employees to provide written accounts of their experiences across various topics, such as

technologies, software development, and living abroad. These experiences were then shared in hard-copy form with all other employees. This early effort ballooned into a full-fledged KM effort supported by e-mail, bulletin boards, and various knowledge repositories. In 1996, a corporate intranet was developed to make BOKs, in HTML format, easily accessible to all. In 1999, Infosys began an organization-wide program to integrate the various knowledge initiatives. A central *knowledge portal* was created, called KShop, and although the KM group developed the technology infrastructure, local groups were encouraged to maintain their own content on KShop.

The content of KShop consisted of different content types—BOKs, case studies, reusable artifacts, and downloadable software—each with its own homepage. Content was carefully categorized by the KM group to ensure that as the amount of content increased, it would still be possible for people to quickly find what they needed.

In early 2000, Infosys appeared to have a very functional KM system, and yet patronage by employees remained low. The KM group therefore initiated a reward scheme to increase both use and contribution. The scheme gave employees who contributed to KShop knowledge currency units (KCUs) that could be accumulated and exchanged for monetary rewards or prizes.

(continued)

CASE 7.2   (continued)

As you can see, KM initiatives are much more than the implementation of technology tools to allow employees to create or document knowledge. Infosys's KM initiatives involved processes to organize knowledge, to categorize knowledge, and to rate knowledge usefulness, as well as strategies to encourage knowledge sharing and reuse.

The Results

Within a year of the introduction of the incentive KCU scheme, 2,400 new knowledge assets had been contributed to KShop by some 20 percent of Infosys's employees. However, as the volume of content increased, so, too, did problems relating to finding the needed information. Moreover, the heavy growth in contributions taxed the limited number of volunteer reviewers, who served an important quality-control function. The KM group therefore modified the KCU incentive scheme. It developed a new KCU scheme

that rated the usefulness of knowledge from the perspective of the users of the knowledge, rather than the reviewers. And, to increase accountability, the KM group requested tangible proof to justify any high ratings. Finally, the KM group raised the bar for cashing in KCU points for monetary awards.

Sources: Compiled from *infosys.com* (accessed October 2008) and Garud and Kumaraswamy (2005).

Questions

1. Why are consulting organizations interested in KM?
2. Identify the KM cycle in this case.
3. Why is a reward system beneficial? Compare the old and new reward systems.
4. Why was using a single portal beneficial?

HOW IS KNOWLEDGE MANAGEMENT RELATED TO E-COMMERCE?

To better perform their EC tasks, organizations need knowledge, which is provided by KM. For example, strategic planning in traditional organizations needs considerable amounts of knowledge. To mitigate this problem, e-commerce can proactively incorporate KM processes to facilitate quick access to different types of knowledge.

By analyzing database marketing data in a timely manner, organizations can learn about their customers and generate useful knowledge for planning and decision making. For these activities to be successful in both B2B and B2C, appropriate knowledge is needed to interpret information and to execute activities.

Core knowledge management activities for companies doing EC should include the following electronically supported activities: identification, creation, capture and codification, classification, distribution, utilization, and evolution of the knowledge needed to develop products and partnerships. *Knowledge creation* involves using various computer based tools and techniques to analyze transaction data and generate new ideas. *Knowledge capture and codification* includes gathering new knowledge and storing it in a machine-readable form. *Knowledge classification* organizes knowledge using appropriate dimensions relating it to its use. *Knowledge distribution* is sharing relevant information with suppliers, consumers, and other internal and external stakeholders through electronic networks—both public and private. *Knowledge utilization* involves appropriate application of knowledge to problem solving. *Knowledge evolution* entails updating knowledge as time progresses.

Some managers believe that a major role of KM is linking EC and business processes. Specifically, knowledge generated in EC contributes to the enhancement of three core processes: CRM, SCM, and product development management. For more on KM-enabling technologies and how they can be applied to business unit initiatives, see kmworld.com and knowledgestorm.com.

KM and Social Networks

A major area of KM is knowledge creation in communities, which is also known as the *wisdom of the crowd* and *communities of practice*. This area has several variations. One variety is limited within a single company (see the Knowledge Network in the opening case of Caterpillar). Another is a public community whose members are interested in a common area of interest. Yet another type is a combination of the two. The major purposes of such communities are:

▶ **Knowledge creation.** The creation of knowledge for a specific problem or area. Individuals are asked to contribute to a solution or offer valuable advice. For example, IBM, GE, and other companies have communities of employees and business partners who contribute to knowledge creations.

▶ **Knowledge sharing.** Members share knowledge by telling other members where to find knowledge of interest to the community. For example, Microsoft Vine is a community that supports those interested in emergency services information exchange.

Web 2.0 applications help aggregate corporate knowledge and simplify the building of repositories of best practices, as demonstrated by the following example.

Example: IBM's Innovation Jam. IBM has long used communities for problem solving. One of its best-known communities is the Innovation Jam, an online brainstorming session. This community of over 150,000 employees and business partners tries to move the latest technologies to the market. IBM has been hosting online brainstorming sessions since 2001. For example, in July 2006 IBM invited employees, partners, and customers to contribute ideas about a certain new product. Within 72 hours, more than 50,000 ideas were posted. These ideas were then winnowed down by using sophisticated analytical software.

Virtual meetings where IBM employees can participate in Innovation Jam launches are conducted in Second Life. IBM's CEO has even created an avatar to represent him. Topics that have been explored by recent Innovation Jams have included new technologies for water filtration, 3D Internet, and branchless banking. For more on IBM's Innovation Jams and use of virtual worlds, see Bjelland and Wood (2008) and en.wikipedia.org/wiki/IBM_Virtual_Universe_Community.

KNOWLEDGE PORTALS

Knowledge portals are single-point-of-access software systems intended to provide easy and timely access to knowledge and to support communities of knowledge workers who share common goals. Knowledge portals can be used for either external or internal use.

Knowledge portals support various tasks performed by knowledge workers: gathering, organizing, searching for, and analyzing information; synthesizing solutions with respect to specific task goals; and then sharing and distributing what has been learned with other knowledge workers. Online File W7.7 describes how IBM uses a knowledge portal to support the work of consultants at IBM and what technologies can be used to support each category of tasks. For further details on how knowledge portals are related to collaborative and intellectual capital management, see Jones et al. (2006).

knowledge portal
A single point of access software system intended to provide timely access to information and to support communities of knowledge workers.

ONLINE ADVICE AND CONSULTING

Another use of knowledge online is offering advice and consulting services. The online advice and consulting field is growing rapidly as tens of thousands of experts of all kinds sell (or provide for free) their expertise over the Internet. The following are some examples:

▶ **Medical advice.** Companies such as WebMD (webmd.com) and others (see liveperson.com) provide health-advice consultations with top medical experts. Consumers can ask specific questions and get an answer from a specialist in a few days. Health sites also offer specialized advice and tips for travelers, for pet owners, and more.

▶ **Management consulting.** Many consultants are selling their accumulated expertise from organizational knowledge bases. A pioneer in this area was Andersen Consulting (now Accenture at accenture.com). Other management consultants that sell knowledge online are Aberdeen (aberdeen.com) and Forrester Research (forresterresearch.com). Because of their high consultation fees, such services mainly are used by corporations.

▶ **Legal advice.** Delivery of legal advice to individuals and businesses by consultation services has considerable prospects. For example, Atlanta-based law firm Alston & Bird coordinates legal counseling with 12 law firms for a large health-care company and for many other clients.

▶ **Gurus and answers to questions.** Several sites provide diversified expert services, some for free. One example is guru.com, which offers general advice and a job board for experts on legal, financial, tax, technical, lifestyle, and other issues. As of 2007, it has aggregated over 480,000 professional "gurus." Expertise is advertised at elance.com, where one can post a required service for experts to bid on. Of special interest is sciam.com, which offers advice from science experts at Scientific American. Some of the most popular services that offer information from experts are answers.com (previously GuruNet), answers.yahoo.com, catholic.com, healthanswers.com, wineanswers.com, and many more. Some provide answers for free; others charge fees for premium services. Answers.com (with its teachers.answers.com) provides free access to over 4 million answers and generates income from advertising.

▶ **Financial advice.** Many companies offer extensive financial advice. For example, Merrill Lynch Online (totalmerrill.com) provides free access to some of the firm's research reports and analyses.

▶ **Social networks.** Several social networks allow users to post questions and get answers. For business-oriented questions, go to linkedin.com.

▶ **Other advisory services.** Many other advisory services are available online—some for free and others for a fee. For example, guestfinder.com makes it easy for people who work in the media to find guests and interview sources.

One word of caution about advice: It is not wise to risk your health, your money, or your legal status on free or even for-fee online advice. Always seek more than one opinion, and carefully check the credentials of any advice provider.

EMPLOYEE KNOWLEDGE NETWORKS AND EXPERT LOCATION SYSTEMS

Expert advice can be provided within an organization in a variety of ways. Human expertise is rare; therefore, companies attempt to preserve it electronically in corporate knowledge bases. Alternatively, electronic expert systems may be used. Although such systems are very useful and they can be used directly by nonexperts, they cannot solve all problems, especially new ones. For such cases, human experts are needed. In large organizations, it may be difficult to locate experts quickly. Recently, social networking is being used.

Finding Experts Electronically

People who need help may post their problem on the corporate intranet (e.g., using blogs) or on public social networks such as LinkedIn (linkedin.com) and ask for help internally and/or externally. Similarly, companies may ask for advice on how to exploit an opportunity. IBM frequently uses this method. Sometimes it obtains hundreds of useful ideas within a few days. It is a kind of brainstorming. The problem with this approach is that it may take days to get an answer, if an answer is even provided, and the answer may not be from the top experts. Therefore, companies employ expert location systems and social networking.

Example. PricewaterhouseCoopers, a large CPA and management services company, has introduced an "Ask the Experts" program that offers users extended access to expertise. Clicking on an expert's picture automatically generates an e-mail to that person—allowing users to ask the experts anything they like. Learners can use the feature to ask questions to facilitate learning. They also can also join discussion forums and consult a glossary of industry terms.

Expert Location Systems

expert location systems
Interactive computerized systems that help employees find and connect with colleagues who have expertise required for specific problems—whether they are across the country or across the room—in order to solve specific, critical business problems in seconds.

Expert location systems (ELS) are interactive computerized systems that help employees find and connect with colleagues with expertise required for specific problems—whether they are across the country or across the room—in order to solve specific, critical business problems in seconds. Expertise location systems are designed to:

▶ Connect people to people
▶ Link people to information about people
▶ Identify people with expertise and link them to those with questions or problems
▶ Identify potential staff for projects requiring specific expertise
▶ Assist in career development
▶ Provide support for teams and communities of practice.

Software for such systems is made by companies such as AskMe, RightNow Technologies, and Tacit Knowledge Systems, Inc. For example, AskMe Enterprise, a software solution for deploying employee knowledge networks, enables organizations to fully leverage employee knowledge and expertise to drive innovations and improve bottom-line performance. The solution is the result of AskMe's collaboration, experience and success with real-world customer deployments and many companies. For benefits, features, and demonstrations, see askmecorp.com. Most expert location systems work similarly, exploring knowledge bases for either an answer to the problem (if it exists there) or locating qualified experts. The generic process is shown in Exhibit 7.8. The four steps of the process are:

1. An employee submits a question to the ELS.

2. The software searches its database to see if an answer to the question already exists. If it does, the information (research reports, spreadsheets, etc.) is returned to the employee. If not, the software searches documents and archived communications for an "expert."

3. Once a qualified candidate is located, the system asks if he or she is able to answer a question from a colleague, If so, the expert submits a response. If the expert is unable to respond, he or she can elect to pass on the question. The question is then routed to the next appropriate candidate until one responds.

4. After the response is sent, it is reviewed for accuracy and sent back to the person who made the query. At the same time, the question and its response are added to the knowledge database. This way, if the question comes up again, it will not be necessary to seek real-time assistance.

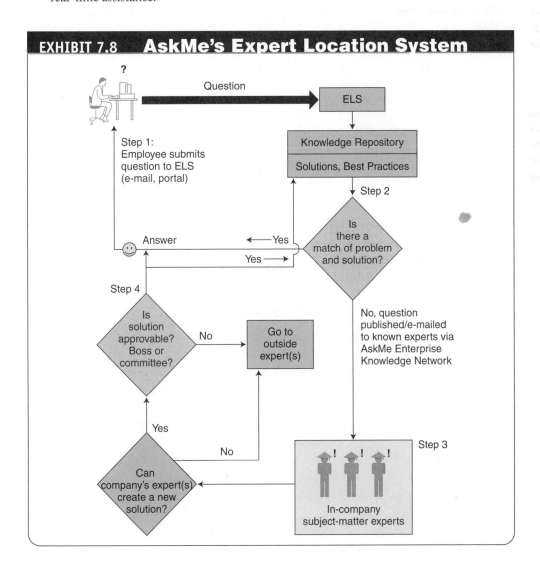

EXHIBIT 7.8   AskMe's Expert Location System

Case 7.3 demonstrates how such a system works for the U.S. government.

EC Application

HOW THE U.S. DEPARTMENT OF COMMERCE USES AN EXPERT LOCATION SYSTEM

The U.S. Commercial Service Division at the Department of Commerce (DOC) conducts approximately 200,000 counseling sessions a year involving close to $40 billion in trade. The division employs many specialists who frequently need to do research or call on experts to answer a question posed by a U.S. corporation.

For example, in May 2004 a U.S.–based software company called Brad Anderson, a DOC specialist, for advice. The software company wanted to close a deal with a customer in Poland, but the buyer wanted to charge the U.S. company a 20-percent withholding tax, a tax it attributed to Poland's recent admission into the European Union. Was the tax legitimate?

To find out, Anderson turned to the DOC Insider, an expertise location system (from AskMe). After typing in his question, Anderson first found some documents that were related to his query, but they did not explain the EU tax code completely. Anderson next asked the system to search the 1,700-strong Commercial Service for a real "live" expert, and within seconds, he was given a list of 80 people in the DOC who might be able to help him. Of those, he chose the six people he felt were most qualified and then forwarded to them his query.

Before the DOC Insider was in place, Anderson says, it would have taken him about 3 days to get an answer to the same question. "You have to make many phone calls and deal with time zones," he says. Thanks to the expertise location system, however, he had three responses within minutes, a complete answer within an hour, and the sale went through the following morning. Anderson estimates that he now uses the system for roughly 40 percent of the work he does.

The DOC Insider is an invaluable tool. Anderson thinks the tool is vital enough to provide it to other units at the agency. In the first 9 months the system was in place, it saved more than 1,000 man hours.

Sources: Compiled from D'Agostino (2004) and *askme.com* (accessed November 2008).

Questions

1. What are the benefits of the expertise location system to the DOC? To U.S. companies?

2. Review Exhibit 7.8 and relate it to this case.

3. What, in your opinion, are the limitations of this system? Can they be overcome? How?

Seeking Expertise in Social Networks

Seeking expertise (and experts) is becoming a very popular activity. People post their problems on bulletin boards, forums, and blogs and wait for response. One of the features of LinkedIn is the free "LinkedIn Answers," where users ask questions for the community to answer.

In many organizations, social networking and the location of expertise are converging. Some organizations use the same internal social networking site, intranet, or portal for internal expertise location as they do for communication and general networking. Many consider expertise location to be an extension of knowledge management, in that the goal is to capture and reuse the skills and experience of internal staff members in order to increase competitive advantage. For discussion and details of when to use social networking for expert location, see kmedge.org/wp/snel-whentouse.html.

Section 7.5 ▶ REVIEW QUESTIONS

1. Define knowledge management.
2. Discuss the relationship between KM and EC.
3. Describe knowledge portals.
4. Describe online advisory services.
5. Describe expert location systems and their benefits.

7.6 CONSUMER-TO-CONSUMER ELECTRONIC COMMERCE

Consumer-to-consumer (C2C) EC, which is sometimes referred to as *peer-to-peer (P2P) networks* or *exchanges*, involve all transactions between and among individual consumers. These transactions can also include third parties, usually in the form of those who facilitate the marketplace, such as eBay or a social network site. C2C networks can include classified ads, music and file sharing, career and job Web sites (linkedin.com and careerone.com.au), and also personal services, such as dating Web sites (match.com).

In C2C EC, consumers sell goods and services to other consumers. There are millions of sellers with different items to sell and an equally large number of buyers. Finding each other may take a long time and can even incur high costs to both buyers and sellers, and this is why intermediaries such as eBay or Craigslist are so important. They simply mediate between consumers who want to buy and sell. Some take small cuts of a seller's profit as a fee for bringing customers to the marketplace.

C2C EC has given online shopping and trading a new dimension. Although this sort of trading is prevalent in the offline world (classified newspaper ads, garage sales, etc.), it was not expected to take off online due to the anonymity of users. This problem was solved by using a third-party payment provider (e.g., Pay-Pal) and insurance provided by eBay and others. One advantage of C2C EC is that it reduces the cost to buyers. It also gives many individuals and small business owners a low-cost way to sell their goods and services.

Social networks have become a popular place for C2C activities such as selling products and services via classified ads, sharing or selling music, bartering, selling virtual properties, and providing personal services.

consumer-to-consumer (C2C) EC
E-commerce model in which consumers sell directly to other consumers.

E-COMMERCE: C2C APPLICATIONS

EC has redefined the traditional structure of business by giving small firms and individuals the same opportunities to conduct business as multinational corporations. As a result, many Web sites have been created that encourage and assist with commerce between consumers. We cover several representative applications next.

C2C Auctions

The most successful example of a C2C application is auctions. In dozens of countries, selling and buying on auction sites is exploding. Most auctions are conducted by intermediaries (the most well-known is eBay). Consumers can visit auctions at general sites such as ebay.com or auctionanything.com or they can use specialized sites such as bidz.com that specializes in exclusive and brand name jewelry. In addition, many individuals are conducting their own auctions with the use of special software. For example, greatshop.com provides software to create C2C reverse auction communities online. Auctions may require intense communication between buyers and sellers. eBay purchased Skype to facilitate P2P communication. In 2009, eBay decided to sell Skype because of lack of profits. Skype will be a spin-off of eBay and each shareholder will get a share in the new company. See Online Chapter 17 for more on auctions.

Classified ADS

People sell to other people every day through classified ads. Internet-based classified ads have several advantages over newspaper classified ads. They offer a national, rather than a local, audience. This greatly increases the supply of goods and services available and the number of potential buyers. One of the most successful sites of C2C classified ads is Craigslist (see Chapter 2). Other examples are iclassifieds2000.com, which contains a list of about 500,000 cars, compared with the much smaller number one might find locally. It also includes apartments for rent across the United States (powered by forrent.com) and personal ads (powered by match.com). Another example is freeclassified.com. Both Google and Yahoo! are expanding their online classifieds. Many newspapers also offer their classified ads online. In many cases, placing an ad on one Web site brings it automatically into the classified sections of numerous partners. This increases ad exposure at no additional cost. To help narrow the search for a particular item, on some sites shoppers can use search engines. In addition, Internet-based classifieds often can be placed for free by private parties, can be edited or changed easily, and in many cases can display photos of the product offered for sale.

The major categories of classified ads are similar to those found in a newspaper: vehicles, real estate, employment, general merchandise, collectibles, computers, pets, tickets, and travel. Classified ads are available through most ISPs (AOL, MSN, etc.), in some portals (Yahoo!, etc.), and from Internet directories, online newspapers, and more. Once a person finds an ad and gets the details, he or she can e-mail or call the other party to find out additional information or to make a purchase. Most classified ads are provided for free. Some classified ad sites generate revenue from advertisers who pay for larger ads, especially when the sellers are businesses. Classified ad Web sites accept no responsibility for the content of any advertisement.

Classified ads appear in thousands of Web sites including popular social networks such as LinkedIn, Facebook, and Second Life.

Personal Services

Numerous personal services are available on the Internet (lawyers, handy helpers, tax preparers, investment clubs, dating services). Some are in the classified ads, but others are listed in specialized Web sites (e.g., hireahelper.com) and directories. Some are free, some charge a fee. Be very careful before purchasing any personal services. Fraud or crime could be involved (e.g., a lawyer online may not be an expert in the area professed or may not deliver the service at all). Online advising and consulting, described in Section 7.5, also are examples of personal services.

Napster and Others—The File-Sharing Utilities

It all started in 2001. By logging onto services such as Napster, people could download files that others were willing to share. Such P2P networks enabled users to search other members' hard drives for a particular file, including data files created by users or copied from elsewhere. Digital music and games were the most popular files accessed. Then came the movies and videos. Napster had more than 60 million members in 2002 before it went out of business.

The Napster server functioned as a directory that listed the files being shared by other users. Once logged into the server, users could search the directory for specific songs and locate the file owner. They could then directly access the owner's computer and download the songs they had chosen. Napster also included chat rooms to connect its millions of users.

However, a U.S. court found Napster to be in violation of copyright laws because it enabled people to obtain music files without paying the creators of the music for access to their material. Following this ruling, in March 2002, Napster closed its free services. Napster continued to operate, with users paying a fee for file sharing and Napster passing along part of the fee to copyright owners.

In December 2002, Roxio, a software maker specializing in CD-burning software, bought Napster's intellectual property assets, including its patents and brand name. Roxio relaunched Napster in 2004 as a for-fee digital music service. Napster was acquired in 2008 by Best Buy. Similarly, Kazaa (kazaa.com) offered music file sharing, and it became very popular. Today, Kazaa offers music downloads for a fee. By 2007, many people were downloading music legally for a fee (e.g., see iTunes at apple.com/itunes).

A number of free file-sharing programs still exist. For example, an even purer version of P2P is Gnutella (downloadable software), a P2P program that dispenses with the central database altogether in connecting the peer computers. To access games over P2P networks, try trustyfiles.com. ICQ (the instant messenger-type chat room) can be considered a hybrid P2P technology because the chatters share the same screen.

Despite the temptation to get "something for nothing," remember that downloading copyrighted materials for free is against the law; violators are subject to penalties if caught. However, in some cases if you are willing to watch a pop-up ad then you can download free music and video clips (see mediaworks.com).

C2C ACTIVITIES IN SOCIAL NETWORKS

C2C activities in social networks include the sharing of photos, videos, music, and other files, trading of virtual properties, and much more. Here we describe trading virtual properties; other activities are described in Chapter 9.

Virtual Properties Trading in Multiplayer Online Games and Virtual Worlds

Believe it or not, millions of online game players, especially in China, are selling and buying online virtual properties in popular massively multiplayer online role-playing games (MMORPG), such as Jianxia Qingyuan or Legend of MIR, and in virtual worlds, especially in Second Life. Users own virtual properties that are registered under their names. They can buy or sell these properties via auctions or classified ads when visiting Second Life or when playing games. According to Ding (2004), who quoted an IDC report, 26.7 percent of the 13.8 million MMORPG players (or about 3.7 million) have bought or sold a virtual property, for about $120 million a year in China, just in 2004. Millions are trading properties at Second Life using special money.

Of course, there are risks. Hackers may steal virtual properties in some sites, and market organizers can sell them. Because the industry is not regulated, users, especially MMORPG players, may have little chance of recovering the virtual property. In addition, there is the risk of the buyer not paying for the item.

SUPPORT SERVICES FOR C2C

When individuals buy products or services from other individuals online, they usually buy from strangers. The issues of ensuring quality, receiving payments, and preventing fraud are critical to the success of C2C. One service that facilitates C2C EC is the handling of payments by intermediaries companies, such as PayPal (paypal.com) (see Chapter 11). Other innovative services and technologies that support C2C EC are described in Chapter 9. For example, tamago.us connects its members' computers into one big network, giving its members the power to buy and sell music that they have created. A major supporting technology is peer-to-peer networks.

Peer-to-Peer Networks

Several C2C applications are based on a computer architecture known as *peer-to-peer*. With a peer-to-peer (P2P) network, each client computer can share files or computer resources (such as processing power) directly with others rather than through a central server. This is in contrast with a client-server architecture in which some computers serve other computers via a central server. (Note that the acronym P2P also can stand for people-to-people, person-to-person, or point-to-point. Our discussion here refers to peer-to-peer networks over which files and other computing resources are shared.) Note that P2P networks may experience problems with security (see Foley 2008). This topic is discussed in Online File W7.8.

peer-to-peer (P2P)
Applications that use direct communications between computers (peers) to share resources, rather than relying on a centralized server as the conduit between client devices.

Other C2C Applications

With P2P, users can sell digital goods directly from their computers rather than going through centralized servers. If users want to sell on eBay, for example, they are required to go through eBay's server, placing an item on eBay's site and uploading a photo. However, if an auction site uses file sharing, it can direct customers to the seller's Web site, where buyers can find an extensive amount of information, photos, and even videos about the items being sold. In this case, an auction site serves as an intermediary making the P2P link between the sellers and buyers.

The following are some more C2C applications using P2P technologies:

▶ **Lending.** Individuals can make loans to creditworthy borrowers (e.g., zopa.com and prosper.com) See details in Chapter 9.

▶ **Bartering.** DVDs are offered for barter at peerflix.com. Also see bookins.com (trade books), and swaptree.com (trade everything).

For additional P2P activities, see Schonfeld (2006).

Section 7.6 ▶ REVIEW QUESTIONS

1. List the major C2C applications.
2. Describe how C2C works in classified online ads.
3. Describe C2C personal services, exchanges, and other support services.

MANAGERIAL ISSUES

Some managerial issues related to this chapter are as follows.

1. **What are the e-government opportunities?** If an organization is doing business with the government, eventually some or all of it may be moved online. Organizations may find new online business opportunities with the government because governments are getting serious about going online; some even mandate it as a major way to conduct B2G and G2B.

2. **How to design the most cost-efficient government e-procurement system?** How much can the governmental e-procurement system save on procurement costs? How can it enhance the transparency of the procurement process and prevent illegal bribery? How should the online and offline procurement systems be designed? How should the portfolio of auctions and desktop purchasing be constructed? Can the government use commercial B2B sites for procurement? Can businesses use the government procurement system for their own procurement? Would the boundary between G2B and B2B blur as the channel of procurement?

3. **How to design the portfolio of e-learning knowledge sources?** There are many sources of e-learning services. The e-learning management office needs to design the portfolio of the online and offline training, internal and external sources, paid and nonpaid sources, and know-how and know-who choices. The internal knowledge management system is an important source for large corporations, whereas external sources will be more cost-effective for small corporations. Obviously,

justification is needed and goes hand-in-hand with the selection of supporting tools (see West 2007). For illustrative case studies, see *brightwave.co.uk*.

4. **How to incorporate social networking based learning and services in our organization?** With the proliferation of social networking initiatives in the enterprise comes the issue of how to integrate these with enterprise systems, including CRM, KM, training, and other business processes. An issue is how to balance the quality of knowledge with the scope of knowledge.

5. **Can we capitalize on C2C EC?** Businesses cannot capture much C2C activity unless they provide secure payment services such as *paypal.com* or an escrow service. Businesses may consider sponsoring C2C activities in order to increase viral marketing and advertising.

6. **How to connect our expert location system and social networking initiatives?** Expert location systems and knowledge management systems can be developed to assist in finding experts both internally and externally. This service can be linked with the job match portal and professional social networks.

7. **What will be the impact of the e-book platform?** If the e-book is widely adopted by readers, the distribution channel of online book sales may be disruptive. This new platform may cannibalize the online book retail business and impact the platform of e-learning as well. A threat is the protection of the intellectual property of digital contents.

SUMMARY

In this chapter, you learned about the following EC issues as they relate to the learning objectives.

1. **E-government activities.** Governments, like any other organization, can use EC applications for great savings. Notable applications are e-procurement using reverse auctions, e-payments to and from citizens and businesses, auctioning of surplus goods, and electronic travel and expense management systems. Governments also conduct electronic business with other governments. Finally, governments can facilitate homeland security with EC tools.

2. **Implementing e-government to citizens, businesses, and its own operations.** Governments worldwide are providing a variety of services to citizens over the Internet. Such initiatives increase citizens' satisfaction and decrease government expenses in providing customer service applications including electronic voting. Governments also are active in electronically trading

with businesses. Finally, EC is done within and between governments.

3. **E-learning and training.** E-learning is the delivery of educational content via electronic media, including the Internet and intranets. Degree programs, lifelong learning topics, and corporate training are delivered by thousands of organizations worldwide. A growing area is distance learning via online university offerings. Some are virtual; others are delivered both online and offline. Online corporate training also is increasing and is sometimes conducted at formal corporate learning centers. Implementation is done in steps starting with just presence and ending with activities on social networks.

4. **Online publishing and e-books.** Online publishing of newspapers, magazines, and books is growing rapidly,

as is the online publishing of other digitizable items, such as software, music, games, movies, and other entertainment. Of special interest are blogging, the publishing of newsletter-like commentaries by individuals on the Internet, and wikis, which enable people to collaborate in writing.

5. **Knowledge management and dissemination as an e-business.** Knowledge has been recognized as an important organizational asset. It needs to be

properly captured, stored, managed, and shared. Knowledge is critical for many e-commerce tasks. Knowledge can be shared in different ways; expert knowledge can be provided to nonexperts (for fee or free) via a knowledge portal or as a personal service (e.g., via e-mail).

6. **C2C activities.** C2C consists of consumers conducting e-commerce with other consumers, mainly in auctions (such as at eBay).

KEY TERMS

Consumer-to-consumer (C2C)	371	Expert location systems (ELS)	368	Knowledge portal	367
Distance learning	352	Government-to-business (G2B)	342	Mobile government (m-government)	347
E-democracy (cyberdemocracy, digital democracy)	338	Government-to-citizens (G2C)	338	Online publishing	359
E-government	338	Government-to-employees (G2E)	343	Peer-to-peer (P2P)	373
E-learning	347	Government-to-government (G2G)	343	Podcast	360
Edutainment	354			Virtual universities	352
Electronic book or E-book	360	Knowledge management (KM)	363	Webcasting	360
				Webinars	360

QUESTIONS FOR DISCUSSION

1. Discuss the advantages and disadvantages of e-government using social networking versus the traditional e-government portal.

2. Discuss the advantages and shortcomings of e-voting.

3. How can online publishing support paper-based publications?

4. Discuss the advantages and disadvantages of e-books.

5. Will paper-based books and magazines be eliminated in the long run? Why or why not?

6. Check an online version of a newspaper or magazine you are familiar with and discuss the differences between the print and online versions.

7. Discuss the advantages of e-learning for an undergraduate student and for an MBA student.

8. Discuss the advantages of e-learning in the corporate training environment.

9. Discuss the relationship between KM and a KM portal.

10. In what ways does KM support e-commerce?

11. Why do you think people trade virtual properties online?

12. Discuss the advantages of expert location systems over corporate databases that contain experts' information and knowledge. What are the disadvantages? Can they be combined? How?

13. Some say that B2G is simply B2B. Explain.

14. Compare and contrast B2E with G2E.

15. Which e-government EC activities are intrabusiness activities? Explain why they are intrabusiness.

16. Identify the benefits of G2C to citizens and to governments.

17. Discuss the benefits of using virtual worlds to facilitate learning.

18. Relate IBM's Innovation Jam to KM and social networks.

19. Relate KM to learning, to e-publishing, and to C2C.

INTERNET EXERCISES

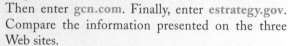

1. Enter tamago.us and nextag.com and learn how they operate. What do they offer? Write a report.

2. Enter pcmag.com, fortune.com, or other online versions of popular magazines. How would you compare reading the electronic magazine against the print version?

3. Enter e-learningcentre.co.uk, elearnmag.org, and elearningpost.com. Identify current issues and find articles related to the effectiveness of e-training. Write a report. Also prepare a list of the resources available on these sites.

4. Enter adobe.com and find the tools they offer for e-learning, knowledge management, and online publishing.

5. Identify a difficult business problem. Post the problem on elance.com, linkedin.com, and answers.com. Summarize the offers to solve the problem.

6. Enter blackboard.com and en.wikipedia.org/wiki/Blackboard and find all the services provided by the company, including its community system. Write a report.

7. Enter whitehouse.gov/government and review the site. Based on the stages presented in Exhibit 7.3, what stage does this site represent? Review the available site tours. Suggest ways the government could improve this portal.

8. Enter oecd.org and identify the studies conducted by the Organization for Economic Cooperation and Development (OECD) on the topic of e-government. What are the organization's major concerns?

9. Enter fcw.com and read the latest news on e-government. Identify initiatives not covered in this chapter. Check the B2G corner. Then enter gcn.com. Finally, enter estrategy.gov. Compare the information presented on the three Web sites.

10. Enter procurement.com and govexec.com. Identify recent e-procurement initiatives and summarize their unique aspects.

11. Enter sbdc.com.au and fcw.com and find the specific G2C information provided. Prepare a list.

12. Enter insight24.com and livelive.com and find the most recent and most popular videos about knowledge management. Prepare a list of five and view one in each category. Prepare a report.

13. Enter learn.gotomeeting.com/forms/G2MC-WBR ARC-100208 or eseminarslive.com/c/a/Service-and-Support/Citrix100208 and find the Webinar titled "How to Build an On-Demand Training Program" Sponsored by Citrix Online. View it (45 min.) and write a report on what it is and what the benefits are.

14. Enter amazon.com and sony.com and find the latest information about their e-book readers. Compare their capabilities and write a report.

15. Enter wi5connect.com and find what product they have for learning in social networking. Prepare a list of capabilities of each product.

TEAM ASSIGNMENTS, PROJECTS, AND CLASS DISCUSSIONS

1. Assign each team to a different country. Each team will explore the e-government offerings of that country. Have each team make a presentation to convince the class that its country's offerings are the most comprehensive. (Exclude Hong Kong and New Zealand.)

2. Create four teams, each representing one of the following: G2C, G2B, G2E, and G2G. Each team will prepare a plan of its major activities in a small country, such as Holland, Denmark, Finland, or Singapore. A fifth team will deal with the coordination and collaboration of all e-government activities in each country. Prepare a report.

3. Have teams search for online universities (e.g., the University of Phoenix, phoenix.edu, Liverpool University in the UK, or ecollege.com). Write a summary of the schools' e-learning offerings.

4. Have each team represent one of the following sites: netlibrary.com, ebooks.com, and cyberread.com. Each team will examine the technology, legal issues, prices, and business alliances associated with its site. Each team will then prepare a report answering the question, "Will e-books succeed?"

5. Have teams explore KM videos and other resources at right24.com and kmworld.com Relate them to the topics of this chapter. Prepare a report.

6. Address the following topics in a class discussion:

   a. Will e-books replace traditional paper books?
   b. Will e-universities replace universities?
   c. Why aren't all firms embracing KM?

A WORLD-CLASS E-GOVERNMENT: SINGAPORE

In 2006, the then Indonesian president described Singapore as "a little red dot." He was comparing Singapore to Indonesia's population of 211 million. Indeed, with a population of about 4.5 million people and a landmass of only 640 square kilometers, the city-state of Singapore lacks a sufficient sizable domestic market for electronic commerce and a critical mass of entrepreneurial ICT talents. In addition, it is positioned in relatively less-developed geographic hinterlands with low e-commerce readiness, political uncertainties, and potential economic rivalries and trade frictions.

Despite these inherent shortcomings, the vision and drive of the government of Singapore has made the country a leader in electronic governance that has invited worldwide recognition. Singapore's government portal has been recognized as "the most developed example of integrated service delivery in the world." In the latest Accenture e-Government ranking, Singapore ranked first. To date, some 1,600 e-government services, constituting 98 percent of all government services, are provided online for businesses and the community. These online services range from seeking approval for major building projects to passport renewals and the filing of income tax returns.

Currently, 90 percent of the people and 95 percent of businesses in Singapore transact with the government online. In 2006 alone, approximately 160 million transactions of such services were made from the base population of 4.5 million people. Online activities such as the electronic filing of income tax returns and renewing road taxes are now commonplace among Singapore residents.

How Did Singapore Do It?

Singapore was among the first countries to develop an integrated and coherent approach to computerizing government services. In 1981, the Civil Service Computerization Program (CSCP) was launched. The CSCP program focused on improving public administration through the effective use of information technology. This was followed in 2000 by the first e-Government Action Plan (2000–2003). The primary objective of the plan was to implement as many public services online as possible. The success resulted in the proliferation of many public online services. In the e-Government Action Plan II (2003–2006), the emphasis was to provide accessible, integrated, and value-added e-services, with the ultimate objective of providing a one-stop service via the Internet. In May 2006, the iGov2010 plan was launched with the aim of bringing the government to the next level of efficiency. This is to be accomplished by integrating back-end processes across the entire government's ministries and organizations. The $1.4 billion, 5-year master plan underscores Singapore's commitment to its goal of achieving a world-class e-government system.

eCitizen Portal

One of the most popular portals is the eCitizen portal (*eCitizen.gov.sg*), which provides a single-entry point to access services from the government and private corporations. Through the portal, users can receive SMS messages from the government on diverse matters, including passport and road-tax renewal reminders, e-government newsletters, and even notifications of overdue library books. As of December 2006, the portal had more than 64,000 subscribers. Users can also personalize their homepages and choose from channels such as MyTravel, MyHome, MyKids, MyFamily, MyCareer, MyInvestment, MyNS, MyRecreation, and MyVehicle.

Access to the portal is via SingPass. Every citizen and permanent resident in Singapore is issued a single online user identification called Singapore Personal Access, better known as SingPass. This enables each person to transact conveniently with the government e-services, while accessing their own confidential information. For example, citizens can use the site to

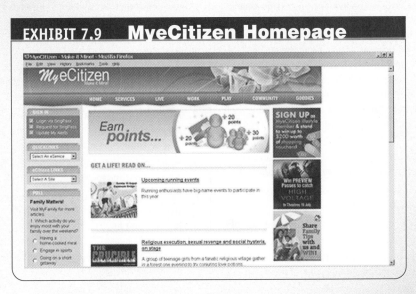

EXHIBIT 7.9   MyeCitizen Homepage

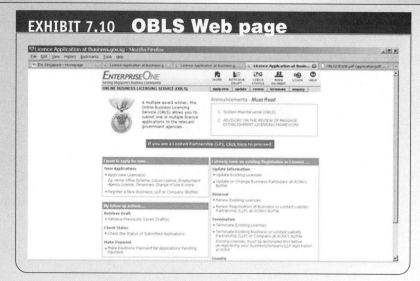

EXHIBIT 7.10   OBLS Web page

plan and calculate the funds required for their retirement using their personal social security funds.

The portal also provides citizens and permanent residents the opportunity to voice their opinions on a number of local issues. Citizens can post their thoughts on issues such as the extension of the smoking ban, reducing government bureaucracy, and the country's national climate change strategy. The topics available for discussion change on a regular basis.

Online Business Licensing Service Portal

Another favorite portal is the Online Business Licensing Service (OBLS), (*licences.business.gov.sg*). This is a one-stop portal to apply for all the relevant government registrations and licenses required to conduct business in Singapore. The portal has won the United Nations Public Service Award for the best application of IT in the e-Government sector.

Through the portal, an applicant only needs to complete one integrated form for multiple licenses. Previously, an applicant had to complete multiple forms at different government agencies, often filling in the same information each time. The system also provides a consolidated online payment mechanism for one-time payments for multiple licence fees. Following the implementation of this system, the average processing time was reduced from 21 days to just 8 days, saving businesses more than $2.1 million annually. Today, OBLS offers more than 80 licenses across 17 agencies for online integrated application. This allows more than 80 percent of all start-up businesses—close to 30,000 businesses annually—to apply for licences with ease.

For example, a restaurant that sells wine and provides a private dining room with a television set is likely to make the following licence applications:

▶ Accounting and Corporate Regulatory Authority's Business Registration or Company Incorporation

▶ National Environment Agency's Food Shop License for the retail sale of food and drinks

▶ Singapore Police Force's Liquor License for the sale of liquor

▶ Media Development Authority's Non-Residential TV License for the television sets capable of receiving broadcasting signals

Before the launch of OBLS, the applicant would have had to make four separate applications to each of the four agencies. With OBLS, the applicant can simply make one application for concurrent processing by these different agencies through one integrated online form. The applicant no longer needs to find out which licenses to apply for and which agency to approach. All the applicant needs to do is access OBLS for one-stop information and service.

Sources: Accenture, "2007 Leadership in Customer Service: Delivering on the Promise," 2007, *accenture.com* (accessed September 8, 2009); America's General Services Administration, "Government and the Internet," 2000; "Habibie: What I Meant by Little 'Red Dot, '" *The Strait Times*, September 20, 2006; Infocommunications Development Authority of Singapore, "Annual e-Government Customer Perception Survey," 2007, *ida.gov.sg* (accessed July 1, 2009); Infocommunications Development Authority of Singapore, 2009, *www.ida.gov.sg* (accessed September 3, 2009); United Nations, "UN E-Government Survey 2008: From E-Government to Connected Governance," 2008, *unpan1.un.org/intradoc/ groups/public/documents/UN/UNPAN028607.pdf* (accessed August 9, 2009); P.-K. Wong, "Globalization and E-Commerce: Growth and Impacts in Singapore," Center for Research on Information Technology and Organizations, University of California, Paper 243, 2001.

Questions

1. Explore the two portals. What are the benefits to both the community and businesses?

2. According to the chapter, there are six stages in the transformation to e-government. Which stage do you think Singapore is in? Why?

3. What could other governments learn from the example of Singapore?

4. Despite the success of its e-government initiatives, Singapore's extremely small domestic market size and environmental factors could impede its goal of becoming a global e-commerce hub. Do you think that Singapore will be successful in achieving this goal? Why or why not? Discuss.

▶ **Knowledge sharing.** Members share knowledge by telling other members where to find knowledge of interest to the community. For example, Microsoft Vine is a community that supports those interested in emergency services information exchange.

Web 2.0 applications help aggregate corporate knowledge and simplify the building of repositories of best practices, as demonstrated by the following example.

Example: IBM's Innovation Jam. IBM has long used communities for problem solving. One of its best-known communities is the Innovation Jam, an online brainstorming session. This community of over 150,000 employees and business partners tries to move the latest technologies to the market. IBM has been hosting online brainstorming sessions since 2001. For example, in July 2006 IBM invited employees, partners, and customers to contribute ideas about a certain new product. Within 72 hours, more than 50,000 ideas were posted. These ideas were then winnowed down by using sophisticated analytical software.

Virtual meetings where IBM employees can participate in Innovation Jam launches are conducted in Second Life. IBM's CEO has even created an avatar to represent him. Topics that have been explored by recent Innovation Jams have included new technologies for water filtration, 3D Internet, and branchless banking. For more on IBM's Innovation Jams and use of virtual worlds, see Bjelland and Wood (2008) and en.wikipedia.org/wiki/IBM_Virtual_Universe_Community.

KNOWLEDGE PORTALS

Knowledge portals are single-point-of-access software systems intended to provide easy and timely access to knowledge and to support communities of knowledge workers who share common goals. Knowledge portals can be used for either external or internal use.

Knowledge portals support various tasks performed by knowledge workers: gathering, organizing, searching for, and analyzing information; synthesizing solutions with respect to specific task goals; and then sharing and distributing what has been learned with other knowledge workers. Online File W7.7 describes how IBM uses a knowledge portal to support the work of consultants at IBM and what technologies can be used to support each category of tasks. For further details on how knowledge portals are related to collaborative and intellectual capital management, see Jones et al. (2006).

knowledge portal
A single point of access software system intended to provide timely access to information and to support communities of knowledge workers.

ONLINE ADVICE AND CONSULTING

Another use of knowledge online is offering advice and consulting services. The online advice and consulting field is growing rapidly as tens of thousands of experts of all kinds sell (or provide for free) their expertise over the Internet. The following are some examples:

▶ **Medical advice.** Companies such as WebMD (webmd.com) and others (see liveperson.com) provide health-advice consultations with top medical experts. Consumers can ask specific questions and get an answer from a specialist in a few days. Health sites also offer specialized advice and tips for travelers, for pet owners, and more.

▶ **Management consulting.** Many consultants are selling their accumulated expertise from organizational knowledge bases. A pioneer in this area was Andersen Consulting (now Accenture at accenture.com). Other management consultants that sell knowledge online are Aberdeen (aberdeen.com) and Forrester Research (forresterresearch.com). Because of their high consultation fees, such services mainly are used by corporations.

▶ **Legal advice.** Delivery of legal advice to individuals and businesses by consultation services has considerable prospects. For example, Atlanta-based law firm Alston & Bird coordinates legal counseling with 12 law firms for a large health-care company and for many other clients.

▶ **Gurus and answers to questions.** Several sites provide diversified expert services, some for free. One example is guru.com, which offers general advice and a job board for experts on legal, financial, tax, technical, lifestyle, and other issues. As of 2007, it has aggregated over 480,000 professional "gurus." Expertise is advertised at elance.com, where one can post a required service for experts to bid on. Of special interest is sciam.com, which offers advice from science experts at Scientific American. Some of the most popular services that offer information from experts are answers.com (previously GuruNet), answers.yahoo.com, catholic.com, healthanswers.com, wineanswers.com, and many more. Some provide answers for free; others charge fees for premium services. Answers.com (with its teachers.answers.com) provides free access to over 4 million answers and generates income from advertising.

▶ **Financial advice.** Many companies offer extensive financial advice. For example, Merrill Lynch Online (totalmerrill.com) provides free access to some of the firm's research reports and analyses.

▶ **Social networks.** Several social networks allow users to post questions and get answers. For business-oriented questions, go to linkedin.com.

▶ **Other advisory services.** Many other advisory services are available online—some for free and others for a fee. For example, guestfinder.com makes it easy for people who work in the media to find guests and interview sources.

One word of caution about advice: It is not wise to risk your health, your money, or your legal status on free or even for-fee online advice. Always seek more than one opinion, and carefully check the credentials of any advice provider.

EMPLOYEE KNOWLEDGE NETWORKS AND EXPERT LOCATION SYSTEMS

Expert advice can be provided within an organization in a variety of ways. Human expertise is rare; therefore, companies attempt to preserve it electronically in corporate knowledge bases. Alternatively, electronic expert systems may be used. Although such systems are very useful and they can be used directly by nonexperts, they cannot solve all problems, especially new ones. For such cases, human experts are needed. In large organizations, it may be difficult to locate experts quickly. Recently, social networking is being used.

Finding Experts Electronically

People who need help may post their problem on the corporate intranet (e.g., using blogs) or on public social networks such as LinkedIn (linkedin.com) and ask for help internally and/or externally. Similarly, companies may ask for advice on how to exploit an opportunity. IBM frequently uses this method. Sometimes it obtains hundreds of useful ideas within a few days. It is a kind of brainstorming. The problem with this approach is that it may take days to get an answer, if an answer is even provided, and the answer may not be from the top experts. Therefore, companies employ expert location systems and social networking.

Example. PricewaterhouseCoopers, a large CPA and management services company, has introduced an "Ask the Experts" program that offers users extended access to expertise. Clicking on an expert's picture automatically generates an e-mail to that person—allowing users to ask the experts anything they like. Learners can use the feature to ask questions to facilitate learning. They also can also join discussion forums and consult a glossary of industry terms.

Expert Location Systems

expert location systems
Interactive computerized systems that help employees find and connect with colleagues who have expertise required for specific problems—whether they are across the country or across the room—in order to solve specific, critical business problems in seconds.

Expert location systems (ELS) are interactive computerized systems that help employees find and connect with colleagues with expertise required for specific problems—whether they are across the country or across the room—in order to solve specific, critical business problems in seconds. Expertise location systems are designed to:

▶ Connect people to people

▶ Link people to information about people

▶ Identify people with expertise and link them to those with questions or problems

▶ Identify potential staff for projects requiring specific expertise

▶ Assist in career development

▶ Provide support for teams and communities of practice.

ONLINE RESOURCES
available at pearsonglobaleditions.com/turban

WWW

Online Files

W7.1 Application Case: A Decade of E-Government Development in Hong Kong (1998 to 2009)

W7.2 Key Issues and Trends of E-Government Development and Implementation

W7.3 The Driving Forces of E-Learning

W7.4 Application Case: Online Global Learning at W. R. Grace

W7.5 Types of E-Books

W7.6 Application Case: Online Knowledge Sharing at Xerox

W7.7 Knowledge Work Tasks with Examples of Supporting Knowledge

W7.8 The Peer-to-Peer Networks

Comprehensive Educational Web Sites

technologyevaluation.com: TEC helps enterprises evaluate and select software solutions that meet their exacting needs by empowering purchasers with the tools, research, and expertise to make an ideal decision.

e-learningcentre.co.uk: A vast collection of selected and reviewed links to e-learning resources.

wwwords.co.uk/elea: An e-learning journal and comprehensive portal.

metakm.com: A portal for KM.

tools.kmnetwork.com: A portal on KM tools and techniques.

portal.brint.com: A portal for KM.

kmworld.com: A collection of KM solutions.

egov.vic.gov.au: A major resource center on e-government.

updates.zdnet.com/tags/e-government.html: A resource center including white papers, case studies, technical articles, and blog posts relating to e-government.

e-democracy.org: A portal focused on e-democracy.

egov.gov: Official e-government site of U.S. government.

REFERENCES

Andersen, K. V. "e-Government: Five Key Challenges for Management." *Electronic Journal of E-Government* (November 2006).

Association of American Publishers. "Book Sales Up Seven Percent in Early '08." AAP press release, March 25, 2008. toc.oreilly.com/ebooks/2008/03 (accessed February 2009).

Bhattacharjee, S., R. D. Gopal, K. Lertchwara, and J. Marsden. "Impact of Legal Threats on Online Music Sharing Activity: An Analysis of Music Industry Legal Actions." *The Journal of Law and Economics* 49 (2006).

Bjelland, O. M., and R. C. Wood. "An Inside View of IBM's Innovation Jam." *MIT Sloan Management Review* (Fall 2008).

Boehle, S. "Caterpillar's Knowledge Network." *Management Smart.com*, October 16, 2007. managesmarter.com/msg/content_display/training/e3iff0e5ee8955eaff00d02da7d36a5b662 (accessed March 2009).

Chan, S. C. H., and E. W. Ngai. "A Qualitative Study of IT Adoption: How Ten Organizations Adopted Web-Based Training." *Information Systems Journal*, 17 (2007).

Chu, K. C., and Q. Lam. "Using an E-Book for Learning." In M. Khosrow-Pour, (Ed.) *Encyclopedia of E-Commerce, E-Government, and Mobile Commerce.* Hershey, PA: Idea Group Reference, 2006.

D'Agostino, D. "Expertise Management: Who Knows About This?" *CIO Insight*, July 1, 2004.

Ding, E. "Virtual Property: Treasure or Trash?" *China International Business*, September 2004.

Epstein, J. "Electronic Voting." *Computer*, August 2007.

Foley, J. "P2P Peril." *InformationWeek*, March 17, 2008.

Galagan, P. A. "Delta Force at Cisco." *Training and Development* (July 2002).

Garud, R., and A. Kumaraswamy. "Vicious and Virtuous Circles in the Management of Knowledge: The Case of Infosys Technologies." *MIS Quarterly*, 29 (2005).

Gibson, R., and C. Brown. "Electronic Voting as the Key to Ballot Reform." In M. Khosrow-Pour, (Ed.). *Encyclopedia of E-Commerce, E-Government, and Mobile Commerce.* Hershey, PA: Idea Group Reference, 2006.

Gibson, S. "Podcasting: An Enterprise Hit." *eWeek*, October 2, 2006.

Glynn, C. E. "Building a Learning Infrastructure." *Training and Development*, January 2008.

Government Technology. "Don't Block Web 2.0 Access, Says Gartner." May 10, 2008. govtech.com/gt/271948 (accessed April 2009).

Henriksen, H. Z. "Fad or Investment in the Future: An Analysis of the Demand of E-Services in Danish Municipalities." *Electronic Journal of e-Government* 4, no. 1 (2006).

Holsapple, C. W. (Ed.) *Handbook on Knowledge Management.* Heidelberg, Germany: Springer Computer Science, 2003.

Huang, W., Y. Chen, and K. L. Wang. "E-Government Development and Implementation." In M. Khosrow-Pour, (Ed.). *Encyclopedia of E-Commerce, E-Government, and Mobile Commerce.* Hershey, PA: Idea Group Reference, 2006.

Hyperion. "Federal Government—Additional Details." 2007. hyperion.com/solutions/federal_division/legislation_summaries.cfm (no longer available online).

Impact Information. "Reducing the High Rates of E-Learning Attrition." July 18, 2006. impact-information.com/impactinfo/newsletter/plwork26.htm (accessed March 2009).

Jones, N. B., D. Provost, and D. Pascale. "Developing a University Research Web-Based Knowledge Portal." *International Journal of Knowledge and Learning*, January–February 2006.

Keen, J. "Politicians' Campaigns Invade MySpace." *USA Today*, October 17, 2006.

Kumar, N., and Q. Peng. "Strategic Alliances in E-Government Procurement." *International Journal of Electronic Business*, 4, no. 2 (2006).

Lagorio, C. "The Ultimate Distance Learning." *New York Times News Service*, published in *Taipei Times*, January 7, 2007.

Lee, S. M., X. Tan, and S. Trimi. "Current Practices of Leading E-Government Countries." *Communications of the ACM* 48, no. 10 (October 2005).

Mark, R. "Election 2.0." *eWeek*, November 12, 2007.

Massey, L. L., and D. W. Taylor, "Out of the Cubicle and into the Field: Mobility Matters in Extending Public Service Delivery." A white paper from BlackBerry Inc. and the center for Digital Government at Republic Inc., 2007.

Morrison, M. "Learner E-Learning: The University of Toyota Case." *Training*, January 2008.

Neal, L. "Predictions for 2007." *eLearn Magazine*, January 12, 2007. elearnmag.org/subpage.cfm?article=42-1&section=articles (accessed March 2009).

New Zealand E-Government. "Networking Government in New Zealand: Agency Initiatives." e.govt.nz/resources/research/progress/agency-initiatives/chapter9.html (accessed March 2009).

New Zealand E-Government. "Networking Government in New Zealand: Web 2.0 Networking Tools." e.govt.nz/resources/research/progress/agency-initiatives/chapter6.html (accessed March 2009).

Perenson, M. J. "Hands-On with Amazon's Kindle 2." *PCWorld.com*, February 9, 2009. pcworld.com/article/159193/handson_with_the_amazon_kindle_2.html (accessed February 2009).

Robbins, S., and M. Bell. *Second Life for Dummies*. Hoboken, NJ: Wiley, 2008.

Roberts, B. "Hard-Facts About Self Skills E-Learning." *HR Magazine*, January 2008.

Rymaszewski, M. et al. *Second Life: The Official Guide*. Hoboken, NJ: Sybex, 2007.

Schonfeld, E. "P2P Gets Personal." *Business 2.0*, November 2006.

Sener, J. "Effectively Evaluating Online Learning Programs." *eLearn Magazine*, May 2006. elearnmag.org/subpage.cfm?section=tutorials&article=23-1 (accessed March 2009).

Shark, A., and S. Toporkoff. *Beyond e-Government and e-Democracy: A Global Perspective*. Scotts Valley, CA: BookSurge Publishing, 2008.

Swisher, J. R., S. H. Jacobson, J. B. Jun, and O. Balci. "Modeling and Analyzing a Physician Clinic Environment Using Discrete-Event (Visual) Simulation." *Computers and Operations Research*, February 2001.

Trimi, S., and H. Sheng. "Emerging Trends in M-Government." *Communications of the ACM* (May 2008).

U.S. Department of Housing and Urban Development. FY 2008 Performance and Accountability Report. November 2008. hud.gov/offices/cfo/reports/hudpar-fy2008.pdf (accessed March 2009).

U.S. Government. "E-Government Strategy." Office of the President of the United States, Special Report, 2003. whitehouse.gov/omb/egov/2003egov_strat.pdf (accessed January 2007).

Wagner, E. "Delivering on the Promise of E-Learning." Adobe Systems, Inc., San Jose, CA. white paper #95010203, May 2008.

Welch, E. W., and S. K. Pandey. "E-Government and Bureaucracy: Toward a Better Understanding of Intranet Implementation and Its Effect on Red Tape." *Journal of Public Administration Research and Theory* (October 2006).

West, E. "Rapid E-learning." Adobe Systems, Inc., San Jose, California, white paper, 2007.

CHAPTER 8

MOBILE COMPUTING AND COMMERCE, AND PERVASIVE COMPUTING

Content

Learning Objectives

Upon completion of this chapter, you will be able to:

1. Discuss the value-added attributes, benefits, and fundamental drivers of m-commerce.

2. Describe the mobile computing environment that supports m-commerce (devices, software, services).

3. Describe the four major types of wireless telecommunications networks.

4. Discuss m-commerce applications in finance.

5. Describe m-commerce applications in shopping, advertising, and provision of content.

6. Discuss the application of m-commerce within organizations and across the supply chain.

7. Describe consumer and personal applications of m-commerce.

8. Understand the technologies and potential application of location-based m-commerce.

9. Describe the major inhibitors and barriers of m-commerce.

10. Discuss the key characteristics, critical technologies, and major applications of pervasive computing.

THE BLOOMING OF FOOD LION

The Problem

Food Lion is a supermarket chain with approximately 1,300 stores in the United States. Like other chains, Food Lion has found it increasingly difficult to compete on price against Wal-Mart. Trying to seek an advantage against low-price competitors like Wal-Mart, Food Lion decided to open a new, upscale chain called "Bloom" in 2004. From the beginning, Bloom stores focused on providing "a more hassle-free shopping experience" that would help consumers find products and check out quicker. This hassle-free experience rested on the creative use of "technology touch points" that improved the level of convenience for the shopper.

The Solution

At the heart of the shopping experience at Bloom are a variety of m-commerce technologies. For the moment, we define *m-commerce* as the ability to conduct commerce using a mobile device (e.g., a mobile or cell phone). Although Bloom utilizes a variety of information technologies, the following are critical to customer convenience:

- **Handheld scanners.** This handheld device (from Symbol Technology) is a point-of-sale (POS) terminal that emulates the system used at checkout. The device is given to the customers. After picking an item from the shelf, the customer scans the item with the device, bags the item (in the cart), and continues shopping. The device shows the price of the item and the running total of all items bagged. Food Lion can also use the personal scanner (from Symbol Technology) to send messages, such as special marketing offers, to customers while they are shopping. When they complete their shopping, customers hand the scanner to a store associate and settle the bill using whatever method they prefer. To deter shoplifting or cheating, customers are randomly picked to check whether items placed in the shopping cart have been scanned. Shoplifting has not been a serious problem.

- **Self-service produce scales.** These scales with specialized printers enable customers to create a bar-coded tag for vegetables, fruits, and other produce items that don't have price tags. Once the bar code is created, the item can be scanned like any other item in the store.

- **Information kiosks.** The meat and liquor departments provide kiosks that shoppers can use to scan items for nutritional and recipe information. The kiosks also enable shoppers to do party planning by generating shopping lists that indicate how much to buy based on the number of people expected to attend.

- **Wireless checkouts.** This is a mobile checkout POS terminal equipped with wheels that can be moved to any location in the store as well as outside (e.g., storefront for special sales). This brings flexibility and the ability to expedite checkout time. These devices can be added whenever checkout lines get long.

The Results

Food Lion began the Bloom chain as an experiment with five stores. During the initial rollout, approximately 20 percent of regular Bloom shoppers used the handheld scanners. Based on their early success, the Bloom chain has expanded to 61 locations. The handheld scanners are available in 26 of these stores.

Overall, Bloom customers indicate that the scanners, and implicitly the associated technologies like the bar code printer, help them keep a running total against their budget and make it easier and faster to shop and check out. It also helps the company control costs, reduce prices, and increase revenue. Those customers who enjoy chatting with cashiers can still shop the old-fashioned way, but most customers, especially those in high-traffic locations, would rather use the scanners to save time.

Food Lion is not the only retailer experimenting with wireless devices. METRO Group is experimenting with in-store mobile devices at its Future Store in Rheinberg, Germany. At the Future Store, customers are provided with special mobile phones known as "Mobile Shopping Assistants (MSAs)." An MSA provides online access to product descriptions and pictures, pricing information, and store maps. It also enables a shopper to scan items as they are placed in the cart and to keep a running list and total cost of the items. At checkout, the MSA allows a shopper to "pay in passing" by using the MSAs to pass scanned data to a payment terminal. METRO has measured the reactions and satisfaction of Future Store shoppers. The results indicate that customers are more satisfied, that customers visit the store more often, that the percentage of new customers has increased, and that customers spend more euros per month.

Sources: Compiled from Bonkoo (2007) and Metro (2008).

WHAT WE CAN LEARN . . .

From a retail perspective, the opening case illustrates that mobile devices have the potential to enhance the shopping experience for in-store customers and to increase the overall financial performance of retailers employing those technologies. This is only one example of the impact of emerging mobile and wireless technologies on commerce and electronic commerce (EC). In this chapter, we will explore a number of these emerging mobile and wireless technologies as well as their potential applications in the commercial arena.

8.1 MOBILE COMMERCE: ATTRIBUTES, BENEFITS, AND DRIVERS

Mobile commerce (m-commerce), also known as **m-business**, includes any business activity conducted over a wireless telecommunications network. This includes B2C and B2B commercial transactions as well as the transfer of information and services via wireless mobile devices. Like regular EC applications, m-commerce can be done via the Internet, via private communication lines, or over other computing networks. M-commerce is a natural extension of e-commerce. Mobile devices create an opportunity to deliver new services to existing customers and to attract new customers. However, the small screen size and reduced bandwidth of most computing devices have limited consumer interest. So even though the mobile computing industry recognizes the potential for B2C m-commerce applications, the number of existing applications is still emerging and consumer uptake has been slow. Instead, intrabusiness and B2B applications are receiving most of the attention and offer the best short-range benefits for businesses. In this chapter, we consider some of the distinguishing attributes and key drivers of m-commerce, the technical underpinnings of m-commerce, and some of the major m-commerce applications. The overall landscape for m-commerce is summarized in Exhibit 8.1.

**mobile commerce
(m-commerce,
m-business)**
Any business activity conducted over a wireless telecommunications network or from mobile devices.

ATTRIBUTES OF M-COMMERCE

Generally speaking, many of the EC applications described in this book also apply to m-commerce. For example, online shopping, Internet banking, e-stock trading, and online gambling are gaining popularity in wireless B2C. Auction sites are starting to use m-commerce (e.g., sending a text message alert when an auction is about to close), and wireless collaborative commerce in B2B EC is emerging. There are, however, some key attributes that offer the opportunity for development of new applications that are possible only in the mobile environment. These include:

▶ **Ubiquity.** *Ubiquity* means being available at any location at any time. A wireless mobile device such as a smartphone or tablet PC can deliver information when it is needed, regardless of the user's location. Ubiquity creates easier information access in a real-time environment, which is highly valued in today's business and consumer markets.

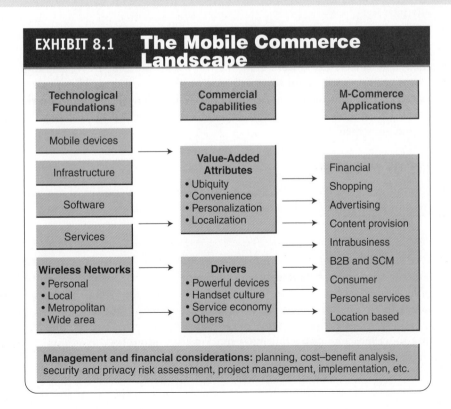

EXHIBIT 8.1 The Mobile Commerce Landscape

Management and financial considerations: planning, cost–benefit analysis, security and privacy risk assessment, project management, implementation, etc.

▶ **Convenience.** It is very convenient for users to operate in the wireless computing environment. Mobile computing devices are increasing in functionality and usability while remaining the same size or becoming smaller. Unlike traditional computers, mobile devices are portable, can be set in a variety of monitoring modes, and most feature instant connectivity (i.e., no need to wait for the device to boot up). Mobile devices enable users to connect easily and quickly to the Internet, intranets, other mobile devices, and online databases.

▶ **Interactivity.** In comparison with the desktop computing environment, transactions, communications, and service provision are immediate and highly interactive in the mobile computing environment. Businesses in which customer support and delivery of services require a high level of interactivity with the customer are likely to find a high value-added component in mobile computing.

▶ **Personalization.** Mobile devices are truly personal computing devices. Whereas a computer in a home, library, or Internet cafe may be used by a number of people, mobile devices are almost always owned and operated by a single individual. This enables consumer personalization—the delivery of information, products, and services designed to meet the needs of individual consumers. For example, users planning a trip can be sent travel-related information for retrieval when and where they want. Consumer personalization applications on mobile devices are still limited. However, the personal nature of the computing device, the increasing availability of personalized services, and transaction feasibility via mobile portals means that the mobile computing device could become the primary EC tool for delivering personalized information, products, and services.

▶ **Localization.** Knowing where a user is physically located at any particular moment is key to offering relevant mobile services in real time. Such services are known as location-based m-commerce (see Section 8.7). Localization may be general—for example, targeting everyone in a certain location (e.g., all shoppers at a shopping mall). Or, even better, it may be targeted so that users get messages that depend both on where they are and what their preferences are, thus combining personalization and localization. For instance, if it is known that a person likes Italian food and that person is strolling in a mall that has an Italian restaurant, the device owner could receive a text message that displays the restaurant's menu offerings and offers a 10 percent discount.

Vendors and carriers can differentiate themselves in the competitive marketplace by offering new, exciting, and useful services based on these attributes. These value-adding attributes can be the basis for businesses to better deliver the value proposition they offer to customers. The services these attributes represent will help e-businesses attract and keep customers and grow their revenues.

DRIVERS OF M-COMMERCE

In addition to the value-added attributes just discussed, the development of m-commerce is being driven by the following technological, business, social, and economic factors:

▶ **Widespread availability of more powerful mobile devices.** By the end of 2008, worldwide mobile telephone subscriptions reached 4 billion—equivalent to half the global population (ITU 2007). By 2011, the overall penetration is forecasted to be 75 percent. These devices are increasing in power, functionality, and features (e.g., color screens, GPS locators, Internet access) that support m-commerce. The potential mass market for conducting m-commerce has emerged.

▶ **The handset culture.** A closely related driver is the widespread use of cell phones among the 15- to 25-year-old age group. These users will constitute a major market of online buyers once they begin to make and spend reasonable amounts of money.

▶ **The service economy.** The transition from a manufacturing to a service-based economy is encouraging the development of mobile-based services, especially when customer service is a differentiator in highly competitive industries. Time-starved, but resource-rich, individuals will pay for mobile services that perform a range of tasks at their convenience (e.g., locating a restaurant or dry cleaner in close proximity to the user's position or mobile banking that allows users to pay bills online from their cell phones).

▶ **Vendor's push.** Both mobile communication network operators and manufacturers of mobile devices are advertising the many potential applications of m-commerce so that they can push new technologies, products, and services to buyers. The advertising expenditure by these companies to encourage businesses to "go mobile" or "mobilize your business" is huge.

▶ **The mobile workforce.** Some workers, such as salespeople and field service employees, have always worked away from an office. Increasingly, other sectors of the workforce also are "going mobile." This is being driven by social trends in the workplace such as telecommuting, employers' concerns about security, employees' desires for improved work–life balance, and a general questioning of where knowledge workers need to be located to conduct their work.

▶ **Increased mobility.** The most widely recognized benefit of increased mobility is the productive use of travel time. Workers who commute long distances, and especially executives who travel frequently, want to make more productive use of time they spend in public transportation vehicles or in airport lounges. However, there also are spatial, temporal, and contextual aspects of increased mobility that introduce business and personal benefits.

▶ **Improved price/performance.** The price of wireless devices and of per-minute pricing of mobile services continues to decline even as available services and functionality are increasing. This is leading to improvements in the price/performance ratio, enticing new owners into the market and encouraging existing owners to increase consumption of services and to upgrade their handsets.

▶ **Improving bandwidth.** To properly conduct m-commerce, sufficient bandwidth is needed to transmit the desired information via text, picture, voice, video, or multimedia. Theoretically, the 3G communications technology supported by newer smartphones (e.g., the iPhone) is providing a data rate of up to 2 Mbps. Empirically, 3G transmission speeds are much slower, with actual rates somewhere between .1 and .5 Mbps. This is in comparison to standard Wi-Fi, which is close to 56 Mbps.

The drivers and attributes of m-commerce underlie most of the applications discussed in later sections of the chapter.

Section 8.1 ▶ REVIEW QUESTIONS

1. Briefly describe the value-added attributes of m-commerce.
2. List and briefly describe eight major drivers of m-commerce.

8.2 COMPONENTS, TECHNICAL INFRASTRUCTURE, AND SERVICES OF MOBILE COMPUTING

In the traditional computing environment, users require a desktop computer and cabled connections to networks, servers, and peripheral devices such as printers. This situation has limited the use of computers to fixed locations and has created difficulties for people who

wireless mobile computing (mobile computing)
Computing that connects a mobile device to a network or another computing device, anytime, anywhere.

either want or need to be connected anytime, anywhere. For instance, salespeople, field service employees, law enforcement agents, inspectors, utility workers, and executives who travel frequently can be more effective if they can use information technology while at their jobs in the field or in transit. A solution to this situation is **wireless mobile computing** (or just **mobile computing**), which enables a real-time connection between a mobile device and computing networks or to another computing device, anytime, anywhere. Mobile computing offers a computing environment suitable for workers who travel outside the boundaries of their workplace or for anyone on the move.

An extensive hardware and software infrastructure underlies mobile computing. First, there are the mobile devices (e.g., smartphones) that enable a user to connect to a mobile network. Next, there are those components (e.g., network access points) that support the wireless connection, as well as parts of the infrastructure (e.g., GPS locators) that support the delivery of services over the connection. Finally, there are those components that support m-commerce activities in the same way they support typical e-commerce activities. For example, a Web server, database server, and enterprise application server offer the same services to a wireless device as they do to a wired computer, with one significant exception. Certain characteristics of mobile devices—small screens, reduced memory, limited bandwidth, and restricted input capabilities—mean that hardware and software designers need to anticipate special requirements and design the system accordingly. For example, a Web server may need two versions of the same Web page—a "normal" page with full graphics for desktop computers and a "mobile" page for PDAs and smartphones—as well as a way to distinguish between devices requesting the Web page.

This section and the next briefly discuss the major components of the mobile computing infrastructure. A more extensive discussion is available in Hu et al. (2006).

MOBILE DEVICES

A few years ago a computer was basically a computer, a cell phone was basically a phone, and a personal digital assistant (PDA) was essentially a stand-alone personal information manager (calendar, contacts, calculator, and the like). Today, all of these devices are converging so that it is difficult from a functional perspective to tell them apart.

Mobile computers come in all shapes and sizes—laptops, thin-and-light notebooks, ultra portables, and ultra-mobile PCs (UMPCs). Most of these have the same basic capabilities (e.g., support for audio and video, e-mail, Internet browsers, and Wi-Fi connections) and run essentially the same operating systems (e.g., some form of Microsoft Windows). What distinguishes one type of mobile computer from another is its physical footprint. Thin notebooks weigh 4 to 6 pounds and have 14-inch displays. In comparison, ultra portables weigh less than 4 pounds and have smaller screens. Most of the major computer manufacturers (HP, Dell, Toshiba, and Lenovo) produce thin notebooks and ultra portables. In contrast, few of the major computer makers currently produce UMPCs. Although UMPCs are also full-blown computers, they tend to have much smaller footprints—either no standard keyboard or much smaller keyboards, weigh between 1 and 2 pounds, and have much smaller screens (5 to 6 inches). Samsung, OQO, and ASUS are some of the manufacturers offering UMPCs.

personal digital assistant (PDA)
A stand-alone handheld computer principally used for personal information management.

Originally, a **personal digital assistant (PDA)**, also known as a *palmtop*, was a stand-alone handheld computer that provided access to a user's address book and calendar and supported calculation and desktop applications such as word processing and spreadsheets. Most of the original PDAs could also be synchronized with a user's desktop computer. This enabled a user to read e-mails offline. Over time, most PDAs have added support for wireless connectivity to the Internet through Wi-Fi. In this way, a PDA can be used to browse the Web and read and send e-mail in real time. Most PDAs also provide multimedia support for audio and video.

The leading producers of PDAs are Palm, Inc. (palm.com) and Hewlett-Packard (hp.com). From a hardware perspective, most PDAs have small screens (2.5 to 4 inches), small memories (64 Mb of RAM), either small keyboards with thumb wheels or a virtual keyboard on the screen, and expansion slots for memory cards (SD or compact flash) that offer additional storage or access to other applications. From a software perspective, most PDAs either run the Palm Operating System (OS) or Microsoft's Windows Mobile operating system.

In recent years, the sales of stand-alone PDAs have declined precipitously. However, the sales of smartphones with PDA capabilities have increased substantially over the same period. For this reason, PDA manufacturers have created PDA models with mobile phone capabilities or have started producing smartphone devices such as the Palm Treo.

Basically, a **smartphone** is a mobile phone with PDA-like or PC-like functionality, including e-mail, Web browsing, multimedia capabilities, address book, calendar, calculator, support for reading Word and PDF documents, a digital camera, and so forth. Unlike PDAs, there is a wide variety of smartphone manufacturers. There is also a wide variety of operating systems, including Symbian, Linux, Palm OS, Windows Mobile, Apple OS/X, and RIM BlackBerry. Like PDAs, smartphones have small screens, keyboards, memory, and storage.

In addition to the full-function mobile devices such as the smartphone and UMPC, there are also specialized devices such as Internet tablets or multimedia players that provide wireless access to the Web. The Nokia N800 series is an example of the former, while the Apple iPod and Archos 604 are examples of the latter. The Nokia N800, for instance, runs a modified version of the Linux operating system, has 128 Mg of RAM and 256 Mg of flash memory, a virtual keyboard, a 4-inch screen, a Web cam, and expansion slots. The device also supports a broad range of applications, including multimedia players and Skype (skype.com).

Clearly, PDAs, smartphones, Internet appliances, and multimedia players appear to be converging toward the same endpoint—a small-footprint, handheld mobile device that combines all the capabilities of these devices in one package. The future of laptops, notebooks, and UMPCs is a little less clear, although these mobile computers will continue to support a broad span of capabilities in a shrinking footprint.

MOBILE COMPUTING SOFTWARE AND SERVICES

Developing software for wireless devices is challenging for several reasons. First, various devices have a number of competing standards for application development. An example is the number of operating systems supported by the various devices. Included in the list are Windows CE (and its many variants) from Microsoft, Palm OS from Palm Computing, EPOC from the Symbian Corporation, and open-source Linux, to name a few. This means that software applications must be customized for each type of device and each type of operating system. Second, software applications have to adapt to match the requirements of the device, not the other way around. Specifically, all software must deal with the technological challenges of small display screens, reduced bandwidth, limited input capabilities, and restricted memory that are common on most mobile devices. For instance, many mobile devices have specialized Web browsers, such as Microsoft's Internet Explorer Mobile or Opera's Mobile browser (opera.com), which have been specifically designed to handle screen and bandwidth limitations.

Although mobile devices such as cell phones and smartphones present a variety of software challenges, they also offer a number of software-enabled services that aren't found in the desktop or even mobile computer worlds. These services provide a foundation for many of the applications described later in the chapter. Included among these services are messaging, location-based, and voice-support services.

Messaging Services

Short message service (SMS), frequently referred to as *text messaging*, or simply *texting*, is a service that supports the transmittal of short text messages (up to 160 characters) between mobile phones on a cellular telephone network. The limited message length means users often use acronyms to convey the message in shorthand text. Examples include "how are you" becomes "how r u," and "great" becomes "gr8." Texting has been immensely popular in Asia and Europe for some time. In the United States, adoption of SMS has been slower than in other parts of the world, although usage has been growing at double-digit rates for the past few years. Based on estimates from the Cellular Telecommunications Industry Association (CTIA), 60 percent of all mobile phone users in Europe use SMS, while the figure is 40 percent for users in the United States (TeleGeography 2006).

Multimedia messaging service (MMS) is the emerging generation of wireless messaging, delivering rich media, including video and audio, to mobile phones and other devices.

smartphone
A mobile phone with PC-like capabilities.

short message service (SMS)
A service that supports the sending and receiving of short text messages on mobile phones.

multimedia messaging service (MMS)
The emerging generation of wireless messaging; MMS is able to deliver rich media.

MMS is an extension of SMS that was commercially introduced in 2002. It allows longer messages and utilizes a special protocol for displaying media content. MMS enables the convergence of mobile devices and personal computers because MMS messages can be sent between PCs, PDAs, and mobile phones that are MMS enabled.

Location-Based Services

Location-based services use the *global positioning system (GPS)* or other positioning techniques to find where customers and clients are located and deliver products and services to them based on the location.

Voice-Support Services

The most natural mode of human communication is voice. Voice recognition and voice synthesizing in m-commerce applications offer advantages such as hands- and eyes-free operation, better operation in dirty or moving environments, faster input (people talk about two-and-a-half times faster than they type), and ease-of-use for disabled people. Most significantly, increased use of voice-support services exploits the built-in audio capabilities of many mobile devices and reduces their dependence on less-than-satisfactory input solutions, such as handwriting recognition, keypads, or virtual touch-screen keyboards.

Voice support applications such as **interactive voice response (IVR)** systems enable users to interact with a computerized system to request and receive information and to enter and change data using a telephone. These systems have been around since the 1980s but are becoming more functional and widespread as artificial intelligence and voice recognition capabilities continue to improve.

The highest level of voice support services is a **voice portal**, a Web site with an audio interface that can be accessed through a telephone call. A visitor requests information by speaking, and the voice portal finds the information on the Web, translates it into a computer-generated voice reply, and provides the answer by voice. For example, tellme.com and bevocal.com allow callers to request information about weather, local restaurants, current traffic, and other handy information. IVR and voice portals are likely to become important ways of delivering m-commerce services over audio.

WIRELESS TELECOMMUNICATIONS NETWORKS

All mobile devices need to connect with a telecommunications network or with another device. How they do this depends on the purpose of the connection, the capabilities and location of the device, and what connection options are available at the time. Included among the various networks are (1) personal area networks for device-to-device connections up to 30 feet; (2) wireless local area networks for medium-range connections up to 300 feet; (3) wireless metropolitan networks for connections up to 30 miles; and (4) wireless wide area networks for connecting to a network with cellular phone coverage.

interactive voice response (IVR)
A voice system that enables users to request and receive information and to enter and change data through a telephone to a computerized system.

voice portal
A Web site with an audio interface that can be accessed through a telephone call.

personal area network (PAN)
A wireless telecommunications network for device-to-device connections within a very short range.

Bluetooth
A set of telecommunications standards that enables wireless devices to communicate with each other over short distances.

▶ **Personal area networks.** A **personal area network (PAN)** is suitable for mobile users who need to make very short-range device-to-device wireless connections within a small space, typically a single room. The most common way to establish a PAN is with Bluetooth. **Bluetooth** is a set of telecommunications standards that enables wireless devices to communicate with each other over short distances of up to 20 meters (60 feet). Bluetooth can be used to pair a number of different devices—wireless keyboards with tablet PCs, PDAs with computers for easy data synchronization, and digital cameras with printers. Bluetooth also can link more than two devices, as is done in connectBlue's operating-room control system (connectblue.se). Equipment that monitors a patient's heartbeat, ECG, respiration, and other vital signs all can be linked via Bluetooth, eliminating obstructive and dangerous cables and increasing the portability of the equipment. For additional information, see Wikipedia (en.wikipedia.org/wiki/Personal_area_network) and bluetooth.org.

▶ **Wireless local area networks and Wi-Fi.** As its name implies, a wireless local area network (WLAN) is equivalent to a wired LAN, but without all the cables. Most WLANs run on a telecommunications standard known as *IEEE 802.11* (e.g., 802.11g) which is commonly called Wi-Fi (for wireless fidelity). Exhibit 8.2 outlines the processes and components underlying Wi-Fi. At the heart of a WLAN is a wireless access point that connects a wireless device to the desired network. The wireless device communicates with the access point by a wireless network card installed by the user or manufacturer of the device. In turn, the access point has a wired connection to the Internet in the same manner as a wired LAN cable. Most public hotspots located in airports, hotels, restaurants, and conference centers rely on Wi-Fi. Similarly, many homeowners have installed Wi-Fi to enable Internet connectivity throughout their home without the need to retrofit the house with cables. Online File W8.1 describes the growing use of Wi-Fi by the traveling public.

▶ **Municipal Wi-Fi networks.** By using a large number of connected hotspots, one can create a wireless city. This is known as a *city-wide* or *municipal Wi-Fi network*. For example, on August 16, 2006, Google created a network of 380 access points posted on lightpoles throughout the city of Mountain View, California. Residents of Mountain View just had to choose the "GoogleWiFi" signal and sign into their

wireless local area network (WLAN)
A telecommunications network that enables users to make short-range wireless connections to the Internet or another network.

Wi-Fi (wireless fidelity)
The common name used to describe the IEEE 802.11 standard used on most WLANs.

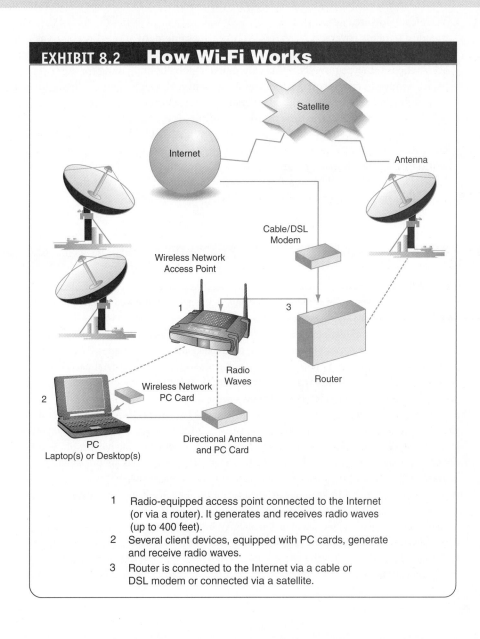

EXHIBIT 8.2   How Wi-Fi Works

1   Radio-equipped access point connected to the Internet (or via a router). It generates and receives radio waves (up to 400 feet).
2   Several client devices, equipped with PC cards, generate and receive radio waves.
3   Router is connected to the Internet via a cable or DSL modem or connected via a satellite.

Google accounts with their user ID and password to access the Web through the free Wi-Fi service. These networks also are known as *grid* or *mesh networks* (see Online File W8.2). Throughout the United States, there have been a number of municipal Wi-Fi projects. Most of these, like Philadelphia, Pennsylvania's "Wireless Philadelphia" project, have experienced cost and schedule overruns only to provide much less coverage than originally envisioned (*Philadelphia Inquirer* 2007).

▶ **WiMax.** Instead of relying on a mesh or grid of multiple access points, like municipal Wi-Fi, WiMax (Worldwide Interoperability for Microwave Access) provides relatively fast (e.g., 70 Mbps) broadband access over a medium-sized area of up to 50 kilometers (31 miles). WiMax works somewhat like a cell phone. More specifically, WiMax coverage is divided into a series of overlapping areas called *cells*. Each of these cells provides broadband Internet coverage within a given geographical area. At the center of each cell is a tower with a base station that is connected to the Internet using high-speed lines. A tower broadcasts radio signals over a set radio frequency called a *spectrum*. Unlike Wi-Fi, the spectrum is restricted to companies who have licensed its usage (e.g., Sprint). This provides wider and more reliable coverage. Again, in order to access a WiMax network, a device (e.g., UMPC) requires a built-in or external card. WiMax is gaining traction in a number of municipal areas throughout the world. The WiMax Forum (wimaxforum.org) provides detailed information about WiMax capabilities and usage.

▶ **Wireless wide area networks.** A Wireless wide area network (WWAN) offers the broadest wireless coverage. WWANs rely on the same network technologies as cell phones. This means that a user with a mobile computer and a WWAN card can access the Internet regionally, nationally, or even globally, depending on the coverage of the wireless service provider the user is accessing. WWANs can be distinguished by their speed (e.g., 2G versus 3G versus 4G networks), by the communication protocols they use (e.g., the time division multiple access [TDMA] protocol used in 2G networks versus the code division multiple access [CDMA] designed for 3G networks), and the cellular standards on which they are based (e.g., much of the world utilizes the Global System for Mobile Communications [GSM] and Personal Digital Cellular [PDC] in Japan). Exhibit 8.3 provides a summary of the differences among the various networks by speed (from 1G to 4G).

WiMax
A wireless standard (IEEE 802.16) for making broadband network connections over a medium-size area such as a city.

wireless wide area network (WWAN)
A telecommunications network that offers wireless coverage over a large geographical area, typically over a cellular phone network.

EXHIBIT 8.3	**Four Generations of WWAN Technologies**
WWAN Generation	**Description**
1G	This was the first generation of wireless technology. It was an analog-based technology in effect from 1979 to 1992 and was used exclusively for voice.
2G	This second generation of digital wireless technology is in widespread existence today. 2G is based on digital radio technology and is able to accommodate text messages (SMS).
2.5G	An interim technology based on new cell phone protocols such as GPRS (general packet radio service) and CDMA2000 (code division multiple access). This generation can communicate limited graphics, such as in picture text messages.
3G	The third generation of digital wireless technology supports rich media, such as video. 3G utilizes packet switching in the high 15 to 20 MHz range. 3G started in Japan in 2001, reached Europe in 2002, and the United States and much of Asia in 2003. As of 2004, the number of 3G-enabled devices was only a tiny fraction of the cell phone market. However, sales are projected to increase gradually as more 3G networks and applications become available.
3.5G	This generation is expected to be about seven times faster than 3G. It promises data download speeds of 14 Mbps and upload speeds of up to 1.8 Mbps. This means major improvement in mobile voice telephony, video telephony, mobile TV, and other media.
4G	The next generation after 3.5G. The arrival of 4G, which will provide faster display of multimedia, is expected by 2010. Information about WWANs can be found at the Web sites of the various service providers (e.g., sprint.com) and at the sites of various mobile or cellular associations (e.g., gsmworld.com).

1. Briefly describe some of the key differences and similarities among the major mobile devices.
2. Why is it difficult to develop software and services for mobile devices?
3. Briefly describe the types of messaging services offered for mobile devices.
4. What are the distinguishing features of PANs, WLANs, WiMax, and WWANs?
5. Define 3G. Why is it important for the adoption of mobile applications and services?

8.3 MOBILE FINANCIAL APPLICATIONS

Most mobile financial applications are simply mobile versions of their wireline counter-parts, but they have the potential to turn a mobile device—cellular phone or personal digital assistant—into a business tool, replacing bank branches, ATMs, and credit cards by letting a user conduct financial transactions with a mobile device, anytime, anywhere. These services fall into two broad categories: mobile banking and mobile payments.

MOBILE BANKING

Throughout Europe, the United States, and Asia, an increasing percentage of banks are offering mobile access to financial and account information. These banks enable their customers to use their mobile devices to check balances, monitor transactions, obtain other account information, transfer funds, locate branches or ATMs, and, sometimes, pay bills.

Most banks deploy these mobile services through a variety of channels, although the Internet and SMS are the most widely used. A blog written by Brandon McGee (brandonmcgee.blogspot.com) provides links to a number of banking Web sites throughout the world that offer these services. Take, for instance, the Chase Mobile services offered by J.P. Morgan Chase Bank. On the one hand, customers can access their accounts at (chase.com) via the browser on their smartphone in much the same way they would access their accounts from their desktop or laptop computers. On the other hand, customers can send Chase Mobile shorthand SMS text messages to inquire about their balances (BAL), payment due dates (DUE), or transaction histories (TRANS).

Historically, the uptake of mobile banking has been relatively low. This is beginning to change. Much of the change is being driven by the world economic crisis. Bank and financial service customers are utilizing their smartphones and cell phones to obtain up-to-the minute financial information and to perform up-to-the-minute transactions. MONILINK, the United Kingdom's mobile money network, which is used by most of the U.K. high-street banks, reported in October 2008 that customers had used the network for approximately 1 million transactions, a substantial increase over the previous months (*M2 Presswire* 2008). IMS Research, a global market research firm, recently forecast that the number of mobile banking users will reach approximately 1 billion in 2012 and that they will complete slightly more than 60 million transactions during that year (IMS Research 2008).

Similar patterns were revealed in a recent survey (PaymentNews 2008) of more than 1,000 cell phone users conducted on behalf of CheckFree (see fiserv.com). Although only 23 percent of the survey respondents currently conduct financial activities over their cell phones, approximately 75 percent indicated that they would be interested in using their phones to check bank and credit card balances, receive and pay bills, transfer money between accounts, etc., if the services were made available. This represents a 50 percent increase over the percent expressing an interest in a survey conducted 2 years prior. Respondents cited anytime, anywhere access as the primary reasons for their interest.

MOBILE PAYMENTS

The term *mobile payment* refers to payment transactions initiated or confirmed using a person's cell phone or smartphone. These transactions include such things as point-of-sale

(POS) purchases, transferring money to a person or business, or purchasing a product or service remotely. Mobile POS payments are also known as *proximity* or *contactless payments*. *Mobile proximity payments* are usually handled using *near field communication (NFC)* technology. NFC is wireless technology that enables data exchange between devices that are within a distance of 10 centimeters (or 4 inches). In contrast, *mobile remote payments* are those initiated and settled through a combination of the cellular and associated payment networks. Like mobile banking, these person-to-person, person-to-business, or business-to-business payments typically rely on either SMS text messaging or the Web to execute the payment.

Mobile Proximity Payments

In the United States, mobile contactless payments have only been used in a handful of pilot projects. For instance, from January 2008 to May 2008 a select group of riders of the San Francisco Bay Area Rapid Transit (BART) were able to pay their fares using their mobile phones (*Wireless and Mobile News* 2008). These phones were outfitted with NFC-enabled chips. Likewise, NFC equipment was installed at the BART turnstiles. In this way, the riders simply tapped their phones on the NFC equipment to gain entrance through the turnstiles. The fare was then deducted via the phone from a prepaid account. These same riders could also use their phones to pay for meals at local Jack in the Box fast-food restaurants. The results of the pilot showed that the BART riders who took part in the trial extensively used their NFC-enabled phones to pay for their BART fares and meals at participating Jack in the Box restaurants.

Although the BART pilot was deemed a success, it points to the "chicken–egg" problem that confronts most EC payment schemes. The problem is discussed at length in Chapter 11. In simple terms, because the consumers' phones require specialized chips, the merchants (in this case BART) require specialized equipment to communicate with the chips. And, because specialized networks are also required to handle the payments, the chances against widespread adoption are substantial, if not overwhelming.

Outside the United States, adoption of mobile contactless payments has been a bit broader, especially in Japan. NTT DoCoMo offers a number of mobile phones with NFC capabilities. DoCoMo has also reported that there are more than 200,000 NFC card readers in Japan (Best 2008). To date, approximately 20 million customers use these phones for debit card transactions. In the future they will also use them as credit cards. Interestingly, taxis in Japan are also starting to install NFC readers.

Mobile Remote Payments

A number of initiatives have been launched to support mobile remote payments. These initiatives offer services that enable clients and consumers to use their mobile devices to pay their monthly bills, to shop on the Internet, to transfer funds to other individuals (P2P payments), and to "top off" their prepaid mobile accounts without having to purchase prepaid phone cards. Case 8.1 provides an example of how mobile remote payments are being used in developing countries like India to service loans to those on the economic margins of the country.

In the case of mobile bill payments, Internet shopping, P2P payments, and "topping off," the processes involved in executing a transaction are basically the same:

1. The payer initiating the payment sets up an account with a mobile payment service provider (MPSP).
2. To make a payment, the payer sends a text message or command to the MPSP that includes the dollar amount and the receiver's mobile phone number.
3. The MPSP receives the information and sends a message back to the payer, confirming the transaction and requesting his or her PIN.
4. The payer receives the request on his mobile device and enters the PIN.
5. When the MPSP receives the payer's PIN, money is transferred to the third party's account (credit or bank account).
6. After the transaction occurs, the payment information is sent to the payer's device.

CASE 8.1
EC Application

CLOSING THE DIGITAL DIVIDE WITH MOBILE MICROFINANCE

The term **digital divide** refers to the gap between people with effective access to digital and information technology and those without. The gap is both a symptom and product of the larger issues of poverty and inequality. In underdeveloped and developing countries, the divide has widened as more of everyday life has moved to the digital arena across the globe. This is especially true in the financial arena. Although many of these countries do not have money to implement wireline phone systems, they can afford WWANs. This provides the opportunity to utilize mobile devices to narrow the widening gap.

The vast majority of the inhabitants in developing countries such as India are "unbanked." Some estimates put the worldwide number of unbanked at 70 percent of the world's population. Basically, they lack access to some of the basic financial services needed to live their daily lives, much less lift them out of poverty. As a consequence, they often turn to local moneylenders who charge exorbitant interest rates (sometimes more than 10 percent per month) in order to handle personal emergencies, life-cycle needs (such as weddings and funerals), or to take advantage of investment opportunities (such as buying land or equipment).

The world of microfinance is aimed at addressing some of these needs. **Microfinance** refers to the provision of financial services to poor or low-income clients, including consumers and the self-employed. Microfinance is also a social movement predicated on the belief that access to a range of financial services will help lift the poor out of poverty. Obviously, financing can come from a variety of sources, both institutional and noninstitutional. However, the term *microfinance* is usually applied to formal financial institutions (such as banks).

A few years back, it was estimated that there were more than 3,000 financial institutions serving the needs of some 665 million poor clients. About a fourth of those serviced were classified as microfinance. In 2007, it was estimated that these institutions were providing more than $25 billion in microfinance loans. Most of these individual loans were for amounts less than US$200.

Grameen Koota, one of these microfinance institutions, is located in Bangalore, India, and is part of a much larger financial institution, Grameen Bank. At the moment, they have more than 40,000 clients and a loan portfolio of more than US$20 million. In order to service their microfinance loans, they maintain a large staff of loan officers. One of the primary jobs of these loan officers is to attend weekly client meetings held within the local communities in order to collect repayments. This is a high-risk process, plagued by theft, fraud, and embezzlement.

Potentially, mobile banking and remote payments could be used to address some of the problems surrounding the collection of loans at Grameen Koota and other microfinance lending institutions. At least this is what Grameen Koota and the founders of start-up mChek, as well as mChek's financial backers at Draper Fisher Juvetson, believe.

Like the rest of India, cell phone use is growing rapidly among Grameen Koota's customers. In countries like India, China, and the Philippines, the penetration of cell phones even among the poor is skyrocketing. In part this is a result of rapidly declining costs of owning and using a cell phone. More than 1 billion people live in India; this is more than 17 percent of the world's population. More than 450 million of these people live in poverty—living on less than 25 rupees a day (a little more than US50¢). It is estimated that midway through 2008, around 300 million Indians had cell phones. At the current growth rate, the number of cell phone owners in India will exceed 750 million by 2012. This makes India the fastest growing cell phone market in the world and the second largest market.

Even though most of the phones owned by the poor inhabitants in India have minimal functionality, they still offer SMS capabilities. These capabilities, in combination with mChek's software, will provide Grameen Koota with the mobile means to make loans and receive payments without the need to send loan officers into the local community. Recently, mChek got a boost when Bharti Airtel (India's leading provider of cell phones) decided to incorporate mChek's software directly into their SIM cards—the device inside a mobile phone that identifies the user and number.

mChek is not the only Indian company focused on providing mobile microfinance capabilities. Obopay India (a branch of the U.S.-based Obopay) is also developing a microfinance mobile platform. Obopay is working with Grameen Solutions, one of the organizations created by Muhammad Yunus, who received the Nobel Peace Prize in 2006 along with Grameen Bank for work done on microcredit.

Sources: Compiled from Talbot (2008) and Mitra (2008).

Questions

1. What is microfinance?

2. What problem is Grameen Koota trying to solve by adopting mobile loans and payments?

3. How will mobile loans and payments work for organizations like Grameen Koota?

digital divide
Refers to the gap between people with effective access to digital and information technology and those without.

microfinance
Refers to the provision of financial services to poor or low-income clients, including consumers and the self-employed.

Similar sorts of steps are used to enable merchants or service providers the opportunity to conduct POS transactions without the need for special POS terminals. These payments have been labeled *mobile POS (mPOS)* transactions. With mPOS, the merchant utilizes a special mobile service to send a payment request from his or her mobile device to the customer's phone number. Once the request is received, the customer enters his or her PIN. At this point, the service sends a confirmation to both the merchant and the customer. The transactions are completed by debiting the customer's account and crediting the merchant's account. Even though the merchant is also charged transaction and communication costs by the service operator, the cost is substantially less than a POS credit card transaction. These services are aimed at small businesses and independent operators such as doctors, dentists, delivery companies, taxis, and plumbers.

Although a number of companies such as Obopay, PayPal Mobile, and TextPayMe offer mobile remote payment services, the worldwide uptake of these services has been minimal. Part of the problem is that few of the companies support a broad range of remote payment services. For instance, with PayPal Mobile, users can only check their PayPal balances, send money to other individuals, and make eBay purchases. Like any other electronic payment system (see Chapter 11), without broader coverage and widely accepted payment methods and standards, most of these services are doomed to failure.

Section 8.3 ❱ REVIEW QUESTIONS

1. Describe some of the services provided by mobile banking.
2. Discuss proximity-based wireless payments. How have they been used in the transportation arena?
3. What are the basic processes used in handling mobile remote payments?

8.4   MOBILE MARKETING AND ADVERTISING

The ratio of mobile handsets to desktop and laptop computers is approximately 2 to 1 and growing. This represents a huge opportunity for online marketing and advertising. Not only has the opportunity been heighted by current economic conditions, but it has also been spurred by the higher response rates to mobile marketing campaigns when compared to more traditional or online campaigns.

MOBILE MARKETING CAMPAIGNS

The holy grail of mobile marketing and advertising is location-based ads (see Section 8.7). Yet, a thorough analysis of prior and current mobile marketing campaigns shows that most are clones of their online, as well as traditional media, counterparts. A review of leading mobile marketing literature (Becker 2006), the analysis of 55 campaigns run by companies such as Coca-Cola and BMW, and interviews with 44 mobile marketing thought leaders determined that there were basically four classes of campaigns focused on one of four types of campaign objectives. The classes included:

1. **Information.** Programs providing information about products, points of interest, news, weather, traffic, horoscopes, and related content.
2. **Entertainment.** Programs that "produce value to the customers" and provide amusement and emotional triggers through videos, music, games, personalization ringtones, wallpapers, and so forth.
3. **Raffles.** Programs that provide prizes such as digital content or physical goods.
4. **Coupons.** Programs that offer monetary incentives (like discounts), trial packages, or free services.

The major objectives of these classes fell into one of six categories:

1. **Building brand awareness.** Increase the customers' ability to recognize and recall a brand in purchase and consumption situations.

2. **Changing brand image.** Change the perception of the brand by customers.

3. **Promoting sales.** Stimulate quicker or greater purchase of a product or service.

4. **Enhancing brand loyalty.** Increase consumers' commitment to repurchase the brand.

5. **Building customer databases.** Collect data about the mobile device or data network or profiles of customers.

6. **Stimulating mobile word of mouth.** Encourage customers to pass on ads from customer to customer via their mobile devices.

Obviously, these are the same types of campaigns and objectives underlying traditional marketing approaches. Currently, SMS and e-mails are the principal technologies used to deliver advertisements to cell phones. However, as more wireless bandwidth becomes available, content-rich advertising involving audio, pictures, and video clips will be generated for individual users with specific needs, interests, and inclinations.

Recent marketing campaigns conducted by high-end clothing retailers are indicative of the types of mobile campaigns. Some examples follow.

Example: Armani Exchange (A/X). In mid-2008 Armani Exchange (A/X) debuted an SMS campaign aimed at building brand awareness and stimulating increased sales (Abramovich 2008). A/X is a youth label of the larger Armani manufacturer and retailer. A/X manufactures, distributes, and retails everything from apparel to eyewear to music. This particular mobile campaign was kicked off with a $1,000 shopping spree sweepstakes. Customers participated by simply sending the text message "AX" to the short code 276264. Once the customer sent the message, they received the reply, "Welcome to TEXT AX! Msgs up to 3x/mo. Std. carrier rates may apply. To opt in, reply w/Postal Code. To opt out, text STOP. For more info, text HELP." Those customers who replied with their postal code received a second message, thanking them and asking them to confirm their sweepstakes entry with a WIN reply. Those customers who opted in were sent SMS promotions up to three times a month.

Example: Dolce & Gabanna (D&G). A similar mobile campaign was recently run by Dolce & Gabanna on the Nokia Media Network (Abramovich 2008). Again, the goal of the campaign was to promote awareness of D&G's overall brand and their teen-focused fashion catalog. Part of the campaign involved a game called "Dee&Gee," which could be downloaded from the D&G mobile Web site. Once at the site, consumers could also view the D&G teen catalog and download D&G-branded wallpaper. The response to the D&G campaign was a 10 percent click-through rate (CTR). According to Nokia, this is typical. CTRs generally range from 2 percent to 20 percent. This may seem low, but it is consistently higher than similar online or traditional media ads. It is one of the main reasons for the growing interest in mobile advertising.

MOBILE MARKETING GUIDELINES

Although organizations such as the Direct Marketing Association have established codes of practice for Internet marketing, including the use of mobile media, most industry pundits agree that they are not well suited for the dynamic nature of mobile commerce. In response, the mobile media industry has established a set of guidelines and best practices for mobile advertising. The Global Code of Conduct from the Mobile Marketing Association (MMA) (mmaglobal.com/codeofconduct.pdf) is indicative of the types of practices promoted by the industry. The basic principles of the code include:

▶ **Notice.** Informing users of the marketer's identity or products and services offered and the key terms and conditions that govern an interaction between the marketer and the user's mobile device.

▶ **Choice and consent.** Respecting the right of the user to control which mobile messages they receive by obtaining consent (opt-in) and implementing a simple termination (opt-out) process.

> ▶ **Customization and constraint.** Ensuring that collected user information is used to tailor communication to the interests of the recipient and is handled responsibly, sensitively, and in compliance with applicable law. Mobile messages should be limited to those requested by the user and provide value such as product and service enhancements, contests, requested information, entertainment, or discounts.
>
> ▶ **Security.** Implementing reasonable technical, administrative, and physical procedures to protect user information from unauthorized use, alteration, disclosure, distribution, or access.
>
> ▶ **Enforcement and accountability.** The MMA expects its members to comply with the MMA Privacy Code of Conduct and has incorporated the code into applicable MMA guidelines, including the U.S. Consumer Best Practice (CBP) guidelines. Until the code can be enforced effectively by a third-party enforcement organization, mobile marketers are expected to use evaluations of their practices to certify compliance with the code.

As the guidelines indicate, actual usage and enforcement is voluntary. For example, the "double opt-in" feature used in the A/X campaign adheres to the principle of "choice and consent." Basically, A/X first asked consumers to send a message indicating their willingness to participate in the campaign (the first opt-in). Once the consumer agreed, they were then asked to confirm their choice a second time with a WIN response (the second opt-in). There was no law or official rule requiring A/X to do this. It was simply smart practice on their part.

Section 8.4 ▶ REVIEW QUESTIONS

1. How are traditional media and mobile marketing campaigns alike?
2. What type of campaign was recently used by Armani Exchange (A/X)? What were the underlying goals of the campaign?
3. Summarize the basic principles in the Global Code of Conduct from the Mobile Marketing Association.

8.5 MOBILE WORKFORCE SOLUTIONS

Although B2C m-commerce gets considerable publicity in the media, for most organizations the greatest short-term benefit from m-commerce is likely to come from intrabusiness applications aimed at supporting the mobile workforce who spend a substantial part of their workday away from corporate premises. Examples include members of sales teams, traveling executives, telecommuters, employees working in corporate yards or warehouses, and repair or installation employees who work at customers' sites or in the field. These individuals need access to the same office and work applications and data as their nonmobile counterparts. This section looks at the mobile devices and technologies that can be used to support mobile workers and the issues that arise in providing this support.

NEEDS OF THE MOBILE WORKFORCE

mobile worker
Any employee who is away from their primary work space at least 10 hours a week or 25 percent of the time.

A mobile worker is usually defined as any employee who is away from their primary work space at least 10 hours a week or 25 percent of the time. Using this definition, IDC forecasts that by 2011 there will be approximately 1 billion mobile workers worldwide (*Business Wire* 2008). This will represent about a third of the total workforce. In the United States alone, they estimate that 75 percent of the workforce will be mobile by that year. This represents a major shift: In 2008, there were more than 150 million workers in the United States, of which approximately 50 million or one-third could be classified as mobile.

Even though the mobile workforce is growing more rapidly, workforce mobility is not a new phenomenon. What is new is the growing recognition within enterprises that a mobile workforce requires and can benefit from specialized mobile solutions and devices.

Toward this end, companies are providing a wide range of mobile devices, including BlackBerry's voice-enabled PDAs and Wi-Fi–enabled laptops, to a substantial percentage of their employees. The percentage varies depending on the industry, as well as the company's size—the percentage is larger in IT and telecommunication firms and in small to midsize enterprises.

Benefits of Mobile Workforce Support

Like other IT investments, many enterprises cite enhanced productivity and reduced costs as the main reasons for the widespread deployment of mobile devices and applications within their organizations. Mobile solutions—devices and applications—provide mobile workers with real-time access to enterprise data and applications. This can reduce, for example, the time required in the field to process orders or to service customer requests. Mobile solutions can also automate existing paper and pen processes and workflows. This can ensure, for instance, that processes are completed in a uniform fashion with minimal data entry errors or data loss.

The specific benefits that accrue by deploying mobile solutions really depend on the segments of the mobile workforce toward which the solutions are aimed. Mobile workers can be divided into three segments: mobile professionals (such as senior executives and consultants), the mobile field force (such as field sales and service technicians), and mobile specialty workers (such as delivery personnel and construction workers). In the United States, for example, these groups represent approximately 45 percent, 35 percent, and 20 percent, respectively. Clearly, the mobile solutions these groups need vary, as do the specific challenges the workers and their companies face in using and deploying these solutions.

Some of the solutions that are widely used by the three segments include the following:

- **Mobile office applications.** According to a worldwide survey of 375 top business executives conducted by the Intelligence Unit of *The Economist* magazine (*The Economist* 2007), e-mail, calendaring, and keeping in touch with colleagues via messaging are the most popular mobile applications. Looking toward 2012, these applications are expected to maintain their popularity with a few minor changes. Executives feel that mobile voice-over-IP (VoIP) and videoconferencing will increase in importance. They also look toward greater use of mobile customer relationship management (CRM) by their sales and services teams.

- **Sales force automation (SFA).** Generally speaking, sales force automation (SFA) systems help guide and automatically record the various stages of the sales process. These stages run the gamut from managing contacts with customers and prospects, tracking sales leads, forecasting sales, and managing orders. Providing mobile access to a company's SFA system can help keep their mobile sales personnel better informed about new product launches, product information, pricing schedules, order status, manufacturing schedules, inventory levels, and delivery schedules. Sales staff can enter sales meetings with the most current and accurate information, perhaps even checking sales and product information during the meeting itself. When it is time to close the deal, the salesperson can wirelessly check production schedules and inventory levels to confirm product availability and even specify a delivery date. This real-time available-to-promise/capacity-to-promise (ATP/CTP) capability reduces the potential for delayed or canceled sales. It also can mean more competitive and realistic offers to prospects and customers. Online File W8.3 provides a detailed example of the use of SFA at a major U.K. retail manufacturer.

- **Field force automation (FFA).** One group of inherently mobile employees are those involved in delivery and dispatch services, as well as services aimed at equipment and service repair, including transportation (e.g., delivery of food, oil, newspapers, and cargo; courier services; tow trucks; taxis), utilities (e.g., gas, electricity, phone, water), field services (e.g., computer, office equipment, home repair), health care (e.g., visiting nurses, doctors, social services), and security (e.g., patrols, alarm installation). FFA, also called *field service management (FSM)*, is designed to support this segment of the mobile workforce. Like SFA, FFA encompasses a wide variety of processes, including managing work orders, scheduling, dispatching, collecting service call information, onsite billing, and ensuring regulatory compliance, to name a few. For most companies, automating these processes involves the integration of a number of enterprise applications and databases, including a company's CRM and ERP systems. Like SFA, providing mobile access to such a system potentially provides the mobile field force personnel with up-to-the-minute information about the service call, shortens the service cycle, eliminates pen and paper processes, and reduces data entry error and loss.

▶ **Mobile CRM (e-CRM).** E-CRM is discussed in detail in Chapter 11. As the chapter notes, *CRM* is an industry term that encompasses methodologies and software that help an enterprise manage customer relationships in an organized fashion. Usually, an extensive database of customer information, including customer contact information, is at the center of a CRM system. In a CRM system, information is entered and accessed by a range of employees through the company, including sales, marketing, customer service, human resource, product engineering and manufacturing, and accounting and finance personnel. In many companies, the SFA and FFA systems are subsystems of their CRM systems. Obviously, the benefits that accrue to providing mobile access to a company's SFA or FFA system also accrue to providing mobile access to their CRM system. In fact, the benefits are probably greater because CRM systems touch a broader audience. Most of the major vendors of these systems also provide mobile capabilities, although quite surprisingly many of these offerings have only been introduced in the recent past. For example, SAP and RIM announced in May 2008 that they were co-developing mobile access capabilities to SAP enterprise applications. The first of these efforts is focused on SAP's CRM.

Challenges of Mobile Workforce Support

Even though most enterprises recognize the need to provide mobile workers with specialized applications and devices, there are many nuts-and-bolts challenges involved in delivering mobile solutions to mobile workers. The challenges include pain points from both the solution provider and solution user point of view:

▶ **Network coverage gaps and interruptions.** Imagine all the places where your cell phone doesn't work or works poorly—on the highway, in large buildings and warehouses, in hospitals and health-care facilities, and in rural areas, to name just a few. Now imagine trying to do critical work in these locations. Not only do these dead spots cause interruptions, but they also result in poor performance for both devices and applications.

▶ **Internetwork roaming.** Cellular networks and devices are designed to support roaming from one cell or network to the next. As users roam or move from one cell or network to another, performance and latency issues can arise. Not only can roaming result in performance and latency issues, but it can also result in application crashes and can force users to reenter lost or corrupt data.

▶ **Mobile network and application performance.** As noted in Section 8.2, developing software and applications for mobile and wireless devices presents a variety of challenges. Many enterprise applications were only designed for desktops or laptops. Most either don't work or perform poorly on mobile devices.

▶ **Device and network management.** While mobile workers see the gaps, interruptions, and poor performance as major frustrations, the teams charged with planning and implementing these mobile solutions are more concerned with managing and securing network access to enterprise data and solutions. This can present a substantial challenge, especially if there are many disparate mobile devices.

▶ **Bandwidth management.** As the number of mobile workers and mobile solutions increases, so does network traffic. Unless the increases are well understood and planned for in a systematic fashion, there can be substantial contention for network bandwidth.

Section 8.5 ▶ REVIEW QUESTIONS

1. Describe the major segments of the mobile workforce. How quickly is this workforce growing?

2. What are some of the common benefits of mobile SFA, FFA, and CRM?

3. What are some of the challenges that companies incur when they try to implement solutions for the mobile workforces?

8.6 MOBILE ENTERTAINMENT

There is some debate about what actually constitutes mobile entertainment and which of its segments falls under the rubric of m-commerce. For example, if you purchase a song on the Web and download it to your PC, then copy it to your MP3 player, is this a form of mobile entertainment? What if you copy it to your smartphone rather than an MP3 player? What if you buy it and download it directly from the Web to your smartphone? What if you buy it and download it from the Web directly to an iPod? What if the song was free? There are a lot of "what if's." By strict definition, **mobile entertainment** is any type of leisure activity that utilizes the wireless telecommunication networks, interacts with service providers, and incurs a cost upon usage. Given that it requires wireless telecommunications, the implication is that mobile entertainment involves devices that operate over these networks.

mobile entertainment
Any type of leisure activity that utilizes wireless telecommunication networks, interacts with service providers, and incurs a cost upon usage.

This section discusses some of the major types of mobile entertainment, including mobile music and video, mobile gaming, and mobile gambling. This discussion is preceded by a look at the mobile entertainment market in general.

GROWTH OF THE MOBILE ENTERTAINMENT MARKET

Juniper Research, headquartered in the United Kingdom, is one of the leading telecom analyst firms covering the mobile entertainment market. Juniper's definition of mobile entertainment corresponds quite closely to the strict definition provided earlier. Also, they further define the mobile entertainment market as encompassing mobile music, games, TV, gambling, adult services, user-generated content, and infotainment. Based on their most recent research findings (Juniper Research 2008), they estimate that the global market for mobile entertainment will jump from worldwide revenues of approximately $21 billion in 2008 to $65 billion in 2012. The 2012 figure is down from previous estimates.

As Exhibit 8.4 shows, Juniper forecasts that mobile music is and will continue to be the largest segment, with approximately $10 billion in revenue in 2007 versus $18 billion in revenue in 2012. However, by 2012 mobile games will produce almost as much revenue as music. From 2007 to 2012, the figures in Exhibit 8.4 indicate that mobile gambling will be the fastest growing segment over the next few years, although this is primarily a function of the small market share that mobile gambling currently has.

Among the various regions of the world, China and the Far East will remain the largest regional market for mobile entertainment. For the period covered by the report, the revenues for this region will grow from $8.5 billion in 2007 to $21.3 billion in 2012.

To put these figures into context, PriceWaterhouseCoopers (2008) forecasts that the global entertainment and media industry as a whole will reach $2.2 trillion in 2012. Although it's hard to combine estimates from different sources, if we assume the various estimates are correct, mobile entertainment will be only 3 percent of the overall entertainment market (i.e., $65 billion versus $2.2 trillion). Among the various segments, traditional distribution methods

EXHIBIT 8.4	Size and Growth of the Mobile Entertainment Market		
Segment	**2007 ($Billion)**	**2012 ($Billion)**	**Compound Annual Growth Rate**
Infotainment	2	6	25 percent
User-generated content	0.5	6	64 percent
Mobile TV (broadcast)	2	43	67 percent
Mobile TV (streaming)	5	4.5	−1.7 percent
Music	10	18	12 percent
Games	5	16	26 percent
Adult	1	4	32 percent
Gambling	0.1	3	97 percent
Images	2.7	2.9	1.2 percent
Total	28.3	103	29.5 percent

Sources: Compiled from *Juniper* (2008) and eMarketer (2008).

will continue to dominate with the exception of music, where digital and mobile distribution will surpass physical distribution in 2011.

MOBILE MUSIC AND VIDEO

When you think of digital and mobile music and video, the first thing that comes to mind is Apple and iTunes. Apple is the clear leader in the digital distribution of music and video. Since 2001, Apple has offered consumers the ability to download songs and videos from the Apple iTunes store. In August 2008, iTunes' customers had purchased and downloaded more than 5 billion songs (Apple 2008). Apple also announced in August 2008 that customers were downloading videos at the rate of 50,000 a day. At the end of 2007, Amazon.com, the largest online store, launched their Amazon MP3 and Amazon Video On Demand (originally called *unBox*) digital download services for music and video, respectively. Outside of market share, the major difference between Apple and Amazon is that the content downloaded from Amazon is not controlled by digital rights management (DRM) technologies, which restrict access, copying, or conversion of the downloaded material.

Although most music and video content is downloaded onto consumers' PCs and then copied to various players or mobile devices, both Apple and Amazon provide the capabilities to download content directly to mobile devices. For example, iPhone owners can download both music and video directly from iTunes. Similarly, Amazon recently announced that owners of T-Mobile G1, the so-called Google phone running Google's Android OS, will have the ability to download music from Amazon MP3.

Although full-track songs and albums represent the major portion of the mobile music segment, there are three other components to this entertainment segment: ringtones, ringback tones, and streaming music and radio. Streaming music and radio represent a very small portion of the overall revenue. This is not the case for ringtones and ringback tones. Ringtones are the tones that play when someone calls you. Ringback tones are the tones that play when you call someone else. These tones come in many varieties. Monophonic tones involve the emission of one note at a time; polyphonic tones are made up of note sequences that play simultaneously and concurrently so the phone emits chords and melodies; and realtones or trutones consist of compressed digital audio files similar to MP3 files. Slowly but surely, realtones are displacing polyphonic tones in all regional markets. These tones represent big business. For some time, the revenues for ringtones have hovered between $2 billion to $4 billion. This market is on the decline. In contrast, the market for ringback tones is on the rise. Some estimate that the market for ringback tones will grow close to $5 billion worldwide in 2012.

MOBILE GAMES

A wide variety of mobile games have been developed to meet the needs and styles of different types of players. They can be classified in several ways:

▶ **Technology**—Embedded, SMS/MMS, Web browsing, J2ME, BREW, native OS
▶ **Number of players**—Soloplay or multiplay
▶ **Genre**—Action, logic/puzzle/skill, sports and racing, arcade, role playing, card and casino, movie, adult, and lifestyle

Several blogs provide information and discussion about the current state of the mobile gaming market, including various game offerings, as well as the technologies and platforms used to develop the games. One of the best is mobilegames.blogs.com.

The potential size and growth of the overall market explains the large number of companies involved in creating, distributing, and running mobile games. Some put the estimate of the number of game developers, aggregator-distributors, publishers, and portals at close to 2,000 enterprises. Many of these reside in Europe and the United States. Although the market is growing, especially in China and India, game publishers are facing some major hurdles. First, there are pressures on margins. Because of a lack of standards, games must be ported to a number of different types of mobile handsets. This is very costly. In addition, telecommunication operators charge game publishers a substantial portion of the retail price of games (up to 60 percent, in some cases). To break even, game publishers need to sell significant volumes for the handsets they support. These volumes are not being met. Second, there are limits to the current technologies and platforms. The coming generation of games requires advanced capabilities of the higher-end handsets and 3G networks. The adoption of these handsets and networks has not been as fast as originally anticipated. Finally, there was a belief that game advertising would generate revenues to offset the costs. The ad spend in mobile games has remained low.

To address these hurdles, some of the more established game publishers such as Sega Corporation, as well as many start-ups, are focusing attention on the Apple iPhone. Not only does the iPhone provide an advanced development platform and 3G delivery capabilities, but Apple also offers more attractive distribution costs. Although Apple charges 30 percent of the proceeds of the sales through its App Store clearinghouse, this is a smaller percentage than other operators charge, which makes it possible to profit on games that sell for just a few dollars or are given away with advertising.

MOBILE GAMBLING

Globally, online gambling is a well-entrenched segment of the overall gambling market. The first online gambling site was established in August 1995. Today, there are approximately 2,000 gambling Web sites worldwide, including sports betting, casino games, and lotteries. Usually, online casino games require good graphics and high-speed connections. In contrast, the technical requirements for lotteries and sports betting are much less stringent. Even SMS can be used to play the lottery or place bets.

The revenue figures for the market size of mobile gambling are a little confusing. Here, market size is sometimes measured by gross win and other times by total wagers. Exhibit 8.4 shows Juniper Research's figures for gross wins (approximately $100 million in 2007 and $3.4 billion in 2012). In comparison, the figures from Juniper Research for total wagers are approximately $1 billion in 2007, rising to around $20 billion in 2012. Regardless of the figures, mobile gambling is the fastest growing segment of mobile entertainment.

Unlike some of the other forms of mobile entertainment, the mobile gambling market has some unique hurdles. First, mobile gambling requires two-way financial transactions. Not only must bettors or gamblers have a way of paying for their online bets, but the online gambling establishment must also have a way of paying off the bettor or gambler if they win. Second, online gambling sites face major trust issues. Gamblers and bettors have to believe that the site is fair, that they have a chance of winning, and that they are not being ripped off. Finally, the legislative picture is very unclear. Most existing gambling legislation was passed prior to the advent of the Web and is outdated. Even if it isn't outdated, the legislative picture is like a patchwork quilt with some forms of gambling barred in certain territories but not in others.

From a legal standpoint, the United Kingdom has some of the least stringent regulations. This is one of the reasons that the United Kingdom is the largest market in terms of gross wagers, accounting for 52 percent of all wagers in 2007. In the future the U.K.'s overall percentage is likely to decline as the markets in other countries, such as China and the Far East, where online gambling is also legal, grow over the next 5 years. It is also one of the reasons that online gambling is not projected to grow much in the near term.

Some countries have attempted to prohibit online gambling altogether or to control the type of online gambling that takes place by making it illegal to operate an online gambling site or a particular type of online gambling site within their jurisdictions. This has simply created a business opportunity for other countries that have encouraged online gambling sites to operate within their borders and have licensed them to do so. For some reason most of the countries taking advantage of this opportunity are located on smaller islands. The islands of Gilbraltar, Malta, Alderney, Antigua, and Costa Rica are all popular hosting destinations for online gambling. Some of these, such as Gilbraltar, Malta, and Alderney, have very strict licensing regulations so that only reputable, well-financed enterprises are awarded licenses. Others, such as Antigua and Costa Rica, have less stringent licensing requirements, meaning that less reputable or underfinanced operations can obtain licenses. Overall, this simply means that even if a country eliminates online gambling sites within their borders, there are plenty of places for gamblers or bettors to place their wagers or bets.

Other countries have attempted to control online gambling by making it illegal either for the individual to gamble online, for the individual and the enterprise to use the "wire" for gambling activity, or for financial institutions to process gambling transactions. In the United States, for example, laws prohibit all three of these types of activities, although the laws don't necessarily apply uniformly across all the states.

Within the United States, some states have laws that ban gambling on the Internet outright, including Michigan, Illinois, Indiana, Louisiana, Massachusetts, Oregon, Washington, Wisconsin, Indiana, Nevada, South Dakota, New Jersey, New York, and Kentucky. Additionally, attorneys general in Florida, Kansas, Minnesota, Oklahoma, and Texas have issued opinions that Internet gambling is illegal in their states. In the other states, online gambling is not directly prohibited but it is controlled by national statutes.

Under U.S. law, there has been some disagreement about whether or not Internet gambling is illegal (American Gaming Association 2007). At issue are two laws: the U.S. Wire Act of 1961, which prohibited gambling over the "wires," and the Professional and Amateur Sports Protection Act of 1992 (PASPA), which banned sports wagering in all states except those with preexisting operations (Nevada, Oregon, and Delaware). The Clinton and Bush presidential administrations interpreted the Wire Act to imply that all forms of Internet gambling are illegal. However, the U.S. Court of Appeals for the Fifth Circuit interpreted the Wire Act differently. In *Thompson v. MasterCard International et al.*, the appeals court in 2002 affirmed a lower court ruling that, under national statutes, sports betting conducted over the Internet is illegal, but casino games are legal. More recently, the U.S. government has relied on the Unlawful Internet Gambling Enforcement Act, which was passed in September 2006. Although this act did not outlaw online gambling per se, it did make it illegal for financial institutions to process gambling transactions. As such, this effectively made it difficult for many U.S. players to deposit or withdraw winnings. In response, some of the offshore sites banned U.S. residents from playing.

Section 8.6 ▶ REVIEW QUESTIONS

1. Briefly describe the growth patterns of the various segments of mobile entertainment.
2. Discuss the basic components of the mobile music market.
3. What are some of the key barriers to the growth of the mobile games market?
4. Discuss some of the key legal issues impeding the growth of mobile gambling.

8.7 LOCATION-BASED MOBILE COMMERCE

**location-based
m-commerce
(l-commerce)**
Delivery of m-commerce transactions to individuals in a specific location, at a specific time.

As noted earlier in this chapter, location-based m-commerce (l-commerce) refers to the use of GPS-enabled devices or similar technologies (e.g., triangulation of radio- or cell-based stations) to find where a customer or client is and deliver products and services based on the customer's location. Location-based services are attractive to both consumers and businesses alike. From a consumer's or business user's viewpoint, localization offers safety (emergency services can pinpoint the mobile device owner's exact location), convenience (a user can locate what is nearby without consulting a directory, pay phone, or map), and productivity (time can be optimized by determining points of interest within close proximity). From a business supplier's point of view, location-based m-commerce offers an opportunity to provide services that more precisely meet a customer's needs.

The services provided through location-based m-commerce focus on five key factors:

1. **Location.** Determining the basic position of a person or a thing (e.g., car or boat)
2. **Navigation.** Plotting a route from one location to another
3. **Tracking.** Monitoring the movement of a person or a thing (e.g., a package or vehicle)
4. **Mapping.** Creating maps of specific geographical locations
5. **Timing.** Determining the precise time at a specific location

The closing case describes how Wal-Mart, in partnership with WeatherBug (weather.weatherbug.com) and Send Word Now (sendwordnow.com), has combined some of these services to ensure the safety of its customers, employees, and stores during weather emergencies.

L-COMMERCE INFRASTRUCTURE

L-commerce rests on an infrastructure made up of five basic components (Steiniger et al. 2006). Included are the following:

▶ **Mobile devices.** These are tools used to request information. Location-based devices can be divided into two categories: single purpose or multipurpose. Single-purpose devices include such things as on-board navigation systems, toll boxes, transceivers, and GPS location devices. Multipurpose devices can be mobile phones, smartphones, PDS, laptops, tablet PCs, and the like.

▶ **Communication network.** The network transfers user data and service requests from the mobile terminal to the service providers, and then the requested information is transferred back to the user.

▶ **Positioning component.** In order to process or service a user's request, the user's position has to be determined. This can be done either through a mobile network or by using a global positioning system (GPS).

▶ **Service or application provider.** Providers are responsible for servicing a user's request. Services can include such things as finding routes, searching yellow pages or other information sources based on the user's location, etc.

▶ **Data or content provider.** Service providers usually rely on geographic data or location-based information to service user requests. More often than not, the location data or information is maintained by a third party, not the service provider.

L-commerce is distinguished from general m-commerce by the positioning component and the geographical information systems on which the various location-based services or applications rest.

Positioning Component

Usually, the positioning component of an l-commerce system is either network-based or terminal-based. Network-based positioning relies on base stations to find the location of a mobile device sending a signal or sensed by the network. For example, the location of a mobile phone can be determined by knowing the location of the nearest mobile phone antenna (base station). In terminal-based positioning, the device calculates the location from signals received from the base stations. For instance, this is how the well-known global positioning system (GPS) works.

The **global positioning system (GPS)** is based on a worldwide satellite tracking system that enables users to determine exact positions anywhere on the earth. GPS was developed by the U.S. Defense Department for military use, but its high value for civilian use was immediately recognized, and the technology was released into the civilian domain, originally for use by commercial airlines and ships. In recent years, GPS locators have become a part of the consumer electronics market and are used widely for business and recreation. Online File W8.4 provides an example of the use of GPS for tracking vehicles.

GPS is supported by 24 U.S. government satellites. Each satellite orbits the earth once every 12 hours on a precise path at an altitude of 10,900 miles. At any point in time, the exact position of each satellite is known, because the satellite broadcasts its position and a time signal from its onboard atomic clock, which is accurate to one-billionth of a second. Receivers on the ground also have accurate clocks that are synchronized with those of the satellites.

GPS locators may be stand-alone units or embedded into a mobile device. At any given time, a GPS locator can receive signals from at least six satellites. Using the fast speed of the satellite signals (186,272 miles, or 299,775 kilometers, per second; the speed of light), the system can determine the location (latitude and longitude) of any GPS locator, to within 50 feet (15 meters) by triangulation, using the distance from the GPS locator to three satellites to make the computation. A fourth satellite can also be used to determine elevation, although not to the same degree of accuracy as longitude or latitude. Advanced forms of GPS can pinpoint a location within a centimeter. GPS software then computes the latitude and longitude of the receiver. More information on how the GPS system works is available at trimble.com/gps.

network-based positioning
Relies on base stations to find the location of a mobile device sending a signal or sensed by the network.

terminal-based positioning
Calculating the location of a mobile device from signals sent by the device to base stations.

global positioning system (GPS)
A worldwide satellite-based tracking system that enables users to determine their position anywhere on the earth.

In 1999 the European Union (EU) proposed the construction of an alternative global navigation satellite system called *Galileo*. Unlike GPS, Galileo is a civilian system, not a military system. As envisioned, Galileo would consist of 30 satellites orbiting at a distance of 23,222 kilometers or 14,429 miles above the earth and would provide positioning to within about a meter. Although the European Union and European Space Agency agreed to fund the project in 2002, the project has been beset by budgetary problems. In April 2008, the EU transportation ministers of 27 countries reached an agreement on funding. Under this agreement, the system will supposedly be operational by 2013 (Parlamentul European 2008).

Location-Based Data

Location-based services and l-commerce revolve around a series of location-based questions or queries. One way to categorize these questions is the following (Steiniger 2006):

▶ **Locating.** Where am I? Where is a specific object or person?
▶ **Navigating.** How do I get to a specific address, place, position, or person?
▶ **Searching.** Where is the nearest or most relevant object or person?
▶ **Identifying.** What, who, or how much is here or there?
▶ **Event checking.** What happens here or there?

Geocoding or *reverse geocoding* is often used to answer these questions. Geocoding translates geographical information (e.g., an address) into geographical coordinates (e.g., longitude and latitude). Reverse geocoding translates geographical coordinates into an associated textual location (e.g., street address). In addition to translating a person's position, location-based queries also rely on static information (e.g., points of interest and road networks), topical and temporal information (e.g., traffic information, weather forecasts, last-minute ticket deals), safety information (e.g., state of the roads or hiking trails, weather changes, emergency situations), and personal information (e.g., recommendations and ratings of places and events).

The data, information, and processes needed to service location-based queries are usually handled by a *geographical information system (GIS)*. A **geographical information system (GIS)** captures, stores, analyzes, manages, and presents data that refers to or is linked to location. For example, suppose a person is using his or her mobile phone to ask an online directory service to provide a list of Italian restaurants that are close by. In order to service this query, the directory service would need access to a GIS containing information about local restaurants by geographical coordinates and type. As noted, location-based service providers usually rely on GISs provided by third parties.

geographical information system (GIS)

A computer system capable of integrating, storing, editing, analyzing, sharing, and displaying geographically-referenced (spatial) information.

LOCATION-BASED SERVICES AND APPLICATIONS

Exhibit 8.5 provides an overview of the main categories of location-based services and applications.

EXHIBIT 8.5	**Location-Based Services and Applications**
Category	**Examples**
Advertising	Banners, advertising alerts
Billing	Road tolling, location-sensitive billing
Emergency	Emergency calls, automotive assistance
Games	Mobile games, geocaching
Information	Infotainment services, travel guides, travel planner, mobile yellow pages, shopping guides
Leisure	Buddy finder, instant messaging, social networking
Management	Facility, infrastructure, fleet, security, environmental
Navigation	Directions, indoor routing, car park guidance, traffic management
Tracking	People/vehicle tracking, product tracking

Source: Compiled from Steiniger et al. (2006).

The following examples illustrate some of the myriad of l-commerce services currently in operation:

Example: Navigation. One of the major problems in many cities is the lack of sufficient parking spaces. This is the situation in Paris, France, where as many as 20 to 25 percent of all vehicles may circulate the city, looking for a parking space at certain times of the day. This causes traffic jams and wastes gasoline. At the end of 2006, Orange, a large mobile telecommunications company, and its partners organized a system that allows drivers to quickly find empty parking spaces in nearby parking garages. Here is how it works: The 120 participating garages collect information electronically about open parking spaces. The information is updated over the Internet to a central server at Orange. Drivers contact the Orange server with their cell phones. Orange can determine the location of the driver either through the location of the antenna being used to make the cell phone call or, if the driver's phone is equipped with a GPS, through the coordinates provided by the GPS (*Taipei Times* 2006; Mullen 2006).

Example: Product Tracking. UltraEx, a West Coast company that specializes in same-day deliveries of items such as emergency blood supplies and computer parts, equips all of its vehicles with @Road's GPS receivers and wireless modems. In addition to giving dispatchers a big-picture view of the entire fleet, @Road helps UltraEx keep clients happy by letting them track the location and speed of their shipments on the Web in real time. This service shows customers a map of the last place the satellite detected the delivery vehicle and how fast it was traveling. Drivers use AT&T's Mobile Data Service to communicate with dispatch, and drivers who own their vehicles, are unable to falsify mileage sheets because @Road reports exact mileage for each vehicle.

Example: Management. The Mexican company Cemex is the third largest cement producer in the world. Concrete is mixed en route to construction sites and must be delivered within a certain time period or it will be unusable. Rather than waiting for orders, preparing delivery schedules, and then sending out the deliveries as most companies do, Cemex has trucks fitted with GPS patrolling the road at all times, waiting for orders; this allows the company to guarantee delivery within 20 minutes of the agreed-upon time. Real-time data on each truck's position are available not only to company managers but also to clients and suppliers, enabling them to plan their schedules to fit in with the next available truck. Digital maps help locate the customers and the trucks, allowing the use of shortcut routes.

Example: Leisure. Want to know where your friends are in real time? The mobile market is swarming with social networking start-ups in partnership with the cell phone behemoths who think they know the answer to the question (Shannon 2008). One of the start-ups is Loopt. Loopt has signed deals with many of the major mobile operators including Sprint Nextel, T-Mobile, Verizon, AT&T, and Boost. Loopt utilizes a cell phone's embedded GPS positioning to show users where friends are located and what they are doing via detailed, interactive maps on their mobile phones. Loopt helps friends connect on the fly and navigate their social lives by orienting them to people, places, and events. Users can also share location updates, geo-tagged photos, and comments with friends in their mobile address book or on online social networks, communities, and blogs. Because of concerns about privacy, Loopt is an opt-in service that can be turned on or off depending on the user's wishes at any given moment. Another of the start-ups is GyPSii, a mobile social network based in Amsterdam. GyPSii offers a collection of capabilities including SpaceMe (real-time location of friends), PlaceMe (geo-tagged photos, video, and audio), and ExploreMe (find nearby places visited by friends). GyPSii has received substantial backing from Nokia.

BARRIERS TO LOCATION-BASED M-COMMERCE

What is holding back the widespread use of location-based m-commerce? Several factors come into play, including the following:

▶ **Lack of GPS in mobile phones.** Last year only about 15 percent of mobile phones sold with GPS. This means that most of the mobile phones in existence lack the feature. Although it is possible to locate a mobile device with other means and GPS-enabled phones are increasing in popularity, this still inhibits the overall adoption of location-based services.

▶ **Accuracy of devices.** Some of the location technologies are not as accurate as people expect them to be. A good GPS provides a location that is accurate up to 15 meters (50 feet).

Less expensive, but less accurate, locators can be used to find an approximate location within 500 meters (1,640 feet).

- **The cost–benefit justification.** For many potential users, the benefits of location-based services do not justify the cost of the devices or the inconvenience and time required to utilize the service. After all, many seem to feel that they can just as easily obtain information the old-fashioned way.

- **Limited network bandwidth.** Wireless bandwidth is currently limited; it will be improved as 3G technology spreads. As bandwidth improves, applications will improve, which will attract more customers.

- **Invasion of privacy.** When "always-on" cell phones are a reality, many people will be hesitant to have their whereabouts and movements tracked throughout the day, even if they have nothing to hide. This issue will be heightened when our cars, homes, appliances, and all sorts of other consumer goods are connected to the Internet and have a GPS device embedded in them.

Section 8.7 ▶ REVIEW QUESTIONS

1. Describe the key elements of the l-commerce infrastructure.
2. What is GPS? How does it work?
3. What are some of the basic questions addressed by location-based services?
4. How are location-based services being integrated with social networking?
5. What are some of the key barriers to l-commerce?

8.8 SECURITY AND OTHER IMPLEMENTATION ISSUES IN MOBILE COMMERCE

Despite the vast potential for mobile commerce to change the way many companies do business, several barriers are either slowing down the spread of m-commerce or leaving many m-commerce businesses and their customers disappointed or dissatisfied. According to Malykhina (2006), the following are the major barriers to enterprise mobile computing (based on the percentage of companies experiencing them): high cost (59 percent), inadequate security (48 percent), lack of integration (46 percent), insufficient broadband (41 percent), inadequate mobile applications development (36 percent), not a high IT priority (34 percent), short battery life (32 percent), management requirements (32 percent), small screens (30 percent), lack of industry standards (21 percent), and inadequate device memory (18 percent). In this section we examine some of these barriers, starting with the issue of the security of mobile communications and mobile computing systems.

M-COMMERCE SECURITY ISSUES

In 2004, Cabir became the first known worm capable of spreading through mobile phones (Laudermilch 2006). Technically, Cabir is a Bluetooth worm that only runs on Series 60 Symbian mobile phones. The worm arrives in the phone's messaging inbox in the guise of a file named *caribe.sis*. When an unsuspecting recipient clicks on the file, the worm activates and is sent to other devices via Bluetooth. To date, the worm has not been launched on a widespread basis. The same is true for other malicious code, such as Brador and Redbrowser (Laudermilch 2006). Brador is a backdoor utility for PocketPCs based on Windows CE or Windows Mobile. Like Cabir, Brador appeared in 2004. Unlike Cabir, when Brador is launched, it creates a special file that enables a malicious user to gain control of the device. Every time the device is connected to the Internet, the malicious user is informed and knows that the backdoor is ready for action. At this point, the backdoor will respond to commands like "list the directory contents" or "download a file," etc. In contrast to Cabir and Brador, RedBrowser is a Trojan Horse that infects mobile phones running Java (J2ME). It was first identified in August 2006. Redbrowser comes in the form of a Java JAR file and is delivered via the Internet or Bluetooth. Once installed, the Trojan sends SMSs to premium-rate numbers, resulting in charges of $5 to $6 per SMS.

These three cases are indicative of the type of malicious code threat that may someday plague mobile computing as much as it does desktop computing. Most Internet-enabled cell phones in operation today have their operating systems and other functional software "burned" into the hardware. This makes them incapable of storing applications and, in turn, incapable of propagating a virus, worm, or other rogue program from one phone to another. However, as the capabilities of cellular phones increase and the functionality of PDAs and cell phones converge, the threat of attack from malicious code will certainly increase. Although m-commerce shares some of the same security issues as general e-commerce, there are some differences between the two.

The basic security goals of confidentiality, authentication, authorization, and integrity are just as important for m-commerce as they are for e-commerce but are more difficult to ensure. Specifically, m-commerce transactions almost always pass through several networks, both wireless and wired. An appropriate level of security must be maintained on each network, in spite of the fact that interoperability among the various networks is difficult. Similarly, post-transactional security issues of auditing and nonrepudiation are more difficult because cell phones do not yet have the capability to store the digital equivalent of a receipt.

Other m-commerce security challenges are unique to mobile computing because of the nature of the mobile computing environment. First, the open-air transmission of signals across multiple networks opens up new opportunities for compromising security. Interception of a communication in a wired network requires physical access to the wires in which the signal is being carried. Interception of a communication in a wireless network can be done with a carefully aimed, even crude, antenna (for example, a legendary war-driving tip is how to use a Pringles potato chip can to hone in on a rogue Wi-Fi signal). Second, because of their small size, mobile devices are easily lost or stolen. Similarly, because they are mobile, cell phones, PDAs, BlackBerries, and other devices are sometimes dropped, crushed, or damaged by water and extreme temperature. A stolen device can provide the thief with valuable data and digital credentials that can be used to compromise an m-commerce network. A lost or damaged device is a security threat because of the loss of any stored data or device settings.

In general, many of the processes, procedures, and technologies used for e-commerce security and for general organizational computer security also apply to m-commerce security. Passwords, encryption, active tokens, and user education are cases in point. However, given the unique nature of mobile security, special security measures for m-commerce may also be required. For example, to prevent the theft of a mobile device, a user might carry a "wireless tether" that sounds a warning if a device is left behind or carried away. Wi-Fi networks have their own built-in security system known as *Wired Equivalent Privacy (WEP)*, which is, as the name suggests, similar to encryption protocols used on wired networks. Similarly, WAP networks depend on the Wireless Transport Layer Security (WTLS), and cell phones can be protected by SIM-based authentication. These three approaches to m-commerce security are discussed in more detail in Online File W8.5. Additional information about mobile commerce security is available in *Commonwealth Telecommunications Organization* (2006).

TECHNOLOGICAL BARRIERS TO M-COMMERCE

When mobile users want to access the Internet, the *usability* of the site is critical to achieve the purpose of the visit and to increase user stickiness (the degree to which users remain at a site). However, current devices have limited usability, particularly with respect to pocket-size screens or data input devices. In addition, because of the limited storage capacity and information access speed of most smartphones and PDAs, it is often difficult or impossible to download large files to these devices.

Mobile visitors to a Web site are typically paying premium rates for Internet connections and are focused on a specific goal (e.g., conducting a stock trade). For visitors to find exactly what they are looking for easily and quickly, the navigation systems have to be fast and designed for mobile devices. Similarly, the information content needs to meet the user's needs. For example, many screens on low-end mobile devices are text based and have only simple black-and-white graphics. This means that mobile users cannot browse an online picture-based catalog, which makes mobile shopping difficult. This situation is improving as devices become more powerful and as 3G bandwidth becomes more commonplace.

Limitation	Description
Insufficient bandwidth	Sufficient bandwidth is necessary for widespread mobile computing, and it must be inexpensive. It will take a few years until 3G and WiMax are available in many places. Wi-Fi solves some of the problems for short-range connections.
Security standards	Universal standards are still under development. It may take 3 or more years for sufficient standards to be in place.
Power consumption	Batteries with long life are needed for mobile computing. Color screens and Wi-Fi consume more electricity, but new chips and emerging battery technologies are solving some of the power-consumption problems.
Transmission interferences	Weather and terrain, including tall buildings, can limit reception. Microwave ovens, cordless phones, and other devices on the free, but crowded, 2.4GHz range interfere with Bluetooth and Wi-Fi 802.11b transmissions.
GPS accuracy	GPS may be inaccurate in a city with tall buildings, limiting the use of location-based m-commerce.
Potential health hazards	Potential health damage from cellular radio frequency emission is not known yet. Known health hazards include cell phone addiction, thumb-overuse syndrome, and accidents caused by people using cell phones while driving.
Human–computer interface	Screens and keyboards are too small, making mobile devices uncomfortable and difficult for many people to use.
Complexity	Too many optional add-ons (e.g., battery chargers, external keyboards, headsets, microphones, cradles) are available. Storing and using the optional add-ons can be a problem.

EXHIBIT 8.6 Technical Limitations of Mobile Computing

Other technical barriers related to mobile computing technology include limited battery life and transmission interference with home appliances. These barriers and others are listed in Exhibit 8.6.

ETHICAL, LEGAL, AND HEALTH ISSUES IN M-COMMERCE

The increasing use of mobile devices in business and society raises new ethical, legal, and health issues that individuals, organizations, and society will have to resolve.

One workplace issue is the isolation that mobile devices can impose on a workforce. The introduction of desktop computing invoked a profound change on social interaction in the workplace, illustrated by the walled cubicles featured in Dilbert cartoons. Some workers had difficulty adjusting to this new environment and sought to replace face-to-face interactions with e-mail interactions, prompting organizational policies against the forwarding of non-business-related e-mail and IM messages.

Equipping the workforce with mobile devices may have similar impacts. Field service employees dispatched remotely and who acquire replacement parts from third-party sources will visit "the office" only briefly at the start and end of each day, if at all. The result could be a reduction in organizational transparency, making it difficult for employees to know what other employees do, how the organization is evolving, and how they fit into it. These changes have powerful implications for individuals and the organization for which they work. Whether the results are good or bad depends on how the change is managed.

The truly personal nature of the mobile device also raises ethical and legal issues in the workplace. Most employees have desktop computers both at home and at work, and separate business and personal work accordingly. However, it is not so easy to separate work and personal life on a cell phone, unless one is willing to carry two phones or two PDAs. And if an organization has the right to monitor e-mail communications on its own network, does it also have the right to monitor voice communications on a company-owned cell phone?

The widespread appearance of mobile devices in society has led to the need for cell phone etiquette, the creation of "cell free" zones in hospitals and airport lounges, and National Cell Phone Courtesy Month. For an insightful essay into the impact of cell phones in work and social spaces, see Rosen (2006).

A widely publicized health issue is the potential, but not yet proven, health damage from cellular radio frequency emissions. Cell phone addiction also is a problem. A study by Seoul National University found that 30 percent of South Korean high school students reported addiction effects, such as feeling anxious when they did not have their phones with them. Many also displayed symptoms of repetitive stress injury from obsessive text messaging (Rosen 2006).

Other ethical, legal, and health issues include the ethics of monitoring staff movements based on GPS-enabled devices or vehicles, maintaining an appropriate work–life balance when work can be conducted anywhere at any time, and the preferred content of an organizational policy to govern use and control of personal mobile computing devices in and out of the workplace.

Section 8.8 ▶ REVIEW QUESTIONS

1. How is m-commerce security similar to e-commerce security? How is it different?
2. Discuss the role that usability plays in the adoption of m-commerce.
3. Discuss a few of the technical limitations of m-commerce.
4. Describe the potential impact of mobile devices on the workplace.

8.9 PERVASIVE COMPUTING

Many experts believe that the next major step in the evolution of computing will be *pervasive computing*. In a pervasive computing environment, almost every object has processing power and a wired or wireless connection to a network. This section provides an overview of pervasive computing and briefly examines a number of pervasive computing initiatives based on RFID and sensor network technologies.

OVERVIEW OF PERVASIVE COMPUTING

Pervasive computing is invisible, everywhere computing; it is computing capabilities being embedded into the objects around us. In contrast, mobile computing is usually represented by devices—handheld computers, handset phones, headsets, and so on—that users hold, carry, or wear. Pervasive computing also is called *embedded computing, augmented computing*, or *ubiquitous computing*. Sometimes a distinction is made between pervasive and ubiquitous computing. The distinction revolves around the notion of mobility. Pervasive computing is embedded in the environment but typically not mobile. In contrast, ubiquitous computing combines a high degree of mobility with a high degree of embeddedness. So, for example, most smart appliances in a smart home represent wired, pervasive computing, and mobile objects with embedded computing, such as in clothes, cars, and personal communication systems, represent ubiquitous computing. In this chapter, however, we treat pervasive and ubiquitous as equivalent terms; pervasive computing devices are embedded in the environment around us, and they may be mobile or stationary.

> **pervasive computing**
> Invisible, everywhere computing; it is computing capabilities being embedded into the objects around us.

The idea of pervasive computing has been around for years. Mark Weiser first articulated the current version in 1988 at Xerox's computer science laboratory, the Palo Alto Research Center (PARC). Weiser and his colleagues were attempting "to conceive a new way of thinking about computers, one that takes into account the human world and allows the computers themselves to vanish into the background." According to Weiser, pervasive computing is the opposite of virtual reality. In virtual reality, the user is immersed in a computer-generated environment. In pervasive computing, the user is immersed in an invisible "computing is everywhere" environment—in cars, clothes, homes, the workplace, and so on.

Invisible Computing

By *invisible*, Weiser did not mean to imply that pervasive computing devices would not be seen but, rather, that, unlike a desktop or handheld computer, these embedded computers would not intrude on our consciousness. As he observed, "The most profound technologies are those that disappear . . . they weave themselves into the fabric of everyday life until they are indistinguishable from it." Think of electric motors. They exist in the devices all around us, but they are invisible to us, and we do not think about using them. This is Weiser's vision for pervasive computing. The user will not think about how to use the processing power in the object; rather, the processing power automatically helps the user perform the task.

Principles of Pervasive Computing

Underlying the embeddedness of pervasive computing are four principles that will define its development:

▶ **Decentralization.** The decentralization of computing that began with the transition from the centralized mainframe computer to the personal computer will continue in pervasive computing. Indeed, computing devices in the future will not be computers but tags, sensors, badges, and commonplace objects all cooperating together in a service-oriented infrastructure.

▶ **Diversification.** Computing devices will evolve from a fully functional one-computer-does-all paradigm to one in which specialized, diversified devices will suit the requirements of an individual for a specific purpose. A person may own several devices that slightly overlap in functionality, but each will be the preferred tool for each specific purpose.

▶ **Connectivity.** The independent pervasive computing devices—tags, sensors, badges—will be seamlessly connected to the network or to each other. Open, common standards will be required to achieve this level of connectivity and interoperability.

▶ **Simplicity.** These devices must be designed for simplicity of use. Intuitive interfaces, speech recognition, one-handed operation, instant on, and always connected are a few of the requirements for high, but simple, usability.

Internet of Things

Early forms of ubiquitous information and communication networks are evident in the widespread use of mobile devices. These devices have become an integral and intimate part of everyday life around the globe. Developments are underway to take this phenomenon even further by embedding short-range mobile transceivers into a wide array of gadgets and everyday items, enabling new forms of communication between people and things and between the things themselves. This will add a new dimension to anytime, anyplace connectivity (Sicari 2006). The dimension is *anything* connectivity. The Internet will become an *Internet of Things (IoT)*.

In order for there to be an IoT, there has to be a way to (1) uniquely identify the things; (2) enable detection of changes in the physical status of those things (e.g., temperature or location); (3) embed intelligence in the things themselves; and (4) enable things to communicate either with one another or with people via the Internet. This is where radio frequency identification (RFID), sensor networks, smart objects, and Internet standards such as the Internet Protocol (IP) come into play.

RADIO FREQUENCY IDENTIFICATION (RFID)

In the world of EC and m-commerce, a number of pervasive computing initiatives revolve around the use of RFID. Simply put, **radio frequency identification (RFID)** is a short-range radio frequency communication technology for remotely storing and retrieving data using devices called *RFID tags* and *RFID readers*. Most RFID tags have a small footprint. They can be embedded or attached to virtually any object—products, people, animals, or vehicles.

RFID Basics

An RFID system consists of two main components: (1) an RFID tag composed of a microchip, antenna, and in some cases a battery, which are enclosed within plastic, silicon, or sometimes glass; and (2) an RFID reader containing a radio transmitter and receiver.

There are three kinds of RFID tags: passive, semiactive, and active. Passive tags have no energy source of their own; semiactive tags have a power source for the chip but not for transmission; and active tags have their own power source for the chip and transmission.

radio frequency identification (RFID)
A short-range radio frequency communication technology for remotely storing and retrieving data using devices called RFID tags and RFID readers.

Essentially, they all work the same way, although they differ in the amount of data they can store and the range at which they can be read:

▶ Data within an RFID tag's microchip waits to be read.

▶ The tag's antenna receives electromagnetic energy from an RFID reader's antenna.

▶ Using power from its internal battery or power harvested from the reader's electromagnetic field, the tag sends radio waves back to the reader.

▶ The reader picks up the tag's radio waves and interprets the frequencies as meaningful data.

Among the three types, passive RFID tags are by far and away the most widely used. Passive tags are manufactured to be disposable, just like the consumer products on which they are often placed. One way to characterize a passive RFID tag is a bar code label on steroids. A passive RFID tag contains three times the amount of information as a bar code label (up to 96 bits). Additionally, RFID readers do not require line-of-sight contact, like a bar code scanner. Passive RFID tags can be read through cardboard, wood, and plastic at a range up to 30 feet. The reader then passes the information, wirelessly or through a docking station, to a computer for processing (see Exhibit 8.7).

For details on all three types of tags, see Meyer (2007).

RFID Applications

Although the principles underlying RFID were articulated more than 60 years ago, it has only been in the last 10 years that RFID has experienced widespread attention and use. In the past, the high cost of RFID tags impeded the adoption of the technology. As their price has dropped, their use has expanded. Today, the average costs for a simple (96 bit) RFID tag is around US$.50, although volume discounts can lower the cost somewhere between US$.07 and US$.15. Even with volume discounts, this makes the use of RFID tags with individual retail items cost-prohibitive, especially in groceries and drugstores. In these situations, bar code labels, which cost pennies or fractions of pennies, are still used with individual items, while RFID tags are being used with pallets or cases of items.

In spite of their current costs, RFID technology is being used in a variety of ways:

▶ **Tracking and identifying people.** In some Japanese schools, tags in backpacks or clothes track students' entry and departure from school buildings. In Denmark, the Legoland amusement park offers parents a child-tracking system that combines RFID and Wi-Fi. As of 2007, RFID tags were being widely used in passports. The first country to employ the tags was Malaysia in 1998. In the mid-2000s, a number of countries followed suit, including New Zealand, Belgium, The Netherlands, Norway, Ireland, Japan, Pakistan, Germany, Portugal, Poland, the United Kingdom, Australia, the United

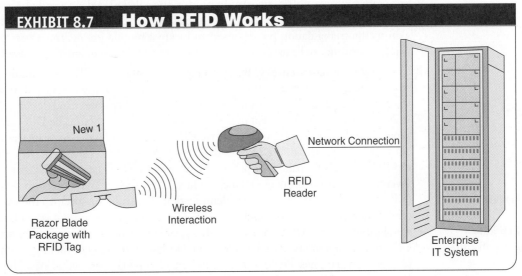

EXHIBIT 8.7 How RFID Works

New 1

Razor Blade Package with RFID Tag

Wireless Interaction

RFID Reader

Network Connection

Enterprise IT System

Source: C. Heinrich, *RFID and Beyond*, Indianapolis: Wiley Publishing, 2005, Figure 3.5, p. 65. Reprinted by permission of John Wiley & Sons, Inc.

States, and the Republic of Korea. Currently, passport tags include the same information as the passport (i.e., name, address, passport number, etc.). Some also hold information about the countries visited and may eventually include a digital picture of the owner, as well as biometric data such as a thumbprint.

▶ **Tracking vehicles and commuters.** In the United States, a number of prepaid toll road systems (e.g., E-Z Pass) rely on RFID tags attached to the windshields inside cars using the roads. When a car with a tag passes a toll facility, an antenna at the toll plaza reads the account information contained in the tag and electronically debits the associated prepaid account. The same sort of system is used with toll roads throughout the world, including Canada, Israel, Chile, Hong Kong, Singapore, France, Italy, and Spain, just to name a few of the countries. RFID tags are also used with a number of transit systems worldwide. In this case, smart cards with embedded RFID chips can be used to pay transit fares. These systems are detailed in Chapter 11, which deals with EC payment systems.

▶ **Tracking animals.** In 2006, Canada mandated that all cattle must be tagged with a CCIA (Canadian Cattle Identification Agency) program–approved RFID tag. The tag makes it possible to identify such things as the animal's age and herd of origin. The program is designed to promote beef consumption through assurance of efficient trace-back and containment of serious animal health and food safety problems. Microchip RFID tags are also implanted under the skin of dogs, cats, and other animals to help identify the animal and its owner. The information can be used by animal shelters to return lost pets. It can also help settle disputes about ownership.

▶ **Tracking assets.** What do manufacturing plants, hospitals, airport terminals, and libraries have in common? They all have problems managing and finding their stuff. All of these operations have tens or even hundreds of millions of dollars of equipment and assets located all over a plant, or building, or campus, and much of it is portable. Many companies or agencies rely on bar codes to manage their inventory, but this doesn't really help locate or track these assets accurately in real time. Take the baggage handling operations at most airports. The number of delayed or lost bags is estimated to run in the millions each year. It cost the airlines billions of dollars to deal with the problem. Most airports rely on bar code labels and equipment to monitor, manage, and track baggage. Given that bar code readers are about 85 percent to 90 percent accurate, this means that a lot of bags will have to be managed manually. Because of the inaccuracy of bar code readers, some airports are beginning to use RFID tags and readers, which are 99 percent accurate. Included in this group of airports are Hong Kong, Las Vegas, Los Angeles, Denver, and Heathrow. In the same vein, a handful of hospitals throughout the world are beginning to use RFID in combination with wireless networks to manage and track equipment. Instead of tagging equipment with bar code labels, RFID tags are attached to the equipment. By themselves, RFID tags and readers do not work with wireless networks. Instead, a special RFID device called a *chokepoint* is needed to read and transmit data about the asset over the IP network. Through a process akin to the triangulation process used to locate a mobile phone, the access points on a wireless network can be used to pinpoint the current location of any tagged asset.

▶ **Tracking product inventory.** By far, the greatest interest in RFID technology revolves around the task of tracking individual products or items to improve inventory and supply chain management. In part this interest was spurred by separate mandates originally issued in 2005 by the U.S. Department of Defense (DoD) and Wal-Mart. The DoD required their suppliers to mark each item with a passive RFID tag, although the mandate was to be rolled out over a 3-year period. Wal-Mart's demands were a little less stringent, requiring only its top 100 suppliers to mark their pallets and cases with RFID tags. RFID tags track product inventory by means of its electronic product code (EPC). The **electronic product code (EPC)** is a relatively new product identification standard that specifies the manufacturer, producer, version, and serial number of each product item. The concept is similar to the universal product code (UPC) that currently appears on almost every consumer product. The UPC is a 12-digit number that is represented by bars and spaces of varying widths, readable by a bar code scanner. The use of an EPC-enabled RFID tag instead of a UPC bar code offers several advantages. First, an RFID tag does not require line-of-sight contact to be read. Second, RFID tags are not printed on paper, so they are less likely to be ripped, soiled,

electronic product code (EPC)

A product identification standard that specifies the manufacturer, producer, version, and serial number of each (product) item.

or lost. Third, the RFID tag identifies the item, not just the manufacturer and product. EPC will provide the ability to track individual items as they move from factories to store shelves, considerably improving supply chain collaboration; eliminating human error from data collection; reducing inventories, loss, and waste; and improving safety and security.

SENSOR NETWORKS AND SMART ITEMS

A question facing many companies interested in becoming more efficient is "How can we sense the important events in the real world and quickly respond with behavior that leads to success?" *Real world awareness* is a concept used to describe the ability (of a company) to sense information in real time from people, IT sources, and physical objects—by using technologies like RFID and sensors—and then respond quickly and effectively (Heinrich 2005).

Sensor Network Basics

At the core of real-world awareness are *sensor networks*. A **sensor network** is a collection of nodes, sometimes as small as millimeters in length or diameter, capable of environmental sensing, local computation, and communication with its peers or with other higher performance nodes. Each node consists of (1) a sensor capable of detecting one or more environmental conditions (e.g., temperature, humidity, vibration, and chemical concentration), (2) a microprocessor for storing and processing data and information, and (3) a weak radio that transmits and receives data and information. The nodes are dispersed throughout some environment of interest (such as a manufacturing plant) and communicate via a *mesh network* in which information is passed bucket-brigade style along the network to a gateway node that transmits the information to a central computer for processing or storage. Today, communications among the nodes are wireless rather than wired.

> **sensor network**
> A collection of nodes, sometimes as small as millimeters in length or diameter, capable of environmental sensing, local computation, and communication with its peers or with other higher performance nodes.

The term *smart item* or *smart object* is sometimes applied to the nodes of a sensory network where they are embedded into physical goods, items, or assets (such as wearing apparel). The reason the term *smart* is applied is because the nodes have embedded intelligence. More accurately, the microprocessor in a node enables it to potentially make autonomous decisions and carry out autonomous actions based on a combination of the logic embedded in the node and the sensory data it receives. In most applications, however, it is better to think of the network of nodes as being collectively *smart* rather than the separate nodes being individually smart.

When coupled with a physical sensing device, active RFIDs can serve as nodes in a sensor network. However, most sensors and sensor networks are based on other technologies. These technologies are provided by companies such as Crossbow Technology, Ember, and Dust Networks. Take, for example, Dust Networks, which was founded in 2002. The name of the company is taken from the concept of *smartdust*, which is used to describe a network of tiny wireless microelectromechanical systems (mems) sensors, robots, or devices installed with wireless communications that can detect (for example) light, temperature, or vibration. The concept was introduced by one of the founders of the company, Kris Pister, at the University of California, Berkley. The idea was that the wireless sensors would so be so small that they could be sprinkled like dust throughout a building, home, or industrial facility—or even in a forest or a field. The networks provided by Dust Networks are called *SmartMesh* and consist of miniature wireless sensors called *motes*. The term *mote* is frequently used to connote the nodes in a sensor network. Currently, motes are about 12 millimeters square (not quite dust) and can run on micro-batteries for years. Dust Networks has focused on selling its products to industrial automation companies for tasks such as monitoring pipelines, valves, tanks for oil refineries, natural gas plants, and product facilities.

Sensor Networking Standards

In order for the nodes in a sensor network to participate in the IoT, the nodes have to be connected to the Internet. In their current configurations, most of the nodes in a sensor network communicate with one another using proprietary methods or other non-Internet standards. For example, *ZigBee* is the name of a specification for a suite of high-level communication protocols enabling low-cost, low-power, wireless mesh networking. The specification supports a mesh network connecting up to 65,000 network nodes. However, the specification does not rely on Internet standards such as the Internet Protocol (IP).

The same can be said for the standards underlying the networking of RFID tags. The standards were originally established by MIT Auto-ID Center. Today, they are managed by EPCGlobal. The standards provide a suite of specifications and protocols governing both RFID hardware and software and the formats of the data they will exchange, store, and process. The standards mimic a number of Internet standards. For instance, one of the keys to the RFID standards is the electronic product code (EPC). In a communication network, the EPC serves the same purpose as an IP address on the Internet, providing a unique identifier for each tagged item. The identifier does not provide detailed information about the item. Instead, this information is contained in a data file (or database) elsewhere on a local network or the Internet. The information about an item is found by interrogating a special database known as the *Object Name Service (ONS)*. The ONS is similar to the Internet's Domain Name Service (DNS), which enables a browser, for example, to locate the server containing a particular Web page of interest (i.e., the URL of the Web page). When an RFID reader obtains the EPC for an item, it passes the EPC to special middleware software. In turn, the middleware queries an ONS on the local network or the Internet to find the data file where the information about the item is stored. Finally, the middleware retrieves the information about the item and passes it to another enterprise application that can use it.

The difficulty with the current set of protocols used with sensor networks is that none of them has widespread adoption nor do they interoperate directly with the Internet. Instead, most sensor networks rely on gateways or centralized servers to connect to the Internet. The situation is similar to the situation that existed with computer networks prior to widespread adoption of Internet protocols. For this reason, some experts have suggested that the nodes in a sensor network should become first-class citizens on the Internet, adopting its underlying protocols. The latest group to make this suggestion is the IPSO (IP for Smart Objects) Alliance. The Alliance is made up of 26 members including Cisco, Sun Microsystems, Texas Instruments, and SAP, among others. As the Alliance notes, "IP has proven itself a long-lived, stable, and highly scalable communication technology that supports both a wide range of application, a wide range of devices, and a wide range of underlying communication technologies" (Dunkels and Vasseur 2008).

In order to use IP with sensor networks, at least two things need to happen. First, Internet (IP) addresses will be needed to handle the billions of nodes that will eventually exist as sensor networks become widely deployed. This means that the current version of the IP address space (IPv4) will have to be replaced by the coming version (IPv6), which can support trillions of addresses. Second, lightweight versions of IP (stack) will have to be adopted. The current standard works well with desktop and laptop computers but is too large to be handled by the small microprocessors found in the nodes of a sensor network.

Smart Applications

Although computer-based instrumentation has existed for a long time, the density of instrumentation made possible by a shift to mass-produced intelligent sensors and the use of pervasive networking technology give wireless sensor networks a new kind of scope that can be applied to a wide range of uses.

M2M magazine (specialtypub.com/m2m), one of the few publications dedicated to covering the machine-to-machine communication market, has constructed a list of more than 180 applications of sensor networks. These have been divided into six major types. Exhibit 8.8 provides a sampling of the list.

In addition to this listing, *M2M* also provides a listing of the major sensor network vendors, as well as key resources for sensor networking (*M2M* 2007).

Another way to differentiate the applications of sensor networks is to categorize the type of monitoring being done by the network. Essentially, there are three types of monitoring:

- Monitoring space
- Monitoring things
- Monitoring the interactions of things with each other and the encompassing space

The first category includes environmental and habitat monitoring, precision agriculture, indoor climate control, surveillance, treaty verification, and intelligent alarms. Case 8.2 provides an example of this category. The second includes structural monitoring, condition-based

EXHIBIT 8.8   Sensor Network Applications

Building control/automation	Automated home technology
	Energy monitoring
	Lighting control
	Museum monitoring
Manufacturing/industrial	How the product operates in the field
	Instrumentation calibration
	Machine health monitoring
	Process control/automation
	Production process
	Pipeline monitoring
	Robot control
Supply chain management	Cold-chain (temperature) monitoring
	Container tracking
	Inventory monitoring
	Tank-level monitoring
Energy/utilities	Automated meter reading
	Oil/gas production monitoring
	Radiation monitoring
Security/public safety	Air quality monitoring
	Border/perimeter security
	Hazardous materials management
	High performance communication with emergency personnel
	Security/alarm systems
Government/military	Battlefield monitoring
	Data storage/image display
	Intelligent vehicle highway systems
	Parking control
	Wastewater management

Source: Compiled from *M2M* (2007), Gross (2007), and Moad (2007).

CASE 8.2
EC Application
WI-FI SENSOR NET AIDS WINEMAKERS

Pickberry, a California vineyard, is using a sensor network to address an age-old conundrum: how to grow better grapes. Grapes that produce good wine sell at a premium, so getting the right conditions for good growth can mean the difference between profit and loss for small vineyards.

One problem Pickberry faces is that the Sonoma County vineyard is spread over a hill, and growing conditions vary over the different parts of the slope. In order to monitor key growing conditions, such as temperature, humidity, and soil moisture, measurements need to be taken at various points throughout the vineyard. Field monitor sensors have been available for some time, but running data cables through the vineyard has been prohibitively expensive and impractical. Pickberry's viticulturists also want information that can help

them work out what grape-growing conditions produce good quality grapes. In the past, they have had to speculate retrospectively why vines growing in one part of the vineyard in one year produced better grapes than vines in another part of the vineyard in another year.

The solution is a sensor net that uses Wi-Fi for data connectivity. Sensors that monitor the conditions known to be key influences on grape quality have been placed throughout the vineyard. A sensor communicates its data to a central server by hopping from one Wi-Fi access point to another. The analysis engine on the server has a series of alerts built in that tells the growers when particular levels of indicators, such as soil moisture or temperature, are reached. Then corrective action can be taken.

(continued)

CASE 8.2 *(continued)*

Wireless was a natural choice for the grape growers, according to Bill Westerman, an associate partner at Accenture who worked on the project. "We are able to get data from 30 acres back to home base without having to run cables and without having to have radio transmitters that are powerful enough to make the leap from one end of the field to the other," said Westerman.

The remote sensor network provides Pickberry with the ability to:

▶ **Make calculated decisions.** Decisions can be made almost vine-by-vine—thanks to the granular level of the data obtained in near real time. For example, Pickberry can use the data to adjust watering schedules for a specific area.
▶ **Combine vineyard data with other data sources.** This enables Pickberry to manage operations and resources, such as water usage, more scientifically. Live data on soil moisture and air humidity can be correlated with weather forecast data to match estimated water demand with well supply.
▶ **Detect potentially devastating events.** Frost, disease, and pests can be detected early on.

What are the results? Obviously the data are helping the Pickberry grape growers know much more about the health of their vines in different parts of the vineyard. They better understand how water is being retained and how much water

needs to be applied, promoting both healthy vines and water conservation. The analysis also has been used to reduce the application of fungicides to control mildew. Now fungicides are applied only when and where they are needed rather than blanket coverage on a regular schedule, as was done before the sensor net.

The data also are helping the viticulturists work out the conditions that produce the best grapes. According to Westerman, "They are using this data in part to verify what they did before and to get details they never had before."

Armed with insight provided from sensor applications, Pickberry can take immediate action. These capabilities lead to more effective crop management, lowering costs while raising product quality.

Sources: Compiled from Ward (2004) and Accenture (2006).

Questions

1. How is the Wi-Fi sensor net contributing to Pickberry's core competency of grape production?
2. Why is Wi-Fi such an important part of this solution?
3. What are the benefits for Pickberry, for the environment, and for the wine industry?

equipment maintenance, medical diagnostics, and urban terrain mapping. The most dramatic applications involve monitoring complex interactions, including wildlife habitats, disaster management, emergency response, ubiquitous computing environments, asset tracking, health care, and manufacturing process flow.

PRIVACY AND PERVASIVE COMPUTING

For pervasive systems to be widely deployed, it is necessary to overcome many of the technical, ethical, and legal barriers associated with mobile computing (see Section 8.8) as well as a few barriers unique to ubiquitous, invisible computing. Ye (2009) provides a comprehensive list of technical challenges, social and legal issues, and economic concerns (including finding appropriate business models) in deploying pervasive computing systems. They also cite research challenges, such as component interaction, adaptation and contextual sensitivity, user interface interaction, and appropriate management mechanisms.

Among the nontechnical issues confronting the deployment of pervasive computing, the prospective loss of individual privacy seems to be at the forefront. In some cases, privacy groups have expressed concern that the tags and sensors embedded in items, especially retail items, make it possible to track the owners or buyers of those items. Although this is a possibility, the larger problem is that the information produced by tags, sensors, and other devices in various networks has the potential to threaten an individual's privacy if misused or mishandled.

With privacy issues, the principle of consent often applies. By law, there are limits to how data may be used by or supplied to third parties. For instance, if you make a purchase with a loyalty card, the information generated during the purchase belongs to the authority that issued the card, which can do what it likes with the data since it was obtained legally and with the explicit and implicit consent of the cardholder. Similarly, if you fill out an online survey in exchange for an online research article, then the information belongs to the enterprise sponsoring the survey and, again, they can do what they want with it, since you have given your consent by participating.

With pervasive computing, the privacy issue is not as straightforward. In most cases, the data are collected in an unobtrusive and invisible fashion. Even though most of the data is low-level, if retained and analyzed it could compromise individual privacy. More importantly, if the data can be tied to specific individuals or groups of individuals, there is often no way for the individual(s) to opt out or provide consent. In the near term, the applications where privacy issues are most likely to arise are medical, retail, and transport systems. For example, equipping the elderly or impaired with wearable devices for monitoring movement, vital signs, usage of facilities and equipment, etc., and transmitting this information regularly over a sensor network can provide the means for people to live safely on their own or with minimal assistance. However, this has privacy implications since access to the data could reveal information about an individual's personal behavior and habits. In the same vein, if a consumer purchases an item at a store and the RFID tag on the item is used to track an individual's movements through the store and throughout the mall of which the store is a part, then this data has been gathered without the individual's consent and potentially violates his or her right to privacy, regardless of how innocuous the data may seem.

In order to protect the privacy of individuals, it must be designed into the tags, nodes, and networks, not addressed in a post hoc fashion. Basically, systems can be engineered in such a way that the data that is gathered is limited to that which is needed to carry out the desired function and nothing else. Identity data can be discarded or coarsened to the maximum extent so that specific users cannot be identified unless there is an absolute need.

Section 8.9 ❱ REVIEW QUESTIONS

1. Define pervasive computing.
2. List four principles of pervasive computing.
3. What is the Internet of Things?
4. Describe how RFID works. What role does EPC play in RFID?
5. Describe some of the current tracking applications of RFID.
6. How does a sensor network work?
7. Describe some of the applications of sensor networks.
8. In what ways can pervasive computing impinge on an individual's right to privacy?

MANAGERIAL ISSUES

Some managerial issues related to this chapter are as follows.

1. **What is your m-commerce strategy?** M-commerce is an amalgamation of three basic market segments: support for internal business processes; an extension of existing e-business services that touch customers, suppliers; and other partners; and extension of Web-based consumer services to a rapidly growing population of "smartphone" users. The key to success in the m-commerce world is to define your overall e-commerce and m-commerce business strategy, determine which segments are critical to the strategy and the order in which they need to be addressed, and which of the available mobile technologies will support the strategy and critical segments.

2. **What is your timetable?** Mobile technologies and applications are undergoing rapid change. It seems like every 6 months new technologies and opportunities emerge. In this accelerated environment, the challenge is to craft an m-commerce strategy that can take advantage of rapidly changing market conditions while at the same time ensuring that choice of mobile solutions and technologies is "future proof."

3. **Are there clear technical winners?** Among mobile devices, the answer is "yes." The all in-one-devices, such as smartphones, have surged to the forefront of the mobile device market and will likely stay there. Among the other components of the mobile infrastructure (e.g., wireless networks such as WiMax, Wi-Fi, and 3G) the answer is "no." There is still a confusing multiplicity of standards, devices, and supporting hardware. The key is to select a well-architected platform and infrastructure that can support in the near term a range of services while at the same time enabling adoption of future technologies as they emerge.

4. **Which applications should be implemented first?** Although there is something of a "cool factor" associated with various m-commerce applications, especially location-based services, mobile applications must be judged like any other business technology—ROI, cost–benefit, cost reductions, and efficiency. Toward these ends, many of the more mundane internal applications supporting the mobile workforce have resulted in the highest returns. Regardless, the application of mobile technology must be based on a realistic view of each situation to determine whether the technology is suitable or not. Recall that the m-commerce platform is the most preferred by younger generations. It is important to understand why Japan has a much higher penetration in m-commerce while other countries with the same level of mobile telecommunication infrastructure do not have a similar level of penetration.

5. **Is pervasive computing real?** Yes. Pervasive computing is invisible, ubiquitous computing that is embedded in the objects around us. The first incarnations of pervasive computing are RFID and sensor networking. Slowly but surely, RFID and other monitoring and tracking technologies based on sensor networking are making their way into our lives. No doubt in the next 5 years they will pervade many aspects of business and personal life, not just the world of the supply chain and inventory control. In some cases, the use of these technologies will be mandated (as with Wal-Mart and the DoD). In other cases, it will be by choice. Regardless, the application of these invisible and unobtrusive technologies will bring to the forefront issues of individual privacy.

SUMMARY

In this chapter, you learned about the following EC issues as they relate to the chapter's learning objectives.

1. **What is m-commerce, its value-added attributes, and fundamental drivers?** M-commerce is any business activity conducted over a wireless telecommunications network. M-commerce is a natural extension of e-commerce. M-commerce can help a business improve its value proposition to customers by utilizing its unique attributes: ubiquity, convenience, interactivity, personalization, and localization. Currently, m-commerce is being driven by large numbers of users of mobile devices; a developing "cell phone culture" among youth; demands from service-oriented customers; vendor marketing; declining prices; a mobile workforce; improved performance for the price; and increasing bandwidth.

2. **What is the mobile computing environment that supports m-commerce?** The mobile computing environment consists of two key elements: mobile devices and wireless networks. Although mobile computing devices vary in size and functionality, they are rapidly moving toward an all-in-one device that is rapidly overcoming some of the limitations associated with poor usability, such as small screen size, limited bandwidth, and restricted input capabilities. Even with their limitations, mobile devices offer a series of support services, principally SMS, voice, and location-based services, which differentiate m-commerce from e-commerce.

3. **Which networks support mobile devices?** Mobile devices connect in a wireless fashion to networks or other devices at a personal, local, metropolitan, or wide area level. Bluetooth (personal), cellular phone networks (WWAN), and wireless LANs (like Wi-Fi) are well-known technologies that are well established in the wireless marketplace. In contrast, municipal Wi-Fi and WiMax (metropolitan) are less well-known and are vying for a broader foothold in the wireless marketplace.

4. **Financial applications.** Many EC applications in the financial services industries (such as banking and electronic bill payment) can be conducted with wireless devices. Most mobile financial applications are simply mobile versions of their wireline counterparts that are conducted via SMS or the mobile Web. Mobile banking and mobile payments are good examples of this. Increasingly, banks throughout the world are enabling their customers to use mobile devices to check balances, monitor transactions, obtain account information, transfer funds, locate brands or ATMs, and sometimes pay bills. In the same vein, some companies are enabling their customers or clients to initiate or confirm payments transactions via their cell phones or smartphones. These transactions are one of two types: mobile proximity payments or mobile remote payments. With mobile proximity payments, also known as "contactless" payments, a cell phone or smartphone is outfitted with a special chip that allows the user to swipe their phone near a payment device (e.g., POS reader), much like a contactless smart card or credit card. With mobile remote payments, the mobile handset can be used to make person-to-person, person-to-business, and business-to-business payments just like they can be used to do mobile banking.

5. **Mobile marketing and advertising.** Like traditional and online media campaigns, mobile marketing and advertising campaigns fall into a variety of categories including information, entertainment, raffles, and coupons. Similarly, their objectives typically fall into one of six categories: building brand awareness, changing brand image, promoting sales, enhancing brand loyalty, building the customer base, and stimulating (mobile) word of mouth. The uptake of mobile marketing has been strong because the response is typically higher than with more traditional or online campaigns. Although there are no strict guidelines for mobile advertising, the success of mobile advertising is linked to some basic principles, including notice, choice and consent, customization and constraint, security, and enforcement and accountability.

6. **Mobile workforce solutions.** Business applications such as mobile office applications, sales force automation (SFA), field force automation (FFA), mobile CRM, inventory management, and wireless job dispatch offer the best opportunities for high

return on investment (ROI) for most organizations, at least in the short term. All of these applications are focused on supporting the mobile worker (someone who is away from their primary work space at least 10 hours a week or 25 percent of the time), although they are aimed at different segments of the mobile workforce (i.e., mobile professionals, mobile field force, and mobile specialty workers). Even though their potential ROI is high, their implementation faces a number of challenges, including interruptions and gaps in network coverage; problems caused by Internet work roaming; performance problems created by slow mobile networks and applications; managing and securing mobile devices; and managing mobile network bandwidth.

7. **Mobile entertainment.** One of the fastest growing markets in m-commerce is mobile entertainment. Mobile entertainment encompasses mobile music, games, TV, gambling, adult services, and user-generated content and infotainment. Among these, mobile music is the largest. Mobile gambling is one of the smallest, although it is the fastest growing in spite of the legal restrictions placed on it by various government bodies.

8. **Location-based commerce.** Location-based m-commerce (l-commerce) refers to the use of positioning devices, such as GPS, to find where a customer or client is and deliver products and services based on his or her location. The services provided by l-commerce companies tend to focus on one or more of the following factors: location, navigation, tracking, mapping, and timing. These services rest on five basic components: mobile devices, communication networks, positioning components, service and application providers, and data or content providers. Among these, the position

and data components, especially geographical information (GIS), are critical. Although l-commerce has been widely hailed, several factors impede its widespread use, including the accuracy of the mobile devices, the cost–benefits of most applications, limited network bandwidth, and the potential invasion of privacy.

9. **Security and other implementation issues.** The mobile computing environment offers special challenges for security, including the need to secure transmission over open air and through multiple connecting networks. The biggest technological changes relate to the usability of devices. Finally, ethical, legal, and health issues can arise from the use of m-commerce, especially in the workplace.

10. **Pervasive computing.** Many experts believe that the next step in the evolution of computing will be pervasive computing—invisible, ubiquitous computing in which computing capabilities are embedded in the objects around us. Pervasive computing is based on four principles: decentralization, diversification, connectivity, and simplicity. Pervasive computing will lead to the Internet of Things (IoT) in which virtually all the embedded objects have the potential to be connected to the Internet. Two technologies that are critical to the spread of pervasive computing and the IoT are RFID and sensor networks. Both technologies, but especially RFID, are already being used in a wide variety of tracking and monitoring applications, although there are still a number of technical hurdles (e.g., using Internet standards to connect small objects) to clear before the IoT will come to fruition. In addition to the technical hurdles, there are also ethical and legal barriers that must be overcome, especially the prospective loss of individual privacy that results from placing wireless tags and sensing devices all around us.

KEY TERMS

QUESTIONS FOR DISCUSSION

1. Discuss how m-commerce can expand the reach of EC.

2. Which of the m-commerce limitations listed in this chapter do you think will have the biggest near-term negative impact on the growth of m-commence? Which ones will be minimized within 5 years? Which ones will not?

3. Describe the ways in which Wi-Fi is affecting the use of cell phones for m-commerce.

4. WiMax, municipal Wi-Fi, and WWAN are all used to provide wide area access to the Internet. Which of these technologies is likely to survive into the future? Why or why not?

5. Discuss the factors that are critical to the overall growth of mobile banking and mobile payments.

6. Suppose you worked for a fashion retailer and were in charge of a new mobile advertising campaign designed to generate sales for a new clothing line. Describe the basic elements of your campaign and guidelines you would use to conduct it.

7. What is the relationship between mobile sales force automation, mobile field force automation, and mobile CRM?

8. Why are many of the more popular mobile gambling sites located on small island countries?

9. How are GPS and GIS related?

10. Location-based services can help a driver find his or her car or the closest gas station. However, some people view location-based services as an invasion of privacy. Discuss the pros and cons of location-based services.

11. Describe some of the activities that are being monitored by RFID and sensor networks.

INTERNET EXERCISES

1. Learn about smartphones by visiting vendors' sites such as Nokia, RIM, Apple, Motorola, and others. List the capabilities the various devices from these vendors offer for supporting m-commerce. In the future, what sorts of new capabilities will be provided by smartphones?

2. Research the status of 3G and the future of 4G by visiting **3gnewsroom.com** (you can find information on 4G by searching for the term at the site). Prepare a report on the status of 3G and 4G based on your findings.

3. You've been asked to put together a directory of Wi-Fi hotspots in your local area. There are a number of sites, such as **hotspot-locations.com**, that offer search capabilities for finding hotpots in a given area. Construct a list of sites that offer this feature. Using these sites, create a directory for your area. Knowing what you do about the Wi-Fi sites in your area, which of the sites seems to produce the best list?

4. Enter **mapinfo.com** and download their white paper on location intelligence (found in the Highlights section of the homepage). Based on the white paper, discuss the role that location intelligence plays in retail, financial applications, insurance, government, and communications.

5. Most of the major social networking sites provide mobile capabilities. The same is true for newer start-ups like Loopt and GyPSii. Compare and contrast the types of social networking capabilities provided by the major sites and the start-ups.

6. Juniper Research has created a variety of white papers dealing with different segments of the mobile entertainment market (e.g., mobile games). Go to **juniperresearch.com/index.php** and download a white paper dealing with one of these segments. Use the white paper to develop a written summary of the market segment you selected—the size of the market, the major vendors, the factors encouraging and impeding its growth, and the future of the market segment.

7. Enter **gpshopper.com**. What sorts of products and services do they provide? One of their products is Slifter. Go to **slifter.com** and run the demo. Enter **nearbynow.com**. Compare the products and services they provide with those offered by GPShopper.

8. Find information about Google Maps for mobile devices. Also review the capabilities of Google SMS and other Google applications. Write a report on your findings.

9. Provide a general description of the EPC identification standard. What role do EPCGlobal (**epcglobalinc.org**) and the Auto-ID Labs (**autoidlabs.org**) play in this standard? EPCGlobal has developed a set of policies for the use of EPCs. What are these policies and how are they enforced?

10. Crossbow (**xbow.com**) and Dust Networks (**dustnetworks.com**) offer products for building sensor technology applications. Compare and contrast the products offered by the two companies, including the types of network protocols used by each and the types of applications to which they are well suited.

TEAM ASSIGNMENTS, PROJECTS, AND CLASS DISCUSSIONS

1. Each team should examine a major vendor of mobile devices (Nokia, Kyocera, Motorola, Palm, BlackBerry, etc.). Each team will research the capabilities and prices of the devices offered by each company and then make a class presentation, the objective of which is to convince the rest of the class to buy that company's products.

2. Each team should explore the commercial applications of m-commerce in one of the following areas: financial services, including banking, stocks, and insurance; marketing and advertising; travel and transportation; human resources management; public services; and health care. Each team will present a report to the class based on their findings. (Start at mobiforum.org.)

3. Each team will investigate a global organization involved in m-commerce, such as gsmworld.com, wimaxforum.org, and openmobilealliance.org. The teams will investigate the membership and the current projects each organization is working on and then present a report to the class based on their findings.

4. Each team will investigate a standards-setting organization and report on its procedures and progress in developing wireless standards. Start with the following: atis.org, etsi.org, and tiaonline.org.

5. Each team should take one of the following areas—homes, cars, appliances, or other consumer goods, such as clothing—and investigate how embedded microprocessors are currently being used and will be used in the future to support consumer-centric services. Each team will present a report to the class based on its findings.

6. Address the following topics in a class discussion:

   a. Discuss how m-commerce can solve some of the problems of the digital divide (the gap within a country or between countries with respect to people's ability to access the Internet).

   b. Discuss what Weiser meant when he said that computers would become invisible.

Closing Case

WAL-MART TURNS TO MOBILE FOR WEATHER ALERTS

The Problem

The benefits of using weather information in the retail industry are numerous. Not only do retailers need to know the impact of weather on specific consumer demands at the store level and in turn on revenue and profitability, but they also need to ensure the safety and well-being of their customers, employees, and stores during weather emergencies. This is why larger retailers often have specialized staff devoted to monitoring weather forecasts and weather emergencies. A case in point is Wal-Mart, the world's largest retailer.

Although the company would not reveal the dollar specifics, Jason Jackson, Wal-Mart's director of emergency management, acknowledges that "weather is the greatest disruption point in Wal-Mart's business." Until 2007, Wal-Mart's emergency operation center monitored watches and warnings from the U.S. National Weather Service (NWS) and Storm Prediction Center, manually calling store managers to warn them of coming weather emergencies. For widespread and drawn out weather emergencies it is difficult to keep up with the level of weather activity in specific locales. A manual system creates too much of a time lag between the time a potential emergency is detected in a given locale and the appropriate store managers are notified.

The Solution

In 2007 Wal-Mart decided to institute an automated system that would deliver locally specific weather emergency information to its 3,800 stores across the United States. They selected the Smart Notification Weather Service. The service generates, authorizes, and delivers severe weather alerts to subscribers when severe weather (hurricanes, lightning, floods, wind gusts, tornadoes) is detected within their proximity. The service is a partnership between WeatherBug and Send Word Now.

The service utilizes information taken from WeatherBug's network of 8,000 tracking stations located throughout the United States, as well as information from the USPLN (United States Precision Lightning Network) and the NWS, to plot weather conditions within a 3 mile area. WeatherBug's stations update information every 2 seconds over the Internet and are far denser than the NWS's 1,200 stations, which are located mainly at major airports and provide updates every hour. The areas covered by the NWS are postal code–based and cover 5 miles to 30+ miles in area.

The Send Word Now network matches standard or customized weather alerts to each subscriber's specific location (based on their GPS-based phone and weather profile). The service formats the appropriate alert to the supported devices and relays the alert to each individual. This provides greater accuracy and relevancy than previous alerting systems. A Java application on the user's mobile device lets the service know the user's location and can be enabled to receive more detailed information. In the case of Wal-Mart, alerts are routed based on a store manager's location. The service also provides two-way messaging, so that local managers can send back a "message received" reply, and it generates an audit log that shows who received the message, when it was received, and on what device they acknowledged it.

The Results

In the summer of 2007, Wal-Mart tested the service in 40 stores. They have since expanded it to 3,000 stores. For most subscribers, the cost of the system is $10 per month, although there is no information on how much Wal-Mart spends per user. Overall, the automated system provided by the Smart Notification Weather Service is

more precise, locally relevant, customized, and reliable than the manual system it replaced. With early warning about local conditions, managers have the information needed to make real-time decisions. As Wal-Mart notes, the faster warning time enables maximum time for proper preparations, which minimizes safety issues and reduces the impact to the bottom line.

Sources: Compiled from McGee (2008) and Rash (2006).

Questions

1. Why was Wal-Mart interested in instituting an automated weather alert system?
2. How does the Smart Notification Weather Service work? Why is it more precise, accurate, and relevant than the NWS tracking system?
3. What are the benefits of the Smart Notification Weather Service for Wal-Mart?

ONLINE RESOURCES
available at pearsonglobaleditions.com/turban

Online Files

W8.1   Wi-Fi and the Traveling Public
W8.2   Wi-Fi Mesh Networks, Google Talk, and Interoperability
W8.3   Application Case: Mobile Sales Solution Results in £1 Million Revenue Boost
W8.4   Application Case: Nextbus: A Superb Customer Service
W8.5   Security Approaches for Mobile Computing

Comprehensive Educational Web Sites

ecommercetimes.com/perl/section/m-commerce
mobile-weblog.com/50226711/mobile_commerce.php
wimaxforum.org
brandonmcgee.blogspot.com
juniperresearch.com/shop/viewreports.php? category=70
mobilegames.blog.com
trimble.com/gps
aimglobal.org/technologies/RFID
rfidjournal.com
epcglobalinc.org/home
ipso-alliance.org/Pages/Front.php
ceng.usc.edu/~anrg/SensorNetBib.html

REFERENCES

Abramovich, G. "A|X Armani Exchange Debuts SMS Campaign." *Mobile Marketer*, August 20, 2008. mobilemarketer.com/cms/news/messaging/1563.html (accessed December 2008).

Accenture. "Pickberry Vineyard: Accenture Prototype Helps Improve Crop Management." 2006. accenture.com/xd/xd.asp?it=enweb&xd=servicespercent5Ctechnologypercent5Ccasepercent5Cpickberry.xml (accessed December 2008).

American Gaming Association. "Internet Gambling." 2007. americangaming.org/Industry/factsheets/issues_detail.cfv?id=17 (accessed December 2008).

Apple. "iTunes Store Tops over Five Billion Songs Sold: Apple Renting and Selling over 50,000 Movies Per Day." June 19, 2008. apple.com/pr/library/2008/06/19itunes.html (accessed December 2008).

Becker, M. "Academic Review: Mobile Marketing Framework Overview." *Mobile Marketing*, 2006. mmaglobal.com/articles/academic-review-mobile-marketing-framework-overview (accessed December 2008).

Best, J. "Around the World in . . . NFC and Contactless Payment." *ZDNet Australia*, January 18, 2008. zdnet.com.au/news/communications/soa/Around-the-world-in-NFC-and-contactless-payments/0,130061791,339285175,00.htm (accessed December 2008).

Bonkoo, T. "Grocery Stores Providing a New Way of Shopping to Customers: Handheld Device Allows Customer to Forgo Long Line." *Associated Content Media*, January 18, 2007. associatedcontent.com/article/284899/grocery_stores_providing_a_new_way.html (accessed December 2008).

Business Wire. "IDC Predicts the Number of Worldwide Mobile Workers to Reach 1 Billion by 2011." *Business Wire*, January 15, 2008. findarticles.com/p/articles/mi_m0EIN/is_2008_Jan_15/ai_n24230213/ (accessed December 2008).

Commonwealth Telecommunications Organization. "Barriers and Enablers to Sustainable Growth in Emerging Markets." *CTO Forum 2006*, London, England, September 4–6, 2006.

Dunkels, A., and J. Vasseur. "IP for Smart Objects." *IPSO Alliances Whitepaper*. September, 2008. ipso-alliance.org/Documents/IPSO-WP-1.pdf (accessed December 2008).

The Economist. "Business in Motion: Managing the Mobile Workforce." *Economist Intelligence Unit*. 2007. a330.g.akamai.net/7/330/25828/20070424135756/graphics.eiu.com/ebf/PDFs/Business_in_motion_Aprilpercent202007_FINAL.pdf (accessed December 2008).

eMarketer. "Mobile Video and Television: Ads Wait for a Clearer Picture." August 2008. emarketer.com/Reports/All/Emarketer_2000507.aspx (accessed May 2009).

Gross, L. A. "Border Security Applications and Solutions." Radio Resource Media Group, October 26, 2007. radioresourcemag.com/onlyonline.cfm?OnlyOnlineID=16 (accessed May 2009).

Heinrich, C. *RFID and Beyond*. New York: Wiley & Sons, 2005.

Hu, W.-C., J.-H. Yeh, H.-J. Yang, and C.-W. Lee. "Mobile Handheld Devices for Mobile Commerce." In M. Khosrow-Pour, (Ed.). *Encyclopedia of E-Commerce, E-Government, and Mobile Commerce*. Hershey, PA: Idea Group Reference, 2006.

IMS Research. "900M Users for Mobile Banking and Payment Services in 2012." May 29, 2008. imsresearch.com/press_release_details.html&press_id=486 (accessed December 2008).

ITU. "ICT Statistics Newslog—Worldwide Mobile Cellular Subscribers to Reach 4 Billion Mark Late 2008." September 29, 2008. itu.int/ITU-D/ict/newslog/Worldwide+Mobile+Cellular+Subscribers+To+Reach+4+Billion+Mark+Late+2008.aspx (accessed December 2008).

Juniper Research. "Mobile—Let Me Entertain You." *Juniper Research*, 2008. juniperresearch.com/shop/viewwhitepaper.php?id=99&whitepaper=57 (accessed December 2008).

Laudermilch, N. "Will Cell Phones Be Responsible for the Next Internet Worm?" *InformIT*, April 28, 2006. informit.com/articles/article.aspx?p=465449 (accessed December 2008).

M2 Presswire. "MONILINK: Monilink Reaches One Million Account Enquiries Per Month." November 11, 2008. ip-pbx.tmcnet.com/news/2008/11/11/3778246.htm (accessed December 2008).

M2M. "Sensor Networking." 2007. specialtypub.com/pdfs/m2msensors.pdf (accessed December 2008).

Malykhina, E. "Leave the Laptop Home." *InformationWeek*, October 30, 2006.

McGee, M. "Track This." *InformationWeek*, February 11, 2008.

Metro. "METRO Group and Real,- Open the Store of the Future." May 2008. metro-link.com/metro-link/html/en/15449208/index.html (accessed December 2008).

Meyer, M. "Tag Knowledge (Part II)—Tag Types." *MoreRFID*, 2007. morerfid.com/details.php?subdetail=Report&action=details&report_id=3668 (accessed December 2008).

Mitra, S. "Mobile Microfinance." *Forbes*, June 6, 2008. forbes.com/home/2008/06/05/mitra-mobile-microfinance-tech-wire-cx_sm_0606mitra.htm (accessed December 2008).

Moad, J. "Start-Up Launches Easy-to-Configure Wireless Sensor Network Technology." *Managing Automation*, April 30, 2007. managingautomation.com/maonline/news/read/StartUp_Launches_EasytoConfigure_Wireless_Sensor_Network_Technology_28618 (accessed May 2009).

Mullen, J. "For Those in Paris About to Park, a Service That Tells Them Where." *The New York Times*, November 21, 2006. nytimes.com/2006/11/20/business/worldbusiness/20garage.html?ex=1321678800&en=9e1908a053b88365&ei=5088&partner=rss-nyt&emc=rss (accessed December 2008).

Parlamentul European. "Getting Galileo into Orbit by 2013." April 17, 2008. newsdesk.se/view/pressrelease/getting-galileo-into-orbit-by-2013-209067 (accessed December 2008).

PaymentNews. "Fiserv Survey Finds Increased Consumer Interest in Mobile Banking." September 2008. paymentsnews.com/2008/09/fiserv-survey-f.html (accessed December 2008).

Philadelphia Inquirer. "It's Getting There: Wi-Fi Baby Steps." December 17, 2007. philly.com/inquirer/opinion/20071217_Editorial___Its_Getting_There.html?adString=inq.news/opinion;!category=opinion;&randomOrd=020408041722 (accessed December 2008).

PriceWaterhouseCoopers. "Global Entertainment & Media to Reach $2.2T in 2012, Driven by Digital, Mobile." *Marketing Charts*, June 20, 2008. marketingcharts.com/television/global-entertainment-media-to-reach-22t-in-2012-driven-by-digital-mobile-5012 (accessed December 2008).

Rash, W. "WeatherBug, Send Word Now Create Emergency Weather Service." June 12, 2006. eweek.com/c/a/Mobile-and-Wireless/WeatherBug-Send-Word-Now-Create-Emergency-Weather-Service (accessed December 2008).

Rosen, C. "Our Cell Phones, Ourselves." *The New Atlantis*, May 29, 2006. thenewatlantis.com/archive/6/TNA06-CRosen.pdf (accessed December 2008).

Shannon, V. "Social Networking Moves to the Cellphone." *The New York Times*, March 6, 2008. nytimes.com/2008/03/06/technology/06wireless.html?_r=2 (accessed December 2008).

Sicari, S. "Internet of Things: It's the Network, Stupid!" *ICST Innovation Society*, 2006. icst.org/portals/content/internet-of-things-its-the-network-stupid (accessed December 2008).

Steiniger, S., M. Neun, and A. Edwardes. "Foundation of Location-Based Services." 2006. spatial.cs.umn.edu/Courses/Fall07/8715/papers/IM7_steiniger.pdf (accessed December 2008).

Taipei Times. "New GPS Parking Hits the Spot for Paris." November 21, 2006. taipeitimes.com/News/world/archives/2006/11/21/2003337287 (accessed December 2008).

Talbot, D. "Upwardly Mobile." *Technology Review*, November–December 2008. technologyreview.com/business/21533 (accessed December 2008).

TeleGeography. "Texting Taking Off." August 31, 2006. telegeography.com/cu/article.php?article_id=14094 (accessed December 2008).

Ward, M. "Wi-fi Sensor Net Aids Winemakers." *BBC News*, July 6, 2004. news.bbc.co.uk/2/hi/technology/3860863.stm (accessed December 2008).

Wireless and Mobile News. "NFC Mobile Phone Trial on SF BART in Jack in the Box Successful." October 7, 2008. wirelessandmobilenews.com/2008/10/nfc_mobile_phone_trial_on_sf_b.html (accessed December 2008).

Ye, J. et al. "Overview of Pervasive Systems." In K. Delaney, (Ed.). *Ambient Intelligence Within Microsystems*. New York: Springer, 2009.

CHAPTER 9

THE WEB 2.0 ENVIRONMENT AND SOCIAL NETWORKS

Content

Learning Objectives

Upon completion of this chapter, you will be able to:

1. Understand the Web 2.0 revolution, social and business networks, and industry and market disruptors.

2. Understand the concept, structure, types, and issues of virtual communities.

3. Understand social networking and social networking sites.

4. Describe the major social networks.

5. Describe business-oriented and enterprise social networks.

6. Understand the commercial aspects of social networking.

7. Describe Web 2.0 entertainment.

8. Describe the potential of Web 3.0 and Web 4.0.

WIKIPEDIA AND ITS PROBLEMS OF CONTENT, QUALITY, AND PRIVACY PROTECTION

The Problem

Wikipedia is a free online collaborative encyclopedia. In 2008, it had over 7 million articles in over 262 languages and generated some 80 million hits per day. By comparison, Wikipedia is 42 times bigger than the *Encyclopedia Britannica*, which contains 120,000 articles.

Wikipedia's greatest strength is also its biggest weakness. Users create the content; therefore, sometimes people with no special expertise on their chosen topics or people with malicious agendas post so-called "facts." For instance, once a contributor to an article on Pope Benedict substituted the Pontiff's photo with that of Emperor Palpatine from the *Star Wars* films. According to Farrell (2007), Microsoft paid experts to write information about the company that was later found to be inaccurate. (For more about the inaccuracy issue, see McNichol 2007a.)

In another, more serious, example, a contributor made the accusation that distinguished journalist and long-time civil rights advocate John Seigenthaler had been involved in the assassinations of President John Kennedy and his brother Bobby Kennedy. The contributor practically fabricated the entire article. Seigenthaler pursued legal action against the anonymous Wikipedia contributor, via the poster's IP address, and charged the unidentified accuser with defamation. For Seigenthaler, Wikipedia is "populated by volunteer vandals with poison-pen intellects" and should not be permitted to exist in its current form.

Another problem is invasion of privacy. Even if information about a certain individual or company is correct (i.e., it is not defamatory), the individual may not want the information to be made public. Because most contributors do not ask permission from those they are writing about, an invasion of privacy occurs. Yet, another problem is that the bulk of Wikipedia is written by only 1,400 of its more than 100,000 contributors (see Blodget 2009), introducing possible bias.

The Solution

In order to avoid false or misleading entries, the Wikimedia Foundation, which operates Wikipedia, along with several other wiki initiatives (such as Wikibooks), has promoted several alternatives to improve the quality of Wikipedia articles. The first step was the creation of a more formal advisory board. The second step was to empower system administrators to block access to the site to certain users who repeatedly vandalized entries. Next, the process of handling complaints was improved.

Ultimately, the owners plan to change the site to Wikipedia 2.0 and are considering the following three options:

1. The editing of mediocre Wikipedia articles by experts in the specific field; especially the use of quality art editors to improve Wikipedia's humanities coverage.

2. The creation of original articles from the ground up. According to Larry Sanger, one of Wikipedia's owners and creators, this could provide a more distinctive culture that will provide more pride in the articles. In this case, the name of the site would change to *citizendium*.

3. Make the users' policy more interactive. Wikipedia is asking readers to notify the company whenever they read inaccurate or incomplete content.

The Results

While the Seigenthaler issue was debated in fall 2005, early quality measures were instituted, and the site's founder, Jimmy Wales, appeared on CNN with Seigenthaler in December 2005. During this time, traffic to Wikipedia nearly tripled, mostly due to the publicity of the CNN presentation and the subsequent publicity in newspapers and TV. Yet problems still exist, with continued complaints against both inaccurate content and privacy invasion. And, after years of enormous growth, the rate of editing articles, new account registration, user blocks, article protection and deletion, and uploads have all declined. In addition, in 2008 Google launched a potential Wikipedia competition with its service called Knol.

Sources: Compiled from Martens (2006), Cone (2007a), Blodget (2009), Riley (2007), Farrell (2007), Wikipedia.org (2008), and McNichol (2007a).

WHAT WE CAN LEARN . . .

The Wikipedia case illustrates a *wiki*, a collaborative online encyclopedia jointly written by volunteers. Murray-Buechner (2006) lists it as one of the 25 sites "we cannot live without" and labeled it as a "real Web wonder." It is a typical Web 2.0 application; it is done for people by people. Also, it illustrates the phenomenon of the "wisdom of the crowd"; namely, many people contributing their knowledge to create better knowledge and to solve problems.

Many companies are now using a similar concept internally; for example, the pharmaceutical company Pfizer implemented an internal wiki, called Pfizerpedia, to accumulate knowledge about its pharmaceutical products and research. Many other companies use the wisdom of the crowd to create corporate knowledge bases.

The Wikipedia case illustrates both the benefits to society and the problems of content created by volunteers. The Wikipedia case also illustrates the potential risk of invasion of privacy, potential of litigation against a site, and the need for financial viability, especially when money is needed to check the content people contribute.

This chapter examines several Web 2.0 applications, namely virtual communities and social networking, and their impact on the way we live and do business. Specific companies, such as LinkedIn, Facebook, YouTube, and Flickr, which have already changed the work and/or lives of millions of people, also are discussed. Finally, the chapter describes the commercialization of social networking and its major implementation issues.

9.1 THE WEB 2.0 REVOLUTION, SOCIAL MEDIA, AND INDUSTRY DISRUPTORS

This chapter deals with the newest areas of EC—social networks and other Web 2.0 applications. Let's see what it is all about.

WHAT IS WEB 2.0?

Web 2.0 is the popular term for describing advanced Web technologies and applications, including blogs, wikis, RSS, mashups, user-generated content, and social networks. A major objective of Web 2.0 is to enhance creativity, information sharing, and collaboration.

One of the most significant differences between Web 2.0 and the traditional Web is the greater collaboration among Internet users and other users, content providers, and enterprises. As an umbrella term for an emerging core of technologies, trends, and principles, Web 2.0 is not only changing what is on the Web, but also how it works. Web 2.0 concepts have led to the evolution of Web-based virtual communities and their hosting services, such as social networking sites, video-sharing sites, and more. Many believe (e.g., Li and Bernoff 2008) that companies that understand these new applications and technologies—and apply the capabilities early on—stand to greatly improve internal business processes and marketing. Among the biggest advantages is better collaboration with customers, partners, and suppliers, as well as among internal users (see the opening case about Eastern Mountain Sports in Chapter 2; en.wikipedia.org/wiki/WEB_2.0, socialcomputingmagazine.com, and Libert et al. 2008).

Web 2.0
The popular term for advanced Internet technology and applications, including blogs, wikis, RSS, and social bookmarking. One of the most significant differences between Web 2.0 and the traditional World Wide Web is greater collaboration among Internet users and other users, content providers, and enterprises.

REPRESENTATIVE CHARACTERISTICS OF WEB 2.0

The following are representative characteristics of the Web 2.0 environment:

▶ The ability to tap into the collective intelligence of users. The more users contribute, the more popular and valuable a Web 2.0 site becomes.

▶ Data is made available in new or never-intended ways. Web 2.0 data can be remixed or "mashed up," often through Web service interfaces, much the way a dance-club DJ mixes music.

▶ Web 2.0 relies on user-generated and user-controlled content and data.

▶ Lightweight programming techniques and tools let nearly anyone act as a Web site developer.

▶ The virtual elimination of software-upgrade cycles makes everything a *perpetual beta* or work-in-progress and allows rapid prototyping, using the Web as an application development platform.

> ▶ Users can access applications entirely through a browser.
>
> ▶ An architecture of participation and *digital democracy* encourages users to add value to the application as they use it.
>
> ▶ A major emphasis on social networks and computing.
>
> ▶ Strong support of information sharing and collaboration.
>
> ▶ Rapid and continuous creation of new business models (Chesbrough 2006).

Other important features of Web 2.0 are its dynamic content, rich user experience, metadata, scalability, open source basis, and freedom (net neutrality).

Most Web 2.0 applications have a rich, interactive, user-friendly interface based on Ajax (Chapter 18) or a similar framework. Ajax (Asynchronous JavaScript and XML) is an effective and efficient Web development technique for creating interactive Web applications. The intent is to make Web pages feel more responsive by exchanging small amounts of data with the server behind the scenes so that the entire Web page does not have to be reloaded each time the user makes a change. This is meant to increase the Web page's interactivity, loading speed, and usability.

WEB 2.0 COMPANIES AND NEW BUSINESS MODELS

Schonfeld (2006a and 2006b) believes that a major characteristic of Web 2.0 is the global spreading of innovative Web sites and start-up companies. As soon as a successful idea is deployed as a Web site in one country, other sites appear around the globe. Schonfeld presents 23 Web 2.0 sites based in 10 different countries. This section presents some of these sites. Others appear in different chapters of this book. For example, approximately 120 companies specialize in providing Twitter-like services in dozens of countries. An excellent source for material on Web 2.0 is Search CIO's *Executive Guide: Web 2.0* (see searchcio.techtarget.com/general/0,295582,sid19_gci1244339,00.html#glossary).

A new business model that has emerged from Web 2.0 is the accumulation of the "power of the crowd," which was discussed in Chapters 2 and 7. The potential of such a business model is unlimited. For example, wikia.com is working on community-developed Web searches. If they can create a successful one, Google may be in trouble. A key point is the new business model is participation, architecture of which is shown in Exhibit 9.1.

Many companies provide the technology for Web 2.0 activities (see the list of activities in Chapter 2), and dozens of firms have emerged as providers of infrastructure and services to social networking. A large number of start-ups appeared in 2005–2008. Sloan (2007) provides a guide to the 25 hottest Web 2.0 companies and the powerful trends that are driving them. Others are described in Gillin (2007). Sloan's 25 sites, broken down by category, are as follows:

> ▶ **Social media:** StumbleUpon (stumbleupon.com), Slide (slide.com), Bebo (bebo.com), Meebo (meebo.com), and Wikia (wikia.com).
>
> ▶ **Video:** Joost (joost.com), Metacafe (metacafe.com), Dabble (dabble.com), Revision3 (revision3.com), and Blip TV (blip.tv).
>
> ▶ **Mobile tools:** Soonr (soonr.com), TinyPicture (tinypicture.com), Fon (fon.com), and Loopt (loopt.com). (For 20 companies in this area, see Longino 2006.)
>
> ▶ **Advertising:** Adify (adify.com), AdMob (admob.com), Turn (turn.com), Spotrunner (spotrunner.com), and Vitrue (vitrue.com).
>
> ▶ **Enterprise:** SuccessFactors (successfactors.com), JanRain (janrain.com), Logoworks (logoworks.com), Simulscribe (simulscribe.com), and ReardenCommerce (reardencommerce.com).

Several of these companies created new business models. For example, Joost invented a P2P service that sends broadcast-quality video over the Internet (disrupting television providers). One of the major phenomena of Web 2.0 is the rise of mass social media.

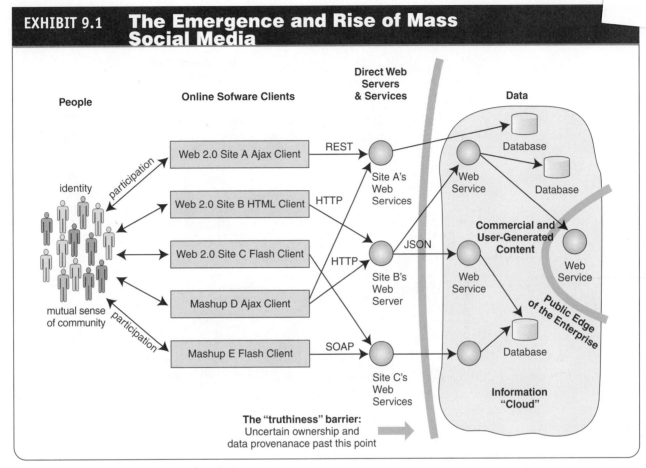

EXHIBIT 9.1   The Emergence and Rise of Mass Social Media

Source: Hinchcliffe, D. *Web 2.0 Blog, web2.wsj2.com.*

SOCIAL MEDIA

Social media refers to the online platforms and tools that people use to share opinions, experiences, insights, and perceptions with each other. Social media can take many different forms, including text, images, audio, or video. The key is that *users*, rather than organizations, control and use the media, often at little or no cost. It is a powerful force of democratization; the network structure enables communication and collaboration on a massive scale. For details on social media, see Hinchcliffe (2006).

Exhibit 9.2 depicts the emergence and rise of mass social media, comparing traditional media with social media. It describes the new tools of social media (e.g., blogs, video blogs, etc.) as being under the consumer's control. With social media, content is produced and consumed by the users. This is in contrast to traditional media, whereby content is created by a company and pushed to or observed by the users. See Blossom (2009) for examples of how social media applications are changing peoples' lives.

Social media and Web 2.0 tools may act as market disruptors.

INDUSTRY AND MARKET DISRUPTORS

Several companies have introduced Web 2.0 innovations that could disrupt and reorder markets, or even entire industries, introducing major changes in the way companies do business. An example is Blue Nile (see case in Chapter 2), which displaced hundreds of jewelers and is changing the jewelry retail industry. Some refer to such companies as disruptors. For example, Zopa (us.zopa.com), which facilitate person-to-person money lending, may disrupt the lending business (see Online File W9.1). Consumer-generated content is disrupting traditional media. Specifically, large numbers of blogs and videos are posted everyday and then viewed by millions around the globe. Content is created continuously by millions of people. The result is that individuals are becoming both publishers of Web-based content and consumers of that content.

social media
The online platforms and tools that people use to share opinions, experiences, insights, perceptions, and various media, including photos, videos, and music, with each other.

disruptors
Companies that introduce a significant change in their industries, thus causing a disruption in normal business operations.

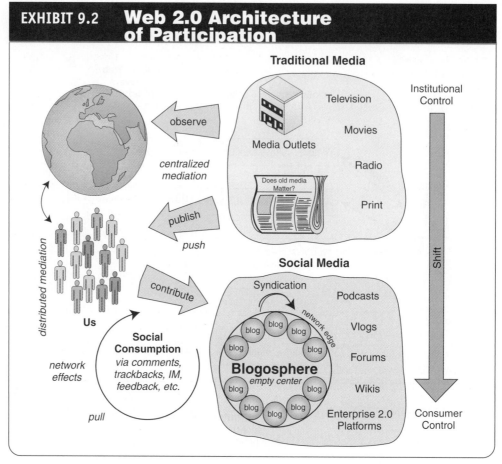

EXHIBIT 9.2   Web 2.0 Architecture of Participation

Source: D. Hinchcliffe, *Web 2.0 Blog, web2.wsj2.com.*

The Disruption Group (see Urlocker 2006) has developed a list of questions to help identify disruptors (see the Disruption Scorecard at ondisruption.com):

1. Is the service or product simpler, cheaper, or more accessible?
2. Does the disruptor change the basis of competition with the current suppliers?
3. Does the disruptor have a different business model?
4. Does the product or service fit with what customers value and pay for?

If the answer to these questions is "yes," service or product may become a major disruptor. Let's look at two examples of industry disruption.

Example: Will Online Wedding Services Disrupt the Traditional Wedding Industry?
Weddings are a big industry. Today, people are using the Internet for a variety of products and services, disintermediating traditional vendors, such as live bands, DJs, and invitation printers.

Couples may create their own playlists on their iPods for use during the wedding ceremony and reception, eliminating the cost of musicians or a band. Couples also save money by using the Internet to comparison shop for wedding supplies (e.g., see theknot.com). Finally, couples can design and buy their wedding rings online (e.g., see bluenile.com).

Many couples create their own wedding sites to keep their guests informed about the wedding plans. They may also create blogs or wikis. Wedding Webcasts are becoming popular, too; couples can broadcast the wedding ceremony on the Web for people who are not able to attend. Wedding videos can be posted on YouTube and pictures on Flickr.

Couples also use the Internet to register for gifts online. Guests can buy the most preferred gifts online from major department stores.

Couples can be very innovative in their use of the Internet. For example, Bernie Peng reprogrammed Tammy Li's favorite video game, "Bejeweled," so that a ring and a marriage proposal would show up on the screen when she reached a certain score. (In this popular game, players score points by swapping gems to form vertical and horizontal chains.) The reprogramming was a tricky task and took him a month. Tammy reached the needed score—and said yes. The couple were married over the 2008 Labor Day weekend and PopCap, the Seattle company that makes "Bejeweled," flew the couple to Seattle as part of their honeymoon. The company also supplied copies of "Bejeweled" to the wedding guests (*CNN.com* 2008).

Example: Real Estate Industry Disruptors. Companies such as Zillow (zillow.com) and HomeGain (homegain.com) are disrupting and real estate industry, providing more services and information than their Web 1.0 counterparts, such as realtor.com and realtytrac.com.

At zillow.com, users can get an estimate of their homes' market value. The market value estimate can be changed by adding extra features to the house's profile. In addition, Zillow provides neighborhood maps that show the estimated values of other homes in the neighborhood (see Team Exercise Problem 1 at the end of this chapter). Users can also list their homes as being for sale. The service is good not only for sellers. For free, buyers can use Zillow to buy a house that is not even on the market, avoiding open houses and bidding wars, and get it cheaper by avoiding commissions.

Will real estate agents be forced to extinction? Some will. More likely, the 6 percent realtor commission paid in the United States will move closer to the 1 percent commission commonly paid in other countries.

Many other disruptors exist. Schonfeld and Morrison (2007) describe 15 disruptors that they believe will change the world (e.g., Blinkx, Zipcar, Expensr). For 10 disruptive IT trends, which include social networks and social media, see the blogs at blogs.cioinsight.com/biztech30/content/future_of_it/top_10_disruptive_it_trends.html and money.cnn.com/galleries/2007/biz2/0708/gallery.next_disruptors.biz2/index.html.

The major application of Web 2.0 is social networks such as MySpace and Facebook. These are based on the concept of *virtual communities*, the topic we present next.

Section 9.1 ▶ REVIEW QUESTIONS

1. Define Web 2.0.
2. List the major characteristics of Web 2.0.
3. Identify the major Web 2.0 technology.
4. Define social media.
5. What is a disruptor? Provide an example.

9.2 VIRTUAL COMMUNITIES

A *community* is a group of people with common interests who interact with one another. A **virtual (Internet) community** is one in which the interaction takes place over a computer network, mainly the Internet. Virtual communities parallel typical physical communities, such as neighborhoods, clubs, or associations, but people do not meet face-to-face. Instead, they meet online. A virtual community is a social network organized around a common interest, idea, task, or goal; members interact across time, geographic, and organizational boundaries to develop personal relationships. Virtual communities offer several ways for members to interact, collaborate, and trade (see Exhibit 9.3). Similar to the EC click-and-mortar model, many physical communities have Web sites to support Internet-related activities that supplement physical activities.

virtual (Internet) community
A group of people with similar interests who interact with one another using the Internet.

CHARACTERISTICS OF TRADITIONAL ONLINE COMMUNITIES AND THEIR CLASSIFICATION

Many thousands of communities exist on the Internet, and the number is growing rapidly. Pure-play Internet communities may have thousands, or even hundreds of millions, of members. MySpace (see Case 1.3 in Chapter 1) grew to 100 million members in just one year. This is one major difference from traditional purely physical communities, which usually are smaller. Another difference is that offline communities frequently are confined to

EXHIBIT 9.3	Elements of Interaction in a Virtual Community
Category	**Element**
Communication	Bulletin boards (discussion groups)
	Chat rooms/threaded discussions (string Q&A)
	E-mail and instant messaging and wireless messages
	Private mailboxes
	Newsletters, "netzines" (electronic magazines)
	Blogging, wikis, and mushups
	Web postings
	Voting
Information	Directories and yellow pages
	Search engine
	Member-generated content
	Links to information sources
	Expert advice
EC element	Electronic catalogs and shopping carts
	Advertisements
	Auctions of all types
	Classified ads
	Bartering online

one geographic location, whereas only a few online communities are geographically confined. For more information on virtual communities, see en.wikipedia.org/wiki/Virtual_community.

Types of Communities

The following are the major types of online communities:

- **Associations.** Many associations have a Web presence. These range from Parent–Teacher Associations (PTAs) to professional associations. An example of this type of community is the Australian Record Industry Association (aria.com.au).

- **Affinity portals.** These are communities organized by interest, such as hobbies, vocations, political parties, unions (e.g., aflcio.org/siteguides/workingfamilies.cfm), and many more. Many communities are organized around a technical topic (e.g., a database) or a product (e.g., Lotus Notes).

- **Ethnic communities.** Many communities are country or language specific. An example of such a site is elsitio.com, which provides content for the Spanish- and Portuguese-speaking audiences in Latin America and the United States. A number of sites, including china.com, hongkong.com, sina.com, and sohu.com, cater to the world's large Chinese-speaking community.

- **Gender communities.** Women.com and ivillage.com, the two largest female-oriented community sites, merged in 2001 in an effort to cut losses and become profitable.

- **Catering to young people (teens and people in their early twenties).** Many companies see unusual opportunities here. Three examples are Alloy.com (alloy.com), Bolt (bolt.com), and BlueSkyFrog (blueskyfrog.com). Alloy.com is based in the United Kingdom and claims to have over 10 million members and reach 17 million more through teen.com, which the company launched in December 2007. Bolt, which operates from the United States, claims to have 12 million members. BlueSkyFrog, which operates from Australia, concentrates on cell phone users and claims to have more than 7 million devoted members.

▶ **Communities of practice.** These can be physical or virtual. Members are professionals and practitioners that share an area of practice (e.g., professors, dentists). Members also share knowledge in discussion groups. An example is Linux Online (linux.org), whose members develop code for the Linux operating system. Learning is an important element of these communities. The community-of-practice concept has become associated with knowledge management, as people have begun to view these communities as a way to develop social capital, nurture new knowledge, stimulate innovation, and share existing knowledge.

▶ **Neighborhood communities.** Some associations and newspapers have created Web sites for local communities. For example, at myadvertiser.com users can check out community events, share photos, and read local news and blogs about seven communities near Honolulu, Hawaii.

▶ **Social networking sites.** These are megacommunities, such as MySpace, Facebook, and Bebo, in which millions of members can express themselves, find friends, exchange photos, view videos, and more. In addition to general-interest communities such as MySpace, interest-based communities have also emerged, such as communities for dog lovers (e.g., doggyspace.com and dogster.com) and cat lovers (catster.com).

▶ **Virtual worlds.** These 3D communities (Chapter 2) are adding many capabilities of social networks (e.g., discussion groups).

Public Versus Private Communities. Communities can be designated as *public*, meaning that their membership is open to anyone. The owner of the community may be a privately held corporation or a public one. Most of the social networks, including MySpace and Facebook belong to the public category.

In contrast, *private* communities belong to a company, an association, or a group of companies and their membership is limited to people who meet certain requirements (e.g., work for a particular employer or work in a particular profession). Private communities may be internal (e.g., only employees can be members) or external.

Example: IBM's Virtual Universe Community. This is a private, internal community of over 5,500 individuals (in January 2009) who are active in virtual worlds. It was launched in 2006 with the goal of moving IBM into a range of new and profitable industries, from the creation of IBM mainframes for virtual worlds to 24-hour virtual service desks staffed by avatars.

Internal and External Private Communities. *Internal communities* exist within organizations. Such communities include employees, retirees, suppliers, and customers who share a common interest. The focus of such communities is on knowledge sharing, collaboration, expert location, and knowledge creation. Companies such as Pfizer, FedEx, Caterpillar, Wells Fargo, and IBM have such communities.

External private communities include one organization and its business partners, government agencies, and prospects. The participants share information on a variety of issues. For example, customers may collaborate around product issues. External private communities have fewer restrictions with regard to participation and security than do internal communities. External communities are used for collaboration, market research, product innovation, or improved customer and suppliers support.

Example: A Virtual World Community. In 2008, Sony launched a virtual community service for its PlayStation 3 (PS3) video game network with 8 million members. The 3D service called Home allows users to create avatars, decorate homes, and interact and socialize with other users in a virtual world. Sony considers this an important part of the game-playing experience. Avatars can interact with each other, and users can play games with friends at a virtual arcade. The community is regional due to language and cultural considerations. As an extension, the service allows downloading of content and movies to PS3.

Other Classifications of Virtual Communities

Virtual communities can be classified in several other ways. One possibility is to classify the members as *traders, players, just friends, enthusiasts,* or *friends in need.* A more common classification recognizes six types of Internet communities: (1) transaction, (2) purpose or interest,

EXHIBIT 9.4   Types of Virtual Communities

Community Type	Description
Transaction and other business activities	Facilitate buying and selling (e.g., *ausfish.com.au*). Combine an information portal with an infrastructure for trading. Members are buyers, sellers, intermediaries, etc., who are focused on a specific commercial area (e.g., fishing).
Purpose or interest	No trading, just exchange of information on a topic of mutual interest. Examples: Investors consult The Motley Fool (*fool.com*) for investment advice; rugby fans congregate at the Fans Room at *nrl.com.au*; music lovers go to *mp3.com*; *geocities.yahoo.com* is a collection of several areas of interest in one place.
Relations or practices	Members are organized around certain life experiences. Examples: *ivillage.com* caters to women and *seniornet.com* is for senior citizens. Professional communities also belong to this category. Examples: *isworld.org* is a space for information systems faculty, students, and professionals.
Fantasy	Members share imaginary environments. Examples: sport fantasy teams at *espn.com*; GeoCities members can pretend to be medieval barons at *dir.yahoo.com/Recreation/games/ role_playing_games/titles*. See *games.yahoo.com* for many more fantasy communities.
Social networks	Members communicate, collaborate, create, share, form groups, entertain, and more. MySpace.com is the leader.
Virtual worlds	Members use avatars to represent them in a simulated 3D environment where they can play, conduct business, socialize, and fantasize.

(3) relations or practices, (4) fantasy, (5) social networks, and (6) virtual worlds. Exhibit 9.4 explains and provides examples of these communities. For issues of participation and design of communities, see en.wikipedia.org/wiki/Virtual_community.

Cashel (2004) proposed another classification of communities, identifying 10 specific niches within the online community space that are bucking the trend and demonstrating strong revenues. These 10 important trends include: (1) search communities, (2) trading communities, (3) education communities, (4) scheduled events communities, (5) subscriber-based communities, (6) community consulting firms, (7) e-mail-based communities, (8) advocacy communities, (9) CRM communities, and (10) mergers and acquisitions activities.

The most popular type of virtual community is the social network, the subject of our next section.

Section 9.2 ▶ REVIEW QUESTIONS

1. Define virtual (Internet) communities and describe their characteristics.
2. List the major types of virtual communities.
3. Distinguish between private and public communities.
4. Distinguish between internal and external communities.

9.3   ONLINE SOCIAL NETWORKING: BASICS AND EXAMPLES

Social networking is built on the idea that there is determinable structure to how people know each other and interact. It has several forms (see Chapter 1). The basic premise is that social networking gives people the power to share, making the world more open and connected. Although social networking is usually practiced in social networks such as MySpace and Facebook, aspects of it also are found in Wikipedia and YouTube.

Let's first define social networks and then look at some of their services provided and capabilities.

A DEFINITION AND BASIC INFORMATION

As you may recall, in Chapter 1 we defined a *social network* as a place where people create their own space, or homepage, on which they write blogs (Web logs); post pictures, videos, or music; share ideas; and link to other Web locations they find interesting. In addition, members of social networks can tag the content they create and post it with keywords they choose themselves, which makes the content searchable. The mass adoption of social networking Web sites points to an evolution in human social interaction (Weaver and Morrison 2008).

A lengthy list of the characteristics and capabilities of social networks was provided in Section 1.3. For more on the definition and history of social networking, see Boyd and Ellison (2007).

The Size of Social Network Sites

Social network sites are growing rapidly, with some having over 100 million members. The typical annual growth of a successful site is 40 to 50 percent in the first few years and 15 to 25 percent thereafter. For a list of the major sites, including user counts, see en.wikipedia.org/wiki/List_of_social_networking_websites. Exhibit 9.5 shows the size of some major social networks as of January 2009.

A Global Phenomenon

Although MySpace and Facebook attract the majority of media attention in the United States, other social networks sites are proliferating and growing in popularity worldwide. For example, Friendster (friendster.com) has gained traction in the Pacific Islands, Orkut (orkut.com) is the premier service in Brazil, Mixi (mixi.jp) has attained widespread adoption in Japan, LunarStorm (lunarstorm.se) has taken off in Sweden, Dutch users have embraced Hyves (hyves.net), and Grono (grono.net) has captured Poland. Hi5 (hi5.com) has been adopted in smaller countries in Latin America, South America, and Europe. Bebo (bebo.com) is very popular in the United Kingdom, New Zealand, and Australia. Additionally, previously popular communication and community services have begun implementing social networking features. For example, the Chinese QQ instant messaging service instantly became the largest social networking service in the world once it added profiles and made friends visible to one another (Boyd and Ellison 2007), and Cyworld cornered the Korean market by introducing homepages and buddies. Note that international entrepreneurs, inspired by the success of the largest social network sites and their capabilities, have created their own local knockoffs. For the copycats of Facebook, LinkedIn, YouTube, and Digg in 10 countries, see *Business 2.0* (2007). For more on social networking around the world, see De Jonghe (2008).

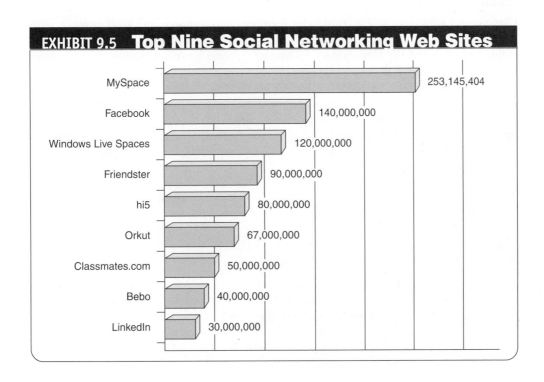

EXHIBIT 9.5 Top Nine Social Networking Web Sites

Site	Members
MySpace	253,145,404
Facebook	140,000,000
Windows Live Spaces	120,000,000
Friendster	90,000,000
hi5	80,000,000
Orkut	67,000,000
Classmates.com	50,000,000
Bebo	40,000,000
LinkedIn	30,000,000

New Business Models

Social networking sites provide innovative business models, ranging from customer reviews of food and night life in India (burrp.com) to users who dress up dolls that look like celebrities (stardoll.com). New revenue models are being created daily. Although some generate limited revenue, others succeed wildly.

Many communities attract advertisers. For example, Vivapets (vivapets.com) attracts pet lovers with Wikipedia-like contributions in its quest to catalog every pet breed. The site attracts about 300,000 unique visitors per month. Obviously, pet-food–related vendors are willing to place ads there.

Social Network Analysis Software

social network analysis software

The mapping and measuring of relationships and information flows among people, groups, organizations, computers, and other information- or knowledge-processing entities. The nodes in the network are the people and groups, whereas the links show relationships or flows between the nodes. SNAs provide both visual and mathematical analyses of relationships.

Social network analysis software is used to identify, represent, analyze, visualize, or simulate network nodes (e.g., agents, organizations, or knowledge) and edges (relationships) from various types of input data (relational and nonrelational), including mathematical models of social networks. Various input and output file formats exist.

Network analysis tools enable researchers to investigate representations of networks of different forms and different sizes, from small (e.g., families, project teams) to very large. Visual representations of social networks are popular and important to understand network data and to convey the results of the analysis.

Some of the representative tools that enable such presentations are:

▶ Business-oriented social network tools such as InFlow and NetMiner
▶ Social Networks Visualizer, or SocNetV, which is a Linux-based open source package

For details, see en.wikipedia.org/wiki/Social_network_analysis_software.

Now let's look at several social networks and sites that provide social networking services.

REPRESENTATIVE SOCIAL NETWORKS SITES AND SERVICES

Here, we provide a sampling of representative social networking sites. Additional information is available at the sites discussed; see Spanbauer (2008) for a list and descriptions of popular social network sites. Some social networking sites are discussed in more detail in Section 9.4. One of the most popular social networking services is YouTube, which is described in detail in Online File W9.2. It is having a large impact on the media and advertising industries.

Classmates Online

Classmates Online (classmates.com) helps members find, connect, and keep in touch with friends and acquaintances they have made throughout their lives, from kindergarten through college, to work and the U.S. military. Classmates Online has more than 40 million active members in the United States and Canada.

The site's basic membership is free and allows users to list themselves to be found and to search the Classmates Online database for friends. Basic members may also post photographs, announcements, and biographies; read community message boards; and learn about upcoming reunions. Gold members, who pay a fee, can also send an e-mail to any member, use Web site tools for planning reunions and events, form private groups, and use My Network to communicate with friends.

The site is owned by United Online, which also operates social networking sites in Germany and Sweden. The site is profitable, generating income from advertisements and membership fees.

Xanga

Xanga (xanga.com), which is operated by Xanga.com, Inc., hosts blogs, photoblogs, and social networking profiles. Users of Xanga are referred to as "Xangans." Xanga's origins can be traced back to 1999, when it was launched as a site for sharing book and music reviews. It has since evolved into one of the most popular blogging and networking services on the Web, with an estimated 40 million users worldwide. In May 2008, Alexa Internet ranked Xanga as the 231st most visited site on the Internet. By April 2009, it was ranked 19th (see vepa.bloggum.com/resim/web20-alexa-rank-changes.html).

A *blogring* connects a circle of Weblogs with a common focus or theme. All Xanga users are given the ability to create a new blogring or join an existing one. Blogrings are searchable by topic. A list of blogrings that the user is associated with appears in a module, typically on the left side of the Web site. Each user is allowed a maximum of eight blogrings.

Digg

Digg (digg.com) is a community-based popularity Web site with an emphasis on technology and science articles (see en.wikipedia.org/wiki/Digg). The site expanded in 2008 to provide a variety of other categories, including politics and videos. It combines social bookmarking, blogging, and syndication with a form of nonhierarchical, democratic editorial control. Users submit news stories and Web sites, and then a user-controlled ranking system promotes these stories and sites to the front page. This differs from the hierarchical editorial system that many other news sites employ. When users read news items, they have the option to "digg it" or "digg that."

Readers can view all the stories that fellow users have submitted in the "digg/All/Upcoming" section of the site. Once a story has received enough "diggs," it appears on Digg's front page. Should the story not receive enough diggs, or if enough users report a problem with the submission, the story will remain in the "digg all" area, from which it may eventually be removed. For additional details, see en.wikipedia.org/wiki/Digg.

Additional Social Networking Sites

The following is a list of interesting social networking sites:

- Piczo.com is a teen-friendly site that is popular in Canada and the United Kingdom.
- Hi5.com is a global, multilanguage, social network popular in Asia and parts of Europe, Africa, and South America.
- Friendsreunited.co.uk connects alumni and helps in organizing reunions. Users can also find dating and employment opportunities.
- Iwiw.net is a Hungarian social networking site with a multilingual interface.
- Migente.com focuses on the American Latino community.
- Blackplanet.com focuses on African American issues and people.
- Grono.net is a Polish social networking site.
- Ning.com provides a platform for users to create their own social networks.

Social networking is strongly related to mobile devices and networks.

MOBILE SOCIAL NETWORKING

Mobile social networking refers to social networking where members converse and connect with one another using cell phones or other mobile devices. A current trend for social networking Web sites such as MySpace and Facebook is to offer mobile services. Some social networking sites offer mobile-only services (e.g., ZYB, Brightkite, and Fon11).

mobile social networking
Members converse and connect with one another using cell phones or other mobile devices.

There are two basic types of mobile social networks. The first type is companies that partner with wireless carriers to distribute their communities via the default start pages on cell phone browsers. For example, users can access MySpace via Cingular's wireless network. The second type is companies that do not have such carrier relationships (also known as "off deck") and rely on other methods to attract users. Examples of this second type include MocoSpace (mocospace.com) and Mobikade (mkade.com).

Windows Live Spaces Mobile can be viewed on mobile devices with limited screen size and slow data connections. It allows users to browse and add photos, blog entries, and comments directly from their mobile devices. However, it has also introduced several other features to improve the user experience with handheld devices. For more information on Windows Live Spaces Mobile, see mobile.spaces.live.com and en.wikipedia.org/wiki/Windows_Live_Spaces_Mobiles.

Mobile social networking is much more popular in Japan, South Korea, and China than it is in the West, generally due to better mobile networks and data pricing (flat rates are widespread in Japan). Most of these Asian networks are extensions of PC-based services, but others are pure mobile-focused offerings. In Japan, where 3G networks have achieved over 80 percent user penetration, the leaders in social networking are mixi (mixi.jp) and Mobage-Town (mbga.jp). Numerous other mobile social networking sites have been launched in Japan.

Experts predict that mobile social networks will experience explosive growth, increasing from 50 million members in 2006 to 174 million in 2011 (Mello 2006). For more predictions, see emarketer.com/reports. The explosion of mobile Web 2.0 services and companies means that many social networks can be based from cell phones and other portable devices, extending the reach of such networks to the millions of people who lack regular or easy access to computers.

With the current software that is available, interactions within mobile social networks are not limited to exchanging simple text messages on a one-to-one basis. In many cases, they are evolving toward the sophisticated interactions of Internet virtual communities.

Mobile Enterprise Networks

Several companies have developed (or fully sponsor) mobile-based social networks. For example, in 2007 Coca-Cola created a social network that could only be accessed by cell phones in an attempt to lure young people to its sodas and other products.

Mobile Community Activities

In many mobile social networks, users can use their mobile devices to create their profiles, make friends, participate in chat rooms, create chat rooms, hold private conversations, and share photos, videos, and blogs. Some companies provide wireless services that allow their customers to build their own mobile community and brand it (e.g., Sonopia at sonopia.com).

Mobile video sharing, which is sometimes combined with photo sharing, is a new technological and social trend. Mobile video-sharing portals are becoming popular (e.g., see myubo.com and myzenplanet.com). Many social networking sites are offering mobile features. For example, MySpace has partnership agreements with a number of U.S. wireless providers to support its MySpace Mobile service. Similarly, Facebook is available in both the United States and Canada via a number of wireless carriers. Bebo has joined forces with O2 Wireless in the United Kingdom and Ireland. This phenomenon is just the next step in the race to establish access to social networking sites across multiple mediums. Some argue that these deals do more to sell mobile phones than to promote the social networking sites; however, the social networks are more than happy to collect the residual attention.

Section 9.3 ▶ REVIEW QUESTIONS

1. Define social network.
2. List some major social network sites.
3. Describe the global nature of social networks.
4. Define social network analysis.
5. Describe Digg.
6. Describe mobile social networking.

9.4 MAJOR SOCIAL NETWORK SERVICES: FROM FACEBOOK TO FLICKR

Now that you are familiar with social network services, let's take a closer look at some of the most popular ones.

FACEBOOK: THE NETWORK EFFECT

Facebook (facebook.com), which was launched in 2004 by former Harvard student Mark Zuckerberg, is the second-largest social network service in the world, with more than 120 million active users worldwide as of January 2009. When Zuckerberg first created Facebook, he had very strong social ambitions and wanted to help people connect to others on the Web.

A primary reason why Facebook has expanded so rapidly is the network effect—more users means more value. As more users become involved in the social space, more people are available to connect with each other. Initially, Facebook was an online social space for college and high school students that automatically connected students to other students at the same school. However,

Facebook realized that it could only keep college and university users for 4 years. In 2006, Facebook opened its doors to anyone age 13 or older with a valid e-mail address. Expanding to a global audience has enabled Facebook to compete directly with MySpace.

The lack of privacy controls (e.g., tools that restrict who sees your profile) was the biggest reason why many people initially resisted joining Facebook. However, in 2008 Facebook introduced controls enabling users to set different levels of access to information about themselves for each of their groups (e.g., family, friends from school, friends from work). For example, only close friends might see your mobile phone number, music favorites, e-mail address, and so forth, whereas other friends might only see the basics of your resume (Abram and Pearlman 2008).

Today, Facebook has a number of applications that support photos, groups, events, marketplaces, posted items, and notes. Facebook also has an application called "People You May Know," which helps users connect with people they might know. More applications are being added constantly. A special feature on Facebook is the News Feed, which enables users to track the activities of friends in their social circles. For example, when a user changes his or her profile, the updates are broadcast to others who subscribe to the feed. Users can also develop their own applications or use any of the millions of Facebook applications that have been developed by other users (Vander Veer 2008).

Facebook is expanding to the rest of the world. In fact, two-thirds of its members are from outside the United States. Even Chinese Premier Wen Jiabao created a profile, and within 2 weeks had more supporters than President Bush. Facebook has adopted a wiki-like approach to translate itself into other languages: Specialists first collect thousands of English words and phrases throughout the site and then members are invited to translate those bits of text into another language. Members then rate the translations, until a consensus is reached. For example, the Spanish version was completed by about 1,500 volunteers in less than a month. The German version was prepared by 2,000 volunteers in less than 2 weeks. In early March 2008, Facebook invited French members to help out. They finished the translations in a few days. The team is continuing to translate to other languages, even relatively small ones (Kirkpatrick 2008).

To generate revenue, Facebook supports advertising for businesses and for developers who offer tools for building applications.

In December 2008, Facebook introduced Facebook Connect, which enables users to login to other sites (e.g., to CitySearch) using their Facebook IDs and to share their activities from these third-party sites with their Facebook friends. For the basics of Facebook and its enterprise efforts, see Abram and Pearlman (2008). For current information, see insidefacebook.com. For a case study, see startup-review.com/blog/facebook-case-study-offline-behavior-drives-online-usage.php.

BEBO

Bebo (bebo.com), an acronym for the phrase "blog early, blog often," was launched in January 2005 and quickly become one of the foremost social networking platforms. Michael and Xochi Birch met in a London bar and started four online businesses that either failed or were minor successes before developing Bebo. Michael, a physicist was the CEO and in charge of programming, and Xochi handled the finance and customer relations. Acknowledging that they had neither business qualifications nor any grasp of marketing, they relied on word-of-mouth for the Web site's popularity. Based in San Francisco, Bebo boasts more than 40 million users who generate billions of page views per month.

Bebo was acquired by AOL for $850 million in March 2008, placing the site alongside MySpace and YouTube, which also were acquired by media conglomerates for enormous sums of money despite possessing mostly intangible property. Similar to Facebook and MySpace, Bebo provides a canvas for users to display personal profiles using such media as photos, diaries, music, embedded video, commercial applications, quizzes, and so forth. It allows its users to add other users as friends who can then view their profiles and post messages. Bebo adopts a private setting whenever a new friend is added, limiting the friend's access to information on the user's profile unless the owner grants special authorization. This tactic ensures more privacy for its users, which has been an issue with social networking sites.

In November 2007, Bebo allowed dozens of business partners (e.g., CBS, BBC, MTV, ESPN) to link to its millions of registered members free of charge. Partners can use Bebo's "channel profiles" to determine how their content is delivered and to encourage communities to grow around it through comments, reviews, forums, blogs, photos, and cross-promotions. In return, users get free and open access to entertainment and news. They can store their favorite music and video content through features such as personal video profiles, which distribute content through "friend networks."

As of January 2009, Bebo faces the challenge of penetrating the North American market, where MySpace and Facebook are both deeply entrenched. Given that social networking sites are so new and that there are so many directions in which they can grow, the idea that this market is becoming mature seems odd. However, the torrid pace at which these sites grow could make it difficult for Bebo to jostle its way into other geographic markets in order to maintain its phenomenal growth rate. This would eventually mean direct competition with sites popular in North America or other foreign market such as Europe, Asia, and Latin America. In 2008 and 2009, Bebo launched a Polish site.

ORKUT: EXPLORING THE VERY NATURE OF SOCIAL NETWORKING SITES

Orkut (orkut.com) was the brainchild of a Turkish Google programmer of the same name. Orkut was to be Google's homegrown answer to MySpace and Facebook. Orkut follows a format similar to that of other major social networking sites; a homepage where users can display every facet of their personal life they desire using various multimedia applications.

A major highlight of Orkut is the individual power afforded to those who create their own groups and forums, which are called "communities." Who can join and how posts are edited and controlled lies solely in the hands of the creator of each community. Moderating an Orkut community is comparable to moderating ones' own Web site, given the authority the creator possesses with regard to design and control of content. Orkut users gain substantial experience with Web 2.0 tools, creating an enormous wave of online proficiency, which is sure to contribute to the development of the online environment.

A number of cultural objections to social networking sites have created controversy for Orkut in various parts of the world, forcing it to make decisions about what the social networking site's rights and responsibilities are, both legally and morally. The nature of the Web allows for freedom of expression; however, some foreign governments and cultures do not cherish this value. Freedom of expression allows people to convey negative comments about governments and to commit what some view as blasphemy. This has caused a number of incidents in India, where local governments have called for the banning of social networking sites, specifically Orkut, which does have hate groups that are difficult to control due to freedom of speech. The Iranian government has banned the use of Orkut, citing national security worries and the dangers of online matchmaking. In response to this state censorship, proxy Orkut sites have emerged in the Middle East, proving that the will of the users ultimately determines how and where online networking takes place. That is the power of the Web.

Orkut recognizes that it is the users who dictate the content of their chosen social networking site. Given this, Orkut has adapted in a number of interesting ways. First, it is adding more languages, expanding the Hindi, Bengali, Marathi, Tamil, and Telugu sites, which expands the popularity of the site and improves the user control over the site. Second, Orkut greets its users on their national and religious holidays with fun features. For example, it wished Indian users a Happy Diwali (en.wikipedia.org/wiki/Diwali) by providing a feature that allowed users to redesign their personal site with Diwali-themed colors and decorations.

Orkut is especially popular in Brazil, where about 30 million members (approximately 67% of all Orkut members) participate in Portuguese (Brazil's official language). Having such a large Brazilian user base has caused legal problems. In 2006, a Brazilian judge ordered Google (the owner of Orkut) to release the user information of more than 20 Brazilians who were suspected of distributing drugs or child pornography or having links to hate speech. The judge ordered that Google be fined $23,000 for every day that the information was not divulged. However, because Google's servers are in the United States and not Brazil, the low court in Brazil agreed that Google is not subject to Brazilian law. Had Google divulged the information, it would have set a precedent and created many questions as to when it would be required to release user information.

Although initially targeted at the U.S. market, Orkut has flourished in some unlikely parts of the world. In addition to Brazil, Orkut receives a large amount of traffic from India, where 15.4 percent of its traffic originates. Orkut also has a strong following in the Middle East (de Mel 2008).

FLICKR TICKS OFF SOME OF ITS USERS

Flickr (flickr.com) was created by a small Vancouver-based company called Ludicorp. The site, which allows for the storage and organization of photos, was launched in 2004 and drew fans who were seeking a place to manage and share their photos. One of the original Web 2.0 applications, Flickr had more than 2 billion images by May 2008, and it continues to grow rapidly.

Initially, users had to have an individual account (free) in order to add friends to their network and to share their photos. When Yahoo! acquired Flickr in 2005, users were not required to obtain a Yahoo! account in order to access their Flickr profile. However, 2 years later Yahoo! required Flickr's users to register with Yahoo!. This stipulation ruffled the feathers of many of Flickr's users, who preferred to have their Flickr content separate from their Yahoo! account. Some users felt that having the accounts remain separate would create a safer and more comfortable environment. Some users were angry because the Yahoo! account requirement would mean that Flickr's users would be bound to Yahoo!'s terms and conditions and be accessible to Yahoo!'s advertisers. Yahoo! claimed the change was largely a strategy to limit the costs of maintaining an independent means of authentication; however, existing users suspect corporate interests are to be credited for the restriction.

Despite some displeasure with corporate ownership and everything that comes with it, Flickr users now enjoy far more applications than could have been provided had the site still been run by Ludicorp, its original owner. The upload restrictions of 2GB have been removed for users with paid ProAccounts, and users with free accounts can now add up to 100MB instead of 20MB. As of April 2008, users can add video clips up to 90 seconds long.

Section 9.4 ▶ REVIEW QUESTIONS

1. Identify the major strategic issues of Facebook (e.g., look at the marketing efforts at insidefacebook.com and at facebook.com).

2. Much of Facebook's early success was due to the close affiliation of its members' networks. How does Facebook expand into new markets *without* losing what originally made the site popular and alienating existing users?

3. What strategies should Bebo pursue in order to compete directly with other social networking sites?

4. What makes Orkut different from other social networks? How should it respond to the demands of local governments that disapprove of some of the ideas and practices associated with social networking sites?

5. Who ultimately deserves the credit for the success of Flickr as a social networking site: the founding developers, the initial users, the corporate backers, Yahoo!, or others?

6. Most social networking sites now offer services similar to those provided by Flickr. Will this cause the demise of Flickr?

9.5 BUSINESS AND ENTERPRISE SOCIAL NETWORKS

Chapter 1 introduced a business-oriented network called Xing (xing.com). This is only one way that enterprises can interact with social networking. Here, we describe other business- and enterprise-oriented networking activities.

DEFINITIONS, CONCEPTS, TYPES, AND EXAMPLES

A **business network** is a group of people who have some kind of commercial or business relationship—for example, the relationships between sellers and buyers, buyers among themselves, buyers and suppliers, and professionals and their colleagues. Such networks of people form enterprise **business social networks**, and they can exist offline or online. Business

business network
A group of people who have some kind of commercial relationship; for example, sellers and buyers, buyers among themselves, buyers and suppliers, and colleagues and other colleagues.

business social network
A social network whose primary objective is to facilitate business connections and activities.

networking can take place outside of traditional corporate physical environments. For example, public places such as airports or golf courses provide opportunities to make new face-to-face business contacts if an individual has good social skills. Similarly, the Internet is also proving to be a good place to network. The most popular business-oriented social network service is LinkedIn (see closing case in this chapter).

Commercial activities related to social networks are on the rise. An increasing number of people and companies are engaged in *business-oriented social networking*, which refers to business activities, especially marketing and operations, by which business opportunities are created through social networks of businesspeople. For example, people might offer to help others to find connections rather than "cold-calling" on prospects themselves (see en.wikipedia.org/wiki/Business_network).

Recall from Chapter 1 that we distinguished *business-oriented social networks* from *enterprise social networks*, which are social networks owned and operated within one enterprise, whose members are usually the employees of that enterprise. An example of an enterprise social network is IBM's Beehive (to be described later).

BUSINESS SOCIAL NETWORKING: CONCEPTS AND BENEFITS

Many professionals contend that business networking is a more cost-effective method of generating new business than advertising or public relations efforts. This is because networking, especially when done online, is a low-cost activity that involves more personal commitment than just the company spending of money.

As an example, a business network may agree to meet weekly or monthly (offline or online) with the purpose of exchanging business leads and referrals with fellow members. To complement this activity, members often meet outside this circle, on their own time, and build their own "one-to-one" relationships with the fellow members. As these relationships become stronger, the exchange of business increases.

The major reasons to use or deploy a business social network are:

- To build better customer relationships
- To improve knowledge management
- To facilitate recruiting and retention
- To increase business opportunities
- To build a community
- To gain expert advice
- To improve tradeshow experiences
- To improve communication and collaboration

Many believe that the ability to communicate and collaborate with people both inside and outside the company via social networking is a key business differentiator that may enable a company to outperform the competition by allowing it to see opportunities that others miss.

Types of Business-Oriented Social Networking

Social networking activities can be conducted both in private and public social networking sites, as well as in internal and external communities. For example, Xing (see Chapter 1) is an example of a public business-oriented network, whereas Facebook is primarily a public social network for social-oriented activities. However, Facebook allows its members to conduct business-oriented activities.

The following are some business-oriented social networks:

- **Ryze.** Similar to LinkedIn, with Ryze (ryze.com) users create profiles that can be viewed and invite friends and business associates into special-interest "tribes."
- **The Business Social Network.** A social network site (thebusinesssocialnetwork.com) that connects businesspeople who want to make connections and identify businesses with similar goals, products, or services. It is a clone of LinkedIn, operating mainly in the UK.
- **Viadeo.** Viadeo (viadeo.com) is a network of over 3 million professionals, mostly in Europe and China. Its primary use is for connecting with business contacts. It is a European clone of LinkedIn, with an emphasis on localization.

▶ **APSense.** APSense (apsense.com) is a business social network where people get paid to come together to share their business through networking, deciding, exploring and creating quality business content. Users build their own social networks by inviting their friends to APSense. Friends of friends can also be placed in users' networks.

Several other networks similar to LinkedIn have been launched: Wealink (wealink.com) in China, Rediff Connexions (connexions.rediff.com) in India, International Jobs and Internships (ihipo.com) in Mexico, and Moikrug (moikrug.ru) in Russia.

ENTERPRISE SOCIAL NETWORKS

An increasing number of companies have created their own social networks for their employees, former employees, and/or customers. Such networks are considered to be "behind the firewall," and are often referred to as *corporate social networks*. For an overview, see McAfee (2006).

Such networks come in several formats, depending on their purpose, the industry, the country, and so forth. McGillicuddy (2006) describes the following guidelines regarding enterprise social networking activities:

> ▶ Allow employees to collaborate and communicate in an employee-driven system (e.g., see the closing case of this chapter).
>
> ▶ Promote the use of enterprise wikis via demonstrations.
>
> ▶ Set up internal blogs and incorporate them into internal directories so users can see who has a blog.
>
> ▶ Set up enterprise social bookmarking systems so users can see what sort of content their colleagues are tagging.
>
> ▶ CIOs should be involved from the beginning to make sure the right infrastructure and tools are in place.

For tutorials on enterprise social networks, see Hinchcliffe (2006) and web2.0central.com. Additional tips and sources are available at cio.com/article/print/115250. Brandel (2008) offers details on Deloitte's DStreet and Best Buy's Blue Shirt Nation.

Let's look at two examples of enterprise social networks.

Example: IBM'S Beehive. IBM's Beehive is an internal social networking site that gives IBMers a rich connection to the people they work with on both a personal and a professional level. Beehive helps employees make new connections, track current friends and coworkers, and renew contacts with people they have worked with in the past. When employees join Beehive, they get a profile page. They can use the status message field and the free-form "About Me" section on their profile page to let other people at IBM know where they are, what they are doing, and even what they are thinking. Employees can use Beehive to find out what team members they spent late nights with a couple of years ago working toward a deadline are doing now by checking out their coworkers' profiles.

Employees can also use Beehive to post photos, create lists, and organize events. If users are hosting an event, they can create an event page in Beehive and invite people to attend. The page can be a place to spread the buzz about the event and get people talking about it through the comments feature.

Users can create top-five lists, called "hive fives," to share their thoughts on any topic they are passionate about. For example, they can add a "hive five" list that outlines their ideas about their project, and then invite their team members to examine the list and voice their opinion.

Beehive can also come in handy when preparing for conference calls. If users do not know the other people on the call, they can check out the participants' Beehive profiles beforehand and find out if they have common interests, either work-related or recreational, or if they have colleagues in common.

In addition to the social goal, the Beehive team created the site to help IBM employees to meet the challenge of building the relationships vital to working in large, distributed enterprises. Beehive can help IBMers discover people with common interests or the right skills for a project. Learning more about someone—personally and professionally—facilitates making contact and might entice people to learn about ongoing projects and activities beyond their immediate project.

Beehive is related to the IBM's Innovation Jam project (see Chapter 7 and Bjelland and Wood 2008). For additional details, see domino.research.ibm.com/cambridge/research.nsf/ 99751d8eb5a20c1f852568db004efc90/8b6d4cd68fc12b52852573d1005cc0fc?OpenDocument and Brandel (2008).

Example: Wachovia/Wells Fargo. Wachovia (wachovia.com) is a large financial holding company (now a part of Wells Fargo Bank). Wachovia introduced its social networking service to its 110,000 employees in early 2008. Like the popular Facebook service, the network allows users to upload photos of themselves—not just corporate ID mug shots either—and personal information. One of the goals of the project is community-building across the vast company.

The network is entirely business oriented. Think of it as a nervous system for the enterprise, one that gets more valuable the more it is used. Wachovia envisions a sophisticated knowledge-management platform integrated with multiple applications to let workers locate information—and the people who use it—simply and intuitively. Employees can look up coworkers and see their relationships to other employees and departments and determine their availability at any given moment. Employees can also search for the best practices by topic and review blogs and wikis written by informed employees. An in-house encyclopedia also is available.

Interfacing with Social Networks

Enterprises can interface with public and/or private social networks in several ways. One way is participating in business-oriented public networks, such as LinkedIn, or in enterprise social networks. Companies can interface with social networking in several other ways as well. The major interfaces are shown in Exhibit 9.6.

Companies can interface with social networks in the following ways:

> ▶ Use existing public social networks, such as Facebook or MySpace, or virtual worlds, such as Second Life to create pages and microcommunities; advertise products or services; and post requests for advice, job openings, and so forth. (For examples, see Weber 2007 and Demopoulos 2007.)
>
> ▶ Create an in-house private social network and then use it for communication and collaboration among employees and retirees or with outsiders (e.g., customers, suppliers, designers). Employees create virtual rooms in their company's social networks where they can use applications to share information (e.g., see wiki.oracle.com).
>
> ▶ Conduct business activities in a business-oriented social network (such as LinkedIn) or sponsor such a site.
>
> ▶ Create services for social networks, such as software development, security, consulting services, and more (e.g., Oracle, IBM, Microsoft).
>
> ▶ Use Web 2.0 tools, mostly blogs, wikis, workspaces, and team rooms, and create innovative applications for both internal and external users (see the opening case for Chapter 2).
>
> ▶ Create and/or participate in a social marketplace (such as fotolia.com).

Many large corporations, including IBM, Wells Fargo, Coca-Cola, Cisco, and Deloitte Touche, have developed innovative in-house social networks. Others create groups within MySpace or other social networks (see Weber 2007, Demopoulas 2007, and Cone 2007b for examples). For a more detailed description of one innovative application used for recruiting, see Online File W9.3.

Some corporate-based social networks do not fly. They simply do not attract enough members and/or visitors. An example is Wal-Mart's failed attempt at a corporate social network (see Section 9.6).

EXHIBIT 9.6 Interactions in Social Networks

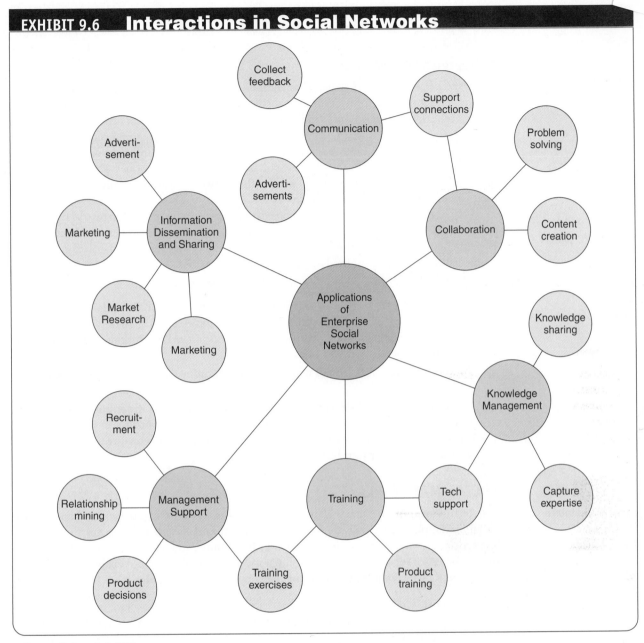

Source: Turban et al. 2008.

OTHER SOCIAL NETWORKING STRUCTURES

Several other social networking structures exist. Here we present three of them.

Enterprise 2.0

Enterprise social networking, including the various ways that companies interact with Web 2.0 tools and social networks, has resulted in an IT strategy where companies are not only digital enterprises, but *enterprises 2.0*. Enterprise 2.0 refers to collaboration within enterprises via Web 2.0 tools such as blogs and wikis. Thousands of companies use Web 2.0. For example, Motorola supports 3,900 blogs. Procter & Gamble uses Microsoft SharePoint and Office Communications for the company's 140,000 employees, many of whom use blogs.

According to an *InformationWeek* survey of business technology experts, the most useful Web 2.0 tools in Enterprise 2.0 are instant messaging (69%), collaborative tools (61%), integrated search tools (56%), unified communication (49%), wikis (47%), and mashups (43%). Also of importance were Ajax (Chapter 18), RSSs, blogs, and presence awareness (30% to 40% each). The experts identified the following major concerns with Enterprise 2.0: security

Enterprise 2.0
Technologies and business practices that free the workforce from the constraints of legacy communication and productivity tools such as e-mail. Provides business managers with access to the right information at the right time through a Web of interconnected applications, services, and devices.

issues (64%), lack of expertise (56%), integration with existing IT systems (52%), and diffi-culty in proving ROI (51%) (Hoover 2007). For more on Enterprise 2.0, see McAfee (2006).

Entrepreneurial Networks

Entrepreneurial networks are social organizations offering various types of resources to start or improve entrepreneurial projects or new businesses. Entrepreneurial networks bring together a broad selection of professionals and resources that complement each others' endeavors (see en.wikipedia.org/wiki/Entrepreneurial_network) with the goal of aiding successful business launches. Entrepreneurs can use such networks to find invaluable information on how to run a business as well as how to differentiate the business from similar ones. Promotion of each member's talents and services both within the network and out in the broader market increases opportunities for all participants.

One of the key needs of any start-up is capital, and entrepreneurial networks often focus help in obtaining financial resources particularly tailored to their membership demographic. Entrepreneurial networks also may be involved in endorsing reforms, legislation, or other municipal drives that accommodate the organization's goals.

The following are examples of entrepreneurial networks:

▶ Ecademy (ecademy.com) is a global social network for business professionals. Participants can build trust with other business professionals; share contacts, knowl-edge, and support; find jobs, prospects, and clients; attend networking events; and trade across the globe.

▶ European Young Professionals (eyplondon.org) promotes links between European busi-ness professionals.

▶ PartnerUp is an online community that helps members find business partners, co-founders, executives, and board members; network with other entrepreneurs and small businesses; and ask for and offer up advice; find commercial real estate; and find service providers for your business.

SOCIAL MARKETPLACES

social marketplace

The term is derived from the combination of *social networking* and *marketplace*. An online community that harnesses the power of one's social networks for the introduc-tion, buying, and selling of products, services, and resources, including one's own creations. Also may refer to a structure that resembles a social net-work but is focused on individual members.

The term **social marketplace** is derived from *social networking* and *marketplaces*. Thus, a social marketplace essentially acts like an online intermediary that harnesses the power of one's social networks for introducing, buying, and selling products and services and mobiliz-ing resources for social networking. Ideally, a social marketplace should enable the marketing of members' own creations. Examples of social marketplaces include:

▶ **Craigslist.** Craigslist can be considered a social network marketplace in that it provides online classifieds in addition to supporting social activities (meetings, dating, events) (see Chapter 2).

▶ **Fotolia.** Fotolia (fotolia.com) is a social marketplace for a huge community of creative people who enjoy sharing, learning, and expressing themselves through images, forums, and blogs. Members provide royalty-free stock images that other individuals and profes-sionals can legally buy and share.

▶ **Flipsy.** Anyone can use Flipsy (flipsy.com) to list, buy, and sell books, music, movies, and games. It was created to fill the need for a free and trustworthy media marketplace. Flipsy does not charge commissions in order to foster increased trading. Payment processing is handled by a third party, such as PayPal.

Section 9.5 ▶ REVIEW QUESTIONS

1. What is a business-oriented network?

2. What is an entrepreneurial network?

3. Define enterprise social network.

4. List six ways organizations can interface with Web 2.0 tools and social networks.

5. What is a social marketplace?

9.6 COMMERCIAL ASPECTS OF WEB 2.0 AND SOCIAL NETWORKING APPLICATIONS

Implementing Web 2.0 applications, especially social networks and similar communities, attracts a large number of visitors. Therefore, it provides an opportunity for vendors to advertise (see Chapter 4) and try to sell to community members.

WHY IS THERE AN INTEREST?

Web 2.0 applications are spreading rapidly, and many of them cater to a specific *segment* of the population (e.g., music lovers, travelers, game lovers, and cars fans), enabling segmented advertising. Finally, many users of Web 2.0 tools are young, and they will grow older and have more money to spend (see Regan 2006). For these reasons, many believe that social networks, blogging, and other Web 2.0 activities will play a major role in the future of e-commerce. In this section, we describe a few areas where success is already evidence.

Retailers stand to benefit from online communities in several important ways:

▶ Consumers can provide feedback on the design of proposed or existing products, on marketing and advertising campaigns, and on how well customer service and support are performing, which can lead to improvements and innovations for manufacturers and retailers.

▶ Word-of-mouth (i.e., *viral marketing*) is free advertising that can increase the visibility of niche retailers and products.

▶ Increased Web site traffic, a common effect of viral marketing, inevitably brings more ad dollars with it.

▶ Increased sales can come from harnessing techniques based on personal preferences such as collaborative filtering. At a more advanced level, retailers strive for a higher degree of relevance in matching the knowledge of one person to someone of like interests who has a need to know (the "twinsumer" concept), as described in Chapter 4.

The strategic use of online communities can increase revenue and profit. Case 9.1 describes some of the potential revenue sources created by EC in social networks.

CASE 9.1

EC Application

REVENUE SOURCES AT YOUTUBE

Some experts think that Google paid too much for YouTube, especially in light of its copyright-related legal problems (see Online File W9.2). However, Google may actually have gotten a bargain. Consider the following:

▶ **2-minute YouTube clips were just the start.** As television comes to the Internet, dozens of companies are competing to become the networks of tomorrow. Whichever networks attract the most viewers will inevitably attract vast numbers of advertisers as well. YouTube's ad revenue in 2007 alone has been valued at $200 million by eMarketer and Citigroup. And wherever there's video programming, viewers will be seeing more video ads. One forecast from eMarketer predicts that overall video advertising on the Web (including video

ads replacing banners on regular Web pages) will reach $4.6 billion in 2013, a sevenfold leap from the 2006 total of $410 million (Seeking Alpha 2009).

▶ **Brand-created entertainment content.** In 2005, Nike produced a pseudo-home video of football star Ronaldinho practicing while wearing his new Nike Gold shoes. In 1 week, the clip was downloaded 3.5 million times on YouTube (worldwide), providing Nike with tremendous exposure to its core, mostly young male, audience. As the younger generation moves away from traditional TV, it is shifting its attention to YouTube and similar offerings.

▶ **User-driven product advertising.** User-generated videos could be leveraged in a similar manner to product placement on TV. For example, although not intentional, a 17-year-old

(continued)

girl's use of Logitech's Webcam features in a short clip on YouTube where she talks about the breakup with her boyfriend greatly contributed to awareness of Logitech's offerings. The product placement trend is also expanding across the blogosphere, with Nokia promoting its new smartphone through the 50 most influential bloggers in Belgium and establishing a blogger-relationship blog.

▶ **Multichannel word-of-mouth campaign.** When Chevrolet decided to combine its *Apprentice* Tahoe Campaign with an online consumer-generated media (CGM) campaign, it did not anticipate the additional viral impact of YouTube. On the Chevrolet site, users could create their own customized video commercial, complete with text and background music. Environmentalists took the opportunity to produce spoof videos and published them on YouTube.

However, the word-of-mouth advertising Chevrolet received on YouTube was ultimately beneficial to Chevrolet. The Chevrolet site generated 4 million page views, 400,000 unique visitors, and 22,000 ad submissions in just 6 months.

Sources: Compiled from Sahlin and Botello (2007) and Seeking Alpha (2009).

Questions

1. List the different advertising models on YouTube.
2. List the success factors from these cases.
3. How do users benefit from using YouTube?

ADVERTISING USING SOCIAL NETWORKS, BLOGS, AND WIKIS

Many advertisers are placing ads on MySpace, Facebook, and YouTube or are using Google AdSense with user searches in social networking sites. Although a social media campaign may have a small impact on actual online retail sales, it may have huge benefits with regard to increasing brand awareness.

Facebook features hundreds of thousands of third-party software applications on its site. One popular application area is travel. For example, one application is "Where I've Been," a map that highlights places where users have visited or hope to visit. You can plan trips, group travel, and find and rate free in-home accommodation (at CouchSwap). This information can be sold to travel-oriented vendors, who in turn advertise their products to Facebook members.

Viral (Word-of-Mouth) Marketing

Young adults are especially good at viral marketing. If members like a certain product or service, word-of-mouth advertising works rapidly. What they like can spread very quickly— sometimes to millions of people at a minimal cost to companies (e.g., see Weber 2007). For example, YouTube conducted almost no advertising in its first few months, but millions joined because of word-of-mouth marketing.

Example. An example of viral marketing on social networks is provided by McNichol (2007b) who describes the story of Stormhoek Vineyards (stormhoek.com). The company first offered a free bottle of wine to bloggers. About 100 of these bloggers posted voluntary comments about the winery on their own blogs within six months. Most had positive comments that were read by other bloggers.

viral blogging
Viral marketing done by bloggers.

According to Megna (2007), many retailers are capitalizing on word-of-mouth marketing by bloggers. When viral marketing is done by bloggers, it is referred to as **viral blogging**. For details, see Demopoulos (2007).

The Stormhoek example raises an interesting question: Can bloggers be bought? The criticism is that bloggers are not required to disclose that they are being paid for their endorsements. According to Wagner (2006), companies can pay bloggers to endorse products via an intermediary such as PayPerPost.

Example: PayPerPost. PayPerPost (payperpost.com) runs a marketplace where advertisers can find bloggers, video bloggers, online photographers, and podcasters willing to endorse the advertisers' products.

A company with a product or a service to advertise registers with PayPerPost and describes what it wants. A sneaker company, for example, might post a request for people willing to write a 50-word blog entry about their sneakers or upload a video of themselves playing basketball wearing the sneakers. The company also says what it is willing to pay for the posting.

Bloggers create the blog post (or whatever content is requested) and inform PayPerPost, which checks to see that the content matches what the advertiser asked for, and PayPerPost arranges payment. Note that the bloggers are required to disclose that they are being paid for their posting.

Classified Ads, Job Listings, and Recruitment

MySpace has provided classifieds and job listings since fall 2005, competing with Craigslist and CareerBuilder. According to O'Malley (2006), MySpace is already a large force in e-commerce, sending more traffic to shopping and classified sites than MSN, and it is fast closing in on Yahoo!, Facebook, LinkedIn, and many other social networks that offer classifieds and job listings as well. Google partnered with eBay in 2006 to roll out "click-to-call" advertising across Google and eBay sites—a deal that is expanding to MySpace's giant network.

One interesting example is Salesforce.com (salesforce.com). The CRM software company has partnered with Facebook to allow Salesforce.com customers to build applications on its Force.com platform inside Facebook. For example, employees could embed a recruitment application within their Facebook page, and then use their social connections to recruit new employees for their company.

Special Advertising Campaigns

Some retailers have successfully used the fall back-to-school season as a social networking focus. For example, in fall 2008 JCPenney created an online game called Dork-Dodge for girls in Facebook. Players had to navigate their way past undesirable boyfriends to get to their dream date. The retailer also had an interactive video (a modern-day take on the movie *The Breakfast Club*) where users could choose clothes from JCPenney for the actors. Similarly, Sears had a fall 2008 marketing campaign that featured actress Vanessa Hudgens from *High School Musical* playing various characters to show the different styles that could be put together with clothing from Sears.

Shoppers at Sears.com have the option of sharing prom dresses with their Facebook friends using a feature called Prom Premier 2008. Sears supplemented the option with an ad campaign on Facebook. Sears is using the program to test the benefits of melding EC with social networking. The company is monitoring the clickstream at the site using Web analytics tools. Many of MySpace's most popular pages are from e-tailers who stock the site with low-cost cosmetics, other Web site ads, and the like. The advertisement value is $140 million or more per year and growing rapidly (Kafka 2007).

MySpace lets brand owners create profile pages for their property. For example, the Burger King mascot, "The King," has a MySpace page. This has been a tremendous success.

MySpace is starting its own *behavioral targeting*, which is similar to collaborative filtering (Chapter 4). Based on the members' voluntary information on what they like and what they do not, MySpace serves up its users to relevant advertisers with the users' permission. For example, DaimlerChrysler's Jeep already has its own MySpace page from which it can conduct sales campaigns to targeted individuals.

Mobile Advertising

Mobile advertising is a rapidly developing area. It refers to advertisement on cell phones and other mobile devices. The competition for mobile ad revenue is intensifying; especially with the increased use of cell phones with access to the Internet. Recently, watching video clips has become popular on cell phones. Advertisers are starting to attach ads to these video clips (see Chapter 4).

SHOPPING IN SOCIAL NETWORKS

Shopping is a natural area for social networks to become involved in. Although shopping in social networks is only beginning to grow, it has enormous potential. Consider the following examples:

- MySpace's music-download service allows the site's independent musicians to sell their work directly from their profile pages. Snocap, a copyright-services company cofounded by Napster creator Shawn Fanning, supports the project. MySpace and Snocap get a cut of every piece of music sold. By allowing users to self-publish, MySpace has become a launching pad for about 3 million musicians, from garage bands to big names. MySpace is also doing it with its Japanese site, where 90,000 musicians and games writers are trying to fulfill the demand for their services.
- The users of this model actually create an EC storefront in their Facebook page in just a few minutes.
- In 2006, Google signed an agreement to pay more than $900 million in ad revenue over 5 years to MySpace for the right to serve searches inside MySpace. The deal includes the extension of Google's checkout payment service (enabling customers to pay once for several vendors) to MySpace.
- YouTube joined Amazon.com and Apple's iTunes in creating the eCommerce Platform. YouTube sells music and games from iTunes and Amazon.com's stores on its site (see the "click-to-buy" icon). YouTube adds more products and vendors continuously.

An overview of selling in social networks is provided by Jefferies (2008), who cites the following drivers (by decreasing level of importance) of selling in social networks:

- Pressure to increase top-line revenue growth
- Efforts to improve overall sales productivity
- Need to compete with increasing customer and prospect knowledge of products and competitive differentiators

For more on social shopping, see genuinevc.com/archives/2006/11/the_meaning_of_2.htm and blog.comtaste.com.

FEEDBACK FROM CUSTOMERS: CONVERSATIONAL MARKETING

Companies are starting to utilize Web 2.0 tools to get feedback from customers. This trend is referred to as *conversational marketing*. In Chapter 4, we described customer feedback via questionnaires, focus groups, and other methods. However, Web 2.0 enables customers to supply feedback via blogs (e.g., see bloombergmarketing.blogs.com/Bloomberg_marketing), wikis, online forums, chat rooms, and social networking sites.

Companies are finding that these tools not only generate faster and cheaper results than traditional focus groups, but also foster closer customer relationships. For example, Macy's quickly removed a metal toothbrush holder from its product line after receiving several complaints about it online (see Gogoi 2007). Companies like Dell are also learning that conversational marketing is less expensive and yields quicker results than focus groups. The computer maker operates a feedback site called IdeaStorm, where it allows customers to suggest and vote on improvements in its offerings.

Cookshack and many other companies operate online forums. Cookshack (forum.cookshack.com/groupee) invites customers to ask and answer questions about barbecue sauces, beef smokers, barbecue ovens, and cooking techniques. The community helps save money by freeing up customer-service personnel who used to answer such questions by phone or e-mail. The community also fosters customer loyalty.

With *enterprise feedback management*, companies are interested not only in collecting information, but also in the interaction between customers and company employees and in properly distributing customer feedback throughout the organization.

According to Gogoi (2007), retailers know that customers, especially the younger and more Net-savvy ones, want to be heard, and they also want to hear what others like them say.

Increasingly, retailers are opening up their Web sites to customers, letting them post product reviews, ratings, and in some cases photos and videos. The result is that *customer reviews* are emerging as a prime place for online shoppers to visit.

Marketing companies have longed for years to have a window on how consumers use their products in order to better develop new product and improve marketing. Customer reviews have long been part of cutting-edge sites such as Amazon.com and Netflix. By the end of 2006, 43 percent of EC sites offered customer reviews and ratings. In addition, as many as 50 percent of customers 18 to 34 years old have posted a comment or review on products they have bought or used. A large part of the reason for this achievement is the influence of social computing and the success of sites such as MySpace, Facebook, and YouTube.

Example: Del Monte. Del Monte, through its "I Love My Dog program," gathers data from pet owners that can help shape its marketing decisions. Its private social network helps Del Monte make decisions about products, test market campaigns, understand buying preferences, and generate discussions about new items and product changes.

Example: PETCO. PETCO operates approximately 800 pet supply stores in the United States. PETCO launched an external enterprise social network, mainly for customers, that included customer reviews as early as October 2005. PETCO noticed that customers who clicked on the highest customer-rated products were 49 percent more likely to buy something. PETCO also noticed that top customer-rated pet toys and other items draw more customers, even if the new customers weren't necessarily planning on buying them; people trust someone else's opinion that is independent of the manufacturer or retailer.

PETCO's experience is not unique. According to an eVoc Insights study, 47 percent of consumers consult reviews before making an online purchase, and 63 percent of shoppers are more likely to purchase from a site if it has ratings and reviews. Negative reviews not only help the retailer address a defect or poorly manufactured item, they also help decrease the number of returns. People are less likely to return an item due to personal expectation because reviews give realistic views of a product and its characteristics (see Gogoi 2007 for details).

COMMERCIAL ACTIVITIES IN BUSINESS AND ENTERPRISE SOCIAL NETWORKS

Although advertising and sales are the major EC activities in public social networks, there are emerging possibilities for commercial activities in business-oriented networks such as LinkedIn and in enterprise social networks.

Recognizing the opportunities, many software vendors are developing Web tools and applications to support enterprise social networking. For example, IBM Lotus (see Chapter 6) is encouraging its 5,000-plus solution providers who are working with Notes/Domino, Sametime, and other Lotus software to add Lotus Connections to their product lineups, building applications based on social networking technology.

Representative areas and examples of enterprise social networking follow.

Finding and Recruiting Workers

Most of the public social networks, especially the business-oriented ones, facilitate recruiting and job finding (see Hoover 2007). For example, recruiting is a major activity at LinkedIn (closing case of this chapter) and was the driver for the site's development. To be competitive, companies must look at the global market for talent, and they can use global social networking sites to find it. Large companies are using their in-house social networks to find in-house talent for vacant positions.

For more on recruitment and job finding in social networks, see Chapter 3, Millard (2008), and blogs.techrepublic.com.com/career/?p=398&tag=nl.e10.

Management Activities and Support

Applications in this category are related to supporting managerial decision making based on analysis of data collected in social networks. Some typical examples include identifying key performers, locating experts and finding paths to access them, soliciting ideas and possible solutions to complex problems, and finding and analyzing candidates for management succession planning. For example, Deloitte Touche Tohmatsu set up a social network to assist its human resources managers in downsizing and regrouping teams. Hoover's has established a social network that uses Visible Path's technology to identify target business users for relationship building and to reach specific users. The Advances in Social Network Analysis and Mining conference on the use of data mining in social networks (July 2009 in Athens, Greece) has been dedicated to the topic.

Training

Several companies use enterprise social networking, and virtual worlds in particular, for training purposes. For example, Cisco is trying to use its virtual campus in Second Life for product training and executive briefings. IBM runs management and customer interaction training sessions in Second Life, too.

Knowledge Management and Expert Location

Applications in this category include activities such as knowledge discovery, creation, maintenance, sharing, transfer, and dissemination. An elaborate discussion on the role of discussion forums, blogs, and wikis for conversational knowledge management can be found in Wagner and Bolloju (2005). Other examples of these applications include expert discovery (see Chapter 7) and mapping communities of expertise.

Consider the following examples of social networking for KM and expert location:

- Innocentive (innocentive.com), a social network with over 150,000 participating scientists, specializes in solving science-related problems (for cash rewards).
- Northwestern Mutual Life created an internal social network where over 7,000 financial representatives share captured knowledge (using Awareness.com blogging software).
- Caterpillar created a knowledge network system for its employees, and it even markets the software to other companies.

Companies also are creating *retiree corporate social networks* to keep retirees connected with each other and with the organization. These people possess huge amounts of knowledge that can be tapped for productivity increases and problem solving (e.g., Alumni Connect from SelectMinds). With 64 million people retiring within the next few years (per the Conference Board), preserving their knowledge is critical.

Enhancing Collaboration

Collaboration in social networking is done both internally, among employees from different units working in virtual teams for example, and externally, when working with suppliers, customers, and other business partners. Collaboration is done mostly in forums and other types of groups and by using wikis and blogs. A list of blogging applications is provided in Section 2.6. For details on collaboration in social networks, see Chapter 6 and Coleman and Levine (2008).

Using Blogs and Wikis Within the Enterprise

In Chapter 2, we provided some examples of blogs and wikis used within enterprises. For examples of how wikis are used within enterprises, see Online File W9.4. The use of these tools is expanding rapidly. Jefferies (2008) reports on a study that shows that 71 percent of the best-in-class companies use blogs and 64 percent use wikis for the following applications:

- Project collaboration and communication (63%)
- Process and procedure document (63%)
- FAQs (61%)
- E-learning and training (46%)
- Forums for new ideas (41%)
- Corporate-specific dynamic glossary and terminology (38%)
- Collaboration with customers (24%)

EXHIBIT 9.7   Generating Revenue from Web 2.0 Applications

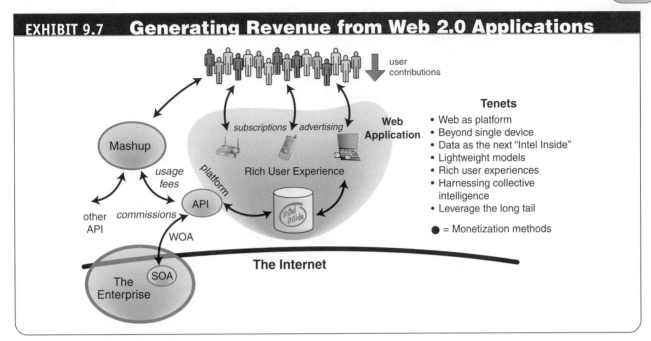

Source: D. Hinchcliffe, *Web 2.0 Blog*, web2.wsj2.com.

REVENUE-GENERATION STRATEGIES IN SOCIAL NETWORKS

The following are some interesting ways social networks generate revenue: (1) offer premium service to individuals for a monthly or per service fee; (2) partner with organizations that pay a monthly service fee; (3) create affiliations with physical venues where members can meet (e.g., meetup.com). Physical venues, such as coffee shops, may pay a fee to be affiliated with the social network.

Exhibit 9.7 illustrates how Web 2.0 applications can generate revenue. It shows users' contributions and the relationships among people, advertising, and Web 2.0 tools, such as mashups. The Web applications may generate revenue via subscription fees and advertisements. To learn more on how a blogs can bring in big money, see Weber (2007) and Zimmerman (2007).

In addition, Web 2.0 tools can generate revenue growth, user growth, and increased resistance to competition in indirect ways, which, in turn, lead to increased subscriptions, advertising, and commission revenue. Consider the following ways that organizations can leverage Web 2.0 tools:

- **Strategic acquisitions.** Identify and acquire Web 2.0 companies on the exponential growth curve before the rest of the market realizes what they are worth.
- **Maintain control of hard-to-recreate data sources.** Let users access everything, but do not let them keep it. For example, users can only access Google's search engine over the Web.
- **Build trust.** By being fair with customer data and leveraging users' loyalty, you can get customers to share more information about themselves, which, in turn, leads to products and services that are tailored to them, thus increasing sales.
- **Turn applications into platforms.** An application that has only a single use is simply a waste of software. Convert applications into online platforms that feature compelling content or services.
- **Automate online customer self-service.** Let users get what they want, when they want it, without help.

RISKS AND LIMITATIONS WHEN INTERFACING WITH SOCIAL NETWORKS

Interfacing with social networks is not without risk. According to Regan (2006), aligning a product or company with sites where content is user-generated and not edited or filtered has its downsides. Another risk is that the company needs to be willing to accept negative reviews and feedback. If a company has really positive customer relationships and strong feedback and is willing to have customers share the good, but possibly some bad, as well as the ugly, it is a good candidate for social networking. If, however, the company worries about what its customers would say, the product or business might not be ready for social networking.

Another key consideration is the 20–80 rule, which posits that a minority of individuals (20%) contribute most of the content (80%) to blogs, wikis, and similar tools. For example, approximately 1,000 of Wikipedia's millions of contributors write most of its content (*Business 2.0* 2007). In an analysis of thousands of submissions over a 3-week period on audience voting sites such as Digg and Reddit, the *Wall Street Journal* reported that one-third of the stories that made it to Digg's homepage were submitted by 30 contributors (out of 900,000 registered members), and that one single person on Netscape, going by the online name "Stoner," was responsible for 13 percent of the top posts on that site. Such distribution may result in biases (reported by Keen 2007).

Any social media site that relies on user contributions may find a similar distribution curve, with a relatively small number of top contributors representing the bulk of submissions. When only a small number of users provide evaluations, the tone of evaluations can change rapidly. One disgruntled customer can generate many posts, evaluations, or reviews. Therefore, it is necessary to monitor what is going on. Companies such as BuzzMetrics offer services that tell corporations what their customers and others are saying on the Internet and what it means to their brands and markets.

Finally, the use of Web 2.0 applications may present a security risk. According to *Innovations* (2006), 74 percent of CIOs surveyed said that Web 2.0 applications will significantly increase their security risk over the next 3 years. For more on security and other Web 2.0 implementation issues, see Chapter 10 and D'Agostino (2006). For a summary of risks in social networking, see Online File W9.5 and MessageLabs (2009).

JUSTIFYING SOCIAL MEDIA AND NETWORKING

Many companies find it difficult to justify social media and networking because most of their benefits are intangible (e.g., positive word-of-mouth). If the costs of using such tools can be kept low and if risk can be contained, then a sophisticated ROI analysis many not be needed. However, a number of companies are developing metrics that can be used in cost–benefit analyses (see Zabin 2008).

Example: Wal-Mart's In-House Social Network. Although many companies have benefited significantly from enterprise social networking (e.g., Nike, Coca-Cola, and Sony), there have been some failures. For example, Wal-Mart's enterprise networking effort was a complete failure.

For the largest retailer in the world, creating its own social network seemed to be natural and simple, but it was not. In 2007, Wal-Mart launched a social network in order to bolster its image with younger consumers. The company hired professional actresses and actors to pose as teens on the site, but they were not convincing. Also, in an attempt to avoid future lawsuits, Wal-Mart allowed parents to control page content. The young viewers were turned off. Because the number of visitors was so small, Wal-Mart pulled down the site after a short period.

Section 9.6 ▶ REVIEW QUESTIONS

1. Why is there so much interest in EC via social communities?
2. How can a social network facilitate viral marketing?
3. How can social networks support shopping?
4. How is customer feedback solicited in social networks?
5. List some risks in enterprise social networking.
6. How do social networks generate revenue?

9.7 ENTERTAINMENT WEB 2.0 STYLE: FROM SOCIAL NETWORKS TO MARKETPLACES

The rich media capabilities of Web 2.0 technologies, the ability to engage millions of young people who are interested in online entertainment, the availability of innovative tools, and the creative and collaborative nature of Web 2.0 all facilitate entertainment. Web 2.0 tools also are aiding in the proliferation of on-demand entertainment. This section describes some of the entertainment-centered social networks as well as other issues related to Web 2.0 entertainment. Note that a major issue with such social networks is copyright violations; this topic will be discussed in more detail in Chapter 16.

ENTERTAINMENT AND SOCIAL NETWORKS

A large number of social networks and communities are fully or partially dedicated to entertainment. In fact, MySpace seems to be morphing into an entertainment portal. MySpace is the second most visited online video site after YouTube. It has a licensing agreement with Sony BMG and other large media companies that gives its members free access to streaming videos, music, and other entertainment in MySpace Music. The companies share in the ad revenue. MySpace is also offering free voice chat in collaboration with Skype. For details see, mediabiz.blogs.cnnmoney.cnn.com.

The following are some additional examples of the use of Web 2.0 applications for entertainment.

Mixi

mixi, Inc. (mixi.co.jp) is a popular invitation-only social networking service in Japan. The focus of mixi is on "community entertainment;" that is, meeting new people by way of common interests. Users can send and receive messages, write in a diary, read and comment on others' diaries, organize and join communities, and invite their friends to join. mixi Station, a client program that detects songs being played in iTunes and Windows Media Player, uploads songs automatically to a communally accessible list in the "Music" section.

The word *mixi* is a combination of *mix* and *I*, referring to the idea that the user, "I," "mixes" with other users through the service. As of March 2009, the site had more than 12.4 million members and about 1,000,000 small communities of friends and interests (en.wikipedia.org/wiki/Mixi).

Last.fm

Last.fm (last.fm) is an Internet radio station and music recommendation system that merged with its sister site, Audioscrobbler, in August 2005. In May 2007, CBS purchased Last.fm in order to extend its online reach. The system builds a detailed profile of each member's musical preferences. Based on this profile, Last.fm recommends artists similar to members' favorites and features their favorite artists and songs on a customizable Web page comprising the songs played on its stations selected via collaborative filtering (Chapter 4) or recorded by a Last.fm plug-in installed into its users' music-playing application.

Last.fm users can build their musical profiles in two ways: by listening to their personal music collection on a music player application with an Audioscrobbler plug-in or by listening to the Last.fm Internet radio service. Songs played are added to a log from which musical recommendations are calculated. Last.fm calls this automatic track logging *scrobbling*. The user's page also displays recently played tracks, allowing users to display them on blogs or as forum signatures.

Regular membership is free; premium membership is $3 per month. The site, which operates in 10 major languages, has won several Best Community awards.

Pandora

Similar to Last.fm, Pandora (pandora.com) is a site for music lovers. The site runs entirely within a Web browser (unlike Last.fm, which requires a plug-in) and relies on people to suggest new music. As users select and listen to songs on Pandora and give them a thumbs-up or thumbs-down, the site offers new songs that human music evaluators have determined to be similar in style. Users can search for a particular artist, song, or genre and Pandora will create an entire personalized "radio station" full of similar music.

eFans

eFans (efans.com) is a social network for sports fans, bringing together millions of fans from all over the world. The site features videos, sports news, blogs, and forums. It also offers event tickets and sports-related products for purchase.

Users can join networks based on teams and athletes, including Tiger Woods, F.C. Barcelona, Manchester United, Ronaldinho, the Boston Red Sox, and thousands more, including local teams. Users can create personal, team, and athlete pages; share photos; and upload videos from YouTube. Users can also get the latest news and live scores and post comments. Users can add to their content, similar to wiki, making it a highly personalized, yet high-profile, interaction.

A new version of eFans includes many exciting features that may change the way sports fans connect on the Internet. For example, the new release has modules that unite fans who have the same favorite athlete or team.

For the Beijing Olympics eFans hosted a special page devoted to the world's best sporting events. The summer games were covered by David Wallenchinsky, author of a series of "The Complete Book of the Olympics," who contributed to eFans live from Beijing.

ADVERTISING MOVIES AND EVENTS IN COMMUNITIES

Advertising movies and special events is becoming popular in social networks. For example, Kevin Smith, the producer of the movie *Clerks II* released in 2006 (reported by Zeigler 2006), used MySpace to promote the film in a true "Indy Guerilla style." The movie characters (e.g., Dante Hicks, Randall Graves) had their own pages at MySpace, which were linked to the movie's hub pages as biographies.

Each week, starting in May 2006 and running until the release of *Clerks II* in August, users went into the "Our Friends" list and picked out fellow MySpacers at random to participate in a contest. Those who had the *Clerks II* MySpace page in their top-eight sites had their names listed at the end of the credits. By word-of-mouth, information about the contest and the movie spread across MySpace, enabling Smith to stay within his limited advertising budget and gross millions from the movie.

ONLINE MARKETPLACE FOR MOVIES

The goal of the start-up company InDplay Inc. (indplay.com) was to connect films with professional buyers through an online marketplace. It can be viewed as occupying the middle ground between the user-generated videos on YouTube and the select world of theatrical distribution.

In the InDplay marketplace, owners of videos could register as sellers and upload preview clips and additional information. Buyers representing theaters, TV networks, cable networks, Internet sites, and other outlets, registered and made e-mail offers to the sellers. Purchases and payments were made via PayPal or wire transfer. InDplay received an 8 percent standard commission. According to Woyke (2006), more than 10 million films and TV programs from around the world were available for sale (or license), and more than 100,000 professional buyers were registered. The site included community features such as ratings and reviews (similar to eBay) and connected people at all stages of a film creation via wikis and blogs. The site was closed in May 2009 due to financial difficulties.

Start-ups such as Lulu (lulu.com) and Zattoo (zattoo.com) also offer unique online markets for music, TV shows, and books.

The Hype Machine

The Hype Machine (hypem.com) is a relatively new concept (Heilemann 2006). Here is how it works: A server scans music blogs for postings with links to MP3 files. When a file is found, it is indexed, and the file is added to a database. The title is posted on the Hype Machine directory. Users can listen to tracks through the site's built-in player or buy music through links to Amazon.com or iTunes. Users can also search the database for their favorite bands.

Internet Series and Movie Streaming

Internet series are similar to soap operas on TV. The number of Internet series is increasing, and some are already on DVD. Examples include *Broken Trail*, *Soup of the Day*, and *Floaters*. For details, see Arnold (2006).

Hulu (hulu.com) offers commercial-supported streaming video of TV shows and movies from NBC, Fox, and many other networks and studios. As of January 2009, Hulu videos were offered only to users in the United States. Hulu provides video in Flash Video Format, including many films and shows. In addition, some TV shows and movies are now offered in high-definition.

Adult Entertainment in Virtual Worlds

The 3D capability of virtual worlds and the ease of manipulating avatars has opened the door to a variety of entertainment options, most notably adult entertainment. All major virtual worlds are full of adult entertainment features, including Second Life, specifically in redlightcenter.com.

MOBILE WEB 2.0 DEVICES FOR ENTERTAINMENT AND WORK

Several mobile devices have been designed with blogs, wikis, and other P2P services in mind. Here are some examples.

iPhone and Its Clones

The iPhone (from apple.com) was introduced in 2007. It is an all-in-one smartphone (see photo of the iPhone 3G). It is considered a disruptor in the cell phone market. Soon after iPhone's release, Samsung announced a new smartphone, BlackBerry introduced the Storm, and Google launched the G1 Google phone. These smartphones are marketed by cell phone carriers such as AT&T and Verizon. The competition among these new smartphones is intense, and new capabilities appear frequently.

The iPhone is also a personal media player, offering all the capabilities of an iPod, with music and video playback, plus the benefits of a high-resolution widescreen display for watching movies and videos. It is a touchscreen smartphone with full-blown Internet communication capabilities; a quad-band, EDGE-capable mobile phone; and it has a brain (i.e., PAD capabilities), making it simple and easy to use. It also has a camera, a headset jack, and a built-in speaker. It also supports online multiplayer gaming.

The iPhone also has a sleep/wake button, and a proximity sensor turns off the screen when users hold the phone to their heads. It features automatic-orientation adjustment, switching between portrait and landscape modes on-the-fly. The iPhone boasts virtually no dedicated controls; instead, everything is driven using a new (patented) multitouch screen that Apple claims is far more accurate than previous touch-sensitive displays. For additional details, see apple.com/iphone and en.wikipedia.org/wiki/iphone.

The iPhone lets companies such as Apple and Google "merge without merging" by delivering Google services through Apple hardware.

YAHOO! GO

Yahoo! Go is optimized for a cell phone's small screen, making it easy and fun to access the Internet. Everything about the Yahoo! Go interface is designed to be both visually striking and to give users what they want with the fewest clicks possible. E-mail, news, photos, and more are "pushed" to users' phones. It includes Yahoo! oneSearch, a new mobile search that provides answers on the spot.

At its core is the carousel, which enables users to navigate intuitively among the various Yahoo! Go widgets, which are personal channels for e-mail, local information and maps, news, sports, finance, entertainment, weather, Flickr photos, and search. Using the carousel,

Source: Courtesy of Digital Trends. Used with permission.

users scroll over the widget they want. Because Yahoo! Go uses advanced caching and background-loading technology, the widget content is automatically and continuously "pushed" to the phone. For details see, mobile.yahoo.com/go.

Nokia's N810 Internet Tablet

Nokia's N810 Internet Tablet which is about the size of a paperback novel, lets users surf the Internet, send and receive e-mail and instant messages, download audio and video, and get RSS feeds. The new model adds a Webcam for videoconferencing and a microphone for Internet phone calls.

As a media player, the N810 handles MP3 and Windows Media files and other common formats, displaying images on a 4.1-inch color screen and playing audio through built-in stereo speakers or a headphone jack. It uses Wi-Fi networking when available, but it can also connect to a compatible Nokia phone via Bluetooth and be used as a wireless modem.

The Internet Tablet, available from retailers and nokiausa.com, has an on-screen keyboard that automatically adjusts its key size and spacing for finger or stylus operation. It recognizes text written on the screen with a stylus.

Section 9.7 ▶ REVIEW QUESTIONS

1. Describe entertainment communities and provide an example.
2. Describe the online marketplaces for music.
3. What is an Internet series?
4. Describe the iPhone.
5. What is unique to the Nokia N810 Internet Tablet?

9.8 THE FUTURE: WEB 3.0 AND WEB 4.0

Web 2.0 is here, but not for long (Hempel 2009). What's next? The answer is a still-unknown entity referred to as **Web 3.0**, the future wave of Internet applications. Some of the characteristics of Web 3.0 are already in the making. Based on nontechnological success factors and technological factors and trends, there is general optimism about the future of the Web and EC.

WEB 3.0: WHAT'S NEXT?

Web 3.0 will not be just about shopping, entertainment, and search. Web 3.0 will deliver a new generation of business applications that will see business and social computing converge on the same fundamentals as on-demand architecture is converging with consumer applications today. Thus, Web 3.0 is just not merely of passing interest to those who work on enterprise EC. The Web 3.0 era could radically change individuals' career paths as well as the organizations where they work, and it may even revolutionize social networking (see Rouch 2006 and Hempel 2009).

According to Stafford (2006) and en.wikipedia.org/wiki/Web_3, the next-generation Internet will not just be more portable and personal, it will also harness the power of people, making it even easier to zero in on precisely what you are looking for.

Web 3.0 has the potential to usher in the following:

> ▶ Faster, far-flung connectivity; richer ways of interacting
> ▶ New Web Services that work entirely within a browser window
> ▶ More powerful search engines
> ▶ More clout for everyday people and more user-friendly application-creation capabilities
> ▶ New artificial intelligence applications
> ▶ 10MB of bandwidth (instead of 1MB in Web 2.0, on average)
> ▶ More uses of 3D tools
> ▶ Greater utilization of wireless and mobile social networks

Web 3.0 Structure

The topology of Web 3.0 can be divided into four distinct layers: *API services, aggregation services, application services,* and *serviced clients* (see Online File W9.6).

Web 3.0 and the Semantic Web

One of the major possible applications of Web 3.0 technologies is the **Semantic Web** (see en.wikipedia.org/wiki/Semantic_Web). The Semantic Web is an evolving extension of the

Web 3.0
A term used to describe the future of the World Wide Web. It consists of the creation of high-quality content and services produced by gifted individuals using Web 2.0 technology as an enabling platform.

Semantic Web
An evolving extension of the Web in which Web content can be expressed not only in natural language, but also in a form that can be understood, interpreted, and used by intelligent computer software agents, permitting them to find, share, and integrate information more easily.

Web in which Web content can be expressed not only in natural language, but also in a form that can be understood, interpreted, and used by intelligent computer software agents, permitting them to find, share, and integrate information more easily. The technology is derived from W3C director Tim Berners-Lee's vision of the Web as a universal medium for data, information, and knowledge exchange. At its core, the Semantic Web comprises a philosophy, a set of design principles, collaborative working groups, and a variety of enabling technologies.

A similar view about the role of the Semantic Web is expressed by Borland (2007), who believes that the role of the Semantic Web in Web 3.0 is certain, and coming soon. Borland believes that new Web 3.0 tools (some of which are already helping developers "stitch" together complex applications) will improve and automate database searches, help people choose vacation destinations, and sort through complicated financial data more efficiently.

According to *The Economist* (2007), by 2010 a Semantic-Web browser may be available that users can use to display data, draw graphs, and so on. An example would be "friend-of-a-friend" networks, where individuals in online communities provide data in the form of links between themselves and friends. The Semantic Web could help to visualize such complex networks and organize them to enable deeper understanding of such communities' structures.

For more on Web 3.0 and the Semantic Web, see en.wikipedia.org/wiki/Web_3.

Web 4.0

The Web generation after Web 3.0. It is still an unknown entity. However, it is envisioned as being based on islands of intelligence and as being ubiquitous.

Web 4.0

Web 4.0 is the next Web generation after Web 3.0. It is still an unknown entity. However, Coleman and Levine (2008) envision it as being based on islands of intelligence and on being ubiquitous. Exhibit 9.8 depicts the relationship of Web 4.0 to Web 1.0, 2.0, and 3.0.

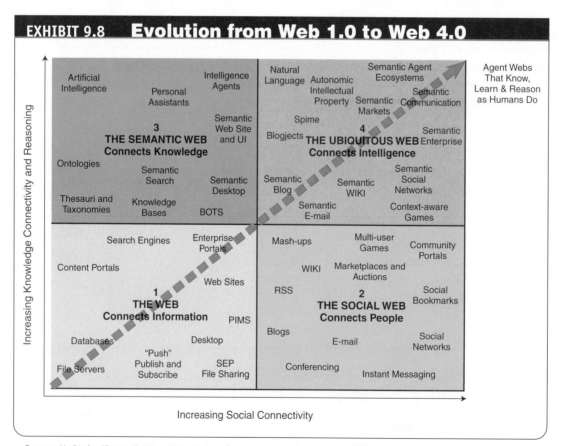

EXHIBIT 9.8 Evolution from Web 1.0 to Web 4.0

Source: M. Davis. "Semantic Wave 2008: Industry Roadmap to Web 3.0 and Multibillion Dollar Market Opportunities." *Project 10X*, 2008. *project10x.com/about.php* (accessed May 2009).

Future Threats

According to Stafford (2006), the following four trends may slow EC and Web 3.0 and even cripple the Internet:

▶ **Security concerns.** Shoppers as well as users of e-banking and other services worry about online security. The Web needs to be made safer.

▶ **Lack of Net neutrality.** If the big telecommunications companies are allowed to charge companies for a guarantee of faster access, critics fear that small innovative Web companies could be crowded out by the Microsofts and Googles that can afford to pay more.

▶ **Copyright complaints.** The legal problems of YouTube, Wikipedia, and others may result in a loss of vital outlets of public opinion, creativity, and discourse.

▶ **Choppy connectivity.** Upstream bandwidths are still constricted, making uploading of video files a time-consuming task. Usable mobile bandwidth still costs a lot, and some carriers impose limitations on how Web access can be employed.

Section 9.8 ▶ REVIEW QUESTIONS

1. What is Web 3.0, and how will it differ from Web 2.0?
2. Define Semantic Web.
3. List the major potential inhibitors of e-commerce and Web 3.0.
4. What is Web 4.0?

MANAGERIAL ISSUES

Some managerial issues related to this chapter are as follows.

1. **How will social networking impact businesses?** The impacts of social networking and the Internet can change the manner in which shoppers make decisions. The impact may be so strong that the entire manner in which companies do business will be changed, with significant impacts on procedures, people, organizational structure, management, and business processes. Strong impact will be felt in advertising, viral marketing, collaboration, and brand recognition.

2. **What are the impacts of the Web 2.0 boom?** In light of the push toward Web 2.0 technologies, *Time* (Grossman 2006/2007) named "you" as the person of the year for 2006. In the information age, no one has more power to influence society than Web 2.0 communities. Yet does this influence truly benefit us, or will we suffer because of it?

3. **Should we explore Web 2.0 collaboration?** Consider whether your corporate culture is ready to experiment with collaboration tools and social networks. Work with your corporate-learning or organization-development department to find areas likely for experimentation.

4. **How shall we start using Web 2.0 tools?** Start small: Determine whether a collaborative tool would benefit a team or group working on a specific project. Marketing groups are often good first targets for information sharing with others because they are usually the ones tasked with sharing corporate information. Try establishing a wiki for a team's collaborative project. Some wikis are hosted on an internal server, whereas others are available as open source or via a hosted service.

5. **Do we need to sponsor a social network?** Although sponsoring a social network might sound like a good idea, it may not be simple to execute. Community members need services, which cost money to provide. The most difficult task is to find an existing community that matches your business. In many cases, the cost of a social network may be justified by its contribution to advertising. However, the social network service providers need to create various revenue models to maintain sustainable services. Creating revenue is the most challenging issue to social network service providers.

6. **How should we deal with Web 2.0 risks?** There are several possible risks, depending on the applications. The knowledge from unreliable participants may downgrade the credibility of knowledge from open sources. To protect the security of the open system, consult your internal security experts and get some outside legal advice. Use a consultant for large projects to examine and evaluate the risks.

7. **Should we have an in-house social network?** This is a debatable issue. Although most companies should probably opt to go into a successful public social network service, there are cases where an in-house service can be much more beneficial. Large companies may use both. It is probably most advantageous to build the knowledge management system using both internal sources and external sources.

SUMMARY

In this chapter, you learned about the following EC issues as they related to the learning objectives.

1. **Web 2.0, social media, and disruptors.** Web 2.0 is about the innovative application of existing technologies. Web 2.0 has brought together the contributions of millions of people and has made their work, opinions, and identity matter. The consequences of the rapid growth of person-to-person computing, such as blogging, are currently hard to understand and difficult to estimate. User-created content is a major characteristic of Web 2.0, as is the emergence of social networking. One impact of Web 2.0 is the creation of industry disruptors.

2. **The structure and role of virtual communities.** Virtual communities create new types of business opportunities—people with similar interests that congregate at one Web site are a natural target for advertisers and marketers. Using chat rooms, members can exchange opinions about certain products and services. Of special interest are communities of transactions, whose interest is the promotion of commercial buying and selling. Virtual communities can foster customer loyalty, increase sales of vendors that sponsor communities, and facilitate customer feedback for improved service and business.

3. **Social networks services.** These are very large Internet communities that enable the sharing of content, including text, videos, and photos, and promote online socialization and interaction. Hundreds of networks are popping up around the world, some of which are global, competing for advertising money.

4. **Representative social networking sites.** In addition to MySpace, we discussed YouTube, Facebook, Bebo, Orkut, Flickr, LinkedIn, hi5, and Cyworld.

5. **Business-oriented social networks.** These communities concentrate on business issues both in one country and around the world (e.g., recruiting, finding business partners). Social marketplaces meld social networks

and some aspects of business. Notable business-oriented social networks are LinkedIn and Xing. Also, some companies own private social networks, whereas others conduct business in public social networks, such as in Facebook. Enterprise social networks are those owned and operated inside one company. Their members are usually employees and retirees. They are used mainly for collaboration, knowledge creation and preservation, training, and socialization. Many large companies have such networks (e.g., IBM, Wells Fargo).

6. **Social networks and e-commerce.** The major areas of interface are online shopping, online advertising, online market research, collaboration, and innovative revenue models. The major attraction is the volume of social networks, the possibility of viral marketing, and the hope that young people in the communities will be online buyers in the future.

7. **Web 2.0, social networking, and entertainment.** Rich media, user-created content, and groups and subgroups with common interests open many possibilities for a second generation of online entertainment. Add to this the wireless revolution and the increased capabilities in mobile devices to support Web 2.0 tools and social networking activities and you will discover a new and exciting world of online entertainment.

8. **Web 3.0.** Web 3.0, the next generation of the Web, will combine social and business computing. It will be more portable and personal, with powerful search engines, increased clout, and greater connectivity with the wireless environment and on-demand applications. Knowledge management will be one of its main pillars. The Semantic Web will play a major role in Web 3.0 applications. Web 4.0 is a futuristic Web that will be built on ubiquitous and intelligent systems. It will connect "islands" of intelligence from different sources.

KEY TERMS

Business network	441	Semantic Web	459	Virtual (Internet) community	431
Business social network	441	Social marketplace	446	Web 2.0	427
Disruptors	429	Social media	429	Web 3.0	459
Enterprise 2.0	445	Social network analysis software	436	Web 4.0	460
Mobile social networking	437	Viral blogging	448		

QUESTIONS FOR DISCUSSION

1. How do business-oriented networks and enterprise social networks differ?

2. What are the major characteristics of Web 2.0? What are some of the advantages of Web 2.0 applications?

3. Discuss the use of virtual communities to do business on the Internet.

4. What are some of the risks companies may face if they decide to use public social networks?

5. Why are social marketplaces considered to be a Web 2.0 application?

6. How can marketers use social networks for viral marketing?

7. Discuss the commercial opportunities presented by public social networks.

8. Why are advertisers so interested in social networks?

9. What are the benefits of conversational marketing?

10. Discuss the nature of industry disrupters.

11. How can wikis be used to facilitate knowledge management?

12. Discuss the relationships among mobile devices, social networking, and EC.

13. Identify and discuss Facebook's revenue model.

14. Search the Internet to find competitors to Wikipedia. How do they compare with Wikipedia?

INTERNET EXERCISES

1. Enter the Web site of a social network service (e.g., myspace.com or facebook.com). Build a homepage. Add a chat room and a message board to your site using the free tools provided. Describe the other capabilities available. Make at least five new friends.

2. Investigate the community services provided by Yahoo! to its members at groups.yahoo.com. List all the services available and assess their potential commercial benefits to Yahoo!.

3. Enter vivapets.com and dogster.com and compare their offerings.

4. Enter classmates.com, myspace.com, and linkedin.com and list their sources of revenue.

5. Enter xing.com and linkedin.com and compare their functionalities (capabilities). Also, enter ryze.com and view the video tutorial networking. Compare Ryze's capabilities with those of LinkedIn.com. Write a report.

6. Enter teenvogue.com and compare its rich media with that of myspace.com and cyworld.com. Prepare a report.

7. Enter clicstar.com. Why is it an online entertainment service? What are the benefits to viewers? Compare this site to starz.com.

8. Enter gnomz.com. What does this site help you accomplish? (Note: translate the page if you don't read French.)

9. Enter advertising.com. Find the innovative/scientific methods that are offered. Relate to Web 2.0 and search.

10. Enter the paulgillin.com blog and find information related to enterprise applications of Web 2.0 technologies. Write a report.

11. Enter pandora.com. Find out how you can create and share music with friends. Why is this a Web 2.0 application?

12. Enter webkinz.com and compare its activities to that of facebook.com. Enter nielsen-online.com and find the average stay time on both social network sites.

13. Enter smartmobs.com. Go to blogroll. Find three blogs related to Web 2.0 and summarize their major features.

14. Enter mashable.com and review the latest news regarding social networks and network strategy. Write a report.

15. Access Hof's "My Virtual Life" (2008) at businessweek.com/print/magazine/content/06_18/b3982001.htm?chang=g1 and meet the seven residents in the slide show. Prepare a table that shows the manner in which they make money, the required skills, and the reason they do it in Second Life.

16. Identify two virtual worlds (other than Second Life). Explore business opportunities there. Join as a member and write a report.

17. Enter secondlife.com and find the commercial activities of the following avatars: Fizik Baskerville, Craig Altman, Shaun Altman, FlipperPA Peregrine, and Anshe Chung. Describe briefly what they represent.

18. Enter alleyinsider.com and find the latest developments in iPhone and similar phones. Relate the developments to social networking. Write a report.

19. Enter en.wikipedia.org/wiki/mixi and look at mixi's features that are similar to those offered by other social networks. Relate it to online entertainment.

20. Enter pixpulseteam.com and explore its capabilities for online communities, mobile commerce, and media networks. Write a report.

21. Enter couchsurfing.com and analyze its activities. Is this a social network? Why or why not? If it is not a social network, what is it?

22. Enter ning.com. Explore its capabilities and discuss how it is related to social network sites.

23. Enter yedda.com and explore its approach to knowledge sharing.

TEAM ASSIGNMENTS, PROJECTS, AND CLASS DISCUSSIONS

1. Each group member selects a single-family house where he or she lives or where a friend lives. Next, enter zillow.com and find the value of a similar house in the neighborhood. Then, add improvements to adjust the value of the first house. Find out how to list the house for sale on Zillow and other sites (e.g., craigslist.org). Write a summary. Compare members' experiences.

2. Each group is assigned to a social network that has business activities on it (e.g., LinkedIn, Xing, Facebook, Second Life, etc.). Each group will then register with hellotxt.com to find out what is going on in the site with regard to recent business activities. Write a report and make a class presentation.

   With Hello TXT, you log on to the site and enter your text message into the dashboard. You then select the sites you want to update with your new status message, and Hello TXT does the rest, reaching out to your various pages to add your new status message. It is a great centralized way to keep all your various profiles as up-to-date as possible, and it is designed to update your LinkedIn status by answering the question "What are you working on?"

3. The group signs in to secondlife.com and creates an avatar(s). Each member is assigned to explore a certain business area (e.g., virtual real estate, educational activities, diplomatic island). Make sure the avatar interacts with other people's avatars. Write a report.

4. Enter facebook.com and myspace.com and find out how 10 well-known corporations use the sites to conduct commercial activities (as per Sections 9.5

   and 9.6). Also, compare the functionalities of the two sites.

5. Address the following topics in a class discussion:

   a. Should companies build in-house social networks for external activities or use existing public social networks (e.g., see Roberts 2008)?

   b. Social networks services, such as Visible Path, can provide social networking services for entire enterprises that are fairly secure. However, security may limit users' creativity and disrupt the business. Should a company use this service?

   c. Some research suggests that the use of public social networks by employees can be good for a business, because employees develop relationships and share information, which increases productivity and innovation. Others say it is a waste of time and ban the use of Facebook, YouTube, and other such sites. Discuss.

   d. Some say that MySpace is turning into an entertainment center, whereas Facebook is becoming a communication center. Discuss.

   e. Discuss the business value of social networking. As a start, read Tom Davenport's "Where's the Working in Social Networks" (blogs.harvardbusiness. org/davenport/2007/10/wheres_the_working_in_social_n.html) and Brett Bonfield's "Should Your Organization Use Social Networking Sites" (techsoup. org/learningcenter/internet/page7935.cfm).

   f. Discuss the opportunities that the faltering economy provides to social networking in assisting enterprises.

Closing Case

LINKEDIN: THE BUSINESS-ORIENTED SOCIAL NETWORK

LinkedIn is a business-oriented social networking site mainly used for professional networking. As of January 2009, it had more than 33 million registered users spanning 150 industries around the world. LinkedIn can be used to find jobs, people, potential clients, service providers, subject experts, and other business opportunities.

A major purpose of LinkedIn is to allow registered users to maintain a list of contact details of people they know and trust in business (see *en.wikipedia.org/ wiki/ LinkedIn*). The people in each list are called *connections.* Users can invite anyone, whether they are a LinkedIn user or not, to become a connection. When people join, they create a profile that summarizes their professional accomplishments. The profile makes it possible to find and be found by former colleagues, clients, and partners.

A *contact network* consists of users' direct connections, each of their connections' connections (called second-degree connections), the connections of second-degree connections (called third-degree connections), and so forth. The contact network makes it possible for a professional to gain an introduction to someone he or she wishes to know through a mutual, trusted contact. LinkedIn's officials are members and have hundreds of connections each (see Elad 2008 and *linkedin.com*).

The "gated-access approach," where contact with any professional requires either a preexisting relationship or the intervention of a contact of theirs, is intended to build trust among the service's users. LinkedIn participates in the EU Safe Harbor Privacy Framework.

The searchable LinkedIn groups feature allows users to establish new business relationships by joining

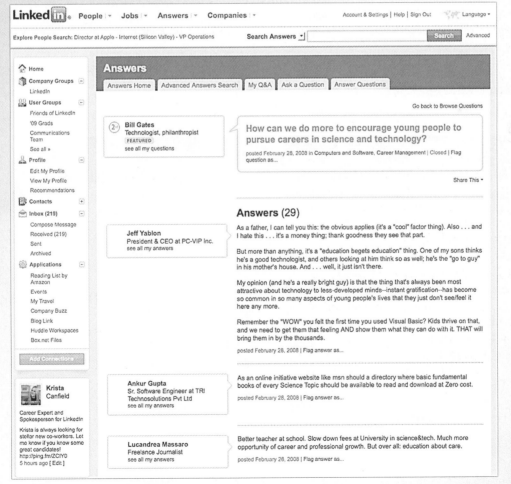

Source: Courtesy of LinkedIn. Used with permission.

alumni, industry, or professional, and other relevant groups. It has close to 100,000 groups in its directory.

LinkedIn is especially useful in helping job seekers and employers find one another. Job seekers can list their resumes, search for open positions, check company profiles, and even review the profiles of hiring managers. Job seekers can also discover inside connections with existing contacts who can introduce them to a specific hiring manager. They can even see who has viewed their profile.

Companies can use the site to post jobs and find and recruit employees, especially those who may not be actively searching for a new position.

As of January 2007, LinkedIn featured "LinkedIn Answers." As the name suggests, the service is similar to Answers.com or Yahoo! Answers. The service allows LinkedIn users to ask questions for the community to answer. "LinkedIn Answers" is free. The identity of the people asking and answering questions is known, so further communication is possible (see *linkedin.com/static?key=press_releases_011607*).

A mobile version of the site was launched in February 2008, which offers access to a reduced feature set over a mobile device. The mobile service is available in six languages: Chinese, English, French, German, Japanese, and Spanish.

In mid-2008, LinkedIn launched LinkedIn DirectAds as a form of sponsored advertising. It is similar to Google's AdWords. For a comparison with Adwords, see *targetinfolabs.com/2008/11/linkedin-directad-vs-google-adwords-ppc.html*.

LinkedIn has also joined forces with the financial news site CNBC. The deal integrates LinkedIn's networking functionality into CNBC.com, allowing LinkedIn users to share and discuss financial and other news with their professional contacts. Community-generated content from LinkedIn, such as survey and poll results, will be broadcast on CNBC, and CNBC will provide LinkedIn with programming, articles, blogs, financial data, and video content. CNBC will be able to draw insights from LinkedIn's global user base to generate new types of business content for CNBC to broadcast.

The following are some useful resources on LinkedIn: *blog.linkedin.com, mylinkedinpowerforum.com,* and *mylinksearch.com*.

Sources: Compiled from Elad (2008) and *en.wikipedia.org/wiki/LinkedIn*.

Questions

1. Enter *linkedin.com* and explore. Why do you think the site is so successful?

2. What features are related to recruiting and job finding?

3. How does "LinkedIn Answers" work? Try to use it by posting a query. Report the results.

4. Why do you think President Obama created a page on LinkedIn while he was running for president?

ONLINE RESOURCES
available at pearsonglobaleditions.com/turban

WWW

Online Files

W9.1   Application Case: Zopa, Prosper, and P2P Lending: Will They Disrupt Banking?

W9.2   Application Case: YouTube and Company—A Whole New World

W9.3   Application Case: Using Intelligent Software and Social Networking to Improve Recruiting Processes

W9.4   How Wikis Are Used

W9.5   Risks in Social Networks

W9.6   Web 3.0 Structure Layers

Comprehensive Educational Web Sites

informationweek.com/shared/printableArticleSrc.jhtml?articleID=202601956: "Growing Pains: Can Web 2.0 Evolve into an Enterprise Technology?"

cioinsight.com/c/a/Past-News/5-Reasons-to-Deploy-a-Corporate-Social-Network: "Five Reasons to Deploy a Corporate Social Network"

bloombergmarketing.blogs.com/Bloomberg_marketing: Diva Marketing Blog

blogs.zdnet.com/Hinchcliffe: Dion Hinchcliffe's Enterprise 2.0 blog

awarenessnetworks.com: Webinars on social media, Web 2.0, ROI, and marketing

blogs.business2.com/business2blog: Videos (combined with blogs)

newsgator.com/enterprise20/Oct2008: Webinar on social computing deployment

REFERENCES

Abram, C., and L. Pearlman. *Facebook for Dummies.* Hoboken, NJ: Wiley 2008.

Arnold, T. K. "From the Internet Straight to DVD." *USA Today*, October 2, 2006.

Bjelland, O. M., and R. C. Wood. "An Inside View of IBM'S Innovation Jam." *MIT Sloan Management Review* (Fall 2008).

Blodget, H. "Who the Hell Writes Wikipedia, Anyway?" *Silicon Alley Insider*, January 3, 2009. alleyinsider.com/2009/1/who-the-hell-writes-wikipedia-anyway (accessed March 2009).

Blossom, J. *Content Nation: Surviving and Thriving as Social Media Technology Changes Our Lives.* Hoboken, NJ: Wiley, 2009.

Borland, J. "A Smarter Web." *Technology Review*, March–April 2007.

Boyd, D. M., and N. B. Ellison. "Social Network Sites: Definition, History and Scholarship." *Journal of Computer-Mediated Communication* (January 2007).

Brandel, M. "Social Networking Behind the Firewall." *Computer World*, August 11, 2008.

Business 2.0. "The Next Net 25 (Web 2.0 Companies)." February 22, 2007.

Cashel, J. "Top Ten Trends for Online Communities." *ProvidersEdge.com.* providersedge.com/docs/km_articles/Top_Ten_Trends_for_Online_Communities.pdf (accessed March 2009).

Chesbrough, H. W. *Open Business Models.* Boston, MA: Harvard Business School Press, 2006.

CNN.com. "Love-Struck Hacker Proposed Using 'Bejeweled.'" April 15, 2008. teamliquid.net/forum/viewmessage.php?currentpage=All&topic_id=69601&show_part= (accessed March 2009).

Coleman, D., and S. Levine. *Collaboration 2.0.* Cupertino CA: Happy About Info, 2008.

Cone, E. "Comment: Put a Fork in the Plan to Fork." *Blog.eweek.com*, January 22, 2007a.

Cone, E. "Social Networks at Work Promise Bottom-Line Results." *CIO Insight*, October 8, 2007b.

D'Agostino, D. "Security in the World of Web 2.0." *Innovations* (Winter 2006).

Davis, M. "Semantic Wave 2008: Industry Roadmap to Web 3.0 and Multibillion Dollar Market Opportunities." *Project 10X,* 2008. project10x.com/about.php (accessed May 2009).

De Jonghe, A. *Social Networks Around the World.* North Charleston, SC: BookSurge, 2008.

de Mel, E. "Google's Orkut Goes Mobile in Stealth Mode." *Mobileopen.com*, April 18, 2008. mobilopen.org/index.php/2008/04/18/101-google-s-orkut-goes-mobile-in-stealth-mode (accessed March 2009).

Demopoulos, T. *Blogging and Podcasting.* Chicago: Kaplan Publishing, 2007.

The Economist. "Watching the Web Grow Up." March 10, 2007.

Elad, J. *LinkedIn for Dummies.* Hoboken, NJ: Wiley, 2008.

Farrell, N. "Microsoft Rumbled over Wikipedia Edits." *The Inquirer*, January 24, 2007. theinquirer.net/gb/inquirer/news/2007/01/24/microsoft-rumbled-over-wikipedia-edits (accessed March 2009).

Gillin, P. *The New Influencers.* Sanger, CA: Quill Driver Books, 2007.

Gogoi, P. "Retailers Take a Tip from MySpace." *BusinessWeek Online*, February 13, 2007. businessweek.mobi/detail.jsp?key=6158&rc=sb&p=4&pv=1 (accessed March 2009).

Grossman, L. "Time Person of the Year—YOU, Power to People." *Time*, December 25, 2006–January 1, 2007.

Heilemann, J. "Digging Up News." *Business 2.0*, April 2006.

Hempel, J. "Web 2.0 Is So Over, Welcome to Web 3.0." *Fortune*, January 8, 2009.

Hinchcliffe, D. "Profitably Running an Online Business in the Web 2.0 Era." *SOA Web Services Journal* (November 29, 2006).

Hof, R. D. "My Virtual Life." *BusinessWeek*, May 1, 2008.

Hoover, J. N. "Enterprise 2.0." *InformationWeek*, February 26, 2007.

Innovations. "Going Beyond Networking." (Winter 2006).

Jefferies, A. "Sales 2.0: Getting Social About Selling." *CRM Buyer,* October 30, 2008.

Kafka, P. "Blue Sky." *Forbes*, February 12, 2007.

Keen, A. *The Cult of the Amateur: How the Internet Is Killing Our Culture.* Portland, OR: Broadway Books, 2007.

Kirkpatrick, D. "Help Wanted: Adults on Facebook." *Fortune,* May 21, 2008. money.cnn.com/2008/03/21/technology/kirkpatrick_facebook.fortune/index.ht (accessed March 2009).

Li, C., and J. Bernoff. *Groundswell: Winning in a World Transformed by Social Technologies.* Boston: Harvard Business School Press, 2008.

Libert, B., J. Spector, and thousands of contributors. *WE Are Smarter Than ME.* Upper Saddle River, NJ: Pearson Education Inc., 2008.

Longino, C. "Your Wireless Future." *Business 2.0*, May 2006.

Martens, C. "Wikipedia to Strive for Higher Quality Content." *PC World*, August 4, 2006.

McAfee, A. P. "Enterprise 2.0: The Dawn of Emergent Collaboration." *MIT Sloan Management Review* (Spring 2006).

McGillicuddy, S. "IT Executives Eager to Exploit 2.0 Wave." *SMB News*, October 24, 2006. searchcio.techtarget.com/originalContent/0,289142,sid182_gci1226050,00.htm (accessed March 2009).

McNichol, T. "Building a Wiki World (Wikia vs. Wikipedia)." *Business 2.0*, March 2007a.

McNichol, T. "Vin Du Blogger." *Business 2.0*, August 2007b.

Megna, M. "Bust or Boon? Calculate Blog ROI." *E-Commerce Guide,* February 8, 2007. ecommerce-guide.com/solutions/article.php/3658776 (accessed March 2009).

Mello, J. P. "Explosive Growth Predicted for Mobile Social Networks." *E-Commerce Times*, December 12, 2006.

MessageLabs. "Social Networking: Brave New World or Revolution from Hell?" White paper. messagelabs.com/whitepaper/US_WP_SocialNetworking_Associate.pdf (accessed February 2009).

Millard, E. "Facebook, LinkedIn: Meet Human Resources." *Baseline*, July 2008.

Murray-Buechner, M. "25 Sites We Can't Live Without." *Time*, August 3, 2006.

O'Malley, G. "MySpace vs. eBay? Site Leaps into E-Commerce." *Advertising Age*, September 11, 2006.

Regan, K. "Plugging In: Can E-Commerce Leverage Social Networks?" *E-Commerce Times*, November 2, 2006.

Riley, D. "Wikipedia Hits Mid Life Slow Down." *TechCrunch*, October 11, 2007. techcrunch.com/2007/10/11/wikipedia-hits-mid-life-slow-down (accessed March 2009).

Roberts, B. "Social Networking at the Office." *HR Magazine*, March 2008.

Rouch, W. "Social Networking 3.0." *Technology Review from MIT's Emerging Technologies Conference*, September 27–29, 2006. technologyreview.com/read_ article.aspx?id=15908&ch=infotech (accessed March 2009).

Roush, W. "Second Earth." *Technology Review*, July–August 2007.

Sahlin, D., and C. Botello. *YouTube for Dummies.* Hoboken, NJ: Wiley, 2007.

Schonfeld, E. "Cyworld Attacks!" *Business 2.0*, August 2006a.

Schonfeld, E. "The Disruptors Get Rowdy." *The.Next.Net*, October 27, 2006b. emedia.blogspot.com/2006/10/next-net-27102006-disruptors-get-rowdy.html (accessed March 2009).

Schonfeld, E., and C. Morrison. "The Next Disruptors." *Business 2.0*, August 21, 2007.

Seeking Alpha. "eMarketer Top 10 Predictions for 2009." January 9, 2009. seekingalpha.com/article/114028-emarketer-top-10-predictions-for-2009 (accessed March 2009).

Sloan, P. "The Next Net 25 (Web 2.0 Companies)." *Business 2.0*, March 2007.

Spanbauer, S. "The Right Social Network for You." *PC World*, February 24, 2008.

Stafford, A. "The Future of the Web." *PC World*, November 2006.

Turban, E., N. Bolloju, and T.-P. Liang. "Enterprise Social Networking: Opportunities and Risks." Working paper, October 2, 2008.

Urlocker, M. "Urlocker on Disruption." The Disruption Group. September 20, 2006. ondisruption.com/my_weblog/2006/09/business_20_top.html (accessed March 2009).

Vander Veer, E. *Facebook: The Missing Manual.* Cambridge, MA: Pogue Press, 2008.

Wagner, M. "Can Bloggers Be Bought?" *InformationWeek*, October 16, 2006.

Wagner, C., and N. Bolloju. "Supporting Knowledge Management in Organizations with Conversational Technologies: Discussion Forums, Weblogs, and Wikis." *Journal of Database Management*, 16, no. 2 (2005).

Weaver, A. C., and B. B. Morrison. "Social Networking." *Computer*, February 2008.

Weber, S. *Plug Your Business.* Falls Church, VA: Weber Books, 2007.

Wikipedia. "About Wikipedia," 2008. en.wikipedia.org/wiki/Wikipedia:About (accessed January 2009).

Woyke, E. "The eBay Model Goes to the Movies." *BusinessWeek*, December 11, 2006.

Wright, J. *Blog Marketing.* New York: McGraw-Hill, 2006.

Zabin, J. "Want to Measure Social Media ROI?: Pick a Metric." *E-Commerce Times*, October 23, 2008.

Zeigler, T. "Clerks II Launches MySpace Promotion." *theBivingsreport,com*, June 30, 2006. bivingsreport.com/2006/313 (accessed May 2009).

Zimmerman, J. *Web Marketing for Dummies.* Hoboken, NJ: Wiley, 2007.

E-COMMERCE FRAUD AND SECURITY

Content

Learning Objectives

Upon completion of this chapter, you will be able to:

1. Understand the importance and scope of security of information systems for EC.

2. Describe the major concepts and terminology of EC security.

3. Learn about the major EC security threats, vulnerabilities, and risks.

4. Understand phishing and its relationship to financial crimes.

5. Describe the information assurance security principles.

6. Identify and assess major technologies and methods for securing EC communications.

7. Describe the major technologies for protection of EC networks.

8. Describe various types of controls and special defense mechanisms.

9. Describe the role of business continuity and disaster recovery planning.

10. Discuss EC security enterprisewide implementation issues.

11. Understand why it is not possible to stop computer crimes.

HOW SEATTLE'S HOSPITAL SURVIVED A BOT ATTACK

The Problem

On a cold Sunday afternoon, many calls reached the help desk at Seattle's Northwest Hospital and Medical Center. PCs were running slow, the hospital staff complained, and documents wouldn't print. On Monday morning, as more employees came to work and logged onto their PCs, the problem spread. Finally, many PCs froze entirely.

By 10 AM, all 50 people in the hospital's information technology (IT) department had been summoned, but their efforts made little difference. Strange things started happening. Operating-room doors stopped opening, and doctors' pagers wouldn't work. Even computers in the intensive care units were shut down.

Everybody was very frightened; hospital communications began to break down. What happened? Northwest was under attack by a *botnet,* a network of PCs infected with code that was controlled, in this case, by a 19-year-old Californian, Christopher Maxwell, and two juveniles. The trio exploited a flaw in Microsoft Windows that let them install pop-ups on the hospital's computers. As the bad code coursed through the network, the hospital's computers started turning into bots. These new bots, in turn, scanned the network, looking for new victims to infect, and the network become clogged with traffic. This kind of attack is known as a *zombie army* (Section 10.3), where computers are set up to attack other computers in the same or other organizations. Initially, Northwest's IT team tried to halt the attack by shutting off the hospital from the Internet. Even though the bots were now contained internally, they still infected PCs faster than the team could clean them.

The Solution

By Monday afternoon, the IT department had figured out which malware the bots were installing on the PCs and wrote a script, directing the PCs to remove the bad code. By Tuesday, Computer Associates—Northwest's antivirus vendor—figured out exactly which malware Maxwell had used to get into the network and wrote a virus protection and removal program that blocked new code from coming in. The attack eventually harmed 150 out of 1,000 PCs—all of which had to have their hard drives wiped clean and their software reinstalled, at an estimated cost of $150,000.

The attack's aftermath lasted for weeks. As computers stopped working, hospital workers relied on *backup systems*—people and paper. Extra workers were brought in to help carry out tasks by hand. Lab results, for instance, were run by a person from the lab to the patients' bedsides on different floors. To save time, elective surgeries were postponed. Every day, department managers met several times to make sure the new security routines were holding and no patients were being endangered.

The Results

The hospital's network is now protected by CA's Pest Patrol, which blocks adware and spyware (Section 10.3), and Cisco MARS, an intrusion detection system (Section 10.3). The Windows flaw that the attacks slipped through has also been fixed.

Northwest wasn't Maxwell and crew's only prey. Among their other victims were the U.S. Department of Defense and Colton

Joint Unified School District in California, according to court papers. Maxwell pleaded guilty to conspiracy and intentionally causing damage to a protected computer. He was sentenced in August 2006 to 37 months in prison. He also was ordered to pay $115,000 to cover the hospital's direct expenses.

Sources: Compiled from Roberts (2006a), Kawamoto (2006), and O'Hagan (2006).

WHAT WE CAN LEARN . . .

Information systems inside organizations can be attacked by criminals that may not even benefit financially from the attacks. This attack was done by using a virus hidden in pop-up ads. This is only one of the many methods used to attack information systems in organizations, disturbing their internal operations. Other attack methods interfere with online trading and other forms of e-commerce. In addition to criminal attacks, information systems may be attacked by natural disasters, human error, equipment malfunction, and more. In this chapter we concentrate on e-commerce attacks and on the defense against them.

10.1 THE INFORMATION SECURITY PROBLEM

If you examine different lists of management concerns regarding the use of EC (and IT), the security issue is and has been among the top concerns. Security is considered to be the backbone of doing business over the Internet. Security-breaching incidents involving all types of organizations (including high-level, secure government agencies such as the CIA, FBI, and the military) appear on the news daily. Few organizations or individuals have not experienced some security breaches in their computerized systems. The damages of security breaches, including crimes, can be substantial and sometimes life-threatening, as was demonstrated in the opening case. Securing data, transactions, and privacy, and protecting people (buyers and sellers) is of utmost importance in conducting EC of any type.

In this chapter, we will provide an overview of the security problems and solutions as they are related to EC and IT. In this section, we look at the nature of the security problems, the magnitude of the problems, and the essential terminology and strategy used in dealing with these issues.

WHAT IS EC SECURITY?

Computer security refers to the protection of data, networks, computer programs, computer power and other elements of computerized information systems (see en.wikipedia.org/wiki/computer_security). It is a very broad concept due to the many methods of attack as well as many modes of defense. The attacks and defense of computers can affect individuals, organizations, countries, or the entire Web. Computer security aims to prevent or at least minimize the attacks. We classify computer security into two categories: *generic*, relating to any information system (e.g., encryption), and *EC-related*, such as buyers' protection. This chapter covers both, but it emphasizes the EC-related side. Attacks on EC Web sites, *identify theft* of both individuals and organizations, and a large variety of fraud schemes, such as phishing, are described in this chapter.

The Status of Computer Security in the United States

Several private and government organizations try to assess the status of computer security in the United States annually. Notable is the CSI report, which is described next.

No one really knows the true impact of online security breaches because, according to the Computer Security Institute (CSI, gocsi.com), only 27 percent of businesses report to legal authorities about computer intrusions. For the 2008 survey, known as the **CSI Computer Crime and Security Survey**, see Richardson (2008). This survey is an annual security survey of U.S. corporations and government agencies; financial, medical, and other institutions; and universities, conducted jointly by the FBI and the Computer Security Institute. Highlights from the 2008 *Security Survey*, which was based on responses from 520 participants, include the following five summary points:

CSI Computer Crime and Security Survey
Annual security survey of U.S. corporations, government agencies, financial and medical institutions, and universities conducted jointly by the FBI and the Computer Security Institute.

1. **The most expensive computer security incidents were those involving financial fraud.** The average reported cost was close to $500,000 per respondent (for those who experienced financial fraud). The second-most expensive, on average, was dealing with "bot" computers within the organization's network (such as in the opening case), reported to cost an average of nearly $350,000 per respondent. The overall average annual loss reported was just under $300,000.

2. **Virus incidents occurred most frequently.** Virus incidents occurred at almost half (49 percent) of the respondents' organizations. Insider abuse of networks was second most frequently occurring, at 44 percent, followed by theft of laptops and other mobile devices (42 percent).

3. **Almost one in ten organizations reported they experienced a domain name system (DNS) incident.** These incidents were up 2 percent from 2007, and noteworthy, given the current focus on vulnerabilities in DNS.

4. **Twenty-seven percent of those surveyed responded positively to a question regarding "targeted attacks."** Respondents had detected at least one such attack, where "targeted attack" was defined as a malware attack aimed exclusively at the respondent's organization or at organizations within a small subset of the general business population.

5. **The vast majority of respondents said their organizations had a security policy.** Sixty-eight percent had policies, while 18 percent were developing a formal information security policy. Only 1 percent said they had no security policy.

Other Interesting Findings. Other findings in the report are:

▶ The budget for IT security is about 10 percent of the total IT budget (on average).

▶ Awareness training is about 3 percent of the total IT budget (on average).

▶ Forty percent of companies use ROI, 20 percent use NPV, and 20 percent use IRR (see Chapter 14) to justify security projects.

▶ About 40 percent outsource some computer security.

▶ About 43 percent experienced security incidents, usually less than 5 but not more than 10 each year.

▶ About half of the attacks are made by insiders.

▶ On average, the number of attacks is declining (50 percent decline over the last 10 years). The most frequent attacks (see Section 10.3) are shown with their occurrence frequency in Exhibit 10.1 and in Chickowski (2008).

The average loss per respondent has been on the decline since 2001. Between 2003 and 2008, average loss was in the range of $168,000 to $526,000. The most commonly used defense technologies in 2008 are shown in Exhibit 10.2 and in Chickowski (2008). Some of these are described in Sections 10.6 through 10.9.

This report indicates that despite the decline in the frequency of incidents and their severity, the security problems still persist.

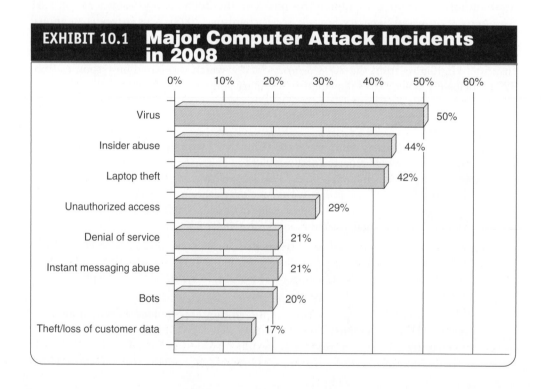

EXHIBIT 10.1 Major Computer Attack Incidents in 2008

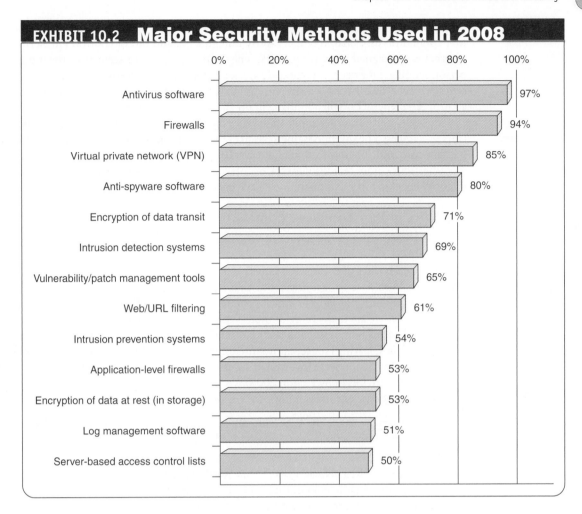

EXHIBIT 10.2 Major Security Methods Used in 2008

Method	Percentage
Antivirus software	97%
Firewalls	94%
Virtual private network (VPN)	85%
Anti-spyware software	80%
Encryption of data transit	71%
Intrusion detection systems	69%
Vulnerability/patch management tools	65%
Web/URL filtering	61%
Intrusion prevention systems	54%
Application-level firewalls	53%
Encryption of data at rest (in storage)	53%
Log management software	51%
Server-based access control lists	50%

National Security

Protection of the U.S. computer networks is in the hands of the Department of Homeland Security (DHS), which coordinates government policies for thwarting cyberthreats. It includes the following programs:

▶ **Cyber Security Preparedness and the National Cyber Alert System.** Computer users can stay up-to-date on cyberthreats through this program.

▶ **U.S.-CERT Operations.** Analyzes and combats cyberthreats and vulnerabilities.

▶ **National Cyber Response Coordination Group.** Comprising 13 U.S. agencies, it coordinates the government response to incidents.

▶ **CyberCop Portal.** Coordination with law enforcement helps capture and convict those responsible for cyberattacks.

On February 9, 2009, President Obama ordered the DHS to review U.S. government cyber security plans.

THE DRIVERS OF EC SECURITY PROBLEMS

Security problems are the results of several drivers. Here, we describe three major ones: the Internet's vulnerable design; the shift to profit-induced crimes and the underground Internet; and the dynamic nature of EC systems and the role of insiders.

The Internet's Vulnerable Design

It is important to recognize that the Internet and its network protocols were never intended for use by untrustworthy people or criminals. They were designed to accommodate computer-to-computer communications in a closed and trusted community. However, the system evolved into an any-to-any means of communication in an open community. As you know, that community is global in scope, mostly unregulated, and out of control. Furthermore, the Internet was designed for maximum efficiency without regard for security or the integrity of a person sending a message or requesting access. Error checking to ensure that the message was sent and received correctly was important at that time but not user authentication or access control. The Internet is still a fundamentally insecure infrastructure.

Virtually every Internet application relies on the reliable operation of *domain name system* (DNS) services. The **domain name system (DNS)** translates (converts) domain names (e.g., pearson.com and fbi.gov) to their numeric IP addresses. An **IP address** is an address that identifies your computer on a network or Internet. The lack of source authentication and data integrity checking in DNS operations leave nearly all Internet services vulnerable to attacks.

domain name system (DNS)

Translates (converts) domain names to their numeric IP addresses.

IP address

An address that uniquely identifies each computer connected to a network or the Internet.

The Shift to Profit-Induced Crimes

There is a clear shift in the nature of the operation of computer criminals (see Symantec 2008, 2009).

In the early days of e-commerce, many hackers simply wanted to gain fame or notoriety by defacing Web sites or "gaining root," that is, root access to a network. The opening case illustrates criminals that did not attack systems to make a profit. Today criminals are profit-oriented, and there are many more of them. Most popular is the theft of personal information such as credit card numbers, bank accounts, and Internet IDs and passwords. According to Privacy Rights ClearingHouse, approximately 250 million records containing personally identifiable information were involved in security breaches in the 3 years between April 2005 and April 2008 (reported by Palgon 2008).

Examples. Some examples follow:

- On February 10, 2008, the U.S. Federal Aviation Administration admitted that someone hacked into their computers and accessed the names and social security numbers of 45,000 employees.

- In January 2008, T. Rowe Price began notifying 35,000 clients that their names and social security numbers might have been compromised. The breach stemmed from the December 2007 theft of computers from the offices of a third-party services provider, which was preparing tax forms on behalf of T. Rowe Price.

- Cybercriminals launched an attack to extort money from StormPay, an online payment processing company. The attack shut down both of StormPay's data centers and its business for 2 days, causing financial losses and upsetting 3 million customers.

- Names, e-mail addresses, and phone numbers of an estimated 1.6 million jobseekers were accessed from Monster.com's resume database in August 2007. Though widely described as a hacking, the data were actually accessed by attackers using legitimate user names and passwords, possibly stolen from professional recruiters or human resources personnel who were using Monster.com to look for job candidates.

Note that laptop computers are stolen for two reasons: selling the hardware and trying to find valuable data on the machine (see Ponemon Institute 2008).

Intrusion access to corporate data occurred at discount retail conglomerate TJX (see Online File W10.1). A major driver of data theft and other crimes is the ability to profit from the theft. Stolen data are sold today in a huge illegal marketplace.

Internet underground economy

E-markets for stolen information made up of thousands of Web sites that sell credit card numbers, social security numbers, other data such as numbers of bank accounts, social network IDs, passwords, and much more.

The Internet Underground Economy

The **Internet underground economy** refers to the e-markets for stolen information. Thousands of Web sites sell credit card numbers, social security numbers, other data such as numbers of bank accounts, social network IDs, passwords, and much more. Such credentials are sold for less than a dollar to several hundred dollars each to spammers or to criminals who are using them for illegal financial transactions such as transferring money to their accounts or paying with someone else's credit card. For example, in August 2008, the FBI arrested a Countrywide employee who stole more than 2 million customer records and sold them on the underground market. A comprehensive study about the underground economy is provided by Holz et al. (2008) and by McCormick and Gage (2005). The Internet security company Symantec released a comprehensive report that provides statistical data about the Internet underground economy (Symantec 2008). The Symantec report provides information on how cybercriminals are getting organized in Russia and other countries. According to this report, about 30 percent of all the transactions in this market deal with credit cards. The value of all unsold items is estimated to be $275 million, while the potential worth of just the credit cards and banking information for sale is $7 billion. Forty-one percent of the underground economy is in the United States, while 13 percent is in Romania. The report also covers the issue of software piracy, which is estimated to be more than $100 million annually. For highlights of the report, see Symantec (2008). Criminals use several methods to steal the information they sell. One popular method is *keystroke logging*.

Keystroke Logging. **Keystroke logging**, often called **keylogging**, is a method of capturing and recording user keystrokes. Such systems are also highly useful for both law enforcement and for law breaking—for instance, by providing a means to obtain passwords or encryption keys and thus bypassing other security measures. Keylogging methods are widely available on the Internet. For more information, see en.wikipedia.org/wiki/Keystroke_logging.

keystroke logging (keylogging)
A method of capturing and recording user keystrokes.

The Dynamic Nature of EC Systems and the Role of Insiders

EC systems are changing all the time due to a stream of innovations. With changes often come security problems. In recent years we have experienced many security problems in the new areas of social networks and wireless systems (some will be explored later in the chapter). Note also that almost half of the security problems are caused by insiders. New insiders are being added frequently and so are the threats they bring.

Example. An insider let two criminals into London's office of Sumitomo Mitsui Bank, where the criminals tampered with the computer system, gaining access to the asset holdings of companies such as Toshiba. Then they tried to steal hundreds of millions of dollars from the bank and its corporate customers. They attempted to electronically transfer $323 million from accounts in the bank to their own account. Fortunately the attempt failed. Otherwise it would have been the biggest theft of its kind (*Taipei Times* 2009).

WHY IS E-COMMERCE SECURITY STRATEGY NEEDED?

Computer security in its simplest form can be divided into three categories: *threats, defenses,* and *management.* As will be seen in Sections 10.3 and 10.4, there are many potential threats. In general, we divide these threats into two categories: unintentional and intentional. The intentional threats are known as *cybercrimes* when they are performed on the Web. These change frequently as the criminals become more sophisticated.

The defense (Sections 10.5 through 10.10) is changing too and is improving in response to new attack methods and to new technological innovations. Yet, neither cybercrime nor cybercriminals can be stopped (see Section 10.10). Like in the physical world, Internet security systems cost money, sometimes a considerable amount. Therefore, one of management's tasks is to determine how much to invest in EC security. In addition, management is responsible to a variety of security programs across the enterprise. This requires a strategy.

The Computer Security Dilemma

Information security departments with big workloads and small budgets are not able to optimize their EC security program for efficiency. Endless worms, spyware, data piracy, and other crimes keep them working reactively rather than strategically; they address security concerns according to attackers' schedules instead of their own. As a result, their security costs and efforts from reacting to crises and paying for damages are greater than if they had an EC security strategy. This is the underlying reason why a comprehensive EC security strategy is necessary.

Section 10.1 ▶ REVIEW QUESTIONS

1. Define computer security.
2. List the major findings of the CSI 2008 survey.
3. Describe the Internet vulnerability design.

business continuity plan
A plan that keeps the business running after a disaster occurs. Each function in the business should have a valid recovery capability plan.

cybercrime
Intentional crimes carried out on the Internet.

exposure
The estimated cost, loss, or damage that can result if a threat exploits a vulnerability.

fraud
Any business activity that uses deceitful practices or devices to deprive another of property or other rights.

malware (malicious software)
A generic term for malicious software.

phishing
A crimeware technique to steal the identity of a target company to get the identities of its customers.

risk
The probability that a vulnerability will be known and used.

social engineering
A type of nontechnical attack that uses some ruse to trick users into revealing information or performing an action that compromises a computer or network.

spam
The electronic equivalent of junk mail.

4. Describe some profit-induced computer crimes.
5. Define the underground Internet.
6. Describe the dynamic nature of EC systems.
7. What makes EC security management so difficult? What is the dilemma?

10.2 BASIC E-COMMERCE SECURITY ISSUES AND LANDSCAPE

In order to better understand security problem, we need to understand some basic concepts in EC and IT security. We begin with some basic definitions, which constitute a vocabulary frequently used in dealing with security issues.

THE SECURITY BASIC TERMINOLOGY

In the opening case and in Section 10.1, we introduced some key concepts and security terms. We begin this section by introducing alphabetically the major terms needed to understand EC security issues:

- Business continuity plan
- Cybercrime
- Exposure
- Fraud
- Malware (malicious software)
- Phishing
- Risk
- Social engineering
- Spam
- Vulnerability
- Zombie

THE EC SECURITY BATTLEGROUND

In Section 10.1 we introduced some results of the CSI computer crime report. Notice the list of attack methods (Exhibit 10.1) and technologies to combat them (Exhibit 10.2). The essence of EC security can be viewed as a battleground between attacks and attackers, defense and defenders, and security requirements. This battleground includes the following components, as shown in Exhibit 10.3:

- The attacks, the attackers, and their strategies
- The items that are being attacked (the targets)
- The defenders and their methods and strategy

Threats and Attacks: Unintentional and Intentional

Information systems including EC are vulnerable to both unintentional and intentional threats.

Unintentional Threats. Unintentional threats fall into three major categories: human error, environmental hazards, and malfunctions in the computer system.

- **Human error.** Human error can occur in the design of the hardware or information system. It can also occur in programming, testing, data collection, data entry, authorization, and instructions. Errors can be a result of negligence or misunderstanding (for example, not changing passwords creates a security hole).

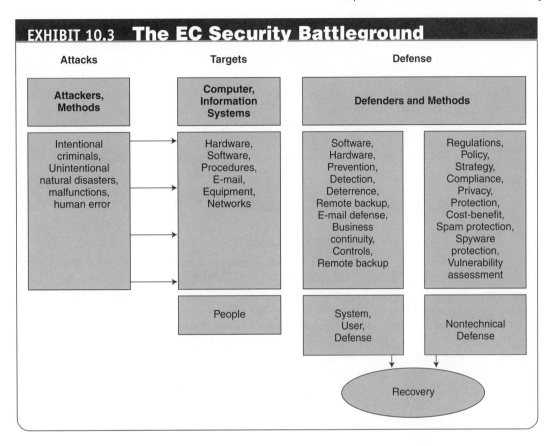

EXHIBIT 10.3 The EC Security Battleground

vulnerability
Weakness in software or other mechanism that threatens the confidentiality, integrity, or availability of an asset (recall the CIA model). It can be directly used by a hacker to gain access to a system or network.

zombies
Computers infected with malware that are under the control of a spammer, hacker, or other criminal.

Example 1. In November 2008, Jefferson County, West Virginia, released a site search engine that gave a new meaning to "open records." The engine exposed social security numbers and other personal information belonging to about 1.6 million citizens. It was a clear programming error made by a person.

▶ **Environmental hazards.** These include earthquakes, severe storms (e.g., hurricanes, blizzards, or sand), floods, power failures or strong fluctuations, fires (the most common hazard), explosions, radioactive fallout, and water-cooling system failures. Computer resources can also be damaged by side effects such as smoke and water.

▶ **Defects in the computer system.** Defects can be the result of poor manufacturing, defective materials, and outdated or poorly maintained networks. Unintentional malfunctions can also happen for other reasons, ranging from lack of experience to inadequate testing.

Example 2. In January 2009, a glitch disabled thousands of Microsoft Zune personal music players. Blogs and social networking sites were unable to listen to music because it would not start properly. The problem occurred when the internal clock on the device moved automatically to January 1, but because 2008 had been a leap year and the programmers had forgotten about it, the glitch occurred.

Intentional Attacks and Crimes. Intentional attacks are done by criminals. Examples of intentional attacks include theft of data; inappropriate use of data (e.g., manipulating inputs); theft of laptops (see Ponemon Institute 2008) and equipment and/or programs; deliberate manipulation in handling, entering, processing, transferring, or programming data; vandalism, sabotage; malicious damage to computer resources; destruction from viruses and similar attacks; miscellaneous computer abuses; and Internet fraud.

Criminals and Social Engineering

Intentional crimes carried out on the Internet are called *cybercrimes*, which are done by **cybercriminals** (*criminals* for short) that include hackers and crackers. **Hacker** describes someone who gains unauthorized access to a computer system. A **cracker** is a *malicious hacker*, such as Maxwell, in the opening case, who may represent a serious problem for a corporation.

Hackers and crackers may implicate unsuspecting insiders in their crimes. In a strategy called *social engineering*, criminals trick unsuspected insiders into giving them information or access that they should not have. Social engineering is a collection of tactics used to manipulate people into performing actions or divulging confidential information. Notorious hacker Kevin Mitnick, who served time in jail for hacking, used social engineering as his primary method to gain access to computer systems. One of the popular recent methods is *scareware*, in which criminals persuade users to download malicious files disguised as security applications.

Vulnerable Areas Are Being Attacked

Any part of an information system can be attacked. PCs can be stolen or attacked by viruses and other malware. They are subject to fraudulent identification and much more. Databases can be attacked by unauthorized access, and data can be copied and stolen. Networks can be attacked, and information flow can be stopped or altered. Terminals, printers, and any other pieces of equipment can be damaged in many ways. Software and programs can be manipulated. Procedures and policies may be altered and much more. Attacks are done on vulnerable areas.

Vulnerability. Mitre Corporation publishes a list of vulnerabilities called *common vulnerabilities and exposures (CVE)* (cve.mitre.org). In 2006, Mitre reported that four of the top five reported vulnerabilities were within Web applications. Vulnerabilities create *risk*, which is the probability that this weakness will be known and used. *Exposure* can result if a threat exploits a vulnerability.

Examples.   Three medical data breaches occurred in May 2008. Unauthorized peer-to-peer (P2P) file sharing led to a data breach at Walter Reed Army Medical Center that exposed the personal data of 1,000 patients. Patients at Staten Island University Hospital in New York were told that a computer with their medical records was stolen. Information on patients of the University of California San Francisco Medical Center was accidentally made accessible on the Internet.

Attacking E-Mail. One of the easiest places to attack is e-mail, since it travels via the unsecured Internet (Baumstein 2008). One example is the ease with which Sarah Palin was hacked in March 2008. For a list of top attack areas, see Online File W10.2.

SECURITY SCENARIOS AND REQUIREMENTS IN E-COMMERCE

EC security involves more than just preventing and responding to cyberattacks and intrusion. Consider, for example, the situation in which users connect to a Web store to obtain some product literature. In return, the users are asked to fill out an electronic form providing information about themselves or their employers before receiving the literature. In this situation, what kinds of security issues arise?

From the user's perspective:

▶ How can the user know whether the Web server is owned and operated by a legitimate company?

▶ How does the user know that the Web page and form have not been compromised by spyware or other malicious code?

▶ How does the user know that an employee won't intercept and misuse the information?

From the company's perspective:

▶ How does the company know the user will not attempt to break into the Web server or alter the pages and content at the site?

▶ How does the company know that the user will not try to disrupt the server so that it is not available to others?

---

cybercriminal

A person who intentionally carries out crimes over the Internet.

hacker

Someone who gains unauthorized access to a computer system.

cracker

A malicious hacker, such as Maxwell, in the opening case, who may represent a serious problem for a corporation.

From both parties' perspectives:

▶ How do both parties know that the network connection is free from eavesdropping by a third party "listening" on the line?

▶ How do they know that the information sent back and forth between the server and the user's browser has not been altered?

Such questions illustrate the kinds of security issues that arise in an EC transaction. For transactions involving e-payments, additional types of security issues must be confronted.

EC Security Requirements

To protect EC transactions, we use the following set of requirements:

▶ **Authentication.** Authentication is a process to verify (assure) the real identity of an entity, which could be an individual, software agent, computer program, or EC Web site. For transmissions, authentication verifies that the sender of the message is who the person or organization claims to be.

▶ **Authorization.** Authorization is the process of determining what an authenticated entity is allowed to access and what operations it is allowed to perform. Authorization of an entity occurs after authentication.

▶ **Auditing.** When a person or program accesses a Web site or queries a database, various pieces of information are recorded or logged into a file. The process of recording information about what was accessed, when, and by whom is known as *auditing*. Audits provide the means to reconstruct what specific actions have occurred and may help EC security investigators identify the person or program that performed unauthorized actions.

▶ **Availability.** Technologies such as load-balancing hardware and software help ensure availability.

▶ **Nonrepudiation.** Closely associated with authentication is nonrepudiation, which is the assurance that online customers or trading partners will not be able to falsely deny (repudiate) their purchase, transaction, or other obligation. Nonrepudiation involves several assurances, including providing:
  ▶ The sender of data with proof of delivery
  ▶ The recipient (EC company) with proof of the sender's identity
  ▶ Authentication and nonrepudiation are potential defenses against phishing and identity theft. To protect and ensure trust in EC transactions, *digital signatures*, or *digital certificates*, are often used to validate the sender and time stamp of the transaction so it cannot be later claimed that the transaction was unauthorized or invalid. A technical overview of digital signatures and certificates and how they provide verification is provided in Section 10.6. Unfortunately, phishers and spammers have devised ways to compromise certain digital signatures (Jepson 2006).

authentication
Process to verify (assure) the real identity of an individual, computer, computer program, or EC Web site.

authorization
Process of determining what the authenticated entity is allowed to access and what operations it is allowed to perform.

nonrepudiation
Assurance that online customers or trading partners cannot falsely deny (repudiate) their purchase or transaction.

THE DEFENSE: DEFENDERS AND THEIR STRATEGY

Security should be the business of everyone. However, in general, the information system department and vendors provide the technical side while management provides the administrative aspects. Such activities are done via security and strategy.

EC Defense Programs and Strategy

An **EC security strategy** consisting of multiple layers of defense is needed. Such a strategy views EC security as the process of deterring, preventing, and detecting unauthorized use of

EC security strategy
A strategy that views EC security as the process of preventing and detecting unauthorized use of the organization's brand, identity, Web site, e-mail, information, or other asset and attempts to defraud the organization, its customers, and employees.

deterring measures
Actions that will make criminals abandon their idea of attacking a specific system (e.g., the possibility of losing a job for insiders).

prevention measures
Ways to help stop unauthorized users (also known as "intruders") from accessing any part of the EC system.

detection measures
Ways to determine whether intruders attempted to break into the EC system; whether they were successful; and what they may have done.

information assurance (IA)
The protection of information systems against unauthorized access to or modification of information whether in storage, processing, or transit, and against the denial of service to authorized users, including those measures necessary to detect, document, and counter such threats.

the organization's brand, identity, Web site, e-mail, information, or other assets and attempts to defraud the organization, its customers, and employees. **Deterring measures** refer to actions that will make criminals abandon their idea of attacking a specific system (e.g., the possibility of losing a job, for insiders). **Prevention measures** help stop unauthorized users (also known as *intruders*) from accessing any part of the EC system (e.g., by requiring a password). **Detection measures** help determine whether intruders attempted to break into the EC system; whether they were successful; and what they may have done.

Making sure that a shopping experience is safe and secure is a crucial part of improving the buyer experience. The ultimate goal of EC security is often referred to as **Information assurance (IA)**. IA is the protection of information systems against unauthorized access to or modification of information whether in storage, processing, or in transit; protection against denial of service to authorized users; and those measures necessary to detect, document, and counter threats (see details in Section 10.5).

Defense Methods and Technologies

There are hundreds defense methods, technologies, and vendors that can be classified in different ways. We introduce them in Sections 10.5 through 10.10 and show one classification in Exhibit 10.4.

Recovery

In security battles there are winners and losers in single episodes, but no one can win the war. As discussed in Section 10.11, there are many reasons for this. On the other hand, after a security breach, organizations and individuals usually recover. Recovery is especially critical in cases of a disaster or a major attack. Organizations need to continue their business until the information systems are fully restored, and they need to restore them fast. This is done by using a *business continuity and disaster recovery plan* (Section 10.10).

Because of the complexity of EC and network security, this topic cannot be covered in a single chapter or even a book. Those readers interested in a more comprehensive discussion should see the *Pearson/Prentice Hall Security Series* (pearsonhighered.com/catalog/series?series_id= 760498&series_name=Prentice%20Hall%20Security%20Series).

Section 10.2 ▶ REVIEW QUESTIONS

1. List five major terms of EC security.
2. Describe the major unintentional security hazards.
3. List five examples of intentional EC security crimes.
4. Describe the security battleground, who participates, and how. What are the possible results?
5. Define hacker, cracker, and social engineering.
6. Define authentication and authorization requirements.
7. What is nonrepudiation?
8. Describe deterring, preventing, and detecting in EC security systems.

10.3 TECHNICAL ATTACK METHODS

Criminals use many methods to attack information systems and users. Here, we cover some major representative methods.

It's helpful to distinguish between two types of attacks—*technical* (which we discuss in this section) and *nontechnical.*

TECHNICAL AND NONTECHNICAL ATTACKS: AN OVERVIEW

Software and systems knowledge are used to perpetrate *technical attacks.* A computer virus is an example of a technical attack.

Nontechnical attacks are those in which a perpetrator uses some form of deception or persuasion to trick people into revealing information or performing actions that can compromise the security of a network. We include in these financial fraud, spam, *social engineering*, and *phishing*. The goals of social engineering are to gain unauthorized access to systems or information. Phishing attacks rely on social engineering.

Many attacks involve a combination of several methods, some of which can be technical and some nontechnical. For instance, an intruder may use an automated tool to post a message to an instant messaging service, offering the opportunity to download software of interest to the members (e.g., software for downloading music or videos) that includes a botnet. When an unsuspecting user downloads the software, the botnet automatically runs on his or her computer, enabling the intruder to turn the machine into a *zombie* to perpetrate a technical attack.

THE MAJOR TECHNICAL ATTACK METHODS

Software and systems knowledge are used to carry out *technical attacks*. Hackers often use several software tools readily and freely available over the Internet, and study hacker and security Web sites to learn of vulnerabilities. Although many of these tools require expertise, novice hackers can easily use many of the existing tools. The major methods are described next.

MALICIOUS CODE: VIRUSES, WORMS, AND TROJAN HORSES

Malware (for *malicious software*) is software designed to infiltrate or damage a computer system without the owner's informed consent. The expression is a general term used by computer professionals to mean a variety of forms of hostile, intrusive, or annoying software or program code.

Software is considered malware based on the perceived intent of the creator rather than any particular features. Malware includes computer viruses, worms, Trojan horses, most rootkits, spyware, dishonest adware, crimeware, and other malicious and unwanted software.

Preliminary results from a study suggested that the release rate of malicious code and other unwanted programs may be exceeding that of legitimate software applications (Symantec 2008). According to F-Secure (f-secure.com), as much malware was produced in 2007 as in the previous 20 years altogether. Malware's most common pathway from criminals to users is through the Internet—primarily by e-mail and the Web.

Viruses

A **virus** is a piece of software code that inserts itself into a host, including the operating systems; running its host program activates the virus. A virus has two components. First, it has a propagation mechanism by which it spreads. Second, it has a payload that refers to what the virus does once it is executed. Sometimes a particular event triggers the virus's execution. For instance, Michelangelo's birth date triggered the Michelangelo virus. Some viruses simply infect and spread. Others do substantial damage (e.g., deleting files or corrupting the hard drive). The process of a virus attack is illustrated in Exhibit 10.4.

For tutorials and information about viruses, see microsoft.com/protect/computer/basics/virus.mspx.

Worms. Unlike a virus, a **worm** can spread itself without any human intervention. Worms use networks to propagate and infect a computer or handheld device (e.g., cell phone) and can even spread via instant messages. Also unlike viruses that generally are confined within a target computer, a worm's ability to self-propagate can degrade network performance. Worms consist of a set of common base elements: a warhead, a propagation engine, a payload, a target-selection algorithm, and a scanning engine. The *warhead* is the piece of code in a worm that exploits some known vulnerability. A huge number of worms have been spread all over the Internet (for example, the Conficker worm in 2009).

In March 2009, the Koobface worm attacked Facebook and other social networks. It created bogus links that looked innocent, but when you clicked them, it gave hackers access to sensitive personal data.

Macro Virus. A **macro virus** or **macro worm** is executed when the application object that contains the macro is opened or a particular procedure is executed. Because worms spread much more rapidly than viruses, organizations need to proactively track new vulnerabilities and apply system patches as a defense against their spread.

Trojan Horse. A **Trojan horse** is a program that appears to have a useful function but contains a hidden function that presents a security risk. The name is derived from the Trojan

virus
A piece of software code that inserts itself into a host, including the operating systems, in order to propagate; it requires that its host program be run to activate it.

worm
A software program that runs independently, consuming the resources of its host in order to maintain itself, that is capable of propagating a complete working version of itself onto another machine.

macro virus (macro worm)
A macro virus or macro worm is executed when the application object that contains the macro is opened or a particular procedure is executed.

Trojan horse
A program that appears to have a useful function but that contains a hidden function that presents a security risk.

EXHIBIT 10.4 How a Computer Virus Can Spread

Just as a biological virus disrupts living cells to cause disease, a computer virus—introduced maliciously—invades the inner workings of computers and disrupts normal operations of the machines.

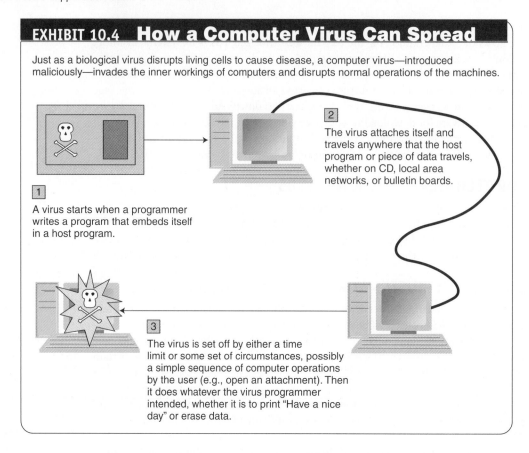

1 A virus starts when a programmer writes a program that embeds itself in a host program.

2 The virus attaches itself and travels anywhere that the host program or piece of data travels, whether on CD, local area networks, or bulletin boards.

3 The virus is set off by either a time limit or some set of circumstances, possibly a simple sequence of computer operations by the user (e.g., open an attachment). Then it does whatever the virus programmer intended, whether it is to print "Have a nice day" or erase data.

horse in Greek mythology. Legend has it that during the Trojan War the city of Troy was presented with a large wooden horse as a gift to the goddess Athena. The Trojans hauled the horse inside the city gates. During the night, Greek soldiers who were hiding in the hollow horse opened the gates of Troy and let in the Greek army. The army was able to take the city and win the war.

There are many variations of Trojan horse programs. The programs of interest are those that make it possible for someone else to access and control a person's computer over the Internet. This type of Trojan horse has two parts: a server and a client. The *server* is the program that runs on the computer under attack. The *client* program is the program used by the person perpetrating the attack. For example, the Girlfriend Trojan is a server program that arrives in the form of a file that looks like an interesting game or program. When the unsuspecting user runs the program, the user unknowingly installs the Trojan program. The installed program executes every time the user turns on the attacked computer. The server simply waits for the associated client program to send a command. This particular Trojan horse enables the perpetrator to capture user IDs and passwords, to display messages on the affected computer, to delete and upload files, and so on. Trojan threads are spread in many ways (e.g., under the guise of Verizon messages). Two examples follow:

Example 1: Spyware researchers at Webroot Software uncovered a stash of tens of thousands of stolen identities from 125 countries that they believe were collected by a new variant of a Trojan program the company named *Trojan-Phisher-Rebery* (Roberts 2006b). The Rebery malicious software is an example of a **banking Trojan**, which is programmed to come to life when computer owners visit one of a number of online banking sites.

Example 2: Bank of America has more than 20 million customers online and processes more transactions online than it does in all of its physical banking centers. According to Gage (2006), Ahlo, a Miami wholesaler of ink and toner cartridges, sued Bank of America for being responsible for an unauthorized transfer of more than $90,000 from Ahlo's account to a bank in Latvia. A Coreflood Trojan infected the company's PC. The Trojan was spread by a phishing attack—fraudulent e-mails that tricked bank customers into giving up their account information and infecting their computers with malware that logged keystrokes.

banking Trojan
A Trojan that comes to life when computer owners visit one of a number of online banking or e-commerce sites.

(The bank does not discuss individual phishing attempts but posted information on its Web site, bofa.com/privacy, to educate customers about online fraud.) Bank of America's battle against phishing shows how hard it is for businesses that have grown by acquiring companies with incompatible information systems to protect gullible and sometimes lazy or "can't happen to me" mentality customers from cybercrime.

The best way to defend against Trojan horses is to implement strict acceptable use policies (AUPs) and procedures for installing new software. In an organization, end users should be forbidden from installing unauthorized programs. Administrators need to check the integrity of programs and patches that are installed. In the same vein, new programs and tools should be installed in a test environment before putting them into a production environment.

Denial of Service

A **denial of service (DOS) attack** is an attack in which a large number of requests for service or access to a site bombard a system, which causes it to crash or become unable to respond in time. In a DOS attack, an attacker uses specialized software to send a flood of data packets to the target computer, with the aim of overloading its resources. Many attackers rely on software created by other hackers that is available over the Internet for free rather than developing it themselves. A common method is the use of zombie PCs to launch DOS attacks.

denial of service (DOS) attack
An attack on a Web site in which an attacker uses specialized software to send a flood of data packets to the target computer with the aim of overloading its resources.

Example: The SCO Group. This attack involved nothing more than having hundreds of thousands of infected machines send page requests to SCO's Web site. The site was brought to a standstill because it was overwhelmed by the large number of requests. It was first thought that SCO was a victim of irate Linux proponents who were angered by SCO's multimillion-dollar lawsuit against IBM for having allegedly included SCO's code in IBM's Linux software. Later, it was suggested that the attack was actually launched by spammers out of Russia.

DOS attacks can be difficult to stop. Fortunately (or unfortunately), they are so commonplace that over the past few years the security community has developed a series of steps for combating these costly attacks. In the case of SCO, the attacks were scheduled to run from February 1, 2004, to February 12, 2004. During that time, SCO shut off its original Web site, sco.com, and set up a new homepage at thescogroup.com. Microsoft, which was the target of MyDoom.B, redirected its Web to specialized security servers run by Akamai Technologies.

Web Server and Web Page Hijacking

Web servers and Web pages can be hijacked and configured to control or redirect unsuspecting users to scam or phishing sites. This exploit allows *any* Webmaster (including criminals) to have his or her own "virtual pages" rank for pages belonging to another Webmaster (e.g., a legitimate EC site). Successfully employed, this technique will allow the offending Webmaster ("the hijacker") to displace the pages of the "target" or victim Web site in the search engine result pages. This causes search engine traffic to the target Web site to vanish or redirects traffic to any other page of choice.

Criminal organizations, crime networks, and terrorist groups have used Web server hijacking and exploited the global information, financial, and transportation networks (Hearing of the Senate Armed Services Committee 2006).

International organized crime syndicates, Al-Qaida groups, and other cybercriminals steal hundreds of billions of dollars every year. Cybercrime is safer and easier than selling drugs, dealing in black market diamonds, or robbing banks. Online gambling offers easy fronts for international money laundering operations. And hack attacks are a key weapon of global jihad.

Example: The Bali Attack. Credit card fraud financed the 2002 explosion that killed more than 200 people at a nightclub in Bali, Indonesia. Imam Samudra, the man behind the attack, wrote a book in jail in which he exhorts followers to "learn to hack." The book continues, "Not just because it makes more money in three to six hours than a policeman makes in six months, but because it is how we can bring America and its cronies to its knees." For details, see Altman (2006).

Botnets

botnet

A huge number (e.g., hundreds of thousands) of hijacked Internet computers that have been set up to forward traffic, including spam and viruses, to other computers on the Internet.

A **botnet** is a huge number (hundreds of thousands) of hijacked Internet computers that have been set up to forward traffic, including spam and viruses (recall the opening case), to other computers on the Internet. An infected computer is referred to as a *computer robot*, or *bot*. Botmasters, or bot herders, control botnets. The combined power of these coordinated networks of computers can scan for and compromise other computers and perpetrate DOS or other attacks. Botnets are used in scams, spams, and frauds.

Example. At the beginning of 2004, the MyDoom. A e-mail virus infected several hundred thousand PCs around the world (Fisher 2004). Like many other e-mail viruses, this virus propagated by sending an official-looking e-mail message with a zip file attached. When the victim opened the zip file, the virus automatically found other e-mail addresses on the victim's computer and forwarded itself to those addresses. However, there was more to MyDoom than simple propagation. When the victim opened the zip file, the virus code also installed a program on the victim's machine that enabled the intruders to automatically launch a DOS attack.

Section 10.3 ▶ REVIEW QUESTIONS

1. Describe the difference between a nontechnical and a technical cyberattack.
2. What are the major forms of malicious code?
3. What factors account for the increase in malicious code?
4. What are some of the major trends in malicious code?
5. Define worm and Trojan horse.
6. How are DOS attacks perpetrated?
7. Describe botnet attacks.

10.4 PHISHING, FINANCIAL FRAUD, AND SPAM

As discussed in Section 10.1, there is a shift to profit-related Internet crimes. These crimes are conducted with the help of both technical methods, such as malicious code that can steal confidential information from your online bank account, and nontechnical methods, such as social engineering and phishing. Exhibit 10.5 illustrates how such cybercrimes are conducted.

Phishers (or other criminals) obtain confidential information by methods ranging from social engineering to physical theft. The stolen information (e.g., credit card numbers, social

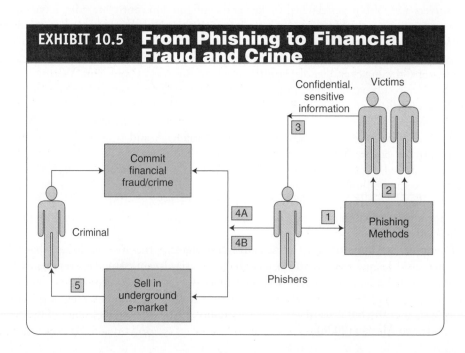

EXHIBIT 10.5 From Phishing to Financial Fraud and Crime

security numbers) is used by thieves to commit financial fraud or is sold in the underground Internet marketplace to another set of criminals, who then use the information to conduct financial crime. In this section, we will describe how such systems work.

PHISHING

In the field of computer security, *phishing* is the criminal, fraudulent process of attempting to acquire confidential information such as user names, passwords, and credit card details by masquerading as a trustworthy entity such as a well-known bank, credit card company, a large social network, or a telecommunication company, in an electronic communication, usually via e-mail or IM. Phishing typically directs users to enter details at a fake Web site that looks and feels almost identical to the legitimate one. Even when using server authentication, it may require skill to detect that the Web site is fake.

For example, "Cyber Monday" is the name retailers gave to the first Monday after the U.S. Thanksgiving holiday weekend because that day kicks off the busiest online shopping period of the year. This 1-day sale grows by 20 percent to 30 percent each year. This growth in sales volume and the number of shoppers has attracted cyber cons aimed at identity theft and fraud.

Online shoppers and those conducting transactions electronically are attractive targets because they typically have higher incomes. Phishers, electronic shoplifters, con artists, and scammers stalk online shoppers because these cyber cons want shoppers' confidential information—today's most valuable form of international currency.

Selling stolen information, like selling any stolen goods, can be profitable and unstoppable. In a 2006 survey, 21 percent of potential customers listed "too much risk of fraud, I don't trust online merchants" as their primary reason for not shopping online. Of the total fraud complaints reported to the FTC, Internet-related fraud complaints jumped from 1 percent in 1996 to 79 percent in 2008 (McMillan 2009). Not only do concerns about cyber cons stunt EC growth, but defending against these cons and compensating for damages also significantly increase the costs of EC. As companies try to expand their e-business in countries where the legal systems are underdeveloped, opportunities for fraud expand with it.

Example. German phishers sent out messages pretending to come from a utility company that provides an electronic invoice as an Adobe PDF file. This social engineering trick worked. Many customers clicked the link to download an "important document," which contained a Trojan horse. The program gave the sender control of the infected machine. The Trojan monitored every Internet connection and keystroke and reported passwords back to the Trojan's creator.

Sophisticated Phishing Methods

RSA Security (rsasecurity.com) reported a powerful new phishing tool fraudsters are selling via online forums and using to dupe consumers. Phishers use a tool called a **universal man-in-the-middle phishing kit** to set up a URL that can interact in real time with the content of a legitimate Web site, such as a bank or e-tailing site. In this way, fraudsters can intercept data entered by customers at log-in or checkout pages. They then send out phishing e-mails containing links that send recipients to the fake URL, where the user can see an organization's legitimate Web site—and where the fraudsters will hijack inputted information being typed. Unfortunately, the trend is toward continuously harder-to-detect online fraud, such as in this example. Phishing is a major provider of information used for financial fraud on the Internet. Exhibit 10.6 illustrates a typical phishing process called "drive-by downloads," a top Web threat (Symantec 2009). For other methods, see en.wikipedia.org/wiki/phishing. For many examples and tips on how to avoid phishing scams, see Microsoft (2008).

universal man-in-the-middle phishing kit
A tool used by phishers to set up a URL that can interact in real time with the content of a legitimate Web site, such as a bank or EC site, to intercept data entered by customers at log-in or check out Web pages.

FRAUD ON THE INTERNET

Phishing is the first step that leads to fraud (recall Exhibit 10.5). An environment where buyers and sellers cannot see each other breeds fraud. Fraud is a problem for online retailers and customers alike. However, even though actual losses per incident are rising, the rate of those losses is flattening out. In other words, the threat actually may be lessening—somewhat. According to the "Tenth Annual Online Fraud Report" released by CyberSource, losses from online fraud in the United States alone in 2007 totaled $1.3 billion, a 5.5 percent increase

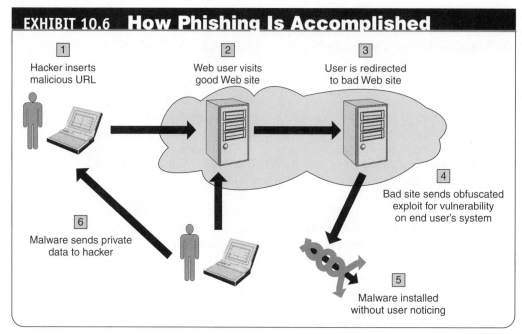

EXHIBIT 10.6 How Phishing Is Accomplished

1. Hacker inserts malicious URL
2. Web user visits good Web site
3. User is redirected to bad Web site
4. Bad site sends obfuscated exploit for vulnerability on end user's system
5. Malware installed without user noticing
6. Malware sends private data to hacker

Source: Symantec, "Web-Based Attacks," ©2009. Used with permission.

over 2005 (U.S. Federal Trade Commission 2008). However, the percentage of revenues lost to fraud dropped to 1.4 percent in 2008, down from 1.6 percent in 2005. Since 2004, the percentage rate of revenue loss has declined. Since e-commerce sales continue to grow by about 20 percent a year, the overall dollar-loss amount showed a rise.

Online merchants reject roughly 4 percent of incoming orders because of suspicion of fraud. An estimated 1 percent of accepted orders turn out to be fraudulent. As an adjustment to a slowing economy, merchants shifted fraud-fighting priorities in 2008, dropping the unaccepted orders from 4.2 percent to 2.9 percent. Among online orders from outside the United States and Canada in 2006, 2.7 percent of the orders were fraudulent. That rate is three times higher than the rate associated with orders from the United States and Canada (*Marketing Charts* 2009).

Special tools enable online merchants to estimate the risk of orders based on information gathered from computer screens. For example, CyberSource's Internet Fraud Screen (IFS) enables merchants to set the level of risk (threshold) that they are willing to accept in an order. IFS assigns a risk score to each transaction. Transactions whose scores fall below the risk threshold are declined.

During the first few years of EC, many types of financial crime came to light, ranging from the online manipulation of stock prices to the creation of a virtual bank that disappeared together with the investors' deposits. Internet fraud has grown even faster than the Internet itself. The following examples demonstrate the scope of the problem. Also visit the Open Directory Project at dmoz.org/Society/Issues/Fraud/Internet for a comprehensive set of fraud resources.

Examples of Typical Online Fraud Attempts

▶ Phishing uses spam e-mails or pop-up messages to deceive victims into disclosing credit card numbers, bank account information, social security numbers, passwords, or other sensitive information. Typically, the e-mail or pop-up message claims to be from a business or organization that the recipient may deal with; for example, an ISP, bank, online payment service, or even a government agency.

▶ When one of the authors advertised online that he had a house to rent, several "doctors" and "nurses" from the United Kingdom and South America applied. They agreed to pay a premium for a short-term lease and said they would pay with a cashier's check. They asked if the author would accept checks for $6,000 to

$10,000 and send them back the balance of $4,000 to $8,000. When advised that this would be fine, but that the difference would be returned only after their checks had cleared, none of the would-be renters followed up.

▶ Extortion rings in the United Kingdom and Russia pried hundreds of thousands of dollars from online sports betting Web sites. Any site refusing to pay protection fees was threatened with zombie computers using DOS attacks.

▶ Fake escrow sites take advantage of the inherent trust of escrow sites, stealing buyers' deposits. Dozens of fake escrow sites on the Internet have convincing names like "Honest-Escrow.net" and use ads such as "Worried about getting scammed in an Internet auction? Just use an escrow service like us."

▶ Click fraud is a common concern for advertisers and search vendors alike. Click fraud occurs in pay-per-click advertising when a person, automated system, or computer program simulates individual clicks on banner or other online advertising methods. These scams and deceptions inflate advertising bills for thousands of companies of all sizes. The spreading scourge poses the single biggest threat to online advertising. It is perpetrated in both automated and human ways. The most common method is the use of online bots, programmed to click on advertisers' links that are displayed on Web sites or listed in search queries. Because advertisers pay fees based on number of clicks, bogus clicks inflate those fees. Google claims to be well equipped to handle the dilemma. They state, "Our Click Quality team investigates every inquiry received from advertisers who believe they may have been affected by undetected click fraud."

click fraud
Type of fraud that occurs in pay-per-click advertising when a person, automated system, or computer program simulates individual clicks on banner or other online advertising methods.

More examples of Internet fraud are provided in Online File W10.3 or see Krebs (2008).

Identity Theft and Identify Fraud

Identity theft refers to stealing an identity of a person; that information is then used by someone pretending to be someone else in order to steal money or get other benefits. The term is relatively new and is actually a misnomer, since it is not inherently possible to steal an identity, only to use it. The person whose identity is used can suffer various consequences when he or she is held responsible for the perpetrator's actions. In many countries, specific laws make it a crime to use another person's identity for personal gain. Identity theft is the number one concern of EC shoppers, according to the U.S. Federal Trade Commission (ftc.gov). The latest statistics indicate (CNNMoney 2009) that identity fraud hit 10 million Americans, who lost $48 billion (a 22 percent increase over 2007).

identity theft
Fraud that involves stealing an identity of a person and then the use of that identity by someone pretending to be someone else in order to steal money or get other benefits.

Identity theft is somewhat different from *identity fraud*, which is related to the unlawful usage of a "false identity" to commit fraud. Examples of identity fraud include

▶ Financial identity theft (using another's identity to obtain goods and services)
▶ Business/commercial identity theft (using another's business name to obtain credit)
▶ Criminal identity theft (posing as another when apprehended for a crime)
▶ Money laundering

Example. No one is immune from identity theft, even the sheriff of Merced County, California. On March 11, 2009, while the sheriff's deputies were searching the home of a woman accused of forging checks, they discovered on her computer the copied signature of their boss. Investigators said the woman lifted the sheriff's signature from a standard check given to departing inmates to reimburse them for pocket money confiscated during booking. She had uploaded the signature to a check-writing program. She used the checks to pay for services she received.

For additional information, see en.wikipedia.org/wiki/Identity_theft.

Other Financial Fraud

Stock fraud is only one of many areas where swindlers are active. Other areas include the sale of bogus investments, phantom business opportunities, and other schemes.

In addition, foreign-currency-trading scams are increasing on the Internet because most online currency exchange shops are not licensed. For many examples see Microsoft (2009) and Symantec (2009).

Spam Attacks

e-mail spam

A subset of spam that involves nearly identical messages sent to numerous recipients by e-mail.

E-mail spam also known as *junk e-mail* or just *spam*, is a subset of spam that involves nearly identical messages sent to numerous recipients by e-mail. A common synonym for spam is *unsolicited bulk e-mail*. Overall, 60 percent to 75 percent of all e-mail is spam. According to Symantec (2008), spam categories include commercial products, health-related products, and financial products (stocks, banking, and so forth). Spam also covers those who conduct financial fraud and Internet scams, illegal gambling, and pornography.

E-mail spam has grown steadily since the early 1990s to several billion messages a day. Spam has frustrated, confused, and annoyed e-mail users. Laws against spam (see Chapter 16) have been sporadically initiated. The total volume of spam (more than 100 billion e-mails per day as of April 2008) has leveled off slightly in recent years and is no longer growing exponentially. But the amount received by most e-mail users has decreased mostly because of better filtering. Approximately 80 percent of all spam is sent by fewer than 200 spammers. Botnets, networks of virus-infected computers, and so forth are used to send about 80 percent of all spam. Since the cost of the spam is borne mostly by the recipient, spam is effective e-mail advertising.

With antispam software and ISP spam filters defeating traditional e-mail spam, spamming tactics have mutated. Those mutations seek to ensure—by any means—a good shopper delivery rate. Spammers use sophisticated botnets and spam zombies to capture a large number of PCs that can generate and disseminate spam messages. Unsolicited junk advertisements are sent via all types of messaging media, including blogs, instant messages (IM), and cell phones. Spammers promote their gambling sites, prescription drugs, get-rich schemes, and the like (see Symantec 2009). There are also those who use spamming for facilitating crime (e.g., identity theft, money laundering, auction fraud).

E-mail addresses are collected from chat rooms, Web sites, newsgroups, and viruses that harvest users' address books. Much spam is sent to invalid e-mail addresses. ISPs have attempted to recover the cost of spam through lawsuits against spammers, although they have been mostly unsuccessful in collecting damages despite winning in court. An example of how spam is used for stock market fraud is provided in Case 10.1.

Automated Blog Spam. Bloggers have found hundreds of automatically generated comments with links to herbal Viagra and gambling vendors on their pages. Software bots that trawl the Internet looking for suitable forms to fill in automatically generate the majority of blog spam. Blog owners can use tools to ensure that humans—and not an automated system—enter comments on their blogs.

Search Engine Spam and Splogs

search engine spam

Pages created deliberately to trick the search engine into offering inappropriate, redundant, or poor-quality search results.

spam site

Page that uses techniques that deliberately subvert a search engine's algorithms to artificially inflate the page's rankings.

splog

Short for *spam blog*. A site created solely for marketing purposes.

Although content spam impacts media users, the greater concern to ethical e-commerce sites is **search engine spam**, which Yahoo! defines as "pages created deliberately to trick the search engine into offering inappropriate, redundant, or poor-quality search results." Those pages, called **spam sites**, use techniques that deliberately subvert a search engine's algorithms to artificially inflate the page's rankings. A similar tactic involves the use of **splogs** (short for *spam blog sites*), which are blogs created solely for marketing purposes. Spammers create hundreds of splogs that they link to the spammer's site to increase that site's search engine ranking. This method makes use of the fact that the number of links found determines a page's rank, as in Google's PageRank system, which calculates a page's position in search results by weighing the links to that page. For information on search engine algorithms and page rankings, see google.com/technology.

Sploggers work on the principle that once Web surfers arrive at their site, a few will click on one of the linked advertisements. Each of these clicks earns a few cents for the splogger. And because any one splogger can run thousands of splogs, the spam can be very profitable. (One splog partnership claimed $71,136.89 in earnings in the 3 months from August to October 2005.)

CASE 10.1
EC Application
INTERNET STOCK FRAUD AIDED BY SPAM

A study reported by Lerer (2007) concluded that stock spam moves markets. The researchers found that the average investor who buys a stock during a spam promotion (campaign) and then sells after the campaign ends loses about 5.5 percent of their investment. In contrast, the spammer who buys stock before the spam campaign and sells during the campaign makes a 5.79 percent return.

The U.S. government made headlines on March 8, 2007, by cracking down on dozens of penny stocks whose prices had been manipulated. The success of *Operation Spamalot*, conducted by the Securities and Exchange Commission (SEC), still will not end spam. There are two reasons spam won't go away: It works and it's profitable. Despite increased enforcement, warnings, and national laws, spam is not only continuing but flourishing. And there's no reason to think the SEC will be able to do much to stop it.

Stock spam has gotten much worse in the last few years. Stock spam messages rose 120 percent during the 6-month period ending March 2007. In total, stock-related messages make up about 20 percent of all e-mail spam. The SEC estimates that 100 million stock spam messages are sent each week.

Technology has increased spammers' ability to send junk e-mail. Spammers used to have to send all their messages from one computer, making them easily blocked by spam filters. Today, spammers send their messages through botnets (linked networks of computers) that they control. With the extra bandwidth, they are sending billions of messages with promotional text embedded in image files—called *image spam*. Image spam looks identical to normal spam but sneaks by antispam programs that look only at text, not pictures or photos.

During 2006, global spam volume tripled. During a 6-week period, Secure Computing Research saw an increase of 50 percent in spam. Spam now accounts for nearly 90 percent of all e-mail. In that same time, the amount of image spam, which today accounts for 30 percent of all spam, tripled.

Sources: Compiled from Lerer (2007) and SecureComputing (2007).

Questions

1. Speculate why people might buy the penny stocks promoted in an e-mail message from an unknown source.
2. Use the Internet (Google) to find what can be done to filter image spam.

Spyware is computer software that is installed surreptitiously on a personal computer to intercept or take partial control over the user's interaction with the computer, without the user's knowledge or consent. Although the term *spyware* suggests software that secretly monitors the user's behavior (Chapter 4), the functions of spyware extend well beyond simple monitoring. Spyware programs can collect various types of personal information, such as Internet surfing habits and sites that have been visited, but they can also interfere with user control of the computer in other ways, such as installing additional (even malicious) software and redirecting Web browser activity. Spyware is known to change computer settings, resulting in slow surfing speeds and/or loss of Internet or functionality of other programs. In an attempt to increase the understanding of spyware, a more formal classification of its included software types is captured under the term *privacy-invasive software*. Although spyware is used mainly by advertisers, it may also be used by criminals.

spyware
Software that gathers user information over an Internet connection without the user's knowledge.

SOCIAL NETWORKING MAKES SOCIAL ENGINEERING EASY

Social engineering tactics have been diversified. In the past, social engineers used cleverly worded e-mail and face-to-face conversations to get information to launch attacks. But now, social networking sites that contain goldmines of information are major targets for new attack methods. Social engineering tactics or scams that depended on user interaction to execute an attack against them rose dramatically in 2006 (LeClaire 2007). As more users take advantage of Web 2.0 applications like social networking sites, blogs, wikis, and RSS feeds, malware authors, identity thieves, and other criminals are going to exploit these users. With the rise of Web 2.0 and more social interaction on social networking sites, security experts warn of an increase in the incidence of hackers inserting malicious code into dynamically generated Web pages.

Social networking sites are creating a means for hackers and con artists to worm their way into the confidence of users, which leaves Internet users and businesses at a greater risk of attack, according to a study by Danish security firm CSIS.

Example. Dennis Rand, a security researcher at CSIS, created a fictitious entry on the LinkedIn network before inviting random and unknown users to LinkedIn to join his private network. By posing as an ex-employee of "targeted" firms, he was able to prompt real workers from these firms into establishing connections. Within a few weeks, Rand created a network of 1,340 trusted connections. In a research paper, Rand explains how information gleaned through this network might be used to harvest e-mail addresses to send messages containing links to malicious codes that are more likely to be accepted because they come from a "trusted" source (Rand 2007).

Despite all the social engineering incidents in 2006, it wasn't until the worm and phishing attack against MySpace in early December 2006 that the public recognized what some security experts are calling "the next big Internet threat." The attack forced MySpace to shut down thousands of user profile pages after a worm converted legitimate links to those that sent users to a phishing site. The phishing site attempted to obtain personal information, including MySpace user names and passwords. During 2008 and 2009, there were many breaches of security in social networks. For example, in March 2008, a Facebook security hole allowed actress Paris Hilton's private pictures to be leaked.

Because successful social engineering attacks depend, in effect, on the cooperation of the victims, stopping social engineering attacks also depends on the victims. Certain positions within an organization are clearly vulnerable, such as those with access to private and confidential information or those that interact with customers or vendors. In the AUP and employee training programs, all users should learn how to avoid becoming a victim of manipulation. Specific policies and procedures need to be developed for securing confidential information, guiding employee behavior with respect to confidential information, and taking the steps needed to respond to and report any social engineering breaches. Social networks are especially vulnerable to spam attacks.

Examples. Some examples of spam attacks in social networks are:

▶ In January 2009, Facebook won $1.3 billion from spammers in Canada who falsely obtained log-in information for Facebook users and then sent spam to those users' friends, violating the CAN-SPAM Act. In 2008, MySpace was awarded $230 million in a similar case (in both cases, the companies were unable to collect).

▶ Twitter became a hot target to hackers who, in January 2009, hijacked the accounts of several high-profile users (now users are protected).

▶ Instant messaging in social networks was found to be very vulnerable to hackers and other cybercriminals.

▶ Hackers are posting content loaded with malicious software that is difficult to detect on YouTube, MySpace, and other social network sites. Other methods are frequently invented.

▶ Chat rooms harbor "fraud as a service" peddlers who use data-harvesting Trojans.

▶ VoIP is used extensively in social networks, yet it is vulnerable to many attacks (products such as VoIPguard can help).

▶ Blogs can be attacked by spammers fairly easily.

▶ Koobface and other worms targeted Facebook, as described earlier. MacMillan (2008) describes the problem and prescribes some solutions.

The discussion so far has concentrated on attacks. Defense mechanisms, including those related to spam and other unsolicited ads, are provided in Sections 10.6 through 10.10. First, let's examine what is involved in assuring information security.

Section 10.4 ▶ REVIEW QUESTIONS

1. Define phishing.
2. Describe the relationship of phishing to financial fraud.
3. Briefly describe some phishing tactics.
4. Describe spam and its methods.
5. Define splogs and explain how sploggers make money.
6. Why and how are social networks being attacked?

10.5 THE INFORMATION ASSURANCE MODEL AND DEFENSE STRATEGY

The *information assurance (IA) model* provides a framework for protection of information systems against unauthorized access to or modification of information that is stored, processed, or sent over a network. The importance of the IA model to EC is that it represents the processes for protecting information by insuring its confidentiality, integrity, and availability. This model is known as the **CIA security triad**, or simply the **CIA triad**, and is shown in Exhibit 10.7.

The model has three components that express the requirements for a secured information system: *confidentiality, integrity,* and *availability*.

CONFIDENTIALITY, INTEGRITY, AND AVAILABILITY

The success and security of EC can be measured by these components: confidentiality, integrity, and availability of information at the business Web site.

1. **Confidentiality** is the assurance of data privacy. The data or transmitted message is encrypted so that it is readable only by the person for whom it is intended. Encryption strength can vary. Depending on the strength of the encryption method, intruders or eavesdroppers might not be able to break the encryption to read the data or text.

2. **Integrity** is the assurance that data are accurate or that a message has not been altered. It means that stored data has not been modified without authorization; a message that was sent is the same message that was received. The integrity function detects and prevents the unauthorized creation, modification, or deletion of data or messages.

3. **Availability** is the assurance that access to data, the Web site, or other EC service is timely, available, reliable, and restricted to authorized users.

Three concepts related to the IA model are *authentication, authorization,* and *nonrepudiation*.

AUTHENTICATION, AUTHORIZATION, AND NONREPUDIATION

All the CIA functions depend on authentication. *Authentication* requires evidence in the form of credentials, which can take a variety of forms, including something known (e.g., a password), something possessed (e.g., a smart card), or something unique (e.g., a signature or fingerprint). *Authorization* requires comparing information about the person or program with access control information associated with the resource being accessed. *Nonrepudiation* is the concept of ensuring that a party in a dispute cannot repudiate or refute the validity of a statement or contract. Although this concept can be applied to any transaction, by far the most common application is in verification and trust of signatures. One nonrepudiation method is the use of a digital signature that makes it difficult for people to dispute that they were involved in an exchange.

CIA security triad (CIA triad)
Three security concepts important to information on the Internet: confidentiality, integrity, and availability.

confidentiality
Assurance of data privacy and accuracy. Keeping private or sensitive information from being disclosed to unauthorized individuals, entities, or processes.

integrity
Assurance that stored data has not been modified without authorization; a message that was sent is the same message that was received.

availability
Assurance that access to data, the Web site, or other EC data service is timely, available, reliable, and restricted to authorized users.

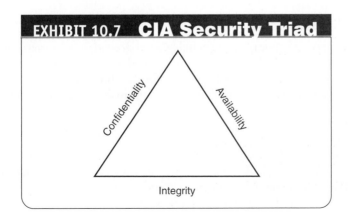

EXHIBIT 10.7 CIA Security Triad

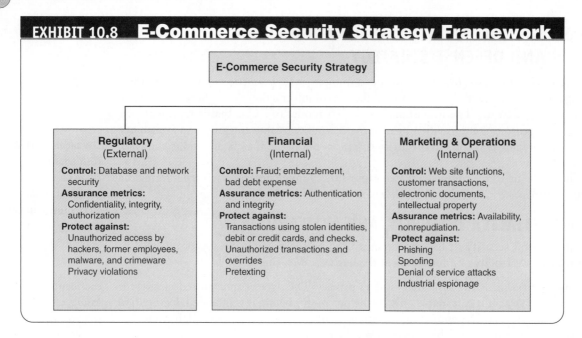

EXHIBIT 10.8   E-Commerce Security Strategy Framework

E-Commerce Security Strategy

Regulatory (External)	Financial (Internal)	Marketing & Operations (Internal)
Control: Database and network security	**Control:** Fraud; embezzlement, bad debt expense	**Control:** Web site functions, customer transactions, electronic documents, intellectual property
Assurance metrics: Confidentiality, integrity, authorization	**Assurance metrics:** Authentication and integrity	**Assurance metrics:** Availability, nonrepudiation.
Protect against: Unauthorized access by hackers, former employees, malware, and crimeware Privacy violations	**Protect against:** Transactions using stolen identities, debit or credit cards, and checks. Unauthorized transactions and overrides Pretexting	**Protect against:** Phishing Spoofing Denial of service attacks Industrial espionage

New or improved methods to ensure the confidentiality of credit card numbers, integrity of entire messages, authentication of the buyer and seller, and nonrepudiation of transactions are being developed as older ones become ineffective.

E-COMMERCE SECURITY STRATEGY

An EC security strategy needs to address the IA model and its components. In Exhibit 10.8, an EC security framework is presented that defines the high-level categories of assurance and their controls. The three major categories are regulatory, financial, and marketing and operations. Only the key areas are listed in the exhibit, but there is overlap in requirements in each category.

The FTC and other regulatory agencies mandate that organizations protect against unauthorized access and privacy violations (see Chapter 16). Given the staggering number of data breaches, these external agencies are imposing increasingly harsh penalties for inadequate database and network security (George 2008).

The financial health of an organization is at risk if fraud, embezzlement, and bad debt expense are not rigorously contained. Doing so requires protecting against the use of stolen identities, checks, debit cards, and credit cards and against unauthorized transactions and overrides of accounting controls. EC marketing depends on the trust and confidence of customers. The ability to operate depends on the availability of the EC site and its ability to provide shopping features and process the transactions. Among the many ways of impairing marketing and operations are phishing, spoofing, denial of service attacks, and industrial espionage. Protection of both buyers and sellers is discussed in Chapter 16.

THE DEFENSE STRATEGY

The defense strategy and controls that should be used depend on what needs to be protected and the cost–benefit analysis. That is, companies should neither underinvest nor overinvest in security. The SEC and FTC impose huge fines for data breaches to deter companies from underinvesting in data protection. The following are the major objectives of defense strategies:

1. **Prevention and deterrence.** Properly designed controls may prevent errors from occurring, deter criminals from attacking the system, and better yet, deny access to unauthorized people. These are the most desirable controls.

2. **Detection.** Like a fire, the earlier an attack is detected, the easier it is to combat, and the less damage is done. Detection can be performed in many cases by using special diagnostic software, at a minimal cost.

3. **Containment (contain the damage).** This objective is to minimize or limit losses once a malfunction has occurred. It is also called *damage control*. This can be accomplished, for example, by including a *fault-tolerant system* that permits operation in a degraded mode until full recovery is made. If a fault-tolerant system does not exist, a quick (and possibly expensive) recovery must take place. Users want their systems back in operation as fast as possible.

4. **Recovery.** A recovery plan explains how to fix a damaged information system as quickly as possible. Replacing rather than repairing components is one route to fast recovery.

5. **Correction.** Correcting the causes of damaged systems can prevent the problem from occurring again.

6. **Awareness and compliance.** All organization members must be educated about the hazards and must comply with the security rules and regulations.

Treating EC Security as a Project

EC security programs have a life cycle, and throughout that life cycle the EC security requirements must be continuously evaluated and adjusted. An **EC security program** is the set of controls over security processes to protect organizational assets. The four high-level stages in the life cycle of an EC security program are:

1. Planning and organizing
2. Implementation
3. Operations and maintenance
4. Monitoring and evaluating

For details, see Online File W10.4.

EC security programs
All the policies, procedures, documents, standards, hardware, software, training, and personnel that work together to protect information, the ability to conduct business, and other assets.

Section 10.5 ▶ REVIEW QUESTIONS

1. What is information assurance? List its major components.
2. Define confidentiality, integrity, and availability.
3. Describe the objectives and elements of EC strategy.

10.6 THE DEFENSE I: ACCESS CONTROL, ENCRYPTION, AND PKI

Most organizations rely on multiple technologies to secure their networks. These technologies can be divided into two major groups: those designed to secure communications across the network and those designed to protect the servers and clients on the network. This section considers the first of these technologies. The second group is the subject of Sections 10.7 and 10.8.

ACCESS CONTROL

Network security depends on access control. **Access control** determines who (person, program, or machine) can legitimately use a network resource and which resources he, she, or it can use. A resource can be anything—Web pages, text files, databases, applications, servers, printers, or any other information source or network component. Typically, access control lists define which users have access to which resources and what rights they have with respect to those resources (i.e., read, view, write, print, copy, delete, execute, modify, or move). Each resource needs to be

access control
Mechanism that determines who can legitimately use a network resource.

considered separately, and the rights of particular users or categories of users (e.g., system administrators, northwest sales reps, product marketing department, trading partners, etc.) need to be established.

Access control involves authorization (having the right to access) and authentication, which is also called *user identification* (proving that the user is who he claims to be). Authentication methods include:

- Something only the user *knows*, such as a password.
- Something only the user *has*, for example, a smart card or a token.
- Something only the user *is*, such as a signature, voice, fingerprint, or retinal (eye) scan. It is implemented via *biometric controls*, which can be physical or behavioral.

Authentication and Passwords

After a user has been *identified*, the user must be *authenticated*. As noted earlier, authentication is the process of verifying that the user is who he or she claims to be. Verification usually is based on one or more characteristics that distinguish the individual from others. The distinguishing characteristics can be based on something one knows (e.g., passwords), something one has (e.g., a token), or something one possesses (e.g., fingerprint). Traditionally, authentication has been based on passwords. Passwords are notoriously insecure because people have a habit of writing them down in easy-to-find places, choosing values that are guessed easily, and willingly telling people their passwords when asked.

Passive Tokens. Combining something a user knows with something a user has, a technique known as *two-factor authentication*, achieves stronger security. Tokens qualify as something a user has. Tokens come in various shapes, forms, and sizes. **Passive tokens** are storage devices that contain a secret code. The most common passive tokens are plastic cards with magnetic strips containing a hidden code. With passive tokens, the user swipes the token through a reader attached to a personal computer or workstation and then enters his or her password to gain access to the network.

Active Tokens. Active tokens usually are small stand-alone electronic devices (e.g., key chain tokens, smart cards, calculators, USB dongles) that generate one-time passwords. In this case, the user enters a PIN into the token, the token generates a password that is only good for a single logon, and the user then logs onto the system using the one-time password. ActivIdentity (actividentity.com) and CRYPTOcard (cryptocard.com) are companies that provide active token authentication devices.

Biometric Systems

A **biometric control** is an automated method for verifying the identity of a person based on physical or behavioral characteristics.

Biometric systems can *identify* a person from a population of enrolled users by searching through a database for a match based on the person's biometric trait, or the system can *verify* a person's claimed identity by matching the individual's biometric trait against a previously stored version. Biometric verification is much simpler than biometric identification, and it is the process used in two-factor authentication (see Online File W10.5).

The most common biometrics are:

- **Thumbprint or fingerprint.** Each time a user wants access, a thumb- or fingerprint (finger scan) is matched against a template containing the authorized person's fingerprint to identify him or her.
- **Retinal scan.** A match is attempted between the pattern of the blood vessels in the retina that is being scanned and a prestored picture of the retina.
- **Voice scan.** A match is attempted between the user's voice and the voice pattern stored on templates.
- **Signature.** Signatures are matched against the prestored authentic signature. This method can supplement a photo-card ID system.

Margin glossary

passive token
Storage device (e.g., magnetic strip) that contains a secret code used in a two-factor authentication system.

active token
Small, stand-alone electronic device that generates one-time passwords used in a two-factor authentication system.

biometric control
An automated method for verifying the identity of a person based on physical or behavioral characteristics.

biometric systems
Authentication systems that identify a person by measurement of a biological characteristic, such as fingerprints, iris (eye) patterns, facial features, or voice.

Other biometrics are:

- Facial recognition
- Facial thermograph
- Hand geometry
- Hand veins
- Keystrokes
- Iris

For details and analysis, see en.wikipedia.org/wiki/Biometrics.

Biometric controls are now integrated into many e-business hardware and software products. Biometric controls do have some limitations: They are not accurate in certain cases, and some people see them as an invasion of privacy.

To implement a biometric authentication system, the physiological or behavioral characteristics of a participant must be scanned repeatedly under different settings. The scans are then averaged to produce a biometric template, or identifier. The template is stored in a database as a series of numbers that can range from a few bytes for hand geometry to several thousand bytes for facial recognition. When a person uses a biometric system, a live scan is conducted, and the scan is converted to a series of numbers that is then compared against the template stored in the database.

ENCRYPTION AND THE ONE-KEY (SYMMETRIC) SYSTEM

Encryption is the process of transforming or scrambling (encrypting) data in such a way that it is difficult, expensive, or time-consuming for an unauthorized person to unscramble (decrypt) it. All encryption has five basic parts (refer to Exhibit 10.9): *plaintext, ciphertext*, an *encryption algorithm*, the *key*, and *key space*. **Plaintext** is a human-readable text or message. **Ciphertext** is not human-readable because it has been encrypted. The **encryption algorithm** is the set of procedures or mathematical functions used to encrypt or decrypt a message. Typically, the algorithm is not the secret piece of the encryption process. The **key** (or **key value**) is the secret value used with the algorithm to transform the message. The **key space** is the large number of possible key values (keys) created by the algorithm to use when transforming messages.

encryption
The process of scrambling (encrypting) a message in such a way that it is difficult, expensive, or time-consuming for an unauthorized person to unscramble (decrypt) it.

plaintext
An unencrypted message in human-readable form.

ciphertext
A plaintext message after it has been encrypted into a machine-readable form.

encryption algorithm
The mathematical formula used to encrypt the plaintext into the ciphertext, and vice versa.

key (key value)
The secret code used to encrypt and decrypt a message.

key space
The large number of possible key values (keys) created by the algorithm to use when transforming the message.

EXHIBIT 10.9 Encryption Components

Component	Description	Example or Description
Plaintext	The original message or document is created by the user, which is in human-readable form.	Credit card number 5342 8765 3652 9982
Encryption algorithm	The set of procedures or mathematical functions to encrypt or decrypt a message. Typically, the algorithm is not the secret piece of the encryption process.	Add a number (the key) to each number in the card. If the resulting number is greater than 9, wrap around the number to the beginning (i.e., modulus arithmetic). For example, add 4 to each number so that 1 becomes 5, 9 becomes 3, etc.
Key or key value	The secret value used with the algorithm to transform the message.	The key dictates what parts (functions) of the algorithm will be used, in what order, and with what values.
Key space	The large number of possible key values (keys) created by the algorithm to use when transforming the message.	The larger the key space, the greater the number of possibilities for the key, which makes it harder for an attacker to discover the correct key.
Ciphertext	Message or document that has been encrypted into unreadable form.	The original 5342 8765 3652 9982 becomes 9786 2109 7096 3326.

Encryption is the foundation for two major security systems: the *symmetric systems*, with one secret key, and *asymmetric systems*, with two keys. The second method is the basis for the PKI system.

Symmetric (Private) Key Encryption

symmetric (private) key encryption

An encryption system that uses the same key to encrypt and decrypt the message.

In a **symmetric (private) key encryption**, the same key is used to encrypt and decrypt the plaintext (see Exhibit 10.10). The sender and receiver of the text must share the same key without revealing it to anyone else—making it a so-called *private* system.

The **Data Encryption Standard (DES)** was at one time the standard symmetric encryption algorithm supported by U.S. government agencies. However, DES became too susceptible to attacks. In 2000, the National Institute of Standards and Technology (NIST) replaced DES with *Rijndael*, the new advanced encryption standard for encrypting sensitive but unclassified government data. Because the algorithms used to encrypt a message are well known, the confidentiality of a message depends on the key. It is possible to guess a key simply by having a computer try all the encryption combinations until the message is decrypted. High-speed and parallel processing computers can try millions of guesses in a second. This is why the length of the key (in bits) is the main factor in securing a message. If a key were 4 bits long (e.g., 1011), there would be only 16 possible combinations (i.e., 2 raised to the fourth power). However, a 64-bit encryption key would take 58.5 years to be broken at 10 million keys per second.

Data Encryption Standard (DES)

The standard symmetric encryption algorithm supported by the NIST and used by U.S. government agencies until October 2000.

PUBLIC KEY INFRASTRUCTURE (PKI)

public key infrastructure (PKI)

A scheme for securing e-payments using public key encryption and various technical components.

Public key infrastructure (PKI) is a scheme for securing e-payments using public key encryption and various technical components. The symmetric one-key encryption requires the movement of a key from the writer of a message to its recipient. Imagine trying to use one-key encryption to buy something offered on a particular Web server. If the seller's key was distributed to thousands of buyers, then the key would not remain secret for long. If the transfer of the key is intercepted, the key may be stolen or changed. The solution was two keys, public and private, and additional features that create the PKI, which is very secure. In addition to the keys, PKI includes *digital signature*, hash digests (function), and digital certificate. Let's see how PKI works.

Public (Asymmetric) Key Encryption

public (asymmetric) key encryption

Method of encryption that uses a pair of matched keys—a public key to encrypt a message and a private key to decrypt it, or vice versa.

Public (asymmetric) key encryption uses a pair of matched keys—a **public key** that is publicly available to anyone and a **private key** that is known only to its owner. If a message is encrypted with a public key, then the associated private key is required to decrypt the message. If, for example, a person wanted to send a purchase order to a company and have the contents remain private, he or she would encrypt the message with the company's public key. When the company received the order, it would decrypt it with the associated private key, being the only one able to read it.

public key

Encryption code that is publicly available to anyone.

A most common public key encryption algorithm is RSA (rsa.com). RSA uses keys ranging in length from 512 bits to 1,024 bits. The main problem with public key encryption is speed. Symmetrical algorithms are significantly faster than asymmetrical key algorithms. Therefore, public key encryption cannot be used effectively to encrypt and decrypt large amounts of data. In practice, a combination of symmetric and asymmetric encryption is used to encrypt messages. Public key encryption is supplemented by digital signature and certificate authority.

private key

Encryption code that is known only to its owner.

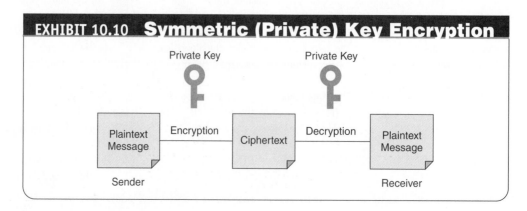

EXHIBIT 10.10   Symmetric (Private) Key Encryption

The PKI Process: Digital Signatures and Certificate Authorities

Digital signatures or **digital certificates** are the electronic equivalent of personal signatures that cannot be forged. Digital signatures are based on public keys for authenticating the identity of the sender of a message or document. They also can ensure that the original content of an electronic message or document is unchanged. Digital signatures have additional benefits in the online world. They are portable, cannot be easily repudiated or imitated, and can be time-stamped. According to the U.S. Federal Electronic Signatures in Global and National Commerce Act of 2000, digital signatures in the United States have the same legal standing as a signature written in ink on paper.

Exhibit 10.11 illustrates how the PKI process works. Suppose a person wants to send a draft of a financial contract to a company with whom he or she plans to do business as an e-mail message. The sender wants to assure the company that the content of the draft has not been changed en route and that he or she really is the sender. To do so, the sender takes the following steps:

1. The sender creates the e-mail message with the contract in it.
2. Using special software, a mathematical computation called a **hash** function is applied to the message, which results in a special summary of the message, converted into a string of digits called a **message digest (MD)**.

digital signature or digital certificate
Validates the sender and time stamp of a transaction so it cannot be later claimed that the transaction was unauthorized or invalid.

hash
A mathematical computation that is applied to a message, using a private key, to encrypt the message.

message digest (MD)
A summary of a message, converted into a string of digits after the hash has been applied.

EXHIBIT 10.11 Digital Signatures

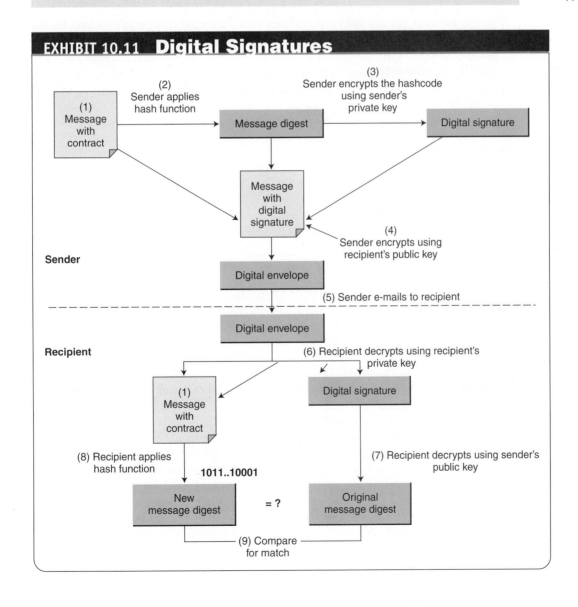

3. The sender uses his or her private key to encrypt the hash. This is the sender's *digital signature*. No one else can replicate the sender's digital signature because it is based on the sender's private key, which no one else knows.

4. The sender encrypts both the original message and the digital signature using the recipient's public key. This couple forms the digital envelope.

5. The sender e-mails the digital envelope to the receiver.

6. Upon receipt, the receiver uses his or her private key to decrypt the contents of the digital envelope. This produces a copy of the message and the sender's digital signature. No one else can do it since there is only one copy of the private key.

7. The receiver uses the sender's public key to decrypt the digital signature, resulting in a copy of the original message digest.

8. Using the same hash function employed in step 2, the recipient then creates a message digest from the decrypted message.

9. The recipient then compares this digest with the original message digest.

10. If the two digests match, then the recipient concludes that the message is authentic.

digital envelope

The combination of the encrypted original message and the digital signature, using the recipient's public key.

In this scenario, the company has evidence that the sender sent the e-mail because the sender is the only one with access to the private key. The recipient knows that the message has not been tampered with because if it had been, the two hashes would not have matched.

certificate authorities (CAs)

Third parties that issue digital certificates.

Certificate Authority. Third parties called certificate authorities (CAs) issue digital certificates. This is a certificate that contains things such as the holder's name, validity period, public key information, and a signed hash of the certificate data (i.e., hashed contents of the certificate signed with the CA's private key). There are different types of certificates, namely those used to authenticate Web sites (*site certificates*), individuals (*personal certificates*), and software companies (*software publisher certificates*).

There are many third-party CAs. VeriSign (verisign.com) is the best known of the CAs. VeriSign issues three classes of certificates: Class 1 verifies that an e-mail actually comes from the user's address. Class 2 checks the user's identity against a commercial credit database. Class 3 requires notarized documents. Companies such as Microsoft offer systems that enable companies to issue their own private, in-house certificates.

Secure Socket Layer (SSL): PKI Systems Are Further Secured with SSL—The Protocol for E-Commerce

Secure Socket Layer (SSL)

Protocol that utilizes standard certificates for authentication and data encryption to ensure privacy or confidentiality.

Transport Layer Security (TLS)

As of 1996, another name for the SSL protocol.

If the average user had to figure out how to use encryption, digital certificates, digital signatures, and the like, there would be few secure transactions on the Web. Fortunately, Web browsers and Web servers handle many of these issues in a transparent fashion. Given that different companies, financial institutions, and governments in many countries are involved in e-commerce, it is necessary to have generally accepted protocols for securing e-commerce. One of the major protocols in use today is Secure Socket Layer (SSL), also known as Transport Layer Security (TLS).

The Secure Socket Layer (SSL) was invented by Netscape to use standard certificates for authentication and data encryption to ensure privacy or confidentiality. SSL became a de facto standard adopted by the browsers and servers provided by Microsoft and Netscape. In 1996, SSL was renamed Transport Layer Security (TLS), but many people still use the SSL name. It is the major standard used for online credit card payments. SSL makes it possible to encrypt credit card numbers and other transmissions between a Web server and a Web browser. In the case of credit card transactions, there is more to making a purchase on the Web than simply passing an encrypted credit card number to a merchant.

In the next section, the focus is on the company's digital perimeter—the network.

Section 10.6 ▶ REVIEW QUESTIONS

1. Define access control.
2. What are the basic elements of an authentication system?
3. What is a passive token? An active token?
4. Define biometric systems and list five of their methods.
5. Describe the five basic components of encryption.
6. What are the key elements of PKI?
7. What are the basic differences between symmetric and asymmetric encryption?
8. What role does a certificate authority play?
9. What is the SSL protocol?

10.7 THE DEFENSE II: SECURING E-COMMERCE NETWORKS

Several technologies exist that ensure that an organization's network boundaries are secure from cyberattack or intrusion and that if the organization's boundaries are compromised, the intrusion is detected quickly and combated. The selection and operation of these technologies should be based on certain design concepts, as described in Online File W10.6.

The major components for protecting internal information flow inside organizations are described next.

FIREWALLS

Firewalls are barriers between a trusted network or PC and the untrustworthy Internet. Technically, it is a network node consisting of both hardware and software that isolates a private network from a public network. On the Internet, the data and requests sent from one computer to another are broken into segments called packets. Each packet contains the Internet address of the computer sending the data, as well as the Internet address of the computer receiving the data. Packets also contain other identifying information that can distinguish one packet from another. A firewall examines all data packets that pass through it and then takes appropriate action—to allow or not to allow. Firewalls can be designed mainly to protect against remote log-in, access via backdoors, spam, and different types of malware (e.g., viruses or macros). For details, see Online File W10.7.

Personal Firewalls

The number of users with high-speed broadband (cable modem or digital subscriber lines [DSL]) Internet connections to their homes or small businesses has increased. These "always-on" connections are much more vulnerable to attack than simple dial-up connections. With these connections, the homeowner or small business owner runs the risk of information being stolen or destroyed, of sensitive information (e.g., personal or business financial information) being stolen, and of the computer being used in a DOS attack against others.

Personal firewalls protect desktop systems by monitoring all the traffic that passes through the computer's network interface card. They operate in one of two ways. With the first method, the owner can create filtering rules (much like packet filtering) that the firewall uses to permit or delete packets. With the other method, the firewall can learn, by asking the user questions, how it should handle particular traffic. For a detailed comparison of several of these products, see firewallguide.com/software.htm.

DEMILITARIZED ZONE

A demilitarized zone (DMZ) is a network area that sits between an organization's internal network and an external network (Internet), providing physical isolation between the two networks that is controlled by rules enforced by a firewall. For example, suppose a company wants to run its own Web site. In a DMZ setup, the company would put the Web server on a publicly accessible network and the rest of its servers on a private internal network.

firewall
A single point between two or more networks where all traffic must pass (choke point); the device authenticates, controls, and logs all traffic.

packet
Segment of data sent from one computer to another on a network.

personal firewall
A network node designed to protect an individual user's desktop system from the public network by monitoring all the traffic that passes through the computer's network interface card.

demilitarized zone (DMZ)
Network area that sits between an organization's internal network and an external network (Internet), providing physical isolation between the two networks that is controlled by rules enforced by a firewall.

A firewall would then be configured to direct requests coming from the outside to the appropriate network and servers. In most cases, a second firewall fronts the internal network to doubly ensure that intrusive requests do not get through to the private (internal or corporate) network.

VPNs

Suppose a company wants to establish a B2B application, providing suppliers, partners, and others access not only to data residing on its internal Web site, but also to data contained in other files (e.g., Word documents) or in legacy systems (e.g., large relational databases). Traditionally, communications with the company would have taken place over a private leased line or through a dial-up line to a bank of modems or a remote access server (RAS) that provided direct connections to the company's LAN. With a private line, the chances of a hacker eavesdropping on the communications between the companies would be minimal, but it is an expensive way to do business. A VPN allows a computer user to access a network via an IP address other than the one that actually connects their computer to the Internet. For details, see en.wikipedia.org/wiki/VPN.

The less expensive alternative would be to use a virtual private network. A **virtual private network (VPN)** uses the public Internet to carry information but remains private by using a combination of encryption to scramble the communications and authentication to ensure that the information has not been tampered with and comes from a legitimate source. A VPN verifies the identity of anyone using the network. In addition, a VPN can also support site-to-site communications between branch offices and corporate headquarters and the communications between mobile workers and their workplace.

VPNs can reduce communication costs dramatically. The costs are lower because VPN equipment is cheaper than other remote solutions; private leased lines are not needed to support remote access; remote users can use broadband connections rather than make long-distance calls to access an organization's private network; and a single access line can be used to support multiple purposes.

The main technical challenge of a VPN is to ensure the confidentiality and integrity of the data transmitted over the Internet. This is where protocol tunneling comes into play. With **protocol tunneling**, data packets are first encrypted and then encapsulated into packets that can be transmitted across the Internet. A special host or router decrypts the packets at the destination address.

INTRUSION DETECTION SYSTEMS (IDSs)

Even if an organization has a well-formulated security policy and a number of security technologies in place, it still is vulnerable to attack. For example, most organizations have antivirus software, yet most are subjected to virus attacks. This is why an organization must continually watch for attempted, as well as actual, security breaches.

An **intrusion detection system (IDS)** is software and/or hardware designed to detect illegal attempts to access, manipulate, and/or disable computer systems through a network. An IDS cannot directly detect attacks within properly encrypted traffic.

An intrusion detection system is used to detect several types of malicious behaviors that can compromise the security and trust of a computer system. This includes network attacks against vulnerable services, data driven attacks on applications, host-based attacks such as privilege escalation, unauthorized log-ins, access to sensitive files, and malware (viruses, Trojan horses, and worms).

The IDS checks files on a regular basis to see if the current signatures match the previous signatures. If the signatures do not match, security personnel are notified immediately. Some examples of commercial host-based systems are Symantec's Intruder Alert (symantec.com), Tripwire Security's Tripwire (tripwiresecurity.com), and McAfee's Entercept Desktop and Server Agents (mcafee.com).

A network-based IDS uses rules to analyze suspicious activity at the perimeter of a network or at key locations in the network. It usually consists of a monitor—a software package that scans the network—and software agents that reside on various host computers and feed information back to the monitor. This type of IDS examines network traffic (i.e., packets) for known patterns

---

virtual private network (VPN)
A network that uses the public Internet to carry information but remains private by using encryption to scramble the communications, authentication to ensure that information has not been tampered with, and access control to verify the identity of anyone using the network.

protocol tunneling
Method used to ensure confidentiality and integrity of data transmitted over the Internet by encrypting data packets, sending them in packets across the Internet, and decrypting them at the destination address.

intrusion detection system (IDS)
A special category of software that can monitor activity across a network or on a host computer, watch for suspicious activity, and take automated action based on what it sees.

of attack and automatically notifies security personnel when specific events or event thresholds occur. A network-based IDS also can perform certain actions when an attack occurs.

HONEYNETS AND HONEYPOTS

Honeynets are another technology that can detect and analyze intrusions. A **honeynet** is a network of honeypots designed to attract hackers like honey attracts bees. In this case, the **honeypots** are information system resources—firewalls, routers, Web servers, database servers, files, and the like—that look like production systems but do no real work. The main difference between a honeypot and the real thing is that the activities on a honeypot come from intruders attempting to compromise the system. In this way, researchers watching the honeynet can gather information about why hackers attack, when they attack, how they attack, what they do after the system is compromised, and how they communicate with one another during and after the attack.

The Honeynet Project is a worldwide, not-for-profit research group of security professionals (see honeynet.org). The group focuses on raising awareness of security risks that confront any system connected to the Internet and teaching and informing the security community about better ways to secure and defend network resources. The project runs its own honeynets but makes no attempt to attract hackers. They simply connect the honeypots to the Internet and wait for attacks to occur.

Before a company deploys a honeynet, it needs to think about what it will do when it becomes the scene of a cybercrime or contains evidence of a crime and about the legal restrictions and ramifications of monitoring legal and illegal activity. Online File W10.8 discusses these issues. A similar technique is *penetration test* (or pen test).

Penetration Test

A **penetration test (pen test)** is a method of evaluating the security of a computer system or a network by simulating an attack from a malicious source (e.g., a cracker). The process involves an active analysis of the system for any potential vulnerabilities and attacks. This analysis is carried out from the position of a potential attacker, and can involve active exploitation of security vulnerabilities. Any security issues that are found will be presented to the system owner, together with an assessment of their impact and often with a proposal for mitigation or a technical solution. The intent of a penetration test is to determine feasibility of an attack and the amount of business impact of a successful exploit, if discovered. It is a component of a full security audit. For details, see en.wikipedia.org/wiki/Penetration_testing.

Section 10.7 ▶ REVIEW QUESTIONS

1. List the basic types of firewalls and briefly describe each.
2. What is a personal firewall?
3. How does a VPN work?
4. Briefly describe the major types of IDSs.
5. What is a honeynet? What is a honeypot?
6. Describe pen testing.

10.8 THE DEFENSE III: GENERAL CONTROLS AND OTHER DEFENSE MECHANISMS

The objective of IT security management practices is to defend all of the components of an information system, specifically data, software applications, hardware, and networks. A defense strategy requires several controls, as shown in Exhibit 10.12. **General controls** are established to protect the system regardless of the specific application. For example, protecting hardware and controlling access to the data center are independent of the specific application. **Application controls** are safeguards that are intended to protect specific

---

honeynet
A network of honeypots.

honeypot
Production system (e.g., firewalls, routers, Web servers, database servers) that looks like it does real work, but that acts as a decoy and is watched to study how network intrusions occur.

penetration test (pen test)
A method of evaluating the security of a computer system or a network by simulating an attack from a malicious source, (e.g., a cracker).

general controls
Controls established to protect the system regardless of the specific application. For example, protecting hardware and controlling access to the data center are independent of the specific application.

application controls
Controls that are intended to protect specific applications.

EXHIBIT 10.12 Major Defense Controls

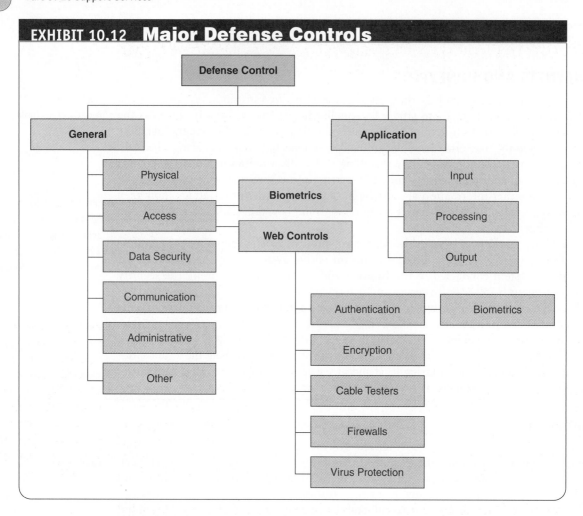

applications. In this and the following sections, we discuss the major types of these two groups of information systems controls.

GENERAL CONTROLS

The major categories of general controls are physical controls, access controls, biometric controls, and administrative controls.

Physical Controls

Physical security refers to the protection of computer facilities and resources. This includes protecting physical property such as computers, data centers, software, manuals, and networks. It provides protection against most natural hazards as well as against some human hazards. Appropriate physical security may include several controls, such as the following:

- Appropriate design of the data center. For example, the site should be noncombustible and waterproof.
- Shielding against electromagnetic fields.
- Good fire prevention, detection, and extinguishing systems, including sprinkler system, water pumps, and adequate drainage facilities.
- Emergency power shutoff and backup batteries, which must be maintained in operational condition.
- Properly designed, maintained, and operated air-conditioning systems.
- Motion detector alarms that detect physical intrusion.

Network access control software is offered by all major security vendors (e.g., see symantec.com/endpoint).

EXHIBIT 10.13 Representative Administrative Controls

- Appropriately selecting, training, and supervising employees, especially in accounting and information systems
- Fostering company loyalty
- Immediately revoking access privileges of dismissed, resigned, or transferred employees
- Requiring periodic modification of access controls (such as passwords)
- Developing programming and documentation standards (to make auditing easier and to use the standards as guides for employees)
- Insisting on security bonds or malfeasance insurance for key employees
- Instituting separation of duties, namely, dividing sensitive computer duties among as many employees as economically feasible in order to decrease the chance of intentional or unintentional damage
- Holding periodic random audits of the system

Administrative Controls

While the previously discussed general controls were technical in nature, administrative controls deal with issuing guidelines and monitoring compliance with the guidelines. Examples of such controls are shown in Exhibit 10.13.

APPLICATION CONTROLS

Sophisticated attacks are aimed at the application level, and many applications were not designed to withstand such attacks. For better survivability, information processing methodologies are being replaced with agent technology. **Intelligent agents,** also referred to as *softbots* or *knowbots*, are highly intelligent applications. The term generally means applications that have some degree of reactivity, autonomy, and adaptability—as is needed in unpredictable attack situations. An agent is able to adapt itself based on changes occurring in its environment, as shown in Exhibit 10.14.

intelligent agents
Software applications that have some degree of reactivity, autonomy, and adaptability—as is needed in unpredictable attack situations. An agent is able to adapt itself based on changes occurring in its environment.

EXHIBIT 10.14 Intelligent Agents

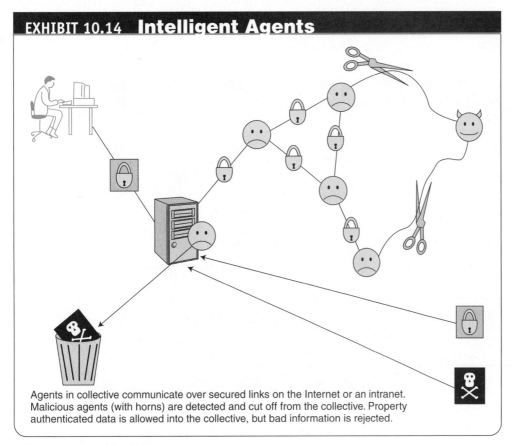

Agents in collective communicate over secured links on the Internet or an intranet. Malicious agents (with horns) are detected and cut off from the collective. Property authenticated data is allowed into the collective, but bad information is rejected.

Source: Courtesy of Sandia Labs.

INTERNAL CONTROL AND COMPLIANCE MANAGEMENT

internal control environment
The work atmosphere that a company sets for its employees.

The **internal control environment** is the work atmosphere that a company sets for its employees. *Internal control (IC)* is a process designed to achieve (1) reliability of financial reporting, (2) operational efficiency, (3) compliance with laws, (4) regulations and policies, and (5) safeguarding of assets. Exhibit 10.15 illustrates how the role of IT in internal control has changed.

PROTECTING AGAINST SPAM

Both legal and technological defenses are used to prevent or punish search engine and other forms of commercial spam. In one case, Verizon Wireless filed a lawsuit against the U.S.-based travel agency Passport Holidays for violating national and state laws by sending 98,000 unsolicited text messages to Verizon Wireless customers. Passport's messages encouraged recipients to call a toll-free number to claim a cruise to the Bahamas. In February 2006, a U.S. court judge granted Verizon Wireless's request for an injunction barring Passport Holidays from sending text message spam. Passport Holidays agreed to pay $10,000 to compensate Verizon Wireless.

Sending spam that disguises a sales pitch to look like a personal e-mail to bypass filters violates the U.S. Controlling the Assault of Non-Solicited Pornography and Marketing (CAN-SPAM) Act of 2003. However, many spammers hide their identity to escape detection by using hijacked PCs, or spam zombies, to send spam.

Filtering achieves more immediate results. Bloggers plagued by comment spam can get help from sites such as SplogSpot (splogspot.com) or Splog Reporter (splogreporter.com), which collect information on such content to help network administrators filter it out.

Evidence shows that unethical and illegal business tactics that exploit or mimic e-commerce operations will not stop. To defend themselves, Google (google.com/contact/spamreport.html), and Yahoo! (add.yahoo.com/fast/help/us/ysearch/cgi_reportsearchspam) have turned to aggressive measures. For example, they have implemented spam site reporting systems, built algorithms that check for and penalize deceptive rank boosting practices, and banned violators' sites outright. In 2006, Google temporarily banned BMW and Ricoh's German Web sites from its search index for using JavaScript redirect, or doorway pages that presented visitors with different content than they had displayed to the search engine.

EXHIBIT 10.15   Increasing Role of IT in Internal Control

Cost	Value	Risk
• Increase efficiency • Improve ROI	• Generate higher revenues • Provide business intelligence and decision support • Improve customer and supplier relationship management • Increase shareholder value	• Safeguard assets • Ensure the integrity of financial reporting • Disclose security breaches in a timely manner • Prevent, detect, and investigate fraud and intrusions • Visibly monitor employee behavior • Retain electronic business records • Provide for recovery from devastating disasters • Provide a defensible basis for investigations and audits
Operational	Strategic	Governance
Pre-1990s	1990–2001	2002–2010

Google has warned that it is expanding its efforts to clamp down on unethical tricks and tactics. As abuses become known or intolerable, additional laws will be passed with varying degrees of effectiveness.

An example is the CAN-SPAM Act (Chapter 16). The **Controlling the Assault of Non-Solicited Pornography and Marketing Act**, or **CAN-SPAM Act**, makes it a crime to send commercial e-mail messages with false or misleading message headers or misleading subject lines. Other provisions of the law:

▶ Require marketers to identify their physical location by including their postal address in the text of the e-mail messages.

▶ Require an opt-out link in each message, which must also give recipients the option of telling senders to stop all segments of their marketing campaigns.

▶ Allow for suits to be brought by ISPs, state attorneys general, and the U.S. government.

▶ Carry penalties of up to $250 per spammed e-mail message, with a cap of $2 million, which can be tripled for aggravated violations. There is no cap on penalties for e-mail sent with false or deceptive headers.

▶ Those found guilty of violating the law may face up to 5 years in prison.

(See spamlaws.com/federal/can-spam.shtml.)

Protection Against Splogs. Blog owners can also use a **Captcha tool** (Completely Automated Public Turing test to tell Computers and Humans Apart), which uses a verification test on comment pages to stop scripts from posting automatically. These tests may require the person to enter sequences of random characters, which automated systems (software scripts) cannot read.

Another potentially effective measure against blog spam and other undesirable content is to only allow comments posted on the blog to be made public after they have been checked. But like the fight against e-mail spam, it is a constant battle in which the spammers seem to have the advantage. Sometimes the only solution to comment spam is for users to turn off their comments function. For more information, see the CAUCE Web site (cauce.org). Online File W10.9 shows an example of how companies fight spamming.

Even with tools such as Captcha turned on, it is risky to simply allow comments to go unchecked. Blog owners may be held responsible for anything illegal or defamatory posted on their blogs.

PROTECTING AGAINST POP-UP ADS

As discussed in Chapter 4, use of pop-ups and similar advertising programs is exploding. Sometimes it is even difficult to close these ads when they appear on the screen. Some of these ads may be part of a consumer's permission marketing agreement, but most are unsolicited. What can a user do about unsolicited pop-up ads? The following tools help stop pop-ups.

Tools for Stopping Pop-Ups. One way to avoid the potential danger lurking behind pop-up ads is to install software that will block pop-up ads and prevent them from appearing in the first place. Several software packages offer pop-up stoppers. Some are free (e.g., panicware.com and adscleaner.com); others are available for a fee. For a list of pop-up blocking software, visit snapfiles.com/Freeware/misctools/fwpopblock.html and netsecurity.about.com/od/popupadblocking/a/aafreepopup.htm.

Many ISPs offer tools to stop pop-ups from appearing. The Mozilla Firefox Web browser does not allow pop-ups. Even the Google Toolbar will block pop-up ads. Microsoft offers pop-up blocking to its Internet Explorer browser.

However, adware or software that gets bundled with other popular applications like person-to-person file sharing is able to deliver the pop-up ads because they originate from the desktop, not the browser, and blocking tools do not govern them.

Like spam, pop-ups have mutated to in-pages ads called *overlays* or *floater ads*. These ads float over a Web page to catch people's attention before reading requested content. Visitors typically cannot manipulate the ads like they can a pop-up by minimizing the window or clicking the exit button.

Controlling the Assault of Non-Solicited Pornography and Marketing (CAN-SPAM) Act
Law that makes it a crime to send commercial e-mail messages with false or misleading message headers or misleading subject lines.

Captcha tool
Completely Automated Public Turing test to tell Computers and Humans Apart, which uses a verification test on comment pages to stop scripts from posting automatically.

Protection Against Phishing

Because there are many phishing attack methods, there are many defense methods as well. Illustrative examples are provided by Microsoft (2008), Symantec (2009), ftc.gov, and en.wikipedia.org/wiki/phishing. For analytical fraud protection, see sas.com/solutions/fraud/index.html.

PROTECTING AGAINST SPYWARE

In response to the emergence of spyware, a large variety of anti-spyware software exists. Running anti-spyware software has become a widely recognized element of computer security best practices for Microsoft Windows desktop computers. A number of jurisdictions have passed anti-spyware laws, which usually target any software that is surreptitiously installed to control a user's computer (see Chapter 16). The U.S. Federal Trade Commission (ftc.gov) has placed on the Internet a page of advice to consumers about how to lower the risk of spyware infection, including a list of "dos" and "don'ts."

Section 10.8 ▶ REVIEW QUESTIONS

1. What are general controls? List the various types.
2. List the various biometric controls. What are their functions?
3. Define access control.
4. Distinguish between application controls and internal controls.
5. How does one protect against spam? Against splogs?
6. How does one protect against pop-ups?

10.9 BUSINESS CONTINUITY, SECURITY AUDITING, AND RISK MANAGEMENT

A major building block in EC security for large companies or companies where EC plays a critical role (e.g., banks, airlines, stock brokerages, e-tailers) is to prepare for natural or man-made disasters. Disasters may occur without warning. The best defense is to be prepared. Therefore, an important element in any security system is the *business continuity plan*, mainly consisting of a disaster recovery plan. Such a plan outlines the process by which businesses should recover from a major disaster. Destruction of all (or most) of the computing facilities can cause significant damage. Therefore, it is difficult for many organizations to obtain insurance for their computers and information systems without showing a satisfactory disaster prevention and recovery plan. The comprehensiveness of a business recovery plan is shown in Exhibit 10.16.

BUSINESS CONTINUITY AND DISASTER RECOVERY PLANNING

Disaster recovery is the chain of events linking the business continuity plan to protection and to recovery. The following are some key thoughts about the process:

> ▶ The purpose of a business continuity plan is to keep the business running after a disaster occurs. Each function in the business should have a valid recovery capability plan.
> ▶ Recovery planning is part of *asset protection*. Every organization should assign responsibility to management to identify and protect assets within their spheres of functional control.
> ▶ Planning should focus first on recovery from a total loss of all capabilities.
> ▶ Proof of capability usually involves some kind of what-if analysis that shows that the recovery plan is current.
> ▶ All critical applications must be identified and their recovery procedures addressed in the plan.

EXHIBIT 10.16 Business Continuity Services and IT Recovery Process

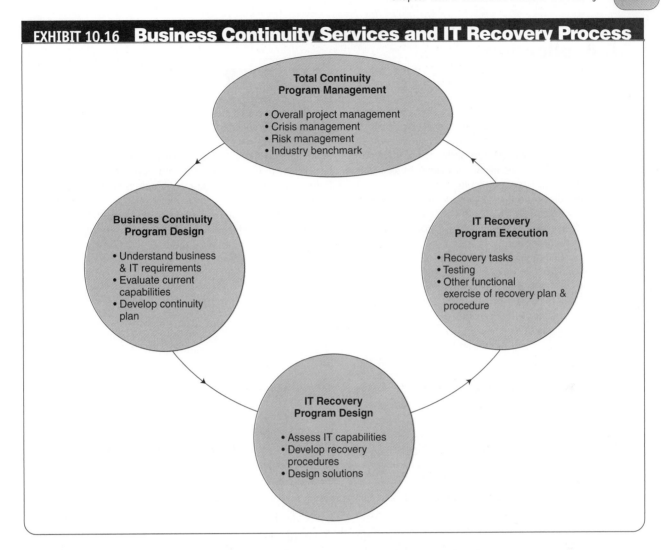

Total Continuity
Program Management

• Overall project management
• Crisis management
• Risk management
• Industry benchmark

Business Continuity
Program Design

• Understand business
  & IT requirements
• Evaluate current
  capabilities
• Develop continuity
  plan

IT Recovery
Program Execution

• Recovery tasks
• Testing
• Other functional
  exercise of recovery plan &
  procedure

IT Recovery
Program Design

• Assess IT capabilities
• Develop recovery
  procedures
• Design solutions

▶ The plan should be written so that it will be effective in case of disaster, not just in order to satisfy the auditors.

▶ The plan should be kept in a safe place; copies should be given to all key managers, or it should be available on the intranet. The plan should be audited periodically.

Disaster recovery planning can be very complex, and it may take several months to complete. Using special software, the planning job can be expedited. See Case 10.2 for a discussion of the importance of business continuity and the ability to recover from a disaster.

Disaster Avoidance. **Disaster avoidance** is an approach oriented toward *prevention*. The idea is to minimize the chance of avoidable disasters (such as fire or other human-caused threats). For example, many companies use a device called *uninterrupted power supply (UPS)*, which provides power in case of a power outage.

AUDITING INFORMATION SYSTEMS

An **audit** is an important part of any control system. Auditing can be viewed as an additional layer of controls or safeguards. It is considered as a deterrent to criminal actions, especially for insiders. Auditors attempt to answer questions such as these:

▶ Are there sufficient controls in the system?

▶ Which areas are not covered by controls?

▶ Which controls are not necessary?

▶ Are the controls implemented properly?

disaster avoidance
An approach oriented toward prevention. The idea is to minimize the chance of avoidable disasters (such as fire or other human-caused threats).

audit
An important part of any control system. Auditing can be viewed as an additional layer of controls or safeguards. It is considered as a deterrent to criminal actions especially for insiders.

EC Application
BUSINESS CONTINUITY AND DISASTER RECOVERY

Ninety-three percent of companies that suffer a significant data loss die within 5 years, according to Freeman Mendel, the chair of the FBI's 2006 Infragard National Conference. Even though business continuity/disaster recovery (BC/DR) is a business survival issue, many managers have dangerously viewed BC/DR as an IT security issue.

Disasters teach the best lessons for both IT managers and corporate executives who have not implemented BC/DR processes. The success or failure of those processes depends on IT, as the following case indicates.

The city of Houston, Texas, and Harris County swung into action by turning Reliant Park and the Houston Astrodome into a "temporary city" with a medical facility, pharmacy, post office, and town square to house more than 250,000 Hurricane Katrina evacuees. Coast Guard Lt. Commander Joseph J. Leonard headed up the operation, drawing on his knowledge of the National Incident Command System. As Leonard explained, ineffective communication between the command staff and those in New Orleans, who could have informed Houston authorities about the number and special needs of the evacuees, caused a serious problem. In addition, agencies and organizations with poor on-scene decision-making authority hampered and slowed efforts to get things done.

Now businesses in hurricane alleys, earthquake corridors, and major cities are deploying BC/DR plans supported with software tools that allow them to replicate, or back up, their mission-critical applications to sites away from their primary data centers. In case of a disaster, companies can transmit vital accounting, project management, or transactional systems and records to their disaster recovery facilities, limiting downtime and data loss despite an outage at the primary location.

Globally, regulators are increasingly paying closer attention to business continuity and recovery times, which are now measured in hours rather than days. The Australian Prudential Regulation Authority (APRA) released its prudential standard on business continuity in April 2005. APRA gave Australian firms only 12 months to fix their compliance gaps.

Sources: Compiled from Fagg (2006), *Fiber Optics Weekly* (2006), and *infragardconferences.com* (accessed March 2009).

Questions

1. Why might a company that had a significant data loss not be able to recover?

2. Why are regulators requiring that companies implement BC/DR plans?

▶ Are the controls effective? That is, do they check the output of the system?

▶ Is there a clear separation of duties of employees?

▶ Are there procedures to ensure compliance with the controls?

▶ Are there procedures to ensure reporting and corrective actions in case of violations of controls?

Auditing a Web site is a good preventive measure to manage legal risk. Legal risk is important in any IT system, but in Web systems it is even more important due to the content of the site, which may offend people or be in violation of copyright laws or other regulations (e.g., privacy protection). Auditing EC is also more complex since in addition to the Web site one needs to audit order taking, order fulfillment, and all support systems.

Auditing involves checking the disaster plan as well (see en.wikipedia.org/wiki/Disaster_recovery_and_business_continuity_auditing).

RISK-MANAGEMENT AND COST–BENEFIT ANALYSIS

It is usually not economical to prepare protection against every possible threat. Therefore, an IT security program must provide a process for assessing threats and deciding which ones to prepare for and which ones to ignore or provide only reduced protection.

Risk-Management Analysis

Risk-management analysis can be enhanced by the use of DSS software packages. A simplified computation is shown here:

$$\text{Expected loss} = P_1 \times P_2 \times L$$

where:

P_1 = probability of attack (estimate, based on judgment)

P_2 = probability of attack being successful (estimate, based on judgment)
L = loss occurring if attack is successful

Example:

$$P_1 = .02, P_2 = .10, L = \$1,000,000$$

Then, expected loss from this particular attack is:

$$P_1 \times P_2 \times L = 0.02 \times 0.1 \times \$1,000,000 = \$2,000$$

The amount of loss may depend on the duration of a system being out of operation. Therefore, some add duration to the analysis.

Ethical Issues

Implementing security programs raises several ethical issues. First, some people are against monitoring any individual's activities. Imposing certain controls is seen by some as a violation of freedom of speech or other civil rights. A Gartner Group study showed that even after the terrorist attacks of September 11, 2001, only 26 percent of Americans approved a national ID database. Using biometrics is considered by many a violation of privacy.

Handling the privacy versus security dilemma is tough. There are other ethical and legal obligations that may require companies to "invade the privacy" of employees and monitor their actions. In particular, IT security measures are needed to protect against loss, liability, and litigation. Losses are not just financial, but also include the loss of information, customers, trading partners, brand image, and ability to conduct business due to the actions of hackers, malware, or employees.

Section 10.9 ▶ REVIEW QUESTIONS

1. Why do organizations need a business continuity plan?
2. List three issues a business continuity plan should cover.
3. Identify two factors that influence a company's ability to recover from a disaster.
4. What types of devices are needed for disaster avoidance?
5. What are auditing information systems?
6. Why should Web sites be audited?
7. How can expected loss be calculated?
8. List two ethical issues associated with security programs.

10.10 IMPLEMENTING ENTERPRISEWIDE E-COMMERCE SECURITY

Now that you have learned about both the threats and the defenses, we can discuss some implementation issues starting with the reason it is difficult, or even impossible, to stop computer crimes and information systems malfunction.

According to an *InformationWeek* survey (Fratto 2008), the major security challenges for corporations are:

▶ Managing the complexity of security (62% of respondents)
▶ Preventing data breaches from outside attackers (35% of respondents)
▶ Enforcing security policies (31% of respondents)

We will discuss these topics in this section.

SENIOR MANAGEMENT COMMITMENT AND SUPPORT

The success of an EC security strategy and program depends on the commitment and involvement of senior management. This is often called the "tone at the top." A genuine and well-communicated executive commitment about EC security and privacy measures is needed to convince users that insecure practices, risky or unethical methods, and mistakes due to ignorance will not be tolerated. Many forms of security are unpopular because they are

EXHIBIT 10.17 Enterprisewide EC Security and Privacy Model

Senior Management Commitment & Support → Security Policies & Training → Security Procedures & Enforcement → Security Tools: Hardware & Software

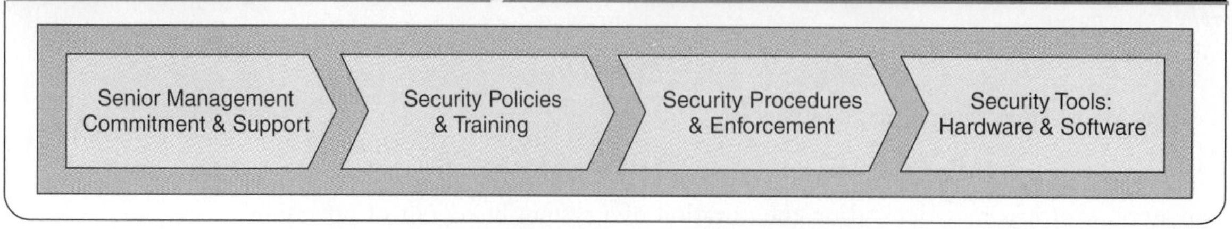

inconvenient, restrictive, time-consuming, and expensive. Security practices tend not to be a priority unless they are mandatory and there are negative consequences for noncompliance (George 2008).

Therefore, an EC security and privacy model for effective enterprisewide security begins with senior management commitment and support, as shown in Exhibit 10.17. The model views EC security (as well as the broader IT security) as a combination of commitment, policy and training, procedures, and tools executed as continuous process. For a comprehensive discussion, see Chickowski (2008).

EC SECURITY POLICIES AND TRAINING

The next step is to develop a general EC security policy, as well as policies that specify acceptable use of computers and networks, access control, enforcement, roles, and responsibilities. The policies need to be disseminated throughout the organization and necessary training provided to ensure that everyone is aware of and understands them. These policies are important because access control rules, access control lists, monitoring, and rules for firewalls and routers are derived from them. For example, to avoid violating privacy legislation when collecting confidential data, policies need to specify that customers:

▶ Know that data is being collected

▶ Give permission, or "opt in," for data to be collected

▶ Have some control over how the information is used

▶ Know the data will be used in a reasonable and ethical manner

acceptable use policy (AUP)
Policy that informs users of their responsibilities when using company networks, wireless devices, customer data, and so forth.

The greater the understanding of how security issues directly impact production levels, customer and supplier relationships, revenue streams, and management's liability, the more security will be incorporated into business projects and proposals. It is essential to have a comprehensive and up-to-date **acceptable use policy (AUP)** that informs users of their responsibilities when using company networks, wireless devices, customer data, and so forth. To be effective, the AUP needs to define the responsibilities of every user by specifying both acceptable and unacceptable computer usage. Access to the company networks, databases, and e-mail should never be given to a user until after this process is completed.

EC SECURITY PROCEDURES AND ENFORCEMENT

business impact analysis (BIA)
An exercise that determines the impact of losing the support of an EC resource to an organization and establishes the escalation of that loss over time, identifies the minimum resources needed to recover, and prioritizes the recovery of processes and supporting systems.

EC security procedures require an evaluation of the digital and financial assets at risk—including cost and operational considerations. To calculate the proper level of protection, managers responsible for a digital asset need to assess its risk exposure. The risk exposure model for digital assets is comprised of five factors, which are shown in Exhibit 10.18.

Another assessment is the *business impact analysis*. **Business impact analysis (BIA)** is an exercise that determines the impact of losing the support of an EC resource to an organization; estimates how that loss may escalate over time; identifies the minimum resources needed to recover from the loss; and prioritizes the steps in the recovery of the processes and supporting systems. After estimating the risk exposure of digital assets, focus resources on the risks that are the greatest.

EXHIBIT 10.18	**Risk Exposure Model for Digital Assets**
Factor	**Cost and Operational Considerations**
Asset's value to the company	What are the costs of replacement, recovery, or restoration? What is the recoverability time?
Attractiveness of the asset to a criminal	What is the asset's value (on a scale of low to high) to identify thieves, industrial spies, terrorists, or fraudsters?
Legal liability attached to the asset's loss or theft	What are the potential legal costs, fines, and restitution expenses?
Operational, marketing, and financial consequences	What are the costs of business disruption, delivery delays, lost customers, negative media attention, inability to process payments or payroll, or a drop in stock prices?
Likelihood of a successful attack against the asset	Given existing and emerging threats, what is the probability the asset will be stolen or compromised?

INDUSTRY STANDARDS FOR CREDIT CARD PROTECTION (PCI DSS)

In addition to legal requirements and technical security measures, a unique industry standard was created in 2008 by industry members to protect their customers' and their members' brand images and revenues. It is called the *Payment Card Industry Data Security Standard (PCI DSS),* created by Visa, MasterCard, American Express, and Discover.

PCI is required for all members, merchants, or service providers that store, process, or transmit cardholder data. In short, PCI DSS requires merchants and card payment providers to make certain their Web applications are secure. If done correctly, it could actually help curb the number of Web-related security breaches. PCI DSS (Section 6.6) mandates that retailers ensure that Web-facing applications are protected against known attacks by applying either of the following two methods:

1. Have all custom supplication code reviewed for vulnerabilities by an application security firm.
2. Install an application layer firewall in front of Web-facing applications. Each application will have its own firewall to protect against intrusions and malware.

The purpose of the PCI DSS is to improve customers' trust in e-commerce, especially when it comes to online payments, and to increase the Web security of online merchants. To motivate the following of these standards, the penalties for noncompliance are severe. The card brands can fine the retailer, and increase transaction fees for each credit or debit card transaction. A finding of noncompliance can be the basis for lawsuits. For details, see en.wikipedia.org/wiki/PCI_DSS.

SECURITY TOOLS: HARDWARE AND SOFTWARE

After the EC security program and policies are defined and risk assessment completed, then the software and hardware needed to support and enforce them can be put in place. Decisions regarding data encryption are implemented at this stage. Although encryption to protect moving or static data is not foolproof, it helps protect a company from customer outrage and public outcry if it suffers a data breach.

Keep in mind that security is an ongoing, multilayered process and not a problem that can be solved only with hardware or software tools. Nor can hardware and software security defenses protect against irresponsible business practices or corrupt management. Managers and employees are potential attack entities, just like hackers and criminal communities. For more information on the reasons for a multilayered security approach, read Online File W10.10. The file concentrates on spyware prevention.

WHY IS IT DIFFICULT TO STOP INTERNET CRIME?

The following are the major reasons Internet crime is so difficult to stop.

Making Shopping Inconvenient

Strong EC security makes online shopping inconvenient and is demanding on customers. The EC industry does not want to enforce safeguards that add friction to the profitable wheels of online commerce. It is possible, for example, to demand passwords or PINs for all credit card transactions, but that could discourage or prevent customers from completing their purchase. It is also possible to demand delivery only to the billing address for a credit card, but that would eliminate an important convenience for gift senders.

Lack of Cooperation from Credit Card Issuers

A second reason is the lack of cooperation from credit card issuers and local and especially foreign ISPs. If the source ISP would cooperate and suspend the hacker's access, it would be very difficult for hackers to do what they do. The hacker would not be able to hack from the comfort of home because that street address would be blacklisted by the ISP.

However, requiring stronger EC standards and information sharing by the credit card companies would not fix the problem. Many cybercriminals, especially ones that do not reside in a G8 nation, do not need to worry about prosecution from their government or even suspension from their ISP. (The Group of Eight [G8] is an international forum for the governments of Canada, France, Germany, Italy, Japan, Russia, the United Kingdom, and the United States.) This situation helps explain why a huge majority of the hackers (some estimate about 95%) reside in Turkey, China, Romania, or Brazil.

Shoppers' Negligence

The third reason pertains to customers. Online shoppers are to blame for not taking necessary precautions to avoid becoming a victim. Some shoppers rely too heavily on fraud protection provided by credit card issuers, ignoring the bigger risk of identity theft. Phishing is rampant because some people respond to it—making it profitable. Although phishing gets most of the media attention, users expose themselves to equally dangerous risks by using debit cards on online gambling sites or revealing themselves in online communities like MySpace, Facebook, and France's Skyblog.

Design and Architecture Issues

A fourth reason arises from information systems (IS) design and security architecture issues. It is well known that preventing vulnerability during the EC design and preimplementation stage is far less expensive than mitigating problems later. The IS staff of a company needs to plan security from the design stage because simple mistakes, such as not ensuring that all traffic into and out of a network pass through a firewall, are often to blame for letting in hackers. If companies don't invest the resources needed to ensure that their applications are secure, they may as well forget about security elsewhere on the Web site. Security needs to be built into an EC site from the very beginning and also into the application level.

There's no doubt that Web applications are attackers' target of choice and that every component in an EC application is subject to some sort of security threat.

Ignoring EC Security Best Practices

The fifth reason is that many companies of all sizes fail to implement basic IT security management, such as best security practices, business continuity plans, and disaster recovery plans. In its fourth annual study on information security and the workforce released in 2008, the **Computing Technology Industry Association (CompTIA)**, a nonprofit trade group, said that the most widespread threats in the United States today stem from spyware, the lack of user awareness, and virus and worm attacks. Because of the known role of human error in information security breaches, 60 percent of the more than 2,000 government, IT, financial, and educational organizations surveyed worldwide had mandatory security training. Nearly 33 percent of all U.S. firms make certification required now, compared to only 25 percent in 2006 and 14 percent in 2005 (CompTIA 2008).

Computing Technology Industry Association (CompTIA)
Nonprofit trade group providing information security research and best practices.

Lack of Due Care in Business Practices

The final reason is the lack of due care in business or hiring practices, outsourcing, and business partnerships. The **standard of due care** comes from the law and is also known as the "duty to exercise reasonable care." Due care in EC is care that a company is reasonably expected to take based on the risks affecting its EC business and online transactions. If managers ignore the standard of due care in business practices, hire criminals, outsource to fraudulent vendors, or partner with unsecured companies, they put their EC business and confidential data at risk, exposing themselves to legal problems. See Online File W10.11 for a discussion of the impacts on ChoicePoint for its negligence for not following reasonable information security and privacy practices. For a description of the PCI standard and requirements, see pcistandard.com.

standard of due care
Care that a company is reasonably expected to take based on the risks affecting its EC business and online transactions.

Section 10.10 ▶ REVIEW QUESTIONS

1. If senior management is not committed to EC security, how might that impact the e-business?
2. What is a benefit of using the risk exposure model for EC security planning?
3. Why should every company implement an acceptable use policy?
4. Why is training required?
5. List the six major reasons why it is difficult to stop computer crimes.

MANAGERIAL ISSUES

Some managerial issues related to this chapter are as follows.

1. **Why is an EC security strategy and life-cycle approach needed?** Without an EC security strategy to guide investments and defenses, security efforts tend to be reactive and more expensive to manage. Ineffective security opens the door to computer and network attacks that can result in damage to technical and information assets; theft of information and information services; temporary loss of a Web site and Internet access; loss of income; litigation brought on by dissatisfied organizational stakeholders; loss of customer confidence; and damaged reputation and credibility. In some cases, attacks literally can put a company out of business, especially if EC is its sole source of revenue.

2. **What is the EC security strategy of your company?** The security strategy of your company should be to deter, prevent, and detect the potential threats in conducting EC whether it is intentional or unintentional. Evaluating the threats, vulnerabilities, and risks of potential criminal attacks and their impacts on business operation is a manager's task. Developing the defense mechanism and disaster recovery plan should be shared throughout the organization. Designing the EC security plan as a part of the overall IT security plan is necessary. Educating senior management about the consequences of poor network security and the best practices in network risk management is essential to the development of a good strategy.

3. **Is the budget for IT security adequate?** To evaluate the adequacy of the IT security budget, it will be useful to compare yours with the national average. If the budget of your company is too low or too high, you will need to seriously review the reasons why. It is reported that the average IT security budget is about 10 percent of the total IT budget, while awareness training is about 3 percent of the total IT budget. Review whether the outsourcing plan for security expertise is adequately balanced with internal effort because about 40 percent of companies outsource some computer security.

4. **What steps should businesses follow in establishing a security plan?** Security risk management is an ongoing process involving three phases: asset identification, risk assessment, and implementation. By actively monitoring existing security policies and measures, companies can determine which are successful or unsuccessful and, in turn, which should be modified or eliminated. However, it also is important to monitor changes in business requirements, changes in technology and the way it is used, and changes in the way people can attack the systems and networks. In this way, an organization can evolve its security policies and measures, ensuring that they continue to support the critical needs of the business.

5. **Should organizations be concerned with internal security threats?** Except for malware, breaches perpetrated by insiders are much more frequent than those perpetrated by outsiders. This is true for both B2C and B2B sites. Security policies and measures for EC

sites need to address these insider threats. Pay special attention to the prevention of social engineering schemes that may allure insiders, and educate the new insiders about such threats.

6. **What is the key to establishing strong e-commerce security?** Most discussions about security focus on technology, with statements like "firewalls are mandatory" or "all transmissions should be encrypted." Although firewalls and encryption can be important technologies, no security solution is useful unless it solves a business problem and is adopted by customers. Determining your business requirements is the most important step in creating a security solution. Business requirements, in turn, determine your information requirements. Once you know your information requirements, you can begin to understand the value of those assets and the steps that you should take to secure those that are most valuable and vulnerable.

SUMMARY

In this chapter, you learned about the following EC issues as they related to the chapter's learning objectives.

1. **The importance and scope of EC information security.** For EC to succeed, it must be secured. Unfortunately this is not an easy task due to many unintentional and intentional hazards. Security incidents and breaches interrupt EC transactions and increase the cost of doing business online. Internet design is vulnerable, and the temptation to commit computer crime is increasing with the increased applications and volume of EC. Criminals are expanding operations, creating an underground economy of stolen valuable information. A strategy is needed to handle the costly defense operation, which includes training, education, project management, and ability to enforce security policy. EC security will remain an evolving discipline because threats change, e-business needs change, and Web-based technologies to provide greater service change. An EC security strategy is needed to optimize EC security programs for efficiency and effectiveness. There are several reasons why. EC security costs and efforts from reacting to crises and paying for damages are greater than if organizations had an EC security strategy. The Internet is still a fundamentally insecure infrastructure. There are many criminals, and they are intent on stealing information for identity theft and fraud. Without a strategy, EC security is treated as a project instead of an ongoing, never-ending process.

2. **Basic EC security issues and perspectives.** The security issue can be viewed as a battleground between attackers and attack and defenders and defense. There are many variations on both sides and many possible collision scenarios. Owners of EC sites need to be concerned with multiple security issues: authentication, verifying the identity of the participants in a transaction; authorization, ensuring that a person or process has access rights to particular systems or data; auditing, being able to determine whether particular actions have been taken and by whom; confidentiality, ensuring that information is not disclosed to unauthorized individuals, systems, or processes; integrity, protecting data from being altered or destroyed; availability, ensuring that data and services are available when needed; and nonrepudiation, the ability to limit parties from refuting that a legitimate transaction took place.

3. **Threats, vulnerabilities, and attacks.** EC sites are exposed to a wide range of attacks. Attacks may be nontechnical (social engineering), in which a perpetrator tricks people into revealing information or performing actions that compromise network security. Or they may be technical, whereby software and systems expertise are used to attack the networks, database, or programs. DOS attacks bring operations to a halt by sending floods of data to target computers or to as many computers on the Internet as possible. Malicious code attacks include viruses, worms, Trojan horses, or some combination of these. Over the past couple of years, various trends in malicious code have emerged, including an increase in the speed and volume of attacks; reduced time between the discovery of a vulnerability and the release of an attack to exploit the vulnerability; the growing use of bots to launch attacks; an increase in attacks on Web applications; and a shift to profit-motivated attacks.

4. **Phishing, financial crimes, and spam.** Phishing attempts to get valuable information from people by masquerading as a trustworthy entity. Personal information is extracted from people (stolen) and sold to criminals who use it to commit financial crimes such as transferring money to illegal accounts. One method of financial crime is to use e-mail spam in an attempt to influence the recipients.

5. **Information assurance.** The importance of the information assurance model to EC is that it represents the processes for protecting information by ensuring its confidentiality, integrity, and availability.

Confidentiality is the assurance of data privacy. Integrity is the assurance that data is accurate or that a message has not been altered. Availability is the assurance that access to data, the Web site, or other EC data service is timely, available, reliable, and restricted to authorized users.

6. **Securing EC access and communications.** In EC, issues of trust are paramount. Trust starts with the authentication of the parties involved in a transaction; that is, identifying the parties in a transaction along with the actions they can perform. Authentication can be established with something one knows (e.g., a password), something one has (e.g., a token), or something one possesses (e.g., a fingerprint). Biometric systems can confirm a person's identity. Fingerprint scanners, iris scanners, facial recognition, and voice recognition are examples of biometric systems. Public key infrastructure (PKI), which is the cornerstone of secure e-payments, also can authenticate the parties in a transaction. PKI uses encryption (private and public) to ensure privacy and integrity and digital signatures to ensure authenticity and nonrepudiation. Digital signatures are themselves authenticated through a system of digital certificates issued by certificate authorities (CAs). For the average consumer and merchant, PKI is simplified because it is built into Web browsers and services. Such tools are secure because security is based on SSL (TSL) communication standards.

7. **Technologies for securing networks.** At EC sites, firewalls, VPNs, and IDSs have proven extremely useful. A firewall is a combination of hardware and software that isolates a private network from a public network. Firewalls are of two general types—packet-filtering routers or application-level proxies. A packet-filtering router uses a set of rules to determine which communication packets can move from the outside network to the inside network. An application-level proxy is a firewall that accepts requests from the outside and repackages a request before sending it to the inside network, thus, ensuring the security of the request. Individuals with broadband access need personal firewalls. VPNs are used generally to support secure site-to-site transmissions across the Internet between B2B partners or communications between a mobile and remote worker and a LAN at a central office. IDSs monitor activity across a network or on a host. The systems watch for suspicious activity and take automated actions whenever a security breach or attack occurs. In the same vein, some companies are installing honeynets and honeypots

in an effort to gather information on intrusions and to analyze the types and methods of attacks being perpetrated.

8. **The different controls and special defense mechanism.** The major controls are general (including physical, access controls, biometrics, administrative controls, application controls, and internal controls for compliance). In addition, there are controls against fraud and spam.

9. **Role of business continuity and disaster recovery planning.** Disaster recovery planning is an integral part of effective internal control and security management. Business continuity planning includes back-up sites and a plan for what to do when disaster strikes. Such plan are required by insurance companies and some lenders. It is necessary to conduct drills that will ensure that people know what to do if disaster strikes.

10. **Enterprisewide EC security.** EC and network security are inconvenient, expensive, tedious, and never-ending. A defensive in-depth model that views EC security as a combination of commitment, people, processes, and technology is essential. An effective program starts with senior management's commitment and budgeting support. This sets the tone that EC security is important to the organization. Other components are security policies and training. Security procedures must be defined with positive incentives for compliance and negative consequences for violations. The last stage is the deployment of hardware and software tools based on the policies and procedures defined by the management team.

11. **Why is it impossible to stop computer crimes?** Responsibility or blame for cybercrimes can be placed on criminals and victimized industries, users, and organizations. The EC industry does not want to enforce safeguards that add friction to the profitable wheels of online commerce. Credit card issuers try to avoid sharing leads on criminal activity with each other or law enforcement. Online shoppers fail to take necessary precautions to avoid becoming a victim. IS designs and security architectures are still incredibly vulnerable. Organizations fail to exercise due care in business or hiring practices, outsourcing, and business partnerships. Every EC business knows that the threats of bogus credit card purchases, data breaches, phishing, malware, and pretexting never end—and that these threats must be addressed comprehensively and strategically.

KEY TERMS

QUESTIONS FOR DISCUSSION

1. Survey results on the incidence of cyberattacks paint a mixed picture; some surveys show increases, others show decreases. What factors could account for the differences in the reported results?

2. Consider how a hacker might trick people into giving him their user IDs and passwords to their Amazon.com accounts. What are some of the ways that a hacker might accomplish this? What crimes can be performed with such information?

3. B2C EC sites continue to experience DOS attacks. How are these attacks perpetrated? Why is it so difficult to safeguard against them? What are some of the things a site can do to mitigate such attacks?

4. All EC sites share common security threats and vulnerabilities. Do you think that B2C Web sites face different threats and vulnerabilities than B2B sites? Explain.

5. How are botnet identity theft attacks and Web site hijacks perpetrated? Why are they so dangerous to e-commerce?

6. A business wants to share its customer account database with its trading partners and customers, while at the same time provide prospective buyers with access to marketing materials on its Web site. Assuming that the business is responsible for running all these network components, what types of security components (e.g., firewalls, VPNs, etc.) could be used to ensure that the partners and customers have access to the account information and others do not? What type of network configuration (e.g., bastion gateway server) will provide the appropriate security?

7. A company is having problems with its password security systems and decides to implement two-factor

authentication. What biometric alternatives could the company employ? What are some of the factors it should consider when deciding among the alternatives?

8. Discuss some of the difficulties of eliminating online financial fraud.

9. Some companies prefer not to have disaster recovery plans. Under what circumstances does this make sense? Discuss.

10. Conduct a Google search on so-called scareware (a social engineering technique). Explain why it is so popular with criminals and how they can profit from it. Discuss some defense mechanisms.

11. Enter idesia.com and look at their product. Discuss these benefits over other biometrics.

12. Enter trendsecure.com and find a tool called "hijack this." Try the free tool. Find an online forum that deals with it. Discuss the benefits and limitations.

INTERNET EXERCISES

1. The National Vulnerability Database (NVD) is a comprehensive cybersecurity database that integrates all publicly available U.S. government vulnerability resources and provides references to industry resources. Visit nvd.nist.gov and review 10 of the recent CVE vulnerabilities. For each vulnerability, list its publish date, CVSS severity, impact type, and the operating system or software with the vulnerability.

2. The Common Vulnerabilities and Exposures Board (cve.mitre.org) maintains a list of common security vulnerabilities. Review the list. How many different vulnerabilities are there? Based on the list, which computer system components appear to be most vulnerable to attack? What impact do these vulnerable components have on EC?

3. Your B2C site has been hacked with a new, innovative method. List two organizations where you would report this incident so that they can alert other sites. How do you do this, and what type of information do you have to provide?

4. The McAfee Avert Labs Threat Library has detailed information on viruses, Trojans, hoaxes, vulnerabilities, and potentially unwanted programs (PUPs), where they come from, how they infect your system, and how to mitigate or remediate them (vil.nai.com). Select one newly discovered malware and one newly discovered PUP. Using other online resources, describe these threats and the steps needed to combat them. Why is adware listed as a PUP?

5. Connect to the Internet. Determine the IP address of your computer by visiting at least two Web sites that provide that feature. You can use a search engine to locate Web sites or visit ip-adress.com or whatis myipaddress.com. What other information does the search reveal about your connection? Based on this information, how could a company or hacker use that information?

6. ICSA Labs (icsalabs.com) provides a detailed list of firewall products for corporate, small business, and residential use. Select three corporate firewall products from the list. Using online materials, research and compare the benefits of each product. Based on the comparison, which product would you choose and why?

7. Select a single type of physiological biometric system. Using the Internet, identify at least two commercial vendors offering these systems. Based on the information you found, what are the major features of the systems? Which of the systems would you select and why?

8. The National Strategy to Secure Cyberspace provides a series of actions and recommendations for each of its five national priorities. Search and download a copy of the strategy online. Selecting one of the priorities, discuss in detail the actions and recommendations for that priority.

9. The Symantec Annual Internet Security Threat Report provides details about the trends in attacks and vulnerabilities in Internet security. Obtain a copy of the latest report and summarize the major findings of the report for both attacks and vulnerabilities.

10. Enter perimeterusa.com and look for a white paper titled "Top 9 Network Security Threats in 2009." Summarize these threats. Then look for a paper titled "The ABC's of Social Engineering." Summarize the suggested defense.

11. Enter security firm finjan.com and find examples of underground Internet activities in five different countries. Prepare a summary.

12. Enter voices.washingtonpost.com/securityfix and identify security breaches in 2009.

13. Enter verisign.com and find information about PKI and encryption. Write a report.

14. Enter gfi.com/emailsecuritytest and similar sites. Write some guidelines for protecting your PC.

TEAM ASSIGNMENTS, PROJECTS, AND CLASS DISCUSSIONS

1. Assign teams to report on the major spam and scam threats. Examine examples provided by ftc.gov, the Symantec report on the state of spam (2009), and white papers from IBM, Verisign, and other security firms.

2. Several personal firewall products are available. A list of these products can be found at firewallguide.com/software.htm. Assign each team three products from the list. Each team should prepare a detailed review and comparison of each of the products they have been assigned.

3. Assign each team member a different B2C or B2B Web site. Have each team prepare a report summarizing the site's security assets, threats, and vulnerabilities. Prepare a brief EC security strategy for the site.

4. Address the following topics in a class discussion:

   a. Some claim that the best strategy is to invest very little and only in proven technologies such as encryption and firewalls. Discuss.

   b. Can the underground Internet marketplace be controlled? Why or why not?

   c. Why is phishing so difficult to control? What can be done? Discuss.

   d. How secure is your e-mail?

Closing Case

UBS PAINEWEBBER'S BUSINESS OPERATIONS DEBILITATED BY MALICIOUS CODE

Employee (Allegedly) Planned to Crash All Computer Networks

In June 2006, a former systems administrator at UBS PaineWebber, Roger Duronio, 63, was charged with building, planting, and setting off a software logic bomb designed to crash the network. His alleged motive was to get revenge for not being paid what he thought he was worth. He designed the logic bomb to delete all the files in the host server in the central data center and in every server in every U.S. branch office. Duronio was looking to make up for some of the cash he felt he had been denied. He wanted to take home $175,000 a year. He had a base salary of $125,000 and a potential annual bonus of $50,000, but the actual bonus was $35,000.

Duronio quit his job, went to a broker within hours, and bought stock options that would only pay out if the company's stock plunged within 11 days. By setting a short expiration date of 11 days instead of a year, the gain from any payout would be much greater. He tried to ensure a stock price crash by crippling the company's network to rock their financial stability. His "put" options expired worthless because the bank's national network did go down, but not UBS stock.

Discovering the Attack

In a U.S. court, UBS PaineWebber's IT manager Elvira Maria Rodriguez testified that on March 4, 2002, at 9:30 AM when the stock market opened for the day, she saw the words "cannot find" on her screen at the company's Escalation Center in Weehawken, New Jersey. She hit the enter key to see the message again, but her screen was frozen. Rodriguez was in charge of maintaining the stability of the servers in the company's branch offices.

When the company's servers went down that day in March 2002, about 17,000 brokers across the country were unable to make trades; the incident affected nearly 400 branch offices. Files were deleted. Backups went down within minutes of being run. Rodriguez, who had to clean up after the logic bomb, said, "How on earth were we going to bring them all back up? How was this going to affect the company? If I had a scale of one to 10, this would be a 10-plus."

The prosecutor, Assistant U.S. Attorney V. Grady O'Malley, told the jury: "It took hundreds of people, thousands of man hours and millions of dollars to correct." The system was offline for more than a day, and UBS PaineWebber (renamed *UBS Wealth Management USA* in 2003) spent about $3.1 million in assessing and restoring the network. The company did not report how much was lost in business downtime and disruption.

Tracking Down the Hacker

A computer forensics expert testified that Duronio's password and user account information were used to gain remote access to the areas where the malicious code was built inside the UBS network. The U.S. Secret Service agent who had investigated the case found a hard copy of the logic bomb's source code on the defendant's bedroom dresser. A computer forensics investigator found electronic copies of the code on two of his four home computers.

Defense Blames UBS Security Holes

Chris Adams, Duronio's defense attorney, offered another scenario. Adams claimed that the code was planted by someone else to be a nuisance or prank. Adams also said the UBS system had many security holes and backdoors that gave easy access to attackers. Adams told the jury:

> UBS computer security had considerable holes. There are flaws in the system that compromise the ability to determine what is and isn't true. Does the ability to walk around in the system undetected and masquerade as someone else affect your ability to say what has happened?

He also claimed that UBS and @Stake, the first computer forensics company to work on the incident, withheld some information from the government and even destroyed some of the evidence. As for the stock options, Adams explained that they were neither risky bets nor part of a scheme, but rather a common investment practice.

Disaster Recovery Efforts

While trying to run a backup to get a main server up and functional, Rodriguez discovered that a line of code (MRM-r) was hanging up the system every time it ran. She renamed the command to hide it from the system and rebooted the server. This action stopped the server from deleting anything else. After testing to confirm the fix, backup tapes brought up the remaining 2,000 servers, and the line of code was deleted from each one. Restoring each server took from 30 minutes to 2 hours unless there was a complication. In those cases, restoration took up to 6 hours. UBS called in 200 IBM technicians to all the branch offices to expedite the recovery.

Many of the servers were down a day and a half, but some servers in remote locations were down for weeks. The incident impacted all the brokers who were denied access to critical applications because the servers were down.

Minimizing Residual Damages

UBS asked the judge to bar the public from Duronio's trial to avoid "serious embarrassment" and "serious injury" to the bank and its clients and possibly reveal sensitive information about the UBS network and operations. UBS argued that documents it had provided to the court could help a criminal hack into the bank's computer systems to destroy critical business information or to uncover confidential client information.

Duronio faced numerous charges, including mail fraud, securities fraud, and computer sabotage, which carry sentences of up to 30 years in jail, $1 million in fines, and restitution for recovery costs. See *informationweek.com/news/security/cybercrime/showArticle.jhtml?articleID=188703100* or *usdoj.gov/usao/nj/press/files/pdffiles/duro1213rel.pdf*.

Sources: Compiled from DOJ (2002), Gaudin (2006), and Whitman (2006).

Questions

1. What "red flags" might have indicated that Duronio was a disgruntled employee? Would any of those red flags also indicate that he would sabotage the network for revenge?

2. How could this disaster have been prevented? What policies, procedures, or technology could have prevented such an attack by an employee with full network access?

3. Did UBS have a disaster recovery plan in place for an enterprisewide network crash?

4. Do you agree with the defense lawyer's argument that anyone could have planted the logic bomb because UBS's computer security had considerable holes?

5. Given the breadth of known vulnerabilities, what sort of impact will any set of security standards have on the rise in cyberattacks?

ONLINE RESOURCES
available at pearsonglobaleditions.com/turban

Online Files

W10.1	Application Case: Hackers Profit from TJX's Corporate Data
W10.2	Top Cyber Security Areas in 2008
W10.3	Examples of Internet Fraud
W10.4	Life Cycle of an EC Security Program
W10.5	Application Case: The Eyes Have It
W10.6	Basic Security Design Concepts
W10.7	What Firewalls Can Protect
W10.8	Application Case: Honeynets and the Law
W10.9	Application Case: How Companies Fight Spamming
W10.10	Cyberassaults Demand a Multilayered Security Approach
W10.11	Application Case: Impacts of ChoicePoint's Negligence in Information Security

Comprehensive Educational Web Sites

nvd.nist.gov: A comprehensive cybersecurity database

itworld.com/security: Comprehensive collection of papers on security

spamlaws.com: News, cases, legal information, and much more; spam, scams, security

microsoft.com/technet/security: Comprehensive collection of papers on security

eseminarslive.com/c/s/topics: Webinars, events, news on security

verisignsecured.com: A major security vendor; tutorials

thebci.org: Business Continuity Institute

drj.com: Disaster recovery journal

webbuyerguide.com/resources: look for security topics

csrc.nist.gov: Computer Security Resource Center

technologyevaluation.com: White papers, etc.; look for security

ic3.gov/crimeschemes.aspx: A comprehensive list of Internet crime schemes and how to deal with them

cbintel.com/auctionfraudreport.pdf: A comprehensive list of Internet auction fraud statistics

REFERENCES

Altman, H. "Jihad Web Snares Online Shops, Buyers." *Tampa Tribune*, February 20, 2006.

Baumstein, A. "E-Peril (E-Mail Attacks)." *InformationWeek*, March 31, 2008.

Chickowski, E. "Closing the Security Gap." *Baseline*, June 2008.

CNNMoney. "Identity Theft Hits Record 10M Americans." February 9, 2009. money.cnn.com/2009/02/09/news/newsmakers/identity_theft.reut/index.htm?postversion=2009020907 (accessed March 2009).

CompTIA. "Trends in Information Security: A CompTIA Analysis of IT Security and the Workforce." 2008. comptia.org/sections/research/reports/200804-SecuritySummary.aspx (accessed March 2009).

Department of Justice (DOJ). "Disgruntled UBS PaineWebber Employee Charged with Allegedly Unleashing 'Logic Bomb' on Company Computers." December 17, 2002. usdoj.gov/criminal/cybercrime/duronioIndict.htm (accessed January 2007).

Fagg, S. "Continuity for the People." *Risk Management Magazine*, March 2006.

Federal Trade Commission. "Consumer Fraud and Identity Theft Complaint Data January—December 2007." February 2008. ftc.gov/opa/2008/02/fraud.pdf (accessed March 2009).

Fiber Optics Weekly. "Telstra Uses NetEx Gear." January 13, 2006.

Fisher, D. "MyDoom E-Mail Worm Spreading Quickly." *eWeek*, January 26, 2004. eweek.com/c/a/Security/MyDoom-EMail-Worm-Spreading-Quickly (accessed March 2009).

Fratto, M. "Secure What Matters." *InformationWeek*, December 1, 2008.

Gage, D. "Bank of America Seeks Anti-Fraud Anodyne." *Baseline*, May 10, 2006. baselinemag.com/article2/0,11040,1962470,00.asp (accessed March 2009).

Gaudin, S. "Nightmare on Wall Street: Prosecution Witness Describes 'Chaos' in UBS PaineWebber Attack." *InformationWeek*, June 6, 2006. informationweek.com/story/showArticle.jhtml?articleID=188702216 (accessed March 2009).

George, R. "Security to Go." *InformationWeek*, May 3, 2008.

Hearing of the Senate Armed Services Committee. "Worldwide Threats to U.S. National Security." Washington, D.C., Federal News Service. February 28, 2006.

Holz, T., M. Engleberth, and F. Freiling. "Learning More About the Underground Economy: A Case Study of Keyloggers and Dropzones." University of Maneheim Laboratory for Dependable System, December 18, 2008. scribd.com/doc/9193817/Learning-More-About-the-Underground-Economy-A-CaseStudy-of-Keyloggers-and-Dropzones (accessed March 2009).

Jepson, K. "Bewear. Bware. Beware. The Typosquatters." *Credit Union Journal*, July 31, 2006.

Kawamoto, D. "California Man Pleads Guilty to Bot Attack." *CNET News*, May 5, 2006. news.cnet.com/California-man-pleads-guilty-to-bot-attack/2100-7348_3-6069238.html (accessed March 2009).

Krebs, B. "Security Fix: Web Fraud 2.0." *Washington Post*, September 12, 2008. voices.washingtonpost.com/securityfix/web_fraud_20 (accessed March 2009).

LeClaire, J. "Social Networking Sites in the Crosshairs?" *TechNewsWorld*, January 3, 2007. technewsworld.com/story/54932.html (accessed March 2009).

Lerer, L. "Why the SEC Can't Stop Spam." *Forbes*, March 8, 2007. forbes.com/2007/03/08/sec-spam-stock-tech-security-cx_ll_0308spam.html (accessed March 2009).

MacMillan, D. "Cyberscams Befriend Social Networks." *BusinessWeek*, November 20, 2008.

Marketing Charts. "Fraudsters Filch $4B Online; Record Losses for U.S. E-Commerce." 2009. marketingcharts.com/interactive/fraudsters-filch-4b-online-record-losses-for-us-e-commerce-7144/cybersource-order-reject-rates-online-segment-fall-2008jpg (accessed March 2009).

McCormick, J., and D. Gage. "Web Mobs." *Baseline*, March 2005.

McMillan, R. "FBI: Internet Fraud Complaints Up 33 Percent in 2008." *IDG News*, March 30, 2009. networkworld.com/news/2009/033009-fbi-internet-fraud-complaints-up.html?page=1 (accessed March 2009).

Microsoft. "Financial Crisis Is a Goldmine for Online Criminals." 2009. blogs.msdn.com/securitytipstalk/archive/2008/11/07/warning-financial-crisis-is-a-goldmine-for-online-criminals.aspx (accessed March 2009).

Microsoft. "What Do You Do If You've Responded to a Phishing Scam?" May 7, 2008. microsoft.com/protect/yourself/phishing/remedy.mspx (accessed March 2009).

O'Hagan, M. "Three Accused of Inducing Ill Effects on Computers at Local Hospital." *Seattle Times*, February 22, 2006. seattletimes.nwsource.com/html/localnews/2002798414_botnet11m.html (accessed March 2009).

Palgon, G. "Simple Steps to Data Security." *Security Management*, June 2008.

Ponemon Institute. "Airport Security: The Case of Lost Laptops." *Special Report*, June 30, 2008.

Prince, K. "Understanding PCI DSS Compliance." perimeterusa.com/wp/PCI_White_Paper.pdf (accessed May 2009).

Rand, D. "Threats When Using Online Social Networks." *CSIS Security Group*, May 16, 2007. (csis.dk/dk/forside/LinkedIn.pdf (accessed March 2009).

Richardson, R. "2008 CSI Computer Crime and Security Survey." Computer Security Institute, 2008. i.zdnet.com/blogs/csisurvey2008.pdf (accessed March 2009).

Roberts, P. F. "DOJ Indicts Hacker for Hospital Botnet Attack." eWeek, February 10, 2006a. eweek.com/c/a/Security/DOJ-Indicts-Hacker-for-Hospital-Botnet-Attack (accessed May 2009).

Roberts, P. F. "Webroot Uncovers Thousands of Stolen Identities." *InfoWorld*, May 8, 2006b. infoworld.com/article/06/05/09/78139_HNTrojanrebery_1.html (accessed March 2009).

SecureComputing. "How to Protect Your Company and Employees from Image Spam." securecomputing.com/image_spam_WP.cfm (accessed March 2009).

Symantec. *Symantec Report on the Underground Economy: July 07–June 08.* Symantec Corp., November 2008 Report #14525717.

Symantec. *Web-Based Attacks.* White paper #20016955, February 2009.

Taipei Times. "Two Convicted in Conspiracy." March 6, 2009. taipeitimes.com/News/world/archives/2009/03/06/2003437699 (accessed March 2009).

Whitman, J. "UBS Wants to Bar Public at Tech 'Bomb' Trial." *New York Post*, June 6, 2006. tmronline.com/A55951/tmrarticles.nsf/b02380a2f0e146ca862569240078f070/0b601788814bab1486257186007a9056!OpenDocument (accessed May 2009).

ELECTRONIC COMMERCE PAYMENT SYSTEMS

Learning Objectives

Upon completion of this chapter, you will be able to:

1. Understand the shifts that are occurring with regard to online payments.

2. Discuss the players and processes involved in using credit cards online.

3. Discuss the different categories and potential uses of smart cards.

4. Discuss various online alternatives to credit card payments and identify under what circumstances they are best used.

5. Describe the processes and parties involved in e-checking.

6. Describe payment methods in B2B EC, including payments for global trade.

Content

PAY-PER-VIEW PAGES: THE NEXT ITUNES

The Problem

The e-book market is heating up. In February 2009, Amazon.com released the second version of its popular Kindle e-book reader. This was followed in March of 2009 with the release of an iPhone application for reading content purchased on Amazon's Kindle Web site and then in May 2009 with the announcement of the Kindle DX with its larger nine inch display format. Around the same time, the Canadian book retailer Indigo Books & Music Inc. launched a Web site, Shortcovers.com, for people who read books and articles online or on mobile devices. The service focuses on providing "bite-sized chunks" of about 5000 words such as individual chapters, short stories, blogs, magazines, newspaper articles, and pieces written and uploaded by users. Free and paid content can be viewed online or transferred to mobile devices using mobile apps that are distributed through iTunes and the Shortcovers Web site.

For the most part, e-books are sold as "exact digital replicas" of their print counterparts. In other words, e-books are not sold a page or chapter at a time. Instead the buyer has to purchase the whole book. This is the way the Kindle online store works. Also, it is the way that the Shortcovers site works. For most of the books in its online catalog, Shortcovers provides the first chapter for free, sells the next two chapters for 99 cents, or offers the entire e-book at a discount of up to half the publisher's list price. This works fine for works of fiction. Most fiction readers are primarily interested in purchasing the entire book, not individual pages or chapters. This isn't the case for nonfiction readers. Plenty of nonfiction readers do not need nor want the complete works. For example:

- A reader is traveling to Rome, Italy, on his or her next vacation and only wants a couple of chapters from Fodor's holiday travel guide to Italy, not the whole guide.

- A software programmer faces a perplexing problem and discovers a solution in a particular chapter of a well-known programming book. The book sells for $80 but the programmer only needs five pages from the 600-page edition.

- A professor wants to assign his or her students a series of chapters from a list of textbooks. Without violating copyright laws or requiring the students to spend a small fortune purchasing the texts, this really isn't really feasible.

A few years ago, Amazon.com and Random House tried to remedy this problem. Amazon announced a plan called "Amazon Pages" that would allow readers to purchase parts of books online. The plan never came to fruition. Instead, they released the Kindle and opened the Kindle online store. Similarly, in February 2008 Random House began testing the idea of selling individual chapters online for $2.99. To date, the first, and only title offered is Chip and Dan Heath's *Made to Stick*.

Selling books online—either hardcopy or electronic—is straightforward. Selling pages, chapters, or any other sections of a book or journal online for under $5 is another story. The barrier is not technical, it is financial. In the online world, the vast majority of consumers use credit cards to make purchases. The financial institutions issuing credit cards charge a fixed percentage for each credit card purchase, as well as a fixed fee. For a purchase under $5, it is difficult for a vendor to break even. It is the same problem faced by merchants in the offline world. Fortunately, the credit card companies, as well as electronic payment companies, such as PayPal, are well aware of the issues associated with small-value purchases and have begun to address the problem.

The Solution

Purchases under $5 are called *micropayments*. In the offline world, "cash has been king of these small sales, because credit card companies charge merchants too much in fees to make the transactions profitable" (D'Agostino 2006). Cash does not work in the online world. In the online world, virtually every attempt to disintermediate cash and credit cards has failed. Yet, ample evidence suggests that consumers are willing to use their credit cards for micropayments.

In the online world, Apple's iTunes has clearly been a success. Originally, iTunes sold individual songs for $0.99. At MacWorld 2009, Apple announced a multitier pricing scheme for iTunes: $0.69, $0.99, or $1.29, depending on a song's age and popularity. Apple also announced that it had sold over 6 billion songs.

Apple has overcome the costs associated with credit and debit card fees by having consumers set up accounts. The purchases of single items are aggregated until the total purchase amount makes it cost-effective to submit the payment to the credit or debit card issuer. Systems that aggregate purchases are also called "closed-loop" systems. The credit card companies are not enamored with these systems and prohibit merchants from aggregating purchases directly. However, they are currently reconsidering their stance because, as Pam Zuercher, Visa's vice president for product innovation, notes "there is an undeniable trend—users want to use their cards for very small purchases" (Mitchell 2007).

The credit and debit card companies, as well as e-payment vendors (e.g., PayPal), are well aware of the difficulties associated with using cards for online micropayments. In response, they have lowered their fees in an effort to entice online (and offline) vendors to permit credit and debit card micropayments. Even with the new fee structure, purchases of less than $2 are still cost-prohibitive for the average merchant. Small-value payments are much less prohibitive for larger vendors, whose large card-purchase volume enables them to negotiate with the card issuers for even smaller fees.

The Results

To date, companies such as Amazon.com and Random House have been unsuccessful with their pay-per-page or chapter plans. Clearly, Amazon.com is in a position to negotiate for smaller credit card fees. Like iTunes, it also has the ability to aggregate purchases for individual buyers. However, Random House does not sell directly to the public. Instead, it relies on other vendors, such as Amazon.com, to do the selling for them. Even with a viable micropayment system, there is no guarantee that pay-per-page or pay-per-chapter will interest consumers, especially given the usual restrictions placed on purchases of this sort.

Consider, for a moment, a few of the restrictions Random House has placed on its viewing programs:

- Books will be available for full indexing, search, and display.

- No downloading, printing, or copying will be permitted.

- Encryption and security measures must be applied to ensure protection of the digital content and compliance with the prescribed usage rules and territorial limitations.

In essence, the only thing the purchaser can do is view the page or chapter online. This is much more onerous than the restrictions placed on music or video downloads, which at least permit the purchaser to copy the content to their PCs or multimedia players. Unless these restrictions are loosened or eliminated, they will likely lead to the long-run failure of the Random House effort and other similar ones.

Sources: CBCNews (2009), D'Agostino (2006), and Mitchell (2007).

WHAT WE CAN LEARN . . .

The overwhelming majority of B2C purchases are paid for by credit card. For merchants, the costs of servicing card payments are high. Transaction costs, potential chargeback fees for fraudulent transactions, and the costs of creating and administering a secure EC site for handling card payments are steep. Over the years, a number of less costly e-payment alternatives to credit cards have been proposed. Digital Cash; PayMe.com; Bank One's eMoneyMail; Flooz; Beenz; Wells Fargo's and eBay's Billpoint; and Yahoo!'s PayDirect are examples of alternatives that failed to gain a critical mass of users and subsequently folded. For a variety of reasons, PayPal is one of the few alternatives to credit cards that has succeeded against significant odds. The same can be said for the world of B2B e-payments. Although a number of diverse payment methods have been proposed, few have survived. This chapter discusses various e-payment methods for B2C and B2B and the underlying reasons why some have been adopted and others have not.

11.1   THE PAYMENT REVOLUTION

Today, we are in the midst of a worldwide payment revolution, with cards and electronic payments taking the place of cash and checks. The tipping point of the revolution occurred in 2003. In that year, the combined use of credit and debit cards for in-store payments for the first time exceeded the combined use of cash and checks. By 2005, debit and credit cards accounted for 55 percent of in-store payments, with cash and checks making up the rest (Simon 2007). The growth in the use of plastic is attributable to the substantial growth in the use of debit cards and the decline in the use of cash. In recent years, debit card use has been spurred by a change in the U.S. Electronic Funds Transfer Act, which eliminated the requirement for merchants to issue receipts for debit purchases of $15 or less.

Similar trends have occurred in noncash payments of recurring bills. In 2001, over 75 percent of all recurring bills were paid by paper-based methods (e.g., paper checks), whereas less than 25 percent of these payments were made electronically. Now, the percent of recurring bills paid electronically hovers around 50 percent.

For decades people have been talking about the cashless society. Although the demise of cash and checks is certainly not imminent, many individuals can live without checks and nearly without cash. In the online B2C world, they already do. Throughout the world, the overwhelming majority of online purchases are made with credit cards, although there are some countries where other payments methods prevail. For instance, consumers in Germany prefer to pay with either direct debit or bank cards, whereas those in China rely on debit cards.

For online B2C merchants, the implications of these trends are straightforward. In most countries, it is hard to run an online business without supporting credit card payments, despite the costs. It also is becoming increasingly important to support payments by debit card. Eventually, the volume of debit card payments may surpass credit card payments in the online world, as they have for offline purchases. For merchants who are interested in international markets, there is a need to support a variety of e-payment mechanisms, including bank transfers, COD, electronic checks, private-label cards, gift cards, instant credit, and other noncard payment systems, such as PayPal. Merchants who offer multiple payment types have lower shopping cart abandonment rates and higher order conversion, on average, resulting in increased revenues.

The short history of e-payments is littered with the remains of companies that have attempted to introduce nontraditional payment systems. It takes years for any payment system to gain widespread acceptance. For example, credit cards were introduced in the 1950s but did not reach widespread use until the 1980s. A crucial element in the success of any e-payment method is the "chicken-and-egg" problem: How do you get sellers to adopt a method when there are few buyers using it? And, how do you get buyers to adopt a method when there are few sellers using it? A number of factors come into play in determining whether a particular method of e-payment achieves critical mass. Some of the crucial factors include the following (Evans and Schmalensee 2005).

Independence. Some forms of e-payment require specialized software or hardware to make the payment. Almost all forms of e-payment require the seller or merchant to install specialized software to receive and authorize a payment. Those e-payment methods that require the payer to install specialized components are less likely to succeed.

Interoperability and Portability. All forms of EC run on specialized systems that are interlinked with other enterprise systems and applications. An e-payment method must mesh with these existing systems and applications and be supported by standard computing platforms.

Security. How safe is the transfer? What are the consequences of the transfer being compromised? Again, if the risk for the payer is higher than the risk for the payee, then the payer is not likely to accept the method.

Anonymity. Unlike credit cards and checks, if a buyer uses cash, there is no way to trace the cash back to the buyer. Some buyers want their identities and purchase patterns to remain anonymous. To succeed, special payment methods, such as e-cash, have to maintain anonymity.

Divisibility. Most sellers accept credit cards only for purchases within a minimum and maximum range. If the cost of the item is too small—only a few dollars—a credit card will not do. In addition, a credit card will not work if an item or set of items costs too much (e.g., an airline company purchasing a new airplane). Any method that can address the lower or higher end of the price continuum or that can span one of the extremes and the middle has a chance of being widely accepted.

Ease of Use. For B2C e-payments, credit cards are the standard due to their ease of use. For B2B payments, the question is whether the online e-payment methods can supplant the existing offline methods of procurement.

Transaction Fees. When a credit card is used for payment, the merchant pays a transaction fee of up to 3 percent of the item's purchase price (above a minimum fixed fee). These fees make it prohibitive to support smaller purchases with credit cards, which leaves room for alternative forms of payment.

International Support. EC is a worldwide phenomenon. A payment method must be easily adapted to local buying patterns and international requirements before it can be widely adopted.

Regulations. A number of international, national, and regional regulations govern all payment methods. Even when an existing institution or association (e.g., Visa) introduces a new payment method, it faces a number of stringent regulatory hurdles. PayPal, for instance, had to contend with a number of lawsuits brought by U.S. state attorneys general that claimed that PayPal was violating state banking regulations.

Section 11.1 ▶ REVIEW QUESTIONS

1. Describe the trends that are occurring in cash and noncash payments in the United States.

2. What types of e-payments should B2C merchants support?

3. What is the "chicken-and-egg" problem in e-payments?

4. Describe the factors that are critical for an e-payment method to achieve critical mass.

11.2 USING PAYMENT CARDS ONLINE

payment card
Electronic card that contains information that can be used for payment purposes.

Payment cards are electronic cards that contain information that can be used for payment purposes. They come in three forms:

▶ **Credit cards.** A credit card provides the holder with credit to make purchases up to a limit fixed by the card issuer. Credit cards rarely have an annual fee. Instead, holders are charged high interest—the annual percentage rate—on their average daily unpaid balances. Visa, MasterCard, and EuroPay are the predominant credit cards.

▶ **Charge cards.** The balance on a charge card is supposed to be paid in full upon receipt of the monthly statement. Technically, holders of a charge card receive a loan for 30 to 45 days equal to the balance of their statement. Such cards usually have annual fees. American Express's Green Card is the leading charge card, followed by the Diner's Club card.

▶ **Debit cards.** With a debit card, the money for a purchased item comes directly out of the holder's checking account (called a demand-deposit account). The actual transfer of funds from the holder's account to the merchant's takes place within 1 to 2 days. MasterCard, Visa, and EuroPay are the predominant debit cards.

PROCESSING CARDS ONLINE

authorization
Determines whether a buyer's card is active and whether the customer has sufficient funds.

settlement
Transferring money from the buyer's to the merchant's account.

The processing of card payments has two major phases: authorization and settlement. **Authorization** determines whether a buyer's card is active and whether the customer has sufficient available credit line or funds. **Settlement** involves the transfer of money from the buyer's to the merchant's account. The way in which these phases actually are performed varies somewhat depending on the type of payment card. It also varies by the configuration of the system used by the merchant to process payments.

There are three basic configurations for processing online payments. The EC merchant may:

▶ **Own the payment software.** A merchant can purchase a payment-processing module and integrate it with its other EC software. This module communicates with a payment gateway run by an acquiring bank or another third party.

▶ **Use a point of sale system (POS) operated by an acquirer.** Merchants can redirect cardholders to a POS run by an acquirer. The POS handles the complete payment process and directs the cardholder back to the merchant site once payment is complete. In this case, the merchant system only deals with order information. In this configuration, it is important to find an acquirer that handles multiple cards and payment instruments. If not, the merchant will need to connect with a multitude of acquirers.

payment service provider (PSP)
A third-party service connecting a merchant's EC system to the appropriate acquiring bank or financial institution. PSPs must be registered with the various card associations they support.

▶ **Use a POS operated by a payment service provider.** Merchants can rely on servers operated by third parties known as **payment service providers (PSPs)**. In this case, the PSP connects with the appropriate acquirers. PSPs must be registered with the various card associations they support.

For a given type of payment card and processing system, the processes and participants are essentially the same for offline (card present) and online (card not present) purchases. Exhibit 11.1 compares the steps involved in making a credit card purchase both online and offline. As the exhibit demonstrates, there is very little difference between the two.

Based on the processes outlined in Exhibit 11.1, the key participants in processing card payments online include the following:

▶ **Acquiring bank.** Offers a special account called an *Internet Merchant Account* that enables card authorization and payment processing.

▶ **Credit card association.** The financial institution providing card services to banks (e.g., Visa and MasterCard).

▶ **Customer.** The individual possessing the card.

▶ **Issuing bank.** The financial institution that provides the customer with a card.

EXHIBIT 11.1 Credit Card Purchases: Online Versus Offline

Online Purchase	Offline Purchase
1. The *customer* decides to purchase a CD on the Web, adding it to the electronic shopping cart and going to the checkout page to enter his or her credit card information.	1. The *customer* selects a CD to purchase, takes it to the checkout counter, and hands his or her credit card to the sales clerk.
2. The *merchant* site receives the customer's information and sends the transaction information to its *payment processing service (PPS)*.	2. The *sales clerk* swipes the card and transfers transaction information to a *point-of-sale (POS)* terminal.
3. The PPS routes information to the *processor* (a large data center for processing transactions and settling funds to the merchant).	3. The POS terminal routes information to the *processor* via a dial-up connection.
4. The processor sends information to the *issuing bank* of the customer's credit card.	4. The processor transmits the credit card data and sales amount with a request for authorization of the sale to the *issuing bank* of the customer's credit card.
5. The issuing bank sends the transaction to the processor, either authorizing the payment or not.	5. If the cardholder has enough credit in his account to cover the sale, the issuing bank authorizes the transaction and generates an authorization code; if not the sale is declined.
6. The processor routes the transaction result to the PPS.	6. The processor sends the transaction code back through the processor to the POS.
7. The PPS passes the results to the merchant.	7. The POS shows the outcome to the merchant.
8. The merchant accepts or rejects transaction.	8. The merchant tells the customer the outcome of the transaction.

Sources: PayPal (2004) and Lamond and Whitman (1996).

▶ **Merchant.** A company that sells products or services.

▶ **Payment processing service.** The service provides connectivity among merchants, customers, and financial networks that enable authorization and payments. Usually these services are operated by companies such as CyberSource (cybersource.com).

▶ **Processor.** The data center that processes card transactions and settles funds to merchants.

FRAUDULENT CARD TRANSACTIONS

Although the processes used for authorizing and settling card payments offline and online are very similar, there is one substantial difference between the two. In the online world, merchants are held liable for fraudulent transactions. In addition to the lost merchandise and shipping charges, merchants who accept fraudulent transactions can incur additional fees and penalties imposed by the card associations. However, these are not the only costs. There also are the costs associated with combating fraudulent transactions. These include the costs of tools and systems to review orders, the costs of manually reviewing orders, and the revenue that is lost from rejecting orders that are valid. In their 10th annual survey of fraudulent online card transactions, CyberSource (2009) indicated that managing online fraud continues to be a significant and growing problem for online merchants of all sizes.

For the past 9 years, CyberSource has sponsored a survey to address the detection, prevention, and management of fraud perpetrated against online merchants. CyberSource's 2008 survey of 400 merchants documented the following trends (CyberSource 2009):

▶ Although the percentage of online revenues lost per merchant has declined slightly since 2004, the total dollars lost to fraud increased substantially, from $1.9 billion in 2003 to $4.0 billion in 2008. The rise was attributable to the increase in the amount of business that was being done online, which grew by 20 percent or more annually over the same time period.

▶ In 2008, merchants estimated that an average of 1.1 percent of their orders were fraudulent. This represented a slight decline from the previous year. The fraudulent orders resulted in merchants' crediting the real cardholder's account (a chargeback). The median value of these fraudulent orders was $200, which was 67 percent higher than the average value of valid orders.

▶ Fifty-two percent of the merchants surveyed accepted international orders outside the United States and Canada. These orders represented 17 percent of the sales for these merchants. The fraud rate for these orders was approximately 4.0 percent, or more than 3.5 times higher than the fraud rate for domestic orders.

▶ Certain merchants were more susceptible to fraud than others. This was due to a number of factors: the merchant's visibility on the Web, the steps the merchant had taken to combat fraud, the ease with which the merchant's products could be sold on the open market, and the merchant's size. Larger firms were less susceptible to fraud than smaller firms.

▶ Although overall security expenditures for online fraud detection remained the same from 2006 to 2007, the amount spent on manual review of orders increased over 30 percent, or by about $100 million. As the number of online orders continues to increase, this is not a viable long-term strategy for merchants.

In addition to tracking cyberfraud trends, the CyberSource surveys also have monitored the steps taken by merchants to combat fraud (CyberSource 2009). In 2008, merchants used more tools than in the past to combat fraud. In 2008, the median number of tools used by merchants was 4.7, compared with 3 in 2003. Merchants are also spending more to combat fraud. The median amount spent to combat fraud in 2008 was 0.2 percent of online revenues. Most of the money was spent on review staff (51%), followed by third-party tools and services (25%) and internally developed tools (24%). The key tools used in combating fraud were:

Address Verification System (AVS)
Detects fraud by comparing the address entered on a Web page with the address information on file with the cardholder's issuing bank.

▶ **Address verification.** Approximately 80 percent of all merchants use the Address Verification System (AVS), which compares the address entered on a Web page with the address information on file with the cardholder's issuing bank. This method results in a number of false positives, meaning that the merchant may reject a valid order. Cardholders often have new addresses or simply make mistakes in inputting numeric street addresses or postal codes. AVS is only available in the United States and Canada.

▶ **Manual review.** Over 80 percent of all merchants use the manual review method, which relies on staff to manually review suspicious orders. For small merchants with a small volume of orders, this is a reasonable method. For larger merchants, this method does not scale well, is expensive, and impacts customer satisfaction. In spite of these limitations, the percentage of merchants using this method is increasing, along with the percentage of items being reviewed. In 2008, the number of orders being reviewed was one in three, versus one in four in 2003.

card verification number (CVN)
Detects fraud by comparing the verification number printed on the signature strip on the back of the card with the information on file with the cardholder's issuing bank.

▶ **Fraud screens and automated decision models.** Larger merchants (those generating over $25 million in revenue) often use fraud screens and automated decision models. These tools are based on automated rules that determine whether a transaction should be accepted, rejected, or suspended. A key element of this method is the ability of the merchant to easily change the rules to reflect changing trends in the fraud being perpetrated against the company.

▶ **Card verification number (CVN).** Approximately 75 percent of all merchants use the card verification number (CVN) method, which compares the verification number printed on the signature strip on the back of the card with the information on file with the cardholder's issuing bank. However, if a fraudster possesses a stolen card, the number is in plain view.

▶ **Card association payer authentication services.** In the last couple of years, the card associations have developed a new set of payer identification services (e.g., Verified by Visa and MasterCard SecureCode). These services require cardholders to register with the systems and merchants to adopt and support both the existing systems and the new systems. In 2004, it was estimated that over 55 percent of merchants would be using this method by 2005. In reality, only 25 percent of merchants in the 2008 survey indicated that they had adopted this method.

▶ **Negative lists.** Thirty-eight percent of all merchants use negative lists. A negative list is a file that includes a customer's information (IP address, name, shipping/billing address, contact numbers, etc.) and the status of that customer. A customer's transaction is matched against this file and flagged if the customer is a known problem.

The overall impact of these tools is that merchants are rejecting a significant number of orders due to suspicion of fraud. In 2003, the average number of rejected orders was over three for every fraudulent order accepted. This represented a rejection rate of 4 percent. The problem with these rejection rates is that a number of the rejected orders are valid, resulting in lost revenue.

Section 11.2 ▶ REVIEW QUESTIONS

1. Describe the three types of payment cards.
2. What options does a merchant have in setting up an e-payment system?
3. List the major participants in processing cards online.
4. What costs does an online merchant incur if it submits a fraudulent card transaction?
5. Describe the major trends in fraudulent orders perpetrated against online merchants.
6. What steps are often taken by online merchants to combat fraudulent orders?

11.3 SMART CARDS

Outside North America, smart cards often are used in place of or in addition to traditional credit and debit cards. They also are used widely to support nonretail and nonfinancial applications. A **smart card** looks like a plastic payment card, but it is distinguished by the presence of an embedded microchip (see Exhibit 11.2). The embedded chip may be a microprocessor combined with a memory chip or just a memory chip with nonprogrammable logic. Information on a microprocessor card can be added, deleted, or otherwise manipulated;

smart card
An electronic card containing an embedded microchip that enables predefined operations or the addition, deletion, or manipulation of information on the card.

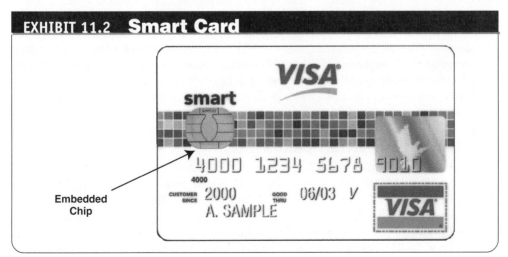

EXHIBIT 11.2 Smart Card

Source: Courtesy of Visa International Service Association.

a memory-chip card is usually a "read-only" card, similar to a credit card. Although the microprocessor is capable of running programs like a computer does, it is not a stand-alone computer. The programs and data must be downloaded from and activated by some other device (such as an ATM machine).

TYPES OF SMART CARDS

contact card

A smart card containing a small gold plate on the face that when inserted in a smart card reader makes contact and passes data to and from the embedded microchip.

contactless (proximity) card

A smart card with an embedded antenna, by means of which data and applications are passed to and from a card reader unit or other device without contact between the card and the card reader.

There are two distinct types of smart cards. The first type is a **contact card**, which is activated when it is inserted into a smart card reader. The second type of card is a **contactless (proximity) card**, meaning that the card only has to be within a certain proximity of a smart card reader to process a transaction. *Hybrid cards* combine both types of cards into one.

Contact smart cards have a small gold plate about one-half inch in diameter on the front. When the card is inserted into the smart card reader, the plate makes electronic contact and data are passed to and from the chip. Contact cards can have electronically programmable, read-only memory (EPROM) or electronically erasable, programmable, read-only memory (EEPROM). EPROM cards can never be erased. Instead, data are written to the available space on the card. When the card is full, it is discarded. EEPROM cards are erasable and modifiable. They can be used until they wear out or malfunction. Most contact cards are EEPROM.

In addition to the chip, a contactless card has an embedded antenna. Data and applications are passed to and from the card through the card's antenna to another antenna attached to a smart card reader or other device. Contactless cards are used for those applications in which the data must be processed very quickly (e.g., mass-transit applications, such as paying bus or train fares) or when contact is difficult (e.g., security-entering mechanisms to buildings). Proximity cards usually work at short range, just a few inches. For some applications, such as payments at highway toll booths, the cards can operate at considerable distances.

With *hybrid* and *dual-interface* smart cards, the two types of card interfaces are merged into one. A hybrid smart card has two separate chips embedded in the card: contact and contactless. In contrast, a dual-interface, or combi, smart card has a single chip that supports both types of interfaces. The benefit of either card is that it eliminates the need to carry multiple cards to support the various smart card readers and applications.

smart card reader

Activates and reads the contents of the chip on a smart card, usually passing the information on to a host system.

With both types of cards, smart card readers are crucial to the operation of the system. Technically speaking, a smart card reader is actually a read/write device. The primary purpose of the **smart card reader** is to act as a mediator between the card and the host system that stores application data and processes transactions. Just as there are two basic types of cards, there are two types of smart card readers—*contact* and *proximity*—which match the particular type of card. Smart card readers can be transparent, requiring a host device to operate, or stand alone, functioning independently. Smart card readers are a key element in determining the overall cost of a smart card application. Although the cost of a single reader is usually low, the cost can be quite high when hundreds or thousands are needed to service a large population of users (e.g., all the passengers traveling on a metropolitan mass transit system).

smart card operating system

Special system that handles file management, security, input/output (I/O), and command execution and provides an application programming interface (API) for a smart card.

Like computers, smart cards have an underlying operating system. A **smart card operating system** handles file management, security, input/output (I/O), and command execution and provides an application programming interface (API). Originally, smart card operating systems were designed to run on the specific chip embedded in the card. Today, smart cards are moving toward multiple and open application operating systems such as MULTOS (multos.com) and Java Card (java.sun.com/products/javacard). These operating systems enable new applications to be added during the life of the card.

APPLICATIONS OF SMART CARDS

The worldwide use of smart cards is growing rapidly. Globally, an estimated 4 billion smart cards were shipped in 2008. This represented an 18 percent increase over the 3.3 billion cards shipped in 2007 (*CardTechnology* 2007). The largest demand for smart cards continues to come from the Asia-Pacific region. The growth in smart card usage, which is somewhere between 20 and 30 percent per annum, is being driven by a variety of financial, transit, mobile phone, health-care, and government applications. A general discussion of these applications can be found at the GlobalPlatform Web site (globalplatform.org). Within EC, smart cards are used in the place of standard credit cards for general retail purchases and for transit fares.

Retail Purchases

The credit card associations and financial institutions are transitioning their traditional credit and debit cards to multi-application smart cards. Of the 4 billion cards shipped in 2008, approximately 600 million were banking (credit and debit) smart cards. In many parts of the world, smart cards have reached mass-market adoption rates. This is especially true in Europe, where all bank cards are slated to be smart cards with strong authentication and digital signature capabilities by 2010 (*EurActiv.com* 2008).

In 2000, the European Commission established an initiative known as the Single Europe Payment Area (SEPA), encompassing 31 European countries. To bring this initiative to fruition, all the EU banks agreed to use the same basic bank cards standard, enabling the use of credit and debit cards throughout the EU. The standard, EMV, is named after the three card associations that developed it (Europay, MasterCard and Visa). It is based on smart cards with a microprocessor chip. The chip is capable of storing not only financial information, but other applications as well, such as strong authentication and digital signatures. The 31 countries have agreed to shift all their magnetic strip cards to EMV smart cards by December 2010 (*EurActiv* 2008). To date, over 50 percent of the cards have been migrated.

One benefit of smart cards versus standard cards is that they are more secure. Because they are often used to store more valuable or sensitive information (e.g., cash or medical records), smart cards often are secured against theft, fraud, or misuse. If someone steals a standard payment card, the number on the card is clearly visible, as is the owner's signature and security code. Although it may be hard to forge the signature, in many situations only the number (and security code) is required to make a purchase. The only protection cardholders have is that there usually are limits on how much they will be held liable for (e.g., in the United States it is $50). If someone steals a stored-value card (or the owner loses it), the original owner is out of luck.

However, if someone steals a smart card, the thief is usually out of luck (with the major exception of contactless, or "wave and go," cards used for retail purchases). Some smart cards show account numbers, but others do not. Before the card can be used, the holder may be required to enter a PIN that is matched with the card. Theoretically, it is possible to "hack" into a smart card. Most cards, however, now store information in encrypted form. The smart cards can also encrypt and decrypt data that is downloaded or read from the card. Because of these factors, the possibility of hacking into a smart card is classified as a "class 3" attack, which means that the cost of compromising the card far exceeds the benefits.

The other benefit of smart cards versus standard payment cards is that they can be extended with other payment services. In the retail arena, many of these services are aimed at those establishments where payments are usually made in cash and speed and convenience are important. This includes convenience stores, gas stations, fast-food or quick-service restaurants, and cinemas. Contactless payments exemplify this sort of value-added service.

A few years ago, the card associations began piloting contactless payment systems in retail operations where speed and convenience are crucial. All these systems utilize the existing POS and magnetic strip payment infrastructure used with traditional credit and debit cards. The only difference is that a special contactless smart card reader is required. To make a purchase, a cardholder simply waves his or her card near the terminal, and the terminal reads the financial information on the card. Data supplied by Bank of America (Simon 2008) supports the contention that contactless credit cards speed things along. The data indicate, for example, that the average contactless fast-food restaurant transaction takes 12.5 seconds, versus 26.7 seconds for the traditional credit card swipe and 33.7 seconds for cash.

In spite of their convenience, the overall uptake of contactless payment cards has been slow. MasterCard's PayPass (mastercard.com/aboutourcards/paypass.html) is a case in point. MasterCard PayPass is an EMV compatible card that supports both magnetic strip and contactless payments. The card was introduced in 2003 in a market trial conducted in Orlando, Florida, with JPMorgan Chase, Citibank, and MBNA. The trial involved more than 16,000 cardholders and more than 60 retailers. The introduction of

PayPass served as a catalyst to increase card usage and loyalty in the Orlando area. During the trial, MasterCard experienced an 18 percent active rate for previously inactive accounts. MasterCard also saw a 23 percent increase in transaction value, a 28 percent increase in total weekly spending, and a 12 percent month-over-month increase in transaction volumes at participating merchants.

Based on the success of this trial, as well as MasterCard survey data indicating that a substantial majority of consumers would be willing to use a contactless card if it were provided, MasterCard began a wider rollout of PayPass in 2005 (*Payments News* 2006a). Today, MasterCard PayPass can be used in over 20 countries and is accepted by more than 80,000 merchants worldwide. In spite of this rollout, to date, only a small fraction of financial institutions have issued the PayPass card. The same fate has also befallen Visa's payWave and American Express' ExpressPay. Worldwide, less than 10 percent of the banking smart cards issued in 2008 were contactless payment cards. Again, it is the same "chicken-and-egg" problem encountered by any new payment system.

Transit Fares

In major cities, commuters often have to drive to a parking lot, board a train, and then change to one or more subways or buses to arrive at work. If the whole trip requires a combination of cash and multiple types of tickets, this can be a major hassle. For those commuters who have a choice, the inconvenience plays a role in discouraging the use of public transportation. To eliminate the inconvenience, most major transit operators in the United States, for example, are implementing smart card fare-ticketing systems. In addition, the U.S. government provides incentives to employers to subsidize the use of public transportation by their employees. In the United States, the transit systems in Washington, D.C.; Baltimore; San Francisco; Oakland; Los Angeles; Chicago; San Diego; Seattle; Minneapolis; Houston; Boston; Philadelphia; Atlanta; and the New York/New Jersey area have all instituted smart card payment systems. Two of the largest implementations to date, Washington, D.C.'s SmarTrip card and Boston's MBTA Charlie Card, have issued over 2.5 million and 1.4 million cards, respectively. The result will be the introduction of an estimated 15 million contactless smart cards and over 20,000 payment processing devices (Smart Card Alliance 2006).

Metropolitan transit operators are moving away from multiple, nonintegrated fare systems to systems that require only a single contactless card regardless of how many modes of transportation or how many transportation agencies or companies are involved. The SmarTrip program run by the Washington Metropolitan Area Transit Authority (WMATA) in the District of Columbia exemplifies this movement (wmata.com/riding/smartrip.cfm). In 1999, WMATA was the first transportation system in the United States to employ smart cards. SmarTrip is a permanent, contactless, rechargeable fare card that can hold up to $300 in fare value. The card can be used with 17 different transit systems, including WMATA-operated parking lots, the Metrorail, Metrobuses, and other regional rail services. SmarTrip handles the complexities associated with the various systems, including zone-based and time-based fares, volume discounts, and bus-to-train and bus-to-bus transfers. To date, close to a half million SmarTrip cards have been issued and well over one-third of Metrorail riders use the cards regularly.

The U.S. smart card transit programs are modeled after those used in Asia. Case 11.1 describes one of these—the TaiwanMoney Card—and Online File W11.1 discusses another Asian implementation. Like their Asian counterparts, some U.S. transit operators are looking to partner with retailers and financial institutions to combine their transit cards with payment cards to purchase goods and services such as snacks, bridge tolls, parking fees, or food in restaurants or grocery stores located near the transit stations.

In addition to handling transit fares, smart cards and other e-payment systems are being used for other transportation applications. For instance, Philadelphia has retooled all its 14,500 parking meters to accept payment from prepaid smart cards issued by the Philadelphia Parking Authority (philapark.org). Similarly, many major toll roads accept electronic payments rendered by devices called transponders that operate much like contactless smart cards.

CASE 11.1

EC Application

TAIWANMONEY CARD

In October 2005, the Kaohsiung City Government (KCG) in Taiwan began, as part of its e-City initiative, the Smart Transport Card Project. Similar to other municipalities in Asia, KCG was interested in utilizing smart card technology to enable contactless payments throughout its transport system. Unlike other municipalities, however, KCG was not interested in introducing a specialized transport card. Typically, transport cards are purchased from a transport authority, and their primary function is to pay transport fares. Occasionally, they can be used at other venues. For example, the Hong Kong metro card known as the Octopus Card can be used at fast-food restaurants and convenience stores. Instead, KCG decided to partner with MasterCard to produce a single card that could be used for both retail and transport payments. In this way, KCG could avoid many of the problems associated with issuing the cards, managing the overall payment systems, and instituting specialized legislation dictating how the cards could be used.

The card, which is produced by MasterCard for KCG, is called the TaiwanMoney Card. Technically, the card was MasterCard's first OneSMART PayPass Chip Combi Card. The card complies with the EMV standard, making it the first EMV-based card to support transport payments. Although KCG is the owner of the Smart Transport Card Project, the cards are marketed, issued, and serviced by Cathay United Bank, E. Sun Bank, and Bank of Kaohsiung.

The KCG system, which is operated by Mondex Taiwan, supports two types of cards. There are *standalone cards* for children and nonlocal and nonbanked customers that are used for single trips. The second card is *Payment Plus*. This type of card is for existing MasterCard holders and new account customers. It is a dual-branded MasterCard credit card or debit card that can be used for both transportation and shopping.

In order for the transportation system to support the cards, contactless TaiwanMoney Card readers had to be installed on all buses. In order for retailers to support the cards, their POS terminals had to be upgraded to accept the TaiwanMoney or MasterCard PayPass contactless cards.

By the end of 2005, there were approximately 100,000 cardholders using the TaiwanMoney Cards to pay fares on buses running in Kaohsiung and six other cities in southern Taiwan. They were also using the cards to make purchases at 5,000 convenience stores, supermarkets, and other retail outlets in the region.

Following the success of the 2005 pilot project, a full-scale rollout of the TaiwanMoney card was initiated in 2007. Because the card is essentially a MasterCard PayPass card, it can be used anywhere PayPass can be used.

Sources: Chen (2008), Hendry (2007), and Tan (2007).

Questions

1. What is the TaiwanMoney Card?
2. Why did KCG decide to use a smart money card for its transportation system rather than a specialized transportation card?
3. What change was required for the PayPass card to work with KCG's metro system?

Section 11.3 ▶ REVIEW QUESTIONS

1. What is a smart card? Contact card? Contactless card?
2. What is a smart card operating system?
3. Describe the use of smart cards in metropolitan transportation systems.

11.4 STORED-VALUE CARDS

What looks like a credit or debit card, acts like a credit or debit card, but isn't a credit or debit card? The answer is a **stored-value card**. As the name implies, the monetary value of a stored-value card is preloaded on the card. From a physical and technical standpoint, a stored-value card is indistinguishable from a regular credit or debit card. It is plastic and has a magnetic strip on the back, although it may not have the cardholder's name printed on it. The magnetic strip stores the monetary value of the card. This distinguishes a stored-value card from a smart card. With smart cards, the chip stores the value. Consumers can use stored-value cards to make purchases, offline or online, in the same way that they use credit and debit cards—relying on the same networks, encrypted communications, and electronic banking protocols. What is different about a stored-value card is that anyone can obtain one without regard to prior financial standing or having an existing bank account as collateral.

Stored-value cards come in two varieties: *closed loop* and *open loop*. Closed-loop, or single-purpose, cards are issued by a specific merchant or merchant group (e.g., a shopping mall) and

stored-value card
A card that has monetary value loaded onto it and that is usually rechargeable.

can only be used to make purchases from that merchant or merchant group. Mall cards, store cards, gift cards, and prepaid telephone cards are all examples of closed-loop cards. Gift cards represent a strong growth area, especially in the United States. Until 2008, spending on gift cards was growing at a rapid rate (*Seeking Alpha* 2008). In 2008, spending retreated to 2006 levels. For example, during the 2008 holiday season gift card spending in the United States fell 6 percent, from a high of $26 billion in 2007 to $24.9 billion. The average spent per card dropped from approximately $156 to $147 during that time. The 2008 figures were slightly above the 2006 figures.

In contrast, an open-loop, or multipurpose, card can be used to make debit transactions at a variety of retailers. Open-loop cards also can be used for other purposes, such as receiving direct deposits or withdrawing cash from ATM machines. Financial institutions with card-association branding, such as Visa or MasterCard, issue some open-loop cards. They can be used anywhere that the branded cards are accepted. Payroll cards, government benefit cards, and prepaid debit cards are all examples of open-loop cards.

Stored-value cards may be acquired in a variety of ways. Employers or government agencies may issue them as payroll cards or benefit cards in lieu of checks or direct deposits. Merchants or merchant groups sell and load gift cards. Various financial institutions and nonfinancial outlets sell preloaded cards by telephone, online, or in person. Cash, bank wire transfers, money orders, cashiers' checks, other credit cards, or direct payroll or government deposits fund preloaded cards.

Stored-value cards have been and continue to be marketed heavily to the "unbanked" and "overextended." Approximately 100 million adults in the United States do not have credit cards or bank accounts—people with low incomes, young adults, seniors, immigrants, minorities, and others (TowerGroup 2008). Among those with credit cards, 40 percent are running close to their credit limits. The expectation is that these groups will be major users of prepaid cards in the future.

For example, individuals in the United States transferred over $12 billion to individuals in Mexico. Instead of sending money orders or cash, programs like the EasySend card from Branch Banking and Trust (BB&T) provide a secure alternative to transferring money to relatives and friends (*Payments News* 2006b). With the EasySend program, an individual establishes a banking account, deposits money in the account, and mails the EasySend card to a relative or friend, who can then withdraw the cash from an ATM machine. When it was introduced in 2004, EasySend was focused primarily on the Hispanic community. Today, it is used by immigrant populations all over the world.

In a slightly different vein, the MasterCard MuchMusic and Visa Buxx cards, which are described in detail in Online File W11.2, provide young people with a prepaid, preloaded card alternative to credit cards or cash. Among other things, these alternatives provide a relatively risk-free way to teach kids fiscal responsibility.

Employers who are using payroll cards as an extension of their direct deposit programs are driving the growth of the prepaid, preloaded card market. Like direct deposit, payroll cards can reduce administrative overhead substantially. Payroll cards are especially useful to companies in the health-care and retail sectors and other industries where the workforce is part time or transient and less likely to have bank accounts.

Section 11.4 ▶ REVIEW QUESTIONS

1. What is a closed-loop stored-value card? What is an open-loop card?
2. Identify the major markets for stored-value cards.

11.5 E-MICROPAYMENTS

Consider the following online shopping scenarios:

▶ A customer goes to an online music store and purchases a single song that costs $0.99.
▶ A person goes online to a leading newspaper or news journal (such as *Forbes* or *BusinessWeek*) and purchases (downloads) a copy of an archived news article for $1.50.

▶ A person goes to an online gaming company, selects a game, and plays it for 30 minutes. The person owes the company $3 for the playing time.

▶ A person goes to a Web site selling digital images and clip art. The person purchases a couple of images at a cost of $0.80.

These are all examples of **e-micropayments**, which are small online payments, usually under $5. From the viewpoint of many vendors, credit and debit cards do not work well for such small payments. Vendors who accept credit cards typically must pay a minimum transaction fee that ranges from $0.25 to $0.35, plus 2 to 3 percent of the purchase price. The same is true for debit cards, where the fixed transaction fees are larger even though there are no percentage charges. These fees are relatively insignificant for card purchases over $5, but can be cost-prohibitive for smaller transactions. Even if the transaction costs were less onerous, a substantial percentage of micropayment purchases are made by individuals younger than 18, many of whom do not have credit or debit cards.

e-micropayments
Small online payments, typically under $10.

Regardless of the vendor's point of view, there is substantial evidence, at least in the offline world, that consumers are willing to use their credit or debit cards for purchases under $5. A random sample telephone survey conducted in 2006 by Ipsos Insight and Peppercoin, an e-micropayment company that was acquired by Chockstone in 2007, examined consumers' spending habits for low-priced items (Ipsos Insight 2006). Based on the survey, more than 67 million Americans had used their credit cards in the 30 days prior to the survey to purchase items priced at $5 or less. For the most part, these purchases were made at convenience stores, quick-service restaurants, and coffee shops or were for subway or other transportation tolls.

In the online world, the evidence suggests that consumers are interested in making small-value purchases, but the tie to credit or debit card payments is less direct. For example, in February 2006 Apple's iTunes music store celebrated its billionth download. A substantial percentage of these were downloads of single songs at $0.99 a piece. Although most of iTunes' customers paid for these downloads with a credit or debit card, the payments were not on a per-transaction basis. Instead, iTunes customers set up accounts and Apple then aggregates multiple purchases before charging a user's credit or debit card. Other areas where consumers have shown a willingness to purchase items under $5 are cell phone ringtones and ring-back tones and online games. As noted in Chapter 8, the market for ringtones and ring-back tones is in the billions of dollars. The download of both types of tones is charged to the consumer's cell phone bill. Similarly, the market for online games is in the billions of dollars. Like songs and tones, the download of a game is usually charged to the consumer's account, which is, in turn, paid by credit or debit card.

As far back as 2000, a number of companies have attempted to address the perceived market opportunity by providing e-micropayment solutions that circumvent the fees associated with credit and debit cards. For the most part, the history of these companies is one of unfulfilled promises and outright failure. Digicash, First Virtual, Cybercoin, Millicent, and Internet Dollar are some of the e-micropayment companies that went bankrupt during the dot-com crash. A number of factors played a role in their demise, including the fact that early users of the Internet thought that digital content should be free.

More recently, Bitpass declared on January 2007 that it was going out of business. As late as fall 2006, Bitpass launched a digital wallet service that enabled consumers to store online downloads of digital content and the payment method used to fund their accounts (i.e., credit cards, PayPal, or Automated Clearing House debits). Bitpass succeeded in partnering with a large number of smaller vendors, as well as a number of larger companies, such as Disney Online and ABC, Inc. However, it purposely focused on the sale of digital content rather than branching out into other markets. Its narrow focus was probably a major factor in its demise.

Currently, there are five basic micropayment models that do not depend solely or directly on credit or debit cards and that have enjoyed some amount of success. Some of these are better suited for offline payments than online payments, although there is nothing that precludes the application of any of the models to the online world. The models include the following (D'Agostino 2006):

- ▶ **Aggregation.** Payments from a single consumer are batched together and processed only after a certain time period has expired (20 business days) or a certain monetary threshold (e.g., $10) is reached. This is the model used by Apple's iTunes. This model is well suited for vendors with a lot of repeat business.

- ▶ **Direct payment.** Micropayments are added to a monthly bill for existing services, such as a phone bill. This is the model used by the cellular companies for ringtone downloads. The payment service provider PaymentOne (paymentone.com) provides a network and e-commerce platform that enable consumers to add purchases of any size to their phone bills. A similar service is offered by Paymo (paymo.com) in 39 countries around the world.

- ▶ **Stored value.** Upfront payments are made to a debit account from which purchases are deducted as they are made. Offline vendors (e.g., Starbucks) often use this model, and music-download services use variants of this model.

- ▶ **Subscriptions.** A single payment covers access to content for a defined period of time. Online gaming companies often use this model, and a number of online newspapers and journals (e.g., *Wall Street Journal*) also use it.

- ▶ **À la carte.** Vendors process purchases as they occur and rely on the volume of purchases to negotiate lower credit and debit card processing fees. The Golden Tee Golf video game uses this model, and quick-service restaurants (QSRs) such as McDonald's and Wendy's also use it.

In the past few years, micropayments have come to represent a growth opportunity for the credit card companies, because credit cards are being used increasingly as a substitute for cash. In response, both Visa and MasterCard have lowered their fees, especially for vendors such as McDonald's with high transaction volumes. In August 2005, PayPal also entered the micropayment market when it announced a new alternative fee structure of 5 percent plus $0.05 per transaction. This is in contrast to its standard fees of 1.9 to 2.9 percent plus $0.30 per transaction. If a PayPal vendor is being charged at a rate of 1.9 percent plus $0.30, then the alternative fee of 5 percent plus $0.05 will be cheaper for any item that costs $7 or less (you can do the math). It is $12 or less for 2.9 percent plus the $0.30 rate. Overall, the movement of the credit card companies and PayPal into the micropayment market does not bode well for those companies that provide specialized software and services for e-micropayments. In the long run, the credit card companies and PayPal will dominate this market.

Section 11.5 ▶ REVIEW QUESTIONS

1. What is a micropayment?
2. List some of the situations where e-micropayments can be used.
3. Outside of using credit or debit cards, what are some of the alternative ways that an online merchant can handle micropayments?

11.6 E-CHECKING

As noted in Section 11.1, in the United States paper checks are the only payment instrument that is being used less frequently now than 5 years ago (Simon 2007). In contrast, e-check usage is growing rapidly. In 2007, the use of online e-checks grew by 27 percent over the previous year, reaching 1.74 billion transactions. Based on a CyberSource survey (2008) of Web merchants, this percentage will continue to grow. Web merchants hope that e-checks will raise sales by reaching consumers who do not have credit cards or who are unwilling to provide credit card numbers online. According to CyberSource, online merchants that implement e-checks experience a 3 to 8 percent increase in sales, on average.

e-check

A legally valid electronic version or representation of a paper check.

An **e-check** is the electronic version or representation of a paper check. E-checks contain the same information as a paper check, can be used wherever paper checks are used, and are based on the same legal framework. An e-check works essentially the same way a paper check works, but in pure electronic form with fewer manual steps. With an online e-check purchase, the buyer simply provides the merchant with his or her account number, the nine-digit bank ABA routing number, the bank account type, the name on the bank account, and the transaction amount. The account number and routing number are found at the bottom of the check in the magnetic ink character recognition (MICR) numbers and characters.

E-checks rely on current business and banking practices and can be used by any business that has a checking account, including small and midsize businesses that may not be able to afford other forms of electronic payments (e.g., credit and debit cards). E-checks or their equivalents also can be used with in-person purchases. In this case, the merchant takes a paper check from the buyer at the point of purchase, uses the MICR information and the check number to complete the transaction, and then voids and returns the check to the buyer (see Case 11.2 for a complete description of the process).

CASE 11.2
EC Application
TO POP OR BOC: DIGITAL CHECKS IN THE OFFLINE WORLD

The use of e-checks is growing in the online world. Paradoxically, the same is true in the offline world, although it is occurring at a slower rate. First, evidence suggests that the use of a special NACHA system known as Purchase Order Processing (POP) is on the uptake. Second, another NACHA system, Back-Office Order Conversion (BOC), went into effect in March 2007. With both systems, merchants convert checks written by consumers into the equivalent of e-checks and process them as ACH debits. The difference between the two systems is whether the check is converted at the POS by a cashier or converted after the sale by other staff in the back office.

The traditional processes used in handling paper checks written by consumers to make purchases in a store involve a number of steps and intermediaries (as many as 28). At a minimum, the checks taken by cashiers are collected periodically throughout the day. After collection, back-office personnel process them. Once this is done, an armored car usually takes them from the store and delivers them to the store's bank. The store's bank processes them and sends them to a clearinghouse. From the clearinghouse, they move to the customer's bank. Not only is this time consuming, but it is also costly. Statistics show that it costs companies $1.25 to $1.55 to handle a paper check. This is in comparison to the administrative costs for an e-check, which can be as low as $0.10 per transaction. Based on these figures, any company stands to save a substantial amount of money by streamlining these traditional processes. This is where POP and BOC come into play.

The Gap, Wal-Mart, Old Navy, and KB Toys are some of the companies that have instituted POP. With POP, consumer checks are converted to ACH transactions at the time of the sale. When a customer writes a check for a purchase at a POS device, an MICR reader scans the check to capture the check details. The reader either keys or inserts the payment amount and the payee name at the time of purchase. At this point, the customer signs a written authorization. The cashier then voids the check and returns it to the customer with a signed receipt. Eligible transactions pass through the ACH system, and a record of payment appears on the customer's bank statement.

POP has a number of benefits:

▶ Back-office and check-handling costs are substantially reduced.
▶ Consumer payments are received more quickly.

▶ Availability of funds is improved.
▶ Notification of insufficient funds happens sooner.

Although POP saves money, it also has a number of costs. Hughes and Edwards (2006) offer the following criticisms of POP:

▶ It requires specialized readers for each checkout counter.
▶ Cashiers need special training to convert the checks to ACH transactions at the POS.
▶ The authorization process can be cumbersome and confusing to consumers.
▶ It slows the purchase process.

For these reasons, some critics suggest that BOC is a better alternative for the average merchant.

With BOC, the customer experience is similar to the traditional process. The customer writes a check for a purchase. The clerk either accepts or rejects the check after the merchant's verification service or guarantee provider verifies it. This process does not require explicit customer authorization to convert the check to an electronic form. Once the checks are collected and moved to the back office, they are scanned into an ACH file and processed electronically. In this way, a merchant only needs one or two scanners and a few personnel to handle the process.

Kohl's, a well-known clothing retailer, began implementing BOC in September 2008. Its implementation is based on an outsourced solution called SPIN from Solutran (*solutran.com*). The solution eliminates all manual check deposits. Solutran provides the facilities required to convert a check to a form of electronic settlement, to create and maintain images of the check, to generate an electronic deposit file, and to submit it to a financial institution. None of these processes require specialized equipment at the POS. The solution eventually will be rolled out across all of Kohl's 957 locations.

Sources: Business Wire (2008), Hughes and Edwards (2006), and Robb (2007).

Questions

1. What does POC stand for and how does it work?
2. What does BOC stand for and how does it work?
3. What are the advantages and disadvantages of POC?

Most businesses rely on third-party software to handle e-check payments. Fiserv (fiserv.com), Chase Paymentech (paymentech.com), and Authorize.Net (authorize.net) are some of the major vendors of software and systems that enable an online merchant to accept and process electronic checks directly from a Web site. For the most part, these software offerings work in the same way regardless of the vendor.

The system shown in Exhibit 11.3 is based on Authorize.Net and is typical of the underlying processes used to support e-checks. Basically, it is a seven-step process. First, the merchant receives written or electronic authorization from a customer to charge his or her bank account (step 1). Next, the merchant securely transmits the transaction information to the Authorize.Net Payment Gateway server (step 2). The transaction is accepted or rejected based on criteria defined by the Payment Gateway. If accepted, Authorize.Net formats the transaction information and sends it as an ACH transaction to its bank (called the Originating Depository Financial Institution, or ODFI) with the rest of the transactions received that day (step 3). The ODFI receives transaction information and passes it to the ACH Network for settlement. The Automated Clearing House (ACH) Network uses the bank account information provided with the transaction to determine the bank that holds the customer's account (which is known as the Receiving Depository Financial Institution, or RDFI) (step 4). The ACH Network instructs the RDFI to charge or refund the customer's account (the customer is the receiver). The RDFI passes funds from the customer's account to the ACH Network (step 5). The ACH Network relays the funds to the ODFI (Authorize.Net's bank). The ODFI passes any returns to Authorize.Net (step 6). After the funds' holding period, Authorize.Net initiates a separate ACH transaction to deposit the e-check proceeds into the merchant's bank account (step 7).

Automated Clearing House (ACH) Network
A nationwide batch-oriented electronic funds transfer system that provides for the interbank clearing of electronic payments for participating financial institutions.

As Exhibit 11.3 illustrates, the processing of e-checks in the United States relies quite heavily on the **Automated Clearing House (ACH) Network**. The ACH Network is a nationwide batch-oriented Electronic Funds Transfer (EFT) system that provides for the interbank clearing of electronic payments for participating financial institutions. The U.S. Federal Reserve and Electronic Payments Network act as ACH operators, which transmit and receive ACH payment entries. ACH entries are of two sorts: credit and debit. An ACH credit entry credits a receiver's account. For example, when a consumer pays a bill sent by a company, the company is the receiver whose account is credited. In contrast, a debit entry debits a receiver's account. For instance, if a consumer preauthorizes a payment to a company,

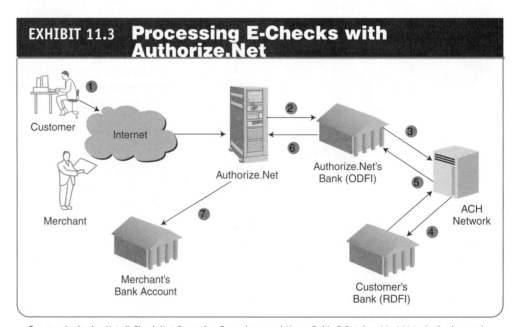

EXHIBIT 11.3 Processing E-Checks with Authorize.Net

Source: Authorize.Net. "eCheck.Net Operating Procedures and Users Guide," October 28, 2004. *Authorize.net/files/echecknetuserguide.pdf.* Copyright 2004. Authorize.Net and eCheck.Net are registered trademarks of Lightbridge, Inc.

then the consumer is the receiver whose account is debited. In 2008, the ACH Network handled an estimated 15 billion transactions worth $30 trillion (NACHA 2009). The vast majority of these were direct payment and deposit entries (e.g., direct deposit payroll). Only 2.1 billion of these entries were Web-based ones, although this represented a 20 percent increase from 2007 to 2008.

E-check processing provides a number of benefits:

▶ It reduces the merchant's administrative costs by providing faster and less paper-intensive collection of funds.

▶ It improves the efficiency of the deposit process for merchants and financial institutions.

▶ It speeds the checkout process for consumers.

▶ It provides consumers with more information about their purchases on their account statements.

▶ It reduces the float period and the number of checks that bounce because of nonsufficient funds (NSFs).

Section 11.6 ▶ REVIEW QUESTIONS

1. What is an e-check?
2. Briefly describe how third-party e-check payment systems work.
3. What is the ACH?
4. List the benefits of e-checking.

11.7 B2B ELECTRONIC PAYMENTS

B2B payments usually are much larger and significantly more complex than the payments made by individual consumers. The dollar values often are in the hundreds of thousands, the purchases and payments involve multiple items and shipments, and the exchanges are much more likely to engender disputes that require significant work to resolve. Simple e-billing or electronic bill presentment and payment (EBPP) systems lack the rigor and security to handle these B2B situations. This section examines the processes by which companies present invoices and make payments to one another over the Internet.

CURRENT B2B PAYMENT PRACTICES

B2B payments are part of a much larger financial supply chain that includes procurement, contract administration, fulfillment, financing, insurance, credit ratings, shipment validation, order matching, payment authorization, remittance matching, and general ledger accounting. From a buyer's perspective, the chain encompasses the procurement-to-payment process. From the seller's perspective, the chain involves the order-to-cash cycle. Regardless of the perspective, in financial supply chain management the goal is to optimize accounts payable (A/P) and accounts receivable (A/R), cash management, working capital, transaction costs, financial risks, and financial administration.

Unlike the larger (physical) supply chain, inefficiencies still characterize the financial supply chains of most companies. A number of factors create these inefficiencies, including (Bolero 2008):

▶ The time required to create, transfer, and process paper documentation

▶ The cost and errors associated with manual creation and reconciliation of documentation

▶ The lack of transparency in inventory and cash positions when goods are in the supply chain

▶ Disputes arising from inaccurate or missing data

▶ Fragmented point solutions that do not address the complete end-to-end processes of the trade cycle

These inefficiencies are evident especially with A/P and A/R processes where payments are still made with paper.

Based on a survey of 375 members of the Association for Financial Professionals (2007) and a comparison of the 2007 results with those from 2004, it appears that the world of B2B payments is slow to change. Approximately 80 percent of B2B payments are still made by check, and the barriers to electronic payments remain essentially the same—IT and constraints posed by the difficulty of integrating various systems, the inability of trading partners to send and receive automated remittance information, and difficulty in convincing customers and suppliers to adopt electronic payments. However, some evidence suggests that companies are beginning to move to B2B e-payments. As the survey results noted, over 40 percent of its members expect to convert the majority of their B2B payments from checks to e-payments in the next 3 years.

ENTERPRISE INVOICE PRESENTMENT AND PAYMENT

enterprise invoice presentment and payment (EIPP)
Presenting and paying B2B invoices online.

The process by which companies present invoices and make payments to one another through the Internet is known as **electronic invoice presentment and payment (EIPP)**. For many firms, presentment and payment are costly and time consuming. It can cost up to $15 to generate a paper invoice and between $25 and $50 to resolve a disputed invoice. On the payment side, it takes 3 to 5 days for a check to arrive by mail. This means that millions of dollars of B2B payments are tied up in floats. This reduces the recipients' cash flow and increases the amount they must borrow to cover the float. In the same vein, manual billing and remittance can result in errors, which in turn can result in disputes that hold up payments. Given that most firms handle thousands of invoices and payments yearly, any reduction in time, cost, or errors can result in millions of dollars of savings. According to a survey by the Credit Research Foundation, the major reasons companies turn to EIPP solutions are improved cash flow, better customer service for billing and remittance, and improved data that can lower invoice processing costs (Lucas 2005).

EIPP Models

EIPP automates the workflow surrounding presentment and payment. Like EBPP, there are three EIPP models: seller direct, buyer direct, and consolidator.

Seller Direct. This solution links one seller to many buyers for invoice presentment. Buyers navigate to the seller's Web site to enroll in the seller's EIPP program. The seller generates invoices on the system and informs the appropriate buyers that they are ready for viewing. The buyers log into the seller's Web site to review and analyze the invoices. The buyers may authorize invoice payment or communicate any disputes. Based on predetermined rules, disputes may be accepted, rejected, or reviewed automatically. Once payment is authorized and made, the seller's financial institution processes the payment transaction.

This model typically is used when there are established relationships between the seller and its buyers. If a seller issues a large number of invoices or the invoices have a high value, then there can be a substantial payoff from implementing an EIPP. For this reason, firms in the manufacturing, telecommunication, utilities, health-care, and financial services industries use this model often.

Buyer Direct. In this model, there is one buyer for many sellers. Sellers enroll in the buyer's EIPP system at the buyer's Web site. Sellers post invoices to the buyer's EIPP, using the buyer's format. Once an invoice is posted, the buyer's staff will be notified. The buyer reviews and analyzes the invoices on the system. The buyer communicates any disputes to the appropriate seller. Based on predetermined rules, disputes may be accepted, rejected, or reviewed automatically. Once an invoice is approved, the buyer will authorize payment, which the buyer's financial institution will process. This is an emerging model based on the buyer's dominant position in B2B transactions. Again, it is used when the buyer's purchases result in a high volume of invoices. Companies such as Wal-Mart are in a strong position to institute buyer-direct EIPPs.

Consolidator. This is a many-to-many model with the consolidator acting as an intermediary, collecting or aggregating invoices from multiple sellers and payments from multiple buyers. Consolidators are generally third parties who not only provide EIPP services but also offer other financial services (e.g., insurance, escrow). In this model, the sellers and buyers register with the consolidator's EIPP system. The sellers generate and transfer invoice information to the EIPP system. The consolidator notifies the appropriate buyer organization that the invoice is ready. The buyer reviews and analyzes the invoice. Disputes are communicated through the consolidator EIPP. Based on predetermined rules, disputes may be accepted, rejected, or reviewed automatically. Once the buyer authorizes the invoice payment, the consolidator initiates the payment. Either the buyer's or the seller's financial institution processes the payment.

The consolidator model eliminates the hassles associated with implementing and running an EIPP. The model has gained ground in those industries where multiple buyers rely on the same suppliers. The JPMorgan Chase Xign Business Settlement Network (jpmorgan.com/xign) and the Global eXchange Services (GXS) Trading Grid (gxs.com) are both third-party consolidators linking thousands of suppliers and buyers. Xign had more than 40,000 active suppliers in its network, generating over $100 billion in transactions. GSX's Trading Grid supports online trading among 40,000 customers in over 60 countries, exchanging over 1 billion electronic transactions representing $1 trillion in goods and services. Each of these networks eliminates the need for point-to-point connections between suppliers and buyers; automates core functions of the A/P process, including invoice receipt, validation, routing, dispute management, approval, and payment; and complements and integrates with the suppliers' and buyers' existing purchasing and procurement systems. The closing case at the end of the chapter details the benefits of the Xign network.

EIPP Options

A variety of online options are available for making payments in an EIPP system. They differ in terms of cost, speed, auditability, accessibility, and control. The selection of a particular mechanism depends on the requirements of the buyers and sellers. Some frequently used B2B payment options follow.

ACH Network. The ACH Network is the same network that underlies the processing of e-checks (described in Section 11.6). The difference is that there are three types of B2B payments, which vary by the amount of remittance information that accompanies the payments. The remittance information enables a buyer or seller to examine the details of a particular invoice or payment. The three types of ACH entries for B2B transactions are: Cash Concentration or Disbursement (CCD), which is a simple payment, usually for a single invoice, that has no accompanying remittance data and is typically initiated by the buyer who credits the seller's account; Cash Concentration or Disbursement with Addenda (CCD+), which is the same as a CCD payment except that it has a small amount of remittance data (up to 80 characters); and Corporate Trade Exchange (CTX), which generally is used to pay multiple invoices and has a large amount of accompanying remittance data (up to a maximum of 9,999 records of 80 characters each).

The ACH Network does not require any special hardware. The cost of the software needed to initiate ACH transactions depends on the volume of CTX transactions. High volumes of CTX transactions require a much larger investment. In addition to hardware and software costs, the buyer's and the seller's financial institutions also charge file, maintenance, transaction, and exception handling fees for ACH transactions.

Purchasing Cards. Although credit cards are the instrument of choice for B2C payments, this is not the case in the B2B marketplace. In the B2B marketplace, the major credit card companies and associations have encouraged businesses and government agencies to rely on *purchasing cards* instead of checks for repetitive, low-value transactions. **Purchasing cards (p-cards)** are special-purpose payment cards issued to a company's employees. They are used solely for the purpose of paying for nonstrategic materials and services (e.g., stationery, office supplies, computer supplies, repair and maintenance services, courier services, and temporary labor services) up to a limit (usually $1,000 to $2,000). These purchases often represent the majority of a company's payments, but only a small percentage of the dollars spent. Purchasing cards operate essentially the same as any other charge card and are used for both offline and online purchases. The major difference between a credit card and a purchase card is that the latter is a nonrevolving account, meaning that it needs to be paid in full each month, usually within 5 days of the end of the billing period.

Purchasing cards enable a company or government agency to consolidate the purchases of multiple cardholders into a single account and, thus, issue a single invoice that can be paid through Electronic Data Interchange (EDI), EFT, or an e-check. This has the benefit of freeing the purchasing department from day-to-day procurement activities and from the

purchasing cards (p-cards)
Special-purpose payment cards issued to a company's employees to be used solely for purchasing nonstrategic materials and services up to a preset dollar limit.

need to deal with the reconciliation of individual invoices. With a single invoice, accounts can be settled more quickly, enabling a company or agency to take advantage of discounts associated with faster payment. A single invoice also enables a company or agency to more easily analyze the spending behavior of the cardholders. Finally, the spending limits make it easier to control unplanned purchases. Some estimates suggest that efficiencies resulting from the use of purchasing cards can reduce transaction costs from 50 to 90 percent. To learn more about purchasing cards, see the National Association of Purchasing Card Professionals (napcp.org) and Purchasing Card News (www.purchasingcardnews.co.uk).

Fedwire or Wire Transfer. Among the forms of online B2B payments, Fedwire is second only to ACH in terms of frequency of use. Fedwire, also known as wire transfer, is a funds transfer system developed and maintained by the U.S. Federal Reserve system. It typically is used with larger dollar payments where time is the critical element. The settlement of real estate transactions, the purchase of securities, and the repayment of loans are all examples of situations where Fedwire is likely to be used. When Fedwire is used, a designated Federal Reserve Bank debits the buyer's bank account and sends a transfer order to the seller's Federal Reserve Bank, which credits the seller's account. All Fedwire payments are immediate and irrevocable.

Letters of Credit for Global Payments. Letters of credit often are used when global B2B payments need to be made, especially when there is substantial risk associated with the payment. A **letter of credit (L/C)**, also called a *documentary credit*, is issued by a bank on behalf of a buyer (importer). It guarantees a seller (exporter) that payment for goods or services will be made, provided the terms of the L/C are met. Before the credit is issued, the buyer and seller agree on all terms and conditions in a purchase and sale contract. The buying company then instructs its bank to issue a documentary credit in accordance with the contract. A credit can be payable at sight or at term. *At sight* means that payment is due upon presentation of documents after shipment of the goods or after a service is provided. Alternatively, if the seller allows the buyer an additional period, after presentation of documents, to pay the credit (30, 60, 90 days, etc.), then the credit is payable *at term*. L/C arrangements usually involve a series of steps that can be conducted much faster online than offline. Online File W11.3 describes the benefits of replacing L/Cs with online payments.

For sellers, the main benefit of an L/C is reduced risk—the bank assures the creditworthiness of the buyer. For those global situations where the buyer is a resident in a country with political or financial instability, the risk can be reduced if the L/C is confirmed by a bank in the seller's country. Reduced risk also is of benefit to buyers who may use this fact to negotiate lower prices.

letter of credit (L/C)
A written agreement by a bank to pay the seller, on account of the buyer, a sum of money upon presentation of certain documents.

Section 11.7 ▶ REVIEW QUESTIONS

1. Describe the financial supply chain.
2. Describe the current state of B2B e-payments.
3. What is electronic invoice presentment and payment (EIPP)?
4. Describe the three models of EIPP.
5. Describe the basic EIPP options.
6. What is a purchasing card?

MANAGERIAL ISSUES

Some managerial issues related to this chapter are as follows.

1. **What payment methods should your B2C site support?** The majority of B2C trades are paid by credit card (about 60%). EFT is the next most popular payment method (about 30%). Most B2C sites use more than one payment gateway to support customers' preferred payment methods. Companies that only accept credit cards rule out a number of potential segments of buyers (e.g., teenagers, non–U.S. customers, and customers who cannot or do not want to use credit cards online). EFT, e-checks, stored-value cards, and PayPal are some possible alternatives to credit cards. The e-check is not used

at all in Asia, because it is not an efficient method in the electronic era; thus, selecting the globally acceptable payment method is important for the globalization of EC.

2. **What e-micropayment strategy should your e-marketplace support?** If your EC site deals with items priced less than $10, credit cards are not a viable solution. Many digital-content products cost less than a dollar. For small-value products, e-micropayments should be supported. Fees may be taken from a prepaid account that is tied to the buyer's bank account or credit card, or the fee may be charged to the buyer's cell phone bill. The use of stored-value smart cards on the Internet has emerged, but has not widely penetrated because buyers need to install the card reader/writer. Your company should support multiple options so that customers can choose their preferred payment method.

3. **What payment methods should B2B exchanges support?** Keep an open mind about online alternatives. When it comes to paying suppliers or accepting payments from partners, most large businesses have opted to stick with EFT or checks over other methods of electronic payment. For MROs, consider using purchasing cards. Some purchases, such as automobiles and large pieces of equipment, are associated with loan services from banks. For global trade, electronic letters of credit are popular. The use of e-checks is another area where cost savings can accrue. With all these methods, a key factor is determining how well they work with existing accounting and ordering systems and with business partners.

4. **What payment methods should a C2C marketplace support?** In C2C sites like eBay, an e-mail payment method such as PayPal is popular. An alternative secure payment service is the escrow service. A buyer pays the e-market operator, and the e-market operator pays the seller once the delivery is confirmed by the buyer. The Internet Auction Corporation site, the leading auctioneer in Korea, which was acquired by eBay, supports an escrow service for the payment of successful bids. The reason they provide the service is because PayPal restricts Korean customers from making purchases with PayPal. However, PayPal does allow Koreans to receive payment for goods they have sold. The bottom line is that it is important to understand popular payment methods in particular markets.

5. **Should we outsource our payment gateway service?** It takes time, skill, money, software, and hardware to integrate the payment systems of all the parties involved in processing any sort of e-payment. For this reason, even a business that runs its own EC site outsources the e-payment service. Many third-party vendors provide payment gateways designed to handle the interactions among the various financial institutions that operate in the background of an e-payment system. Also, if a Web site is hosted by a third party (e.g., Yahoo! Store), an e-payment service will be provided.

6. **How secure are e-payments?** Security and fraud continue to be major issues in making and accepting e-payments of all kinds. This is especially true with regard to the use of credit cards for online purchases. B2C merchants are employing a wide variety of tools (e.g., address verification and other authentication services) to combat fraudulent orders. These and other measures that are employed to ensure the security of e-payments have to be part of a broader security scheme that weighs risks against issues such as the ease of use and the fit within the overall business context.

7. **What is the required security to use Internet banking?** EFT is one of the primary methods of electronic payment, thus Internet banking is one of the most important entities for EC. In Korea, digital certificates based on public key infrastructure are required for all financial transactions; thus, virtually all Internet bank users have digital certificates. Today, most certificates are stored on PCs. However, certificates are increasingly being stored in smart cards or in cell phone chips. In addition, two-factor authentication is required for bank account access in many countries; so other authentication schemes have been developed to complement password-authentication measures.

SUMMARY

In this chapter, you learned about the following EC issues as they relate to the learning objectives.

1. **Payment revolution.** Cash and checks are no longer kings. Debit and credit cards now rule—both online and offline. This means that online B2C businesses need to support debit and credit card purchases. In international markets outside of Western Europe, buyers often favor other forms of e-payment (e.g., bank transfers). With the exception of PayPal, virtually all the alternatives to charge cards have failed. None have gained enough traction to overcome the "chicken-and-egg" problem. Their failure to gain

critical mass has resulted from the confluence of a variety of factors (e.g., they required specialized hardware or setup or they failed to mesh with existing systems).

2. **Using payment cards online.** The processing of online card payments is essentially the same as it is for brick-and-mortar stores and involves essentially the same players and the same systems—banks, card associations, payment processing services, and the like. This is one of the reasons why payment cards predominate in the online world. The major difference is that the rate of fraudulent orders is much higher online. Surveys, such as those conducted annually by CyberSource, indicate that merchants have adopted a wide variety of methods over the past few years to combat fraudulent orders, including address verification, manual review, fraud screens and decision models, card verification numbers, card association authentication services, and negative files. In the same vein, some consumers have turned to virtual or single-use credit cards to avoid using their actual credit card numbers online.

3. **Smart cards.** Smart cards look like credit cards but contain embedded chips for manipulating data and have large memory capacity. Cards that contain microprocessor chips can be programmed to handle a wide variety of tasks. Other cards have memory chips to which data can be written and from which data can be read. Most memory cards are disposable, but others—smart cards—can hold large amounts of data and are rechargeable. Smart cards have been and will be used for a number of purposes, including contactless retail payments, paying for mass transit services, identifying cardholders for government services, securing physical and network access, and storing health-care data and verifying eligibility for health-care and other government services. Given the sensitive nature of much of the data on smart cards, public key encryption and other cryptographic techniques are used to secure their contents.

4. **Stored-value cards.** A stored-value card is similar in appearance to a credit or debit card. The monetary value of a stored value card is housed in a magnetic strip on the back of the card. Closed-loop stored-value cards are issued for a single purpose by a specific merchant (e.g., a Starbucks gift card). In contrast, open-loop stored-value cards are more like standard credit or debit cards and can be used for multiple purposes (e.g., a payroll card). Those segments of the population without credit cards or bank accounts—people with low incomes, young adults, seniors, and minorities—are spurring the substantial growth of stored-value cards. Specialized cards, such as EasySend, make it simple for immigrant populations to transfer funds to family members in other countries. Similarly, specialized cards, such as MasterCard's MuchMusic, provide teens and preteens with prepaid debit cards that function like standard credit or debit cards while helping parents monitor and maintain control over spending patterns.

5. **E-micropayments.** When an item or service being sold online costs less than $5, credit cards are too costly for sellers. A number of other e-payment systems have been introduced to handle these micropayment situations. For the most part, they have failed. Yet, ample evidence indicates that consumers are interested in using their credit and debit cards for small-value online purchases (e.g., songs on iTunes, online games, and ringtone sales). In response, a number of newer micropayment models, such as aggregated purchases, have been developed to reduce the fees associated with credit and debit cards.

6. **E-checking.** E-checks are the electronic equivalent of paper checks. They are handled in much the same way as paper checks and rely quite heavily on the ACH Network. E-checks offer a number of benefits, including speedier processing, reduced administrative costs, more efficient deposits, reduced float period, and fewer "bounced" checks. These factors have resulted in the rapid growth of e-check usage. The rapid growth is also being spurred by the use of e-checks for in-store purchases. Purchase Order Processing (POP) and Back-Office Order Conversion (BOC) are two systems, established by the NACHA, that enable retailers to convert paper checks used for in-store purchases to ACH debits (i.e., e-checks) without the need to process the checks using traditional procedures.

7. **B2B electronic payments.** B2B payments are part of a much larger financial supply chain that encompasses the range of processes from procurement to payment and order to cash. Today, the vast majority of B2B payments are still made by check, although many organizations are moving to EIPP. There are three models of EIPP: seller direct (buyers go to the seller's Web site), buyer direct (sellers post invoices at the buyer's Web site), and consolidator (many buyers and many sellers are linked through the consolidator's Web site). Two of the largest consolidators are Xign Payment Services and GSX Trading Grid. In addition to these models, there are several EIPP payment options, including the ACH Network, purchasing cards, wire transfers, and letters of credit (L/C). The move to EIPP is being inhibited by the shortage of IT staff, the lack of integration of payment and account systems, the lack of standard formats for remittance information, and the inability of trading partners to send or receive electronic payments with sufficient remittance information.

KEY TERMS

QUESTIONS FOR DISCUSSION

1. PayMo recently introduced a system enabling buyers to charge their purchases to their cell phone accounts. Do you think PayMo's system will succeed? What factors will play a major role in its success or failure?

2. A textbook publisher is interested in selling individual book chapters on the Web. What types of e-payment methods would you recommend to the publisher? What sorts of problems will the publisher encounter with the recommended methods?

3. Recently, a merchant who accepts online credit card payments has experienced a wave of fraudulent orders. What steps should the merchant take to combat the fraud?

4. A retail clothing manufacturer is considering e-payments for both its suppliers and its buyers. What sort of e-payment method should it use to pay for office supplies? How should it pay suppliers of raw materials? How should its customers—both domestic and international clothing retailers—pay?

5. A metropolitan area wants to provide riders of its public transportation system with the ability to pay transit fares, as well as make retail purchases, using a single contactless smart card. What sorts of problems will they encounter in setting up the system, and what types of problems will the riders encounter in using the cards?

INTERNET EXERCISES

1. Use various online sources to research the dispute involving the Authors' Guild, various book publishers (e.g., Penguin), and Google over Google's Book Search Library Project. Describe some of the details of the settlement that was reached among these parties.

2. A number of years ago, eBay offered a payment system called Billpoint. It was a head-to-head competitor with PayPal. Use online sources to research why PayPal succeeded and Billpoint failed. Write a report based on your findings.

3. Select a major retail B2C merchant in your country and another country. Detail the similarities and differences in the e-payment systems they offer. According to Cyber-Source's "Insider's Guide to ePayment Management" (**cybersource.com/cgi-bin/pages/prep.cgi?page=/promo/Insiders Guide2008/index.html**), what other payment systems could the sites offer?

4. Go to **cybersource.com**. Identify the services it provides for B2B e-payments. Describe the features of CyberSource's major products that provide these merchant services.

5. Download "Transit and Contactless Financial Payments" from **smart cardalliance.org/pages/publications-**

transit-financial. What are the key requirements for an automated fare-collection system? Based on the report, what type of payment system did the Utah Transit Authority (UTA) pilot? What factors helped determine the type of system to be piloted? How did the pilot work? What was the role of contactless payment in the UTA system (if any)?

6. Kohl's utilizes Solutran's SPIN for its BOC system. So does Walgreens. Based on information provided at Solutran's Web site (**solutran.com**) and information found in online articles about the system, what sorts of capabilities and benefits does the system provide? What is unique about the system?

7. Go to **nacha.org**. What is NACHA? What is its role? What is the ACH? Who are the key participants in an ACH e-payment?

8. Go to MasterCard's RPSS site (**mastercardintl.com/rpps**). What type of system is RPSS, EPBB or EIPP? How does it work? What are the benefits of a system like RPSS?

TEAM ASSIGNMENTS, PROJECTS, AND CLASS DISCUSSIONS

1. Select some B2C sites that cater to teens and others that cater to older consumers. Have team members visit these sites. What types of e-payment methods do they provide? Do the methods used differ based on the target market? What other types of e-payment would you recommend for the various sites and why?

2. Write a report comparing smart card applications in two or more European and/or Asian countries. In the report, discuss whether those applications would succeed in North America.

3. Have one team represent MasterCard PayPass and another represent Visa payWave. The task of each team is to convince a company that its product is superior.

4. Have each team member interview three to five people who have made a purchase or sold an item via an online auction. Find out how they paid. What security and privacy concerns did they have regarding the payment? Is there an ideal payment method?

5. Go to the NACHA Web site for the Council on Electronic Billing and Payment (**ebilling.org/EIPP/eipp.htm**). The site provides information on various forms of EIPP. Compare and contrast two of the forms detailed on the site.

6. Address the following topics in a class discussion:

   a. Apple's iTunes clearly dominates the online music business. In the long run, which company has the best chance of dominating the e-book business, Google or Amazon.com? Explain.

   b. If you were running an online retail store would you permit purchases with e-checks? Why or why not?

Closing Case

THE CHECK IS IN THE NETWORK

In May 2008, KeySpan Energy Delivery became part of National Grid, an international electricity and gas company. National Grid, one of the largest investor-owned companies in the world, supplies energy and gas to millions of customers across Great Britain and the Northeastern United States. The U.S. division of National Grid has over 17,000 employees who provide gas and electric service to more than 7 million customers across 30,000 square miles in the New York Metropolitan area, upstate New York, Massachusetts, New Hampshire, and Rhode Island. In providing service to its customers, the U.S. division relies heavily on a number of outside service companies supplying energy-related products, services, and solutions to homes and businesses.

Given the number of service suppliers, the U.S. division was inundated with paperwork. The accounts payable group (AP) of National Grid was manually handling over 22,000 invoices per month, over 260,000 per year. The AP staff was buried in paperwork, taking up to 45 days to pay bills, with an average invoice backlog of 5 days. Not only was it costing National Grid thousands of dollars to perform these processes manually, but, just as important, it was losing out on supplier discounts because it was not able to pay its bills on time. Many suppliers offer discounts in order to get paid sooner. Companies that rely on paper processing, such as National Grid did, cannot process their orders and payments fast enough to qualify for the discounts.

In 2007, the U.S. division of National Grid launched a series of initiatives to address these problems. It decided to move to a shared-services organization, relying on an overall corporate AP staff rather than its own division staff. Just as importantly, it replaced manual and paper-based processes with an electronic settlement solution. Lacking the necessary skills to build the solution in-house, it undertook a comprehensive vendor evaluation process that involved not only the AP group, but also the treasury, procurement, and information technology groups. As a result of the cross-team evaluation, National Grid selected JPMorgan's Xign service.

As noted in Section 11.7, Xign helps businesses pay bills electronically via a hosted online payments network (called the Business Settlement Network). The network consists of thousands of suppliers, buyers, and their associated banks and enables buyers and suppliers to manage the purchasing process from the initial order to final payment. The network eliminates the need for the suppliers or buyers to install any special hardware or software on their premises. The network automates purchase order delivery, invoice presentment, and payment. To send invoices, a supplier must be invited by a buyer to enter the network. Xign helps recruit, enroll, and train suppliers. On average, a buyer can expect about 80 percent of its suppliers to be on board within 8 to 10 weeks. In the case of National Grid, 750 of its suppliers participate in the network.

Suppliers can connect to the network in a variety of ways. At a minimum, all suppliers and buyers can use the browser-based interface to send purchase orders, invoices, and payments. This is fine for buyers who work with a small number of suppliers. However, most enterprises use more direct server-to-server connections. With server-to-server connections, once a purchase order is sent by a buyer's server the supplier's server immediately turns it into an invoice and sends it back to the buyer. This guarantees that not only does the purchase order and invoice match, but also that the invoice was received. With the traditional paper-based system, these steps can take a substantial amount of time. The Xing system can also dynamically handle supplier discounts and prorate them based on when an invoice is paid.

In addition to handling the coordination of the activities between the suppliers and the buyers, the network can also manage the interactions with their banks. When a supplier enrolls with the network, it provides bank account information to Xign. Suppliers keep this information updated. The buyer has no specific knowledge of this information. When the buyer sends a payment data file to Xign, the file contains information about the suppliers that need to be paid along with the amounts. The Xign network matches the information in the payment file to the appropriate supplier's bank account information and sends the associated payment data to the bank. The bank then initiates an ACH payment to the suppliers.

Xign also offers a JPMorgan Chase purchasing card. The purchasing card works like ACH payments. In this case, when the buyer sends in the payment data file it requests that the supplier be paid by the purchasing card rather than by ACH. The network then routs the payment information to the credit card network rather than the supplier's bank, eliminating the need for the supplier to process the card payments.

After a year of operation, 75 to 80 percent of the suppliers of the U.S. division of National Grid were on the Xign network. The U.S. division was managing 50 percent of its payments through the service. The overall benefits to National Grid have been substantial and include:

▸ A 30 percent increase in AP processing efficiency and a $500,000 reduction in AP processing costs.

▸ A reduction in the bill payment window from 45 days to 10 days.

▸ A reduction in the invoice backlog window from 5 days to 1 day.

▸ A fivefold increase in the number of discounts, with an average discount of 1.6 percent and a total payback of over $1 million.

From National Grid's supplier's standpoint, participation in the network has produced faster cycle times, visibility into the payment status, as well as fewer exceptions and disputes. The system also provides suppliers with detailed remittance information that enables them to simplify the reconciliation between orders and payments.

Sources: Edwards (2007), JPMorgan (2007), and Simons (2007).

Questions

1. Enter the Xign site (*jpmorgan.com/xign*). Describe the five best practices embodied in the Xign network. In addition to National Grid (i.e., KeySpan), Xign also provides case study information on a number of other companies. Read two of these other case studies and summarize the basic benefits these companies have realized from their use of the network.

2. One of the benefits of the Xign network for suppliers is the ability to perform electronic payment reconciliation (EPR). Enter the CyberSource Web site and download its document on EPR (*cybersource.com/resources/collateral/Resource_Center/product_briefs/Cybs_Reconciliation.pdf*). Based on this document, what is EPR? Compare and contrast manual and automated reconciliation. What are the major benefits of electronic reconciliation?

3. Ariba (*ariba.com*) and Harbor Payments (*harborpayments.com*) both offer EIPP solutions that compete with Xign. Using information from their Web sites, in what ways are these offerings similar to or different from the Xign solution? Do you think one of these other offerings would have provided greater benefits to National Grid?

ONLINE RESOURCES
available at pearsonglobaleditions.com/turban

Online Files

W11.1   Application Case: Hong Kong's Octopus Card
W11.2   Application Case: Stored-Value Cards: Tapping the Teen and Preteen Markets
W11.3   Application Case: Eliminating Letters of Credit— Rite Aid Deploys the TradeCard Solution

Comprehensive Educational Web Sites

afponline.org: Association for Financial Professionals Web site.
cardtechnology.com: Source for news about smart cards and such related payment and identification technologies as biometrics, PKI, mobile commerce, physical access control,

and computer network security. Keep track of upcoming smart card conferences and find smart card vendors.

cybersource.com: CyberSource is focused on services that optimize business results through active management of the payment process from payment acceptance and order screening, through reconciliation and payment security.

globalplatform.org: Driven by its member organizations, with cross-industry representation from all world continents, GlobalPlatform is the worldwide leader in smart card infrastructure development.

nacha.org: NACHA—Electronic Payments Association

paymentsnews.com: Web site maintained by Glenbrook Partners. Glenbrook Partners continuously scan for news stories of interest to payments professionals and make them available on this site.

purchasingcardnews.co.uk: *Purchasing Card News* has become an essential read and a primary source of information for companies and key company personnel wishing to gain further knowledge of best practice procurement initiatives, purchasing card solutions, and e-commerce transaction technology.

smartcardalliance.org: The Smart Card Alliance is a nonprofit, multi-industry association working to stimulate the understanding, adoption, use, and widespread application of smart card technology.

REFERENCES

Association for Financial Professionals (AFP). "2007 Electronic Payments Survey." 2007. afponline.org/pub/pdf/2007_AFP_Electronic_Payments_Survey.pdf (accessed March 2009).

Bolero. "The Financial Supply Chain." 2008. bolero.net/solutions/finacial_supply_chain.html (accessed March 2009).

Business Wire. "Kohl's Successfully Implements Back-Office Conversion with Solutran." September 9, 2008. allbusiness.com/company-activities-management/operations-back/11553648-1.html (accessed March 2009).

Card Technology. "Eurosmart: 2008 Shipments to Approach 4 Billion." November 13, 2007. cardtechnology.com/article.html?id=200711130Q64SQXC (accessed March 2009).

CBCNews. "Indigo Books Targets E-Book Market Chapter by Chapter." March 2, 2009. cbc.ca/arts/books/story/2009/03/02/tech-shortcovers.html (accessed March 2009).

Chen, J. "KCG Ticketing Project in Southern Taiwan." March 2008. multos.com/downloads/10-years/taiwanmoneycard.pdf (accessed March 2009).

CyberSource. "10th Annual Online Fraud Report." 2009. forms.cybersource.com/forms/FraudReport2009NACYBSwww020309 (accessed March 2009).

CyberSource. "Insider's Guide to ePayment Management." 2008. cybersource.com/cgi-bin/pages/prep.cgi?page=/promo/InsidersGuide2008/index.html (accessed March 2009).

D'Agostino, D. "Pennies from Heaven." *CIO Insight*, January 2006. cioinsight.com/c/a/Trends/In-ECommerce-Small-is-the-New-Big/ (accessed March 2009).

Edwards, J. "The Check Is in the Web." *CFO.com*, January 17, 2007. cfo.com/article.cfm/8468144 (accessed March 2009).

EurActiv.com. "Payment Services Directive: The End of the Cash Era?" April 30, 2008. euractiv.com/en/financial-services/payment-services-directive-cash-era/article-171979 (accessed March 2009).

Evans, D., and R. Schmalensee. *Paying with Plastic: The Digital Revolution in Buying and Borrowing*, 2nd ed. Cambridge, MA: MIT Press, 2005.

Hendry, M. *Multi-Application Smart Cards: Technology and Applications.* Cambridge, UK: Cambridge University Press, 2007.

Hughes, S., and N. Edwards. "Best Practices for a Successful POP Implementation." *Epson.com*, May 9, 2006. pop.epson.com/checks/pdfs/walmartpres.ppt (accessed March 2009).

Ipsos Insight. "More Than 67 Million Americans Have Used Credit or Debit Cards for Purchases of Less Than $5 in the Past 30 Days." June 2006. ipsos-na.com/news/pressrelease.cfm?id=3284 (accessed August 2009).

JPMorgan. "KeySpan Energizes Working Capital Performance with JPMorgan Xign." July 2007. jpmorgan.com/tss/General/Testimonials_and_Case_Studies/1159317518897 (accessed March 2009).

Lamond, K., and D. Whitman. "Credit Card Transactions: Real World and Online." *VirtualSchool.edu*, 1996. virtualschool.edu/mon/ElectronicProperty/klamond/credit_card.htm (accessed May 2008).

Lucas, P. "Taming the Paper Tiger." *Collectionsworld.com*, February 2005. collectionsworld.com/cgi-bin/readstory2.pl?story=20040601CCRV263.xml (accessed March 2009).

Mitchell, D. "In Online World, Pocket Change Is Not Easily Spent." *New York Times*, August 27, 2007. nytimes.com/2007/08/27/technology/27micro.html?scp=1&sq=In+Online+World%2C+Pocket+Change+Is+Not+Easily+Spent&st=nyt (accessed March 2009).

NACHA. "ACH Transaction Volume Grew in 4th Quarter Despite Tough Economy." NACHA press release. February 11, 2009. nacha.org/docs/News%20 Release %20Q4%202008%20ACH%20Volume.pdf (accessed March 2009).

Payments News. "MasterCard Reports PayPass Increases Customer Loyalty." July 10, 2006a. paymentsnews. com/ 2006/07/mastercard_repo.html (accessed March 2009).

Payments News. "BB&T Makes EasySend Money Transfer Free." June 2006b. paymentsnews.com/2006/06/bbt_ makes_easys.html (accessed March 2009).

PayPal. "Business Guide to Online Payment Processing." 2004. paypal.com/cgi-bin/webscr?cmd=_pp-promo& CID=MTJGKXB4URU33ANS (accessed March 2009).

Robb, S. "The Benefits of Back-Office Conversion." *gtnews.com*, February 19, 2007. gtnews.com/article/ 6638.cfm (accessed March 2009).

Seeking Alpha. "Gift Card Spending to Drop as Holiday Shoppers Look for Bargains." November 20, 2008. seekingalpha.com/article/107099-gift-card-spending- to-drop-as-holiday-shoppers-look-for-bargains (accessed March 2009).

Simon, J. "Issuers Look to Future with Contactless Credit Cards." May 9, 2008. creditcards.com/credit-card-news/ contactless-credit-card-changes-spending-habits- 1273.php (accessed March 2009).

Simon, J. "Paper to Plastic: Checks and Cash Losing to Debit and Credit." October 3, 2007. creditcards.com/ credit-card-paper-vs-plastic.php (accessed March 2009).

Simons, P. "JPMorgan Chase Acquires Xign." June 2007. ibspublishing.com/index.cfm?section=news&action= view&id=10867 (accessed March 2009).

Smart Card Alliance. "Transit and Contactless Financial Payments: New Opportunities for Collaboration and Convergence." October 2006. smartcardalliance.org/ pages/publications-transit-financial (accessed March 2009).

Tan, G. "MasterCard Announces the Full-Scale Roll-Out of the Internationally Recognized TaiwanMoney Card." MasterCard press release, June 1, 2007. mastercard. com/us/company/en/newsroom/pr_taiwanmoney- card.html (accessed March 2009).

TowerGroup. "As U.S. 'Unbanked' Population Grows, Financial Institutions Must Develop New Approaches and Products for Underserved Markets." July 30, 2008. towergroup.com/research/news/news.htm?newsId=4 540 (accessed March 2009).

12

FULFILLING E-COMMERCE ORDERS AND OTHER EC SUPPORT SERVICES

Learning Objectives

Upon completion of this chapter, you will be able to:

1. Describe the role of support services in electronic commerce (EC).

2. Define EC order fulfillment and describe the EC order fulfillment process.

3. Describe the major problems of EC order fulfillment.

4. Describe various solutions to EC order fulfillment problems.

5. Describe the integration of enterprise systems and e-commerce.

6. Describe enterprise resource planning (ERP) and its benefits.

7. Describe intelligent agents as supporters of EC.

8. Describe other EC support services.

9. Discuss the drivers of outsourcing support services.

Content

Opening Case: How Amazon.com Fulfills Orders

12.1 Order Fulfillment and Logistics— An Overview

12.2 Problems in Order Fulfillment

12.3 Solutions to Order Fulfillment Problems

12.4 Integration and Enterprise Resource Planning

12.5 Intelligent Agents and Their Role in E-Commerce

12.6 Other E-Commerce Support Services

Managerial Issues

Closing Case: How Mass Customization EC Orders Are Fulfilled—Multibras of Brazil

HOW AMAZON.COM FULFILLS ORDERS

The Problem

With traditional retailing, customers go to a physical store and purchase items that they then take home. Large quantities are delivered to each store or supermarket; there are not too many delivery destinations. With e-tailing, customers want the goods quickly and to have them shipped to their homes. Deliveries of small quantities need to go to a large number of destinations. Too, items must be available for immediate delivery. Therefore, maintaining an inventory of items becomes critical. Maintaining inventory and shipping products cost money and take time, which may negate some of the advantages of e-tailing. Let's see how Amazon.com, the "king" of e-tailing, handles the situation.

When Amazon.com launched in 1995, its business model called for virtual retailing—no warehouses, no inventory, no shipments. The idea was to take orders and receive payments electronically and then let others fill the orders. It soon became clear that this model, although appropriate for a small company, would not work for a giant e-tailer.

The Solution

Amazon.com decided to change its business model and handle its own inventory. The company spent close to $2 billion to build warehouses around the country and became a world-class leader in warehouse management, warehouse automation, packaging, and inventory management. Amazon.com outsources the actual shipment of products to UPS and the U.S. Postal Service (USPS).

How is Amazon.com able to efficiently fulfill millions of orders every month?

- **Step 1.** When a customer places an order online, a computer program checks the location of the item. It identifies the Amazon.com distribution center that will fulfill the order. Alternatively, it may identify the vendor that will fulfill the order in those cases where Amazon.com acts only as an intermediary. The program transmits the order automatically and electronically to the appropriate distribution center or vendor. Here, we describe what happens in Amazon.com's distribution centers, such as the 800,000-square-foot facility in Fernley, Nevada.

- **Step 2.** A "flowmeister" at the distribution center receives all orders and assigns them electronically to specific employees.

- **Step 3.** The items (such as books, games, and CDs) are stocked in bins. Each bin has a red light and a button. When an order for an item is assigned, the red light turns on automatically. Pickers move along the rows of bins and pick an item from the bins with red lights; they press the button to reset the light. If the light returns, they pick another unit until the light goes off.

- **Step 4.** The picked items are placed into a crate moving on a conveyor belt, which is part of a winding belt system that is more than 10 miles long in each warehouse. Each crate can reach many destinations; bar code readers (operated automatically or manually) identify items in the crate at 15 different points in the conveyor maze. This tracks the location of an item at any given time and reduces errors to zero.

- **Step 5.** All crates arrive at a central location where bar codes are matched with order numbers. Items are moved from the crates to chutes, where they slide into cardboard boxes. Sophisticated technology allows items picked by several people in different parts of the warehouse to simultaneously arrive in the same chute and be packed in one box.

- **Step 6.** If gift wrapping was selected, this is done by hand.

- **Step 7.** Boxes are packed, taped, weighed, labeled, and routed to one of 40 truck bays in the warehouse. From there, they go to UPS or the USPS. The items are scanned continuously.

Amazon.com rents out space in its warehouse and provides logistic services to other companies. It takes orders for them, too. How does it work?

1. Sellers label, pack, and ship items to Amazon.com.

2. When Amazon.com receives sellers' items, they store them until an order is placed.

3. When an order is placed, Amazon.com will pick, pack, and ship the item, and may combine it with other items in the same order.

4. Amazon.com manages postorder customer service and handles returns as needed.

The Results

Each warehouse can deliver 200,000 or more pieces a day. All five warehouses must handle more than 3 million pieces a day during the busiest part of the holiday season. However, in 2004, the warehouses were able to deliver only 1 million pieces a day, creating some delays during peak periods. Amazon.com leases space to other retailers with online businesses, such as Target and Toys "R" Us. The system gives Amazon.com the ability to offer lower prices and stay competitive, especially because the company is becoming a huge online marketplace that sells thousands of items. As of 2007, profitability was increasing steadily.

To increase efficiency, Amazon.com combines items into one shipment if they are small enough. Shipping warehouses do not handle returns of unwanted merchandise—the Altrec.com warehouse in Auburn, Washington, handles returns.

Sources: Compiled from news items at *amazon.com* (accessed March 2009), Heizer and Render (2007), and LaMonica (2006).

WHAT WE CAN LEARN . . .

The Amazon.com case illustrates the complexity of order fulfillment by a large e-tailer and some of the solutions employed. Order fulfillment is a major EC support service, and it is the topic of this chapter. This chapter examines other support services, primarily acquisition of products and services, finance and accounting services, and customer services and customer relationship management (CRM).

12.1 ORDER FULFILLMENT AND LOGISTICS— AN OVERVIEW

The implementation of most EC applications requires the use of support services. The most obvious support services are security (Chapter 10), payments (Chapter 11), infrastructure and technology (Online Chapter 18), and order fulfillment and logistics (this chapter). Most of the services are relevant for both B2C and B2B. Exhibit 12.1 summarizes the major services described in these chapters, which organizes services into the following categories, as suggested by the Delphi Group (delphigroup.com): e-infrastructure, e-process, e-markets, e-content, e-communities, and e-services. The exhibit shows representative topics in each category.

The first three sections of the chapter give an overview of order fulfillment and logistics.

Taking orders over the Internet could well be the easy part of B2C. Fulfillment and delivery to customers' doors can be the tricky parts. Many e-tailers have experienced fulfillment problems, especially during the 1990s. Amazon.com, for example, which initially operated as a totally virtual company, added physical warehouses with thousands of employees in order to expedite deliveries and reduce order fulfillment costs.

EXHIBIT 12.1   E-Commerce Services

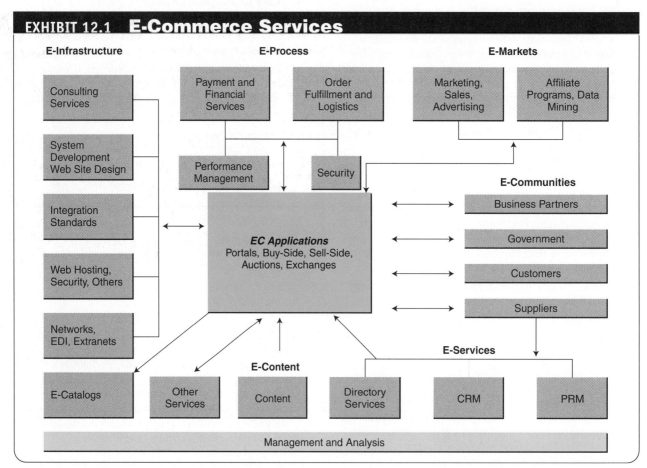

Sources: Adapted from Chio (1997), p. 18, from Murphy (2004), and from Natural Fusion (naturalfusion.com).

ACQUIRING GOODS AND SERVICES

Sellers need to acquire what they sell. They produce it if they are manufacturers. They buy it if they are retailers, or they just refer buyers to sellers if they are intermediaries. In either case, efficient and effective acquisition needs to be done.

Deliveries to retailers and customers may be delayed for several reasons. These range from an inability to accurately forecast demand to ineffective e-tailing supply chains. Many of the same problems affect offline businesses. One issue typical to EC is that EC is based on the concept of "pull" operations that begin with an order, frequently a customized one. This is in contrast with traditional retailing, which usually begins with production to inventory that is then "pushed" to customers (see Exhibit 2A.1 on page 97). In the EC pull case, it is more difficult to forecast demand because of lack of experience and changing consumer tastes. Another reason for delays is that, in a B2C pull model, many small orders need to be organized to be delivered to the customers' doors, whereas in brick-and-mortar retailing, the goods are shipped in large quantities to retail stores where customers pick them up.

Before we analyze the order fulfillment problems and describe some solutions, we need to introduce some basic order fulfillment and logistics concepts.

BASIC CONCEPTS OF ORDER FULFILLMENT AND LOGISTICS

The key objectives of order fulfillment are delivery of materials or services at the right time, to the right place, and at the right cost.

Order fulfillment refers not only to providing customers with what they have ordered and doing so on time, but also to providing all related customer services. For example, a customer must receive assembly and operation instructions when purchasing a new appliance. This can be done by including a paper document with the product or by providing the instructions on the Web. (A nice example of this is available at safemanuals.com.) In addition, if the customer is not happy with a product, an exchange or return must be arranged.

Order fulfillment involves back-office operations, which are the activities that support the fulfillment of orders, such as packing, delivery, accounting, inventory management, and shipping. It also is strongly related to the front-office operations, or *customer-facing activities*, which are activities, such as advertising and order taking, that are visible to customers.

OVERVIEW OF LOGISTICS

The Council of Supply Chain Management Professionals defines logistics as "the process of planning, implementing, and controlling the efficient and effective flow and storage of goods, services, and related information from point of origin to point of consumption for the purpose of conforming to customer requirements" (*Logistics World* 2008). Note that this definition includes inbound, outbound, internal, and external movement and the return of materials and goods. It also includes order fulfillment. However, the distinction between logistics and order fulfillment is not always clear, and the terms are sometimes used interchangeably, as we do in this text.

Traditional Versus EC Logistics

EC logistics, or e-logistics, refers to the logistics of EC systems mainly in B2C. The major difference between e-logistics and traditional logistics is that the latter deals with the movement of large amounts of materials to a few destinations (e.g., to retail stores). E-logistics shipments typically are small parcels sent to many customers' homes. Other differences are shown in Exhibit 12.2.

THE EC ORDER FULFILLMENT PROCESS

In order to understand why there are problems in order fulfillment, it is beneficial to look at a typical EC fulfillment process, as shown in Exhibit 12.3. The process starts on the left, when an order is received and after verification that it is a real order. Several activities take

---

order fulfillment
All the activities needed to provide customers with their ordered goods and services, including related customer services.

back-office operations
The activities that support fulfillment of orders, such as packing, delivery, accounting, and logistics.

front-office operations
The business processes, such as sales and advertising, which are visible to customers.

logistics
The operations involved in the efficient and effective flow and storage of goods, services, and related information from point of origin to point of consumption.

e-logistics
The logistics of EC systems, typically involving small parcels sent to many customers' homes (in B2C).

EXHIBIT 12.2 How E-Logistics Differs from Traditional Logistics

Characteristic	Traditional Knowledge	EC Logistics
Type, quantity	Bulk, large volume	Small, parcels
Destinations	Few	Large number, highly dispersed
Demand type	Push	Pull
Value of shipment	Very large, usually more than $1,000	Very small, frequently less than $50
Nature of demand	Stable, consistent	Seasonal (holiday season), fragmented
Customers	Business partners (in B2B), usually repeat customers (B2C), not many	Usually unknown in B2C, many
Inventory order flow	Usually unidirectional, from manufacturers	Usually bidirectional
Accountability	One link	Through the entire supply chain
Transporter	Frequently the company, sometimes outsourced	Usually outsourced, sometimes the company
Warehouse	Common	Only very large shippers (e.g., Amazon.com) operate their own

place, some of which can be done simultaneously; others must be done in sequence. These activities include the following steps:

▶ **Activity 1: Making sure the customer will pay.** Depending on the payment method and prior arrangements, the validity of each payment must be determined. In B2B, the company's finance department or financial institution (i.e., a bank or a credit card issuer, such

EXHIBIT 12.3 Order Fulfillment and the Logistics Process

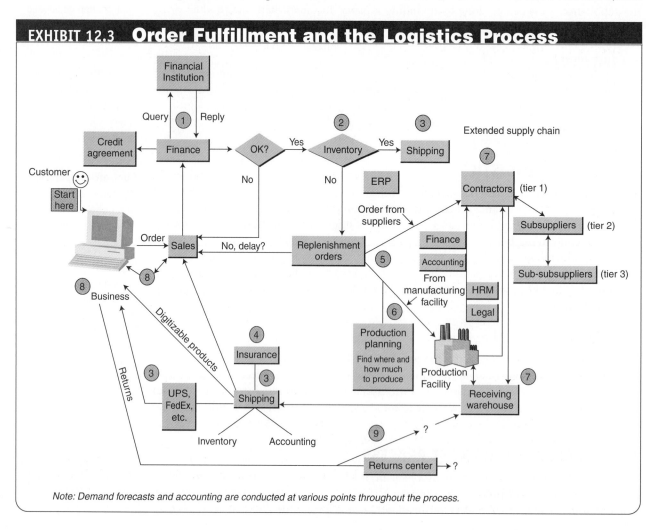

Note: Demand forecasts and accounting are conducted at various points throughout the process.

as Visa) may do this. Any holdup may cause a shipment to be delayed, resulting in a loss of goodwill or a customer. In B2C, the customers usually prepay, frequently by credit card or by using services such as PayPal (Chapter 11).

▶ **Activity 2: Checking for in-stock availability.** Regardless of whether the seller is a manufacturer or a retailer, as soon as an order is received, an inquiry needs to be made regarding stock availability. Several scenarios are possible that may involve the material management and production departments, as well as outside suppliers and warehouse facilities. In this step, the order information needs to be connected to the information about in-stock inventory availability or manufacturing capability.

▶ **Activity 3: Arranging shipments.** If the product is readily available, it can be shipped to the customer right away (otherwise, go to activity 5). Products can be digital or physical. If the item is physical and it is readily available, packaging and shipment arrangements need to be made. It may involve both the packaging and shipping department and internal shippers or outside logistics services. Digital items are usually available because their "inventory" is not depleted. However, a digital product, such as software, may be under revision, and unavailable for delivery at certain times. In either case, information needs to flow among several partners.

▶ **Activity 4: Insurance.** Sometimes the contents of a shipment need to be insured. This could involve both the finance department and an insurance company, and again, information needs to flow, not only inside the company, but also to and from the customer and insurance agent.

▶ **Activity 5: Replenishment.** Customized orders (build-to-order, Appendix 2A in Chapter 2) will always trigger a need for some manufacturing or assembly operation. Similarly, if standard items are out of stock, they need to be produced or procured. In both cases, production can be done in-house or by contractors. The suppliers involved may have their own suppliers (subsuppliers or tier-2 suppliers).

▶ **Activity 6: In-house production.** In-house production needs to be planned. Production planning involves people, materials, components, machines, financial resources, and possibly suppliers and subcontractors. In the case of assembly, manufacturing, or both, plant services may be needed, including possible collaboration with business partners. Services may include scheduling of people and equipment, shifting other products' plans, working with engineering on modifications, getting equipment, and preparing content. The actual production facilities may be in a different country than the company's headquarters or retailers. This may further complicate the flow of information and communication. All this needs to be done efficiently and effectively, as described in Section 12.4.

▶ **Activity 7: Use contractors.** A manufacturer may opt to buy products or subassemblies from contractors. Similarly, if the seller is a retailer, such as in the case of amazon.com or walmart.com, the retailer must purchase products from its manufacturers. Several scenarios are possible. Warehouses can stock purchased items, which is what Amazon.com does with its best-selling books, toys, and other commodity items. However, Amazon.com does not stock books for which it receives only a few orders. In such cases, the publishers or intermediaries must make the special deliveries. In either case, appropriate receiving and quality assurance of incoming materials and products must take place.

Once production (activity 6) or purchasing from suppliers (activity 7) is completed, shipments to the customers (activity 3) are arranged.

▶ **Activity 8: Contacts with customers.** Sales representatives need to keep in constant contact with customers, especially in B2B, starting with notification of orders received and ending with notification of a shipment or a change in delivery date (for other customer services, see Insights and Additions 12.1). These contacts are usually done via e-mail and are frequently generated automatically (e.g., using RFID).

▶ **Activity 9: Returns.** In some cases, customers want to exchange or return items. Such returns can be a major problem, as more than $100 billion in North American goods are returned each year (Kuzeljevich 2004) for both online and offline situations, combined. The movement of returns from customers back to vendors is called **reverse logistics**.

reverse logistics
The movement of returns from customers to vendors.

Insights and Additions 12.1 What Services Do Customers Need?

Insights on online customer services:

▶ **Customer preferences.** Customers tend not to do much self-service in terms of getting information from companies (e.g., only 19% use FAQs), so they require attention. As more companies offer online self-service, though, this situation is changing. When contacting companies for information, customers use e-mail more than the telephone (71% versus 51%).

▶ **Types of service.** Four types of service exist, based on where the customer is in the purchase experience: *during shopping* (search products, compare, find product attributes); *during buying* (questions on warranties, billing, receipt, payment); *after placing the order* (checking status in processing and in shipping); and *after receiving the item* (checking return procedures, how to use the item).

▶ **Problem resolution.** Customers expect quick resolutions to problems, and expect problems to be resolved to their satisfaction. Therefore, easy returns and order tracking are desirable.

▶ **Shipping options.** Several shipping options are usually needed to make customers happy.

▶ **Fraud protection.** Customers need to make sure that sellers or others are not going to cheat them (Chapters 10 and 16).

▶ **Order status and updates.** Customers want to have some way to check on the status of their order, which involves tracking either by phone or online. These services are highly desired, including order notification and a clear return policy.

▶ **Developing customer relationships.** This includes building trust, providing security, and ensuring privacy protection (see Chapters 4, 10, and 16).

▶ **Agent profiling.** The process of matching service agents directly with the needs and personalities of customers is a win-win situation for businesses, customers, and employees.

Order fulfillment processes may vary, depending on the product and the vendor. The order fulfillment process also differs between B2B and B2C activities, between the delivery of goods and of services, and between small and large products. Furthermore, certain circumstances, such as in the case of perishable materials or foods, require additional steps and administrative activities.

Such a complex process may have problems (see Section 12.2); automating the various steps can minimize or eliminate several of these problems.

The Administrative Activities of Order Taking and Fulfillment

The administrative activities of order taking and fulfillment may involve (according to Wikipedia 2009) the following:

▶ **Product inquiry**—Initial inquiry about offerings, visit to the Web site, catalog request

▶ **Sales quote**—Budgetary or availability quote

▶ **Order configuration**—Where ordered items need a selection of options or order lines need to be compatible with each other

▶ **Order booking**—The formal order placement or closing of the deal

▶ **Order acknowledgment or confirmation**—Confirmation that the order is booked or received

▶ **Order sourcing or planning**—Determining the source or location of item(s) to be shipped

▶ **Order changes**—Changes to orders, if needed

▶ **Shipment release**—Process step where the warehouse/inventory stocking point starts the shipping process; may be comprised of picking, packing, and staging for shipment

▶ **Shipment**—The shipment and transportation of the goods

▶ **Delivery**—The delivery of the goods to the consignee or customer

▶ **Settlement**—The payment of the charges for goods, services, and delivery

▶ **Returns**—In case the goods are unacceptable or not required

Order Fulfillment and the Supply Chain

The 9-activity order fulfillment process previously described, as well as order taking, are integral parts of the supply chain. The flows of orders, payments, information, materials, and parts need to be coordinated among all the company's internal participants, as well as with and among external partners. The principles of supply chain management (SCM) must be considered when planning and managing the order fulfillment process, which due to its complexity may have problems.

Section 12.1 ▶ REVIEW QUESTIONS

1. Define order fulfillment and logistics.
2. Compare traditional logistics with e-logistics.
3. List the nine steps of the order fulfillment process.
4. Compare logistics with reverse logistics.

12.2 PROBLEMS IN ORDER FULFILLMENT

During the 1999 holiday season, logistics problems plagued the B2C e-tailers, especially those that sold toys. Price wars boosted demand, and neither the e-tailers nor the manufacturers were ready for it. As a result, supplies were late in coming from manufacturers. Toys "R" Us, for example, had to stop taking orders around December 14. The manufacturers, warehouses, and distribution channels were not in sync with the e-tailers. As a result, many customers did not get their holiday gifts on time. (For more on the order fulfillment troubles experienced by Toys "R" Us, see Online File W12.1.) Although most of these problems were solved, some still exist for certain sellers.

TYPICAL SUPPLY CHAIN PROBLEMS

The inability to deliver products on time is a typical problem in both offline and online commerce. Several other problems have been observed along the supply chain: Some companies grapple with high inventory costs; quality problems exist due to misunderstandings; shipments of wrong products, materials, and parts occur frequently; and the cost to expedite operations or shipments is high. The chance that such problems will occur in EC is even higher due to the lack of appropriate infrastructure and the special characteristics of EC. For example, most manufacturers' and distributors' warehouses are designed to ship large quantities to several stores; they cannot optimally pack and ship many small packages to many customers' doors. Improper inventory levels are typical in EC, as are poor delivery scheduling and mixed-up shipments.

Another major activity related to the supply chain problem is the difficulty in demand forecasting. In the case of standard or commodity items, such as toys, a demand forecast must be done in order to determine appropriate inventories of finished goods at various points in the supply chain. Such a forecast is difficult in the fast-growing field of online ordering. In the case of customized products, it is necessary to forecast the demand for the components and materials required for fulfilling customized orders. Demand forecasting must be done with business partners along the supply chain, as described in Chapter 6. Supply chain problems jeopardize order fulfillment.

WHY SUPPLY CHAIN PROBLEMS EXIST

Many problems along the EC supply chain stem from uncertainties and from the need to coordinate several activities, internal units, and business partners.

A major source of uncertainty in EC, as noted earlier, is the demand forecast. Factors such as consumer behavior, economic conditions, competition, prices, weather conditions, technological developments, and consumer taste and confidence influence demand. Any one of these factors may change quickly. The demand forecast should be conducted frequently, in conjunction with collaboration among business partners along the supply chain, in order to correctly gauge demand and make plans to meet it. As shown in Chapter 6, companies attempt to achieve accurate demand forecasts by methods such as information sharing using collaborative commerce.

third-party logistics suppliers (3PL)
External, rather than in-house, providers of logistics services.

Pure EC companies are likely to have more problems because they do not have a logistics infrastructure already in place and are forced to use external logistics services rather than in-house departments for these functions. These external logistics services are often called **third-party logistics suppliers (3PL)**, or *logistics service providers*. Outsourcing such services can be expensive, and it requires more coordination and dependence on outsiders who may not be reliable. For this reason, large virtual retailers such as Amazon.com have or are developing their own physical warehouses and logistics systems. Other virtual retailers are creating strategic alliances with logistics companies or with experienced mail-order companies that have their own logistics systems.

In addition to uncertainties, lack of coordination and an inability or refusal to share information among business partners also creates EC supply chain fulfillment problems. One of the most persistent order fulfillment problems is the bullwhip effect (see Chapter 6).

EC (and IT) can provide solutions to these order fulfillment problems, as the next section will show.

Section 12.2 ▶ REVIEW QUESTIONS

1. List some problems along the EC supply chain.
2. Explain how uncertainties create order fulfillment problems. List some of these problems.
3. Describe the role of 3PLs.

12.3 SOLUTIONS TO ORDER FULFILLMENT PROBLEMS

Many EC logistics problems are generic; they can be found in the non-Internet world as well. Therefore, many of the solutions that have been developed for these problems in brick-and-mortar companies also work for e-tailers. IT and EC technologies, as shown in Chapter 6, facilitate most of these solutions. They also provide for automation of various operations along the supply chain that usually improve its operation. In this section, we will discuss some of the specific solutions to EC order fulfillment problems.

IMPROVEMENTS IN THE ORDER-TAKING ACTIVITY

One way to improve order fulfillment is to improve the order-taking activity and its links to fulfillment and logistics. Order taking can be done via EDI, EDI/Internet, the Internet, or an extranet, and it may be fully automated. For example, in B2B, orders can be generated and transmitted automatically to suppliers when inventory levels fall below a certain threshold. It is a part of the vendor-managed inventory (VMI) strategy described in Chapter 6. The result is a fast, inexpensive, and more accurate (no need to rekey data) order-taking process. In B2C, Web-based ordering using electronic forms expedites the process, makes the process more accurate (e.g., intelligent agents can check the input data and provide instant feedback), and reduces processing costs for sellers. When EC order taking can interface or integrate with a company's back-office system, it shortens cycle times and eliminates errors.

Order-taking improvements also can take place within an organization, for example, when a manufacturer orders parts from its own warehouse. When delivery of such parts runs smoothly, it minimizes disruptions to the manufacturing process, reducing losses from downtime. For example, as detailed in Online File W12.2, Dell has improved the flow of parts in its PC repair operations, resulting in greater efficiency and cost savings.

Implementing linkages between order-taking and payment systems also can be helpful in improving order fulfillment. Electronic payments can expedite both the order fulfillment cycle and the payment delivery period. With such systems, payment processing can be significantly less expensive, and fraud can be better controlled.

warehouse management system (WMS)
A software system that helps in managing warehouses.

WAREHOUSING AND INVENTORY MANAGEMENT IMPROVEMENTS

A popular EC inventory management solution is a **warehouse management system (WMS)**. WMS refers to a software system that helps in managing warehouses. It has several components. For example, in the case of Amazon.com, the system supports item

EC Application

HOW WMS HELPS SCHURMAN IMPROVE ITS INTERNAL AND EXTERNAL ORDER FULFILLMENT SYSTEM

Schurman Fine Papers (*papyrusonline.com*) is a manufacturer and retailer of greeting cards and related products. It sells through its own 170 specialty stores (Papyrus), as well as through 30,000 independent retail outlets.

Using RedPrairie (*redprairie.com*) integrated logistics software solutions, Schurman improved its demand forecast and minimized both out-of-stocks and overstocking. The system also allows physical inventory counts to be conducted without the need to shut down the two central warehouses for a week three times a year.

The central warehouses receive shipments from about 200 suppliers worldwide (500 to 1,000 orders per day). Until 2003, all inventory and logistics management was done manually. One problem solved by the software is picking products from multiple stock-keeping unit (SKU) locations. Picking is faster now, with a minimum of errors.

Customers' orders come directly from the EDI and ignite the fulfillment and shipment process. This system automatically generates an advanced shipping notice (replacing the lengthy process of manual scanning). The new system also automates the task of assessing the length, width, height, and weight of each item before it goes into a box (to determine which item goes into what box). The system also improved inventory replenishment allocations. In the past, the list of items to be picked up included items not available in the primary location. Pickers wasted time looking for these items, and unfound items had to be picked up later from the reserve storage center, resulting in delays. The WMS simultaneously created two lists, expediting fulfillment. This tripled the number of orders fulfilled per picker per day. The system also generates automatic replenishment orders for items falling below a minimum level at any storage location.

In addition, special software provides Schurman's customer service department with real-time access to inventory and distribution processes, allowing the department to track the status of all orders. The WMS also tracks the status of all orders and sends alerts when an order problem occurs (e.g., delay in downloading). An e-mail goes to all necessary parties in the company so they can fix the problem. Finally, information collected about problems can be analyzed so remedies can be made quickly. All this helps to reduce both overstocks and out-of-stocks.

Sources: Compiled from Parks (2004), *papyrusonline.com* (accessed May 2009), Maloney (2006), and *redprairie.com* (accessed January 2009).

Questions

1. Identify what the WMS automates, both in receiving and shipping.

2. In the future, RFID tags could replace the bar codes that are currently used. What would be the advantages of using RFID? Where can it be used?

3. How has inventory management been improved?

---

pickers as well as packaging. Amazon.com's B2C WMS can handle hundreds of millions of packages. In Case 12.1, we describe a B2B WMS at Schurman Fine Papers, which demonstrates several applications.

Other Inventory Management Improvements

WMS is useful in reducing inventory and decreasing the incidence of out-of-stocks. Such systems also are useful in maintaining an inventory of repair items so repairs can be expedited (e.g., Dell, see Online File W12.2); picking items out of inventory in the warehouse (e.g., Amazon.com and Schurman); communicating (e.g., Schurman); managing product inventory (e.g., Schurman); receiving items at the warehouse (e.g., Schurman); and automating the warehouse (e.g., Amazon.com). For example, introducing a make-to-order (pull) production process and providing fast and accurate demand information to suppliers can minimize inventories. Allowing business partners to electronically track and monitor inventory levels and production activities can improve inventory management and inventory levels, as well as minimize the administrative expenses of inventory management. In some instances, the ultimate inventory improvement is to have no inventory at all; for products that can be digitized (e.g., software), order fulfillment can be instantaneous and can eliminate the need for inventory. Two methods of inventory improvements are VMI and the use of RFID (Chapter 6). Next, we describe some other methods.

Automated Warehouses

Automated warehouses may include robots and other devices that expedite the pickup of products. An example of a company that uses such warehouses is Amazon.com (see the opening case).

A large EC/mail-order warehouse in the United States was operated by a mail-order company, Fingerhut. This company handled its own order fulfillment process for mail orders and online orders, as well as orders for Wal-Mart, Macy's, KbKids, and many others. Other companies (e.g., fosdickfulfillment.com and efulfillmentservice.com) provide similar order fulfillment services. The keys to successful inventory management, in terms of order fulfillment, are efficiency and speed, which wireless devices can facilitate.

Using Wireless Technologies

Wireless technologies have been used in warehouses for more than a decade—RFID being a new one. Online File W12.3 provides an example of how wireless supports WMS.

Using RFID to Improve WMS. In Chapter 6, we introduced the potential uses of RFID in supply chains. We provided an example of how RFID can track items as they move from the manufacturers' to the customers' warehouses. Once inside a customer's warehouse, RFID can track the whereabouts of the items (see Case 12.1, question 2). This can facilitate inventory counts and save pickers' trips.

SPEEDING DELIVERIES

In 1973, an innovative, then tiny company initiated the concept of "next-day delivery." It was a revolution in door-to-door logistics. A few years later, that company, FedEx, introduced its "next-morning delivery" service. In 2008, FedEx moved more than 6.7 million packages a day all over the globe, using several hundred airplanes and several thousand vans. Incidentally, by one report, 70 percent of these packages were the result of EC.

Same-Day, Even Same-Hour, Delivery

In the digital age, however, even the next morning may not be fast enough. Today, we talk about same-day delivery, and even delivery within an hour. Deliveries of urgent materials to and from hospitals are an example of such a service. Two of the newcomers to this area are eFullfillment Service (efulfillmentservice.com) and OneWorld Direct (owd.com). These companies have created networks for the rapid distribution of products, mostly EC-related ones. They offer national distribution systems across the United States in collaboration with shipping companies, such as FedEx and UPS.

Delivering groceries is another area where speed is important, as discussed in Chapter 3. Quick pizza deliveries have been available for a long time (e.g., Domino's Pizza). Today, many pizza orders can be placed online. Also, many restaurants deliver food to customers who order online, a service called "dine online." Examples of this service can be found at dineonline.com and gourmetdinnerservice.com.au. Some companies even offer aggregating supply services, processing orders from several restaurants and then making deliveries (e.g., dialadinner.com.hk in Hong Kong).

Supermarket Deliveries

Supermarket deliveries are done same day or next day. Arranging and making such deliveries may be difficult, especially when fresh or perishable food is to be transported, as discussed in Chapter 3. Buyers may need to be home at certain times to accept the deliveries. Therefore, the distribution systems for such enterprises are critical. For an example of an effective distribution system, see Online File W12.4 about Woolworths of Australia.

One of the most comprehensive delivery systems is that of GroceryWorks (now a subsidiary of Safeway USA). Online File W12.5 illustrates this system. Note that the delivery trucks can pick up other items (such as rented videos and dry cleaning). Using wireless control, tracking, and management of delivery trucks, the global corporation successfully manages its supply chain in more than 100 supermarkets.

A Speedier Superstore Using a Drive-In Model

AutoCart (autocart.biz) allows you to pick up orders of groceries, dry cleaning, prescription medicine, DVD rentals, and more without leaving your car. Here is how it works. Customers make their selection online, by phone, or onsite using a touchscreen tablet PC. Each driver is assigned to a pickup station. The orders show up on-screen inside a specialized warehouse, where a computer directs employees to products via headset. After items are picked, they are placed on a high-speed conveyor belt and travel to the consolidation zone, where purchases are placed into bags. Shoppers waiting at the pickup station can watch television while receiving the audio on their car radio. A shopping card icon at each parking station indicates the progress of the driver's order. Approximately 15 minutes after the order is placed (on average), it is ready for delivery via a conveyor belt to the customer. The customer pays with credit card, cash, or check and picks up the goods. There are other delivery models (see autocart.biz).

Failed Delivery Companies

As cited in Chapters 1 and 3, one of the most publicized dot-com failures was Webvan, an express-delivery company that lost $1.2 billion (the largest of any failed dot-com loss). Another well-publicized failure was that of Kozmo.com, described in Online File W12.6.

PARTNERING EFFORTS AND OUTSOURCING LOGISTICS

An effective way to solve order fulfillment problems is for an organization to partner with other companies. For example, several EC companies partner with UPS or FedEx, which may own part of the EC company.

Logistics-related partnerships can take many forms. For example, marketplaces may be managed by one of many freight forwarders (forwarders.com) such as A & A Contract Customs Brokers (aacb.com), companies that help other companies find "forwarders"—the intermediaries that prepare goods for shipping. Forwarders can find the best prices on air carriers, and the carriers bid to fill the space with forwarders' goods that need to be shipped.

SkyMall (skymall.com), now a subsidiary of Gem-Star TV Guide International, is a retailer that sells from catalogs on airplanes, over the Internet, and by mail order. It relies on its catalog partners to fill the orders. For small vendors that do not handle their own shipments and for international shipments, SkyMall contracts distribution centers owned by fulfillment outsourcer Sykes Enterprise. As orders come in, SkyMall conveys the data to the appropriate vendor or to a Sykes distribution center. A report is then sent to SkyMall.

Comprehensive Logistics Services

Major shippers, notably UPS and FedEx, offer comprehensive logistic services. These services are for B2C, B2B, G2B, and other types of EC. See Insights and Additions 12.2 for a description of the broad EC services that UPS offers.

Outsourcing Logistics

Instead of a joint venture or equity ownership with partners, many companies simply outsource logistics. One advantage of outsourcing is that it is easy to change the logistics provider, as can be seen in the case of National Semiconductor Corporation, described in Online File W12.7. Outsourcing is especially appealing to small companies.

INTEGRATED GLOBAL LOGISTICS SYSTEMS

An increase in global trading created a need for an effective global logistics system. Order fulfillment problems described earlier tend to be even larger in longer supply chains that cross country borders. The number of partners in such situations is usually larger (e.g., custom brokers, global carriers), and so is the need for coordination, communication, and collaboration. Furthermore, such systems require a high level of security, especially when the Internet is the centric technology platform. Integrating separate segments of the supply chain can be very beneficial for minimizing problems in long global chains.

Insights and Additions 12.2 UPS Provides Broad EC Services

UPS is not only a leading transporter of goods sold on the Internet, but it also is a provider of expertise, infrastructure, and technology for managing global commerce—synchronizing the flow of goods, information, and funds for its customers.

UPS has a massive infrastructure to support these efforts. For example, it has a more than 500-terabyte database that contains customer information and shipping records. More than 100,000 UPS customers have incorporated UPS online tools into their own Web sites to strengthen their customer services. In addition, UPS offers the following EC applications:

▶ Electronic supply chain services for corporate customers, by industry. This includes a portal page with industry-related information and statistics.

▶ Calculators for computing shipping fees.

▶ Helping customers manage their electronic supply chains (e.g., expediting billing and speeding up accounts receivable).

▶ Improved inventory management, warehousing, and delivery.

▶ A shipping management system that integrates tracking systems, address validation, service selection, and time-in-transit tools with Oracle's ERP application suite (similar integration with SAP exists).

▶ Notification of customers by e-mail about the status and expected arrival time of incoming packages.

Representative Tools

UPS's online tools—a set of seven transportation and logistics applications—let customers do everything from tracking packages to analyzing their shipping history using customized criteria to calculate exact time-in-transit for shipments between any two postal codes in the continental United States.

The tools, which customers can download to their Web sites, let customers query UPS's system to get proof that specific packages were delivered on schedule. For example, if a company is buying supplies online and wants

them delivered on a certain day, a UPS customer can use an optimal-routing feature to ensure delivery on that day, as well as automatically record proof of the delivery in its accounting system.

UPS offers logistics services tailored for certain industries. For example, UPS Logistics Group provides supply chain reengineering, transportation network management, and service parts logistics to vehicle manufacturers, suppliers, and parts distributors in the auto industry worldwide. UPS Autogistics improves automakers' vehicle delivery networks. For example, Ford reduced the time to deliver vehicles from plants to dealers in North America from an average of 14 days to about 6 days. UPS Logistics Group offers similar supply chain and delivery tracking services to other kinds of manufacturers.

UPS also is expanding into another area important to e-business—delivery of digital documents. The company was the first conventional package shipper to enter this market in 1998 when it launched UPS Document Exchange. This service monitors delivery of digitally delivered documents and provides instant receipt notification, encryption, and password-only access.

UPS offers many other EC-related services. These include allowing customers to enter the UPS system from wireless devices; helping customers configure and customize services; and providing for electronic bill presentation and payment (for B2B), EFT, and processing of COD payments.

Sources: Compiled from Violino (2000), Farber (2003), and *ups.com* (accessed May 2009).

Questions

1. Why would a shipper, such as UPS, expand to other logistics services?

2. Why would shippers want to handle payments?

3. Why does UPS provide software tools to customers?

4. What B2B services does UPS provide? (Note: Check *ups.com* to make sure that your answers are up-to-date.)

ORDER FULLFILLMENT IN MASS CUSTOMIZATION

As you may recall from Chapters 1 and 2, one of the advantages of EC is the ability to easily customize products and personalize services. Although taking customized orders is easily done online (recall the Dell case, Online File W1.2, and the Nike case in Exhibit 2.12), the fulfillment of such orders may not be simple. Mass production enabled companies to reduce the price per unit. Customization may cost lots of money, since each item must be handled separately. Consumers, on the other hand, want customized products at a price that is not much higher than that of similar products produced by mass production. Another problem is the frame. Customized products, especially big ones such cars, may take a long time to produce. Customers are not willing to wait.

The question is how to deliver large numbers of customized products (mass customization, or build-to-order, see Appendix 2A in Chapter 2, and en.wikipedia.org/wiki/mass_customization) at a reasonable cost and in a reasonable time.

Fulfilling Orders

The pioneering approach by Dell was to produce the components of computers via mass production and to offer customization in the manner in which they were assembled. This solution has been adopted by many other manufacturers (e.g., see the closing case of this chapter regarding customized refrigerators). Most customized cars, shoes, toys, textbooks, and wedding rings are made this way. Of course, when you talk about millions of computers at Dell, the supply chain, the logistics, and the delivery of components become critical (see the Dell case [Online File W12.2], the Dell example later in this chapter, and Online File W1.2 in Chapter 1). You also need to closely collaborate with your suppliers. In addition, you need to have flexible production lines where changes are made quickly and inexpensively (e.g., painting cars at Toyota), and you need tools that enable quick and not-so-expensive changes (usually driven by computerized systems). This is usually a part of intelligent factories or production lines. For sources on intelligent factories and mass customization, see the International Institute on Mass Customization & Personalization (iimcp.org), the *International Journal of Mass Customization* (inderscience.com/ijmassc), The Smart Factory KL, (smartfactory.eu), and managingchange.com/masscust/overview.htm.

Here, we present an example of how customization is accomplished by these methods.

Example 1: Intelligent Factories. These factories work on a totally integrated automation that enables mass customization to be executed at a reasonable cost and speed. Major developers are Siemens AG (siemens.com), IBM, and General Electric. Selectron Corp. developed a virtual factory floor—MyFactory@SLR.com, which helps to manage its worldwide trading partners. Another company that develops intelligent factories is Anterus (see anterus.com/pages/intelligencefactory.html).

Example 2: Distributed Mass Customization. Etsy (etsy.com) is a market maker for handmade goods, many of which are customized and sold online. Thousands of small producers custom produce on demand. Etsy aggregates them into one electronic marketplace. For details, see en.wikipedia.org/wiki/Etsy.

HANDLING RETURNS (REVERSE LOGISTICS)

Allowing for the return of unwanted merchandise and providing for product exchanges are necessary to maintaining customers' trust and loyalty. The Boston Consulting Group (2001) found that the "absence of a good return mechanism" was the number-two reason shoppers cited for refusing to buy on the Web frequently. A good return policy is a must in EC.

Dealing with returns is a major logistics problem for EC merchants. Several options for handling returns exist:

- **Return the item to the place of purchase.** This is easy to do with a purchase from a brick-and-mortar store, but not a virtual one. To return a product to a virtual store, a customer needs to get authorization, pack everything up, pay to ship it back, insure it, and wait up to two billing cycles for a credit to show up on his or her statement. The buyer is not happy and neither is the seller, who must unpack, check the paperwork, and resell the item, usually at a loss. This solution is workable only if the number of returns is small or the merchandise is expensive (e.g., Blue Nile, Case 2.2 in Chapter 2).

- **Separate the logistics of returns from the logistics of delivery.** With this option, returns are shipped to an independent returns unit and are handled separately. This solution may be more efficient from the seller's point of view, but it does not ease the returns process for the buyer.

- **Completely outsource returns.** Several outsourcers, including UPS and FedEx, provide logistics services for returns. The services deal not only with delivery and returns but also with the entire logistics process. FedEx, for example, offers several options for returning goods (see fedex.com).

⬤ **Allow the customer to physically drop the returned item at a collection station.** Offer customers locations (such as a convenience store or the UPS Store) where they can drop off returns. In Asia and Australia, returns are accepted in convenience stores and at gas stations. For example, BP Australia Ltd. (gasoline service stations) teamed up with wishlist.com.au, and Caltex Australia is accepting returns at the convenience stores connected to its gasoline stations. The accepting stores may offer in-store computers for ordering and may also offer payment options, as at Japanese 7-Eleven's (7dream.com). And in Taiwan, you can pay, pick up books and other item orders, and return unwanted items at a 7-Eleven store. Click-and-mortar stores usually allow customers to return merchandise that was ordered from the online outlet to their physical stores (e.g., walmart.com, and eddiebauer.com).

⬤ **Auction the returned items.** This option can go hand-in-hand with any of the previous solutions.

For strategy and guidelines on returns, see Ellis (2006). The Reverse Logistics Executive Council (rlec.org) is a major portal on reverse logistics.

ORDER FULFILLMENT IN B2B

Exhibit 12.4 shows the B2B fulfillment options. The exhibit shows how the buy options (gold lines) relate to the shipping options (blue lines). For another overview of B2B fulfillment, see *Supplychainer.com* (2006). B2B fulfillment may be more complex than that of B2C because it has at least six dimensions of complexity (versus two in B2C): shipment size, multiple distribution channels, more variety of shipment frequency, uneven breadth of carrier services, fewer carrier EC offerings, and complex EC transaction paths.

Using BPM to Improve Order Fulfillment

B2B order fulfillment commonly uses business processes management (BPM) software to automate various steps in the process, as done by Daisy Brand (Case 12.2). The case also demonstrates how customers pressure suppliers to improve the order fulfillment process.

Online File W12.8 lists some representative B2B fulfillment players and challenges.

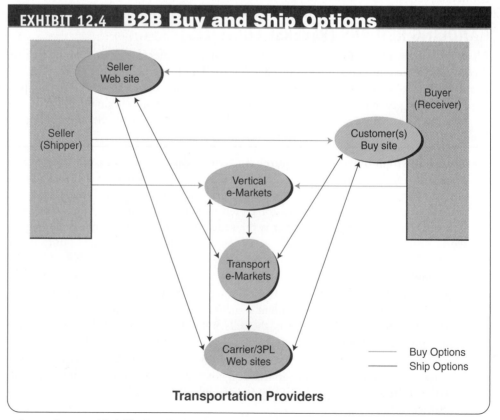

EXHIBIT 12.4 B2B Buy and Ship Options

Source: Courtesy of Norbridge Inc., © 2003.

CASE 12.2
EC Application
HOW DAISY BRAND FULFILLS B2B ORDERS

Daisy Brand, a large U.S. producer of sour cream products, is known for its quality products. Its major customers are supermarkets that operate in a very competitive environment. Many of their customers require that Daisy Brand provide certain services that will improve the efficiency of the customers' operations—for example, vendor-managed inventory, collaborative planning, and forecasting. The customers pressured Daisy Brand to improve its services along the supply chain; order processing became a prime target for improvement.

The Daisy Brand information systems (IS) team sought technology that would improve the efficiency of its existing order fulfillment process. Customers submit orders electronically. Every order that Daisy Brand handles travels through multiple applications: Customers submit orders through an electronic data interchange (EDI) transaction. From there, orders flow to an Invensys Protean enterprise resource planning (ERP) system and various other systems for fulfillment and ultimately to shipping. The company sought to implement a workflow solution that could integrate and automate this order-to-delivery process.

Using TIBCO's business integration and business process management (BPM) solution (see *tibco.com*), the EC team designed, developed, tested, and deployed a workflow that manages order processing from inception all the way to the point of delivery to ensure that orders move forward within the set time frame. The company can also send notifications about shipping activity back to the customer.

If an order is to ship within a certain number of hours, but it hasn't shipped, TIBCO's solution can trace the order and get it moving faster. TIBCO's solution also helps stop problems before they start by auditing customer order information before it enters the ERP system.

In addition to improving the efficiency of order processing at Daisy Brand, TIBCO's solution also enables the company to more flexibly accommodate customer needs. For example, a retail customer might change an order after the order is sent to the warehouse—perhaps to request that the order ship on a different day or with a different amount. In these cases, the TIBCO-based system sends an alert to the logistics management workbench to immediately notify the warehouse that the order has been modified. Thus, the logistics team can quickly implement the change, ensuring minimum impact on the order cycle time.

The workflow software is part of TIBCO's BPM software suite, which includes other applications for control of business processes and to improve agility. Future projects include automation of new customer entry; integration of plant control systems; support for collaborative planning, forecasting, and replenishment (CPFR) and vendor-managed inventory (VMI); and implementation of a real-time electronic order-arrival board.

Sources: Compiled from Tibco (2006) and Smith (2006).

Note: A video supporting this case is available at *tibco.com*.

Questions

1. Describe the steps in order fulfillment at Daisy Brand.
2. How is the automation of order fulfillment done?
3. How can supermarkets benefit from introducing electronic processing by Daisy Brand?
4. Enter *tibco.com* and find information about their BPM and workflow products. How can they support order fulfillment?
5. How can Daisy Brand improve its agility?

Using E-Marketplaces and Exchanges to Ease Order Fulfillment Problems in B2B

In Chapter 5, we introduced a variety of e-marketplaces and exchanges. One of the major objectives of these entities is to improve the operation of the B2B supply chain. Let's see how this works with different business models.

- A company-centric marketplace can solve several supply chain problems. For example, CSX Technology developed an extranet-based EC system for tracking cross-country train shipments as part of its supply chain initiative and was able to effectively identify bottlenecks and more accurately forecast demand.
- Using an extranet, Toshiba America provides an ordering system for its dealers to buy replacement parts for Toshiba's products. The system smoothes the supply chain and delivers better customer service.
- *Supplychainer.com* (2006) suggested taking into consideration the following seven elements (per High Jump Software) for optimal order fulfillment:
  1. Integrate your systems.
  2. Automate your pickings.

3. Incorporate automated shipment planning (ASP).

4. Automate shipment verification.

5. Reduce or eliminate paperwork.

6. Source orders based on facility workloads.

7. Incorporate sales and marketing into the process.

For additional discussion on how fulfillment is done in B2B, see fedex.com, ups.com, and supplychainer.com.

Order Fulfillment in Services

Thus far, we have concentrated on order fulfillment with physical products. Fulfilling service orders (e.g., buy or sell stocks, process insurance claims) may involve more information processing, which requires more sophisticated EC systems. Case 12.3 describes a reservation system used by Sundowner Motor Inns.

INNOVATIVE E-FULFILLMENT STRATEGIES

merge-in-transit

Logistics model in which components for a product may come from two (or more) different physical locations and are shipped directly to the customer's location.

Several innovative e-fulfillment strategies exist. For example, supply chain partners can move information flows and hold off shipping actual physical goods until a point at which they can make more-direct shipments. Two examples of logistics postponement are (1) merge-in-transit and (2) rolling warehouses.

Merge-in-transit is a model in which components for a product may come from two different physical locations. For example, in shipping a desktop PC, the monitor may come from eastern Asia and the CPU from western Asia. Instead of shipping the components to a central location and then shipping both together to the customer, the

---

CASE 12.3

EC Application

HOW SUNDOWNER MOTOR INNS FULFILLS ITS ONLINE RESERVATIONS

Based in Shepparton, Victoria, Australia, Sundowner Motor Inns owns and franchises 24 large motels throughout rural Australia. Sundowner Motor Inns initiated a customer supply chain system to automate the management of room inventory. Software was developed to enable two existing systems to "talk" to each other: (1) the online booking systems and (2) the offline property management system (PMS). The system has worked successfully since then and is continuously being improved.

Here is how the system fulfills orders:

1. Customers make a reservation inquiry at the company's Web site (*constellationhotels.com.au/sundowner*) or at independent online reservation portals (e.g., *wotif.com*, *expedia.com*).
2. Customers are connected automatically to a Web server, and the PMS provides graphic files, pricing, and room availability information.
3. In real time, the customer reviews room details.
4. The customer confirms the reservation by submitting their credit card details via the secure Web page.
5. Upon confirmation of the reservation, the PMS is updated automatically for room availability.
6. The company sends an automatic e-mail confirmation to the customer.

A significant internal process change was the shifting of a large network of rural motel managers from manually interacting with customers over the Internet to allowing an automated system to do it for them. Sundowner Motor Inns plan to continually deliver more customer value using the Web site as a central transaction platform. "Packaged" online deals are now available, offering a whole range of customized offers.

Sources: Compiled from Multimedia Victoria (2004) and from *constellationhotels.com.au/sundowner* (accessed March 2009).

Questions

1. Once you automate order fulfillment and your data are online, you can generate additional revenue. How?
2. What are the criteria for good order fulfillment in online hotel reservations?
3. Why is it advantageous to integrate the front-end and back-end systems?

components are shipped directly to the customer and merged into one shipment by the local deliverer (so the customer gets all the parts in one delivery), reducing unnecessary transportation.

With a **rolling warehouse**, products on the delivery truck are not preassigned to a destination, but the decision about the quantity to unload at each destination is made at the time of unloading. Thus, the latest order information can be taken into account, assisting in inventory control and lowering logistics costs (by avoiding repeat delivery trips). The rolling warehouse method also works in the ocean shipping industry, where it is called a *floating warehouse*.

rolling warehouse
Logistics method in which products on the delivery truck are not preassigned to a destination, but the decision about the quantity to unload at each destination is made at the time of unloading.

Example: A World-Class Supply Chain and Order Fulfillment System Works at Dell

One of the most sophisticated order fulfillment systems is at Dell. On one hand, Dell needs to fulfill both orders from individual customers and from businesses. On the other hand, Dell's suppliers need to fulfill Dell's orders for components and subassemblies. Here is how it is done.

Dell has completely automated its ability to take thousands of orders, translate them into millions of component requirements, and work directly with its suppliers to build and deliver products to meet customer requirements. More than 90 percent of Dell's component purchases now are handled online: Suppliers use an Internet portal to view Dell's requirements and changes to forecasts based on marketable activity and to confirm their ability to meet Dell's delivery requirements. Then, as Dell factories receive orders and schedule assemblies, a "pull" signal to the supplier triggers the shipment of only the materials required to build current orders, and suppliers deliver the materials directly to the appropriate Dell assembly lines.

Using Web Services (Chapter 18), Dell now schedules every line in every factory around the world every 2 hours, and only brings 2 hours' worth of materials into the factory. This has decreased the cycle time at Dell's assembly factories and reduced warehouse space—space that has been replaced by more manufacturing lines.

The project has produced more than just enhanced supply chain efficiencies and accelerated, highly reliable order fulfillment. At any given time, there is less than 4 days of inventory in the entire Dell operation, whereas many competitors routinely carry 30 days or more. In addition, automation has helped Dell react more quickly to correct potentially out-of-balance situations, made it much easier to prevent components from becoming obsolete, and improved response times across the supply chain by providing a global view of supply and demand at any specific Dell location at any time.

For another example, see Online File W12.9 about Ingram Micro.

Section 12.3 ▶ REVIEW QUESTIONS

1. List the various order-taking solutions.
2. List solutions for improved delivery.
3. Describe same-day shipments.
4. Describe some innovative e-strategies for order fulfillment.
5. Describe how to effectively manage the return of items.
6. Describe issues in B2B fulfillment.

12.4 INTEGRATION AND ENTERPRISE RESOURCE PLANNING

If you review Exhibit 12.3 for the order fulfillment process, you will notice that certain activities involve interfacing with other information systems, such as finance, inventory management, production schedule, vendor and customer contact, and logistics. Most of these interfaces are internal, but some are external (most with suppliers and customers). For the sake of effectiveness and efficiency, such interfaces need to be done quickly and without errors. The fewer manual interfaces we need to make, the better. How wonderful it would be if we used only one interface, and if it was automated! This is exactly what an enterprise resource planning (ERP) system does.

ENTERPRISE RESOURCE PLANNING: AN OVERVIEW

enterprise resource planning (ERP)
An enterprisewide information system designed to coordinate all the resources, information, and activities needed to complete business processes such as order fulfillment or billing.

Enterprise resource planning (ERP) is an enterprisewide information system designed to coordinate all the resources, information, and activities needed to complete business processes such as order fulfillment or billing.

An ERP system supports most of the business systems using a single database that contains the data needed for a variety of business functions such as manufacturing, supply chain management, financials, projects, human resources, and customer relationship management. The database in a large organization is the data warehouse (Chapter 4, Online File W4.1).

An ERP system is based on a modular software design. The common database allows every department of a business to store and retrieve information in real time. The information should be reliable, accessible, and easily shared. The modular software design means that a business can select the modules they need, mix and match modules from different vendors, and add new modules of their own to improve business performance. E-commerce can be a module, or its software (e.g., shopping cart, Web analytics) can be easily integrated with the ERP modules.

Ideally, the data for the various business functions are integrated. In practice, the ERP system may comprise a set of discrete applications, each maintaining a discrete data store within one physical database.

A variation of this ERP that operates in an open-source environment is known as ERP5 (see erp5.org).

ERP's Structure

ERP is used for planning and managing all resources and their use in the entire enterprise. ERP is a software program comprised of a set of applications that automate routine back-end and some front-end operations such as financial transactions, inventory management, and scheduling—all of which are critical in EC. For example, there are application modules for cost control, accounts payable and receivable, fixed assets, logistics management, supply chain management, and treasury management (see Exhibit 12.5). The leading ERP software is a SAP R/3, and it includes about 120 different business activities modules.

Objectives and Vendors

ERP's major objective is to integrate all departments and functions across a company by using a single computer system that can serve all of the enterprise's needs. For example, improved order entry allows immediate access to accurate information about inventory, product data, customer credit history, and prior order information. The availability of such information raises productivity and enables improved customer service, thus increasing customer satisfaction. For success stories about ERP implementation, see erpwire.com. ERP systems are in use in thousands of large and medium-sized companies worldwide. Some are producing dramatic results (see erp.ittoolbox.com).

The leading software for ERP is SAP AG. Oracle is SAP's major competitor for ERP for large businesses, whereas Microsoft, Great Plains, and IBM are competing in the market for small and medium enterprises.

ADVANTAGES AND BENEFITS OF ERP SYSTEMS

In the absence of an ERP system, a large manufacturer may find itself with many software applications that neither talk to each other nor interface effectively. Tasks that need to interface with one another may involve (with their EC interfaces in parenthesis):

- Integration among different functional areas to ensure proper communication, productivity, and efficiency (c-commerce, e-supply chains)
- Design engineering (how to best make the product and e-collaboration)
- Order tracking, from acceptance through fulfillment (for B2B and B2C)
- The revenue cycle, from invoice through cash receipt (for e-payment)
- Managing interdependencies of complex processes such as billing of materials (for digital enterprise)
- Tracking the three-way match between purchase orders (what was ordered), inventory receipts (what arrived), and costing (what the vendor invoiced); (e-supply chain)

EXHIBIT 12.5   Basic ERP Solution Model

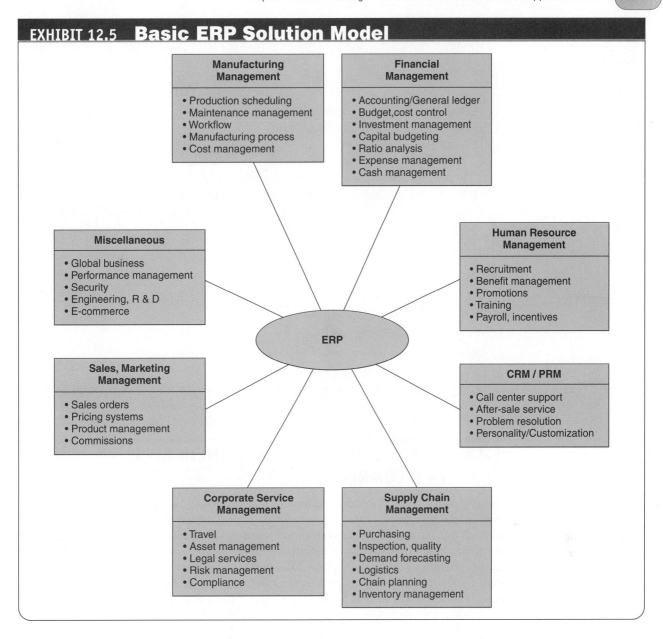

The accounting for all these tasks: tracking the revenue, cost, and profit at a granular level (better performance)

For limitations and implementation issues, see en.wikipedia.org/wiki/Enterprise_resource_planning.

Some Specific Benefits

The following are the major potential benefits of ERP systems:

- Buyers can reach more vendors, producing from more competitive bids and lowering the cost of products and services purchased. Sellers and vendors can widen participation in government contracts.
- Potential for substantial yearly savings to buyers from cost reduction. For example, significant paper and postage cost reduction.
- Faster product/service look-up and ordering; saving time and money (for buyers, for internal operation).

> ▶ Automated ordering and payment, lowering payment processing and paper costs (for buyers and sellers).

> ▶ Fast access to detailed account histories, providing more abundant information and improved planning and analysis (for buyers and sellers).

> ▶ Ability to distribute, receive, and award contracts out for bid much faster (for buyers and sellers).

> ▶ Link the budget system to payroll, accounting, control and legal personnel and other departments, allowing nearly instant data exchange and ensuring such information is consistent and uniform across the board (for buyers).

> ▶ Provide easy access to trend data; financial information from previous years is quickly combined into an up-to-date long-term view (for buyers and sellers).

> ▶ Empower departments to more closely measure program performance and results (for internal operations).

Section 12.4 ▶ REVIEW QUESTIONS

1. Why do we need to integrate EC in the enterprise?
2. Define ERP.
3. Describe the ERP modular design.
4. How can ERP interface with EC?
5. List five specific benefits of ERP that are related to EC.

12.5 INTELLIGENT AGENTS AND THEIR ROLE IN E-COMMERCE

As various chapters in the text have demonstrated (especially Chapter 4), intelligent or software agents have come to play an increasingly important role in EC—providing assistance with Web searches, helping consumers comparison shop, making shopping recommendations, matching buyers to sellers, monitoring activities, and automatically notifying users of recent events (e.g., new job openings). This section is provided for those readers who want to learn a little more about the general features and operation of software and intelligent agents in a networked world such as the Web.

For an extensive list of resources, see Online File W12.10.

DEFINITIONS AND BASIC CONCEPTS

There are several definitions of intelligent agents.

Definition

intelligent agent (IA)
An autonomous entity that perceives its environment via sensors, and acts upon that environment directing its activity toward achieving a goal(s) (i.e., acting rationally) using its actuators.

An **intelligent agent (IA)** is an autonomous entity that perceives its environment via sensors, and acts upon that environment by directing its activity toward achieving a goal(s) (i.e., acting rationally) using its actuators. The process is illustrated in Exhibit 12.6. Intelligent agents may also learn or use knowledge to achieve their goals. They may be very simple or very complex: A thermostat, for example, is an intelligent agent, as is a human being, as is a community of human beings working together toward a goal. Our attention here is directed to computer-based software agents.

Examples of IA elements include:

> ▶ **Sensors.** Eyes, nose, camera, sonar, laser range finder, search engine

> ▶ **Percepts.** Electronic signals, noise level, temperature level, e-mail volume

> ▶ **Actuators.** Limbs (artificial, real), digits, electronic commands

> ▶ **Actions.** Move an arm (real, artificial), activate electronic command, move, close, or open switch

EXHIBIT 12.6   A Simple Intelligent Agent

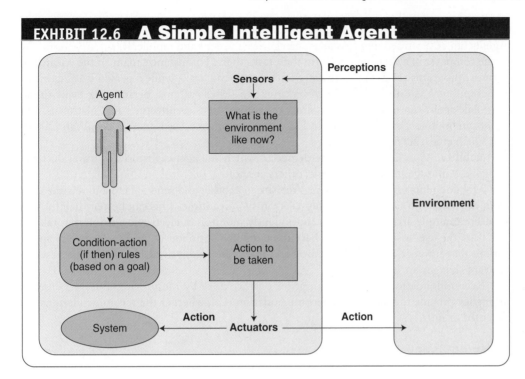

Types of Agents

Some definitions of intelligent agents emphasize their autonomy, and so prefer the term *autonomous intelligent agents*. Still others consider goal-directed behavior as the essence of intelligence and so prefer a term borrowed from economics, *rational agent*.

Intelligent agents in artificial intelligence are closely related to agents in economics, and versions of the intelligent agent paradigm are studied in cognitive science, ethics, and the philosophy of practical reason, as well as in many interdisciplinary sociocognitive modeling and computer social simulations.

Software Agents

Intelligent agents are also closely related to **software agents**, which are autonomous software programs that carry out tasks on behalf of users. In computer science, the term *intelligent agent* may be used to refer to a software agent that has some intelligence, regardless of whether it is or is not a rational agent. For example, autonomous programs used for operator assistance or data mining (sometimes referred to as *bots*) are also called *intelligent agents*. The two terms are often confused and used interchangeably. Note that most EC agents are software agents, but several have some intelligence.

software agents
Autonomous software programs that carry out tasks on behalf of users.

Following are the major types of software agents:

- **Simple reflex agents.** Simple reflex agents act only on the basis of the current precept. The agent's function is based on the *condition-action rule*: if condition, then action.
- **Model-based reflex agents.** Model-based agents can handle partially observable environments. Its current state is stored inside the agent, maintaining some kind of structure that describes the part of the world that cannot be seen. This behavior requires information on how the environment behaves and works.
- **Goal-based agents.** Goal-based agents are model-based agents that store information regarding situations that are desirable. This allows the agent a way to choose among multiple possibilities, selecting the one that reaches a goal state.
- **Utility-based agents.** Goal-based agents distinguish only between goal states and non-goal states. It is possible to define a measure of how desirable a particular state is. This measure can be obtained through the use of a *utility function* (or value function), which maps a state to a measure of the utility of the state.

The essential traits of software agents are described in Online File W12.11.

Mobile Agents

resident agents
Software agents that stay in the computer or system and perform their tasks.

Agents can be classified into two major categories: resident and mobile. **Resident agents** stay in the computer or system and perform their tasks there. For instance, many of the wizards in software programs are designed to carry out very specific tasks while a person is using his or her computer. **Mobile agents**, however, move to other systems, performing tasks there. A mobile agent can transport itself across different system architectures and platforms. EC agents are mobile. For applications in EC and m-commerce, see Guan (2006), Wan (2006), and Quah et al. (2006).

mobile agents
Software agents that move to other systems, performing tasks there. A *mobile agent* can transport itself across different system architectures and platforms.

Mobility. **Mobility** refers to the degree to which the agents themselves travel over the network. Some agents are very mobile; others are not.

Mobile agents can move from one Web site to another and send data to and retrieve data from the user, who can focus on other tasks in the meantime. This can be very helpful to a user. For example, if a user wants to continuously monitor an electronic auction that takes a few days, the user essentially would have to be online continuously for days. Software applications that automatically watch auctions and stocks are readily available, alerting users when relevant changes are being made.

mobility
The degree to which the agents themselves travel over the network. Some agents are very mobile; others are not.

Recommendation agents can improve performance by monitoring a user's behavior after they provide the user with a recommendation (i.e., whether the recommendations are accepted or not).

Learning Agents

learning agents
Software agents that have the capacity to adapt or modify their behavior— that is, to learn.

Software agents are called **learning agents** if they have the capacity to adapt or modify their behavior—that is, to learn. Simple software agents, such as e-mail agents, lack this capacity. If a simple software agent has any intelligence at all, it is found in the subroutine or methods that the agent uses to perform its tasks. Learning agents can act as assistants to humans.

A learning agent can modify its behavior in four ways:

1. **"Look over the shoulder" of the user.** An agent can continually monitor the user's interactions with the computer. By keeping track of the user's actions over an extended period of time, the agent can discern regularities or recurrent patterns and offer to correct or automate these patterns.

2. **Provide direct and indirect user feedback.** The user can provide the agent with negative feedback either in a direct or an indirect fashion. Directly, the user can tell the agent not to repeat a particular action. Indirectly, the user can neglect the advice offered by an agent and take a different course of action.

3. **Learn from examples given by the user.** The user can train the agent by providing it with hypothetical examples of events and actions that indicate how the agent should behave in similar situations.

4. **Ask the agents of other users.** If an agent encounters a situation for which it has no recommended plan of action, it can ask other agents what actions they would recommend for that situation.

Examples of commercial personal learning assistants are Cybelle (see agentland.com) and Imp (see inchain.com.au).

MULTIAGENT SYSTEMS

Agents can communicate, cooperate, and negotiate *with other agents*. The basic idea of multiagent systems is that it is easy to build an agent that has a small amount of specialized knowledge and then group several agents to create a system where each agent is assigned to a simple subtask. However, in executing complex tasks that require much knowledge, it frequently is necessary to employ several software agents in one application. These agents need to *share* their knowledge, otherwise the results of applying this knowledge together may fail (see en.wikipedia.org/wiki/Multiagent_system).

Multiagent Systems at Work

With **multiagent systems (MASs)**, no single designer stands behind all of the agents. Each agent in the system may be working toward different goals, even contradictory ones. Agents either compete or cooperate. For example, a customer may want to place a long-distance call. Once this information is known, agents representing the carriers submit bids simultaneously. The bids are collected, and the best bid wins. In a complex system, the customer's agent may take the process one step further by showing all bidders the offers, allowing them to rebid or negotiate.

A complex task is broken into subtasks, each of which is assigned to an agent that works on its task independently of others and is supported by a knowledge base. Acquiring and interpreting information is done by knowledge processing agents that use deductive and inductive methods, as well as computations. The data are defined, interpreted, and sent to the coordinator, who transfers whatever is relevant to a specific user's inquiry or need to the user interface. If no existing knowledge is available to answer an inquiry, knowledge creating and collecting agents of various types are triggered.

Of the many topics related to MASs, ones that are related to EC, are negotiation, coordination, collaboration, communities of agents, and agent networking.

Example: MultiAgent in E-Commerce. Consider a situation in which agents cooperate to arrange for a person's summer vacation in Hawaii. The person's agent notifies sellers' agents about the potential traveler's needs for a hotel, plane tickets, and a rental car; the sellers' agents submit bids. The person's agent collects the bids and tries to get lower rebids. The sellers' agents can use rules for a negotiation. Related to negotiation is intermediation (see Bohte and La Poutre 2006).

multiagent systems (MASs)

Computer systems in which there is no single designer who stands behind all the agents; each agent in the system can be working toward different, even contradictory, goals.

APPLICATIONS OF SOFTWARE AND INTELLIGENT AGENTS IN E-COMMERCE

In addition to applications cited in the various chapters, or to supplement the description there, we provide a comprehensive list.

- **Mundane personal activity.** In a fast-paced society, time-strapped people need new ways to minimize the time spent on routine personal tasks, such as shopping for groceries or travel planning, so that they can devote more time to professional and leisure activities. An agent can help in several tasks.

- **Search and retrieval.** Shoppers need to find information and then compare and analyze it. It is not possible to directly manipulate a distributed database system containing millions of data objects for such activities. Users will have to delegate the tasks of searching and cost comparison to agents. Such agents perform the tedious, time-consuming, and repetitive tasks of searching databases, retrieving and filtering information, and delivering results back to the user.

- **Repetitive office activity.** There is a pressing need to automate tasks performed by administrative and clerical personnel in functions such as online sales, desk purchasing, or customer support in order to reduce labor costs and increase office productivity. Labor costs were estimated to be as much as 60 percent of the total cost of information delivery in EC.

- **Decision support.** Increased support for tasks performed by knowledge workers, especially in the decision-making arena, is needed. Timely and knowledgeable decisions made by EC professionals greatly increase their effectiveness and the success of their businesses in the marketplace.

- **Domain experts.** It is advisable to model costly expertise and make it widely available. Expert software agents could model real-world agents such as EC consultants, EC system developers, EC site translators, EC lawyers, and so forth.

- **Data mining.** Finding patterns and relationships in data, including Web data, can be done by data mining agents, even in real time. This is especially important in market research and personalization. For a discussion, see en.wikipedia.org/data_mining.

- **Web and text mining.** Web mining—the analysis of Web data—can be facilitated by agents that can analyze large volumes of data very rapidly. The results can be used to improve Internet advertising and customer service.

Section 12.5 ▶ REVIEW QUESTIONS

1. Define intelligent agents.

2. List and describe the major components of an intelligent agent.

3. Define a software agent.

4. Describe a mobile agent.

5. Define a learning agent.

6. Define multiagents and describe some of their applications.

12.6 OTHER E-COMMERCE SUPPORT SERVICES

Depending on the nature and magnitude of its EC initiatives, a company may require several other support services.

CONSULTING SERVICES

How does a firm learn how to do something that it has never done before? Many firms, both start-up and established companies, are turning to consulting firms that have established themselves as experts in guiding their clients through the maze of legal, technical, strategic, and operational problems and decisions that must be addressed in order to ensure success in this new business environment. Some of these firms have established a reputation in one area of expertise, whereas others are generalists. Some consultants even take equity (ownership) positions in the firms they advise. Some consultants will build, test, and deliver a working Web site and may even host it and maintain it for their clients. There are three broad categories of consulting firms.

The first type of consulting firm includes those that provide expertise in the area of EC but not in traditional business. Some of the consultants that provide general EC expertise are Agency.com, Virtusa (virtusa.com), Sun Microsystems (sun.com), Inforte (inforte.com), Sapient (sapient.com), Autonomy (autonomy.com), and WebTrends (webtrends.com).

The second type of consulting firm is a traditional consulting company that maintains divisions that focus on EC. These include the so-called Big Four U.S. accounting firms and the large established U.S. national management consulting firms. These firms leverage their existing relationships with their corporate clients and offer EC value-added services. Representative companies are Accenture, Computer Service Corporation, Cambridge Technology Partners, Boston Consulting Group, Booz Allen Hamilton, Deloitte & Touche, Ernst and Young, EDS, KPMG, McKinsey, and PricewaterhouseCoopers.

The third category of consulting firms is EC hardware and software vendors that provide technology-consulting services. These include SAP, IBM, Oracle, Sun Microsystems, Cisco, Intel, and many more.

Online Consulting. Guideline (guideline.com) sells instant consulting. For an ad hoc fee starting at $500 or an annual fee of up to $10,000, clients can reach more than 70 consultants for phone- or Web-based queries. Answers to business questions are produced within 24 hours, with backup documents. Experts give advice on product launches, market segmentation, and potential competitors' moves. A Web-only service to small and medium enterprises (SMEs) is available.

It is imperative that any firm seeking help in devising a successful online strategy select not only an experienced and competent consulting firm but also one with sufficient synergies with the client firm. For a discussion of vendor selection and management, see Online Chapter 18.

DIRECTORY SERVICES, NEWSLETTERS, AND SEARCH ENGINES

The EC landscape is huge, with hundreds of thousands of companies online selling products and services. How can a buyer find all suitable sellers? How can a seller find all suitable buyers? In B2B, vertical exchanges can help with this matching process, but even vertical exchanges include only a limited number of potential partners, usually located in one country. To overcome the problem of finding buyers or sellers online, a company may use directory services.

Directory Services

There are several types of directory services. Some simply list companies by categories; others provide links to companies. In many cases, the data are classified in several different ways for easy search purposes. In others, special search engines are provided. Finally, value-added services, such as matching buyers and sellers, are available. The following are some popular directories:

▶ B2Business.net (b2business.net) is a major resource for B2B professionals. It includes listings of business resources in about 30 functional areas, company research resources (e.g., credit checks, customs research, and financial reviews), information on start-up (business plans, domain names, recruiting, patents, incubators, and even a graveyard), general EC information (e.g., books, articles, reports, events, and research), e-marketplace directories (e.g., enablers and builders, services, support services, and major markets), and infrastructure resources (e.g., security, connectivity, catalogs, content, portal builders, and ASPs).

▶ B2BToday.com (b2btoday.com) is a directory that contains listings of B2B services organized by type of service (e.g., Web site creation, B2B marketing, and B2B software) and product category (e.g., automotive and books). Each part of the directory highlights several companies at the start of the list that pay extra fees to be listed on the top; after the premium slots, the directory is organized in alphabetical order. The directory listings are hyperlinked to the companies' Web sites. Many of the sites are involved in B2C.

▶ A2Z of B2B (a2zofb2b.com) is a directory of B2B companies organized in alphabetical order or industry order. It specifies the type and nature of the company, the venture capital sponsor of the B2B, and the stock market ticker (if the company's stock is listed on a publicly traded stock exchange).

▶ i-Stores.co.uk (istores.com) is a directory that targets online stores. The company provides Web site design and creation with emphasis on e-commerce solutions affordable for small businesses.

▶ Websters, (webstersonline.com) is a large business directory organized by location and by product or service. In addition, it provides listings by industry and subindustry (according to SIC and NAICS codes).

▶ ThomasNet (thomasnet.com) provides a directory of more than 150,000 manufacturers of industrial products and services.

▶ Yahoo! Small Business (smallbusiness.yahoo.com/index) provides business directories. As of 2009, it listed more than 320,000 companies (dir.yahoo.com/Business_ and_Economy).

Newsletters

There are many B2B newsletters to choose from. Several are e-mailed to individuals free of charge. Examples of B2B newsletters are shown at emarketer.com/newsletters (look for B2B Weekly) and line56.com. Many companies (e.g., Ariba, Intel) issue corporate newsletters and e-mail them to people who request them. Also, companies can use software from onlinepressreleases.com to send online press releases to thousands of editors.

Directories and newsletters are helpful, but they may not be sufficient. Therefore, one may need specialized search engines.

Search Engines and News Aggregators

Several search engines can be used to discover B2B-related information. Some of these are embedded in the directories. Here are some examples:

▶ Moreover (w.moreover.com) is a search engine that locates information and aggregates B2B (and other business) news.

▶ Google offers a directory of components for B2B and B2C Web sites. These range from currency exchange calculators to server performance monitors (see directory.google.com).

▶ iEntry (ientry.com) provides B2B search engines, targeted "niche engines," and several industry-focused newsletters. iEntry operates a network of Web sites and e-mail newsletters that reaches more than 2 million unique opt-in subscribers. Newsletters are available in each of the following categories: Web Developers, Advice, Technology, Professional, Sports & Entertainment, Leisure & Lifestyles, and Web Entrepreneurs. Click on a newsletter to get a brief description and view sample content.

MORE EC SUPPORT SERVICES

Many other service providers support e-commerce in different ways. Each service provider adds a unique value-added service. This section describes only several representative examples.

Trust Services. Chapter 4 introduced the role of trust in B2C. Trust also is important in B2B because one cannot touch the seller's products and because buyers may not be known to sellers. Trust-support services such as TRUSTe, BBBOnline, and Ernst & Young's trust service are used both in B2C and B2B.

Trademark and Domain Names. A number of domain name services are available. Examples are verisign.com, mydomain.com, register.com, easyspace.com, and whois.net.

Digital Photos. Companies such as IPIX (ipix.com) provide innovative pictures for Web sites.

Global Business Communities. The e-commerce portal from Wiznet (wiznet.net) is a global, Web-based "business community" that supports the unique requirements of buying organizations, including cross-catalog searches, RFQ development and distribution, and decision support, while simultaneously enabling suppliers to dictate the content and presentation of their own product catalogs.

Access to Commercial Databases. Subscribers to Thomson Dialog (dialog.com) can access about 900 databases, including those containing patents, trademarks, government reports, and news articles.

Knowledge Management. Lotus Domino, a major knowledge management and collaboration company, offers the capability to manage Web content with its Domino product (see Chapter 6).

Client Matching. TechRepublic (techrepublic.com) matches business clients with firms that provide a wide variety of IT services. It works like a matchmaking service. Clients define what they want, and TechRepublic performs the searching and screening, checking against some general parameters and criteria. This reduces the risk of clients' making bad choices. Buyers also save time and have greater exposure to a larger number of IT service providers.

E-Business Rating Sites. A number of sites are available for businesses to research rankings of potential partners and suppliers. Bizrate.com, forrester.com, gomez.com, and consumersearch.com all provide business ratings.

Security and Encryption Sites. VeriSign (verisign.com) provides valuable encryption tools for all types of EC organizations. It provides domain site registration and several security mechanisms.

Web Research Services. A number of Web research providers help companies learn more about technologies, trends, and potential business partners and suppliers. Some of these are IDC (idc.com), ZDNet (zdnet.com), and Forrester (forrester.com).

Coupon-Generating Sites. A number of vendors help companies generate online coupons. Some of these are Q-pon.com (q-pon.com), CentsOff (centsoff.com), and TheFreeSite.com (thefreesite.com).

Exhibit 12.7 presents additional services available for B2B operations.

OUTSOURCING EC SUPPORT SERVICES

Most companies do not maintain in-house support services. Instead, they outsource many of these services.

Why Outsource EC Services?

Historically, early businesses were vertically integrated—they owned or controlled their own sources of materials, manufactured components, performed final assembly, and managed the

EXHIBIT 12.7 Other B2B Services

Category	Description	Examples
Marketplace concentrator (aggregator)	Aggregates information about products and services from multiple providers at one central point. Purchasers can search, compare, shop, and sometimes complete the sales transaction.	InternetMall, Dealernet, Insweb, Industrial Marketplace
Information brokers (infomediaries)	Provide product, pricing, and availability information. Some facilitate transactions, but their main value is the information they provide.	PartNet, Travelocity, Autobytel
Transaction brokers	Buyers can view rates and terms, but the primary business activity is to complete the transaction.	E*TRADE, Ameritrade
Digital product delivery	Sells and delivers software, multimedia, and other digital products over the Internet.	Regards.com, PhotoDisc, SonicNet
Content provider	Creates revenue by providing content. The customer may pay to access the content, or revenue may be generated by selling advertising space or by having advertisers pay for placement in an organized listing in a searchable database.	*The Wall Street Journal* Interactive, Tripod
Online service provider	Provides service and support for hardware and software users.	CyberMedia, TuneUp.com
Specialized directories	Provide leads to a variety of B2B services categories.	Business.com, Knowledgestorm, Searchedu.com

distribution and sale of their products to consumers. Later, nearly all firms began to contract with other firms to execute various activities along the supply chain, from manufacturing to distribution and sales, in order to concentrate their activities in their *core competency*. This contracting practice is known as *outsourcing*.

When EC emerged, it became obvious that it would be necessary to outsource some of the support services involved in its deployment. Many companies prefer to do this due to:

▶ A desire to concentrate on the core business
▶ The need to have services up and running rapidly
▶ Lack of expertise (experience and resources) for many of the required support services
▶ The inability to have the economies of scale enjoyed by outsourcers, which often results in high costs for in-house options
▶ The inability to keep up with rapidly fluctuating demands if an in-house option is used
▶ The number of required services, which usually are simply too many for one company to handle

To show the importance of outsourcing, we will look at the typical process of developing and managing EC applications (the e-infrastructure), a topic we address in detail in Online Chapter 18. The process includes the following major steps:

1. EC strategy formulation
2. Application design
3. Building (or buying) the systems
4. Hosting, operating, and maintaining the EC site

Each of these steps may include several activities, as shown in Exhibit 12.8. A firm may execute all the activities of this process internally, or it may outsource some or all of them. In

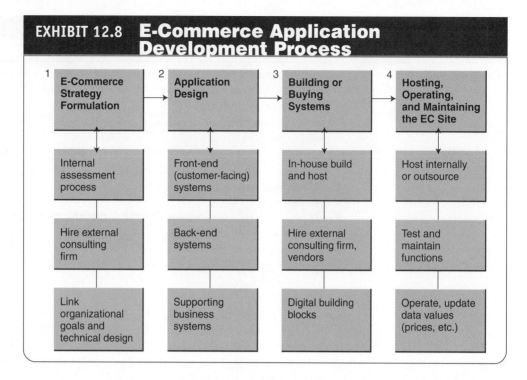

EXHIBIT 12.8 **E-Commerce Application Development Process**

1 E-Commerce Strategy Formulation	2 Application Design	3 Building or Buying Systems	4 Hosting, Operating, and Maintaining the EC Site
Internal assessment process	Front-end (customer-facing) systems	In-house build and host	Host internally or outsource
Hire external consulting firm	Back-end systems	Hire external consulting firm, vendors	Test and maintain functions
Link organizational goals and technical design	Supporting business systems	Digital building blocks	Operate, update data values (prices, etc.)

addition to design and maintenance of technical systems, many other system design issues and business functions related to using a Web site also must be addressed. For example, a firm doing EC must design and operate its order fulfillment system and outbound logistics (delivery) functions; it must provide dynamic content on the site; and it must also provide services to its customers and partners.

IT Outsourcing and Application Service Providers

IT is the most frequently outsourced business activity. Most enterprises engaged in EC practice a very large degree of IT outsourcing. While concentrating on core competencies, they develop strategic alliances with partner firms in order to provide activities such as payment processing, order fulfillment, outbound logistics, Web site hosting, and customer service.

Outside contractors best serve SMEs with few IT staff and smaller budgets. Outside contractors also have proven to be a good choice for large companies wanting to experiment with EC without a great deal of up-front investment. In addition, outsourcing allows them to protect their own internal networks or to rely on experts to establish sites over which they will later assume control. Some of the best-known B2C sites on the Web (e.g., eddiebauer.com and 1800flowers.com) are run by third-party vendors.

Several types of providers offer services for creating and operating electronic storefronts.

One of the most interesting types of EC outsourcing is the use of application service providers. An **application service provider (ASP)** is an agent or vendor who assembles the functions needed by enterprises and packages them with outsourced development, operation, maintenance, and other services (see Online Chapter 18 for details).

application service provider (ASP)
An agent or vendor who assembles the functions needed by enterprises and packages them with outsourced development, operation, maintenance, and other services.

Section 12.6 ▶ REVIEW QUESTIONS

1. Describe the role of EC consultants and list their major types.
2. Describe the value offered by directory services. Provide three examples of what value they add.
3. Explain why specialized search engines are needed.
4. List some other EC support services.
5. List the major reasons why companies outsource EC support services.
6. Which types of services are outsourced the most?
7. Define ASPs.

MANAGERIAL ISSUES

Some managerial issues related to this chapter are as follows.

1. **If you are an EC vendor, what is the bottleneck in the order fulfillment process?** Order fulfillment is a critical task, especially for virtual EC vendors. The problem is not only the physical shipment but also the efficient execution of the entire order fulfillment process, which may be complex along a long supply chain. To enhance the order fulfillment process, the vendor needs to identify the bottleneck that needs improvement. Potential issues are the delayed delivery date, high return rate, high inventory cost, high shipping cost, and poor integration along the supply chain and demand chain. The EC vendor should identify its own problem first.

2. **For which items should we keep our own inventory?** As Amazon.com has experienced, online vendors try to avoid keeping inventory because it is expensive. However, we should not neglect the fact that retailing with appropriate inventory is a source of extra profit as well. In addition, for certain items, it is not possible to assure on-time delivery without having controllable inventory; the no-inventory policy is not always the best policy. A company has to design the portfolio plan of inventory and distribution centers for the items that have a positive effect of having inventory. A CPFR scheme may be adopted to minimize the burden of holding inventories. The plan for distribution centers must be balanced with the plan of outsourced items through partners.

3. **What is the alliance strategy in order fulfillment?** Partnerships and alliances can improve logistics and alleviate supply chain problems. We need to decide in which part of order fulfillment we should count on partners. The typical activities that may be outsourced are shipping, warehousing, inventory holding, return management, and so on. Decide on the appropriate third-party logistic supplier that can provide reliable service on these activities. For certain items that you cannot supply well, a partner may take care of the entire merchandising as well as order fulfillment, especially if you have leverage on the online brand image. An example is Amazon.com's software corner, which is handled by Egghead.com.

4. **How should we manage returns?** Dealing with returns can be a complex issue. Reverse logistics is very costly, and most companies cannot continue online business if the return rate is too high. Use the CRM system to identify the items with higher return rates and resolve the reason or stop the online sales of such items. A company should estimate its percentage of returns and plan a process for receiving and handling them. The logistics of returns may be executed through an external logistic service provider.

5. **What logistic information should we provide to customers?** Customers, particularly business customers, want to know the availability of inventory and delivery date at the time of order. To meet these needs, the EC system should be integrated with the back-end information system. Customers may also want to trace the status of order processing, which should be managed by more than one company along the order fulfillment process. To provide seamless information beyond the boundary of the vendor, the partners should collaborate while developing their information systems.

6. **What integration policy of EC with ERP, SCM, and CRM should be in place?** To enhance the services to EC customers, it is essential to integrate EC with ERP, SCM, and CRM. One issue is how to integrate these systems. One strategy is to buy the entire system from one software vendor. The other strategy is to integrate the best breed—purchasing separate modules of the system from different vendors. The former assures integrated services, while the latter may provide the best service for each function. The integration of systems designed by different vendors is not an easy task because integration requires more than interfacing different modules. Integration with external partners requires following the B2B standard such as XML, EDI, and RosettaNet.

7. **Can we use intelligent agents?** To provide personalized service to customers, intelligent agents may be used. For business purposes, this means software that can conduct intelligent roles such as customized configuration, search and comparison capability, relevant product information provision, and personalized information services. It will not be easy or cost-effective for small and medium enterprises to provide these kinds of services through their own system; it is recommended that they use external EC system services to benefit these functions.

8. **Should we use RFID for the order fulfillment?** If your buyer requires you to use RFID tags, there is no choice but to follow the request; however, the experts and equipment on RFID are not always available within a company. Some third-party logistics service providers support the tagging service. One question is who pays for the cost and who gets the benefit. So far, big buyers such as Wal-Mart and large government agencies get the benefit, while the suppliers pay the cost. In the long run, suppliers may be able to share the benefit in inventory management. However, it will take time until the cost of RFID chips becomes cost-effective and the penetration becomes pervasive enough to maximize the benefit of RFID technology.

SUMMARY

In this chapter, you learned about the following EC issues as they relate to the chapter's learning objectives.

1. **The role of support services in EC.** Support services are essential to the success of EC. They range from order fulfillment to providing customer service. They can be done by the companies or they can be outsourced.

2. **The order fulfillment process.** Large numbers of support services are needed for EC implementation. Most important are payment mechanisms and order fulfillment. On-time delivery of products to customers may be a difficult task, especially in B2C. Fulfilling an order requires several activities ranging from credit and inventory checks to shipments. Most of these activities are part of back-office operations and are related to logistics. The order fulfillment process varies from business to business and also depends on the product. Generally speaking, however, the following steps are recognized: payment verification, inventory checking, shipping arrangement, insurance, production (or assembly), plant services, purchasing, customer contacts, and return of products.

3. **Problems in order fulfillment.** It is difficult to fulfill B2C orders due to uncertainties in demand and potential delays in supply and deliveries. Problems also result from lack of coordination and information sharing among business partners.

4. **Solutions to order fulfillment problems.** Automating order taking (e.g., by using forms over the Internet) and smoothing the supply chain are two ways to solve order fulfillment problems. Several other innovative solutions exist, most of which are supported by software that facilitates correct inventories, coordination along the supply chain, and appropriate planning and decision making.

5. **Integrating EC and enterprise systems.** Large and medium EC projects should be integrated with the company back end, especially with inventory management, finance, billing, production management, and marketing. Tight integration expedites business processes and increases customer satisfaction. Integration is done with all relevant enterprise systems.

6. **ERP systems contain integrated modules of all routine business operations.** Therefore, if EC is connected to ERP it will be connected to all major information systems in the enterprise. ERP standardizes operation and communication and enables better collaboration internally and with business partners.

7. **Intelligent agents in EC.** EC may involve considerable mundane activities ranging from search and comparison to price monitoring and inventory availability. Intelligent agents can deal with the large volume of information involved in EC transactions.

8. **Other support services.** EC support services include consulting services, directory services, infrastructure providers, and many more. One cannot practice EC without some of them. These support services need to be coordinated and integrated. Some of them can be done in-house; others must be outsourced.

9. **Outsourcing EC services.** Selective outsourcing of EC services usually is a must. Lack of time and expertise forces companies to outsource, despite the risks of doing so. Using ASPs is a viable alternative, but they are neither inexpensive nor risk-free. (See Online Chapter 18.)

KEY TERMS

QUESTIONS FOR DISCUSSION

1. Discuss the problem of reverse logistics in EC. What types of companies may suffer the most?

2. Explain why UPS defines itself as a "technology company with trucks" rather than as a "trucking company with technology."

3. Chart the supply chain portion of returns to a virtual store. Check with an e-tailer to see how it handles returns. Prepare a report based on your findings.

4. Under what situations might the outsourcing of EC services not be desirable?

5. Why does it make sense to use a consultant to develop an e-strategy?

6. UPS and other logistics companies also provide financial services. Discuss the logic behind this.

7. Differentiate order fulfillment in B2C from that of B2B.

8. Discuss the pros and cons of using ASPs.

9. Discuss the motivation of suppliers to improve the supply chain to customers.

10. Discuss the need to integrate EC with enterprise systems.

11. Discuss the need to integrate EC with partners' systems.

12. Explain how ERP facilitates integration and discuss its benefits.

13. Discuss the need for intelligent and software agents.

14. Why might we need multiagent systems?

15. Discuss the benefits of mobile intelligent agents.

INTERNET EXERCISES

1. The U.S. Postal Service is also in the EC logistics field. Examine its services and tracking systems at usps.com/shipping. What are the potential advantages of these systems for EC shippers?

2. Enter redprairie.com and find their order fulfillment–related products and services. Prepare a list. Also, review the RFID products that can be used for order fulfillment.

3. Visit ups.com and find its recent EC initiatives. Compare them with those of fedex.com. Then go to wwwapps.ups.com/ctc/request and simulate a purchase. Report your experiences.

4. Visit freightquote.com and the sites of one or two other online freight companies. Compare the features offered by these companies for online delivery.

5. Enter efulfillmentservice.com. Review the products you find there. How does the company organize the network? How is it related to companies such as FedEx? How does this company make money?

6. Enter categoric.com and find information about products that can facilitate order fulfillment. Write a report.

7. Enter kewill.com. Find the innovations offered there that facilitate order fulfillment. Compare it with shipsmo.com. Write a report.

8. Enter b2byellowpages.com and a2zofb2b.com. Compare the information provided on each site. What features do both sites share? How do the sites differ?

9. Visit b2btoday.com. Go to the B2B Communities area and identify the major vendors there. Then select three vendors and examine the services they provide to the B2B community.

10. Enter ahls.com and find out what services it offers. Comment on the uniqueness of the services.

11. Enter support.dell.com and examine all the services available. Examine the tracking services Dell provides to its customers. Finally, examine Dell's association with bizrate.com. Write a report about customer service at Dell.

12. Review Insights and Additions 12.2, enter ups.com, and answer the following questions:

   a. Why would a shipper such as UPS expand to other logistics services?

   b. Why would shippers want to handle payments?

   c. Why does UPS provide software tools to customers?

   d. What B2B services does UPS provide?

13. Enter rlec.org and summarize the differences between reverse and forward logistics. Also include returns management.

14. Enter autocart.biz and review the different classifications (options) available. Write a summary report.

15. Enter chainanalytics.com and find how they can improve logistics and solve supply chain and other fulfillment difficulties. Write a report.

16. Enter freshdirect.com and examine the methods they use to improve order fulfillment of online grocery.

17. Enter zoovy.com and find how they provide data integration. Click on the areas that inhibit EC growth (see diagram there). Write a report.

TEAM ASSIGNMENTS, PROJECTS, AND CLASS DISCUSSIONS

1. Each team should investigate the order fulfillment process offered at an e-tailer's site, such as amazon.com, staples.com, or landsend.com. Contact the company, if necessary, and examine any related business partnerships. Based on the content of this chapter, prepare a report with suggestions for how the company can improve its order fulfillment process. Each group's findings will be discussed in class. Based on the class's findings, draw some conclusions about how companies can improve order fulfillment.

2. FedEx, UPS, the U.S. Postal Service, DHL, and others are competing in the EC logistics market. Each team should examine one such company and investigate the services it provides. Contact the company, if necessary, and aggregate the team's findings into a report that will convince classmates or readers that the company in question is the best. (What are its best features? What are its weaknesses?)

3. Each team selects a product/service that can be managed by an intelligent agent (or group of agents), such as a self-driving car. Identify the IA major components: sensors, actuators, and so forth, as well as its environment and the goal(s) that direct its operation.

4. Address the following topics in a class discussion:

   a. Should a B2B EC company outsource its shipments?
   b. Some say outsourcing B2B services may hurt the competitive edge. Others disagree. Discuss.
   c. Which activities are most critical in order fulfillment of B2C (check Exhibit 12.3)? For B2B? Discuss the differences.
   d. Should we buy ERP or lease (on-demand)?

Closing Case

HOW MASS CUSTOMIZATION EC ORDERS ARE FULFILLED—MULTIBRAS OF BRAZIL

Introduction

Multibras S.A. is a subsidiary of the Whirlpool Corporation in Brazil. It manufactures and sells a variety of household appliances. Brastemp is the leading brand name of the company, and it is a pioneer of EC in Brazil (see *brastemp.com.br*).

Multibras has had an e-commerce department since 2001, providing customer service and selling its commodity-type products. In a very competitive global market, new marketing ideas are a must. Multibras became the first company in the world to sell made-to-order refrigerators on the Internet under the Brastemp name. You can see photos of these products at *flickr.com/photos/brastempyou*.

The Customized Product

The Brastemp "You" refrigerator is a niche product, built to order and available in only one size. It is a product that serves to strengthen the brand in terms of superior quality, and as one that launches market trends.

It also serves to reinforce the brand with frost-free functionality: The company chose this basic model for *You* as the model that sells most among the large refrigerator models. From the basic model, the consumer can configure a series of accessories, such as color, external opening of the doors, outer accessories (water dispenser, external electronic control), and internal accessories (door bottle, can and goblet cooler), with a total of 19,000 possible combinations. It is a highly profitable product.

The purchase can be made only on the company's Web site. There, the consumer chooses each item and adds it to the product, and that adds to the final price, which varies between R$3,200 and R$4,800 (US$1,330 to US$2,000 in March 2009), nearly 10 to 15 percent higher than for similar refrigerators in the series. It is not necessary to conclude the whole purchase in one step. The consumer can store his "creation" and return to it to make alterations. If there are any doubts about color (on the computer screen, the shades are not always very true), Brastemp will send small samples of painted steel to the consumer's home.

Fulfilling the Orders

Problems arose on the factory floor: In an automated mass-assembly line, with a production capacity of 20,000 units a day, would it be possible to manufacture a specific refrigerator without hindering the other products' production flow? That is, when an order for a *You* arrives on the production floor, the refrigerator enters and leaves the assembly line on the orders of a quality auditor. At each point he indicates to the assembler what items have been ordered by the customer—some, like wine bottle shelves and vegetable separators, are only available on the *You* refrigerator—and so on, until the end of the process, in a kind of parallel handcrafted assembly line. The customized refrigerator is identified by a name chosen by the customer when buying it, and this is the name by which it will be recognized, even at the customer call center.

After placing a buy order, the consumer can check the manufacturing status on the Web site in real time and monitor what is happening with regard to the production of both the product and its instruction manual (because the latter is also customized).

With this model of sales of customized products via the Internet, Mutibras is seeking to achieve two strategic objectives. The first is to increase profitability through innovation (the Web site already serves to measure consumer preferences and strengthen Brastemp's image as a brand that launches new trends). The second is to reach the end customer without depending fully on the traditional distribution channels—the company sells refrigerators in several countries as well.

There used to be a myth that no one would buy without seeing and touching these products. Because the *You* line sold via the Web site comprises products whose prices are relatively high, this myth was dispelled the moment the site went live. Today it not only sells, but also ensures that Brastemp provides its buyers with a service that lives up to its name.

For Brastemp, it does not matter how the buyer acquires a product—whether it is online or in a retail outlet; what matters is that they want a Brastemp product. The site is not meant to compete with the retail area, but rather to complement it. The Internet is used to help in those more remote locations where retailers do not operate; thus, the company avoids channel conflict with its distributors.

In addition to the pre-sale and sales areas, the site also offers an after-sales service; in a private chat room, the user can use live chat (Chapter 6) with Brastemp's contact center employee via the Web site without the need to use a toll-free number. Because the contact center and the service team are basically the same, customer service is available 24 hours a day, 7 days a week, and a large number of consumers' problems are solved in this way.

Sources: Compiled from Zilber and Nohara (2009) and from *brastemp.com.br* (accessed May 2009).

Questions

1. What are the drivers of the make-to-order project?
2. How are orders taken?
3. How are orders handled on the assembly line?
4. How are channel conflicts eliminated?
5. How is customer service provided?

ONLINE RESOURCES
available at pearsonglobaleditions.com/turban

Online Files

W12.1 Order Fulfillment Troubles in Toyland (Supply Chain)

W12.2 Application Case: How Dell Fulfills Customer Repair Orders (Logistic, Supply Chain)

W12.3 Application Case: Peacocks Uses Wireless WMS to Smooth Its Internal Supply Chain (Supply Chain)

W12.4 Application Case: Grocery Supermarket Keeps It Fresh: Woolworth's of Australia (Grocery Delivery)

W12.5 Order Fulfillment at GroceryWorks (Grocery Delivery, Warehousing)

W12.6 Application Case: The Rise and Fall of Kozmo.com (A Failing EC Logistic Company)

W12.7 Application Case: Outsourcing Logistics at National Semiconductor Corporation (Supply Chain, Order Fulfillment, Collaboration)

W12.8 Players and Challenges in B2B Fulfillment

W12.9 Application Case: Ingram Micro: World-Class Computer Products Distributor and E-Commerce Provider (B2B Aggregator)

W12.10 General Resources about Intelligent Agents

W12.11 Characteristics of Software Agents: The Essentials

Comprehensive Educational Web Sites

A list of resources is available in Online File W12.10.

REFERENCES

Bohte, S. M., and H. La Poutre. "Emergent Intelligence in Competitive Multi-Agent Systems." *ERCIM News*, January 2006.

Boston Consulting Group. "Winning the Online Consumer: The Challenge of Raised Expectations." 2001. bcg.com/impact_expertise/publications/files/Winning_Online_Consumer_Jun_01_ofa.pdf (accessed March 2009).

Chio, S. Y., et al. *The Economics of Electronic Commerce.* Indianapolis, IN: Macmillan Technical Publishing, 1997.

Ellis, D. "Seven Ways to Improve Returns Processing." *Multichannelmerchant.com*, January 4, 2006. multichannelmerchant.com/opsandfulfillment/returns/improve_returns_processing_01042006 (accessed March 2009).

Farber, D. "UPS Takes Wireless to the Next Level." *ZDNet.com*, April 25, 2003. techupdate.zdnet.com/techupdate/stories/main/0,14179,2913461,00.html (accessed March 2009).

Guan, S. U. "Mobile Agent–Based Auction Services." In M. Khosrow-Pour, (Ed.). *Encyclopedia of E-Commerce, E-Government, and Mobile Commerce.* Hershey, PA: Idea Group Reference, 2006.

Heizer, J., and B. Render. *Operations Management*, 9th ed. Upper Saddle River, NJ: Prentice Hall, 2007.

Kuzeljevich, J. "Targeting Reverse Logistics." *Canadian Transportation Logistics*, 107, no. 9 (2004).

LaMonica, M. "Amazon: Utility Computing Power Broker." *CNET News*, November 16, 2006. news.com.com/Amazon+Utility+computing+powe+broker/2100-7345_3-6135977.html (accessed March 2009).

Logistics World. "What Is Logistics?" 2008. logisticsworld.com/logistics.htm (accessed May 2008).

Maloney, D. "More Than Paper Savings." *DC Velocity*, January 2006. dcvelocity.com/articles/20060101/pdfs/06_01techreview.pdf (no longer available online).

Multimedia Victoria. "Sundowner Motor Inns." eCommerce Case Studies. Victoria Government, Australia, 2004. mmv.vic.gov.au/Search (accessed March 2009).

Murphy, J. V. "Advanced Order Fulfillment Requires Warehouses with 'On Demand' Capability." *Global Logistics and Supply Chain Strategies*, June 2004. scvisions.com/articles/advanced order4.pdf accessed May 2009.

Parks, L. "Schurman Fine Papers Rack Up Labor Savings." *Stores*, February 2004.

Quah, J. T. S., W. C. H. Leow, and Y. K. Soh. "Mobile Agent Assisted E-Learning." In M. Khosrow-Pour, (Ed.). *Encyclopedia of E-Commerce, E-Government, and Mobile Commerce.* Hershey, PA: Idea Group Reference, 2006.

Smith, A. "Daisy Brand Uses BPM to Improve Agility." *Staffware.com.* staffware.com/resources/customers/successstory_daisybrand.pdf (no longer available online).

Supplychainer.com. "Seven Ways to Immediately Increase Fulfillment Speed." June 22, 2006. supplychainer.com/50226711/seven_ways_to_immediately_increase_order_fulfillment_speed.php (accessed March 2009).

Tibco. "Daisy Brand Uses TIBCO's Solution to Deliver Fresh Services." 2006. bpmleader.tibco.com/docs/successstory_daisybrand.pdf (no longer available online).

Violino, B. "Supply Chain Management and E-Commerce." *InternetWeek*, May 4, 2000.

Wan, Y. "Comparison-Shopping Agents and Online Small Business." In M. Khosrow-Pour, (Ed.). *Encyclopedia of E-Commerce, E-Government, and Mobile Commerce.* Hershey, PA: Idea Group Reference, 2006.

Wikipedia. "Order Fulfillment." 2009. en.wikipedia.org/wiki/Order_fulfillment (accessed January 2009).

Zilber, N. S., and J. J. Nohara. "Mass Customization and Strategic Benefits: A Case Study in Brazil." *Electronic Journal Information Systems in Developing Countries*, 36, no. 5 (2009).

E-COMMERCE STRATEGY AND GLOBAL EC

Content

Learning Objectives

Upon completion of this chapter, you will be able to:

1. Describe the strategic planning process.

2. Describe the purpose and content of a business plan and a business case.

3. Understand how e-commerce impacts the strategic planning process.

4. Understand how to formulate, justify, and prioritize EC applications.

5. Describe strategy implementation and assessment, including the use of metrics.

6. Evaluate the issues involved in global EC.

7. Analyze the impact of EC on small and medium-sized businesses.

THE SUCCESS OF TRAVELOCITY'S E-STRATEGY

The Problem

Travelocity (*travelocity.com*), which is owned by American Airlines and Sabre, was the first online travel company. Its initial strategy was to concentrate on airline ticketing and some hotel booking and to sell advertisements on its Web site. This business model worked very well initially, making the company the leading online travel service. However, this business model became ineffective when the airlines reduced, and then eliminated, travel agents' commissions and competitors entered the market successfully.

Expedia (*expedia.com*) emerged as the new market leader; by 2002 it pulled in nearly five times more revenue than Travelocity. The losses in market share resulted in mounting financial losses for Travelocity.

The Solution

Guided by rigorous study of customer behavior, the company developed new strategies and business and revenue models. Specifically, instead of focusing on airline tickets Travelocity moved toward selling customized packages that incorporated more hotel bookings and car rentals. Instead of being a commission-based intermediary, it started to buy blocks of airline tickets and hotel rooms (discounted wholesale) and then selling them to individual customers in customized "merchant travel" packages. Another strategy was to create a fast and effective search engine so that its customers could find the lowest prices for their travel needs.

To better understand customer behavior and to set performance standards for its e-strategy, the company used business analyses performed by the operations research department of Sabre Holding, Travelocity's parent company. The results of the research pointed out a need for better customer service.

Improving the performance of the overall system meant setting performance goals for each of the subsystems and then improving them through the use of several software packages. Quantitative targets and goals formed the basis for system enhancement. Once these goals were set, the company then planned how best to achieve them. The performance standard was related to a mathematical model of how customers choose between travel options, based on the utility of each option (utility is a function of criteria such as price, departure time, trip time, and airline name). Different customers prioritize the criteria differently, and Travelocity attends to the needs of all of its customers.

Travelocity implemented data mining and Web mining tools and data warehouses so that customers can execute flight searches easier and 30 percent faster. When there are airfare price discounts, customers on mailing lists receive e-mail alerts. Cost-conscious travelers receive e-mails about price drops of more than 20 percent (from or to favorite destinations). This program, known as "Good Day to Buy," is a major CRM contributor.

The Results

By the first quarter of 2006, revenue grew to almost half of Expedia's (versus 20% in 2002), a 300 percent improvement over of its performance in 2002. The acquisition of Lastminute.com, a strategic acquisition completed in 2005, contributed to part of this growth.

Using three performance metrics, Travelocity made the following progress against its competitors:

- **Brand impact index.** This index measures the image people have of the company. Travelocity moved from sixth place in 2004 to third in 2008.

- **Conversion impact index.** Conversion of customers from browsing to purchasing showed a 55 percent improvement between 2004 and 2005. Travelocity was in second place in 2008.

- **Customer satisfaction with the Web site.** Travelocity moved from fourth to second place from 2004 to 2005. Only 6 percent of customers said they could not find the lowest fares in 2005, versus 18 percent in 2004. In 2008, Travelocity ranked first in satisfaction with rental car reservations.

Overall, Travelocity is turning itself back into a winner. With its customer-driven focus, Travelocity has become one of the largest travel companies in the world, with annual gross bookings of more than $10 billion.

Sources: Compiled from Carr (2006), Keynote Competitive Research (2008), and Travelocity (2008).

WHAT WE CAN LEARN . . .

Proper strategy, including IT and EC strategies, can help companies survive and excel. For pure-play companies, it may be even more important to change strategies quickly. Strategies are based on performance indices, which are used as targets as well as measures of success. Once performance targets are set, including quantitative measures, improvement plans can be initiated; then the strategy can be implemented. Later progress can be assessed. These are the basic steps in EC strategy, which is the main subject of this chapter. The chapter also presents the related topics of global EC and EC in small and medium-sized enterprises (SMEs).

13.1 ORGANIZATIONAL STRATEGY: CONCEPTS AND OVERVIEW

An organizational **strategy** is a broad-based formula for how a business is going to accomplish its mission, what its goals should be, and what plans and policies it will need to accomplish these goals. An organization's strategy has to start with understanding where the company is today and where it wants to go in the future. The economic/financial crisis of 2008–2009 makes it even more important to have an EC and IT strategy (see transformationenablers.com).

strategy
A broad-based formula for how a business is going to accomplish its mission, what its goals should be, and what plans and policies will be needed to carry out those goals.

STRATEGY AND THE WEB ENVIRONMENT

Strategy is more than deciding what a company should do next. Strategy also is about making tough decisions about what not to do. Strategic positioning is making decisions about trade-offs, recognizing that a company must abandon or not pursue some products, services, and activities in order to excel at others. How are these trade-offs determined? Not merely with a focus on growth and increases in revenue, but also on profitability and increases in shareholder value over the long run. How is this profitability and economic value determined? By establishing a unique value proposition and the configuration of a tailored value chain that enables a company to offer unique value to its customers. Therefore, strategy has been, and remains, focused on questions about organizational fit, trade-offs, profitability, and value (Porter 2001).

Any contemporary strategy-setting process must include the Internet. Strategy guru Michael Porter (2001) argues that a coherent organizational strategy that includes the Internet is more important than ever before: "Many have argued that the Internet renders strategy obsolete. In reality, the opposite is true . . . it is more important than ever for companies to distinguish themselves through strategy. The winners will be those that view the Internet as a complement to, not a cannibal of, traditional ways of competing" (p. 63).

Porter's Competitive Forces Model and Strategies

Porter's competitive forces model has been used to develop strategies for companies to increase their competitive edge. It also demonstrates how IT and EC can enhance competitiveness.

The model recognizes five major forces that could endanger a company's position in a given industry. Other forces, such as those cited in Chapter 1, including the impact of government, affect all companies in the industry, and therefore may have less impact on the relative success of a company within its industry. Although the details of the model differ from one industry to another, its general structure is universal. The five major forces in an industry that affect the degree of competition and, ultimately, the degree of profitability are:

1. Threat of entry of new competitors
2. Bargaining power of suppliers
3. Bargaining power of customers or buyers
4. Threat of substitute products or services
5. Rivalry among existing firms in the industry

The strength of each force is determined by the industry's structure. Existing companies in an industry need to protect themselves against the forces; alternatively, they can use the forces to improve their position or to challenge the leaders in the industry. The relationships are shown in Exhibit 13.1. The definitions and details are provided by Porter (1980).

While implementing Porter's model, companies can identify the forces that influence competitive advantage in their marketplace and then develop a strategy. Porter (1985) proposed three such strategies: cost leadership, differentiation, and niche strategies.

In Exhibit 13.2, we first list Porter's three classical strategies, plus nine other general strategies, for dealing with competitive advantage. Each of these strategies can be enhanced by EC, as shown throughout the book.

EXHIBIT 13.1   Porter's Competitive Forces Model

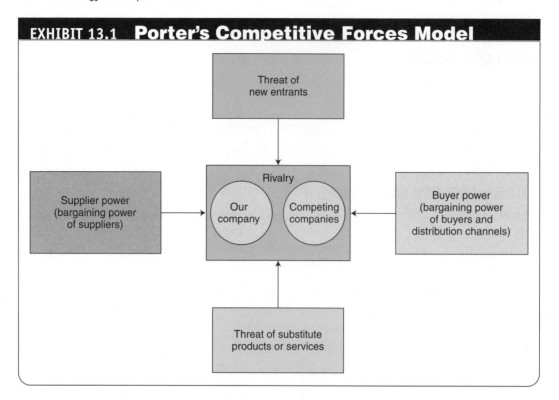

EXHIBIT 13.2   Strategies for Competitive Advantage

Strategy	Description
Classic Strategies	
Cost leadership	Produce product/service at the lowest cost in the industry.
Differentiation	Offer different products, services, or product features.
Niche	Select a narrow-scope segment (market niche) and be the best in quality, speed, or cost in that segment.
General Strategies	
Growth	Increase market share, acquire more customers, or sell more types of products.
Alliance	Work with business partners in partnerships, alliances, joint ventures, or virtual companies.
Innovation	Introduce new products/services; put new features in existing products/services; develop new ways to produce products/services.
Operational effectiveness	Improve the manner in which internal business processes are executed so that the firm performs similar activities better than rivals.
Customer orientation	Concentrate on customer satisfaction.
Time	Treat time as a resource, then manage it and use it to the firm's advantage.
Entry barriers	Create barriers to entry. By introducing innovative products or using EC business models to provide exceptional service, companies can create entry barriers to discourage new entrants.
Customer or supplier lock-in	Encourage customers or suppliers to stay with you rather than going to competitors. Reduce customers' bargaining power by locking them in.
Increase switching costs	Discourage customers or suppliers from going to competitors for economic reasons.

The Impact of the Internet

Porter (2001) has identified several ways that the Internet impacts each of the five forces of competitiveness—bargaining power of consumers and suppliers, threats from substitutes and new entrants, and rivalry among existing competitors—that were originally described in one of his seminal works on strategy (Porter 1980). These five forces and associated Internet impacts are shown in Exhibit 13.3. The majority of impacts are negative, reflecting Porter's view that "The great paradox of the Internet is that its very benefits—making information widely available; reducing the difficulty of purchasing, marketing, and distribution; allowing buyers and sellers to find and transact business with one another more easily—also make it more difficult for companies to capture those benefits as profits" (Porter 2001, p. 66).

The impact of the Internet on strategic competitiveness and long-term profitability will differ from industry to industry. Accordingly, many businesses are taking a focused look at the impact of the Internet and EC on their future. For these firms, an **e-commerce strategy**, or **e-strategy**, is the formulation and execution of a vision of how a new or existing company intends to do business electronically. The process of building an e-strategy is explained in

e-commerce strategy (e-strategy)

The formulation and execution of a vision of how a new or existing company intends to do business electronically.

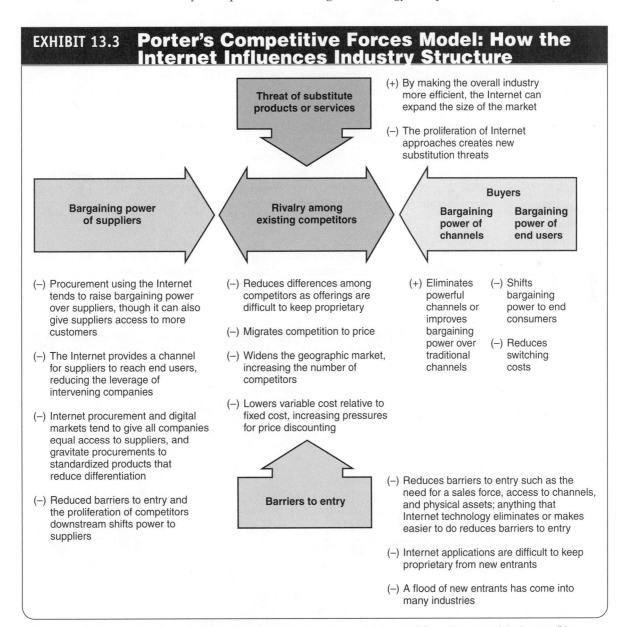

EXHIBIT 13.3 Porter's Competitive Forces Model: How the Internet Influences Industry Structure

Threat of substitute products or services

(+) By making the overall industry more efficient, the Internet can expand the size of the market

(−) The proliferation of Internet approaches creates new substitution threats

Bargaining power of suppliers

Rivalry among existing competitors

Buyers

Bargaining power of channels   **Bargaining power of end users**

(−) Procurement using the Internet tends to raise bargaining power over suppliers, though it can also give suppliers access to more customers

(−) The Internet provides a channel for suppliers to reach end users, reducing the leverage of intervening companies

(−) Internet procurement and digital markets tend to give all companies equal access to suppliers, and gravitate procurements to standardized products that reduce differentiation

(−) Reduced barriers to entry and the proliferation of competitors downstream shifts power to suppliers

(−) Reduces differences among competitors as offerings are difficult to keep proprietary

(−) Migrates competition to price

(−) Widens the geographic market, increasing the number of competitors

(−) Lowers variable cost relative to fixed cost, increasing pressures for price discounting

(+) Eliminates powerful channels or improves bargaining power over traditional channels

(−) Shifts bargaining power to end consumers

(−) Reduces switching costs

Barriers to entry

(−) Reduces barriers to entry such as the need for a sales force, access to channels, and physical assets; anything that Internet technology eliminates or makes easier to do reduces barriers to entry

(−) Internet applications are difficult to keep proprietary from new entrants

(−) A flood of new entrants has come into many industries

Source: "Porter's Competitive Forces Model: How the Internet Influences Industry Structure" from "Strategy and the Internet," by M. E. Porter, March 2001 © 2001 by the Harvard Business School Publishing Corp. *Harvard Business Review.* Reprinted by permission.

detail later in this chapter. First, though, we continue our overview of organizational strategy and IT strategy, of which e-commerce strategy is a component.

Strategic Planning for IT and EC

strategic information systems planning (SISP)
A process for developing a strategy and plans for aligning information systems (including e-commerce applications) with the organization's business strategies.

Strategic information systems planning (SISP) refers to a process for developing a strategy and plans for aligning information systems (including e-commerce applications) with the business strategies of an organization. Researchers have suggested that more extensive SISP in an uncertain environment produces greater planning success. Managers must decide whether, and if so when, to perform such SISP. For further details, see bizplan.com/sisp.html. The SISP process is discussed next.

THE STRATEGIC PLANNING PROCESS

A strategy is important, but the process of developing a strategy is even more important. (See Online File W13.1 for what some famous people have said about the planning process.) No matter how large or how small the organization, the strategic planning process forces corporate executives, a company's general manager, or a small business owner to assess the current position of the firm, where it should be, and how to get from here to there. The process also involves primary stakeholders, including the board of directors, employees, and strategic partners. This involvement ensures that stakeholders buy into the strategy and reinforces stakeholder commitment to the future of the organization.

Strategy development will differ depending on the type of strategy, the implementation method, the size of the firm, and the approach that is taken. Nevertheless, any strategic planning process has four major phases, as shown in Exhibit 13.4. (Note that the phases in Exhibit 13.4 correspond to section numbers in this chapter.) The major phases of the strategic planning process, and some identifiable activities and outcomes associated with each phase, are discussed briefly in the following text. The phases are then discussed more extensively as part of the e-commerce strategic planning process in Sections 13.4 through 13.7. Note that the process is cyclical and continuous.

Strategy Initiation

strategy initiation
The initial phase of strategic planning in which the organization examines itself and its environment.

In the **strategy initiation** phase, the organization examines itself and its environment. The principal activities include setting the organization's mission and goals, examining organizational strengths and weaknesses, assessing environmental factors impacting the business, and

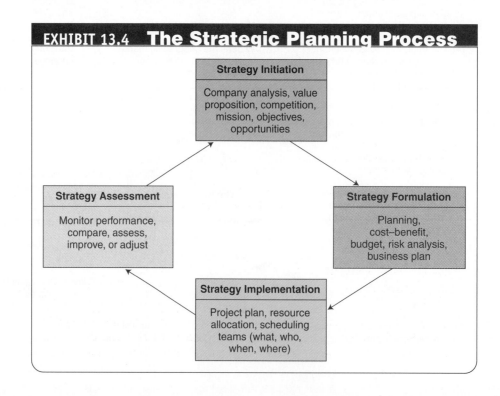

EXHIBIT 13.4 The Strategic Planning Process

Strategy Initiation
Company analysis, value proposition, competition, mission, objectives, opportunities

Strategy Formulation
Planning, cost–benefit, budget, risk analysis, business plan

Strategy Implementation
Project plan, resource allocation, scheduling teams (what, who, when, where)

Strategy Assessment
Monitor performance, compare, assess, improve, or adjust

conducting a competitor analysis. As emphasized throughout this chapter, this includes an examination of the potential contribution that the Internet and other emerging technologies can make to the business.

Specific outcomes from this phase include:

▶ **Company analysis and value proposition.** The *company analysis* includes the vision, mission, value proposition, goals, capabilities, constraints, strengths, and weaknesses of the company. Questions typically asked in a company analysis are: What business are we really in? Who are our future customers? Do our mission statement and our goals adequately describe our intended future? What opportunities, and threats, do our business and our industry face? One key outcome from this analysis should be a clear statement of the company's **value proposition**—the benefit that a company's products or services provide to a company and its customers. Value proposition is actually a statement that summarizes the customer segment, competitor target, and the core differentiation of one's product from the offering of competitors. It describes the value added by the company (or the e-commerce projects), and usually is included in the business plan. It is only by knowing what benefits a business is providing to customers that chief-level executives can truly understand "what business they are in" and who their potential competitors are. For example, Amazon.com recognizes that it is not just in the book-selling business, but that it also is in the information-about-books business. Amazon.com's strategists know this is where customers find value in shopping at Amazon.com and where a great deal of Amazon.com's competitive advantage lies. So Amazon.com has introduced new services such as "search inside the book" to deliver on that value proposition to its customers.

▶ **Core competencies.** A *core competency* refers to the unique combination of the resources and experiences of a particular firm. It takes time to build these core competencies, and they can be difficult to imitate. For example, Google's core competency is its expertise in information search technology, and eBay's core competency is in conducting online auctions. A company uses its core competency to deliver a product or service. Google's products are AdWords and AdSense, and Intel produces chips.

▶ **Forecasts.** *Forecasting* means identifying business, technological, political, economic, and other relevant trends that are currently affecting the business or that have the potential to do so in the future.

▶ **Competitor (industry) analysis.** *Competitor analysis* involves scanning the business environment to collect and interpret relevant information about direct competitors, indirect competitors, and potential competitors. Several methodologies are available to conduct such an analysis, including a strengths, weaknesses, opportunities, and threats (SWOT) analysis and competitor analysis grid.

value proposition
The benefit that a company's products or services provide to a company and its customers.

Strategy Formulation

Strategy formulation is the development of strategies to exploit opportunities and manage threats in the business environment in light of corporate strengths and weaknesses. In an EC strategy, the end result is likely to be a list of EC applications or projects to be implemented.

Specific activities and outcomes from this phase include:

strategy formulation
The development of strategies to exploit opportunities and manage threats in the business environment in light of corporate strengths and weaknesses.

▶ **Business opportunities.** If the strategy initiation has been done well, a number of scenarios for future development of the business will be obvious. How well these scenarios fit with the future direction of the company are assessed. Similarly, the first phase may also have identified some current activities that are no longer relevant to the company's future and are candidates for divestiture, outsourcing, or elimination.

▶ **Cost–benefit analysis.** Each proposed opportunity must be assessed in terms of the potential costs and benefits to the company in light of its mission and goals.

These costs and benefits may be financial or nonfinancial, tangible or intangible, or short-term or long-term. More information about conducting a cost–benefit analysis is included in Chapter 14.

▶ **Risk analysis, assessment, and management.** The risks of each proposed EC initiative (project) must be analyzed and assessed. If a significant risk is evident, then a risk management plan is required. Of particular importance in an EC strategy are business risk factors such as transition risk and partner risk, which are discussed in Section 13.5.

▶ **Business plan.** Many of the outcomes from these first two phases—goals, competitor analysis, strategic opportunities, risk analysis, and more—come together in a business plan. As described in Section 13.2, every business—large or small, new or old, successful or not—needs a business plan to acquire funding and to ensure that a realistic approach is being taken to implement the business strategy. According to Access eCommerce (2006), a business plan for EC is likely to include these activities: introduction, technology audit, check out the competition, set goals, identify the audience, build a team, create a budget, locate resources, use a Web site planning checklist, try a Web site promotion checklist, send a press release, evaluate the plan, prepare appendices to the plan, and identify related resources. The value proposition part of a business plan includes, these four phases: (1) value definition, (2) value development, (3) value measurement, and (4) value communication (see en.wikipedia.org/wiki/Value_proposition for details).

Strategy Implementation

strategy implementation
The development of detailed, short-term plans for carrying out the projects agreed on in strategy formulation.

In this phase, the emphasis shifts from "what do we do?" to "how do we do it?" In the **strategy implementation** phase, detailed, short-term plans are developed for carrying out the projects agreed on in strategy formulation. Specifically, decision makers evaluate options, establish specific milestones, allocate resources, and manage the projects.

Specific activities and outcomes from this phase include:

▶ **Project planning.** Inevitably, strategy implementation is executed through an EC project or a series of projects. Project planning includes setting specific project objectives, creating a project schedule with milestones, and setting measurable performance targets. Normally, a project plan would be set for each project and application.

▶ **Resource allocation.** Organizational resources are those owned, available to, or controlled by a company. They can be human, financial, technological, managerial, or knowledge based. This phase includes business process outsourcing (BPO) consideration and use.

▶ **Project management.** This is the process of making the selected applications and projects a reality—hiring staff; purchasing equipment; licensing, purchasing, or writing software; contracting vendors; and so on.

Strategy Assessment

strategy assessment
The continuous evaluation of progress toward the organization's strategic goals, resulting in corrective action and, if necessary, strategy reformulation.

Just as soon as implementation is complete, assessment begins. **Strategy assessment** is the continuous evaluation of progress toward the organization's strategic goals, resulting in corrective action and, if necessary, strategy reformulation. In strategy assessment, specific measures called metrics (discussed in Section 13.7) assess the progress of the strategy. In some cases, data gathered in the first phase can be used as baseline data to assess the strategy's effectiveness. If not, this information will have to be gathered. For large EC projects, business performance management tools can be employed (see oracle.com/hyperion).

What happens with the results from strategy assessment? As shown in Exhibit 13.4, the strategic planning process starts over again, immediately. Note that a cyclical approach is required—a strategic planning process that requires constant reassessment of today's strategy while preparing a new strategy for tomorrow.

A major organizational restructuring and transformation was the reason for the development of a new strategic plan for InternetNZ, as Case 13.1 describes.

STRATEGIC PLANNING TOOLS

Strategists have devised a number of strategic planning tools and techniques that can be used in strategic planning. Online File W13.2 provides a representative list of these tools. This section briefly describes a few of the most popular tools. A strategic management textbook or handbook can provide more information about these and other strategic planning tools.

Representative Strategic Planning Tools

SWOT analysis is a methodology that surveys the opportunities (O) and threats (T) in the external environment and relates them to the organization's internal strengths (S) and weaknesses (W) (see en.wikipedia.org/wiki/SWOT). SWOT analysis diagrams are available at smartdraw.com/specials/swotanalysis.htm.

A competitor analysis grid is a strategic planning tool that highlights points of differentiation between competitors and the target firm. The grid is a table with the company's most significant competitors entered in the columns and the key factors for comparison entered in the rows. Factors might include mission statements, strategic partners, sources of competitive advantage (e.g., cost leadership, global reach), customer relationship strategies, and financial resources. An additional column includes the company's data on each factor so

SWOT analysis
A methodology that surveys external opportunities and threats and relates them to internal strengths and weaknesses.

competitor analysis grid
A strategic planning tool that highlights points of differentiation between competitors and the target firm.

CASE 13.1
EC Application
STRATEGIC PLANNING AT INTERNETNZ

InternetNZ is not only an Internet-based business; its business is the Internet. An incorporated, nonprofit organization, InternetNZ describes itself as "the guardian of the Internet for New Zealand," and its primary business activity is management of the .nz country code top-level domain (ccTLD).

After a somewhat turbulent transition from its predecessor organization, the Internet Society of New Zealand, in early 2004 InternetNZ embarked on a comprehensive strategic planning exercise. In 2007, InternetNZ released a second strategic plan, which is a model of the content that should be in every strategic plan.

▶ **Vision statement.** Sixteen visionary goals (e.g., "Benefits of the Internet have been extended to all New Zealanders") follow a vision statement for 2009 ("The Internet, open and uncaptureable").

▶ **Mission statement.** "To protect and promote the Internet for New Zealand" captures many of the characteristics—visionary, realistic, easily understood, short, and concise—of a good mission statement.

▶ **SWOT analysis.** A SWOT analysis lists 13 strengths (e.g., "Committed, involved, clever volunteers" and "Has created a best practice model for .nz ccTLD"), 13 weaknesses (e.g., "Perception of InternetNZ as mainly 'geeks' or 'techies'" and "Lack of internal resources to respond to rapidly changing environment"), 14 opportunities (e.g., "A leader in the fight against spam" and "Help ensure widespread broadband access"), and 11 threats (e.g., "Unnecessary government intervention or regulation" and "Low level of membership, hence, providing little funding and vulnerable to take over").

▶ **Core values.** Four core values—openness and transparency, leadership, ethical behavior, and stewardship—are identified and described briefly.

▶ **Goal statements.** Four strategies are listed (e.g., country code manager for the .nz ccTLD, advocacy and public policy, technical policy and innovation, and organizational capability). For each strategy, one to four goals are listed that clearly identify that the InternetNZ committee is accountable for achievement of the strategy. The 2007–2009 InternetNZ business plan identifies goals, a statement of purpose, projected outcomes, and specific examples for execution for each goal.

▶ **Business plan.** Separate from, but an integral part of the InternetNZ strategic plan, is the InternetNZ business plan. This document lists, describes, and prioritizes the specific activities that are necessary to achieve the goals, with associated income and expenses.

The InternetNZ Council adopted the strategic plan and the business plan at its April 2008 meeting, and both plans are in the process of being implemented.

Sources: Compiled from InternetNZ (2006) and (2007).

Questions

1. Why would a nonprofit organization, such as InternetNZ, need a strategic plan or a business plan?

2. What is the difference between a vision statement and a mission statement?

scenario planning
A strategic planning methodology that generates plausible alternative futures to help decision makers identify actions that can be taken today to ensure success in the future.

balanced scorecard
A management tool that assesses organizational progress toward strategic goals by measuring performance in a number of different areas.

that significant similarities and differences (i.e., points of differentiation) will be obvious. A competitor analysis grid template is available in the Online Tutorial ("An E-Business Plan Tutorial") on the book's Web site.

Scenario planning offers an alternative to traditional planning approaches that rely on straight-line projections of current trends. These approaches fail when low-probability events occur that radically alter current trends. The aim of scenario planning is to generate several plausible alternative futures, giving decision makers the opportunity to identify actions that can be taken today to ensure success under varying future conditions (see en.wikipedia.org/wiki/Scenario_planning).

The basic method in scenario planning is that a group of analysts generates simulation games for policy makers (see en.wikipedia.org/wiki/Scenario_planning). The games combine projected factors about the future, such as demographics, geography, military, political, and industrial information, with plausible alternative social, technical, economic, and political (STEP) trends, which are key driving forces. Scenario planning can include anticipatory thinking (futures) elements that are difficult to formalize, such as subjective interpretations of facts, shifts in values, new regulations, or inventions.

Balanced scorecard is a tool that assesses organizational progress toward strategic goals by measuring performance in a number of different areas. Originally proposed by Kaplan and Norton (1996) as an alternative to narrowly focused financial assessments, the balanced scorecard seeks more balance by measuring organizational performance in four areas: finance, customers' assessments, internal business processes, and learning and growth. For more information about the balanced scorecard, see en.wikipedia.org/wiki/Balanced_scorecard and Section 13.7.

Section 13.1 ▶ REVIEW QUESTIONS

1. What is strategy?
2. Describe the strategic planning process.
3. Describe the four phases of strategic planning.
4. Why is a cyclic approach to strategic planning required?
5. Describe four tools that can be used for strategic planning.

13.2 BUSINESS PLANNING IN E-COMMERCE

business plan
A written document that identifies a company's goals and outlines how the company intends to achieve the goals and at what cost.

One almost inevitable outcome of strategy setting is a business plan. A business plan is a written document that identifies the company's goals and outlines how the company intends to achieve those goals. Exhibit 13.5 shows a typical outline of a business plan. This outline follows the Online Tutorial ("An E-Business Plan Tutorial") at the book's Web site, where detailed information about each section of the outline is available.

BUSINESS PLAN FUNDAMENTALS

Business plans are written for a variety of purposes. The customary reason why a business needs a business plan is to acquire funding. Entrepreneurs in start-up companies use business plans to get funding from investors, such as a venture capitalist or a bank. An existing company may write a business plan to get funding from a bank, the financial markets, or a prospective business partner.

A second reason to write a business plan is to acquire nonfinancial resources. A prospective landlord, equipment supplier, or ASP may want to see a viable business plan before entering into a contract. Similarly, a business plan can be useful for recruiting senior management. Any person truly capable of leading a medium-sized or large business will want to see an organization's business plan before accepting the position.

Another purpose for writing a business plan is to obtain a realistic approach to the business. The process of writing the plan forces the business owner to think ahead, set achievable goals, seek out and analyze competitors, figure out how to reach target markets, anticipate problems, and compare projected revenue streams against realistic expense statements. As with strategy setting, the process, not the plan itself, increases the likelihood that the business will be a success.

EXHIBIT 13.5 Outline of a Business Plan

- **Executive summary.** The executive summary is a synopsis of the key points of the entire business plan. Its purpose is to explain the fundamentals of the business in a way that both informs and excites the reader.
- **Business description.** The business description describes the nature and purpose of the business and includes the firm's mission statement, goals, and value proposition and a description of the products and services it provides. The purpose of the business description is to objectively explain and justify the business idea in a positive and enthusiastic manner.
- **Operations plan.** The operations section of the business plan describes the inputs, processes, procedures, and activities required to create what products the business will sell or what services it will deliver.
- **Financial plan.** The financial plan estimates the monetary resources and flows that will be required to carry out the business plan. The financial plan also indicates when and by how much the business intends to be profitable. Finally, the financial statements (e.g., balance sheet, cash-flow statement) tell a lot about the entrepreneur in terms of business commitment and financial wherewithal to make the business a profitable success.
- **Marketing plan.** The central part of the marketing plan is the market analysis, which defines the firm's target markets and analyzes how the organization will position its products or services to arouse and fulfill the needs of the target markets in order to maximize sales. Other aspects of the marketing plan include pricing strategy, promotion plan, distribution plan, and a demand forecast.
- **Competitor analysis.** The competitor analysis (a) outlines the competitive strengths and weaknesses of rivals in the industry and (b) reveals the firm's competitive position in the marketspace.

A realistic approach also means that sometimes the most successful outcome of writing a business plan is a decision not to proceed. Researching and writing a plan can reveal the realities of tough competition, a too-small target market, or an income and expense statement that is awash in red ink. Many owners of failed start-ups would have saved considerable time, money, and heartbreak if a proper business plan had been done.

When to do a business plan? The most obvious time is when a new business is seeking start-up funds and other resources. However, a business plan may also be required if an existing company is planning to create a separate division, reengineer or restructure the existing company, or launch the company in a new direction. A plan also is required when the existing plan is reaching its use-by date. If the original plan set forth a 3-year plan and the business just celebrated its second birthday, it is time to write a new plan.

Several software packages are available for the creation of business plans (e.g., see bplans.com and planware.org). Insights and Additions 13.1 highlights the differences between a traditional business plan and an e-business plan.

BUSINESS CASE

A distinctive type of business plan is the business case. As described in the previous section, a business plan often is used when launching a new business. A business case is a business plan for a new initiative or a large, new project inside an existing organization. Its purpose is the same as with a business plan—to justify a specific investment of funds—but the audience is the company's board of directors and senior management, not an external funding agency. The business case helps clarify how the organization will use its resources by identifying the strategic justification ("Where are we going?"), technical justification ("How will we get there?"), operational justification ("When will we get there?"), and financial justification ("Why will we win?").

For example, a business case that describes how *business intelligence (BI)* will be used to improve business results should provide a description of BI-driven business improvement opportunities (BIOs). Each BIO comprises the following specific details: the targeted business process, how BI will improve that process, when BI will be used, what kind of BI is needed, who will use the BI, what units will use the BI, how improvement will be measured, and links (if any) to a balanced scorecard (Williams 2008).

business case
A business plan for a new initiative or large, new project inside an existing organization.

Insights and Additions 13.1 Putting the "E" in E-Business

How is an e-business plan different from any other business plan? First, it must be said that there are far more similarities than differences. A business is a business and a plan is a plan, so most of what one would expect to see in a business plan also will be in an e-business plan. Beyond adding an *e* to the title, what are some of the differences that make writing an e-business plan different from writing a business plan?

▶ **The Internet is unlike any other sales channel.** The Internet allows companies to distribute information at the speed of light and at almost zero cost, reach out to customers with both reach and range, introduce new and innovative business models, and reduce costs and generate savings. There are many, many more differences, as discussed elsewhere in this book. However, the Internet also increases customers' bargaining power; creates a more perfect information market, to the customer's benefit; and makes it easier for competitors to invade a company's marketplace. So the first, and biggest, difference in e-business planning is the need for the entrepreneur to recognize the different and unique capabilities of the Internet and to begin to think differently, and creatively, about the opportunities and problems the Internet presents.

▶ **The Internet is global.** Being on the Web means a business will be visible to an international audience. This introduces complexity for payment options (e.g., show prices in U.S. dollars or local currency?), distribution channels, Web site design, and the logistics of product returns.

▶ **Web storefronts never close.** Being on the Web means a store will be open 24/7. The e-business plan must account for this difference in Web hosting and customer service requirements.

▶ **E-commerce is conducted at Internet speed.** This means that Web site deployment must be planned in months, or even weeks, not years. Companies will lose first-mover advantage if they are unable to move at Internet speed, and e-business plan readers know that. Also, changes must be done quickly.

▶ **The Web allows greater opportunities for personalization of content, one-to-one marketing, and customer self-service.** A company must incorporate these into its e-commerce strategy, because its serious competitors certainly will.

▶ **The Internet facilitates serious customer relationship management.** Business has always been about "getting close to the customer," but that was in a world without the potential of personalization, one-on-one marketing, data mining, concurrent reach and range, and customer relationship management. The Internet, and the customer-oriented applications that the Internet makes possible, means that every e-business must totally focus on the customer.

In all these ways, and more, writing a business plan for an e-business is different, new, exciting, and difficult (see Online Tutorial T1).

As a special cases of a business plan, the content of a business case is similar to that of a business plan. One difference is that the business plan concentrates on the viability of a company, whereas a business case assesses both viability of individual projects and the fit of the initiative with the firm's mission and goals. A business case also will almost certainly have more operational detail and a justification that it is the best way for the organization to use its resources to accomplish the desired strategy. An example of a structure of a business case is shown in Exhibit 13.6. The Online Tutorial highlights other differences between a business plan and a business case.

With a firm foundation of organizational strategy and business planning in place, we now turn our attention to the details of e-commerce strategy.

Section 13.2 ▶ REVIEW QUESTIONS

1. What is a business plan?
2. List three situations that require a business plan.
3. How is an e-business plan different from a traditional business plan?
4. What is a business case? How is it different from a business plan?

13.3 E-COMMERCE STRATEGY: CONCEPTS AND OVERVIEW

What is the role of the Internet in organizational strategy? According to Ward and Peppard (2002), strategy setting begins with the business strategy—determining an organization's vision, mission statement, and overall goals (see Exhibit 13.7). Then the information systems

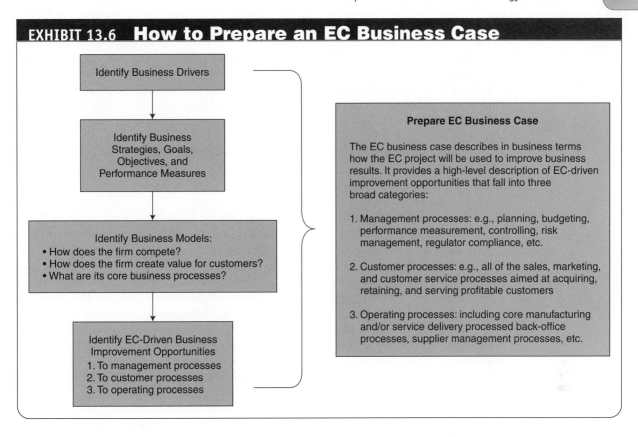

EXHIBIT 13.6 How to Prepare an EC Business Case

Identify Business Drivers

↓

Identify Business Strategies, Goals, Objectives, and Performance Measures

↓

Identify Business Models:
• How does the firm compete?
• How does the firm create value for customers?
• What are its core business processes?

↓

Identify EC-Driven Business Improvement Opportunities
1. To management processes
2. To customer processes
3. To operating processes

Prepare EC Business Case

The EC business case describes in business terms how the EC project will be used to improve business results. It provides a high-level description of EC-driven improvement opportunities that fall into three broad categories:

1. Management processes: e.g., planning, budgeting, performance measurement, controlling, risk management, regulator compliance, etc.

2. Customer processes: e.g., all of the sales, marketing, and customer service processes aimed at acquiring, retaining, and serving profitable customers

3. Operating processes: including core manufacturing and/or service delivery processed back-office processes, supplier management processes, etc.

(IS) strategy is set, primarily by determining what information and associated information systems are required to carry out the business strategy. The information and communications technology (ICT) strategy is decided based on how to deliver the information and information systems via technology. The EC strategy is a derivative of both the IS strategy and the ICT strategy. The solid downward pointing arrows in Exhibit 13.7 depict the top-down portion of the process. The broken line indicates possible bottom-up activities, which means that lower-level strategies cause adjustments in higher-level strategies.

The Internet impacts all levels of organizational strategy setting, as shown by the shaded boxes in Exhibit 13.7. Business strategists need to consider the Internet's role in creating or

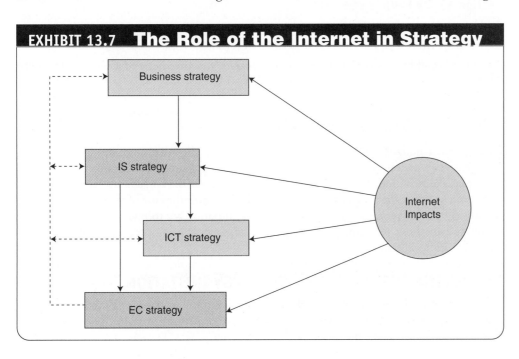

EXHIBIT 13.7 The Role of the Internet in Strategy

Business strategy

IS strategy

ICT strategy

EC strategy

Internet Impacts

innovating products, in product and service delivery, in supplier and customer relationships, and its impact on competition in the marketplace. Generally, strategic planners need to view the Internet as a complement to traditional ways of competing, not as a source of competitive advantage in and of itself (Porter 2001). IS strategists need to consider the Internet as a tool for collecting information and distributing it to where it is required. ICT planners will need to plan the integration of the Internet-based technologies into the existing ICT infrastructure. Thinking about and planning for the Internet should be subsumed into each of the four strategy levels.

Using the process just described, businesses continue to evolve their own e-commerce strategies, defined as the formulation and execution of a vision of how a new or existing company intends to do business electronically.

Consider the following two examples of e-strategies.

Example: China Southern Airlines. On March 2, 2006, China Southern Airlines announced a plan to improve its in-house e-ticketing system and cooperate with more online travel agencies and metasearch companies (per Zhuhai Flight Training Center 2006).

Example: Nike. On October 26, 2006, Nike created a position of vice president, global e-commerce, who reports directly to the company's president and CEO. The vice president is responsible for driving an integrated global e-commerce strategy for the Nike brand and Nike Inc. subsidiaries, including Converse and Cole Haan.

According to a press release (PRNewswire 2006), Nike's e-commerce sites represent an incredible opportunity for building deeper consumer connections and for supporting the overall growth of the Nike Inc. brand portfolio. The vice president will accelerate the company's efforts to create an integrated global e-commerce strategy across the company portfolio and deliver consistent and compelling brand experiences for consumers.

Nike has been a leader in creating unique personalized shopping experiences for consumers through innovative sites such as Nike iD, which gives consumers the opportunity to design their own Nike product. Nike also relaunched its global nikestore.com e-commerce site with new leading-edge technology. The changes in the store are designed to introduce better product descriptions, faster functionality, and enhanced customer service; they encompass the first major renovation of Nike's online store since its launch in 1999. The result is a new, more dynamic online shopping experience, in which the common conventions of e-commerce are adapted to the unique character of the Nike brand. The site offers more than 30,000 products.

The following sections explain in detail the process of building an e-strategy.

Section 13.3 ▶ REVIEW QUESTIONS

1. Describe the process of deriving an EC strategy.
2. Describe the role of the Internet in setting EC strategy.
3. How should business strategic planners consider the Internet and EC? IS strategists? ICT planners?

13.4 E-STRATEGY INITIATION

In the strategy initiation phase, the organization prepares the initial steps needed for starting the cycle, such as collecting information about itself, its competitors, and its environment. EC can make two fundamental contributions to the business: (1) facilitate value creation or value enhancement for company stakeholders and (2) lower the cost of providing goods and services to the marketplace. The steps in strategy initiation are to review the organization's vision and mission; to analyze its industry, company, and competitive position; and to consider various initiation issues.

REPRESENTATIVE ISSUES IN E-STRATEGY INITIATION

With company, competitor, and trend data in hand, the company faces a number of questions about its approach to and operation of its EC strategy that need to be explored prior to strategy formulation. These include the following.

Be a First Mover or a Follower?

The business, IT, and e-commerce worlds all have examples of companies that succeeded with first-mover advantage, companies that failed despite first-mover advantage, and late movers that are now success stories. Generally, the advantages of being first include an opportunity to make a first and lasting impression on customers, to establish strong brand recognition, to lock in strategic partners, and to create switching costs for customers. The risks of being a first mover include the high cost of pioneering EC initiatives, making mistakes, the chance that a second wave of competitors will eliminate a first mover's lead through lower cost and innovation, and the risk that the move will be too early. Although the importance of a speedy market entry cannot be dismissed, some research suggests that over the long run first movers are substantially less profitable than followers (Kalamas et al. 2006).

So what determines whether a first mover succeeds or fails? Rangan and Adner (2001) suggest that the following factors are important determinants of EC marketplace success: (1) the size of the opportunity (i.e., the first-mover company must be big enough for the opportunity, and the opportunity must be big enough for just one company); (2) the nature of the product (i.e., first-mover advantage is easier to maintain in commodity products in which later entrants have a hard time differentiating their product); and (3) whether the company can be the best in the market.

Born-on-the-Net or Move-to-the-Net?

Another key distinction in EC strategy at the initiation phase is whether the company is a born-on-the-Net or a move-to-the-Net business (also called brick-and-click or click-and-mortar). Born-on-the-Net and move-to-the-Net firms both start with substantial assets and liabilities that influence their ability to formulate and execute an e-commerce strategy (see Online File W13.3). However, the difference between success and failure is rarely the assets and liabilities on the company's strategy balance sheet but rather in the company's ability to capitalize on its strengths. For example, the customer, product, and market knowledge in the move-to-the-Net firm is worthless unless processes and systems are in place to acquire, store, and distribute this knowledge to where it is needed, and innovative management direction is required to recognize its use for competitive advantage in the marketplace. Similarly, whereas the lack of a logistics channel and value chain partnerships is a born-on-the-Net liability, it is frequently easier to build a brand-new Web-based value chain than to change an established one with flawed practices and processes.

Lonely Planet is a move-to-the-Net firm that is using its strengths—a superb reputation, a community of independent travelers, and an immense database of maps and travel information—to find new opportunities on the Internet (see Online File W13.4). Wal-Mart is attempting to leverage its physical presence and iconic brand name into a powerful move-to-the-Net strategy, as described in Chapter 3. Sears is trying to do it, too, but with less success than Wal-Mart.

Determining Scope

Inevitably, most e-strategy efforts are intended to grow the business. This can be done in a variety of ways, primarily by expanding the firm's appeal to a new set of customers, by increasing the size or scale of the business, or by broadening the scope through a wider range of products and services. Chapter 4 discusses expanding the customer base, and Chapter 14 discusses economies of scale. This section offers a few comments on the proper determination of scope.

When determining scope, the organization considers the number of products or services it sells. The most efficient way to expand an organization's scope is to introduce new products or services into new or existing markets without increasing production facilities or staff. This way, revenues and profits grow while production costs increase only slightly. This strategy is usually most effective when the expanded scope is consistent with the firm's existing core competencies and value proposition to its customers. For example, almost all of Google's expanding scope is based on its core competency in search technology.

Expanding scope as an e-strategy usually is less effective when it requires a large investment and when it threatens the existing value proposition. Sears discovered this when it expanded from a retail store into financial services and real estate. Neither strategy was profitable, and Sears eventually withdrew from these markets. In summary, the critical question that businesses contemplating an EC strategy that involves expanding products and services should ask is: What else do our customers want to buy in addition to the products and services we currently offer?

Have a Separate Online Company?

Separating a company's online operations into a new company makes sense when: (1) the volume of anticipated e-business is large, (2) a new business model needs to be developed apart from the constraints of current operations, (3) the subsidiary can be created without dependence on current operations and legacy systems, and (4) the online company is given the freedom to form new alliances, attract new talent, set its own prices, and raise additional funding. Barnes & Noble, Halifax in the United Kingdom (online banking), and the ASB Bank in New Zealand are a few examples of companies that have established separate companies or subsidiaries for online operations. The advantages of creating a separate company include reduction or elimination of internal conflicts; more freedom for the online company's management in pricing, advertising, and other decisions; the ability to create a new brand quickly (see the next section); the opportunity to build new, efficient information systems that are not burdened by the legacy systems of the old company; and an influx of outside funding if the market likes the e-business idea and buys the company's stock. The disadvantages of creating an independent division are that it may be very costly, risky, or both, and the new company will not benefit from the expertise and spare capacity in the business functions (marketing, finance, distribution) unless it gets superb collaboration from the parent company.

Have a Separate Online Brand?

A company faces a similar decision when deciding whether to create a separate brand for its online offerings. Generally, companies with strong, mature, international brands will want to retain and promote those brands online. Google has chosen extensions or variations of its strong brand name—Google Desktop, Google Print, Gmail, Google Maps—in introducing new products and services.

However, existing firms with a weak brand or a brand that does not reflect the intent of the online effort may decide to create a new brand. An analysis from an e-commerce strategic planning effort identified an opportunity to deliver an integrated e-commerce solution in the marketplace (see Case 13.2). To capitalize on this opportunity and retain its reputation, Axon created a new division and launched a new brand, Quality Direct, to distinguish the effort within the parent company.

CASE 13.2

EC Application

MEASURING PROFIT ON THE WEB

Axon (*axon.co.nz*) is an IT solutions company with locations in New Zealand's four largest cities. Axon's goal is "to be New Zealand's most recommended IT Services Company."

In 2002, as part of an examination of the success of its Quality Direct service, Axon issued a white paper that examined business profitability on the Web. Specifically the white paper listed four areas of potential profits from Web activities and the metrics that Axon used to assess the impact of the Web on business profits. This case provides a real example of a small business that is profiting from its Web-based delivery of services and has collected some quantitative data to demonstrate its EC success.

Metrics were applied in four areas. Here we describe each of the four areas, followed by some of the metrics (a partial list) Axon used to assess goal achievement.

Cost Avoidance and Reduction

Web technologies can enhance profitability by reducing or eliminating transaction costs (e.g., product purchase) or interaction costs (e.g., a meeting, a phone call). Cost avoidance and reduction happens through activities such as improved access to information, customer self-help, and error reduction.

(continued)

CASE 13.2   (continued)

The following metrics demonstrated cost avoidance and reduction by Axon:

▸ Selling costs were reduced by 40 percent for each dollar of margin generated.
▸ Call volume to sales support increased at less than 50 percent of the traditional rate.
▸ Warehouse space was reduced by 40 percent, while volume increased by 40 percent.
▸ Obsolete stock write-offs as percentage of revenue were reduced by 93 percent.

Customer Service Enhancements

Delivering information to customers on all aspects of their transactions helps make the product or service more visible. Increased visibility generates increased value from a customer's perspective.

The following metrics demonstrated customer service enhancements by Axon:

▸ Average days to delivery were reduced by 20 percent over 2 years.
▸ Satisfaction with the delivery process is consistently greater than 80 percent.

New Market Opportunities

New market opportunities include new services to existing clients, changing the value proposition for existing clients, and targeting new markets.

The following metrics demonstrated new market opportunities by Axon:

▸ Product revenue increased over 40 percent in the first 12 months of full operation.
▸ New customers were added at twice the rate that previously was being achieved.

New Media Options

"New media" includes improved communication, advertising, and marketing efforts through lower collateral costs, improved target marketing, subscriber lists, and sold advertising space.

The following metrics demonstrated the use of new media options by Axon:

▸ Cost per item for e-mail was less than 1 percent of the cost per item for postal mail.
▸ Response rate to e-mail was five times the response rate to postal mail.
▸ Expenditures on brochure design and production were reduced by 45 percent.

IT Best Investment Opportunities for 2005 and Beyond

The following were identified as the best EC-related investment opportunities for the future:

▸ Application management and access to applications
▸ Desktop and server management
▸ Information collaboration
▸ Mobile and convergence technologies
▸ Server and storage consolidation
▸ Service optimization

Sources: Compiled from Green (2002) and from *axon.co.nz* (accessed March 2009).

Questions

1. List four areas in which Axon demonstrates increased profitability through the use of the Web.
2. Describe the characteristics of the metrics listed here (e.g., financial, customer service, quantitative, time based).
3. What other metrics might apply? (Hint: Consult Chapter 14.)

STRATEGY IN THE WEB 2.0 ENVIRONMENT AND IN SOCIAL NETWORKING

Social networking technologies are the hottest applications in today's business environment. A 2007 study conducted by McKinsey & Company found that 75 percent of respondents (executives from global companies) plan to maintain or increase investments in Web 2.0 technologies in coming years. Similarly, Forrester reported that 24 percent of businesses would implement Web 2.0 software throughout 2008. The use of Web 2.0 tools and technologies to help employees, partners, suppliers, and customers work together to build networks of like-minded people and share information in the enterprise is called *Enterprise 2.0* (as reported by Miller 2007).

Plenty of employees are using Web 2.0 tools throughout enterprises. In particular, they create profiles and connect with one another in ways similar to LinkedIn, Facebook, and MySpace. Shuen (2008) offers four major reasons for why employees should use internal social networks: (1) quick access to knowledge, know-how, and know-who; (2) expansion of social connections and broadening of affiliations; (3) self-branding and expression of a personal digital identity and reputation; and (4) viral distribution of knowledge through referrals, testimonials, benchmarking, and RSS updating. Deloitte, IBM, and Best Buy are three early adopters of internal social networking. All three companies believe that the easier and faster connections among employees facilitate cross-division collaboration and greater innovation (Brandel 2007).

Consider the following examples of internal social networking:

▶ In January 2007, Deloitte created a business case for the social networking environment. Getting the support of Deloitte leadership and partnering with internal IT, communications, and knowledge management groups, the team launched the alpha version of D Street in June 2007. D Street shared some similar functions as Facebook (e.g., personal profile, group memberships, and blogs). Currently, all 46,000 employees are in the system.

▶ Beehive is a collaborative platform at IBM that emulates the physical work environment. For instance, employees can display personal items such as photographs and trophies. They can also chat about last night's game. The user population grew to 38,000 in its first 9 months, mainly through viral adoption. Adoption is the strongest in the areas of product management, human resources, talent management, and the global services consulting business.

▶ Best Buy implemented BlueShirt Nation (BSN) in 2006. The company's senior managers use the social network to harvest marketing ideas from store employees. The technology was promoted virally. Now all Best Buy's employees use BSN to exchange ideas and discuss company policies.

Miller (2007) suggests that companies should start small so that they can observe how people react to the tools, learn how to manage the process, and develop a social system. For instance, companies can start with a small internal project that addresses a real business problem around knowledge sharing. Blogs or wikis are self-contained tools with content management, structure, and tagging capability built right in. They can also start in one department by providing blogs to employees to share ideas around a particular project, such as customer development in sales, competitive analysis in marketing, and so forth. After the companies complete the internal "beta" project, they can expand the effort to include other Enterprise 2.0 tools, as well as to bring other departments onboard and even move outside the organization to involve customers, partners, and suppliers. For example, Dell first launched internal blogs before creating IdeaStorm, which is offered to external customers.

Marketers are increasingly using social networking tools in a wide range of activities, including advertising, public relations, customer service, and product development. For example, Brewtopia (brewtopia.com.au) initially invited 140 of its friends to describe their ideal beer. Within weeks, more than 10,000 people from over 20 countries joined the community and voted for their favorite beer's style, color, and alcohol content; the shape of the bottle; and the color printed on the label. In 2007, the company offered a platform for its customers to discuss and create their own beers.

Cookshack (cookshack.com) has implemented various forums for its customers to ask and answer questions about barbecue sauces, smokers and barbecue ovens, and cooking techniques. The online customer community saves the company money for freeing customer-service personnel for other work. At the same time, it creates a cohesive and loyal community of repeat customers who can be tapped for other purposes (e.g., to test new products). Although there are a number of successful examples, there is a lack of well-established Web 2.0 strategies.

Shenkan and Sichel (2007) suggest a top-down approach for marketers: start with a conceptual map that links a company's brand, industry, and customer characteristics with its core marketing activities that could benefit from the social network. Adopting this approach, companies can establish priorities, identify the most relevant initiatives, evaluate their potential business impact, and invest more heavily in the most promising ones. For example, marketers in industries where R&D is a competitive differentiator should focus on getting consumers involved in the product-development process.

Siteworx (2008) proposes an "outside-in" perspective in developing social networking strategies. Its four-part methodology includes the following steps:

1. Collect and analyze assumptions about the target audience and business objectives.
2. Validate assumptions through research, analysis, and testing.

3. Examine the current IT infrastructure and make key decisions regarding whether to upgrade the existing technology or build or buy a solution.

4. Plan the initiative.

A comprehensive guide to Web 2.0 strategy is provided by Shuen (2008). A strategic guide for m-commerce is provided by Gold (2009). For a guide on how to develop a business-aligned social media and social networking strategy, see ddmcd.com/managing-technology/how-to-develop-a-business-aligned-social-media-social-networ.html.

Section 13.4 ▶ REVIEW QUESTIONS

1. Describe the advantages, risks, and success factors that first movers face.
2. What are the advantages and disadvantages of creating a separate online company?
3. Why would an existing company want to create a new brand for its e-commerce initiative?

13.5 E-STRATEGY FORMULATION

The outcome of the strategy initiation phase should be a number of potential EC initiatives that exploit opportunities and manage threats in the business environment in light of corporate strengths and weaknesses. In the strategy formulation phase, the firm must decide which initiatives to implement and in what order. Strategy formulation activities include evaluating specific EC opportunities and conducting cost–benefit and risk analyses associated with those opportunities. Specific outcomes include a list of approved EC projects or applications, risk management plans, pricing strategies, and a business plan that will be used in the next phase of strategy implementation.

SELECTING EC OPPORTUNITIES

More productive strategy selection approaches can be used when compelling internal or external forces drive the strategy selection process. A problem-driven strategy may be best when an organization has a specific problem that an EC application can solve. For example, the use of forward e-auctions using e-auctioneers such as Liquidation.com (liquidation.com) may be the best solution to dispose of excess equipment. A technology-driven strategy can occur when a company owns technology that it needs to use. A market-driven strategy can occur when a company waits to see what competitors in the industry do. As noted earlier, this late-mover strategy can be effective if the company can use its brand, technology, superior customer service, or innovative products and strategies to overcome any lost first-mover advantage.

Most times, however, it is best to use a systematic methodology that determines which initiatives to pursue and when. The next section describes such an approach.

DETERMINING AN APPROPRIATE EC APPLICATION PORTFOLIO MIX

For years, companies have tried to find the most appropriate portfolio (group) of projects among which an organization should share its limited resources. The classic portfolio strategy attempts to balance investments with different characteristics. For example, the company would combine long-term speculative investments in new potentially high-growth businesses with short-term investments in existing profit-making businesses.

The BCG Model and an Internet Portfolio Map

One well-known framework of this strategy is the Boston Consulting Group's (BCG) growth-share matrix with its star, cash cow, wild card, and dog opportunities. In the 1970s, BCG created the popular "growth-share" matrix to assist corporations in deciding how to allocate cash among their business units and projects. The matrix has two dimensions: "Market growth rate," which can be low or high, and relative "market share," which can be low or high. This results in four cells: stars (high growth, high share), cash cows (high share, low growth), question marks (high growth, low share), and dogs (low growth, low share). The corporation would then categorize its business units (or projects) as stars, cash cows, question marks, and dogs, and allocate budgets accordingly, moving money from cash cows to stars and to question marks that had higher market growth rates, and hence higher upside potential (see en.wikipedia.org/wiki/Boston_Consulting_Group#BCG_growth-share_matrix for details).

Tjan (2001) adapted the BCG approach to create what he calls an "Internet portfolio map." Instead of evaluating market potential and market share, the Internet portfolio map is based on company fit and project viability, both of which can be either low or high. Various criteria, including market value potential, time to positive cash flow, time to implementation, and funding requirements, can be used to assess viability. Similarly, metrics such as alignment with core capabilities, alignment with other company initiatives, fit with organizational structure, and ease of technical implementation can be used to evaluate fit. Together, these create an Internet portfolio map (see Exhibit 13.8).

Each company will want to determine for itself the criteria used to assess viability and fit. Senior managers and outside experts evaluate each proposed EC initiative (e.g., a B2B procurement site, a B2C store, an enterprise portal) on each of these criteria, typically on a quantitative (e.g., 1 to 100) or qualitative (e.g., high, medium, low) scale. If some criteria are more important than others, these can be weighted appropriately. The scores are combined, and average fit and viability scores are calculated for each initiative. Initiatives in which there is high agreement on rankings can be considered with more confidence.

The various initiatives are then mapped onto the Internet portfolio map. If both viability and fit are low, the project is rejected. If both are high, the project is adopted. If fit is high but viability is low, the project is redesigned (to get higher viability). Finally, if the fit is low but the viability is high, the project is not adopted, or sold. (An example of this process is shown in Online File W13.5.) Senior management must also consider factors such as cost-benefit (discussed in Chapter 14) and risk (discussed next) in making the final decision about what initiatives get funded and in what order. However, the Internet portfolio map can be an invaluable guide for navigating an e-commerce strategy through uncharted waters.

RISK ANALYSIS AND MANAGEMENT

e-commerce (EC) risk
The likelihood that a negative outcome will occur in the course of developing and operating an electronic commerce strategy.

E-commerce (EC) risk is the likelihood that a negative outcome will occur in the course of developing and operating an e-commerce initiative. Risk on the Internet and in EC environments has special characteristics (Muncaster 2006), one of which is Internet security threats and vulnerabilities.

Mention e-commerce risk and most business professionals think of information security—the threat posed by hackers and negligent loss of data. This is the most obvious, but not the

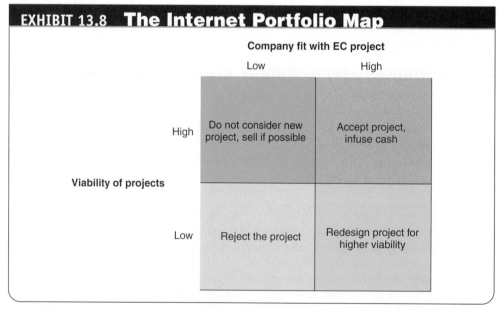

EXHIBIT 13.8 The Internet Portfolio Map

		Company fit with EC project	
		Low	High
Viability of projects	High	Do not consider new project, sell if possible	Accept project, infuse cash
	Low	Reject the project	Redesign project for higher viability

Sources: Compiled from Tjan, A. K. "Finally, a Way to Put Your Internet Portfolio in Order." *Harvard Business Review* (February 2001); Sons, J. "Resolving the Complexity Dilemma in E-Commerce Firms through Objective Organization." *Logistics Information Management* (January 2001); and authors' experience.

most threatening, aspect of EC risk. The most dangerous risk to a company engaged in e-commerce is business risk—the possibility that developing and operating an e-commerce strategy could negatively impact the well-being of the organization itself. Chapter 10 focuses on information security and its risks; here the emphasis is on business risk.

The first step in any risk assessment is risk analysis—identifying and evaluating the sources of risk. Deise et al. (2000), for example, list 15 sources of e-business risk: dependence on partners, competitive environment, operations, human resources, legal and regulatory, reputation, strategic direction, technology, security, culture, project management, governance, business process controls, tax, and currency exchange rate. Once sources of risk have been identified, the next step is risk assessment, namely to assess the potential damage. If it is large enough, we move to risk management—to put in place a plan that reduces the threat posed by the risk. Risk management involves taking steps to reduce the probability that the threat will occur, minimizing the consequences if it occurs anyway, or both. Many risk management strategies in the offline world also apply to e-commerce risk management. For example, commonly used control systems can mitigate risk factors in e-commerce sourcing. In other risk areas, new and innovative risk management strategies are necessary. For example, putting trust-generating policies and procedures in place can minimize customer-induced risk.

For risks involved in using Web 2.0 and social networking, see Chapter 9. Various methods can be used to conduct risk assessment (e.g., see Wheelen and Hunger 2003). A number of sources offer specific advice about analyzing and managing e-commerce risk (e.g., Minsky 2006).

Security Issues

According to Tennant Risk Services (2004), the following security issues need to be addressed in an EC strategy:

> ▶ Fraudulent and malicious acts committed by either employees or third parties against the company's computer systems
> ▶ Computer virus attacks that hinder or even close down the company's operations
> ▶ Accidental alterations to or destruction of electronic information and records
> ▶ Loss of intellectual property when trade secrets are copied or recorded
> ▶ Extortion
> ▶ Business interruption and extra expense caused by a computer virus or other malicious acts
> ▶ Accidental or malicious destruction of electronic information
> ▶ Costs to mitigate a covered loss
> ▶ Multimedia liability, such as libel, slander, invasion of privacy, infringement of copyright, plagiarism, and false advertising
> ▶ Liability for damage to a third-party's computer system

ISSUES IN STRATEGY FORMULATION

A variety of issues exist in strategy formulation, depending on the company, industry, nature of the applications, and so forth. This section discusses some representative issues.

How to Handle Channel Conflict

As discussed in Chapters 2 and 3, channel conflict may arise when an existing company creates an additional distribution channel online. Several options exist for handling channel conflict:

> ▶ Let the established distributors handle e-business fulfillment, as the auto industry is doing. Buyers can order online, or they can provide directions to distributors online.
> ▶ Provide online services to intermediaries (e.g., by building portals for them) and encourage them to reintermediate themselves in other ways.

> Sell some products only online, such as LEGO (lego.com) is doing. Other products may be advertised online but sold exclusively offline. Another example is the case of Brastemp (Chapter 12).

> Avoid channel conflict entirely by not selling online. In such a case, a company could still have an EC presence by offering promotion and customer service online, as BMW (bmw.com) is doing.

How to Handle Conflict Between the Offline and Online Businesses

In a click-and-mortar business, the allocation of resources between offline and online activities can create difficulties. Especially in sell-side projects, the two activities can be viewed as competitors. In this case, personnel in charge of offline and online activities may behave as competitors. This conflict may cause problems when the offline side needs to handle the logistics of the online side or when prices need to be determined. For example, Sears lessened this conflict by offering a sales commission to its retail stores on all online sales based on the postal code of the online customers.

Corporate culture, the ability of top management to introduce change properly, and the use of innovative processes that support collaboration will all determine the degree of collaboration between offline and online activities in a business. Clear support by top management for both the offline and online operations and a clear strategy of "what and how" each unit will operate are essential.

Pricing Strategy

Traditional methods for determining price are the cost-plus and competitor models. Cost-plus means adding up all the costs involved—material, labor, rent, overhead, and so forth—and adding a percentage mark-up as profit. The competitor model determines price based on what competitors are charging for similar products in the marketplace.

Pricing products and services for online sales changes these pricing strategies in subtle ways:

> **Price comparison is easier.** In traditional markets, either the buyer or, more often, the seller has more information than the other party, and this situation is exploited in determining a product's price. By facilitating price comparison, the Internet helps create what economists call a perfect market—one in which both the buyer and the seller have ubiquitous and equal access to information, usually in the buyer's favor. On the Internet, search engines, price comparison sites (e.g., mysimon.com, kelkoo.co.uk), infomediaries, and intelligent agents make it easy for customers to find who offers the product at the best price.

> **Buyers sometimes set the price.** Name-your-own-price models such as Priceline.com and auction sites mean that buyers do not necessarily just take the price; sometimes they make the price.

> **Online and offline goods are priced differently.** Pricing strategy may be especially difficult for a click-and-mortar company. Setting prices lower than those offered by the offline business may lead to internal conflict, whereas setting prices at the same level will hurt competitiveness.

> **Differentiated pricing can be a pricing strategy.** For decades, airline companies have maximized revenues with yield management—charging different prices for the same product. In the B2C EC marketplace, one-on-one marketing can extend yield management from a class of customer (e.g., buying an airline seat early or later) to individual customers. In the B2B EC marketplace, extranets with customized pricing pages present different prices to different customers based on purchasing contracts, the customer's buying history, and other factors. **Versioning**, which is selling the same goods but with different selection and delivery characteristics, is especially effective in selling digitized goods. For example, time-critical information such as stock market prices can be sold at a higher price if delivered in real time rather than with a 20-minute delay. As with all forms of differentiated pricing, versioning information is based on the fact that some buyers are willing to pay more to receive some additional advantage.

versioning
Selling the same good, but with different selection and delivery characteristics.

Internet technologies tend to provide consumers with easier access to pricing information, which increases their bargaining power. To remain competitive and profitable, sellers will have to adopt smarter pricing strategies. Specifically, businesses will have to look at ways of using the Internet to optimize prices, primarily through greater precision in setting prices, more adaptability in changing prices, and new ways of customer segmentation for differentiated pricing.

Section 13.5 ▶ REVIEW QUESTIONS

1. Describe how a company should *not* select EC applications.
2. Explain Tjan's Internet portfolio map.
3. List four sources of business risk in EC. What questions exemplify each source of risk?
4. Discuss three strategies for smarter pricing online.
5. How can a company handle channel conflict?

13.6   E-STRATEGY IMPLEMENTATION

The execution of the strategic plan takes place in the strategy implementation phase, in which detailed, short-term plans are developed for carrying out the projects agreed on in strategy formulation. Decision makers evaluate options, establish specific milestones, allocate resources, and manage the projects.

Typically, the first step in strategy implementation is to establish a Web team, which then initiates and manages the execution of the plan. As EC implementation continues, the team is likely to introduce changes in the organization. Thus, during the implementation phase, it also becomes necessary to develop an effective change management program, including the possibility of business process management.

In this section, we examine some of the topics related to this implementation process. Chapter 15 continues the implementation discussion with an overview of many of the practical considerations involved in launching an online business.

E-STRATEGY IMPLEMENTATION PROCESS

Create a Web Team

In creating a Web (project) team, the organization should carefully define the roles and responsibilities of the team leader, team members, the Webmaster, and the technical staff. The purpose of the Web team is to align business goals and technology goals and to implement a sound EC plan with available resources.

Every Web project, and every Web team, also requires a project champion. In his study of EC strategy in 43 companies, Plant (2000) found, "In every successful e-commerce project studied, a strong project champion was present in the form of a senior executive or someone in a position to demonstrate to a senior executive the potential added value such a project could bring to the organization" (pp. 34–35). Similarly, "top management championship" was identified as a critical factor for organizational assimilation of Web technologies. The **project champion** is the person who ensures that the project gets the time, attention, and resources required and defends the project from detractors at all times. The project champion may be the Web team leader or a senior executive.

project champion
The person who ensures the EC project gets the time, attention, and resources required and defends the project from detractors at all times.

Start with a Pilot Project

Implementing EC often requires significant investments in infrastructure. Therefore, a good way to start is to undertake one or a few small EC pilot projects. Pilot projects help uncover problems early, when the plan can easily be modified before significant investments are made.

General Motors' pilot program (GM BuyPower) is an example of the successful use of a pilot project. On its Web site, gm.com/vehicles, shoppers can choose car options, check local dealer inventory, schedule test drives, arrange financing, and get best-price quotes by e-mail or telephone. GM BuyPower started as a pilot project in four U.S. states before expanding to all states. Similarly, when Home Depot decided to go online in 2000 it started in six stores in Las Vegas, then moved to four other cities, and eventually went nationwide.

Allocate Resources

The resources required for EC projects depend on the information requirements and the capabilities of each project. Some resources—software, computers, warehouse capacity, staff—will be new and unique to the EC project. Even more critical for the project's success is effective allocation of infrastructure resources that many applications share, such as data-bases, the intranet, and possibly an extranet.

Manage the Project

A variety of tools can assist in resource allocation. Project management tools, such as Microsoft Project, assist with determining project tasks, milestones, and resource require-ments. Standard system design tools (e.g., data flow diagrams) can help in executing the resource-requirement plan.

STRATEGY IMPLEMENTATION ISSUES

There are many strategy implementation issues, depending on the circumstances. Here we describe some common ones.

Application Development

Implementation of an EC application requires access to the construction of the Web site and integration of the site with the existing corporate information systems (e.g., front end for order taking, back end for order processing). At this point, a number of decisions of whether to build, buy, or outsource various construction aspects of the application implementation process face the company. Some of these decisions include the following:

- Should site development be done internally, externally, or by a combination of internal and external development?
- Should the software application be built or will commercially available software be satisfactory?
- If a commercial package will suit, should it be purchased from the vendor or rented from an application service provider (ASP)? Should it be modified?
- Will the company or an external ISP (Internet service provider) host the Web site?
- If hosted externally, who will be responsible for monitoring and maintaining the infor-mation and system?

Each option has its strengths and weaknesses, and the correct decisions will depend on factors such as the strategic nature of the application, the skills of the company's technology group, and the need to move fast or not.

Outsource: What? When? To Whom?

Successful implementation of EC projects often requires careful considerations of outsourcing strategies, which involve: (1) evaluating when outsourcing should take place; (2) deciding which part(s) to outsource and which to keep in-house; and (3) choosing an appropriate vendor(s).

outsourcing
The use of an external vendor to provide all or part of the products and services that could be provided internally.

Outsourcing is generally defined as the process of contracting out the company's prod-ucts or services to another organization that agrees to provide and manage these products/ services for a set fee over a set period (Kern and Willcocks 2002). These services could be otherwise carried out in-house by the company's own employees. In the context of EC, outsourcing means the use of external vendors to acquire EC applications. Outsourcing deci-sions for organizations, both large and small, are often made during EC project implementa-tion. Large companies may choose outsourcing when they want to experiment with new EC technologies without a great deal of up-front investment. Outsourcing also allows large firms to protect their internal networks and to gain expert advice. Small firms with limited IT expertise and tight budgets also find outsourcing advantageous.

Depending on the availability of cutting-edge resources and facilities, organizations may decide to develop EC applications in-house or work with external vendors or consultants. A comparison of the in-house and outsourcing approaches is provided in Exhibit 13.9. Sometimes, after an evaluation of both approaches, a hybrid approach is taken to leverage the

EXHIBIT 13.9	In-House Development Versus Outsourcing	
Criteria	**In-House Development**	**Outsourcing**
Accessibility to the project	Greater	Limited
Knowledge of the systems and its development	More	Less
Retention of knowledge and skills in staff	Higher	Lower
Ownership cost	Higher	Lower
Self-reliance for maintenance, update, and expansion	Greater	Lower
Development times	Longer	Shorter
Experienced staff with technical know-how and specialized areas	Less	More

benefit of both. Organizations may choose to outsource part or all of the EC implementation process or keep parts of the process in-house. For example, a company may have an external ISP host a Web site that is developed internally.

ISPs, ASPs, and consultants are external vendors (business partners) that are commonly involved in EC application developments:

▶ ISPs offer Web site design, Web hosting, and maintenance service for a monthly or yearly fee. It can be more cost-effective to host Web sites with heavy traffic with an ISP.

▶ ASPs offer application development service. They write programs and lease them to clients. ASPs can be an attractive alternative for small businesses with small technology budgets.

▶ Consultants offer consulting services in various aspects (e.g., security, system integration) that aim to streamline and smoothen the EC implementation process.

Online Chapter 18 discusses in more detail many of these options—build or buy, in-house or outsource, host externally or internally.

Partners' Strategy

Another important issue is that many EC application developments involve business partners—ASPs, ERP vendors and consultants, and ISPs—with different organizational cultures and their own EC strategies and profit motives. A key criterion in choosing an EC partner is finding one whose strategy aligns with or complements the company's own.

When negotiating a partnership, the partner's goal is to make a profit, and it is the negotiator's responsibility to make sure that is not being done at the expense of the company's bottom line. One popular EC partner strategy is *outsourcing*, which is the use of an external vendor to provide all or part of the products and services that could be provided internally. For example, many firms in developed countries have found it advantageous to outsource call center functions offshore.

The bottom line here is that partnerships can be an effective way to develop and implement an EC strategy, but they require a realistic evaluation of the potential risks and rewards.

Business Alliances and Virtual Corporations

In the EC strategic planning process, a large-scale EC application that is too difficult or complex for one company to undertake alone, an idea that works best across the industry rather than within a single firm, or a strategy that requires a variety of competencies to implement may be identified. In these cases, an alliance may be formed with other businesses, perhaps even competitors.

One type of business alliance is a B2B e-marketplace. For example, Sears was one of the founding members of GlobalNetXchange (GNX). The purpose of GNX was to reduce procurement costs and product prices for its members while making the purchase process more efficient. Eventually Sears, Carrefour (a global retailer), Kroger (United States), Metro AG (Europe), Coles Myer (Australia), and others joined GNX. GNX later was expanded under the name Agent Rick (Chapter 5).

virtual corporation (VC)
An organization composed of several business partners sharing costs and resources for the production or utilization of a product or service.

Another form of business alliance is a virtual corporation (VC), an organization composed of several business partners sharing costs and resources for the production or utilization of a product or service. A virtual corporation typically includes several companies, each creating a portion of the product or service in an area in which it has a superior core competency (e.g., product development, manufacturing, marketing) or special advantage (e.g., exclusive license, low cost). VCs may be permanent (designed to create or assemble a broad range of productive resources on an ongoing basis) or temporary (created for a specific purpose and existing for only a short time).

co-opetition
Two or more companies cooperate together on some activities for their mutual benefit, even while competing against each other in the marketplace.

A particularly interesting type of business alliance is *co-opetition*. Co-opetition is a combination of the words *cooperate* and *competition*. It describes when two or more companies cooperate on some activities for mutual benefit, even while competing against each other in the marketplace. A global airline alliance, such as OneWorld or Star Alliance, is an example of co-opetition. Individually, the airlines compete against each other for passengers. However, when flights can be combined to save costs without compromising customer service, the airlines cooperate through the alliance. The most visible aspect of this is code-share flights, in which passengers who bought tickets from a number of different airlines fly together on the same flight. Through co-opetition, the airlines are reducing inefficiencies in their competing supply chains, and the result is an excellent example of strategic supply chain alignment.

Redesigning Business Processes and BPR

An internal issue many firms face at the implementation stage is the need to change business processes to accommodate the changes an EC strategy brings. Sometimes these changes are incremental and can be managed as part of the project implementation process. Sometimes the changes are so dramatic that they affect the manner in which the organization operates. In this instance, business process reengineering is usually necessary. Business process reengineering (BPR) is a methodology for conducting a one-time comprehensive redesign of an enterprise's processes. BPR may be needed for the following reasons:

business process reengineering (BPR)
A methodology for conducting a comprehensive redesign of an enterprise's processes.

▶ To fix poorly designed processes (e.g., processes are not flexible or scalable)
▶ To change processes so that they will fit commercially available software (e.g., ERP, e-procurement)
▶ To produce a fit between systems and processes of different companies that are partnering in e-commerce (e.g., e-marketplaces, ASPs)
▶ To align procedures and processes with e-services such as logistics, payments, or security

On its way to becoming an e-business, IBM instituted a comprehensive BPR initiative for several of the reasons cited previously. The results were dramatic improvements in IBM's global operations, as described in Online File W13.6.

business process management (BPM)
Method for business restructuring that combines workflow systems and redesign methods; covers three process categories—people-to-people, systems-to-systems, and systems-to-people interactions.

Business Process Management

The term business process management (BPM) refers to activities performed by businesses to improve their processes. While such improvements are hardly new, software tools called business process management systems have made such activities faster and cheaper. BPM systems monitor the execution of the business processes so that managers can analyze and change processes in response to analysis rather than just a hunch. BPM differs from BPR in that it deals not just with one-time change to the organization but rather long-term-consequences and repetitive actions. The activities that constitute business process management can be grouped into three categories: design, execution, and monitoring. For details, see en.wikipedia.org/wiki/business_process_management.

Section 13.6 ▶ REVIEW QUESTIONS

1. Describe a Web (project) team and its purpose.
2. What is the role of a project champion?
3. What is the purpose of a pilot project?
4. Discuss the major strategy implementation issues of application development, partners' strategy, business alliances, and BPR.
5. Describe BPM and the need for it in EC development.

13.7 E-STRATEGY AND PROJECT ASSESSMENT

The last phase of e-strategy begins as soon as the implementation of the EC application or project is complete. Strategy assessment includes both the continual assessment of EC metrics and the periodic formal evaluation of progress toward the organization's strategic goals. Based on the results, corrective actions are taken and, if necessary, the strategy is reformulated.

THE OBJECTIVES OF ASSESSMENT

Strategic assessment has several objectives. The most important ones are:

▶ Measure the extent to which the EC strategy and ensuing projects are delivering what they were supposed to deliver. If they are not delivering, apply corrective actions to ensure that the projects are able to meet their objectives.

▶ Determine if the EC strategy and projects are still viable in the current environment.

▶ Reassess the initial strategy in order to learn from mistakes and improve future planning.

▶ Identify failing projects as soon as possible and determine why they failed to avoid the same problems on subsequent projects.

Web applications often grow in unexpected ways, expanding beyond their initial plan. For example, Genentec Inc., a biotechnology giant, wanted merely to replace a homegrown bulletin-board system. It started the project with a small budget but soon found that the intranet had grown rapidly and had become very popular in a short span of time, encompassing many applications. Another example is Lockheed Martin, which initially planned to put its corporate phone directory and information about training programs on its intranet. Within a short time, it placed many of its human resources documents on the intranet as well, and soon thereafter, the use of the Web for internal information expanded from administrative purposes to collaborative commerce and partner relationship management (PRM) applications.

MEASURING RESULTS AND USING METRICS

Each company measures success or failure by a different set of standards. Some companies may find that their goals were unrealistic, that their Web servers were inadequate to handle demand, or that expected cost savings were not realized. Others may experience so much success that they have to respond to numerous application requests from various functional areas in the company.

Assessing EC is difficult because of the many configurations and impact variables involved and the sometimes intangible nature of what is being measured. However, a review of the requirements and design documents should help answer many of the questions raised during the assessment. It is important that the Web team develop a thorough checklist to address both the evaluation of project performance and the assessment of a changing environment. One way to measure a project's performance is to use metrics.

EC Metrics

A **metric** is a specific, measurable standard against which actual performance is compared. Metrics assist managers in assessing progress toward goals, communicating the strategy to the workforce through performance targets (Rayport and Jaworski 2004), and identifying where corrective action is required. Exhibit 14.1 (p. 632) lists a number of tangible and intangible metrics for various EC users, and a number of financial metrics are suggested by

metric
A specific, measurable standard against which actual performance is compared.

Maxwell (2006). An example of a company that has implemented a comprehensive EC metrics approach is Axon, as described in Case 13.2 (p. 600).

Corporate (Business) Performance Management and Balanced Scorecards

corporate (business) performance management (CPM, BPM)
Advanced performance measuring and analysis approach that embraces planning and strategy.

Corporate (business) performance management (CPM, BPM) is a closed-loop process that links strategy to execution in order to optimize business performance. The major steps of the process are:

1. Setting goals and objectives
2. Establishing initiatives and plans to achieve those goals.
3. Monitoring actual performance against the goals and objectives
4. Taking corrective action

It is a real-time system that alerts managers to potential opportunities, impending problems and threats, and then empowers them to react through models and collaboration. Strategic planning in CPM includes the following eight steps:

1. Conduct a current situation analysis.
2. Determine the planning horizon.
3. Conduct an environment scan.
4. Identify critical success factors.
5. Complete a gap analysis (performance vs. goals).
6. Create a strategic vision.
7. Develop a business strategy.
8. Identify strategic objectives and goals.

This provides an answer to the question: "Where do we want to go?" The CPM tells the company "how to get there." Then the firm monitors its performance, usually using the balanced scorecard. This answers the question "how are we doing?" Finally, by comparing actual performance to the strategy and goal, the company can decide "what needs to be done differently," and then act and adjust plans and execution.

Balanced Scorecards. Probably the best-known and most widely used performance management system is the balanced scorecard (see en.wikipedia.org/wiki/Balanced_scorecard and in Online File W13.7). Kaplan and Norton first articulated this methodology in their 1992 *Harvard Business Review* article "The Balanced Scorecard: Measures That Drive Performance." For an overview, see Kaplan and Norton (1996) and Person (2009), balancedscorecard.org/basics/bsc/html.

From a high-level viewpoint, the balanced scorecard is both a performance measurement and a management methodology that helps an organization translate its financial, customer, internal process, learning, and growth objectives and targets into a set of actionable initiatives. As a measurement methodology, the balanced scorecard is designed to overcome the limitations of systems that are financially focused. It does this by translating an organization's vision and strategy into a set of interrelated financial and nonfinancial objectives, measures, targets, and initiatives. The nonfinancial objectives fall into one of three perspectives:

▶ **Customer.** These objectives define how the organization should appear to its customers if it is to accomplish its vision.

▶ **Internal business process.** These objectives specify the processes the organization must excel at in order to satisfy its shareholders and customers.

▶ **Learning and growth.** These objectives indicate how an organization can improve its ability to change and improve in order to achieve its vision.

With the balanced scorecard approach, the term *balance* arises because the combined set of measures is supposed to encompass indicators that are:

▶ Financial and nonfinancial
▶ Leading and lagging

▶ Internal and external

▶ Quantitative and qualitative

▶ Short term and long term

Balanced Scorecards and Metrics. The balanced scorecard can be viewed as a method for evaluating the overall health of organizations and projects (including EC ones) by looking at metrics in four areas: finance, customer satisfaction, learning and growth for employees, and internal business processes (see Chapter 12 and en.wikipedia.org/wiki/balanced_scorecard). It is an advanced method for EC justification. Each of the four areas can be defined by organizational goals and corresponding measurable metrics (e.g., see Beasley et al. 2008).

Aligning Strategies and Actions. As a strategic management methodology, the balanced scorecard enables an organization to align its actions with its overall strategies and with risk analysis (e.g., see Beasley et al. 2008). It accomplishes this task through a series of interrelated steps. The specific steps that are involved vary from one book to the next. In our case, the process can be captured in five steps:

1. Identify strategic objectives for each of the perspectives (about 15 to 25 in all).

2. Associate measures with each of the strategic objectives; a mix of quantitative and qualitative should be used.

3. Assign targets to the measures.

4. List strategic initiatives to accomplish each of the objectives (i.e., responsibilities).

5. Link the various strategic objectives through a cause-and-effect diagram called a *strategy map*.

Strategy Maps

A **strategy map** delineates the relationships among the key organizational objectives for all four balanced scorecard perspectives. In this instance, the map specifies the relationships among seven objectives that cover four different perspectives. Like other strategy maps, this one begins at the top with a financial objective (i.e., exceed growth in key segments). This objective is driven by a customer objective (i.e., build strong customer relationships). In turn, the customer objective is the result of an internal (i.e., process) objective (i.e., identify/capture new business opportunities). The map continues down to the bottom of the hierarchy, where the learning objectives are found (e.g., develop key skills).

Each objective that appears in a strategy map has an associated measure, target, and initiative. For example, the objective "build strong customers relationships" might be measured by customer satisfaction. For this measure, we might be targeting a 15 percent improvement over last year's figure in our customer service index. One of the ways of accomplishing this improvement is by implementing the customer feedback database.

Overall, strategy maps represent a hypothetical model of a segment of the business. When specific names (of people or teams) are assigned to the various initiatives, the model serves to align the bottom-level actions of the organization with the top-level strategic objectives. When actual results are compared with targeted results, a determination can be made about whether the strategy that the hypothesis represents should be called into question or whether the actions of those responsible for various parts of the hypothesis need to be adjusted.

strategy map
A tool that delineates the relationships among the key organizational objectives for all four BSC perspectives.

Web Analytics

One large and growing area of EC strategy assessment is **Web analytics**, the analysis of clickstream data to understand visitor behavior on a Web site. (See Chapter 4 for details.) Web analytics begins by identifying data that can assess the effectiveness of the site's goals and objectives (e.g., frequent visits to a site map may indicate site navigation problems). Next, analytics data are collected, such as where site visitors are coming from, what pages they look at and for how long while visiting the site, and how they interact with the site's information. The data can reveal the impact of search engine optimization or an advertising campaign, the effectiveness of Web site design and navigation, and, most important, visitor conversion. Because the goal of most EC Web sites is to sell product, the most valuable Web

Web analytics
The analysis of clickstream data to understand visitor behavior on a Web site.

analytics are those related to step-by-step conversion of a visitor to a customer down the so-called purchase funnel.

Information about Web analytics is available from Sostre and LeClaire (2007), emetrics.org, and jimnovo.com. Two of many Web analytics tools include WebTrends (webtrends.com) and ClickTracks (clicktracks.com).

Section 13.7 ▶ REVIEW QUESTIONS

1. Describe the need for assessment.
2. Define metrics and describe their contribution to strategic planning.
3. Describe the corporate performance management approach to strategy assessment.
4. What is a balanced scorecard?
5. Define a strategy map.
6. Define Web analytics.

13.8 GLOBAL E-COMMERCE

Global electronic activities have existed for more than 25 years, mainly EFT and EDI in support of B2B and other repetitive, standardized financial transactions. However, these activities required expensive and inflexible private telecommunications lines and, therefore, were limited mostly to large corporations. The emergence of the Internet and technologies such as extranets and XML has resulted in an inexpensive and flexible infrastructure that can greatly facilitate global trade.

A global electronic marketplace is an attractive thrust for an EC strategy. "Going global" means access to larger markets, mobility (e.g., to minimize taxes), and flexibility to employ workers anywhere. However, going global is a complex and strategic decision process due to a multiplicity of issues. Geographic distance is the most obvious dimension of conducting business globally, but, frequently, it is not the most important dimension. Instead cultural, political, legal, administrative, and economic dimensions are equally likely to threaten a firm's international ambitions. This section briefly examines the opportunities, problems, and solutions for companies using e-commerce to go global.

BENEFITS AND EXTENT OF OPERATIONS

The major advantage of EC is the ability to do business at any time, from anywhere, and at a reasonable cost. These are also the drivers behind global EC, and there have been some incredible success stories in this area. For example:

- eBay conducts auctions in hundreds of countries worldwide.
- Alibaba.com (Chapter 5) provides B2B trading services to thousands of companies in hundreds of countries.
- Amazon.com sells books and hundreds of other items to individuals and organizations in over 190 countries.
- Small companies, such as ZD Wines (zdwines.com), sell to hundreds of customers worldwide. Hothothot (hothothot.com) reported its first international trade only after it went online; within 2 years global sales accounted for 25 percent of its total sales. By 2007, the company had over 10,000 hits per day (up from 500 in 1997), and its annual growth rate is over 125 percent, selling to customers in 45 countries.
- Major corporations, such as GE and Boeing, have reported an increasing number of out-of-the-country vendors participating in their electronic RFQs. These electronic bids have resulted in a 10 to 15 percent cost reduction and an over 50 percent reduction in cycle time.
- Many international corporations have considerably increased their success in recruiting employees for foreign locations when they use online recruiting (see xing.com and linkedin.com).

BARRIERS TO GLOBAL EC

Despite the benefits and opportunities offered by globalization, there are several barriers to global EC. Some of these barriers face any EC venture but become more difficult when international impacts are considered. These barriers include authentication of buyers and sellers (Chapter 10), generating and retaining trust (Chapter 4), order fulfillment and delivery (Chapter 11), security (Chapter 10), and domain names. Others are unique to global EC. We will use the culture, administration, geography, economics (CAGE) distance framework proposed by Ghemawat (2001) to identify areas in which natural or manmade barriers hinder global EC.

Cultural Issues

The Internet is a multifaceted marketplace made up of users from many cultures. The multicultural nature of global EC is important, because cultural attributes determine how people interact with companies, agencies, and each other based on social norms, local standards, religious beliefs, and language. Cultural and related differences include spelling differences (e.g., American vs. British spelling), information formatting (e.g., dates can be mm/dd/yy or dd/mm/yy), graphics and icons (e.g., mailbox shapes differ from country to country), measurement standards (e.g., metric vs. imperial system), the use of color (e.g., European Web sites tend to use brighter and bolder colors than U.S. sites do), protection of intellectual property (e.g., Chinese tolerance of copyright infringement has Confucian roots), time standards (e.g., local time zones vs. Greenwich Mean Time), styles of navigation (e.g., people in the Middle East tend to scan from right to left rather than left to right), and information density on homepages (e.g., Asian homepages tend to have a higher density of information than U.S. homepages).

Culture and Language Translation

Solutions for overcoming cultural barriers begin with an awareness of the cultural identities and differences in the target markets. Many companies are globalizing their Web sites by creating different sites for different cultural groups, taking into account site design elements, pricing and payment infrastructures, currency conversion, customer support, and language translation. Language translation is one of the most obvious and most important aspects of maintaining global Web sites. On average, the number of languages supported by the top 20 global Web sites (according to Yunker's annual ranking) is 45, and the site with the most supported languages is Wikipedia, with 250 (reported by Brandel 2007). Byte Level Research suggests that to reach 80 percent of the world's Internet users, a Web site should support at least 10 languages. The primary problems with language translation are speed and cost. It may take a human translator a week to translate a medium-sized Web site into another language. For large sites, the cost can be upwards of $500,000, depending on the complexity of the site and languages of translation, and it may take a long time. Some companies address the cost and time problems by translating their Web pages into different languages through so-called machine translators (a list of these translator programs is available in Online File W13.8). Recently, more and more companies are using globalization management systems or translation providers that keep previously translated content in a translation memory so as to cut costs and increase consistency. For an organization that is successfully using machine translation, see Online File W13.9.

Administrative Issues

One of the most contentious areas of global EC is the resolution of international legal issues. A number of national governments and international organizations are working together to find ways to avoid uncoordinated actions and encourage uniform legal standards.

An ambitious effort to reduce differences in international law governing EC is the United Nations Commission on International Trade Law (UNCITRAL) Model Law on Electronic Commerce. Its purpose is to "offer national legislators a set of internationally acceptable rules which detail how a number of legal obstacles to the development of e-commerce may be removed, and how a more secure legal environment may be created" (*e-Business World* 2000).

The Model Law has been adopted in some form in many countries and legal jurisdictions, including Singapore, Australia, Canada, Hong Kong, and some American states (e.g., California, Colorado, Iowa, and Kentucky).

International trade organizations, such as the World Trade Organization (WTO) and the Asia-Pacific Economic Cooperation (APEC) forum, have working groups that are attempting to reduce EC trade barriers in areas such as pricing regulations, customs, import/export restrictions, tax issues, and product specification regulations.

Geographic Issues and Localization

The geographic issues of shipping goods and services across international borders are well known. Barriers posed by geography differ based on the transportation infrastructure between and within countries and the type of product or service being delivered. For example, geographic distance is almost irrelevant with online software sales.

Example: Matrix Denture Systems International, Inc. Matrix Denture Systems International, Inc., provides its global customers with an advanced multilanguage e-commerce site (manta.com/coms2/dnbcompany_79gxs5). Revenues from Europe and Asia increased significantly since the introduction of the native languages.

Localization. Many companies use different names, colors, sizes, and packaging for their overseas products and services. This practice is referred to as *localization*. In order to maximize the benefits of global information systems, the localization approach should also be used in the design and operation of the supporting information systems. For example, many Web sites offer different language or currency options, as well as special content. Europcar (europcar.com), for example, offers portals in 118 countries, each with an option for 1 of 10 languages.

Economic Issues

Economic and financial issues encompassing global EC include government tariffs, customs, and taxation. In areas subject to government regulation, tax and regulatory agencies have attempted to apply the rules used in traditional commerce to electronic commerce, with considerable success. Exceptions include areas such as international tariff duties and taxation. Software shipped in a box would be taxed for duties and tariffs when it arrives in the country. However, software downloaded online relies on self-reporting and voluntary payment of tax by the purchaser, something that does not happen very often.

The key financial barrier to global EC is electronic payment systems. To sell effectively online, EC firms must have flexible payment methods that match the ways different groups of people pay for their online purchases. Although credit cards are used widely in the United Kingdom and the United States, many European and Asian customers prefer to complete online transactions with offline payments. Even within the category of offline payments, companies must offer different options depending on the country. For example, French consumers prefer to pay with a check, Swiss consumers expect an invoice by mail, Germans commonly pay for products only upon delivery, and Swedes are accustomed to paying online with debit cards.

Pricing is another economic issue. A vendor may want to price the same product at different prices in different countries in consideration of local prices and competition. However, if a company has one Web site, differential pricing will be difficult or impossible. Similarly, what currency will be used for pricing? What currency will be used for payment?

BREAKING DOWN THE BARRIERS TO GLOBAL EC

A number of international organizations and experts have offered suggestions on how to break down the barriers to global EC. Some of these suggestions include the following:

▶ **Be strategic.** Identify a starting point and lay out a globalization strategy. Remember that Web globalization is a business-building process. Consider what languages and countries it makes sense for the company to target and how the company will support the site for each target audience.

▶ **Know your audience.** Carefully consider the target audience. Be fully informed of the cultural preferences and legal issues that matter to customers in a particular part of the world.

▶ **Localize.** As much as practical and necessary, offer Web sites in national languages; offer different sites in different countries (e.g., "Yahoo! Japan" is at yahoo.co.jp); price products in local currencies; and base terms, conditions, and business practices on local laws and cultural practices.

▶ **Think globally, act consistently.** An international company with country Web sites managed by local offices must make sure that areas such as brand management, pricing, corporate information, and content management are consistent with company strategy.

▶ **Value the human touch.** Trust the translation of the Web site content only to human translators, not machine translation programs. Involve language and technical editors in the quality assurance process. One slight mistranslation or one out-of-place graphic can turn off customers forever.

▶ **Clarify, document, explain.** Pricing, privacy policies, shipping restrictions, contact information, and business practices should be well documented and located on the Web site and visible to the customer. To help protect against foreign litigation, identify the company's location and the jurisdiction for all contract or sales disputes.

▶ **Offer services that reduce barriers.** It is not feasible to offer prices and payments in all currencies, so link to a currency exchange service (e.g., xe.com) for the customer's convenience. In B2B e-commerce, be prepared to integrate the EC transaction with the accounting/finance internal information system of the buyer.

Section 13.8 ▶ REVIEW QUESTIONS

1. Describe globalization in EC and the advantages it presents.
2. Describe the major barriers to global EC in each dimension of the CAGE framework.
3. What can companies do to overcome the barriers to global EC?

13.9 E-COMMERCE IN SMALL AND MEDIUM-SIZED ENTERPRISES

Some of the first companies to take advantage of Web-based electronic commerce were small and medium-sized enterprises (SMEs). While larger, established, tradition-bound companies hesitated, SMEs moved onto the Web because they realized there were opportunities in marketing, business expansion, business launches, cost-cutting, and tighter partner alliances. Some examples are virtualvine.com, hothothot.com, and philaprintshop.com.

SMEs consider the Internet to be a valuable business tool. According to a 2004 survey by Interland (*eMarketer* 2004), 28 percent of small businesses expect more than three-quarters of their annual sales to come from the Internet. And it isn't only online sales that are being used to measure success. Although one-third of respondents measure site success by sales, almost half (47%) measure site success based on measures such as customer comments about the site and the volume of site traffic.

However, many SMEs have found it difficult to formulate or implement an EC strategy, mainly because of low use of EC and IT by customers and suppliers, lack of knowledge or IT expertise in the SME, and limited awareness of the opportunities and risks. Exhibit 13.10 provides a more complete list of major advantages and disadvantages of EC for SMEs. For critical success factors for SMEs, see Online File W13.10.

When analyzing e-commerce for SMEs when integration or use of RFID or XML may be necessary, one should distinguish between B2C, which may be simple, and B2B, which may be complex when the SME is a supplier to a large company.

EXHIBIT 13.10 Advantages and Disadvantages of EC for Small and Medium-Sized Businesses

Advantages/Benefits	Disadvantages/Risks
• Inexpensive sources of information. A Scandinavian study found that over 90 percent of SMEs use the Internet for information search (OECD 2001). • Inexpensive ways of advertising and conducting market research. Banner exchanges, newsletters, chat rooms, and so on are nearly zero-cost ways to reach customers. • Competitor analysis is easier. The Scandinavian study found that Finnish firms rated competitor analysis third in their use of the Internet, after information search and marketing. • Inexpensive ways to build (or rent) a storefront. Creating and maintaining a Web site is relatively easy and cheap (see Chapter 16). • SMEs are less locked into legacy technologies and existing relationships with traditional retail channels. • Image and public recognition can be generated quickly. A Web presence makes it easier for a small business to compete against larger firms. • An opportunity to reach worldwide customers. No other medium is as efficient at global marketing, sales, and customer support. • Other advantages for SMEs include increased speed of customer payments, closer ties with business partners, reduced errors in information transfer, lower operating costs, and other benefits that apply to all businesses.	• Lack of financial resources to fully exploit the Web. A transactional Web site may entail relatively high up-front fixed costs in terms of cash flow for an SME. • Lack of technical staff or insufficient expertise in legal issues, advertising, etc. These human resources may be unavailable or prohibitively expensive to an SME. • Less risk tolerance than a large company. If initial sales are low or the unexpected happens, the typical SME does not have a large reserve of resources to fall back on. • When the product is not suitable or is difficult for online sales (e.g., experiential products such as clothes or beauty products; perishable products, such as certain foods), the Web opportunity is not as great. • Reduced personal contact with customers represents the dilution of what is normally a strong point for a small business. • Inability to afford entry to or purchase enough volume to take advantage of digital exchanges.

Example: How SMEs Are Using E-Commerce in Australia. According to Fisher et al., (2007), 57 percent of small business in Australia use a Web site to promote their business. Having an effective Web site is an important step for small business owners moving toward e-commerce. The researchers suggest that once a business has a clear online strategy through a Web site, they are more likely to move to e-commerce. Although many small business owners have a business strategy, it is often the case that this strategy does not include their Web presence. The researchers identified elements that are important for small business owners developing an e-strategy. The research indicates that many owners see their Web sites mainly as an advertising medium and only few are ready for the move to actual selling and other e-commerce activities. Identifying the level of maturity of a small business owner's e-strategy however can help us understand how prepared a small business owner is to move to e-commerce. For another example of successful implementation of an EC strategy see Case 13.3.

SUPPORTING SMES

SMEs have a variety of support options. Almost every developed country in the world has a government agency devoted to helping SMEs become more aware of and able to participate in electronic commerce (e.g., sba.gov, business.gov.au).

Vendors realized the opportunity represented by thousands of businesses going online, and many have set up a variety of service centers that typically offer a combination of

CASE 13.3
EC Application
NETWORX EVENTS USES E-COMMERCE

Networx Events (*networxevents.com.au*) is a relatively new, small business (two full-time and one part-time staff member) that arranges professional events in Melbourne and Sydney, Australia. Networx's founder, Kimberly Palmer, started by sending e-mail invitations to 20 of her friends and colleagues. The mailing list grew rapidly, and orders for tickets exploded. This required a sophisticated and secure transaction-enabled ticketing system. By 2004, sales over the Internet reached AU$140,850, for a gross profit of $100,350. The system also saved $3,240 on reduced postage, telephone calls, and so on. The initial investment was only $13,100, and the operating expenses $4,040. Thus, the system net profit was $86,450, an amazing return on the investment (see more on ROI calculations in Chapter 14). The system also provides CRM and payment arrangement.

Here is how the ticket-purchasing process works:

1. Prospects "opt-in" to receive e-mail invitations to future events (permission e-mail, Chapter 4).
2. Personalized invitations are e-mailed to the opt-in database of recipients.
3. If accepting, the recipient fills out an online form to register for the event.
4. Once booking details are confirmed, the recipient fills in credit card details (if it is not stored already).
5. The recipient uses a credit card to pay via a Secure Socket Layer payment system (Chapter 11).
6. Upon successful transmission, the e-ticket and receipt are automatically returned to the recipient via e-mail.

For a small business, it made sense to outsource for the technology involved in the process. Invitee and member contact details are stored in a third-party database. E-mails are delivered via an ASP on a cost per e-mail basis. The Eventix (*eventix.com.au*) ticketing system provides the ticketing, e-mail, and payment component. In addition to the setup cost, Networx pays a percentage of its ticket price to the operator.

The ASP model reduces up-front costs. Networx has avoided much of the negative publicity surrounding spam due to careful adherence to its privacy policy. Networx has always sought permission to send e-mails and, therefore, was not obligated to make any major changes once the Australian Government's Spam Act was introduced in April 2004. However, Networx has always promoted the notion of "forwarding" invitations to other friends and colleagues (viral marketing, Chapter 4), which does not contravene the current Spam Act requirements.

Networx Events plans to expand in both territory and range. It is about to launch its first franchise in Queensland—a move set to be replicated in other territories while expanding from marketing into entrepreneurship and other vertical professions. Both of these plans will continue to be underpinned by opt-in e-mail, electronic customer relationship management, and online ticketing infrastructures.

Sources: Compiled from *networxevents.com.au* (accessed February 2009), Victoria Online (2007), and APT Strategies (2007).

Questions

1. What were the drivers of e-commerce in this case?
2. Discuss the strategy of dealing with technological issues.
3. Discuss the strategies of permission and viral marketing.
4. Does the planned expansion make sense?

---

free information and fee-based support. Examples are IBM's Small Business Center (ibm.com/businesscenter) and Microsoft's Small Business Center (microsoft.com/smallbusiness). Professional associations, Web resource services (e.g., smallbusiness.yahoo.com, workz.com), and small businesses that are in the business of helping other small businesses go online sponsor other small business support centers. For more on e-commerce barriers for SMEs, see Sharma (2006).

SMEs and Social Networks

Social network sites are growing in popularity across the board, so it is no surprise that SMEs also view social networking as a means to improve customer relationships, build community, and create feedback loops regarding their products and services.

Social networking sites are a particularly good fit for smaller businesses because SMEs often do not have a peer group nearby with which to discuss relevant topics. On the Internet, SMEs would turn to a community site catering to small businesses that provides them with access to peers, information on starting up, and advice (e.g., linkedin.com/talkbiznow.com/zaabiz.com).

In addition to using these sites to make contacts and get advice (e.g., at LinkedIn), they can be very useful in a B2B context as a way to build relationships with partners or build contact networks with other small businesses.

It has always been the case that business success is intimately linked to how well an organization taps into its relationships across employees, customers, partners, and suppliers. Social networking is just a means to that end—it helps humanize the organization and enables people to establish relationships and participate from a community sense.

Although there is no doubt that the use of social networking among small businesses will grow, managing expectations is key. SMEs have to live up to the anticipated outcomes people have when they participate in such social networks; it must be bidirectional. If it seems like just another marketing or PR ploy, or if the company exploits the community, then the results will be worse than having not participated at all. For more details and statistics, see Maddox (2008).

Section 13.9 ▶ REVIEW QUESTIONS

1. What are the advantages or benefits of EC for small businesses?
2. What are the disadvantages or risks of EC for small businesses?
3. What are the CSFs for small businesses online?
4. Relate SMEs to social networks.

MANAGERIAL ISSUES

Some managerial issues related to this chapter are as follows.

1. **What is the strategic value of EC to the organization?** Management needs to understand how EC can improve marketing and promotions, customer services and sales, and the supply chain and procurement processes. More significantly, the greatest potential of EC is realized when management views EC from a strategic perspective, not merely as a technological advancement. Management should determine the primary goals of EC, such as new market creation, cost avoidance and reduction, and customer service enhancement.

2. **What is the scope of e-business planning?** Planning e-business entails deciding the scope of EC activities and their priority to encompass marketing, procurement, operations, process innovation, information technology, and all other areas of the business. The synergy between online and offline channels should be maximized, while the issue of channel conflict should be coped with strategically. Strategy is ultimately the responsibility of senior management. But participation in setting an e-commerce strategy is something that should happen at all levels in all areas of the organization because e-business is related to the entire business.

3. **How to relate the EC activities with business objectives and metrics?** Companies first must choose objectives and design appropriate metrics to measure the goals and actual achievement. The companies need to exercise this with caution because the metrics may accidentally lead employees to behave in the opposite direction of the intended objectives. The balanced scorecard is a popular framework adopted to define objectives, establish performance metrics, and then map them. EC planning needs to identify what the role of EC is in achieving the goals in BSC metrics.

4. **Should the dot-com activities be spun off as a separate company?** This is a debatable issue. Sometimes it is useful in eliminating conflicts of prices and strategy. Also, using the spin-off as an IPO can be rewarding. Lotte Department Store in Korea has spun off Lotte.com because of its unique growth. However, it created the *lotteshopping.com* site to assist traditional shopping. In other cases, the spin-off can create problems and administrative expenses. Wal-Mart and Barnes and Noble have suffered from the spin-offs and have merged them into the offline part of their companies.

5. **How should the e-business scope evolve?** As Amazon.com experienced, a company may handle a certain item in the beginning stage. But the number of items will expand to include many kinds. As the scope of items expands, the order fulfillment plan has to evolve accordingly considering the alliance strategy with partners who have strong sourcing capability. The key competitors will be changed as the scope of business evolves. Management has to envision the prospect of e-business that can create justifiable revenue and profit so that investors can join the funding and patiently wait. The community in the social network needs to be linked with the revenue creation eventually.

6. **What are the benefits and risks of EC?** Strategic moves have to be carefully weighed against potential risks. Identifying CSFs for EC and doing a cost–benefit analysis should not be neglected. Benefits can be derived not only from the adoption of EC, but also from the reengineering of traditional business process. Benefits often are hard to quantify,

especially because gains tend to be strategic. In such an analysis, risks should be addressed with contingency planning (deciding what to do if problems arise).

7. **Why do we need an EC planning process?** A strategic plan is both a document and a process. Dwight D. Eisenhower, former U.S. president, once said "Plans are nothing, planning is everything." A planning process that includes management, employees, business partners, and other stakeholders not only produces a planning document that will guide the business into the future but also achieves buy-in among the participants about where the company is going and how it intends to get there. The same can be said for e-business planning—the process is as important as the plan itself.

8. **How can EC go global?** Going global with EC is a very appealing proposition, but it may be difficult to do, especially on a large scale. We need to identify what are the barriers to globalization such as culture, language, and law as well as customers and suppliers. The e-business needs to decide on a localization strategy. Some companies, such as eBay, acquire or establish local companies to support local customers, whereas other companies, such as Amazon.com, only support the English site. In B2B, one may create collaborative projects with partners in other countries.

9. **How to manage the EC project?** Forming an effective team is critical for EC project success. The team's leadership, the balance between technical and business staff, getting the best staff representation on the team, and having a project champion are essential for success. Reconciling the business objectives and system design is critical. IT sourcing needs to be considered, particularly for SMEs.

SUMMARY

In this chapter, you learned about the following EC issues as they relate to the learning objectives:

1. **The strategic planning process.** Four major phases compose this cyclical process: initiation, formulation, implementation, and assessment. A variety of tools are available to carry out this process.

2. **Writing a business plan and a business case.** A business plan is an essential outcome of a strategic planning process. Writing the business plan may produce more significant outcomes than the plan itself. The purpose of the plan is to describe the operation of the business, and its content includes revenue sources, business partners, and trading procedures. A business case is a distinctive type of business plan. It refers to a business plan for a new initiative or large, new project inside an existing organization.

3. **The EC strategic process.** Considering e-commerce in strategy development does not radically change the process, but it does impact the outcome. Move-to-the-Net firms must approach the process differently than born-on-the-Net firms, but both types of firms must recognize the way electronic technologies, such as the Internet, make an e-difference. Because of the comprehensiveness of EC, formal strategic planning is a must.

4. **E-strategy initiation and formulation.** The strategy initiation phase involves understanding the company, the industry, and the competition. Companies must consider questions such as "Should we be a first mover?" "Should we go global?" and "Should we create a separate company or brand?" With the proliferation of the Web 2.0 tools, companies should also consider strategies related to Web 2.0 and social networking. In strategy formulation, specific opportunities are selected for implementation based on project viability, company fit, cost–benefit, risk, and pricing.

5. **E-strategy implementation and assessment.** Creating an effective Web team and ensuring that sufficient resources are available initiate the implementation phase. Other important implementation issues are whether to outsource various aspects of development and the need to redesign existing business processes. Immediately after implementation, assessment begins. Metrics provide feedback, and management acts by taking corrective action and reformulating strategy, if necessary.

6. **Issues in global EC.** Going global with EC can be done quickly and with a relatively small investment. However, businesses must deal with a number of different issues in the cultural, administrative, geographic, legal, and economic dimensions of global trading.

7. **Small and medium-sized businesses and EC.** Depending on the circumstances, innovative small companies have a tremendous opportunity to adopt EC with little cost and to expand rapidly. Being in a niche market provides the best chance for small business success, and a variety of Web-based resources are available that small and medium-sized business owners can use to help ensure success.

KEY TERMS

QUESTIONS FOR DISCUSSION

1. How would you identify competitors for a small business that wants to launch an EC project?

2. How would you apply Porter's five forces and Internet impacts in Exhibit 13.3 to the Internet search engine industry?

3. Why must e-businesses consider strategic planning to be a cyclical process?

4. How would you apply the SWOT approach to a small, local bank that is evaluating its e-banking services?

5. Discuss how writing an e-business plan differs from writing a traditional business plan.

6. Offer some practical suggestions as to how a company can include the impact of the Internet in all levels of planning.

7. Explain the logic of Tjan's Internet portfolio map.

8. Amazon.com decided not to open physical stores, whereas First Network Security Bank (FNSB), which was the first online bank, opened its first physical bank in 1999. Compare and discuss the two strategies.

9. Discuss the pros and cons of going global with a physical product.

10. For each part of the CAGE framework, briefly discuss one barrier that may negatively impact e-commerce companies doing business globally.

11. Find some SME EC success stories and identify the common elements in them.

INTERNET EXERCISES

1. Survey several online travel agencies (e.g., travelocity.com, orbitz.com, cheaptickets.com, priceline.com, expedia.com, bestfares.com, and so on) and compare their business strategies. How do they compete against physical travel agencies? (See Chapter 18.)

2. Enter digitalenterprise.org and go to Web analytics. Read the material on Web analytics and prepare a report on the use of Web analytics for measuring advertising success.

3. Check the music CD companies on the Internet (e.g., cduniverse.com, musica.co.uk). Do any companies focus on specialized niche markets as a strategy?

4. Enter ibm.com/procurement and go to the e-procurement section. Prepare a report on how IBM's Supplier Integration Strategy can assist companies in implementing an EC strategy.

5. Compare the following search engines: google.com, search.yahoo.com, search.ask.com, and mooter.com. Conduct a comparative search (i.e., search for the same term at each site), learn more about how each search engine works (e.g., click on "about us" or similar link), and look for comparative articles at Web sites such as searchenginewatch.com. Consider the strengths and weaknesses of each site, when one would be more useful than another, and what special features distinguish it in the search engine marketplace. Prepare a report based on your findings.

6. One of the most global companies is Amazon.com (amazon.com). Find stories about its global

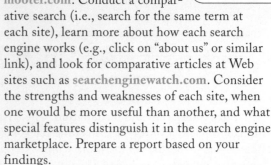

strategies and activities (try google.com and forbes.com). What are the most important lessons you learned?

7. Visit business.com/guides/startup and find some of the EC opportunities available to small businesses. Also, visit the Web site of the Small Business Administration (SBA) office in your area. Summarize recent EC-related topics for SMEs.

8. Enter alloy.com and bolt.com. Compare the sites on functionality, ease of use, message boards, homepage layout, and so on. Prepare a report based on your findings.

9. Find out how Web sites such as tradecard.com facilitate the conduct of international trade over the Internet. Prepare a report based on your findings.

10. Use a currency conversion table (e.g., xe.com/ucc) to find out the exchange rate of US$100 with the currencies of Brazil, Canada, China, India, Sweden, the European Union, and South Africa.

11. Conduct research on small businesses and their use of the Internet for EC. Visit sites such as microsoft.com/smallbusiness/hub.mspx and uschamber.org. Also, enter google.com or yahoo.com and type "small businesses + electronic commerce." Use your findings to write a report on current small business EC issues.

12. Enter businesscase.com and review its products. What are the benefits of case builders to people conducting e-commerce strategy development?

13. Enter advisorzones.com/adv/e-commerceAdvisor. Find the services provided for areas related to this chapter. Write a summary.

14. Enter languageweaver.com and locate its product for language translation for multinational corporations. Write a report.

TEAM ASSIGNMENTS, PROJECTS, AND CLASS DISCUSSIONS

1. Have three teams represent the following units of one click-and-mortar company: (1) an offline division, (2) an online division, and (3) top management. Each team member represents a different functional area within the division. The teams will develop a strategy in a specific industry (a group of three teams will represent a company in one industry). Teams will present their strategies to the class.

2. The relationship between manufacturers and their distributors regarding sales on the Web can be very strained. Direct sales may cut into the distributors' business. Review some of the strategies available to handle such channel conflicts. Each team member should be assigned to a company in a different industry. Study the strategies, compare and contrast them, and derive a proposed generic strategy.

3. Each team must find the latest information on one global EC issue (e.g., cultural, administrative, geographic, economic). Each team will offer a report based on their findings.

4. Survey google.com and isworld.org to find out about EC efforts in different countries. Assign a country or two to each team. Relate the developments to each country's level of economic development and to its culture.

5. Enter strassmann.com and find 10 entries related to e-strategy (including videos). Prepare summaries of them relating to this chapter.

6. Compare the services provided by Yahoo!, Microsoft, and Website Pros Inc. to SMEs in the e-commerce area. Each team should take one company and make a presentation.

7. Address the following topics in a class discussion:

   a. Should a small business be on a social network (such as Facebook)?

   b. Is Amazon eBay's biggest challenge? (See Ackerman 2008.)

Closing Case

PIERRE LANG EXPANDS INTO EASTERN EUROPE

Pierre Lang Europe (*pierrelang.com*) sells designer jewelry throughout Western Europe. Its traditional business model was to sell earrings, pendants, necklaces, and other jewelry through the firm's 5,500 sales representatives. When Pierre Lang decided to expand into Eastern Europe, the firm decided it needed to change this business model and the underlying information systems and business processes.

The company knew it was losing business because it was unable to keep track of customers and it did not have direct contact with them. If sales representatives left the company for any reason, they would take their customers with them. Pierre Lang Europe wanted more than sales from its customers, it wanted customer relationships for follow-on sales and customer support.

Like many companies expanding globally, Pierre Lang also anticipated that this expansion could double its revenues and order volume. The company needed better information about its finances, improved control of its order process, and a system that could handle the multiple legal and language requirements of doing business in many different countries.

Pierre Lang selected mySAP after evaluating several competing solutions. Installation began in July 2003; early rollout projects were in place by November; and financial and controlling capabilities went live in all company locations in January 2004.

Today, Pierre Lang uses country-specific versions of mySAP to handle invoicing, tax, language, and fiscal issues. France, for example, has unique requirements for tracking the import and export of gold and silver. "Lots of small things like that have to be considered because they're vital for Pierre Lang. It has to work perfectly in every country, so they have to know whom they will charge what, and do that automatically," says Rudolf Windisch, one of Pierre Lang's consulting partners on this project. "They also have to deal with all the tax issues, which vary considerably from one country to another. There are no homogeneous tax systems in Europe."

Pierre Lang expects to increase the accuracy of its information and eliminate the need for manual transfers of tax data to develop reports. Executives also anticipate decreased inventory costs through improved material disposition as well as better information about sales efforts and costs that will lead to improved forecasting and planning.

As noted in this chapter, expanding regionally or globally can have a dramatic impact on a company's bottom line but only if it is prepared to deal with the heterogeneous legal and financial systems in different countries. Pierre Lang knew this and met the challenge.

To safeguard its multinational enterprise network, the company uses an integrated network security platform (from Fortinet). The system protects both the headquarters in Vienna and 65 sales offices throughout Europe. The centrally managed system protects every remote user. The system is updated in real time.

Sources: SAP AG (2005) and Fortinet (2005).

Questions

1. Why was it necessary for Pierre Lang to look at fundamental changes in its business model and information systems?

2. Relate the facts of this case to the CAGE framework discussed in Section 13.8.

3. What have been the results of implementing mySAP at Pierre Lang?

4. Why is security so important to the company and how is it protected?

5. Enter *fortinet.com* and examine the capabilities of its FortiGate products.

ONLINE RESOURCES
available at pearsonglobaleditions.com/turban

Online Files

W13.1 Words of Wisdom About the Importance of Planning

W13.2 Strategic Planning Tools

W13.3 An EC Strategy Balance Sheet for Born-on-the-Net and Move-to-the-Net Firms

W13.4 Application Case: Lonely Planet Travels from Place to Space

W13.5 Application Portfolio Analysis for a Toy Distributor

W13.6 Application Case: IBM's E-Business Strategy

W13.7 The Balanced Scorecards

W13.8 Automatic Translation of Web Pages

W13.9 Application Case: Web Page Translation at the Denver Metro Convention and Visitors Bureau

W13.10 Critical Success Factors for SMEs

Comprehensive Educational Web Sites

bizauto.com/net.htm

net-strat.com/portfolio.htm

monitus.com/internet.htm

sazbean.com/2008/10/06/creating-an-internet-business-strategy-implementation

r0.unctad.org/ecommerce/event_docs/estrategies.htm
tutorialized.com/tutorials/eCommerce/Strategy/1
ecommerce-digest.com/strategies.html

A series of comprehensive educational Web sites about social networking strategies are available

bmighty.com/ebusiness/showArticle.jhtml?article-ID=206902611
macnewsworld.com/story/64639.html
articlesbase.com/seo-articles/simple-social-networking-strategies-to-increase-traffic-to-your-site-634029.html

REFERENCES

Access eCommerce. "Developing Your Internet Business Plan." 2006. access-ecom.info/section.cfm?sid=bp&%20xid=MN (accessed March 2009).

Ackerman E. "Amazon Is eBay's Biggest Challenge." *Maui News*, August 28, 2008.

APT Strategies. "Networx Case Study." aptstrategies.com.au/case_studies/Networx ebusiness Case Study by APT Strategies.pdf (accessed March 2009).

Beasley M., A. Chen, K. Nunez, and L. Wright. "Working Hand in Hand: Balanced Scorecards and Enterprise Risk Management." *Strategic Finance*, March 2008.

Brandel, M. "The Global/Local Web Site: Why You Need It; How to Build It." *ComputerWorld*, November 19, 2007.

Carr, D. F. "Changing Course amid Turbulence." *Baseline*, September 2006.

Deise, M. V., et al. *Executive's Guide to E-Business—From Tactics to Strategy*. New York: Wiley, 2000.

e-Business World. "Global Imperative . . . and the Pitfalls of Regionalism." January–February 2000.

eMarketer. "Small Businesses Expecting E-Sales." December 14, 2004. emarketer.com/article.aspx?1003177 (no longer available online).

Fisher, J., A. Craig, and J. Bentley. "Moving from a Web Presence to E-Commerce: The Importance of a Business-Web Strategy for Small-Business Owners." *Electronic Markets*, 17, no. 4 (2007).

Forrester. "Top Enterprise Web 2.0 Predictions for 2008." January 25 2008. forrester.com/Research/Document/Excerpt/0,7211,43882,00.html (accessed May 2009)

Fortinet. "Pierre Lang Jewelers Safeguards Multi-National Enterprise Network." March 30, 2005. fortinet.com/news/pr/2005/pr033005.html (accessed March 2009).

Ghemawat, P. "Distance Still Matters: The Hard Reality of Global Expansion." *Harvard Business Review* (September 2001).

Gold, J. E. "E-Guide: A Strategic Approach to Enabling Mobile Business Applications." Sponsored by BlackBerry. searchmobile_computing.com (accessed March 2009).

Green, S. *Profit on the Web*. Auckland, New Zealand: Axon Computertime, 2002.

InternetNZ. *InternetNZ Strategic Plan: 2006*. February 23, 2006. internetnz.net.nz/reports/plans/archive/2006/2006-03-04-strategicplan (accessed March 2009).

InternetNZ. *InternetNZ Strategic Plan: 2007–2009*. July 2007. internetnz.net.nz/reports/plans/2008-2009/2007-07-27-strategicplan (accessed March 2009).

Kalamas, M., M. Cleveland, M. Laroche, and R. Laufer. "The Critical Role of Congruency in Prototypical Brand Extensions." *Journal of Strategic Marketing*, 14, no. 3 (2006).

Kaplan, R. S., and D. P. Norton. *The Balanced Scorecard: Translating Strategy into Action*. Boston: Harvard Business School Press, 1996.

Keynote Competitive Research. "Airline Travel Study." 2008. keynote.com/docs/kcr/KCR_Airlines.pdf (accessed May 2009)

Kern, T., and L. Willcocks. "Exploring Relationships in Information Technology Outsourcing: The Interaction Approach." *European Journal of Information Systems*, 11, 2002.

Maddox, K. "Looking for Small-Business Owners? Try Advertising on Social Networks." *B2B Magazine*, June 9, 2008.

Maxwell, S. "Show Me the Metrics!" *Posts from an Expansion Stage Venture Capitalist*. January 30, 2006. scottmaxwell.wordpress.com/2006/01/30/show-me-the-metrics (accessed March 2009).

Miller, R. "ABC: An Introduction to Enterprise 2.0." *CIO.com*, July 12, 2007. cio.com/article/123550/ABC_An_Introduction_to_Enterprise (accessed March 2009).

Minsky, S. "The Power of Expert Opinion: A Lesson in Risk Management" *eBizQ.net*, October 17, 2006. ebizq.net/blogs/chief_risk_officer/2006/10/the_power_of_expert_opinion_a.php (accessed March 2009).

Muncaster, P. "Risk Policy Needs Rethink." *IT Week*, June 30, 2006. itweek.co.uk/itweek/news/2159522/risk-policyneeds-rethink (accessed March 2009).

OECD (Organization for Economic Cooperation and Development). Enhancing SME Competitiveness: The OECD. Bologna, Italy, Ministerial Conference, 2001.

Person, R. *Balanced Scorecards and Operational Dashboards with Microsoft Excel*. Hoboken, NJ: Wiley, 2009.

Plant, R. T. *E-Commerce: Formulation of Strategy*. Upper Saddle River, NJ: Prentice Hall, 2000.

Porter, M. E. *Competitive Strategy: Techniques for Analyzing Industries and Competitors*. New York: The Free Press, 1980.

Porter, M. E. *Competitive Advantage: Creating and Sustaining Superior Performance*. New York: The Free Press, 1985.

Porter, M. E. "Strategy and the Internet." *Harvard Business Review* (March 2001).

PRNewswire. "Nike, Inc., Elevates Global E-Commerce Strategy." October 24, 2006. nikebiz.com/media/pr/2006/10/24_ecommerce.html (accessed March 2009).

Rangan, S., and R. Adner. "Profits and the Internet: Seven Misconceptions." *MIT Sloan Management Review*, 42, no. 4 (2001).

Rayport, J., and B. J. Jaworski. *Introduction to E-Commerce*, 2nd ed. Boston: McGraw-Hill, 2004.

SAP AG. "Pierre Lang Europe." 2005. sap.com/solutions/business-suite/erp/pdf/cs_pierre_lang.pdf (accessed March 2009).

Sharma, S. K. "E-Commerce in a Digital Economy." In M. Khosrow-Pour, (Ed.). *Encyclopedia of E-Commerce, E-Government, and Mobile Commerce*. Hershey, PA: Idea Group Reference, 2006.

Shenkan, A. G., and Sichel, B. "Marketing with User-Generated Content." *McKinsey Quarterly*, November 2007.

Shuen, A. *Web 2.0: A Strategy Guide: Business Thinking and Strategies Behind Successful Web 2.0 Implementations*. Sebastopol, CA: O'Reilly, 2008.

Siteworx. Inc. "Developing a Social Networking Strategy: A Strategic Approach to Applying Social Media to Sales, Marketing, and Operations." 2008. siteworx.com/static/docs/webinar/SiteworxSocialNetworking.pdf (accessed March 2009).

Sostre, P., and J. LeClaire. *Web Analytics for Dummies*. Hoboken, NJ: Wiley, 2007.

Tennant Risk Services. "Technology and Cyber-Risk Insurance." 2004. tennant.com/p-cyber.php#ecom (no longer available online).

The Mckinsey Quarterly. "How Businesses Are Using Web 2.0: A Mckinsey Global Survey." March 2007. mckinseyquarterly.com/How_businesses_are_using_Web_20_A_McKinsey_Global_Survey_1913 (accessed May 2009).

Tjan, A. K. "Finally, a Way to Put Your Internet Portfolio in Order." *Harvard Business Review* (February 2001).

Travelocity. "Travelers Find Doing Good More Difficult with Tighter Budgets." December 22, 2008. Press release. phx.corporate-ir.net/phoenix.zhtml?c=75787&p=irol-newsArticle&ID=1238477&highlight= (accessed March 2009).

Victoria Online. "Network Events." mmv.vic.gov.au/uploads/downloads/ICT_projects/eCommerce/NetworxEvets.pdf (no longer available online).

Ward, J., and J. Peppard. *Strategic Planning for Information Systems*, 3rd ed. Chichester, UK: John Wiley & Sons, 2002.

Wheelen, T., and J. Hunger. *Cases in Strategic Management and Business Policy*, 9th ed. Upper Saddle River, NJ: Prentice Hall, 2003.

Williams, S. "Business Requirements for BI and the BI Portfolio: How to Get It Right." *DM Review* (July 2008).

Zhuhai Flight Training Center. "Southern China Planning Aggressive E-Commerce Strategy." March 2, 2006. zhftc.com/news_detailEN.asp?id=86 (accessed March 2009).

CHAPTER 14

ECONOMICS AND JUSTIFICATION OF ELECTRONIC COMMERCE

Content

Learning Objectives

Upon completion of this chapter, you will be able to:

1. Describe the need for justifying electronic commerce (EC) investments, how it is done, and how metrics are used to determine justification.

2. Understand the difficulties in measuring and justifying EC investments.

3. Recognize the difficulties in establishing intangible metrics and describe how to overcome them.

4. List and briefly describe traditional and advanced methods of justifying IT investments.

5. Understand how e-CRM, e-learning, and other EC projects are justified.

6. Describe some economic principles of EC.

7. Understand how product, industry, seller, and buyer characteristics impact the economics of EC.

8. Recognize key factors in the success of EC projects and the major reasons for failures.

JUSTIFYING INVESTMENT IN IT AND EC AT CALIFORNIA STATE AUTOMOBILE ASSOCIATION

The Problem

California State Automobile Association (CSAA) is a 7,000-employee, not-for-profit organization serving residents across northern California, Nevada, and Utah. Focusing on membership, travel, and insurance, CSAA provides services for more than 5 million members and annually processes 3 billion documents and scans 1.6 million images.

To support its members and employees, CSAA had a major IT infrastructure based on 600 servers. However, these servers were 4.5 years old; vendors were no longer supporting their operating systems; there were security patches and outages; and disk failures and crashes were common. In short, the existing infrastructure was nearing the end of its life. This created numerous problems, not to mention the inability to launch or improve e-commerce projects such as automated member self-service capabilities and enterprise-level customer service.

The Solution

To support existing and future EC and IT applications, it was necessary to replace the 600 servers. The upgrade would reduce the number of servers to 136 for less maintenance and better utilization. Also, the solution would ensure that CSAA received the latest security patches and antivirus updates for its 8,500 PCs. The solution also called for innovations such as Web farms (or Web servers), which increase the capabilities of the individual servers.

CSAA developed a business case for the solution and its outsourcing. EDS, a large outsourcer, won the bid. The projected cost of the project was $5 million for hardware and $2.5 million for EDS's services. A 5-year return-on-investment (ROI) projection justified the project (see the spreadsheet calculations below). This was part of the business case submitted to top management.

Projected Costs and Benefits for the CSAA Infrastructure Proposal

Project Costs	Year 1	Year 2	Year 3	Year 4	Year 5	Total
Hardware	$5,000,000	$0	$0	$0	$0	$5,000,000
EDS Charge	$2,500,000	$0	$0	$0	$0	$2,500,000
Total Project Costs	$7,500,000	$0	$0	$0	$0	$7,500,000

Benefits	Year 1	Year 2	Year 3	Year 4	Year 5	Total
Productivity	$270,000	$270,000	$270,000	$270,000	$270,000	$1,350,000
Cost Avoidance	$1,680,000	$1,680,000	$1,680,000	$1,680,000	$1,680,000	$8,400,000
Hardware Savings	$3,644,800	$3,644,800	$3,644,800	$3,644,800	$3,644,800	$18,224,000
Support Improvement	$1,795,200	$1,795,200	$1,795,200	$1,795,200	$1,795,200	$8,976,000
Total Benefits	$7,390,000	$7,390,000	$7,390,000	$7,390,000	$7,390,000	$36,950,000

Financial Analysis	Year 1	Year 2	Year 3	Year 4	Year 5
Net Value	($110,000)	$7,390,000	$7,390,000	$7,390,000	$7,390,000
Cumulative Net Value	($110,000)	$7,280,000	$14,670,000	$22,060,000	$29,450,000
Net Present Value	$21,863,789				

The Results

The results of the spreadsheet analysis indicated extremely positive return on the investment. The required investment of $7.5 million would be paid back in slightly more than 12 months. The total accumulated tangible realized net benefits of almost $29.5 million translated into almost $22 million NPV (based on a 9% interest rate). The computed ROI of 493 percent was extremely high, and it convinced management to approve the project. In addition to the financial results, CSAA could deliver better and faster customer service; reduce the total cost of ownership of its IT infrastructure; support the company's growth; and offer EC services such as automated self-service capabilities. Finally, security and privacy protection would improve dramatically, all of which would make the 5 million members and the 7,000 employees much happier.

Sources: Compiled from EDS (2006a), EDS (2006b), and *csaa.com* (accessed January 2009).

WHAT WE CAN LEARN . . .

The case illustrates a situation in which an organization needed to decide on upgrading and restructuring its infrastructure used for several EC and IT applications. Once the goals and the technical solution were specified, CSAA prepared a business case that was used both for conducting a bid among competing vendors and for getting approval from top management. To justify the investment, CSAA used a 5-year projection utilizing three traditional tools to assess the ROI, NPV, and payback period. Although the justification included only measurable tangible benefits, the analysis recognized significant intangible benefits, such as improved customer service.

In this case, there was no need to quantify the intangible benefits because the return of the tangible benefits was more than sufficient to justify the investment. Furthermore, several quantifiable results, such as total cost of operation (TCO) and increased response time, were excluded from the financial spreadsheet for the same reason.

The previous concepts are the main topics described in this chapter. Other topics described are more advanced tools that can be used for more complex justification situations and for handling the intangible benefits and costs. This chapter also presents the topics of the economics of EC and the conditions necessary to ensure its success.

14.1 WHY JUSTIFY E-COMMERCE INVESTMENTS? HOW CAN THEY BE JUSTIFIED?

Companies need to justify their EC investments for a number of different reasons.

INCREASED PRESSURE FOR FINANCIAL JUSTIFICATION

Once upon a time, or so the story goes, the beggars of New York City decided to conduct a competition as to who could collect the most money in one day. Many innovative ideas were employed, and several beggars collected almost $1,000 each. The winner, however, collected $5 million. When asked how he did it, the beggar replied: "I made a sign that said 'EC experts need funding for an innovative electronic marketplace' and put the sign in front of the New York Stock Exchange."

This story symbolizes what happened from 1995 through 2000, when EC projects and start-up companies were funded with little analysis of their business viability or finances. The result of the rush to invest was the 2001 to 2003 "dot-com bust," when hundreds of EC start-up went out of business and the stock market crashed. Some companies and individual investors lost more than 90 to 100 percent of their investments! Furthermore, many companies, even large ones such as Disney, Merrill Lynch, and Sears, terminated EC projects after losing considerable amounts of money and realizing few benefits from huge investments. The positive result of the crash was the "back-to-basics" movement, namely, a return to carefully checking and scrutinizing any request for EC funding.

Today, companies are holding the line on IT and EC budgets. According to Pisello (2006a), IT executives feel the pressure for financial justification and planning from top executives, but most face an uphill battle to address this new accountability, as demonstrated by the following statistics:

- Sixty-five percent of companies lack the knowledge or tools to do EC ROI calculations.
- Seventy-five percent have no formal processes or budgets in place for measuring EC ROI.
- Sixty-eight percent do not measure how EC projects coincide with promised benefits 6 months after completion.

At the same time, demand for expanding or initiating e-business projects remains strong. In order to achieve the optimal level of investment, CIOs will need to calculate and effectively communicate the value of proposed EC projects in order to gain approval. For further discussion, see Keen and Joshi (2009).

OTHER REASONS WHY EC JUSTIFICATION IS NEEDED

The following are some additional reasons for conducting EC justification:

▶ Companies now realize that EC is not necessarily the solution to all problems. Therefore, EC projects must compete for funding and resources with other internal and external projects, as described in Chapter 13. Analysis is needed to determine when funding of an EC project is appropriate.

▶ Some large companies, and many public organizations, mandate a formal evaluation of requests for funding (e.g., see the Closing Case at the end of this chapter).

▶ Companies are required to assess the success of EC projects after completion (and later, on a periodic basis).

▶ The success of EC projects may be assessed in order to pay bonuses to those involved with the project.

Reasons for IT and EC justification reported by *CIO Insight* (2004) are as follows: pressure from top management, internal competition for funding, the large amount of money involved, and weak business conditions. The same study found that justification forces EC and IT into better alignment with the corporate business strategy. Finally, justification increases the credibility of EC projects. Similar reasons exist for justifying new EC start-ups.

EC INVESTMENT CATEGORIES AND BENEFITS

Before we look at how to justify EC investments, let's examine the nature of such investments. One basic way to categorize different EC investments is to distinguish between investment in infrastructure and investment in specific EC applications.

IT infrastructure provides the foundation for EC applications in the enterprise. IT infrastructure includes intranets, extranets, data centers, data warehouses, knowledge bases, and many applications throughout the enterprise that share the infrastructure. Infrastructure investments are made for the long term.

EC applications are specific systems and programs for achieving certain objectives—for example, taking a customer order online or providing e-CRM. The number of EC applications can be large. They may be in one functional department or several departments may share them, which makes evaluation of their costs and benefits more complex.

Ross and Beath (2002) propose another way to look at EC and investment categories. They base their categories on the *purpose of the investment*. They also suggest a cost justification (funding) approach as well as the probable owner of each application (e.g., specific department or corporate ownership). The variety of EC investment categories demonstrates the complex nature of EC investments.

The basic reasons that companies invest in IT and EC are to improve business processes, lower costs, increase productivity, increase customer satisfaction and retention, increase revenue, reduce time-to-market, and increase market share.

Specific Benefits

According to a *CIO Insight* (2004) survey, companies want to get the following benefits from an IT (including EC) investment: cost reduction (84%); productivity improvement (77%); improved customer satisfaction (66%); improved staffing (57%); higher revenues (45%); higher earnings (43%); better customer retention (42%); more return on equity (33%); and faster time-to-market (31%). (Note that separate data for EC are not available.)

HOW IS AN EC INVESTMENT JUSTIFIED?

cost–benefit analysis
A comparison of the costs of a project against the benefits.

Justifying an EC investment means comparing the costs of each project against its benefits in what is known as a cost–benefit analysis. To conduct such an analysis, it is necessary to define and measure the relevant EC benefits and costs. Cost–benefit analysis is frequently assessed by *return on investment (ROI)*, which is also the name of a specific method for evaluating investments.

A number of different methods are available to measure the *business value* of EC and IT investments. Traditional methods that support such analyses are *net present value (NPV)* and ROI (see Online File W14.1).

Business Justification and Business Case

The cost–benefit analysis and the business value are part of the business case. Several vendors provide templates, tools, guidelines, and more for preparing the business case for specific areas. For example, itbusinessedge.com provides an SOA Business Case Resource Kit (the templates are in Microsoft Word). ROI is calculated with Excel's templates (see itbusinessedge. com/premiumtools/0069-soabizcase-0002.aspx).

WHAT NEEDS TO BE JUSTIFIED? WHEN SHOULD JUSTIFICATION TAKE PLACE?

Not all EC investments need to be formally justified. In some cases, a simple one-page qualitative justification will do. The following are cases where formal evaluation may not be needed:

- When the value of the investment is relatively small for the organization
- When the relevant data are not available, are inaccurate, or are too volatile
- When the EC project is mandated—it must be done regardless of the costs and benefits involved

However, even when formal analysis is not required, an organization should have at least some qualitative analysis to explain the logic of investing in the EC project.

USING METRICS IN EC JUSTIFICATION

A metric is a specific, measurable standard against which actual performance is compared. Metrics are used to describe costs, benefits, or the ratio between them. They are used not only for justification but also for other economic activities (e.g., to compare employee performance in order to reward specific employees). Metrics can produce very positive results in organizations by driving behavior in a number of ways. Metrics can:

metric
A specific, measurable standard against which actual performance is compared.

- Be the basis for specific goals and plans
- Define the value proposition of business models
- Communicate a business strategy to the workforce through performance targets
- Increase accountability when metrics are linked with performance appraisal programs and rewards
- Align the objectives of individuals, departments, and divisions to the enterprise's strategic objectives
- Track the performance of EC systems, including usage, types of visitors, page visits, conversion rate, etc.
- Assess the health of companies by using tools such as balanced scorecards and performance dashboards

EC metrics can be tangible or intangible; see Exhibit 14.1 for examples.

Metrics, Measurements, and Key Performance Indicators

Metrics need to be defined properly with a clear way to measure them. For example, revenue growth can be measured in total dollars, in percentage change over time, or in percentage growth as compared to that of the entire industry. *Cost avoidance*, for example, can be achieved in many ways, one of which may be "decrease obsolete stock write-offs as percentage of revenue." Defining the specific measures is critical; otherwise, what the metrics actually measure may be open to interpretation.

The *balanced scorecard method* (en.wikipedia.org/wiki/balanced_scorecard) uses customer metrics, financial metrics, internal business processes metrics, and learning and growth metrics. Metrics are related to the goals, objectives, vision, and plans of the organization.

EXHIBIT 14.1 Sample EC Metrics for Various Entities of Users

EC User	Tangible Metrics	Intangible Metrics
Buyer (B2C)	• Cost/price of the product • Time in executing the transaction • Number of available alternatives	• Ease of use of EC • Convenience in purchasing • Information availability • Reliability of the transaction • Privacy of personal data
Seller (B2C)	• Profit per customer • Conversion rate of visitors • Customer retention rate • Inventory costs • Profit per item sold • Market share	• Customer satisfaction • Customer loyalty • Transaction security
Net-enhanced organization (B2B)	• From design-to-market (time) • Cash-to-cash cycle • Percentage of orders delivered on time or early • Profit per item sold	• Flexibility in changing purchase orders • Agility to sustain unplanned production increase • Risk reduction • Improved quality of products/services
Government (G2C)	• Reduction in cost of transactions • Reduction in licensing fees • Increase in participation in government programs • Lower tax rates	• Citizen satisfaction • Reelection of candidates • Choice of interacting with elected officials • Promoting democratic principles • Disseminating more information quickly

Additional Examples of Measurements Made Using Metrics

- More than one-third of consumers use the same password for online banking as they do for other online activities.
- More than 50 brands were targeted by phishing scams in November 2004.
- More than half of consumers say they are less likely to respond to an e-mail from their bank because of phishing threats.
- Experts say that 80 percent of the infrastructures of large industries are likely to be hit by cyberattacks.
- Some consumers of financial products say phishing has turned them away from Web transactions.
- Consumers are slightly more likely to receive permission-based e-mails from online merchants than other retail businesses.
- Two-thirds of computers have spyware on them.
- Spam messages are considerably shorter than legitimate e-mails.
- eBay tops the list of online destinations on Black Friday (the day after Thanksgiving).
- Spam takes up volume, but not bandwidth.

Sources: Compiled from *cio.com/topic/1406/Metrics* (accessed December 2004–March 2009) and Borenstein et al. (2005).

key performance indicators (KPIs)
The quantitative expression of critically important metrics.

Key performance indicators (KPIs), which are the quantitative expression of critically important metrics (known as *critical success factors*), frequently use metrics that deal directly with performance (e.g., sales, profits). Frequently, one metric has several KPIs.

Any organization, private or public, can use metrics. Let's look at an example. In Australia, the government of Victoria is one of the leaders in exploiting the Internet to provide a one-stop service center called "Do It Online." It employs many metrics (see vic.gov.au). In the United States, CA.gov (my.ca.gov) offers many services for the citizens of California. In both cases, the metrics of "travel" and "wait time" for citizens who would otherwise have to visit a physical office was used in justifying offering the EC service of renewing driver's licenses.

We limit our discussion here mainly to individual EC projects or initiatives. EC projects deal most often with the automation of business processes, and as such, they can be viewed as capital investment decisions. Chapter 15 discusses investment in a start-up company.

Now that we understand the need for conducting EC justification and the use of metrics, let's see why EC justification is so difficult to accomplish.

Section 14.1 ▶ REVIEW QUESTIONS

1. List some of the reasons for justifying an EC investment.
2. Describe the risks of not conducting an EC justification study.
3. Describe how an EC investment is justified.
4. List the major EC investment categories.
5. When is justification of EC investments unnecessary?
6. What are metrics? What benefits do they offer?

14.2 DIFFICULTIES IN MEASURING AND JUSTIFYING E-COMMERCE INVESTMENTS

Justifying EC (and IT) projects can be a complex and, therefore, difficult process. Let's see why.

THE EC JUSTIFICATION PROCESS

The EC justification process varies depending on the situation and the methods used. However, in its extreme, it can be very complex. As shown in Exhibit 14.2, five areas must be considered in the justification of IT projects. In this section, we discuss the intangible and tangible areas. In Chapter 13, we discussed some strategic and tactical considerations.

Next, we provide other difficulties in conducting justifications.

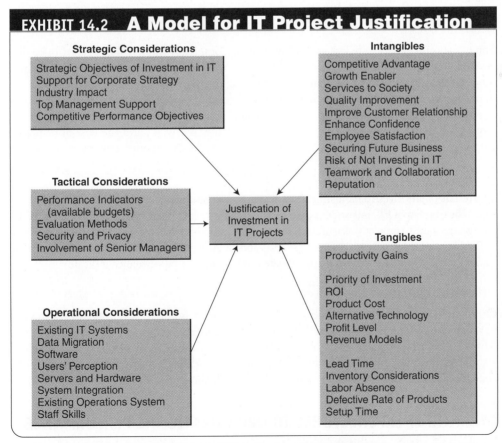

EXHIBIT 14.2 A Model for IT Project Justification

Strategic Considerations
- Strategic Objectives of Investment in IT
- Support for Corporate Strategy
- Industry Impact
- Top Management Support
- Competitive Performance Objectives

Tactical Considerations
- Performance Indicators (available budgets)
- Evaluation Methods
- Security and Privacy
- Involvement of Senior Managers

Operational Considerations
- Existing IT Systems
- Data Migration
- Software
- Users' Perception
- Servers and Hardware
- System Integration
- Existing Operations System
- Staff Skills

Justification of Investment in IT Projects

Intangibles
- Competitive Advantage
- Growth Enabler
- Services to Society
- Quality Improvement
- Improve Customer Relationship
- Enhance Confidence
- Employee Satisfaction
- Securing Future Business
- Risk of Not Investing in IT
- Teamwork and Collaboration
- Reputation

Tangibles
- Productivity Gains
- Priority of Investment
- ROI
- Product Cost
- Alternative Technology
- Profit Level
- Revenue Models
- Lead Time
- Inventory Considerations
- Labor Absence
- Defective Rate of Products
- Setup Time

Sources: Compiled from *International Journal of Information Management*, March 2001, Gunasekaran A., P. Love, F. Rahimi, and R. Miele. "A Model for Investment Justification in Information Technology Projects," © 2006, with permission from Elsevier, and R. Misra, "Evolution of the Philosophy of Investments in IT Projects," *Issues in Informing Sciences and Information Technology*, Vol. 3, 2006.

DIFFICULTIES IN MEASURING PRODUCTIVITY AND PERFORMANCE GAINS

One of the major benefits of using EC is increased productivity. However, productivity increases may be difficult to measure for a number of different reasons.

Data and Analysis Issues

Data, or the analysis of the data, may hide productivity gains. Why is this so? For manufacturing, it is fairly easy to measure outputs and inputs. For example, Toyota produces motor vehicles—a relatively well-defined product that shows gradual quality changes over time. It is not difficult to identify the inputs used to produce these vehicles with reasonable accuracy. However, in service industries, such as finance or health-care delivery, it is more difficult to define what the products are, how they change in quality, and how they may be related to corresponding benefits and costs.

For example, banks now use EC to handle a large portion of deposit and withdrawal transactions through ATMs. The ability to withdraw cash from ATMs 24/7 is a substantial benefit for customers compared to the limited hours of the physical branch. But, what is the value of this to the bank in comparison with the associated costs? If the incremental value exceeds the incremental costs, then it represents a productivity gain; otherwise, the productivity impact is negative.

EC Productivity Gains May Be Offset by Losses in Other Areas

Another possible difficulty is that EC gains in certain areas of the company may be offset by losses in other areas. For example, increased online sales may decrease offline sales, a situation known as *cannibalism*. Or consider the situation where an organization installs a new EC system that makes it possible to increase output per employee. If the organization reduces its production staff but has to increase its IT staff, the productivity gains from EC could be small, or even negative.

Hidden Costs and Benefits

Some costs and benefits are less visible, or even are completely hidden. These need to be discovered and considered. Examples of hidden costs or benefits include currency fluctuations; the need to upgrade software or hardware over time; the cost of underestimation or benefits of overestimation; the cost of supporting changes; the cost of paying employees who were forced to retire due to the EC project (e.g., pension, health care); the cost of headcount reduction; the cost of the transition period for employees used to the "old way"; and the cost of displaced employees who leave before the EC project is completed and temporary employees are hired.

Incorrectly Defining What Is Measured

The results of any investment justification depend on what is actually measured. For example, to assess the benefits of EC investment, one should usually look at productivity improvement in the area where the EC project was installed. However, productivity increase may not necessarily be a profitable improvement (e.g., due to large costs and/or losses in other areas). The problem of definitions can be overcome by using appropriate metrics and key performance indicators.

Other Difficulties

Other performance measurement difficulties also have been noted. A number of researchers have pointed out, for example, that time lags may throw off productivity measurements (e.g., Misra 2006). Many EC investments, especially those in e-CRM, take 5 to 6 years to show significant positive results, but many studies do not wait that long to measure productivity changes. For a list of other factors that impact performance, see Devaraj and Kohli (2002).

RELATING IT EXPENDITURES TO ORGANIZATIONAL PERFORMANCE

Exhibit 14.3 shows some of the difficulties in finding the relationship between EC investment and organizational performance. The exhibit shows that the relationship between investment and performance is indirect; factors such as shared IT assets and how they are

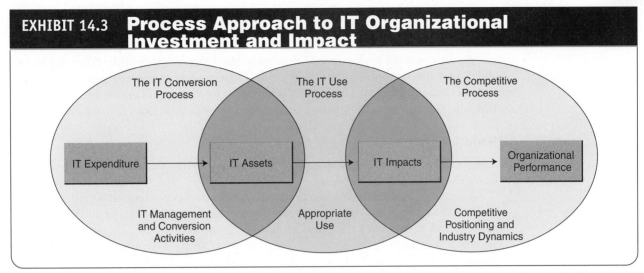

EXHIBIT 14.3   Process Approach to IT Organizational Investment and Impact

Source: Soh, C., and L. M. Markus, "How IT Creates Business Value: A Process Theory Synthesis," *Proceedings of the 16th International Conference on Information System*, Amsterdam, December 1995. Used with permission of the authors.

used can impact organizational performance and make it difficult to assess the value of an IT (or EC) investment.

Furthermore, changes in organizational performance may occur years after installing an EC application. Thus, proper evaluation must be done over the entire life cycle of the system. This requires forecasting, which may be difficult. In EC, it is even more difficult because investors often require that risky and fast-changing EC systems pay for themselves within 3 years. For further discussion, see Keystone Strategy, Inc. (2006). For difficulties in measuring intangible costs and benefits, see Online File W14.2.

In many cases, EC projects generate intangible benefits, such as faster time-to-market, increased employee and customer satisfaction, easier distribution, greater organizational agility, and improved control. These are very desirable benefits, but it is difficult to place an accurate monetary value on them. For example, many people would agree that e-mail improves communications, but it is not at all clear how to measure the value of this improvement. Managers are very conscious of the bottom line, but no manager can prove that e-mail is responsible for so many cents per share of the organization's total profits.

INTANGIBLE COSTS AND BENEFITS

Broadly speaking, EC costs and benefits can be classified into two categories: tangible and intangible. *Tangible* costs and benefits are easier to measure once metrics, such as the cost of software (cost) and the amount of labor saved (benefit), are determined. *Intangible* costs and benefits are usually more difficult to measure.

Tangible Costs and Benefits

Tangible costs are those that are easy to measure and quantify and that relate directly to a specific investment. The costs involved in purchasing hardware, software, consulting, and support services usually are tangible, as are the costs of telecommunication services, maintenance, and labor. These costs can be measured through accounting information (e.g., from the general ledger). Similarly, tangible benefits, including increased profitability, improved productivity, and greater market share, can be measured with relative ease.

Intangible Costs and Benefits

When it comes to *intangible* costs and benefits, organizations must develop innovative metrics to track them as accurately as possible. Intangible costs may include the learning curve of the firm's customer service employees to incorporate an EC system to respond to customer inquiries. Another intangible cost may involve having to change or adapt other business processes or information systems, such as processing items returned by customers or building and operating an inventory tracking system. An additional difficulty is separating EC costs from the costs of routine maintenance of inventory and other relevant IT systems.

An analyst could ignore intangible benefits, but doing so implies that their value is zero, which may lead an organization to reject EC investments that could indirectly increase revenues and profitability. Therefore, it is necessary to consider intangible benefits in a way that reflects their potential impact. The question is how to do it (see Hubbard 2007).

Handling Intangible Benefits

The first step in dealing with intangible benefits is to define them and, if possible, specify how they are going to be measured.

The most straightforward solution to the problem of evaluating intangible benefits in cost–benefit analysis is to make *rough estimates* of the monetary values of all the intangible benefits and then conduct an ROI or similar financial analysis. The simplicity of this approach is attractive, but in many cases the simplification assumptions used in these estimates are debatable. If an organization acquires the EC technology because decision makers assigned too high a value to intangible benefits, the organization could find that it has wasted some valuable resources. On the other hand, if the valuation of intangible benefits is too low, the organization may reject the EC investment and later find itself losing market share to competitors who did implement the technology.

Intangible costs and benefits may be approached in a number of different ways. Several of the methods presented in Section 14.3 also can be used to evaluate intangible benefits. For more on intangible costs and benefits, see Online File W14.2.

One way to deal with intangible benefits is to develop a balanced scorecard (Chapter 13) for the proposal investment. The approach requires listing both tangible and intangible goals and their measures. For an example of how this works, see Person (2009).

The problems of measuring intangible costs and benefits become more complex as companies try to justify large investments in EC because of the special characteristics of EC. Intuitively, we know that EC provides significant benefits of flexibility, ease of use, and low transaction costs. However, how can management quantify these intangible benefits? Nucleus Research (2002) suggests that ROI justification metrics should provide management with a consistent, reliable, and repeatable process that can compare the relative impact of investment opportunities on the company's bottom line.

THE PROCESS OF JUSTIFYING EC AND IT PROJECTS

Justifying large-scale investments is not only about selecting a method; it is also about how to execute it. The appropriate process is not simple. The major steps of this process, according to *Baseline* (2006) and the authors' experience, are:

- Lay an appropriate foundation for analysis with your vendor, and then conduct your ROI.
- Conduct a good research on metrics (including internal and external metrics) and validate them.
- Justify and document the cost and benefit assumptions.
- Document and verify all figures used in the calculation. Clarify all assumptions.
- Do not leave out strategic benefits, including long-term ones. Is the project really bolstering the company's competitive and strategic advantage?
- Be careful not to underestimate cost and overestimate benefits (a tendency of many managers).
- Make figures as realistic as possible and include risk analysis.
- Commit all partners, including vendors and top management.

These difficulties cause many companies not to measure the value of IT and EC projects (Alter 2006). This can be a risky approach. For those companies that like to try a formal justification, we present a number of methods in Sections 14.3 and 14.4.

1. How do organizations measure performance and productivity? What are the difficulties in measuring performance and productivity?

2. Why is it difficult to relate EC (IT) investments to organizational performance? List the major reasons.

3. Define tangible costs and benefits.

4. Define intangible costs and benefits and explain why they must be considered when justifying an IT investment.

5. How should management handle the intangibles and uncertainties of benefits?

14.3 METHODS AND TOOLS FOR EVALUATING AND JUSTIFYING E-COMMERCE INVESTMENTS

Now that we have an understanding of the difficulties of EC justification and how organizations evaluate EC investments, let's examine the methods and tools used for such evaluation and justification. Companies use commercially available tools or develop in-house tools. And as with the economic justification of non-EC investments, a number of different methods can be applied to EC investments.

At their core, all economic justification approaches attempt to account for the costs and benefits of investments. They differ in their ability to account for the tangible and intangible costs and benefits of EC, particularly when compared to other corporate investments.

OPPORTUNITIES AND REVENUE GENERATED BY EC INVESTMENT

A major difficulty in assessing the EC value is the measurement of possible benefits (tangible and intangible) that drive EC investment. Furthermore, some of these are opportunities that may or may not materialize, so there is only a certain probability for return on the EC investment.

In preparing the business case for EC investment, as we will describe later, one should examine the potential *additional revenues* created by the EC investments. Chapter 1 presented the typical revenue models generated by EC and the Web. Additional examples are:

❱ Companies that allow people to play games for a fee or watch a sports competition in real time for a fee (e.g., see espn.com)

❱ Increased revenues via products or services from a larger global market because of more effective product marketing on the Web

❱ Increased margins attained by using processes with lower cost

❱ Increased revenues as a consequence of becoming an online portal

❱ Increased value-added content from selling searches, access to data, and electronic documents

❱ Commission generated from affiliated marketing

METHODOLOGICAL ASPECTS OF JUSTIFYING EC INVESTMENTS

Before presenting the specific methods for EC justification, let's examine some methodological issues that are common to most of these methods.

Types of Costs

Although costs may appear to be the simple side of a cost–benefit analysis, they may not be so simple. Here are a few things to consider:

❱ **Distinguish between initial (up-front) costs and operating costs.** The initial costs may be a one-time investment or they may spread over several months or a year. In addition, system operating cost needs to be considered.

❱ **Direct and indirect shared costs.** Direct costs can be related directly to a specific project. Indirect costs usually are shared infrastructure-related costs. In addition, the costs may be related to several EC and IT projects. Therefore, one needs to allocate these costs to the specific projects. Such allocation may not be easy to perform; a number of approaches to cost allocation are available (consult an accountant).

▶ **In-kind costs.** Although it is easy to track monetary payments, costs also may be in kind; for example, contributions of a manager, contribution of machine time, and so on. These frequently are indirect shared costs (e.g., overhead), which complicates their calculation.

TRADITIONAL METHODS FOR EVALUATING EC INVESTMENTS

The following are the most popular methods for evaluating IT and EC investments. For details, see Online File W14.1 and Wattemann (2007).

The ROI Method

The *ROI method* uses a formula that divides the total net benefits (revenues less costs, for each year) by the initial cost. The result is a ratio that measures the ROI for each year or for an entire period; also, see Keen and Joshi (2009). Online File W14.1 provides the ROI formula and an example. In calculating ROI, one should consider the following techniques.

Payback Period

With the payback-period method, the company calculates how long it will take for the net benefits to pay back the entire initial investment. Online File W14.1 also provides the details of this method.

NPV Analysis

In an *NPV analysis*, analysts convert future values of benefits to their present-value equivalents by discounting them at the organization's cost of funds. This requires that analysts determine a discount rate, which can be the average or the marginal interest rate paid by a company to obtain loans. Then the analyst can compare the present value of the future benefits with the present value of the costs required to achieve those benefits to determine whether the benefits exceed the costs. A project with estimated NPV greater than zero may be a candidate for acceptance. One with an estimated NPV less than zero would probably be rejected. One needs to consider the intangible benefits. For more specific guidelines and decision criteria on how NPV analysis works, consult a financial management textbook and Online File W14.1.

Internal Rate of Return (IRR)

For an investment that requires and produces a number of cash flows over time, people use the *internal rate of return (IRR)* method. The IRR is the discount rate that makes the NPV of those cash flows equal to zero. Some companies set a minimum acceptable IRR (or hurdle rate) based on their own cost of capital and the minimum percentage return they'd like to see from their investments.

Break-Even Analyses

A *break-even point* is the point at which the benefits of a project are equal to the costs. Firms use this type of analysis to determine the point at which the EC investment starts to pay for itself.

The Total Costs and Benefits of Ownership

total cost of ownership (TCO)
A formula for calculating the cost of owning, operating, and controlling an IT system.

The costs of an IT system may accumulate over many years. An interesting approach for IT cost evaluation is the *total cost of ownership*. Total cost of ownership (TCO) is a formula for calculating the cost of owning, operating, and controlling an IT system, even one as simple as a PC. The cost includes acquisition costs (hardware and software), operations costs (maintenance, training, operations, evaluation, technical support, installation, downtime, auditing, virus damage, and power consumption), and control costs (standardization, security, central services). The TCO may be 100 percent higher than the cost of the hardware, especially for PCs.

By identifying these various costs, organizations can make more accurate cost–benefit analyses. David et al. (2002) offer a methodology for calculating TCO. They also provide a detailed example of the items to include in TCO calculations. For further discussion, see Bothama (2006). For a comprehensive study of TCO, see Ferrin and Plank (2002). For calculations in an open-source environment, see Spector (2006).

A similar concept is **total benefits of ownership (TBO)**. This calculation includes both tangible and intangible benefits. By calculating and comparing TCO and TBO, one can compute the payoff of an IT investment (i.e., payoff = TBO − TCO).

total benefits of ownership (TBO)
Benefits of ownership that include both tangible and intangible benefits.

Economic Value Added

Economic value added (EVA) attempts to quantify the net value added by an investment. It is the return on invested capital (i.e., after-tax cash flow) generated by a company minus the cost of the capital used in creating the cash flow. For example, if the earnings per share are 10 percent and the cost of capital is 12 percent per share, the investment reduces rather than adds economic value.

For a comparison of some of these methods, see Exhibit 14.4 and Pisello (2006a).

Using Several Traditional Methods

As you may recall from the opening case, CSAA used the ROI, NPV, and payback period to justify the investment. Each of these measures, as well as the other traditional ones, provides us with a different dimension of the analysis.

The ROI is measured over 3 years (5 in the CSAA case due to infrastructure nature). It is expressed as a percentage and helps assess the net benefits of a project relative to the initial investment. The NPV indicates the magnitude of the project and whether it generated a profit. It is expressed in terms of a currency (e.g., dollars, pounds, yuan). The payback period provides information about the risk. The longer the projected period, the longer the risk of obsolescence. It also measures the positive cumulative cash flow. The IRR is frequently used to decide whether to commit to an investment. In many cases, an investment is accepted when the IRR is greater than the opportunity cost.

EXHIBIT 14.4 Evaluating EC and IT Traditional Investments Methods

Method	Advantages	Disadvantages
Internal rate of return (IRR)	Brings all projects to common footing. Conceptually familiar.	Assumes reinvestment at same rate. Can have multiple roots. No assumed discount rate.
Net present value (NPV) or net worth (NW)	Very common. Maximizes value for unconstrained project selection.	Difficult to compare projects of unequal lives or sizes.
Payback period	May be discounted or nondiscounted. Measure of exposure.	Ignores flows after payback is reached. Assumes standard project cash flow profile.
Benefit-to-cost analysis or ratio	Conceptually familiar.	May be difficult to classify outlays as expenses or investments.
Economic value added	Measures net value created for the stakeholder.	The true benefits can be difficult to measure.

IMPLEMENTING TRADITIONAL METHODS

When implementing traditional methods, one may encounter some difficulties. Therefore, the methods discussed earlier are frequently implemented by using calculators.

Business ROI Versus Technology ROI

When implementing ROI, one should look both at the business side and the technology side of the project to be justified. For details, see Online File W14.3. Related to this is the issue of measuring the quality of EC projects (see Smith 2006).

ROI CALCULATORS

The traditional methods of calculating ROI involve fairly simple formulas and are available as Excel functions or other calculators. Calculators are also available for complex and proprietary formulas.

ROI calculator

Calculator that uses metrics and formulas to compute ROI.

Vendors and consulting companies have accumulated quite a bit of experience in developing metrics and tools called ROI calculators to evaluate investments. Recently, companies specializing in ROI also have developed ROI calculators, some of which are in the public domain.

The Offering from *Baseline* Magazine

One of the major sources of simple calculators is *Baseline* (baselinemag.com). They offer several dozen Excel-based calculators (for free or for a fee). Examples of calculators they offer include:

▶ Calculating ROI (*Baseline* 2006)
▶ Figuring the ROI of RFID
▶ Comparing smartphones and laptops
▶ Figuring the ROI of application performance management
▶ Determining your true total cost of ownership (TCO)
▶ Calculating the ROI of VoIP
▶ Determining the cost of videoconferencing solutions

In addition, *Baseline* offers tutorials, guides, statistical data, and more related to these calculators.

Other Calculators

Nucleus Research Inc. (nucleusresearch.com), a research and advisory company, uses several ROI calculators in helping businesses evaluate IT investments. Nucleus Research argues that if a company must make frequent justifications for EC and has unique intangible costs and benefits, it may be necessary to custom build an ROI evaluation tool. ROI calculators for e-services are also available. For instance, StreamingMedia (streamingmedia.com) provides an ROI calculator to measure the costs and benefits of telecommunication bandwidth for videoconferencing, streaming video, and video file servers.

Few organizations have attempted to assess the ROI on e-learning, perhaps because it is so difficult to calculate and justify. However, Learnativity.com (learnativity.com) provides resources such as ROI calculators, methodologies, a bibliography, and online communities to support the assessment of e-learning (see learnativity.com/roi-learning.html).

ROI calculators also are available from various other companies, such as Phoenix Technologies (phoenix.com), Citrix's XenDesktop (citrix.com/English/ps2/products/product.asp?contentID=163057&ntref=3_nav), and Alinean, Inc. (alinean.com). CovalentWorks Corporation (covalentworks.com) specializes in B2B calculators. For more examples of ROI calculators, see roi-calc.com, gantrygroup.com, and phormion.com.

ADVANCED METHODS FOR EVALUATING IT AND EC INVESTMENTS

According to Sidana (2006), traditional methods that are based only on tangible financial factors may not be sufficient for many IT and EC justifications. Therefore, new methods have evolved with time and now include intangible factors such as customer satisfaction (e.g., see Smith and Laurent 2008). These methods may supplement the ROI traditional methods or replace them.

Renkema (2000) presents a comprehensive list of more than 60 different appraisal and justification methods for IT investments. For details of some of these and other methods, see McKay and Marshall (2004). Most justification methods can be categorized into the following four types:

- **Financial approaches.** These appraisal methods consider only those impacts that can be valued monetarily. They focus on incoming and outgoing cash flows as a result of the investment made. Traditional methods with modifications are examples of financial approach methods.

- **Multicriteria approaches.** These methods consider both financial impacts and non-financial impacts that cannot be (or cannot easily be) expressed in monetary terms. These methods employ quantitative and qualitative decision-making techniques. Examples include information economics, balanced scorecard, and value analysis (see Online File W14.4). For a further description, see Borenstein et al. (2005).

- **Ratio approaches.** These methods use several ratios to assist in EC investment evaluation (e.g., EC expenditures versus total turnover). The metrics used usually are financial in nature, but other types of metrics can be used as well. An example of this would be EC expenditures divided by annual sales or EC expenditures as a percentage of the operating budget.

- **Portfolio approaches.** These methods apply portfolios (or grids) to plot several investment proposals against decision-making criteria. Portfolio methods are more informative than multicriteria methods and generally use fewer evaluation criteria. These are very complex; for more information, see Hovenden et al. (2005).

Exhibit 14.5 summarizes representative advanced methods useful in evaluating EC investments.

EXHIBIT 14.5 Advanced Methods for EC Justification and Evaluation

- **Value analysis.** With the value analysis method, the organization evaluates intangible benefits using a low-cost, trial EC system before deciding whether to commit a larger investment in a complete system.
- **Information economics.** Using the idea of critical success factors, this method focuses on key organizational objectives and the potential impacts of the proposed EC project on each of them.
- **Scoring methodology.** This method assigns weights and scores to various aspects of the evaluated project (e.g., weights to each metric) and then calculates a total score. Information economics methods are used to determine the aspects to include in the scoring.
- **Benchmarks.** This method is appropriate for evaluating EC infrastructure. Using industry standards, for example, the organization can determine what the industry is spending on e-CRM. Then the organization can decide how much it should spend.
  Benchmarks may be industry metrics or best practices recommended by professional associations or consultants.
- **Management by maxim.** An organization may use this method to determine how much it should invest in large EC (and IT) infrastructures. It is basically a combination of brainstorming and consensus-reaching methodologies.
- **Real-options valuation.** This is a fairly complex assessment method, and it is used only infrequently. It can be fairly accurate in certain situations. The idea behind this method is to look at future opportunities that may result from the EC investment and then place monetary values on them.
- **Balanced scorecard.** This method evaluates the health or performance of the organization by looking at a broad set of factors, not just financial ones. It is becoming a popular tool for assessing EC projects. (See Beasley et al. 2006, and Pearlson and Sounders 2006.)
- **Performance dashboard.** This is a variant of the balanced scorecard that is used widely in e-business situations. A dashboard is a single view that provides the status of multiple metrics. (See Pearlson and Sounders 2006.)
- **Activity-based costing and justification.** This managerial accounting concept was adapted for assessing EC investments in recent years and has been proven to be fairly successful. (See Peacock and Tanniru 2005.)

Unfortunately, none of these methods is perfect or universal. Therefore, one needs to look at the advantages and disadvantages of each. Exhibit 14.6 shows the popularity (or use) of the major methods.

Justification methods are usually included in a business plan or business case (see Chapter 13 and the Online Tutorial). Business case software for EC is available from bplans.com and paloalto.com.

Section 14.3 ▶ REVIEW QUESTIONS

1. Briefly define ROI, NPV, payoff period, NVP/IRR, and break-even methods of evaluation.
2. What are ROI calculators?
3. Describe TCO and TBO.

14.4 EXAMPLES OF E-COMMERCE PROJECT JUSTIFICATION

The methods and tools described in the previous section can be used alone, in combination, or with modifications to justify different EC projects. Here, we provide a few examples of how these methods and tools can be used to justify different types of EC projects.

JUSTIFYING E-PROCUREMENT

E-procurement (see Chapter 5) is not limited to just buying and selling; it also encompasses the various processes involved in buying and selling: selecting suppliers, submitting formal requests for goods and services to suppliers, getting approval from buyers, processing purchase orders, fulfilling orders, delivering and receiving items, and processing payments.

Given the diversity of activities involved in e-procurement, the metrics used to measure the value of e-procurement must reflect how well each process is accomplished. However, the focus on the metrics used will differ for buyers and sellers. For example, *buyers* will be interested in metrics such as how quickly they can locate a seller; *sellers* will be most interested in

EXHIBIT 14.6	**Popularity of the Various Justification Methods**	
Technique	Percentage Who Use It (2004)	Percentage Who Use It (2006)
ROI	44	52
Internal ROI	40	47
Activity-based costing	37	32
Company-specific measure	36	57
Net present value	35	33
Economic value added	29	31
Balanced scorecard	24	NA
Return on assets	24	35
Return on equity	18	19
Portfolio management	16	NA
Applied information economics	9	9
Real options	6	NA
Time to payback	NA	60

NA = Not available

Sources: Compiled from *CIO Insight* (2004) and Alter (2006).

Insights and Additions 14.1 E-Procurement Metrics

Measuring the success of e-procurement is in many ways similar to measuring the success of the purchasing department. Some direct measures involve the company's ability to secure quality, cost-effective materials and supplies that are delivered on time. The following metrics indicate progress in e-procurement:

▸ Increased order fulfillment rate

▸ Increased on-time deliveries

▸ Decreased number of rejects received from suppliers

▸ Decreased purchase order processing time

▸ Decreased prices due to increased supplier visibility and order aggregation

▸ Decreased ratio of freight costs to purchases

Indirect metrics include minimizing costs, such as:

▸ Reduced inventory costs

▸ Reduced raw material costs

▸ Reduced rework costs

▸ Reduced operating costs

▸ Reduced freight costs

E-procurement can directly or indirectly affect these metrics. Measuring and monitoring e-procurement activities is crucial to identifying both problematic and successful areas. It provides insight into what an organization is doing right and wrong so that it can pinpoint which activities it needs to investigate and adjust.

The University of Pennsylvania measures e-procurement performance through several metrics, as shown in Online File W14.6.

click-to-release time (i.e., the time that elapsed from when the customer clicked to buy an item online until the warehouse staff had a ticket to pick and pack the order). For examples of e-procurement metrics, see Insights and Additions 14.1. Setting metrics for e-procurement is especially difficult when procurement is done in exchanges. One solution to ease such problems is the use of Web Services (see Chapter 18).

CUSTOMER SERVICE AND E-CRM

Customer service and e-CRM (Chapter 11) can be provided in a number of different ways. For example, Lowe's seeks to improve customer service on its Web site (lowes.com) by providing a "do it yourself" information portal (e.g., offering information about how to install a ceiling fan or fix paint problems). Such information may already be available online, and the company also uses it to train service personnel. EC-based banking sites often add customer value by lowering risks and providing information relating to the last successful log-on and the number of unsuccessful log-on attempts. Online prescription drug companies, such as Medco Health Solutions (medcohealth.com), proactively provide information on their Web sites and via e-mail concerning prescription refills and drug recalls.

Recent surveys of e-CRM applications have continued to show mixed payoffs. Only a fraction of companies have demonstrated a significantly positive ROI for their e-CRM investments. What can we learn from those companies that have successfully deployed e-CRM and have extracted significant business value? For answers, look at Online File W14.5.

e-CRM Metrics

A report from a survey of SMEs conducted by the Yankee Group, an IT consulting company, also echoes the issues in assessing the ROI of e-CRM. The Yankee Group found that CRM-based EC applications are effective only when they are part of a company's overall business plan and not just an EC investment (Kingstone 2004). The Yankee Group report outlines key e-CRM metrics in three areas: sales, marketing, and service, as shown in Exhibit 14.7. These CRM success metrics can also be viewed as tangible,

EXHIBIT 14.7   Key Metrics for Measuring CRM Success

Sales	Marketing	Service
Revenue per salesperson; cost per sales made	Marketing dollars as a percentage of revenue	First-call resolution rate
Average sale cycle; average deal size	Average return on marketing	Call quality (as measured by quality monitoring)
Sales representative turnover rate	Total leads generated	Voice service level (by type of call)
New rep ramp time	Average response rate	E-mail service level (by type of e-mail)
Average administrative time per representative	Lead qualification rate	Average speed of answer
Percentage of representatives that achieve quota	Lead close rate	Abandon rate
Average time to close	Percent of marketing collateral used by sales representatives	Average handle time
Average price discount	Change in market penetration	Cost per contact (calls, e-mail)
Percentage of accurate forecasted opportunities	Improved time-to-market; percentage of customer retention	Average call value
Average number of calls to close deal	Number of feedback points	Average close rate
Average number of presentations necessary to close deal	Marketing execution time	Agent turnover
Average number of proposals needed to close deal	Message close rate	Customer satisfaction
Average win rate	Marketing dollars as a percentage of revenue	Accuracy of data entered (e.g., trouble tickets)

Sources: Compiled from Kingstone (2004), exhibit, p. 7; Alter (2006); and *teradata.com* (accessed January 2009).

intangible, and risk-related measures. For instance, revenue per salesperson represents financial tangible metrics; marketing dollars and efficiency metrics are captured in the average time to close and average response time. Intangible metrics are captured as customer satisfaction and call quality. Although financial and efficiency measures are also classified as risk measures, risk metrics in the Yankee Group report are captured through the first-call resolution rate and the accuracy of the data entered (listed under the "Service" column of Exhibit 14.7). These metrics constitute what is of value to the EC sellers and buyers.

JUSTIFYING A PORTAL

In making the case for investing in a Web portal, Bisconti (2004) suggests that the fundamental business case should be made from the internal and external perspectives of the business. The internal payoff must result in productivity improvements, whereas revenue generation determines the external value. Although several commercial portal development environments are available, large companies may consider building theirs in-house. Bisconti argues that metrics and ROI analysis can serve as a prerequisite to the build-versus-buy decision.

Some of the tangible benefits from investment in portal technology include revenue growth, call center productivity increases, and increased customer loyalty and retention. Adopters also report much improved trading relationships with suppliers and business partners. However, most of the benefits of portals are intangible. For example, employee portals have the potential to fundamentally change and improve employer–employee relationships—a desirable benefit, although somewhat difficult to measure. Portals offer the following benefits, which are difficult to quantify:

▶ They offer a simple user interface for finding and navigating content via a browser.

▶ They improve access to business content and increase the number of business users who can access information, applications, and people.

▶ They offer access to common business applications from anywhere in a geographically distributed enterprise and beyond. Using Web-enabled mobile or wireless devices, content can be accessed from anywhere.

▶ They offer the opportunity to use platform-independent software (Java) and data (XML).

However, given that portals are relatively low-cost, low-risk devices, it is not surprising that they are being adopted by thousands of organizations worldwide. Large companies often have an array of intranet and other information systems; the integration of these systems becomes key to the success of the portal. Thus, the compatibility and flexibility of the portal technology becomes paramount. Bisconti asserts that justification for a portal must focus on *business* ROI as well as *technology* ROI. For examples of ROI of portals, see *Baseline* (2006).

JUSTIFYING E-TRAINING PROJECTS

End-user training that helps employees acquire or improve their EC and IT skills plays a key role in ensuring the smooth operation of organizations in the information economy. However, such training and retraining can be expensive, slow, and ineffective. Therefore, a large number of organizations are considering e-training (Chapter 7) to supplement or substitute traditional classroom training.

When comparing e-training and traditional training methods, several factors, most of which are intangible, must be evaluated. Mahapatra and Lai (2005) developed a framework for evaluating end-user training. Exhibit 14.8 shows some of the metrics that may be included in such an evaluation. In executing such a justification, the organization also needs to consider the financial factors of e-training versus traditional training methods.

EXHIBIT 14.8 Factors to Consider in Evaluating E-Training

Evaluation Level	Evaluator	Factors to Evaluate
Technology	Training provider	• Effectiveness of IT in supporting training-related tasks • Ease of use and usefulness of IT-based tools used by training providers
	Trainee	• Delivery and presentation of training materials • Ease of use and usefulness of communication tools
Reaction	Trainee	• Relevance of the course to the trainee's job • Satisfaction with course content and presentation • Quality of instruction • Effectiveness of instructor • Overall satisfaction with the training experience
Skill acquisition	Trainee	• Knowledge and skill learned
Skill transfer	Trainee	• Ability to apply the skill learned at work
	Manager	• Effect of the training on the trainee's performance
Organizational effect	Manager	• Effect of the training on organizational goal achievement

Sources: Compiled from Mahapatra and Lai (2005) and Hughes and Atwell (2003).

JUSTIFYING AN INVESTMENT IN MOBILE COMPUTING AND IN RFID

Justifying the cost of mobile computing may be difficult due to cost sharing and intangible benefits (e.g., see MacDonald 2003). *Baseline* (baselinemag.com) offers tutorials and several calculators to help companies do the following:

▶ Calculate the return on the wireless workforce

▶ Calculate the return on outsourcing mobile device management

▶ Calculate the cost of the wireless networks

Vendors of wireless and mobile hardware, software, and services offer tutorials and calculators, as well (e.g., Symbol Technology—now a Motorola company, Sybase, and Intel). For a comprehensive discussion of the justification of mobile computing, see MobileInfo.com (2009).

Many medium and large corporations are considering implementing RFID systems to improve their supply chain operations (see Chapter 5). Although such systems offer many tangible benefits that can be defined, many measures cannot be developed due to the fact that the technology is new and that legal requirements (for privacy protection) are still evolving. For a discussion of RFID justification, see Chapter 8, Online File W14.7, and Pisello (2006b). For a fee, baselinemag.com offers an RFID justification calculator.

An example justifying investment in wireless computing is provided in Case 14.1.

CASE 14.1

EC Application

PAESANO RESTAURANT JUSTIFIES WIRELESS E-COMMERCE

The Business
Paesano, a restaurant located in Knox City, Australia, services 400 seats. The restaurant employs 40 floor staff and 20 kitchen staff and is strategically positioned outside the Knox City cinema complex. On weekends, 1,200 customers walk through Paesano's doors, so the waiters are very busy all the time.

The System
Paesano purchased a wireless point-of-sale (POS) system called OrderMate (from *ordermate.com.au*), which allows waiters to place orders using their handheld devices without the need to return to the bar or kitchen areas, saving time and improving efficiency. Paesano installed four terminals in the main restaurant area and one terminal in the pizza area. The terminals are connected wirelessly to the waiters and are wired to the kitchen and bar.

How the Technology Works
The OrderMate POS system runs on a touchscreen terminal (Waitermate) and the wireless, handheld HP PDA devices (Pocketmate).

The simple and intuitive screen layout and minimal input mean that staff immediately feel confident using the POS system—making OrderMate quick to learn (10 minutes) and easy to use.

The screen on the handheld PDA is split into the relevant sections of drinks and kitchen. Orders entered into PocketMate are instantly relayed to printers in relevant preparation areas.

The technology is suited to all restaurant sizes and can operate 50 meters (approximately 54 yards) externally, allowing the staff to move outside the restaurant to take orders.

Results
The wireless ordering system allows the waiters more customer time and, therefore, more time for extra foods and drinks to be ordered—and more customers to be accommodated each day.

After costs, Paesano's total return on investment of the wireless application is $46,682 (see the accompanying table).

Cost and Benefit Calculations (in Australian Dollars)
Paesano invested more than $32,000 in up-front costs for computer hardware, handheld digital assistants, printers, and software licenses. Training was a low $300, and ongoing costs amount to $4,000 per annum.

(continued)

CASE 14.1 (continued)

Paesano management estimate conservatively that an additional $48,750 in net sales resulted from floor staff being in front of customers longer. Increased efficiency also allows reduced staff hours and customer service costs amounting to $34,000.

Challenges and Process Change

The implementation of the wireless devices has been very well received by staff at Paesano. Staff noted that customers found the wireless devices to be novel and a talking point, making their job more enjoyable while improving customer satisfaction.

Future Plans

Paesano introduced a touchscreen, paperless kitchen system that is likened to a virtual docket rail. This enables waiters to inform customers about the estimated time of arrival for orders!

Home delivery using a global positioning system is also planned for the future. This will automatically optimize the drivers' routes and allow management to know where each driver is at all times.

Sources: Compiled from *ordermate.com.au* (accessed March 2009) and MultiMedia Victoria (2009).

Questions

1. Identify the intangible benefits in this case.
2. Calculate the return on investment (ROI) and the internal rate of return (IRR) (take 6% interest rate).
3. Compute the NPV.

Assumptions: Assume sales and cost of goods sold occur in the middle of the year, up-front costs occur on day 1; expense reduction occurs in the middle of the year.

Annual Costs and Benefits (in Australian Dollars)

Additional Revenue from E-Commerce

Increased sales		81,250
Less: Cost of Goods Sold		(32,500)
Net Profit for E-Commerce		48,750

Add: E-Commerce Expenses Reductions

Wages and overheads		17,000
Reduced customer services costs		17,000
Total E-Commerce Expense Reduction		34,000
Gross Benefit from E-Commerce	48,750 + 34,000	82,750

Less: Up-Front Fixed Expenses

Computer hardware, including modem		
OrderMate server		1,342
5 × WaiterMate—touch PC client		12,342
6 × Kitchen/bar order printers		3,177
4 × PocketMate handheld devices		2,587
9 × Software licenses		11,020
Training, creation, and installation		1,600
Total E-Commerce Fixed Expenses		(32,068)

Less: Annual Operational Expenses

OrderMate support		1,000
OrderMate printer consumables		3,000
Total E-Commerce Operational Expenses		(4,000)
Total E-Commerce Costs		(36,068)
Total E-Commerce Benefits	82,750–36,068	46,682

JUSTIFYING SECURITY PROJECTS

More than 85 percent of viruses enter business networks via e-mail. Cleaning up infections is labor intensive, but antivirus scanning is not. ROI calculators are available (e.g., at baselinemag.com) to judge the cost of using an expert to decontaminate a system versus the use of software to keep the system virus free (Keepmedia.com 2005).

Employee security training is usually poorly done. Companies tell employees what to do, with little or no time devoted to why specific security rules are in place. ROI calculators are available to estimate the cost for training sessions with enough time to explain "why," allowing workers to understand the consequences of ignoring or misusing security procedures.

JUSTIFYING SOCIAL NETWORKING AND THE USE OF WEB 2.0 TOOLS

Justifying social networking initiatives and the use of Web 2.0 can be difficult due to the intangible benefits and the potential risks (Chapter 9). However, in many cases the cost is relatively low and so companies embark on such projects without formal justification, especially in cases of experiments. The major issue could be that of risk assessment. Some of the tools are available for free or are being added by vendors to communication and collaboration tools.

Section 14.4 ▶ REVIEW QUESTIONS

1. List five success factors for e-procurement.
2. List five performance metrics for e-procurement.
3. List three tangible and three intangible benefits of e-CRM.
4. List some metrics that can justify e-training and learning.

14.5   THE ECONOMICS OF E-COMMERCE

EC business models and applications have capabilities that may change several economic factors and trade-off relationships. These, in turn, provide the advantages of EC over traditional commerce. For example, with online purchases the incremental or variable costs of delivering digital content to individual customers or of processing transactions are very low, and therefore, the market for EC is large and growing rapidly.

The economic environment of e-commerce is broad and diversified. In this section, we present only representative topics that relate to the traditional economic microeconomic theory and formula, such as:

$$\text{Profit} = \text{Revenues} - \text{Production costs} - \text{Transaction costs}$$

E-commerce helps to decrease costs and increase revenues, resulting in increased profits.

REDUCING PRODUCTION COSTS

Production costs are the costs to produce the product or service a company is selling. E-commerce makes a major contribution to lowering production costs. For example, e-procurement may result in cost reductions. Much of intrabusiness EC deals with cost reductions. The following economic principles express these reductions.

Product Cost Curves

The *average-cost curve (AVC)* represents the behavior of average costs as quantity changes. The AVC of many physical products and services is U shaped (see as Exhibit 14.9). This curve indicates that, at first, as quantity increases, the average cost declines (part a). As quantity increases still more, the cost goes back up due to increasing variable costs (especially marketing costs) and fixed costs (more management is needed) in the short run. However, the variable cost per unit of digital products is very low (in most cases) and almost fixed (once the initial investment is recovered), regardless of the quantity. Therefore, as Exhibit 14.9 shows, with digital products the average cost per unit (part b) declines as quantity increases because the fixed costs are spread (prorated) over more units. This relationship results in increasing returns with increased sales. It provides competitive advantage because EC users can sell at lower prices.

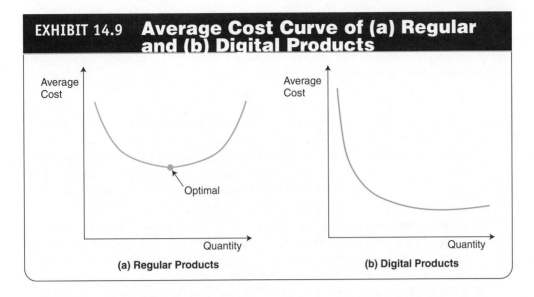

EXHIBIT 14.9   Average Cost Curve of (a) Regular and (b) Digital Products

(a) Regular Products

(b) Digital Products

Production Function

The **production function**, shown in Exhibit 14.10 (part a), represents a mathematical formula that indicates that for the same quantity of production, Q, companies either can use a certain amount of labor or invest in more automation (e.g., they can substitute IT capital for labor). For example, for a quantity $Q = 1,000$, the lower the amount of labor needed the higher the required IT investment (capital costs). When EC enters the picture, it *shifts* the function inward (from L_1 to L_2), lowering the amount of labor and/or capital needed to produce the same $Q = 1,000$. Again, EC provides competitive advantage, allowing companies to sell at lower prices than the competition.

production function
An equation indicating that for the same quantity of production, Q, companies either can use a certain amount of labor or invest in more automation.

Agency Costs

Exhibit 14.10 (part b) shows the economics of the firm's **agency costs** (or *administrative costs*). These are the costs incurred in ensuring that certain support and administrative tasks related to production are performed as intended (e.g., by an agent). In the "old economy," agency costs (A_1) grew with the size (and complexity) of the firm, reaching a high level of cost quickly and frequently preventing companies from growing to a very large size. In the digital economy, the agency costs curve shifts outward, to A_2. This means that as a result of EC, companies can significantly expand their business without too much of an increase in administrative costs. Again, this is a competitive advantage for the rapidly growing companies.

agency costs
Costs incurred in ensuring that the agent performs tasks as expected (also called *administrative costs*).

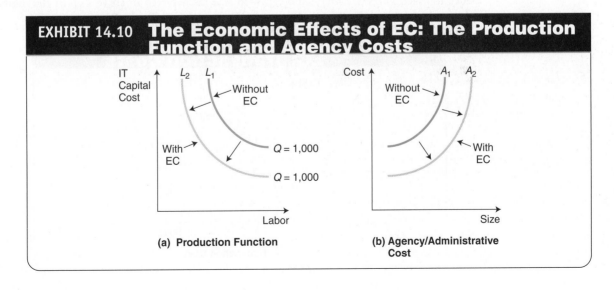

EXHIBIT 14.10   The Economic Effects of EC: The Production Function and Agency Costs

(a) Production Function

(b) Agency/Administrative Cost

Transaction Costs

Transaction costs cover a wide range of costs that are associated with the distribution (sale) and/or exchange of products and services. Most economists (e.g., Chen 2005) divide these costs into the following six categories:

1. **Search costs.** Buyers and sellers incur costs in locating each other and in locating specific products and services.

2. **Information costs.** For buyers, this includes costs related to learning about the products and services of sellers and the basis for their cost, profit margins, and quality. For sellers, this includes costs related to learning about the legitimacy, financial condition, and needs of the buyer, which may lead to a higher or lower price.

3. **Negotiation costs.** Buyers and sellers need to agree on the terms of the sale (e.g., quantity, quality, shipments, financing, etc.). Negotiation costs result from meetings, communication-related expenses, exchanges of technical data or brochures, entertainment, and legal fees.

4. **Decision costs.** for buyers, decision costs result from the evaluation of sellers and their internal processes, such as purchasing approval, to ensure that they meet the buyers' policies. For sellers, decision costs arise in the determination of whether to sell to one buyer instead of another buyer, or not at all.

5. **Monitoring costs.** Buyers and sellers need to ensure that the goods or services purchased translate into the goods or services exchanged. In addition, they need to make sure that the exchange proceeds according to the terms under which the sale was made. This may require transaction monitoring, inspection of goods, and negotiations over late or inadequate deliveries or payments.

6. **Legal-related costs.** Buyers and sellers need to ensure that they remedy unsatisfied terms. Legal-related costs include costs that arise from fixing defects and providing substitutions and agreeing on discounts and other penalties. They also include litigation costs in the event of a legal dispute.

As we have seen throughout the book, e-commerce can reduce all these costs. Reducing transaction cost benefits mostly customers by providing competitive advantage through better customer service. For example, search engines and comparison bots can reduce search costs and information costs. EC also can drastically reduce the costs of monitoring, collaborating, and negotiating.

Exhibit 14.11 reflects one aspect of transaction costs. As seen in the exhibit, there is a trade-off between transaction cost and size (volume) of business. Traditionally, in order to reduce transaction costs, firms had to grow in size (as depicted in curve T_1). In the digital

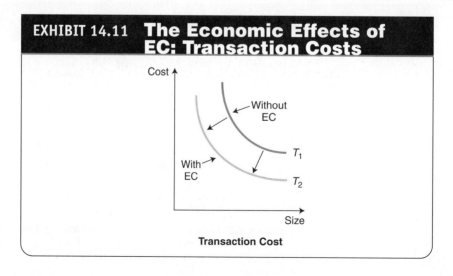

EXHIBIT 14.11 The Economic Effects of EC: Transaction Costs

Transaction Cost

economy, the transaction cost curve shifts downward to position T_2. This means that EC makes it possible to have low transaction costs even with smaller firm size and to enjoy much lower transaction costs as firm size increases.

INCREASED REVENUES

Throughout the text, we have demonstrated how an organization can use EC to increase revenues through online storefronts, auctions, cross-selling opportunities, multichannel distribution arrangements, and so on. EC can also be used to increase revenues by improving reach and richness.

Reach Versus Richness

Another economic impact of EC is the trade-off between the number of customers a company can reach (called *reach*) and the amount of interactions and information services it can provide to them (*richness*). According to Evans and Wurster (2000), for a given level of cost (resources), there is a trade-off between reach and richness. The more customers a company wants to reach, the fewer services it can provide to them for a given amount of money used in the transaction cost. Exhibit 14.12 depicts this economic relationship.

The case of stockbroker Charles Schwab illustrates the implementation of the reach versus richness trade-off. Initially, Schwab attempted to increase its reach. To do so, the company went downward along the curve (see Exhibit 14.12), reducing its richness. However, with its Web site (schwab.com), Schwab was able to drastically increase its reach (moving from point A to B) and at the same time provide more richness in terms of customer service and financial information to customers, moving from point B to point C. For example, Schwab's Mutual Fund Screener allows customers to design their own investment portfolios by selecting from an array of mutual funds. Providing such services (richness) allows Schwab to increase the number of customers (reach), as well as charge higher fees than competitors that provide few value-added services. In summary, the Internet pushes the curve outward toward the upper right-hand corner of the chart, allowing more reach with the same cost. For additional details, see Jelassi and Enders (2005).

Other Ways to Increase Revenues

EC can also increase revenues by:

▶ Providing products or services from a larger global market because of more effective product marketing on the Web

▶ Allowing customers to order anytime from any place via the use of m-commerce and l-commerce

▶ Using processes with lower internal cost (e.g., using lower cost computers) and with higher prices because of value-added services to the customer (e.g., information attached to product)

▶ Becoming an online portal

▶ Creating value-added content from selling searches, access to data, and electronic documents

The remainder of this section deals with some other issues related to the economics of EC.

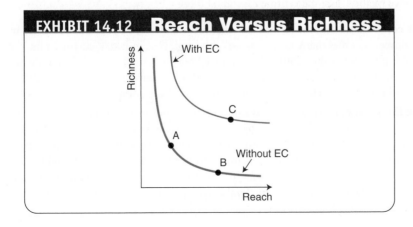

EXHIBIT 14.12 Reach Versus Richness

REDUCING TRANSACTION FRICTION OR RISK

Allowing the customer to utilize an EC-based calculator and avoid potentially embarrassing situations can reduce psychological risks. For example, online tracking tools reduce psychological concerns by allowing customers to check the status of a package. By publishing specifications and providing product comparison engines, EC can help reduce a customer's risk of purchasing an unwanted product or one of poor quality. EC also has been instrumental in providing customers with an accurate picture of product availability, helping them to avoid the risk of unexpected delays. Proper explanation can mitigate customer concerns over the security of EC transactions. Finally, linking the transaction to third-party security providers, such as the Better Business Bureau or VeriSign, can address customer concerns over privacy and security. In this way, EC can provide value by lowering the transaction friction or risk and providing the customer with *economic value*. For more on risk analysis and its reduction, see Beasley et al. (2006).

FACILITATING PRODUCT DIFFERENTIATION

product differentiation
Special features available in products that make them distinguishable from other products. This property attracts customers that appreciate what they consider an added value.

Organizations can use EC to provide **product differentiation**—products with special features. For example, McAfee allows users of its VirusScan virus-detection software to automatically update the latest security patches online, differentiating itself from those that require manual upgrades. Differentiation does not necessarily require a physical product; services also can be differentiated. EC can provide differentiation through better product information, informing users on how to use the product, how to replenish it, and how to provide feedback.

EC INCREASES AGILITY

agility
An EC firm's ability to capture, report, and quickly respond to changes happening in the marketplace and business environment.

EC can provide firms with the **agility** to monitor, report, and quickly respond to changes in the marketplace and the business environment. Companies with agile systems can respond to customer requests quickly, improving customer service. FedEx, UPS, and other delivery companies can provide location information because they use EC to connect with customers and make available package tracking information. EC systems enable companies to learn more about customers and understand their buying habits. This enables a company to better predict trends for better planning and quickly introduce changes when needed. Similarly, e-procurement has given firms the ability to quickly locate sellers and place orders. Sellers, in turn, use e-fulfillment to quickly locate products in their warehouses and fill customer orders.

VALUATION OF EC COMPANIES

valuation
The fair market value of a business or the price at which a property would change hands between a willing buyer and a willing seller who are both informed and under no compulsion to act. For a publicly traded company, the value can be readily obtained by multiplying the selling price of the stock by the number of available shares.

Valuation is the process of trying to determine the value or worth of a company. It is done for the purpose of selling a company or determining its value for going public (an IPO) or for a proposed merger. In the EC context, valuation often is conducted to determine a reasonable IPO price when a start-up company goes public.

Many valuation methods exist (e.g., see Smith and Laurent 2008). The three most common ones, according to Rayport and Jaworski (2004), are the comparable method, the financial performance method, and the venture capital method:

- ▶ **The comparable method.** With this method, analysts compare the company with similar companies on as many factors as possible (e.g., size, industry, customer base, products, growth rate, book value, debt, sales, financial performance). In addition, they may look at performance trends, management teams, and other features. A major difficulty with this method is finding such information for privately held companies.
- ▶ **The financial performance method.** This method uses projections of future earnings (usually 5 years), cash flows, and so on to find the NPV of a company. With this method, the analyst needs to discount future cash flows using a discount or interest rate. The major problem with this method is in determining the discount rate, which is based on future interest rates. Analysts may use pro forma income statements, free cash flow values, and the company's terminal value (the value of the company, if sold, 3 to 5 years in the future) to generate a valuation.

▶ **The venture capital method.** Venture capital (VC) firms (Chapter 16) invest in start-ups and usually take them through to their IPOs. They may use combinations of the first two methods, concentrating on terminal value. The VC firm then discounts the terminal value of the company, using a very high discount rate (e.g., 30% to 70%). When companies pay using their stocks, they have high valuation so they can afford to buy a high-valuation EC company. An example is IAC/Interactive Corp., which purchased AskJeeves in March 2005 in an all-stock acquisition. This compensates them for the high risk they assume.

Let's look at one of the most successful IPOs of an EC company—Google. Google floated its IPO in fall 2004, targeting it at $85 per share. Within a few weeks, the share price more than doubled, reaching more than $450 in late 2005, $500 in 2006, and more than $700 in 2007, giving Google a market capitalization of $200 billion a year. In 2008, the price declined to $300 when the stock market crashed. Does it make any sense?

The increase in share price indicated that investors were willing to pay huge premiums for anticipated future performance and valuation. Many acquisitions and mergers from 1996 through 2001 involved unrealistically high valuations, and so did the acquisition of social networks from 2005 to 2007. For example, Google paid $1.65 billion for YouTube.com in 2006. Note that when EC companies acquire other EC companies, they frequently pay in the form of stock, not cash, so such high valuations are more appropriate. Google uses this same strategy to acquire other companies.

The too-high valuation associated with the dot-com failures between 2000 and 2003 are back for highly trafficked Web 2.0 sites. The validation at that period in terms of price per monthly unique visitor reached several hundred dollars (e.g., $385 for Lycos, $384 for Excite). In 2008, the price was still low (e.g., $36 for MySpace, $44 for Ask Jeeves), but since 2003 it is increasing. News Corp. paid $580 million for MySpace; Google paid $1.65 billion for YouTube, and IAC/InterActive paid almost $2 billion for a relatively small search engine company, Ask.com. Although this seems like too much of an investment, it allows IAC/InterActive to use Ask.com to integrate a $20 billion Web portfolio of companies. IAC/InterActive based the high valuation on the expectation of online ads, which went from $6 billion in 2002 to $15 billion in 2006, and is estimated to be about $20 billion by 2009.

In summary, the economics of EC enable companies to be more competitive and more profitable. It also enables them to grow faster, collaborate better, provide superb customer service, and innovate more quickly. As in any economic environment, here, too, those that capitalize on these opportunities will excel; the rest are doomed to mediocrity or failure.

Section 14.5 ▶ **REVIEW QUESTIONS**

1. How does EC impact the production cost curve?
2. Define transaction costs. List the major types and explain how EC can reduce such costs.
3. How can EC increase revenues?
4. How can EC increase the competitive advantage for a firm?
5. What are the benefits of increasing reach? How can EC help?
6. How can organizations reduce psychological risk?
7. Explain the impact of EC on product differentiation and agility.
8. Define valuation. Why is it so high for some EC start-ups?

14.6 OPPORTUNITIES FOR SUCCESS IN E-COMMERCE AND AVOIDING FAILURE

Now that EC has been around for several years, it is possible to observe certain patterns that contribute to its success or failure. By examining EC patterns, one can find indications of the opportunities that lie ahead and avoid pitfalls along the way. This section examines EC failures, the key factors to EC success, how EC is creating digital options, and the complementary investments that are needed to enable EC success. But first, let's look at the determinants of success and failure.

FACTORS THAT DETERMINE E-COMMERCE SUCCESS

The economic capabilities of EC described earlier influence some industries more than others. The success factors of EC depend on the industry, the sellers and buyers, and the products sold. Furthermore, the ability of sellers to create economic value for consumers will also determine EC success. When deciding to sell online, looking at the major factors that determine the impact of EC can assist in evaluating the chances for success.

Four categories of e-market success factors commonly exist: product, industry, seller, and consumer characteristics.

Product Characteristics

Selecting the right product to sell is a critical success factor for e-tailing. Digitized products, such as software, documents, music, and videos, are particularly well suited for e-markets because they can be distributed to customers electronically, resulting in instant delivery and very low distribution costs. Digitization also decreases the amount of time involved in the order-taking cycle because automation can be introduced to help customers search for, select, and pay for a product, anyplace and anytime, without the intervention of a sales or technical person. Finally, product updates can be communicated to customers rapidly.

A product's price may also be an important determinant of its success. The higher the product price, the greater the level of risk involved in the market transaction between buyers and sellers who are geographically separated and who may have never dealt with each other before. Therefore, some of the most common items currently sold through e-markets are low-priced items such as CDs and books. Logically, for expensive products, such as fine wines, diamonds, and perfumes, or service-based products, such as hotel and vacation packages, customers often rely on the e-marketplace's *reputation* or information availability rather than just on price. In either case, EC can play a significant role in facilitating business.

Another product characteristic is the cost and speed of *product customization*. Millions of consumers configure computers, cars, toys, clothes, shoes, and services to their liking, and if sellers can fulfill such requests at a reasonable cost and in a short amount of time, they can assure success (e.g., Dell). Finally, computers, electronic products, consumer products, and even cars can be sold online because consumers know exactly what they are buying. The more product information that is available, the easier it is to sell. The use of multimedia and product tutorials (e.g., see bluenile.com) can dramatically facilitate product description.

Another aspect of a product's characteristics is *cross-selling* and *up-selling*. EC enables efficient and effective cross-selling and up-selling of many (but not all) products and services.

Industry Characteristics

Electronic markets are most useful when they are able to match buyers and sellers directly. However, some industries require transaction brokers. E-markets affect these industries less than those that do not require brokers. Stockbrokers, insurance agents, and travel agents may provide needed services, but in some cases, software may reduce the need for these brokers. This is particularly true as intelligent systems become more available to assist consumers.

Other important industry characteristics include the following: Who are the major players (corporations) in the industry? How many companies in the industry are well managed? How strong is the competition, including foreign companies?

Seller Characteristics

Electronic markets reduce *search costs*, allowing consumers to find sellers that offer lower prices, better service, or both. As in the case of the motion picture industry, this may reduce profit margins for sellers that compete in e-markets, but it may increase the number of transactions that take place (i.e., people watching more movies). However, if sellers are unwilling to participate in this environment, it may reduce the impact of e-markets. In highly competitive industries with low *barriers to entry*, sellers may not have a choice but to join in; if they do not, online customers' searches will lead them to an online competitor's distribution channel.

Consumer Characteristics

Consumers can be classified as impulse, patient, or analytical. Electronic markets may have little impact on industries in which impulse buyers make a sizable percentage of purchases. Because e-markets require a certain degree of effort and preparation on the part of the consumer, e-markets are more conducive to consumers who do some comparisons before buying (i.e., the patient and analytical buyers). Mobile devices are changing this situation because real-time information is available now while shoppers are in physical stores.

Analytical buyers can use the Internet to evaluate a wide range of information before deciding where to buy. On the other hand, *m-commerce* and especially *l-commerce*, which provides and even customizes services based on a customer's location, are banking on impulse buyers—on the customer's being in the right place at the right time. However, m-commerce also offers indirect benefits to consumers through improved location services. Team Assignment 2 presents a case where you can identify costs and benefits of a mobile computing system.

E-COMMERCE FAILURES

By examining the economic history of previous innovations, the failure of EC initiatives and EC companies (see discussions in Chapters 1 through 3 and 5) should come as no surprise. Three economic phenomena suggest why this is the case:

1. At a macroeconomic level, technological revolutions, such as the railroad and the automobile industries, have had a boom–bust–consolidation cycle. For example, between 1904 and 1908, more than 240 companies entered the then-new automobile manufacturing business in the United States. In 1910, the shakeout began. Today, there are only three U.S. automakers, but the size of the auto industry has grown several hundred times.

   Arthur (1996) compared the Internet revolution with the railroad revolution and found that both followed a similar pattern. First, there was the excitement over the emerging technology, then irrational euphoria followed by inflated market values of anything related to the new technology, and then the bust. However, Arthur notes that following the bust, the railroads saw their golden period, in which railroad activities in England grew tenfold. Why was this the case? Arthur believes that the real benefits of a technology come when organizations structure their activities around the cluster of technologies (e.g., after railroads emerged, steel rails, track safety systems, traffic control systems, and so on were needed). Similarly, businesses relocated to where the cost and availability of raw materials were favorable along the railroad lines.

2. At a mid-economic level, the bursting of the dot-com bubble from 2000 through 2003 is consistent with periodic economic downturns that have occurred in real estate, precious metals, currency, and stock markets.

3. At a microeconomic level, the "Web rush" reflected an over allocation of scarce resources—venture capital and technical personnel—and too many advertising-driven business models. This is analogous to the influx of people and resources to specific places during a "gold rush."

Chapters 3 and 13 provide some of the specific reasons for failure in B2C EC: lack of profitability, excessive risk exposure, the high cost of customer acquisition, poor performance, and static Web site design. Two additional financial reasons are lack of funding and incorrect revenue models (discussed in Chapter 2). With EC, B2B businesses have been trying to improve interfirm operations and customer service by allowing customers and partners to interact directly with the Web sites to do self-service. However, Schultze and Orlikowski (2004) found that in click-and-mortar EC applications, the use of the self-serve technology made it more difficult for sales representatives to build and maintain customer relationships. The use of IT and EC altered the nature and quality of information shared by the participants, undermined the ability of sales representatives to provide consulting services to customers, reduced the frequency of their interaction, and prompted sales representatives to expend social capital to promote the customers' technology adoption. These changes produced intended and unintended shifts in the network relations and raised serious challenges to the viability of their business model.

E-COMMERCE SUCCESSES

Despite the failure of hundreds of start-ups and thousands of EC projects, EC is alive and well and continues to grow rapidly after a short pause from 2000 through 2002, as discussed throughout the text.

EC success stories abound, primarily in specialty and niche markets. One example is Puritan's Pride (puritan.com), a successful vitamin and natural health-care product store. Another is campusfood.com, which allows college students to order take-out food online (Chapter 1). Also doing very well are employment sites, such as Monster (monster.com). Alloy (alloy.com) is a successful shopping and entertainment portal for young adults. As pointed out in Chapter 3, online services such as stock trading, travel reservations, online banking, and more are commanding a major part of the business in their industries. For a comparison of how these and other thriving online businesses have translated critical success factors (CSFs) from the old economy into EC success, see Exhibit 14.13.

Following are some of the reasons for EC success and suggestions from EC experts and consultants on how to succeed in EC.

Strategies for EC Success

Thousands of brick-and-mortar companies are adding online marketing and/or procurement channels with great success. Examples are uniglobe.com, staples.com, homedepot.com, walmart.com, clearcommerce.com, 1800flowers.com, and Southwest Airlines (iflyswa.com). Existing firms can use organizational knowledge, brand recognition, infrastructure, and other "morphing strategies" to migrate from the offline marketplace to the online marketspace. The following are strategies and critical success factors that can help EC succeed.

> ▸ Kauffman et al. (2006) assert strategies that include moving to higher-quality customers, changing products or services in their existing market, and establishing an offline presence (e.g., moving from pure-play dot-com to click-and-mortar). The authors provide guidelines for understanding successful e-business strategy.
>
> ▸ Pavlou and Gefen (2004) found that institutional-based trust, which is derived from buyers' perceptions that effective third-party institutional mechanisms are in place, is critical to EC success. These mechanisms include (1) feedback mechanisms, (2) third-party escrow services, and (3) credit card guarantees. This helps explain why, despite the inherent uncertainty that arises when buyers and sellers are separated in time and in space, online marketplaces are proliferating.

EXHIBIT 14.13   Critical Success Factors: Old Economy and EC

Old Economy CSFs	EC CSFs
Vertically integrate or do it yourself	Create new partnerships and alliances; stay with core competency
Deliver high-value products	Deliver high-value service offerings that encompass products
Build market share to establish economies of scale	Optimize natural scale and scope of business; look at mass customization
Analyze carefully to avoid missteps	Approach with urgency to avoid being locked out; use proactive strategies
Leverage physical assets	Leverage intangible assets, capabilities, and relationships—unleash dormant assets
Compete to sell product	Compete to control access and relationships with customers; compete with Web sites

▶ A group of Asian CEOs recommend the following EC CSFs: select robust business models, anticipate the dot-com future, foster e-innovation, carefully evaluate a spin-off strategy, co-brand, employ ex–dot-com staffers, and focus on the e-generation, as alloy.com and bolt.com have done. Kambil and van Heck (2002) found that for an EC exchange to be successful, it has to create value for *all* participants, not just the sellers, the market maker, or the buyers. The issue of value in an online exchange is the subject of debate among the many suppliers in the electronic marketplace. In Team Assignment 3, you will learn more about electronic hubs and have the opportunity to participate in identifying collaborative opportunities. These authors also recommend that for EC to be successful, it should support and enrich human interactions through technologies such as virtual reality (i.e., increase richness).

▶ Pricing in EC has continued to be a challenge for sellers because of handling and shipping costs. Often the seller and market maker will see the potential for profits and ignore the fact that the buyers will subscribe to EC only if they see the benefit in price or product variety. For example, in January 2005, Amazon.com decided to absorb such costs for orders above a certain level (e.g., $25). Free shipping is available at Dell, HP, and many other e-tailers.

▶ New technologies can boost the success of EC. For example, RFID has great potential for improving the supply chain (Chapter 6); however, it will take a large investment in EC infrastructure and applications to realize its full potential (see Section 14.4).

Wikipedia (2009) and others provide guidelines for success in the following areas:

▶ Technical and organizational aspects of good management
▶ Customer-oriented approach
▶ Handling problems properly and quickly
▶ Product suitability for online sale (especially digital products)
▶ Consumer acceptance of electronic shopping
▶ Peters (2006) offered 15 steps to EC success at websitecm.com. Peters supports several of Wikipedia's guidelines.
▶ Veneeva (2006) suggests that the current improvements in Internet services and their inherent characteristics, like improved security, reliability, user friendliness, two-way communication, low costs, accessibility, and customizability, have been the driving forces for successful e-commerce.

A number of experts and consultants have proposed many more keys to success.

Additional Guidelines for EC Success. A research study of 30 organizations identified the following factors that contributed to the successful implementation of B2C and B2B EC projects (Esichaikul and Chavananon 2001):

▶ The top three factors for successful B2C e-commerce were effective marketing management, an attractive Web site, and building strong connections with the customers.

▶ The top three factors for successful B2B e-commerce were the readiness of trading partners, information integration inside the company and in the supply chain, and the completeness of the EC system.

▶ The top three factors for the overall success of an e-business were a proper business model, readiness of the firm to become an e-business, and internal enterprise integration.

At this still-early stage of the EC revolution, success cannot be assured, and failure rates will remain high. However, if companies learn from the mistakes of the past and follow the guidelines offered by experts and researchers, their chances for success are greatly enhanced.

In the remaining parts of this section, we will discuss important strategies and factors that should be considered to assure EC success. The first one is the creation of digital options.

OPPORTUNITIES FOR SUCCESS: CREATING DIGITAL OPTIONS

Firms have welcomed the EC project evaluation process, including the tools of economic justification, because it allows them to justify an EC investment, compare it with other potential investments, and evaluate the potential risk or payoff. However, EC and information technologies play an innate role in supporting business projects that may not be well suited for the types of economic justification that work well for other types of investments. Researchers and practitioners are rethinking the extent to which ROI and related financial measures should play a role in the decision to invest in EC.

Sawhney (2002) argues that increased focus on ROI in evaluating e-business initiatives can lead to the bias of looking inward only and forcing out initiatives with little immediate and tangible ROI but with significant long-term value to the company. He suggests that firms should think broadly and follow the unanticipated benefits of EC projects, as in the example of Eli Lilly & Co., which created a Web site called InnoCentive (innocentive.com) to attract scientists to solve chemistry problems in exchange for financial rewards. In doing so, Eli Lilly has established contact with more than 8,000 scientists that the human resources department can tap into for future hiring and consulting needs.

digital options

A set of IT-enabled capabilities in the form of digitized enterprise work processes and knowledge systems.

Sambamurthy et al. (2003) refer to such opportunities from EC applications as *digital options*, a set of IT-enabled capabilities in the form of digitized enterprise work processes and knowledge systems. They refer to these capabilities as *options* because, as in the case of Eli Lilly, the firm has an option to exploit the project for other purposes. They suggest that exploiting such options increases agility. Had Eli Lilly only used the ROI justification approach, it might not have invested in the EC-based Web site. However, the "value" it provides in identifying and establishing contact with more than 8,000 scientists may be significant and last for the long term.

Online File W14.8 describes how GE Aircraft Engines has created digital options from a data collection system created to improve manufacturing operations.

CULTURAL DIFFERENCES IN EC SUCCESSES AND FAILURES

Chapter 1 mentioned culture as a possible barrier to the use of EC. In Chapter 13, we discussed the need to understand cultural issues such as differences in social norms, measurement standards, and nomenclature. Here, we raise the issue of cultural differences so that appropriate metrics can be developed.

One of the strengths of EC is the ease with which its adopters can reach a global population of consumers or suppliers. However, EC-driven businesses must consider the cultural differences in this diverse global consumer base because without the broad acceptance of the EC channel, consumers may choose not to participate in online transactions. Critical elements that can affect the value of EC across cultures are perceived trust, consumer loyalty, regulation, and political influences. Even the content of online ads can mean different things in different cultures. Due to these differences, the transaction costs, including coordination costs, may vary among the consumer base.

EC success factors differ among countries and so do adoption strategies (see Online File W14.9).

CAN EC SUCCEED IN DEVELOPING ECONOMIES?

Similar to cultural differences, developed and developing economies vary in how EC is used and whether the economics favor this channel of commerce. Developing economies struggle with various issues taken for granted in developed economies, such as the United Kingdom or Singapore.

Developing economies often face power blackouts, unreliable telecommunications infrastructure, undependable delivery mechanisms, and the fact that only a few customers own computers and credit cards. Such limitations make it difficult for firms to predict whether EC investments will pay off, and when. However, developing economies, such as China and India, represent a significant opportunity for EC to connect businesses to customers, as well as other businesses. The potential volume of transactions in developed countries can make EC investments more attractive for established firms. This is because much of the cost of EC systems development would have already been recovered because EC initiatives frequently can use existing IT infrastructures.

The traditional EC assumption is that every computer user has the investment capacity to own a computer and maintain a dedicated Internet connection, as is the case in developed economies. In developing economies, the assumption will have to be revised to incorporate low-cost access, pay for use only, a community of users, and mass coverage. The payoffs from EC use in developing countries are likely to go beyond financial returns. Enabling people to take advantage of EC technology without disrupting their traditions may be the most valuable, yet intangible, return.

A major booster for EC in developing countries is the increasing use of low-cost laptop computers in a wireless environment. With computer cost less than $200 (in 2008, and declining) and the wide spread of cell phones with Internet access and free access in public places, it is likely that EC use will increase significantly in developing countries.

Section 14.6 ▶ REVIEW QUESTIONS

1. Describe product characteristics in EC.
2. What are industry characteristics in EC?
3. What are seller characteristics in EC?
4. What are consumer characteristics in EC?
5. List three reasons why EC failure should not come as a surprise.
6. What are some reasons for EC success?
7. What are digital options?
8. Relate EC to cultural differences.

MANAGERIAL ISSUES

Some managerial issues related to this chapter are as follows.

1. **How should the value of EC investment be justified?** EC investments must be measured against their contribution to business objectives. The best justification may come from the behavior of competitors. If EC has a strategic value to customers, there is no choice but to invest as long as competitors provide EC services. EC investments will involve direct and indirect costs as well as tangible and intangible benefits. The impact of EC on reengineering the existing processes and systems must not be ignored.

   Automated transactions in EC may replace human roles in sales, procurement, and services. However, in some applications like customer services and knowledge management, EC may supplement rather than replace the human element. The measurement of EC value, including both tangible and intangible benefits, should occur against the backdrop of metrics that define business performance and success. To identify the intangible benefits, refer to the business performance indicators in the balanced scorecard, which may not be easily measured in tangible metrics.

2. **Which investment analysis method should we adopt for EC justification?** The precise estimation of total cost of ownership is a good starting point for financial investment analysis. If an intangible benefit is the primary source of benefit, such as enhanced customer services and quality assurance of purchased material, management has to judge the tangible cost with an intangible benefit. However, if the tangible benefit can be precisely measured, such as creation of new revenue and/or reduced purchase cost, the net present value and ROI can be computed with tangible benefits and costs. Based on the investment analysis, the intangible factors may be considered additionally for managers' multicriteria judgments. Since there is high uncertainty in estimating the future revenue creation, the best or worst case analysis may supplement the most-likely analysis.

3. **Shift from tangible to intangible benefits.** Few opportunities remain for automation projects that simply replace manual labor with IT on a one-for-one basis. Therefore, the economic justification of EC applications will increasingly depend on intangible benefits such as increased quality or improved customer service. It is very difficult to accurately estimate

the value of intangible benefits prior to the actual implementation. Some intangible benefits are difficult to measure even after the implementation. Therefore, managers need to understand and use tools that bring intangible benefits into the decision-making processes for the sensitivity analysis of IT investments.

4. **What complementary investments will be followed?** Companies should consider the complementary investments in other functional areas to ensure EC success because the goal of EC may not be attained simply by implementing the EC system. If a brick-and-mortar company becomes click-and-mortar, the traditional organization will be severely influenced and restructuring costs will be incurred. For instance, banking sectors have opened their online services, and the Internet has become the primary channel. This implies that the traditional branch office has to transform its functions to differentiate its roles focusing on VIP customers. A strong CRM system should be implemented to identify and retain VIP customers. This is an example of follow-on investment.

5. **Who should conduct the justification?** For small projects, the project team possibly in cooperation with the finance department can do the analysis. For a large or complex project, we may use the unbiased outside consultant although it may be expensive. The justification should include both tangible and intangible benefits and costs. However, some vendors may provide ROI calculators as a part of a proposal that may fit with your application without extra charge.

6. **How does one know if the valuation of EC companies is justifiable?** During the early stage of EC companies, the high growth rate and market share are the primary origin of justification. Thus the loss may be excused for awhile. Establishment of a large customer base and community can be another origin of justification, particularly for the social network service providers. However, eventually the profit is attained from solid revenue sources. E-businesses should cultivate and show the diverse sources of revenue to justify the future value of EC companies.

7. **Is it possible to predict EC success?** The more comprehensive the analysis, the more accurate the justification of the EC project; its chances for approval will be greater even though management cannot precisely know the future success of the project. The procurement innovation using EC is almost risk free in achieving the goals. Refer to the fee strategy of iMarketKorea (IMK) for their procurement services in the closing case in Chapter 5. IMK does not charge a fee, but shares the discount effect with their customers. This kind of project is almost risk free. However, using EC for sales increase is uncertain. Opening new independent e-marketplaces takes high investment and is very risky because the entry barrier is already very high. This kind of EC investment may fail. The risk depends upon the type of EC being used.

SUMMARY

In this chapter, you learned about the following EC issues as they relate to the chapter's learning objectives.

1. **The need for EC justification.** Like any other investment, EC investment (unless it is small) needs to be justified. Many start-up EC companies have crashed because of no or incorrect justification. In its simplest form, justification looks at revenue minus all relevant costs. Analysis is done by defining metrics related to organizational goals.

2. **The difficulties in justifying EC investment.** The nature of EC makes it difficult to justify due to the presence of many intangible costs and benefits. In addition, the relationship between investment and results may be complex, extending over several years. Also, several projects may share both costs and benefits; several areas may feel the impacts (sometimes negative).

3. **Difficulties in established intangible metrics.** Intangible metrics may be difficult to define. Some of these benefits change rapidly; others have different values to different people or organizational units.

Intangible metrics have qualitative measures that are difficult to compare. One solution is to quantify the qualitative measures. Scoring methodology, value analysis, and other advanced methods, as described in Online File W14.4, can do this.

4. **Traditional methods for evaluating EC investments.** Evaluating EC involves a financial analysis, usually the ROI analysis, as well as an assessment of the technology and its architecture. Future costs and benefits need to be discounted, using the NPV method, especially if the costs and benefits will extend over several years. A payback period describes how long it will take to recover the initial investment. However, financial ROI alone can lead to an incomplete and misleading evaluation. Tools to integrate the various ROI aspects of EC investment include the balanced scorecard (BSC), which also focuses on the internal business processes and learning and growth

perspective of the business. EC ROI should take into account the risk of reducing possible failures or adverse events that can drain the financial ROI. No method is universal or perfect, so selecting a method (or a mix of methods) is critical.

5. **Understand how to justify specific EC projects.** All EC projects include intangible and tangible benefits and costs that must be identified. Then, a method(s) must be selected to match the particular characteristics of the EC application.

6. **EC investment evaluation.** Economic fundamentals must be kept in mind when evaluating an EC investment. With nondigital products, the cost curve shows that average per unit costs decline as quantity increases. However, with digital products, the variable cost per unit usually is low, and thus, the evaluation will differ. Similar differences are evident in EC's ability to lower transaction costs, agency costs, and transaction risks. EC can also enable the firm to be agile in responding faster to changing market conditions and ensure increasing returns to scale regardless of the volume involved. Finally, EC enables increased reach with multimedia richness at a reasonable cost.

7. **E-marketplace economics.** Products, industry, seller, and consumer characteristics require different metrics of EC value. With the growing worldwide connectivity to the Internet, EC economics will play a major role in supporting buyers and sellers. As compared with traditional commerce, EC can quickly succeed due to its ability to create network effects, lock-in effects, and disintermediation, especially in the case of digital products.

8. **Reasons for EC success and failure.** Like other innovations, EC is expected to go through the cycle of enormous success, followed by speculation, and then disaster before the reality of the new situation sets in. Some EC failures were the result of problematic Web site design, lack of sustained funding, and weak revenue models. Success in EC has come through automating and enhancing familiar strategies, such as branding, morphing, trust building, and creating value for all trading partners by enriching the human experience with integrated and timely information. EC investments can go beyond the traditional business models by creating digital options. To ensure success, complementary investments must be made in managing change and responding to cultural differences among EC users.

KEY TERMS

Agency costs	649	Metric	631	Total cost of ownership		
Agility	652	Product differentiation	652	(TCO)	638	
Cost–benefit analysis	630	Production function	649	Transaction costs	650	
Digital options	658	ROI calculator	640	Valuation	652	
Key performance indicators		Total benefits of ownership				
(KPIs)	632	(TBO)	639			

QUESTIONS FOR DISCUSSION

1. A mail-order catalog company that is adding online selling has hired you. Develop EC success metrics for the company. Develop a set of metrics for the company's customers.

2. Your government is considering an online vehicle registration system. Develop a set of EC metrics and discuss how these metrics differ from those of an online catalog company (see the previous question).

3. Consider the various economic justification methods. Are there conditions under which one may be more useful than the others?

4. Discuss the advantage of using several methods (e.g., ROI, payback period) to justify investments.

5. Enter businesscase.com and find material on ROI analysis. Discuss how ROI is related to a business case.

6. A craftsperson operates a small business making wooden musical instruments in a small town. The business owner is considering using EC to increase the business's reach to the nation and the world. How can the business owner use EC to increase richness to make the products more attractive to consumers?

7. You are considering moving your bank account to an online bank. What features and services can the bank provide to reduce your psychological risk in making EC transactions?

8. A company is planning a wireless-based CRM system. Almost all the benefits are intangible. How can you justify the project to top management?

9. Discuss the value of TCO and TBO concepts for EC investment evaluation.

INTERNET EXERCISES

1. Enter idc.com and find how they evaluate ROI on intranets, supply chains, and other EC and IT projects. Enter nucleusresearch.com. Go to "Research," "Latest Research," and then click "View ROI Scorecards." Open the PDF file titled "Market ROI Scorecard: Hosted CRM" for a review of hosted CRM vendors. Summarize your findings in a report. (Note: Use Google to find this information.)

2. Enter schwab.com. Examine the list of online services available for planning and retirement, and advised investment services. Relate them to richness and reach.

3. Go to google.com and search for articles dealing with the ROI of RFID. List the key issues in measuring the ROI of RFID.

4. Enter citrix.com/English/ps2/products/product.asp?contentID=163057&ntref=3_nav, sharkfinesse.com, and covalentworks.com. Review their calculators. Write a report.

5. Go to alinean.com/P_ROIcalculator.asp and follow the walk-through of the calculators. Find the capabilities of the calculators. Calculate the ROI of a project of your choice as well as the TCO.

7. Enter sas.com, corvu.com, balancedscorecard.org, and cio.com. Find demos and examples of how to use the various tools and methods to evaluate EC projects. Write a report.

8. Enter solutionmatrix.com and find information about ROI, metrics, and cost–benefit tools. Write a report based on your findings.

9. Enter roi-calc.com. View the demos. What investment analysis services does the company provide?

10. Enter zebra.com and find their ROI calculators (go to resource library). What analysis do the calculators provide?

11. Enter google.com and baselinemag.com. Find information related to EC investment evaluation. Summarize your findings in a report.

12. Enter sap.com and use the "casebuilder calculator" for a hypothetical (or real) IT project. Write a report on your experience.

13. Enter searchcio.techtarget.com and find free ROI analysis tools. Download a tool of your choice and identify its major components. Write a report.

14. Enter peaksalesconsulting.com/crm_roi.htm and use their free calculator to examine a CRM project of your choice.

15. Enter apc.com and find information about the Efficiency Quotient tool. Write a report on how the tool works and its benefits.

TEAM ASSIGNMENTS, PROJECTS, AND CLASS DISCUSSIONS

1. Download the ROI case study "Venda Xerox Document Supplies (Case Study E11)" from the Nucleus Research (nucleusresearch.com) Web site. Read the Venda Xerox case study. While you are connected to the Internet, click "ROI Help Tutorial" in the NR_Standard_ROI_Tool.xls file and read modules 1 through 4. Enter your assumptions of costs and benefits into the calculator and examine how they impact the overall ROI, payback period, NPV, and average yearly cost of ownership (under the Summary tab).

   Answer the following questions based on the Venda Xerox Document Supplies ROI case study.

   a. What were the key reasons why Xerox developed an EC system?

   b. What were the areas in which Xerox could benefit from EC?

   c. How did Xerox calculate the ROI of the EC system?

2. In this activity, you will measure the business value of a mobile computing system for the field service representatives at Alliance Insurance Company (AIC), a fictitious company name based on some actual companies. See Online File W14.10 for details.

3. Explore the business value of EC. Each member enters a different site (e.g., nicholasgcarr.com, baselinemag.com, strassmann.com, etc.). Prepare a presentation on issues, value, and directions.

4. Address the following topics in a class discussion:

   a. A cost–benefit analysis may be inaccurate, so why should it be done?

   b. Why is traditional ROI so popular since it does not include intangibles?

   c. How should we deal with intangible benefits of CRM? KM? Exchanges?

JUSTIFYING EC AND IT INVESTMENT IN THE U.S. STATE OF IOWA

The Problem

For years, there was little planning or justification for EC and IT projects by the government of the state of Iowa. Any state agency that needed money for an EC or IT project slipped it into its budget request. State agencies requested many projects, knowing that only a few would be funded. Bargaining, political favors, pressures, and other outside influences determined which agencies' requests were honored. As a result, some important projects were not funded, and unimportant ones were. In addition, there was very little incentive to save money. This was the situation in Iowa until 1999, and it still exists in many other states, countries, cities, and other public institutions. However, in Iowa, everything changed in 1999 when a request for $22.5 million to resolve the Y2K problem was made.

The Solution

Iowa's solution to its IT planning and spending program, the Iowa Return on Investment Program (ROI Program), is an IT value model. The basic idea is to promote *performance-based government*, an approach that measures the results of government programs. The state of Iowa developed the ROI Program to justify investment in the Y2K solution. The basic principles of the model follow.

First, a pot of money called the Pooled Technology Account, which is appropriated by the legislature and controlled by the state's IT department, primarily funds new investments. Pooling of funds makes budget oversight easier and prevents duplications. Second, agencies submit requests for funding future EC and IT projects from the pooled account. To support their requests, agency managers must document the expected costs and benefits of the project based on a set of factors. The maximum score for each factor ranges from 5 to 15 points, for a maximum total score of 100 points. In addition, they must specify metrics related to those factors in order to determine the project's success. The scores are based on 10 criteria that are used to determine value (for details on these criteria, see Varon 2003).

The ROI Program requires agencies to detail their technology requirements and functional needs. This enforces standards, and it also helps officials identify duplicate projects and expenditures. For example, in 2001 several agencies proposed building pieces of an ERP system that would handle e-procurement and human resources management. The IT department suggested that the state deploy a single, more cost-effective ERP system that several agencies could

share. The project, which had an estimated cost of $9.6 million, could easily have cost many times that amount if agencies had been allowed to go it alone. Once a project is funded, the state saves money by scrutinizing expenses. Agencies must submit their purchase orders and invoices to the Enterprise Quality Assurance Office for approval before they can be reimbursed. This IT value model is universal and fits EC projects as well. The IT department reimburses agencies for expenses from the Pooled Technology Account only after verifying that the expenses were necessary. If an agency's expenditures are not in line with the project schedule, it presents a red flag for auditors that the project could be in trouble.

The Results

Iowa's ROI Program became a national model for documenting value and prioritizing IT and EC investments in the public sector. In 2002, the National Association of State Chief Information Officers (NASCIO) named the program the "Best State IT Management Initiative." It saved taxpayers more than $5 million in less than 4 years (about 16% of the spending on new IT projects).

The process also changed users' behavior. For example, during fiscal year 2003, seventeen EC and IT projects were requested through the budget approval process, and only six were approved. For the year 2004, four projects were requested, and all were approved. Also, there is considerable collaboration and use of cross-functional teams to write applications. State agencies are now thinking through their IT and EC investments more carefully. Another improvement is collaboration among agencies that submit joint proposals, thereby eliminating duplicate projects. Finally, the methodology minimizes political pressure. The success of Iowa's ROI Program led to the Iowa Accountable Government Act of 2001, which requires establishing a similar methodology for all state investments, not just EC or IT projects.

Sources: Compiled from Varon (2003) and State of Iowa (2007).

Questions

1. List the major deficiencies of the old method of project funding.
2. How are projects justified under the new method?
3. List the advantages of the new program.
4. What are the limitations of the method?

ONLINE RESOURCES
available at pearsonglobaleditions.com/turban

Online Files

W14.1 Nucleus Research's ROI Methodology

W14.2 Handling Intangible Benefits

W14.3 Issues in Implementing Traditional Justification Methods

W14.4 Advanced Methods for Justifying EC and IT Investments Value Analysis

W14.5 Assessing e-CRM ROI

W14.6 E-Procurement Complexities in Marketplaces

W14.7 The ROI on RFID

W14.8 Application Case: GE Aircraft Engines' Digital Options

W14.9 Application Case: The Success Story of E-Choupal

W14.10 Application Case: Alliance Insurance Exercise

Comprehensive Educational Web Sites

mmv.vic.gov.au/ecommerce: Case studies
nucleuresearch.com: Metrics, ROI
roi-calc.com: Calculators, metrics
baselinemag.com: Calculators, metrics
strassmann.com: ROI, justification, metrics

REFERENCES

Alter, A. "The Bitter Truth About ROI." *CIO Insight*, July 2006.

Arthur, W. B. "Increasing Returns and the New World of Business." *Harvard Business Review*, 74, no. 4 (1996).

Baseline. "How to Calculate ROI." September 6, 2006. baselinemag.com/article2/0,1540,2012723,00.asp (accessed January 2009).

Beasley, M., A. Chen, K. Nunez, and L. Wright. "Balanced Scorecard and Enterprise Risk Management." *Strategic Finance*, March 2006.

Bisconti, K. "Determining the Value and ROI of an Enterprise Portal, Part 2." *Enterprise Systems*, November 16, 2004. esj.com/enterprise/article.aspx?EditorialsID=1197 (accessed January 2009).

Borenstein, D., P. Betencourt, and R. Baptista. "A Multi-Criteria Model for the Justification of IT Investments." *INFOR*, February 2005.

Bothama, H. "State of the Art in TCO." SAP white paper with ASUG, January 2006.

Chen, S. *Strategic Management of E-Business*, 2nd ed. West Sussex, England: John Wiley & Sons, Ltd., 2005.

CIO Insight. "Top Trends for 2005." December 2004.

David, J. S., D. Schuff, and R. St. Louis. "Managing Your IT Total Cost of Ownership." *Communications of the ACM*, 45, no. 1 (2002).

Devaraj, S., and R. Kohli. *The IT Payoff: Measuring Business Value of Information Technology Investment*. Upper Saddle River, NJ: Prentice Hall, 2002.

EDS. "Case Study: California State Automobile Association." 2006a. eds.com/insights/casestudies/ca_state_auto.aspx (accessed January 2009).

EDS. "EDS Exceeds Expectation for CSAA." EDS press release, August 14, 2006b. eds.com/multimedia/ videos/downloads/2895_CSAATranscript.pdf (accessed January 2009).

Esichaikul, V., and S. Chavananon. "Electronic Commerce and Electronic Business Implementation Success Factors." *Proceedings of the 14th Bled Electronic Commerce Conference*, Bled, Slovenia, June 25–26, 2001.

Evans, P., and T. S. Wurster. *Blown to Bits: How the New Economics of Information Transforms Strategy*. Boston, MA: Harvard Business School Press, 2000.

Ferrin, B. G., and R. E. Plank. "Total Cost of Ownership Models: An Exploratory Study." *Journal of Supply Chain Management* (Summer 2002).

Hovenden, D., D. St. Clair, and M. Potter. "From Projects to Portfolios: A Strategic Approach to IT Investment." *ATKearney Executive Agenda*, 6, no. 1 (March 2005). atkearney.com/res/shared/pdf/EAv6n1_projects_port folios_S.pdf (accessed January 2009).

Hubbard, D.W. *How to Measure Anything: Finding the Value of Intangible in Business*. Hoboken, NJ: John Wiley and Sons, 2007.

Hughes, J., and G. Atwell. "A Framework for the Evaluation of E-Learning." Seminar series on Exploring Models and Partnerships for eLearning in SMEs, Brussels, Belgium, February 2003.

Jelassi, T., and A. Enders. *Strategies for E-Business*. Harlow, England: Prentice Hall, 2005.

Kambil, A., and E. van Heck. *Making Markets: How Firms Can Design and Profit from Online Auctions and Exchanges*. Boston, MA: Harvard Business School Press, 2002.

Kauffman, R. J., T. Miller, and B. Wang. "When Internet Companies Morph: Understanding Organizational Strategy Changes in the 'New' New Economy." *Special Issue: Commercial Applications of the Internet*, July 2006.

Keen, J. M., and R. Joshi. *Making Technology Investment Profitable: ROI Roadmap to Better Business Cases*, 2nd ed. Hoboken, NJ: John Wiley & Sons, 2009.

Keepmedia.com. "Tool: The Return on Stopping Viruses." February 7, 2005. keepmedia.com/pubs/baseline/2005/02/07/721943 (no longer available online).

Keystone Strategy, Inc. *Enterprise IT Capabilities and Business Performance Study*. March 16, 2006.

Kingstone, S. "The Financial Realities of CRM: A Guide to Best Practices, TCO, and ROI." The Yankee Group, 2004.

MacDonald, D. "Foundations for Anytime, Anywhere Computing." Montgomery Research, Inc. May 23, 2003.

Mahapatra, R., and V. S. Lai. "Evaluating End-User Training Programs." *Communications of the ACM* (January 2005).

McKay, J., and P. Marshall. *Strategic Management of E-Business*. Milton, Australia: Wiley, 2004.

Misra, R. "Evolution of the Philosophy of Investments in IT Projects." *Issues in Informing Sciences and Information Technology*, 3 (2006).

MobileInfo.com. "Mobile Computing Business Cases." mobileinfo.com/business_cases.htm (accessed January 2009).

MultiMedia Victoria. *eCommerce Case Studies*. mmv.vic. gov.au/ecommercecasestudies (accessed January 2009).

Nucleus Research. "Manifesto: Separating ROI Fact from Fiction." Research Note C51, 2002. nucleusresearch. com/research/notes-and-reports/manifesto-separating-roi-fact-from-fiction (accessed January 2009).

Pavlou, P. A., and D. Gefen. "Building Effective Online Marketplaces with Institution-Based Trust." *Information Systems Research*, 15, no. 1 (2004).

Peacock, E., and M. Tanniru. "Activity-Based Justification of IT Investments." *Information Management*, March 2005.

Pearlson, K. E., and C. S. Sounders. *Managing and Using Information Systems*. Hoboken, NJ: John Wiley & Sons, 2006.

Person, R. *Balanced Scorecards and Operational Dashboards with Microsoft Excel*. Hoboken, NJ: John Wiley & Sons, 2009.

Peters, J. "15 Steps to E-Commerce Success." *Website CM.com*, August 1, 2006. websitecm.com/news/26/15-Stepsto-ECommerce-Success-Part-1-of-3.html (accessed January 2009).

Pisello, T. "Metrics: ROI, IRR, NPV, Payback, Discounted Payback." *Techtarget*, September 15, 2006a. searchcrm. techtarget.com/expert/KnowledgebaseAnswer/0,2896 25,sid11_gci1216028,00.html (accessed January 2009).

Pisello, T. "The ROI of RFID in the Supply Chain." *RFID Journal*, August 21, 2006b. rfidjournal.com/article/articleview/2602/1/2 (accessed January 2009).

Rayport, J., and B. J. Jaworski. *Introduction to E-Commerce*, 2nd ed. New York: McGraw-Hill, 2004.

Renkema, T. J. W. *The IT Value Quest: How to Capture the Business Value of IT-Based Infrastructure*. Chichester (UK) and New York: John Wiley & Sons, 2000.

Ross, J. W., and C. M. Beath. "Beyond the Business Case: New Approaches to IT Investment." *MIT Sloan Management Review* (Winter 2002).

Sambamurthy, V., A. Bharadwaj, and V. Grover. "Shaping Agility Through Digital Options: Reconceptualizing the Role of Information Technology in Contemporary Firms." *MIS Quarterly*, 27, no. 2 (2003).

Sawhney, M. "Damn the ROI, Full Speed Ahead: 'Show Me the Money' May Not Be Right Demand for E-Business Projects." *CIO Magazine* (2002).

Schultze, U., and W. J. Orlikowski. "A Practice Perspective on Technology-Mediated Network Relations: The Use of Internet-Based Self-Serve Technologies." *Information Systems Research*, 15, no. 1 (2004).

Sidana, N. "The ROI on IT Investment." *Network Magazine*, December 2006. networkmagazineindia.com/200612/analyst'scorner01.shtml (accessed February 2007).

Smith, R. "Are You Meeting Quality Goals?" *Baseline*, October 2006.

Smith, A. C., and J. Laurent. "Allocating Value Among Different Classes of Equity." *Journal of Accountancy* (March 2008).

Soh, C., and L. M. Markus. "How IT Creates Business Value: A Process Theory Synthesis." *Proceedings of the 16th International Conference on Information Systems*, Amsterdam, Netherlands, December 10–13, 1995.

Spector, D. H. M. "Calculating TCO and ROI in Open Source Platforms." *TechRepublic*, April 6, 2006. search. techrepublic.com.com/index.php?q=Calculating+TCO +and+ROI+in+Open+Source+Platforms&go=Search (accessed January 2009).

State of Iowa. "ROI Program." 2007. state.ia.us/itd/roi (accessed January 2009).

Varon, E. "R.O. Iowa: By Centralizing Its State IT Budget Process, Establishing a Scoring Method and Instituting Value Metrics, Iowa Has Become a National Model for Gauging Project ROI." *CIO Magazine* (2003).

Veneeva, V. "E-Business: Success or Failure?" *Ezinearticles. com*, June 29, 2006. ezinearticles.com/?E-Business:-Successof-Failure?&id=232635 (accessed January 2009).

Wattemann, R. "ROI 101: Making the Business Case for Technology Investment." *CIO.com*, Analyst Report #1344 (by Nucleus Research). cio.com/analyst/report1344.html (accessed January 2007).

Wikipedia. "Electronic Commerce." 2009. en.wikipedia. org/wiki/Electronic_commerce (accessed January 2009).

LAUNCHING A SUCCESSFUL ONLINE BUSINESS AND EC PROJECTS

Learning Objectives

Upon completion of this chapter, you will be able to:

1. Understand the fundamental requirements for initiating an online business.

2. Describe the process of initiating and funding a start-up e-business or large e-project.

3. Understand the process of adding EC initiatives to an existing business.

4. Describe the issues and methods of transforming an organization into an e-business.

5. Describe the process of acquiring Web sites and evaluating building versus hosting options.

6. Understand the importance of providing and managing content and describe how to accomplish this.

7. Evaluate Web sites on design criteria, such as appearance, navigation, consistency, and performance.

8. Understand how search engine optimization may help a Web site obtain high placement in search engines.

9. Understand how to provide some support e-services.

10. Understand the process of building an online storefront.

11. Know how to build an online storefront with templates.

Content

OBO SETS ITS GOALS FOR SUCCESS

The Problem

OBO of New Zealand (*obo.co.nz*) is a small company that sells protective gear for field hockey goalkeepers. The leg guards, helmets, gloves, and other products protect goalies from the hard hockey ball without inhibiting the goalie's need to move quickly and easily. OBO's protective foam has a tighter and more consistent cell structure than competitors' products to provide maximum, long-wearing protection, and OBO's unique three-dimensional thermo-bonding manufacturing process produces equipment that reflects the way the body moves. By manufacturing a quality product and listening to its customers, OBO has become the market leader in most of the 20 countries in which its products are sold. In the 2008 Olympics, all the medal-winning teams wore OBO gear.

OBO is based in Palmerston North, a small provincial town in New Zealand that is a very long way from its principal markets in Europe and the Americas. OBO produces a niche product that it sells best through agents or stores to ensure a proper fit. How does OBO use its Web site to market an experiential product to a global market from New Zealand?

The Solution

The goals of the *obo.co.nz* Web site are community building, product sales, and research and development. As the "About OBO" Web page proudly boasts, "OBO loves the Web because it lets us have contact with the people we exist to serve."

Community building happens through online discussion forums, sponsored players, and an image gallery. In addition, OBO sponsors goalkeepers. It e-mails 900 to 1,000 people biweekly and gives goalkeepers the opportunity to ask an expert about the game and the equipment, join a group, link to other hockey sites, and offer opinions. The company tries to get people involved by having their photo on the Web site. By getting people involved, they come to love the brand name, image, and the feelings that go with it.

OBO also sells goalie equipment through the Web site. The main marketing and sales goal of the Web site is to convince the visitor of the value of the product and direct the customer to a store or agent to make the purchase. The Web site is a support mechanism for the brand and the sale of equipment through the agents, and the company picks up the odd sale here and there.

OBO meets its marketing and development goals through online surveys, solicitation of players' opinions of the products, and focus groups. The company also uses the Web site for research and development through online focus groups. For example, OBO might offer a topic such as goalkeeping shoes—Is there a need for them? What features should they have? What pricing? The focus group is carefully selected from the database, given the brief (the purpose of the questions), and asked to respond by the end of the week with their opinions.

The Results

The OBO Web site is most successful at community building. In 2000, over 100,000 people visited the Web site, many of them first-time OBO equipment buyers who must register their product warranty online. Many become registered "team players" and contribute to discussion forums as well as create their own "favorites" section and online address book. The site also builds community by promoting a goalie-friendly approach to OBO's customers. The most special thing about OBO is its employees, who are dedicated to the work.

Online product sales are modest and growing slowly. This is in line with the company's expectation that the Web site should support, not compete with, OBO's agent network. For example, prices at the Web site are slightly higher than in retail stores. However, online sales are expected to grow, because OBO has introduced a new line of clothes designed specifically for goalies that is sold *exclusively* through the Web site.

The focus groups deliver high-value feedback at almost no cost, and the discussion forums contribute to both community building and a constant stream of feedback about OBO's products in the marketplace.

Sources: Compiled from New Zealand Ministry of Economic Development (2000) and from *obo.co.nz* (accessed February 2009).

WHAT WE CAN LEARN . . .

OBO's use of the Web matches many of the expectations that online business owners have for their own Web sites. A small company with a great product is using its Web site to reach its target markets in distant countries. Like many successful online businesses, OBO uses its site to support business goals and to meet the needs and expectations of its target audience. The Web site is simple and well designed: It includes "attractors" that encourage customer interaction and keep customers coming back, it contains content that promotes cross-selling, and it effectively promotes sustainable customer relationships. OBO is one of tens of thousands of small businesses successfully using the Web for e-commerce. The purpose of this chapter is to describe the requirements for creating and maintaining a successful e-business or EC initiative. It also teaches you how to build a small storefront quickly.

15.1   GETTING INTO E-COMMERCE AND STARTING A NEW ONLINE BUSINESS

As described in Chapter 1 and throughout the book, it is a terrific time to be an entrepreneur. The availability of cheap computer hardware, free or inexpensive software, and high-speed Internet access has created a powerful base from which to launch new business and expand or transform existing ones. Belew and Elad (2009) provide a complete guide on how to start an online business. This chapter describes some of the steps involved in setting up an e-business.

GETTING INTO E-COMMERCE

Now that you are familiar with EC and its potential, you may want to know how to get into EC yourself. You can start an e-commerce venture in any number of ways; your only limit is your imagination. In this chapter, we will discuss some of the most common ways of starting an e-business. Specifically, this chapter presents the following topics:

- Starting a new online business (a start-up; see Section 15.2)
- Adding e-commerce initiative(s) to an existing business (i.e., becoming a click and-mortar organization; see Section 15.3)
- Transforming to an e-business (Section 15.3)
- Opening a storefront on the Web (Section 15.9)

Almost any e-commerce initiative will require support activities and services, as well as plans for attracting visitors to a Web site. This chapter presents the following with regards to these types of activities:

- Developing a Web site (Section 15.4)
- Hosting the Web site and selecting and registering a domain name (Section 15.5)
- Developing, updating, and managing the content of a Web site (Section 15.6)
- Designing a Web site for maximum usability (Section 15.7)
- Providing support services (Section 15.8)

According to Hise (2009), becoming an owner of a business has become a national obsession in the United States, and the percentage of Internet businesses is increasing.

STARTING A NEW ONLINE BUSINESS

Success in the online marketplace is never an assured outcome. As in the brick-and-mortar marketplace, the failure rate for online companies is high. Why do so few online companies succeed while many others fail? What does the entrepreneur need to know to launch a profitable online business?

Online businesses may be pure-play companies or click-and-mortar companies that add online projects, such as e-procurement or selling online, as an additional marketing channel.

AN E-START-UP IS A START-UP

Before we start our discussion, we need to emphasize that an e-start-up is basically a start-up and, as such, must consider all the issues faced by a physical start-up. Many books, magazines, and articles are dedicated to starting a new business. Magazines such as *Entrepreneur* are fully dedicated to start-ups. Copeland and Malik (2006) provide a 16-step process and guidelines for building a bulletproof start-up. They also provide a list of "things to avoid," "tools you need," "tips for success," and more. The Internet is contributing to what Hise (2007) calls "America's love affair with entrepreneurship." In 2005, 672,000 new companies were developed versus 642,000 in 2004. However, not all are e-businesses. Also, note that 544,800 small businesses closed in 2005 (Hise 2007). In 2008 and 2009, more failures were recorded than newly created companies, mainly due to the economic crisis. For a case of an e-start-up that failed after 2 years see Craig (2006). Several centers for information technology start-ups exist, some sponsored by major software companies.

Example: Microsoft Startup Center. The Microsoft Startup Center offers free step-by-step guidance, tips, and resources for starting a business, including an e-business. A wealth of information is provided under eight general headings: "The Rules," "Office Setup," "Your Brand," "Marketing," "Sales," "Finances," "The Details," and, last but not the least, "Employees."

The Startup Center provides links to the IRS, the U.S. Patent and Trademark Office, Startup Nation, and other resources, including Bank of America's Small Business Resource Center, which also offers valuable step-by-step tips. From furniture resources to how to jumpstart marketing with a free Web site from Office Live, the Microsoft Startup Center is worth viewing.

Remember, new business owners should always seek the guidance of a professional tax consultant, accountant, and/or attorney to verify that all legal requirements have been met before starting and operating a business. For more information, see microsoft.com/small business/startup-toolkit.

Many physical start-ups are click-and-mortars or use the Web for support services. For example, Sloan (2006) describes how some entrepreneurs use the Web to build a large customer base before they even have the ability to deliver what they plan to sell.

One of the major steps in launching any start-up is to find a viable product (service). This may take a long time, because the concept comes first, followed by a prototype, and then a market test. Also, finding the correct business model is critical (Chapter 1 and the Online Tutorial).

Umesh et al. (2005) provide some interesting guidelines to avoid dot-com failures. Specifically, they suggest looking at: (1) the growth rate of the intended market, (2) the timing of market entry, (3) revenue flow, and (4) what part of the cycle a market is in. Maier (2005) suggests that starting small with two founders is the best option, although as many as four founders can work. For a free 14-session guide to starting a business, see myownbusiness.org/course_list.html.

CREATING A NEW COMPANY OR ADDING AN ONLINE PROJECT

Most new businesses—brick-and-mortar, pure play, or click-and-mortar—begin in a similar manner. The following three steps describe the process:

1. **Identify a consumer or business need in the marketplace.** Many businesses simply begin with a good idea. A magazine article, a personal observation, an unsolved problem, a small irritation, or a friend's suggestion may trigger an idea, and the prospective business owner sees a gap between what people want and what is available. For an example, see Case 15.1. Note that the key here is *innovation*. For many examples of innovations, see Williams (2006).

CASE 15.1

EC Application

INNOVATION AND CREATIVITY AT AMAZON.COM

Call it fate or call it the right person having the right idea at the right time. Whatever you call it, the idea behind Amazon.com and its founder, Jeff Bezos, seemed destined for each other.

Bezos was born in January 1964 in Albuquerque, New Mexico. Even as a boy, his cleverness, intelligence, and entrepreneurial skills were obvious. At the age of 12, Bezos built a motorized mirrored Infinity Cube because he couldn't afford the $20 to buy one. A few years later, he graduated as valedictorian of his Florida high school. As a young entrepreneur, he created a summer camp for middle-school students and

promoted it by saying that it "emphasizes the use of new ways of thinking in old areas," which was in many ways a prediction of his future success.

Bezos graduated from Princeton University with a degree in computer science, and his first employment was in electronic commerce, building an EDI network for settling cross-border equity transactions. A few jobs later, he was a senior vice president at the hedge fund firm D. E. Shaw, responsible for exploring new business opportunities on the Internet. It was then that his intelligence, entrepreneurial talents, computing education, and e-commerce experience all came together in a

(continued)

CASE 15.1 (continued)

brilliant idea: The most logical thing to sell over the Internet was books. Several years later he added dozens of other products.

Why books? Behind the thousands of brick-and-mortar bookstores are just two large book distributors, with an extensive list of books already online in the distributors' databases. Bezos was willing to bet that book buyers would be willing to give up the cozy, coffee-shop, browsing environment of the local bookstore if he could offer them the "earth's biggest bookstore," fantastic customer service, and features that no physical bookstore could match—customer book reviews, author interviews, personalized book recommendations, and more.

The rest of the story is the stuff of legend. Bezos left his six-figure Wall Street salary and wrote the Amazon.com business plan during a cross-country move to Seattle, Washington. The Amazon.com Web site was built in a cramped, poorly insulated garage. When Amazon.com launched in July 1995, a bell would ring every time the server recorded a sale. Within a few weeks the constant bell ringing became unbearable, and they turned it off. Today, on a busy day, Amazon.com sells hundreds of thousands of products to about 3 million customers.

In the late 1990s and early 2000s, Amazon.com invested $2 billion in physical warehouses (see the opening case to Chapter 12) and other expansion opportunities. This was in line with Bezos's vision for Amazon.com as "broader than books and music."

After years of large losses, Amazon.com announced its first small profit in the fourth quarter of 2001. By 2005, the company had become increasingly more profitable. In 2009, Amazon.com was one of the few companies to report increased sales and earnings.

During its first decade of operation, Amazon.com changed its business model several times, adding innovative

ideas. It also acquired other companies or stakes in companies in several countries (e.g., *joyo.com*—the largest e-tailer of books, music, and videos in China). Amazon Services, Inc., a subsidiary of Amazon.com, has projects with a number of different partners (e.g., American Express). Amazon Theater offers film viewing from its Web site, as well as many more innovations. In 2008, Amazon.com expanded into downloadable books (recall the Kindle 2 e-book reader, Chapter 7), music, and movies.

Bezos is indeed an innovator. His most original idea is his vision of Blue Origin, a futuristic center for suborbital spaceships. In the last few years, he has worked on commercializing space trips. Bezos's Blue Origin commercial space venture is developing a vehicle to take occupants on a 10-minute ride to the edge of space, nearly 60 miles (96 km) above the earth and back (see Quitter 2008). Perhaps it will only be a matter of time before customers can purchase tickets for space trips from Amazon.com. It all began with a smart entrepreneur whose life experiences gave him a brilliant idea that led to the founding of a legendary e-tailing company.

Sources: Compiled from Business Wire (2004), Klotz (2005), and Quitter (2008).

Questions

1. What were the opportunities and needs in the consumer market that inspired Bezos to create Amazon.com?

2. What factors, at both personal and business levels, led Bezos to his brilliant idea?

3. Visit Amazon.com and find some of their recent innovations.

---

2. **Investigate the opportunity.** Just because a person perceives that an opportunity exists does not mean that it is real. Perhaps the potential number of individuals interested in purchasing the proposed product or service is too small. Perhaps the cost of manufacturing, marketing, and distributing the product or providing the service is too large. The revenue model may be wrong, others may have tried already and failed, satisfactory substitute products may be available, and so on. For example, online grocery shopping would seem like a wonderful opportunity—relieving busy professionals of the time-consuming and tiresome task of regular visits to a grocery store. Many have tried to provide large- and small-scale online grocery ventures (e.g., NetGrocer, Peapod, HomeGrocer, Webvan), but most have failed or continue to lose money because they misjudged the logistical problems associated with grocery warehousing and delivery. This is why it is so important to develop a business plan. One of the purposes of a *business plan* is to determine the feasibility and viability of a business opportunity in the marketplace.

3. **Determine the business owner's ability to meet the need.** Assuming that realistic business opportunity exists, does the prospective business owner have the ability to convert the opportunity into success? Some personal qualities are important: Is the business in an industry the prospective business owner knows well? Is it something the entrepreneur loves doing? Are family and friends supportive? Business skills in staff recruitment, management, negotiation, marketing, and financial management are

required, as well as entrepreneurial attitudes such as innovation, risk taking, and being proactive. Many good ideas and realistic initiatives have failed in the execution stage because the owners or other principals of the business lacked sufficient business skills to make it a reality. Boo.com, for example, seemingly had a great concept (retailing ultra-modern, designer clothing) and superior software, but it failed because of the inability of management to organize the business and manage the projects necessary to bring Boo.com online before it burned through $120 million of start-up capital (Cukier 2000).

The process for developing EC projects in existing companies is similar, except that step 3 changes to: "Determine the organization's ability to meet the need."

Some Tips for Success

Winnick (2006) provides the following five "secrets" to help you come up with the next big thing:

1. **Do your homework.** Research what's really happening in the world. Simple innovations are not understated. They have to be tangibly more effective than anything already on the market. For example, attend ExpoMart, where the annual Innovation New Product Exposition (INPEX), takes place (see Williams 2006).

2. **Aim for excitement.** Make your customers say "wow" or "finally," such as Bezos's initiative to take customers into space.

3. **Whittle, shape, iterate, repeat.** Test and improve the ideas and prototypes several times. Your designers and developers can do this.

4. **Get real.** Build physical prototypes to get feedback from friends, suppliers, and customers (see Copeland and Malik 2006).

5. **Avoid creating a gizmo.** Beware of creating a product (service) with obvious faults, even if it looks like a brilliant design. Even though a product (service) must be attractive to customers, it must also work.

For additional guidelines, see Williams (2006).

Beyond these general platitudes about what it takes to start a prosperous business, the owner of an online business must consider some requirements that reflect the online nature of the business. The first of these is the need to understand Internet culture. Activities such as spam, extensive use of graphics, forced visitor registration, and intrusive pop-up browser windows are counter to the accepted norms of behavior on the Internet.

A second requirement that the owner of an online business must consider is the nature of appropriate products and services. Although virtually anything is available for sale on the Internet, the degree of sales success is somewhat dependent on the type of item or service being offered. For example, digitized products (e.g., information, music, software) sell well and are delivered easily. Similarly, services (e.g., stock brokering, travel ticket sales), and commodities (e.g., books, CDs) also have been quite successful. In contrast, experiential products, such as expensive clothes, do not sell well online. One of the greatest opportunities the Internet offers is in niche marketing (see the JetPens case in Chapter 1). Rare and quirky sales ideas, such as antique Coke bottles (antiquebottles.com), gadgets for left-handed individuals (anythingleft-handed.co.uk), Swedish gourmet food (wikstromsgourmet.com), toys for cats and dogs (cattoys.com and dogtoys.com), and gift items from Belize (belizenet.com), would rarely succeed in a physical storefront, but the Internet offers the owners of these sites an opportunity to pursue their business idea and be successful.

Cloning

Entrepreneurs all over the globe try to clone or copycat the Web's most successful Web sites, such as eBay, Amazon.com, MySpace, and YouTube. Examples are Amazon.gr called itself "Greece's Biggest Bookstore," and had much the same look and feel as Amazon.com's site at the time when Amazon.com referred to itself as the "Earth's biggest bookstore." This site is no longer live. CarSpace.com, is a site with content provided by Edmunds for people who like cars. It has all the features you'd expect on a site like MySpace, but geared toward letting people make car friends and is still a popular site.

PLANNING ONLINE BUSINESSES

Planning an online business is similar to planning for any start-up venture in that it centers on a business plan (see Rutgers 2009).

Business Plan

business plan

A written document that identifies a company's goals and outlines how the company intends to achieve the goals and at what cost.

Every new online business needs at least an informal business plan. As defined in Chapter 13, a **business plan** is a written document that identifies a company's goals and outlines how the company intends to achieve those goals and at what cost. A business plan includes both strategic elements (e.g., mission statement, business model, value proposition, and competitive positioning statement) and operational elements (e.g., operations plan, financial statements) of how a new business intends to do business. Medium and large businesses, or those seeking external funding, must have a formal business plan.

The primary reason an entrepreneur writes a business plan is to use it to acquire funding from a bank, an angel investor, a venture capitalist, or the financial markets. Similarly, in an existing business a business case needs to be written for any new large EC project so management can decide whether to fund it. A business plan also is important for a new venture as a tool to recruit senior management and to convince business partners to make a commitment to the business. A business plan helps ensure a thriving business by encouraging an entrepreneur to set goals, anticipate problems, set measures for success, and keep the business on track after starting it. A business plan forces the entrepreneur to be realistic about the business's prospects. Sometimes the most successful outcome of a business plan is a decision not to proceed. For all aspects of business plans for start-up companies, see hjventures.com.

For a sample of business plan software, see planware.org, planmagic.com, and abs-usa.com. Palo Alto Software (paloalto.com) offers Business Plan Pro 2007, which includes more than 500 sample plans. Another resource is Microsoft's Small Business Center at microsoft.com/smallbusiness/hub.mspx. For more on getting started with a business plan in a small company, see smallbusiness.yahoo.com (search for Yahoo! answers). The Online Tutorial on the book's Web site explores this topic in further depth and offers a detailed explanation of how to prepare a business plan. Also see en.wikipedia.org/wiki/Business_plan and Session 2 at myownbusiness.org/course_list.html.

The Business Case

business case

A document that justifies the investment of internal, organizational resources in a specific application or project.

An existing brick-and-mortar business looking to move online (either to add EC projects or to transform itself to an e-business) needs a **business case**—a document that is used to *justify* the investment of organizational resources in a specific application or project (see discussion in Chapter 13). A business case for a large, resource-intensive EC project resembles a business plan. The Online Tutorial includes details on how to write a business case and the similarities and differences in writing such a business case and business plan. For a small or medium-size project, the business case can be much simpler. Online File W15.1 presents a high-level template for a business case that you can use to justify new online applications, such as a new e-procurement, e-learning, an extranet, or participation in a social network.

FUNDING A NEW ONLINE BUSINESS

Launching an online business can be expensive. The brave entrepreneur is usually willing to invest personal funds from savings, personal lines of credit, or taking a second house mortgage, but these sources of "bootstrap funding" are unlikely to be sufficient. According to Maier (2005), entrepreneurs should "bootstrap" as long as possible, but not wait too long to tap into the venture community.

If the new venture involves significant risk, traditional sources of debt financing, such as a bank loan, can be difficult or impossible to get. For other sources of funding for a start-up business, see Pearlson and Sounders (2006) and Rutgers (2009). For an introduction to sources of e-business funding, see businesspartners.com.

First Round of Initial Funding: Angel Investors and Incubators

When the entrepreneur's personal funds are insufficient, the entrepreneur will go to friends, family members, or to *angel investors*. An **angel investor** is a wealthy individual who contributes personal funds and possibly expertise at the earliest stage of business development. Angel investors can be found through organizations such as the Angel Capital Association (angelcapitalassociation.org) and newspapers, magazines, and business-oriented social networks (e.g., LinkedIn).

A typical angel investor scenario begins with, for example, a young software developer who has identified a niche in the market for a new software application and has used his own money to get started but has insufficient funding to continue. An angel investor may provide the developer with an office, hardware, software, salary, and access to the human and financial resources required to write the software application. In most cases, the angel investor also provides guidance or access to management expertise. In addition to sometimes-altruistic goals, the angel investor is looking for a reasonable return on the investment. In other words, the angel investor is almost always a pre-venture-capital funding source and may be paid later from the infusion of venture capital funds. An angel investor is an excellent source of funding for the entrepreneur; however, angel funding is scarce and difficult to find.

Another important source of support, if not direct funding, for pre-venture-capital firms is an incubator. An **incubator** is a company, university, or nonprofit organization that supports promising businesses in their initial stages of development. Although some incubators offer start-up funding, the primary purpose of most incubators is to offer a variety of support services—office space, accounting services, group purchasing schemes, reception services, coaching, and information technology consulting—at little or no cost. In return, the incubator receives a modest fee, start-up equity in the company, or both (en.wikipedia.org/wiki/Business_incubator).

angel investor
A wealthy individual who contributes personal funds and possibly expertise at the earliest stage of business development.

incubator
A company, university, or nonprofit organization that supports businesses in their initial stages of development.

Second Round Financing: Venture Capital

One major source of funding new ventures is *venture capital*. **Venture capital (VC)** is money invested in a business by an individual, a group of individuals (venture capitalists), or a funding company in exchange for equity in the business. Venture capitalists tend to invest in companies that have identified what seems to be an outstanding business opportunity, have taken some action to make the opportunity happen (e.g., written a new software application, secured a patent, built an interesting social network that attracts many visitors, conducted some promising experiments, or recruited key personnel), and need an infusion of funds and management expertise to expand and launch the business. Some venture capitalists may have connections with CEOs who would be good strategic guides for the business; others may be more market specific (e.g., experts on software development). It is therefore important to match your VC with your business. Venture capitalists usually invest large sums of money and expect, in return, some management control and a profit on their investment within 3 to 5 years, when the successful start-up goes public (an IPO) or when a larger company merges with it or acquires it. The start-up company receives the funds and experienced management guidance it needs during its launch and expansion stages.

The downside for the start-up business to acquire VC is minimal; it loses some control over the business in return for funds it is unlikely to acquire from any other source. The more difficult problem is finding VC. Due to the many dot-com failures in 2000 and onward, many VC sources have disappeared, and competition for venture capital is fierce.

Some well-known VC companies are vFinance Capital (vfinance.com), the Capital Network (westlakesecurities.com), and Garage Technology Ventures (garage.com), which was founded by personal-computing guru Guy Kawasaki. Venture capitalists may be start-ups. Most of them lost large amounts of money for their investors during the dot-com bust. For more information, see the National Venture Capital Association (nvca.org), the Venture Capital Marketplace (v-capital.com.au), Mobius Venture Capital (mobiusvc.com), and VC Fodder (vcfodder.com).

venture capital (VC)
Money invested in a business by an individual, a group of individuals (venture capitalists), or a funding company in exchange for equity in the business.

Additional Funding: A Large Partner

As part of a VC investment or after the depletion of VC money, one or more large companies may step into the process. For example, Yahoo!, IBM, Microsoft, Motorola, Google, Time

Warner News Corp., and Oracle have invested in hundreds of EC start-up companies. Eventually, they may acquire the start-up completely. Such investments are frequently done in complementary or competing areas. For example, Yahoo! is a major investor in Google and in Baidu in China; News Corp. acquired the start-up MySpace; and Google invested in dozens of companies related to advertising, including the purchase of YouTube in 2006. Microsoft purchased a part in Facebook in 2008, and eBay owns 25 percent of Craigslist. Google and other EC companies are buying companies even before they try to get the VC support.

The IPO

Once the company is well known and successful, it will go to a stock exchange to raise money via an initial public offer (IPO). In such offerings, investors will pay a much larger amount of money per share than that paid by the initial and secondary funding source, sometimes 5 or 10 times more per share. A vivid example is the launch of Alibaba (Chapter 5); its IPO was valued in the billions of dollars on the Hong Kong stock exchange in October 2007.

Section 15.1 ▶ REVIEW QUESTIONS

1. List the major steps in the process of building an online business.
2. Describe the formation process of a typical online business.
3. What special requirements must an online business consider in its formation? In e-business planning?
4. What is a business case and how does it contribute to business success?
5. Describe initial, secondary, and IPO funding options available to a start-up.
6. What is an angel investor? An incubator?
7. How does a VC company support a start-up?

15.2 ADDING E-COMMERCE INITIATIVES OR TRANSFORMING TO AN E-BUSINESS

Creating an e-business start-up certainly is exciting, but it also is very risky. As with any other business, the failure rate is very high. However, in cyberspace the risks and uncertainties, plus lack of experience, may result in an even higher rate of failure. Nevertheless, thousands of new online businesses have been created since 1995, mostly small ones (see Chapter 13). A much more common strategy is adding one or several EC initiatives to an existing business.

ADDING EC INITIATIVES TO AN EXISTING BUSINESS

Almost all medium-to-large organizations have added or plan to add EC initiatives to the existing business. The most common additions are:

▶ **A storefront.** Adding an online sales channel is common in both B2C (e.g., godiva.com, walmart.com) and B2B (e.g., ibm.com). The required investment is fairly low, because inexpensive storefront hosting and software is available from many vendors (see Sections 15.5 and 15.9). A storefront can be built fairly quickly, and the damage in case of failure may not be too large. Because the required investment is not large, it may not be necessary to expend the time and money in developing a formal business case. This is a practical strategy for an SME. For a large-scale storefront, a company will need to follow the steps suggested in Section 15.1, especially the preparation of a business case, in order to secure internal funding and blessings from the top management. For further details on developing storefronts, see the "Getting Started" guide at smallbusiness.yahoo.com. A major issue in developing a storefront is deciding what support services to offer and how to provide them. Note that some well-known companies may create a special subsidiary for online activities using external funding. Such a strategy often results in an IPO.

▶ **A portal.** As discussed in Chapter 6, there are several types of corporate portals. Almost all companies today have one or several portals that they use for external and/or internal collaboration and communication. A storefront for employees or for external customers will include a portal. Adding a portal (or several portals) may be a necessity, and it may not be preceded by a formal business case. Issues of content and design, as well as security, are of utmost importance. Because many vendors offer portal-building services, vendor selection may be an important issue (see Online Chapter 18).

▶ **E-procurement.** This EC initiative is popular with large companies, as described in Chapter 5. E-procurement frequently requires a business plan and extensive integration (both internally and externally), so an EC architecture must be in place.

▶ **Auctions and reverse auctions.** Large corporations need to consider building their own auction or reverse auction (for e-procurement) sites. Although forward auctions can be added to a storefront at a reasonable cost, a reverse auction usually requires more integration with business partners and, consequently, a larger investment and a business case.

▶ **M-commerce.** Many companies are embarking on wireless applications inside the organization and on selling and advertising via m-commerce technologies.

▶ **Enterprise social networks and Web 2.0 tools.** Many large companies now offer blogs and wikis; others (e.g., Toyota, Coca-Cola, Wells Fargo Bank) operate enterprise social networks.

Organizations may consider many other EC initiatives, following the business models presented in Chapter 1. For example, Qantas (qantas.com.au) sells tickets online directly from its Web site and from a B2B exchange; it buys supplies and services from its e-procurement site as well as from several exchanges; it provides e-training for its employees; operates several corporate portals; offers online banking services to its employees; provides e-CRM and ePRM; manages its frequent-flier program; supports a wireless notification system to customers; and so on. Large companies, such as GE and IBM, have hundreds of active EC projects.

TRANSFORMATION TO AN E-BUSINESS

As the brick-and-mortar organization implements more EC projects, it becomes a click-and-mortar organization, and eventually an e-business. Being an e-business does not imply that the organization is a pure-play company, it just means that it conducts as many processes as possible online. A rapid or large-scale change from brick-and-mortar to e-business involves organizational transformation. For planning such a transformation, see Basu and Muylle (2007), who outline a detailed process for such a transformation.

What Is Organizational Transformation?

Organizational transformation is a comprehensive concept that implies a major organizational change. According to McKay and Marshall (2004), a *transformation* is not only a major change, but also a sharp break from the past. The key points in understanding organizational transformation are as follows:

▶ The organization's ways of thinking and vision will fundamentally change.

▶ There will be revolutionary changes to the process and context involved in creating a new organizational vision and rethinking business models and business strategy.

▶ The change must involve a substantial break from previous ways of acting. It will likely involve discovering and developing new opportunities and new ways of doing things.

▶ The change must permeate through and impact on the behavior of a majority of organizational members.

▶ The change will involve creating new systems, procedures, and structures that not only enable and dictate how new processes function, but that will also impact on the deeply embedded business models and understandings that drive the organization.

An e-business transformation is not solely about technology. Technologies must be integrated with possible changes in business strategy, processes, organizational culture, and infrastructure.

How an Organization Can Be Transformed into an E-Business

Transforming an organization, especially a large company, into an e-business can be a very complex endeavor. For an organization to transform itself into an e-business, it must transform several major processes, such as procurement, sales, CRM, and manufacturing, as well as deal with *change management*.

Such a transformation involves several strategic issues. Lasry (2002) raised several of these issues in an investigation of the rate at which brick-and-mortar retail firms adopt the Web as an additional sales channel. He examined organizational strategies, such as internal restructuring, the formation of joint ventures, and outsourcing. He concluded that implementing EC requires a disruptive and potentially hazardous change in core features. He suggests that companies spin off EC activities as part of the transformation process. Müller-Lankenau et al. (2006) provide a comprehensive description of the transformation to e-business, describing both the internal and external processes supported by IT, as shown in Exhibit 15.1. They then show the support of IT at each stage. Finally, they describe the necessary *change management* activities. *Baseline* (baselinemag.com) offers a calculator to measure the cost and value of business transformation. For details on business transformation, see Strassmann (2007).

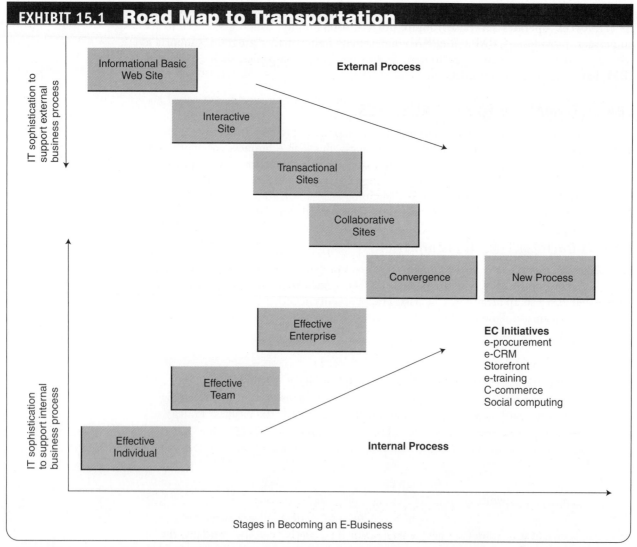

EXHIBIT 15.1   Road Map to Transportation

Source: Ginige, A. et al. "A Road Map for Successfully Transforming SMEs into E-Business." *Cutter IT Journal*, May 2001. Used with permission of the author.

Business Process Reengineering

Several studies have examined the transformation to e-business. For example, Chen and Ching (2002) have explored the relationship of BPR and e-business and the change process both for individuals and organizations. They propose a process of redesigning an organization for e-business, providing several research propositions. Others have explored the use of simulation modeling for enabling transformation to e-business, examining the BPR process and using simulation and process maps to support the process. Turban et al. (2008) describe the use of business intelligence in BPR. Finally, organizational change issues in transformation to e-business need to be addressed.

Business Process Management

Business process management has been used to facilitate organizational transformation. The term **business process management (BPM)** refers to activities performed by businesses to improve their processes. Although such improvements are hardly new, software tools called *business process management systems* have made such activities faster and cheaper. BPM systems monitor the execution of the business processes so that managers can analyze and change processes in response to data, rather than in response to a hunch. BPM differs from BPR in that it deals not just with one-time changes to the organization, which is what BPR does, but with long-term consequences. The major activities of BPM are process design, process execution, and process monitoring. For details, see en.wikipedia.org/wiki/Business_ process_management and Jeston and Nelis (2008).

business process management (BPM)
Method for business restructuring that combines workflow systems and redesign methods; covers three process categories—people-to-people, systems-to-systems, and systems-to-people interactions.

Software Tools for Facilitating Transformation to E-Business

Several vendors offer methodologies and tools to facilitate transformation to e-business (e.g., see IBM 2006 and Ould 2003). Using special methodologies, organizations in the public sector as well as public utilities, can achieve dramatic cost and cycle time reductions.

Change Management

Transforming an existing business to an e-business or adding a major e-commerce initiative means a manager must change business processes and the manner in which people work, communicate, and are promoted and managed. According to Ash and Burn (2006), this requires systematic attention to learning processes, organizational culture, technology infrastructure, people's thinking, and systems. Employees, business partners, and even customers may resist such a change. Ash and Burn have developed a model of e-business change as well as a model for managing e-business change. Chu and Smithson (2007) provided a case study for organizational change in an automobile manufacturer. For more on change management, see en.wikipedia.org/wiki/Change_management.

Section 15.2 ▶ REVIEW QUESTIONS

1. Which EC initiatives are brick-and-mortar organizations most likely to add?
2. Describe the steps in becoming an e-business and the major activities involved in the process.
3. List some of the issues involved in transforming to an e-business.
4. Define BPR and BPM.
5. Describe the major characteristics (key points) of organizational transformation.

15.3 BUILDING OR ACQUIRING A WEB SITE

Every online business needs a Web site. A Web site is the primary way any firm doing business on the Internet advertises its products or services and attracts customers. Many Web sites also sell products and services. The Web site may be a storefront, a portal, an auction site, and so on. How can an organization build or acquire such a site (see Rutgers 2009)? First, let's examine the major different types of Web sites that exist. An entrepreneur can start a business for just $300 (Swanhill 2009).

CLASSIFICATION OF WEB SITES

Web sites come in all shapes and sizes. One of the major distinctions made in Web site classification is the level of functionality inherent in the site:

informational Web site
A Web site that does little more than provide information about the business and its products and services.

interactive Web site
A Web site that provides opportunities for the customers and the business to communicate and share information.

▶ An **informational Web site** does little more than provide information about the business and its products and services. For many brick-and-mortar businesses, an informational "brochureware" Web site is perfectly satisfactory. The major purpose is to have a *presence* on the Web.

▶ An **interactive Web site** provides opportunities for the customers and the business to communicate and share information. An interactive site will contain all the information about products and services that an informational site does, but it also delivers informational features intended to encourage interaction between the business and customers or among customers, such as an e-newsletter, product demonstrations, blogs, and customer discussion forums. An interactive Web site will strongly encourage feedback by including contact e-mail addresses; providing feedback forms, wikis, and blogs; and promoting completion of online surveys. Features such as the ability to search the site, a well-designed site map, and mouseovers (clickable buttons that change shape or color when a visitor passes a mouse cursor over the button) make navigation more interactive. Value-added tools such as currency converters, price comparisons, calendars, and various types of calculators (e.g., a mortgage calculator on a bank's Web site) can enhance interactivity.

attractors
Web site features that attract and interact with visitors in the target stakeholder group.

▶ At a higher level of interactivity are **attractors**—Web site features that attract and interact with site visitors. Attractors such as games, puzzles, prize giveaways, contests, and electronic postcards (e-cards) encourage customers to find the Web site, visit again, and recommend the site to their friends. For example, Ragu's Web site does not sell spaghetti sauce or other Ragu products, but the recipes, customer interaction ("talk to Mama"), unforgettable domain name (eat.com), and other features make this an attractor-loaded site that increases *brand awareness* and sells Ragu's products in the customer's next trip to the grocery store. Coca-Cola and Disney have similar sites.

transactional Web site
A Web site that sells products and services.

▶ A **transactional Web site** sells products and services. These Web sites typically include information and interactivity features but also have sell-side features, such as a shopping cart, a product catalog, a customer-personalized account, a shipping calculator, and the ability to accept credit cards to complete the sale.

collaborative Web site
A site that allows business partners to collaborate.

▶ A **collaborative Web site** is a site that allows business partners to collaborate (i.e., it includes many supportive tools; see Chapter 6). B2B exchanges may also provide collaboration capabilities.

BUILDING A WEB SITE

Assuming that a business has completed the preparatory work of business formation—writing a business plan, deciding what type of site they want to build, and acquiring initial funding—it is ready to build a site. The process of building the site is illustrated in Exhibit 15.2 and in Online File W15.2. Templates are available at smallbusiness.yahoo.com/webhosting/websitetemplates.php.

The forthcoming sections discuss each of the steps illustrated in Exhibit 15.2.

Section 15.3 ▶ REVIEW QUESTIONS

1. Distinguish among informational, interactive, transactional, and collaborative Web sites.
2. List the six steps in building a Web site. (*Hint:* See Online File W15.2.)

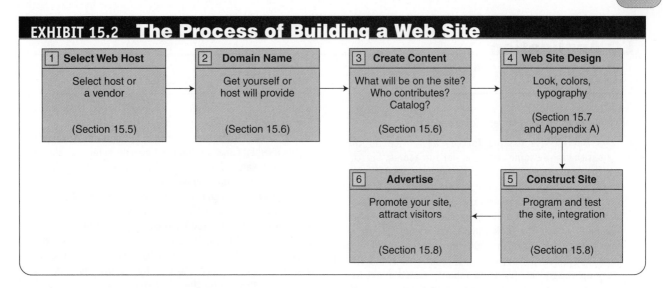

EXHIBIT 15.2 The Process of Building a Web Site

1 Select Web Host	2 Domain Name	3 Create Content	4 Web Site Design
Select host or a vendor (Section 15.5)	Get yourself or host will provide (Section 15.6)	What will be on the site? Who contributes? Catalog? (Section 15.6)	Look, colors, typography (Section 15.7 and Appendix A)

6 Advertise	5 Construct Site
Promote your site, attract visitors (Section 15.8)	Program and test the site, integration (Section 15.8)

15.4 WEB SITE HOSTING AND OBTAINING A DOMAIN NAME

Every retail business—online or offline—has a storefront from which it sells goods and/or services. The business either owns or rents the storefront in a mall or at an independent location. The decisions about whether to own (self-host) or rent, where to host the Web site (storebuilder service, ISP, pure Web hosting service, or self-hosting), and the site's domain name are some of the first important decisions an online business owner has to make. This section discusses the considerations in making these decisions. For details, see Rutgers (2009).

WEB HOSTING OPTIONS

The following are the major Web hosting options.

Storebuilder Service

A **storebuilder service** (also called a *design-and-host service*) provides Web hosting as well as storage space, templates, and other services to help small businesses build a Web site quickly and inexpensively.

An example of a company that offers comprehensive storebuilding hosting services and software is Yahoo! Web Hosting. Yahoo!'s base service offers Web hosting as well as customized templates and other support for $11.95 per month; the next plan up, which is offered for $19.95 a month, offers additional services; a package for professionals that includes security features is available for $39.95 a month. All levels of Yahoo! Web Hosting include access to template-based software, SiteBuilder, which offers more than 330 customizable templates. The software can be used to build a storefront quickly and easily (see Section 15.9 and Team Assignment 4). Yahoo!'s Web Hosting package also provides marketing tools, domain name selection assistance, a payment gate, storage (disk) space, and shipment services. The package also works with the Yahoo! Merchant Solutions, which is described in Section 15.9. Yahoo! Web Hosting usually offers a Web site address (e.g., a URL, such as smallbusiness.yahoo.com/mybusiness), management tools, security features, and Internet connection maintenance. Yahoo! combines Web hosting and store building, but other vendors may separate the two functions, as shown later in this section.

The advantage of a storebuilder service is that it is a quick, easy, and inexpensive way to build a Web site. The disadvantages are the lack of a strong online identity, limited functionality (e.g., accepting credit cards may not be possible), dependence on the service for proper management of connectivity to the site, and some lack of differentiation (the Web site tends to look like other sites because everyone is using the same set of templates). Despite the disadvantages, storebuilder services are the prime choice of small and sometimes medium-size businesses (see Case 15.2).

storebuilder service
A hosting service that provides disk space and services to help small and microbusinesses build a Web site quickly and cheaply.

CASE 15.2

EC Application

HOW SMALL COMPANIES USE A STOREBUILDER

The following are illustrative examples of how small companies build e-stores using storebuilding services.

▶ Laura Modrell was looking for the best price for the Thomas the Tank Engine character her son adored. Searching the Web, she discovered that people were buying these toy trains and reselling them online at a huge profit. So she built a simple storefront in 1999 using free templates and began selling unique educational toys, including Thomas the Tank Engine and Friends. The business grew rapidly, and in 2000 she switched to Yahoo! Store. She not only needed the professional look, but also the support services. By using Yahoo! Store, Modrell has complete control over her site (*trains4tots.com*) with regards to product descriptions, prices, orders, and so on at a minimal cost and with limited computer knowledge. Revenues grew from $100,000 in 2000 to about $2,000,000 in 2005.

▶ Kristine Wylie started writing ads and Web content in 2002. As a freelance writer, she needed to promote her writing and copyediting services. She selected Yahoo!'s Web Hosting and its e-mail service. Using SiteBuilder, she constructed a site (*mswrite.com*) in 2003, and within a year she obtained clients in several countries around the world. Income tripled in a year, enabling Wylie to hire helpers and expand the business further.

▶ Ken and Pat Gates retired in 2001. While surfing the Internet, they discovered how easy it was to go into e-commerce. The couple decided to sell online products related to their favorite collegiate sports teams. Using Yahoo!'s Web Hosting service and templates, in 2003 they built their store, College Sports Stuff (*collegesportsstuff. com*), and generated $35,000 in sales. By 2005, they covered

62 teams, including noncollege ones, tripling their sales. Their store ships customers' orders within an hour.

▶ Using Yahoo!'s SiteBuilder software, Springwater Woodcraft, an established Canadian furniture manufacturer, was able to add a new sales channel (*springwaterwoodcraft.com*). The software helped not only with sales but also with accounting. It also led the company into the international market.

▶ TailorMade-adidas Golf (TMaG) is the world's leading manufacturer of metal and wood golf clubs. When it launched the revolutionary r7 Quad, TMaG had to make sure that its customers (golf retailers) would understand the new product and its benefits in order to transform those benefits into customer sales. To do that, TMaG created courses that it offered online to educate the golf retailers. Using Yahoo! Merchant Solutions, it rapidly launched the e-training B2B project (*tmagconnection.com*). Participation in the course was high, and when the store opened online it attracted 15 percent of all TMaG customers, who placed $600,000 in orders in the first 3 months. The company has created several other storefronts (e.g., one for selling its products to employees of TMaG's parent company).

Sources: Compiled from Yahoo! (2006) and authors' experience.

Questions

1. What benefits did the owners of these businesses derive from using Yahoo!'s services?

2. Identify the common elements in all these cases.

3. Why would a large company, such as TMaG, use templates to create a B2B site?

---

eBay also offers storefront software tools for its merchants. For more on eBay stores, see pages.ebay.com/storefronts/seller-landing.html. Amazon.com offers a similar service (see webstore.amazon.com/WebStore-for-eCommerce-Business). The advantage of going with storebuilders is that hosting at Yahoo! Store, Amazon.com, or e-Bay exposes the sellers to the large number of potential buyers who visit these sites (e.g., see Elms 2006). Storebuilders are a special case of a pure hosting service.

A Dedicated Hosting Service

Web hosting service
A dedicated Web site hosting company that offers a wide range of hosting services and functionality to businesses of all sizes.

A **Web hosting service** is a dedicated Web site hosting company that offers a wide range of hosting services and functionality to businesses of all sizes. Companies such as Hostway (hostway.com), Go Daddy (godaddy.com), Mosso (mosso.com), and 1&1 (1and1.com) offer more and better services than a storebuilder service because Web site hosting is their core business. Almost all Web hosting companies have internal Web design departments to ensure the cooperation between the designer and the host. Also, functionality such as database integration, shipping and tax calculators, sufficient bandwidth to support multimedia files, shopping carts, site search engines, and comprehensive site statistics are likely to be readily available. Major services are offered by IBM Global service (ibm.com/services/us/gbs/bus/html/bcs_index.html) and Microsoft (see microsoft.com/smallbusiness/startup-toolkit).

A Web hosting service can be the best option for an online business that needs one or more *mirror sites*. A **mirror site** is an exact duplicate of the original Web site, but it is physically located on a Web server located in another province or country. A business may decide that it needs a mirror site when large numbers of customers are a far distance from the original site. A mirror site reduces telecommunications costs and improves the speed of customer access, because the site reduces the distance between the Web server and the customer's browser. Typically, customers do not know, or care, that they are accessing a mirror site.

ISP Hosting Combined with Web Designer

The same company that delivers e-mail and Web access to a business probably can host the company's Web site. An **ISP hosting service** provides an independent, stand-alone Web site for small and medium-sized businesses. The ISP will probably provide additional hosting services (e.g., more storage space, simple site statistics, credit card gateway software) at the same or a slightly higher cost than the storebuilder services. The List of ISPs (thelist.com) provides lists of ISPs and providers of commercial Internet access.

The major difference between a storebuilder and an ISP hosting service is that with the ISP service, the time-consuming and sometimes expensive task of designing and constructing the Web site becomes the responsibility of the EC business. The business owners, usually with the help of a contracted Web designer, must use a Web site construction tool to create the Web site (e.g., Ibuilt at ibuilt.net) or a Web page editor (e.g., Dreamweaver at adobe.com or FrontPage at microsoft.com). This is not necessarily a bad thing. Compared with a storebuilder template, the combination of an ISP hosting service and a Web designer or builder offers the business increased flexibility as to what it can do with the site, so the site can be distinctive and stand out from the competition. Sites hosted by an ISP also will have a branded domain name. However, one disadvantage of using an ISP is that most providers have limited functionality (e.g., an ISP may be unwilling to host a back-end database). Another consideration is the commitment of the ISP to maintaining quality service and keeping its hosting services up-to-date. Remember that the main business of an ISP is providing *Internet access*, not hosting Web sites.

Self-Hosting

With **self-hosting**, the business acquires the hardware, software, staff, and dedicated telecommunications services necessary to set up and manage its own Web site. Self-hosting is beneficial when a business has special requirements, such as maximum data security, protection of intellectual property, or, most likely, when the business intends to have a large and complex site.

The disadvantages of self-hosting are the cost and the speed of construction. The other Web-hosting options allow the hosting company to amortize the costs of site hosting across hundreds or thousands of customers. A business that hosts its own Web site will have to bear these costs alone, not to mention concerns about security and full-time Web site management. These costs must be weighed against the benefits of better control over site performance and increased flexibility in site design, improvement, and functionalities.

REGISTERING A DOMAIN NAME

Selecting a domain name is an important marketing and branding consideration for any business. The domain name will be the business's online address, and it provides an opportunity to create an identity for the business.

Domain Names

A **domain name** is a name-based address that identifies an Internet-connected server. Usually, it is designated by the portion of the address that comes to the left of .com or .org and includes the .com or .org. The domain name should be an easy-to-remember name (e.g., congress.gov) that the *domain name system* (DNS) maps to a corresponding IP address (e.g., 140.147.248.209). Each domain name must include a top-level domain (TLD). This is

mirror site
An exact duplicate of an original Web site that is physically located on a Web server on another continent or in another country.

ISP hosting service
A hosting service that provides an independent, stand-alone Web site for small and medium-sized businesses.

self-hosting
When a business acquires the hardware, software, staff, and dedicated telecommunications services necessary to set up and manage its own Web site.

domain name
A name-based address that identifies an Internet-connected server. Usually it refers to the portion of the address to the left of .com and .org, etc.

either a general top-level domain (e.g., .com or .biz for commercial businesses, .org for non-profit organizations, .name for individuals), or it is a country-code Top-Level Domain (ccTLD) (e.g., .au for Australia, .jp for Japan). Most ccTLDs also have a *second-level domain name* that indicates the type of organization (e.g., redcross.org.au, yahoo.co.jp). At the left side of the domain name is the organization's name (e.g., dell.com), a brand name (e.g., coke.com for Coca-Cola), or a generic name (e.g., plumber.com).

Domain Name System and Its Implementation

Domain Name System (DNS)

A hierarchical naming system for computers, services, or any resource participating in the Internet; it is like a directory.

The **Domain Name System (DNS)** is a hierarchical naming system for computers, services, or any resource participating in the Internet; it is like a directory. An often used analogy to explain the DNS is that it serves as the "phone book" for the Internet by translating human-friendly computer hostnames into IP addresses.

The DNS makes it possible to assign domain names to groups of Internet users in a meaningful way, independent of each user's physical location.

Domain name assignment is under the authority of the Internet Corporation for Assigned Names and Numbers (ICANN; icann.org). ICANN has delegated responsibility for domain name registration procedures and database administration in the general TLDs to top-level domain administrators such as Afilias (for .info), Public Interest Registry (for .org), and VeriSign Global Registry Services (for .com and .net). Similarly, regional Internet registries administer the ccTLDs (e.g., Nominet for the .uk domain, Japan Registry Service for .jp).

Hundreds of ICANN-accredited registrars carry out the actual registration of domain names. These are located in various countries, but most are in the United States. A list of these registrars is available at icann.org/registrars/accredited-list.html. A domain name registrar is a business that assists prospective Web site owners with finding and registering a domain name of their choice.

Some investors and speculators have made a fortune from buying domain names and then selling them. Sloan (2007) provides an overview of how this is done, including how the domain owner collects money from advertisers. Some domain name owners have over 5,000 names, and one owner built a $30 million empire.

A useful resource for learning more about domain names and the registration process is About Domains (aboutdomains.com), which offers "guides and resources for successful Internet presence," including a domain name glossary, a registration FAQ file, and "horror stories" from domain name owners who have had bad experiences with registrars. Also see "How to Register a Domain Name" at 2 Create a Website (2CreateaWebsite.com). You can also get a domain name at smallbusiness.yahoo.com/domains.

Section 15.4 ▶ REVIEW QUESTIONS

1. What are the advantages and disadvantages of the different Web hosting options?
2. What is a mirror site? Why would a company use a mirror site?
3. What criteria should an online business consider in choosing a Web hosting service?
4. What is a domain name? Why is selecting a domain name an important step for going online?
5. How are domain names controlled in order to avoid duplication?

15.5 CONTENT CREATION, DELIVERY, AND MANAGEMENT

content

The text, images, sound, and video that make up a Web page.

Content is the text, images, sound, and video that comprises Web pages. Creating and managing content is critical to Web site success because content is what a visitor is looking for at a Web site, and content is what the Web site owners use to sell the site, the product or service, and the company that stands behind the site. A successful Internet presence has always been about effective delivery of the information the visitor wants—"Content is king!" This section describes the role content plays in successful online business operations and the key aspects of creating, delivering, and managing Web site content. For details, see Rutgers (2009).

CATEGORIES AND TYPES OF CONTENT

Providing content to EC sites may be a complex job because of the variety and quantity of sources from which to acquire content and the fact that the content must be updated frequently. Also, B2B content, especially in online catalogs, may include pictures, diagrams, and even sound. In addition, content may involve security, quality, and permission issues.

One of the difficulties in Web content management is that some content needs to be kept up-to-the-minute (e.g., news, stock prices, weather). This is referred to as **dynamic Web content**, as distinguished from *static Web content*, which is updated infrequently.

For each type of content, companies may use a different approach for content creation and delivery. Exhibit 15.3 shows the content life cycle. As shown in the exhibit, once content is created, it may appear in different formats (e.g., text, video, music). Then, it moves to a content syndicator. A syndicator (to be described later in this section) moves the content to a portal or news site. From there, a hosting service moves the content, possibly via an optimizer (such as akamai.com). The optimizer delivers the content to the final consumer. We will discuss this process and its elements in more detail a bit later.

Content may be in the public domain, or it may be proprietary in nature (e.g., information about the company and its employees and services). The sites that offer content may be general-purpose public portals, such as Yahoo! or Google, or they may be specialized portals designed to appeal to a specific audience, such as espn.com or ski.com.

Up-to-the-minute dynamic content is what attracts new and returning customers ("eyeballs") and makes them stay longer ("stickiness"). Therefore, dynamic content contributes to customer loyalty.

dynamic Web content
Content that must be kept up-to-date.

Primary and Secondary Content

Content should include more than information about the product itself (the *primary content*). A Web site also should include *secondary content* that offers marketing opportunities, such as the following:

▸ **Cross-selling.** Using content for **cross-selling** means offering similar or complementary products and services to increase sales. In the offline world, the McDonald's question, "Would you like your burger supplemented with fries?" exemplifies cross-selling. In the online world, Amazon.com offers book buyers options such as "customers who bought this book also bought . . . " and "look for similar books by subject." Accessories, add-on products, extended warranties, and gift wrapping are other examples of cross-selling opportunities that companies can offer to buyers on the product pages or in the purchase process. Another example is that if you buy a car online, you may be offered insurance and financing.

cross-selling
Offering similar or complementary products and services to increase sales.

EXHIBIT 15.3 Digital Content Delivery Life Cycle

Original Sources of Digital Content	Content Syndicator	EC Portal or News Site
• Text, video, music • News, scores, data • Stock quotes, etc.	(Intermediary, content broker)	• General portals • Niche sites (financial, sports)

Broadband or Dial-up ISP	Digital Content Delivery Optimizer	Web Site Hosting Service
Connection to Virtual Visitor, personalized content	(Cache, streaming)	(Server mgmt.)

▶ **Up-selling.** Creating content for **up-selling** means offering an upgraded version of the product in order to boost sales and profit. McDonald's practices up-selling every time a sales clerk asks a combo-meal buyer, "Would you like to super-size that?" Amazon.com offers "great buy" book combinations (buy two complementary books for slightly more than the price of one). (It also practices *down-selling* by offering visitors cheaper, used copies of a book directly under the new book price.) Up-selling activities usually include offering products with a different design, color, fabric, or size.

▶ **Promotion.** A coupon, rebate, discount, or special service is secondary content that can increase sales or improve customer service. Amazon.com frequently offers reduced or free shipping charges, and it promotes this offer on each product page.

▶ **Comment.** Reviews, testimonials, expert advice, or further explanation about the product can be offered after introducing the product. Amazon.com book pages always have editorial and customer reviews of the book, and the "look inside this book" feature sometimes allows Web site visitors to preview book contents online.

Creating effective content also means fulfilling the information needs and experiential expectations of the visitor.

CREATION OR ACQUISITION OF CONTENT

Where does content come from? The site's owners and developers create the content on most sites. Typically, it begins by collecting all the content that is currently available (e.g., product information, company information, logos). Then the value of additional content—e-newsletters, discussion forums, customer personalization features, FAQ pages, and external links—is assessed for inclusion in the Web site. Customers can generate content—through product reviews, testimonials, discussion forums, and other ways. Business partners downstream in the supply chain also can provide content (e.g., a chemical industry digital exchange would not need to duplicate product information but could simply source it from the chemical manufacturers).

Buying Content

Content can be purchased or licensed. Lonely Planet, the Australian travel guide company, and the popular Mobile Travel Guide both sell travel information to Web sites such as Travelocity. *Content syndicators* such as Wilson Internet Services (wilsonweb.com/syndicate) serve as intermediaries that link content creators with businesses interested in acquiring content. Finally, some individuals and businesses, such as Mike Valentine's WebSite 101 (website101.com/freecontent.html), provide free content and ask only for proper attribution in return.

Buying from a Syndicator

Syndication involves the sale of the same content (good) to many customers, who then integrate it with other offerings and resell it or give it away for free. Syndication has been extremely popular in the world of entertainment and publishing but was rare elsewhere until the arrival of the Internet. The digitization of products and services, and the resulting ease with which information can flow, makes syndication a popular business model (e.g., see yellowbrix.com). Exhibit 15.4 shows the syndication supply chain. A few examples are available on Online File W15.3. Web syndication is done in many cases by using RSS feeds. In such a case, content is arranged into a standardized structure of heading, content summary, and links to original sources. For details on RSS feeds, see Cong and Du (2008).

Representative Content-Related Vendors

A large number of vendors support content creation and management that facilitates the sharing of an organization's digital assets. Thus far, we have discussed the role of intermediaries and other third-party B2B providers in channeling digital content to the sites that display the content to consumers. Our discussion now turns to the next step in the content delivery chain, the task of delivering digital content to customers.

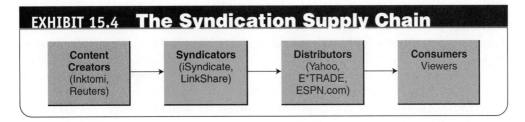

EXHIBIT 15.4 The Syndication Supply Chain

Content Delivery Networks

Content delivery is a service that hosting companies sometimes offer to help customers manage their content. Using *content delivery networks (CDNs)*, companies can update content, improve the quality of the site, increase consistency, control content, and decrease the time needed to create or maintain a site. Akamai (akamai.com) provides CDNs. Later in this section, we will discuss the case of Akamai.

In B2B, the information contained in electronic catalogs is of extreme importance. Companies can create and maintain the content in-house, or they can outsource such tasks.

Personalizing Content

Personalized content is Web content that is prepared to match the needs and expectations of the individual visitor. Such content enables visitors to find the information they need faster than at traditional sites, resulting in more visitors coming to the site. The process begins by tracking the visitor's behavior on the Web site via cookies. This information is provided to server software that generates dynamic Web pages that contain content the visitor can use. Amazon.com's Web site is the king of personalized content, offering content such as recommendations for products based on previous purchases, recently viewed items, and even a personalized "Welcome Back" message for repeat visitors. The downside of personalization is that it is expensive and can slow performance.

personalized content
Web content that matches the needs and expectations of the individual visitor.

Delivering Content by E-Newsletter

One of the most effective strategies for delivering content of interest to potential customers is an e-mail newsletter. An **e-newsletter** is a collection of short, informative content sent at regular intervals via e-mail to individuals who have an interest in the newsletter's topic. Examples are *E-Marketer Daily* and *Commerce Minutes*. An e-newsletter can support the business and the product.

e-newsletter
A collection of short, informative articles sent at regular intervals by e-mail to individuals who have an interest in the newsletter's topic.

CONTENT MANAGEMENT AND MAINTENANCE

Content management is the process of collecting, publishing, revising, updating, and removing content from a Web site to keep content fresh, accurate, compelling, and credible. Almost all sites begin with a high level of relevant content, but over time material becomes dated, irrelevant, or incorrect. Content management makes sure a site remains relevant and accurate long after the initial push to launch the site is over. For details on content management, see Henri and Heroux (2008).

content management
The process of adding, revising, and removing content from a Web site to keep content fresh, accurate, compelling, and credible.

Content Testing and Updating

An obvious task in content management is testing the content. Web managers need to make extensive and frequent checks of material for accuracy, clarity, typos, poor punctuation, misspelled words, and inconsistencies. Employees knowledgeable about the content should read site material to test it for accuracy; customer focus groups and professional editors should read it to check for clarity; and everyone should read new content to find mistakes. For more on content testing, see kefra.com and optimost.com.

Measuring Content Quality

How does a company know if the content on its Web site is meeting its e-commerce goals? How does a company know if it is delivering what its customers need? They do it by comparing the content to quality standards. In addition, content must meet privacy requirements, copyright and other legal requirements, language translation needs, and much more. You may use guidelines for knowledge management as well. Metrics are available from W3C (w3c.org/PICS) and periodically in *Baseline* magazine. Measuring the quality of content also requires appropriate Web traffic measurement tools. For specific suggestions on how to effectively use metrics to measure content quality, see Norguet et al. (2006). For a comprehensive discussion of data quality in e-business systems, see Kim et al. (2005).

Pitfalls of Content Management

According to Byrne (2002), companies face various content management pitfalls. The top six content management pitfalls and the best practices for avoiding them are found in Exhibit 15.5.

Content Removal

An important task within content management is removing old, out-of-date pages from the Web server. Even if all references to the page in the Web site have been removed, the page is still visible to search engines, searches on the site itself, and links from other Web pages. Delete or remove expired pages to an offline location that can serve as an archive.

Content Management Software

Content management software allows nontechnical staff to create, edit, and delete content on the company's Web site. The driving forces behind content management software (CMS) include the desire for companies to empower content owners to manage their own content and the inability of the computing services staff to keep up with demands for new or changed content on the Web site.

Even a small EC site may be content extensive, and in such a case software can help, as in the case of Anglesea Online (Case 15.3).

The closing case about Telecom New Zealand at the end of this chapter gives an example of comprehensive content management. For more on CMS, see emc.com and vignette.com.

CATALOG CONTENT AND ITS MANAGEMENT

Much of the content in B2B and B2C sites is catalog based. Chapter 2 discussed the benefits of electronic catalogs. Although there are many positive aspects of electronic catalogs, poorly

EXHIBIT 15.5 Content Management Pitfalls and Their Solutions

Problem or Pitfall	Solution
Picking content management software before developing solid requirements and the business case	Convert some of the resources currently being expended on software evaluation to a deeper examination of the company's own content and business needs.
Not getting a clear mandate from the top to proceed	Get business leaders onboard; you will need their strategic direction and a mandate for change.
Underestimating integration and professional service needs	Budget two to four times the cost of software license for consulting, customization, and integration.
Hiring inexperienced developers to integrate and extend the software	Hire good developers with content management software experience to implement mediocre software. This is always preferable to excellent software in the hands of novice integrators.
Depending entirely on an outside company to make changes to the system	Involve your own technical people closely in the initial development, even if you are outsourcing the integration. Do not skimp on training.
Thinking your migration will be painless despite what the content management system provider tells you	Start to prepare yourself for a content management system by cleaning up your HTML code and organizing your content. This takes longer than you might think!

Sources: Compiled from Byrne (2002) and Nielsen (2005).

EC Application

ANGLESEA ONLINE USES CONTENT MANAGEMENT SOFTWARE FOR SUCCESS

Anglesea Online is a really small business of one employee (owner), Nicholas Soames. It is an online community and business directory in rural Australia (*anglesea-online.com.au*). Launched in December 2002, the online directory became popular, providing information about the community, its life, community news, and so on. Business advertisers, who can use rich media ads, support the site. The owner and three casual contributors create most of the content. The site grew rapidly, reaching over 2,600 pages by 2007. Anglesea is located on Victoria's western surf coast, and it is blessed with tourists who also use the site. The surge in popularity increased dramatically after the demise of Anglesea's local newspaper. Soames soon realized that he could no longer manage the rapid growth of the Web site without some technological improvement. As a result, he developed a *content management system* (using a Microsoft Access database) to streamline the management of the more dynamic sections of the site, such as the business directories, gig guides, events listings, and classifieds. (Note: the site was temporarily closed in April 2009.)

How Does the Technology Work?

The content management system takes items such as classified listings and publishes them in a standard format within Web page templates. The following steps are carried out to amend sections of the Web site listings and to add, move, or delete listings.

1. Soames accesses the content management system databases, keying the elements into the prescribed template fields.
2. The CMS then identifies each element by which field it is entered into and places it into the required format, depending on the section of the site.

3. The CMS then publishes this content to the site in the appropriate section, which can then be reviewed and either saved or amended.
4. Once the content is correct and approved, it is published on the live site.

The content management system gave Soames more time to write content and pursue advertising revenue from the community.

For such a small company, cost is important. Computer hardware and software amounted to a one-time expenditure of $12,000 and operational expenses of $2,300 per year, whereas annual revenue from the EC business was $29,000 in 2003 and $35,000 in 2006.

Sources: Victorian Government (2007) and *anglesea-online.com.au* (accessed January 2009).

Questions

1. List the improvements to content management generated by the software.
2. Discuss the social and cultural aspects of the site.
3. Soames used a self-developed content management system, and it worked well. Why do most companies buy or lease systems from vendors, such as Vignette (*vignette.com*)?
4. Soames said that his site is no longer a hobby, but rather a revenue-generating business. Comment on his statement.
5. Online photograph sales and online advertising have become major revenue sources. Relate this to content management.

organized ones may deter buyers. Companies need to make sure that their catalog content is well managed.

For B2B buyers who aggregate suppliers' catalogs on their own Web sites, content management begins with engaging suppliers and then collecting, standardizing, classifying, hosting, and continually updating their catalog data. That is no small task, considering that most large buying organizations have hundreds, or even thousands, of suppliers, each using different data formats and nomenclature to describe their catalog items. The management of catalog content has some unique aspects and options.

CONTENT MAXIMIZATION AND STREAMING SERVICES

Many companies provide media-rich content, such as video clips, music, or Flash media, in an effort to reach their target audience with an appealing marketing message. For example, automakers want to provide a virtual driving experience as seen from the car's interior; realtors want to provide 360-degree views of their properties; and music sellers want to provide easily downloadable samples of their songs. Public portals and others are using considerable amounts of media-rich information as well. Finally, B2B e-catalogs may include thousands of photos.

These and other content providers are concerned about the download time from the user's perspective. Impatient or fickle Web surfers may click "Stop" before the multimedia has had a chance to fully download. Remember that B2C and B2B customers not only want their news stories, music, video clips, reference information, financial information, and sports scores delivered to them over the Web, but they also want them delivered quickly and effortlessly.

Therefore, it is important that content providers and marketers use technical delivery solutions that will not cause "traffic jams" during downloading. Several technical solutions are available from vendors who are referred to as *content maximizers* or *streaming services*. They use what is called "content delivery networks" (see Pallis and Vakali 2006). The leading vendor is Akamai, described in Case 15.4. To manage content that includes multimedia, one can use products such as those offered by Kontiki (kontiki.com).

CASE 15.4

EC Application

AKAMAI TECHNOLOGIES

An Internet company decided to name itself after a Hawaiian word that means "intelligent, clever, or cool"—Akamai (AH-kuh-my). And indeed, the company has created a clever product. Let's explain.

As user interest in high-speed Internet connections has grown, demand for bandwidth-heavy applications and media also has begun to surge. Paul Kagen Associates estimate that revenues from streaming media services totaled $1.5 billion in 2002 and will reach $70 billion by 2014. Similarly, AccuStream iMedia Research reports that the streaming video market was over $25 billion in 2006.

However, user connection speeds are only part of the streaming media picture. How will the networks handle the influx of bandwidth-chewing material? With a growing number of users and an abundance of rich media, the Internet is becoming extremely congested. Network traffic control is needed. Akamai and its competitors (Digital Island, Ibeam, and Mirror Image) are stepping in to manage Internet traffic.

Akamai products act as Internet traffic cops by using complicated mathematical algorithms to speed Web pages from the closest Akamai-owned server to a customer's location, thereby passing through fewer router hops. This process also helps to eliminate Internet gridlock. Today, caching and content distribution are the only practical ways to reduce network delay.

How does it work? To provide the service, Akamai maintains a global network of over 48,000 servers in 70 countries with almost 1,000 networks (in 2009) and leases space on them to giant portals, such as Yahoo! and CNN. These sites use the servers to store graphic-rich information closer to Internet users' computers in order to circumvent Web traffic jams and enable faster page loads, reducing delivery time to users by 20 to 30 percent.

Using Akamai's FreeFlow Launcher, Web site designers "Akamaize" their sites by marking content for delivery using the Akamai network. FreeFlow takes this content and stores it on Akamai Web servers around the world. When a user visits a Web site that has been "Akamaized," the images and multimedia content are downloaded from an Akamai server near the user for faster content delivery. Akamai allows customer data to move to and from big Web sites through its global network for a fee.

Unfortunately, the service is not 100 percent reliable. The speed for the end user depends on how many people are using the user's LAN at any given point in time and also on the speed of the server downloading any given Web site. A number of competing technologies are trying to provide the same solutions, and only a limited number of large companies that use lots of rich media are willing to pay for the service.

Another advantage of using Akamai or a similar service is the added security. For example, on June 15, 2004, a cybercriminal attacked some of Akamai's major clients, including Microsoft, Google, and Apple, using a DoS attack (see Chapter 10). Within minutes, Akamai deleted the attacks and solved the problem. According to Pallis and Vakali, Akamai controls 80 percent of the content delivery networks.

In 2001, Akamai started to diversify, offering a comprehensive suite of content delivery, streaming audio and video, traffic management, and other services, such as dynamic page view, bundled in a package called EdgeAdvantage. Akamai and its competitors were losing money in early 2001, but their revenues were increasing rapidly. In 2009 Akamai delivers between 15 to 20 percent of all Web traffic; delivers daily Web traffic greater than a Tier-1 ISP, at times reaching more than 2 Terabits per second; delivers hundreds of billions of daily Internet interactions; and helps enable more than $100 billion in secure annual e-commerce for its online retail customers.

Sources: Compiled from Pallis and Vakali (2006), *Internet Marketing Newswatch* (2007), Jones (2008), Akamai Technologies (2009a and 2009b), and *akamai.com/html/technology/index.html* (accessed January 2009).

Questions

1. What services does Akamai provide?

2. What is the company's revenue model?

3. What are the services' limitations?

Content for Large EC Sites

Content creation and management for a large EC site can be slow and expensive. Many software vendors provide content management tools. One example is Oracle, whose content management system is illustrated in Exhibit 15.6.

Section 15.5 ▶ REVIEW QUESTIONS

1. What is content? Dynamic content? Personalized content?

2. How can a business use content for cross-selling? For up-selling? For promotion?

3. Where does content come from? Identify four sources of Web site content. What is content creation?

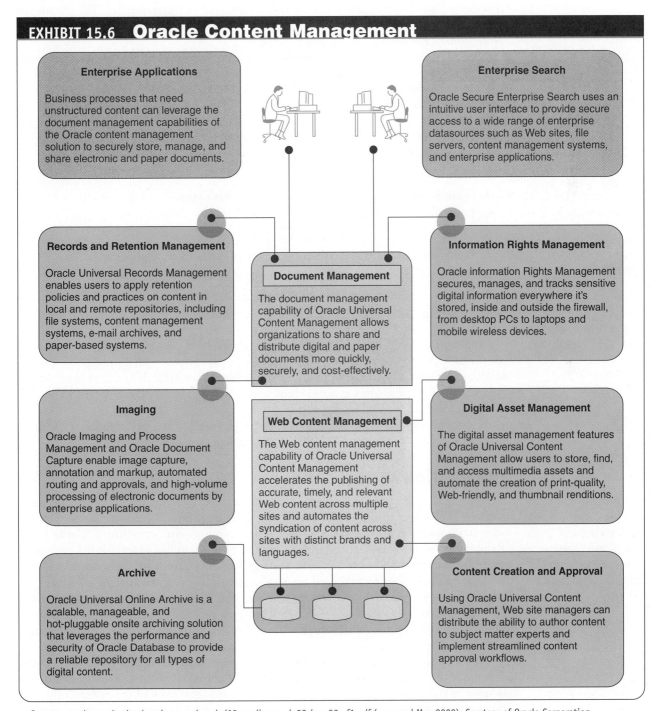

EXHIBIT 15.6 Oracle Content Management

Enterprise Applications

Business processes that need unstructured content can leverage the document management capabilities of the Oracle content management solution to securely store, manage, and share electronic and paper documents.

Enterprise Search

Oracle Secure Enterprise Search uses an intuitive user interface to provide secure access to a wide range of enterprise datasources such as Web sites, file servers, content management systems, and enterprise applications.

Records and Retention Management

Oracle Universal Records Management enables users to apply retention policies and practices on content in local and remote repositories, including file systems, content management systems, e-mail archives, and paper-based systems.

Document Management

The document management capability of Oracle Universal Content Management allows organizations to share and distribute digital and paper documents more quickly, securely, and cost-effectively.

Information Rights Management

Oracle information Rights Management secures, manages, and tracks sensitive digital information everywhere it's stored, inside and outside the firewall, from desktop PCs to laptops and mobile wireless devices.

Imaging

Oracle Imaging and Process Management and Oracle Document Capture enable image capture, annotation and markup, automated routing and approvals, and high-volume processing of electronic documents by enterprise applications.

Web Content Management

The Web content management capability of Oracle Universal Content Management accelerates the publishing of accurate, timely, and relevant Web content across multiple sites and automates the syndication of content across sites with distinct brands and languages.

Digital Asset Management

The digital asset management features of Oracle Universal Content Management allow users to store, find, and access multimedia assets and automate the creation of print-quality, Web-friendly, and thumbnail renditions.

Archive

Oracle Universal Online Archive is a scalable, manageable, and hot-pluggable onsite archiving solution that leverages the performance and security of Oracle Database to provide a reliable repository for all types of digital content.

Content Creation and Approval

Using Oracle Universal Content Management, Web site managers can distribute the ability to author content to subject matter experts and implement streamlined content approval workflows.

Source: *oracle.com/technology/oramag/oracle/08-sep/images/o58share20_f1.pdf* (accessed May 2009). Courtesy of Oracle Corporation. Used with permission.

4. What is syndication? How does it relate to content?

5. What e-newsletter content does a subscriber value most?

6. What is the purpose of content management?

7. Describe content maximization.

15.6 WEB SITE DESIGN

The goal of any Web site is to deliver quality content to its intended audience and to do so with an elegant design (Wiedemann 2007). With the Web site's content in hand, the Web site owner's next task is Web site design, which includes information architecture, navigation design, use of colors and graphics, and maximizing site performance. The purpose of this section is to enable you to contribute to the design of a Web site when working with professionals. For details, see Rutgers (2009).

Successful Web site design is about meeting customer expectations. Design starts with identifying customer needs, expectations, and problems. Then a site is designed to meet those needs and expectations or to solve the customers' problems. Pratt (2007) provides the following guideline for a successful Web site:

1. Build it for users (useful for the user, not necessarily the company).

2. Make it useful (e.g., usability test).

3. Make information easy to find.

4. Accommodate all users, including those with disabilities.

5. Build a comprehensive, responsive, and effective site.

6. Measure the site against the best of its peer group.

7. Build trust; be up front about security, privacy, and marketing policies.

8. Assign ownership to users, but work as a team with the technical people.

9. Set priorities; do the most beneficial stuff first.

10. Watch for new developments and encourage innovation.

Online File W15.4 shows a list of important Web site design criteria, with relevant questions. This and other chapters discuss some of these criteria, such as interactivity, scalability, and security. The focus of this section is on the fundamental design criteria of navigation, consistency, performance, appearance, and quality assurance. For a detailed Web site design process, see the Online Appendix.

Examples of well-designed sites are those of Intel, Sears, HP, Medco, Procter & Gamble, Johnson & Johnson, IBM, Pfizer, and Bank of America.

INFORMATION ARCHITECTURE

information architecture
How the site and its Web pages are organized, labeled, and navigated to support browsing and searching throughout the Web site.

A Web site's **information architecture** determines how a site organizes, labels, and navigates its Web pages to support browsing and searching. Information architecture begins with designing the site's structure. The most common site structure is hierarchical. Exhibit 15.7 shows a typical hierarchical structure for an online store. Most hierarchical Web sites are built wide and shallow, putting 3 to 10 sections in the second level and limiting most sections to two or three levels. Other, less frequently used structures are circular and linear ones. A circular structure is useful when presenting training materials. A linear structure is useful when telling a story or presenting a tutorial. For example, Online File W15.5 presents an abbreviated version of the linear structure of the e-business plan in the Online Tutorial.

A Web site typically includes a *homepage* that welcomes a visitor and introduces the site; *help* pages that assist the visitor to use or navigate through the site; *company* pages that inform the visitor about the online business; *transaction* pages that lead the customer through the purchase process; and *content* pages that deliver information about products and services

EXHIBIT 15.7   A Simple Hierarchical Web Site Structure

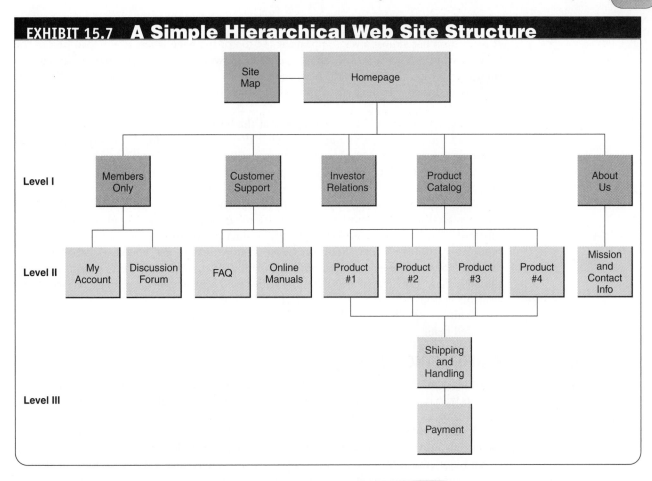

at all stages of the purchase process, from information search to postpurchase service and evaluation.

SITE NAVIGATION

The purpose of **site navigation** is to help visitors quickly and easily find the information they need on a Web site. Among the questions considered in site navigation are: How will visitors enter a site? How will visitors use the site? How will they find what is available at the site? How will they get from one page to another and from one section to another? How will visitors find what they are looking for? Site navigation has to help visitors find information quickly, because visitors do not want to take the time to figure out how to move around on a site. Site navigation has to be easy; visitors want moving around the site to be predictable, consistent, and intuitive enough that they do not have to think about it.

The simplest navigation aid is a *navigation bar* (see example in Exhibit 15.8). A navigation bar provides the visitor an opportunity to link to likely destinations (e.g., homepage, "about us") and major sections of the Web site (e.g., product catalog, customer support).

site navigation
Aids that help visitors find the information they need quickly and easily.

EXHIBIT 15.8   A Typical Navigation Bar

Site Map and Navigation

A navigation bar almost always appears at the top of the page where it will load first in the browser window and be visible "above the fold." However, if the page contains banner ads, then the navigation bar should be placed prominently below the ads. Why? Frequent Web users develop "banner ad blindness" in which they ignore banner ads and everything above them.

A second navigation bar should appear at the bottom of every page. Then, visitors who have read the page and have not found what they are looking for can easily be guided to where they need to go next. An effective navigation scheme is to offer a simple, attractive, graphical navigation bar at the top of the page and a longer, text navigation bar at the bottom of each page.

If the site's contents need more options than what can fit on a navigation bar, subsections can be placed in each section of the navigation bar (e.g., customer support might include subsections such as customer service FAQ, product information, order status). The subsections can appear on the navigation bar via a pull-down menu or a mouseover (when a visitor passes a mouse cursor over the button, a submenu will pop up). Large and medium-size sites should include a site map page so that the visitor who is unsure of where to go can see all the available options.

Exhibit 15.9 illustrates the major information architecture and navigation concepts discussed here.

PERFORMANCE (SPEED)

Speed ranks at or near the top of every list of essential design considerations, for good reason. Visitors who have to wait more than a few seconds for a Web page to load are likely to hit the "stop" or "back" button and go somewhere else.

A number of factors affect the speed at which the page transfers from the Web server to the client's browser. Factors out of the control of the Web designer and site owner are the visitor's modem speed, the bandwidth available at the customer's ISP, and, to some degree, the current bandwidth available at the Web host's location. The critical factor that is under the control of the Web designer is the content and design of the page. A competent Web designer will know what can be done to improve a page's download speed or at least give it the appearance of loading fast.

The most widely recognized cause of long download times is a large graphic or a large number of small graphics on a single page. Create graphics at the lowest possible resolution so that the visitor can clearly see the picture, art, or icon so that the graphic file is only a few kilobytes in size. If a large, high-resolution graphic image is important, thumbnail images can be put on the page and linked to full-size, higher-resolution images available at the visitor's discretion.

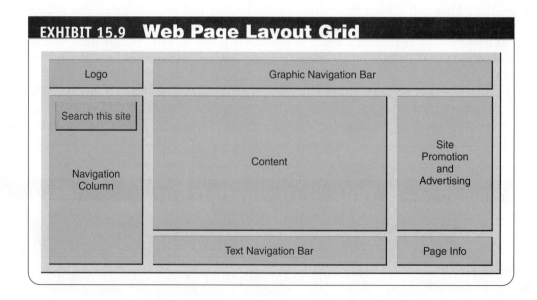

EXHIBIT 15.9 Web Page Layout Grid

COLORS AND GRAPHICS

The Web is a colorful and graphic world, and colors, pictures, artwork, and video can be used effectively if used correctly.

The key to effective use of color and graphics is to design the site to match the expectations of the target audience. Financial services sites tend to use formal colors (e.g., green, blue) with simple charts to illustrate the text but not many pictures. Sites directed at a female audience tend to feature lighter colors, usually pastels, with many pictures and an open design featuring lots of white space. Game sites are one type of site that can get away with in-your-face colors, Flash effects, and highly animated graphics.

WEB SITE USABILITY

Usability measures the quality of a user's experience when interacting with a product or system—whether a Web site, software application, mobile technology, or any user-operated device.

In general, **usability** refers to how well users can learn and use a product or a Web site to achieve their goals as well as how satisfied they are with that process. Usability means that people who use the Web site can do so quickly and easily to accomplish their tasks and may also consider such factors as cost-effectiveness and usefulness.

According to Nielsen (2005) and usability.gov, the following factors determine usability:

> **usability (of Web site)**
> The quality and usefulness of the user's experience when interacting with the Web site.

> ▶ **Ease of learning.** How fast can a user who has never seen the user interface before learn it sufficiently well to accomplish basic tasks? How easy and intuitive is it to learn to use the Web site?
>
> ▶ **Efficiency of use.** Once an experienced user has learned to use the system, how fast can he or she accomplish tasks?
>
> ▶ **Memorability.** If a user has used the system before, can he or she remember enough to use it effectively the next time, or does the user have to start over again learning everything?
>
> ▶ **Error frequency and severity.** How often do users make errors while using the system, how serious are these errors, and how can users recover from these errors?
>
> ▶ **Subjective satisfaction.** How much does the user like using the system? How pleasant is it to use the Web site design?

On the Web, usability is a necessary condition for survival. If a Web site is difficult to use, people leave. This results in negative financial performance. For further details, see usability.gov and useit.com/alertbox. Usable sites need to meet customer demands (see Stoller 2008).

What Annoys EC Customers?

One approach to a good Web design is to eliminate things that annoy customers—pop-up ads, the need to install extra software, deal links, mandatory registration requirements, confusing navigation, slow moves from page to page, obsolete content, and a poor search tool. See the Online Appendix for details.

Section 15.6 ▶ REVIEW QUESTIONS

1. Describe 10 criteria used to judge Web site design.
2. Name four site navigation aids.
3. Why is performance a key design criterion? What slows performance? What can decrease download time?
4. Describe some issues for proper use of color and graphics on a Web site.
5. What is usability? List the major criteria used to determine usability.

15.7 PROVIDING E-COMMERCE SUPPORT SERVICES

Creating content and designing the Web site are the creative aspects of building a Web site. Determining how the Web site actually will be built and by whom are the implementation parts of Web site construction. Web site construction is usually about three options—internal development, outsourcing, and partnering—spread over two time periods—start-up construction and ongoing maintenance (see Online Chapter 18).

WHO BUILDS THE WEB SITE?

Early in the Web site development process, the online business owner has to decide whether to build the Web site with internal staff, an outside contractor, or a combination of these two options. This involves managerial considerations such as control, speed, and desired organizational competencies, as generally described in information technology textbooks.

PAYMENTS: ACCEPTING CREDIT CARDS

Another important service is payments (see Chapter 11). You can't do business if you can't get paid. This truism means that every online business has to face decisions about electronic payment systems. The dominant form of B2C payment is accepting credit cards over the Internet.

Chapter 11 described the process for accepting credit card payments. As noted there, processing credit card payments on the Internet differs only slightly from the process in traditional, face-to-face transactions. What are these differences from a merchant's perspective? What are the basic requirements for an online business to be able to accept credit cards for payment?

First, in the online process, the credit card reader in the store is replaced with credit card processing software (a credit card gateway) that is capable of accepting input from a Web page and submitting it into the credit card system (the merchant's bank, the customer's bank, and the credit card interchange, such as Visa or MasterCard).

card-not-present (CNP) transaction

A credit card transaction in which the merchant does not verify the customer's signature.

Second, with online transactions, a signature and verification of the signature by the merchant is not required, resulting in what is known as a **card-not-present (CNP) transaction**. This situation removes a considerable amount of certainty and security from the process. In response to this increased risk, banks are more selective about who gets an online merchant account, and they require that the entire process be as secure as possible (e.g., checking that the shipping address provided by the customer matches the billing address on file at the customer's bank). In addition, banks charge higher transaction fees for CNP transactions to offset the increased risks.

An online business that wants to accept credit cards for payment generally has to do the following:

▶ **Open a merchant account.** It is likely that the business's current bank will be happy to extend banking privileges for the business to accept credit cards online. However, some small, regional banks may not offer this service; other banks may establish thresholds that are too high for the business to qualify (i.e., banks are more selective about CNP merchant accounts).

▶ **Purchase credit card processing software.** Credit card gateway companies such as authorize.net, cybersource.com, and charge.com provide credit card processing software and services that accept credit card numbers and manage their transfer into and back from the credit card system. Factors to consider in deciding which gateway company to use include companies that the site developer has worked with before and what software the organization hosting the Web site will accept. A business typically pays the credit card gateway a setup fee and a per-transaction fee.

▶ **Integrate the credit card processing software into the transaction system.** To work effectively, the software must be able to manage the flow of data between the transaction and customer databases and the credit card systems. The site developer writes scripts that enable the different components in the credit card transaction to share data they require.

For best practices regarding merchants' protection against fraud, see Chapter 10, fbi.gov/majcases/fraud/Internetschemes.htm, ic3.gov, fraud.org/internet/intinfo.htm, and en.wikipedia.org/credit_card_fraud.

WEB SITE PROMOTION

Every successful online business needs a highly visible Web site. Chapter 4 discussed Web site promotion through advertising (e.g., banner ads, pop-up ads) and marketing strategies (e.g., banner swapping; use of blogs, chat rooms, or groups in social networks and virtual worlds). This section focuses on internal Web site promotion ("selling" the Web site on the site) and search engine optimization (getting the Web site to the top of the search engine listings).

Internal Web Site Promotion

Internal Web site promotion begins by including content that establishes the site as a useful site for customers so that they remember the site and return and make a purchase. To do this, the Web site should become not only a place to buy something, but also an indispensable resource with compelling content, useful links to other Web sites, and features that will make customers want to return.

Promoting the Web site internally often includes a page of testimonials from satisfied customers. If the site or the business has received any awards, draw the visitor's attention to them. If the business owner's background or credentials relate to the business, then list any degrees, professional affiliations, and awards that relate to the online business.

Site promotion continues with a marketing plan that includes the URL on every product, business card, letterhead, package, and e-mail message that leaves the business. A **signature file** is a simple text message that an e-mail program adds automatically to outgoing messages. A typical signature file includes the person's name, title, contact details, and name and URL of the business.

Promotions can be based on Web analytics. **Web analytics** is the measurement, collection, analysis, and reporting of Internet data for the purposes of understanding and optimizing Web usage (en.wikipedia.org/wiki/Web_analytics). An example of Web analytics reports and a case study are provided in Online File W15.6. For interesting customer success stories, see Webtrends (webtrends.com).

There are two categories of Web analytics: offsite and onsite. Offsite Web analytics refers to Web measurement and analysis of the Web in general. It includes the measurement of a Web site's potential audience (opportunity), share of voice (visibility), and buzz (comments) that is occurring on the Internet as a whole. Onsite Web analytics measure a visitor's journey once the visitor is on the company's Web site. Such Web analytics measure the site's drivers and conversions; for example, which pages encourage people to make a purchase. Onsite Web analytics measures the performance of the Web site in a commercial context. This data is typically compared against key performance indicators for performance and is used to improve a site or marketing campaign's audience response. For more details, see Sostre and LeClaire (2008).

Web analytics vendors include IBM, Oracle, Microsoft, MicroStrategy, SAS, Applix, and Webtrends.

Search Engine Optimization

How is a Web site found by customers in the vast world of cyberspace? How does a new online business get noticed ahead of its more well-established competitors? In addition to promotional and advertising strategies discussed in this and other chapters, perhaps the most important and cost-effective way to attract new customers is search engine optimization. **Search engine optimization (SEO)** is the use of strategies intended to position a Web site at the top of Web search engines' results such as Google, AllTheWeb, and Teoma. Search engines are the primary way many Web users find relevant Web sites; an online business cannot ignore SEO strategies. For details on SEO, see Kay 2007 and en.wikipedia.org/search_engine_optimization.

The strategies to optimize a Web site's ranking in search engines should be part of content creation, Web site design, and site construction. Optimizing search engine rankings through keyword placement and link building is much easier, less time consuming, and less expensive if it is integrated into the Web site development process. Online File W15.7 provides a comprehensive guide to SEO.

signature file
A simple text message an e-mail program automatically adds to outgoing messages.

Web analytics
The measurement, collection, analysis, and reporting of Internet data for the purposes of understanding and optimizing Web usage.

search engine optimization (SEO)
The application of strategies intended to position a Web site at the top of Web search engines.

Several SEO services, such as WebPosition (webposition.com) and Search Summit (searchsummit.com), will supervise the entire SEO process for a Web site. However, SEO requires constant monitoring to be effective, and decisions such as which companies are acceptable linking partners are management decisions that should not be left to neutral parties. SEO services can assist, but successful SEO requires supervision and involvement by the site owner. For further details, see Covel (2007) and en.wikipedia.org/SEO.

CUSTOMER RELATIONSHIP MANAGEMENT

Customer relationship management (CRM) is a customer service approach that focuses on building long-term and sustainable customer relationships that add value for the customer and the company. This section focuses on what every start-up online business needs to know in order to initiate an effective CRM program. After getting these fundamentals right, successful online firms will be ready to move into more advanced CRM techniques, which include services such as contact management, data mining, and personalization.

Using Content to Build Customer Relationships

The first step to building customer relationships is to give customers good reasons to visit and return to the Web site. In other words, the site should be rich in information and have more content than a visitor can absorb in a single visit. The site should include not just product information, but also value-added content from which visitors can get valuable information and services for free. Exhibit 15.10 lists some ways in which online businesses can build customer relationships through content.

EXHIBIT 15.10 Building CRM Through Content

Content Strategy	Description	CRM Benefits
Provide membership	Offer registration at the site to gain access to premium content and services.	Community building, targeted marketing, paid subscription opportunity
Personalize the user experience	Present content that the site visitor has indicated an interest in through previous browsing or member profiles.	Community building, targeted commerce offers, customer and site loyalty
Attract visitors	Provide free games, shows, and blogs.	Customer loyalty, revisits, tell friends
Support users	Provide responsive and convenient customer service.	Community building, customer and site loyalty, repeat purchases
Communicate via the community	Allow visitors to communicate with each other and the publisher through the site.	Community building, customer and site loyalty
Reward visitors	Provide visitors with rewards for visiting and using the Web site.	Customer and site loyalty, promotional product up-sell and cross-sell opportunities
Consumer education	Educate consumer on important topics (e.g., medical, diets).	Community building
Market effectively	Promote the site's content and products without alienating current and potential customers.	Customer and site loyalty, promotional product up-sell and cross-sell opportunity
Set up smart affiliate relationships	Establish affiliate relationships with both private (consumer) and commercial Web publishers.	Customer and site loyalty, new revenue stream

Sources: Tomsen (2000) and Ariguzo et al. (2006).

Section 15.7 ▶ REVIEW QUESTIONS

1. List the three options for Web site construction.
2. What factors favor internal development of a Web site? What factors favor external development?
3. Describe the process required for an online business to accept credit cards over the Internet.
4. List four types of Web site content that can promote the Web site internally.
5. What is search engine optimization? Why is it important?
6. List some ways Web sites can use content to manage customer relationships.

15.8 OPENING A WEB STOREFRONT

The most common EC project on the Internet is the *storefront* (also known as the *Webstore*). Millions of storefronts exist on the Internet, mostly those of small businesses. However, large corporations, as well as many individuals, including students and even children, have storefronts as well. As we have seen throughout the book, most online entrepreneurs, such as the initiators of Campusfood.com, Amazon.com, CatToys.com, and JetPens, started with a storefront. Storefronts appear in all different shapes, and their construction and operating expenses vary greatly. Storefronts primarily sell products or services (see en.wikipedia.org/wiki/Electronic_commerce), yet their functionalities differ considerably (for a list of functionalities, see Online Chapter 18).

OPTIONS FOR ACQUIRING STOREFRONTS

Storefronts can be acquired in several ways:

▶ **Build them from scratch.** Pioneering storefronts, such as hothothot.com, wine.com, and amazon.com, built their stores from scratch. Specifically, they designed them and then hired programmers to program all the necessary software. The major advantage of this approach is that the site owner can customize the site to his or her liking. The disadvantages are that the process is slow, expensive, and error prone and requires constant maintenance. Consequently, today only large corporations build their storefronts from scratch. See Online Chapter 18 for more on how to build a storefront from scratch. Most companies use other alternatives (see Bracken 2006).

▶ **Build them from components.** This option is faster and less expensive than the first one. The site owner purchases off-the-shelf components (or sometimes obtains them for free), such as a shopping cart, an e-catalog, and a payment gate, and then assembles them. The site owner can replace the components if they become obsolete; therefore, the site owner can save on maintenance. The downside is that the resulting site may not fit the online business owner's needs very well. See Online Chapter 18 for information on how to build a site from components. An example of this type of solution is Microsoft's Site Server Commerce Edition, which has a built-in wizard that helps users model their own online business processes graphically. This approach, however, is usually more costly than building from templates and may take longer. In addition, it usually requires some in-house technical expertise for installation of the required hardware and software as well as for continued operation and maintenance. Network Solutions (networksolutions.com) provides many such components.

▶ **Build with templates (storebuilders).** As described earlier in the chapter, using storebuilders is one of the most viable options for starting an online business. Several vendors provide storebuilding templates. Some provide them free, free for 30 days, or for a nominal monthly fee that includes hosting the site on their servers. Using this approach is especially attractive to small businesses because the cost is relatively low (usually $10 to $99 per month), the business can construct the store in one or a few days, and it does not require extensive programming skills. The site owner basically fills out forms and attaches pictures. Another major benefit of this approach is that hosting is usually provided, as well as support services such as payment collection, shipments, and security.

Furthermore, the vendor will take care of all software maintenance. Many vendors also offer store and inventory management as well as other features, as described later in this section. Finally, and perhaps most important, if the site owner uses a vendor such as Yahoo!, eBay, or Amazon.com the site will be included in the vendor's e-marketplace, which provides a great deal of exposure. The downside of this approach is that it limits the site owner to the available templates and tools. However, some vendors provide a professional version that allows customization. Representative vendors that provide templates are:

- Yahoo! Small Business offers Yahoo! Merchant Solutions (smallbusiness. yahoo.com/ecommerce/)
- eBay ProStores (prostores.com; see Elms 2006)
- Hostway (hostway.com)
- GoEmerchant (goemerchant.com)
- StoreFront eCommerce (storefront.net)
- 1 & 1 Hosting (1and1.com)
- Go Daddy (godaddy.com)
- Shopping.com (shopping.com)
- Amazon.com ProMerchant (amazonservices.com)
- ShoppingCartsPlus (shoppingcartsplus.com)

For a comparison and evaluation of these vendors and others, see ecommerce-software-review.toptenreviews.com. To compare this and other products go to: ecommerce-software-review.toptenreviews.com/goemerchant-review. The major criteria used are: Feature set, ease of use, ease of installation, ease of set up, documentation, and fraud protection.

Selecting a Development Option

Before choosing the appropriate development option, you need to consider a number of issues in order to generate a list of requirements and capabilities. The following is a list of representative questions that need to be addressed when defining requirements:

- **Customers.** Who are the target customers? What are their needs? What kind of marketing tactics should a business use to promote the store and attract customers? How can a business enhance customer loyalty?
- **Merchandising.** What kinds of products or services will the business sell online? Are soft (digitized) goods or hard goods sold? Are soft goods downloadable?
- **Sales service.** Can customers order online? How? Can they pay online? Can they check the status of their order online? How are customer inquiries handled? Are warranties, service agreements, and guarantees available for the products? What are the refund procedures?
- **Promotion.** How are the products and services promoted? How will the site attract customers? Are coupons, manufacturer's rebates, or quantity discounts offered? Is cross-selling possible?
- **Transaction processing.** Is transaction processing in real time? How are taxes, shipping and handling fees, and payments processed? Are all items taxable? What kinds of shipping methods will the site offer? What kinds of payment methods, such as checks, credit cards, or cybercash, will the site accept? How will the site handle order fulfillment?
- **Marketing data and analysis.** What information, such as sales, customer data, and advertising trends, will the site collect? How would the site use such information for future marketing?
- **Branding.** What image should the storefront reinforce? How is the storefront different from those of the competition?

The initial list of requirements should be as comprehensive as possible. It is preferable to validate the identified requirements through focus-group discussions or surveys with potential customers. The business can then prioritize the requirements based on the customers' preferences. The final list of prioritized requirements serves as the basis for selecting and customizing the appropriate package or designing a storefront from scratch.

In the remainder of this section, we will introduce the Yahoo! package for small business.

YAHOO! SMALL BUSINESS

Yahoo! offers one of the most popular storefront packages at smallbusiness.yahoo.com. It offers three levels of merchant solutions: starter, standard, and professional. The capabilities and fees of each plan are available on Yahoo!'s Web site. Yahoo! offers a step-by-step guide that explains how Yahoo! Merchant Solutions ("sell online") works and how you can use it to build, manage, and market an online business. Yahoo! also offers three related services: Web hosting, sponsored advertising, and posting of job ads. Read on to gain valuable tips and guidance that will help you succeed in developing your own online storefront.

Getting Started

Online File W15.8 provides a summary of the e-commerce basics guide (as of January 2009), do the walk-through at smallbusiness.yahoo.com/ecommerce/basics.php. Also see Snell (2006).

Take a Tour and See the Videos

To see all the features that come with Yahoo! Merchant Solutions, take a tour (click "Tour"). Once welcomed, you will see a slideshow that lists its capabilities. Notable features include the following: Web hosting and domain name registration; e-mail; EC tools (shopping cart, payment processing, inventory management); business tools and services (site design, marketing, site management); order processing tools; site development tools (site editor, templates, uploading content, for example, with Yahoo! SiteBuilder); finding and keeping customers (per Chapter 4; from e-mail campaigns to cross-selling suggestions); payment acceptance tools; tax calculators; order notification and confirmations; and performance-tracking tools (statistics, drill-downs, measuring the effectiveness of marketing campaigns). Finally, watch the videos about success stories of small businesses.

Using the Templates

You can build your store in several ways. Your primary tool is the easy-to-use Store Editor. You can create a homepage, set up various store sections, and add to them. You can upload content developed in Microsoft FrontPage, Macromedia Dreamweaver, or Yahoo! SiteBuilder.

Section 15.8 ▶ REVIEW QUESTIONS

1. List the various options for acquiring a storefront.
2. What are the advantages of building with templates? What are the disadvantages?
3. List the typical features of a storefront.
4. What are some of the selection criteria for a software option?

MANAGERIAL ISSUES

Some managerial issues related to this chapter are as follows.

1. **What does it take to create a successful online business?** The ability of a business to survive, and thrive, in the marketplace depends on the strength of the business concept, the capabilities of the entrepreneur, and successful execution of the business plan. Creativity, entrepreneurial attitudes, and management skills represent a human capital investment that every potentially successful business needs (Umesh et al. 2005). This is

true for both online and offline businesses. However, to succeed in online business, management needs to consider additional factors, such as e-business models, revenue models, synergy and conflict between the online and offline channels, Web site management, and integration of information systems for EC and back-end systems.

2. **Is creating a Web site a technical task or a management task?** It is both. Although somewhat expensive, the technical skills required to build a Web site are readily available in the marketplace. The prerequisite managerial skills are somewhat more difficult to find. Online business owners need to possess traditional business skills as well as understand the technical aspects of building a Web site in order to be able to hire and work with information architects, Web designers, and Web site hosting services. Management should be able to map the business goals with a combination of solution sets, such as e-marketplaces, CRM, SCM, and ERP. The integration policy should connect the internal entities and enable collaboration with external partners.

3. **How do we attract visitors to the Web site?** Search engine optimization is important, but the key to attracting visitors, getting them to return, and encouraging them to tell others about the site is to offer credible content that fulfills a value-exchange proposition. That is, both the site owner and the customer must receive value from the visit. What the site says (content) is important, but so is how it says it. Web design delivers content in a compelling manner that enhances the readability of the content and the quality of the customer experience. Personalized services support will be important in order to provide relevant information and to motivate users to visit again.

4. **How do we turn visitors into buyers?** Getting people to come to the Web site is only half the battle. Visitors become buyers when a Web site offers products and services that customers need, with promotions and a price that entice visitors to buy there rather than go somewhere else, in an environment that promotes trust. Customer contact services for resolution of complaints will contribute to retaining the customer and generating repurchases. A well-designed CRM system needs to support the services.

5. **Are best practices useful?** For an inexperienced EC person or company, the best practices of others can be extremely useful (see Maguire 2005). The experiences of vendors, companies, academicians, and others are most useful. Free advice is available from many sources, including ECommercePartners.net (*ecommercepartners.net*). A comprehensive set of benchmark e-business cases can be found in Lee et al. (2006).

6. **What should my new business give to funders?** It depends on the stage of the business. In the early stage, funders are concerned about the sales growth rate and market share. Losses may be tolerated as long as the growth is high and the vision of future profit is clear. However, the eventual concern will be the realized profit and stock price. The important thing is to maintain control by keeping 51 percent of the shares (at least up to the IPO).

7. **What are important factors for successful Web management?** To manage the Web site successfully, the online business owner needs to select an appropriate Web hosting service, maintain value-creating contents, and promote the Web site so that new customers will visit. The alternatives to Web hosting are storebuilder services, dedicated hosting, ISP hosting services, and self-hosting. To maintain the quality of the site's content, a policy for acquiring, testing, and updating content should be established. Personalization is also important. Social networking may be adopted as an important source of content collection from the open public.

SUMMARY

In this chapter, you learned about the following EC issues as they relate to the learning objectives.

1. **Fundamental requirements for initiating an online business.** A good idea becomes a successful online business when owners with the required skills, attitudes, and understanding of Internet culture execute a powerful business plan.

2. **Funding options for a start-up online business.** Incubators usually provide support services, whereas angel investors and venture capitalists provide funds for a prospective online business. The business and business owners usually benefit greatly from these arrangements, but the funding sources are scarce and competition for funds is stiff.

3. **Adding e-initiatives.** Adding e-initiatives (or projects) is common. A large project requires a business case. Additions are made gradually that eventually make the business a click-and-mortar one. Common projects are e-procurement, e-CRM, and a storefront.

4. **Transformation to e-business.** In an e-business, all possible processes are conducted online. Achieving such a state in a large organization is a complex process involving change management.

5. **Web site hosting options for an online business.** Storebuilder services, ISPs, dedicated Web site hosting services, and self-hosting give online business owners a range of options in deciding how and where to host the Web site. A well-chosen domain name is an "address for success," a way of making the site easy to find and remember. Choosing a domain name is an important step in setting up the hosting site.

6. **Provide content that attracts and keeps Web site visitors.** Content is king. Content can be created, purchased, or acquired for free and used for site promotion, sales, and building customer relationships. Successful Web sites offer content that the site's target audience wants and expects.

7. **Design a visitor-friendly site.** Although text is content rich and inexpensive, a text-only site is a barren and unmemorable site. Select graphics and colors with the site's business goals and visitors' needs in mind. Web site owners and designers should never overestimate the attention span of the site visitor, so it is best to include small graphics that are few in number so that the end result is an attractive page but one that also will load fast. The key to visitor-friendly navigation is to project a visitor's mental map on the Web site: where they are, where they were, where they should go next, and how to get to where they want to be.

8. **High placement in search engines is key.** Keyword occurrence and placement on a merchants' site and promoting link popularity are the fundamental strategies for search engine optimization. High placement on search engine keyword searches will guarantee visitors, the essential first step toward online business success.

9. **Provision of support services.** Like offline businesses, online businesses need support services. These include payment, security, content creation, Web site design, advertisement (promotion), search engine optimization, and CRM.

10. **The process of building a storefront.** Assuming that you know what you want to sell and how to do it, you need to obtain a domain name and arrange for hosting. Then you need to design the site and fill it with appropriate content. Your storefront needs to have support services (such as payment) and be secure. You must also promote the site in order to attract buyers.

11. **Using templates to build a storefront.** Small sites can be built quickly, easily, and inexpensively using templates. The disadvantages are that the site will look like many others that use the same templates and it might not fit the needs of the company.

KEY TERMS

Term	Page	Term	Page	Term	Page
Angel investor	673	Domain Name System (DNS)	682	Self-hosting	681
Attractors	678	Dynamic Web content	683	Signature file	695
Business case	672	E-newsletter	685	Site navigation	691
Business plan	672	Incubator	673	Storebuilder service	679
Business process management (BPM)	677	Information architecture	690	Syndication	684
Card-not-present (CNP) transaction	694	Informational Web site	678	Transactional Web site	678
		Interactive Web site	678	Up-selling	684
Collaborative Web site	678	ISP hosting service	681	Usability (of a Web site)	693
Content	682	Mirror site	681	Venture capital (VC)	673
Content management	685	Personalized content	685	Web analytics	695
Cross-selling	683	Search engine optimization (SEO)	695	Web hosting service	680
Domain name	681				

QUESTIONS FOR DISCUSSION

1. Compare and contrast setting up a traditional, brick-and-mortar business and an online business. Consider factors such as entrepreneurial skills, facilities and equipment, and business processes.

2. Compare and contrast the creation of a new online business and the establishment of an online initiative in an existing company. Consider factors such as resource acquisition, start-up processes, and competitor analysis.

3. How is an e-business plan different from a traditional business plan?

4. Describe organizational transformation, and discuss some of the difficulties involved.

5. How would you decide which Web site hosting option an online business should use? List and briefly explain factors to consider in your decision.

6. Who should be on a Web site development team for a small business? For a large business?

7. Several times in this chapter we advise online business owners to gather competitive intelligence from competitors (e.g., in SEO, what sites link to competitor sites). Is this ethical? Why or why not?

8. Why is a store such as cattoys.com not economically feasible offline?

9. What are the advantages and disadvantages of using templates to build a storefront?

10. Yahoo! provides many services, including Web site hosting, storebuilding tools, and an online mall. List the benefits of these services. What are the drawbacks, if any?

11. How is usability related to Web site design?

12. Relate Web analytics to search engine optimization.

INTERNET EXERCISES

1. Go to vFinance Capital (vfinance.com) and the National Venture Capital Association (nvca.com) and identify any trends or opportunities in acquiring start-up funding.

2. Go to a Yahoo! category, such as tourist agencies or insurance companies, and pick 10 sites. Classify them as informational, interactive, or transactional Web sites. Make a list of any informational, interactive, or transactional features.

3. Many individuals try to make a living simply by buying and selling goods on eBay. Visit ebay.com and make a list of the ways in which these entrepreneurs use cross-selling and up-selling in their sales activities.

4. Visit the Webmaster Forums (webmaster-forums. net). Register (for free) and visit the Web site critique area. Compare the design rules offered in this chapter with some of the Web sites offered for critique at the site. Offer at least one design suggestion to a Webmaster who is soliciting feedback.

5. Explore the Web to find five dedicated Web site hosting services. Compare them using the criteria listed in this chapter. Write a report based on your findings.

6. Enter networksolutions.com. View the shopping cart demo. What features impress you the most and why?

What related services does it provide? Compare it to storefront.net and nexternal.com.

7. Compare the shopping malls of Yahoo!, amazon.com, and internetmall.com.

8. Go to godaddy.com. Examine its Traffic Blazer product. How can it help you with an online business?

9. Enter 1and1.com. Examine its hosting, development, and other tools. Take the Test Drive. Compare it with services offered by jstreettech.com. Write a report.

10. Enter willmaster.com. View its tutorials and comment on its usefulness to EC site builders.

11. Enter omniture.com. How does it help with site optimization? What other services does it provide?

12. Go to checkout.google.com and find the services offered to buyers. Why is shopping here faster than at Amazon.com or Yahoo!?

13. Enter documentum.com and find its enterprise content management products. Write a report.

14. Enter nichemarketsolutions.com/template.asp and find the offering of visually dynamic merchandise presentation. Why is it so special?

15. Enter enquiro.com and find the search engine product(s). Find how they do search engine optimization. Write a report.

TEAM ASSIGNMENTS, PROJECTS, AND CLASSROOM DISCUSSIONS

1. Enter entrepreneurs.about.com. Each team member should select two or three of the "browse topics" and relate it to online businesses. Make a presentation to the class.

2. Enter myownbusiness.org/s2/index.html. Obtain a template and design a business plan for your class EC project.

3. Form two teams, a client team and a Web design team. After suitable preparation, both teams meet for their first Web site planning meeting. Afterward, both teams critique their own and the other team's performance in the meeting.

4. Enter webhosting.yahoo.com/ps/sb/index.php and download the SiteBuilder. As a team, build a storefront for your dream business. You can try it for free for 30 days. Use the design features available. Have visitors check out the site. The instructor and class will review the sites for design and usability. Awards will be given to the best stores. Alternatively, you may use the equivalent tools from eBay or 1and1.com.

5. Address the following topics in a class discussion:

   a. Discuss the logic of outsourcing the combined Web hosting and site construction. What are some of the disadvantages?

   b. Should a small business maintain its own Web site? Why or why not? Should a large business maintain its own Web site? Why or why not?

   c. What are the trade-offs in giving the customer everything possible (e.g., personalized content, high-resolution graphics, a feature-full site) and the fundamental rules of Web design?

Closing Case

HOW TELECOM NEW ZEALAND (TNZ) EXCELS WITH CONTENT MANAGEMENT

Telecom New Zealand (TNZ) is a major telecommunication and online provider offering a full range of advanced services to most of the population in New Zealand. The company wants its customers to use its Web site (*telecom.co.nz*) not only for customer service, but also as the primary marketing and sales channel for both standard and complex products and services. To do so, TNZ is using a comprehensive solution called Enterprise Content Management from Vignette (*vignette.com*) that supports Web site creation, management, process automation, publishing, and analysis. Vignette provides a suite of products that help TNZ control, manage, and share content; optimize business processes; integrate the site content with existing enterprise applications; and deliver the entire inventory of content in a personalized fashion to TNZ's choice of devices.

The solution also enables TNZ to run segment-focused marketing campaigns, to save time and money in site development to support marketing campaigns, and to develop one-to-one relationships with customers by delivering relevant and tailored content. The solution enables TNZ to continuously increase the sophistication of its marketing campaigns by supporting appropriate results-based analysis.

To attract customers, the company needed to provide site content related to products and services, which are provided both to individuals and organizations (B2B), in such a way that the content is current, comprehensive, and easy to find and understand—all of which needed to be done in a cost-effective manner.

Working with IT software and service provider Sybase (including wireless technologies), TNZ implemented Vignette's products in 2000. By 2007, TNZ developed several applications that make Web site content delivery faster and more manageable. Improvements were registered in:

▶ Manageability of all content.

▶ Easier online publishing (using templates to automate the process).

▶ Faster training of employees in online publishing.

▶ Improved efficiency of online publishing (reduction from days to hours).

▶ The number of staff publishing online.

▶ Consistency in style and design of pages by different employees (template-based content is also more accurate).

▶ Easier self-service by customers (e.g., customers can enter their phone number to find if broadband Internet access is available in their areas, as well as the waiting time and cost).

▶ Site visits increased 25 percent in 6 months, and online sales grew by 150 percent in a 1-year period.

▶ The online call center operates much more efficiently and effectively.

To ensure that users were gaining maximum benefits from the Web site, TNZ conducted a content audit. The audit indicated that customers wanted more personalization, so using the software, TNZ provided it. Also, the 3,000 different pieces of content are now presented in about 6,000 different ways. Now content can be presented to please each customer.

Using integration with back-end customer information (e.g., billing), TNZ offers very detailed and personalized service regarding its usage and accounts. Finally, the data collected on content usage (clickstream analysis) were analyzed to provide TNZ information about customer behavior and behavioral changes due to marketing campaigns.

To ensure that the company is working together as one entity, the entire content of the intranet (35,000 pages on 220 disparate sites) was moved to a content management system. This aligned with TNZ's business objectives.

In early 2007, TNZ joined forces with Yahoo! to provide an enhanced suite of online content and application services to New Zealanders.

Sources: Compiled from *CRM Advocate* (2002), Vignette (2006), and Myle (2004).

Questions

1. What are the benefits to TNZ from offering the advanced services, and how does better content management help achieve these benefits?

2. Enter *vignette.com/us/products* and look at the product categories. List each category and explain how it supports TNZ's needs.

3. How does better content increase sales of TNZ products and services?

4. How can better content provide better service to TNZ's customers?

5. How can the system improve marketing campaigns?

6. What were the objectives of moving the entire intranet to a content management system?

ONLINE RESOURCES
available at pearsonglobaleditions.com/turban

WWW

Online Files

W15.1 A High-Level Business Case Template
W15.2 Steps in Building a Web Site
W15.3 Examples of Syndication
W15.4 Web Site Design Criteria
W15.5 A Simple Linear Web Site Structure
W15.6 Web Analytics Reports
W15.7 A Comprehensive Guide to Search Engine Optimization
W15.8 Yahoo!'s Steps on Starting an E-Business

Comprehensive Educational Web Sites

bplans.com: Sample business plans
libserv2.rutgers.edu/rul/rr_gateway/research_guides/busi/ecomm.shtml: A comprehensive EC guide

microsoft.com/smallbusiness/startup-toolkit: Software for small start-ups
smallbusiness.yahoo.com/ecommerce/features.php: E-store templates
sba.gov/smallbusinessplanner: Business plan advice
entrepreneur.com: Information on starting a business
onlinebusiness.about.com: A guide for beginners
networksolutions.com: Domain names and hosting
entrepreneurs.about.com: All about starting a business
ecommercesourcecenter.com/plan/createonlinebusiness.html: All about starting an online business
myownbusiness.org/s2/index/html: How to write a business plan (templates provided)

REFERENCES

Akamai Technologies. "Akamai Reports Fourth Quarter 2008 and Full-Year 2008 Financial Results." February 4, 2009a. akamai.com/html/investor/quarterly_releases/2009/press_020409.html (accessed March 2009).

Akamai Technologies. "Akamai Facts and Figures." 2009b. akamai.com/html/about/facts_figures.html (accessed April 2009).

Ariguzo, G. C., E. G. Mallach, and D. S. White. "The First Decade of E-Commerce." *International Journal of Business Information Systems*, 1, no. 3 (2006).

Ash, C. G., and J. M. Burn. "Managing E-Business Change." In M. Khosrow-Pour (Ed.). *Encyclopedia of E-Commerce, E-Government, and Mobile Commerce*. Hershey, PA: Idea Group Reference, 2006.

Basu, A., and S. Muylle. "How to Plan E-Business Initiatives in Established Companies." *MIT Sloan Management Review* (Fall 2007).

Belew, S., and J. Elad. *Starting an Online Business All-In-One Desk Reference for Dummies*, 2nd ed. Hoboken, NJ: John Wiley & Sons, 2009.

Bracken, B. "The eCommerce Solution Guide—Easy UK eCommerce on a Budget." September 14, 2006. ebyro.com/read-article/the-ecommerce-solution-guide-easy-ukecommerce-on-a-budget/912 (no longer available online).

Business Wire. "Amazon Services to Provide American Express Merchants with Special Offer for Selling Through Amazon.com." July 24, 2004. accessmylibrary.com/coms2/summary_0286-1279385_ITM (accessed January 2009).

Byrne, T. "Top Six Content Management Pitfalls." *PC Magazine*, September 17, 2002.

Chen, J. S., and R. K. H. Ching. "A Proposed Framework for Transition to an e-Business Model." *Quarterly Journal of E-Commerce* (October–December 2002).

Chu, C., and S. Smithson. "E-Business and Organizational Change: A Structural Approach." *Information Systems Journal* (2007).

Cong, Y., and H. Du. "Web Syndication Using RSS." *Journal of Accountancy* (June 2008).

Copeland, M. V., and O. Malik. "How to Build a Bulletproof Startup. *Business 2.0*, June 2006.

Covel, S. "Keyword Play: How an Acronym Helped Unlock Marketing Puzzle." *Wall Street Journal*, August 27, 2007.

Craig, R. "Developing a Viable Product for an Emerging Market." In M. Khosrow-Pour (Ed.). *Encyclopedia of E-Commerce, E-Government, and Mobile Commerce*. Hershey, PA: Idea Group Reference, 2006.

CRM Advocate. "Case Study: Telecom New Zealand Improves Content Management, Online Marketing and Delivers Personalized Content with Vignette." April 2002. crmadvocate.com/casestudy/vignette/telecomnz_70.pdf (accessed March 2009).

Cukier, K. N. "Boo's Blues." *Red Herring*, May 4, 2000. redherring.com/vc/2000/0504/vc-boo050400.html (no longer available online).

Elms, J. "Good Things in (eBay) Store." *Entrepreneur*, April 2006.

Henri, J-F., and S. Heroux. "Developing Control for Managing Website Content." *CMA Management* (June–July 2008).

Hise, P. "Everyone Wants to Start a Business." *Fortune Small Business*, January 23, 2007. money.cnn.com/2007/01/22/magazines/fsb/entrepreneurship.boom.fsb (accessed March 2009).

IBM. "Web Cast: Leveraging Information for Business Transformation." April 4, 2006.

Internet Marketing Newswatch. "Streaming Media Growth and Content Category Share: 2006–2010." March 8, 2007. imnewswatch.com/archives/2007/03/streaming_media.html?visitFrom=1 (accessed April 2007).

Jeston, J., and Nelis, J. *Business Process Management: Practical Guides to Successful Implementation*, 2nd ed. Burlington, MA: Butterworth-Heinemann, 2008.

Joch, A. "Share 2.0." *Oracle Magazine*, September/October 2008. oracle.com/technology/oramag/oracle/08-sep/o58share20.html (accessed May 2009).

Jones, K. C. "Streaming Media to Draw $70 Billion in Revenue Before 2014." *InformationWeek*, April 1, 2008. informationweek.com/news/internet/webdev/showArticle.jhtml?articleID=207001008 (accessed April 2009).

Kay, R. "Search Engine Optimization." *Computerworld*, June 4, 2007.

Kim, Y. J., R. Kishore, and G. L. Sanders. "From DQ to EQ: Understanding Data Quality in the Context of E-Business Systems." *Communications of the ACM* (October 2005).

Klotz, I. "Space Race 2: Bezos and Life Beyond Amazon." *Washington Times*, January 18, 2005.

Lasry, E. M. "Inertia.com: Rates and Processes of Organizational Transformation in the Retail Industry." *Quarterly Journal of E-Commerce* (July–September 2002).

Lee, J. K., et al. *Premier eBusiness Cases from Asia*. Upper Saddle River, NJ: Prentice Hall, 2006.

Maguire, J. "E-Commerce Best Practices: Ten Rules of the Road." *Ecommercepartners.net*, January 11, 2005. ecommerce-guide.com/solutions/advertising/article.php/3457431 (accessed May 2009).

Maier, M. "Building the Next Google." *Business 2.0*, November 2005.

McKay, J., and P. Marshall. *Strategic Management of e-Business*. Milton, Australia: John Wiley & Sons, 2004.

Müller-Lankenau, K., K. Wehmeyer, and S. Klein. "Strategic Channel Alignment: An Analysis of the Configuration of Physical and Virtual Marketing Channels." *Information Systems and E-Business Management* (April 2006).

Myle, S. "Content Management Helps Us to Work Smarter at Telecom New Zealand." *The Electronic Library*, 22, no. 6 (2004).

New Zealand Ministry of Economic Development (MED). "E-Commerce: A Guide for New Zealand Business." Wellington, New Zealand: New Zealand Ministry of Economic Development, 2000.

Nielsen, J. "Top Ten Mistakes in Web Design," 2005. useit.com/alertbox/9605.html (accessed March 2009).

Norguet, J.-P., E. Zimányi, and R. Steinberger. "Improving Web Sites with Web Usage Mining, Web Content Mining, and Semantic Analysis." *Proceedings of the 32nd Conference on Current Trends in Theory and Practice of Computer Science*, Merín, Czech Republic, January 21–27, 2006.

Ould, M. A. *Business Process*. Chichester, UK: John Wiley & Sons, 2003.

Pallis, G., and A. Vakali. "Insights and Perspectives for Content Delivery Networks." *Communications of the ACM* (January 2006).

Pearlson, K. E., and C. S. Sounders. *Managing and Using Information Systems*, 3rd ed. Hoboken, NJ: John Wiley & Sons, 2006.

Pratt, M. K. "How to Build a Better Web Site." *Computerworld*, May 21, 2007.

Quitter, J. "The Charmed Life of Amazon's Jeff Bezos." *Fortune*, April 15, 2008. cnnmoney.printhis. clicka bility.com/pt/cpt?action=cpt&title=The+charmed+ dot-com (accessed March 2009).

Rutgers. "Electronic Commerce." 2009. libraries.rutgers. edu/rul/rr_gateway/research_guides/busi/ecomm. shtml (accessed April 2009).

Sloan, P. "The Man Who Owns the Internet." *Business 2.0*, June 2007.

Sloan, P. "The Startup Façade." *Business 2.0*, October 2006.

Snell, R. *Starting a Yahoo! Store for Dummies*. Hoboken, NJ: John Wiley & Sons, 2006.

Sostre, P., and J. LeClaire. *Web Analytics for Dummies*. Hoboken, NJ: John Wiley & Sons, 2008.

Stoller, J. "More Companies Tailor Website Design to Meet Customer Demands." *CMA Management* (June–July 2008).

Strassmann, P. A. "Calculator: Measuring Business Transformation." *Baseline*, January 25, 2007.

Swanhill, J. "Start a Business for Just $300—Start an E-Commerce Website." Ezine @rticles, 2009. ezinearticles .com/?Start-a-Business-For-Just-$300—Start-an-Ecommerce-Website&id=1705830 (accessed April 2009).

Tomsen, M. *Killer Content: Strategies for Web Content and E-Commerce*. Boston: Addison-Wesley, 2000.

Turban, E., et al. *Business Intelligence: A Managerial Approach*. Upper Saddle River, NJ: Prentice Hall, 2008.

Umesh, U. N., M. Huynh, and L. Jessup. "Creating Successful Entrepreneurial Ventures in IT." *Communications of the ACM* (June 2005).

Victoria Government. "Online Business." business.vic. gov.au/BUSVIC/STANDARD//pc=PC_62525.html (accessed March 2009).

Vignette. "Telecom New Zealand Customer Story." 2006. vignette.com/dafiles/docs/Downloads/CS-Telecom-NZ.pdf (accessed March 2009).

Wiedemann, J. *Web Design: E-Commerce*. London: Taschen UK, 2007.

Williams, G. "Mother of Invention." *Entrepreneur*, May 2006.

Winnick, M. "5 Secrets to a Successful Launch." *Business 2.0*, October 2, 2006.

Yahoo! "6 Tips for Easy Web Site Navigation." 2006. smallbusiness.yahoo.com/r-article-a-70123-m-6-sc-37-6_tips_for_easy_web_site_navigation-i (accessed March 2009).

CHAPTER 16

REGULATORY, ETHICAL, AND COMPLIANCE ISSUES IN EC

Content

Learning Objectives

Upon completion of this chapter, you will be able to:

1. Understand the foundations for legal and ethical issues in EC.

2. Describe civil, intellectual property, and common law.

3. Understand legal and ethical challenges and how to contain them.

4. Explain privacy, free speech, and defamation and their challenges.

5. Describe types of fraud on the Internet and how to protect against them.

6. Describe the needs and methods to protect sellers.

7. Describe EC-related societal issues.

8. Describe Green EC and IT.

WHY IS DISNEY FUNDING CHINESE PIRATES?

Disney's funding arm, Steamboat Ventures, invested $10 million in a popular Chinese video- and file-sharing site called *56.com*. The site had 33 million registered members in 2009. Note that the words for "56" in Chinese sound similar to "I'm Happy."

The Problem

In May 2008, The Walt Disney Company released its animated film *Wall-E*; the film was released on DVD in November 2008. However, immediately after the movie release in May, the robot love story was available for free on the Chinese video site *56.com*. In other words, Disney is funding a Chinese site that bootlegs it own work.

The problem is that pirated movies are difficult to detect because they appear under different names. Although 56.com managed to remove some of the full-length bootlegged copies, many others remain. The 56.com site is often referred to as a Chinese version of YouTube. But unlike YouTube, 56.com and similar sites like *Toudou* and *Youku* don't impose 10-minute limits on uploaded videos. And that makes them a haven for illegally uploaded videos, including full-length movies and TV episodes.

If 56.com were in any country but China, we'd expect the Recording Industry Association of America (RIAA) and similar organizations to put pressure on the company to remove copyrighted materials. But China doesn't have a very strong record of enforcing Western copyright laws.

The Solution

One reason that Disney invested in 56.com was that it hoped that Steamboat Ventures, as a major investor, would influence 56.com to take action against copyright violators. In other words, Steamboat Ventures is trying to help 56.com curb pirated videos.

In the United States, you can take legal action against companies such as 56.com. For example, media giant Viacom is suing YouTube for $1 billion. However, that is not an option (yet) in China. At best, the Chinese government will provide a warning to violators.

The Results

Although 56.com is still facilitating free movies, video games, and the like, Disney seems not to be too concerned with these actions. Its investment provides the company a channel of distribution for its products that may provide a strategic advantage to Disney in China. In March 2009, Disney allowed YouTube to run short videos as well as full episodes of its ABC (a television station) and ESPN (Internet and television sports channel) networks under an ad-revenue sharing arrangement.

Sources: Compiled from McBride and Chao (2008) and *en.wikipedia.org/wiki/56.com* (accessed March 2009).

WHAT WE CAN LEARN . . .

Violation of copyrights on the Internet is a major problem for creators and distributors of intellectual property such as movies, music, and books. The problem arises not only because it is difficult to monitor millions of postings, but also because in many countries there is not much legal protection of copyright, and even if there is, it is difficult to enforce. Protection of intellectual property is one of the major EC legal issues presented in this chapter, which provides an introduction to legislation and court decisions to help you understand the liability exposure and risks that arise from attempts to manipulate EC operations, defraud customers or sellers, and violate privacy. Such an overview of the legal system provides a foundation for assessing whether current and controversial proposals for government regulations, such as Internet neutrality, are good for e-business. A full analysis of the legal and ethical issues is far beyond the scope of one chapter. For a comprehensive treatment, see Mann and Winn (2008). This chapter also deals with several societal issues related to EC and especially the potential environmental impacts known as *"Green EC."*

16.1 THE COMPLEXITY OF LEGAL AND REGULATORY ISSUES

Consumer and commercial use of the World Wide Web began in the mid-1990s with the commercialization of the Internet. Those uses continue to reshape business, marketing, and communications in diverse ways, including unethical or illegal ones. The Internet has empowered widespread and immediate dissemination of information more than any other technological development. This raises a crucial question: Why should EC companies comply with ethical and legal practices? One answer centers on trust. Customers need to trust the online marketplace and its businesses. Unethical and illegal business practices have long-lasting negative business consequences that cannot be repaired. Violators expose themselves to harsh penalties from various government agencies and victimized customers, as well as bloggers and consumer interest groups (e.g., privacy groups).

New tactics that are deployed on the Web to maximize competitive advantage or attract customers raise a number of questions about what constitutes illegal, unethical, intrusive, or undesirable behavior. In the world of commerce, copyright, trademark, and patent infringement; freedom of thought and speech; theft of property; and fraud are not new issues. However, EC has added to the scope and scale of these issues.

Violation of copyright as demonstrated in the opening case is a major issue on the Internet, and the problem is growing rapidly with the growth of social media and mobile computing. As we will see, companies like 56.com have few controls on the content its members place on the site. It is not only a question of copyright; it is also a source of possible defamation of character, distribution of false information, and privacy violation.

Regulation in cyberspace does not consist only of laws that government issues and enforces. Private-sector regulations may have positive impacts (e.g., Google filtering out search engine spam) or potentially lead to abusive behavior or illegal acts—and interfere with free speech, privacy, or intellectual property. **Intellectual property** is a creation of the mind, such as inventions, literary and artistic works, symbols, names, images, and designs, that is used in commerce. Its violation is a major problem in EC, as demonstrated in the opening case.

intellectual property
Creations of the mind, such as inventions, literary and artistic works, and symbols, names, images, and designs, used in commerce.

LAWS ARE SUBJECT TO INTERPRETATION

Keep in mind that most laws and regulations are broadly written and, therefore, only provide outlines to guide public policy. Even physical crime laws that sound specific, such as killing a human being is illegal, do not apply in all situations, such as in self-defense.

Specific disputes (such as the scope of free speech) cannot be resolved by simply referring to relevant laws for two reasons. First, the scope of a law (i.e., whether it applies to a specific situation) needs to be interpreted by looking at the intent of the lawmakers. Second, laws may conflict with each other. For example, how companies use information collected from customers via their Web sites is subject to privacy laws. One privacy law may prohibit a company from sharing customers' social security numbers with business partners, whereas a homeland security law may require revealing the identity (i.e., social security number) of customers. (Banks with CRM programs often encounter these legal conflicts.) Another example of legal conflict is the debate between free speech and protection of children from offensive content (see details in Section 16.4).

For another example of the courts resolving novel conflicts, see the story of *Ticketmaster v. Microsoft* in Online File W16.1. Political spam is discussed in Online File W16.2. An example of the legal conflict with ethics is provided in Case 16.1.

For the moment it seems that we will continue to rely on conflicting legal systems and obsolete precedents, which means that EC traders may not be able to avoid lawsuits. Therefore, CIOs and company lawyers should be intimately involved in corporate strategy.

The previous discussion and online files should give you a better understanding of the complexity and conflicts surrounding legal, ethical, and regulatory issues, particularly those involving online conduct. Fundamentally, laws protect the rights and guarantees described in a nation's constitution. That sounds simple enough. But as you've learned, getting agreement on whose rights and determining which rights are being protected and whose rights are being violated may not be possible. You will see other examples of such dilemmas throughout the chapter.

EC Application

IS eBAY A STORE OR A BULLETIN BOARD?

Let's look at two 2008 court decisions testing eBay's liability for counterfeit merchandise sold by its users. Courts in the United States and France reached opposite conclusions on nearly identical facts, demonstrating just how fractured and confused the developing law of Internet commerce can be.

The luxury jeweler Tiffany & Co. sued eBay for refusing to comply with its demands to eliminate the sale of fake Tiffany merchandise on eBay. Citing eBay's multimillion-dollar program to control the sale of fakes, as well as extensive tools provided to Tiffany and other brands to identify and report suspicious listings, the judge ruled in favor of eBay in 2008. "It is the trademark owner's burden to police its mark," he concluded.

The Paris Commercial Court reached the opposite conclusion a week earlier, and ordered eBay to pay more than $60 million in damages to a European jeweler. A particularly disturbing feature of the French case is that some of the merchandise was not alleged to be counterfeit, but was simply being sold or resold without permission from the jeweler.

Both decisions are being appealed. eBay has lost similar cases in Europe. In the United States, an American software trade association has threatened to sue eBay over allowing unauthorized or unlicensed software sales.

The difficulty here is that the legal system does not define what an electronic marketplace is. Also, eBay never takes possessions of the goods that are sold through its Web site. Thus, eBay argues that it is simply a host for classified ads, like a newspaper. The truth is that electronic markets are something new and are not covered properly by the legal system.

Sources: Compiled from Downes (2008) and Arden-Besunder and Sherwin (2009).

Questions

1. In your opinion is eBay a store or an electronic board? Why?

2. Can such conflicting court decisions happen in the same country? Why or why not?

3. Why is it said that a corporate strategy can help an EC vendor?

4. Some say that the jewelers are suing eBay because it interferes with their illegal price-fixing practices. Comment on this issue.

THE LAW: A SYSTEM FOR SOCIAL CONTROL AND PROTECTION

Law provides a *system* for social control. As with all systems, the formation of laws is a dynamic process that responds to ever-changing conditions. The nature of law is dynamic, in part, because it must be responsive to new threats or abuses that violate a nation's constitution. That is why significant changes in the nature of business and its environment or crimes lead to new laws.

Due Process, Rights, and Duties

due process
A guarantee of basic fairness and fair procedures in legal action.

Without knowledge of the basics of the legal system, nature of law, and due process, those involved in EC risk fines, prison times, or other penalties. Due process is essentially a guarantee of basic fairness and fair procedures. In a legal system, the government produces a set of rules and regulations and has the power to enforce them, as shown in the legal framework in Exhibit 16.1. These rules and regulations create both rights and duties. A right is a legal claim that others not interfere with an individual's or organization's protected interest. In broad terms, protected interests are interests, such as *life*, *liberty*, and *property*, that are protected by national constitutions.

right
Legal claim that others not interfere with an individual's or organization's protected interest.

Privacy, intellectual property, and free speech are examples of protected interests. Those interests are not absolute. For example, a person convicted of a felony crime is going to jail—and cannot claim that being confined to jail violates his or her right to liberty. To learn more about protected interests, see FindLaw (2009). A duty is a legal obligation imposed on individuals and organizations that prevents them from interfering with another's protected interest or right. See World Intellectual Property Organization (WIPO) (2009) for a global perspective on these rights and duties.

protected interests
Interests, such as life, liberty, and property, which a national constitution protects.

duty
Legal obligation imposed on individuals and organizations that prevents them from interfering with another's protected interest or right.

PERSONAL AND PROPERTY RIGHTS

Rights are divided into two categories: personal rights and property rights (see Exhibit 16.1). Generally, the interests of *life* and *liberty* fall into the personal rights category. *Property* interests

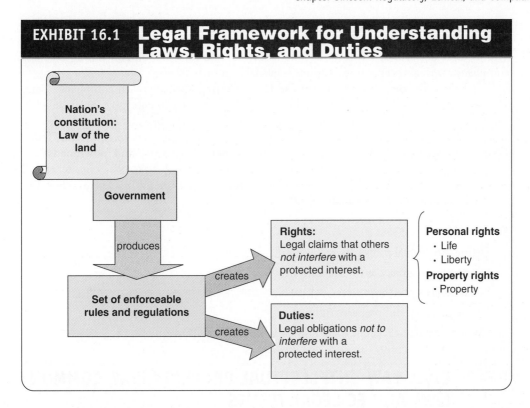

EXHIBIT 16.1 Legal Framework for Understanding Laws, Rights, and Duties

are in the category of property rights. Internet business Web sites, proprietary systems, and customer lists are examples of property. The major property rights relevant to EC and Web sites are:

1. Control of the use of the property
2. The right to any benefit from the property
3. The right to transfer or sell the property
4. The right to exclude others from the property

Referring to Exhibit 16.1 and the previous list, it is clear that an online business has the legal right, for example, to prevent spammers or other people from interfering with or harming the benefits (profits) from its EC site—and can file lawsuits against them. Lawsuits are one type of civil litigation, an adversarial proceeding in which a party (the plaintiff) sues another party (the defendant) to get compensation for a wrong committed by the defendant. For example, the entertainment industry has the right to its intellectual property (IP) and can file lawsuits (*civil litigation*) against online businesses, such as YouTube or 56.com, for any interference with its operation. In contrast, law enforcement brings *criminal litigation*. Section 16.2 discusses criminal and civil laws further. You will also learn the terminology needed to understand legal issues.

REGULATORY COMPLIANCE IN EC

In general, compliance means conforming to a specification or policy, standard, or law that has been clearly defined. Corporate scandals, such as the financial crisis in 2008–2009 or the Enron case in 2001, have highlighted the need for stronger compliance regulations for publicly listed companies. One of the most significant regulations in this context is the Sarbanes-Oxley Act, which defines significantly tighter personal responsibility of corporate top management for the accuracy of reported financial statements.

Regulatory compliance refers to systems or departments in an organization whose job is to ensure that personnel are aware of and take steps to comply with relevant laws, standards,

civil litigation
An adversarial proceeding in which a party (the plaintiff) sues another party (the defendant) to get compensation for a wrong committed by the defendant.

regulatory compliance
Systems or departments in an organization whose job is to ensure that personnel are aware of and take steps to comply with relevant laws, standards, policies, and regulations.

policies, and regulations. These laws can have criminal or civil penalties. Unfortunately, the definition of what constitutes an effective compliance plan has been elusive.

A single point of access to government services and information concerning business compliance with government regulations is available at business.gov.

To help with compliance, one can use EC software, especially with compliance data. Compliance data is defined as all data belonging or pertaining to enterprise or included in the law, which can be used for the purpose of implementing or validating compliance. Compliance software is available from all major software companies (e.g., Oracle, IBM, EMC, and Computer Associates). For white papers, Webcasts, and downloads, see search.techrepublic.com.com/searchcompliance+and+it+management.html, en.wikipedia.org/wiki/regulatory_compliance, and regulatorycompliance.com. For IT-oriented compliance, see Fineagan (2009).

compliance data

Pertaining to enterprise included in the law that can be used for the purpose of implementing or validating compliance.

Section 16.1 ▶ REVIEW QUESTIONS

1. Define intellectual property.
2. Why are laws subject to interpretation?
3. What do laws protect?
4. Define personal and property rights.
5. Describe regulatory compliance. How is it related to EC?

16.2 CIVIL LAW, INTELLECTUAL PROPERTY LAW, COMMON LAW, AND EC LEGAL ISSUES

The legal system is faced with the task of maintaining a delicate balance between preserving social order and protecting individual rights. Keep in mind that the term *individual* when used in law is broadly defined to mean a person, group of people, or other legal entity such as an organization. In this section, we explain the various types of laws.

CRIMINAL LAW AND CIVIL LAW

Laws are divided into two major categories: *criminal* and *civil*.

Characteristics of Criminal and Civil Laws

crime

Offensive act against society that violates a law and is punishable by the government.

There are several important legal concepts to understand. First, a crime is an offensive act against society that violates a law and is punishable by the government. Second, in order for an act to be a crime, the act must violate at least one criminal law. Third, an act can violate both criminal and civil law. For example, spammers who violate the CAN-SPAM law (Section 16.5) can be charged with a crime and punished under criminal law, and they also can be sued under civil law if the spam causes an identifiable loss to an online business.

Criminal laws are laws that protect the public, human life, or private property. Rules called statutes define criminal laws. In contrast, civil laws are laws that enable a party (individual or organization) that has suffered harm or a loss to bring a lawsuit against whoever is responsible for the harm or loss (e.g., spammers).

An offensive act or omission, such as failing to take reasonable care to prevent the loss of personal data, typically violates both criminal law and civil law. Exhibit 16.2 presents a comparison of key characteristics of criminal and civil laws.

criminal laws

Laws to protect the public, human life, or private property.

statutes

Rules that define criminal laws.

civil laws

Laws that enable a party (individual or organization) that has suffered harm or a loss to bring a lawsuit against who is responsible for the harm or loss.

Civil Law

Civil law deals with noncriminal injuries. Civil law gives an injured party the opportunity to bring a lawsuit (a civil charge) against a violator to get compensated for the injury or harm caused by the violator. Certain conditions must be met for a lawsuit to proceed. For example, to sue for breach of contract, there must be proof that the party failed to perform any term of the contract without a legitimate legal excuse. Lawsuits also serve to warn and deter others from similar violations, particularly violations of intellectual property law in e-commerce.

EXHIBIT 16.2	**Differences Between Criminal and Civil Laws**	
Characteristics	**Criminal Law**	**Civil Law**
Objective	To protect society's interests by defining offenses against the public	To provide an injured private party the opportunity to bring a lawsuit for the injury
Purpose	To deter crime and punish criminals	To deter injuries and compensate injured party
Wrongful act	It violates a statute	It causes harm or loss to an individual, group of people, or legal entity (e.g., organization)
Who brings charges against an offender	A local, regional, or national government body	A private party, which may be a person, company, or group of people, as in a class-action lawsuit
Deals with	Criminal violations	Noncriminal harm or loss
burden of proof	Beyond a reasonable doubt	Preponderance of the evidence
Principal types of penalties or punishment	Capital punishment, fines, or imprisonment	Monetary damages paid to victims or some equitable relief

INTELLECTUAL PROPERTY LAW

Intellectual property law is the area of the law that includes *patent law, copyright law, trademark law, trade secret law,* and other relevant branches of the law, such as licensing and unfair competition.

Intellectual property law may also be concerned with the regulation of mental products, including creativity. It affects such diverse subjects as the visual and performing arts, electronic databases, advertising, and video games. Creativity is an integral part of the entire business world, as is the protection of innovation. Visit Online File W16.3 for related intellectual property Web sites.

There are various intellectual property law specialties, as shown in Exhibit 16.3. Those specialty laws are interrelated and may even overlap.

Copyright Violation and Protection

Numerous high-profile lawsuits already have been filed regarding online copyright infringement. A **copyright** is an exclusive right of the author or creator of a book, movie, musical composition, or other artistic property to print, copy, sell, license, distribute, transform to another medium, translate, record, perform, or otherwise use. In the United States, as soon as a work is created in a tangible form, such as through writing or recording, the work automatically has national copyright protection. A copyright does not last forever; it is good for a fixed number of years after the death of the author or creator (e.g., 50 years in the United Kingdom). In the United States in 1998, copyright was extended to 70 years after the death of the author by the Sonny Bono Copyright Extension Act. After the copyright expires, the work reverts to the public domain. Copyrights are owned in many cases by corporations (e.g., the copyrights to this book). In such a case, the copyrights will last forever unless legally reassigned. The legal term for the use of the work without permission or contracting for payment of a royalty is **infringement**.

intellectual property law
Area of the law that includes patent law, copyright law, trademark law, trade secret law, and other branches of the law such as licensing and unfair competition.

copyright
An exclusive right of the author or creator of a book, movie, musical composition, or other artistic property to print, copy, sell, license, distribute, transform to another medium, translate, record, perform, or otherwise use.

infringement
Use of the work without permission or contracting for payment of a royalty.

EXHIBIT 16.3 Intellectual Property Laws and Their Protections	
Laws	**Protection Provided by the Law**
Intellectual property law	Protects creations of the human mind
Patent law	Protects inventions and discoveries
Copyright law	Protects original works of authorship, such as music and literary works, and computer programs
Trademark law	Protects brand names and other symbols that indicate the source of goods and services
Trade secret law	Protects confidential business information
Law of licensing	Enables owners of patents, trademarks, copyrights, and trade secrets to share them with others on a mutually agreed-upon basis
Law of unfair competition dealing with counterfeiting and piracy	Protects against those who try to take a free ride on the efforts and achievements of creative people

Examples of Infringement

To protect its interests, the Recording Industry Association of America (RIAA), the recording industry's trade group, uses lawsuits to stamp out rampant music piracy on the Internet. RIAA launched a lawsuit-settlement Web site, p2plawsuits.com, and sent a mass mailing to college and university presidents across the United States, asking for their cooperation in its ongoing war against file sharing. RIAA sought compensation from university students for losses that it alleged were caused by copyright infringement. For example, in February 2007, RIAA announced that it would give 400 college students suspected of illegally pirating music online at 13 universities the option to reach discounted settlements before being sued for greater damages for copyright infringement. According to Mitch Bainwol, RIAA chairman and CEO, "theft of music remains unacceptably high and undermines the industry's ability to invest in new music" (Veiga 2007). Judges' decisions on legal cases, such as this one, can have an immediate and long-lasting impact because they become common law.

Universal Music Group, the world's largest music company, filed a lawsuit against MySpace for copyright infringement of thousands of artists' work (Reuters 2007). French media giant Vivendi owns Universal Music Group; it filed a lawsuit at the U.S. District Court of California. Universal estimated maximum damages for each copyrighted work at $150,000.

YouTube avoided a similar lawsuit by reaching a licensing agreement with Universal Music. However, in 2007 Viacom found more than 100,000 illegal clips. The company asked YouTube to remove them. In 2008, the courts ordered YouTube to give Viacom video logs. One solution is to allow consumers to stream music and videos for free to their computers if they are supported by advertisements.

The entertainment industry, led primarily by the Motion Picture Association of America (MPAA) and RIAA, is also attempting technical solutions via the legal system to protect its interests. It is actively pursuing digital rights management policy initiatives through legislation and the courts.

Digital Rights Management (DRM)

digital rights management (DRM)
An umbrella term for any of several arrangements that allow a vendor of content in electronic form to control the material and restrict its usage.

Digital rights management (DRM) is an umbrella term for any of several arrangements that allow a vendor of content in electronic form to control the material and restrict its usage. These arrangements are technology-based protection measures. Typically, the content is a copyrighted digital work to which the vendor holds rights.

In the past, when content was analog in nature, it was easier to buy a new copy of a copyrighted work on a physical medium (e.g., paper, film, tape) than to produce such a copy independently. The quality of most copies often was inferior. Digital technologies make it possible to produce and distribute a high-quality duplicate of any digital recording with minimal effort and cost. The Internet virtually has eliminated the need for a physical medium to transfer a work, which has led to the use of DRM systems for protection.

However, DRM systems may restrict the *fair use* of material by individuals. In law, **fair use** refers to the use of copyrighted material for *noncommercial* purposes. Several DRM technologies were developed without regard for privacy protection. Many systems require the user to reveal his or her identity and rights to access protected content. Upon authentication of identity and rights to the content, the user can access the content for free (see epic.org/privacy/drm).

fair use
The legal use of copyrighted material for noncommercial purposes without paying royalties or getting permission.

Patents

A **patent** is a document that grants the holder exclusive rights to an invention for a fixed number of years (e.g., 20 years in the United Kingdom). Patents serve to protect tangible technological inventions, especially in traditional industrial areas. They are not designed to protect artistic or literary creativity. Patents confer monopoly rights to an idea or an invention, regardless of how it may be expressed. An invention may be in the form of a physical device or a method or process for making a physical device. Similar to a patent is a **trademark**, which is a symbol businesses use to identify their goods and services; government registration of the trademark confers exclusive legal right to its use.

patent
A document that grants the holder exclusive rights to an invention for a fixed number of years.

Certain patents granted in the United States deviate from established practices in Europe. For example, Amazon.com successfully obtained a U.S. patent on its "1-Click" ordering and payment procedure. Using this patent, Amazon.com sued Barnes & Noble in 1999 and in 2000, alleging that its rival had copied its patented technology. Barnes & Noble was enjoined by the courts from using the procedure. Similarly, in 1999, Priceline.com filed a suit against Expedia.com, alleging that Expedia was using Priceline's patented reverse-auction business model. The suit was settled in 2001 when Expedia.com agreed to pay Priceline.com royalties for use of the model. However, in Europe and many Asian, African, and South American countries, it is almost impossible to obtain patents on business methods or computer processes. For a sample of EC patents, see Online File W16.4.

trademark
A symbol used by businesses to identify their goods and services; government registration of the trademark confers exclusive legal right to its use.

Many people question the eligibility of EC programs to be patented. For years, the U.S. Patent and Trademark Office (PTO) has granted patents covering e-commerce business methods, and companies have made use of such patents to gain a competitive advantage in the marketplace. One example is Amazon.com's suit against Barnes & Noble, alleging infringement of the company's "1-Click" shopping cart patent. The court found in favor of Amazon. Although the validity of Amazon's patent was later questioned, thousands of other e-commerce patents are held by companies doing business on the Internet. These patents give companies a valuable resource for obtaining venture capital and protecting research and development investments.

In May 2008, a U.S. court of appeals held a full-court hearing to decide whether to limit "process patents." Attorneys argued that a *process* should be patentable as long as it produces a practical result, regardless of whether it is tied to a machine or transforms something tangible. The U.S. Supreme Court years ago had made it clear that a patentable process must either be tied to a machine or must transform something physical.

Depending on how the court rules, the decision may have a wide-ranging effect on the patenting practices of e-commerce companies and may call into question the validity of thousands of patents granted on business methods since the 1990s. (For more details, see Wright 2008.)

COMMON LAW IN E-COMMERCE

Despite what seems like an endless number of criminal and civil laws, statutes do not cover all situations. When statutes do not cover certain situations, judges create laws through their court decisions. Judges' court decisions set *precedents* and become **common law** or **case law**. Even though common laws do not have a statutory basis, when judges create laws through written opinions, they become binding on future decisions of lower courts—that is, until new common laws or precedents are set.

common law (case law)
Law created by judges in court decisions.

Laws primarily relating to property, contracts, and torts typically are part of the common law. A **tort** is a civil wrong that can be grounds for a lawsuit. The main types of torts

tort
Civil wrong that can be grounds for a lawsuit.

EXHIBIT 16.4   Common Types of Torts in E-Commerce

Torts	Definitions	Examples
Negligence	The failure to exercise reasonable care toward others, or taking action that results in an accident that causes physical or property damage. Not practicing the standard of due care can be considered negligence.	ChoicePoint was charged with multiple counts of negligence for failing to follow *reasonable* information security practices that resulted in the compromise of the personal and financial information of 145,000 individuals.
Nuisance	The unreasonable, unwarranted, or unlawful use of property that causes inconvenience or damage to others, either to individuals or the general public.	Universal Tube and Rollform Equipment, a company with the domain name *uTube* since 1996, filed a lawsuit against YouTube Inc. for illegal acts that resulted in the direction of millions of nuisance Internet visitors to the uTube Web site. According to the lawsuit, due to confusion in the minds of consumers, the spillover of nuisance traffic to utube.com has destroyed the value of their trademark and Internet property, repeatedly caused the shutdown of their Web site, increased Internet costs by thousands of dollars a month, and damaged the company's good reputation. The full text of the complaint is available at *pub.bna.com/eclr/062628.pdf*.
Defamation	Making an untrue statement (expressly stated or implied to be factual) about a person, company, or product that damages their reputation. If the defamatory statement is printed or broadcast over the media, it is libel, If the statement is oral (or transitory), it is slander.	The first British Internet libel case, *Keith-Smith v. Williams* (2006), resulted in the successful prosecution of an individual poster in a chat room. The case involved an ex-teacher, Tracy Williams, who had falsely accused Michael Keith Smith of being a sexual offender and racist bigot. The court ordered her to pay £10,000 plus costs. The accusations were made in a Yahoo! discussion group with about 100 members, but damages were awarded based on the remarks being available throughout the world. For further reading, see *lvl9.org/article.htm*.

are *negligence*, *nuisance*, and *defamation*. Exhibit 16.4 explains these three types of torts, with EC examples.

FAN AND HATE SITES

Fan and hate Web sites are part of the Internet self-publishing phenomenon that includes blogging (see Chapters 7 and 9). Fan sites may violate intellectual property rights. For example, some people get advanced copies of new movies or TV programs and create sites that compete with the legal sites of the movie or TV producer, even before the legal site is activated. Although the producers can get a court order to close such sites, new sites can appear the next day. Although the intention of the fans may be good, they may cause damage to the creators of the intellectual property.

Hate Web sites can cause problems for corporations as well. Many hate sites are directed against large corporations (e.g., Wal-Mart, Microsoft, Nike). Associated with hate sites is the idea of **cyberbashing**, which is the registration of a domain name that criticizes an organization or person (e.g., paypalsucks.com, walmartblows.com). As long as these Web sites contain legitimate complaints that are not libelous, defamatory in character, sponsored by competitors, or do not infringe upon trademark rights by confusing consumers, they probably fall within the protections of the First Amendment.

cyberbashing
Domain name that criticizes an organization or person.

Material published on fan sites, hate sites, and newsgroups may violate the copyrights of the creators or distributors of intellectual property. This issue is another example of the conflict between protection of intellectual property and free speech, as discussed in Section 16.4.

OTHER E-COMMERCE LEGAL ISSUES

In the previous sections, we provided an overview of some of the legal complexities as they relate to EC and provided some generic concepts required for understanding how the regulatory system in the United States and several other countries work. We also introduced a specific EC issue, *copyright infringement*.

Hundreds of laws are related to EC, and it is not possible to list all of them in this book. For coverage of some of the important issues, see Mann and Winn (2008). In this chapter, we only cover the following issues:

▶ Intellectual property and copyright (Section 16.2)
▶ Ethical challenges as compared to legal ones (Section 16.3)
▶ Privacy, free speech, and defamation (Section 16.4)
▶ Fraud and fraud protection (Section 16.5)

Other significant EC legal issues are illustrated in Exhibit 16.5.

EXHIBIT 16.5   Summary of Important EC Legal Issues

Issue	Description
E-filings in court	Litigation means a large quantity of paper. Some courts allow electronic filing of such documents.
Evidence, electronic evidence (e-evidence)	Some electronic documents can be used as evidence in court. The State of New York, for example, allows e-mails to be used as evidence. For an overview of electronic evidence, see Volonino et al. (2007).
Jurisdiction	Ability to sue in other states or countries: Whose jurisdiction prevails when litigants are in different states or countries? Who can sue for Internet postings done in other countries?
Liability	The use of multiple networks and trading partners makes the documentation of responsibility difficult. How can liability for errors, malfunctions, or fraudulent use of data be determined?
Defamation	Is the ISP liable for material published on the Internet because of services they provide or support? (Usually not.) Who else is liable for defamation? What if the publisher is in another country?
Identity fraud	The Identity, Theft, and Assumption Deterrence Act of 1998 makes identity fraud a felony carrying a 3- to 25-year prison sentence.
Computer crime	The Information Infrastructure Protection Act (IIP Act, 1996) protects information in all computers.
Digital signature	Digital signatures are recognized as legal in the United States and some other countries, but not in all countries (see Chapter 11).
Regulation of consumer databases	The United States allows the compilation and sale of customer databases; the European Union Directive on Data Protection prohibits this practice.
Encryption technology	Export of U.S. encryption technology was made legal in 1999. (Countries still restricted from export are Iran, Syria, Sudan, North Korea, and Cuba.)
Time and place	An electronic document signed in Japan on January 5 may have the date January 4 in Los Angeles. Which date is considered legal if disputes arise?
Location of files and data	Much of the law hinges on the physical location of files and data. With distributed and replicated databases, it is difficult to say exactly where data are stored at any given time.
Electronic contracts	If all the elements to establish a contract are present, an electronic contract is valid and enforceable.
E-communications privacy	The Electronic Communications Privacy Act (ECPA) of 1986 makes it illegal to access stored e-mail or e-mail in transmission.
IPOs online	Web sites with the necessary information on securities offerings are considered a legal channel for selling stock in a corporation.

(continued)

EXHIBIT 16.5   (continued)

Issue	Description
Antitrust	*U.S. DOJ v. Microsoft* found that (1) Microsoft used predatory and anticompetitive conduct to illegally maintain the monopoly in Windows OS; (2) Microsoft illegally attempted to monopolize the market for Internet browsing software; and (3) Microsoft illegally bundled its Web browser with Windows OS, engaging in a tying arrangement in violation of the Sherman Act.
Taxation	Taxation of sales transactions by states is on hold in the United States and some (not all) countries, but the issue will be revised.
Money laundering	How can money laundering be prevented when the value of the money is in the form of a smart card?

Sources: Compiled from Cheeseman (2008), FTC.gov, Volonino et al. (2007), and Volonino and Robinson (2004).

Section 16.2 ▶ REVIEW QUESTIONS

1. Define criminal and civil laws.
2. What is an intellectual property law?
3. Define DRM. Describe one potential impact on privacy.
4. What is common law? How does it differ from criminal and civil law?
5. What is meant by "fair use"?
6. List the legal rights of a copyright owner.
7. Define tort and explain three types of torts.
8. Describe fan and hate sites.
9. Define cyberbashing.

16.3   ETHICAL CHALLENGES AND GUIDELINES

ethics
The branch of philosophy that deals with what is considered to be right and wrong.

Ethics describes how individuals choose to interact with one another. It is the branch of philosophy that deals with what is considered to be right and wrong. Ethics define the nature of duties that people owe themselves and one another. One duty is to not intrude on a person's privacy, which is the right to be left alone and free of unreasonable personal intrusions.

ETHICAL PRINCIPLES AND GUIDELINES

privacy
The right to be left alone and free of unreasonable personal intrusions.

Law (that is, public law) embodies ethical principles, but they are not the same. Acts that are generally considered unethical may not be illegal. Lying to a friend may be unethical, but it is not illegal. Conversely, the law is not simply the coding of ethical norms, nor are all ethical codes incorporated into public law.

A common agreement in a society as to what is right and wrong determines ethics, but they are not subject to legal sanctions except when they overlap with activities that also are illegal. Online File W16.5 shows a framework for ethical issues.

An example of one ethical issue is the Facebook fiasco of 2009.

Example: Who Owns User-Generated Content?

In February 2009, Facebook casually slipped into its terms of service an updated clause that users must sign before joining, announcing that users give Facebook an irrevocable, perpetual, nonexclusive, transferable, fully paid, worldwide license to use, retain, and display content posted to the site. In other words, anything you upload to Facebook can be used by Facebook in any way they deem fit, forever, no matter what you do later. Consumer watchdog groups and privacy experts immediately cried foul.

The objective of this change was to enable Facebook to sell customer data to marketers: Facebook needed more revenue sources. As a result, Facebook pointed out that the company wouldn't use information in a way that goes against the privacy settings outlined by users. Facebook also claimed that the new policy was consistent with how other services (like e-mail) work. However, according to MacMillan (2009), legal and privacy experts say that Facebook is giving itself wider latitude in how it can use content than several other companies that rely on user-generated content. Retaining rights to content after the user has left is unprecedented for a social media site.

Facebook did not do a good enough job of communicating the changes to the terms of service, privacy experts say. Rather than asking users to agree to the new terms, or even sending an e-mail alert to all users, the company quietly added this line to its terms: Your continued use of the Facebook Service after any such changes constitutes your acceptance of the new terms. That may not be good business practice, but is it unethical?

BUSINESS ETHICS

Business ethics is a form of applied ethics that examines ethical principles and moral or ethical problems that arise in a business environment.

In the increasingly conscience-focused marketplaces of the twenty-first century, the demand for more ethical business processes and actions (known as *ethicism*) is increasing. Simultaneously, pressure is being applied on industries to improve business ethics through new public initiatives and laws (e.g., higher U.K. road tax for higher-emission vehicles).

For example, today most major corporate Web sites lay emphasis on commitment to promoting noneconomic social values under a variety of headings (e.g., ethics codes, social responsibility charters).

Business ethics defines how a company integrates the core values of honesty, trust, respect, and fairness into its policies and practices—and complies with legal standards and regulations. The scope of business ethics has expanded to encompass a company's actions with regard not only to how it treats employees and obeys laws but to the nature and quality of the relationships with shareholders, customers, business partners, suppliers, the community, the environment, and even future generations, as well. European companies especially have embraced this expanded definition of ethics. Under recent clarifications of the U.S. Federal Sentencing Guidelines (ussc.gov/guidelin.htm), companies with credible ethics programs, as opposed to merely *paper* programs such as that of Enron, may reduce penalties or avoid prosecution for crimes committed by managers or employees.

Because of the worldwide scope and universal accessibility of the Internet, there are serious questions as to which ethical rules and laws apply. These questions involve an appreciation of the law that is constantly changing. Lawsuits and criminal charges are very disruptive, expensive, and may damage customer relations. The best strategy is to avoid behaviors that expose the company to these types of risks.

Businesspeople engaging in e-commerce need guidelines as to what behaviors are reasonable and what risks are foreseeable under a given set of circumstances. Based on what you have read, it is clear that the two major risks are a criminal charge or lawsuit (civil charge). Exhibit 16.6 lists examples of safeguards to minimize exposure to those risks. (Also see Yamamura and Grupe 2008.)

business ethics
A form of applied ethics that examines ethical principles and moral or ethical problems that arise in a business environment.

EXHIBIT 16.6 Safeguards to Minimize Exposure to Risk of Criminal or Civil Charges

1. Does the Web site clearly post shipment policies and guarantees? Can the company fulfill those policies and guarantees? Does the Web site explain what happens in case of a missed deadline? Does it comply with the law?

2. Does the Web site clearly articulate procedures for customers to follow when returning gifts or seeking a refund for services not received?

3. Has the company checked backgrounds before entering agreements with third-party vendors and supply chain partners? Do those agreements with vendors and partners indemnify (i.e., protect) the company against their failure to deliver goods or process transactions on time and correctly?

4. If a third-party ISP or Web-hosting service is used, are there safeguards if the site crashes, is infected by malware, or if bandwidth is insufficient to meet all of your customers' needs?

5. Is there sufficient customer support staff, and are they knowledgeable and adequately trained to process inquiries from customers?

EC ETHICAL ISSUES

There are many EC- and Internet-related ethical issues (Himma and Tavani 2008). Examples of ethical issues discussed elsewhere in this book are channel conflict (Chapter 3), pricing conflict (Chapter 3), disintermediation (Chapters 2, 3, and 5), and trust (Chapter 4). Two additional EC-related ethical issues are non–work-related use of the Internet and codes of ethics.

Non–Work-Related Use of the Internet

A majority of employees use e-mail and surf the Web for non-work-related purposes. The use of company property for e-mail and Internet use creates risk and wastes time. The degree of risk depends on the extent to which the company has implemented policies and procedures to prevent and detect illegal uses. For example, companies may be held liable for their employees' use of e-mail to harass another employee, participate in illegal gambling, or distribute child pornography.

Codes of Ethics

A practical and necessary approach to limiting non–work-related Internet surfing is an Internet acceptable use policy (AUP) to which all employees must conform. It includes EC, social networks, and any IT-related topics. Without a formal AUP, it is much more difficult to enforce acceptable and eliminate unacceptable behaviors and punish violators. Whenever a user signs on to the corporate network, the user should see a reminder of the AUP and be notified that online activities are monitored. Such notification should be a part of a code of ethics.

Corporate *codes of ethics* state the rules and expected behaviors and actions. Typically, the ethics code should address the use of offensive content and graphics, as well as proprietary information. It should encourage employees to think about who should and who should not have access to information before they post it on the Web site. The code should specify whether the company allows employees to set up their own Web pages on the company intranet and state policies regarding private e-mail usage and non–work-related surfing during working hours. A company should formulate a general idea of the role it wants Web sites to play in the workplace. This should guide the company in developing an AUP and provide employees with a rationale for that policy. Finally, do not be surprised if the code of ethics looks a lot like simple rules of etiquette; it should. Exhibit 16.7 lists several useful guidelines for a corporate Web policy. For a list of Web site quality guidelines, see Online File W16.6. For ethics case studies, see harpercollege.edu/~tmorris/ekin/home.htm.

Section 16.3 ❱ REVIEW QUESTIONS

1. What does business ethics define?
2. Give an example of an EC activity that is unethical but not illegal.

EXHIBIT 16.7   Corporate Web Policy Guidelines

- Issue written AUP guidelines about employee use of the Internet and communication systems including e-mail and instant messaging.
- Make it clear to employees that they cannot use copyrighted or trademarked material without permission.
- Post disclaimers concerning content, such as sample code, that the company does not support.
- Post disclaimers of responsibility concerning content of online forums and chat sessions.
- Make sure that Web content and activity comply with the laws in other countries, such as those governing contests and privacy.
- Make sure that the company's Web content policy is consistent with other company policies.
- Appoint someone to monitor Internet legal and liability issues and have that person report to a senior executive or legal counsel.
- Have attorneys with cyber law expertise review Web content to make sure that there is nothing unethical or illegal on the company's Web site and that all required statements and disclaimers are properly included.

3. Identify an employee activity that exposes a company to legal risk.

4. List the major issues that a code of ethics should include.

16.4 PRIVACY RIGHTS, PROTECTION AND FREE SPEECH

The explosion in online communications technologies has created complex new ethical dilemmas for businesses. As transaction costs for processing, storing, and transmitting data dropped dramatically and sophisticated tracking and monitoring software became widespread, concerns rose around online consumer privacy, free speech, and defamation. For example, there is an increasing risk of personal privacy invasion from compromising photos that digital cameras or cell phones capture, particularly when they are posted on the Internet (Puente 2007). Related to this is the possible misuse of personal information, whether public or secret (see Weitzner et al. 2008).

PRIVACY RIGHTS AND PROTECTION

Privacy means different things to different people. In general, privacy is the right to be left alone and the right to be free of unreasonable personal intrusions. (For other definitions of privacy, see the Privacy Rights Clearinghouse at privacyrights.org.) Privacy has long been a legal, ethical, and social issue in most countries.

Today, virtually all U.S. states and the national government, either by statute or by common law, recognize the right to privacy. The definition of privacy can be interpreted quite broadly. However, the following two rules have been followed fairly closely in past U.S. court decisions: (1) The right of privacy is not absolute. Privacy must be balanced against the needs of society. (2) The public's right to know is superior to the individual's right of privacy. These two rules show why it is sometimes difficult to determine and enforce privacy regulations.

Section 5 of the U.S. Federal Trade Commission Act prohibits unfair or deceptive practices and gives the commission (FTC; a regulatory agency) authority to take action against companies whose lax security practices could expose the personal financial information of customers to theft or loss; it also protects privacy. For explanation of the act, see ftc.gov/privacy/privacyinitiatives/promises.html. Those practices extend to privacy, free speech, and defamation if the company does not fulfill its duty to protect the rights of others.

Opt-In and Opt-Out

To some extent, privacy concerns have been overshadowed by post–September 11 terrorism efforts, but consumers still expect and demand that companies behave as responsible custodians of their personal data. One way to manage this issue is *opt-in* and *opt-out* information practices. Opt-out is a business practice that gives consumers the opportunity to refuse to share information about themselves. Offering opt-out is a good customer practice, but it is difficult to opt out in some industries either because consumer demand for opt-out is low or the value of the customer information is high. In contrast, opt-in is based on the principle that information sharing should not occur unless customers affirmatively allow it or request it.

According to IBM (2008), a successful privacy project should include the following six practices:

1. **Get organized.** Form a cross-functional privacy team to help guide your endeavor.

2. **Define requirements.** Define the requirements of your privacy project and identify the types of applications/hardware/data that must be protected.

3. **Perform data inventory.** Analyze and catalog your data stores, flows, processes, dependencies, and business rules to help simplify the scope of your privacy project.

4. **Select solution.** Choose and implement a data privacy solution that provides the techniques needed to protect privacy in all environments.

5. **Test, test, test.** Develop a prototype and methodology for your project and then test the prototype for validation.

6. **Widen the scope.** Expand your data privacy project to encompass other applications across your organization.

opt-out
Business practice that gives consumers the opportunity to refuse sharing information about themselves.

opt-in
Agreement that requires computer users to take specific steps to allow the collection of personal information.

FREE SPEECH ONLINE VERSUS PRIVACY PROTECTION

As with all rights, the right of free speech is not unlimited. Free speech does not mean any speech. Some of the traditional restrictions on what may be freely said or published are defamation laws (including privacy violation), contempt of court, and national security. For example, it is illegal to scream "fire" in a crowded theater or make bomb threats in an airport. Free speech often clashes with privacy, protection of children, indecency, and so forth.

Free Speech Online Versus Child Protection Debate

Children's Internet Protection Act (CIPA)
Law that mandates the use of filtering technologies in schools and libraries that received certain types of U.S. federal funding.

legal precedent
A judicial decision that may be used as a standard in subsequent similar cases.

The conflict over free speech versus child protection erupted after the Children's Internet Protection Act (CIPA) was signed into law in December 2000. CIPA mandated the use of filtering technologies in schools and libraries that received certain types of U.S. national funding. CIPA was immediately challenged in court, so it did not go into effect at that time.

Opponents of the law relied on earlier court cases (that is, a legal precedent), saying that government-imposed limitations on the public's right to freely read and learn at public libraries violated the free speech protections of the First Amendment. A legal precedent is a judicial decision that may be used as a standard in subsequent similar cases. For details of the debate, see ACLU (2006). It was a major victory for proponents of free speech online in May 2002 when a district court declared the CIPA as unconstitutional. The district court judges ruled that CIPA was overbroad and would violate the First Amendment rights of library patrons, both adults and minors. That court ordered that CIPA not be enforced. The conflict did not end there. The district court's decision was appealed to the Supreme Court. In June 2003, Supreme Court judges declared that the CIPA was constitutional. Their review represented the third time justices had heard arguments pitting free speech against attempts to protect children from offensive online content. CIPA went into effect in 2004, but efforts to defeat it still continue and, of course, the issue of enforcing it is debatable, too. An example of protecting children versus privacy can be seen in Online File W16.7.

THE PRICE OF PROTECTING AN INDIVIDUALS' PRIVACY

In the past, the complexity of collecting, sorting, filing, and accessing information manually from several different government agencies was a built-in protection against misuse of private information. It was simply too expensive, cumbersome, and complex to invade a person's privacy. The Internet, in combination with large-scale databases, eliminated those barriers.

The inherent power in systems that can access vast amounts of data can be used for the good of society. For example, by matching records with the aid of a computer, it is possible to eliminate or reduce fraud, crime, government mismanagement, tax evasion, welfare fraud, employment of illegal aliens, and so on. The question is: What price must every individual pay in terms of loss of privacy so that the government can better apprehend these types of criminals? A related issue is the control of content in classified ads (as illustrated in Case 16.1 and as described in the following Craigslist example).

Example: Sheriff Sues Craigslist to Curb Prostitution. A sheriff in the U.S. state of Illinois filed a federal lawsuit in March 2009, alleging that Craigslist has become the top provider of prostitution services in the United States and claiming that missing children, runaways, abused women, and women trafficked in from foreign countries are routinely forced to have sex with strangers because they're being pimped on Craigslist.

The sheriff wanted Craigslist to shut down the erotic services category of its Web site and to compensate his department for the cost of prosecuting Web site–related prostitution cases. But Web free speech advocates say that existing laws insulate Craigslist from any illegal activities related to its ads, and they predict a quick defeat for the sheriff's legal efforts. For details, see San Miguel (2009).

In May 2009 Craigslist decided to eliminate its "erotic services" category and screen all submissions to a new "adult services" section before they are posted. Sheriff Dart said his lawsuit would stay on file until he sees changes online.

HOW INFORMATION ABOUT INDIVIDUALS IS COLLECTED

The Internet offers a number of opportunities to collect private information about individuals. Exhibit 16.8 lists several ways that the Internet can be used to find information about an individual; the last three are the most common ways of gathering information on the Internet.

Web Site Registration

Virtually all B2C sites, marketing Web sites, online magazines, vendors, government sites, and social networks ask visitors to fill out registration forms. During the process, individuals voluntarily provide their names, addresses, phone numbers, e-mail addresses, hobbies and likes or dislikes, and other personal information to participate, receive a download, win a lottery, or receive some other item in exchange. There are few restraints on the ways in which the site can use this information. The site might use it to improve customer service. Or the site could just as easily sell the information to another company, which could use it in an inappropriate or intrusive manner.

Internet users are skeptical of the necessity of giving such information to online businesses. Most people dislike registering at Web sites they visit; 15 percent refuse to register at all. Many do not trust companies not to share their personal information.

Cookies

Another way that a Web site can gather information about an individual is by using cookies. As described in Chapter 4, a *cookie* contains data that are passed back and forth between a Web site and an end user's browser as the user navigates the site. Cookies enable sites to keep track of users without having to constantly ask the users to identify themselves. Web bugs described in Section 4.6 are similar to cookies.

Originally, cookies were designed to help with personalization and market research; however, cookies can also be used to invade an individual's privacy. Cookies allow Web sites to collect detailed information about a user's preferences, interests, and surfing patterns. The personal profiles created by cookies often are more accurate than self-registration because users have a tendency to falsify information in a registration form.

Although the ethics of the use of cookies are still being debated, concerns about cookies reached a pinnacle in 1997 at the U.S. FTC hearings on online privacy. Following those hearings, Netscape and Microsoft introduced options enabling users to *block cookies*. Since that time, the uproar has subsided because most users accept cookies rather than fight them. The problem with deleting or disabling cookies is that the user will have to keep reentering information and, in some instances, may be blocked from viewing useful pages.

Spyware as a Threat to Privacy and Intellectual Property

In Chapter 10, we discussed *spyware* as a tool that some merchants use to spy on users without their knowledge. Spyware infections are a major threat to privacy and intellectual property, according to 62 percent of corporate IT security professionals that responded to

---

EXHIBIT 16.8 How to Use the Internet to Find Information

- By reading an individual's blogs or newsgroup postings
- By looking up an individual's name and identity in an Internet directory
- By reading an individual's e-mail, IM, or text messages
- By monitoring and conducting surveillance on employees
- By wiretapping wireline and wireless communication lines
- By asking an individual to complete a registration form on a Web site
- By recording an individual's actions as they navigate the Web with a browser, usually using cookies
- By using spyware, keystroke loggers, and similar methods

"Survey on the Corporate Response to Spyware," a study conducted by the Ponemon Institute (ponemon.org) (Burns 2006). **Spyware**, also referred to as *crimeware*, is defined in the study as "all unwanted software programs designed to steal proprietary information, or that target data stores containing confidential information."

Spyware may enter the user's computer as a virus or as a result of the user's clicking an option in a deceptive pop-up window. Sometimes when users download and install legitimate programs, they get spyware as well. Spyware is very effective in tracking users' Web surfing habits. It can scan computer hard drives for sensitive files and send the results to hackers or spammers. Spyware use is clearly a violation of the computer user's privacy. It can also slow down computer performance. Spyware writers are getting more innovative and are trying to avoid detection. For example, *Keystroke Logger* runs in the background of the user's computer and records every keystroke the user makes. A hacker can then identify confidential information and then steal the user's social security number, bank account number, and password, all of which can be used in identify theft (see Chapter 10).

Antivirus software and Internet firewalls cannot "see" spyware; special protection is needed. Many free and low-cost antispyware software packages are on the market. Representative free programs are Ad-Aware, Spybot, SpyKiller, and PestPatrol. For-fee programs include SpySubtract, Spy Sweeper, Ad-Aware Plus, and SpyWasher. Spyware protection is provided also by Symentec and other companies that provide Internet security software.

RFID's Threat to Privacy

As mentioned in earlier chapters, privacy advocates fear that the information stored on RFID tags or collected with them may be used to violate an individual's privacy. To protect the individual, RSA Security Corp. and others are developing locking technologies that protect consumers from being tracked after buying products with RFID tags. Several U.S. states mandated or are considering legislation to protect customers from a loss of privacy due to the tags.

Other Methods

Other methods of collecting data about people are:

- **Site transaction logs.** These logs show the usage patterns of people surfing the Internet.
- **EC ordering systems and shopping carts.** These features permit others to know what you ordered, when, from whom, and how much you paid for the item.
- **Search engines.** Search engines can be used to collect information about your searches. Also, specialized searches (e.g., maps), blogging, chatting, and Web conferences are sources of privacy information.
- **Behavioral targeting.** Behavioral targeting uses tools for collaborative filtering and analysis of user-entered data.
- **Polling and surveys.** Personal data may be revealed by participating in online voting, completing questionnaires, and so forth.
- **Payment information and e-wallets.** These may include information that can be leaked or sold to others.

Privacy of Employees

There are also issues concerning employee privacy. In addition to wasting time online, employees may disclose trade secrets and possibly make employers liable for defamation based on what they do on the corporate Web site. In response to these concerns, most companies monitor their employees' usage of e-mail and Web surfing. One tool that allows companies to spy on their employees is Google's Latitude, which works in combination with a GPS/cell phone (see Coursey 2009). For more about Internet usage monitoring, see Wen et al. (2007) and Harbert (2007).

PRIVACY PROTECTION BY INFORMATION TECHNOLOGIES

Dozens of software programs and IT procedures are available to protect your privacy. Some were described in Chapter 10. Representative examples are:

> **Platform for Privacy Preferences Project (P3P)**—software that communicates privacy policies (described later in this chapter)
>
> **Encryption**—software programs such as PKI (Chapter 10) for encrypting e-mail, transactions, and other documents
>
> **Spam blocking**—built into browsers and e-mail; blocks pop-up and unwanted mail (Chapter 10)
>
> **Spyware blocking**—detects and removes spyware and adware; built into some browsers (Chapter 10)
>
> **Cookie managers**—prevents the computer from accepting cookies; disables cookies (Chapter 10)
>
> **Anonymous e-mail and surfing**—allows you to send e-mail and surf without a trace (Chapter 10)

PRIVACY ISSUES IN WEB 2.0 TOOLS AND SOCIAL NETWORKS

The explosion of social networks raises some special issues in privacy and free speech. Here are a few examples.

Presence, Location, and Privacy

Presence in the social networking world is in progress. For example, Facebook added instant messaging (IM) to its Web site, enabling users to know when friends are online. IBM Lotus also supports presence capabilities tied into "Connections," while Microsoft offers similar capabilities with SharePoint. The iPhone E2.0 Impact includes two applications, Loopt and Whrrl, which enable users to see both the real-time presence and the location of others by leveraging iPhone's built-in location awareness capabilities.

What happens when LinkedIn, Facebook, or MySpace provides the ability for a GPS-enabled mobile device or iPhone to dynamically share their location status with others? Will or how will businesses begin to take advantage of these same capabilities to build applications to enable tracking of field sales and support personnel by leveraging the location status capabilities already present in their mobile devices? What are the privacy implications? Who will be held responsible or legally liable for unforeseen harm resulting from so much awareness and connectivity?

Free Speech via Wikis and Social Networks

Free speech and privacy rights collide in a world populated by anonymous critics and cyberbullies. But the attacks are not always from competitors or others outside the company. The nature of the Internet ensures that we may become our own worst enemies personally and professionally, based on the content or images we post on blogs, or the friends we keep on social networking pages.

Companies victimized by online gossip and rumor have legal recourse, but against whom? What if the identity of the sender or poster is not known? Who is responsible for restricting troublesome content? Furthermore, companies face legal action if they are found to be negligent for not restricting harmful content.

PRIVACY PROTECTION BY ETHICAL PRINCIPLES

The ethical principles commonly applied to the collection and use of personal information also apply to information collected in e-commerce. These principles include the following:

> **Notice or awareness.** Consumers must be given notice of an entity's information practices prior to the collection of personal information. Consumers must be able to make informed decisions about the type and extent of their disclosures based on the intentions of the party collecting the information.

▶ **Choice or consent.** Consumers must be made aware of their options as to how their personal information may be used, as well as any potential secondary uses of the information. Consent may be granted by the consumers through opt-out clauses.

▶ **Access or participation.** Consumers must be able to access their personal information and challenge the validity of the data.

▶ **Integrity or security.** Consumers must be assured that their personal data are secure and accurate. It is necessary for those collecting the data to take whatever precautions are required to ensure that they protect data from loss, unauthorized access or alteration, destruction, and fraudulent use, and to take reasonable steps to gain information from reputable and reliable sources. This principle has been extended to digital property, as described in Case 16.2.

▶ **Enforcement or redress.** A method of enforcement and remedy must be available. Otherwise, there is no real deterrent or enforceability for privacy issues.

In the United States, the broadest law in scope is the Communications Privacy and Consumer Empowerment Act (1997), which requires, among other things, that the FTC enforce online privacy rights in EC, including the collection and use of personal data. For existing U.S. privacy legislation, see Online File W16.8. (For the status of pending

---

CASE 16.2

EC Application

PROPERTY RIGHTS EXTENDED TO DOMAIN NAMES AND DIGITAL PROPERTY

In 2005, Mexican authorities arrested Stephen Cohen when he tried to renew his Mexican work visa and handed him over to U.S. Marshals. After a $65 million ruling against him, Cohen, a con man, had hidden outside the United States for 6 years. Cohen had stolen what was considered the most valuable domain name in the world, *sex.com*.

After a 5-year court battle, Judge James Ware found Cohen guilty of hijacking the *sex.com* domain name from plaintiff Gary Kremen, the founder of Match.com. Kremen had registered Sex.com in 1994. In 1995, Cohen stole the domain name by defrauding the domain registrar, VeriSign/Network Solutions, Inc. (NSI).

In a separate court case, Kremen filed a lawsuit against NSI for transferring ownership of the Sex.com domain name—property that belonged to Kremen—to Cohen. This unauthorized transfer was obtained using forged letters. NSI had switched domain name registry records without bothering to check the veracity of these documents. In a hearing before an appeals court panel in San Francisco, lawyers representing Sex.com argued that NSI, which runs the central database for the dot-com addresses, committed a breach of contract when it failed to verify a forged request to transfer the domain with its owner.

A Ninth Circuit Court of Appeals judge ruled that Gary Kremen had a property right to the stolen domain and that NSI was potentially liable for giving it away without proper authorization.

Internet activists praised the appeal court's ruling in the case, which set an important legal precedent. The court's Sex.com decision provides Internet domain registrants with protection from inappropriate domain name seizures. NSI paid Kremen an out-of-court settlement thought to be worth up to $20 million.

The Sex.com decision is likely to influence legal developments in the handling of intangible (digital) property. The Ninth Circuit's decision is an important step in applying settled principles to this new realm of digital property rights. Some believe that Sex.com single-handedly caused the courts to define domain names as property and, thus, changed the laws governing the World Wide Web.

Sources: Compiled from Boyle (2005), McCarthy (2005), and Posner (2004).

Questions

1. Why is a domain name considered property?
2. What is the difference between tangible property and intangible property?
3. What precedent was set by the decision of the Ninth Circuit Court of Appeals?

legislation in the United States, visit the Center for Democracy and Technology at cdt.org/privacy/guide/protect.)

Online Privacy Clarification

Consumers think that online privacy policies mean that the Web site will not sell or use data in specific ways. But there may be a disconnect between business practices and consumer expectations. Consumers think privacy notices mean certain default protections; they do not understand that privacy policies are just notices. They do not guarantee any rights.

Customers are willing to share all kinds of information when they see firms using it to enhance their experience. But some data-driven interactions can easily cross the line from customer delight into customer despair, and oftentimes this despair is caused by the following pitfalls:

1. Asking customers for data and then neglecting to use it for the customer's benefit or expectation.

2. Failing to protect the data collected; losing customer data in a security breach quickly drives despair.

3. Customers perceiving that their data was somehow used to harm them, either by wasting their time with an avalanche of unwanted solicitations or by cornering them with hidden costs or restrictions.

Therefore, a clarification of how data will be used and protected is necessary for a good EC relationship.

THE USA PATRIOT ACT

The USA PATRIOT Act (officially, Uniting and Strengthening America by Providing Appropriate Tools Required to Intercept and Obstruct Terrorism) was passed in October 2001, in the aftermath of the September 11 terrorist attacks. Its intent is to give law enforcement agencies broader range in their efforts to protect the public. The American Civil Liberties Union (ACLU), the Electronic Freedom Foundation (EFF), and other organizations have grave concerns, including (1) expanded surveillance with reduced checks and balances, (2) overbreadth with a lack of focus on terrorism, and (3) rules that would allow U.S. foreign intelligence agencies to more easily spy on Americans.

On March 9, 2007, the U.S. Department of Justice (DOJ) said that the FBI had improperly used provisions of the USA PATRIOT Act to obtain thousands of telephone, business, and financial records without prior judicial approval (Johnson and Lipton 2007). The report is available on the DOJ's Web site at justice.gov/oig/new.htm. The result of this report is that the government may restrain some parts of the act that allow expanded surveillance in the following areas:

- E-mail and Internet searches
- Nationwide roving wiretaps
- Requirement that ISPs hand over more user information
- Expanded scope of surveillance based on new definitions of terrorism
- Government spying on suspected computer trespassers with no need for court order
- Wiretaps for suspected violations of the Computer Fraud and Abuse Act
- Dramatic increases in the scope and penalties of the Computer Fraud and Abuse Act
- General expansion of Foreign Intelligence Surveillance Act (FISA) authority
- Increased information sharing between domestic law enforcement and intelligence
- FISA detours around U.S. domestic surveillance limitations; domestic surveillance detours around FISA limitations

For details and discussions see en.wikipedia.org/wiki/USA_PATRIOT_ACT.

P3P Privacy Platform

The **Platform for Privacy Preferences Project (P3P)** is a protocol allowing Web sites to declare their intended use of information they collect about browsing users. It is designed to give users

Platform for Privacy Preferences Project (P3P)
A protocol allowing Web sites to declare their intended use of information they collect about browsing users.

more control of their personal information when browsing by communicating a Web site's privacy policies to its users, allowing them to compare the policies to their preferences or to other standards. P3P was developed by the World Wide Web Consortium (W3C) in April 2002.

P3P is a mechanism that helps to express a Web site's data management practices. P3P manages information through privacy policies. When a Web site uses P3P, they set up a set of policies that allows them to state their intended uses of personal information that may be gathered from their site visitors.

P3P provides a standard XML format that Web sites can use to encode their privacy policies. Sites also provide XML "policy reference files" to indicate which policy applies to which part of the site. Sites can optionally provide a "compact policy" by configuring their servers to issue a special P3P header when cookies are set.

The Purpose of P3P. As the Web became an acceptable medium in which to sell products and services, electronic commerce Web sites tried to collect more information about the people who purchased their merchandise. Some companies used controversial practices such as tracker cookies to ascertain the users' demographic information and buying habits, using this information to provide specifically targeted advertisements. Users who saw this as an invasion of privacy would sometimes turn off the cookies or use proxy servers to keep their personal information secure. P3P is designed to give users more precise control of the kind of information. According to the W3C, the main goal of P3P is to increase user trust and confidence in the Web through technical empowerment.

When users decide to use P3P, they set their own policies and state what personal information they will allow to be seen by the sites that they visit. For implementation details, see w3.org/P3P/details.html.

The process of P3P is shown in Exhibit 16.9. It is based on the following five points: (1) GET: request P3P policy files, (2) send P3P policy files, (3) GET: request Web page, (4) send Web page, and (5) display page and policy to user (U.S. Department of Commerce 2009).

PRIVACY PROTECTION IN COUNTRIES OTHER THAN THE UNITED STATES

In 1998, the European Union passed a privacy directive (EU Data Protection Directive) reaffirming the principles of personal data protection in the Internet age. This directive protects privacy more than U.S. protection laws. Member countries are required to put this directive into effect by introducing new laws or modifying existing laws in their respective countries. The directive aims to regulate the activities of any person or company that controls the collection, storage, processing, or use of personal data on the Internet.

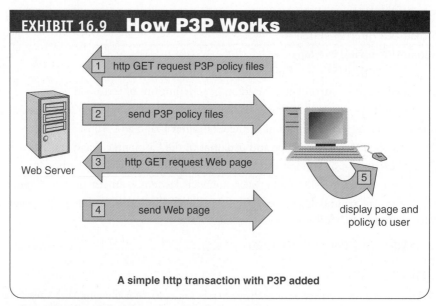

EXHIBIT 16.9   How P3P Works

1   http GET request P3P policy files

2   send P3P policy files

3   http GET request Web page

4   send Web page

5

Web Server

display page and policy to user

A simple http transaction with P3P added

Source: U.S. Department of Commerce (2009).

In many countries, the debate continues about the rights of the individual versus the rights of society. In some countries there is little privacy protection.

Section 16.4 ▶ REVIEW QUESTIONS

1. Define privacy and free speech.
2. List some of the ways that the Internet can collect information about individuals.
3. What are cookies and spyware, and what do they have to do with online privacy?
4. List four common ethical principles related to the gathering of personal information.
5. Describe privacy issues in social networks.
6. Define P3P and describe its objectives and procedures.
7. How has the USA PATRIOT Act expanded the government's reach?

16.5 CONSUMER AND SELLER PROTECTION FROM ONLINE FRAUD

An FBI report released in March 2009 revealed that the number of EC fraud complaints reached 275,285 in 2008 (a 35% increase from 2007), at a price tag of $265 million. Therefore, it is necessary to defend EC consumers.

CONSUMER (BUYER) PROTECTION

Consumer protection is critical to the success of any commerce, especially electronic, where buyers do not see sellers. The FTC enforces consumer protection laws in the United States (see ftc.gov). The FTC provides a list of 10 scams that are most likely to arrive by bulk e-mail (see onguardonline.gov/spam.html). In addition, the European Union and the United States are attempting to develop joint consumer protection policies. For details, see the TransAtlantic Consumer Dialogue Web site at tacd.org.

Representative Tips and Sources for Your Protection

Protecting consumers is an important topic for government agencies, vendors, professional associations, and consumer protection organizations. They provide many tips on how to protect consumers online. A representative list follows.

> ▶ Users should make sure that they enter the real Web site of well-known companies, such as Wal-Mart, Disney, and Amazon.com, by going directly to the site, rather than through a link, and should shop for reliable brand names at those sites.
>
> ▶ Check any unfamiliar site for an address and telephone and fax numbers. Call and quiz a salesperson about the seller.
>
> ▶ Check out the seller with the local chamber of commerce, Better Business Bureau (bbbonline.org), or TRUSTe.
>
> ▶ Investigate how secure the seller's site is and how well it is organized.
>
> ▶ Examine the money-back guarantees, warranties, and service agreements before making a purchase.
>
> ▶ Compare prices online with those in regular stores—too-low prices may be too good to be true.
>
> ▶ Ask friends what they know. Find testimonials and endorsements.
>
> ▶ Find out what redress is available in case of a dispute.
>
> ▶ Consult the National Consumers League Fraud Center (fraud.org).
>
> ▶ Check the resources available at consumerworld.org.

In addition to these tips, consumers also have shopper's rights on the Internet, as described in the following list of sources:

▶ The FTC (ftc.gov): Abusive e-mail should be forwarded to uce@ftc.gov; ftc.gov/bcp/menus/consumer/tech/online.shtm provides tips for online shopping and Internet auctions.
▶ National Consumers League Fraud Center (fraud.org)
▶ Federal Citizen Information Center (pueblo.gsa.gov)
▶ U.S. Department of Justice (usdoj.gov)
▶ The FBI's Internet Crime Complaint Center (ic3.gov/default.aspx)
▶ The American Bar Association provides online shopping tips at safeshopping.org.
▶ The Better Business Bureau (bbbonline.org)
▶ The U.S. Food and Drug Administration for buying medicine and medical products online (fda.gov/oc/buyonline)
▶ The Direct Marketing Association (the-dma.org)

Disclaimer: This is general information on consumer rights. It is not legal advice on how any particular individual should proceed. If you require specific legal advice, consult an attorney.

Third-Party Assurance Services

Several public organizations and private companies attempt to protect consumers. The following are just a few examples.

TRUSTe's "Trustmark." TRUSTe (truste.org) is a nonprofit group whose mission is to build users' trust and confidence in the Internet by promoting the policies of disclosure and informed consent. TRUSTe certifies and monitors Web site privacy, e-mail policies, and practices, and resolves thousands of consumer privacy problems every year (TRUSTe 2009). Sellers who become members of TRUSTe can add value and increase consumer confidence in online transactions by displaying the TRUSTe Advertising Affiliate "Trustmark" (a seal of quality). This mark identifies sites that have agreed to comply with responsible information-gathering guidelines. In addition, the TRUSTe Web site provides its members with a "privacy policy wizard," which helps companies create their own privacy policies. The site offers several types of seals such as privacy, children, e-health, safe harbor, wireless, e-mail services, and international services.

The TRUSTe program is voluntary. The licensing fee for use of the Trustmark ranges from $500 to $10,000, depending on the size of the online organization and the sensitivity of the information it is collecting. Many Web sites are certified as TRUSTe participants, including AT&T, CyberCash, Excite, IBM, Buena Vista Internet Group, CNET, Google, Infoseek, the *New York Times*, and Yahoo!. However, there still seems to be a fear that signing with TRUSTe could expose firms to litigation from third parties if they fail to live up to the letter of the TRUSTe pact, and that fear is likely to deter some companies from signing up.

Better Business Bureau. The Better Business Bureau (BBB), a private nonprofit U.S. organization supported largely by membership, provides reports on businesses that consumers can review before making a purchase. The BBB responds to millions of inquiries each year. Its BBBOnLine program (bbbonline.com) is similar to TRUSTe's Trustmark. The goal of the program is to promote confidence on the Internet through two different seals. Companies that meet the BBBOnLine standards for the Reliability Seal are members of the local BBB and have good truth-in-advertising and consumer service practices. Those that exhibit the BBBOnLine Privacy Seal on their Web sites have an online privacy protection policy and standards for handling consumers' personal information. In addition, consumers are able to click on the BBBOnLine seals and instantly get a BBB report on the participating company.

WHICHonline. Supported by the European Union, WHICHonline (which.co.uk) gives consumers protection by ensuring that online traders under its Which? Web Trader Scheme abide by a code of proactive guidelines. These guidelines outline issues such as product information, advertising, ordering methods, prices, delivery of goods, consumer privacy, receipting, dispute resolution, and security.

Web Trust Seal and Others. The Web Trust seal program is similar to TRUSTe. The American Institute of Certified Public Accountants (cpawebtrust.com) sponsors it. Another program, Gomez (gomez.com), monitors customer complaints and provides merchant certification.

Evaluation by Consumers. A large number of sites include product and vendor evaluations offered by consumers. For example, Deja.com, now part of Google, is home to many communities of interest whose members trade comments about products at groups.google.com. In addition, epubliceye.com allows consumers to give feedback on reliability, privacy, and customer satisfaction. It makes available a company profile that measures a number of elements, including payment options.

The Computer Fraud and Abuse Act (CFAA)

The Computer Fraud and Abuse Act (CFAA) was passed in 1984 and amended several times and is an important milestone in EC legislation. Initially, the scope and intent of CFAA was to protect government computers and financial industry computers from criminal theft by outsiders. In 1986, the CFAA was amended to include stiffer penalties for violations, but it still only protected computers used by the U.S. government or financial institutions. Then, as the Internet expanded in scope, so did the CFAA. In 1994 and in 1996, there were significant revisions of CFAA that added a civil law component and civil charges to this criminal law. In 2001 it was amended by the USA PATRIOT Act (Section 16.4), which provides for counterterrorism activities.

> **Computer Fraud and Abuse Act (CFAA)**
> Major computer crime law to protect government computers and other Internet-connected computers.

SELLER PROTECTION

The Internet makes fraud by customers or others easier because of user anonymity. It must protect sellers against:

▶ Customers who deny that they placed an order

▶ Customers who download copyrighted software and/or knowledge and sell it to others

▶ Customers who give false payment (credit card or bad checks) information in payment for products and services provided

▶ Use of their name by others (e.g., imposter sellers)

▶ Use of their unique words and phrases, names, and slogans and their Web addresses by others (trademark protection)

Sellers also can be attacked illegally or unethically by competitors.

Example. Discount online retailer SmartBargains was using pop-up ads on its rival Overstock.com's Web site. Overstock filed a lawsuit alleging violations of the U.S. state of Utah's antispyware statute. The court ruled that insertion of unwanted competitive pop-up advertisements does not constitute unfair competition or tortious interference in favor of SmartBargains in August 2008.

What Can Sellers Do?

The Web site cardcops.com provides a database of credit card numbers that have had chargeback orders recorded against them. Sellers who have access to the database can use this information to decide whether to proceed with a sale. In the future, the credit card industry is planning to use biometrics to deal with electronic shoplifting. Also, sellers can use PKI and digital certificates, especially the SET protocol, to help prevent fraud (see Chapter 10).

Other possible solutions include the following:

▶ Use intelligent software to identify possibly questionable customers (or do this identification manually in small companies). One technique, for example, involves comparing credit card billing and requested shipping addresses.

▶ Identify warning signals—that is, red flags—for possible fraudulent transactions.

▶ Ask customers whose billing address is different from the shipping address to call their bank and have the alternate address added to their bank account. Retailers agree to ship the goods to the alternate address only if this is done.

For further discussion of what merchants can do to protect themselves from fraud, see OnGuard Online at onguardonline.gov/spam.html.

PROTECTING BUYERS AND SELLERS: ELECTRONIC AND DIGITAL SIGNATURES

One method to help distinguish between legitimate and fraudulent transactions is electronic signatures. Electronic signature legislation is designed to accomplish two goals: (1) to remove barriers to e-commerce and (2) to enable and promote the desirable public policy goal of e-commerce by helping to build trust and predictability needed by parties doing business online.

A signature, whether electronic or on paper, is a symbol that signifies intent to be bound to the terms of the contract or transaction. Thus, the definition of "signed" in the Uniform Commercial Code includes "any symbol" so long as it is "executed or adopted by a party with present intention to authenticate a writing."

electronic signature
A generic, technology-neutral term that refers to the various methods by which one can "sign" an electronic record.

Electronic signature is a generic term that refers to the various methods by which one can "sign" an electronic record. Although all electronic signatures are represented digitally (i.e., as a series of ones and zeroes), many different technologies can create them. Examples of electronic signatures include a name typed at the end of an e-mail message by the sender; a digitized image of a handwritten signature attached to an electronic document; a secret code or PIN to identify the sender to the recipient; a code or "handle" that the sender of a message uses to identify himself; a unique biometrics-based identifier, such as a fingerprint or a retinal scan; and a digital signature created through the use of public key cryptography (see Chapter 10). Digital signatures have generated the most business and technical usage, as well as legislative initiatives.

Authentication and Biometric Controls

In cyberspace, buyers and sellers do not see each other. Even when videoconferencing is used, the authenticity of the person on the other end must be verified unless the person has been dealt with before. However, if one can assure the identity of the person on the other end of the line, one can imagine improved and new EC applications. For example, students will be able to take exams online from any place without the need for proctors. Fraud among recipients of government entitlements and transfer payments will be reduced to a bare minimum. Buyers will be assured who the sellers are, and sellers will know who the buyers are, with a very high degree of confidence. Arrangements can be made so that only authorized people in companies can place (or receive) purchasing orders. Interviews for employment and other matching applications will be accurate because it will be almost impossible for imposters to represent other people. Overall, trust in online transactions and in EC in general will increase significantly.

As discussed in Chapter 10, the solution for such authentication is provided by information technologies known as *biometric controls*. Biometric controls provide access procedures that match every valid user with a *unique user identifier (UID)*. They also provide an authentication method that verifies that users requesting access to the computer system are really who they claim to be. Authentication and biometric controls are valid for both consumer and merchant protection.

Section 16.5 ▶ REVIEW QUESTIONS

1. Describe consumer protection measures.
2. Describe assurance services.
3. What must a seller do to protect itself against fraud? How?
4. Describe types of electronic signatures.
5. Describe authentication and biometric controls.

16.6 SOCIETAL ISSUES AND GREEN EC

At this point in the chapter, our attention turns to several societal issues of EC. The first topic is one of concern to many—the digital divide.

THE DIGITAL DIVIDE

Despite the factors and trends that contribute to future EC growth, since the inception of the Internet, and e-commerce in particular, a gap has emerged between those who have and those who do not have the ability to use the technology. This gap is referred to as the digital divide.

The gap exists both *within* and *between* countries. The U.S. federal and state governments are attempting to close this gap within the country by encouraging training and supporting education and infrastructure. In the United States, the number of "disconnected" households dropped from 29 percent in 2006, but 20 million households (18%) still have no Internet access (Linder 2008).

The gap among countries, however, may be widening rather than narrowing. Many government and international organizations are trying to close the digital divide, including the United Nations and Citizens Online. Developed countries should reach a broadband penetration rate of 28 percent in 2008, while developing countries will be at only 3 percent. However, with the use of mobile phone technology, developing countries reached nearly 50 percent in 2008 (*American Free Press* 2008).

digital divide
The gap that has emerged between those who have and those who do not have the ability to use the technology.

ELECTRONIC DISCOVERY

Electronic discovery (e-discovery) refers to discovery in civil litigation that deals with information in electronic format, which is also referred to as *electronically stored information (ESI)*. In this context, *electronic form* is the representation of information as binary numbers. Electronic information is different from paper information because of its intangible form, volume, transience, and persistence. Also, electronic information is usually accompanied by *metadata* (data about data), which is never present in paper information unless manually coded. Electronic discovery poses new challenges and opportunities for attorneys, their clients, technical advisors, and the courts, as electronic information is collected, reviewed, and produced.

Examples of the types of data included in e-discovery are e-mail, instant messaging chats, documents (such as MS Office), accounting databases, CAD/CAM files, Web sites, and any other electronically-stored information that could be relevant evidence in a lawsuit. Also included in e-discovery is "raw data," which forensic investigators can review for hidden evidence.

E-discovery deals frequently with e-mail archives. According to Conry-Murray (2008), e-mail is the prime target of e-discovery requests, and it must have features such as full-content index, keyword search, and metadata index.

electronic discovery (e-discovery)
Discovery in civil litigation that deals with information in electronic format; also referred to as *electronically stored information* (ESI).

OPERATING GREENER BUSINESSES AND ECO-FRIENDLY DATA CENTERS

The growing power consumption of computing technology and high energy costs are having a direct negative impact on business profitability. Enterprises are trying to reduce energy costs and increase the use of recyclable materials. Green computing is the study and practice of eco-friendly computing resources (e.g., see en.wikipedia.org/wiki/Green_computing. In this section, we focus on how EC is *going green* by adopting environmentally friendly practices.

With an increased awareness about the damage to the physical environment and ecosystem, organizations and individuals are looking at potential improvements and savings that can be made in the EC and IT industry. These efforts are known as Green IT. For example, energy use in data centers (a data center is a facility used to house computer systems and associated components, such as storage) is a major concern to corporations. Green EC/IT is a growing movement (see Nelson 2008).

Data center servers are known to be both power hungry and heat generating. PC monitors consume about 80 to 100 billion kilowatt hours of electricity every year in the United States.

Green computing
The study and practice of eco-friendly computing resources; is now a key concern of businesses in all industries—not just environmental organizations.

Green IT
Green IT begins with manufacturers producing environmentally friendly products and encouraging IT departments to consider more friendly options like virtualization, power management, and proper recycling habits.

Both Intel and AMD are producing new chips aimed at reducing this amount of energy usage. Note that PCs should be turned off when not in use. PCs generate CO_2 (carbon dioxide) that damages the atmosphere. Finally, discarded PCs and other computer equipment cause waste disposal problems. An important issue is how to recycle old equipment and whose responsibility (the manufacturers? the users?) it is to take care of the problem. *Green software* refers to software products that help companies save energy or comply with EPA requirements.

HOW TO OPERATE GREENER BUSINESSES, DATA CENTERS, AND SUPPLY CHAINS

Are eco-friendly computing and business growth compatible? Yes, they are. According to Gartner Group, 80 percent of the world's data centers are constrained by heat, space, and power requirements. In addition to the demand on processing capability to satisfy the growth of the business, there is enormous demand on power consumption and space requirements for computing platforms. Data center configurations are no longer based on one dimension (e.g., price or performance)—meaning that factors other than affordability or performance must be considered. The equation is much more complicated. Gartner estimates that by 2008, 50 percent of current data centers will have insufficient power and cooling capacity to meet the demands of high-density equipment that traditionally accounted for less than 10 percent of an overall IT budget; demand could soon account for more than half. All of these factors must be taken into consideration when deciding on the design of a data center (reported by Sun Microsystems 2007).

An enterprise can cut energy costs in half, double space efficiency, and increase server utilization levels to as high as 85 percent. Gaining these efficiencies requires dealing with these four issues: the desktop, data center computing power, data center power/cooling, and data center storage. For more details on Green computing, see Online File W16.9.

Example 1. Wells Fargo is a large financial institution that offers a wide range of services, including consumer and corporate banking, insurance, investments, and mortgages. Its revenue in 2008 exceeded $42 billion. The company is data-dependent and known for its eco-friendliness. In 2007, with the increase in energy costs, the company decided to go "green" in its two new data centers. Data centers must ensure security and availability of their services, and when they are planned from scratch, they can be energy efficient with low power consumption. The two new facilities have more than 8,000 servers that consume considerable power and generate heat.

Several energy-saving features were introduced, including water-based economizers that regulate energy usage and cool the physical environment, a computer-controlled central fan system for cooling the floors, direct air to cool specific hot spaces, and semiconductor chips that automatically shut off power until it is needed. With increasing volumes of data, Wells Fargo constantly expands and renovates its data centers, taking environmental concerns into consideration. The company experimented with a solar system for making hot water, with motion-detector lights, and with variable-speed fans.

Example 2. Monsanto, Inc., a large global provider of agriculture products with 2008 revenues of $11 billion, is building an energy-efficient data center that supports analysis of its worldwide operations. Two factors driving investment in the new center were the 50 percent annual growth in data usage and high cooling costs for the old data center. The new energy-efficient center houses 900 servers and uses air for cooling rather than water. Another feature is the exterior glass shield that deflects 90 percent of the sun's heat.

Both companies have their data centers certified by the Leadership in Energy and Environmental Design (LEED) of the U.S. Green Building Council. In the United States, data centers consume about 20 to 30 billion kilowatt hours per year, and the number of servers is growing at 50 percent every 3 years. In both Wells Fargo and Monsanto, virtualization technologies increase the speed of data processing. For further details, see Duvall (2007a) and Watson (2007).

GLOBAL GREEN REGULATIONS

Global regulations also are influencing green business practices. Sustainability regulations such as RoHS (rohs.eu and rohs.gov.uk) in the European Union (EU) will increasingly impact how supply chains function regardless of location. The RoHS directive stands for "the restriction of the use of certain hazardous substances in electrical and electronic equipment." For example, EU member states ensured that beginning in July 2006, new electrical and electronic equipment put on the market would not contain any of six banned substances—lead, mercury, cadmium, hexavalent chromium, poly-brominated biphenyls (PBB), and polybrominated diphenyl ethers (PBDE)—in quantities exceeding maximum concentration values. Moreover, China has passed its own RoHS legislation.

Similar legislation is developing elsewhere. For example, California's Electronic Waste Recycling Act (EWRA) prohibits the sale of electronic devices banned by the EU's RoHS, including CRTs, LCDs, and other products that contain the four heavy metals restricted by RoHS. In addition, many states have enacted mercury and PBDE bans, and several are considering bills similar to EWRA. For example, Seattle has issued many regulations related to eliminating paper-based manuals and mandating recycling.

Eco-friendly practices reduce costs and improve public relations in the long run. Not surprisingly, demand for green computers is on the rise. A tool to help companies find such hardware is the Electronic Product Environmental Assessment Tool, or EPEAT.

Electronic Product Environmental Assessment Tool

Maintained by the Green Electronics Council (GEC), the **Electronic Product Environmental Assessment Tool (EPEAT)** is a searchable database of computer hardware that meets a strict set of environmental criteria. Among other criteria, products registered with EPEAT comply with the U.S. government's Energy Star 4.0 rating (see energystar.gov); have reduced levels of cadmium, lead, and mercury; and are easier to upgrade and recycle. Energy Star–qualified products use less energy. Depending on how many criteria they meet, products receive a gold, silver, or bronze certification rating.

EPEAT rates computers and monitors on a number of environmental criteria, including energy efficiency, materials used, product longevity, takeback programs, and packaging. Twenty-two percent of the 109 million computers shipped worldwide in 2007 were registered on EPEAT (epeat.net). In contrast, in 2006, only 10 percent of computers were registered. Regarding monitors, in 2008, all nine of Lenovo's ThinkVision LCD monitors were EPEAT gold certified, the highest eco-friendly ranking awarded by EPEAT. In addition, more than 280 monitors met the lower silver and bronze certifications.

Electronic Product Environmental Assessment Tool (EPEAT)
A searchable database of computer hardware that meets a strict set of environmental criteria.

The Field of Green Technology and Telecommuting

The field of green technology covers a broad range of issues. Green technology focuses on reducing the harmful environmental impacts of computing and industrial processes and innovative technologies caused by the needs of the growing worldwide population. The objective is to minimize damaging the environment or depleting natural resources by creating fully recyclable products, reducing pollution, and designing energy-efficient or alternative technologies.

Telecommuting or virtual work also offers many green benefits, including reducing rush-hour traffic, improving air quality, improving highway safety, and even improving health care (see Exhibit 16.10).

OTHER SOCIETAL ISSUES

Many other societal issues can be related to EC. Three in which EC has had a generally positive impact are mentioned here: education, public safety, and health.

Education

E-commerce has had a major impact on education and learning, as described in Chapter 7. Virtual universities are helping to reduce the digital divide. Companies can use the Internet to retrain employees much more easily, enabling them to defer retirement if they so choose. Homebound individuals can get degrees from good institutions, and many vocational professions can be learned from home.

EXHIBIT 16.10 Potential Benefits of Telecommuting or Virtual Work

Individuals	Organizational	Community and Society
• Reduces or eliminates travel-related time and expenses. • Improves health by reducing stress related to compromises made between family and work responsibilities • Allows closer proximity to and involvement with family • Allows closer bonds with the family and the community • Decreases involvement in office politics • Increases productivity despite distractions	• Reduces office space needed • Increases labor pool and competitive advantage in recruitment • Provides compliance with the Americans with Disabilities Act • Decreases employee turnover, absenteeism, and sick leave usage • Improves job satisfaction and productivity	• Conserves energy and lessens dependence on foreign oil • Preserves the environment by reducing traffic-related pollution and congestion • Reduces traffic accidents and resulting injuries or deaths • Reduces the incidence of disrupted families when people do not have to quit their jobs if they need to move because of a spouse's new job or family obligations • Increases employment opportunities for the homebound • Allows the movement of job opportunities to areas of high unemployment

Public Safety, Criminal Justice, and Homeland Security

With increased concerns about public safety after September 11, 2001, many organizations and individuals have started to look at technologies that will help to deter, prevent, or detect criminal activities of various types. Various e-commerce tools can help increase our safety at home and in public. These include e-911 systems; global collaborative commerce technologies (for collaboration among national and international law enforcement units); e-procurement (of unique equipment to fight crime); e-government efforts at coordinating, information sharing, and expediting legal work and cases; intelligent homes, offices, and public buildings; and e-training of law enforcement officers.

Health Aspects

Is EC a health risk? Generally speaking, it is probably safer and healthier to shop from home than in a physical store. However, some believe that exposure to cellular mobile communication radiation may cause health problems. It may take years before the truth of this claim is known. Even if communication radiation does cause health problems, the damage could be insignificant due to the small amount of time most people spend on wireless shopping and other wireless activities. However, given the concern of some about this issue, protective devices may soon be available that will solve this problem.

EC technologies such as collaborative commerce can help improve health care. For example, using the Internet, the approval process of new drugs has been shortened, saving lives and reducing suffering. Pervasive computing helps in the delivery of health care. Intelligent systems facilitate medical diagnoses. Health-care advice can be provided from a distance. Finally, intelligent hospitals, doctors, and other health-care facilities use EC tools (see Europe's Information Society 2009).

Section 16.6 ▶ REVIEW QUESTIONS

1. Define the digital divide.
2. Describe electronic discovery and its uses.
3. Describe how EC can improve education.
4. Describe how EC can improve safety and security.
5. Describe the impact of EC on health services.
6. What is Green computing?
7. List three ways in which computing can help protect the environment or conserve resources.
8. What is a Green supply chain? Give one example.
9. How do the new data centers help us "go green"?
10. How does telecommuting or virtual work conserve the environment?

MANAGERIAL ISSUES

Some managerial issues related to this chapter are as follows.

1. **What legal and ethical issues should be of major concern to an EC enterprise?** Key issues to consider include the following: (1) What type of proprietary information should we allow and disallow on our site? (2) Who will have access to information that visitors post to our site? (3) Do the content and activities on our site comply with laws in other countries? (4) What disclaimers do we need to post on our Web site? (5) Are we using trademarked or copyrighted materials without permission? Regardless of the specific issues, an attorney should periodically review the content on the site, and someone should be responsible for monitoring legal and liability issues.

2. **What are the most critical ethical issues?** Negative or defamatory articles published about people, companies, or products on Web sites or blogs can lead to charges of libel—and libel can stretch across countries. Issues of privacy, ethics, and legal exposure may seem tangential to running a business, but ignoring them puts the company at risk of fines, customer anger, and disruption of the operation of an organization. Privacy protection is a necessary investment.

3. **How can intellectual property rights be protected when it comes to digital content?** To protect intellectual property rights such as video, music, and books online, we need to monitor what copyrights, trademarks, and patents are infringed upon over the Internet. Portal sites that allow pirated video and music files should be monitored. This monitoring may require a vast amount of work, so software agents may be employed to continually inspect the pirated material. The risk to the business that can be caused by the infringement and the possibility of legal protection as well as technical protection by current regulation and potential new common law should be analyzed. Consider settling any suit for damages by negotiation. If the violator is not controllable, consider owning the origin of the challenge by acquiring it, as Disney did in China.

4. **How can patent cost be monitored effectively?** Some people claim that patents should not be awarded to business or computer processes related to EC (as is the case in Europe). Therefore, investing large amounts of money in developing or buying patents may be financially unwise in cases where patents may not hold. Some companies that own many business model patents have been unable to create business value out of the patents.

5. **What is the ethical principle of protecting the privacy of customers?** To provide personalized services, companies need to collect and manage customers' profile data. In practice, the company has to decide whether they would use spyware to collect data. This process may easily cross the line from customer delight into customer despair. The company needs a well-established principle of protecting customer privacy: Notify customers before collecting their personal information; inform and get consent on the type and extent of disclosures; allow customers to access their personal data and make sure the data are accurate and securely managed; and apply some method of enforcement and remedy to deter privacy breaches. In this manner, the company can avoid legal suits and gain the long-term trust of customers.

6. **How can a company create opportunities in the global trend toward Green EC?** Reducing carbon emissions and saving energy are global issues that can be serious threats but can also provide opportunities for businesses during the next decade. (1) EC can save carbon emission by reducing physical transportation. This is a generic contribution of EC. (2) EC can provide the exchange platform that trades the CO_2 emission rights with the clean development mechanism projects conducted in developing countries. This is a new business opportunity. (3) The IT hardware platform for EC is vying for the Energy Star Excellence Award from the Environmental Protection Agency to prove that their products are contributing to the protection of the environment and to gain consumer preference. This is a threat and an opportunity for platform manufacturers.

SUMMARY

In this chapter, you learned about the following EC issues as they relate to the chapter's learning objectives.

1. **Understanding the foundation for legal and ethical issues.** Laws and regulations are broadly written and can only provide outlines to guide public policy. Ethics also are generally defined. Simply referring to relevant laws or philosophical principles cannot resolve specific legal disputes or ethical dilemmas. Law and ethics provide systems for achieving both social control and the greater good. As with all systems, the formation of laws is a dynamic process that responds to ever-changing conditions. The nature of law is dynamic so that it can be responsive to new threats to individual rights or failures to perform one's duties. The Net not only offers freedom of speech but also widens opportunities for irresponsible activity. Despite laws and technical defenses, new types of spam have emerged to capture customer traffic. The legal framework for EC—both statutory and common law—continues to evolve. To date, the major legal issues in EC have involved rights of privacy, intellectual property, freedom of speech and censorship, and fraud. In the absence of legal constraints, ethical codes help to fill the gap. Differences in interpretations of what is legal or illegal often lead to rigorous and even contentious debate.

2. **Civil law, intellectual property, and common law.** EC operations are subject to various types of laws—some of which judges create in landmark court cases. Civil law provides companies with ways to get compensated for damages or misuse of their property rights. Laws are being amended to better protect EC. These protections are needed because it is easy and inexpensive to copy or steal intellectual works on the Internet (e.g., music, photos, movies) and to distribute or sell them without the permission of the owner. These actions violate or infringe upon copyrights, trademarks, and patents. Although the legal aspects seem fairly clear, monitoring and catching violators remains difficult.

3. **Understanding legal and ethical challenges and how to contain them.** The global scope and universal accessibility of the Internet create serious questions as to which ethical rules and laws apply. Ignoring laws exposes companies to lawsuits or criminal charges that are disruptive, expensive, and damaging to customer relations. The best strategy is to avoid behaviors that expose the company to these types of risk. Important safeguards are a corporate code of ethics stating the rules and expected behaviors and actions and an Internet acceptable use policy.

4. **Privacy, free speech, defamation, and their challenges.** B2C companies use CRM and depend on customer information to improve products and services. Registration and cookies are two of the ways used to collect this information. The key privacy issues are who controls this information and how private it should remain. Strict privacy laws have been passed recently that carry harsh penalties for any negligence that exposes personal or confidential data. There is ongoing debate about censorship on the Internet. The proponents of censorship feel that it is up to the government and various ISPs and Web sites to control inappropriate or offensive content. Others oppose any form of censorship; they believe that control is up to the individual. In the United States, for example, most legal attempts to censor content on the Internet have been found unconstitutional. The debate is not likely to be resolved.

5. **Fraud on the Internet and how to protect consumers against it.** Protection is needed because there is no face-to-face contact; there is great possibility for fraud; there are insufficient legal constraints; and new issues and scams appear constantly. Several organizations, private and public, attempt to provide the protection needed to build the trust that is essential for the success of widespread EC. Of special importance are electronic contracts (including digital signatures), the control of gambling, and what taxes should be paid to whom on interstate and international transactions. Although the trend is not to have a sales tax or a value-added tax, this may not be the case for too much longer. Many procedures are used to protect consumers. In addition to legislation, the FTC tries to educate consumers so they know the major scams. The use of seals on sites (such as TRUSTe) can help, as well as tips and measures taken by vendors.

6. **Protection of sellers.** Sellers can be cheated by buyers and by other sellers or thieves. Protective measures include using contacts and encryption (PKI, Chapter 10), keeping databases of potential criminals and sharing the information with other sellers, educating employees, and using intelligent software.

7. **Societal impacts of EC.** EC brings many societal benefits, ranging from improved security, transportation, and education to better health-care delivery and international collaboration. Although the digital divide still exists between developed and developing countries, the advent of mobile computing, especially through cell phones, is beginning to close the gap.

8. **Green EC.** EC requires large data centers that waste energy and create pollution. Other environmental concerns are also caused by the use of EC. There are several ways to make EC greener, including working from home (telecommuting).

KEY TERMS

Business ethics	719	Due process	710	Opt-in	721
Children's Internet		Duty	710	Opt-out	721
Protection Act (CIPA)	722	Electronic discovery		Patent	715
Civil laws	712	(e-discovery)	733	Platform for Privacy Preferences	
Civil litigation	711	Electronic Product		Project (P3P)	727
Common law (case law)	715	Environmental Assessment Tool		Privacy	718
Compliance data	712	(EPEAT)	735	Protected interests	710
Computer Fraud and		Electronic signature	732	Regulatory compliance	711
Abuse Act (CFAA)	731	Ethics	718	Right	710
Copyright	713	Fair use	715	Spyware	724
Crime	712	Green computing	733	Statutes	712
Criminal laws	712	Green IT	733	Tort	715
Cyberbashing	716	Infringement	713	Trademark	715
Digital divide	733	Intellectual property	709		
Digital rights management		Intellectual property law	713		
(DRM)	714	Legal precedent	722		

QUESTIONS FOR DISCUSSION

1. What can EC Web sites do to ensure the safeguarding of personal information?

2. Privacy is the right to be left alone and free of unreasonable personal intrusions. What are some intrusions that you consider "unreasonable"?

3. Who should control minors' access to "offensive" material on the Internet—parents, the government, or ISPs? Why?

4. Discuss the conflict between freedom of speech and the control of offensive Web sites.

5. Discuss what the RIAA hopes to achieve by using lawsuits (civil law) against college students for copyright infringement.

6. Discuss the possible insufficient protection of opt-in and opt-out options. What would you be happy with?

7. The IRS buys demographic market research data from private companies. These data contain income statistics that could be compared with tax returns. Many U.S. citizens feel that their rights within the realm of the Electronic Communications Privacy Act (ECPA) are being violated; others say that this is an unethical behavior on the part of the government. Discuss.

8. Clerks at 7-Eleven stores enter data regarding customers (gender, approximate age, and so on) into the computer. These data are then processed for improved decision making. Customers are not informed about this, nor are they being asked for permission. (Names are not keyed in.) Are the clerks' actions ethical? Compare this with the case of cookies.

9. Many hospitals, health maintenance organizations, and government agencies are converting, or plan to convert, all patient medical records from paper to electronic storage (using imaging technology). Once completed, electronic storage will enable quick access, any time and from any place, to most records. However, the availability of these records in a database or on networks or smart cards may allow people, some of whom are unauthorized, to view another person's private medical data. To protect privacy fully may cost too much money or may considerably slow the speed of access to the records. What policies could health-care administrators use to prevent unauthorized access? Discuss.

10. Why do many companies and professional organizations develop their own codes of ethics? After all, ethics are ethics.

11. Cyber Promotions, Inc., attempted to use the First Amendment in defense of its flooding of AOL subscribers with junk e-mail. AOL tried to block the junk e-mail. A judge agreed with AOL that unsolicited e-mail is annoying, a costly waste of Internet time, and often inappropriate and, therefore, should not be sent. Discuss some of the issues involved, such as freedom of speech, how to distinguish between junk and nonjunk e-mail, and the analogy with regular mail.

12. The U.S. Communications Decency Act, which was intended to protect children and others from pornography and other offensive material online, was ruled unconstitutional by the courts. Discuss the importance and implications of this incident.

13. Why does the government warn customers to be careful with their payments for EC products and services?

14. Why so some people feel that the USA PATRIOT Act is weakening the protection of civil liberties?

INTERNET EXERCISES

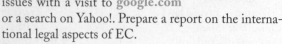

1. You want to set up an ethical blog. Using sites such as CyberJournalist.net: A Bloggers' Code of Ethics at cyberjournalist.net/news/000215.php, review the suggested guide to publishing on a blog. Make a list of the top 10 ethical issues for blogging.

2. You want to set up a personal Web site. Using legal sites such as cyberlaw.com, prepare a report summarizing the types of materials you can and cannot use (e.g., logos, graphics, etc.) without breaking copyright law.

3. Use google.com to prepare a list of industry and trade organizations involved in various computer privacy initiatives. One of these groups is the World Wide Web Consortium (W3C). Describe its Privacy Preferences Project (w3.org/tr/2001/wd-p3p-20010928).

4. Enter pgp.com. Review the services offered. Use the free software to encrypt a message.

5. Enter calastrology.com. What kind of community is this? Check the revenue model. Then enter astrocenter.com. What kind of site is this? Compare and comment on the two sites.

6. Enter nolo.com. Try to find information about various EC legal issues. Find information about international EC issues. Then go to legalcompliance.com or cybertriallawyer.com. Try to find information about international legal aspects of EC. Locate additional information on EC legal issues with a visit to google.com or a search on Yahoo!. Prepare a report on the international legal aspects of EC.

7. Find the status of the latest copyright legislation. Try fairuse.stanford.edu. Is there anything regarding the international aspects of copyright legislation?

8. Enter ftc.gov and identify some of the typical types of fraud and scams on the Internet. List 10 of them.

9. Enter usispa.org and ispa.org.uk, two organizations that represent the ISP industry. Identify the various initiatives they have undertaken regarding topics discussed in this chapter.

10. Visit consumers.com. What protection can this group give that is not provided by BBBOnLine?

11. Download freeware from junkbuster.com/ijb.htm and learn how to prohibit unsolicited e-mail. Describe how your privacy is protected.

12. Enter scambusters.com and identify and list its antifraud and antiscam activities.

TEAM ASSIGNMENTS, PROJECTS, AND CLASS DISCUSSIONS

1. The number of lawsuits around the world involving EC has increased. Have each team prepare a list of five recent EC legal cases on each topic in this chapter (e.g., privacy, digital property, defamation, domain names). Prepare a summary of the issues of each case, the parties, the courts, and dates. What were the outcomes of these cases? What was (or might be) the impact of each decision?

2. Form three teams. Have a debate on free speech versus protection of children between two teams. The third team acts as judges. One team is for complete freedom of speech on the Internet; the other team advocates protection of children by censoring offensive and pornographic material. After the debate, have the judges decide which team provided the most compelling legal arguments.

3. It is legal to monitor employees' Internet activity, e-mail, and instant messages. At the same time, it is illegal to open letters addressed to individuals and sent to the company's address. Why is that necessary? To what extent is it ethical? Are employees' rights being violated? Have two teams debate these issues.

4. Enter whatis.techtarget.com, wikipedia.org, wikia.com, or similar resource sites. Read about spam and splogs. Find how spam and splog filters work (also see ironport.com and other vendors). Finally, take the self-assessment quiz at searchcrm.techtarget.com. Prepare a report and class presentation.

5. Debate the issue of ownership of user-generated content (the Facebook example). One group should be for and one against.

6. Address the following topics in a class discussion:
   a. Is net neutrality good for EC?
   b. Should exchange of songs between individuals be allowed over the Internet?
   c. Is the USA PATRIOT Act too loose or too tight?
   d. It may too expensive for some companies to "go green." If they "go green," they may not be able to compete against companies in countries that do not practice Green EC. Should the government subsidize Green EC?
   e. Who should own content created by employees during their regular work hours?
   f. Are privacy standards tough enough to protect electronic health records?

Closing Case

NET NEUTRALITY: GOOD FOR E-BUSINESS?

Internet neutrality (also *network neutrality, net neutrality,* or *NN*) is a hotly debated topic that will shape the future of the Internet (see *en.wikipedia.org/wiki/Net_neutrality*). It became a high-profile topic when telecommunications network operators (telcos) AT&T and Verizon stated that they should have the right to charge extra for premium placement on their network to recoup vast investments in their infrastructure. Currently, all Internet traffic is being treated equally (or "neutrally") by telecommunication providers. In response, numerous grassroots campaigns emerged to try to stop such a practice.

Basically, net neutrality (NN) would be a new government regulation. The regulation would prohibit telcos from prioritizing any content or services that traveled across their networks. For example, without NN, a telco could charge the social network Web site YouTube extra fees to have its site delivered faster than the Web site of a company who could not afford the premium service fees.

It is a major issue as the United States considers new telecommunications laws. In May 2006, the U.S. House of Representatives passed telecom bill H.R. 5252, without net neutrality protections. As of March 2007, the debate was in the Senate, where advocates were working to get strong net neutrality language in the bill, known as the *Snowe-Dorgan legislation*. It would bar network operators from blocking or degrading access to Internet content and services and from preventing consumers from connecting external devices to the network, with exceptions for security and other consumer protection purposes.

Supporters of Net Neutrality

Those in favor view net neutrality as a necessity to keep the Internet a level playing field. They argue that if net neutrality does not pass, there is no restriction on the telcos, which enables them to prioritize traffic according to the level of service (e.g., basic or premium) that the customer bought. (An analogy is the airline industry offering different classes of service—first class, business class, and coach—at different prices.)

Internet giants Google and Amazon.com are strong supporters of net neutrality. In a prepared statement to the U.S. Senate Committee Hearing on Network Neutrality on February 7, 2006, Vinton G. Cerf, codeveloper of the Internet Protocol and Google's chief Internet evangelist, stated:

Allowing broadband carriers to control what people see and do online would fundamentally undermine the principles that have made the Internet such a success. . . . A number of justifications have been created to support carrier control over consumer choices online; none stand up to scrutiny.

Opponents of Net Neutrality

Those opposed to net neutrality warn that it would eliminate incentives to invest and upgrade networks and next-generation network services. One of the primary inventors, Bob Kahn criticizes net neutrality as a slogan that would halt experimentation and improvement in the Internet's core. Except for Vinton Cerf (employed by Google—a major proponent of NN), most senior internetworking engineers agree with Kahn.

Some NN opponents believe NN is too important to be left to government regulators because of mistakes in past attempts to regulate Internet activities and technology. They cite the CAN-SPAM and Digital Millennium Copyright Act as examples of laws that did not achieve their intended objectives. As such, they fear that legislation with the stated purpose of preserving network neutrality would have precisely the opposite effect. Their contempt is evident in the following:

Legislators would sit in back rooms with representatives of big business and emerge with network neutrality laws that favor companies with revenues greater than $1 billion. The laws would protect the Yahoo!s, Microsofts, and Googles of the world, while leaving innovative startups out in their cold garage (Wagner 2007).

Related issues are as follows: Who really owns the Internet (see Goldsmith and Wu 2008)? How can one solve the bandwidth problem that may clog the Internet (see McDowell 2008)?

Sources: Ford et. al (2007), Wagner (2007), Goldsmith and Wu (2008), and Google (2007).

Questions

1. Why is net neutrality a hotly debated issue?
2. How do proponents support their position? Do you agree with their position? Explain.
3. How do opponents support their position? Do you agree with their position? Explain.
4. What is the current state of net neutrality?

ONLINE RESOURCES
available at pearsonglobaleditions.com/turban

Online Files

W16.1 Application Case: Linking to a Web Site: The Ticketmaster Case

W16.2 Controversial Issues Regarding Political Spam

W16.3 Intellectual Property Web Sites—International Sites

W16.4 Representative EC Patents

W16.5 Framework of Ethical Issues

W16.6 Web Site Quality Guidelines

W16.7 Application Case: Protection Pitted Against Privacy

W16.8 Representative U.S. Federal Privacy Legislation

W16.9 How to Go Green in a Data Center and the Related Supply Chain

Comprehensive Educational Web Sites

ftc.gov: Major source on consumer fraud and protection

dmoz.org/society/issues/fraud/Internet: Comprehensive resources on fraud

fraud.org: The National Consumers League Fraud Center

ic3.gov: The FBI's Internet crime complaint center

fda.gov/oc/buyonline: Food and Drug Administration center for buying medicine and medical products online

regulatorycompliance.com: A private company with a comprehensive collection

business.gov: A single point of access to government services

sba.gov/advo/laws/law_modeleg.html: Small business government legal (advocate) staying current with federal regulations

law.com: A comprehensive legal collection

privacy.org: A comprehensive source of privacy information

epic.org: A privacy watchdog site

privacyrights.org: An educational clearinghouse

itworld.com/green-it: A comprehensive source for IT-related issues, including Green EC and IT

digitaldivide.org: A comprehensive collection of related material

greenit.net: A comprehensive collection of related material

techworld.com/green-it: A comprehensive collection of related material

REFERENCES

ACLU. "Libraries, the Internet, and the Law: Adults Must Have Unfiltered Access." November 16, 2006. aclu-wa.org/detail.cfm?id=556 (accessed April 2009).

American Free Press. "Digital Divide Widens Between Rich and Poor Countries: UN." February 7, 2008. afp.google.com/article/ALeqM5jr4ayXdu2K-oN5TyOywARrQBtvZg (accessed April 2009).

Arden-Besunder, A., and L. J. Sherwin. "Who Should Monitor Online Counterfeiters?" *New York Law Journal* (March 18, 2009).

Boyle, M. "Sex.com, Drugs, and a Rocky Road." *Fortune*, December 12, 2005. money.cnn.com/magazines/fortune/fortune_archive/2005/12/12/8363122/index.htm (accessed April 2009).

Burns, E. "Intellectual Property Threatened by Spyware." *ClickZ Stats*, November 14, 2006. clickz.com/showPage.html?page=3623943 (accessed April 2009).

Cheeseman, H. R. *Business Law*, 7th ed. Upper Saddle River, NJ: Prentice Hall, 2008.

Conry-Murray, A. "IT Fought the Law . . . " *InformationWeek*, June 23, 2008.

Coursey, D. "Spy on Your Workers with Google Latitude." *PCWorld*, February 5, 2009.

Department of Commerce. "How Does P3P Work?" 2009. osec.doc.gov/webresources/P3P_User_Admin_files/TextMostly/Slide7.html (accessed April 2009).

Downes, L. "eBay and the Legal Problems with Online Marketplaces." *CIO Insight*, August 13, 2008.

Duvall, M. "Monsanto Grows Green." *Baseline*, November 29, 2007.

Europe's Information Society. "Telemedicine for the Benefit of Patients, the Healthcare System, and Society." 2009. ec.europa.eu/information_society/activities/health/policy/telemedicine/index_en.htm (accessed April 2009).

FindLaw. "U.S. Constitution: Fourth Amendment: Annotations." 2007. caselaw.lp.findlaw.com/data/constitution/amendment04/01.html (accessed March 2009).

Fineagan, C. "How to Meet Unique Information Management and Compliance Challenges." February 18, 2009. eweek.com/c/a/Data-Storage/How-to-Meet-Unique-Information-Management-and-Compliance-Challenges (accessed April 2009).

Ford, G. S., T. Koutsky, and L. Spiwak. "Network Neutrality and Foreclosing Market Exchange." *Phoenix Center Policy Paper Series*, March 2007. phoenix-center.org/ pcpp/PCPP28Final.pdf (accessed April 2009).

Goldsmith, J., and T. Wu. *Who Controls the Internet? Illusions of a Borderless World*. New York: Oxford University Press, 2008.

Google. "A Guide to Net Neutrality for Google Users." 2007. google.com/help/netneutrality.html (accessed April 2009).

Harbert, T. "Dark Secrets and Ugly Truths: When Ethics and IT Collide."*Computerworld*, February 17, 2007.

Himma, K. E., and H. T. Tavani. *The Handbook of Information and Computer Ethics*. Hoboken, NJ: Wiley & Sons, 2008.

IBM. "Data Privacy Best Practices: Time to Take Action." White paper, *IBM Information Management Software*, September 2008.

Johnson, D., and E. Lipton. "Justice Department Says F.B.I. Misused Patriot Act." *The New York Times*, March 9, 2007.

Linder, B. "Study: Digital Divide Still Alive and Well in the U.S." *Download Squad*, May 18, 2008. download squad.com/2008/05/18/study-digital-divide-is-alive-and-well-in-the-us (accessed April 2009).

MacMillan, D. "Facebook's Fine-Print Fiasco." *BusinessWeek*, February 17, 2009.

Mann, R. J., and J. K. Winn. *Electronic Commerce* (*Law in Commerce*), 3rd ed. New York: Aspen Publishers, 2008.

McBride, S., and L. Chao. "Disney Battles Pirates at China Affiliate." *The Wall Street Journal-Asia*, November 24, 2008.

McCarthy, K. "Sex.com Thief Arrested." *The Register* (UK). October 28, 2005. theregister.co.uk/2005/10/28/sexdotcom_cohen_arrested (accessed April 2009).

McDowell, R. "Who Should Solve This Internet Crisis?" July 28, 2008. Washington.com/wp-dyn/content/article/2008/07/27/AR2008072701172.ht . . . (accessed July 2008).

Nelson, N. "How to Estimate Energy Efficiency." *eWeek*, July 7, 2008.

Posner, J. "Sex.com Settles Monumental Case Against VeriSign/Network Solutions." *CircleID*, April 20, 2004. circleid.com/posts/sexcom_settles_monumental_case_against_verisign_network_solutions (accessed April 2009).

Puente, M. "Hello to Less Privacy." *USA Today*, February 28, 2007.

Reuters. "Universal Music Sues MySpace over Copyrights." *The Financial Express*, January 8, 2007.

San Miguel, R. "Sheriff Sues Craigslist to Curb Prostitution." *E-Commerce Times*, March 6, 2009.

Sun Microsystems. "The Economics of 'Green IT.'" 2007. technologysolutionssimplified.com/report_ecogreenit.pdf (accessed April 2009).

TRUSTe. "About TRUSTe." truste.org/about/index.php (accessed April 2009).

Veiga, A. "Music Industry Group Targets Students." *FindLaw.com*, February 28, 2007. news.corporate.findlaw.com/ap/f/66/02-28-2007/2538000b9e255e43.html (no longer available online).

Volonino, L., and S. Robinson. *Principles and Practices of Information Security*. Upper Saddle River, NJ: Prentice Hall, 2004.

Volonino, L., R. Anzaldua, and J. Godwin. *Computer Forensics: Principles and Practices*. Upper Saddle River, NJ: Prentice Hall, 2007.

Wagner, M. "Net Neutrality Is Too Important to Leave to the Government." *InformationWeek*, March 8, 2007. informationweek.com/blog/main/archives/2007/03/net_neutrality_4.html (accessed April 2009).

Watson, B. "Cool Cash." *Baseline*, October 29, 2007.

Weitzner, D. J., H. Abelson, T. Berners-Lee, J. Feigenbaum, J. A. Hendler, and G. J. Sussman. "Information Accountability." *Communications of the ACM* (June 2008).

Wen, H. J., D. Schwieger, and P. Gershuny. "Internet Usage Monitoring in the Workplace." *Information Systems Management*, January 2007.

Wikipedia. "Network Neutrality." en.wikipedia.org/wiki/Network_neutrality (accessed March 2009).

World Intellectual Property Organization (WIPO). "Splot Alert." *Wilson Quarterly*, 30, no. 4 (Autumn 2006). wipo.int/portal/index.html.en (accessed January 2009).

Wright, B. C. "End of the Road for E-Commerce Patents?" *E-Commerce Times*, May 26, 2008. ecommercetimes.com/story/63107.html (accessed April 2009).

Yamamura, J. H., and F. Grupe. "Ethical Considerations for Providing Professional Services Online." *The CPA Journal* (May 2008).

DYNAMIC TRADING: E-AUCTIONS, BARTERING, AND NEGOTIATIONS

Learning Objectives

Upon completion of this chapter, you will be able to:

1. Define the various types of e-auctions and list their characteristics.
2. Describe forward and reverse auctions.
3. Describe the benefits and limitations of e-auctions.
4. Describe some unique e-auction models.
5. Describe the various services that support e-auctions.
6. Describe bartering and negotiating.
7. Describe the hazards of e-auction fraud and discuss possible countermeasures.
8. Describe e-auction deployment and implementation issues.
9. Analyze mobile auctions and future directions of e-auctions.

Content

A complete version of this chapter is available on the textbook's Web site.

BUILDING E-COMMERCE APPLICATIONS AND INFRASTRUCTURE

Content

Learning Objectives

Upon completion of this chapter, you will be able to:

1. Discuss the major steps in developing an EC system.

2. Describe the major EC development strategies and list their major advantages and disadvantages.

3. List the various EC application development methods along with their benefits and limitations.

4. Discuss various EC application outsourcing options, including application service providers (ASPs), software as a service (SaaS), and utility computing.

5. Discuss the major EC software packages and EC application suites.

6. Discuss the value and technical foundation of Web Services and Web 2.0.

7. Understand service-oriented architecture (SOA) and virtualization and their relationship to EC application development.

8. Describe the criteria used in selecting software vendors and packages.

9. Describe various methods for connecting an EC application to back-end systems and databases.

10. Understand the value and uses of EC application log files.

11. Discuss the importance of usage analysis and site management.

745

A complete version of this chapter is available on the textbook's Web site.

GLOSSARY

acceptable use policy (AUP) Policy that informs users of their responsibilities when using company networks, wireless devices, customer data, and so forth. 510

acceptance testing Determining whether a Web site meets the original business objectives and vision. W18-7

access control Mechanism that determines who can legitimately use a network resource. 493

access log A record kept by a Web server that shows when a user accesses the server; kept in a common log file format, each line of this text file details an individual access. W18-43

active token Small, stand-alone electronic device that generates one-time passwords used in a two-factor authentication system. 494

ad management Methodology and software that enable organizations to perform a variety of activities involved in Web advertising (e.g., tracking viewers, rotating ads). 224

ad views The number of times users call up a page that has a banner on it during a specific period; known as *impressions* or *page views*. 208

Address Verification System (AVS) Detects fraud by comparing the address entered on a Web page with the address information on file with the cardholder's issuing bank. 528

admediaries Third-party vendors that conduct promotions, especially large-scale ones. 223

advanced planning and scheduling (APS) systems Programs that use algorithms to identify optimal solutions to complex planning problems that are bound by constraints. 307

advergaming The practice of using computer games to advertise a product, an organization, or a viewpoint. 216

advertising networks Specialized firms that offer customized Web advertising, such as brokering ads and targeting ads to select groups of consumers. 209

affiliate marketing A marketing arrangement by which an organization refers consumers to the selling company's Web site. 219

agency costs Costs incurred in ensuring that the agent performs tasks as expected (also called *administrative costs*). 649

agility An EC firm's ability to capture, report, and quickly respond to changes happening in the marketplace and business environment. 652

Ajax A Web development technique for creating interactive Web applications. W18-24

angel investor A wealthy individual who contributes personal funds and possibly expertise at the earliest stage of business development. 673

application controls Controls that are intended to protect specific applications. 501

application service provider (ASP) (1) A company that provides business applications to users for a small monthly fee. (2) An agent or vendor who assembles the functions needed by enterprises and packages them with outsourced development, operation, maintenance, and other services. 578, W18-12

Atom RSS Internet standard created by the Internet Engineering Task Force (IETF) and formally known as the Atom Syndication Format. W18-24

attractors Web site features that attract and interact with visitors in the target stakeholder group. 678

auction (1) A competitive process in which a seller solicits consecutive bids from buyers (forward auctions) or a buyer solicits bids from sellers (backward auctions). Prices are determined dynamically by the bids. (2) Market mechanism by which buyers make bids and sellers place offers; characterized by the competitive and dynamic nature by which the final price is reached. 106, W17-3

auction vortals Another name for a vertical auction vertical portal. W17-7

audit An important part of any control system. Auditing can be viewed as an additional layer of controls or safeguards. It is considered as a deterrent to criminal actions especially for insiders. 507

authentication Process to verify (assure) the real identity of an individual, computer, computer program, or EC Web site. 479

authorization (1) Determines whether a buyer's card is active and whether the customer has sufficient funds. (2) Process of determining what the authenticated entity is allowed to access and what operations it is allowed to perform. 479, 526

Automated Clearing House (ACH) Network A nationwide batch-oriented electronic funds transfer system that provides for the interbank clearing of electronic payments for participating financial institutions. 538

availability Assurance that access to data, the Web site, or other EC data service is timely, available, reliable, and restricted to authorized users. 491

avatars Animated computer characters that exhibit humanlike movements and behaviors. 117, W4-32

B2B portals Information portals for businesses. 265

back end The activities that support online order fulfillment, inventory management, purchasing from suppliers, payment processing, packaging, and delivery. 96

back-office operations The activities that support fulfillment of orders, such as packing, delivery, accounting, and logistics. 553

balanced scorecard A management tool that assesses organizational progress toward strategic goals by measuring performance in a number of different areas. 594, W14-7

banking Trojan A Trojan that comes to life when computer owners visit one of a number of online banking or e-commerce sites. 482

banner On a Web page, a graphic advertising display linked to the advertiser's Web page. 210

banner exchanges Markets in which companies can trade or exchange placement of banner ads on each other's Web sites. 211

banner swapping An agreement between two companies to each display the other's banner ad on its Web site. 211

bartering The exchange of goods and services. 110, W17-19

bartering exchange An intermediary that links parties in a barter; a company submits its surplus to the exchange and receives points of credit, which can be used to buy the items that the company needs from other exchange participants. 111, 259

behavioral targeting Targeting that uses information collected about an individual's Web-browsing behavior, such as the pages they have visited or the searches they have made, to select an advertisement to display to that individual. 195

benchmarks An approach to evaluating infrastructure that focuses on *objective* measures of performance. W14-6

best-practice benchmarks Benchmarks that emphasize how information system activities are actually performed rather than on numeric measures of performance. W14-6

bid shielding Having phantom bidders bid at a very high price when an auction begins; they pull out at the last minute, and the real bidder who bid a much lower price wins. W17-23

biometric control An automated method for verifying the identity of a person based on physical or behavioral characteristics. 494

biometric systems Authentication systems that identify a person by measurement of a biological characteristic, such as fingerprints, iris (eye) patterns, facial features, or voice. 494

biometrics An individual's unique physical or behavioral characteristics that can be used to identify an individual precisely (e.g., fingerprints). 206

blog A personal Web site that is open to the public to read and to interact with; dedicated to specific topics or issues. 112

Bluetooth A set of telecommunications standards that enables wireless devices to communicate with each other over short distances. 388

botnet A huge number (e.g., hundreds of thousands) of hijacked Internet computers that have been set up to forward traffic, including spam and viruses, to other computers on the Internet. 484

brick-and-mortar (old economy) organizations Old-economy organizations (corporations) that perform their primary business off-line, selling physical products by means of physical agents. 48

brick-and-mortar retailers Retailers who do business in the non-Internet, physical world in traditional brick-and-mortar stores. 149

build-to-order (pull system) A manufacturing process that starts with an order (usually customized). Once the order is paid for, the vendor starts to fulfill it. 128

bullwhip effect Erratic shifts in order up and down supply chains. 293

bundle trading The selling of several related products and/or services together. W17-18

business case (1) A business plan for a new initiative or large, new project inside an existing organization. (2) A document that justifies the investment of internal, organizational resources in a specific application or project. 595, 672

business continuity plan A plan that keeps the business running after a disaster occurs. Each function in the business should have a valid recovery capability plan. 476

business ethics A form of applied ethics that examines ethical principles and moral or ethical problems that arise in a business environment. 719

business impact analysis (BIA) An exercise that determines the impact of losing the support of an EC resource to an organization and establishes the escalation of that loss over time, identifies the minimum resources needed to recover, and prioritizes the recovery of processes and supporting systems. 510

business intelligence Activities that not only collect and process data, but also make possible analysis that results in useful—intelligent—solutions to business problems. W4-2

business model A method of doing business by which a company can generate revenue to sustain itself. 72

business network A group of people who have some kind of commercial relationship; for example, sellers and buyers, buyers among themselves, buyers and suppliers, and colleagues and other colleagues. 441

business plan A written document that identifies a company's goals and outlines how the company intends to achieve the goals and at what cost. 594, 672

business process management (BPM) Method for business restructuring that combines workflow systems and redesign methods; covers three process categories—people-to-people, systems-to-systems, and systems-to-people interactions. 610, 677

business process reengineering (BPR) A methodology for conducting a comprehensive redesign of an enterprise's processes. 610

business social network A social network whose primary objective is to facilitate business connections and activities. 441

business-to-business (B2B) E-commerce model in which all of the participants are businesses or other organizations. 51

business-to-business e-commerce (B2B EC) Transactions between businesses conducted electronically over the Internet, extranets, intranets, or private networks; also known as eB2B (electronic B2B) or just B2B. 237

business-to-business-to-consumer (B2B2C) E-commerce model in which a business provides some product or service to a client business that maintains its own customers. 51

business-to-consumer (B2C) E-commerce model in which businesses sell to individual shoppers. 51

business-to-employees (B2E) E-commerce model in which an organization delivers services, information, or products to its individual employees. 51

button A small banner that is linked to a Web site; may contain downloadable software. 208

buy-side e-marketplace (1) A corporate-based acquisition site that uses reverse auctions, negotiations, group purchasing, or any other e-procurement method. (2) A private e-marketplace in which one company makes purchases from invited suppliers. 97, 251

Captcha tool Completely Automated Public Turing test to tell Computers and Humans Apart, which uses a verification test on comment pages to stop scripts from posting automatically. 505

card verification number (CVN) Detects fraud by comparing the verification number printed on the signature strip on the back of the card with the information on file with the cardholder's issuing bank. 528

card-not-present (CNP) transaction A credit card transaction in which the merchant does not verify the customer's signature. 694

Cascading Style Sheets (CSS) A standard that uses text files to specify formatting characteristics (styles) for various elements in an HTML document, allowing styles to be controlled and changed easily. WA-14

certificate authorities (CAs) Third parties that issue digital certificates. 498

channel conflict Situation in which an online marketing channel upsets the traditional channels due to real or perceived damage from competition. 174

chatterbots Animation characters that can talk (chat). W4-32

Children's Internet Protection Act (CIPA) Law that mandates the use of filtering technologies in schools and libraries that received certain types of U.S. federal funding. 722

CIA security triad (CIA triad) Three security concepts important to information on the Internet: confidentiality, integrity, and availability. 491

ciphertext A plaintext message after it has been encrypted into a machine-readable form. 495

civil laws Laws that enable a party (individual or organization) that has suffered harm or a loss to bring a lawsuit against who is responsible for the harm or loss. 712

civil litigation An adversarial proceeding in which a party (the plaintiff) sues another party (the defendant) to get compensation for a wrong committed by the defendant. 711

click (click-through or **ad click)** A count made each time a visitor clicks on an advertising banner to access the advertiser's Web site. 208

click fraud Type of fraud that occurs in pay-per-click advertising when a person, automated system, or computer program simulates individual clicks on banner or other online advertising methods. 487

click-and-mortar (click-and-brick) organizations Organizations that conduct some e-commerce activities, usually as an additional marketing channel. 48

click-and-mortar retailers Brick-and-mortar retailers that offer a transactional Web site from which to conduct business. 148

clickstream behavior Customer movements on the Internet. 204

clickstream data Data that occur inside the Web environment; they provide a trail of the user's activities (the user's clickstream behavior) in the Web site. 205

click-through rate The percentage of visitors who are exposed to a banner ad and click on it. 208

click-through ratio The ratio between the number of clicks on a banner ad and the number of times it is seen by viewers; measures the success of a banner in attracting visitors to click on the ad. 208

cloud computing Internet (cloud)-based development coupled with the use of computer technology (computing). W18-36

Collaboration 2.0 The technology and tools used for collaboration in the Web 2.0 world and in Enterprise 2.0 that are in sync with social networking and user-generated content. 323

collaboration hub (c hub) The central point of control for an e-market. A single c-hub, representing one e-market owner, can host multiple collaboration spaces (c-spaces) in which trading partners use c-enablers to exchange data with the c-hub. 301

collaborative commerce (c-commerce) (1) E-commerce model in which individuals or groups communicate or collaborate online. (2) The use of digital technologies that enable companies to collaboratively plan, design, develop, manage, and research products, services, and innovative EC applications. 52, 301

collaborative filtering A market research and personalization method that uses customer data to predict, based on formulas derived from behavioral sciences, what other products or services a customer may enjoy; predictions can be extended to other customers with similar profiles. 195

collaborative planning A business practice that combines the business knowledge and forecasts of multiple players along a supply chain to improve the planning and fulfillment of customer demand. 291

collaborative planning, forecasting, and replenishment (CPFR) Project in which suppliers and retailers collaborate in their planning and demand forecasting to optimize flow of materials along the supply chain. 307

collaborative portals Portals that allow collaboration. 313

collaborative Web site A site that allows business partners to collaborate. 678

collaborative workspace An interconnected environment in which all the participants in dispersed locations can access and interact with each other just as inside a single entity. 323

common law (case law) Law created by judges in court decisions. 715

company-centric EC E-commerce that focuses on a single company's buying needs (many-to-one, or buy-side) or selling needs (one-to-many, or sell-side). 238

competitor analysis grid A strategic planning tool that highlights points of differentiation between competitors and the target firm. 593

compliance data Pertaining to enterprise included in the law that can be used for the purpose of implementing or validating compliance. 712

Computer Fraud and Abuse Act (CFAA) Major computer crime law to protect government computers and other Internet-connected computers. 731

Computing Technology Industry Association (CompTIA) Nonprofit trade group providing information security research and best practices. 512

confidentiality Assurance of data privacy and accuracy. Keeping private or sensitive information from being disclosed to unauthorized individuals, entities, or processes. 491

consortium trading exchange (CTE) An exchange formed and operated by a group of major companies in an industry to provide industry-wide transaction services. 268

consumer-to-business (C2B) E-commerce model in which individuals use the Internet to sell products or services to organizations or individuals who seek sellers to bid on products or services they need. 51

consumer-to-consumer (C2C) E-commerce model in which consumers sell directly to other consumers. 51, 371

contact card A smart card containing a small gold plate on the face that when inserted in a smart card reader makes contact and passes data to and from the embedded microchip. 530

contactless (proximity) card A smart card with an embedded antenna, by means of which data and applications are passed to and from a card reader unit or other device without contact between the card and the card reader. 530

content The text, images, sound, and video that make up a Web page. 682

content management The process of adding, revising, and removing content from a Web site to keep content fresh, accurate, compelling, and credible. 685

Controlling the Assault of Non-Solicited Pornography and Marketing (CAN-SPAM) Act Law that makes it a crime to send commercial e-mail messages with false or misleading message headers or misleading subject lines. 505

conversion rate The percentage of clickers who actually make a purchase. 208

cookie A data file that is placed on a user's hard drive by a remote Web server, frequently without disclosure or the user's consent, which collects information about the user's activities at a site. 194

co-opetition Two or more companies cooperate together on some activities for their mutual benefit, even while competing against each other in the marketplace. 610

copyright An exclusive right of the author or creator of a book, movie, musical composition, or other artistic property to print, copy, sell, license, distribute, transform to another medium, translate, record, perform, or otherwise use. 713

corporate (business) performance management (CPM, BPM) Advanced performance measuring and analysis approach that embraces planning and strategy. 612

corporate (enterprise) portal (1) A major gateway through which employees, business partners, and the public can enter a corporate Web site. (2) A gateway for entering a corporate Web site, enabling communication, collaboration, and access to company information. 63, 310

cost–benefit analysis A comparison of the costs of a project against the benefits. 630

CPM (cost per thousand impressions) The fee an advertiser pays for each 1,000 times a page with a banner ad is shown. 208

cracker A malicious hacker, who may represent a serious problem for a corporation. 478

crime Offensive act against society that violates a law and is punishable by the government. 712

criminal laws Laws to protect the public, human life, or private property. 712

cross-selling Offering similar or complementary products and services to increase sales. 683

CSI Computer Crime and Security Survey Annual security survey of U.S. corporations, government agencies, financial and medical institutions, and universities conducted by the Computer Security Institute. 471

customization Creation of a product or service according to the buyer's specifications. 121

cyberbashing Domain name that criticizes an organization or person. 716

cybercrime Intentional crimes carried out on the Internet. 476

cybercriminal A person who intentionally carries out crimes over the Internet. 478

cybermediation (electronic intermediation) The use of software (intelligent) agents to facilitate intermediation. 174

data conferencing Virtual meeting in which geographically dispersed groups work on documents together and exchange computer files during videoconferences. 319

Data Encryption Standard (DES) The standard symmetric encryption algorithm supported by the NIST and used by U.S. government agencies until October 2000. 496

data mart A small data warehouse designed for a strategic business unit (SBU) or department. W4-4

data mining The process of searching a large database to discover previously unknown patterns; automates the process of finding predictive information. W4-7

data warehouse (DW) A single, server-based data repository that allows centralized analysis, security, and control over data. W4-2

demilitarized zone (DMZ) Network area that sits between an organization's internal network and an external network (Internet), providing physical isolation between the two networks that is controlled by rules enforced by a firewall. 499

denial of service (DOS) attack An attack on a Web site in which an attacker uses specialized software to send a flood of data packets to the target computer with the aim of overloading its resources. 483

desktop purchasing Direct purchasing from internal marketplaces without the approval of supervisors and without the intervention of a procurement department. 257

desktop search Search tools that search the contents of a user's or organization's computer files, rather than searching the Internet. The emphasis is on finding all the information that is available on the user's PC, including Web browser histories, e-mail archives, and word-processed documents, as well as in all internal files and databases. 105

detection measures Ways to determine whether intruders attempted to break into the EC system; whether they were successful; and what they may have done. 480

deterring measures Actions that will make criminals abandon their idea of attacking a specific system (e.g., the possibility of losing a job for insiders). 480

differentiation Providing a product or service that is unique. 120

digital divide Refers to the gap between people with effective access to digital and information technology and those without. 394, 733

digital economy An economy that is based on digital technologies, including digital communication networks, computers, software, and other related information technologies; also called the *Internet economy*, the *new economy*, or the *Web economy*. 62

digital enterprise A new business model that uses IT in a fundamental way to accomplish one or more of three basic objectives: reach and engage customers more effectively, boost employee productivity, and improve operating efficiency. It uses converged communication and computing technology in a way that improves business processes. 62

digital envelope The combination of the encrypted original message and the digital signature, using the recipient's public key. 498

digital options A set of IT-enabled capabilities in the form of digitized enterprise work processes and knowledge systems. 658

digital products Goods that can be transformed to digital format and delivered over the Internet. 96

digital rights management (DRM) An umbrella term for any of several arrangements that allow a vendor of content in electronic form to control the material and restrict its usage. 714

digital signature or **digital certificate** Validates the sender and time stamp of a transaction so it cannot be later claimed that the transaction was unauthorized or invalid. 497

direct marketing Broadly, marketing that takes place without intermediaries between manufacturers and buyers; in the context of this book, marketing done online between any seller and buyer. 148

direct materials Materials used in the production of a product (e.g., steel in a car or paper in a book). 240

disaster avoidance An approach oriented toward prevention. The idea is to minimize the chance of avoidable disasters (such as fire or other human-caused threats). 507

disintermediation (1) Elimination of intermediaries between sellers and buyers. (2) The removal of organizations or business process layers responsible for certain intermediary steps in a given supply chain. 128, 173

disruptors Companies that introduce a significant change in their industries, thus causing a disruption in normal business operations. 429

distance learning Formal education that takes place off campus, usually, but not always, through online resources. 352

document type definition (DTD) In XML, a file that defines the tags that are allowed and the manner in which they can be used; basically, a set of grammar rules for the tags in a particular document. WA-16

domain name A name-based address that identifies an Internet-connected server. Usually it refers to the portion of the address to the left of .com and .org, etc. 681

Domain Name System (DNS) (1) A hierarchical naming system for computers, services, or any resource participating in the Internet; it is like a directory. (2) Translates (converts) domain names to their numeric IP addresses. 474, 682

double auction Auction in which multiple buyers and sellers may be making bids and offers simultaneously; buyers and their bidding prices and sellers and their asking prices are matched, considering the quantities on both sides. 109, W17-18

due process A guarantee of basic fairness and fair procedures in legal action. 710

duty Legal obligation imposed on individuals and organizations that prevents them from interfering with another's protected interest or right. 710

dynamic pricing Fluctuating prices that are determined based on supply and demand relationships at any given time. 108, 262, W17-4

dynamic Web content Content that must be kept up-to-date. 683

e-bartering (electronic bartering) Bartering conducted online, usually in a bartering exchange. 110

e-book A book in digital form that can be read on a computer screen or on a special device. 360

e-business A broader definition of EC that includes not just the buying and selling of goods and services, but also servicing customers, collaborating with business partners, and conducting electronic transactions within an organization. 47

EC architecture A plan for organizing the underlying infrastructure and applications of a site. W18-5

EC security programs All the policies, procedures, documents, standards, hardware, software, training, and personnel that work together to protect information, the ability to conduct business, and other assets. 493

EC security strategy A strategy that views EC security as the process of preventing and detecting unauthorized use of the organization's brand, identity, Web site, e-mail, information, or other asset and attempts to defraud the organization, its customers, and employees. 479

EC suite A type of merchant server software that consists of an integrated collection of a large number of EC tools and components that work together for EC applications development. W18-31

e-check A legally valid electronic version or representation of a paper check. 536

e-commerce (EC) risk The likelihood that a negative outcome will occur in the course of developing and operating an electronic commerce strategy. 604

e-commerce strategy (e-strategy) The formulation and execution of a vision of how a new or existing company intends to do business electronically. 589

e-democracy (cyberdemocracy, digital democracy) The use of EC and electronic communications technologies such as the Internet in enhancing democratic processes within a democratic country. 338

e-distributor An e-commerce intermediary that connects manufacturers with business buyers (customers) by aggregating the catalogs of many manufacturers in one place—the intermediary's Web site. 102

edutainment The combination of education and entertainment, often through games. 354

e-government E-commerce model in which a government entity buys or provides goods, services, or information from or to businesses or individual citizens. 53, 338

e-grocer A grocer that takes orders online and provides deliveries on a daily or other regular schedule or within a very short period of time. 166

e-learning The online delivery of information for purposes of education, training, or knowledge management. 53, 347

electronic auctions (e-auctions) Auctions conducted online. 107, W17-3

electronic (online) banking or **e-banking** Various banking activities conducted from home or the road using an Internet connection; also known as cyberbanking, virtual banking, online banking, and home banking. 162

electronic bartering (e-bartering) Bartering conducted online, usually by a bartering exchange. W17-19

electronic catalogs (e-catalogs) (1) The virtual-world equivalent of a traditional product catalog; contains product descriptions and photos, along with information about various promotions, discounts, payment methods, and methods of delivery. (2) The presentation of product information in an electronic form; the backbone of most e-selling sites. 102, W18-30

electronic commerce (EC) The process of buying, selling, or exchanging products, services, or information via computer. 46

electronic discovery (e-discovery) Discovery in civil litigation that deals with information in electronic format; also referred to as *electronically stored information* (ESI). 733

electronic market (e-marketplace) An online marketplace where buyers and sellers meet to exchange goods, services, money, or information. 48

electronic product code (EPC) A product identification standard that specifies the manufacturer, producer, version, and serial number of each (product) item. 412

Electronic Product Environmental Assessment Tool (EPEAT) A searchable database of computer hardware that meets a strict set of environmental criteria. 735

electronic retailing (e-tailing) Retailing conducted online, over the Internet. 143

electronic shopping cart An order-processing technology that allows customers to accumulate items they wish to buy while they continue to shop. 105

electronic signature A generic, technology-neutral term that refers to the various methods by which one can "sign" an electronic record. 732

e-logistics The logistics of EC systems, typically involving small parcels sent to many customers' homes (in B2C). 553

e-loyalty Customer loyalty to an e-tailer or loyalty programs delivered online or supported electronically. 197

e-mail spam A subset of spam that involves nearly identical messages sent to numerous recipients by e-mail. 488

e-mall (online mall) An online shopping center where many online stores are located. 98

e-marketplace An online market, usually B2B, in which buyers and sellers exchange goods or services; the three types of e-marketplaces are private, public, and consortia. 95

e-micropayments Small online payments, typically under $10. 535

encryption The process of scrambling (encrypting) a message in such a way that it is difficult, expensive, or time-consuming for an unauthorized person to unscramble (decrypt) it. 495

encryption algorithm The mathematical formula used to encrypt the plaintext into the ciphertext, and vice versa. 495

e-newsletter A collection of short, informative articles sent at regular intervals by e-mail to individuals who have an interest in the newsletter's topic. 685

Enterprise 2.0 Technologies and business practices that free the workforce from the constraints of legacy communication and productivity tools such as e-mail. Provides business managers with access to the right information at the right time through a Web of interconnected applications, services, and devices. 445

enterprise application integration (EAI) Class of software that integrates large systems. W18-9

enterprise invoice presentment and payment (EIPP) Presenting and paying B2B invoices online. 540

enterprise-oriented networks Social networks whose primary objective is to facilitate business. 59

enterprise resource planning (ERP) An enterprisewide information system designed to coordinate all the resources, information, and activities needed to complete business processes such as order fulfillment or billing. 568

enterprise search The practice of identifying and enabling specific content across the enterprise to be indexed, searched, and displayed to authorized users. 104

e-procurement The use of Web-based technology to support the key procurement processes, including requisitioning, sourcing, contracting, ordering, and payment. E-procurement supports the purchase of both direct and indirect materials and employs several Web-based functions such as online catalogs, contracts, purchase orders, and shipping notices. 253, 290

e-sourcing The process and tools that electronically enable any activity in the sourcing process, such as quotation/tender submittance and response, e-auctions, online negotiations, and spending analyses. W5-12

e-supply chain A supply chain that is managed electronically, usually with Web technologies. 288

e-supply chain management (e-SCM) The collaborative use of technology to improve the operations of supply chain activities as well as the management of supply chains. 289

e-tailers Retailers who sell over the Internet. 143

e-tailing Online retailing, usually B2C. 51

ethics The branch of philosophy that deals with what is considered to be right and wrong. 76, 718

exchanges (trading communities or **trading exchanges)** Many-to-many e-marketplaces, usually owned and run by a third party or a consortium, in which many buyers and many sellers meet electronically to trade with each other. 238

expert location systems (ELS) Interactive computerized systems that help employees find and connect with colleagues who have expertise required for specific problems—whether they are across the country or across the room—in order to solve specific, critical business problems in seconds. 368

exposure The estimated cost, loss, or damage that can result if a threat exploits a vulnerability. 476

eXtensible Markup Language (XML) An open standard for defining data elements. Like HTML, it uses a set of tags along with content (or values), but, unlike HTML, the tags are defined by the Web designer (i.e., there are no fixed tags). WA-15

eXtensible Style Language Transformations (XSLT) A special type of style sheet defines how the contents of an XML document are to be displayed. WA-17

extranet A network that uses a virtual private network to link intranets in different locations over the Internet; an "extended intranet." 49, W5-2

fair use The legal use of copyrighted material for noncommercial purposes without paying royalties or getting permission. 715

firewall A single point between two or more networks where all traffic must pass (choke point); the device authenticates, controls, and logs all traffic. 499

folksonomy (collaborative tagging, social classification, social indexing, social tagging) The practice and method of collaboratively creating, classifying, and managing tags to annotate and categorize content. 116

forward auction An auction in which a seller entertains bids from buyers. Bidders increase price sequentially. 108, W17-4

fraud Any business activity that uses deceitful practices or devices to deprive another of property or other rights. 476

front end The portion of an e-seller's business processes through which customers interact, including the seller's portal, electronic catalogs, a shopping cart, a search engine, and a payment gateway. 96

front-office operations The business processes, such as sales and advertising, which are visible to customers. 553

general controls Controls established to protect the system regardless of the specific application. For example, protecting hardware and controlling access to the data center are independent of the specific application. 501

geographical information system (GIS) A computer system capable of integrating, storing, editing, analyzing, sharing, and displaying geographically-referenced (spatial) information. 404

global positioning system (GPS) A worldwide satellite-based tracking system that enables users to determine their position anywhere on the earth. 403

government-to-business (G2B) E-government category that includes interactions between governments and businesses (government selling to businesses and providing them with services and businesses selling products and services to government). 342

government-to-citizens (G2C) E-government category that includes all the interactions between a government and its citizens. 338

government-to-employees (G2E) E-government category that includes activities and services between government units and their employees. 343

government-to-government (G2G) E-government category that includes activities within government units and those between governments. 343

Green computing The study and practice of eco-friendly computing resources; is now a key concern of businesses in all industries—not just environmental organizations. 733

Green IT Green IT begins with manufacturers producing environmentally friendly products and encouraging IT departments to consider more friendly options like virtualization, power management, and proper recycling habits. 733

group decision support system (GDSS) An interactive computer-based system that facilitates the solution of semi-structured and unstructured problems by a group of decision makers. 317

group purchasing The aggregation of orders from several buyers into volume purchases so that better prices can be negotiated. 258

groupware Software products that support groups of people who share common tasks or goals and collaborate on their accomplishment. 315

hacker Someone who gains unauthorized access to a computer system. 478

hash A mathematical computation that is applied to a message, using a private key, to encrypt the message. 497

hit A request for data from a Web page or file. 208

honeynet (1) A network of honeypots. 501

honeypot Production system (e.g., firewalls, routers, Web servers, database servers) that looks like it does real work, but that acts as a decoy and is watched to study how network intrusions occur. 501

horizontal marketplaces Markets that concentrate on a service, material, or a product that is used in all types of industries (e.g., office supplies, PCs). 240

Hypertext Markup Language (HTML) The language used to create Web pages. WA-2

identity theft Fraud that involves stealing an identity of a person and then the use of that identity by someone pretending to be someone else in order to steal money or get other benefits. 487

incubator A company, university, or nonprofit organization that supports businesses in their initial stages of development. 673

indirect materials Materials used to support production (e.g., office supplies or lightbulbs). 240

infomediaries Electronic intermediaries that provide and/or control information flow in cyberspace, often aggregating information and selling it to others. 100

information architecture How the site and its Web pages are organized, labeled, and navigated to support browsing and searching throughout the Web site. 690

information assurance (IA) The protection of information systems against unauthorized access to or modification of information whether in storage, processing, or transit, and against the denial of service to authorized users, including those measures necessary to detect, document, and counter such threats. 480

information economics An approach similar to the concept of critical success factors in that it focuses on key organizational objectives, including intangible financial benefits, impacts on the business domain, and impacts on IT itself. W14-5

information portals Portals that store data and enable users to navigate and query these data. 313

information visibility The process of sharing critical data required to manage the flow of products, services, and information in real time between suppliers and customers. 290

informational Web site A Web site that does little more than provide information about the business and its products and services. 678

infringement Use of a work without permission or contracting for payment of a royalty. 713

insourcing In-house development of applications. W18-8

instant messaging Technologies that create the possibility of real-time text-based communication between two or more participants over the Internet/intranet. 323

integration testing Testing the combination of application modules acting in concert. W18-7

integrity Assurance that stored data has not been modified without authorization; a message that was sent is the same message that was received. 491

intellectual property Creations of the mind, such as inventions, literary and artistic works, and symbols, names, images, and designs, used in commerce. 709

intellectual property law Area of the law that includes patent law, copyright law, trademark law, trade secret law, and other branches of the law such as licensing and unfair competition. 713

intelligent agent (IA) (1) An autonomous entity that perceives its environment via sensors, and acts upon that environment directing its activity toward achieving a goal(s) (i.e., acting rationally) using its actuators. (2) Software applications that have some degree of reactivity, autonomy, and adaptability—as is needed in unpredictable attack situations. An agent is able to adapt itself based on changes occurring in its environment. 503, 570

interactive marketing Online marketing, facilitated by the Internet, by which marketers and advertisers can interact directly with customers, and consumers can interact with advertisers/vendors. 207

interactive voice response (IVR) A voice system that enables users to request and receive information and to enter and change data through a telephone to a computerized system. 388

interactive Web site A Web site that provides opportunities for the customers and the business to communicate and share information. 678

intermediary A third party that operates between sellers and buyers. 96

internal control environment The work atmosphere that a company sets for its employees. 504

internal procurement marketplace The aggregated catalogs of all approved suppliers combined into a single internal electronic catalog. 257

Internet radio A Web site that provides music, talk, and other entertainment, both live and stored, from a variety of radio stations. 225

Internet underground economy E-markets for stolen information made up of thousands of Web sites that sell credit card numbers, social security numbers, other data such as numbers of bank accounts, social network IDs, passwords, and much more. 474

interoperability Connecting people, data, and diverse systems; the term can be defined in a technical way or in a broad way, taking into account social, political, and organizational factors. W18-8

interorganizational information systems (IOSs) Communications systems that allow routine transaction processing and information flow between two or more organizations. 48

intrabusiness EC E-commerce category that includes all internal organizational activities that involve the exchange of goods, services, or information among various units and individuals in an organization. 51

intranet An internal corporate or government network that uses Internet tools, such as Web browsers, and Internet protocols. 49

intraorganizational information systems Communication systems that enable e-commerce activities to go on within individual organizations. 48

intrusion detection system (IDS) A special category of software that can monitor activity across a network or on a host computer, watch for suspicious activity, and take automated action based on what it sees. 500

IP address An address that uniquely identifies each computer connected to a network or the Internet. 474

ISP hosting service A hosting service that provides an independent, stand-alone Web site for small and medium-sized businesses. 681

key (key value) The secret code used to encrypt and decrypt a message. 495

key performance indicators (KPIs) The quantitative expression of critically important metrics. 632

key space The large number of possible key values (keys) created by the algorithm to use when transforming the message. 495

keystroke logging (keylogging) A method of capturing and recording user keystrokes. 475

keyword banners Banner ads that appear when a predetermined word is queried from a search engine. 210

knowledge discovery in databases (KDD)/knowledge discovery (KD) The process of extracting useful knowledge from volumes of data. W4-5

knowledge management (KM) The process of capturing or creating knowledge, storing it, updating it constantly, disseminating it, and using it whenever necessary. 363

knowledge portal A single point of access software system intended to provide timely access to information and to support communities of knowledge workers. 367

latency The time required to complete an operation, such as downloading a Web page. W18-22

learning agents Software agents that have the capacity to adapt or modify their behavior—that is, to learn. 572

legal precedent A judicial decision that may be used as a standard in subsequent similar cases. 722

letter of credit (L/C) A written agreement by a bank to pay the seller, on account of the buyer, a sum of money upon presentation of certain documents. 542

localization The process of converting media products developed in one environment (e.g., country) to a form culturally and linguistically acceptable in countries outside the original target market. 224

location-based m-commerce (l-commerce) Delivery of m-commerce transactions to individuals in a specific location, at a specific time. 402

logistics The operations involved in the efficient and effective flow and storage of goods, services, and related information from point of origin to point of consumption. 553

macro virus (macro worm) A macro virus or macro worm is executed when the application object that contains the macro is opened or a particular procedure is executed. 481

malware (malicious software) A generic term for malicious software. 476

management by maxim A 5-step process that brings together corporate executives, business-unit managers, and IT executives in planning sessions to determine appropriate infrastructure investments. W14-7

market segmentation The process of dividing a consumer market into logical groups for conducting marketing research and analyzing personal information. 192

marketspace A marketplace in which sellers and buyers exchange goods and services for money (or for other goods and services), but do so electronically. 95

mashup Combination of two or more Web sites into a single Web site that provides the content of both sites (whole or partial) to deliver a novel product to consumers. W18-21

mass customization A method that enables manufacturers to create specific products for each customer based on the customer's exact needs. 128

maverick buying Unplanned purchases of items needed quickly, often at non-pre-negotiated higher prices. 253

merchant brokering Deciding from whom (from what merchant) to buy a product. 189

merchant server software Software for selling over the Internet that enables companies to establish selling sites relatively easily and inexpensively. W18-30

merge-in-transit Logistics model in which components for a product may come from two (or more) different physical locations and are shipped directly to the customer's location. 566

message digest (MD) A summary of a message, converted into a string of digits after the hash has been applied. 497

metadata Data about data, including software programs about data, rules for organizing data, and data summaries. W4-2

metric A specific, measurable standard against which actual performance is compared. 611, 631

metric benchmarks A method that provides numeric measures of performance. W14-6

micro-blogging A form of blogging that allows users to write messages (usually up to 140 characters) and publish them, either to be viewed by anyone or by a restricted group that can be chosen by the user. These messages can be submitted by a variety of means, including text messaging, instant messaging, e-mail, MP3, or just on the Web. 114

microfinance Refers to the provision of financial services to poor or low-income clients, including consumers and the self-employed. 394

middleware Separate products that serve as the glue between two applications; sometimes called plumbing because it connects two sides of an application and passes data between them. W18-42

mirror site An exact duplicate of an original Web site that is physically located on a Web server on another continent or in another country. 681

mobile advertising Ads sent to and presented on mobile devices. 221

mobile agents Software agents that move to other systems, performing tasks there. A *mobile agent* can transport itself across different system architectures and platforms. 572

mobile commerce (m-commerce, m-business) Any business activity conducted over a wireless telecommunications network or from mobile devices. 383

mobile entertainment Any type of leisure activity that utilizes wireless telecommunication networks, interacts with service providers, and incurs a cost upon usage. 399

mobile government (m-government) The wireless implementation of e-government mostly to citizens but also to business. 347

mobile instant messaging Messaging service that transposes the desktop messaging experience to the usage scenario of being on the move. 324

mobile portals Portals accessible via mobile devices, especially cell phones and PDAs. 100, 313

mobile social networking Members converse and connect with one another using cell phones or other mobile devices. 437

mobile worker Any employee who is away from their primary work space at least 10 hours a week or 25 percent of the time. 396

mobility The degree to which the agents themselves travel over the network. Some agents are very mobile; others are not. 572

MRO (maintenance, repair, and operation) Indirect materials used in activities that support production. 240

multiagent systems (MASs) Computer systems in which there is no single designer who stands behind all the agents; each agent in the system can be working toward different, even contradictory, goals. 573

multichannel business model A business model where a company sells in multiple marketing channels simultaneously (e.g., both physical and online stores). 149

multimedia messaging service (MMS) The emerging generation of wireless messaging; MMS is able to deliver rich media. 387

multi-tiered application architecture EC architecture consisting of four tiers: Web browsers, Web servers, application servers, and database servers. W18-41

"name-your-own price" model Auction model in which would-be buyers specify the price (and other terms) they are willing to pay to any willing seller; a C2B model pioneered by Priceline.com. 109, W17-6

network-based positioning Relies on base stations to find the location of a mobile device sending a signal or sensed by the network. 403

nonrepudiation Assurance that online customers or trading partners cannot falsely deny (repudiate) their purchase or transaction. 479

on-demand delivery service Express delivery made fairly quickly after an online order is received. 166

one-to-one marketing (relationship marketing) Marketing that treats each customer in a unique way. 192

online analytical processing (OLAP) End-user analytical activities, such as DSS modeling using spreadsheets and graphics, that are done online. W4-6

online intermediary An online third party that brokers a transaction online between a buyer and a seller; may be virtual or click-and-mortar. 239

online negotiation A back-and-forth process of bargaining until a buyer and seller reach a mutually agreeable price. W17-20

online publishing The electronic delivery of newspapers, magazines, books, news, music, videos, and other digitizable information over the Internet. 359

operational data store A database for use in transaction processing (operational) systems that uses data warehouse concepts to provide clean data. W4-4

opt-in Agreement that requires computer users to take specific steps to allow the collection of personal information. 721

opt-out Business practice that gives consumers the opportunity to refuse sharing information about themselves. 721

order fulfillment All the activities needed to provide customers with their ordered goods and services, including related customer services. 553

outsourcing (1) A method of transferring the management and/or day-to-day execution of an entire business function to a third-party service provider. (2)The use of an external vendor to provide all or part of the products and services that could be provided internally. 608, W18-9

packet Segment of data sent from one computer to another on a network. 499

page An HTML (Hypertext Markup Language) document that may contain text, images, and other online elements, such as Java applets and multimedia files; may be generated statically or dynamically. 208

partner relationship management (PRM) Business strategy that focuses on providing comprehensive quality service to business partners. 271

passive token Storage device (e.g., magnetic strip) that contains a secret code used in a two-factor authentication system. 494

patent A document that grants the holder exclusive rights to an invention for a fixed number of years. 715

payment card Electronic card that contains information that can be used for payment purposes. 526

payment service provider (PSP) A third-party service connecting a merchant's EC system to the appropriate acquiring bank or financial institution. PSPs must be registered with the various card associations they support. 526

peer-to-peer (P2P) Applications that use direct communications between computers (peers) to share resources, rather than relying on a centralized server as the conduit between client devices. 373

penetration test (pen test) A method of evaluating the security of a computer system or a network by simulating an attack from a malicious source, (e.g., a cracker). 501

permission advertising (permission marketing) Advertising (marketing) strategy in which customers agree to accept advertising and marketing materials (known as *opt-in*). 222

personal area network (PAN) A wireless telecommunications network for device-to-device connections within a very short range. 388

personal digital assistant (PDA) A stand-alone handheld computer principally used for personal information management. 386

personal firewall A network node designed to protect an individual user's desktop system from the public network by monitoring all the traffic that passes through the computer's network interface card. 499

personalization (1) The ability to tailor a product, service, or Web content to specific user preferences. (2) The matching of services, products, and advertising content with individual consumers and their preferences. 121, 194

personalized content Web content that matches the needs and expectations of the individual visitor. 685

person-to-person lending Lending done between individuals circumventing the bank traditional role in this process. W9-1

pervasive computing Invisible, everywhere computing; it is computing capabilities being embedded into the objects around us. 409

phishing A crimeware technique to steal the identity of a target company to get the identities of its customers. 476

plaintext An unencrypted message in human-readable form. 495

Platform for Privacy Preferences Project (P3P) A protocol allowing Web sites to declare their intended use of information they collect about browsing users. 727

podcast A media file that is distributed over the Internet using syndication feeds for playback on mobile devices and personal computers. As with the term *radio*, it can mean both the content and the method of syndication. A collection of audio files in MP3 format. 360, W15-4

policy-based resource management tools Automate and standardize all types of IT management best practices, from initial configuration to ongoing fault management and asset tracking. W18-12

policy-based service-level management tools Coordinate, monitor, and report on the ways in which multiple infrastructure components come together to deliver a business service. W18-12

pop-under ad An ad that appears underneath the current browser window, so when the user closes the active window the ad is still on the screen. 211

pop-up ad An ad that appears in a separate window before, after, or during Internet surfing or when reading e-mail. 211

presence information Status indicator that conveys ability and willingness of a potential communication partner. 324

prevention measures Ways to help stop unauthorized users (also known as "intruders") from accessing any part of the EC system. 480

privacy The right to be left alone and free of unreasonable personal intrusions. 718

private key Encryption code that is known only to its owner. 496

procurement The process made up of a range of activities by which an organization obtains or gains access to the resources (materials, skills, capabilities, facilities) they require to undertake their core business activities. 289

procurement management The planning, organizing, and coordinating of all the activities relating to purchasing goods and services needed to accomplish the organization's mission. 252

product brokering Deciding what product to buy. 189

product differentiation Special features available in products that make them distinguishable from other products. This property attracts customers that appreciate what they consider an added value. 652

product lifecycle management (PLM) Business strategy that enables manufacturers to control and share product-related data as part of product design and development efforts. 308

production function An equation indicating that for the same quantity of production, Q, companies either can use a certain amount of labor or invest in more automation. 649

project champion The person who ensures the EC project gets the time, attention, and resources required and defends the project from detractors at all times. 607

protected interests Interests, such as life, liberty, and property, which a national constitution protects. 710

protocol tunneling Method used to ensure confidentiality and integrity of data transmitted over the Internet by encrypting data packets, sending them in packets across the Internet, and decrypting them at the destination address. 500

proxy bidding Use of a software system to place bids on behalf of buyers; when another bidder places a bid, the software (the proxy) will automatically raise the bid to the next level until it reaches the buyer's predetermined maximum price. W17-16

public (asymmetric) key encryption Method of encryption that uses a pair of matched keys—a public key to encrypt a message and a private key to decrypt it, or vice versa. 496

public e-marketplaces Third-party exchanges open to all interested parties (sellers and buyers). 238

public key Encryption code that is publicly available to anyone. 496

public key infrastructure (PKI) A scheme for securing e-payments using public key encryption and various technical components. 496

purchasing cards (p-cards) Special-purpose payment cards issued to a company's employees to be used solely for purchasing nonstrategic materials and services up to a preset dollar limit. 541

radio frequency identification (RFID) (1) A short-range radio frequency communication technology for remotely storing and retrieving data using devices called RFID tags and RFID readers. (2) Tags that can be attached to or embedded in objects, animals, or humans and use radio waves to communicate with a reader for the purpose of uniquely identifying the object or transmitting data and/or storing information about the object. 295, 410

random banners Banner ads that appear at random, not as the result of the user's action. 210

Really Simple Syndication (RSS) A family of Web-feed formats used to publish frequently updated digital content. W18-24

regulatory compliance Systems or departments in an organization whose job is to ensure that personnel are aware of and take steps to comply with relevant laws, standards, policies, and regulations. 711

reintermediation The process whereby intermediaries (either new ones or those that had been disintermediated) take on new intermediary roles. 174

Representational State Transfer (REST) Refers to a collection of architectural principles. W18-20

request for quote (RFQ) The "invitation" to participate in a tendering (bidding) system. 255, W18-39

request for proposal (RFP) Notice sent to potential vendors inviting them to submit a proposal describing their software package and how it would meet the company's needs. W18-39

resident agents Software agents that stay in the computer or system and perform their tasks. 572

reusability The likelihood a segment of source code can be used again to add new functionalities with slight or no modification. W18-8

reverse auction (bidding or **tendering system)** Auction in which the buyer places an item for bid (tender) on a request for quote (RFQ) system, potential suppliers bid on the job, with the price reducing sequentially, and the lowest bid wins; primarily a B2B or G2B mechanism. 108, W17-6

reverse logistics The movement of returns from customers to vendors. 555

right Legal claim that others not interfere with an individual's or organization's protected interest. 710

risk The probability that a vulnerability will be known and used. 476

ROI calculator Calculator that uses metrics and formulas to compute ROI. 640

rolling warehouse Logistics method in which products on the delivery truck are not preassigned to a destination, but the decision about the quantity to unload at each destination is made at the time of unloading. 567

RSS An XML format for syndicating and sharing Web content. W15-4

RuBee Bidirectional, on-demand, peer-to-peer radiating transceiver protocol under development by the Institute of Electrical and Electronics Engineers. 300

scalability How big a system can grow in various dimensions to provide more service; measured by total number of users, number of simultaneous users, or transaction volume. W18-6

scenario planning A strategic planning methodology that generates plausible alternative futures to help decision makers identify actions that can be taken today to ensure success in the future. 594

scoring methodology A method that evaluates alternatives by assigning weights and scores to various aspects and then calculating the weighted totals. W14-5

screen-sharing software Software that enables group members, even in different locations, to work on the same document, which is shown on the PC screen of each participant. 319

sealed-bid auction Auction in which each bidder bids only once; a silent auction, in which bidders do not know who is placing bids or what the bid prices are. W17-5

search engine A computer program that can access databases of Internet resources, search for specific information or keywords, and report the results. 105

search engine optimization (SEO) (1) The application of strategies intended to position a Web site at the top of Web search engines. (2) The craft of increasing site rank on search engines; the optimizer uses the ranking algorithm of the search engine (which may be different for different search engines) and best search phases, and tailors the ad accordingly. 213, 695

search engine spam Pages created deliberately to trick the search engine into offering inappropriate, redundant, or poor-quality search results. 488

Secure Socket Layer (SSL) Protocol that utilizes standard certificates for authentication and data encryption to ensure privacy or confidentiality. 498

self-hosting When a business acquires the hardware, software, staff, and dedicated telecommunications services necessary to set up and manage its own Web site. 681

sell-side e-marketplace (1) A private e-marketplace in which one company sells either standard and/or customized products to qualified companies. (2) A Web-based marketplace in which one company sells to many business buyers from e-catalogs or auctions, frequently over an extranet. 97, 243

Semantic Web An evolving extension of the Web in which Web content can be expressed not only in natural language, but also in a form that can be understood, interpreted, and used by intelligent computer software agents, permitting them to find, share, and integrate information more easily. 459

sensor network A collection of nodes, sometimes as small as millimeters in length or diameter, capable of environmental sensing, local computation, and communication with its peers or with other higher performance nodes. 413

service-level agreement (SLA) A formal agreement regarding the division of work between a company and a vendor. W18-40

service-oriented architecture (SOA) An application architecture in which executable components, such as Web Services, can be invoked and executed by client programs based on business rules. W18-20

settlement Transferring money from the buyer's to the merchant's account. 526

shopping portals Gateways to e-storefronts and e-malls; may be comprehensive or niche oriented. 170

shopping robots (shopping agents or **shopbots)** Tools that scout the Web on behalf of consumers who specify search criteria. 170

short message service (SMS) A service that supports the sending and receiving of short text messages on mobile phones. 387

signature file A simple text message an e-mail program automatically adds to outgoing messages. 695

single auction Auction in which at least one side of the market consists of a single entity (a single buyer or a single seller). W17-18

site navigation Aids that help visitors find the information they need quickly and easily. 691

smart card An electronic card containing an embedded microchip that enables predefined operations or the addition, deletion, or manipulation of information on the card. 529

smart card operating system Special system that handles file management, security, input/output (I/O), and command execution and provides an application programming interface (API) for a smart card. 530

smart card reader Activates and reads the contents of the chip on a smart card, usually passing the information on to a host system. 530

smartphone A mobile phone with PC-like capabilities. 387

sniping Entering a bid during the very last seconds of an auction and outbidding the highest bidder. W17-16

social bookmarking A Web Service for sharing Internet bookmarks. It is a popular way to store, classify, share, and search links through folksonomy techniques on the Internet and intranets. 116, W18-26

social computing An approach aimed at making the human–computer interface more natural. 55

social engineering A type of nontechnical attack that uses some ruse to trick users into revealing information or performing an action that compromises a computer or network. 476

social marketplace The term is derived from the combination of *social networking* and *marketplace*. An online community that harnesses the power of one's social networks for the introduction, buying, and selling of products, services, and resources, including one's own creations. Also may refer to a structure that resembles a social network but is focused on individual members. 446

social media The online platforms and tools that people use to share opinions, experiences, insights, perceptions, and various media, including photos, videos, music, with each other. 429

social network A category of Internet applications that help connect friends, business partners, or individuals with specific interests by providing free services such as photos presentation, e-mail, blogging, and so on using a variety of tools. 56

social network advertising Online advertising that focuses on social networking sites. 217

social network analysis (software) The mapping and measuring of relationships and information flows among people, groups, organizations, computers, and other information- or knowledge-processing entities. The nodes in the network are the people and groups, whereas the links show relationships or flows between the nodes. SNAs provide both visual and a mathematical analyses of relationships. 436

social network service (SNS) A service that builds online communities by providing an online space for people to build free homepages and that provides basic communication and support tools for conducting different activities in the social network. 57

social networking The creation or sponsoring of a social network service and any activity, such as blogging, done in a social network (external or internal). 57

social software A software product that enables people to rendezvous, connect, and collaborate through computer-mediated communication. W18-24

software agents Autonomous software programs that carry out tasks on behalf of users. 571

software as a service (SaaS) A model of software delivery where the software company provides maintenance, daily technical operation, and support for the software provided to their client. SaaS is a model of software delivery rather than a market segment. W18-13

spam The electronic equivalent of junk mail. 476

spam site Page that uses techniques that deliberately subvert a search engine's algorithms to artificially inflate the page's rankings. 488

spamming Using e-mail to send unwanted ads (sometimes floods of ads). 222

splog Short for *spam blog*. A site created solely for marketing purposes. 488

spot buying The purchase of goods and services as they are needed, usually at prevailing market prices. 239

spyware All unwanted software programs designed to steal proprietary information, or that target data stores containing confidential information without the user's knowledge. 205, 489, 724

standard of due care Care that a company is reasonably expected to take based on the risks affecting its EC business and online transactions. 513

statutes Rules that define criminal laws. 712

stickiness Characteristic that influences the average length of time a visitor stays in a site. 209

storebuilder service A hosting service that provides disk space and services to help small and microbusinesses build a Web site quickly and cheaply. 679

stored-value card A card that has monetary value loaded onto it and that is usually rechargeable. 533

storefront A single company's Web site where products or services are sold. 97

strategic information systems planning (SISP) A process for developing a strategy and plans for aligning information systems (including e-commerce applications) with the organization's business strategies. 590

strategic (systematic) sourcing Purchases involving long-term contracts that usually are based on private negotiations between sellers and buyers. 239

strategy A broad-based formula for how a business is going to accomplish its mission, what its goals should be, and what plans and policies will be needed to carry out those goals. 587

strategy assessment The continuous evaluation of progress toward the organization's strategic goals, resulting in corrective action and, if necessary, strategy reformulation. 592

strategy formulation The development of strategies to exploit opportunities and manage threats in the business environment in light of corporate strengths and weaknesses. 591

strategy implementation The development of detailed, short-term plans for carrying out the projects agreed on in strategy formulation. 592

strategy initiation The initial phase of strategic planning in which the organization examines itself and its environment. 590

strategy map A tool that delineates the relationships among the key organizational objectives for all four BSC perspectives. 613

supplier relationship management (SRM) A comprehensive approach to managing an enterprise's interactions with the organizations that supply the goods and services it uses. W5-18

supply chain The flow of materials, information, money, and services from raw material suppliers through factories and warehouses to the end customers. 287

supply chain management (SCM) A complex process that requires the coordination of many activities so that the shipment of goods and services from supplier right through to customer is done efficiently and effectively for all parties concerned. SCM aims to minimize inventory levels, optimize production and increase throughput, decrease manufacturing time, optimize logistics and distribution, streamline order fulfillment, and overall reduce the costs associated with these activities. 289

SWOT analysis A methodology that surveys external opportunities and threats and relates them to internal strengths and weaknesses. 593

symmetric (private) key encryption An encryption system that uses the same key to encrypt and decrypt the message. 496

syndication The sale of the same good (e.g., digital content) to many customers, who then integrate it with other offerings and resell it or give it away free. 684

tag A nonhierarchical keyword or term assigned to a piece of information (such as an Internet bookmark, digital image, video clip, or any computer document). 116

teleconferencing The use of electronic communication that allows two or more people at different locations to have a simultaneous conference. 319

tendering (bidding) system Model in which a buyer requests would-be sellers to submit bids; the lowest bidder wins. 75

terminal-based positioning Calculating the location of a mobile device from signals sent by the device to base stations. 403

text mining The application of data mining to nonstructured or less-structured text files. W4-8

third-party logistics suppliers (3PL) External, rather than in-house, providers of logistics services. 558

throughput The number of operations completed in a given period of time; indicates the number of users that a system can handle. W18-22

tort Civil wrong that can be grounds for a lawsuit. 715

total benefits of ownership (TBO) Benefits of ownership that include both tangible and intangible benefits. 639

total cost of ownership (TCO) A formula for calculating the cost of owning, operating, and controlling an IT system. 638

trademark A symbol used by businesses to identify their goods and services; government registration of the trademark confers exclusive legal right to its use. 715

transaction costs Costs that are associated with the distribution (sale) or exchange of products and services including the cost of searching for buyers and sellers, gathering information, negotiating, decision making, monitoring the exchange of goods, and legal fees. 650

transaction log A record of user activities at a company's Web site. 204

transactional Web site A Web site that sells products and services. 678

Transport Layer Security (TLS) As of 1996, another name for the SSL protocol. 498

Trojan horse A program that appears to have a useful function but that contains a hidden function that presents a security risk. 481

trust The psychological status of willingness to depend on another person or organization. 198

turnkey approach Ready to use without further assembly or testing; supplied in a state that is ready to turn on and operate. W18-9

tweets Text-based posts up to 140 characters in length posted to Twitter. 114

Twitter A free micro-blogging service that allows its users to send and read other users' updates. 114

unified communication (UC) Simplification of all forms of communication in the enterprise. 320

unique visit A count of the number of visitors entering a site, regardless of how many pages are viewed per visit. 209

unit testing Testing application software modules one at a time. W18-7

universal man-in-the-middle phishing kit A tool used by phishers to set up a URL that can interact in real time with the content of a legitimate Web site, such as a bank or EC site, to intercept data entered by customers at log-in or check out Web pages. 485

up-selling Offering an upgraded version of the product in order to boost sales and profit. 684

usability (of Web site) The quality and usefulness of the user's experience when interacting with the Web site. 693

usability testing Testing the quality of the user's experience when interacting with a Web site. W18-7

user profile The requirements, preferences, behaviors, and demographic traits of a particular customer. 194

utility (on-demand) computing Unlimited computing power and storage capacity that can be used and reallocated for any application—and billed on a pay-per-use basis. W18-11

valuation The fair market value of a business or the price at which a property would change hands between a willing buyer and a willing seller who are both informed and under no compulsion to act. For a publicly traded company, the value can be readily obtained by multiplying the selling price of the stock by the number of available shares. 652

value proposition The benefit that a company's products or services provide to a company and its customers from using EC. 75, 591

vendor-managed inventory (VMI) The practice of retailers' making suppliers responsible for determining when to order and how much to order. 304

venture capital (VC) Money invested in a business by an individual, a group of individuals (venture capitalists), or a funding company in exchange for equity in the business. 673

versioning Selling the same good, but with different selection and delivery characteristics. 606

vertical auction Auction that takes place between sellers and buyers in one industry or for one commodity. W17-7

vertical marketplaces Markets that deal with one industry or industry segment (e.g., steel, chemicals). 240

Vickrey auction Auction in which the highest bidder wins but pays only the second highest bid. W17-5

video teleconference Virtual meeting in which participants in one location can see participants at other locations on a large screen or a desktop computer. 319

viral blogging Viral marketing done by bloggers. 448

viral marketing Word-of-mouth marketing by which customers promote a product or service by telling others about it. 218

viral video Video clip that gains widespread popularity through the process of Internet sharing, typically through e-mail or IM messages, blogs, and other media-sharing Web sites. W18-29

virtual (Internet) community A group of people with similar interests who interact with one another using the Internet. 431

virtual corporation (VC) An organization composed of several business partners sharing costs and resources for the production or utilization of a product or service. 610

virtual (pure-play) e-tailers Firms that sell directly to consumers over the Internet without maintaining a physical sales channel. 148

virtual meetings Online meetings whose members are in different locations, even in different countries. 317

virtual (pure-play) organizations Organizations that conduct their business activities solely online. 48, 148

virtual private network (VPN) A network that uses the public Internet to carry information but remains private by using encryption to scramble the communications, authentication to ensure that information has not been tampered with, and access control to verify the identity of anyone using the network. 500, W5-2

virtual team A group of employees using information and communications technologies to collaborate from different work bases. 316

virtual university An online university from which students take classes from home or other offsite locations, usually via the Internet. 352

virtual world A user-defined world in which people can interact, play, and do business. The most publicized virtual world is Second Life. 60

virtualization A technique for hiding the physical characteristics of computing resources from the way in which other systems, applications, or end users interact with those resources. W18-35

virtualization tools Enable server, storage, and network resources to be deployed and managed as giant pools and seamlessly changed as needs change. W18-12

virus A piece of software code that inserts itself into a host, including the operating systems, in order to propagate; it requires that its host program be run to activate it. 481

visibility The knowledge about where materials and parts are at any given time, which helps solving problems such as delay, combining shipments, and more. 294

visit A series of requests during one navigation of a Web site; a pause of a certain length of time ends a visit. 209

vlog (video blog) A blog with video content. 113

voice commerce (v-commerce) An umbrella term for the use of speech recognition to allow voice activated e-commerce services, including Internet browsing ad email retrieval. W9-10

voice portal (1) A portal accessed by telephone or cell phone. (2) A Web site with an audio interface that can be accessed through a telephone call. 100, 388

voice-over-IP (VoIP) Communication systems that transmit voice calls over Internet Protocol–based networks. 324

vortals B2B portals that focus on a single industry or industry segment; "vertical portals." 265

vulnerability Weakness in software or other mechanism that threatens the confidentiality, integrity, or availability of an asset (recall the CIA model). It can be directly used by a hacker to gain access to a system or network. 477

warehouse management system (WMS) A software system that helps in managing warehouses. 558

Web 2.0 The popular term for advanced Internet technology and applications, including blogs, wikis, RSS, folksonomies, and social bookmarking. One of the most significant differences between Web 2.0 and the traditional World Wide Web is greater collaboration among Internet users and other users, content providers, and enterprises. 55, 427, W18-17

Web 3.0 A term used to describe the future of the World Wide Web. It consists of the creation of high-quality content and services produced by gifted individuals using Web 2.0 technology as an enabling platform. 459

Web 4.0 The Web generation after Web 3.0. It is still an unknown entity. However, it is envisioned as being based on islands of intelligence and as being ubiquitous. 460

Web analytics (1) The analysis of clickstream data to understand visitor behavior on a Web site. (2) The measurement, collection, analysis, and reporting of Internet data for the purposes of understanding and optimizing Web usage. 613, 695

Web bugs Tiny graphics files embedded in e-mail messages and in Web sites that transmit information about users and their movements to a Web server. 205

Web hosting service A dedicated Web site hosting company that offers a wide range of hosting services and functionality to businesses of all sizes. 680

Web mining Data mining techniques for discovering and extracting information from Web documents; explores both Web content and Web usage. 205, W4-8

Web portal A single point of access, through a Web browser, to critical business information located inside and outside (via Internet) of an organization. 99

Web Services (1) An architecture enabling assembly of distributed applications from software services and tying them together. (2) Self-contained, self-describing business and consumer modular applications, delivered over the Internet that users can select and combine through almost any device, ranging from personal computers to mobile phones. 310, W18-16

Web syndication A form of syndication in which a section of a Web site is made available for other sites to use. W15-3

Web video analytics A way of measuring what viewers do when they watch an online video. 218

Webcasting A free Internet news service that broadcasts personalized news and information, including seminars, in categories selected by the user. 220, 360

Webinars Seminars on the Web (Web-based seminars). 360

Web-oriented architecture (WOA) A set of Web protocols (e.g., HTTP and plain XML) as the most dynamic, scalable, and interoperable Web Service approach. W18-20

widget A Web page feature or a small Web toolbox often designed on top of Web applications. W18-21

Wi-Fi (wireless fidelity) The common name used to describe the IEEE 802.11 standard used on most WLANs. 389

wiki (wikilog) A blog that allows everyone to participate as a peer; anyone may add, delete, or change content. 117

WiMax A wireless standard (IEEE 802.16) for making broadband network connections over a medium-size area such as a city. 390

wireless local area network (WLAN) A telecommunications network that enables users to make short-range wireless connections to the Internet or another network. 389

wireless mobile computing (mobile computing) Computing that connects a mobile device to a network or another computing device, anytime, anywhere. 386

wireless wide area network (WWAN) A telecommunications network that offers wireless coverage over a large geographical area, typically over a cellular phone network. 390

workflow The movement of information as it flows through the sequence of steps that make up an organization's work procedures. 314

workflow management The automation of workflows, so that documents, information, and tasks are passed from one participant to the next in the steps of an organization's business process. 315

workflow systems Business process automation tools that place system controls in the hands of user departments to automate information processing tasks. 314

worm A software program that runs independently, consuming the resources of its host in order to maintain itself, that is capable of propagating a complete working version of itself onto another machine. 481

zombies Computers infected with malware that are under the control of a spammer, hacker, or other criminal. 477

Index

Note: Page references with A indicate appendix pages, those with E represent exhibits, and those with W represent Web pages.